Trees and Shrubs

A GARDENER'S ENCYCLOPEDIA

Trees and Shrubs

A GARDENER'S ENCYCLOPEDIA

SENIOR CONSULTANTS

Geoff Bryant and Tony Rodd

FIREFLY BOOKS

A FIREFLY BOOK

Published by Firefly Books Ltd. 2011

Photographs from the Global Book
Publishing Photo Library © Global
Book Publishing Pty Ltd 2011
Text © Global Book Publishing Pty
Ltd 2011
Maps © Global Book Publishing Pty
Ltd 2011

First printing

**Publisher Cataloging-in-Publication
Data (U.S.)**
A CIP record of this book is available
from the Library of Congress.

**Library and Archives Canada
Cataloguing in Publication**
Bryant, Geoff
    Trees and shrubs : a gardener's
encyclopedia / Geoff Bryant and Tony
Rodd.
Includes index.
ISBN-13: 978-1-55407-836-3
ISBN-10: 1-55407-836-9
    1. Trees–Encyclopedias.   2. Shrubs–
Encyclopedias.   I. Rodd, Tony II. Title.
SB435.B79 2010   635.9'7603
C2010-906709-6

Published in the United States by
Firefly Books (U.S.) Inc.
P.O. Box 1338, Ellicott Station
Buffalo, New York 14205

Published in Canada by
Firefly Books Ltd.
66 Leek Crescent
Richmond Hill, Ontario L4B 1H1

The moral rights of the contributors
have been asserted.

Printed in China by 1010 Printing
International Ltd
Color separation Pica Digital Pte Ltd,
Singapore

Developed by Global Book Publishing
Level 8, 15 Orion Road, Lane Cove,
NSW 2066, Australia
Ph: (612) 9425 5800
Fax: (612) 9425 5804
E: rightsmanager@globalpub.com.au

MANAGING DIRECTOR
Chryl Campbell

EDITORIAL DIRECTOR
Sarah Anderson

ART DIRECTOR
Kylie Mulquin

PROJECT MANAGER
Dannielle Viera

SENIOR CONSULTANTS
Tony Rodd, Geoff Bryant

CONTRIBUTORS
David Austin, Don Blaxell, David
Bond, Peter Brownless, Geoff Bryant,
Kate Bryant, Ian Connor, Penny Dunn,
Richard Francis, William Grant, Ken
Grapes, Sarah Guest, Sean Hogan,
Melanie Kinsey, Folko Kullmann,
Todd Lasseigne, Marilyn S. Light,
Tony Lord, David Mabberley, Valda
Paddison, Ron Parsons, Lee Reich,
Tony Rodd, Stephen Ryan, Julie Silk,
Wendy Thomas, R. G. Turner, Jr.,
Marion Tyree, Ben-Erik van Wyk,
Rachel Vogan, Scott Williams

EDITORS
Loretta Barnard, Kate Etherington,
Janet Parker, Marie-Louise Taylor,
Dannielle Viera

DESIGNERS
Stan Lamond, Kylie Mulquin,
Jacqueline Richards

PROOFREADER
Puddingburn Publishing Services

INDEXER
Dannielle Viera

PUBLISHING COORDINATOR
Jessica Luca

PUBLISHING ASSISTANT
Kristen Donath

CAPTIONS
Front cover: *Pinus bungeana*. Spine: *Rosa*,
Old Rose, Alba, 'Alba Maxima'. Back cover
(left to right): *Rosa*, Modern Rose, Cluster-
flowered, 'Chinatown'; *Prunus maackii*;
Magnolia grandiflora; *Liquidambar stryraciflua*;
Amelanchier lamarckii.

Page 1 (top to bottom): *Spiraea japonica*
'Goldflame'; *Rosa*, Large-flowered (Hybrid
Tea), 'Jason'; *Euptelea pleiosperma*.
Page 2: *Lavandula angustifolia* 'Lodden
Blue'. Page 3 (top to bottom): *Chaenomeles
japonica*; *Aralia spinosa*. Pages 4–5: *Ulmus*
x *hollandica* 'Modolina'.

Contents

How This Book Works

Stunningly illustrated with hundreds of full-color photographs, this book provides a wealth of up-to-date information on over 1,500 trees and shrubs suitable for gardens of all sizes from all parts of the world. Because the great majority of garden enthusiasts live in the temperate zones, there is a more complete coverage of temperate plants than of tropical or alpine species.

The book is divided into two chapters: Trees and Shrubs; and Fruit Trees, Nut Trees, and Other Fruits. Each chapter begins with a short introduction to the plant group, followed by a comprehensive table of all the species in the chapter, with at-a-glance information on height, spread, plant type, climate, frost tolerance, aspect, and more. Directly after the table are the extensive individual plant entries, arranged alphabetically by genus name.

The symbol × before a genus or species name usually indicates a hybrid genus or species. The genus entries give the family to which the plant belongs, as well as geographical range, number of species, distinguishing features, commercial uses, and propagation and cultivation requirements of the genus as a whole.

Under every genus entry are a number of species entries (which include synonyms and common names, if applicable), each containing information such as the growth habit, flowering season, flower color, forms, and hardiness zones, with symbols denoting aspect, frost hardiness, spread, and height. The spread and height given apply to a mature plant in cultivation. The hardiness zones show the climatic areas in which plants can be grown.

Page heading
The heading on the left-hand page names the first genus or species entry on that page; the right-hand page heading names the last entry on that page.

Forms
Includes well-known or award-winning subspecies, varieties, forms, and cultivars of the species.

Species entry
Contains detailed information on particular species and forms, and includes hardiness rating by zones.

Common names
The non-botanical names by which the plant is generally known, usually in its native region.

Place of origin
The particular countries or regions of the world where the plant is naturally found.

Hardiness zones
The regions in which the plant can be successfully cultivated. See page 7 for more information.

Genus entry
Contains information about the genus as a whole, including geographical range, and cultivation and propagation requirements.

Family name
The name of the group to which the genus belongs; related plant genera are placed in the same family.

Cultivation
General information on growing and propagating the members of the genus as a whole.

Symbols
At-a-glance information about the plant—see the list of symbols on page 7 for their meaning.

Synonyms
Incorrect botanical names by which the plant may have been known in the past.

---

82   *Amelanchier laevis*

Angophora costata, in the wild, New South Wales, Australia

Amelanchier laevis
syn. *Amelanchier canadensis* of gardens
ALLEGHENY SERVICEBERRY, SARVIS TREE
◐ ❈ ↔ 25 ft (8 m) ↕ 25 ft (8 m)
Found mainly in Appalachian mountains of eastern USA, extending into Canada. Bronzy purple slightly downy new leaves; sweet, juicy, blue-black fruit. Flowers as leaves unfold in late spring. Zones 4–9.

Amelanchier lamarckii
LAMARCK SERVICEBERRY
◐ ❈ ↔ 35 ft (10 m) ↕ 30 ft (9 m)
Probable hybrid origin. Small tree with spreading branches, leaves silky-haired, bronzy red when new. Loose sprays of flowers open with new leaves. Fruit purple-black. Zones 4–9.

AMHERSTIA
The 1 species of this genus, of the cassia subfamily of legumes (Fabaceae), is from the lowlands of southern Myanmar, and almost unknown in the wild. It has long pinnate leaves with glossy leaflets and may be briefly deciduous. At the start of the wet season pale bronzy pink new leaves emerge, changing through brown to green. On long stalks, flowers are orchid-like with a pair of large pink bracts at the base, up to 4 in (10 cm) across, pinkish red with darker red and yellow markings. Rarely produced are the curved woody pods.
CULTIVATION: *Amherstia* has been successfully cultivated only in the lowland wet tropics. Its growth is fairly slow, and it needs a sheltered but sunny situation and deep moist soil. Propagate from seed if it can be obtained; an alternative is layering of low branches.

Amherstia nobilis
PRIDE OF BURMA
◐ ➤ ↔ 50 ft (15 m) ↕ 40 ft (12 m)
Lovely tree with broad low-branching canopy of foliage. Mature specimens may flower for much of year, but flowering season is spring–early summer. Red orchid-like flowers. Zone 12.

ANDROMEDA
Two fully hardy, low-growing, evergreen shrub species make up this genus of the heath (Ericaceae) family, found growing in the acid peat bogs of the Northern Hemisphere. The somewhat leathery, smooth-edged, small oblong leaves form a deep green background to the tiny, white or pink, bell-like flowers held in terminal clusters during spring.
CULTIVATION: *Andromeda* species require an acid soil where constant moisture is assured, and are best grown in peat beds, shady woodlands, or rock gardens. They can be propagated from suckers, by layering, or from softwood cuttings.

Andromeda polifolia
BOG ROSEMARY, MARSH ANDROMEDA
◐ ❈ ↔ 22 in (55 cm) ↕ 4–18 in (10–45 cm)
Variable growing shrub, either erect or prostrate. Small, pointed, oblong leaves with clusters of bell-like flowers in spring or early summer. 'Alba', low-growing prostrate shrub with pure white flowers; 'Compacta', compact growth habit, pink flowers; and 'Macrophylla', larger leaves and pink flowers. Zones 2–9.

ANGOPHORA
This eastern Australian genus of the myrtle (Myrtaceae) family is closely allied to *Eucalyptus* and *Corymbia*. Its 15 species of evergreen trees have separate sepals and petals enclosing the buds. Most are medium to large trees of open forest, woodland, and heath. Bark is usually rough, rather corky or flaky, though smooth in some species. Leaves, in opposite pairs, vary from narrow pointed to broad heart-shaped. Flowers have masses of white to cream stamens, in terminal clusters at the branch tips. Blooms are followed by ribbed woody capsules.
CULTIVATION: These trees are light-loving and fast growing, preferring sandy moderately fertile soils and shelter from strong winds. Most tolerate a degree or two of overnight frost as long as days are warm and sunny. Propagate from seed, to be collected just as capsules discharge.

Amelanchier lamarckii

Angophora costata
syn. *Angophora lanceolata*
ANGOPHORA, RUSTY GUM, SYDNEY RED GUM
○ ❅ ↔ 80 ft (24 m) ↕ 100 ft (30 m)
From sandy forest country of coastal New South Wales, Australia. Pinkish gray bark sheds in early summer to reveal bright orange-brown bark. Deep wine red new foliage. Clusters of white flowers in spring–early summer. Zones 9–11.

Angophora hispida
syn. *Angophora cordifolia*
DWARF APPLE
○ ❅ ↔ 12 ft (3.5 m) ↕ 12 ft (3 m)
Localized to sandstone ridges around Sydney, Australia. Broad, harsh-textured leaves. Flowers in large heads, in mid-spring–summer. New shoots and flower buds have deep red bristles. Zones 10–11.

Symbols

Each species entry in this book features symbols that provide at-a-glance information about the species.

★   Flora Award—the plant is recommended by our consultants as outstanding in its group

↔   Spread—the width of the mature plant in cultivation

↑   Height—the height of the mature plant in cultivation

☼   Full Sun—the plant thrives in sunny conditions

☽   Half Sun—the plant thrives in dappled sunlight or part-shade

☀   Shade—the plant thrives in shady conditions

❋   Frost Tolerance—the plant is fully hardy

❄   Frost Tolerance—the plant is frost hardy

❅   Frost Tolerance—the plant is half-hardy

✈   Frost Tolerance—the plant is frost tender

World Hardiness Zones

This world map is divided into Plant Hardiness Zones, which indicate how well cultivated plants survive the minimum winter temperature expected for each zone. The system was developed by the U.S. Department of Agriculture, originally for North America, but it now includes other geographical areas. Zone 1 applies to the cold subarctic climates of Alaska and Siberia, for example, whereas Zone 12 covers the warmest areas around the equator.

Both a minimum and maximum zone is given for every plant species listed in this book. A European native, *Rosa canina* will withstand the winter frosts occurring in parts of Zone 3, in which temperatures fall below –30°F (–34°C); it will also thrive up to Zone 10, where the minimum winter temperatures are above 30°F (–1°C). It is important to note that maximum temperatures also have an effect, and plants that can survive the cold of Zone 3 are unlikely to succeed in the heat of Zones 10 and 11.

Other climatic factors also affect plant growth. Humidity, day length, season length, wind, soil temperature, and rainfall all need to be considered.

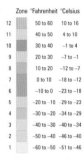

Zone	°Fahrenheit	°Celsius
12	50 to 60	10 to 16
11	40 to 50	4 to 10
10	30 to 40	–1 to 4
9	20 to 30	–7 to –1
8	10 to 20	–12 to –7
7	0 to 10	–18 to –12
6	–10 to 0	–23 to –18
5	–20 to –10	–29 to –23
4	–30 to –20	–34 to –29
3	–40 to –30	–40 to –34
2	–50 to –40	–46 to –40
1	–60 to –50	–51 to –46

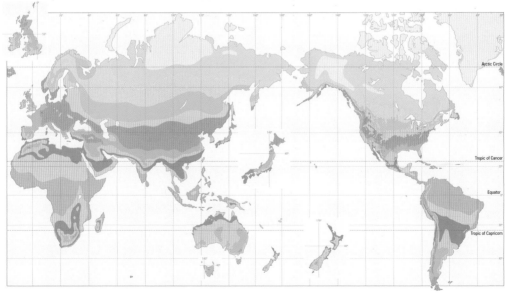

Trees and Shrubs

Trees are defined as woody perennial plants that are distinguished from other woody plants such as shrubs by the presence of usually, but not always, a single woody stem—the trunk. Shrubs are defined as woody perennial plants that possess multiple stems arising from a common point known as the crown. Both trees and shrubs inhabit virtually all climates and soil types, with a large variation in form, adaptability, and stress tolerance from species to species.

Most trees are long lived, with some living for many centuries, such as the bristlecone pine *(Pinus longaeva)* of California that reaches ages of 4,500 years or more. Some trees can attain a great height—reaching over 320 ft (96 m) tall—such as the Australian mountain ash *(Eucalyptus regnans)*; other trees might grow to only 3 ft (0.9 m) tall due to the harsh climate in which they live.

Not merely existing as miniature trees, shrubs instead display completely different growth habits— some can creep or sucker, such as *Deutzia* species and *Viburnum tinus,* while others rarely or never spread in this fashion. Many shrubs, such as *Choisya* species, are very tolerant of hard pruning, wherein the entire crown can be cut back to ground level—this is a natural adaptation to fire or browsing by animals.

The oriental photinia *(Photinia villosa)* is native to China, Korea, and Japan. Its dark green leaves take on attractive shades of yellow, orange, and red in autumn.

Trees and Shrubs Finder

The following cultivation table features at-a-glance information for every species or hybrid with an individual entry in the Trees and Shrubs chapter of this book. Simply find the plant you wish to know more about, and run your eye along the row to discover its height and spread, whether it is frost tolerant or not, the aspect it prefers, and more.

The type of plant is abbreviated to **T**, **S**, or **C**:
T – the plant is a tree.
S – the plant is a shrub.
C – the plant is a conifer.

The climate(s) that each plant needs to thrive in the outdoors are given (some plants will grow in more than one climate), abbreviated to **C**, **W**, or **T**:
C – the plant prefers a cool climate.
W– the plant prefers a warm-temperate or subtropical climate.
T – the plant prefers a tropical climate.

The flowering season is abbreviated to **A**, **W**, **Sp**, or **Su**:
A – the plant bears flowers in autumn.
W– the plant bears flowers in winter.
Sp – the plant bears flowers in spring.
Su – the plant bears flowers in summer.

Plant name	Height	Spread	Type	Climate	Deciduous	Evergreen	Showy flowers	Showy foliage	Scented flowers	Flowering season	Grow in pot/tub	Indoor use	Frost tolerant	Full sun	Half sun	Heavy shade
Abelia floribunda	6 ft (1.8 m)	6 ft (1.8 m)	S	W		♦	♦			Su/A				♦		
Abelia × grandiflora	6 ft (1.8 m)	6 ft (1.8 m)	S	C/W		♦	♦	♦	♦	Su/A				♦	♦	
Abelia schumannii	4 ft (1.2 m)	8 ft (2.4 m)	S	C/W		♦	♦			Su/A				♦	♦	
Abeliophyllum distichum	3 ft (0.9 m)	6 ft (1.8 m)	S	C/W	♦		♦		♦	W/Sp				♦	♦	
Abies balsamea	50 ft (15 m)	15 ft (4.5 m)	C	C		♦		♦		Sp				♦	♦	
Abies cephalonica	100 ft (30 m)	25 ft (8 m)	C	C/W		♦		♦		Sp				♦	♦	
Abies concolor	120 ft (36 m)	25 ft (8 m)	C	C		♦		♦		Sp				♦	♦	
Abies fargesii	60 ft (18 m)	12 ft (3.5 m)	C	C		♦		♦		Sp				♦	♦	
Abies fraseri	60 ft (18 m)	20 ft (6 m)	C	C		♦		♦		Sp				♦	♦	
Abies grandis	300 ft (90 m)	25 ft (8 m)	C	C		♦		♦		Sp				♦	♦	
Abies homolepis	80 ft (24 m)	25 ft (8 m)	C	C		♦		♦		Sp				♦	♦	
Abies koreana	50 ft (15 m)	5 ft (1.5 m)	C	C		♦		♦		Sp				♦	♦	
Abies pinsapo	80 ft (24 m)	15 ft (4.5 m)	C	C		♦		♦		Sp				♦	♦	
Abies procera	150 ft (45 m)	30 ft (9 m)	C	C		♦		♦		Sp				♦	♦	
Abutilon × hybridum	6–15 ft (1.8–4.5 m)	5–10 ft (1.5–3 m)	S	W		♦	♦			Sp–A	♦			♦	♦	♦
Abutilon megapotamicum	8 ft (2.4 m)	8 ft (2.4 m)	S	W		♦	♦			Sp–A	♦			♦	♦	
Abutilon × suntense	12 ft (3.5 m)	8 ft (2.4 m)	S	W	♦		♦			Sp/Su				♦	♦	
Abutilon vitifolium	15 ft (4.5 m)	8 ft (2.4 m)	S	W	♦		♦			Sp/Su				♦	♦	
Acacia adunca	20 ft (6 m)	12 ft (3.5 m)	S	W		♦	♦		♦	W/Sp				♦		
Acacia baileyana	6–20 ft (1.8–6 m)	20 ft (6 m)	T	W		♦	♦	♦		W/Sp				♦		
Acacia binervia	50 ft (15 m)	35 ft (10 m)	T	W		♦	♦		♦	Sp				♦		

Plant name	Height	Spread	Type	Climate	Deciduous	Evergreen	Showy flowers	Showy foliage	Scented flowers	Flowering season	Grow in pot/tub	Indoor use	Frost tolerant	Full sun	Half sun	Heavy shade
Acacia cardiophylla	3–10 ft (0.9–3 m)	5–8 ft (1.5–2.4 m)	T	W		♦	♦	♦	♦	W/Sp			♦	♦		
Acacia cultriformis	6–10 ft (1.8–3 m)	6–10 ft (1.8–3 m)	S	W		♦	♦	♦	♦	Sp			♦	♦		
Acacia cyclops	7–15 ft (2–4.5 m)	7–15 ft (2–4.5 m)	S	W		♦	♦			Sp–A			♦	♦		
Acacia dealbata	50 ft (15 m)	25 ft (8 m)	T	W		♦	♦		♦	W/Sp			♦	♦		
Acacia elata	100 ft (30 m)	40 ft (12 m)	T	W		♦	♦	♦		Su				♦		
Acacia farnesiana	15 ft (4.5 m)	15 ft (4.5 m)	S	W/T		♦	♦		♦	W/Sp			♦	♦		
Acacia giraffae	40–60 ft (12–18 m)	40 ft (12 m)	T	W		♦	♦		♦	W/Sp				♦		
Acacia howittii	25 ft (8 m)	10 ft (3 m)	T	W		♦	♦		♦	Sp				♦		
Acacia karroo	25 ft (8 m)	25 ft (8 m)	T	W	♦		♦		♦	Su/A				♦		
Acacia longifolia	6–25 ft (1.8–8 m)	15 ft (4.5 m)	T	W		♦	♦			W/Sp				♦		
Acacia melanoxylon	100 ft (30 m)	20 ft (6 m)	T	W		♦	♦			W/Sp			♦	♦		
Acacia podalyriifolia	10–15 ft (3–4.5 m)	15 ft (4.5 m)	S	W		♦	♦	♦	♦	W/Sp				♦		
Acacia pravissima	10–25 ft (3–8 m)	10 ft (3 m)	S	W		♦	♦	♦		Sp			♦	♦		
Acacia pycnantha	10–25 ft (3–8 m)	15 ft (4.5 m)	S	W		♦	♦		♦	W/Sp				♦		
Acacia riceana	10–20 ft (3–6 m)	10 ft (3 m)	S	W		♦	♦			Sp			♦	♦		
Acacia verticillata	10 ft (3 m)	7 ft (2 m)	S	W		♦	♦	♦		W/Sp						♦
Acacia vestita	6–15 ft (1.8–4.5 m)	6–15 ft (1.8–4.5 m)	S	W		♦	♦	♦		Sp				♦		
Acacia xanthophloea	50 ft (15 m)	20–40 ft (6–12 m)	T	W	♦		♦	♦	♦	Sp				♦		
Acalypha amentacea subsp. *wilkesiana*	10 ft (3 m)	10 ft (3 m)	S	W/T		♦		♦		Su/A	♦			♦		
Acalypha hispida	12 ft (3.5 m)	5 ft (1.5 m)	S	W/T		♦	♦			Su	♦	♦			♦	
Acalypha reptans	12 in (30 cm)	12 in (30 cm)	S	W/T		♦	♦			Su	♦	♦			♦	
Acca sellowiana	10 ft (3 m)	10 ft (3 m)	S	W		♦	♦			Su				♦	♦	
Acer buergerianum	30 ft (9 m)	25 ft (8 m)	T	C/W	♦			♦		Sp				♦	♦	
Acer campestre	30 ft (9 m)	12 ft (3.5 m)	T	C	♦			♦		Sp				♦	♦	
Acer capillipes	40 ft (12 m)	35 ft (10 m)	T	C	♦			♦		Sp				♦	♦	
Acer cappadocicum	60 ft (18 m)	50 ft (15 m)	T	C	♦			♦		Sp				♦	♦	
Acer circinnatum	15 ft (4.5 m)	15 ft (4.5 m)	T	C	♦			♦		Sp				♦	♦	
Acer davidii	30 ft (9 m)	25 ft (8 m)	T	C	♦			♦		Sp				♦	♦	
Acer forrestii	25–40 ft (8–12 m)	20–30 ft (6–9 m)	T	C	♦			♦		Sp				♦	♦	
Acer griseum	40 ft (12 m)	35 ft (10 m)	T	C	♦			♦		Sp				♦	♦	

Plant name	Height	Spread	Type	Climate	Deciduous	Evergreen	Showy flowers	Showy foliage	Scented flowers	Flowering season	Grow in pot/tub	Indoor use	Frost tolerant	Full sun	Half sun	Heavy shade
Acer japonicum	30 ft (9 m)	30 ft (9 m)	T	C	◆			◆		Sp			◆	◆		
Acer macrophyllum	80 ft (24 m)	80 ft (24 m)	T	C	◆			◆		Sp			◆	◆		
Acer maximowiczianum	60 ft (18 m)	40 ft (12 m)	T	C	◆			◆		Sp			◆	◆		
Acer negundo	60 ft (18 m)	30 ft (9 m)	T	C/W	◆		◆	◆		Sp			◆	◆		
Acer palmatum	20 ft (6 m)	25 ft (8 m)	T	C	◆			◆		Sp	◆		◆	◆		◆
Acer pensylvanicum	30 ft (9 m)	35 ft (10 m)	T	C	◆			◆		Sp			◆	◆		◆
Acer platanoides	80 ft (24 m)	50 ft (15 m)	T	C	◆			◆		Sp			◆	◆		
Acer pseudoplatanus	100 ft (30 m)	80 ft (24 m)	T	C	◆			◆		Sp			◆	◆		
Acer rubrum	100 ft (30 m)	35 ft (10 m)	T	C	◆		◆	◆		Sp			◆	◆		
Acer saccharinum	100 ft (30 m)	80 ft (24 m)	T	C	◆			◆		Sp			◆	◆		
Acer saccharum	100 ft (30 m)	40 ft (12 m)	T	C	◆			◆		Sp			◆	◆		
Acmena ingens	100 ft (30 m)	15–30 ft (4.5–9 m)	T	W		◆	◆			Su				◆		
Acmena smithii	60 ft (18 m)	35 ft (10 m)	T	W/T		◆	◆			Su				◆		
Acokanthera oblongifolia	10 ft (3 m)	5–8 ft (1.5–2.4 m)	S	W		◆	◆	◆	◆	Sp/Su				◆		
Adenium obesum	5 ft (1.5 m)	5 ft (1.5 m)	S	W/T		◆	◆			Su/A	◆	◆		◆		
Aesculus californica	15 ft (4.5 m)	30 ft (9 m)	S	C/W	◆		◆			Su			◆	◆		
Aesculus × carnea	30 ft (9 m)	15 ft (4.5 m)	T	C/W	◆		◆			Sp			◆	◆		
Aesculus hippocastanum	100 ft (30 m)	70 ft (21 m)	T	C	◆		◆			Sp			◆	◆		
Aesculus parviflora	10 ft (3 m)	15 ft (4.5 m)	S	C/W	◆		◆			Su			◆	◆		
Aesculus pavia	15 ft (4.5 m)	10 ft (3 m)	T	C/W	◆		◆			Su			◆	◆		
Afrocarpus falcatus	60–200 ft (18–60 m)	25–50 ft (8–15 m)	C	W		◆		◆		Su/A				◆		
Agathis australis	150 ft (45 m)	50 ft (15 m)	C	W		◆		◆					◆	◆		
Agathis robusta	180 ft (55 m)	40 ft (12 m)	C	W/T		◆		◆		Sp				◆		
Agonis flexuosa	30 ft (9 m)	15 ft (4.5 m)	T	W		◆	◆	◆		Sp/Su				◆		
Ailanthus altissima	40 ft (12 m)	40 ft (12 m)	T	C/W	◆			◆		Su			◆	◆		
Albizia julibrissin	20–40 ft (6–12 m)	15–20 ft (4.5–6 m)	T	C/W/T	◆		◆	◆		Su			◆	◆		
Albizia saman	100 ft (30 m)	50–100 ft (15–30 m)	T	W/T	◆		◆	◆		Su				◆	◆	
Aleurites fordii	25 ft (8 m)	10 ft (3 m)	T	W	◆		◆			Sp			◆	◆		
Aleurites moluccana	80 ft (24 m)	35 ft (10 m)	T	W/T		◆		◆		Sp				◆		
Allamanda schottii	6 ft (1.8 m)	6 ft (1.8 m)	S	W/T		◆	◆	◆		Su	◆			◆		
Allocasuarina torulosa	40–80 ft (12–24 m)	20 ft (6 m)	T	W		◆		◆		A			◆	◆	◆	

Plant name	Height	Spread	Type	Climate	Deciduous	Evergreen	Showy flowers	Showy foliage	Scented flowers	Flowering season	Grow in pot/tub	Indoor use	Frost tolerant	Full sun	Half sun	Heavy shade
Alloxylon flammeum	60 ft (18 m)	20 ft (6 m)	T	W		◆	◆	◆		W/Sp				◆		
Alnus acuminata	40 ft (12 m)	20 ft (6 m)	T	W		◆	◆			W/Sp			◆	◆		
Alnus glutinosa	60 ft (18 m)	35 ft (10 m)	T	C	◆		◆			W/Sp			◆	◆		
Alnus incana	70 ft (21 m)	30 ft (9 m)	T	C	◆		◆			W/Sp			◆	◆		
Alnus rubra	50 ft (15 m)	30 ft (9 m)	T	C	◆		◆			W/Sp			◆	◆		
Alyogyne huegelii	3–6 ft (0.9–1.8 m)	3–6 ft (0.9–1.8 m)	S	W		◆	◆			Sp/Su	◆			◆		
Amelanchier alnifolia	3–6 ft (0.9–1.8 m)	12 ft (3.5 m)	S	C	◆		◆			Sp/Su				◆		◆
Amelanchier arborea	60 ft (18 m)	30 ft (9 m)	T	C	◆		◆			Sp			◆	◆		
Amelanchier canadensis	25 ft (8 m)	10 ft (3 m)	T	C	◆		◆			Sp				◆		◆
Amelanchier laevis	25 ft (8 m)	25 ft (8 m)	T	C	◆		◆			Sp				◆		◆
Amelanchier lamarckii	30 ft (9 m)	35 ft (10 m)	T	C	◆		◆			Sp				◆		◆
Amherstia nobilis	40 ft (12 m)	50 ft (15 m)	T	T		◆	◆	◆		Sp/Su				◆		
Andromeda polifolia	4–18 in (10–45 cm)	22 in (55 cm)	S	C		◆	◆			Sp/Su				◆		◆
Angophora costata	100 ft (30 m)	80 ft (24 m)	T	W		◆	◆	◆		Sp/Su				◆		
Angophora hispida	10 ft (3 m)	12 ft (3.5 m)	S/T	W		◆	◆	◆		Sp/Su				◆		
Anisodontea capensis	3 ft (0.9 m)	30 in (75 cm)	S	W		◆	◆			Sp–A				◆		
Aphelandra sinclairiana	15 ft (4.5 m)	10 ft (3 m)	S	W/T		◆	◆			Sp–A	◆	◆				◆
Aphelandra squarrosa	6 ft (1.8 m)	5 ft (1.5 m)	S	W/T		◆	◆	◆		Sp–A	◆	◆				◆
Aralia elata	40 ft (12 m)	30 ft (9 m)	S	C	◆		◆	◆		Su/A				◆		◆
Aralia spinosa	20 ft (6 m)	15 ft (4.5 m)	S	C	◆		◆	◆		Su				◆		◆
Araucaria araucana	80 ft (24 m)	35 ft (10 m)	C	C/W		◆		◆		Sp			◆	◆		
Araucaria bidwillii	150 ft (45 m)	35 ft (10 m)	C	W		◆		◆		Sp				◆		
Araucaria cunninghamii	150 ft (45 m)	12 ft (3.5 m)	C	W		◆		◆		Sp				◆		
Araucaria heterophylla	200 ft (60 m)	25 ft (8 m)	C	W		◆		◆		Sp	◆	◆		◆		
Arbutus andrachne	20 ft (6 m)	20 ft (6 m)	T	C/W		◆	◆			Sp			◆	◆		
Arbutus 'Marina'	25–50 ft (8–15 m)	20–40 ft (6–12 m)	T	C/W		◆	◆			All			◆	◆		
Arbutus menziesii	30 ft (9 m)	30 ft (9 m)	T	C/W		◆	◆			Su			◆	◆		
Arbutus unedo	25 ft (8 m)	20 ft (6 m)	T	C/W		◆	◆			A/W			◆	◆		
Arctostaphylos densiflora	5 ft (1.5 m)	6 ft (1.8 m)	S	W		◆	◆			Sp			◆	◆	◆	
Arctostaphylos hookeri	6–48 in (15–120 cm)	4–15 ft (1.2–4.5 m)	S	W		◆	◆			W/Sp			◆	◆		
Arctostaphylos manzanita	15 ft (4.5 m)	10 ft (3 m)	S	W		◆	◆			Sp			◆	◆		

Plant name	Height	Spread	Type	Climate	Deciduous	Evergreen	Showy flowers	Showy foliage	Scented flowers	Flowering season	Grow in pot/tub	Indoor use	Frost tolerant	Full sun	Half sun	Heavy shade
Arctostaphylos pumila	1–5 ft (0.3–1.5 m)	3–10 ft (0.9–3 m)	S	W		◆	◆			W/Sp			◆	◆		
Arctostaphylos uva-ursi	4 in (10 cm)	20 in (50 cm)	S	C		◆	◆			Sp			◆	◆		
Arctostaphylos Hybrid Cultivars	6 in–10 ft (15 cm–3 m)	5–15 ft (1.5–4.5 m)	S	W		◆	◆	◆		Sp			◆	◆	◆	
Ardisia crenata	6 ft (1.8 m)	18 in (45 cm)	S	W		◆	◆			Sp/Su			◆			◆
Ardisia japonica	12 in (30 cm)	unlimited	S	W		◆	◆			Su			◆			◆
Argyranthemum frutescens	3 ft (0.9 m)	3 ft (0.9 m)	S	W		◆	◆			All	◆			◆		
Argyranthemum Hybrid Cultivars	12–30 in (30–75 cm)	18–36 in (45–90 cm)	S	W		◆	◆			All	◆			◆	◆	
Argyrocytisus battandieri	12 ft (3.5 m)	12 ft (3.5 m)	S	C/W		◆	◆	◆	◆	Sp/Su			◆	◆		
Aronia arbutifolia	6 ft (1.8 m)	5 ft (1.5 m)	S	C	◆		◆	◆		Sp			◆		◆	
Artemisia arborescens	5 ft (1.5 m)	5 ft (1.5 m)	S	W		◆		◆		Su			◆	◆		
Atherosperma moschatum	100 ft (30 m)	15 ft (4.5 m)	T	W		◆	◆			Sp			◆	◆		
Atriplex canescens	5 ft (1.5 m)	5 ft (1.5 m)	S	C/W		◆		◆		Su			◆	◆		
Atriplex halimus	6 ft (1.8 m)	10 ft (3 m)	S	W		◆		◆		Su			◆	◆		
Aucuba japonica	6 ft (1.8 m)	6 ft (1.8 m)	S	C/W		◆		◆		Sp/Su	◆		◆			◆
Auranticarpa rhombifolia	20–60 ft (6–18 m)	10–20 ft (3–6 m)	T	W		◆	◆		◆	Su			◆			
Azara microphylla	25 ft (8 m)	15 ft (4.5 m)	T	W		◆	◆		◆	Sp			◆		◆	
Azara serrata	12 ft (3.5 m)	8 ft (2.4 m)	S	W		◆	◆			Sp			◆		◆	
Baccharis 'Centennial'	3 ft (0.9 m)	5 ft (1.5 m)	S	W		◆				W/Sp			◆	◆		
Baccharis pilularis	20 in (50 cm)	20 in (50 cm)	S	W		◆				Sp			◆	◆		
Backhousia citriodora	20–25 ft (6–8 m)	10–15 ft (3–4.5 m)	T	W		◆	◆		◆	Su			◆			
Banksia ericifolia	8–20 ft (2.4–6 m)	15 ft (4.5 m)	S	W		◆	◆			A/W			◆	◆		
Banksia 'Giant Candles'	15 ft (4.5 m)	12 ft (3.5 m)	S	W		◆	◆			A/W				◆		
Banksia integrifolia	20–80 ft (6–24 m)	20 ft (6 m)	T	W		◆	◆			Su–W			◆	◆		
Banksia marginata	8–30 ft (2.4–9 m)	15–20 ft (4.5–6 m)	S/T	W		◆	◆			Su–W			◆	◆		
Banksia menziesii	50 ft (15 m)	15 ft (4.5 m)	T	W		◆	◆			A/W				◆		
Banksia robur	10 ft (3 m)	7 ft (2 m)	S	W		◆	◆			Su–W				◆		
Banksia serrata	15–30 ft (4.5–9 m)	5–10 ft (1.5–3 m)	T	W		◆	◆			Su–W				◆		
Banksia spinulosa	3 ft (0.9 m)	5 ft (1.5 m)	S	W		◆	◆			A/W				◆	◆	
Barleria albostellata	5 ft (1.5 m)	5 ft (1.5 m)	S	W/T		◆	◆	◆		Sp/Su				◆		
Barleria cristata	3 ft (0.9 m)	5 ft (1.5 m)	S	W/T		◆	◆			All					◆	
Barleria obtusa	3 ft (0.9 m)	3 ft (0.9 m)	S	W		◆	◆			A				◆		

Plant name	Height	Spread	Type	Climate	Deciduous	Evergreen	Showy flowers	Showy foliage	Scented flowers	Flowering season	Grow in pot/tub	Indoor use	Frost tolerant	Full sun	Half sun	Heavy shade
Bartlettina sordida	10 ft (3 m)	7 ft (2 m)	S	W/T		♦	♦		♦	Su–W				♦		
Bauera rubioides	2–6 ft (0.6–1.8 m)	7 ft (2 m)	S	W		♦	♦			W/Sp						♦
Bauera sessiliflora	6 ft (1.8 m)	6 ft (1.8 m)	S	W		♦	♦			Sp/Su						♦
Bauhinia × blakeana	30 ft (9 m)	15 ft (4.5 m)	T	W/T		♦	♦			A/W				♦		
Bauhinia galpinii	10–20 ft (3–6 m)	8 ft (2.4 m)	S	W/T		♦	♦			Su/A				♦		
Bauhinia tomentosa	15 ft (4.5 m)	10 ft (3 m)	S	W/T		♦	♦			All				♦		
Bauhinia variegata	25 ft (8 m)	25 ft (8 m)	T	W/T	♦		♦			W–Su				♦		
Berberis buxifolia	8 ft (2.4 m)	10 ft (3 m)	S	C		♦	♦			Sp			♦	♦		
Berberis × carminea	5 ft (1.5 m)	8 ft (2.4 m)	S	C	♦		♦			Sp/Su			♦	♦		
Berberis darwinii	10 ft (3 m)	10 ft (3 m)	S	C		♦	♦			Sp			♦	♦		
Berberis julianae	10 ft (3 m)	10 ft (3 m)	S	C		♦	♦			Sp			♦	♦		
Berberis × macracantha	12 ft (3.5 m)	12 ft (3.5 m)	S	C	♦		♦			Sp			♦	♦		
Berberis × ottawensis	8 ft (2.4 m)	8 ft (2.4 m)	S	C	♦		♦	♦		Sp			♦	♦		
Berberis × rubrostilla	5 ft (1.5 m)	8 ft (2.4 m)	S	C	♦		♦			Sp/Su			♦	♦		
Berberis × stenophylla	10 ft (3 m)	15 ft (4.5 m)	S	C		♦	♦			Sp			♦	♦		
Berberis thunbergii	3 ft (0.9 m)	8 ft (2.4 m)	S	C	♦		♦	♦		Sp			♦	♦		
Berberis valdiviana	15 ft (4.5 m)	15 ft (4.5 m)	S	C/W		♦	♦			Sp/Su			♦	♦		
Berberis wilsoniae	3 ft (0.9 m)	6 ft (1.8 m)	S	C	♦		♦	♦		Su			♦	♦		
Betula albosinensis	80 ft (24 m)	30 ft (9 m)	T	C	♦		♦	♦		Sp			♦	♦		
Betula ermanii	70 ft (21 m)	40 ft (12 m)	T	C	♦			♦		Sp			♦	♦		
Betula lenta	50 ft (15 m)	40 ft (12 m)	T	C	♦		♦	♦		Sp			♦	♦		
Betula mandschurica	70 ft (21 m)	30 ft (9 m)	T	C	♦			♦		Sp			♦	♦		
Betula nigra	30 ft (9 m)	15 ft (4.5 m)	T	C/W	♦			♦		Sp			♦	♦		
Betula papyrifera	60 ft (18 m)	30 ft (9 m)	T	C	♦			♦		Sp			♦	♦		
Betula pendula	80 ft (24 m)	35 ft (10 m)	T	C	♦			♦		Sp			♦	♦		
Betula platyphylla	70 ft (21 m)	40 ft (12 m)	T	C	♦		♦	♦		Sp			♦	♦		
Bixa orellana	30 ft (9 m)	10–15 ft (3–4.5 m)	T	W/T		♦	♦			Sp				♦		
Bocconia arborea	25 ft (8 m)	15 ft (4.5 m)	T	W/T		♦	♦			Su				♦	♦	
Bombax ceiba	60 ft (18 m)	30–40 ft (9–12 m)	T	W/T	♦		♦			Sp				♦		
Boronia heterophylla	6 ft (1.8 m)	4 ft (1.2 m)	S	W		♦	♦		♦	W/Sp	♦					♦
Boronia megastigma	3 ft (0.9 m)	3 ft (0.9 m)	S	W		♦	♦		♦	W/Sp	♦					♦

Plant name	Height	Spread	Type	Climate	Deciduous	Evergreen	Showy flowers	Showy foliage	Scented flowers	Flowering season	Grow in pot/tub	Indoor use	Frost tolerant	Full sun	Half sun	Heavy shade
Boronia pinnata	5 ft (1.5 m)	5 ft (1.5 m)	S	W		♦	♦		♦	W/Sp					♦	
Bouvardia longiflora	3 ft (0.9 m)	3 ft (0.9 m)	S	W		♦	♦		♦	A/W	♦				♦	
Bouvardia ternifolia	3 ft (0.9 m)	3 ft (0.9 m)	S	W		♦	♦			Su/A	♦				♦	
Brachychiton acerifolius	40 ft (12 m)	20 ft (6 m)	T	W		♦				Sp/Su				♦		
Brachychiton discolor	80 ft (24 m)	30 ft (9 m)	T	W		♦				Su				♦		
Brachychiton populneus	30 ft (9 m)	15 ft (4.5 m)	T	W		♦				Sp/Su			♦	♦		
Brachyglottis greyi	5 ft (1.5 m)	10 ft (3 m)	S	W		♦	♦	♦		Su			♦	♦		
Brachyglottis laxifolia	3 ft (0.9 m)	7 ft (2 m)	S	W		♦	♦	♦		Su			♦	♦		
Breynia disticha	4 ft (1.2 m)	3 ft (0.9 m)	S	W/T		♦		♦		Su					♦	
Broussonetia papyrifera	50 ft (15 m)	30 ft (9 m)	S	W/T	♦			♦		Su			♦	♦		
Brugmansia arborea	15 ft (4.5 m)	5–8 ft (1.5–2.4 m)	S	W/T		♦	♦			Su/A				♦		
Brugmansia × candida	10 ft (3 m)	6 ft (1.8 m)	S	W/T		♦	♦		♦	Su/A	♦			♦		
Brugmansia 'Charles Grimaldi'	6 ft (1.8 m)	4 ft (1.2 m)	S	W/T		♦	♦		♦	A–Sp	♦			♦		
Brugmansia × insignis	12 ft (3.5 m)	8–10 ft (2.4–3 m)	S	W/T		♦	♦			Su/A	♦			♦		
Brugmansia sanguinea	12 ft (3.5 m)	12 ft (3.5 m)	S	W/T		♦	♦			Su/A				♦		
Brugmansia suaveolens	15 ft (4.5 m)	10 ft (3 m)	S	W/T		♦	♦		♦	Su/A				♦		
Brunfelsia americana	15 ft (4.5 m)	4–7 ft (1.2–2 m)	S	W/T		♦	♦		♦	Su	♦				♦	
Brunfelsia pauciflora	8 ft (2.4 m)	5 ft (1.5 m)	S	W/T		♦	♦			Su	♦			♦	♦	
Buckinghamia celsissima	30 ft (9 m)	12 ft (3.5 m)	T	W/T		♦	♦			A				♦		
Buddleja alternifolia	15 ft (4.5 m)	15 ft (4.5 m)	S	C	♦		♦		♦	Sp/Su				♦	♦	
Buddleja colvilei	20 ft (6 m)	20 ft (6 m)	S	C	♦		♦	♦		Sp				♦	♦	
Buddleja davidii	10–17 ft (3–5 m)	17 ft (5 m)	S	C	♦		♦		♦	Sp/Su				♦	♦	
Buddleja globosa	10–20 ft (3–6 m)	10 ft (3 m)	S	C		♦	♦		♦	Sp/Su				♦	♦	
Buddleja salviifolia	12–25 ft (3.5–8 m)	15 ft (4.5 m)	S	C		♦	♦		♦	A/W				♦	♦	
Buddleja × weyeriana	15 ft (4.5 m)	12 ft (3.5 m)	S	C	♦		♦		♦	Sp/Su				♦	♦	
Burchellia bubalina	10 ft (3 m)	8 ft (2.4 m)	S	W		♦	♦			Sp/Su				♦		
Buxus microphylla	8 ft (2.4 m)	7 ft (2 m)	S	C/W		♦		♦		Sp				♦	♦	
Buxus sempervirens	5–30 ft (1.5–9 m)	5–15 ft (1.5–4.5 m)	S	C/W		♦		♦		Sp				♦	♦	
Buxus, Sheridan Hybrids	18–24 in (45–60 cm)	18–24 in (45–60 cm)	S	C/W		♦		♦		Sp				♦	♦	
Buxus sinica	3–20 ft (0.9–6 m)	2–12 ft (0.6–3.5 m)	S	C/W		♦		♦	♦	Sp				♦	♦	♦
Caesalpinia ferrea	50 ft (15 m)	20 ft (6 m)	T	W/T	♦		♦			Su				♦		

Plant name	Height	Spread	Type	Climate	Deciduous	Evergreen	Showy flowers	Showy foliage	Scented flowers	Flowering season	Grow in pot/tub	Indoor use	Frost tolerant	Full sun	Half sun	Heavy shade
Caesalpinia gilliesii	10 ft (3 m)	4–8 ft (1.2–2.4 m)	S	W		◆	◆	◆		Su				◆		
Caesalpinia pulcherrima	10 ft (3 m)	6–12 ft (1.8–3.5 m)	S	W		◆	◆	◆		All				◆		
Calliandra haematocephala	10 ft (3 m)	20 ft (6 m)	S	W/T		◆	◆			A/W				◆	◆	
Calliandra surinamensis	10 ft (3 m)	10 ft (3 m)	S	W/T		◆	◆			All				◆		
Calliandra tweedii	6 ft (1.8 m)	6 ft (1.8 m)	S	W		◆	◆			Sp–A				◆		
Callicarpa americana	10 ft (3 m)	7 ft (2 m)	S	C/W		◆	◆			Sp			◆	◆	◆	◆
Callicarpa bodinieri	10 ft (3 m)	8 ft (2.4 m)	S	C/W	◆		◆			Sp			◆	◆	◆	
Callicarpa japonica	6 ft (1.8 m)	5 ft (1.5 m)	S	W	◆		◆			Sp				◆	◆	
Callicoma serratifolia	12–30 ft (3.5–9 m)	10 ft (3 m)	S	W		◆	◆	◆		Sp/Su				◆		
Callistemon citrinus	10 ft (3 m)	10 ft (3 m)	S	W		◆	◆			Sp/Su				◆		
Callistemon phoeniceus	10 ft (3 m)	5 ft (1.5 m)	S	W		◆	◆			Sp/Su				◆		
Callistemon salignus	15–30 ft (4.5–9 m)	15–20 ft (4.5–6 m)	S	W		◆	◆			Sp/Su				◆		
Callistemon viminalis	25 ft (8 m)	7–10 ft (2–3 m)	S	W		◆	◆			Sp/Su				◆		
Callistemon Hybrid Cultivars	6–20 ft (1.8–6 m)	5–10 ft (1.5–3 m)	S	W		◆	◆			Sp/Su				◆		
Callitris rhomboidea	50 ft (15 m)	10–15 ft (3–4.5 m)	C	W		◆		◆		Sp			◆	◆		
Calluna vulgaris	24 in (60 cm)	30 in (75 cm)	S	C		◆	◆	◆		Su/A	◆		◆	◆		
Calocedrus decurrens	120 ft (36 m)	30 ft (9 m)	C	C		◆		◆		Sp			◆	◆		
Calodendrum capense	30 ft (9 m)	30 ft (9 m)	T	W		◆	◆			Sp/Su				◆		
Calothamnus quadrifidus	8 ft (2.4 m)	8 ft (2.4 m)	S	W		◆	◆			W/Sp				◆		
Calothamnus validus	8 ft (2.4 m)	8 ft (2.4 m)	S	W		◆	◆			W/Sp				◆		
Calycanthus floridus	10 ft (3 m)	7 ft (2 m)	S	C/W	◆		◆		◆	Sp/Su			◆	◆	◆	
Calycanthus occidentalis	10 ft (3 m)	7 ft (2 m)	S	C/W	◆		◆		◆	Sp/Su			◆	◆	◆	
Camellia grijsii	10 ft (3 m)	8 ft (2.4 m)	S	C/W		◆	◆		◆	W/SP	◆		◆		◆	
Camellia japonica	30 ft (9 m)	25 ft (8 m)	S/T	C/W		◆	◆			W/SP	◆		◆		◆	
Camellia nitidissima	10 ft (3 m)	8 ft (2.4 m)	S	W		◆	◆			W/SP					◆	
Camellia pitardii	20 ft (6 m)	12 ft (3.5 m)	S	C/W		◆	◆			W/SP	◆		◆		◆	
Camellia reticulata	30 ft (9 m)	15 ft (4.5 m)	S/T	W		◆	◆			W/SP				◆		
Camellia saluenensis	4–15 ft (1.2–4.5 m)	4–15 ft (1.2–4.5 m)	S	C/W		◆	◆			W/SP	◆		◆		◆	
Camellia sasanqua	10–25 ft (3–8 m)	5 ft (1.5 m)	S	C/W		◆	◆		◆	A	◆		◆		◆	
Camellia sinensis	8–20 ft (2.4–6 m)	10 ft (3 m)	S	C/W/T		◆	◆			W/SP	◆		◆		◆	
Camellia × *williamsii*	7–15 ft (2–4.5 m)	4–10 ft (1.2–3 m)	S/T	C/W		◆	◆			W/SP			◆		◆	

Plant name	Height	Spread	Type	Climate	Deciduous	Evergreen	Showy flowers	Showy foliage	Scented flowers	Flowering season	Grow in pot/tub	Indoor use	Frost tolerant	Full sun	Half sun	Heavy shade
Camellia Hybrid Cultivars	3–20 ft (0.9–6 m)	3–20 ft (0.9–6 m)	S	C/W		◆	◆			W/SP	◆		◆			◆
Cantua buxifolia	12 ft (3.5 m)	8 ft (2.4 m)	S	W		◆	◆			Sp/Su	◆				◆	
Caragana arborescens	10 ft (3 m)	4 ft (1.2 m)	S	C	◆		◆			Sp				◆	◆	
Caragana frutex	10 ft (3 m)	8 ft (2.4 m)	S	C	◆		◆			Sp				◆	◆	
Carica × heilbornii	6–12 ft (1.8–3.5 m)	10 ft (3 m)	S	W		◆	◆			Su	◆			◆		
Carissa edulis	5 ft (1.5 m)	5 ft (1.5 m)	S	W		◆	◆		◆	Sp/Su	◆	◆		◆	◆	
Carissa macrocarpa	7–10 ft (2–3 m)	10 ft (3 m)	S	W/T		◆	◆		◆	Sp/Su	◆	◆		◆		
Carmichaelia odorata	6 ft (1.8 m)	6 ft (1.8 m)	S	C/W		◆	◆		◆	Sp/Su				◆	◆	
Carmichaelia stevensonii	12 ft (3.5 m)	10 ft (3 m)	S	C/W		◆	◆			Sp/Su				◆	◆	
Carpenteria californica	8 ft (2.4 m)	8 ft (2.4 m)	S	W/T		◆	◆			Su				◆	◆	
Carpinus betulus	80 ft (24 m)	60 ft (18 m)	T	C	◆			◆		Sp				◆	◆	
Carpinus caroliniana	40 ft (12 m)	40 ft (12 m)	T	C	◆			◆		Sp				◆	◆	
Carya cordiformis	80 ft (24 m)	50 ft (15 m)	T	C	◆			◆		Sp				◆	◆	
Caryopteris × clandonensis	5 ft (1.5 m)	5 ft (1.5 m)	S	C/W	◆		◆			Su				◆	◆	
Caryopteris incana	5 ft (1.5 m)	5 ft (1.5 m)	S	C/W	◆		◆			Su				◆	◆	
Cassia fistula	60 ft (18 m)	20 ft (6 m)	T	W/T	◆		◆		◆	Su				◆		
Cassia javanica	50 ft (15 m)	10 ft (3 m)	T	W/T	◆		◆			Su				◆		
Cassia × nealiae	25–50 ft (8–15 m)	20–30 ft (6–9 m)	T	W/T	◆		◆		◆	Sp/Su				◆		
Cassiope lycopodioides	3 in (8 cm)	10 in (25 cm)	S	C		◆	◆			Sp/Su	◆			◆	◆	
Cassiope mertensiana	6–12 in (15–30 cm)	10 in (25 cm)	S	C		◆	◆			Sp	◆			◆	◆	
Castanospermum australe	40 ft (12 m)	40 ft (12 m)	T	W/T		◆	◆			Su				◆		
Casuarina cunninghamiana	100 ft (30 m)	25 ft (8 m)	T	W		◆		◆		Su				◆		
Casuarina equisetifolia	60 ft (18 m)	20 ft (6 m)	T	W/T		◆		◆		Su				◆		
Casuarina glauca	70 ft (21 m)	20 ft (6 m)	T	W/T		◆		◆		Su				◆		
Catalpa bignonioides	50 ft (15 m)	40 ft (12 m)	T	C/W	◆		◆	◆		Su				◆	◆	
Catalpa bungei	30 ft (9 m)	25 ft (8 m)	T	C/W	◆		◆	◆		Su				◆	◆	
Catalpa speciosa	120 ft (36 m)	90 ft (27 m)	T	C/W	◆		◆	◆		Su				◆	◆	
Ceanothus arboreus	20 ft (6 m)	12 ft (3.5 m)	S	C		◆	◆			Sp				◆	◆	
Ceanothus × delileanus	5 ft (1.5 m)	5 ft (1.5 m)	S	C	◆		◆			Su				◆	◆	
Ceanothus diversifolius	4–12 in (10–30 cm)	3–6 ft (0.9–1.8 m)	S	C		◆	◆			Sp/Su				◆	◆	
Ceanothus gloriosus	12 in (30 cm)	12 ft (3.5 m)	S	C		◆	◆			Sp				◆	◆	

Plant name	Height	Spread	Type	Climate	Deciduous	Evergreen	Showy flowers	Showy foliage	Scented flowers	Flowering season	Grow in pot/tub	Indoor use	Frost tolerant	Full sun	Half sun	Heavy shade
Ceanothus griseus	10 ft (3 m)	10 ft (3 m)	S	C		♦	♦			Sp			♦	♦		
Ceanothus hearstiorum	12 in (30 cm)	6 ft (1.8 m)	S	C		♦	♦			Sp/Su			♦	♦		
Ceanothus impressus	10 ft (3 m)	10 ft (3 m)	S	C		♦	♦			Sp			♦	♦		
Ceanothus prostratus	3 in (8 cm)	8 ft (2.4 m)	S	C		♦	♦			Sp			♦	♦		
Cedrus atlantica	80 ft (24 m)	30 ft (9 m)	C	C/W		♦		♦		A			♦	♦		
Cedrus deodara	200 ft (60 m)	30 ft (9 m)	C	C/W		♦		♦		A			♦	♦		
Cedrus libani	150 ft (45 m)	90 ft (27 m)	C	C/W		♦		♦		A			♦	♦		
Ceiba insignis	60 ft (18 m)	40 ft (12 m)	T	W/T	♦		♦			Su–W				♦		
Ceiba pentandra	230 ft (70 m)	80 ft (24 m)	T	W/T	♦		♦			Su–W				♦		
Celtis australis	60 ft (18 m)	60 ft (18 m)	S	W				♦		Sp			♦	♦		
Celtis laevigata	80 ft (24 m)	60 ft (18 m)	S	C/W				♦		Sp			♦	♦		
Celtis occidentalis	60 ft (18 m)	60 ft (18 m)	S	C/W				♦		Sp			♦	♦		
Celtis reticulata	25 ft (8 m)	25 ft (8 m)	S	C/W	♦					Sp			♦	♦		
Cephalotaxus fortunei	20 ft (6 m)	10 ft (3 m)	C	C/W		♦				Sp			♦	♦		
Cephalotaxus harringtonia	15 ft (4.5 m)	10 ft (3 m)	C	C/W		♦				Sp			♦	♦		
Ceratonia siliqua	40 ft (12 m)	25 ft (8 m)	T	W		♦	♦		♦	A			♦			
Ceratopetalum gummiferum	15 ft (4.5 m)	6 ft (1.8 m)	S	W		♦	♦			Su					♦	♦
Ceratostigma plumbaginoides	18 in (45 cm)	12 in (30 cm)	S	C	♦		♦			Su/A			♦	♦		
Ceratostigma willmottianum	3 ft (0.9 m)	5 ft (1.5 m)	S	C/W	♦		♦			Su/A			♦	♦		
Cercidiphyllum japonicum	60 ft (18 m)	35 ft (10 m)	T	C/W	♦			♦		Sp			♦	♦		
Cercis canadensis	30 ft (9 m)	30 ft (9 m)	T	C	♦		♦	♦		Sp			♦	♦		
Cercis siliquastrum	35 ft (10 m)	35 ft (10 m)	T	C/W	♦		♦	♦		Sp			♦	♦		
Cestrum aurantiacum	10 ft (3 m)	6 ft (1.8 m)	S	W		♦	♦			Sp/Su			♦	♦		
Cestrum × cultum	10 ft (3 m)	6 ft (1.8 m)	S	W		♦	♦			Sp/Su			♦	♦		
Cestrum elegans	10 ft (3 m)	8 ft (2.4 m)	S	W		♦	♦			Su/A			♦	♦		
Cestrum 'Newellii'	10 ft (3 m)	10 ft (3 m)	S	W		♦	♦			All	♦		♦	♦		
Cestrum nocturnum	10 ft (3 m)	10 ft (3 m)	S	W		♦	♦		♦	Su/A	♦		♦	♦		
Chaenomeles × californica	6 ft (1.8 m)	5 ft (1.5 m)	S	C/W	♦		♦			Sp			♦	♦	♦	
Chaenomeles japonica	3 ft (0.9 m)	6 ft (1.8 m)	S	C	♦		♦			W/Sp			♦	♦	♦	
Chaenomeles speciosa	10 ft (3 m)	15 ft (4.5 m)	S	C	♦		♦			W/Sp			♦	♦	♦	♦
Chaenomeles × superba	5 ft (1.5 m)	6 ft (1.8 m)	S	C/W	♦		♦			Sp			♦	♦	♦	♦

Plant name	Height	Spread	Type	Climate	Deciduous	Evergreen	Showy flowers	Showy foliage	Scented flowers	Flowering season	Grow in pot/tub	Indoor use	Frost tolerant	Full sun	Half sun	Heavy shade
Chamaecyparis lawsoniana	100 ft (30 m)	10–15 ft (3–4.5 m)	C	C		♦		♦		Sp			♦	♦		
Chamaecyparis obtusa	60 ft (18 m)	20 ft (6 m)	C	C/W		♦		♦		Sp			♦	♦		
Chamaecyparis pisifera	75 ft (23 m)	15 ft (4.5 m)	C	C/W		♦		♦		Sp			♦	♦		
Chamaecyparis thyoides	50 ft (15 m)	12 ft (3.5 m)	C	C		♦		♦		Sp			♦	♦		
Chamaecytisus purpureus	18 in (45 cm)	24 in (60 cm)	S	C/W	♦		♦			Su	♦		♦	♦		
Chamelaucium uncinatum	8 ft (2.4 m)	8 ft (2.4 m)	S	W		♦	♦			W	♦			♦		
Chilopsis linearis	10–20 ft (3–6 m)	8 ft (2.4 m)	S	W	♦		♦			Sp/Su			♦	♦		
Chimonanthus praecox	12 ft (3.5 m)	10 ft (3 m)	S	C/W	♦		♦		♦	W			♦	♦		
Chionanthus retusus	15–30 ft (4.5–9 m)	10 ft (3 m)	T	C/W	♦		♦			Su			♦	♦		
Chionanthus virginicus	12–25 ft (3.5–8 m)	10 ft (3 m)	T	C/W	♦		♦			Su			♦	♦		
Choisya 'Aztec Pearl'	8 ft (2.4 m)	8 ft (2.4 m)	S	W		♦	♦		♦	Sp/Su	♦			♦	♦	
Choisya ternata	6 ft (1.8 m)	6 ft (1.8 m)	S	W		♦	♦		♦	Sp/Su	♦			♦	♦	
Chorizema cordatum	4 ft (1.2 m)	4 ft (1.2 m)	S	W		♦	♦			Su–W	♦				♦	♦
Chrysophyllum cainito	50 ft (15 m)	15 ft (4.5 m)	T	W/T		♦		♦		Su				♦		
Cinnamomum camphora	60 ft (18 m)	30 ft (9 m)	T	W		♦		♦		Sp				♦		
Cistus albidus	3 ft (0.9 m)	4 ft (1.2 m)	S	W		♦	♦			Sp/Su			♦	♦		
Cistus creticus	3 ft (0.9 m)	3 ft (0.9 m)	S	W		♦	♦			Sp/Su	♦		♦	♦		
Cistus ladanifer	5 ft (1.5 m)	5 ft (1.5 m)	S	W		♦	♦			Sp/Su			♦	♦		
Cistus × pulverulentus	2 ft (0.6 m)	6 ft (1.8 m)	S	W		♦	♦			Sp/Su			♦	♦		
Cistus salviifolius	30 in (75 cm)	30 in (75 cm)	S	W		♦	♦			Sp/Su			♦	♦		
Cistus Hybrid Cultivars	2–5 ft (0.6–1.5 m)	3–6 ft (0.9–1.8 m)	S	W		♦	♦			Sp/Su	♦		♦	♦		
Citrus trifoliata	15 ft (4.5 m)	15 ft (4.5 m)	S	C/W	♦				♦	Sp/Su			♦	♦		
Cladrastis kentukea	25–40 ft (8–12 m)	30 ft (9 m)	T	C	♦		♦			Su			♦	♦		
Clematis heracleifolia	3–6 ft (0.9–1.8 m)	2–5 ft (0.6–1.5 m)	S	C	♦				♦	Su/A	♦		♦	♦	♦	
Clerodendrum bungei	8 ft (2.4 m)	8 ft (2.4 m)	S	W	♦		♦		♦	Su	♦		♦	♦	♦	
Clerodendrum trichotomum	15 ft (4.5 m)	15 ft (4.5 m)	S	W	♦		♦		♦	Su	♦			♦		♦
Clethra acuminata	12 ft (3.5 m)	12 ft (3.5 m)	S	C/W	♦		♦		♦	Su				♦		♦
Clethra alnifolia	6 ft (1.8 m)	6 ft (1.8 m)	S	C/W	♦		♦		♦	Su					♦	♦
Clethra arborea	25 ft (8 m)	20 ft (6 m)	S	W		♦	♦		♦	Su						♦
Clethra barbinervis	10 ft (3 m)	10 ft (3 m)	S	C/W	♦		♦		♦	Su/A			♦			♦
Clianthus puniceus	6 ft (1.8 m)	6 ft (1.8 m)	S	W		♦	♦			Sp/Su	♦		♦	♦	♦	

Plant name	Height	Spread	Type	Climate	Deciduous	Evergreen	Showy flowers	Showy foliage	Scented flowers	Flowering season	Grow in pot/tub	Indoor use	Frost tolerant	Full sun	Half sun	Heavy shade
Clusia major	50 ft (15 m)	50 ft (15 m)	T	W/T		♦	♦			Su				♦		
Coccoloba uvifera	20 ft (6 m)	10 ft (3 m)	T	W		♦	♦		♦	Su				♦		
Codiaeum variegatum	3–12 ft (0.9–3.5 m)	2–4 ft (0.6–1.2 m)	S	W/T		♦		♦		Su	♦	♦			♦	♦
Coffea arabica	10 ft (3 m)	10 ft (3 m)	S	W/T		♦	♦	♦	♦	A	♦	♦			♦	♦
Coleonema pulchellum	2–5 ft (0.6–1.5 m)	3–4 ft (0.9–1.2 m)	S	W		♦	♦			W/Sp	♦			♦		
Colletia hystrix	10–15 ft (3–4.5 m)	10–15 ft (3–4.5 m)	S	C/W		♦	♦		♦	Su/A			♦	♦		
Colletia paradoxa	6 ft (1.8 m)	8 ft (2.4 m)	S	C/W		♦	♦			Su/A			♦	♦		
Colutea arborescens	15 ft (4.5 m)	10 ft (3 m)	S	C/W	♦		♦	♦		Sp			♦	♦		
Combretum kraussii	40 ft (12 m)	15 ft (4.5 m)	T	W		♦	♦		♦	W/Sp				♦		
Coprosma 'Coppershine'	3–5 ft (0.9–1.5 m)	3–4 ft (0.9–1.2 m)	S	W		♦		♦		Sp	♦		♦	♦	♦	
Coprosma × *kirkii*	3 ft (0.9 m)	7 ft (2 m)	S	W		♦		♦		Sp				♦		
Coprosma repens	20 ft (6 m)	12 ft (3.5 m)	S	W		♦		♦		Sp				♦		
Coprosma rugosa	6 ft (1.8 m)	6 ft (1.8 m)	S	W		♦		♦		Sp			♦	♦		
Cordia boissieri	8 ft (2.4 m)	8 ft (2.4 m)	S	W		♦	♦			Su			♦	♦		
Cordyline australis	20 ft (6 m)	8 ft (2.4 m)	T	C/W		♦	♦	♦	♦	Su	♦		♦	♦	♦	
Cordyline fruticosa	10 ft (3 m)	4 ft (1.2 m)	S	W/T		♦	♦	♦		Su	♦				♦	
Cordyline rubra	10–15 ft (3–4.5 m)	3–7 ft (0.9–2 m)	S	W		♦	♦	♦		Su	♦				♦	
Cordyline stricta	15 ft (4.5 m)	3 ft (0.9 m)	S	W/T		♦	♦	♦		Sp/Su	♦	♦				♦
Cornus alba	10 ft (3 m)	10 ft (3 m)	S	C	♦			♦		Sp			♦	♦	♦	
Cornus capitata	30 ft (9 m)	30 ft (9 m)	T	C/W		♦	♦			Sp/Su			♦	♦		
Cornus controversa	60 ft (18 m)	50 ft (15 m)	T	C	♦		♦			Sp			♦	♦		
Cornus 'Eddie's White Wonder'	15 ft (4.5 m)	15 ft (4.5 m)	S	C	♦		♦	♦		Sp			♦	♦		
Cornus florida	30 ft (9 m)	25 ft (8 m)	T	C	♦		♦	♦		Sp			♦	♦		
Cornus kousa	25 ft (8 m)	15 ft (4.5 m)	T	C	♦		♦			Su			♦	♦		
Cornus mas	25 ft (8 m)	20 ft (6 m)	T	C	♦		♦	♦		W/Sp			♦	♦		
Cornus nuttallii	60 ft (18 m)	40 ft (12 m)	T	C	♦		♦	♦		Sp/Su			♦	♦		
Cornus sanguinea	15 ft (4.5 m)	10 ft (3 m)	T	C	♦			♦		Sp			♦	♦		
Corokia buddlejoides	10 ft (3 m)	7 ft (2 m)	S	C/W		♦		♦		Sp			♦	♦	♦	
Corokia cotoneaster	10 ft (3 m)	10 ft (3 m)	S	C/W		♦	♦			Sp			♦	♦		
Corokia × *virgata*	6 ft (1.8 m)	6 ft (1.8 m)	S	C/W		♦		♦		Sp			♦	♦		
Correa alba	3 ft (0.9 m)	6 ft (1.8 m)	S	W		♦	♦			W/Sp	♦		♦	♦	♦	

Plant name	Height	Spread	Type	Climate	Deciduous	Evergreen	Showy flowers	Showy foliage	Scented flowers	Flowering season	Grow in pot/tub	Indoor use	Frost tolerant	Full sun	Half sun	Heavy shade
Correa backhouseana	6 ft (1.8 m)	6 ft (1.8 m)	S	W		◆	◆			W/Sp	◆		◆	◆		
Correa pulchella	3 ft (0.9 m)	3 ft (0.9 m)	S	W		◆	◆			W/Sp	◆		◆	◆	◆	
Correa reflexa	2–6 ft (0.6–1.8 m)	1–7 ft (0.3–2 m)	S	W		◆	◆			W/Sp	◆		◆	◆	◆	
Correa Hybrid Cultivars	18 in–6 ft (45 cm–1.8 m)	2–4 ft (0.6–1.2 m)	S	W		◆	◆			W/Sp	◆					◆
Corylopsis sinensis	15 ft (4.5 m)	15 ft (4.5 m)	S	C	◆		◆			Sp/Su			◆			◆
Corylopsis spicata	6 ft (1.8 m)	10 ft (3 m)	S	C	◆		◆			Sp			◆			◆
Corymbia citriodora	100 ft (30 m)	35 ft (10 m)	T	W/T		◆	◆			Su/A				◆		
Corymbia ficifolia	30 ft (9 m)	15 ft (4.5 m)	T	W		◆	◆	◆	◆	Su				◆		
Corynocarpus laevigata	50 ft (15 m)	25 ft (8 m)	T	W		◆			◆	Sp	◆			◆		
Cotinus coggygria	15 ft (4.5 m)	15 ft (4.5 m)	S	C/W	◆		◆	◆		Su			◆	◆		
Cotinus 'Grace'	20 ft (6 m)	15 ft (4.5 m)	S	C/W	◆		◆	◆		Su			◆	◆		
Cotinus obovatus	30 ft (9 m)	20 ft (6 m)	T	C/W	◆		◆	◆		Su			◆	◆		
Cotoneaster dammeri	8 in (20 cm)	6 ft (1.8 m)	S	C/W		◆	◆			Su			◆	◆		
Cotoneaster franchetii	10 ft (3 m)	10 ft (3 m)	S	C/W		◆	◆			Su			◆	◆		
Cotoneaster frigidus	30 ft (9 m)	30 ft (9 m)	S	C/W	◆		◆			Su			◆	◆		
Cotoneaster horizontalis	3 ft (0.9 m)	5 ft (1.5 m)	S	C/W	◆		◆			Sp			◆	◆		
Cotoneaster lacteus	12 ft (3.5 m)	12 ft (3.5 m)	S	C/W		◆	◆			Su			◆	◆		
Cotoneaster microphyllus	3 ft (0.9 m)	3 ft (0.9 m)	S	C/W		◆	◆			Sp/Su			◆	◆		
Cotoneaster salicifolius	15 ft (4.5 m)	15 ft (4.5 m)	S	C/W		◆	◆			Su			◆	◆		
Cotoneaster simonsii	8 ft (2.4 m)	6 ft (1.8 m)	S	C/W	◆		◆			Su			◆	◆		
Cotoneaster × watereri	15 ft (4.5 m)	15 ft (4.5 m)	S	C/W		◆	◆			Su			◆	◆		
Couroupita guianensis	100 ft (30 m)	15 ft (4.5 m)	T	W/T		◆	◆			Sp				◆		
Crataegus 'Autumn Glory'	10 ft (3 m)	10 ft (3 m)	S	C/W	◆		◆			Su			◆	◆		
Crataegus crus-galli	30 ft (9 m)	35 ft (10 m)	T	C/W	◆		◆	◆		Sp			◆	◆		
Crataegus laciniata	20 ft (6 m)	20 ft (6 m)	T	C	◆		◆			Su			◆	◆		
Crataegus laevigata	25 ft (8 m)	25 ft (8 m)	T	C	◆		◆			Sp			◆	◆		
Crataegus × lavalleei	20 ft (6 m)	20 ft (6 m)	T	C/W	◆		◆			Su			◆	◆		
Crataegus monogyna	25 ft (8 m)	25 ft (8 m)	T	C	◆		◆			W/Sp			◆	◆		
Crataegus persimilis 'Prunifolia'	20 ft (6 m)	25 ft (8 m)	T	C	◆		◆			Sp/Su			◆	◆		
Crataegus phaenopyrum	30 ft (9 m)	30 ft (9 m)	T	C	◆		◆	◆	◆	Su			◆	◆		
Crataegus punctata	30 ft (9 m)	30 ft (9 m)	T	C	◆		◆			Su			◆	◆		

Plant name	Height	Spread	Type	Climate	Deciduous	Evergreen	Showy flowers	Showy foliage	Scented flowers	Flowering season	Grow in pot/tub	Indoor use	Frost tolerant	Full sun	Half sun	Heavy shade
Crescentia cujete	30 ft (9 m)	20 ft (6 m)	T	W/T		♦	♦	♦		Sp				♦	♦	
Crowea exalata	18–36 in (45–90 cm)	12–60 in (30–150 cm)	S	W		♦	♦			All	♦				♦	
Crowea saligna	3 ft (0.9 m)	3 ft (0.9 m)	S	W		♦	♦			A/W	♦				♦	
Cryptomeria japonica	90 ft (27 m)	20 ft (6 m)	C	C/W		♦		♦		Sp				♦	♦	
Cunninghamia lanceolata	70 ft (21 m)	20 ft (6 m)	C	C/W		♦		♦		Sp				♦	♦	
Cunonia capensis	50 ft (15 m)	15 ft (4.5 m)	S	W		♦	♦		♦	Su/A					♦	
Cupaniopsis anacardioides	50 ft (15 m)	15–30 ft (4.5–9 m)	S	W		♦	♦	♦		Sp/Su					♦	
Cuphea hyssopifolia	18 in (45 cm)	15 in (38 cm)	S	W/T		♦	♦			Sp–A	♦	♦			♦	
Cuphea ignea	24 in (60 cm)	30 in (75 cm)	S	W/T		♦	♦			Sp–A	♦	♦			♦	
Cuphea micropetala	30 in (75 cm)	30 in (75 cm)	S	W/T		♦	♦			Su/A	♦				♦	
Cuphea × purpurea	18 in (45 cm)	18 in (45 cm)	S	W		♦	♦			Sp/Su	♦	♦			♦	
Cupressus arizonica	40 ft (12 m)	15 ft (4.5 m)	C	C/W		♦		♦		Sp			♦	♦		
Cupressus cashmeriana	30 ft (9 m)	20 ft (6 m)	C	C/W		♦		♦		Sp				♦	♦	
Cupressus funebris	70–80 ft (21–24 m)	25–30 ft (8–9 m)	C	C/W		♦		♦		Sp				♦	♦	
Cupressus lusitanica	40 ft (12 m)	20 ft (6 m)	C	C/W		♦		♦		Sp				♦	♦	
Cupressus macrocarpa	100 ft (30 m)	35 ft (10 m)	C	C/W		♦		♦		Sp				♦	♦	
Cupressus sempervirens	50 ft (15 m)	15 ft (4.5 m)	C	C/W		♦		♦		Sp	♦			♦	♦	
Cupressus torulosa	60 ft (18 m)	15 ft (4.5 m)	C	C/W		♦		♦		Sp				♦	♦	
× Cuprocyparis leylandii	120 ft (36 m)	15 ft (4.5 m)	C	C/W		♦		♦		Sp				♦	♦	
Cussonia spicata	30 ft (9 m)	12 ft (3.5 m)	T	W		♦	♦			Sp/Su					♦	
Cytisus ardoinoi	10–24 in (25–60 cm)	10–24 in (25–60 cm)	S	C	♦		♦			Sp/Su	♦			♦	♦	
Cytisus × kewensis	18 in (45 cm)	5 ft (1.5 m)	S	C		♦	♦			Sp/Su	♦			♦	♦	
Cytisus multiflorus	10 ft (3 m)	8 ft (2.4 m)	S	C		♦	♦			Su				♦	♦	
Cytisus × praecox	5 ft (1.5 m)	5 ft (1.5 m)	S	C/W	♦		♦		♦	Sp/Su				♦	♦	
Cytisus scoparius	7 ft (2 m)	7 ft (2 m)	S	C	♦		♦			Su				♦	♦	
Cytisus Hybrid Cultivars	3–8 ft (0.9–2.4 m)	3–6 ft (0.9–1.8 m)	S	C/W	♦	♦	♦		♦	Sp/Su	♦			♦	♦	
Daboecia cantabrica	15 in (38 cm)	26 in (65 cm)	S	C		♦	♦			Su/A				♦	♦	
Dacrydium cupressinum	90–200 ft (27–60 m)	30 ft (9 m)	C	W		♦		♦		Sp				♦	♦	
Dais cotinifolia	10 ft (3 m)	10 ft (3 m)	T	W		♦	♦			Su					♦	
Daphne bholua	10 ft (3 m)	4 ft (1.2 m)	S	C/W		♦	♦		♦	W/Sp				♦		♦
Daphne cneorum	8 in (20 cm)	24 in (60 cm)	S	C/W		♦	♦		♦	Sp	♦			♦		♦

Plant name	Height	Spread	Type	Climate	Deciduous	Evergreen	Showy flowers	Showy foliage	Scented flowers	Flowering season	Grow in pot/tub	Indoor use	Frost tolerant	Full sun	Half sun	Heavy shade
Daphne genkwa	5 ft (1.5 m)	5 ft (1.5 m)	S	C/W	◆		◆		◆	Sp			◆		◆	
Daphne gnidium	6 ft (1.8 m)	4 ft (1.2 m)	S	W		◆	◆		◆	Sp/Su	◆		◆		◆	
Daphne laureola	5 ft (1.5 m)	5 ft (1.5 m)	S	C/W		◆	◆		◆	W/Sp			◆		◆	
Daphne mezereum	4 ft (1.2 m)	3 ft (0.9 m)	S	C/W	◆		◆		◆	W/Sp			◆		◆	
Daphne odora	5 ft (1.5 m)	5 ft (1.5 m)	S	W		◆	◆		◆	W/Sp	◆		◆		◆	
Daphne pontica	5 ft (1.5 m)	5 ft (1.5 m)	S	C/W		◆	◆		◆	Sp	◆		◆		◆	
Daphne tangutica	6 ft (1.8 m)	5 ft (1.5 m)	S	C/W		◆	◆		◆	Sp/Su	◆		◆		◆	
Darwinia citriodora	5 ft (1.5 m)	5 ft (1.5 m)	S	W		◆	◆	◆		W–Su	◆				◆	
Davidia involucrata	60 ft (18 m)	30 ft (9 m)	T	C	◆		◆			Sp			◆	◆		
Delonix regia	30 ft (9 m)	30 ft (9 m)	T	W/T	◆		◆	◆		Su				◆		
Dendromecon rigida	10 ft (3 m)	10 ft (3 m)	S	W		◆	◆			Su			◆	◆		
Desfontainia spinosa	10 ft (3 m)	10 ft (3 m)	S	C/W		◆	◆	◆		Su/A	◆		◆		◆	
Deutzia × elegantissima	5 ft (1.5 m)	5 ft (1.5 m)	S	C	◆		◆			Su			◆	◆		
Deutzia gracilis	3–6 ft (0.9–1.8 m)	3–6 ft (0.9–1.8 m)	S	C	◆		◆			Sp/Su			◆	◆		
Deutzia × kalmiiflora	5 ft (1.5 m)	5 ft (1.5 m)	S	C	◆		◆			Su			◆	◆		
Deutzia × magnifica	6 ft (1.8 m)	7 ft (2 m)	S	C	◆		◆			Su			◆	◆		
Deutzia × rosea	3 ft (0.9 m)	3 ft (0.9 m)	S	C	◆		◆			Su			◆	◆		
Deutzia scabra	10 ft (3 m)	7 ft (2 m)	S	C	◆		◆		◆	Su			◆	◆		
Dillenia alata	25 ft (8 m)	12 ft (3.5 m)	T	W/T		◆	◆	◆		Sp/Su				◆		
Dillenia indica	30–50 ft (9–15 m)	12 ft (3.5 m)	T	W/T		◆	◆	◆		Sp/Su					◆	
Dimocarpus longan	40 ft (12 m)	20 ft (6 m)	T	W/T		◆	◆	◆		Sp					◆	
Disanthus cercidifolius	20 ft (6 m)	10 ft (3 m)	S	C	◆			◆		A			◆	◆		
Dodonaea viscosa	10 ft (3 m)	5 ft (1.5 m)	S	W		◆		◆		Sp			◆	◆	◆	
Dombeya cacuminum	40 ft (12 m)	20 ft (6 m)	T	W/T		◆	◆	◆		Su/A				◆		
Dombeya tiliacea	25 ft (8 m)	12 ft (3.5 m)	T	W/T		◆	◆	◆		Su/A				◆		
Dracaena draco	30 ft (9 m)	12 ft (3.5 m)	T	W/T		◆		◆		Su	◆			◆		
Dracaena fragrans	10–30 ft (3–9 m)	6 ft (1.8 m)	T	W/T		◆	◆	◆		Su	◆			◆	◆	
Dracaena marginata	7–17 ft (2–5 m)	3–10 ft (0.9–3 m)	T	W/T		◆		◆		Su	◆			◆	◆	◆
Dracaena reflexa	8 ft (2.4 m)	3 ft (0.9 m)	T	W/T		◆	◆	◆	◆	Sp	◆			◆		
Dracaena sanderiana	5 ft (1.5 m)	16–32 in (40–80 cm)	T	W/T		◆		◆		Su	◆			◆		
Drimys winteri	50 ft (15 m)	30 ft (9 m)	T	W		◆	◆		◆	Sp/Su			◆	◆	◆	

Plant name	Height	Spread	Type	Climate	Deciduous	Evergreen	Showy flowers	Showy foliage	Scented flowers	Flowering season	Grow in pot/tub	Indoor use	Frost tolerant	Full sun	Half sun	Heavy shade
Dryandra formosa	10 ft (3 m)	7 ft (2 m)	S	W		◆	◆	◆		W/Sp				◆		
Dryandra quercifolia	10 ft (3 m)	10 ft (3 m)	S	W		◆	◆	◆		W/Sp				◆		
Duranta erecta	15 ft (4.5 m)	8 ft (2.4 m)	T	W/T		◆	◆			A				◆		
Duranta stenostachya	4–6 ft (1.2–1.8 m)	4–5 ft (1.2–1.5 m)	S	W/T		◆	◆		◆	Su	◆			◆		
Edgeworthia chrysantha	8 ft (2.4 m)	6 ft (1.8 m)	S	C/W	◆		◆		◆	W/Sp	◆		◆			◆
Elaeagnus × ebbingei	12 ft (3.5 m)	12 ft (3.5 m)	S	C		◆	◆	◆	◆	A			◆	◆		
Elaeagnus macrophylla	10 ft (3 m)	12 ft (3.5 m)	S	C/W		◆	◆	◆	◆	A			◆	◆		
Elaeagnus multiflora	10 ft (3 m)	10 ft (3 m)	S	C		◆	◆	◆	◆	Sp			◆	◆		
Elaeagnus pungens	15 ft (4.5 m)	20 ft (6 m)	S	C/W		◆		◆		A			◆	◆		
Elaeagnus umbellata	30 ft (9 m)	30 ft (9 m)	S	C		◆	◆	◆	◆	Sp/Su			◆	◆		
Elaeocarpus hookerianus	40–80 ft (12–24 m)	15–30 ft (4.5–9 m)	T	W		◆		◆		Sp/Su						◆
Elaeocarpus reticulatus	15–30 ft (4.5–9 m)	15 ft (4.5 m)	S	W		◆	◆	◆		Sp/Su						◆
Embothrium coccineum	40 ft (12 m)	20 ft (6 m)	T	W		◆	◆			Sp/Su				◆		
Empetrum nigrum	12 in (30 cm)	15 in (38 cm)	S	C		◆		◆		Sp/Su	◆		◆	◆		
Enkianthus campanulatus	15 ft (4.5 m)	15 ft (4.5 m)	S	C	◆		◆	◆		Sp/Su			◆	◆		
Enkianthus cernuus	8 ft (2.4 m)	8 ft (2.4 m)	S	C	◆		◆	◆		Sp/Su			◆	◆		
Enkianthus perulatus	7 ft (2 m)	7 ft (2 m)	S	C	◆		◆			Sp			◆	◆		
Epacris impressa	3 ft (0.9 m)	30 in (75 cm)	S	W		◆	◆			W/Sp			◆			◆
Epacris longiflora	3 ft (0.9 m)	3 ft (0.9 m)	S	W		◆	◆			W/Sp	◆					◆
Ephedra distachya	3 ft (0.9 m)	3 ft (0.9 m)	S	C		◆		◆		Sp				◆		
Ephedra viridis	4 ft (1.2 m)	3 ft (0.9 m)	S	C/W		◆		◆		Sp			◆	◆		
Epigaea repens	4–8 in (10–20 cm)	12–24 in (30–60 cm)	S	C		◆	◆		◆	Sp	◆		◆			◆
Eranthemum pulchellum	4 ft (1.2 m)	3 ft (0.9 m)	S	W/T		◆	◆			Sp				◆		
Eremophila maculata	3–8 ft (0.9–2.4 m)	3–10 ft (0.9–3 m)	S	W		◆	◆			A–Sp	◆			◆		
Eremophila nivea	5 ft (1.5 m)	5 ft (1.5 m)	S	W		◆	◆	◆		W/Sp	◆			◆		
Erica arborea	15 ft (4.5 m)	10 ft (3 m)	S	C/W		◆	◆		◆	Sp			◆	◆		
Erica canaliculata	6 ft (1.8 m)	4 ft (1.2 m)	S	W		◆	◆			W/Sp				◆		
Erica carnea	12 in (30 cm)	22 in (55 cm)	S	C/W		◆	◆			W/Sp			◆	◆	◆	
Erica cerinthoides	2–5 ft (0.6–1.5 m)	3 ft (0.9 m)	S	W		◆	◆			W/Sp	◆			◆		
Erica cinerea	24 in (60 cm)	30 in (75 cm)	S	C/W		◆	◆	◆		Su/A			◆	◆		
Erica × darleyensis	12 in (30 cm)	24 in (60 cm)	S	C/W		◆	◆	◆		W/Sp			◆	◆		

Plant name	Height	Spread	Type	Climate	Deciduous	Evergreen	Showy flowers	Showy foliage	Scented flowers	Flowering season	Grow in pot/tub	Indoor use	Frost tolerant	Full sun	Half sun	Heavy shade
Erica erigena	8 ft (2.4 m)	3 ft (0.9 m)	S	C/W		♦	♦	♦	♦	W/Sp			♦	♦		
Erica lusitanica	5–10 ft (1.5–3 m)	3 ft (0.9 m)	S	W		♦	♦			W/Sp			♦	♦		
Erica mammosa	5 ft (1.5 m)	6 ft (1.8 m)	S	W		♦	♦			Sp/Su	♦			♦		
Erica manipuliflora	3 ft (0.9 m)	3 ft (0.9 m)	S	W		♦	♦			Su/A			♦	♦		
Erica melanthera	24 in (60 cm)	18 in (45 cm)	S	W		♦	♦			Sp/Su	♦			♦		
Erica regia	3 ft (0.9 m)	3 ft (0.9 m)	S	W		♦	♦			Sp	♦			♦		
Erica scoparia	6 ft (1.8 m)	3 ft (0.9 m)	S	W		♦	♦			Su				♦		
Erica tetralix	12 in (30 cm)	20 in (50 cm)	S	C		♦	♦	♦		Su/A			♦	♦		
Erica vagans	30 in (75 cm)	30 in (75 cm)	S	C		♦	♦			Su/A			♦	♦		
Erica ventricosa	20 in (50 cm)	20 in (50 cm)	S	W		♦	♦			Sp	♦			♦		
Erica × williamsii	30 in (75 cm)	18 in (45 cm)	S	C		♦	♦			Su/A			♦	♦		
Eriostemon australasius	6 ft (1.8 m)	3 ft (0.9 m)	S	W		♦	♦			W/Sp					♦	♦
Erythrina acanthocarpa	6 ft (1.8 m)	6 ft (1.8 m)	S	W	♦		♦			Sp/Su				♦		
Erythrina × bidwillii	12 ft (3.5 m)	10 ft (3 m)	S	W/T	♦		♦			Sp/Su				♦		
Erythrina crista-galli	30 ft (9 m)	12–40 ft (3.5–12 m)	T	W	♦		♦			Sp/Su				♦		
Erythrina humeana	12 ft (3.5 m)	7 ft (2 m)	S	W	♦		♦			Su				♦		
Erythrina × sykesii	50 ft (15 m)	30 ft (9 m)	T	W	♦		♦			W/Sp				♦		
Erythrina variegata	30–60 ft (9–18 m)	30 ft (9 m)	T	T	♦		♦			W				♦		
Escallonia bifida	15–30 ft (4.5–9 m)	10–20 ft (3–6 m)	T	W		♦	♦		♦	A			♦	♦		
Escallonia × exoniensis	15–20 ft (4.5–6 m)	12 ft (3.5 m)	T	W		♦	♦			Sp–A			♦	♦		
Escallonia rubra	15 ft (4.5 m)	15 ft (4.5 m)	S	W		♦	♦			Su			♦	♦		
Escallonia Hybrid Cultivars	5–10 ft (1.5–3 m)	6–12 ft (1.8–3.5 m)	S	W		♦	♦			Su/A			♦	♦		
Eucalyptus bicostata	120 ft (36 m)	25–50 ft (8–15 m)	T	W		♦		♦		Sp/Su			♦	♦		
Eucalyptus caesia	20 ft (6 m)	15 ft (4.5 m)	T	W/T		♦	♦			Sp–A				♦		
Eucalyptus camaldulensis	150 ft (45 m)	50 ft (15 m)	T	W/T		♦	♦			Sp/Su				♦		
Eucalyptus cinerea	50 ft (15 m)	30 ft (9 m)	T	W/T		♦		♦		Su			♦	♦		
Eucalyptus erythrocorys	25 ft (8 m)	10 ft (3 m)	T	W/T		♦	♦			Su/A				♦		
Eucalyptus forrestiana	15 ft (4.5 m)	12 ft (3.5 m)	T	W/T		♦	♦	♦		Su/A				♦		
Eucalyptus glaucescens	20–70 ft (6–21 m)	20 ft (6 m)	T	W		♦		♦		A			♦	♦		
Eucalyptus globulus	180 ft (55 m)	40 ft (12 m)	T	W/T		♦		♦		Sp				♦		
Eucalyptus grandis	200 ft (60 m)	30–50 ft (9–15 m)	T	W/T		♦		♦		W				♦		

Plant name	Height	Spread	Type	Climate	Deciduous	Evergreen	Showy flowers	Showy foliage	Scented flowers	Flowering season	Grow in pot/tub	Indoor use	Frost tolerant	Full sun	Half sun	Heavy shade
Eucalyptus gunnii	80 ft (24 m)	25 ft (8 m)	T	C/W		◆		◆		Sp/Su			◆	◆		
Eucalyptus leucoxylon	100 ft (30 m)	20–40 ft (6–12 m)	T	W		◆	◆			A–Sp				◆		
Eucalyptus macrocarpa	6–12 ft (1.8–3.5 m)	12 ft (3.5 m)	S	W		◆	◆		◆	W/Sp				◆		
Eucalyptus mannifera	70 ft (21 m)	30 ft (9 m)	T	W		◆		◆		Su/A			◆	◆		
Eucalyptus microcorys	60–180 ft (18–55 m)	40 ft (12 m)	T	W/T		◆	◆	◆		W–Su				◆	◆	◆
Eucalyptus nicholii	50 ft (15 m)	20–40 ft (6–12 m)	T	W/T		◆		◆		A			◆	◆		
Eucalyptus pauciflora	60 ft (18 m)	20 ft (6 m)	T	C/W		◆		◆		Sp/Su			◆	◆		
Eucalyptus perriniana	20–40 ft (6–12 m)	10–20 ft (3–6 m)	T	C/W		◆	◆	◆		Su			◆	◆		
Eucalyptus polyanthemos	25–80 ft (8–24 m)	20 ft (6 m)	T	W/T		◆		◆		Sp			◆	◆		
Eucalyptus pulverulenta	15–30 ft (4.5–9 m)	12 ft (3.5 m)	T	W		◆		◆		Sp			◆	◆		
Eucalyptus regnans	320 ft (96 m)	30–60 ft (9–18 m)	T	W		◆		◆		Su			◆	◆		
Eucalyptus rhodantha	10 ft (3 m)	10 ft (3 m)	S	W/T		◆	◆	◆		Sp/A				◆		
Eucalyptus urnigera	40 ft (12 m)	15–30 ft (4.5–9 m)	T	C/W		◆	◆			Su/A			◆	◆		
Eucalyptus viminalis	80–180 ft (24–55 m)	35 ft (10 m)	T	W		◆		◆		Su			◆	◆		
Eucryphia glutinosa	30 ft (9 m)	20 ft (6 m)	T	W		◆	◆			Su			◆	◆		
Eucryphia × intermedia	30 ft (9 m)	15 ft (4.5 m)	T	W		◆	◆			Sp–A			◆	◆		
Eucryphia lucida	25 ft (8 m)	15 ft (4.5 m)	T	W		◆	◆			Su			◆	◆		
Eucryphia × nymansensis	30 ft (9 m)	15 ft (4.5 m)	T	W		◆	◆			Sp–A			◆	◆		
Eugenia uniflora	10–30 ft (3–9 m)	8 ft (2.4 m)	S	W/T		◆	◆		◆	Su						◆
Euonymus alatus	6 ft (1.8 m)	10 ft (3 m)	S	C/W	◆			◆		Su			◆	◆		
Euonymus americanus	8 ft (2.4 m)	6 ft (1.8 m)	S	C/W	◆			◆		Su			◆	◆		
Euonymus europaeus	20 ft (6 m)	8 ft (2.4 m)	S	C/W	◆			◆		Sp			◆	◆		
Euonymus fortunei	1–10 ft (0.3–3 m)	3–10 ft (0.9–3 m)	S	C/W		◆		◆		Su			◆	◆		
Euonymus japonicus	12 ft (3.5 m)	6–12 ft (1.8–3.5 m)	S	C/W		◆		◆		Su			◆	◆		
Euphorbia fulgens	5 ft (1.5 m)	30 in (75 cm)	S	W		◆		◆		W	◆	◆		◆		
Euphorbia pulcherrima	10 ft (3 m)	7 ft (2 m)	S	W/T		◆		◆		W	◆	◆		◆		
Euptelea pleiosperma	15–30 ft (4.5–9 m)	15 ft (4.5 m)	T	C	◆			◆		Sp			◆	◆		
Euryops acraeus	12–36 in (30–90 cm)	36 in (90 cm)	S	W		◆	◆	◆		Sp/Su	◆			◆		
Euryops chrysanthemoides	4 ft (1.2 m)	5 ft (1.5 m)	S	W/T		◆	◆			W/Sp				◆		
Euryops pectinatus	4 ft (1.2 m)	5 ft (1.5 m)	S	W/T		◆	◆	◆		All	◆			◆	◆	
Exochorda giraldii	10 ft (3 m)	10 ft (3 m)	S	C	◆		◆			Sp				◆	◆	

Plant name	Height	Spread	Type	Climate	Deciduous	Evergreen	Showy flowers	Showy foliage	Scented flowers	Flowering season	Grow in pot/tub	Indoor use	Frost tolerant	Full sun	Half sun	Heavy shade
Exochorda × macrantha	7 ft (2 m)	10 ft (3 m)	S	C	◆		◆			Sp			◆	◆		
Exochorda racemosa	10 ft (3 m)	10 ft (3 m)	S	C	◆		◆		◆	Sp			◆	◆		
Fabiana imbricata	8 ft (2.4 m)	7 ft (2 m)	S	W		◆	◆			Su			◆	◆		
Fagus crenata	30 ft (9 m)	20 ft (6 m)	T	C	◆			◆		Sp			◆	◆		
Fagus grandifolia	80 ft (24 m)	35 ft (10 m)	T	C	◆			◆		Sp			◆	◆		
Fagus japonica	80 ft (24 m)	25 ft (8 m)	T	C	◆			◆		Sp			◆	◆	◆	
Fagus sylvatica	100 ft (30 m)	50 ft (15 m)	T	C	◆			◆		Sp			◆	◆		
× Fatshedera lizei	6 ft (1.8 m)	8 ft (2.4 m)	S	C/W/T		◆		◆		A	◆	◆	◆		◆	◆
Fatsia japonica	6–12 ft (1.8–3.5 m)	6–12 ft (1.8–3.5 m)	S	C/W		◆	◆	◆		Su/A	◆		◆		◆	◆
Ficus benghalensis	30–40 ft (9–12 m)	75–400 ft (23–120 m)	T	T		◆		◆		Sp				◆		
Ficus benjamina	80 ft (24 m)	50 ft (15 m)	T	W/T		◆		◆		Sp	◆	◆		◆		
Ficus elastica	40–100 ft (12–30 m)	40–100 ft (12–30 m)	T	T		◆		◆		Sp	◆	◆		◆		
Ficus lyrata	30 ft (9 m)	30 ft (9 m)	T	W/T		◆		◆		Sp	◆	◆		◆		
Ficus macrophylla	80–100 ft (24–30 m)	130 ft (40 m)	T	W/T		◆		◆		Sp				◆		
Ficus microcarpa	40–70 ft (12–21 m)	20–50 ft (6–15 m)	T	W/T		◆		◆		Sp				◆		
Ficus religiosa	30–40 ft (9–12 m)	25 ft (8 m)	T	W/T	◆			◆		Sp				◆		
Ficus rubiginosa	30–80 ft (9–24 m)	35–70 ft (10–21 m)	T	W/T		◆		◆		Sp				◆		
Firmiana simplex	60 ft (18 m)	35 ft (10 m)	T	C/W	◆		◆	◆		Sp			◆	◆		
Forsythia × intermedia	15 ft (4.5 m)	7 ft (2 m)	S	C	◆		◆			Sp			◆	◆		
Forsythia ovata	5 ft (1.5 m)	8 ft (2.4 m)	S	C	◆		◆			Sp			◆	◆		
Forsythia suspensa	12 ft (3.5 m)	10 ft (3 m)	S	C	◆		◆			Sp			◆	◆		
Forsythia viridissima	10 ft (3 m)	10 ft (3 m)	S	C	◆		◆			Sp			◆	◆		
Forsythia Hybrid Cultivars	5–10 ft (1.5–3 m)	10 ft (3 m)	S	C	◆		◆			Sp			◆	◆		
Fothergilla gardenii	3 ft (0.9 m)	3 ft (0.9 m)	S	C	◆		◆		◆	Sp			◆	◆		
Fothergilla major	5–10 ft (1.5–3 m)	6 ft (1.8 m)	S	C	◆		◆		◆	Sp/Su			◆	◆		
Franklinia alatamaha	20 ft (6 m)	12 ft (3.5 m)	T	C/W	◆		◆	◆		Su/A			◆		◆	
Fraxinus americana	80 ft (24 m)	50 ft (15 m)	T	C/W	◆			◆		Sp			◆	◆		
Fraxinus angustifolia	80 ft (24 m)	40 ft (12 m)	T	C/W	◆			◆		Sp			◆	◆		
Fraxinus chinensis	80 ft (24 m)	25 ft (8 m)	T	C	◆		◆	◆		Sp			◆	◆		
Fraxinus excelsior	100 ft (30 m)	60 ft (18 m)	T	C/W	◆		◆	◆		Sp			◆	◆		
Fraxinus nigra	50 ft (15 m)	25 ft (8 m)	T	C/W	◆			◆		Sp			◆	◆		

Plant name	Height	Spread	Type	Climate	Deciduous	Evergreen	Showy flowers	Showy foliage	Scented flowers	Flowering season	Grow in pot/tub	Indoor use	Frost tolerant	Full sun	Half sun	Heavy shade
Fraxinus ornus	50 ft (15 m)	40 ft (12 m)	T	C/W	♦		♦	♦		Sp			♦	♦		
Fraxinus pennsylvanica	70 ft (21 m)	70 ft (21 m)	T	C/W	♦		♦	♦		Sp			♦	♦		
Fraxinus uhdei	25 ft (8 m)	15 ft (4.5 m)	T	W		♦	♦	♦		Sp			♦	♦		
Fraxinus velutina	30 ft (9 m)	30 ft (9 m)	T	C/W	♦			♦		Sp			♦	♦		
Fremontodendron californicum	12–25 ft (3.5–8 m)	15 ft (4.5 m)	S	W		♦	♦			Sp/Su			♦	♦		
Fremontodendron mexicanum	20 ft (6 m)	12 ft (3.5 m)	S	W/T		♦	♦			Sp–A				♦		
Fremontodendron Hybrid Cultivars	12–20 ft (3.5–6 m)	10–15 ft (3–4.5 m)	S	W		♦	♦			Sp/Su			♦	♦		
Fuchsia arborescens	6 ft (1.8 m)	5 ft (1.5 m)	S	W/T		♦	♦			Su	♦			♦	♦	
Fuchsia boliviana	12 ft (3.5 m)	3–4 ft (0.9–1.2 m)	S	W/T		♦	♦	♦		Su/A	♦			♦		
Fuchsia coccinea	5–20 ft (1.6–6 m)	4 ft (1.2 m)	S	W/T		♦	♦			Su				♦	♦	
Fuchsia fulgens	5 ft (1.5 m)	30 in (75 cm)	S	T		♦	♦	♦		Su/A	♦			♦	♦	
Fuchsia magellanica	10 ft (3 m)	6 ft (1.8 m)	S	C/W	♦		♦	♦		Su/A				♦	♦	
Fuchsia procumbens	6 in (15 cm)	3 ft (0.9 m)	S	W/T		♦	♦			Su	♦	♦		♦	♦	
Fuchsia splendens	8 ft (2.4 m)	3 ft (0.9 m)	S	W/T		♦	♦			Su	♦			♦	♦	
Fuchsia thymifolia	36 in 90 cm)	20 in (50 cm)	S	W/T		♦	♦			Su/A	♦		♦	♦	♦	♦
Fuchsia triphylla	6 ft (1.8 m)	2 ft (0.6 m)	S	T		♦	♦	♦		Su/A	♦	♦		♦	♦	♦
Fuchsia Hybrid Cultivars	1–7 ft (0.3–2 m)	18–36 in (45–90 cm)	S	C/W	♦	♦	♦	♦		Su/A	♦	♦		♦	♦	♦
Garcinia mangostana	50 ft (15 m)	15 ft (4.5 m)	T	T		♦		♦		Sp					♦	
Gardenia augusta	5–8 ft (1.5–2.4 m)	5 ft (1.5 m)	S	W/T		♦	♦	♦	♦	Su	♦	♦		♦	♦	
Gardenia thunbergia	12 ft (3.5 m)	7 ft (2 m)	S	W/T		♦	♦	♦	♦	Su				♦		
Garrya elliptica	8–12 ft (2.4–3.5 m)	6 ft (1.8 m)	S	W		♦	♦			W/Sp			♦	♦		
Garrya fremontii	7–10 ft (2–3 m)	6 ft (1.8 m)	S	W		♦	♦			Su/A			♦	♦		
Gaultheria depressa	4 in (10 cm)	10 in (25 cm)	S	C/W		♦	♦			Su				♦	♦	
Gaultheria mucronata	18–60 in (45–150 cm)	48 in (120 cm)	S	C/W		♦	♦			Sp			♦	♦	♦	
Gaultheria procumbens	6 in (15 cm)	36 in (90 cm)	S	C/W		♦	♦			Su			♦	♦	♦	
Gaultheria shallon	5 ft (1.5 m)	5 ft (1.5 m)	S	C/W		♦	♦			Sp			♦	♦	♦	
Gaultheria × wisleyensis	3 ft (0.9 m)	3 ft (0.9 m)	S	C/W		♦	♦			Su			♦	♦	♦	
Geijera parviflora	40 ft (12 m)	35 ft (10 m)	T	W/T		♦	♦			Sp			♦	♦		
Genista aetnensis	25 ft (8 m)	25 ft (8 m)	S	W		♦	♦		♦	Su/A			♦	♦		
Genista lydia	24 in (60 cm)	36 in (90 cm)	S	C/W	♦		♦			Sp/Su			♦	♦		
Genista sagittalis	6 in (15 cm)	36 in (90 cm)	S	C/W	♦		♦			Sp/Su			♦	♦		

Plant name	Height	Spread	Type	Climate	Deciduous	Evergreen	Showy flowers	Showy foliage	Scented flowers	Flowering season	Grow in pot/tub	Indoor use	Frost tolerant	Full sun	Half sun	Heavy shade
Genista × spachiana	10–20 ft (3–6 m)	17 ft (5 m)	S	W/T		◆	◆			W/Sp	◆	◆		◆		
Genista tinctoria	3 ft (0.9 m)	3 ft (0.9 m)	S	C/W	◆		◆			Su			◆	◆		
Ginkgo biloba	100 ft (30 m)	25 ft (8 m)	T	C/W	◆			◆		Sp			◆	◆		
Gleditsia triacanthos	150 ft (45 m)	70 ft (21 m)	T	C/W	◆			◆		Sp			◆	◆		
Glyptostrobus pensilis	80 ft (24 m)	20 ft (6 m)	C	W	◆					Sp			◆	◆		
Gordonia axillaris	12–20 ft (3.5–6 m)	12 ft (3.5 m)	S	W		◆	◆			W/Sp	◆			◆		◆
Gordonia lasianthus	50 ft (15 m)	30 ft (9 m)	S	W		◆	◆			Su	◆					◆
Graptophyllum pictum	6 ft (1.8 m)	30 in (75 cm)	S	W/T		◆		◆		Su	◆			◆		
Grevillea aquifolium	6 ft (1.8 m)	6 ft (1.8 m)	S	W		◆	◆			W–Su			◆	◆		
Grevillea banksii	10–30 ft (3–9 m)	7 ft (2 m)	S/T	W/T		◆	◆	◆		Sp				◆		
Grevillea curviloba	6 ft (1.8 m)	4 ft (1.2 m)	S	W		◆	◆		◆	Sp			◆	◆		
Grevillea × gaudichaudii	4 in (10 cm)	10 ft (3 m)	S	W		◆	◆	◆		Sp/Su	◆		◆	◆		
Grevillea juniperina	8 ft (2.4 m)	7 ft (2 m)	S	W		◆	◆			Sp/Su			◆	◆		
Grevillea lanigera	5 ft (1.5 m)	4 ft (1.2 m)	S	C/W		◆	◆			W/Sp			◆	◆		
Grevillea lavandulacea	3 ft (0.9 m)	3 ft (0.9 m)	S	W		◆	◆			Sp/Su			◆	◆		
Grevillea robusta	60 ft (18 m)	30 ft (9 m)	T	W/T		◆	◆	◆		Sp/Su			◆	◆		
Grevillea rosmarinifolia	6 ft (1.8 m)	6 ft (1.8 m)	S	W		◆	◆			W–Su			◆	◆		
Grevillea thelemanniana	3 ft (0.9 m)	6 ft (1.8 m)	S	W/T		◆	◆			W/Sp				◆		
Grevillea victoriae	6 ft (1.8 m)	6 ft (1.8 m)	S	W		◆	◆	◆		Sp/Su			◆	◆		
Grevillea Hybrid Cultivars	6 in–20 ft (15 cm–6 m)	4–15 ft (1.2–4.5 m)	S	W		◆	◆			W–Su				◆	◆	
Grewia occidentalis	10 ft (3 m)	10 ft (3 m)	S	W/T		◆	◆			Sp/Su	◆					
Greyia sutherlandii	15 ft (4.5 m)	7 ft (2 m)	S	W/T	◆		◆	◆		W/Sp						
Griselinia littoralis	25 ft (8 m)	15 ft (4.5 m)	S	W/T		◆		◆		Sp	◆			◆	◆	
Gymnocladus dioica	75 ft (23 m)	12 ft (3.5 m)	T	C	◆			◆		Su			◆	◆		
Hakea bucculenta	8 ft (2.4 m)	7 ft (2 m)	S	W		◆	◆			W/Sp				◆		
Hakea cristata	12 ft (3.5 m)	8 ft (2.4 m)	S	W/T		◆	◆			W				◆		
Hakea laurina	25 ft (8 m)	8 ft (2.4 m)	S	W/T		◆	◆			A/W				◆		
Hakea microcarpa	6 ft (1.8 m)	6 ft (1.8 m)	S	C/W		◆	◆			W/Sp			◆	◆		
Hakea myrtoides	18 in (45 cm)	15 in (38 cm)	S	W/T		◆	◆			W/Sp				◆		
Hakea purpurea	6–10 ft (1.8–3 m)	6–10 ft (1.8–3 m)	S	W/T		◆	◆			W/Sp				◆		
Hakea salicifolia	20 ft (6 m)	12 ft (3.5 m)	S	C/W		◆	◆			Sp			◆	◆		

Plant name	Height	Spread	Type	Climate	Deciduous	Evergreen	Showy flowers	Showy foliage	Scented flowers	Flowering season	Grow in pot/tub	Indoor use	Frost tolerant	Full sun	Half sun	Heavy shade
Halesia carolina	25 ft (8 m)	25–30 ft (8–10 m)	T	C	◆		◆			Sp			◆	◆		
Halesia monticola	30 ft (9 m)	20 ft (6 m)	T	C	◆		◆			Sp			◆	◆		
× *Halimiocistus wintonensis*	24 in (60 cm)	30 in (75 cm)	S	C/W		◆	◆			Su	◆		◆	◆		
Halimium halimifolium	3 ft (0.9 m)	3 ft (0.9 m)	S	C/W		◆	◆			Sp/Su			◆	◆		
Halimium lasianthum	3 ft (0.9 m)	4 ft (1.2 m)	S	W		◆	◆			Sp/Su			◆	◆		
Halimium Hybrid Cultivars	3 ft (0.9 m)	3 ft (0.9 m)	S	W		◆	◆			Su			◆	◆		
Halleria lucida	35 ft (10 m)	12 ft (3.5 m)	T	W		◆	◆			W/Sp			◆	◆		
Hamamelis × *intermedia*	12 ft (3.5 m)	12 ft (3.5 m)	S	C	◆		◆	◆	◆	W/Sp				◆		◆
Hamamelis japonica	15 ft (4.5 m)	12 ft (3.5 m)	S	C/W	◆		◆		◆	W/Sp				◆		◆
Hamamelis mollis	15 ft (4.5 m)	12 ft (3.5 m)	S	C	◆		◆		◆	W/Sp				◆		◆
Hamamelis virginiana	12–15 ft (3.5–4.5 m)	8–12 ft (2.4–3.5 m)	S	C	◆		◆		◆	A				◆		◆
Harpephyllum caffrum	30 ft (9 m)	25 ft (8 m)	T	W/T		◆		◆		Sp				◆		
Hebe albicans	18–24 in (45–60 cm)	27 in (70 cm)	S	W		◆	◆	◆		Su/A	◆		◆	◆		
Hebe × *andersonii*	3–7 ft (0.9–2 m)	4 ft (1.2 m)	S	W/T		◆	◆			Su/A	◆			◆		
Hebe armstrongii	3 ft (0.9 m)	3 ft (0.9 m)	S	C/W		◆		◆		Su			◆	◆		
Hebe cupressoides	3 ft (0.9 m)	3 ft (0.9 m)	S	C/W		◆		◆		Su			◆	◆		
Hebe diosmifolia	36 in (90 cm)	24 in (60 cm)	S	W/T		◆	◆			Sp	◆			◆		
Hebe elliptica	3–7 ft (0.9–2 m)	4 ft (1.2 m)	S	W/T		◆	◆	◆		Su/A				◆		
Hebe × *franciscana*	3 ft (0.9 m)	4 ft (1.2 m)	S	W/T		◆	◆	◆		Su/A	◆			◆		
Hebe odora	3 ft (0.9 m)	4 ft (1.2 m)	S	C/W		◆	◆			Sp/Su				◆		
Hebe pinguifolia	10 in (25 cm)	30 in (75 cm)	S	C/W		◆	◆	◆		Sp–A			◆	◆		
Hebe salicifolia	8 ft (2.4 m)	7 ft (2 m)	S	C/W		◆	◆			Su			◆	◆		
Hebe speciosa	3 ft (0.9 m)	3 ft (0.9 m)	S	W/T		◆	◆			Su/A	◆			◆		
Hebe topiaria	3 ft (0.9 m)	3 ft (0.9 m)	S	W/T		◆		◆		Su				◆		
Hebe Hybrid Cultivars	12 in–5 ft (30 cm–1.5 m)	12 in–5 ft (30 cm–1.5 m)	S	W/T		◆	◆	◆		Sp–A	◆			◆		
Helianthemum croceum	12–14 in (30–35 cm)	16–20 in (40–50 cm)	S	C/W		◆	◆			Sp/Su			◆	◆		
Helianthemum nummularium	20 in (50 cm)	24 in (60 cm)	S	C/W		◆	◆			Sp/Su				◆		
Helianthemum Hybrid Cultivars	6–12 in (15–30 cm)	18–36 in (45–90 cm)	S	C/W		◆	◆	◆		Sp/Su			◆	◆		
Heptacodium miconioides	10–15 ft (3–4.5 m)	7–10 ft (2–3 m)	S	C	◆		◆		◆	Su/A				◆		◆
Heteromeles arbutifolia	12 ft (3.5 m)	12 ft (3.5 m)	S	W		◆	◆		◆	Su				◆	◆	
Hibbertia miniata	15 in (38 cm)	8 in (20 cm)	S	W/T		◆	◆			Sp/Su	◆					◆

Plant name	Height	Spread	Type	Climate	Deciduous	Evergreen	Showy flowers	Showy foliage	Scented flowers	Flowering season	Grow in pot/tub	Indoor use	Frost tolerant	Full sun	Half sun	Heavy shade
Hibbertia stellaris	30 in (75 cm)	30 in (75 cm)	S	W/T		◆	◆			Sp–A	◆					◆
Hibiscus coccineus	7 ft (2 m)	2–3 ft (0.6–0.9 m)	S	W/T	◆		◆			Su			◆	◆		
Hibiscus heterophyllus	10–20 ft (3–6 m)	6–10 ft (1.8–3 m)	S	W/T		◆	◆			All				◆		
Hibiscus moscheutos	8 ft (2.4 m)	40 in (100 cm)	S	C/W	◆		◆			Sp/Su			◆	◆		
Hibiscus mutabilis	10–15 ft (3–4.5 m)	6–8 ft (1.8–2.4 m)	S	W	◆		◆			Su/A			◆	◆		
Hibiscus pedunculatus	4–6 ft (1.2–1.8 m)	5 ft (1.5 m)	S	W/T		◆	◆			All				◆		
Hibiscus rosa-sinensis	8–30 ft (2.4–9 m)	5 ft (1.5 m)	S	W/T		◆	◆			Su–W	◆			◆		
Hibiscus schizopetalus	10 ft (3 m)	6 ft (1.8 m)	S	W/T		◆	◆			Su/A				◆		
Hibiscus syriacus	8–20 ft (2.4–6 m)	6–10 ft (1.8–3 m)	S	C/W	◆		◆			Su/A			◆	◆		
Hibiscus tiliaceus	25 ft (8 m)	10–20 ft (3–6 m)	S	W/T		◆	◆			Su				◆		
Hibiscus trionum	12–24 in (30–60 cm)	12 in (30 cm)	S	W/T	◆		◆			Su/A				◆		
Hoheria lyallii	7–12 (2–3.5 m)	10 ft (3 m)	T	W	◆		◆			Su/A			◆	◆		
Hoheria sexstylosa	15–25 ft (4.5–8 m)	20 ft (6 m)	T	W/T		◆	◆		◆	Su/A			◆	◆		
Holmskioldia sanguinea	3–6 ft (0.9–1.8 m)	6 ft (1.8 m)	S	W/T		◆	◆			Sp–A	◆			◆	◆	
Holodiscus discolor	12 ft (3.5 m)	12 ft (3.5 m)	S	C/W	◆		◆			Su			◆	◆	◆	
Homalocladium platycladum	6–10 ft (1.8–3 m)	6 ft (1.8 m)	S	W/T		◆	◆			Sp				◆		
Hydrangea arborescens	3–12 ft (0.9–3.5 m)	8 ft (2.4 m)	S	C/W	◆		◆			Su				◆	◆	
Hydrangea aspera	10 ft (3 m)	10 ft (3 m)	S	C/W	◆		◆	◆		Su/A				◆	◆	
Hydrangea heteromalla	10–15 ft (3–4.5 m)	10 ft (3 m)	S	C/W	◆		◆			Su				◆	◆	
Hydrangea macrophylla	10 ft (3 m)	8 ft (2.4 m)	S	C/W	◆		◆	◆		Su/A				◆	◆	◆
Hydrangea paniculata	6–20 ft (1.8–6 m)	10 ft (3 m)	S	C/W	◆		◆			Su/A				◆	◆	
Hydrangea 'Preziosa'	5 ft (1.5 m)	5 ft (1.5 m)	S	C/W	◆		◆	◆		Su	◆			◆	◆	◆
Hydrangea quercifolia	3–8 ft (0.9–2.4 m)	8 ft (2.4 m)	S	C/W	◆		◆			Su				◆	◆	◆
Hydrangea serrata	3–6 ft (0.9–1.8 m)	5 ft (1.5 m)	S	C/W	◆			◆		Su				◆	◆	◆
Hymenosporum flavum	30 ft (9 m)	12 ft (3.5 m)	T	W/T		◆	◆			Sp				◆		
Hypericum balearicum	10 in (25 cm)	10 in (25 cm)	S	C/W		◆	◆			Su	◆			◆	◆	
Hypericum beanii	2–6 ft (0.6–1.8 m)	6 ft (1.8 m)	S	C/W		◆	◆			Su			◆			
Hypericum calycinum	8–24 in (20–60 cm)	5 ft (1.5 m)	S	C/W		◆	◆			Su/A	◆			◆		◆
Hypericum empetrifolium	2 ft (0.6 m)	3 ft (0.9 m)	S	C/W		◆	◆	◆		Su				◆	◆	
Hypericum 'Hidcote'	4 ft (1.2 m)	4 ft (1.2 m)	S	C/W		◆	◆			Su/A			◆	◆		
Hypericum lancasteri	3 ft (0.9 m)	3 ft (0.9 m)	S	C/W	◆		◆			Su				◆	◆	

Plant name	Height	Spread	Type	Climate	Deciduous	Evergreen	Showy flowers	Showy foliage	Scented flowers	Flowering season	Grow in pot/tub	Indoor use	Frost tolerant	Full sun	Half sun	Heavy shade
Hypericum × moserianum	12–16 in (30–40 cm)	24–32 in (60–80 cm)	S	C/W		◆	◆	◆		Su/A			◆	◆		
Hypericum olympicum	10 in (25 cm)	15 in (38 cm)	S	C/W	◆		◆			Su			◆	◆		
Hypericum prolificum	6 ft (1.8 m)	5 ft (1.5 m)	S	C/W	◆		◆			Su			◆	◆		
Hypericum 'Rowallane'	6 ft (1.8 m)	4 ft (1.2 m)	S	C/W		◆	◆			Su/A			◆	◆		
Hypoestes aristata	3 ft (0.9 m)	26 in (65 cm)	S	W/T		◆	◆			A					◆	
Hypoestes phyllostachya	3 ft (0.9 m)	30 in (75 cm)	S	W/T		◆		◆		A	◆	◆			◆	
Idesia polycarpa	50 ft (15 m)	35 ft (10 m)	T	C/W	◆		◆		◆	Su			◆	◆		
Ilex × altaclerensis	70 ft 921 m)	20 ft (6 m)	T	C/W		◆	◆	◆		Sp/Su			◆	◆		
Ilex aquifolium	40–80 ft (12–24 m)	25 ft (8 m)	T	C/W		◆	◆	◆		Sp/Su			◆	◆		
Ilex × aquipernyi	20 ft (6 m)	12 ft (3.5 m)	T	C/W		◆	◆			Sp/Su			◆	◆		
Ilex cassine	40 ft (12 m)	15 ft (4.5 m)	T	C/W		◆	◆			Sp/Su			◆	◆		
Ilex cornuta	6–12 ft (1.8–3.5 m)	6–12 ft (1.8–3.5 m)	S	C/W		◆	◆			Sp/Su			◆	◆		
Ilex crenata	15 ft (4.5 m)	12 ft (3.5 m)	S	C/W		◆	◆			Sp/Su			◆	◆		
Ilex decidua	6–20 ft (1.8–6 m)	6–15 ft (1.8–4.5 m)	S	C/W	◆		◆			Sp/Su			◆	◆		
Ilex glabra	10 ft (3 m)	10 ft (3 m)	S	C/W		◆	◆			Sp/Su			◆	◆		
Ilex × koehneana	20 ft (6 m)	12 ft (3.5 m)	T	C/W		◆	◆	◆		Sp			◆	◆		
Ilex × meserveae	6–15 ft (1.8–4.5 m)	10 ft (3 m)	S	C/W		◆	◆			Sp/Su			◆	◆		
Ilex mitis	30 ft (9 m)	20 ft (6 m)	T	W/T		◆	◆			Sp/Su			◆	◆		
Ilex opaca	50 ft (15 m)	35 ft (10 m)	T	C/W		◆	◆	◆		Sp/Su			◆	◆		
Ilex pedunculosa	30 ft (9 m)	20 ft (6 m)	T	C/W		◆	◆			Sp/Su			◆	◆		
Ilex pernyi	30 ft (9 m)	12 ft (3.5 m)	S	C/W		◆	◆			Sp/Su			◆	◆		
Ilex serrata	15 ft (4.5 m)	10 ft (3 m)	S	C/W	◆		◆	◆		Sp/Su			◆	◆		
Ilex verticillata	15 ft (4.5 m)	15 ft (4.5 m)	S	C/W	◆		◆	◆		Sp/Su			◆	◆		
Ilex vomitoria	20 ft (6 m)	12 ft (3.5 m)	S	C/W		◆	◆			Sp/Su			◆	◆		◆
Ilex Hybrid Cultivars	8–20 ft (2.4–6 m)	5–15 ft (1.5–4.5 m)	S/T	C/W		◆	◆	◆		Sp/Su	◆		◆	◆		
Illicium anisatum	25 ft (8 m)	20 ft (6 m)	S	W/T		◆	◆		◆	Sp			◆			◆
Illicium floridanum	10 ft (3 m)	8 ft (2.4 m)	S	W/T		◆	◆		◆	Sp/Su			◆			◆
Indigofera australis	6 ft (1.8 m)	6 ft (1.8 m)	S	W/T		◆	◆	◆		Su				◆		
Indigofera decora	30 in (75 cm)	4 ft (1.2 m)	S	C/W	◆		◆			Su/A	◆		◆	◆		
Indigofera heterantha	8 ft (2.4 m)	8 ft (2.4 m)	S	C/W	◆		◆			Su			◆	◆		
Indigofera kirilowii	2–5 ft (0.6–1.5 m)	3–6 ft (0.9–1.8 m)	S	C/W	◆		◆			Su			◆	◆		

Plant name	Height	Spread	Type	Climate	Deciduous	Evergreen	Showy flowers	Showy foliage	Scented flowers	Flowering season	Grow in pot/tub	Indoor use	Frost tolerant	Full sun	Half sun	Heavy shade
Indigofera potaninii	3–5 ft (0.9–1.5 m)	4 ft (1.2 m)	S	C/W	◆		◆	◆		Su/A			◆	◆		
Iochroma coccineum	10 ft (3 m)	6 ft (1.8 m)	S	W/T		◆	◆			Su				◆		
Iochroma cyaneum	10 ft (3 m)	5 ft (1.5 m)	S	W/T		◆	◆	◆		Su				◆		
Iochroma grandiflorum	8 ft (2.4 m)	6 ft (1.8 m)	S	W/T		◆	◆			Su/A				◆		
Isopogon dubius	5 ft (1.5 m)	5 ft (1.5 m)	S	W/T		◆	◆			W/Sp				◆		
Isopogon formosus	6 ft (1.8 m)	6 ft (1.8 m)	S	W/T		◆	◆			W/Sp				◆		
Itea ilicifolia	15 ft (4.5 m)	10 ft (3 m)	S	C/W		◆	◆		◆	Su			◆	◆		
Itea virginica	4–10 ft (1.2–3 m)	5 ft (1.5 m)	S	C	◆		◆	◆	◆	Sp/Su			◆	◆		
Ixora chinensis	6 ft (1.8 m)	5 ft (1.5 m)	S	W/T		◆	◆			Sp–A	◆	◆				
Ixora coccinea	8 ft (2.4 m)	8 ft (2.4 m)	S	T		◆	◆			All	◆	◆				
Ixora Hybrid Cultivars	1–6 ft (0.3–1.8 m)	1–3 ft (0.3–0.9 m)	S	T		◆	◆			All	◆	◆				
Jacaranda cuspidifolia	15–40 ft (4.5–12 m)	30 ft (9 m)	T	W/T	◆		◆	◆		Sp/Su				◆		
Jacaranda mimosifolia	25–50 ft (8–15 m)	20–35 ft (6–10 m)	T	W/T	◆		◆	◆		Sp/Su				◆		
Jasminum humile	12 ft (3.5 m)	12 ft (3.5 m)	S	W		◆	◆		◆	Su			◆	◆	◆	
Jasminum mesnyi	10 ft (3 m)	10 ft (3 m)	S	W		◆	◆			Su			◆	◆	◆	
Jasminum nudiflorum	10 ft (3 m)	10 ft (3 m)	S	C/W	◆		◆		◆	W			◆	◆	◆	
Jatropha integerrima	10–20 ft (3–6 m)	4–8 ft (1.2–2.4 m)	S	W/T		◆	◆		◆	Sp–A	◆			◆		
Jatropha multifida	12 ft (3.5 m)	10 ft (3 m)	S	W/T		◆	◆	◆		Su	◆			◆		
Juglans ailanthifolia	50 ft (15 m)	40 ft (12 m)	T	C/W	◆			◆		Sp			◆	◆		
Juglans californica	30 ft (9 m)	30 ft (9 m)	T	C/W	◆			◆		Sp			◆	◆		
Juglans cinerea	60 ft (18 m)	50 ft (15 m)	T	C/W	◆			◆		Sp			◆	◆		
Juniperus chinensis	30 ft (9 m)	15 ft (4.5 m)	C	C/W		◆		◆		Sp	◆		◆	◆		
Juniperus communis	20 ft (6 m)	3–15 ft (0.9–4.5 m)	C	C		◆		◆		Sp			◆	◆		
Juniperus conferta	2 ft (0.6 m)	5–8 ft (1.5–2.4 m)	C	C		◆		◆		Sp			◆	◆		
Juniperus deppeana	20 ft (6 m)	7 ft (2 m)	C	C		◆		◆		Sp			◆	◆		
Juniperus horizontalis	18 in (45 cm)	12 ft (3.5 m)	C	C/W		◆		◆		Sp			◆	◆		
Juniperus osteosperma	12–20 ft (3.5–6 m)	20 ft (6 m)	C	C		◆		◆		Sp			◆	◆		
Juniperus × pfitzeriana	4–10 ft (1.2–3 m)	5–15 ft (1.5–4.5 m)	C	C/W		◆		◆		Sp	◆		◆	◆		
Juniperus procumbens	30 in (75 cm)	12 ft (3.5 m)	C	C		◆		◆		Su/Sp			◆	◆		
Juniperus recurva	30 ft (9 m)	15 ft (4.5 m)	C	C		◆		◆		Sp			◆	◆		
Juniperus sabina	12 ft (3.5 m)	15 ft (4.5 m)	C	C/W		◆		◆		Sp			◆	◆		

Plant name	Height	Spread	Type	Climate	Deciduous	Evergreen	Showy flowers	Showy foliage	Scented flowers	Flowering season	Grow in pot/tub	Indoor use	Frost tolerant	Full sun	Half sun	Heavy shade
Juniperus scopulorum	30 ft (9 m)	15 ft (4.5 m)	C	C		◆		◆		Sp	◆		◆	◆		
Juniperus squamata	2–20 ft (0.6–6 m)	15 ft (4.5 m)	C	C		◆		◆		Sp				◆	◆	
Juniperus virginiana	40 ft (12 m)	12–20 ft (3.5–6 m)	T	C/W		◆		◆		Sp				◆	◆	
Justicia adhatoda	6–8 ft (1.8–2.4 m)	3–5 ft (0.9–1.5 m)	S	W/T		◆	◆			Su				◆	◆	
Justicia aurea	3–5 ft (0.9–1.5 m)	3 ft (0.9 m)	S	W/T		◆	◆			Su/A	◆	◆				◆
Justicia brandegeeana	36 in (90 cm)	26 in (65 cm)	S	W/T		◆	◆			Sp–A	◆	◆		◆	◆	
Justicia carnea	3–6 ft (0.9–1.8 m)	3 ft (0.9 m)	S	W/T		◆	◆			Su/A	◆				◆	
Justicia rizzinii	10–22 in (25–55 cm)	10–22 in (25–55 cm)	S	W/T		◆	◆			W/Sp	◆	◆		◆	◆	
Justicia spicigera	6 ft (1.8 m)	5 ft (1.5 m)	S	W/T		◆	◆			Sp–A	◆			◆		
Kalmia angustifolia	3 ft (0.9 m)	5 ft (1.5 m)	S	C		◆	◆			Su				◆		◆
Kalmia latifolia	10 ft (3 m)	10 ft (3 m)	S	C		◆	◆			Sp/Su	◆			◆		
Kalmia polifolia	2 ft (0.6 m)	3 ft (0.9 m)	S	C		◆	◆			Sp				◆		◆
Kalopanax septemlobus	20–60 ft (6–18 m)	10–30 ft (3–9 m)	T	C/W	◆			◆		Su			◆	◆		
Kerria japonica	6 ft (1.8 m)	5 ft (1.5 m)	S	C/W	◆		◆			Sp			◆	◆	◆	
Kigelia africana	40 ft (12 m)	12 ft (3.5 m)	T	W/T		◆	◆	◆	◆	Su				◆		
Koelreuteria bipinnata	30 ft (9 m)	25 ft (8 m)	T	W/T	◆		◆		◆	Su/A				◆		
Koelreuteria paniculata	30 ft (9 m)	30 ft (9 m)	T	C/W	◆		◆		◆	Su				◆		
Kolkwitzia amabilis	12 ft (3.5 m)	12 ft (3.5 m)	S	C/W	◆		◆			Sp/Su				◆	◆	
Kunzea ambigua	12 ft (3.5 m)	12 ft (3.5 m)	S	W/T		◆	◆			Sp/Su				◆		
Kunzea baxteri	8 ft (2.4 m)	8 ft (2.4 m)	S	W/T		◆	◆			W/Sp				◆		
Kunzea parvifolia	5 ft (1.5 m)	5 ft (1.5 m)	S	W		◆	◆			Sp/Su			◆	◆		
Kunzea pulchella	6 ft (1.8 m)	6 ft (1.8 m)	S	W/T		◆	◆			W/Sp				◆		
+ *Laburnocytisus adamii*	25 ft (8 m)	15 ft (4.5 m)	T	C	◆		◆			Sp			◆	◆		
Laburnum alpinum	25 ft (8 m)	25 ft (8 m)	T	C	◆		◆			Su				◆	◆	
Laburnum anagyroides	25 ft (8 m)	25 ft (8 m)	T	C	◆		◆			Sp/Su				◆	◆	
Laburnum × watereri	25 ft (8 m)	25 ft (8 m)	T	C	◆		◆			Sp/Su				◆	◆	
Lagerstroemia floribunda	40 ft (12 m)	15 ft (4.5 m)	T	T	◆		◆			Su/A				◆		
Lagerstroemia indica	20 ft (6 m)	20 ft (6 m)	T	W/T	◆		◆	◆		Su/A				◆	◆	
Lagerstroemia speciosa	30–50 ft (9–15 m)	30 ft (9 m)	T	W/T	◆		◆	◆		Su/A				◆		
Lagerstroemia Hybrid Cultivars	15–25 ft (4.5–8 m)	8–25 ft (2.4–8 m)	T	W/T	◆		◆	◆		Su/A	◆			◆	◆	
Lagunaria patersonia	25–50 ft (8–15 m)	15 ft (4.5 m)	T	W/T		◆	◆			Su	◆			◆		

Plant name	Height	Spread	Type	Climate	Deciduous	Evergreen	Showy flowers	Showy foliage	Scented flowers	Flowering season	Grow in pot/tub	Indoor use	Frost tolerant	Full sun	Half sun	Heavy shade
Lantana camara	4–12 ft (1.2–3.5 m)	8–30 ft (2.4–9 m)	S	W/T		♦	♦			All	♦			♦		
Lantana montevidensis	3 ft (0.9 m)	10 ft (3 m)	S	W/T		♦	♦		♦	All	♦			♦		
Larix decidua	165 ft (50 m)	12–20 ft (3.5–6 m)	C	C	♦			♦		Sp			♦	♦		
Larix kaempferi	100 ft (30 m)	12–20 ft (3.5–6 m)	C	C	♦			♦		Sp			♦	♦		
Larix laricina	60 ft 918 m)	12–20 ft (3.5–6 m)	C	C	♦			♦		Sp			♦	♦		
Larix × marschlinsii	90 ft (27 m)	20 ft (6 m)	C	C	♦			♦		Sp			♦	♦		
Larix occidentalis	180 ft (55 m)	15 ft (4.5 m)	C	C	♦			♦		Sp			♦	♦		
Lavandula × allardii	3 ft (0.9 m)	3 ft (0.9 m)	S	W/T		♦	♦	♦	♦	Su	♦		♦	♦		
Lavandula angustifolia	2–3 ft (0.6–0.9 m)	4 ft (1.2 m)	S	C/W		♦	♦	♦	♦	Sp/Su	♦		♦	♦		
Lavandula dentata	3–5 ft (0.9–1.5 m)	5 ft (1.5 m)	S	W/T		♦	♦	♦	♦	Sp/Su	♦			♦		
Lavandula × intermedia	3 ft (0.9 m)	3 ft (0.9 m)	S	C/W		♦	♦	♦	♦	Sp/Su	♦		♦	♦		
Lavandula lanata	3 ft (0.9 m)	3 ft (0.9 m)	S	C/W		♦	♦	♦	♦	Su	♦		♦	♦		
Lavandula latifolia	3 ft (0.9 m)	4 ft (1.2 m)	S	C/W		♦	♦	♦	♦	Su	♦			♦		
Lavandula pinnata	3 ft (0.9 m)	3 ft (0.9 m)	S	W/T		♦	♦	♦	♦	Sp–A	♦			♦		
Lavandula stoechas	24 in (60 cm)	24 in (60 cm)	S	W/T		♦	♦	♦	♦	Su	♦		♦	♦		
Lavandula viridis	36 in (90 cm)	30 in (75 cm)	S	W/T		♦	♦	♦	♦	Su	♦		♦	♦		
Lavatera olbia	6 ft (1.8 m)	5 ft (1.5 m)	S	W		♦	♦			Su			♦	♦		
Leptospermum laevigatum	10–20 ft (3–6 m)	10–15 ft (3–4.5 m)	S	W/T		♦	♦			Sp					♦	
Leptospermum nitidum	8 ft (2.4 m)	6 ft (1.8 m)	S	W		♦	♦			Su			♦	♦		
Leptospermum petersonii	20 ft (6 m)	10 ft (3 m)	S	W/T		♦	♦			Su				♦		
Leptospermum rotundifolium	6 ft (1.8 m)	10 ft (3 m)	S	W		♦	♦			Sp			♦	♦		
Leptospermum scoparium	6 ft (1.8 m)	6 ft (1.8 m)	S	W		♦	♦			Sp/Su			♦	♦		
Leptospermum spectabile	10 ft (3 m)	6 ft (1.8 m)	S	W/T		♦	♦			Sp				♦		
Leptospermum squarrosum	6 ft (1.8 m)	5 ft (1.5 m)	S	W/T		♦	♦			A			♦	♦		
Leschenaultia biloba	24 in (60 cm)	24 in (60 cm)	S	W/T		♦	♦			W		♦		♦		
Leschenaultia formosa	12 in (30 cm)	24 in (60 cm)	S	W/T		♦	♦			W		♦		♦		
Leucadendron argenteum	20–30 ft (6–9 m)	6–12 ft (1.8–6 m)	T	W		♦		♦		Su				♦		
Leucadendron eucalyptifolium	20 ft (6 m)	8 ft (2.4 m)	S	W		♦	♦	♦		W/Sp			♦	♦		
Leucadendron salicifolium	10 ft (3 m)	6 ft (1.8 m)	S	W		♦	♦	♦		W/Sp			♦	♦		
Leucadendron sessile	5 ft (1.5 m)	3 ft (0.9 m)	S	W		♦	♦	♦		W			♦	♦		
Leucadendron tinctum	4 ft (1.2 m)	4 ft (1.2 m)	S	W		♦	♦	♦	♦	W			♦	♦		

Plant name	Height	Spread	Type	Climate	Deciduous	Evergreen	Showy flowers	Showy foliage	Scented flowers	Flowering season	Grow in pot/tub	Indoor use	Frost tolerant	Full sun	Half sun	Heavy shade
Leucadendron Hybrid Cultivars	4–8 ft (1.2–2.4 m)	4–8 ft (1.2–2.4 m)	S	W/T		♦	♦	♦		A–Sp	♦			♦		
Leucaena leucocephala	30 ft (9 m)	15 ft (4.5 m)	T	W/T		♦	♦	♦		Sp				♦		
Leucophyta brownii	3 ft (0.9 m)	3 ft (0.9 m)	S	W/T		♦		♦		Su/A				♦		
Leucospermum bolusii	5–6 ft (1.5–1.8 m)	5–6 ft (1.5–1.8 m)	S	W		♦	♦			Sp			♦	♦		
Leucospermum cordifolium	6 ft (1.8 m)	6 ft (1.8 m)	S	W		♦	♦			Sp	♦		♦	♦		
Leucospermum tottum	5 ft (1.5 m)	5 ft (1.5 m)	S	W		♦	♦			Sp/Su			♦	♦		
Leucospermum 'Veldfire'	5 ft (1.5 m)	5 ft (1.5 m)	S	W		♦	♦			Sp/Su	♦		♦	♦		
Leucothoe fontanesiana	6 ft (1.8 m)	7 ft (2 m)	S	C/W		♦	♦	♦		Sp			♦			♦
Leucothoe racemosa	3–8 ft (0.9–2.4 m)	5 ft (1.5 m)	S	C/W	♦		♦	♦		Sp/Su			♦			♦
Leycesteria formosa	6 ft (1.8 m)	6 ft (1.8 m)	S	C/W		♦	♦			Su/A			♦	♦		
Libocedrus plumosa	40 ft (12 m)	10 ft (3 m)	T	W/T		♦		♦		Sp	♦		♦	♦		
Ligustrum japonicum	10 ft (3 m)	8 ft (2.4 m)	S	C/W		♦	♦		♦	Su/A			♦	♦		
Ligustrum lucidum	30 ft (9 m)	30 ft (9 m)	S	W/T		♦	♦	♦	♦	A			♦	♦		
Ligustrum ovalifolium	12 ft (3.5 m)	12 ft (3.5 m)	S	C/W		♦	♦	♦	♦	Su			♦	♦		
Lindera obtusiloba	30 ft (9 m)	25 ft (9 m)	T	C/W	♦			♦		Sp			♦	♦		
Liquidambar formosana	60 ft (18 m)	30 ft (9 m)	T	W/T	♦			♦		Sp			♦	♦		
Liquidambar orientalis	25–50 ft (8–15 m)	15 ft (4.5 m)	T	W/T	♦			♦		Sp			♦	♦		
Liquidambar styraciflua	70 ft (21 m)	35 ft (10 m)	T	C/W/T	♦			♦		Sp			♦	♦		
Liriodendron tulipifera	100 ft (30 m)	40 ft (12 m)	T	C/W	♦		♦	♦		Sp			♦	♦		
Lithodora diffusa	6–12 in (15–30 cm)	24–36 in (60–90 cm)	S	C/W		♦	♦			Sp/Su			♦	♦		♦
Lomatia ferruginea	30 ft (9 m)	15 ft (4.5 m)	T	W		♦	♦	♦		Su				♦		
Lomatia polymorpha	6–12 ft (1.8–3.5 m)	5 ft (1.5 m)	T	W		♦	♦	♦		Sp/Su			♦	♦		
Lonicera fragrantissima	6 ft (1.8 m)	8 ft (2.4 m)	S	C/W	♦		♦		♦	W/Sp			♦	♦		
Lonicera involucrata	3 ft (0.9 m)	3 ft (0.9 m)	S	C/W	♦		♦			Sp			♦	♦		
Lonicera maackii	15 ft (4.5 m)	15 ft (4.5 m)	S	C/W	♦		♦		♦	Sp/Su			♦	♦		
Lonicera nitida	12 ft (3.5 m)	10 ft (3 m)	S	C/W		♦	♦			Sp			♦	♦		
Lonicera × *purpusii*	10 ft (3 m)	8 ft (2.4 m)	S	C/W	♦		♦		♦	W/Sp			♦	♦		
Lonicera syringantha	10 ft (3 m)	7 ft (2 m)	S	C/W	♦		♦		♦	Sp/Su			♦	♦	♦	
Lonicera tatarica	10 ft (3 m)	7 ft (2 m)	S	C/W	♦		♦		♦	Sp/Su			♦	♦		
Lophomyrtus bullata	8–12 ft (2.4–3.5 m)	8 ft (2.4 m)	S	W		♦		♦		Su				♦		
Lophomyrtus × *ralphii*	6 ft (1.8 m)	5 ft (1.5 m)	S	W/T		♦		♦		Su				♦		

Plant name	Height	Spread	Type	Climate	Deciduous	Evergreen	Showy flowers	Showy foliage	Scented flowers	Flowering season	Grow in pot/tub	Indoor use	Frost tolerant	Full sun	Half sun	Heavy shade
Lophostemon confertus	130 ft (40 m)	30 ft (9 m)	T	W/T		◆	◆			Su				◆		
Loropetalum chinense	6–15 ft (1.8–4.5 m)	8 ft (2.4 m)	S	W/T		◆	◆	◆		Sp	◆		◆	◆		
Luculia grandifolia	12–20 ft (3.5–6 m)	7 ft (2 m)	S	W		◆	◆		◆	Su	◆			◆	◆	
Luculia gratissima	10–20 ft (3–6 m)	10–15 ft (3–4.5 m)	S	W		◆	◆		◆	A/W	◆			◆	◆	
Luma apiculata	20 ft (6 m)	20 ft (6 m)	T	W		◆	◆			Sp/Su				◆	◆	
Lupinus arboreus	3–7 ft (0.9–2 m)	4–8 ft (1.2–2.4 m)	S	W		◆	◆			Sp/Su			◆	◆		
Mackaya bella	8 ft (2.4 m)	4 ft (1.2 m)	S	W/T		◆	◆			Sp–A	◆			◆	◆	
Maclura pomifera	50 ft (15 m)	30 ft (9 m)	T	C/W	◆			◆		Su			◆	◆	◆	
Magnolia acuminata	100 ft (30 m)	30 ft (9 m)	T	C/W	◆		◆			Su			◆	◆		
Magnolia campbellii	100 ft (30 m)	30 ft (9 m)	T	C/W	◆		◆			W/Sp			◆	◆		
Magnolia denudata	30 ft (9 m)	30 ft (9 m)	T	C/W	◆		◆		◆	Su				◆	◆	
Magnolia fraseri	40 ft (12 m)	30 ft (9 m)	T	C/W	◆		◆		◆	Sp/Su				◆		
Magnolia grandiflora	35 ft (10 m)	35 ft (10 m)	T	C/W		◆	◆	◆	◆	Su				◆		
Magnolia kobus	40 ft (12 m)	30 ft (9 m)	T	C	◆		◆		◆	Sp				◆		
Magnolia liliiflora	10 ft (3 m)	15 ft (4.5 m)	S	C/W/T	◆		◆		◆	Sp/Su	◆		◆	◆		
Magnolia × loebneri	30 ft (9 m)	20 ft (6 m)	T	C	◆		◆			Sp/Su				◆		
Magnolia macrophylla	50 ft (15 m)	30 ft (9 m)	T	C	◆		◆	◆		Su					◆	
Magnolia salicifolia	40 ft (12 m)	20 ft (6 m)	T	C/W	◆		◆			Sp				◆		
Magnolia sargentiana	60 ft (18 m)	25 ft (8 m)	T	C/W	◆		◆	◆		Sp				◆		
Magnolia sieboldii	20 ft (6 m)	25 ft (8 m)	S	C/W	◆		◆		◆	Sp/Su				◆		
Magnolia × soulangeana	20 ft (6 m)	20 ft (6 m)	S	C/W	◆		◆			Sp/Su				◆		
Magnolia sprengeri	40 ft (12 m)	25 ft (8 m)	T	C/W	◆		◆		◆	Sp				◆		
Magnolia stellata	15 ft (4.5 m)	10 ft (3 m)	S	C/W	◆		◆		◆	W/Sp	◆			◆		
Magnolia × veitchii	100 ft (30 m)	15 ft (4.5 m)	T	C/W	◆		◆			Sp	◆			◆		
Magnolia virginiana	30 ft (9 m)	20 ft (6 m)	T	C/W	◆	◆	◆	◆	◆	Su				◆		
Magnolia wilsonii	20 ft (6 m)	20 ft (6 m)	S	C/W	◆		◆		◆	Sp/Su				◆		
Magnolia Hybrid Cultivars	20–40 ft (6–12 m)	20–30 ft (6–9 m)	S/T	C/W	◆		◆			W–Su	◆			◆	◆	
Mahonia aquifolium	6 ft (1.8 m)	8 ft (2.4 m)	S	C/W		◆	◆	◆		W				◆		◆
Mahonia fortunei	7 ft (2 m)	3 ft (0.9 m)	S	C/W		◆	◆	◆		A				◆		◆
Mahonia fremontii	12 ft (3.5 m)	7 ft (2 m)	S	W/T		◆	◆	◆		Su				◆	◆	
Mahonia 'Golden Abundance'	6–8 ft (1.8–2.4 m)	3 ft (0.9 m)	S	C/W		◆	◆	◆		Su	◆			◆	◆	

Plant name	Height	Spread	Type	Climate	Deciduous	Evergreen	Showy flowers	Showy foliage	Scented flowers	Flowering season	Grow in pot/tub	Indoor use	Frost tolerant	Full sun	Half sun	Heavy shade
Mahonia japonica	6 ft (1.8 m)	10 ft (3 m)	S	C/W		♦	♦	♦	♦	W			♦			♦
Mahonia lomariifolia	10 ft (3 m)	8 ft (2.4 m)	S	C/W		♦	♦	♦	♦	A–Sp	♦		♦			♦
Mahonia × media	15 ft (4.5 m)	12 ft (3.5 m)	S	C/W		♦	♦	♦		Su	♦		♦			♦
Mahonia repens	18 in (45 cm)	36 in (90 cm)	S	C/W		♦	♦	♦	♦	Sp			♦			♦
Malpighia coccigera	30 in (75 cm)	30 in (75 cm)	S	W/T		♦	♦			Su	♦	♦				♦
Malpighia glabra	10 ft (3 m)	4 ft (1.2 m)	S	W/T		♦	♦			Su	♦	♦				♦
Malus baccata	40 ft (12 m)	40 ft (12 m)	T	C/W	♦		♦		♦	Sp				♦	♦	
Malus coronaria	30 ft (9 m)	30 ft (9 m)	T	C/W	♦		♦		♦	Sp				♦	♦	
Malus floribunda	12 ft (3.5 m)	20 ft (6 m)	T	C/W	♦		♦			Sp				♦	♦	
Malus × gloriosa	10 ft (3 m)	8–10 ft (2–3 m)	T	C/W	♦		♦	♦		Sp				♦	♦	
Malus halliana	15 ft (4.5 m)	10 ft (3 m)	T	C/W	♦		♦	♦		Sp				♦	♦	
Malus hupehensis	15 ft (4.5 m)	25 ft (8 m)	T	C/W	♦		♦		♦	Sp				♦	♦	
Malus ioensis	20 ft (6 m)	20 ft (6 m)	T	C	♦		♦		♦	Sp				♦	♦	
Malus × micromalus	15 ft (4.5 m)	15 ft (4.5 m)	T	C/W	♦		♦			Sp				♦	♦	
Malus × purpurea	20 ft (6 m)	25 ft (8 m)	T	C/W	♦		♦	♦		Sp				♦	♦	
Malus sargentii	6 ft (1.8 m)	15 ft (4.5 m)	T	C/W	♦		♦			Sp				♦	♦	
Malus × scheideckeri	15 ft (4.5 m)	8 ft (2.4 m)	T	C/W	♦		♦			Sp				♦	♦	
Malus sieboldii	15 ft (4.5 m)	10 ft (3 m)	T	C/W	♦		♦			Sp				♦	♦	
Malus sylvestris	30 ft (9 m)	10 ft (3 m)	T	C	♦		♦			Sp				♦	♦	
Malus tschonoskii	40 ft (12 m)	20 ft (6 m)	T	C/W	♦		♦			Sp				♦	♦	
Malus × zumi	15 ft (4.5 m)	10 ft (3 m)	T	C	♦		♦			Sp				♦	♦	
Malus Hybrid Cultivars	10–40 ft (3–12 m)	5–25 ft (1.5–8 m)	T	C	♦		♦		♦	Sp				♦	♦	
Malvaviscus arboreus	12–15 ft (3.5–4.5 m)	10 ft (3 m)	S	W/T		♦	♦			Su/A					♦	
Malvaviscus penduliflorus	12–15 ft (3.5–4.5 m)	10 ft (3 m)	S	W/T		♦	♦			Su					♦	
Maytenus boaria	70 ft (21 m)	30 ft (9 m)	T	W/T		♦		♦		Sp				♦	♦	
Megaskepasma erythrochlamys	10 ft (3 m)	4 ft (1.2 m)	S	W/T		♦	♦		♦	All	♦				♦	
Melaleuca armillaris	25 ft (8 m)	12 ft (3.5 m)	T	W/T		♦	♦			Sp/Su					♦	
Melaleuca bracteata	30 ft (9 m)	20 ft (6 m)	S	W/T		♦	♦			Sp					♦	
Melaleuca fulgens	10 ft (3 m)	6 ft (1.8 m)	S	W/T		♦	♦			Sp/Su	♦			♦	♦	
Melaleuca hypericifolia	15 ft (4.5 m)	15 ft (4.5 m)	S	W/T		♦	♦			Sp/Su					♦	
Melaleuca incana	10 ft (3 m)	10 ft (3 m)	S	W/T		♦	♦	♦		Sp/Su					♦	

Plant name	Height	Spread	Type	Climate	Deciduous	Evergreen	Showy flowers	Showy foliage	Scented flowers	Flowering season	Grow in pot/tub	Indoor use	Frost tolerant	Full sun	Half sun	Heavy shade
Melaleuca lateritia	6 ft (1.8 m)	3 ft (0.9 m)	S	W/T		♦	♦			Sp/Su				♦		
Melaleuca leucadendra	90 ft (27 m)	30 ft (9 m)	T	W/T		♦	♦	♦		A/W				♦		
Melaleuca linariifolia	20 ft (6 m)	10 ft (3 m)	T	W/T		♦	♦			Su			♦	♦		
Melaleuca pulchella	6 ft (1.8 m)	6 ft (1.8 m)	S	W/T		♦	♦			Sp/Su			♦	♦		
Melaleuca quinquenervia	30–50 ft (9–15 m)	20 ft (6 m)	T	W/T		♦	♦	♦		Sp				♦		
Melaleuca radula	6 ft (1.8 m)	6 ft (1.8 m)	S	W/T		♦	♦			W/Sp			♦	♦		
Melaleuca thymifolia	3 ft (0.9 m)	3 ft (0.9 m)	S	W/T		♦	♦			All			♦	♦		
Melastoma malabathricum	6–8 ft (1.8–2.4 m)	5 ft (1.5 m)	S	W/T		♦	♦	♦		All				♦		
Melia azederach	20–80 ft (6–24 m)	25 ft (8 m)	T	W/T	♦		♦			Su			♦	♦		
Melianthus major	6–10 ft (1.8–3 m)	3 ft (0.9 m)	S	W/T		♦		♦		Sp/Su				♦	♦	♦
Metasequoia glyptostroboides	70 ft (21 m)	20 ft (6 m)	T	C/W	♦			♦		Sp				♦	♦	
Metrosideros excelsa	15–50 ft (4.5–15 m)	25 ft (8 m)	T	W/T		♦	♦			Su	♦			♦		
Metrosideros kermadecensis	20 ft (6 m)	15 ft (4.5 m)	T	W/T		♦	♦			Any	♦			♦		
Metrosideros polymorpha	20–50 ft (6–15 m)	20 ft (6 m)	T	T		♦	♦			Sp/Su				♦		
Michelia champaca	100 ft (30 m)	10 ft (3 m)	T	W/T		♦	♦		♦	Su/A				♦		
Michelia doltsopa	30 ft (9 m)	20 ft (6 m)	T	W/T		♦	♦			W/Sp				♦		
Michelia figo	15 ft (4.5 m)	10 ft (3 m)	S	W/T		♦	♦		♦	Sp/Su	♦			♦		
Michelia yunnanensis	15 ft (4.5 m)	7 ft (2 m)	S	W/T		♦	♦			W/Sp	♦			♦		
Microbiota decussata	2 ft (0.6 m)	5 ft (1.5 m)	C	C		♦				Sp	♦		♦	♦	♦	
Millettia grandis	20–40 ft (6–12 m)	30 ft (9 m)	T	W/T	♦		♦			Su				♦		
Mimosa pudica	3 ft (0.9 m)	3 ft (0.9 m)	S	W/T		♦	♦	♦		Su	♦	♦		♦		
Montanoa bipinnatifida	10–20 ft (3–6 m)	7 ft (2 m)	S	W/T		♦	♦			A				♦		
Morella cerifera	30 ft (9 m)	15 ft (4.5 m)	T	C/W		♦		♦		Su				♦		♦
Morella pensylvanica	6–10 ft (1.8–3 m)	4 ft (1.2 m)	S	C	♦			♦		Su				♦	♦	
Murraya paniculata	10 ft (3 m)	10 ft (3 m)	S	W/T		♦	♦	♦	♦	Sp	♦	♦		♦		
Mussaenda erythrophylla	10 ft (3 m)	5 ft (1.5 m)	S	T		♦	♦	♦		Sp	♦			♦		
Mussaenda Hybrid Cultivars	10 ft (3 m)	5–7 ft (1.5–2 m)	S	T		♦	♦	♦		Sp	♦			♦		
Myoporum floribundum	10 ft (3 m)	8 ft (2.4 m)	S	W		♦	♦	♦	♦	W–Su				♦		
Myoporum laetum	15–30 ft (4.5–9 m)	10 ft (3 m)	S	W		♦				Su				♦		
Myrica gale	3–6 ft (0.9–1.8 m)	4 ft (1.2 m)	S	C	♦		♦	♦		Su			♦	♦	♦	♦
Myrtus communis	10 ft (3 m)	10 ft (3 m)	S	W/T		♦	♦	♦		Sp	♦			♦	♦	

Plant name	Height	Spread	Type	Climate	Deciduous	Evergreen	Showy flowers	Showy foliage	Scented flowers	Flowering season	Grow in pot/tub	Indoor use	Frost tolerant	Full sun	Half sun	Heavy shade
Nageia nagi	70 ft (21 m)	15 ft (4.5 m)	C	W		♦		♦		Sp			♦			♦
Nandina domestica	7 ft (2 m)	4 ft (1.2 m)	S	C/W		♦		♦		Su	♦		♦	♦		
Neillia sinensis	10 ft (3 m)	7 ft (2 m)	S	C/W	♦		♦			Sp/Su			♦	♦		
Neillia thibetica	6 ft (1.8 m)	6 ft (1.8 m)	S	C/W	♦		♦			Su			♦	♦		
Nerium oleander	10 ft (3 m)	8 ft (2.4 m)	S	W/T		♦	♦			Sp–A	♦		♦	♦		
Neviusia alabamensis	5 ft (1.5 m)	5 ft (1.5 m)	S	C/W	♦		♦			Sp			♦	♦	♦	
Nothofagus antarctica	40 ft (12 m)	20 ft (6 m)	T	C/W	♦			♦		Sp			♦	♦		
Nothofagus cunninghamii	5–100 ft (1.5–30 m)	8–30 ft (2.4–9 m)	T	C/W		♦		♦		Sp			♦	♦		
Nothofagus fusca	100 ft (30 m)	25 ft (8 m)	T	C/W		♦		♦		Sp			♦	♦		
Nothofagus menziesii	60 ft (18 m)	30 ft (9 m)	T	C/W		♦		♦		Sp			♦	♦		
Nothofagus solanderi	60 ft (18 m)	25 ft (8 m)	T	C/W		♦		♦		Sp			♦	♦		
Nyssa aquatica	50 ft (15 m)	15 ft (4.5 m)	T	C/W	♦					Su			♦	♦		
Nyssa sinensis	40 ft (12 m)	30 ft (9 m)	T	C/W	♦					Su			♦	♦		
Nyssa sylvatica	50 ft (15 m)	30 ft (9 m)	T	C/W	♦					Su			♦	♦		
Ochna kirkii	10 ft (3 m)	7 ft (2 m)	S	W/T		♦	♦			Sp				♦		
Ochna serrulata	12 ft (3.5 m)	7 ft (2 m)	S	W/T		♦	♦		♦	Sp/Su				♦		
Odontonema callistachyum	6 ft (1.8 m)	3–6 ft (0.9–1.8 m)	S	W/T		♦	♦			All	♦	♦		♦		
Odontonema schomburgkianum	6 ft (1.8 m)	2 ft (0.6 m)	S	W/T		♦	♦			Sp	♦	♦		♦		
Olea capensis	50 ft (15 m)	15 ft (4.5 m)	T	W/T		♦		♦		Sp				♦		
Olearia albida	10 ft (3 m)	7 ft (2 m)	S	W		♦	♦		♦	Su/A			♦	♦		
Olearia furfuracea	8–15 ft (2.4–4.5 m)	7 ft (2 m)	S	W/T		♦	♦		♦	Su			♦	♦		
Olearia insignis	3–7 ft (0.9–2 m)	3–7 ft (0.9–2 m)	S	W/T		♦	♦		♦	Su				♦		
Olearia macrodonta	7 ft (2 m)	7 ft (2 m)	S	W/T		♦	♦		♦	Su			♦	♦		
Olearia phlogopappa	8 ft (2.4 m)	7 ft (2 m)	S	W		♦	♦			Sp	♦		♦	♦		
Olearia × scilloniensis	10 ft (3 m)	8 ft (2.4 m)	S	W		♦	♦			Sp			♦	♦		
Olearia traversii	15 ft (4.5 m)	10 ft (3 m)	S	W/T		♦		♦		Su			♦	♦		
Oncoba spinosa	6–10 ft (1.8–3 m)	6 ft (1.8 m)	S	W/T		♦	♦		♦	Sp–A				♦		
Oplopanax horridus	3–10 ft (0.9–3 m)	5 ft (1.5 m)	S	C/W	♦			♦		Sp/Su			♦		♦	♦
Orphium frutescens	24 in (60 cm)	18 in (45 cm)	S	W/T		♦	♦			Su				♦		
Osmanthus × burkwoodii	10 ft (3 m)	10 ft (3 m)	S	C/W		♦	♦		♦	Sp			♦	♦		
Osmanthus delavayi	8 ft (2.4 m)	8 ft (2.4 m)	S	C/W		♦	♦		♦	W/Sp			♦	♦		

Plant name	Height	Spread	Type	Climate	Deciduous	Evergreen	Showy flowers	Showy foliage	Scented flowers	Flowering season	Grow in pot/tub	Indoor use	Frost tolerant	Full sun	Half sun	Heavy shade
Osmanthus × fortunei	10 ft (3 m)	10 ft (3 m)	S	C/W		♦	♦		♦	A			♦	♦		
Osmanthus fragrans	20 ft (6 m)	20 ft (6 m)	S	C/W		♦	♦		♦	W/Sp/A			♦	♦		
Osmanthus heterophyllus	12 ft (3.5 m)	12 ft (3.5 m)	S	C/W		♦	♦	♦	♦	A/W			♦	♦		
Ostrya carpinifolia	70 ft (21 m)	70 ft (21 m)	T	C/W	♦		♦	♦		Sp			♦	♦		
Ostrya virginiana	50 ft (15 m)	35 ft (10 m)	T	C/W	♦		♦	♦		Sp			♦	♦		
Oxydendrum arboreum	6–10 ft (1.8–3 m)	10 ft (3 m)	T	C/W	♦		♦	♦	♦	Su			♦	♦		
Pachira aquatica	20 ft (6 m)	10 ft (3 m)	T	W/T		♦	♦	♦		Su				♦		
Pachystachys lutea	36 in (90 cm)	20 in (50 cm)	S	W/T		♦	♦			Sp-A	♦	♦				♦
Paeonia delavayi	7 ft (2 m)	5 ft (1.5 m)	S	C	♦					Sp			♦	♦	♦	
Paeonia × lemoinei	6 ft (1.8 m)	6 ft (1.8 m)	S	C	♦					Sp/Su			♦	♦	♦	
Paeonia rockii	7 ft (2 m)	3 ft (0.9 m)	S	C/W	♦					Sp/Su			♦	♦	♦	
Paeonia suffruticosa	7 ft (2 m)	7 ft (2 m)	S	C	♦					Sp			♦	♦	♦	♦
Pandanus tectorius	12–25 ft (3.5–8 m)	10–20 ft (3–6 m)	T	W/T		♦	♦	♦	♦	Sp				♦		
Paraserianthes lophantha	25 ft (8 m)	10 ft (3 m)	T	W		♦	♦			Sp				♦		
Parmentiera cereifera	20 ft (6 m)	10 ft (3 m)	T	W/T		♦	♦			Sp				♦		
Parrotia persica	25–40 ft (8–12 m)	20 ft (6 m)	T	C/W	♦			♦		W/Sp			♦	♦		
Paulownia fortunei	60 ft (18 m)	40 ft (12 m)	T	C/W	♦		♦	♦		Sp			♦	♦		
Paulownia tomentosa	50 ft (15 m)	30 ft (9 m)	T	C/W	♦		♦	♦		Sp			♦	♦		
Pavonia × gledhillii	5 ft (1.5 m)	3 ft (0.9 m)	S	W/T		♦	♦			Sp-A	♦	♦		♦		
Pavonia hastata	36 in (90 cm)	24 in (60 cm)	S	W/T		♦	♦			Sp-A	♦	♦		♦		
Peltophorum pterocarpum	50 ft (15 m)	30 ft (9 m)	T	T		♦	♦		♦	Su				♦		
Persoonia pinifolia	10–15 ft (3–4.5 m)	10 ft (3 m)	S	W/T		♦	♦			Su/A						♦
Phellodendron amurense	50 ft (15 m)	40 ft (12 m)	T	C	♦			♦		Su			♦	♦		
Philadelphus coronarius	10 ft (3 m)	8 ft (2.4 m)	S	C/W	♦		♦	♦	♦	Su			♦	♦		
Philadelphus inodorus	10 ft (3 m)	4 ft (1.2 m)	S	C/W	♦		♦			Su			♦	♦		
Philadelphus lewisii	10 ft (3 m)	10 ft (3 m)	S	C/W	♦		♦		♦	Su			♦	♦		
Philadelphus mexicanus	15 ft (4.5 m)	8 ft (2.4 m)	S	C/W		♦	♦		♦	Su			♦	♦		
Philadelphus Hybrid Cultivars	30 in–10 ft (75 cm–3 m)	6–8 ft (1.8–2.4 m)	S	C/W	♦		♦	♦	♦	Su			♦	♦		
Philodendron bipinnatifidum	10 ft (3 m)	10 ft (3 m)	S	W/T		♦		♦		Su	♦	♦	♦		♦	♦
Phlomis chrysophylla	4 ft (1.2 m)	3 ft (0.9 m)	S	W		♦	♦	♦		Su			♦	♦		
Phlomis fruticosa	30 in (75 cm)	30 in (75 cm)	S	C/W		♦	♦	♦		Su			♦	♦		

Plant name	Height	Spread	Type	Climate	Deciduous	Evergreen	Showy flowers	Showy foliage	Scented flowers	Flowering season	Grow in pot/tub	Indoor use	Frost tolerant	Full sun	Half sun	Heavy shade
Photinia davidiana	25 ft (8 m)	20 ft (6 m)	S	W		◆	◆	◆		Su			◆	◆		
Photinia × fraseri	15 ft (4.5 m)	15 ft (4.5 m)	S	C/W		◆	◆	◆		Sp			◆	◆		
Photinia glabra	15 ft (4.5 m)	12 ft (3.5 m)	T	C/W		◆	◆	◆		Su			◆	◆		
Photinia villosa	15 ft (4.5 m)	15 ft (4.5 m)	T	C	◆		◆	◆		Sp			◆	◆		
Phygelius aequalis	3 ft (0.9 m)	3 ft (0.9 m)	S	W		◆	◆			Su			◆		◆	
Phygelius capensis	6 ft (1.8 m)	22 in (55 cm)	S	W		◆	◆			Su			◆		◆	
Phygelius × rectus	4 ft (1.2 m)	4 ft (1.2 m)	S	W		◆	◆			Su			◆		◆	
Phylica plumosa	3–6 ft (0.9–1.8 m)	3 ft (0.9 m)	S	W/T		◆	◆	◆		W				◆		
Phyllocladus glaucus	35–50 ft (10–15 m)	10–15 ft (3–4.5 m)	C	W/T		◆				Sp				◆	◆	
Phyllocladus trichomanoides	70 ft (21 m)	20 ft (6 m)	C	W				◆		Sp			◆	◆		
Physocarpus monogynus	4 ft (1.2 m)	4 ft (1.2 m)	S	C	◆		◆			Sp/Su			◆	◆		
Physocarpus opulifolius	10 ft (3 m)	15 ft (4.5 m)	S	C	◆		◆	◆		Sp/Su			◆	◆		
Phytolacca dioica	50 ft (15 m)	30 ft (9 m)	T	W/T		◆	◆			Sp/Su				◆		
Picea abies	200 ft (60 m)	20 ft (6 m)	C	C		◆				Sp			◆	◆		
Picea engelmannii	150 ft (45 m)	15 ft (4.5 m)	C	C		◆		◆		Sp			◆	◆		
Picea glauca	80 ft (24 m)	12–20 ft (3.5–6 m)	C	C		◆				Sp			◆	◆		
Picea jezoensis	120 ft (36 m)	25 ft (8 m)	C	C/W		◆		◆		Sp			◆	◆		
Picea mariana	60 ft (18 m)	10 ft (3 m)	C	C		◆				Sp			◆	◆		
Picea omorika	100 ft (30 m)	20 ft (6 m)	C	C		◆		◆		Sp			◆	◆		
Picea orientalis	100 ft (30 m)	20 ft (6 m)	C	C		◆				Sp			◆	◆		
Picea pungens	100 ft (30 m)	20 ft (6 m)	C	C		◆		◆		Sp			◆	◆		
Picea sitchensis	100 ft (30 m)	25 ft (8 m)	C	C		◆				Sp			◆	◆		
Picea smithiana	75 ft (23 m)	20 ft (6 m)	C	C		◆				Sp			◆	◆		
Pieris floribunda	6 ft (1.8 m)	7 ft (2 m)	S	C/W		◆	◆	◆		Sp			◆	◆	◆	
Pieris 'Forest Flame'	12 ft (3.5 m)	6 ft (1.8 m)	S	C/W		◆	◆	◆		Sp			◆	◆		
Pieris formosa	10–20 ft (3–6 m)	7 ft (2 m)	S	C/W		◆	◆	◆		Sp			◆	◆		
Pieris japonica	8–10 ft (2.4–3 m)	8 ft (2.4 m)	S	C/W		◆	◆	◆		Sp	◆		◆	◆		
Pimelea ferruginea	3 ft (0.9 m)	3 ft (0.9 m)	S	W		◆	◆			Sp	◆		◆	◆		
Pimelea nivea	6 ft (1.8 m)	3 ft (0.9 m)	S	W		◆	◆			Su			◆			◆
Pimelea physodes	3 ft (0.9 m)	2 ft (0.6 m)	S	W		◆	◆			Sp				◆		
Pimelea prostrata	6 in (15 cm)	36 in (90 cm)	S	W		◆	◆			Su			◆	◆		

Plant name	Height	Spread	Type	Climate	Deciduous	Evergreen	Showy flowers	Showy foliage	Scented flowers	Flowering season	Grow in pot/tub	Indoor use	Frost tolerant	Full sun	Half sun	Heavy shade
Pinus banksiana	60 ft (18 m)	20 ft (6 m)	C	C		◆		◆		Sp			◆	◆		
Pinus bungeana	60 ft (18 m)	20 ft (6 m)	C	C		◆		◆		Sp			◆	◆		
Pinus canariensis	130 ft (40 m)	25 ft (8 m)	C	W/T		◆		◆		Sp			◆	◆		
Pinus cembra	30 ft (9 m)	15 ft (4.5 m)	C	C		◆		◆		Sp			◆	◆		
Pinus contorta	75 ft (23 m)	25 ft (8 m)	C	C		◆		◆		Sp			◆	◆		
Pinus coulteri	100 ft (30 m)	30 ft (9 m)	C	C/W		◆		◆		Sp			◆	◆		
Pinus densiflora	70 ft (21 m)	20 ft (6 m)	C	C		◆		◆		Sp			◆	◆		
Pinus halepensis	60 ft (18 m)	20 ft (6 m)	C	C/W		◆		◆		Sp			◆	◆		
Pinus heldreichii	60 ft (18 m)	20 ft (6 m)	C	C		◆		◆		Sp			◆	◆		
Pinus lambertiana	150 ft (45 m)	20 ft (6 m)	C	C/W		◆		◆		Sp			◆	◆		
Pinus longaeva	60 ft (18 m)	15 ft (4.5 m)	C	C		◆		◆		Sp			◆	◆		
Pinus merkusii	150 ft (45 m)	20 ft (6 m)	C	W/T		◆		◆		Sp				◆		
Pinus monticola	100 ft (30 m)	20 ft (6 m)	C	C		◆		◆		Sp			◆	◆		
Pinus mugo	25 ft (8 m)	12 ft (3.5 m)	C	C		◆		◆		Sp	◆		◆	◆		
Pinus nigra	120 ft (36 m)	25 ft (8 m)	C	C		◆		◆		Sp			◆	◆		
Pinus palustris	100 ft (30 m)	15 ft (4.5 m)	C	C/W		◆		◆		Sp			◆	◆		
Pinus parviflora	80 ft (24 m)	20 ft (6 m)	C	C		◆		◆		Sp			◆	◆		
Pinus patula	50 ft (15 m)	30 ft (9 m)	C	W		◆		◆		Sp			◆	◆		
Pinus pinaster	100 ft (30 m)	30 ft (9 m)	C	C/W		◆		◆		Sp			◆	◆		
Pinus pinea	80 ft (24 m)	20 ft (6 m)	C	C/W		◆		◆		Sp			◆	◆		
Pinus ponderosa	130 ft (40 m)	20 ft (6 m)	C	C		◆		◆		Sp			◆	◆		
Pinus radiata	100 ft (30 m)	25 ft (8 m)	C	C/W		◆		◆		Sp			◆	◆		
Pinus resinosa	100 ft (30 m)	20 ft (6 m)	C	C		◆		◆		Sp			◆	◆		
Pinus roxburghii	100 ft (30 m)	15 ft (4.5 m)	C	W		◆		◆		Sp			◆	◆		
Pinus strobus	165 ft (50 m)	20 ft (6 m)	C	C		◆		◆		Sp			◆	◆		
Pinus sylvestris	100 ft (30 m)	20 ft (6 m)	C	C		◆		◆		Sp			◆	◆		
Pinus taeda	100 ft (30 m)	25 ft (8 m)	C	C/W		◆		◆		Sp			◆	◆		
Pinus thunbergii	130 ft (40 m)	20 ft (6 m)	C	C		◆		◆		Sp				◆	◆	
Pinus wallichiana	150 ft (45 m)	20 ft (6 m)	C	C		◆		◆		Sp			◆	◆		
Piper aduncum	17–25 ft (5–8 m)	8–17 ft (2.4–5 m)	S	W/T		◆		◆		Sp–A				◆		
Pistacia chinensis	25–50 ft (8–15 m)	15 ft (4.5 m)	T	C/W	◆			◆		Su			◆	◆		

Plant name	Height	Spread	Type	Climate	Deciduous	Evergreen	Showy flowers	Showy foliage	Scented flowers	Flowering season	Grow in pot/tub	Indoor use	Frost tolerant	Full sun	Half sun	Heavy shade
Pistacia lentiscus	12 ft (3.5 m)	12 ft (3.5 m)	S	W/T		◆		◆		Sp			◆	◆		
Pittosporum crassifolium	10–20 ft (3–6 m)	8 ft (2.4 m)	S	W/T		◆		◆	◆	Sp/Su				◆		
Pittosporum eugenioides	40 ft (12 m)	12 ft (3.5 m)	T	W/T		◆		◆	◆	Sp/Su			◆	◆		
Pittosporum 'Garnettii'	7–10 ft (2–3 m)	7 ft (2 m)	S	W/T		◆		◆	◆	Sp				◆		
Pittosporum tenuifolium	15–20 ft (4.5–6 m)	15 ft (4.5 m)	S	W/T		◆		◆	◆	Sp			◆	◆		
Pittosporum tobira	20 ft (6 m)	7 ft (2 m)	S	W/T		◆	◆	◆	◆	Sp/Su	◆			◆		
Pittosporum undulatum	15–40 ft (4.5–12 m)	20 ft (6 m)	T	W/T		◆	◆	◆	◆	Sp				◆		
Platanus × hispanica	100 ft (30 m)	60 ft (18 m)	T	C	◆			◆		Sp			◆	◆		
Platanus occidentalis	150 ft (45 m)	70 ft (21 m)	T	C	◆			◆		Sp			◆	◆		
Platanus orientalis	100 ft (30 m)	70 ft (21 m)	T	C	◆			◆		Sp			◆	◆		
Platanus racemosa	100 ft (30 m)	75 ft (23 m)	T	C/W	◆			◆		Sp				◆		
Platycladus orientalis	40 ft (12 m)	15 ft (4.5 m)	C	C/W		◆		◆		Sp	◆		◆	◆		
Plumbago auriculata	15 ft (4.5 m)	7 ft (2 m)	S	W/T		◆	◆			Sp–A				◆		
Plumbago indica	5 ft (1.5 m)	3 ft (0.9 m)	S	W/T		◆	◆			Sp–A					◆	
Plumeria obtusa	25 ft (8 m)	12 ft (3.5 m)	T	W/T		◆	◆	◆	◆	Sp–A				◆		
Plumeria rubra	25 ft (8 m)	15 ft (4.5 m)	T	W/T	◆		◆	◆	◆	Su/A	◆			◆		
Podalyria calyptrata	12 ft (3.5 m)	12 ft (3.5 m)	S	W		◆	◆			Sp/Su				◆		
Podocarpus elatus	50 ft (15 m)	20 ft (6 m)	C	W/T		◆		◆		Sp	◆			◆		
Podocarpus latifolius	90 ft (27 m)	15 ft (4.5 m)	C	W/T		◆		◆		Sp				◆		
Podocarpus lawrencei	12 ft (3.5 m)	4 ft (1.2 m)	C	C/W		◆		◆		Sp			◆	◆		
Podocarpus macrophyllus	60 ft (18 m)	20 ft (6 m)	C	W/T		◆		◆		Sp	◆		◆	◆		
Podocarpus totara	80 ft (24 m)	25 ft (8 m)	C	W/T		◆		◆		Sp			◆	◆		
Polyalthia longifolia	50 ft (15 m)	3–10 ft (0.9–3 m)	T	W/T		◆	◆	◆		Su						
Polygala × dalmaisiana	3–10 ft (0.9–3 m)	3 ft (0.9 m)	S	W/T		◆	◆			All				◆		
Polygala myrtifolia	6 ft (1.8 m)	3–6 ft (0.9–1.8 m)	S	W/T		◆	◆			All				◆		
Polyscias elegans	100 ft (30 m)	15 ft (4.5 m)	T	W/T		◆	◆	◆		A/W						◆
Polyscias filicifolia	15 ft (4.5 m)	4 ft (1.2 m)	T	W/T		◆	◆	◆		Su						◆
Polyscias guilfoylei	20 ft (6 m)	8 ft (2.4 m)	T	W/T		◆	◆	◆		Su						◆
Populus alba	80 ft (24 m)	40 ft (12 m)	T	C/W	◆			◆		Sp			◆	◆		
Populus balsamifera	80 ft (24 m)	25 ft (8 m)	T	C	◆			◆		Sp			◆	◆		
Populus × canadensis	80 ft (24 m)	35 ft (10 m)	T	C	◆			◆		Sp			◆	◆		

Plant name	Height	Spread	Type	Climate	Deciduous	Evergreen	Showy flowers	Showy foliage	Scented flowers	Flowering season	Grow in pot/tub	Indoor use	Frost tolerant	Full sun	Half sun	Heavy shade
Populus deltoides	100 ft (30 m)	60 ft (18 m)	T	C/W	◆			◆		Sp			◆	◆		
Populus fremontii	100 ft (30 m)	40 ft (12 m)	T	C/W	◆			◆		Sp			◆	◆		
Populus grandidentata	60 ft (18 m)	30 ft (9 m)	T	C	◆			◆		Sp			◆	◆		
Populus lasiocarpa	50–80 ft (15–24 m)	35 ft (10 m)	T	C/W	◆			◆		Sp			◆	◆		
Populus nigra	100 ft (30 m)	60 ft (18 m)	T	C/W	◆			◆		Sp			◆	◆		
Populus simonii	80–100 ft (24–30 m)	25 ft (8 m)	T	C	◆			◆		Sp			◆	◆		
Populus tremuloides	50 ft (15 m)	30 ft (9 m)	T	C	◆			◆		Sp			◆	◆		
Populus trichocarpa	80–120 ft (24–36 m)	35 ft (10 m)	T	C/W	◆			◆		Sp			◆	◆		
Posoqueria latifolia	6–20 ft (1.8–6 m)	15 ft (4.5 m)	T	W/T		◆	◆	◆	◆	Sp				◆		
Potentilla fruticosa	5 ft (1.5 m)	5 ft (1.5 m)	S	C	◆		◆			Su/A			◆	◆		
Pouteria cainito	35 ft (10 m)	15 ft (4.5 m)	T	W/T		◆		◆		Sp				◆		
Pouteria campechiana	60 ft (18 m)	25 ft (8 m)	T	W/T		◆		◆		Sp				◆		
Prinsepia sinensis	6 ft (1.8 m)	6 ft (1.8 m)	S	C	◆		◆		◆	Sp			◆	◆		
Prinsepia uniflora	5 ft (1.5 m)	6 ft (1.8 m)	S	C	◆		◆		◆	Sp			◆	◆		
Prosopis glandulosa	30 ft (9 m)	25 ft (8 m)	T	W/T	◆		◆			Sp/Su			◆	◆		
Prosopis velutina	15–40 ft (4.5–12 m)	15–40 ft (4.5–12 m)	T	W/T	◆		◆			Sp/Su			◆	◆		
Prostanthera cuneata	3 ft (0.9 m)	5 ft (1.5 m)	S	W		◆	◆			Su	◆		◆	◆	◆	
Prostanthera lasianthos	15 ft (4.5 m)	12 ft (3.5 m)	S	W		◆	◆			Su			◆		◆	
Prostanthera nivea	12 ft (3.5 m)	7 ft (2 m)	S	W/T		◆	◆			Sp				◆	◆	
Prostanthera ovalifolia	6 ft (1.8 m)	6 ft (1.8 m)	S	W/T		◆	◆			Sp					◆	
Protea aurea	10 ft (3 m)	10 ft (3 m)	S	W		◆	◆	◆		A/W			◆	◆		
Protea cynaroides	7 ft (2 m)	7 ft (2 m)	S	W		◆	◆	◆		W–Su				◆		
Protea eximia	10 ft (3 m)	10 ft (3 m)	S	W		◆	◆	◆		Any			◆	◆		
Protea grandiceps	5 ft (1.5 m)	5 ft (1.5 m)	S	W		◆	◆	◆		W–Su			◆	◆		
Protea lacticolor	7–15 ft (2–4.5 m)	7 ft (2 m)	S	W		◆	◆	◆		A/W			◆	◆		
Protea magnifica	5 ft (1.5 m)	5 ft (1.5 m)	S	W		◆	◆	◆		Sp/Su			◆	◆		
Protea neriifolia	7 ft (2 m)	7 ft (2 m)	S	W		◆	◆	◆		A–Sp			◆	◆		
Protea repens	8 ft (2.4 m)	7 ft (2 m)	S	W		◆	◆	◆		A/W			◆	◆		
Protea scolymocephala	3 ft (0.9 m)	3 ft (0.9 m)	S	W		◆	◆	◆		W/Sp			◆	◆		
Protea speciosa	3 ft (0.9 m)	3 ft (0.9 m)	S	W		◆	◆	◆		Su/A			◆	◆		
Protea venusta	30 in (75 cm)	8 ft (2.4 m)	S	W		◆	◆	◆		Su/A			◆	◆		

Plant name	Height	Spread	Type	Climate	Deciduous	Evergreen	Showy flowers	Showy foliage	Scented flowers	Flowering season	Grow in pot/tub	Indoor use	Frost tolerant	Full sun	Half sun	Heavy shade
Protea Hybrid Cultivars	5–8 ft (1.5–2.4 m)	10 ft (3 m)	S	W		♦	♦		♦	Any			♦	♦		
Prunus × *amygdalo-persica*	20 ft (6 m)	20 ft (6 m)	T	C	♦		♦			W/Sp			♦	♦		
Prunus × *blireana*	15 ft (4.5 m)	15 ft (4.5 m)	T	C/W	♦		♦			Sp			♦	♦		
Prunus campanulata	30 ft (9 m)	25 ft (8 m)	T	C/W	♦		♦			W/Sp			♦	♦		
Prunus caroliniana	40 ft (12 m)	20 ft (6 m)	T	C/W	♦		♦			Sp			♦	♦		
Prunus cerasifera	30 ft (9 m)	30 ft (9 m)	T	C/W	♦		♦	♦		Sp			♦	♦		
Prunus glandulosa	5 ft (1.5 m)	5 ft (1.5 m)	S	C			♦			Sp			♦	♦		
Prunus ilicifolia	25 ft (8 m)	20 ft (6 m)	S	W/T	♦	♦				Sp				♦		
Prunus incisa	15–20 ft (4.5–6 m)	15 ft (4.5 m)	T	C	♦		♦	♦		Sp			♦	♦		
Prunus laurocerasus	20 ft (6 m)	30 ft (9 m)	T	C/W	♦	♦	♦			Sp			♦	♦		
Prunus lusitanica	20 ft (6 m)	30 ft (9 m)	T	C/W	♦	♦				Sp			♦	♦		
Prunus maackii	50 ft (15 m)	25 ft (8 m)	T	C	♦		♦			Sp			♦	♦		
Prunus padus	30–50 ft (9–15 m)	25 ft (8 m)	T	C	♦		♦			Sp			♦	♦		
Prunus pensylvanica	30 ft (9 m)	30 ft (9 m)	T	C	♦		♦			Sp			♦	♦		
Prunus sargentii	50 ft (15 m)	35 ft (10 m)	T	C	♦		♦			Sp			♦	♦		
Prunus, Sato-zakura Group	20–40 ft (6–12 m)	30 ft (9 m)	T	C	♦		♦	♦		Sp			♦	♦		
Prunus serotina	100 ft (30 m)	30 ft (9 m)	T	C	♦		♦			Sp			♦	♦		
Prunus spinosa	20 ft (6 m)	15 ft (4.5 m)	S	C/W	♦		♦			Sp			♦	♦		
Prunus × *subhirtella*	50 ft (15 m)	25 ft (8 m)	T	C	♦		♦			Sp			♦	♦		
Prunus tenella	5 ft (1.5 m)	5 ft (1.5 m)	S	C	♦		♦			Sp			♦	♦		
Prunus triloba	12 ft (3.5 m)	12 ft (3.5 m)	S	C	♦		♦			Sp			♦	♦		
Prunus × *yedoensis*	40 ft (12 m)	30 ft (9 m)	T	C	♦		♦	♦		Sp			♦	♦		
Pseuderanthemum atropurpureum	4 ft (1.2 m)	3 ft (0.9 m)	S	W/T		♦	♦	♦		Su	♦					♦
Pseuderanthemum reticulatum	3 ft (0.9 m)	3 ft (0.9 m)	S	W/T		♦	♦	♦		Su	♦					♦
Pseudolarix amabilis	100 ft (30 m)	25 ft (8 m)	T	C	♦			♦		Sp			♦	♦		
Pseudopanax arboreus	10–20 ft (3–6 m)	15 ft (4.5 m)	T	W/T		♦		♦		W				♦		
Pseudopanax ferox	15 ft (4.5 m)	7 ft (2 m)	S	W/T		♦		♦		Sp				♦		
Pseudopanax lessonii	12 ft (3.5 m)	7 ft (2 m)	T	W/T		♦		♦		Sp				♦		
Pseudotsuga menziesii	80–150 ft (24–45 m)	15–30 ft (4.5–9 m)	T	C/W		♦		♦		Sp			♦	♦		
Psidium cattleianum	10–20 ft (3–6 m)	8 ft (2.4 m)	S	W/T		♦		♦		Sp				♦		
Psoralea pinnata	6–10 ft (1.8–3 m)	7 ft (2 m)	S	W/T		♦	♦			Sp/Su				♦		

Plant name	Height	Spread	Type	Climate	Deciduous	Evergreen	Showy flowers	Showy foliage	Scented flowers	Flowering season	Grow in pot/tub	Indoor use	Frost tolerant	Full sun	Half sun	Heavy shade
Ptelea angustifolia	12 ft (3.5 m)	12 ft (3.5 m)	S	W	♦		♦		♦	Su			♦	♦		
Ptelea trifoliata	25 ft (8 m)	12 ft (3.5 m)	S	C/W	♦		♦		♦	Su			♦	♦		
Pterocarpus indicus	80 ft (24 m)	35 ft (10 m)	T	W/T		♦	♦		♦	Sp				♦		
Pterocarya fraxinifolia	80 ft (24 m)	60 ft (18 m)	T	C	♦		♦	♦		Sp			♦	♦		
Pterocarya stenoptera	70 ft (21 m)	40 ft (12 m)	T	C	♦			♦		Sp			♦	♦		
Pterostyrax corymbosa	40 ft (12 m)	20 ft (6 m)	T	C/W	♦		♦		♦	Sp			♦	♦		
Pterostyrax hispida	25 ft (8 m)	20 ft (6 m)	T	C/W	♦		♦			Sp			♦	♦		
Pycnostachys urticifolia	8 ft (2.4 m)	4 ft (1.2 m)	S	W/T		♦	♦			Su/A				♦		
Pyracantha angustifolia	12 ft (3.5 m)	12 ft (3.5 m)	S	C/W		♦	♦			Su			♦	♦		
Pyracantha coccinea	15 ft (4.5 m)	15 ft (4.5 m)	S	C/W		♦	♦			Su			♦	♦		
Pyracantha crenulata	15 ft (4.5 m)	12 ft (3.5 m)	S	C/W		♦	♦			Su			♦	♦		
Pyracantha koidzumii	12–15 ft (3.5–4.5 m)	12 ft (3.5 m)	S	C/W		♦	♦			Su			♦	♦		
Pyracantha rogersiana	12 ft (3.5 m)	12 ft (3.5 m)	S	W		♦	♦			Sp			♦	♦		
Pyracantha Hybrid Cultivars	5–10 ft (1.5–3 m)	6–10 ft (1.8–3 m)	S	C/W		♦	♦	♦		Su			♦	♦		
Pyrus calleryana	40 ft (12 m)	40 ft (12 m)	T	C/W	♦		♦	♦	♦	Sp			♦	♦		
Pyrus nivalis	30 ft (9 m)	20 ft (6 m)	T	C	♦		♦		♦	Sp			♦	♦		
Pyrus salicifolia	25 ft (8 m)	15 ft (4.5 m)	T	C	♦		♦	♦	♦	Sp			♦	♦		
Pyrus ussuriensis	50 ft (15 m)	20 ft (6 m)	T	C	♦		♦	♦	♦	Sp			♦	♦		
Quercus acutissima	80 ft (24 m)	40 ft (12 m)	T	C/W	♦			♦		Sp			♦	♦		
Quercus agrifolia	40 ft (12 m)	35 ft (10 m)	T	W		♦		♦		Sp			♦	♦		
Quercus alba	100 ft (30 m)	100 ft (30 m)	T	C	♦			♦		Sp			♦	♦		
Quercus bicolor	80 ft (24 m)	40 ft (12 m)	T	C/W	♦			♦		Sp			♦	♦		
Quercus canariensis	80 ft (24 m)	40 ft (12 m)	T	W	♦			♦		Sp			♦	♦		
Quercus castaneifolia	100 ft (30 m)	60 ft (18 m)	T	C/W	♦			♦		Sp			♦	♦		
Quercus cerris	100 ft (30 m)	75 ft (23 m)	T	C/W	♦			♦		Sp			♦	♦		
Quercus chrysolepis	70 ft (21 m)	30 ft (9 m)	T	W		♦		♦		Sp			♦	♦		
Quercus coccinea	70 ft (21 m)	40 ft (12 m)	T	C	♦			♦		Sp			♦	♦		
Quercus dentata	50 ft (15 m)	30 ft (9 m)	T	C	♦			♦		Sp				♦	♦	
Quercus douglasii	70 ft (21 m)	20 ft (6 m)	T	C/W	♦			♦		Sp				♦	♦	
Quercus falcata	80 ft (24 m)	35 ft (10 m)	T	W	♦			♦		Sp			♦	♦		
Quercus frainetto	100 ft (30 m)	60 ft (18 m)	T	C/W	♦			♦		Sp			♦	♦		

Plant name	Height	Spread	Type	Climate	Deciduous	Evergreen	Showy flowers	Showy foliage	Scented flowers	Flowering season	Grow in pot/tub	Indoor use	Frost tolerant	Full sun	Half sun	Heavy shade
Quercus gambelii	30 ft (9 m)	25 ft (8 m)	T	C	◆			◆		Sp			◆	◆		
Quercus garryana	15 ft (4.5 m)	15 ft (4.5 m)	T	C/W	◆			◆		Sp			◆	◆		
Quercus × hispanica	100 ft (30 m)	25 ft (8 m)	T	C/W	◆			◆		Sp			◆	◆		
Quercus ilex	70 ft (21 m)	60 ft (18 m)	T	W		◆		◆		Sp			◆	◆		
Quercus kelloggii	60–90 ft (18–27 m)	40 ft (12 m)	T	C/W	◆			◆		Sp			◆	◆		
Quercus laurifolia	60 ft (18 m)	60 ft (18 m)	T	C/W		◆		◆		Sp			◆	◆		
Quercus lyrata	60 ft (18 m)	30 ft (9 m)	T	W	◆			◆		Sp			◆	◆		
Quercus macrocarpa	120 ft (36 m)	40 ft (12 m)	T	C	◆			◆		Sp			◆	◆		
Quercus mongolica	100 ft (30 m)	40 ft (12 m)	T	C	◆			◆		Sp			◆	◆		
Quercus muehlenbergii	100 ft (30 m)	40 ft (12 m)	T	C	◆			◆		Sp			◆	◆		
Quercus nigra	50 ft (15 m)	40 ft (12 m)	T	C/W	◆			◆		Sp			◆	◆		
Quercus palustris	100 ft (30 m)	60 ft (18 m)	T	C/W	◆			◆		Sp			◆	◆		
Quercus petraea	150 ft (45 m)	75 ft (23 m)	T	C/W	◆			◆		Sp			◆	◆		
Quercus phellos	100 ft (30 m)	40 ft (12 m)	T	C/W	◆			◆		Sp			◆	◆		
Quercus robur	100 ft (30 m)	70 ft (21 m)	T	C/W	◆			◆		Sp			◆	◆		
Quercus rubra	100 ft (30 m)	70 ft (21 m)	T	C/W	◆			◆		Sp			◆	◆		
Quercus shumardii	100 ft (30 m)	40 ft (12 m)	T	C/W	◆			◆		Sp			◆	◆		
Quercus suber	70 ft (21 m)	70 ft (21 m)	T	W		◆		◆		Sp			◆	◆		
Quercus texana	50–70 ft (15–21 m)	50–70 ft (15–21 m)	T	C/W	◆			◆		Sp			◆	◆		
Quercus velutina	100 ft (30 m)	75 ft (23 m)	T	C/W	◆			◆		Sp			◆	◆		
Quercus virginiana	70 ft (21 m)	35 ft (10 m)	T	C/W		◆		◆		Sp			◆	◆		
Quercus wislizeni	80 ft (24 m)	35 ft (10 m)	T	W		◆		◆		Sp			◆	◆		
Quillaja saponaria	50–60 ft (15–18 m)	15–25 ft (4.5–8 m)	T	W		◆	◆			Sp			◆			◆
Radermachera sinica	30 ft (9 m)	15 ft (4.5 m)	T	W/T		◆	◆	◆	◆	Sp/Su				◆		
Rehderodendron macrocarpum	25–35 ft (8–10 m)	15–17 ft (4.5–5 m)	T	W	◆		◆	◆	◆	Sp			◆			◆
Reinwardtia indica	3 ft (0.9 m)	2 ft (0.6 m)	S	W		◆	◆			A/W/Sp				◆		
Retama monosperma	10 ft (3 m)	10 ft (3 m)	S	W		◆			◆	Sp				◆		
Rhamnus alaternus	15 ft (4.5 m)	12 ft (3.5 m)	S	C/W		◆		◆		Sp/Su			◆	◆		
Rhamnus californica	12 ft (3.5 m)	10 ft (3 m)	S	C/W		◆		◆		Sp/Su				◆	◆	
Rhamnus cathartica	20 ft (6 m)	15 ft (4.5 m)	S	C	◆			◆		Sp/Su			◆	◆		
Rhamnus crocea	6 ft (1.8 m)	7 ft (2 m)	S	C/W		◆		◆		Sp/Su				◆	◆	

Plant name	Height	Spread	Type	Climate	Deciduous	Evergreen	Showy flowers	Showy foliage	Scented flowers	Flowering season	Grow in pot/tub	Indoor use	Frost tolerant	Full sun	Half sun	Heavy shade
Rhamnus frangula	15 ft (4.5 m)	15 ft (4.5 m)	S	C	◆			◆		Sp/Su			◆	◆		
Rhamnus imeretina	10 ft (3 m)	15 ft (4.5 m)	S	C	◆			◆		Sp/Su			◆	◆		
Rhamnus prinoides	25 ft (8 m)	15 ft (4.5 m)	S	C/W		◆		◆		Sp/Su				◆		
Rhaphiolepis × delacourii	6 ft (1.8 m)	8 ft (2.4 m)	S	W/T		◆	◆		◆	Sp/Su			◆	◆		
Rhaphiolepis indica	8 ft (2.4 m)	8 ft (2.4 m)	S	W/T		◆	◆		◆	Sp			◆	◆		
Rhaphiolepis umbellata	6 ft (1.8 m)	7 ft (2 m)	S	W/T		◆	◆		◆	Sp/Su			◆	◆		
Rhododendron aberconwayi	6 ft (1.8 m)	4 ft (1.2 m)	S	C/W		◆	◆			Sp/Su					◆	
Rhododendron albrechtii	7 ft (2 m)	4 ft (1.2 m)	S	C	◆		◆			Sp					◆	
Rhododendron alutaceum	7–15 ft (2–4.5 m)	5–12 ft (1.5–3.5 m)	S	C/W		◆	◆			Sp			◆	◆	◆	
Rhododendron arborescens	10 ft (3 m)	8 ft (2.4 m)	S	C	◆		◆		◆	Sp/Su					◆	
Rhododendron arboreum	60 ft (18 m)	15 ft (4.5 m)	T	C/W		◆	◆			Sp					◆	
Rhododendron arizelum	6–25 ft (1.8–8 m)	6–25 ft (1.8–8 m)	S	C/W		◆	◆	◆		Sp/Su					◆	
Rhododendron augustinii	3–20 ft (0.9–6 m)	2–10 ft (0.6–3 m)	S	C/W		◆	◆			Sp/Su					◆	
Rhododendron austrinum	10 ft (3 m)	10 ft (3 m)	S	C	◆		◆			Sp					◆	
Rhododendron calophytum	15 ft (4.5 m)	20 ft (6 m)	T	C/W		◆	◆	◆		Sp					◆	
Rhododendron campanulatum	15 ft (4.5 m)	15 ft (4.5 m)	S	C		◆	◆	◆		Sp					◆	
Rhododendron campylogynum	18 in (45 cm)	30 in (75 cm)	S	C/W		◆	◆			Sp/Su	◆				◆	
Rhododendron canescens	15 ft (4.5 m)	8 ft (2.4 m)	S	C/W	◆		◆		◆	Sp					◆	
Rhododendron catawbiense	10 ft (3 m)	10 ft (3 m)	S	C/W		◆	◆			Sp/Su					◆	
Rhododendron ciliatum	6 ft (1.8 m)	6 ft (1.8 m)	S	W		◆	◆			Sp					◆	
Rhododendron cinnabarinum	10 ft (3 m)	7 ft (2 m)	S	C/W		◆	◆	◆		Sp/Su					◆	
Rhododendron concinnum	6–20 ft (1.8–6 m)	6–10 ft (1.8–3 m)	S	C/W		◆	◆			Sp					◆	
Rhododendron dauricum	8 ft (2.4 m)	8 ft (2.4 m)	S	C/W		◆	◆			W/Sp					◆	
Rhododendron decorum	20 ft (6 m)	8 ft (2.4 m)	S	C/W		◆	◆	◆	◆	Su					◆	
Rhododendron degronianum	8 ft (2.4 m)	7 ft (2 m)	S	C/W		◆	◆	◆		Sp/Su	◆				◆	
Rhododendron edgeworthii	6 ft (1.8 m)	6 ft (1.8 m)	S	W		◆	◆	◆	◆	Sp	◆				◆	
Rhododendron falconeri	40 ft (12 m)	30 ft (9 m)	T	W		◆	◆	◆	◆	Sp/Su					◆	
Rhododendron flammeum	6 ft (1.8 m)	3 ft (0.9 m)	S	W/T	◆		◆			Sp/Su				◆		
Rhododendron forrestii	4 in (10 cm)	48 in (120 cm)	S	W		◆	◆	◆		Sp/Su	◆				◆	
Rhododendron fortunei	15 ft (4.5 m)	8 ft (2.4 m)	S	C/W		◆	◆		◆	Su					◆	
Rhododendron griffithianum	60 ft (18 m)	10 ft (3 m)	T	W		◆	◆		◆	Sp/Su					◆	
Rhododendron haematodes	5 ft (1.5 m)	5 ft (1.5 m)	S	C/W		◆	◆	◆		Sp/Su					◆	

Plant name	Height	Spread	Type	Climate	Deciduous	Evergreen	Showy flowers	Showy foliage	Scented flowers	Flowering season	Grow in pot/tub	Indoor use	Frost tolerant	Full sun	Half sun	Heavy shade
Rhododendron impeditum	12 in (30 cm)	12 in (30 cm)	S	C/W		♦	♦			Sp	♦		♦		♦	
Rhododendron indicum	3 ft (0.9 m)	2 ft (0.6 m)	S	C/W		♦	♦			Sp	♦		♦		♦	
Rhododendron intricatum	5 ft (1.5 m)	5 ft (1.5 m)	S	C		♦	♦			Sp/Su			♦		♦	
Rhododendron jasminiflorum	22 in (55 cm)	22 in (55 cm)	S	W/T		♦	♦		♦	W	♦	♦			♦	
Rhododendron kaempferi	4 ft (1.2 m)	4 ft (1.2 m)	S	C	♦	♦	♦			Sp			♦		♦	
Rhododendron kiusianum	3 ft (0.9 m)	3 ft (0.9 m)	S	C/W		♦	♦			Sp	♦		♦		♦	
Rhododendron konori	12 ft (3.5 m)	6 ft (1.8 m)	S	W/T		♦	♦			W	♦	♦			♦	
Rhododendron lacteum	12 ft (3.5 m)	12 ft (3.5 m)	S	C/W		♦	♦			Sp			♦		♦	
Rhododendron laetum	10 ft (3 m)	4 ft (1.2 m)	S	W/T		♦	♦			A–Sp	♦	♦			♦	
Rhododendron leucaspis	4 ft (1.2 m)	4 ft (1.2 m)	S	C/W		♦	♦	♦		W/Sp			♦		♦	
Rhododendron lochiae	3 ft (0.9 m)	2 ft (0.6 m)	S	W/T		♦	♦			W	♦	♦			♦	
Rhododendron luteiflorum	12–36 in (30–90 cm)	18–32 in (45–80 cm)	S	C/W		♦	♦			Sp			♦	♦	♦	
Rhododendron lutescens	20 ft (6 m)	15 ft (4.5 m)	S	C/W		♦	♦			W/Sp			♦		♦	
Rhododendron luteum	12 ft (3.5 m)	8 ft (2.4 m)	S	C/W	♦		♦	♦		Sp			♦		♦	
Rhododendron macgregoriae	15 ft (4.5 m)	7 ft (2 m)	S	W/T		♦	♦			W	♦	♦			♦	
Rhododendron macrophyllum	12 ft (3.5 m)	12 ft (3.5 m)	S	C/W		♦	♦			Su			♦		♦	
Rhododendron maddenii	25 ft (8 m)	8 ft (2.4 m)	T	W		♦	♦		♦	Sp					♦	
Rhododendron mallotum	20 ft (6 m)	12 ft (3.5 m)	S	C/W		♦	♦			Sp			♦		♦	
Rhododendron maximum	6 ft (1.8 m)	7 ft (2 m)	S	C		♦	♦			Sp/Su			♦		♦	
Rhododendron megeratum	15–30 in (38–75 cm)	15 in (38 cm)	S	W		♦	♦			W/Sp	♦				♦	
Rhododendron minus	3–5 ft (0.9–1.5 m)	3–5 ft (0.9–1.5 m)	S	C		♦	♦			Sp/Su			♦		♦	
Rhododendron molle	4 ft (1.2 m)	4 ft (1.2 m)	S	C/W	♦		♦			Sp			♦		♦	
Rhododendron mucronulatum	6 ft (1.8 m)	3 ft (0.9 m)	S	C	♦		♦			Sp			♦		♦	
Rhododendron neriiflorum	10–20 ft (3–6 m)	6–12 ft (1.8–3.5 m)	S	C/W		♦	♦	♦		Sp/Su			♦	♦	♦	
Rhododendron nuttallii	35 ft (10 m)	20 ft (6 m)	T	W		♦	♦	♦	♦	Su					♦	
Rhododendron × obtusum	3 ft (0.9 m)	3 ft (0.9 m)	S	C/W		♦	♦			Sp	♦		♦		♦	
Rhododendron occidentale	5 ft (1.5 m)	5 ft (1.5 m)	S	C/W	♦		♦	♦	♦	Sp			♦		♦	
Rhododendron orbiculare	10 ft (3 m)	10 ft (3 m)	S	C/W		♦	♦	♦		Sp			♦		♦	
Rhododendron orbiculatum	3 ft (0.9 m)	3 ft (0.9 m)	S	W/T		♦	♦			A–Sp	♦	♦			♦	
Rhododendron pachysanthum	4 ft (1.2 m)	3 ft (0.9 m)	S	C/W		♦	♦	♦		Sp					♦	
Rhododendron periclymenoides	10 ft (3 m)	8 ft (2.4 m)	S	C/W	♦		♦		♦	Sp			♦		♦	
Rhododendron ponticum	25 ft (8 m)	20 ft (6 m)	S	C/W		♦	♦			Sp			♦	♦		

Plant name	Height	Spread	Type	Climate	Deciduous	Evergreen	Showy flowers	Showy foliage	Scented flowers	Flowering season	Grow in pot/tub	Indoor use	Frost tolerant	Full sun	Half sun	Heavy shade
Rhododendron protistum	100 ft (30 m)	15 ft (4.5 m)	T	W		♦	♦	♦		W/Sp					♦	
Rhododendron quinquefolium	8–25 ft (2.4–8 m)	4–8 ft (1.2–2.4 m)	S	C/W	♦		♦	♦		Sp			♦		♦	
Rhododendron racemosum	5 ft (1.5 m)	5 ft (1.5 m)	S	C		♦	♦			Sp			♦		♦	
Rhododendron reticulatum	4 ft (1.2 m)	4 ft (1.2 m)	S	C/W	♦		♦			Sp			♦		♦	
Rhododendron rubiginosum	30 ft (9 m)	20 ft (6 m)	S	C/W		♦	♦			Sp			♦		♦	
Rhododendron schlippenbachii	15 ft (4.5 m)	15 ft (4.5 m)	S	C	♦		♦	♦		Sp			♦		♦	
Rhododendron scopulorum	15 ft (4.5 m)	8 ft (2.4 m)	S	W		♦	♦		♦	Sp/Su					♦	
Rhododendron sinogrande	50 ft (15 m)	30 ft (9 m)	S	W		♦	♦	♦		Sp					♦	
Rhododendron spinuliferum	10 ft (3 m)	8 ft (2.4 m)	S	W		♦	♦			Sp					♦	
Rhododendron stamineum	10 ft (3 m)	10 ft (3 m)	S	W		♦	♦			Sp					♦	
Rhododendron thomsonii	2–20 ft (0.6–6 m)	2–20 ft (0.6–6 m)	S	C/W		♦	♦			Sp					♦	
Rhododendron tomentosum	1–4 ft (0.3–1.2 m)	3 ft (0.9 m)	S	C		♦	♦			Sp/Su					♦	♦
Rhododendron trichostomum	5 ft (1.5 m)	3 ft (0.9 m)	S	C/W		♦	♦			Sp					♦	
Rhododendron veitchianum	8 ft (2.4 m)	8 ft (2.4 m)	S	W		♦	♦		♦	Sp/Su					♦	
Rhododendron viscosum	8 ft (2.4 m)	8 ft (2.4 m)	S	C/W	♦		♦		♦	Sp/Su					♦	
Rhododendron wardii	25 ft (8 m)	15 ft (4.5 m)	S	C/W		♦	♦			Sp					♦	
Rhododendron williamsianum	5 ft (1.5 m)	4 ft (1.2 m)	S	C/W		♦	♦	♦		Sp					♦	
Rhododendron yedoense	3 ft (0.9 m)	3 ft (0.9 m)	S	C	♦		♦	♦	♦	Sp					♦	
Rhododendron zoelleri	6 ft (1.8 m)	3 ft (0.9 m)	S	W/T		♦	♦			A–Sp	♦	♦			♦	
Rhododendron, Hardy Small Hybrids	12–40 in (30–100 cm)	12–40 in (30–100 cm)	S	C/W		♦	♦	♦		Sp/Su	♦				♦	
Rhododendron, Hardy Medium Hybrids	3–6 ft (0.9–1.8 m)	2–6 ft (0.6–1.8 m)	S	C/W		♦	♦			Sp/Su					♦	
Rhododendron, Hardy Tall Hybrids	6–35 ft (1.8–10 m)	5–17 ft (1.5–5 m)	S	C/W		♦	♦	♦		Sp/Su					♦	
Rhododendron, Tender Hybrids	3–17 ft (0.9–5 m)	3–10 ft (0.9–3 m)	S	W		♦	♦	♦	♦	Sp/Su				♦	♦	
Rhododendron, Vireya Hybrids	18–72 in (45–180 cm)	12–60 in (30–150 cm)	S	W/T		♦	♦			A–Sp	♦	♦			♦	♦
Rhododendron, Yak Hybrids	1–6 ft (0.3–1.8 m)	2–5 ft (0.6–1.5 m)	S	C/W		♦	♦			Sp/Su	♦				♦	
Rhododendron, Ghent Hybrids	5–8 ft (1.5–2.4 m)	3–6 ft (0.9–1.8 m)	S	C/W	♦		♦			Sp/Su				♦	♦	
Rhododendron, Ilam and Melford Hybrids	4–10 ft (1.2–3 m)	4–7 ft (1.2–2 m)	S	C/W	♦		♦			Sp/Su				♦	♦	♦
Rhododendron, Knap Hill and Exbury Hybrids	4–10 ft (1.2–3 m)	4–7 ft (1.2–2 m)	S	C/W	♦		♦			Sp/Su				♦	♦	♦

Plant name	Height	Spread	Type	Climate	Deciduous	Evergreen	Showy flowers	Showy foliage	Scented flowers	Flowering season	Grow in pot/tub	Indoor use	Frost tolerant	Full sun	Half sun	Heavy shade
Rhododendron, Mollis Hybrids	5–8 ft (1.5–2.4 m)	5–7 ft (1.5–2 m)	S	C/W	♦		♦			Sp/Su			♦	♦	♦	
Rhododendron, Occidentale Hybrids	6–10 ft (1.8–3 m)	6–10 ft (1.8–3 m)	S	C/W	♦		♦		♦	Sp			♦	♦	♦	
Rhododendron, Belgian Indica Hybrids	2–5 ft (0.6–1.5 m)	3–6 ft (0.9–1.8 m)	S	W		♦	♦			W/Sp	♦	♦	♦	♦	♦	
Rhododendron, Rutherford Indica Hybrids	3–8 ft (0.9–2.4 m)	4–8 ft (1.2–2.4 m)	S	W		♦	♦			W/Sp	♦	♦		♦	♦	
Rhododendron, Southern Indica Hybrids	5–10 ft (1.5–3 m)	6–12 ft (1.8–3.5 m)	S	W		♦	♦			Sp			♦	♦	♦	
Rhododendron, Kaempferi or Malvatica Hybrids	2–8 ft (0.6–2.4 m)	3–7 ft (0.9–2 m)	S	C/W		♦	♦			Sp			♦	♦	♦	
Rhododendron, Vuyk Hybrids	2–8 ft (0.6–2.4 m)	3–7 ft (0.9–2 m)	S	C/W		♦	♦			Sp	♦		♦	♦	♦	
Rhododendron, Kurume Hybrids	2–4 ft (0.6–1.2 m)	2–4 ft (0.6–1.2 m)	S	C/W		♦	♦			Sp			♦	♦	♦	
Rhododendron, Satsuki Hybrids	12–36 in (30–90 cm)	24–48 in (60–120 cm)	S	C/W		♦	♦			Sp/Su	♦		♦	♦	♦	
Rhododendron, Azaleodendron Hybrids	2–8 ft (0.6–2.4 m)	2–7 ft (0.6–2 m)	S	C/W	♦	♦	♦		♦	Sp/Su	♦		♦	♦	♦	
Rhodoleia championii	20 ft (6 m)	12 ft (3.5 m)	T	W		♦	♦			W/Sp			♦			♦
Rhus aromatica	3–5 ft (0.9–1.5 m)	5 ft (1.5 m)	S	C	♦			♦	♦	Sp				♦	♦	
Rhus chinensis	20 ft (6 m)	15 ft (4.5 m)	T	W/T	♦			♦	♦	Su/A				♦	♦	
Rhus copallina	5 ft (1.5 m)	5 ft (1.5 m)	S	C/W	♦			♦	♦	Su				♦	♦	
Rhus glabra	8 ft (2.4 m)	8 ft (2.4 m)	S	C/W	♦			♦	♦	Su				♦	♦	
Rhus lancea	25 ft (8 m)	25 ft (8 m)	T	W/T		♦		♦		Su				♦		
Rhus lucida	12 ft (3.5 m)	12 ft (3.5 m)	S/T	W		♦		♦		Sp				♦		
Rhus microphylla	6–10 ft (1.8–3 m)	4–6 ft (1.2–1.8 m)	S	W	♦			♦	♦	Sp				♦	♦	
Rhus pendulina	15 ft (4.5 m)	15 ft (4.5 m)	T	W		♦		♦		Su				♦		
Rhus typhina	15 ft (4.5 m)	15 ft (4.5 m)	T	C	♦			♦	♦	Su				♦	♦	
Ribes alpinum	3–6 ft (0.9–1.8 m)	3 ft (0.9 m)	S	C	♦		♦			Sp				♦	♦	
Ribes aureum	6 ft (1.8 m)	6 ft (1.8 m)	S	C/W	♦		♦			Sp				♦	♦	
Ribes fasciculatum	5 ft (i.5 m)	4 ft (1.2 m)	S	C/W	♦		♦			Sp				♦	♦	
Ribes magellanicum	6–8 ft (1.8–2.4 m)	6 ft (1.8 m)	S	C/W	♦		♦			Sp				♦	♦	
Ribes sanguineum	10 ft (3 m)	10 ft (3 m)	S	C/W	♦		♦			Sp				♦	♦	
Ribes speciosum	12 ft (3.5 m)	10 ft (3 m)	S	W		♦	♦		♦	Su				♦	♦	
Ricinocarpos pinifolius	3 ft (0.9 m)	3 ft (0.9 m)	S	W/T		♦	♦			Sp						♦
Ricinus communis	5–15 ft (1.5–4.5 m)	3 ft (0.9 m)	S	W/T	♦			♦		Su					♦	

Plant name	Height	Spread	Type	Climate	Deciduous	Evergreen	Showy flowers	Showy foliage	Scented flowers	Flowering season	Grow in pot/tub	Indoor use	Frost tolerant	Full sun	Half sun	Heavy shade
Robinia hispida	10 ft (3 m)	10 ft (3 m)	T	C/W	♦		♦			Sp			♦	♦		
Robinia pseudoacacia	50 ft (15 m)	35 ft (10 m)	T	C/W	♦		♦	♦		Sp			♦	♦		
Robinia × slavinii	15 ft (4.5 m)	10 ft (3 m)	S	C/W	♦		♦			Sp			♦	♦		
Robinia viscosa	30 ft (9 m)	20 ft (6 m)	T	C/W	♦		♦			Sp			♦	♦		
Roella ciliata	3 ft (0.9 m)	2 ft (0.6 m)	S	W		♦	♦			Sp/Su				♦		
Roldana petasitis	6–10 ft (1.8–3 m)	6–10 ft (1.8–3 m)	S	W/T	♦	♦	♦	♦		W				♦		
Rondeletia amoena	10 ft (3 m)	8 ft (2.4 m)	S	W/T		♦	♦		♦	Sp				♦		
Rondeletia odorata	5 ft (1.5 m)	3 ft (0.9 m)	S	W/T		♦	♦		♦	Su/A	♦			♦		
Rosa acicularis	6 ft (1.8 m)	4 ft (1.2 m)	S	C/W	♦		♦		♦	Su			♦	♦		
Rosa beggeriana	8 ft (2.4 m)	8 ft (2.4 m)	S	C	♦		♦			Su			♦	♦		
Rosa blanda	3–7 ft (0.9–2 m)	3 ft (0.9 m)	S	C/W	♦		♦		♦	Su			♦	♦		
Rosa californica	7 ft (2 m)	6 ft (1.8 m)	S	C/W	♦		♦		♦	Su			♦	♦		
Rosa canina	10 ft (3 m)	10 ft (3 m)	S	C/W	♦		♦		♦	Su			♦	♦		
Rosa chinensis	20 ft (6 m)	8 ft (2.4 m)	S	W	♦		♦			Su				♦	♦	
Rosa cinnamomea plena	6 ft (1.8 m)	5 ft (1.5 m)	S	C/W	♦		♦			Su			♦	♦		
Rosa davurica	3–5 ft (0.9–1.5 m)	4 ft (1.2 m)	S	C/W	♦		♦			Su			♦	♦		
Rosa ecae	4 ft (1.2 m)	4 ft (1.2 m)	S	C/W	♦		♦			Sp			♦	♦		
Rosa eglanteria	10 ft (3 m)	10 ft (3 m)	S	C/W	♦		♦		♦	Su			♦	♦		
Rosa elegantula	3–7 ft (0.9–2 m)	8 ft (2.4 m)	S	C/W	♦		♦			Su			♦	♦		
Rosa foetida	3–10 ft (0.9–3 m)	6 ft (1.8 m)	S	C/W	♦		♦			Su			♦	♦		
Rosa gallica	4 ft (1.2 m)	4 ft (1.2 m)	S	C/W	♦		♦		♦	Su			♦	♦		
Rosa gigantea	30–60 ft (9–18 m)	20–40 ft (6–12 m)	S	C/W	♦	♦	♦		♦	Su			♦	♦		
Rosa glauca	6 ft (1.8 m)	6 ft (1.8 m)	S	C/W	♦		♦	♦		Su			♦	♦		
Rosa hemisphaerica	7 ft (2 m)	7 ft (2 m)	S	C/W	♦		♦			Su			♦	♦		
Rosa hugonis	7 ft (2 m)	6 ft (1.8 m)	S	C/W	♦		♦		♦	Sp/Su			♦	♦		
Rosa laxa	7–8 ft (2–2.4 m)	5–10 ft (1.5–3 m)	S	C/W	♦		♦			Su			♦	♦	♦	♦
Rosa macrophylla	10 ft (3 m)	10 ft (3 m)	S	C/W	♦		♦		♦	Su			♦	♦		
Rosa marginata	3–8 ft (0.9–2.4 m)	8 ft (2.4 m)	S	C/W	♦		♦			Su			♦	♦		
Rosa minutifolia	4 ft (1.2 m)	4 ft (1.2 m)	S	W	♦	♦	♦			Su				♦	♦	
Rosa moyesii	10 ft (3 m)	10 ft (3 m)	S	C/W	♦		♦			Su			♦	♦		
Rosa multiflora	10–15 ft (3–4.5 m)	10 ft (3 m)	S	C/W	♦		♦			Su			♦	♦		
Rosa nitida	3 ft (0.9 m)	4 ft (1.2 m)	S	C/W	♦		♦	♦	♦	Su				♦	♦	

Plant name	Height	Spread	Type	Climate	Deciduous	Evergreen	Showy flowers	Showy foliage	Scented flowers	Flowering season	Grow in pot/tub	Indoor use	Frost tolerant	Full sun	Half sun	Heavy shade
Rosa nutkana	6–10 ft (1.8–3 m)	7 ft (2 m)	S	C/W	♦		♦		♦	Su			♦	♦		
Rosa pendulina	2–7 ft (0.6–2 m)	5 ft (1.5 m)	S	C/W	♦		♦			Su			♦	♦		
Rosa pisocarpa	3–7 ft (0.9–2 m)	4 ft (1.2 m)	S	C/W	♦		♦			Su			♦	♦		
Rosa primula	5–10 ft (1.5–3 m)	5 ft (1.5 m)	S	C/W	♦		♦		♦	Su			♦	♦		
Rosa roxburghii	7 ft (2 m)	7 ft (2 m)	S	C/W	♦		♦		♦	Su			♦	♦		
Rosa rugosa	5–8 ft (1.5–2.4 m)	5–8 ft (1.5–2.4 m)	S	C/W	♦		♦		♦	Su/A			♦	♦		
Rosa sempervirens	1–6 ft (0.3–1.8 m)	20–35 ft (6–10 m)	S	C/W		♦	♦			Su			♦	♦		
Rosa sericea	10 ft (3 m)	8 ft (2.4 m)	S	C/W	♦		♦			Sp			♦	♦		
Rosa setipoda	8 ft (2.4 m)	5 ft (1.5 m)	S	C/W	♦		♦			Su			♦	♦		
Rosa spinosissima	3–7 ft (0.9–2 m)	4 ft (1.2 m)	S	C/W	♦		♦			Sp			♦	♦		
Rosa stellata	3 ft (0.9 m)	3 ft (0.9 m)	S	C/W	♦		♦			Su			♦	♦		
Rosa sweginzowii	12 ft (3.5 m)	15 ft (4.5 m)	S	C/W	♦		♦			Su			♦	♦		
Rosa virginiana	5 ft (1.5 m)	5 ft (1.5 m)	S	C/W	♦		♦			Su			♦	♦		
Rosa wichurana	6 ft (1.8 m)	20 ft (6 m)	S	C/W	♦		♦		♦	Su			♦	♦		
Rosa willmottiae	6 ft (1.8 m)	5 ft (1.5 m)	S	C/W	♦		♦			Su			♦	♦		
Rosa woodsii	3–7 ft (0.9–2 m)	5 ft (1.5 m)	S	C/W	♦		♦			Su			♦	♦		
Rosa, Cluster-flowered (Floribunda) Roses	4–7 ft (1.2–2 m)	3–6 ft (0.9–1.8 m)	S	C/W	♦		♦		♦	Su/A			♦	♦		
Rosa, Large-flowered (Hybrid Tea) Roses	5–8 ft (1.5–2.4 m)	3–6 ft (0.9–1.8 m)	S	C/W	♦		♦		♦	Su/A			♦	♦		
Rosa, Patio (Dwarf Cluster-flowered) Roses	18–30 in (45–75 cm)	18–36 in (45–90 cm)	S	C/W	♦		♦		♦	Su/A	♦		♦	♦		
Rosa, Polyantha Roses	2–4 ft (0.6–1.2 m)	2–3 ft (0.6–0.9 m)	S	C/W	♦		♦		♦	Su			♦	♦		
Rosa, Hybrid Rugosa Roses	2–7 ft (0.6–2 m)	5–10 ft (1.5–3 m)	S	C/W	♦		♦	♦	♦	Su			♦	♦		
Rosa, Modern Shrub Roses	4–8 ft (1.2–2.4 m)	4–8 ft (1.2–2.4 m)	S	C/W	♦		♦		♦	Su			♦	♦		
Rosa, Miniature Roses	8–24 in (20–60 cm)	12–18 in (30–45 cm)	S	C/W	♦		♦			Su	♦		♦	♦		
Rosa, Alba Roses	2–8 ft (0.6–2.4 m)	6–10 ft (1.8–3 m)	S	C/W	♦		♦		♦	Su			♦	♦		
Rosa, Bourbon Roses	4–7 ft (1.2–2 m)	5–8 ft (1.5–2.4 m)	S	C/W	♦		♦		♦	Su/A			♦	♦		
Rosa, Centifolia Roses	2–8 ft (0.6–2.4 m)	4–8 ft (1.2–2.4 m)	S	C/W	♦		♦		♦	Su			♦	♦		
Rosa, China Roses	3–6 ft (0.9–1.8 m)	3–6 ft (0.9–1.8 m)	S	C/W	♦		♦		♦	Su/A			♦	♦		
Rosa, Damask Roses	3–7 ft (0.9–2 m)	5–8 ft (1.5–2.4 m)	S	C/W	♦		♦		♦	Su			♦	♦		
Rosa, Gallica Roses	4–6 ft (1.2–1.8 m)	4–6 ft (1.2–1.8 m)	S	C/W	♦		♦		♦	Su			♦	♦		
Rosa, Hybrid Perpetual Roses	4–7 ft (1.2–2 m)	3–6 ft (0.9–1.8 m)	S	C/W	♦		♦		♦	Su/A			♦	♦		

Plant name	Height	Spread	Type	Climate	Deciduous	Evergreen	Showy flowers	Showy foliage	Scented flowers	Flowering season	Grow in pot/tub	Indoor use	Frost tolerant	Full sun	Half sun	Heavy shade
Rosa, Moss Roses	3–7 ft (0.9–2 m)	5–8 ft (1.5–2.4 m)	S	C/W	◆		◆		◆	Su			◆	◆		
Rosa, Portland Roses	2–4 ft (0.6–1.2 m)	3–5 ft (0.9–1.5 m)	S	C/W	◆		◆		◆	Su			◆	◆		
Rosa, Scots Roses	3–7 ft (0.9–2 m)	5–8 ft (1.5–2.4 m)	S	C/W	◆		◆	◆	◆	Su			◆	◆		
Rosa, Sweet Briar Roses	4–8 ft (1.2–2.4 m)	5–10 ft (1.5–3 m)	S	C/W	◆		◆		◆	Su			◆	◆		
Rosa, Tea Roses	3–7 ft (0.9–2 m)	3–6 ft (0.9–1.8 m)	S	C/W	◆		◆			Su/A			◆	◆		
Rosa, Miscellaneous Old Garden Roses	2–6 ft (0.6–1.8 m)	20–48 in (50–120 cm)	S	C/W	◆		◆			Su			◆	◆	◆	
Rothmannia globosa	12–20 ft (3.5–6 m)	6–10 ft (1.8–3 m)	S	W		◆	◆	◆	◆	Sp				◆		
Rubus biflorus	10 ft (3 m)	10 ft (3 m)	S	C/W	◆			◆		Su			◆	◆		
Rubus cockburnianus	8 ft (2.4 m)	8 ft (2.4 m)	S	C/W	◆		◆	◆		Su			◆	◆		
Rubus crataegifolius	8 ft (2.4 m)	5 ft (1.5 m)	S	C/W	◆		◆	◆		Su			◆	◆		
Rubus fruticosus	3–6 ft (0.9–1.8 m)	10–25 ft (3–8 m)	S	C	◆		◆			Sp/Su			◆	◆		
Rubus odoratus	8 ft (2.4 m)	8 ft (2.4 m)	S	C/W	◆		◆		◆	Su/A			◆	◆		
Rubus pentalobus	4 in (10 cm)	3–7 ft (0.9–2 m)	S	W		◆	◆	◆		Su			◆	◆		
Rubus thibetanus	6–8 ft (1.8–2.4 m)	6–8 ft (1.8–2.4 m)	S	C/W	◆			◆		Su			◆	◆		
Rubus tricolor	2 ft (0.6 m)	8–15 ft (2.4–4.5 m)	S	C/W		◆	◆	◆		Su			◆	◆		
Rubus ursinus	20–36 in (50–90 cm)	3–10 ft (0.9–3 m)	S	C/W	◆		◆			Sp/Su			◆	◆		
Ruellia macrantha	6 ft (1.8 m)	20 in (50 cm)	S	W/T		◆	◆			W	◆				◆	
Ruspolia hypocrateriformis	3 ft (0.9 m)	3 ft (0.9 m)	S	W/T		◆	◆			Sp–A	◆				◆	
Russelia equisetiformis	5 ft (1.5 m)	8 ft (2.4 m)	S	W/T		◆	◆			All				◆		
Ruttya fruticosa	12 ft (3.5 m)	5 ft (1.5 m)	S	W/T		◆	◆			Sp–A				◆		
Salix alba	80 ft (24 m)	30 ft (9 m)	T	C/W	◆			◆		Sp			◆	◆		
Salix amygdaloides	70 ft (21 m)	25 ft (8 m)	T	C/W	◆			◆		Sp			◆	◆		
Salix babylonica	40 ft (12 m)	35 ft (10 m)	T	C/W	◆			◆		Sp			◆	◆		
Salix 'Boydii'	3 ft (0.9 m)	2 ft (0.6 m)	S	C	◆			◆		Sp			◆	◆		
Salix caprea	15–35 ft (4.5–10 m)	10–20 ft (3–6 m)	T	C/W	◆		◆			Sp			◆	◆		
Salix cinerea	10 ft (3 m)	8 ft (2.4 m)	S	C	◆				◆	W/Sp			◆	◆		
Salix daphnoides	35 ft (10 m)	20 ft (6 m)	T	C/W	◆		◆	◆		W/Sp			◆	◆		
Salix discolor	25 ft (8 m)	15 ft (4.5 m)	T	C	◆		◆			W/Sp			◆	◆		
Salix elaeagnos	20 ft (6 m)	20 ft (6 m)	T	C/W	◆			◆		W/Sp			◆	◆		
Salix fargesii	10 ft (3 m)	10 ft (3 m)	S	C/W	◆			◆		Sp			◆	◆		
Salix 'Flame'	20 ft (6 m)	20 ft (6 m)	T	C	◆			◆		Sp			◆	◆		

Plant name	Height	Spread	Type	Climate	Deciduous	Evergreen	Showy flowers	Showy foliage	Scented flowers	Flowering season	Grow in pot/tub	Indoor use	Frost tolerant	Full sun	Half sun	Heavy shade
Salix fragilis	50 ft (15 m)	35 ft (10 m)	T	C/W	◆					Sp			◆	◆		
Salix gracilistyla	10–15 ft (3–4.5 m)	10–15 ft (3–4.5 m)	S	C/W	◆		◆			W/Sp			◆	◆		
Salix hastata	5 ft (1.5 m)	7 ft (2 m)	S	C/W	◆		◆			Sp			◆	◆		
Salix helvetica	2–5 ft (0.6–1.5 m)	3 ft (0.9 m)	S	C	◆		◆			Sp			◆	◆		
Salix integra	10–15 ft (3–4.5 m)	12 ft (3.5 m)	S	C/W	◆			◆		W/Sp			◆	◆		
Salix lanata	2–4 ft (0.6–1.2 m)	6 ft (1.8 m)	S	C/W	◆		◆	◆		Sp			◆	◆		
Salix lindleyana	2 in (5 cm)	30 in (75 cm)	S	C/W	◆		◆			Sp			◆	◆		
Salix magnifica	20 ft (6 m)	10 ft (3 m)	T	C/W	◆		◆			Sp			◆	◆		
Salix nakamurana	12 in (30 cm)	36 in (90 cm)	S	C/W	◆			◆		Sp			◆	◆		
Salix nigra	10–30 ft (3–9 m)	15 ft (4.5 m)	T	C/W	◆		◆			Sp			◆	◆		
Salix purpurea	15 ft (4.5 m)	15 ft (4.5 m)	S	C/W	◆		◆	◆		Sp			◆	◆		
Salix repens	8 in–5 ft (20 cm–1.5 m)	5 ft (1.5 m)	S	C/W	◆		◆			Sp			◆	◆		
Salix reptans	2 in (5 cm)	18–36 in (45–90 cm)	S	C	◆		◆	◆		Sp			◆	◆		
Salix reticulata	6 in (15 cm)	15 in (38 cm)	S	C/W	◆			◆		Sp			◆	◆		
Salix × rubens	35 ft (10 m)	25 ft (8 m)	T	C/W	◆		◆	◆		Sp			◆	◆		
Salix × sepulcralis	40 ft (12 m)	40 ft (12 m)	T	C/W	◆					Sp			◆	◆		
Salix taxifolia	10–15 ft (3–4.5 m)	7–10 ft (2–3 m)	S	W	◆					Sp			◆	◆		
Salix viminalis	8–20 ft (2.4–6 m)	15 ft (4.5 m)	S	C/W	◆					Sp			◆	◆		
Salvia apiana	4 ft (1.2 m)	3 ft (0.9 m)	S	W/T		◆	◆	◆		Sp				◆		
Salvia aurea	3–5 ft (0.9–1.5 m)	3 ft (0.9 m)	S	W/T		◆	◆	◆		Su/A				◆		
Salvia canariensis	4–7 ft (1.2–2 m)	3 ft (0.9 m)	S	W/T		◆	◆			Sp/Su				◆		
Salvia clevelandii	24–48 in (60–120 cm)	15–26 in (38–65 cm)	S	W		◆	◆		◆	Su			◆	◆		
Salvia fruticosa	3 ft (0.9 m)	2 ft (0.6 m)	S	W		◆	◆			Su			◆	◆		
Salvia × jamensis	27–40 in (70–100 cm)	27–40 in (70–100 cm)	S	W/T		◆	◆			Su/A				◆		
Salvia karwinskii	8 ft (2.4 m)	4 ft (1.2 m)	S	W/T		◆	◆	◆		W				◆		
Salvia leucophylla	5 ft (1.5 m)	3 ft (0.9 m)	S	W/T		◆	◆	◆		A			◆	◆		
Salvia mexicana	10 ft (3 m)	7 ft (2 m)	S	W/T		◆	◆			A				◆		
Salvia regla	4 ft (1.2 m)	3 ft (0.9 m)	S	W		◆	◆			A				◆		
Sambucus canadensis	8–12 ft (2.4–3.5 m)	12 ft (3.5 m)	S	C	◆		◆	◆		Su			◆	◆		
Sambucus ebulus	5–7 ft (1.5–2 m)	3–7 ft (0.9–2 m)	S	C/W	◆					Su			◆	◆		
Sambucus nigra	8–30 ft (2.4–9 m)	10–20 ft (2–6 m)	S	C/W	◆		◆	◆	◆	Sp/Su			◆	◆		
Sambucus racemosa	12 ft (3.5 m)	12 ft (3.5 m)	S	C/W	◆		◆	◆		Sp/Su			◆	◆		

Plant name	Height	Spread	Type	Climate	Deciduous	Evergreen	Showy flowers	Showy foliage	Scented flowers	Flowering season	Grow in pot/tub	Indoor use	Frost tolerant	Full sun	Half sun	Heavy shade
Sanchezia speciosa	5 ft (1.5 m)	5 ft (1.5 m)	S	W/T		♦	♦	♦		Su	♦			♦		
Santalum acuminatum	20 ft (6 m)	12 ft (3.5 m)	S	W/T		♦	♦			Any				♦		
Santalum lanceolatum	20 ft (6 m)	15 ft (4.5 m)	S	W/T		♦	♦			Sp/Su				♦		
Santolina rosmarinifolia	12–24 in (30–60 cm)	36 in (90 cm)	S	W		♦	♦	♦		Su			♦	♦		
Sapindus drummondii	50 ft (15 m)	30 ft (9 m)	T	W	♦			♦		Su			♦	♦		
Sapindus mukorossi	40–80 ft (12–24 m)	20 ft (6 m)	T	W	♦			♦		Su				♦		
Sapindus saponaria	30 ft (9 m)	20 ft (6 m)	T	W/T		♦	♦			Su				♦		
Sapium integerrinum	10–20 ft (3–6 m)	20 ft (6 m)	T	W/T	♦		♦			Sp/Su				♦		
Saraca cauliflora	30 ft (9 m)	25 ft (8 m)	T	W/T		♦	♦		♦	Su/A						♦
Sarcobatus vermiculatus	6 ft (1.8 m)	7 ft (2 m)	S	C/W	♦			♦		Su			♦	♦		
Sarcococca confusa	7 ft (2 m)	7 ft (2 m)	S	C/W		♦	♦	♦	♦	W			♦			♦
Sarcococca hookeriana	5 ft (1.5 m)	6 ft (1.8 m)	S	C/W		♦	♦	♦	♦	A/W			♦			♦
Sarcococca ruscifolia	3 ft (0.9 m)	3 ft (0.9 m)	S	W		♦	♦	♦	♦	W	♦		♦			
Sarcococca saligna	3 ft (0.9 m)	3 ft (0.9 m)	S	C/W		♦	♦	♦	♦	W/Sp	♦		♦			♦
Sassafras albidum	50 ft (15 m)	30 ft (9 m)	T	C/W	♦					Sp			♦	♦		
Schefflera actinophylla	30 ft (9 m)	12 ft (3.5 m)	T	W/T		♦	♦	♦		A–Sp				♦		
Schefflera arboricola	3–5 ft (0.9–1.5 m)	3 ft (0.9 m)	T	W/T		♦		♦		Sp/Su	♦	♦		♦		
Schefflera elegantissima	50 ft (15 m)	10 ft (3 m)	T	W/T		♦		♦		Sp/Su	♦	♦		♦		
Schefflera umbellifera	30 ft (9 m)	25 ft (8 m)	T	W/T		♦		♦		Sp/Su				♦		
Schima wallichii	25 ft (8 m)	20 ft (6 m)	T	W		♦	♦	♦	♦	Su	♦	♦		♦		
Schinus molle	50–60 ft (15–18 m)	50 ft (15 m)	T	W/T		♦		♦		Sp				♦		
Schinus terebinthifolius	20 ft (6 m)	15 ft (4.5 m)	T	W/T		♦		♦		Sp				♦		
Schotia brachypetala	50 ft (15 m)	15–25 ft (4.5–8 m)	S	W/T	♦		♦		♦	Su				♦		
Schotia latifolia	50 ft (15 m)	25 ft (8 m)	S	W/T	♦		♦			Su				♦		
Sciadopitys verticillata	70 ft (21 m)	20 ft (6 m)	C	C/W		♦		♦		Sp	♦		♦	♦		
Senna alata	30 ft (9 m)	15 ft (4.5 m)	T	W/T		♦	♦	♦		Su/A				♦		
Senna artemisioides	7 ft (2 m)	7 ft (2 m)	S	W/T		♦	♦			Sp–A				♦		
Senna corymbosa	10 ft (3 m)	8 ft (2.4 m)	S	W/T		♦	♦			Sp–A			♦	♦		
Senna didymobotrya	10 ft (3 m)	10 ft (3 m)	S	W/T		♦	♦			Sp–A				♦		
Senna multijuga	25 ft (8 m)	20 ft (6 m)	T	W/T		♦	♦			Su/A				♦		
Senna polyphylla	25 ft (8 m)	12 ft (3.5 m)	T	W/T		♦	♦			Any				♦		
Senna siamea	40 ft (12 m)	35 ft (10 m)	T	W		♦	♦			Sp/Su				♦		

Plant name	Height	Spread	Type	Climate	Deciduous	Evergreen	Showy flowers	Showy foliage	Scented flowers	Flowering season	Grow in pot/tub	Indoor use	Frost tolerant	Full sun	Half sun	Heavy shade
Senna splendida	10–15 ft (3–4.5 m)	8–12 ft (2.4–3.5 m)	T	W/T		♦	♦			A				♦		
Sequoia sempervirens	150 ft (45 m)	15–25 ft (4.5–8 m)	C	W		♦		♦		Sp			♦	♦		
Sequoiadendron giganteum	150–165 ft (45–50 m)	20–35 ft (6–9 m)	C	C/W		♦				Sp			♦	♦		
Serruria 'Sugar 'n' Spice'	4 ft (1.2 m)	4 ft (1.2 m)	S	W		♦	♦			W/Sp				♦		
Sesbania punicea	6 ft (1.8 m)	4 ft (1.2 m)	S	W/T		♦	♦			Su				♦		
Shepherdia argentea	12 ft (3.5 m)	12 ft (3.5 m)	S	C	♦			♦		Sp			♦	♦		
Shepherdia canadensis	8 ft (2.4 m)	8 ft (2.4 m)	S	C	♦		♦	♦		Su				♦		
Simmondsia chinensis	8 ft (2.4 m)	6 ft (1.8 m)	S	W/T		♦	♦			Su				♦		
Skimmia × confusa	2–10 ft (0.6–3 m)	4 ft (1.2 m)	S	C/W		♦	♦	♦	♦	W	♦		♦	♦	♦	♦
Skimmia japonica	20 ft (6 m)	20 ft (6 m)	S	C/W		♦	♦	♦	♦	Sp	♦		♦	♦	♦	
Skimmia laureola	2–40 ft (0.6–12 m)	3–10 ft (0.9–3 m)	S	C/W		♦	♦	♦	♦	Sp	♦		♦	♦		
Solanum aviculare	3–12 ft (0.9–3.5 m)	3–12 ft (0.9–3.5 m)	S	W/T		♦	♦	♦		Su/A						♦
Solanum capsicastrum	12–24 in (30–60 cm)	24 in (60 cm)	S	W/T		♦		♦		Su/A	♦	♦		♦		
Solanum giganteum	12 ft (3.5 m)	10 ft (3 m)	S	W/T		♦	♦	♦		Su/A				♦		
Solanum mammosum	5 ft (1.5 m)	3 ft (0.9 m)	S	W/T		♦		♦		Su/A	♦	♦		♦		
Solanum pseudocapsicum	3–6 ft (0.9–1.8 m)	4 ft (1.2 m)	S	W/T		♦				Su/A	♦	♦		♦		
Solanum pyracanthum	3–6 ft (0.9–1.8 m)	2–3 ft (0.6–0.9 m)	S	W/T		♦		♦		Su	♦	♦		♦		
Solanum rantonnetii	6 ft (1.8 m)	7 ft (2 m)	S	W/T		♦	♦		♦	Su	♦	♦		♦		
Sophora arizonica	10–15 ft (3–4.5 m)	8–10 ft (2.4–3 m)	S	W		♦	♦		♦	Sp			♦	♦		
Sophora davidii	10 ft (3 m)	10 ft (3 m)	S	C/W	♦		♦			Su			♦	♦		
Sophora japonica	50 ft (15 m)	35 ft (10 m)	T	C/W	♦		♦			Su			♦	♦		
Sophora microphylla	20–30 ft (6–9 m)	20 ft (6 m)	T	W		♦	♦			Sp				♦		
Sophora prostrata	6 ft (1.8 m)	7 ft (2 m)	S	W		♦	♦	♦		W/Sp			♦	♦		
Sophora secundiflora	30 ft (9 m)	15 ft (4.5 m)	T	W/T		♦	♦		♦	Sp			♦	♦		
Sophora tetraptera	15–40 ft (4.5–12 m)	15 ft (4.5 m)	T	W		♦	♦			Sp			♦	♦		
Sophora tomentosa	30 ft (9 m)	8 ft (2.4 m)	T	W/T		♦	♦			Sp/Su				♦		
Sorbaria kirilowii	17 ft (5 m)	20 ft (6 m)	S	C	♦		♦		♦	Su			♦	♦		
Sorbaria sorbifolia	10 ft (3 m)	10 ft (3 m)	S	C/W	♦		♦			Su			♦	♦		
Sorbaria tomentosa	20 ft (6 m)	15 ft (4.5 m)	S	C/W	♦		♦			Su			♦	♦		
Sorbus alnifolia	50 ft (15 m)	25 ft (8 m)	T	C	♦		♦	♦		Sp			♦	♦		
Sorbus americana	20–30 ft (6–9 m)	20 ft (6 m)	T	C	♦		♦			Sp			♦	♦		
Sorbus aria	20–40 ft (6–12 m)	25 ft (8 m)	T	C	♦		♦	♦		Sp			♦	♦		

Plant name	Height	Spread	Type	Climate	Deciduous	Evergreen	Showy flowers	Showy foliage	Scented flowers	Flowering season	Grow in pot/tub	Indoor use	Frost tolerant	Full sun	Half sun	Heavy shade
Sorbus × arnoldiana	15–40 ft (4.5–12 m)	20 ft (6 m)	T	C	◆		◆			Sp			◆	◆		
Sorbus aucuparia	15–40 ft (4.5–12 m)	20 ft (6 m)	T	C	◆		◆		◆	Sp			◆	◆		
Sorbus cashmiriana	30 ft (9 m)	20 ft (6 m)	T	C/W	◆		◆	◆		Sp			◆	◆		
Sorbus chamaemespilus	3–6 ft (0.9–1.8 m)	3–6 ft (0.9–1.8 m)	T	C/W	◆		◆			Sp			◆	◆		
Sorbus commixta	20–30 ft (6–9 m)	20 ft (6 m)	T	C/W	◆		◆	◆		Sp			◆	◆		
Sorbus decora	30 ft (9 m)	15 ft (4.5 m)	T	C	◆		◆			Sp			◆	◆		
Sorbus esserteauiana	50 ft (15 m)	35 ft (10 m)	T	C/W	◆		◆	◆		Sp			◆	◆		
Sorbus forrestii	25 ft (8 m)	20 ft (6 m)	T	C/W	◆		◆			Sp			◆	◆		
Sorbus × hostii	12–15 ft (3.5–4.5 m)	10 ft (3 m)	T	C/W	◆		◆			Sp			◆	◆		
Sorbus hupehensis	30 ft (9 m)	20 ft (6 m)	T	C/W	◆		◆	◆		Sp			◆	◆		
Sorbus intermedia	20–30 ft (6–9 m)	20 ft (6 m)	T	C	◆		◆	◆		Sp			◆	◆		
Sorbus latifolia	30–50 ft (9–15 m)	20 ft (6 m)	T	C	◆		◆	◆		Sp			◆	◆		
Sorbus megalocarpa	30 ft (9 m)	8 ft (2.4 m)	T	C/W	◆		◆			Sp			◆	◆		
Sorbus mougeotii	40 ft (12 m)	15 ft (4.5 m)	T	C/W	◆		◆			Sp			◆	◆		
Sorbus pohuashanensis	70 ft (21 m)	20 ft (6 m)	T	C	◆		◆			Sp			◆	◆		
Sorbus reducta	15 in (38 cm)	6 ft (1.8 m)	S	C/W	◆				◆	Sp			◆	◆		
Sorbus sargentiana	20–30 ft (6–9 m)	20 ft (6 m)	T	C/W	◆		◆			Sp			◆	◆		
Sorbus thibetica	50 ft (15 m)	30 ft (9 m)	T	W	◆		◆	◆		Sp			◆	◆		
Sorbus × thuringiaca	30–40 ft (9–12 m)	25 ft (8 m)	T	C/W	◆		◆			Sp			◆	◆		
Sorbus torminalis	30–50 ft (9–15 m)	25 ft (8 m)	T	C/W	◆		◆	◆		Sp			◆	◆		
Sorbus vilmorinii	20 ft (6 m)	15 ft (4.5 m)	T	C/W	◆		◆	◆		Sp			◆	◆		
Sorbus Hybrid Cultivars	10–25 ft (3–8 m)	7–15 ft (2–4.5 m)	T	C/W	◆		◆	◆		Sp			◆	◆		
Sparmannia africana	20 ft (6 m)	10 ft (3 m)	T	W/T		◆	◆	◆		Sp/Su				◆		
Spartium junceum	10 ft (3 m)	10 ft (3 m)	S	W	◆		◆		◆	Sp/Su			◆	◆		
Spathodea campanulata	25–35 ft (8–10 m)	25 ft (8 m)	T	W/T	◆		◆			Sp/Su				◆		
Spiraea 'Arguta'	5–7 ft (1.5–2 m)	4 ft (1.2 m)	S	C/W	◆		◆			Sp			◆	◆		
Spiraea betulifolia	3 ft (0.9 m)	3 ft (0.9 m)	S	C/W	◆		◆			Su			◆	◆		
Spiraea × billardii	7 ft (2 m)	7 ft (2 m)	S	C/W	◆		◆			Su			◆	◆		
Spiraea × brachybotrys	8 ft (2.4 m)	6 ft (1.8 m)	S	C/W	◆		◆			Su			◆	◆		
Spiraea cantoniensis	6 ft (1.8 m)	8 ft (2.4 m)	S	C/W	◆		◆			Su			◆	◆		
Spiraea × cinerea	5 ft (1.5 m)	5 ft (1.5 m)	S	C/W	◆		◆			Sp			◆	◆		
Spiraea douglasii	6 ft (1.8 m)	6 ft (1.8 m)	S	C/W	◆		◆			Su			◆	◆		

Plant name	Height	Spread	Type	Climate	Deciduous	Evergreen	Showy flowers	Showy foliage	Scented flowers	Flowering season	Grow in pot/tub	Indoor use	Frost tolerant	Full sun	Half sun	Heavy shade
Spiraea fritschiana	3 ft (0.9 m)	5 ft (1.5 m)	S	C/W	◆		◆			Su			◆	◆		
Spiraea japonica	6 ft (1.8 m)	4 ft (1.2 m)	S	C/W	◆		◆	◆		Su			◆	◆		
Spiraea nipponica	6 ft (1.8 m)	6 ft (1.8 m)	S	C/W	◆		◆			Su			◆	◆		
Spiraea prunifolia	7 ft (2 m)	7 ft (2 m)	S	C/W	◆		◆			Sp			◆	◆		
Spiraea thunbergii	5 ft (1.5 m)	7 ft (2 m)	S	C/W	◆		◆			Sp			◆	◆		
Spiraea tomentosa	7 ft (2 m)	7 ft (2 m)	S	C/W	◆		◆			Su			◆	◆		
Spiraea trichocarpa	6 ft (1.8 m)	4 ft (1.2 m)	S	C/W	◆		◆			Su			◆	◆		
Spiraea × vanhouttei	6 ft (1.8 m)	4 ft (1.2 m)	S	C/W	◆		◆			Su			◆	◆		
Stachyurus chinensis	8 ft (2.4 m)	8 ft (2.4 m)	S	C/W	◆		◆		◆	Sp			◆	◆		
Stachyurus praecox	6–12 ft (1.8–3.5 m)	6–12 ft (1.8–3.5 m)	S	C/W	◆		◆			W/Sp			◆	◆		
Staphylea bumalda	7 ft (2 m)	6 ft (1.8 m)	S	C/W	◆		◆			Sp			◆	◆		
Staphylea colchica	10–15 ft (3–4.5 m)	10 ft (3 m)	S	C/W	◆		◆		◆	Sp			◆	◆		
Staphylea holocarpa	15 ft (4.5 m)	10 ft (3 m)	S	C/W	◆		◆			Sp			◆	◆		
Staphylea pinnata	15 ft (4.5 m)	15 ft (4.5 m)	S	C/W	◆		◆			Sp			◆	◆		
Staphylea trifolia	15 ft (4.5 m)	15 ft (4.5 m)	S	C/W	◆		◆	◆	◆	Sp			◆	◆		
Stenocarpus salignus	100 ft (30 m)	10–15 ft (3–4.5 m)	T	W/T		◆	◆			Sp/Su				◆		
Stenocarpus sinuatus	120 ft (36 m)	15 ft (4.5 m)	T	W/T		◆	◆		◆	Sp/Su				◆		
Stephanandra incisa	6 ft (1.8 m)	10 ft (3 m)	S	C/W	◆		◆	◆		Su			◆	◆		
Stephanandra tanakae	10 ft (3 m)	8 ft (2.4 m)	S	C/W	◆			◆		Su			◆	◆		
Sterculia murex	20–40 ft (6–12 m)	10–20 ft (3–6 m)	T	W	◆		◆	◆		Sp				◆		
Sterculia quadrifida	40 ft (12 m)	20 ft (6 m)	T	W/T		◆	◆	◆	◆	Su				◆		
Stewartia malacodendron	15–30 ft (4.5–9 m)	10 ft (3 m)	T	C/W	◆		◆	◆		Su			◆	◆		
Stewartia monadelpha	50 ft (15 m)	20 ft (6 m)	T	C/W	◆		◆	◆		Su			◆	◆		
Stewartia ovata	15–20 ft (4.5–6 m)	15 ft (4.5 m)	T	C/W	◆		◆	◆		Su			◆	◆		
Stewartia pseudocamellia	20–50 ft (6–15 m)	15 ft (4.5 m)	T	C/W	◆		◆	◆		Sp			◆	◆		
Stewartia pteropetiolata	20 ft (6 m)	12 ft (3.5 m)	T	C/W	◆		◆			Su			◆	◆		
Stewartia sinensis	15–30 ft (4.5–9 m)	20 ft (6 m)	T	C/W	◆		◆	◆	◆	Su			◆	◆		
Strelitzia nicolai	30 ft (9 m)	15 ft (4.5 m)	T	W/T		◆	◆	◆		Sp/Su				◆		
Streptosolen jamesonii	7 ft (2 m)	5 ft (1.5 m)	S	W/T		◆	◆			Sp	◆			◆		
Strychnos decussata	30 ft (9 m)	15 ft (4.5 m)	T	W/T		◆	◆			Sp/Su						◆
Strychnos spinosa	20 ft (6 m)	12 ft (3.5 m)	T	W/T		◆	◆			Sp				◆		
Styphelia tubiflora	24 in (60 cm)	30 in (75 cm)	S	W		◆	◆			W				◆		◆

Plant name	Height	Spread	Type	Climate	Deciduous	Evergreen	Showy flowers	Showy foliage	Scented flowers	Flowering season	Grow in pot/tub	Indoor use	Frost tolerant	Full sun	Half sun	Heavy shade
Styrax americanus	10 ft (3 m)	8 ft (2.4 m)	S	C/W	◆		◆	◆		Sp			◆	◆		
Styrax benzoin	20 ft (6 m)	10–20 ft (3–6 m)	T	W/T		◆	◆	◆		Sp				◆		
Styrax grandifolius	15 ft (4.5 m)	15 ft (4.5 m)	S	W	◆		◆	◆	◆	Sp			◆	◆		
Styrax japonicus	20–30 ft (6–9 m)	15 ft (4.5 m)	S	C/W	◆		◆		◆	Sp/Su			◆	◆		
Styrax obassia	35 ft (10 m)	20 ft (6 m)	S	C/W	◆		◆		◆	Sp			◆	◆		
Sutherlandia frutescens	5 ft (1.5 m)	5 ft (1.5 m)	S	W/T		◆	◆	◆		W/Sp			◆			
Swietenia macrophylla	150 ft (45 m)	25 ft (8 m)	T	W/T		◆		◆		Sp				◆		
Swietenia mahogani	80 ft (24 m)	15 ft (4.5 m)	T	W/T		◆		◆		Sp				◆		
Symphoricarpos albus	4–6 ft (1.2–1.8 m)	4–6 ft (1.2–1.8 m)	S	C/W	◆			◆		Sp			◆	◆		
Symphoricarpos × chenaultii	6–8 ft (1.8–2.4 m)	5 ft (1.5 m)	S	C/W	◆			◆		Su			◆	◆		
Symphoricarpos mollis	3 ft (0.9 m)	3 ft (0.9 m)	S	C/W	◆					Sp			◆	◆		
Symphoricarpos orbiculatus	6 ft (1.8 m)	6 ft (1.8 m)	S	C/W	◆			◆		Su			◆	◆		
Symplocos paniculata	15 ft (4.5 m)	15 ft (4.5 m)	T	C/W	◆			◆	◆	Sp/Su			◆	◆		
Syncarpha vestita	12–20 in (30–50 cm)	12–20 in (30–50 cm)	S	W		◆	◆	◆		Sp/Su				◆		
Syncarpia glomulifera	100 ft (30 m)	25 ft (8 m)	T	W/T		◆	◆			Sp/Su				◆		
Syringa × chinensis	12 ft (3.5 m)	12 ft (3.5 m)	S	C/W	◆			◆	◆	Sp			◆	◆		
Syringa emodi	15 ft (4.5 m)	12 ft (3.5 m)	S	C/W	◆		◆	◆	◆	Su			◆	◆		
Syringa × hyacinthiflora	15 ft (4.5 m)	15 ft (4.5 m)	S	C/W	◆			◆	◆	Sp			◆	◆		
Syringa × josiflexa	8–10 ft (2.4–3 m)	7 ft (2 m)	S	C/W	◆			◆	◆	Su			◆	◆		
Syringa josikaea	12 ft (3.5 m)	10 ft (3 m)	S	C/W	◆		◆	◆	◆	Su			◆	◆		
Syringa laciniata	12 ft (3.5 m)	10 ft (3 m)	S	C/W	◆		◆	◆	◆	Sp			◆	◆		
Syringa meyeri	5 ft (1.5 m)	4 ft (1.2 m)	S	C/W	◆			◆	◆	Sp–A			◆	◆		
Syringa oblata	12 ft (3.5 m)	10 ft (3 m)	S	C/W	◆			◆	◆	Sp			◆	◆		
Syringa pekinensis	15 ft (4.5 m)	12 ft (3.5 m)	S	C/W	◆			◆	◆	Su			◆	◆		
Syringa potaninii	6–8 ft (1.8–2.4 m)	6 ft (1.8 m)	S	C/W	◆			◆	◆	Sp			◆	◆		
Syringa × prestoniae	12 ft (3.5 m)	12 ft (3.5 m)	S	C/W	◆			◆	◆	Su			◆	◆		
Syringa pubescens	12 ft (3.5 m)	12 ft (3.5 m)	S	C/W	◆			◆	◆	Sp/Su			◆	◆		
Syringa reflexa	12 ft (3.5 m)	12 ft (3.5 m)	S	C/W	◆		◆		◆	Su				◆	◆	
Syringa reticulata	30 ft (9 m)	15 ft (4.5 m)	S	C/W	◆			◆	◆	Su			◆	◆		
Syringa × swegiflexa	10 ft (3 m)	5 ft (1.5 m)	S	C/W	◆			◆	◆	Sp			◆	◆		
Syringa sweginzowii	10 ft (3 m)	6 ft (1.8 m)	S	C/W	◆			◆	◆	Sp/Su			◆	◆		
Syringa tigerstedtii	8 ft (2.4 m)	8 ft (2.4 m)	S	C/W	◆			◆	◆	Su			◆	◆		

Plant name	Height	Spread	Type	Climate	Deciduous	Evergreen	Showy flowers	Showy foliage	Scented flowers	Flowering season	Grow in pot/tub	Indoor use	Frost tolerant	Full sun	Half sun	Heavy shade
Syringa tomentella	10 ft (3 m)	10 ft (3 m)	S	C/W	◆		◆		◆	Su			◆	◆		
Syringa vulgaris	20 ft (6 m)	20 ft (6 m)	S	C/W	◆		◆		◆	Sp/Su			◆	◆		
Syringa wolfii	15 ft (4.5 m)	12 ft (3.5 m)	S	C/W	◆		◆			Sp			◆	◆		
Syzygium australe	25 ft (8 m)	20 ft (6 m)	T	W/T		◆	◆			Su				◆		
Syzygium francisii	80 ft (24 m)	70 ft (21 m)	T	W/T		◆	◆			Su				◆		
Syzygium jambos	20 ft (6 m)	15 ft (4.5 m)	T	W/T		◆	◆		◆	Su				◆		
Syzygium luehmannii	50 ft (15 m)	30 ft (9 m)	T	W/T		◆	◆	◆		Su				◆		
Syzygium paniculatum	25 ft (8 m)	20 ft (6 m)	T	W/T		◆	◆			Su				◆		
Syzygium wilsonii	6 ft (1.8 m)	7 ft (2 m)	S	W/T		◆	◆	◆		Sp/Su				◆		
Tabebuia chrysantha	20–50 ft (6–15 m)	20 ft (6 m)	T	W/T		◆	◆			Sp				◆		
Tabebuia rosea	90 ft (27 m)	30 ft (9 m)	T	W/T		◆	◆			Sp				◆		
Tabernaemontana divaricata	6 ft (1.8 m)	5 ft (1.5 m)	S	W/T		◆	◆	◆	◆	Su	◆	◆		◆		
Tabernaemontana elegans	10–20 ft (3–6 m)	10 ft (3 m)	S	W/T	◆		◆	◆	◆	Sp/Su						
Taiwania cryptomerioides	180 ft (55 m)	35 ft (10 m)	C	W		◆		◆		Sp			◆	◆		
Tamarindus indica	90 ft (27 m)	35 ft (10 m)	T	W/T		◆	◆	◆		Su				◆		
Tamarix chinensis	15 ft (4.5 m)	10 ft (3 m)	S	C/W	◆		◆			Su			◆	◆		
Tamarix gallica	12 ft (3.5 m)	10 ft (3 m)	S	C/W	◆		◆			Su			◆	◆		
Tamarix parviflora	15 ft (4.5 m)	20 ft (6 m)	T	C/W	◆		◆			Sp			◆	◆		
Tamarix ramosissima	15 ft (4.5 m)	15 ft (4.5 m)	S	C/W	◆		◆			Su/A			◆	◆		
Taxodium distichum	75 ft (23 m)	20 ft (6 m)	C	C/W	◆			◆		Sp			◆	◆		
Taxodium mucronatum	100 ft (30 m)	50 ft (15 m)	C	W	◆	◆		◆		Sp			◆	◆		
Taxus baccata	50 ft (15 m)	25 ft (8 m)	C	C/W		◆		◆		Su			◆	◆		
Taxus chinensis	20 ft (6 m)	15 ft (4.5 m)	C	C/W		◆		◆		Su			◆	◆		
Taxus cuspidata	50 ft (15 m)	20 ft (6 m)	C	C/W		◆		◆		Sp			◆	◆		
Taxus × media	25 ft (8 m)	20 ft (6 m)	C	C/W		◆		◆		Sp			◆	◆		
Tecoma capensis	10 ft (3 m)	7 ft (2 m)	S	W/T		◆	◆			Sp–A				◆		
Tecoma castaneifolia	15–25 ft (4.5–8 m)	8–12 ft (2.4–3.5 m)	T	W/T		◆	◆			Sp–A				◆		
Tecoma stans	15–30 ft (4.5–9 m)	10 ft (3 m)	T	W/T		◆	◆			W–Su				◆		
Telanthophora grandifolia	20 ft (6 m)	12 ft (3.5 m)	S	W/T		◆	◆	◆		Sp/Su				◆		
Telopea mongaensis	10 ft (3 m)	10 ft (3 m)	S	W		◆	◆			Sp/Su			◆	◆		
Telopea oreades	10–30 ft (3–9 m)	10 ft (3 m)	S	W		◆	◆			Su				◆		
Telopea speciosissima	10 ft (3 m)	5 ft (1.5 m)	S	W		◆	◆			Sp				◆		

Plant name	Height	Spread	Type	Climate	Deciduous	Evergreen	Showy flowers	Showy foliage	Scented flowers	Flowering season	Grow in pot/tub	Indoor use	Frost tolerant	Full sun	Half sun	Heavy shade
Telopea truncata	10 ft (3 m)	10 ft (3 m)	S	W		◆	◆			Sp			◆	◆		
Tephrosia grandiflora	2–5 ft (0.6–1.5 m)	3 ft (0.9 m)	S	W		◆	◆			Sp/Su				◆		
Terminalia arostrata	17–35 ft (5–10 m)	6–10 ft (1.8–3 m)	T	W	◆			◆		Su				◆		
Ternstroemia japonica	12 ft (3.5 m)	10 ft (3 m)	T	W		◆	◆	◆	◆	Su			◆			◆
Tetraclinis articulata	50 ft (15 m)	25 ft (8 m)	C	W/T		◆		◆		Sp				◆		
Tetradenia riparia	8–10 ft (2.4–3 m)	8 ft (2.4 m)	S	W/T		◆	◆		◆	W/Sp				◆		
Tetradium daniellii	50 ft (15 m)	40 ft (12 m)	T	W	◆		◆	◆	◆	Su/A			◆	◆		
Tetradium ruticarpum	30 ft (9 m)	15 ft (4.5 m)	T	W	◆		◆	◆	◆	Su				◆		
Tetratheca thymifolia	2 ft (0.6 m)	2 ft (0.6 m)	S	W		◆	◆			Sp						◆
Teucrium fruticans	4 ft (1.2 m)	6 ft (1.8 m)	S	W		◆	◆	◆		Su			◆	◆		
Thevetia peruviana	15 ft (4.5 m)	8 ft (2.4 m)	S	W/T		◆	◆		◆	Su				◆		
Thryptomene saxicola	3–5 ft (0.9–1.5 m)	5 ft (1.5 m)	S	W		◆	◆			W/Sp				◆		
Thuja occidentalis	30–70 ft (9–21 m)	15 ft (4.5 m)	C	C/W		◆		◆		Sp			◆	◆		
Thuja plicata	70–120 ft (21–36 m)	15 ft (4.5 m)	C	C/W		◆		◆		Sp			◆	◆		
Thuja standishii	100 ft (30 m)	20 ft (6 m)	C	C/W		◆		◆		Sp			◆	◆		
Thujopsis dolabrata	100 ft (30 m)	20 ft (6 m)	C	C/W		◆		◆		Sp			◆	◆		
Thunbergia erecta	6–8 ft (1.8–2.4 m)	7 ft (2 m)	S	W/T		◆	◆			Su	◆			◆		
Tibouchina granulosa	12–35 ft (3.5–10 m)	10 ft (3 m)	S	W/T		◆	◆	◆		A	◆			◆		
Tibouchina lepidota	12 ft (3.5 m)	10 ft (3 m)	S	W/T		◆	◆	◆		Su/W	◆			◆		
Tibouchina urvilleana	15 ft (4.5 m)	10 ft (3 m)	S	W/T		◆	◆	◆		Su				◆		
Tilia americana	100 ft (30 m)	40 ft (12 m)	T	C/W	◆			◆	◆	Su			◆	◆		
Tilia cordata	80–100 ft (24–30 m)	40 ft (12 m)	T	C/W	◆			◆	◆	Su			◆	◆		
Tilia × euchlora	70 ft (21 m)	40 ft (12 m)	T	C/W	◆				◆	Su			◆	◆		
Tilia × europaea	100 ft (30 m)	40 ft (12 m)	T	C/W	◆				◆	Su			◆	◆		
Tilia japonica	50 ft (15 m)	20 ft (6 m)	T	C/W	◆			◆	◆	Su			◆	◆		
Tilia oliveri	100 ft (30 m)	30 ft (9 m)	T	C/W	◆		◆	◆		Su			◆	◆		
Tilia platyphyllos	100 ft (30 m)	50 ft (15 m)	T	C/W	◆				◆	Su			◆	◆		
Tilia tomentosa	80–100 ft (24–30 m)	50 ft (15 m)	T	C/W	◆				◆	Su			◆	◆		
Tipuana tipu	100 ft (30 m)	25 ft (8 m)	T	W/T		◆	◆			Sp				◆		
Toona ciliata	120 ft (36 m)	20 ft (6 m)	T	W/T	◆		◆	◆	◆	Sp				◆		
Toona sinensis	40 ft (12 m)	30 ft (9 m)	T	W	◆		◆	◆	◆	Sp			◆	◆		
Torreya californica	80 ft (24 m)	25 ft (8 m)	C	C/W		◆		◆		Su			◆	◆		

Plant name	Height	Spread	Type	Climate	Deciduous	Evergreen	Showy flowers	Showy foliage	Scented flowers	Flowering season	Grow in pot/tub	Indoor use	Frost tolerant	Full sun	Half sun	Heavy shade
Torreya nucifera	50–80 ft (15–24 m)	25 ft (8 m)	C	C/W		◆		◆		Su			◆	◆		
Toxicodendron diversilobum	8 ft (2.4 m)	7 ft (2 m)	S	C/W	◆			◆		Su			◆	◆		
Toxicodendron succedaneum	30 ft (9 m)	20 ft (6 m)	S	C/W	◆			◆		Su			◆	◆		
Toxicodendron vernix	10 ft (3 m)	10 ft (3 m)	S	C/W	◆			◆		Su			◆	◆		
Trevesia palmata	30 ft (9 m)	12 ft (3.5 m)	S	C/W		◆	◆	◆		Su						◆
Triadica sebifera	20–30 ft (6–9 m)	15–20 ft (4.5–6 m)	T	W/T	◆			◆		Sp/Su			◆	◆		
Tristania neriifolia	15 ft (4.5 m)	7 ft (2 m)	S/T	W		◆	◆			Su				◆		
Tristaniopsis laurina	60 ft (18 m)	20 ft (6 m)	T	W/T		◆	◆	◆		Su				◆		
Trochodendron aralioides	70 ft (21 m)	25 ft (8 m)	T	W		◆	◆			Sp			◆			◆
Tsuga canadensis	80–120 ft (24–36 m)	30 ft (9 m)	C	C		◆		◆		Sp			◆	◆		
Tsuga heterophylla	60–120 ft (18–36 m)	20–30 ft (6–9 m)	C	C/W		◆		◆		Sp			◆			
Tsuga mertensiana	50 ft (15 m)	20 ft (6 m)	C	C		◆		◆		Sp			◆	◆		
Tsuga sieboldii	50–100 ft (15–30 m)	25 ft (8 m)	C	C/W		◆		◆		Sp			◆	◆		
Ulex europaeus	8 ft (2.4 m)	7 ft (2 m)	S	C/W		◆	◆		◆	W/Sp			◆	◆		
Ulmus americana	100 ft (30 m)	100 ft (30 m)	T	C	◆			◆		Sp			◆	◆		
Ulmus carpinifolia	50–70 ft (15–21 m)	70 ft (21 m)	T	C/W	◆			◆		Sp			◆	◆		
Ulmus crassifolia	70–100 ft (21–30 m)	40 ft (12 m)	T	C/W	◆			◆		Sp			◆	◆		
Ulmus glabra	100 ft (30 m)	70 ft (21 m)	T	C	◆			◆		Sp			◆	◆		
Ulmus × hollandica	100 ft (30 m)	80 ft (24 m)	T	C/W	◆		◆	◆		Sp			◆	◆		
Ulmus japonica	100 ft (30 m)	60 ft (18 m)	T	C/W	◆			◆		Sp			◆	◆		
Ulmus laevis	70 ft (21 m)	30 ft (9 m)	T	C/W	◆			◆		Sp			◆	◆		
Ulmus parvifolia	70 ft (21 m)	30 ft (9 m)	T	C/W	◆			◆		Sp			◆	◆		
Ulmus procera	70–100 ft (21–30 m)	50 ft (15 m)	T	C/W	◆		◆	◆		Sp			◆	◆		
Ulmus pumila	20–35 m (6–10 m)	20–30 ft (6–9 m)	T	C/W	◆			◆		Tree			◆	◆		
Ulmus 'Sapporo Autumn Gold'	50 ft (15 m)	35 ft (10 m)	T	C/W	◆			◆		Sp			◆	◆		
Ulmus 'Sarniensis'	75–80 ft (23–24 m)	23–25 ft (7–8 m)	T	C/W	◆		◆	◆		Sp			◆	◆		
Ulmus thomasii	100 ft (30 m)	40 ft (12 m)	T	C	◆		◆	◆		Sp			◆	◆		
Umbellularia californica	50–70 ft (15–21 m)	35 ft (10 m)	T	W		◆	◆	◆		Sp			◆	◆		
Vaccinium crassifolium	15 in (38 cm)	3 ft (0.9 m)	S	C/W		◆	◆			Sp			◆	◆		
Vaccinium nummularia	12–15 in (30–38 cm)	12–15 in (30–38 cm)	S	C/W		◆	◆			Sp			◆	◆		
Vaccinium stamineum	5 ft (1.5 m)	3 ft (0.9 m)	S	C/W	◆		◆			Sp			◆	◆		
Vaccinium vitis-idaea	6 in (15 cm)	2–4 ft (0.6–1.2 m)	S	C		◆	◆			Sp			◆	◆		

Plant name	Height	Spread	Type	Climate	Deciduous	Evergreen	Showy flowers	Showy foliage	Scented flowers	Flowering season	Grow in pot/tub	Indoor use	Frost tolerant	Full sun	Half sun	Heavy shade
Verticordia chrysantha	2 ft (0.6 m)	2 ft (0.6 m)	S	W		♦	♦			Sp			♦	♦		
Verticordia grandis	7 ft (2 m)	3 ft (0.9 m)	S	W		♦	♦			Sp			♦	♦		
Verticordia plumosa	20 in (50 cm)	20 in (50 cm)	S	W		♦	♦			Sp			♦	♦		
Vestia foetida	6 ft (1.8 m)	5 ft (1.5 m)	S	W		♦	♦			Sp/Su						♦
Viburnum betulifolium	10 ft (3 m)	10 ft (3 m)	S	C/W	♦		♦			Su			♦	♦		
Viburnum × bodnantense	10 ft (3 m)	7 ft (2 m)	S	C/W	♦		♦		♦	A–Sp			♦	♦		
Viburnum × burkwoodii	8 ft (2.4 m)	8 ft (2.4 m)	S	C/W		♦	♦		♦	Sp			♦	♦		
Viburnum × carlcephalum	8 ft (2.4 m)	8 ft (2.4 m)	S	C/W	♦		♦	♦	♦	Sp			♦	♦		
Viburnum carlesii	8 ft (2.4 m)	7 ft (2 m)	S	C/W	♦		♦	♦	♦	Sp			♦	♦		
Viburnum 'Cayuga'	6 ft (1.8 m)	6 ft (1.8 m)	S	C/W	♦		♦			Sp			♦	♦		
Viburnum davidii	4 ft (1.2 m)	4 ft (1.2 m)	S	C/W		♦	♦	♦		Sp			♦	♦		
Viburnum dentatum	10 ft (3 m)	10 ft (3 m)	S	C	♦		♦	♦		Sp/Su			♦	♦		
Viburnum dilatatum	10 ft (3 m)	8 ft (2.4 m)	S	C	♦		♦	♦		Sp/Su			♦	♦		
Viburnum erubescens	20 ft (6 m)	10 ft (3 m)	S	C/W	♦		♦			Su			♦	♦		
Viburnum farreri	10 ft (3 m)	8 ft (2.4 m)	S	C/W	♦		♦	♦	♦	A–Sp			♦	♦		
Viburnum × globosum	3–4 ft (0.9–1.2 m)	3–4 ft (0.9–1.2 m)	S	C/W		♦	♦	♦		Sp			♦	♦		
Viburnum × hillieri	6–8 ft (1.8–2.4 m)	7 ft (2 m)	S	C/W		♦	♦	♦		Su			♦	♦		
Viburnum japonicum	8 ft (2.4 m)	8 ft (2.4 m)	S	C/W		♦	♦	♦	♦	Su			♦	♦		
Viburnum × juddii	6 ft (1.8 m)	7 ft (2 m)	S	C/W	♦		♦	♦	♦	Sp			♦	♦		
Viburnum lantana	15 ft (4.5 m)	12 ft (3.5 m)	S	C	♦		♦	♦		Sp/Su			♦	♦		
Viburnum lantanoides	15 ft (4.5 m)	15 ft (4.5 m)	S	C	♦		♦	♦		Sp/Su			♦	♦		
Viburnum lentago	20 ft (6 m)	10 ft (3 m)	S	C	♦		♦	♦		Sp/Su			♦	♦		
Viburnum macrocephalum	15 ft (4.5 m)	15 ft (4.5 m)	S	C/W	♦		♦			Sp			♦	♦		
Viburnum nudum	10 ft (3 m)	6 ft (1.8 m)	S	C/W	♦		♦	♦		Su			♦	♦		
Viburnum opulus	15 ft (4.5 m)	15 ft (4.5 m)	S	C/W	♦		♦	♦		Sp/Su			♦	♦		
Viburnum plicatum	8 ft (2.4 m)	10 ft (3 m)	S	C/W	♦		♦	♦		Sp/Su			♦	♦		
Viburnum prunifolium	20 ft (6 m)	12 ft (3.5 m)	S	C/W	♦		♦	♦		Sp/Su			♦	♦		
Viburnum rhytidophyllum	10 ft (3 m)	8 ft (2.4 m)	S	C		♦	♦	♦		Su			♦	♦		
Viburnum sieboldii	10 ft (3 m)	15 ft (4.5 m)	S	C	♦		♦	♦		Sp/Su			♦	♦		
Viburnum tinus	8–10 ft (2.4–3 m)	8–10 ft (2.4–3 m)	S	C/W		♦	♦	♦	♦	W/Sp			♦	♦		
Viburnum trilobum	10 ft (3 m)	10 ft (3 m)	S	C	♦		♦	♦		Su			♦	♦		

Plant name	Height	Spread	Type	Climate	Deciduous	Evergreen	Showy flowers	Showy foliage	Scented flowers	Flowering season	Grow in pot/tub	Indoor use	Frost tolerant	Full sun	Half sun	Heavy shade
Viburnum utile	6 ft (1.8 m)	5 ft (1.5 m)	S	C/W		♦	♦			Sp			♦	♦		
Viburnum veitchii	5 ft (1.5 m)	5 ft (1.5 m)	S	C/W	♦		♦		♦	Sp/Su			♦	♦		
Virgilia oroboides	30 ft (9 m)	15 ft (4.5 m)	T	W	♦		♦		♦	Sp/Su				♦		
Vitex agnus-castus	15 ft (4.5 m)	15 ft (4.5 m)	S	C/W	♦		♦		♦	Su/A			♦	♦		
Vitex lucens	30–50 ft (9–15 m)	10–15 ft (3–4.5 m)	T	W		♦	♦	♦		A/W				♦		
Warszewiczia coccinea	15 ft (4.5 m)	10 ft (3 m)	S	W/T		♦	♦			All				♦		
Weigela decora	10–15 ft (3–4.5 m)	5–7 ft (1.5–2 m)	S	C/W	♦		♦			Sp/Su			♦	♦		
Weigela floribunda	10 ft (3 m)	8 ft (2.4 m)	S	C/W	♦		♦		♦	Sp/Su			♦	♦		
Weigela florida	8 ft (2.4 m)	8 ft (2.4 m)	S	C/W	♦		♦		♦	Sp/Su			♦	♦		
Weigela japonica	10 ft (3 m)	10 ft (3 m)	S	C/W	♦		♦			Sp			♦	♦		
Weigela middendorffiana	5 ft (1.5 m)	5 ft (1.5 m)	S	C/W	♦		♦			Su			♦			♦
Weigela praecox	8 ft (2.4 m)	7 ft (2 m)	S	C/W	♦		♦	♦	♦	Sp/Su			♦	♦		
Weigela Hybrid Cultivars	5–12 ft (1.5–3.5 m)	5–8 ft (1.5–2.4 m)	S	C/W	♦		♦		♦	Sp/Su			♦	♦		
Weinmannia racemosa	30 ft (9 m)	8–15 ft (2.4–4.5 m)	T	W		♦	♦	♦		Su				♦		
Weinmannia trichosperma	70 ft (21 m)	5–12 ft (1.5–3.5 m)	T	W		♦	♦			Su				♦		
Westringia fruticosa	6 ft (1.8 m)	7 ft (2 m)	S	W		♦	♦			Any				♦		
Westringia 'Wynyabbie Gem'	4 ft (1.2 m)	5 ft (1.5 m)	S	W		♦	♦			Any	♦			♦		
Widdringtonia nodiflora	40 ft (12 m)	6–12 ft (1.8–3.5 m)	C	W		♦		♦		Sp				♦		
Widdringtonia schwarzii	120 ft (36 m)	15–30 ft (4.5–9 m)	C	W		♦		♦		Sp			♦	♦		
Wigandia caracasana	15 ft (4.5 m)	12 ft (3.5 m)	T	W/T		♦	♦	♦		Sp/Su	♦	♦		♦		
Wollemia nobilis	120 ft (36 m)	4–10 ft (1.2–3 m)	C	W		♦				Sp				♦		
Xanthoceras sorbifolium	25 ft (8 m)	10 ft (3 m)	T	C/W	♦		♦		♦	Sp/Su			♦	♦		
Zanthoxylum americanum	25 ft (8 m)	15 ft (4.5 m)	T	C/W	♦			♦		Sp			♦	♦		
Zanthoxylum piperitum	20 ft (6 m)	10 ft (3 m)	T	C/W	♦			♦		Sp			♦	♦		
Zanthoxylum planispinum	12 ft (3.5 m)	8 ft (2.4 m)	S	C/W	♦			♦		Sp			♦	♦		
Zanthoxylum simulans	7–25 ft (2–8 m)	7–25 ft (2–8 m)	T	C	♦			♦		Su			♦	♦		
Zelkova carpinifolia	100 ft (30 m)	25 ft (8 m)	T	C/W	♦		♦	♦		Sp			♦	♦		
Zelkova serrata	60–100 ft (18–30 m)	50 ft (15 m)	T	C/W	♦			♦		Sp			♦	♦		
Zenobia pulverulenta	3–10 ft (0.9–3 m)	4 ft (1.2 m)	S	C/W	♦		♦		♦	Sp/Su				♦		♦
Ziziphus mucronata	17–35 ft (5–10 m)	10–20 ft (3–6 m)	T	W	♦			♦		Sp			♦	♦		

Abelia × grandiflora

ABELIA

This decorative genus from the woodbine (Caprifoliaceae) family has about 30 ornamental shrubs, both evergreen and deciduous, and occurs in eastern Asia and Mexico. The leaves are glossy and opposite or whorled, while the funnelform or tubular flowers, white or pinkish, sometimes with orange blotches, appear in summer. Some species have persistent reddish sepals that provide an additional ornamental feature after the flowers have faded.
CULTIVATION: *Abelia* species are moderately frost hardy, and perform best when planted in a sunny spot in any well-drained, moderately fertile soil. Pruning should be carried out in winter, removing some of the basal shoots to make room for new growth, plus the cane ends. Care should be taken to preserve the plant's naturally arching habit. Propagate from soft-tip cuttings in spring or summer, or half-hardened cuttings in late autumn or winter.

Abelia floribunda
☼ ⚘ ↔ 6 ft (1.8 m) ↕ 6 ft (1.8 m)
From Mexico. Generally evergreen with an open habit. Leaves smaller and less glossy than *A. × grandiflora*. Pendulous clusters of pale rose to deep red flowers in summer–autumn. Persistent sepals. Zones 9–11.

Abelia × grandiflora ★
GLOSSY ABELIA
☼ ❄ ↔ 6 ft (1.8 m) ↕ 6 ft (1.8 m)
Evergreen shrub with arching canes, hybrid between *A. chinensis* and *A. uniflora*. Reddish brown stems. Leaves dark green, turning red to orange in winter. Perfumed flowers flushed mauve-pink.

'Francis Mason', leaves heavily margined and suffused with yellow; 'Prostrata', low growing, to 24 in (60 cm) high; 'Sherwoodii', compact habit, to 3–4 ft (0.9–1.2 m) high; 'Sunrise', to 6 ft (1.8 m) tall, attractive autumn foliage color. Zones 7–10.

Abelia schumannii
syn. *Abelia longituba*
SCHUMANN'S ABELIA
☼ ❄ ↔ 8 ft (2.4 m) ↕ 4 ft (1.2 m)
From China. Nearly evergreen shrub with pale green to dull green leaves. Pale rosy mauve flowers in clusters, with broad white stripe and some orange spots on lower lobe, in summer–autumn. Zones 7–10.

ABELIOPHYLLUM

The name of this genus, of the olive (Oleaceae) family, is derived from *Abelia*, which it is said to resemble. It contains just one species of small deciduous shrub, closely related to *Forsythia*, bearing similar flowers in white. The shrub is native to the mountains of Korea, where it is becoming scarce.
CULTIVATION: The species will grow in a range of soil conditions but in cool temperate climates should be given a warm site. It can be trained against a wall if desired. Less vigorous old canes should be cut out. Prune every 2 to 3 years to maintain shape. Propagation is usually by half-hardened cuttings taken in summer or by layering in spring or autumn.

Abeliophyllum distichum
WHITE FORSYTHIA
☼ ❄ ↔ 6 ft (1.8 m) ↕ 3 ft (0.9 m)
Arching, straggly, deciduous shrub from Korea. In late winter, bare branches are smothered in fragrant, white, forsythia-like flowers that burst from pink-tinged buds. In some forms buds are deeper shade with flowers emerging pale pink. Zones 5–10.

ABIES

This genus in the pine (Pinaceae) family consists of about 50 species occurring in the northern temperate zones of Europe, North Africa, Asia, and North America. Mostly long lived and medium to very tall, these evergreen conifers have narrow smooth leaves. The leaves are mid- to dark green, often with a grayish white band. The female

Abies homolepis

cones are carried erect on upper branches, while the hanging male cones grow throughout the crown. *Abies* species are fully hardy, although frost damage can occur on juvenile foliage.
CULTIVATION: They do best in neutral to acid, moist, fertile soil with good drainage in full sun; most tolerate some shade. Some, including *A. pinsapo*, tolerate alkaline soils. Some juvenile trees need shelter from cold winds. Adelgids and honey fungus can be a problem. Sow seed as it ripens, but it needs to be stratified for 3 weeks for better germination. Graft cultivars in winter.

Abies balsamea

BALSAM FIR, DWARF BALSAM FIR

☼ ❄ ↔ 15 ft (4.5 m) ↑ 50 ft (15 m)

Conical tree from northeastern USA, east and central Canada. Sleek gray bark, fragrant resin. Leaves dark green, whitish beneath. Cones cylindrical, purplish blue. Fairly short lived in gardens. Dwarf cultivars include '**Nana**' and **Hudsonia Group**. Zones 3–8.

Abies cephalonica

syn. *Abies apollinis*

GREEK FIR

☼ ❄ ↔ 25 ft (8 m) ↑ 100 ft (30 m)

Pyramidal tree, native to central and southern Greece. Dark green, rigid, slightly curved leaves, greenish white beneath. Cylindrical greenish brown cones are resinous. '**Meyer's Dwarf**', with shorter leaves, forms mound only 20 in (50 cm) high, with diameter of 10 ft (3 m). Zones 7–10.

Abies concolor

BLUE FIR, COLORADO WHITE FIR, SILVER FIR, WHITE FIR

☼ ❄ ↔ 25 ft (8 m) ↑ 120 ft (36 m)

Grows in western USA down to northern Mexico. Statuesque tree with pyramidal crown, dull greenish gray leaves, mid-green to brown cylindrical cones. Cultivars include '**Compacta**', '**Masonic Broom**', and **Violacea Group** ★. Dwarf cultivars grow no more than 30 in (75 cm) in height and spread. Zones 5–9.

Abies fargesii

syn. *Abies sutchuenensis*

☼ ❄ ↔ 12 ft (3.5 m) ↑ 60 ft (18 m)

Statuesque tree from central China. Leaves dark green with silver-striped undersides. Egg-shaped cones violet-purple in color, with protruding, slightly resinous bracts. Zones 7–9.

Abies fraseri

☼ ❄ ↔ 20 ft (6 m) ↑ 60 ft (18 m)

Pyramidal tree, native to southwestern Virginia, western North Carolina, and eastern Tennessee, USA. Leaves 1 in (25 mm) long, mid- to dark green with silvery to greenish white band on underside. Cylindrical cones green to dark purple, ripening to brown; pronounced bracts. Zones 6–9.

Abies grandis

GIANT FIR

☼ ❄ ↔ 25 ft (8 m) ↑ 300 ft (90 m)

Giant conical to columnar tree from western North America. Dark green, soft, shiny leaves, with whitish banding on undersides. Cones smallish, ripening to gray-brown. '**Johnsonii**', reaches height of 60–70 ft (18–21 m). Zones 6–9.

Abies homolepis

syn. *Abies brachyphylla*

MANCHURIAN FIR, NIKKO FIR

☼ ❄ ↔ 25 ft (8 m) ↑ 80 ft (24 m)

Conical tree native to southern and central Japan. Leaves dull grayish green with silver banding. Branches tiered up trunk. Cones cylindrical and violet-blue, turning brown with age. Zones 5–9.

Abies koreana ★

KOREAN FIR

☼ ❄ ↔ 5 ft (1.5 m) ↑ 50 ft (15 m)

From mountains of South Korea. Narrow, pyramid-shaped, slow-growing tree; striking purple cones. Leaves dark green above, shiny white beneath. Cultivars include '**Compact Dwarf**', '**Flava**', and '**Silberlocke**' (syn. '**Horstmann's Silberlocke**'). Zones 5–8.

Abies pinsapo

SPANISH FIR

☼ ❄ ↔ 15 ft (4.5 m) ↑ 80 ft (24 m)

From dry mountain slopes of southern Spain. Rigid, short, linear, dark green leaves. Purplish brown cylindrical cones. Cultivars include '**Glauca**', with gray-blue leaves; and '**Kelleriis**', robust dwarf. Zones 6–8.

Abies procera

syn. *Abies nobilis*

NOBLE FIR

☼ ❄ ↔ 30 ft (9 m) ↑ 150 ft (45 m)

Native to high-rainfall areas of western USA. Pyramidal tree becomes broader with age. Leaves gray-green to blue-silver, banded gray underneath. Barrel-shaped green cones ripen to brown. **Glauca Group** features cultivars (including '**Glauca Prostrata**') with blue leaves. Zones 4–9.

Abies koreana

Abies pinsapo

Abies procera, Glauca Group cultivar

ABUTILON

CHINESE LANTERN

This genus of the mallow (Malvaceae) family is represented in warmer parts of South or Central America, Australia, and Africa. Most are shrubs with slender tough-barked twigs but a few are annuals, perennials, or even small trees. Leaves vary from heart-shaped to jaggedly lobed with toothed margins. The common name alludes to the pendent bell-shaped flowers of some species with 5 petals. Colors range from white to pink, and from yellow and orange to deep bronzy red. Fruit is a capsule. In mild climates they flower almost throughout the year, in cooler climates from spring to autumn. **CULTIVATION:** Plant Chinese lanterns in well-drained moderately fertile soil, in light shade or bright sun. Extra water is needed if they are planted in an exposed position. In cool climates keep indoors until the worst frosts are past, then plant out for summer display; newer dwarf cultivars are suitable for this purpose. Prune leading shoots in late winter for a compact form, although some cultivars display their blooms best on long arching branches. Propagate from tip cuttings in late summer.

Abutilon vitifolium

Abutilon × hybridum

CHINESE LANTERN, GARDEN ABUTILON

☼/◐ ✳ ↔ 5–10 ft (1.5–3 m) ↑ 6–15 ft (1.8–4.5 m)
Wide-ranging group of hybrids with unclear origins, although most show *A. pictum* influence. Leaves usually dark green, smooth, 3–6 in (8–15 cm) long, toothed or with up to 5 lobes. Flowers to 3 in (8 cm) wide, one per leaf axil, mainly yellow, orange, and red shades, appear most of the year. Popular hybrids include 'Apricot', 'Ashford Red', 'Bartley Schwartz', 'Boule de Neige', 'Canary Bird', 'Cannington Carol', 'Cannington Skies', 'Cerise Queen', 'Clementine', 'Crimson Belle', 'Dwarf Red', 'Kentish Belle', 'Linda Vista Peach', 'Mobile Pink', 'Moonchimes', 'Moritz', 'Nabob' ★, 'Souvenir de Bonn', and 'Summer Sherbet'. Zones 9–11.

Abutilon × hybridum
'Cannington Skies'

Abutilon megapotamicum

Abutilon megapotamicum

syn. *Abutilon vexillarium*

CHINESE LANTERN, TRAILING ABUTILON

☼ ✳ ↔ 8 ft (2.4 m) ↑ 8 ft (2.4 m)
From southern Brazil. Has several forms, from an erect shrub with arching branches to an almost prostrate form. Bell-shaped flowers, red calyx, pale yellow petals. 'Marianne', tangerine flowers; 'Variegatum', yellow mottled leaves; 'Victory' ★, smaller, with darker yellow leaves. Zones 8–10.

Abutilon × suntense

☼ ✳ ↔ 8 ft (2.4 m) ↑ 12 ft (3.5 m)
Deciduous shrub with bright green leaves and violet flowers. Dislikes hot/humid summer areas. Cultivars include 'Gorer's White', large pure white flowers; and 'Jermyns', clear mauve-purple flowers. Zones 8–10.

Abutilon vitifolium

syn. *Corynabutilon vitifolium*

☼ ✳ ↔ 8 ft (2.4 m) ↑ 15 ft (4.5 m)
Weak-branched deciduous shrub from Chile. Maple-like toothed leaves. Flowers saucer-shaped, white to violet-purple, in spring–summer. Dislikes hot/humid summer areas. 'Veronica Tennant', slightly larger pale mauve-pink flowers. Zones 8–10.

ACACIA

From the mimosa subfamily of the legume (Fabaceae) family, *Acacia* consists of at least 1,200 species. It comes mainly from Australia, but is also found in Africa, the tropical Americas, Asia, and islands of the Pacific and Indian Oceans. There are shrubs, small to medium-sized trees, a few large forest trees, and a few climbers. Flowers are very small, but densely crowded into spikes or globular heads in colors of yellow, cream, or white. Leaf structure is bipinnate—but in many species the leaves change to phyllodes. The acacia fruit is a typical legume pod, splitting open when ripe to reveal a row of hard seeds. Fast-growing acacias enrich the soil by converting nitrogen from the air into soil nitrogen. **CULTIVATION:** Most acacias require well-drained soil and full sun. In mild climates they can become environmental weeds. They are often short lived. Propagate from seeds, treated to soften the hard case. Give a light prune after flowering.

Acacia adunca

WALLANGARRA WATTLE

☼ ◑ ↔ 12 ft (3.5 m) ↑ 20 ft (6 m)
Bushy shrub or small tree from southeastern Australia. Phyllodes narrow, light green. Long sprays of ball-shaped, sweetly scented, golden yellow flowers in late winter and spring. Zones 9–11.

Acacia baileyana

COOTAMUNDRA WATTLE

☼ ◑ ↔ 20 ft (6 m) ↑ 6–20 ft (1.8–6 m)
Widely naturalized in most Australian States. Small elegant tree occurs naturally around Cootamundra, New South Wales. Leaves

Acacia adunca

feathery silver-gray. Flowers bright yellow, globular, in racemes, in winter–spring. '**Purpurea**', attractive purplish foliage and new growth. Zones 9–10.

Acacia binervia
syn. *Acacia glaucescens*
COAST MYALL
☀ ❧ ↔ 35 ft (10 m) ↑ 50 ft (15 m)
From tablelands and coast of New South Wales, Australia. Handsome tree; large compact crown of silvery gray curved phyllodes. Masses of bright yellow flower spikes in early spring. Young foliage may be poisonous to stock. Zones 9–11.

Acacia cardiophylla
WYALONG WATTLE
☀ ❁ ↔ 5–8 ft (1.5–2.4 m) ↑ 3–10 ft (0.9–3 m)
Beautiful free-flowering shrub from mallee country of inland New South Wales, Australia. Leaves bipinnate with tiny heart-shaped leaflets on long arching branches. Panicles of small, sweetly scented, bright yellow, ball-shaped flowers. '**Gold Lace**' (syn. 'Kuranga Gold Lace') differs from species by its prostrate and trailing habit and earlier flowering time (late winter–early spring). Stems become twisted with age. Zones 8–11.

Acacia cultriformis
KNIFE-LEAF WATTLE, PLOUGHSHARE WATTLE
☀ ❁ ↔ 6–10 ft (1.8–3 m) ↑ 6–10 ft (1.8–3 m)
Widely cultivated tall shrub from eastern Australia. Drooping branches with blue-gray almost triangular phyllodes. Perfumed, bright yellow, globular flowers, on long sprays, in spring. Excellent plant for hedging. '**Cascade**' (syn. 'Austraflora Cascade'), prostrate habit, with flowers similar in size and color to species. Zones 8–11.

Acacia cyclops
ROOIKRANS, WESTERN COASTAL WATTLE
☀ ❁ ↔ 7–15 ft (2–4.5 m) ↑ 7–15 ft (2–4.5 m)
Occurs along coastal fringe of southern and southwestern Australia. Dense shrub, spreading, branching near ground level. Thick, slightly curved phyllodes, 1½–4 in (3.5–10 cm) long, with 3 to 5 prominent veins. Heads of about 40 lemon yellow flowers during spring–autumn. Grayish brown leathery pods. Has naturalized in southern Africa and is serious environmental weed. Zones 9–11.

Acacia dealbata
MIMOSA, SILVER WATTLE
☀ ❁ ↔ 25 ft (8 m) ↑ 50 ft (15 m)
From southeastern Australia. Trunk has dark gray to black bark. Silvery branchlets, gray-green bipinnate leaves. Pale lemon to bright yellow globular flowers on extended racemes in late winter–spring. Known in Europe as mimosa. '**Gaulois Astier**', deep green foliage; '**Kambah Karpet**', dense, prostrate habit. Drought tolerant. Zones 8–10.

Acacia elata
CEDAR WATTLE
☀ ❧ ↔ 40 ft (12 m) ↑ 100 ft (30 m)
From moist sheltered forests in coastal eastern Australia. Dark green bipinnate leaves, long individual leaflets. Clusters of fluffy, pale yellow, ball-shaped flowers in summer. Zones 9–11.

Acacia farnesiana
MIMOSA BUSH
☀ ✴ ↔ 15 ft (4.5 m) ↑ 15 ft (4.5 m)
Can be spreading shrub or small tree, native to tropical zones of Americas. Bipinnate leaves with strong spines in leaf axils.
Golden, sweetly scented, globular flowers in winter–spring. Zones 11–12.

Acacia farnesiana

Acacia giraffae
syn. *Acacia erioloba*
CAMEL THORN
☀ ❧ ↔ 40 ft (12 m) ↑ 40–60 ft (12–18 m)
Shapely tree with wide-spreading crown, widespread in southern Africa. Straight thorns, bipinnate leaves. Sweetly scented, yellow, ball-shaped flowers in late winter–early spring. Sickle-shaped pod. Good shade. Zones 9–11.

Acacia howittii
HOWITT'S WATTLE
☀ ❧ ↔ 10 ft (3 m) ↑ 25 ft (8 m)
From southeastern Australia. Small tree with dense weeping habit. Sticky dark green phyllodes; displays masses of scented lemon flower balls in spring. Makes very good hedge plant. Low-spreading form is in cultivation. Zones 9–11.

Acacia karroo
KARROO THORN, SWEET THORN
☼ ⁂ ↔ 25 ft (8 m) ↑ 25 ft (8 m)
Common and widespread tree from southern Africa. Spreading rounded crown of deciduous, dark green, bipinnate leaves. Smooth brownish gray bark, paired straight thorns. Dark yellow, sweetly scented, globular flowers in summer–autumn. Zones 9–11.

Acacia longifolia
SYDNEY GOLDEN WATTLE
☼ ⁂ ↔ 15 ft (4.5 m) ↑ 6–25 ft (1.8–8 m)
From eastern Australia. Small bushy tree, low spreading branches. Bright green thick phyllodes. Bright yellow flower spikes along branches in winter–spring. Useful as hedge. Zones 9–11.

Acacia melanoxylon
BLACKWOOD
☼ ❄ ↔ 20 ft (6 m) ↑ 100 ft (30 m)
From mainland eastern Australia and Tasmania. Spreading bushy crown of dull green phyllodes with longitudinal veins. Clusters of pale yellow globular flowers in late winter–early spring. Best in moist sheltered situation. Weed in South Africa. Zones 8–11.

Acacia podalyriifolia
QUEENSLAND WATTLE
☼ ⁂ ↔ 15 ft (4.5 m) ↑ 10–15 ft (3–4.5 m)
Native to coastal southern Queensland, Australia. Large shrub or slender small tree. Rounded silvery phyllodes and profuse, fragrant, golden flower balls, in clusters, in early winter–spring. Zones 9–11.

Acacia melanoxylon

Acacia longifolia

Acacia podalyriifolia

Acacia pravissima
OVENS WATTLE, WEDGE-LEAFED WATTLE
☼ ❄ ↔ 10 ft (3 m) ↑ 10–25 ft (3–8 m)
Native to hilly country in southeastern Australia. Spreading shrub or small tree, drooping branches and small, roughly triangular, olive green phyllodes. Profuse, golden yellow, globular flowers, in extended racemes, in spring. Prostrate form, '**Golden Carpet**', spreads to 15 ft (4.5 m). Zones 8–10.

Acacia pycnantha
GOLDEN WATTLE
☼ ⁂ ↔ 15 ft (4.5 m) ↑ 10–25 ft (3–8 m)
Tall shrub or small open-branched tree; Australia's national floral emblem. Pendulous branches, bright green phyllodes. Racemes of large, perfumed, golden yellow, ball-shaped flowers in late winter–spring. Zones 9–11.

Acacia riceana ★
RICE'S WATTLE
☼ ❄ ↔ 10 ft (3 m) ↑ 10–20 ft (3–6 m)
Native to Tasmania, Australia. Prickly shrub or small tree, often with drooping branches. Narrow, dark green, sharply pointed phyllodes. Profuse pale yellow flower balls, in loose sprays, in early spring. Zones 8–10.

Acacia verticillata
PRICKLY MOSES
◑ ⁂ ↔ 7 ft (2 m) ↑ 10 ft (3 m)
Shrub from southeastern mainland Australia and Tasmania. May be low and spreading or upright with arching branches. Very sharp needle-like phyllodes in whorls. Bright yellow flower spikes in late winter–spring. *A. v.* var. *latifolia* covers a range of forms with broader, flatter, and often blunt-tipped phyllodes. Zones 9–11.

Acacia vestita
WEEPING BOREE
☼ ⁂ ↔ 6–15 ft (1.8–4.5 m) ↑ 6–15 ft (1.8–4.5 m)
From eastern Australia. Dense shrub, widely cultivated, attractive pendulous branches, green phyllodes. Masses of golden yellow

ball-shaped flowers, in clusters, in spring. Good screen, hedge, or low windbreak. Prune after flowering to maintain shape. Zones 9–11.

Acacia xanthophloea
FEVER TREE

☼ ☘ ↔ 20–40 ft (6–12 m) ↑ 50 ft (15 m)

Native to southeastern Africa. Deciduous tree with somewhat sparse wide-spreading crown. Bark smooth, powdery, yellow-green; straight sharp thorns and small bipinnate leaves. Fragrant, golden yellow, rounded flowers in spring. This is fever tree of Rudyard Kipling's story, "The Elephant's Child." Zones 9–11.

ACALYPHA

This pantropical genus of the spurge or euphorbia (Euphorbiaceae) family contains over 400 species of perennials, shrubs, and trees best known for their long catkins or spikes of flowers, often bright magenta to red shades. Their leaves are simple, fairly large, and oval-shaped with toothed edges. Individually the flowers are minute, but those of the female plants form densely packed catkins that in some species can be as much as 18 in (45 cm) long.
CULTIVATION: Warm, almost frost-free conditions are essential as is plenty of moisture during the growing season. Plant in moist, humus-rich, well-drained soil, and feed well to keep the foliage lush and the plants flowering freely. Pinch back the young shoots and deadhead the flowers to keep the growth compact; otherwise little pruning is required. Propagate from cuttings and, if growing indoors, watch for mealybugs and white flies.

Acalypha amentacea subsp. *wilkesiana*
syn. *Acalypha wilkesiana*
COPPERLEAF, FIJIAN FIRE PLANT, JACOB'S COAT

☼ ☘ ↔ 10 ft (3 m) ↑ 10 ft (3 m)

From Fiji and nearby Pacific islands. Shrub with striking foliage colors and patterns. Colors range from green to bronze, and in tapestries of pink, rosy red, cream, or yellow, sometimes with contrasting margins that are coarsely serrated. Flowers in summer–autumn are upstaged by foliage. 'Ceylon', bronze-purple leaves, edged in pink or white; 'Marginata', coppery leaves edged in red. Zones 10–12.

Acalypha hispida
CHENILLE PLANT, RED-HOT CAT-TAIL

☀ ☘ ↔ 5 ft (1.5 m) ↑ 12 ft (3.5 m)

Famed for its long tassels of blood red flowers, this species is most likely a native of tropical East Asia. Leaves bright green, with toothed edges, and covered in fine hairs. Excellent in hanging baskets where the tassels can be seen from below. Zones 11–12.

Acalypha reptans
RED CAT-TAILS

☀ ☘ ↔ 12 in (30 cm) ↑ 12 in (30 cm)

Native of Florida, USA, and nearby Caribbean islands, often grown as hanging basket plant. Soft light to mid-green leaves.

Acalypha reptans

Flower catkins deep pink to pale red in summer, spot flowering at other times. Zones 10–12.

ACCA
syn. *Feijoa*

This South American genus of the myrtle (Myrtaceae) family consists of 6 species of evergreen shrubs and small trees that bear a guava-like fruit. Simple, smooth-edged leaves are paler on the underside. The attractive single flowers have fleshy petals and conspicuous stamens. Only one species, *A. sellowiana* (syn. *Feijoa sellowiana*), is commonly cultivated, for its tasty fruit or for ornament, and is grown in the same kinds of warm-temperate climates that suit oranges.

CULTIVATION: The feijoa likes a sunny position and well-drained soil of moderate fertility. It is tolerant of exposure and even salt-laden winds, and can be clipped to form a dense hedge. Mature plants tolerate moderate winter frosts but in cooler climates will thrive better against a wall that traps the sun's heat. Cross-pollination, preferably by another plant not of the same clone, is needed for good fruit production. Named varieties are propagated from cuttings or grafting, but seed-raised plants are just as ornamental, if lacking fruit quality, and are more reliable pollinators.

Acca sellowiana

Acca sellowiana ★
syn. *Feijoa sellowiana*
FEIJOA, PINEAPPLE GUAVA

☼ ❄ ↔ 10 ft (3 m) ↑ 10 ft (3 m)

Native from southern Brazil to northern Argentina. Leathery, oval, glossy green leaves, whitish beneath. Flowers have cupped petals, pale carmine, with dark crimson stamens. Fruit elliptical with sweet, aromatic, cream flesh. 'Beechwood', smooth-skinned fruit; 'Coolidge', abundant fruit; 'Mammoth', bearing large wrinkled-skinned fruit; 'Nazemetz', bearing large fruit to 4 in (10 cm) long; and 'Trask', thick-skinned fruit. Zones 8–11.

ACER

MAPLE

This genus of mostly deciduous trees was formerly treated as a family of its own, but is now included in the soapberry (Sapindaceae) family. It consists of around 120 species, most from the Northern Hemisphere. Maples are forest or woodland trees of moist climates. The majority have simple leaves, mostly toothed or lobed, borne on slender leaf stalks attached to the twigs in opposite pairs. A small number have compound leaves with 3, 5, or 7 leaflets. Flowers are small, in clusters or dense spikes. Fruits consist of two small nuts (samaras), joined where attached to the flower stalk, each terminating in an elongated wing.
CULTIVATION: Maples thrive best in cooler temperate climates with adequate rainfall, aided by warm humid summers and sharply demarcated winters. They are best in deep well-drained soil with permanent subsoil moisture. Some need dappled shade to preserve their foliage from summer scorching, but some can tolerate exposure to drying winds. Propagation of species is from seed, cultivars by grafting.

Acer japonicum

Acer buergerianum

TRIDENT MAPLE

☼ ❄ ↔ 25 ft (8 m) ↑ 30 ft (9 m)

From eastern China and Korea. Usually seen as sturdy small tree; popular bonsai subject. Leaves have 3 short lobes, turning yellowish often flushed with red in autumn. Bark flaky, pale gray. Winged fruits persist through winter. Zones 6–10.

Acer campestre

FIELD MAPLE, HEDGE MAPLE

☼ ❄ ↔ 12 ft (3.5 m) ↑ 30 ft (9 m)

Spreading tree from western Asia, Europe, and North Africa. Leaves turn clear golden yellow in autumn; bark becomes thick and furrowed with age. *A. c.* subsp. *tauricum*, smaller leaves with downy undersides. *A. c.* 'Carnival', slow-growing to 10 ft (3 m) high and wide, leaves heavily margined white; 'Elsrijk', rich dark green foliage, conical habit; 'Queen Elizabeth' ★, erect habit, lustrous foliage; and 'Schwerinii', reddish foliage, turning purple. Zones 3–9.

Acer capillipes

RED SNAKEBARK MAPLE

☼ ❄ ↔ 35 ft (10 m) ↑ 40 ft (12 m)

From Japan. Young stems bright pinkish red ageing to white-striped green-brown bark. Leaves dark green with serrated edges and prominent red stalks. Zones 5–9.

Acer cappadocicum

CAPPADOCIAN MAPLE

☼ ❄ ↔ 50 ft (15 m) ↑ 60 ft (18 m)

Fast-growing species from highlands of Turkey and southwest Asia to Himalayas. Leaves with 5 or 7 very regular, triangular lobes and flat base. Unfolding leaves may be reddish, and turn butter yellow in autumn. *A. c.* subsp. *lobelii*, columnar form; *A. c.* subsp. *sinicum*, more sharply pointed leaf lobes and rougher bark. *A. c.* 'Aureum', golden new foliage in spring; 'Rubrum', deep red young foliage. Zones 5–9.

Acer circinnatum

VINE MAPLE

☼ ❄ ↔ 15 ft (4.5 m) ↑ 15 ft (4.5 m)

Shrub or low-branching tree from western North America. Leaves rounded, 7 to 9 lobes, turn orange-scarlet to deep red in autumn. Purple flowers. Red horizontal winged fruits. 'Monroe', deeply cut leaves. Zones 4–9.

Acer davidii ★

PERE DAVID'S MAPLE

☼ ❄ ↔ 25 ft (8 m) ↑ 30 ft (9 m)

Elegant fast-growing tree from central and western China. Open habit with arching branches, striped greenish bark. Leaves pointed, toothed, some with small lobes near base. Small reddish fruits in long pendent spikes. 'Ernest Wilson', compact tree, narrow orange leaves; 'George Forrest', dark red young foliage, almost unlobed leaves; and 'Serpentine', smaller-leafed than species. Zones 5–9.

Acer forrestii

syn. *Acer pectinatum* subsp. *forrestii*

☼ ❄ ↔ 20–30 ft (6–9 m) ↑ 25–40 ft (8–12 m)

Medium-sized tree with spreading branches from western China. Bark reddish or purplish on young branches, striped with white. Leaves dull dark green, long-pointed, 2 to 4 lateral lobes. 'Alice', large strong-veined leaves variegated pink in summer. Zones 5–9.

Acer griseum

CHINESE PAPERBARK MAPLE, PAPERBARK MAPLE

☼ ❄ ↔ 35 ft (10 m) ↑ 40 ft (12 m)

Slender tree from central and western China. Outstanding bark texture and color. Leaves turn orange, scarlet, and crimson in autumn. Winged fruits with large seeds. Zones 4–9.

Acer japonicum

FULL-MOON MAPLE

☼ ❄ ↔ 30 ft (9 m) ↑ 30 ft (9 m)

Broadly spreading small tree from mostly dry and sunny mountain forests of Japan. Leaves rounded; 7 to 11 sharp-toothed, pointed lobes turn yellow, orange, and crimson in autumn. 'Aconitifolium', leaves deeply dissected and toothed turning crimson in autumn; 'Vitifolium', large leaves, bronzy when young. Zones 6–9.

Acer macrophyllum

OREGON MAPLE

☼ ❄ ↔ 80 ft (24 m) ↑ 80 ft (24 m)

Tall broadly columnar tree from western North America. Leaves largest of all maples, 5-lobed, dark green, glossy, turning bright orange in autumn. Large pendulous fruit clusters. Zones 6–9.

Acer maximowiczianum ★

syn. *Acer nikoense*

NIKKO MAPLE

☼ ❋ ↔ 40 ft (12 m) ↑ 60 ft (18 m)

Broadly spreading tree from China and Japan; 3-part dark green leaves, brilliant red in autumn. Green winged fruits in spreading pairs. Zones 4–9.

Acer negundo

BOX ELDER, BOX ELDER MAPLE, MANITOBA MAPLE

☼ ❋ ↔ 30 ft (9 m) ↑ 60 ft (18 m)

Fast-growing hardy tree from North America with several popular variegated forms. Green species is rounded to broadly columnar tree. Colored forms are smaller and less vigorous. All have compound leaves with 3 to 5 or 7 large leaflets. *A. n.* var. *violaceum,* red to purple flowers on dark branches. *A. n.* 'Aureovariegatum', gold-edged leaflets; 'Elegans', broad gold margin, male clone; 'Flamingo', pink-margined in early spring, fading to white; 'Sensation', rich pink autumn color; and 'Variegatum' ★, white-margined, sterile, female clone. Zones 5–10.

Acer palmatum

GREENLEAF JAPANESE MAPLE, JAPANESE MAPLE

☼ ❋ ↔ 25 ft (8 m) ↑ 20 ft (6 m)

Tree from Japan, Korea, and China with more than 1,000 cultivars. The 5- to 7-lobed leaves turn yellow, amber, crimson, and purple. Cultivars must be propagated by grafting or cuttings to be true to type. *A. p.* var. *coreanum* 'Korean Gem' has black bark and spectacular autumn foliage.

Many cultivars belong to *A. p.* **Dissectum Group**, which consists of shrubs with narrow

Acer platanoides 'Drummondii'

leaf lobes, which themselves are strongly lobed. Most are low growing with cascading branches, giving mature plants an umbrella-like or dome-like form. Further subdivisions include the **Dissectum Viride Group** and the **Dissectum Atropurpureum Group**; 'Crimson Queen', vigorous growth, bright red autumn foliage; 'Dissectum Nigrum' (syn. 'Ever Red'), bright red in autumn; 'Inabe-shidare', burgundy foliage; 'Ornatum', deeply dissected leaves, turning red, amber, and gold in autumn.

A. p. 'Akaji-nishiki' (syn. 'Bonfire'), pinkish foliage in spring and autumn; 'Butterfly', vase-shaped with cream-white margined 5-lobed leaves; 'Garnet', deep red spring foliage turning fiery red in autumn; 'Higasayama', cream and pink variegated leaves; 'Kotohime', dwarf to 5 ft (1.5 m) high, green-brown leaves turning golden in autumn; 'Nigrum', dark purple shrub with light green winged fruits; 'Osakazuki', 7-lobed brown-green leaves, turning russet in autumn; 'Red Dragon', rich purple foliage; 'Red Filigree Lace', the most finely divided leaves of all maples of this type; 'Sango-kaku', remarkable for its glowing red bark in winter; 'Seiryu', distinctive vigorous growth and upright habit; 'Shishi-gashira', the "lion's head maple," good for seaside gardens; 'Trompenburg', unique among maples for its mature foliage; and 'Waterfall', a classic, cascading, dome-shaped shrub. Other cultivars include 'Atrolineare' (syns 'Filiferum Purpureum', 'Linearilobium Rubrum'), 'Atropurpureum', 'Bloodgood', 'Burgundy Lace', 'Chishio', 'Chitoseyama', 'Heptalobum Rubrum', 'Katsura', 'Linearilobum', 'Moonfire', 'Nicholsonii', 'Red Pygmy', 'Shigitatsu-sawa', 'Shindeshojo', 'Suminagashi', and 'Villa Taranto'. Zones 6–10.

Acer pensylvanicum

GOOSEFOOT MAPLE, MOOSEWOOD, STRIPED MAPLE

☼ ❋ ↔ 35 ft (10 m) ↑ 30 ft (9 m)

Only North American snakebark maple, with branches marked like markings found on garter snake. Broadly columnar tree from moist woodlands. White and red-brown stripes pattern green bark. 'Erythrocladum', winter bark coral to salmon red, striped white. Leaves turn golden amber. Zones 4–9.

Acer platanoides

NORWAY MAPLE

☼ ❋ ↔ 50 ft (15 m) ↑ 80 ft (24 m)

Fast-growing broadly columnar tree. Leaves 5-lobed, bright green, on long slender stalks, color clear yellow in autumn. Yellow-green flower clusters. Large winged fruits. Cultivars include 'Cavalier', 'Cleveland', 'Columnare', 'Crimson King', 'Deborah', 'Drummondii', 'Emerald Queen', 'Faassen's Black', 'Globe', 'Goldsworth Purple', 'Green Lace', 'Jade Gem', 'Laciniatum', 'Palmatifidum', 'Schwedleri', 'Undulatum', and 'Walderseei'. Zones 4–8.

Acer palmatum

Acer pseudoplatanus
SYCAMORE MAPLE

☼ ❄ ↔ 80 ft (24 m) ↑ 100 ft (30 m)

Large-domed tree native to central and southern Europe. Leaves mid-green, 5 rounded lobes, turn burnt yellow in autumn. Greenish yellow flowers. Large winged fruit. Seeds prolifically. '**Atropurpureum**', leaves dark green above and reddish purple underneath; '**Brilliantissimum**', striking salmon pink spring foliage; '**Erectum**', upright branches; '**Leopoldii**', gold-flecked leaves; and '**Prinz Handjery**', similar to 'Brilliantissimum', with purplish reverse to leaves. Zones 4–8.

Acer rubrum
CANADIAN MAPLE, RED MAPLE, SCARLET MAPLE, SWAMP MAPLE

☼ ❄ ↔ 35 ft (10 m) ↑ 100 ft (30 m)

Large tree native to eastern North America. Appreciated for its fast growth, spectacular autumn color, and tolerance of wet soils and atmospheric pollution. Leaves 3- to 5-lobed, dark green, bluish beneath, changing to yellow, amber, or fiery red. Dense red flower clusters. Red winged fruit. *A. r.* var. *drummondii*, larger flowers and thicker leaves, whitish beneath. *A. r.* '**Autumn Flame**', dense rounded crown, crimson autumn foliage; '**Gerling**', broad conical shape, fiery red autumn color; '**October Glory**', spectacular "Lipstick" tree; '**Scanlon**', leaves turn gold-orange and speckled crimson in autumn; '**Scarsen**', upright habit, yellow-orange to vivid red color in autumn; and '**Sunshine**', popular cultivar. Zones 4–8.

Acer saccharinum
RIVER MAPLE, SILVER MAPLE, SOFT MAPLE, WHITE MAPLE

☼ ❄ ↔ 80 ft (24 m) ↑ 100 ft (30 m)

Large tree found on moist riverbanks in eastern North America. Fast growing but can be short lived, easily damaged by wind. Deep angularly lobed leaves, silvery beneath, turn clear yellow in autumn. Coppery green winged fruits fall early. *A. s.* f. *lutescens*, yellow spring foliage turns light green then yellow in autumn; *A. s.* f. *pyramidale*, narrower form with deeply cut leaves, ideal street tree. Cultivars include *A. s.* '**Beebe's Cutleaf Weeping**' and '**Skinneri**'. Zones 4–9.

Acer saccharum
HARD MAPLE, ROCK MAPLE, SUGAR MAPLE

☼ ❄ ↔ 40 ft (12 m) ↑ 100 ft (30 m)

This North American species produces the best sap, extracted to make maple syrup. Tree and foliage resemble *A. platanoides*. Leaves turn yellow-orange and crimson in autumn. Stylized interpretation of leaf is national symbol of Canada. *A. s.* subsp. *grandidentatum* (syn. *A. grandidentatum*) grows 35–40 ft (10–12 m) high; *A. s.* subsp. *leucoderme* (syn. *A. leucoderme*) grows to 25 ft (8 m) high; and *A. s.* subsp. *nigrum* (syn. *A. nigrum*) is known as the black maple for its black bark; '**Green Column**', light green foliage turning yellow to apricot orange in autumn; '**Temple's Upright**', narrow upright form. Cultivars include *A. s.* '**Flax Hill Majesty**', '**Green Mountain**', '**Legacy**', and '**Seneca Chief**'. Zones 4–9.

ACMENA

Fifteen species make up this genus from the myrtle (Myrtaceae) family of evergreen rainforest trees, native to eastern Australia and New Guinea. All *Acmena* species were once included in *Eugenia*, but that name is now restricted almost entirely to the American species. Acmenas have simple smooth-edged leaves. Small white flowers are borne in panicles terminating the branches. They are followed by globular edible fruit. A cavity at the fruit apex has a sharp circular rim, a feature that distinguishes the genus from *Syzygium*.

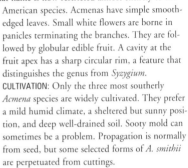

Acer saccharinum 'Beebe's Cutleaf Weeping'

CULTIVATION: Only the three most southerly *Acmena* species are widely cultivated. They prefer a mild humid climate, a sheltered but sunny position, and deep well-drained soil. Sooty mold can sometimes be a problem. Propagation is normally from seed, but some selected forms of *A. smithii* are perpetuated from cuttings.

Acmena ingens
syns *Acmena australis*, *Eugenia brachyandra*
RED APPLE

☼ ⚘ ↔ 15–30 ft (4.5–9 m) ↑ 100 ft (30 m)

Tree from northeastern New South Wales to southeastern Queensland, Australia. Narrow pointed leaves. White flowers in summer. Large magenta or crimson fruit. Zones 9–11.

Acmena smithii
syn. *Eugenia smithii*
LILLYPILLY

☼ ⚘ ↔ 35 ft (10 m) ↑ 60 ft (18 m)

Found along whole length of east Australian coast and ranges. Medium-sized tree with dense bushy crown, glossy green leaves, and tiny white flowers in summer. White to dull mauve fruit, edible, ripen in winter. Zones 9–12.

Acmena smithii

ACOKANTHERA

There are 7 species in this genus of evergreen shrubs and small trees, generally occurring in open forest and scrub from south-eastern Africa to southern Arabia. The genus belongs to the dog-bane (Apocynaceae) family and has similar poisonous properties. However, *Acokanthera* has been widely cultivated for ornament, with accidental poisoning being rare. Leaves are smooth, leathery, in opposite pairs or whorls of three. Sweet-scented, tubular, white flowers in the leaf axils are followed by fruit the shape and size of olives. Fruit, leaves, and bark all bleed a thick white sap. CULTIVATION: These are tough shrubs and trees that are adapted to growing in exposed positions, and they are fairly drought and salt tolerant. In the garden they tolerate neglect as long as they are not too shaded by other trees or shrubs. Heavy pruning results in vigorous resprouting. Propagate from seed or soft tip cuttings.

Acokanthera oblongifolia

Acokanthera oblongifolia
syn. *Carissa spectabilis*
DUNE POISON BUSH, WINTERSWEET
☼ ❄ ↔ 5–8 ft (1.5–2.4 m) ↑ 10 ft (3 m)
Shrub native to coastal zone of eastern South Africa and adjacent Mozambique. Foliage often tinged purple, coloring more deeply in winter. Clusters of sweet-scented flowers, pink in bud, opening white. Fruit reddish, ripening black. 'Variegata', leaves marbled in white and gray-green, flushed pink. Zones 9–11.

ADENIUM

The current view is that this genus, which belongs to the dog-bane (Apocynaceae) family, consists of a single variable species ranging from southern Arabia through eastern and central Africa to northeastern South Africa. There are a number of subspecies, some with swollen succulent stems. Less succulent forms are popular ornamentals in tropical gardens around the world, dis-playing their striking trumpet-shaped blooms. The milky sap is believed to be poisonous. The fleshy leaves, widest toward the apex, are spirally arranged rather than opposite or whorled. CULTIVATION: Drought and heat tolerant, adeniums are grown outdoors in the tropics, in containers or well-drained garden beds. In warm-temperate climates they can be grown against a hot sunny wall but in cool climates they require a greenhouse or conservatory with high light levels. Watering through summer and autumn promotes leaf growth and prolongs flowering. Propagation is from seed (if obtainable) or cuttings allowed to callus before planting.

Adenium obesum
syn. *Adenium multiflorum*
DESERT ROSE, IMPALA LILY, SABI STAR
☼ ❄ ↔ 5 ft (1.5 m) ↑ 5 ft (1.5 m)
Usually a shrub, branching into multiple stems with age, but can be more tree-like, reaching 15 ft (4.5 m) or more. Growing on sunny rock outcrops, roots are swollen and succulent, as are stem bases. Forms grown for showy flowers all belong to *A. o.* subsp. *obesum* ★; flower color of cultivars varies from pink to deep crim-son, commonly with white or paler zone, late summer–autumn.

Adenium obesum subsp. *swazicum*

A. o. subsp. *oleifolium*, tuberous and largely underground; *A. o.* subsp. *somaliense*, small tree, smooth hairless leaves; *A. o.* subsp. *swazicum*, also largely underground. Zones 10–12.

AESCULUS

BUCKEYE, HORSE CHESTNUT
There are about 15 species of deciduous shrubs to tall trees in this genus of the soap-berry (Sapindaceae) family. Half are native to North America, commonly called buck-eye; the remainder spread from Asia to south-eastern Europe. Growing in sheltered valleys, they have large compound leaves of 5 to 11 leaflets palmately arranged, and in spring–summer showy upright panicles of cream to reddish flowers are borne. Inedible fruits are held in big smooth to spiny seed capsules, and give rise to the other common name, horse chestnut. CULTIVATION: These trees do best in cool-temperate climates with marked differences in summer and winter temperatures. The larger species suit parks and open landscapes where their pyramidal crowns can develop fully. They need a deep, fertile, and moisture-retentive soil. Propagation is from seed, which is best sown fresh, and cultivars are grafted in late winter.

Aesculus californica
CALIFORNIA BUCKEYE
☼ ❄ ↔ 30 ft (9 m) ↑ 15 ft (4.5 m)
From California and Oregon, USA. Spreading shrub with grayish green leaves. Cylindrical panicles of creamy white flowers, pink tinged, in summer, followed by fig-shaped fruit. Can stand hot dry summers. Deciduous in summer in dry areas. Zones 7–10.

Aesculus × carnea
syn. *Aesculus rubicunda*
RED HORSE CHESTNUT
☼ ❄ ↔ 15 ft (4.5 m) ↑ 30 ft (9 m)
Hybrid of *A. hippocastanum* and *A. pavia*. Erect panicles of deep reddish pink flowers with yellow blotches in spring. 'Briotii' (syn. *A. hippocastanum* 'Briotii'), bigger and darker flowers. Zones 6–9.

Aesculus hippocastanum
COMMON HORSE CHESTNUT, EUROPEAN HORSE CHESTNUT, HORSE CHESTNUT
☼ ❄ ↔ 70 ft (21 m) ↑ 100 ft (30 m)
Spreading tree from Greece, Albania, and Bulgaria. Best suited to large gardens. Erect panicles of white flowers with yellow to red basal blotches in late spring, followed by round prickly fruits commonly known as conkers. **'Baumannii'**, rounded crown and showy, white, double flowers; **'Pyramidalis'**, pyramidal growth habit. Zones 6–9.

Aesculus parviflora
BOTTLEBRUSH BUCKEYE
☼ ❄ ↔ 15 ft (4.5 m) ↑ 10 ft (3 m)
Shrub growing in woodland areas of southeastern USA. Leaves downy beneath, buff-colored when young. Slender panicles of white summer flowers with protruding pink stamens. *A. p. f. serotina*, leaves less downy, bluish green. Zones 6–10.

Aesculus pavia
syn. *Aesculus splendens*
RED BUCKEYE
☼ ❄ ↔ 10 ft (3 m) ↑ 15 ft (4.5 m)
From woodlands on coastal plains of eastern USA. Shrub or small tree. Leaves reddish in autumn. Crimson flowers on short erect panicles in early summer. **'Atrosanguinea'**, deep red flowers. Zones 6–10.

AFROCARPUS
The 6 or so species of this African genus of conifers, of the podocarp or plum-pine (Podocarpaceae) family, were formerly included in *Podocarpus*. In their native habitats they are tall forest trees with massive trunks, seen in mountainous regions of central, eastern, and southern Africa. All have attractive bark that peels off in flakes or strips. Leaves are leathery and narrow. Male (pollen) and female (seed) organs are on different trees; female cones have a thin stalk with a single, usually larger seed with a thick juicy outer layer.
CULTIVATION: These slow-growing trees suit parks and avenues in warm-temperate and subtropical climates with adequate rainfall. Plant in deep, well-drained, reasonably fertile soil. They are affected by few pests or diseases and require little shaping. Propagate from seed, sown fresh after removing the fleshy coating.

Afrocarpus falcatus
syns *Nageia falcata*, *Podocarpus falcatus*
OUTENIQUA YELLOWWOOD
☼ ❄ ↔ 25–50 ft (8–15 m) ↑ 60–200 ft (18–60 m)
One of South Africa's largest trees. In cultivation reaches 30–50 ft (9–15 m). Peeling and flaky bark, purplish brown to paler red-brown. Fine dense foliage, drab green. Female trees covered in pale yellow "fruit" in summer–autumn. Zones 9–11.

AGATHIS
KAURI
These conifers, which grow into massive trees, are from the araucaria (Araucariaceae) family. This genus is of great evolutionary interest because it dates back to the temperate rainforests that

Aesculus parviflora

covered much of the southern supercontinent of Gondwana. The species are scattered from Sumatra in the northwest to New Zealand and Fiji in the southeast. Kauri trees have a straight smooth trunk, developing massive ascending limbs with age. Peeling bark produces distinctive patterns. Broad leathery leaves, with no midrib, are arranged in almost opposite pairs. Cones are almost globular with tightly packed scales.
CULTIVATION: *Agathis* grow readily in the wet tropics and in warmer temperate climates. They prefer deep soil with reliable subsoil moisture. Height growth may be quite fast, but a large trunk diameter takes many decades to achieve. Propagate only from seed, gathered as soon as it falls and sown immediately.

Agathis australis
NEW ZEALAND KAURI
☼ ❄ ↔ 50 ft (15 m) ↑ 150 ft (45 m)
New Zealand's largest native tree. Found in swampy lowland forests in North Island. Small leaves, 1½ in (35 mm) long, closely crowded on adult branches. Slow growing, dense conical or columnar form. Bark dappled gray and brown with small thick scales detaching. Bluish cones in summer. Zones 8–10.

Agathis robusta
QUEENSLAND KAURI
☼ ❄ ↔ 40 ft (12 m) ↑ 180 ft (55 m)
Huge tree with orange-tan bark finely dappled with gray, becoming flaky with age. Fast growing in cultivation, with pole-like trunk and short side branches. At full size stem diameter increases rapidly. Zones 9–12.

AGONIS
This small genus consists of 12 evergreen species growing naturally in temperate regions of southwest Western Australia. All have white or pink flowers. Like other members of the myrtle (Myrtaceae) family, the leaves contain aromatic oil, released when the leaves are crushed. The fibrous bark is a feature of the genus.

Afrocarpus falcatus

Agathis robusta

CULTIVATION: An adaptable, almost pest-free genus, suited to full sun in a range of well-drained soils and climates. Some species can be damaged by frost. Tip prune at any time for bushier growth; trees also respond to pruning after flowering. Propagate species from seed or cuttings, cultivars from cuttings only.

Agonis flexuosa ★

PEPPERMINT TREE, WILLOW MYRTLE

☼ ⚘ ↔ 15 ft (4.5 m) ↑ 30 ft (9 m)

Dome shape and weeping habit when mature. White flowers resemble tea-tree. 'Nana', to 10 ft (3 m); dwarf form 'Weeping Wonder', to 3 ft (0.9 m); 'Belbra Gold' and 'Variegata', dainty variegated foliage forms. Zones 9–11.

Albizia saman

AILANTHUS

There are 5 or 6 species of medium-sized to large trees in this genus, in the quassia (Simaroubaceae) family, occurring from India to northern China and Australia. They include both evergreen tropical and deciduous cold-hardy species. Leaves are pinnate, mostly with a long midrib and many leaflets arranged in 2 regular rows. Flowers, of different sexes on different trees, are small and greenish yellow, in large stalked clusters in leaf axils toward tips of branches, followed by clusters of flat elongated fruits.
CULTIVATION: Easily cultivated if their respective climatic requirements are met, they make fast growth when young. Propagate from seed (may need cold stratification) or root cuttings.

Ailanthus altissima

syn. *Ailanthus glandulosa*

TREE OF HEAVEN

☼ ❄ ↔ 40 ft (12 m) ↑ 40 ft (12 m)

Deciduous tree from China. Long pinnate leaves with unpleasant smell. Female trees flower in mid-summer, fruit in early autumn. Profuse suckers; a weed in many areas. Zones 5–10.

ALBIZIA

This genus contains trees, shrubs, and vines in the mimosa subfamily of the legumes. Most have feathery foliage of bipinnate compound leaves and showy flowerheads of prominent stamens in pink, cream, or white followed by flattened pods.
CULTIVATION: Tolerant of poor soils, they perform best on well-drained loam in a sheltered position, requiring moisture and warmth in summer. As seeds have impermeable coats, soak in sulfuric acid for half an hour, then wash thoroughly prior to sowing. In early spring, root cuttings of at least ½ in (12 mm) diameter planted immediately are also successful.

Albizia julibrissin

PERSIAN SILK TREE, PINK SIRIS, SILK TREE

☼ ❄ ↔ 15–20 ft (4.5–6 m) ↑ 20–40 ft (6–12 m)

Deciduous tree from Japan and western Asia. Pinkish inflorescences with silky stamens in summer. Feathery compound leaves dark green, paler beneath, yellowish in autumn. Zones 6–12.

Albizia saman

syn. *Samanea saman*

MONKEY POD, RAIN TREE, SAMAN

☼/◐ ⚘ ↔ 50–100 ft (15–30 m) ↑ 100 ft (30 m)

Evergreen or briefly deciduous tree found from Caribbean and Central America to Brazil. Broad spreading crown of pinnate leaves with fine leaflets. Pink flowerheads, clustered, followed by edible black-brown seed pods. Zones 10–12.

ALEURITES

This genus in the spurge (Euphorbiaceae) family includes 5 evergreen and deciduous Asian–Australasian species, 3 of which are important for the oils obtained from their large seeds. They are medium-sized to large trees with a straight central trunk and tiered branches. Leaves are large and heart-shaped. Flowers are mostly funnel-shaped with 5 white or cream petals, in large clusters at branch tips. Fruits are globular, the husk enclosing 2 to 5 large nut-like seeds, which may cause violent vomiting if eaten.
CULTIVATION: Best in climates with long humid summers, they thrive in deep fertile soils but will grow in poorer soils. Deciduous species tolerate moderate winter frosts. Propagate from fresh seed in autumn, or from hardwood cuttings for deciduous species.

Aleurites fordii

syn. *Vernicia fordii*

TUNG-OIL TREE

☼ ❄ ↔ 10 ft (3 m) ↑ 25 ft (8 m)

Deciduous tree from China, cultivated for seed oil. Compact crown, broad heart-shaped leaves. White flowers with red centers in spring. Fruit green, ripening black, in summer. Zones 8–11.

Aleurites moluccana

syn. *Aleurites triloba*

CANDLENUT TREE

☼ ⚘ ↔ 35 ft (10 m) ↑ 80 ft (24 m)

Evergreen forest tree from tropical Asia to islands of western Pacific. Glossy heart-shaped leaves. Small cream flowers in spring. Green fruit in summer. Zones 10–12.

ALLAMANDA

This genus, a member of the dogbane (Apocynaceae) family, consists of around 12 evergreen shrubs, including both upright and semi-climbing species. They are tropical American natives and are lush, colorful, and flamboyant. The large, glossy, deep green leaves are the perfect foil to the flowers, usually a deep golden yellow. The flowers appear mainly in summer and autumn and are trumpet-shaped with a widely flared throat and 5 large, overlapping petals. CULTIVATION: Protection from frost is paramount, and a moist subtropical to tropical climate is best, though it is possible to grow allamandas in sheltered areas in cooler zones. For a prolific flower display give them rich well-drained soil and plenty of summer moisture. They also do well in conservatories but watch out for insects. Propagation is usually from half-hardened cuttings.

Allamanda schottii
syn. *Allamanda neriifolia*
BUSH ALLAMANDA
☼ ✿ ↔6ft(1.8m) ↑6ft(1.8m)
South American species, kept neat with regular pinching back and annual spring trim. Glossy deep green leaves, bright golden yellow flowers streaked light orange, large green seed pods. Zones 11–12.

ALLOCASUARINA
SHE-OAK
Allocasuarina, part of the she-oak (Casuarinaceae) family, has 59 species entirely confined to Australia, all trees or shrubs with a pine-like appearance. The fine twigs appear leafless, but in fact have whorls of narrow leaves fused flat against their surfaces, with only tips remaining free and appearing as rings of minute teeth at regular intervals along the twig. The number of teeth per ring is a characteristic feature of each species. Flowers are mostly of different sexes on different plants. Fruits are fused into a cone-like spike, splitting apart to release the "seeds." CULTIVATION: Most species are adapted to poor sandy or stony soils, low in essential nutrients; however taller tree species adapt to more fertile soils. Propagation is from seed, which quickly falls out of gathered cones and germinates readily.

Alnus glutinosa

Allocasuarina torulosa
syn. *Casuarina torulosa*
FOREST OAK, FOREST SHE-OAK
☼/☀ ❄ ↔20ft(6m) ↑40–80ft(12–24m)
Native to eastern Australian coast. Coppery drooping branches and branchlets in winter. Corky light brown bark. Male flowers golden orange in autumn. Rounded warty cones. Zones 8–11.

ALLOXYLON

Belonging to the protea (Proteaceae) family, *Alloxylon* comprises 4 species of evergreen rainforest trees native to tropical and subtropical eastern Australia and New Guinea. Conspicuous red or pinkish flowers in large terminal clusters attract nectar-feeding birds. The leaves are irregularly lobed or pinnate, though tending

Alloxylon flammeum

to become unlobed and simple on flowering branches. The fruit is a large follicle that splits to release winged seeds. CULTIVATION: They are demanding, requiring a subtropical climate with year-round rainfall, or tropical hill conditions with a not too severe dry season. Soil must be well drained and moderately fertile, and the trees sheltered from strong winds. Young plants less than 10–15 ft (3–4.5 m) tall are prone to sudden wilting and death. Propagation is from seed, sown as soon as collected.

Alloxylon flammeum
syn. *Oreocallis wickhamii* of gardens
WARATAH TREE
☼ ❄ ↔20ft(6m) ↑60ft(18m)
From Atherton Tableland of far northeastern Queensland, Australia. Dark green sapling leaves to 18 in (45 cm) long with 3 to 7 large lobes, smaller on flowering shoots. Bright scarlet flower clusters in late winter–spring. Zones 10–11.

ALNUS
ALDER
Alnus, of the birch (Betulaceae) family, is an essentially Northern Hemisphere genus. Of the 25 alder species only 2 extend across the equator. All are deciduous or semi-evergreen. In the wild, alders are fast-growing pioneer trees of disturbed ground. Alders mostly have darker brownish or blackish bark, with leaves usually larger and slightly thicker than birches; leaf margins vary from smooth and wavy to jaggedly toothed, winter buds sticky and aromatic. The flowers are tiny and arranged in catkins; the male is long and thin, while the female is short and barrel-shaped. CULTIVATION: These plants are easily grown in their appropriate climate. Sapling growth is often very fast but they mature early and are sometimes not very long lived. Many are able to thrive in soils of low fertility and poor drainage, aided by nitrogen-fixing fungi in the roots. Propagation is normally from seed, which may need stratification over winter and should not be covered, as germination is stimulated by light. Some cultivars require grafting.

Alnus acuminata

syn. *Alnus jorullensis* of gardens

EVERGREEN ALDER, MEXICAN ALDER

☼ ❋ ↔ 20 ft (6 m) ↕ 40 ft (12 m)

Often misidentified as *A. jorullensis,* a close relation. Evergreen broad-crowned tree in warm climates. Narrow drooping leaves tapering to long points, jaggedly toothed. Brownish yellow male catkins. *A. a.* subsp. *glabrata* is the form in cultivation. Zones 8–11.

Alnus glutinosa

BLACK ALDER, COMMON ALDER

☼ ❋ ↔ 35 ft (10 m) ↕ 60 ft (18 m)

From Europe to Siberia and North Africa. Deciduous tree, may reach 30 ft (9 m) in cultivation. Leaves dark green, rounded, shallowly toothed. Buds and twigs sticky. Male catkins dull purple to yellow. Female catkins purple to burgundy to green to brown. '**Imperialis**', open habit; '**Laciniata**', dissected leaves. Zones 4–8.

Alnus incana

GRAY ALDER

☼ ❋ ↔ 30 ft (9 m) ↕ 70 ft (21 m)

Found in Caucasus and mountains of Europe. Bark smooth gray. Gray down on young shoots and undersides of leaves. *A. i.* subsp. *tenuifolia* (syn. *A. tenuifolia*), smaller with red downy young shoots that are soon smooth. *A. i.* '**Aurea**', yellowish foliage; '**Laciniata**', narrow-lobed leaves; and '**Pendula**', weeping form. Zones 3–9.

Alnus rubra

syn. *Alnus oregona*

OREGON ALDER, RED ALDER

☼ ❋ ↔ 30 ft (9 m) ↕ 50 ft (15 m)

From canyons and riverbanks of North America. Fast growing tree, pyramidal crown, somewhat pendulous habit. Young shoots dark red; reddish brown down on new leaves, turning dark green above and blue-gray beneath. Zones 4–9.

ALYOGYNE

Once included within the genus *Hibiscus*, the 4 species that make up this genus, of the mallow (Malvaceae) family, are distinctive, evergreen, Australian shrubs which, despite their delicate silky blooms, are native to the drier regions of the western half of the continent. Leaves are variable; in some species they are smooth-edged, in others palmately lobed. They are fast growing and, as though to make up for their short-lived single blooms, usually in pinks or mauves, they flower profusely over a long period. CULTIVATION: These are hardy plants for non-humid areas. Most are able to survive frost. They do best planted in full sun and can survive in all soil types but appreciate good drainage. Pruning is sometimes necessary. Propagate from cuttings or seed.

Alyogyne huegelii ★

BLUE HIBISCUS

☼ ❂ ↔ 3–6 ft (0.9–1.8 m) ↕ 3–6 ft (0.9–1.8 m)

Fast growing. Flowers pale mauve to purplish with overlapping petals set against pale green, slightly felty, deeply lobed leaves. '**Monterey Bay**' and '**Santa Cruz**' are popular cultivars. Zones 9–10.

AMELANCHIER

SERVICEBERRY

Amelanchier, a member of the rose (Rosaceae) family, consists of 30 or so species of deciduous shrubs and small trees from North America and Mexico, with one species in China, and another in Europe and Turkey. All have smallish oval or elliptical leaves with finely toothed margins. Flowers, each with 5 white narrow petals, are borne in small sprays; the small hawthorn-like fruit has sepals at the apex. The fruit ripens to blue-black and is edible. CULTIVATION: These are mostly woodland plants preferring moist sheltered sites, while some species do well at the edge of a pond or stream. They are prone to the same pests and diseases as apples, pears, and hawthorns, including fireblight. Propagation is normally from seed, germination being aided by cold stratification, or by layering of low branches or suckers. Cultivars are often grafted.

Amelanchier alnifolia

syn. *Amelanchier florida*

ALDERLEAF SERVICEBERRY, JUNEBERRY, SASKATOON SERVICEBERRY

☼ ❋ ↔ 12 ft (3.5 m) ↕ 3–6 ft (0.9–1.8 m)

North American species found on banks of rivulets or on sheltered mountainsides. Leaves rounded, toothed mainly in upper half, 1 in (25 mm) long. Flowers in late spring–early summer, dark purple edible fruit. *A. a.* var. *semiintegrifolia* (syn. *A. florida*), from southern Alaska to northern California. Zones 3–9.

Amelanchier arborea

syn. *Amelanchier canadensis* of gardens

DOWNY SERVICEBERRY

☼ ❋ ↔ 30 ft (9 m) ↕ 60 ft (18 m)

From eastern USA. Narrow rounded crown. Silver-gray smooth bark, rough with age. Leaves abruptly pointed, turn red or yellow in autumn. Flowers early spring. Small purple-black fruit. Zones 4–9.

Amelanchier canadensis

syn. *Amelanchier oblongifolia*

JUNEBERRY, SERVICEBERRY, SHADBLOW SERVICEBERRY

☼ ❋ ↔ 10 ft (3 m) ↕ 25 ft (8 m)

Upright suckering shrub or small tree mainly from boggy ground in eastern North America. Woolly new leaves, spring flowers in upright sprays, juicy blue-black fruit about ½ in (12 mm) wide. Cultivars include '**Glenn Form**' and '**Sprizam**'. Zones 5–9.

Alyogyne huegelii

Angophora costata, in the wild, New South Wales, Australia

Amelanchier laevis
syn. *Amelanchier canadensis* of gardens
ALLEGHENY SERVICEBERRY, SARVIS TREE

◐ ❉ ↔ 25 ft (8 m) ↕ 25 ft (8 m)

Found mainly in Appalachian mountains of eastern USA, extending into Canada. Bronzy purple slightly downy new leaves; sweet, juicy, blue-black fruit. Flowers as leaves unfold in late spring. Zones 4–9.

Amelanchier lamarckii
LAMARCK SERVICEBERRY

◐ ❉ ↔ 35 ft (10 m) ↕ 30 ft (9 m)

Probable hybrid origin. Small tree with spreading branches, leaves silky-haired, bronzy red when new. Loose sprays of flowers open with new leaves. Fruit purple-black. Zones 4–9.

AMHERSTIA
The 1 species of this genus, of the cassia sub-family of legumes (Fabaceae), is from the lowlands of southern Myanmar, and almost unknown in the wild. It has long pinnate leaves with glossy leaflets and may be briefly deciduous. At the start of the wet season pale bronzy pink new leaves emerge, changing through brown to green. On long stalks, flowers are orchid-like with a pair of large pink bracts at the base, up to 4 in (10 cm) across, pinkish red with darker red and yellow markings. Rarely produced are the curved woody pods.
CULTIVATION: *Amherstia* has been successfully cultivated only in the lowland wet tropics. Its growth is fairly slow, and it needs a sheltered but sunny situation and deep moist soil. Propagate from seed if it can be obtained; an alternative is layering of low branches.

Amherstia nobilis
PRIDE OF BURMA

☼ ✦ ↔ 50 ft (15 m) ↕ 40 ft (12 m)

Lovely tree with broad low-branching canopy of foliage. Mature specimens may flower for much of year, but flowering season is spring–early summer. Red orchid-like flowers. Zone 12.

Amelanchier lamarckii

ANDROMEDA
Two fully hardy, low-growing, evergreen shrub species make up this genus of the heath (Ericaceae) family, found growing in the acid peat bogs of the Northern Hemisphere. The somewhat leathery, smooth-edged, small oblong leaves form a deep green background to the tiny, white or pink, bell-like flowers held in terminal clusters during spring.
CULTIVATION: *Andromeda* species require an acid soil where constant moisture is assured, and are best grown in peat beds, shady woodlands, or rock gardens. They can be propagated from suckers, by layering, or from softwood cuttings.

Andromeda polifolia
BOG ROSEMARY, MARSH ANDROMEDA

◐ ❉ ↔ 22 in (55 cm) ↕ 4–18 in (10–45 cm)

Variable growing shrub, either erect or prostrate. Small, pointed, oblong leaves with clusters of bell-like flowers in spring or early summer. '**Alba**', low-growing prostrate shrub with pure white flowers; '**Compacta**', compact growth habit, pink flowers; and '**Macrophylla**', larger leaves and pink flowers. Zones 2–9.

ANGOPHORA
This eastern Australian genus of the myrtle (Myrtaceae) family is closely allied to *Eucalyptus* and *Corymbia*. Its 15 species of evergreen trees have separate sepals and petals enclosing the buds. Most are medium to large trees of open forest, woodland, and heath. Bark is usually rough, rather corky or flaky, though smooth in some species. Leaves, in opposite pairs, vary from narrow pointed to broad heart-shaped. Flowers have masses of white to cream stamens, in terminal clusters at the branch tips. Blooms are followed by ribbed woody capsules.
CULTIVATION: These trees are light-loving and fast growing, preferring sandy moderately fertile soils and shelter from strong winds. Most tolerate a degree or two of overnight frost as long as days are warm and sunny. Propagate from seed, to be collected just as capsules discharge.

Angophora costata
syn. *Angophora lanceolata*
ANGOPHORA, RUSTY GUM, SYDNEY RED GUM

☼ ❧ ↔ 80 ft (24 m) ↕ 100 ft (30 m)

From sandy forest country of coastal New South Wales, Australia. Pinkish gray bark sheds in early summer to reveal bright orange-brown bark. Deep wine red new foliage. Clusters of white flowers in spring–early summer. Zones 9–11.

Angophora hispida
syn. *Angophora cordifolia*
DWARF APPLE

☼ ❧ ↔ 12 ft (3.5 m) ↕ 10 ft (3 m)

Localized to sandstone ridges around Sydney, Australia. Broad, harsh-textured leaves. Flowers in large heads, in mid-spring–summer. New shoots and flower buds have deep red bristles. Zones 10–11.

ANISODONTEA

This genus of 20 species of shrubs and subshrubs in the mallow (Malvaceae) family is native to South Africa. They are half-hardy evergreen species with toothed leaves that can be palmately lobed or elliptic and toothed. Flowers are 5-petalled with shallow cups. CULTIVATION: Plants do best in loam-based gritty compost. Grown indoors, they need maximum light. Outdoors they need full sun and should be fed in spring. Pot-grown specimens should receive a balanced fertilizer once a month. In winter, watering should be reduced and feeding stopped. New plants can be tip pruned for bushiness, pruning old wood in spring. Pot plants are prone to red spider mite and white fly. Seeds should be sown in spring. Take half-hardened cuttings in summer, but they need bottom heat.

Anisodontea capensis

syn. *Malvastrum capensis*

☼ ⬧ ↔ 30 in (75 cm) ↕ 3 ft (0.9 m)

Erect shrub with hairy stems and ovate to triangular leaves. Flowers pale red to deep red-purple, up to 1 in (25 mm) across, most of year in warm climates, all summer in cool-temperate. Zones 9–11.

APHELANDRA

This genus, a member of the acanthus (Acanthaceae) family, consists of about 170 species of shrubs and subshrubs. Short-lived red and yellow flowers appear year-round. Native to tropical North, Central, and South America, all species are frost tender and live in the wild as understory plants in moist woodland. CULTIVATION: To grow in pots, combine loam-based compost in the ratio 2:1, with one part of leaf mold. These plants thrive when watered with rainwater (soft water). They should be fed regularly through the growing season, with food and water reduced throughout dormancy. Avoid drafts and direct sun. After flowering, cut back plants to encourage side shoots, which can be used for propagation. Spider mites, aphids, and scale insects can be a problem under glass.

Aphelandra sinclairiana

☼ ⬧ ↔ 10 ft (3 m) ↕ 15 ft (4.5 m)

Central America species, often grown as house plant. Deep pink flowers open from candle-like, orange-pink-bracted flower spikes. Leaves bright mid-green, covering of fine hairs. Zones 10–12.

Aphelandra squarrosa

SAFFRON SPIKE, ZEBRA PLANT

☼ ⚡ ↔ 5 ft (1.5 m) ↕ 6 ft (1.8 m)

Native to Brazil. Leaves 12 in (30 cm) long, heavy cream veining, pronounced midrib. Flower spikes of generally yellow flowers with cream, yellow, or maroon bracts. '**Claire**', broad cream zones along leaf veins; '**Leopoldii**', yellow or orange flowers; '**Louisae**', white veins against dark green background; and '**Snow Queen**', silvery white veins and lemon flowers. Zones 11–12.

ARALIA

From the ivy (Araliaceae) family, this genus of trees, shrubs, and herbaceous perennials consists of around 40 species mostly from Southeast Asia and North, Central, and South America. Most are deciduous and nearly all have large compound leaves. Flowers are small, numerous, usually cream, carried in umbels arranged in panicles terminating the branches, followed by black fruits. Some species have prickly stems, and suckering can occur. Roots and bark of several species are used in traditional medicine. CULTIVATION: All species known in cultivation will tolerate at least light frosts, but most need a warm humid summer for best growth. They prefer deep reasonably fertile soil and shelter from strong winds. Though shade tolerant, they grow and flower better in sun. Propagate from seed, which for tree species may need cold stratification, or from root cuttings or basal suckers.

Aralia elata

JAPANESE ANGELICA TREE

☼ ❄ ↔ 30 ft (9 m) ↕ 40 ft (12 m)

Native to Japan, shrub spread by root suckers, with prickly corky trunk. Bipinnate leaves, to 4 ft (1.2 m) long, yellow-purplish in autumn. Large panicles of near-white flowers in late summer. '**Aureomarginata**', yellow leaf margins, turning to creamy white; '**Variegata**' ★ (syn. '**Albomarginata**'), white leaf margins. Zones 4–9.

Aralia spinosa

AMERICAN ANGELICA TREE, DEVIL'S WALKING-STICK, HERCULES CLUB

☼ ❄ ↔ 15 ft (4.5 m) ↕ 20 ft (6 m)

Occurring wild in damp woodland from Pennsylvania, USA, southward. Bipinnate leaves, up to 3 ft (0.9 m) long, turning yellow in autumn. Panicles of flowers in mid- to late summer. Zones 5–9.

Anisodontea capensis

Aphelandra sinclairiana

Aralia spinosa

ARAUCARIA

This ancient conifer genus from the araucaria (Araucariaceae) family consists of 19 species—13 from New Caledonia, 2 from South America, 2 from Australia, 2 from New Guinea (1 also in Australia), and 1 from Norfolk Island. Araucarias have a distinctive growth habit with a straight trunk and usually whorled branches; the spirally arranged leaves are densely crowded and often overlapping on flexible branchlets. Male and female organs are on the same tree, the tassel-like pollen cones on the side branches, and egg-shaped seed cones with spine-tipped scales near the top of the crown. The seeds, which may be quite large and nut-like, are embedded in the tough cone scales, a feature unique to this genus. CULTIVATION: Cold tolerance varies, and these plants cannot be grown outdoors in severe climates. They are best grown as conservatory plants and may be kept in tubs for many years. In warmer climates araucarias are grown in large gardens, parks, and avenues. Propagation is from fresh seed, which germinates readily; cuttings tend to retain sideways growth if taken from lower branches.

Arbutus unedo

Araucaria araucana
syn. *Araucaria imbricata*
MONKEY PUZZLE TREE
☼ ❄ ↔ 35 ft (10 m) ↑ 80 ft (24 m)
From Andean slopes of south-central Chile. Young trees have tangle of upcurved branches, developing broad crown with age. Leaves densely overlapping, rigid, sharp pointed. Globular seed cones 3–6 in (8–15 cm) in diameter. Zones 7–9.

Araucaria araucana, in the wild, Chile

Araucaria bidwillii
BUNYA BUNYA, BUNYA PINE
☼ ❄ ↔ 35 ft (10 m) ↑ 150 ft (45 m)
From Queensland, Australia. Sharp-pointed leaves, up to 2 in (5 cm) long, glossy dark green, arranged on branchlets that are soon shed. Large seed cones up to 12 in (30 cm) in diameter. Zones 9–11.

Araucaria cunninghamii
HOOP PINE
☼ ❄ ↔ 12 ft (3.5 m) ↑ 150 ft (45 m)
Native to eastern Australia. Dark gray bark often furrowed into "hoops" encircling trunk. Juvenile foliage prickly. Adult leaves small, densely overlapping, very dark green. Bluish-leafed forms are known. *A. c.* var. *papuana*, from New Guinea. Zones 9–12.

Araucaria heterophylla
syn. *Araucaria excelsa*
NORFOLK ISLAND PINE
☼ ❄ ↔ 25 ft (8 m) ↑ 200 ft (60 m)
From Norfolk Island. Very symmetrical form, with regularly whorled branches on which branchlets form 2 neat rows with V-shaped trough between. Best near seashores in subtropical regions; not pollution tolerant. Zones 10–11.

ARBUTUS

This small genus contains about 8 to 10 species of small evergreen trees belonging to the heath or erica (Ericaceae) family, which are known as strawberry trees due to their strawberry-like fruit. They occur in the Mediterranean region, western Asia, and southwestern USA, with a few species in Central America and Mexico. All have attractive bell-shaped flowers and red or yellow fruit, and in some cases have red or cinnamon-colored, stringy, peeling bark. CULTIVATION: *Arbutus* like a well-drained soil, preferably free of lime, and an open sunny position protected from cold winds. Most species are tolerant of sustained cold winters. Little pruning is required. Propagation is from half-hardened cuttings taken in autumn or winter; scions can also be top-grafted on seedling understocks. Seeds can be sown in spring.

Arbutus andrachne
GRECIAN STRAWBERRY TREE
☼ ❄ ↔ 20 ft (6 m) ↑ 20 ft (6 m)
From eastern Mediterranean. Cinnamon brown bark flakes away to reveal greenish cream bark beneath. White pitcher-shaped flowers, in upright clusters, in spring, followed by orange-red fruit. Protect from frost when young. Zones 7–10.

Arbutus 'Marina'
☼ ❄ ↔ 20–40 ft (6–12 m) ↑ 25–50 ft (8–15 m)
Possibly clone of *A.* × *andrachnoides* or with some hybrid influence of *A. canariensis*. First noticed in a San Francisco garden in 1984. Smooth reddish bark, bronze new leaves, pink-flushed flowers nearly all year, yellow fruit ageing red, edible. Zones 8–10.

Arbutus menziesii ★

MADRONA, MADRONE, PACIFIC MADRONE

☼ ❉ ↔30 ft (9 m) ↑30 ft (9 m)

From Pacific coast of northern USA. Spreading, shrubby. Bright brick red bark peels to reveal green new layer. White flowers, in drooping clusters. Fruit orange-red. Zones 7–10.

Arbutus unedo

IRISH STRAWBERRY TREE, STRAWBERRY TREE

☼ ❉ ↔20 ft (6 m) ↑25 ft (8 m)

Occurring in Mediterranean region and Ireland. Red stringy bark, often arranged in spiral fashion. Flowers white, flushed with pink, in autumn–winter. Fruit ripening green to orange-red to bright red, edible though bland. Tolerant of pollution. *A. u.* f. *rubra,* 4–6 ft (1.2–1.5 m) tall. *A. u.* 'Compacta', smaller form; 'Elfin King', bushy form; and 'Oktoberfest', pink-flowered form. Zones 7–10.

ARCTOSTAPHYLOS

There are about 50 species in this genus of mostly evergreen small shrubs and trees in the heath or erica (Ericaceae) family. The genus is found only in North America, except for 2 species from the alpine-arctic regions of the Northern Hemisphere. They have reddish brown ornamental bark, smooth or peeling in flakes. Leaves are alternate, smooth or toothed. White or pink bell- or urn-shaped flowers are in terminal racemes or panicles. Fruits are spherical. In the UK, leaves of *A. uva-ursi* have been used as a urinary antiseptic since the thirteenth century.
CULTIVATION: They need lime-free soil, and are mostly disease-free except for leaf spot. In pots water freely and feed in the growing season. Withhold water and fertilizer from western North American species in summer. Put seed in boiling water for 15–20 seconds before sowing in autumn with protection against frosts. Layer prostrate species in autumn. Plant half-hardened cuttings in summer.

Arctostaphylos densiflora

☼/◐ ❉ ↔6 ft (1.8 m) ↑5 ft (1.5 m)

Native to Sonoma County, California, USA. Procumbent shrub with dark red to nearly black, smooth bark. Flowers in small short panicles, white with tinge of pink. Leaves glossy, mid-green, elliptical. 'Emerald Carpet', dense ground cover up to 12 in (30 cm) high; 'Howard McMinn', denser than species. Zones 8–10.

Arctostaphylos hookeri

MONTEREY MANZANITA

☼ ❉ ↔4–15 ft (1.2–4.5 m) ↑6–48 in (15–120 cm)

Coastal species found from San Francisco Bay to near Monterey, California, USA, often on dunes. Forms extensive dense mat, mounding with age. Leaves small, shiny green. Flowers white to pink, in winter–spring. Fruit shiny red, in summer. *A. h.* subsp. *franciscana* (Franciscan manzanita), mat-forming, from San Francisco Peninsula, extinct in wild but preserved in cultivation; *A. h.* subsp. *hearstiorum* (Hearsts' manzanita), quite prostrate, rooting along stems, leaves under ½ in (12 mm) long; *A. h.* subsp. *montana* (Tamalpais manzanita), more erect or mounding form, sometimes to 6 ft (1.8 m) high. *A. h.* 'Monterey Carpet', compact cultivar. Zones 8–10.

Arctostaphylos pumila   *Arctostaphylos uva-ursi*

Arctostaphylos manzanita

MANZANITA

☼ ❉ ↔10 ft (3 m) ↑15 ft (4.5 m)

From California and Oregon, USA. Bark red to brown, tending to peel. Leaves leathery, hairy, oval, green to gray-green. Deep pink flowers in early spring. White fruit, ripening to red-brown, in autumn. 'Doctor Hurd', upright cultivar. Zones 8–10.

Arctostaphylos pumila

DUNE MANZANITA, SANDMAT MANZANITA

☼ ❉ ↔3–10 ft (0.9–3 m) ↑1–5 ft (0.3–1.5 m)

From coastal dunes around Monterey Bay, California, USA. Prostrate to mound-forming shrub, ascending branches. Dull green leaves. Small groups of white, sometimes pale pink, flowers in late winter–early spring. Pea-sized, brown fruit in summer. Zones 8–10.

Arctostaphylos uva-ursi

BEARBERRY, KINNIKINICK

☼ ❉ ↔20 in (50 cm) ↑4 in (10 cm)

Native of cool-temperate regions of Northern Hemisphere. White flowers flushed pink, followed by red fruit. Leaves are traditionally smoked in North America and used for herbal tea in Europe. 'Massachusetts', vigorous mat-former, to 12 in (30 cm) high and 15 ft (4.5 m) wide; 'Vancouver Jade', glossy leaves, vigorous habit, ability to resist diseases; and 'Wood's Red', dwarf cultivar with pink flowers, large shiny red fruit, red young shoots. Zones 4–9.

Arctostaphylos Hybrid Cultivars

☼/◐ ❉ ↔5–15 ft (1.5–4.5 m) ↑6 in–10 ft (15 cm–3 m)

Nearly all these hybrids originated in wild or as accidental crosses in gardens. They range from low mat-forming plants to tall shrubs. 'Indian Hill', possible form of *A. edmundsii*, extensive mat of glossy bright green foliage, new shoots attractive bronze, white flowers in winter; 'John Dourley' ★, of uncertain classification, mound-forming shrub, dense bluish green foliage, bronze new growths, pale pink flowers; 'Pacific Mist', mat-forming to mound-forming shrub, pink young branches, narrow gray-green leaves, white flowers; 'Sunset', densely mounding shrub, dark red branches, deep gray-green foliage, bright new growths, pink flowers. Zones 8–10.

ARDISIA

Over 250 species of evergreen shrubs and small trees make up this Myrsinaceae family genus, occurring in the tropics and subtropics of all continents except Africa. They occur mainly in high-rainfall mountain areas. Leaves are simple with margins sometimes toothed or crinkled, crowded at the ends of branchlets. A common feature is translucent brownish spots or streaks in the leaves, more easily seen in thinner leaves. The small flowers are mostly star-shaped, borne in stalked umbels among the outer leaves; the 5 petals are often patterned with tiny spots. Fruits are small one-seeded berries.
CULTIVATION: Most are shade-loving plants and prefer humid conditions protected from the wind. Soil should be well drained, humus rich, and moisture retentive. Indoor plants should be kept away from hot sunny positions. They can be cut back near the base, resulting in renewal by vigorous shoots. Propagation is usually from seed; cuttings can also be used.

Argyranthemum, Hybrid Cultivar, Butterfly/'Ulyssis'

Argyranthemum, Hybrid Cultivar, 'Petite Pink'

Ardisia crenata

CORAL ARDISIA, CORALBERRY

☀ ❈ ↔ 18 in (45 cm) ↑ 6 ft (1.8 m)

From southern Japan, China, and eastern Himalayas. Side branches in tiers form bushy dark green foliage. White starry flowers in umbels, in spring–summer. Coral red fruits persist into winter. Zones 8–11.

Ardisia japonica

☀ ❈ ↔ unlimited ↑ 12 in (30 cm)

Native to Japan and China. Leaves in whorls of 3 in (8 cm), glossy, dark green, saw-toothed margins. White to pale pink flowers in summer. Fruit pink to red. 'Nishiki', variegated with irregular cream margins, translucent pink on new leaves. Zones 7–10.

ARGYRANTHEMUM

From the Canary Islands and Madeira and often treated as perennials, the 24 members of this genus, of the daisy (Asteraceae) family, are evergreen shrubs. There are numerous cultivars, most with "double" or "semi-double" flowerheads over a long season. All branch low, with brittle stems and crowded leaves from coarsely toothed to deeply dissected. Leaves have a slightly aromatic, bitter smell when bruised. Long-stalked flowerheads are borne in groups of 2 to 5.
CULTIVATION: Marginally frost hardy, in cold climates these shrubs need to be brought under shelter in winter. They prefer a temperate climate with a distinct cool winter. Soil should be very well drained and not too rich; a sunny position is needed. Pinch out young plants to shape. Propagate from tip cuttings at any time, preferably in autumn for spring–summer display.

Ardisia crenata

Argyranthemum frutescens

syn. *Chrysanthemum frutescens*

MARGUERITE, MARGUERITE DAISY

❈ ❈ ↔ 3 ft (0.9 m) ↑ 3 ft (0.9 m)

Original wild form of this Canary Islands native is low spreading shrub with leaves dissected into few narrow segments. Single white flowerheads, golden yellow centers, for much of year. Most recent cultivars have generally been included in this species, but are in fact of hybrid origin, with other species in parentage. Zones 9–10.

Argyranthemum Hybrid Cultivars

❈/❈❈ ❈ ↔ 18–36 in (45–90 cm) ↑ 12–30 in (30–75 cm)

Though many references have included all *Argyranthemum* cultivars under *A. frutescens*, most present-day cultivars are of hybrid origin. Apart from *A. frutescens*, likely parent species include *A. foeniculaceum* and *A. maderense*. Single cultivars include Butterfly/'Ulyssis', compact, rich yellow flowers; 'California Gold' ★, dwarf habit, large golden yellow blooms, leaf segments few and broad; 'Donnington Hero', low and spreading, coarsely lobed leaves, neat white flowers; 'Gill's Pink', pale pink rays, deeper at base, and broad leaf lobes; 'Jamaica Primrose', pale to mid-yellow blooms; and 'Petite Pink', pink flowers. Doubles include 'Blizzard', rather tangled white rays and some disc florets showing. Anemone-form or semi-double group includes 'Mary Wootton', older cultivar with pale pink center; 'Tauranga Star', white rays, slightly quilled, white "button" grading with pale gold center; and 'Vancouver', similar to 'Mary Wootton' but with bright pink domed central "button" and paler rays like the spokes of a wheel. Zones 9–10.

ARGYROCYTISUS

A monotypic genus of the pea-flower subfamily of legumes (Fabaceae), its sole species is an evergreen shrub native to the Rif and Atlas Mountains of Morocco. The name is a combination of *argyros* (silver) and *Cytisus* (the plant's former genus). It refers to the silvery foliage, which derives its color from a dense covering of fine, silvery, reflective hairs that give the plant a metallic sheen. Spikes of bright golden yellow flowers open in late spring–early summer.
CULTIVATION: Left alone, this species can become rather spindly, though it bushes up if trimmed regularly. It is quite hardy and prefers a gritty well-drained soil in full sun. Propagate from seed or half-hardened late summer and autumn cuttings.

Argyrocytisus battandieri

syn. *Cytisus battandieri*

SILVER BROOM

☼ ❄ ↔ 12 ft (3.5 m) ↑ 12 ft (3.5 m)

Shrub with silvery trifoliate foliage. Bright yellow flowers, scented. Pea-pod-like seed capsules, covered with fine silvery hair. '**Yellow Tail**', richer yellow flowers. Zones 7–10.

ARONIA

CHOKEBERRY

This genus of deciduous shrubs from woodlands of eastern USA contains 2 species and a naturally occurring hybrid. In the rose (Rosaceae) family, it is closely allied to *Photinia*—in fact current opinion suggests it should be in that genus, though this has not gained wide acceptance. The shrubs are of compact size bearing white or pale pink spring blossoms that are followed by small berry-like fruits of red, purple, or black. The foliage colors in autumn in shades of red and crimson. CULTIVATION: These shrubs are well suited to informal plantings and woodland edges. They need deep, moist, well-drained soil and will grow in part-shade or sun. Sunnier sites encourage better fruiting and autumn coloring. The shiny black cherry and pear slug can cause damage to the foliage but can be controlled with a carbaryl or pyrethrin preparation. Propagate from half-hardened cuttings, layering, removal of suckers, or seed sown in autumn.

Aronia arbutifolia

syn. *Photinia pyrifolia*

AMELANCHIER, RED CHOKEBERRY

◑ ❄ ↔ 5 ft (1.5 m) ↑ 6 ft (1.8 m)

Downy young branches. Clusters of small white to pale pink flowers in spring. Bright red berries, persisting into winter. '**Brilliantissima**', vivid red autumn leaves. Zones 4–9.

ARTEMISIA

This genus of about 300 species of evergreen herbs and shrubs is spread throughout northern temperate regions with some also found in southern Africa and South America. It is a member of the daisy (Asteraceae) family but they bear small dull white or yellow flowerheads without ray florets. Foliage is palest gray to silver. The plants are frequently aromatic. CULTIVATION: These shrubs are ideal for hot dry areas as most can withstand drought. They should be grown in full sun in well-drained soil. Their silvery leaves provide a foliage contrast in borders; when clipped some species can be used as a low hedge. Prune hard in spring and lightly clip at flowering time if the flowers are not wanted. Propagate from softwood or half-hardened cuttings in summer.

Argyrocytisus battandieri

Artemisia arborescens

SHRUB WORMWOOD

☼ ❄ ↔ 5 ft (1.5 m) ↑ 5 ft (1.5 m)

Attractive Mediterranean species that grows into rounded shrub. Finely divided silver foliage, aromatic. More frost tender than most species in genus but its cultivar '**Faith Raven**' is much hardier. Zones 8–11.

ATHEROSPERMA

The sole species in this genus is a large evergreen tree native to the States of New South Wales, Victoria, and Tasmania in Australia. It is a member of the family Monimiaceae. Although not closely related to the true sassafras *(Sassafras albidum),* the tree yields similar oils, most intensely from the bark. It has dark green, aromatic, lance-shaped leaves. Dainty white flowers are produced during spring, with male and female flowers borne on separate plants. CULTIVATION: Although a little tender when young, *Atherosperma* adapts well to cultivation and seems happy in any well-drained soil with at least a half-day of sun. For the best results grow it in a moist climate with rich soil. Seedlings are slow to develop but are usually more reliable than cuttings.

Atherosperma moschatum ★

BLACK SASSAFRAS, SOUTHERN SASSAFRAS

☼ ❄ ↔ 15 ft (4.5 m) ↑ 100 ft (30 m)

Under cultivation this species rarely reaches 50 ft (15 m) tall. Leathery foliage, deep green above with pale hairs below. Pendulous white flowers open in spring. Female flowers have a covering of silky hairs. Zones 8–10.

Atherosperma moschatum, in the wild, Tasmania, Australia

Aucuba japonica 'Gold Dust'   Auranticarpa rhombifolia

ATRIPLEX

SALTBUSH

From all continents except Antarctica, there are around 300 species included in this genus in the goosefoot or saltbush (Chenopodiaceae) family. *Atriplex* includes many shrubs, as well as annuals and perennials, that are multi-branched with wiry crooked twigs. The leaves are fleshy, and may be covered in fine whitish scales giving the foliage a silvery or pale bluish cast. They frequently grow in saline soils and the leaf sap is then salty. Flowers are small, of different sexes often on different plants.
CULTIVATION: These plants are suited to hot, dry, or saline environments, including exposed seashores. All require full sun and do best in a well-drained soil of moderate fertility. They can be cut back hard, responding with thicker foliage, and trained into hedges. Propagate from softwood cuttings or seed. Soak seed to simulate the effect of rain needed for these plants to germinate.

Atriplex canescens

CHAMIZO, FOUR-WING SALTBUSH

☼ ❄ ↔ 5 ft (1.5 m) ↑ 5 ft (1.5 m)
From western USA and Mexico. Densely massed stems. Narrow blunt-tipped leaves of mealy whitish appearance. Tiny yellowish flowers give way to 4-winged papery fruit bracts crowded onto short spikes, in late summer. Zones 6–10.

Atriplex halimus ★

TREE PURSLANE

☼ ❄ ↔ 10 ft (3 m) ↑ 6 ft (1.8 m)
Shrub from saltmarshes of southern Europe. Slightly larger, more silvery leaves than other species. Irregular spikes of greenish white flowers in late summer. Zones 8–10.

AUCUBA

This genus of dioecious plants in the silk-tassel (Garryaceae) family originates from the Himalayas and eastern Asia. It contains 3 or 4 species of evergreen shrubs or small trees, frequently used in garden situations, as they tolerate deep shade. Spotted forms are most popular. The glossy leaves are lance-shaped, smooth or serrate, and grow in an alternate arrangement along the branches. Flowers, either green or maroon, are in leaf axils or at the ends of terminal shoots and are of different sexes on different plants. Fruit are red, orange, or whitish yellow.
CULTIVATION: *Aucuba* grows best in moist soil. The spotted forms require partial shade—in sun they can scorch, while in deep shade the spotting fades. Both male and female plants are required to ensure berries. Cut back in spring. If grown in containers, use loam-based compost, and feed monthly when in growth. Sow seed in spring. Take half-hardened cuttings in summer.

Aucuba japonica

JAPANESE AUCUBA, JAPANESE LAUREL

☀ ❄ ↔ 6 ft (1.8 m) ↑ 6 ft (1.8 m)
Evergreen shrub from Japan. Purplish flowers and red berries. 'Crotonifolia', strongly gold-variegated cultivar; 'Gold Dust', female, variegated leaves; 'Rozannie', self-fruiting form; 'Salicifolia', female, narrow long-pointed leaves; and 'Variegata' ★, gold variegated, preferring deep shade. Zones 7–10.

AURANTICARPA

Close study of the large genus *Pittosporum* by some Australian botanists revealed that a group of northern Australian species is not closely related to the remainder of the species. As a result they named it as a new genus, *Auranticarpa* ("gold fruit"), though it is still in the pittosporum (Pittosporaceae) family. It is distinguished by a much-branched inflorescence with small bright orange fruit with blackish seeds. It consists of 6 species of evergreen trees, 3 transferred from *Pittosporum* and 3 new to science. Five of them are confined to the tropical north, while one extends from north Queensland to northeastern New South Wales.
CULTIVATION: Only A. *rhombifolia* is widely cultivated, popular as a street and park tree and adapting well to drier and cooler regions. It prefers moderately fertile, moist but well-drained soil and tolerates exposure to strong winds as well as part-shade, but full sun is required for a good display of its fruit. Propagate from seed.

Auranticarpa rhombifolia

syn. *Pittosporum rhombifolium*

DIAMOND-LEAF LAUREL, HOLLY WOOD

☼ ❄ ↔ 10–20 ft (3–6 m) ↑ 20–60 ft (6–18 m)
Eastern Australian native, young growth covered in dense rusty hairs. Glossy green leaves, roughly diamond-shaped. Small, sweetly scented, white flowers in summer. Showy orange seed capsules. Zones 9–11.

AZARA

One of temperate South America's gifts to horticulture, this genus in the governor's plum (Flacourtiaceae) family contains 10 species of evergreen trees and shrubs with attractive foliage, graceful growth habits, and easy culture. Mostly native to Chile, their foliage varies in size but is generally glossy and leathery. Each main leaf is appended with one or two smaller "accessory leaves." Flowers tend to be golden yellow, small, fluffy pompons without petals. Fleshy fruits follow.
CULTIVATION: Most species will tolerate repeated light frosts but are damaged by severe cold. They do not tolerate extreme heat

and generally prefer a temperate climate with cool moist soil. Otherwise, they are easy-care plants that can be kept compact with routine trimming. Propagate from seed or half-hardened cuttings.

Azara microphylla
VANILLA TREE

☀ ❄ ↔ 15 ft (4.5 m) ↕ 25 ft (8 m)

Tree from Chile and Argentina. Small leaves on frond-like branches in ferny spray. Vanilla-scented, tiny, dull yellow flowers in spring, red fruit. '**Variegata**', golden variegated foliage. Zones 8–10.

Azara serrata ★
◑ ❄ ↔ 8 ft (2.4 m) ↕ 12 ft (3.5 m)

Shrub from Chile. Sharply toothed foliage. Golden flowers open later than other azaras. With age can become rather sparse. Zones 8–10.

BACCHARIS
Of the daisy (Asteraceae) family, this genus of about 350 species is native to North, Central, and South America. These shrub or herb perennials are deciduous or evergreen and bear male and female flowers on separate plants. Some species have no leaves, so photosynthesis takes place in the green stems. The flowers are carried in panicles or corymbs.
CULTIVATION: Fully frost hardy to frost tender, these plants do best in good soil in full sun. Softwood cuttings can be taken in summer, while seed can be sown in spring. In colder areas plants may behave as perennials.

Baccharis 'Centennial'
COYOTE BRUSH, DESERT BROOM
☼ ❄ ↔ 5 ft (1.5 m) ↕ 3 ft (0.9 m)

Female cross between *B. pilularis* and *B. sarothroides* from USA. Evergreen sprawling shrub, narrow leaves. Inconspicuous white flowers in winter–spring. Tan seed pods, white fluffy seeds. Zones 8–10.

Banksia 'Giant Candles'

Baccharis pilularis
CHAPARRAL BROOM
☼ ❄ ↔ 20 in (50 cm) ↕ 20 in (50 cm)

Evergreen shrub native to western coast of USA. Leaves broad to ovate, hairless. Flowers white with green spot, found at branch tips. Cultivars include '**Pigeon Point**' and '**Twin Peaks**' ★. Zones 8–10.

BACKHOUSIA
This genus, a member of the myrtle (Myrtaceae) family, consists of 7 evergreen species of both shrubs and trees, all of which occur in the subtropical and tropical rainforests of east coast Australia. All species have a neat habit, white or cream flowers that have prominent stamens, and smooth-edged leaves in opposite pairs.
CULTIVATION: These rainforest plants do best in rich well-composted soil, in which sufficient moisture is retained. Although partial shade is best while young, plants often flower more profusely in full sun. Propagate from cuttings or fresh seed.

Backhousia citriodora
LEMON-SCENTED MYRTLE, SWEET VERBENA TREE
☼ ◐ ↔ 10–15 ft (3–4.5 m) ↕ 20–25 ft (6–8 m)

Neat small tree with foliage from ground level. Dense dull green leaves scented lemon when crushed. Oil contained in leaves used for food flavoring. Flowers strongly lemon scented, creamy white, in summer. Zones 9–11.

BANKSIA
From the protea (Proteaceae) family, the 75 or so species are endemic to Australia, with just one, *B. dentata*, extending to New Guinea. They vary from prostrate shrubs to low-branching trees. Thick leathery leaves are variously toothed. Large cylindrical or globular flower spikes are rich in nectar and are followed by woody cones. Species from southwest Western Australia are not always easy to cultivate, especially in summer-rainfall areas. Species from eastern Australia are more adaptable.
CULTIVATION: Most species prefer an open sunny position and well-drained sandy soil low in phosphorus. Some are moderately frost tolerant and, once established, most will withstand dry conditions. Harvest flowers to encourage flower production. To propagate, extract seed from the cone after it has been heated in a hot oven.

Banksia ericifolia
HEATH BANKSIA, HEATH-LEAFED BANKSIA
☼ ❄ ↔ 15 ft (4.5 m) ↕ 8–20 ft (2.4–6 m)

Australian east coast shrub. Narrow leaves, bright green above, furry beneath. Flower spikes to 10 in (25 cm) long, pale yellow to orange-red, yellow or orange-brown styles, in autumn–winter. Zones 8–10.

Banksia 'Giant Candles' ★
HYBRID BANKSIA
☼ ◐ ↔ 12 ft (3.5 m) ↕ 15 ft (4.5 m)

Shrub from eastern Australia. *B. ericifolia* and *B. spinulosa* hybrid, branching to near ground level. Bright green foliage. Orange flower spikes to 15 in (38 cm) long, in autumn–winter. Zones 9–10.

Banksia integrifolia ★

COAST BANKSIA

☀ ❄ ↔ 20 ft (6 m) ↑ 20–80 ft (6–24 m)

Fast-growing tree from east coast of Australia. Bark has roughly square pattern. Leaves dull green above, silvery woolly beneath. Flowers pale yellow-green, in summer–winter. Persistent fruits. Tolerates clay soils. 'Roller Coaster', prostrate form. Zones 8–11.

Banksia marginata ★

SILVER BANKSIA

☀ ❄ ↔ 15–20 ft (4.5–6 m) ↑ 8–30 ft (2.4–9 m)

From southeast Australia, variable banksia species found as shrub, tree, or prostrate form. Leaves narrow, silvery furry beneath. Flowers in short, pale yellow, cylindrical spikes, in late summer– winter. Hard prune plants with underground stems, others only lightly shape. Zones 8–10.

Banksia menziesii

FIREWOOD BANKSIA

☀ ✂ ↔ 15 ft (4.5 m) ↑ 50 ft (15 m)

Gnarled tree from Western Australia, much smaller and more compact in cultivation. Leaves long and toothed. Flowers silvery pink and gold, in acorn-shaped spikes, in autumn–winter. Patterned seed cones. Best in areas with dry summer. Zones 10–11.

Banksia robur

LARGE-LEAF BANKSIA, SWAMP BANKSIA

☀ ✂ ↔ 7 ft (2 m) ↑ 10 ft (3 m)

Found on east coast of Australia, usually in swampy woodlands. Leaves large, stiff, coarsely serrated, smooth above, furry beneath. Persistent golden flowers in summer–winter. Zones 9–10.

Barleria albostellata

Banksia serrata ★

OLD MAN BANKSIA, SAW BANKSIA

☀ ✂ ↔ 5–10 ft (1.5–3 m) ↑ 15–30 ft (4.5–9 m)

From Australian east coast. Gnarled trunk and branches. Leaves stiff, coarsely serrated. Large, cylindrical, creamy flower spikes in summer–winter. Persistent woody fruits, immortalized by children's author May Gibbs as "big bad Banksia Men." Fire tolerant. 'Pygmy Possum', ground cover to 2 ft (0.6 m) tall and 8 ft (2.4 m) wide; 'Superman', to 20 ft (6 m) in height. Zones 9–10.

Banksia spinulosa

HAIRPIN BANKSIA

☀/◐ ✂ ↔ 5 ft (1.5 m) ↑ 3 ft (0.9 m)

From east coast of Australia. Branchlets furry. Leaves linear, woolly undersides. Flower spikes cylindrical to 5 in (12 cm), golden yellow with gold, red, or orange styles, in autumn–winter. Fire tolerant. *B. s.* var. *collina* (syn. *B. collina*), bright yellow flowers, yellow to red styles. *B. s.* var. *cunninghamii*, large yellow spikes; 'Lemon Glow', pale yellow-flowered form. *B. s.* 'Honeypots', open-branched shrub, flowers golden, red styles, in summer–winter. Zones 9–10.

BARLERIA

Barleria belongs to the acanthus (Acanthaceae) family, and consists of around 250 species of shrubs, subshrubs, and scrambling climbers. From tropical continents, except Australia, many occur in dry rocky habitats. Leaves are simple and smooth edged, arranged in opposite pairs on the stems. Flowers are more or less trumpet-shaped but distinctly 2-lipped, in shades from white through yellow, orange, pink, mauve, and violet. They emerge from between stiff bracts that are often edged by spiny teeth. Flowers appear over a long season, followed by club-shaped seed capsules. CULTIVATION: Easily cultivated in warm climates, these plants are fast growing but short lived. Grow in fertile well-drained soil, in a sunny but sheltered position. In cool climates they make good conservatory plants, but need strong light. They can be trimmed as hedges or cut back hard, responding to this treatment with denser, more vigorous foliage. Propagate from cuttings.

Barleria albostellata

GRAY BARLERIA

☀ ✂ ↔ 5 ft (1.5 m) ↑ 5 ft (1.5 m)

Evergreen shrub from northeastern South Africa, Zimbabwe, and Mozambique. Gray foliage due to dense coating of hairs on 2–3 in (5–8 cm) long oval leaves. Flowers white, 1 in (25 mm) wide, at branch tips, in spring–summer. Zones 9–12.

Barleria cristata

PHILIPPINE VIOLET

◐ ✂ ↔ 5 ft (1.5 m) ↑ 3 ft (0.9 m)

Widely grown ornamental species from Myanmar. Densely branching from ground level with soft deep green foliage. Flowers white, mauve, or violet from bristly edged green bracts, most of year. Tip prune to encourage denser growth. Zones 10–12.

Banksia menziesii

Bartlettina sordida

Bauera rubioides

Bauhinia × blakeana

Barleria obtusa

BUSH VIOLET

☼ ❅ ↔ 3 ft (0.9 m) ↑ 3 ft (0.9 m)

Native to southern Africa. Spreading shrub, twiggy habit, small silky-haired leaves. Profuse white-pink or violet flowers, 1 in (25 mm) wide, from small furry bracts, in autumn. Zones 9–11.

BARTLETTINA

Found in tropical and Central America and Mexico, this daisy (Asteraceae) family genus comprises 23 species of evergreen shrubs and small trees. They form a dense, many-branched crown with young stems that are usually covered with fine hairs. The leaves are lance-shaped to oval, often with toothed edges; the corymbs or panicles of crowded small flowerheads occur in a variety of shades.
CULTIVATION: Most species grow extremely freely and may be somewhat invasive. Plant in moist well-drained soil with a position in full sun or partial shade. If necessary, trim to shape after flowering. Propagate from seed or half-hardened cuttings.

Bartlettina sordida

syns Bartlettina megalophylla, Eupatorium megalophyllum, E. sordidum

☼ ❅ ↔ 7 ft (2 m) ↑ 10 ft (3 m)

Very vigorous shrub from Mexico. Young stems covered with red hairs; leaves oval with toothed edges, to 4 in (10 cm) long. Fragrant violet flowers in corymbs in warmer months. Zones 10–11.

BAUERA

Bauera is an eastern Australian genus of just 4 species. Once included in the saxifrage (Saxifragaceae) family, these evergreen wiry-stemmed shrubs are now included in the spoonbush (Cunoniaceae) family. The small leaves, borne in opposite pairs, are trifoliate but stalkless, their leaflets appearing like a whorl of 6 small leaves at each node. Bowl-shaped flowers arise from leaf axils in spring and early summer.
CULTIVATION: Apart from being fairly frost tender, Bauera plants are easily grown and undemanding. They do best in well-drained, light, sandy soil with added humus. They prefer to avoid extremes of heat and cold, so some shade from the hottest sun is appreciated, as is winter shelter. Occasional trimming will keep the bushes compact. Propagate from seed or half-hardened cuttings.

Bauera rubioides ★

DOG ROSE, RIVER ROSE

◐ ❅ ↔ 7 ft (2 m) ↑ 2–6 ft (0.6–1.8 m)

Shrub from moister regions of southeastern Australia. Leaves ½ in (12 mm) long, often covered in fine hairs. Flowers white or pink, to 1 in (25 mm) wide, with 6 to 8 radiating petals, in late winter–spring. 'Luina Gem', pale pink double flowers. Zones 9–11.

Bauera sessiliflora

GRAMPIANS BAUERA

◐ ❅ ↔ 6 ft (1.8 m) ↑ 6 ft (1.8 m)

Native to the Grampians, a mountain range in western Victoria, Australia. Flowers rosy pink to magenta, in late spring–early summer. Various cultivars are available. Zones 9–10.

BAUHINIA

This genus of around 300 species, many confined to the tropics, occurs in all continents except Europe, and on larger tropical islands. They belong to the caesalpinia subfamily of the legume (Fabaceae) family and include shrubs, climbers, and small to medium-sized trees, many deciduous. A characteristic feature is the compound leaf consisting of only 2 broad leaflets, their inner edges often fused. Flowers have 5 petals, borne in the leaf axils or in terminal sprays. Seed pods are slightly woody and flattened. Bauhinias are ornamental trees and shrubs, but some are used in traditional medicine or as a source of fiber; a few species have seeds that can be eaten.
CULTIVATION: These plants are easily cultivated in warm climates, though often slow growing. Species from tropical climates with a long dry season do not grow or flower well in wetter climates. Deep rooted, they do not like being transplanted, but will often tolerate hot exposed positions and hard dry soils. Few grow well in shade. Propagate from seed; half-hardened cuttings can also be taken.

Bauhinia × blakeana

HONG KONG ORCHID TREE

☼ ❅ ↔ 15 ft (4.5 m) ↑ 30 ft (9 m)

This hybrid, probably between B. purpurea and B. variegata, is floral emblem of Hong Kong. Leaves broad, reliably evergreen. Flowers purple-red, slightly scented, 4–6 in (10–15 cm) wide, in autumn–winter. Zones 10–12.

Berberis buxifolia

Berberis × macracantha

Berberis × ottawensis f. purpurea

Bauhinia galpinii

syn. *Bauhinia punctata*

PRIDE OF DE KAAP, SOUTH AFRICAN ORCHID-BUSH

☼ ⚘ ↔ 8 ft (2.4 m) ↑ 10–20 ft (3–6 m)

Horizontally branching evergreen shrub or scrambling climber from South Africa. Leaves rounded with 2 distinct lobes, paler undersides. Flowers light to brick red, in summer–autumn. Fruits woody, persistent, flattened, green-brown pods. Zones 9–11.

Bauhinia tomentosa

YELLOW BELL BAUHINIA

☼ ⚘ ↔ 10 ft (3 m) ↑ 15 ft (4.5 m)

From tropical Africa and Asia, usually a multi-stemmed evergreen shrub. Leaves light green, 3 in (8 cm) long, hairy beneath. Flowers bell-shaped, cream to pale yellow, throughout year. Zones 10–12.

Bauhinia variegata

BUTTERFLY BUSH, ORCHID TREE

☼ ⚘ ↔ 25 ft (8 m) ↑ 25 ft (8 m)

From tropical foothills of Himalayas through to Malay Peninsula, small tree with short trunk and spreading canopy. Semi-deciduous in warm areas, fully in cool areas. Orchid-like flowers, pale to deep pink. White form also seen. Zones 9–10.

BERBERIS

BARBERRY

This Berberidaceae family genus consists of more than 450 species of evergreen and deciduous shrubs, mainly seen across the Northern Hemisphere. with a smaller group in the South American Andes. They are variable in size, with spines on their branches, and are generally cultivated for the ornamental value of their leaves, flowers, and berries. All of the plant parts are supposed to cause mild stomach upsets if eaten. *B.* × *stenophylla* has become a serious pest in New Zealand. Many North American botanists now include all of the *Mahonia* species in *Berberis*. CULTIVATION: *Berberis* will grow in most well-drained to fairly heavy soils. Tropical African species prefer rocky soil in mountainous areas. Plants can be grown in full sun or partial shade but autumn color is better in full sun. Propagate from softwood cuttings in early summer, or half-hardened cuttings later in summer. Site with care as branch spines can be hazardous.

Berberis buxifolia

☼ ❉ ↔ 10 ft (3 m) ↑ 8 ft (2.4 m)

Native to Chile and Argentina. Erect evergreen or semi-evergreen species with arching branches. Leaves leathery, dark green, spiny tips. Flowers deep orange-yellow in upper leaf axils, in mid- to late spring. Dark purple fruits. **'Pygmaea'** (syn. 'Nana'), dwarf form to 3 ft (0.9 m) tall. Zones 6–9.

Berberis × *carminea*

☼ ❉ ↔ 8 ft (2.4 m) ↑ 5 ft (1.5 m)

Hybrid of *B. aggregata* and *B. wilsoniae*. Leaves egg-shaped, dull gray-green. Flowers yellow, arranged in clusters of 10 to 16 blooms per panicle, in late spring–early summer. Fruits red or orange, in dense clusters. **'Barbarossa'**, showy bright red fruits; **'Pirate King'**, dense foliage. Zones 6–9.

Berberis darwinii

DARWIN BARBERRY

☼ ❉ ↔ 10 ft (3 m) ↑ 10 ft (3 m)

Evergreen shrub native to Chile and Argentina. Leaves dark green, toothed, with spines, pale green beneath. Flowers deep yellow or orange in pendulous racemes. Oblong purplish black fruits with bloom. **'Flame'**, grows to half the height of the species. Zones 7–10.

Berberis julianae

WINTERGREEN BARBERRY

☼ ❉ ↔ 10 ft (3 m) ↑ 10 ft (3 m)

Evergreen shrub found in western Hubei Province, China. Spiny stems, leaves oval shaped with narrow end at base, serrated margins, dark green above, paler undersurface. Juvenile foliage with copper tints. Flowers yellow or tinged red, in clusters, in early spring. Fruits black with white bloom. **'Lombarts Red'**, leaves tinged red underneath. Zones 5–9.

Berberis × *macracantha*

☼ ❉ ↔ 12 ft (3.5 m) ↑ 12 ft (3.5 m)

Garden hybrid between *B. aristata* and *B. vulgaris;* deciduous shrub. Stems well protected by thorns more than 1 in (25 mm) long. Long racemes of bright yellow flowers in spring, followed by deep purple-red berries in autumn. Zones 5–9.

Berberis × *ottawensis*

HYBRID PURPLE BARBERRY

☼ ❄ ↔ 8 ft (2.4 m) ↑ 8 ft (2.4 m)

Cross between *B. thunbergii* and *B. vulgaris*. Leaves mid-green, egg-shaped. Flowers pale yellow, in clusters, in spring. Fruits egg-shaped red berries. *B.* × *o.* f. *purpurea*, purple-red foliage; 'Superba' (syn. 'Purpurea'), new growth almost bronze. *B.* × *o.* 'Silver Miles', dark purplish red leaves marked silvery gray. Zones 5–10.

Berberis × *rubrostilla*

☼ ❄ ↔ 8 ft (2.4 m) ↑ 5 ft (1.5 m)

Deciduous hybrid, possibly cross of *B. aggregata* and *B. wilsoniae*. Leaves narrow, egg-shaped, mid-green above, gray undersides, 1¼ in (30 mm) long, with marginal spines. Pale yellow flowers. Egg-shaped, translucent, red fruits. Zones 6–9.

Berberis × *stenophylla*

☼ ❄ ↔ 15 ft (4.5 m) ↑ 10 ft (3 m)

Hybrid of *B. darwinii* and *B. empetrifolia*. Leaves narrow, elliptical, ¾ in (18 mm) long, dark green above, bluish green beneath. Flowers deep yellow, in late spring. Fruits black with blue bloom. Cultivars include 'Corallina Compacta', 'Crawley Gem', 'Irwinii', and 'Lemon Queen' (syn. 'Cornish Cream'). Zones 6–9.

Berberis thunbergii

JAPANESE BARBERRY

☼ ❄ ↔ 8 ft (2.4 m) ↑ 3 ft (0.9 m)

Deciduous shrub native to Japan. Compact foliage and rounded shape. Leaves egg-shaped, smooth, fresh green above, bluish green beneath. Flowers pale yellow, can be tinged red, in racemes, in mid-spring. Fruits glossy red. *B. t.* f. *atropurpurea*, purple-red stems and leaves. *B. t.* 'Helmond Pillar', to 5 ft (1.5 m) tall, dark red foliage; 'Red Chief', to 6 ft (1.8 m) tall, pink-variegated leaves; 'Rose Glow' ★, red-purple foliage flecked with white; 'Sparkle', persistent bright red fruit. Zones 4–9.

Berberis thunbergii 'Sparkle'

Berberis valdiviana

☼ ❄ ↔ 15 ft (4.5 m) ↑ 15 ft (4.5 m)

Native to Chile. Leaves 2 in (5 cm) long, elliptical, smooth, dark green above, yellow-green beneath. Saffron yellow flowers in drooping racemes in late spring. Fruits black with blue bloom. Zones 8–10.

Berberis wilsoniae

WILSON BARBERRY

☼ ❄ ↔ 6 ft (1.8 m) ↑ 3 ft (0.9 m)

Deciduous or semi-evergreen shrub from western Sichuan and Yunnan Provinces, China. Branches dense, spiny, arching. Leaves gray-green, oval to linear, orange-red in autumn. Pale yellow flowers in summer. Pink to red fruits. Zones 5–10.

BETULA

BIRCH

This genus gives its name to the birch family, Betulaceae, and consists of about 60 deciduous small shrubs or tall trees occurring throughout temperate and arctic zones of the Northern Hemisphere. Tree trunks are often marked in different shades; in many species the outer layer of bark peels off. Pendulous male catkins and erect female catkins are carried on the same tree in early spring. Leaves are mid- to dark green, ovate in shape, with indented margins.

Betula albosinensis

CULTIVATION: Birches are hardy trees, withstanding extreme cold and exposure to wind. They are best in well-drained fertile soil, with some moisture and full sun or light shade. Take softwood cuttings in summer, or half-hardened cuttings in autumn. Birches are susceptible to fungi such as *Armillaria melea* and *Piptoporus betulinus;* the latter, specific to the birch family, will destroy the tree.

Betula albosinensis

CHINESE RED BIRCH

☼ ❄ ↔ 30 ft (9 m) ↑ 80 ft (24 m)

Native to Provinces of Sichuan, Gansu, and Shaanxi, southwestern China. New bark gray-cream turning orange or red-brown. Leaves glossy, green above, paler beneath, to 2½ in (6 cm) long, turn yellow in autumn. Showy male catkins. Zones 6–9.

Betula ermanii

ERMAN'S BIRCH, GOLD BIRCH, RUSSIAN ROCK-BIRCH

☼ ❄ ↔ 40 ft (12 m) ↑ 70 ft (21 m)

Native to Japan and mainland Asia. Bark pink or creamy white turning pinkish. Tapered oval leaves, dark green, margins serrated. Male catkins in groups of 3. Zones 2–8.

Betula lenta

BLACK BIRCH, CHERRY BIRCH, SWEET BIRCH

☼ ❄ ↔ 40 ft (12 m) ↑ 50 ft (15 m)

Native to eastern North America. Bark crimson, becomes scaly and gray ageing to black. Leaves egg-shaped, chartreuse, 4 in (10 cm) long, autumn color. Male catkins pendulous, 3 in (8 cm) long. Female catkins erect. Zones 3–9.

Betula papyrifera, in the wild, USA

Betula mandschurica

syn. *Betula platyphylla* var. *japonica*
MANCHURIAN BIRCH

☼ ❋ ↔ 30 ft (9 m) ↕ 70 ft (21 m)

Native to northeastern China and southeastern Siberia. Bark dusty milky white. Leaves mid-green, egg-shaped, to 3 in (8 cm) long, deeply indented, heavily veined. Male and female catkins pendulous, 1 in (25 mm) long. *B. m.* var. *japonica*, with white bark, to 80 ft (24 m) tall; 'Whitespire' (syn. *B. platyphylla* 'Whitespire'), narrowly conical habit. Zones 2–9.

Betula nigra

RIVER BIRCH, TROPICAL BIRCH

☼ ❋ ↔ 15 ft (4.5 m) ↕ 30 ft (9 m)

Deciduous tree from along rivers in eastern USA. Bark white, smooth then thin flaking plates of cream, salmon, and pale brown. Dark and furrowed with age. Tolerates heat and dryness. 'Heritage', peeling cream to pale brown bark; 'Little King', dwarf cultivar, to 10 ft (3 m) tall. Zones 4–9.

Betula papyrifera

CANOE BIRCH, PAPER BIRCH, WHITE BIRCH

☼ ❋ ↔ 30 ft (9 m) ↕ 60 ft (18 m)

Deciduous North American tree. White papery bark peeling to orange-brown. Light canopy allows sunlight through. Tolerates cold and drought. Zones 2–8.

Betula pendula

EUROPEAN SILVER BIRCH, EUROPEAN WHITE BIRCH

☼ ❋ ↔ 35 ft (10 m) ↕ 80 ft (24 m)

Deciduous tree from northern Europe, commonly found on poor soils. Foliage turns clear yellow in autumn. Arching habit, white bark. Trunk blackens with age. 'Dalecarlica' (weeping birch), dissected foliage; 'Fastigiata', erect tree to 70 ft (21 m); 'Laciniata', loses leaves earlier in autumn than species; 'Purpurea', with thin

pendulous branches; 'Tristis', narrowly conical habit; 'Youngii' ★, usually sold as grafted tree with strongly weeping head. Zones 2–8.

Betula platyphylla

☼ ❋ ↔ 40 ft (12 m) ↕ 70 ft (21 m)

Native to Siberia, northeastern China, Korea, and Japan. Bark pure white. Leaves chartreuse, 4 in (10 cm) long, egg-shaped with serrated margins. Male catkins to 3 in (8 cm) long; female catkins to 1¼ in (3 cm) long. Zones 4–9.

BIXA

This genus of a single species gives its name to the family Bixaceae. The sole member is a small tree from tropical South America. Cultivated as an ornamental, it is also commercially grown for an orange food and fabric dye, annatto, obtained from its seeds. It features pretty flowers, lush foliage, and distinctive bristly red seed pods.

CULTIVATION: Most at home in moist humid tropics, *Bixa* can be grown in a frost-free temperate climate if sheltered from cool winds. It prefers year-round moisture, good drainage, and moderately fertile soil in full sun or partial shade. Cutting-grown plants flower at a younger age than seedlings.

Bixa orellana

Bixa orellana

ANNATTO, LIPSTICK PLANT

☼ ✦ ↔ 10–15 ft (3–4.5 m) ↕ 30 ft (9 m)

Large shrub or small tree. Leaves oval, leathery, bright green. Pink or pinkish white flowers in panicles. Clusters of red to red-brown spiny seed pods persist after seeds released. Zones 10–12.

BOCCONIA

This genus of 9 species from subtropical and tropical America is part of the poppy (Papaveraceae) family. The leaves, while very large, are at least reminiscent of garden poppies, but the flowers are not what would commonly be thought of as poppy-like. They lack petals and are carried in large plume-like terminal racemes. The plants normally start as a single trunk topped with a head of leaves, but with age, side shoots and suckers develop to form multiple trunks. All parts release a yellow latex if cut.

CULTIVATION: *Bocconia* plants can tolerate light frosts but need a mild climate to thrive. They grow best in moist, well-drained, humus-rich soil with a sunny or partly shaded exposure. They are very vigorous plants and care should be taken to plant them only where their seeding and suckering can be controlled.

Bocconia arborea

☼/◐ ✦ ↔ 15 ft (4.5 m) ↕ 25 ft (8 m)

Found in Central America. Leaves deeply cut and divided, 18 in (45 cm) long, 12 in (30 cm) wide, toothed, often downy beneath. Flowers in racemes, up to 8 in (20 cm) long, in summer. Zones 10–12.

BOMBAX

This genus of large tropical deciduous trees, a member of the mallow (Malvaceae) family, consists of around 20 species from tropical Africa, southern Asia, and northern Australia. They grow around rock outcrops or along river valleys. Trunks are thick and straight, with tiered branches, often buttressed at the base. Bark is often armed with conical prickles. Leaves are compound with 5 or more leaflets attached to a common stalk. Appearing on leafless branches in the dry season, the large flowers have 5 tongue-shaped red, white, or yellow petals and a central mass of stamens. Large fruits split when ripe to release oily seeds embedded in white hairs. CULTIVATION: Easily grown in the tropics, plants prefer a sheltered site; deep, fertile, well-drained soil; and subsoil moisture. Fast growing when young, they can be short lived if attacked by insects. Propagate from fresh seed or tip cuttings, planted in the wet season.

Bombax ceiba

syn. *Bombax malabaricum*

SILK COTTON TREE

☀ ❄ ↔ 30–40 ft (9–12 m) ↑ 60 ft (18 m)

Broadly spreading, heavy-limbed tree from Asia. Trunk prickly when young. Flowers profuse, deep scarlet, appear in tropical dry season (spring). In Asia, fiber obtained from bark. Zones 10–12.

BORONIA

Noted for its sweet fragrance, early spring blooms, and aromatic foliage, this genus is a member of the rue (Rutaceae) family and consists of approximately 100 species of small to medium-sized, compact, evergreen shrubs, nearly all from Australia. They have simple or pinnate leaves and small 4-petalled flowers that may be open and star-shaped or bell-like with overlapping petals. Flowers come in a range of colors from white, pink, and bluish mauve to red, yellow, yellow-green, and brown. CULTIVATION: Locate boronias in sheltered positions with the protection of other plants in sun or part-shade. The soil should be well drained with a fairly high organic content; avoid drying out. If growing in pots, ensure that the potting mix does not contain added fertilizers with high phosphorus levels. The flowers generally last well when picked. After flowering, up to half of the plant can be removed to prolong life and improve bushiness. Propagate from half-hardened tip-cuttings. Some species can be short lived.

Boronia heterophylla

KALGAN BORONIA, RED BORONIA

☀ ❄ ↔ 4 ft (1.2 m) ↑ 6 ft (1.8 m)

Evergreen shrub native to southern Western Australia. Leaves bright green, aromatic. Flowers fragrant, deep pink, bell-shaped, in late winter–early spring. Zones 9–10.

Boronia megastigma ★

BROWN BORONIA

☀ ❄ ↔ 3 ft (0.9 m) ↑ 3 ft (0.9 m)

From southwest Western Australia. Popular species with light green foliage, slender stems, spicy aromatic leaves. Flowers reddish brown outside, yellow inside, pendent, bell-like, highly fragrant, in late winter–early spring. Often short lived; best in well-drained moist

soil. 'Harlequin', yellow and brown flowers; 'Heaven Scent', compact dwarf, brown flowers; 'Jack Maguire's Red', scarlet flowers; 'Lutea', clear greenish yellow flowers, foliage lighter green than species; 'Virtuoso', near-black petals. Zones 9–11.

Boronia pinnata

PINNATE BORONIA

☀ ❄ ↔ 5 ft (1.5 m) ↑ 5 ft (1.5 m)

Erect shrub from temperate east coast Australia. Pinnate leaves, strongly aromatic. Fragrant, pink to mauve, starry flowers, in loose sprays, in late winter–spring. Best in sheltered partially shaded position. 'Spring White', profuse white flowers. Zones 9–11.

BOUVARDIA

This genus, reaching from southern North America to northern South America, includes several evergreen shrubs among its 30 or so species, and belongs to the madder (Rubiaceae) family. *Bouvardia* tend to be rather sprawling, weak-stemmed plants that need support to keep them upright. Their leaves are not large but they are a pleasant shade of deep green and are usually glossy. The long-tubed flowers are the main attraction. The brighter colors are visually striking, while those in lighter shades or white are fragrant. CULTIVATION: *Bouvardia* species tolerate light frost only and need a mild climate with rich well-drained soil to flower well. They are best in partial shade and also perform well as greenhouse plants. Light trimming helps to keep them compact and bushy.

Bouvardia longiflora

SCENTED BOUVARDIA

☀ ❄ ↔ 3 ft (0.9 m) ↑ 3 ft (0.9 m)

Shrub from Mexico. Weak stems, easily damaged. Highly fragrant, waxy white, long-tubed, 4-petalled flowers, in autumn–winter. 'Albatross' (syn. *B. humboldtii* 'Albatross'), larger flowers. Zones 10–11.

Bouvardia ternifolia

☀ ❄ ↔ 3 ft (0.9 m) ↑ 3 ft (0.9 m)

Soft-stemmed evergreen shrub native to Arizona and Texas, USA, and Mexico. Flowers vivid red, tubular, in corymbs. Cultivars available with flowers in various pink and red shades. Zones 9–11.

Boronia megastigma

Bouvardia ternifolia

BRACHYCHITON

This genus in the mallow (Malvaceae) family contains around 30 species of evergreen or partially deciduous trees, mostly native to Australia, and found chiefly in northern tropical and subtropical regions with a few extending to arid regions. They have large smooth or lobed leaves and showy sprays or clusters of colorful flowers often appearing just ahead of the new foliage in spring and summer. All species have shapely, sometimes swollen trunks and large, boat-shaped, woody seed follicles.
CULTIVATION: Although moderately frost hardy when established, most species are relatively slow growing in the initial stages and require a warm climate to bring out their best display of flowers. They do best in a well-drained acidic soil in full sun. Propagate from fresh seed in spring, or by grafting in the case of hybrids.

Brachychiton acerifolius
syn. *Sterculia acerifolia*
FLAME KURRAJONG, ILLAWARRA FLAME TREE
☼ ❄ ↔ 20 ft (6 m) ↕ 40 ft (12 m)
Deciduous tree from Australian east coast. Flowers crimson, on bare branches. For gardens, grafted trees desirable because seedlings take many years to flower. Very drought tolerant. Zones 9–10.

Brachychiton discolor
syn. *Sterculia discolor*
LACEBARK KURRAJONG
☼ ❄ ↔ 30 ft (9 m) ↕ 80 ft (24 m)
Conical deciduous tree from eastern Australian rainforests. Leaves dark green, lobed, paler beneath. Bark very green. Flowers pink, velvety, on leafless branches, in early summer. Zones 9–11.

Brachychiton populneus
syn. *Sterculia diversifolia*
KURRAJONG
☼ ❄ ↔ 15 ft (4.5 m) ↕ 30 ft (9 m)
Semi-deciduous, with greenish bark. Glossy, ovate, deeply 3-lobed leaves. Flowers white, bell-shaped, in spring–early summer. Woody boat-shaped fruits. Zones 8–11.

Brachychiton discolor

Brachychiton populneus

Brachyglottis laxifolia

BRACHYGLOTTIS

This genus of about 30 evergreen trees, shrubs, climbers, and perennials is part of the large daisy (Asteraceae) family. They are found in New Zealand and Tasmania, Australia, in habitats ranging from coastal to alpine. Most were previously included in the genus *Senecio*. They are usually grown for their attractive gray foliage which is covered in white or buff down in varying degrees. Generally the yellow or white daisies are of little significance but in a small number of species they are quite showy.
CULTIVATION: Most species prefer a well-drained soil and a sunny site, and many tolerate harsh coastal conditions. In cool-temperate climates the more tender species are cultivated in the greenhouse and the hardier species against a sunny wall. Prune to maintain a compact bushy shape. Species are propagated from seed or half-hardened cuttings in autumn, and cultivars from cuttings only.

Brachyglottis greyi
syn. *Senecio greyi*
☼ ❄ ↔ 10 ft (3 m) ↕ 5 ft (1.5 m)
From Wellington on New Zealand's North Island. Leaves oblong, grayish green, wavy margins, white down beneath. Flowers bright yellow, in summer. Suitable for hedging. Zones 8–10.

Brachyglottis laxifolia
syn. *Senecio laxifolius*
☼ ❄ ↔ 7 ft (2 m) ↕ 3 ft (0.9 m)
Found in mountains of northern South Island of New Zealand. Lax habit. Leaves narrow, oblong, close set, slightly leathery, covered with dense gray down beneath. Zones 8–10.

BREYNIA

Part of the spurge (Euphorbiaceae) family, the 25 or so species in this genus of evergreen shrubs and small trees range from Australia and the Pacific Islands northward to Southeast and East Asia. Often suckering from the roots, they have delicate twigs and small oval leaves arranged alternately and tending to form 2 rows. Leaves often turn black before falling. Inconspicuous greenish flowers, both male and female on the same plant, appear in the leaf axils followed by small, flattened, white, red, or black berries.

CULTIVATION: Use as border shrubs in tropical and subtropical gardens; in cooler climates, grow indoors in pots or plant out for summer in bedding schemes or patio tubs. Species prefer a sunny but sheltered spot and well-drained soil. Propagate from cuttings.

Breynia disticha
syns *Breynia nivosa*, *Phyllanthus nivosus*
SNOW BUSH

☀ ↔ 3 ft (0.9 m) ↕ 4 ft (1.2 m)

From islands of western Pacific. Ovate leaves, 1 in (25 mm) long, spotted white or cream, or some all green, others all white. 'Roseopicta', pink new growth, many leaves pink-flushed, has largely replaced white-spotted form in gardens. Zones 10–12.

BROUSSONETIA
From the mulberry (Moraceae) family, *Broussonetia* consists of 8 species of deciduous trees and shrubs with milky sap, from tropical and eastern Asia; 1 species is endemic to Madagascar. Deeply lobed leaves are broad, heart-shaped, with toothed edges. Small male and female flowers are borne on separate trees, males in long catkins, females in globular heads. Male flowers expel pollen explosively, visible as tiny spurts of white dust. Small fleshy fruits are clustered on a globular fruiting head.
CULTIVATION: Only the more cold-hardy species from East Asia are known in cultivation. Moderately frost tolerant, they prefer hot humid summers. Heavy pruning creates vigorous resprouting. Propagate from cuttings of short shoots taken in summer; seed can be used if available.

Broussonetia papyrifera
PAPER MULBERRY

☀ ❀ ↔ 30 ft (9 m) ↕ 50 ft (15 m)

From China and Japan. Young branches softly hairy. Leaves variably lobed or unlobed to 8 in (20 cm). Male catkins whitish, female purplish. Fruiting heads red. Zones 6–12.

BRUGMANSIA
This genus in the Solanaceae family contains 5 species of small trees or shrubs native to South America, particularly the Andes. They are grown for their drooping tubular or funnelform flowers, which are fragrant, with a 2- to 5-lobed cylindrical calyx. Fruits are ovoid or elliptical. All plant parts are poisonous; seeds are hallucinogenic.
CULTIVATION: Brugmansias need a sunny protected position with no more than light frost. Moderately fertile, free-draining soil is suitable. Plants are best trained to a single trunk by removing any competing leaders; branchlets should be shortened annually in late winter or early spring. Propagation is from soft-tip cuttings taken in spring or summer, or hardwood cuttings in autumn or winter.

Brugmansia arborea
syn. *Brugmansia cornigera*

☀ ↔ 5–8 ft (1.5–2.4 m) ↕ 15 ft (4.5 m)

Small evergreen tree from Ecuador and northern Chile. Leaves irregularly alternate. Flowers white, solitary, with extended green tip, in summer–autumn. Fruits green, ovoid, with numerous

seeds. 'Knightii' (syn. *B. × candida* 'Double White'), off-white double flowers, gray-green leaves. Zones 10–12.

Brugmansia × candida
ANGEL'S TRUMPET

☀ ↔ 6 ft (1.8 m) ↕ 10 ft (3 m)

Hybrid of *B. aurea* and *B. versicolor*, sometimes labelled *B. knightii*. Small evergreen tree from Ecuador. Leaves bright green, paler below. Flowers greenish white, fragrant at night, in summer–autumn. Fruit green capsule. 'Grand Marnier', peach flowers. Zones 10–12.

Brugmansia 'Charles Grimaldi'

☀ ↔ 4 ft (1.2 m) ↕ 6 ft (1.8 m)

Cross between 'Doctor Seuss' and 'Frosty Pink'. Leaves large. Flowers long, widely flared, fragrant, salmon pink to yellow-orange, in autumn–spring. Compact plant, flowers heavily. Zones 10–12.

Brugmansia × insignis
syn. *Brugmansia sanguinea* 'Rosea'

☀ ↔ 8–10 ft (2.4–3 m) ↕ 12 ft (3.5 m)

Hybrid of *B. suaveolens* and *B. versicolor*, a multi-stemmed shrub. Flowers slender, tubular, flared petals, white ageing to pink or apricot. 'Betty Marshall', compact growth habit, white flowers; 'Jamaica Yellow', pale yellow blooms. Zones 9–10.

Brugmansia sanguinea ★
RED ANGEL'S TRUMPET

☀ ↔ 12 ft (3.5 m) ↕ 12 ft (3.5 m)

Small tree or shrub native to Colombia, Ecuador, and Peru. Leaves long. Flowers solitary, persistent calyx. Corolla yellowish, turning orange-scarlet. Fruits ovoid, smooth skinned. Zones 9–11.

Breynia disticha

Brugmansia sanguinea

Brugmansia suaveolens

ANGEL'S TRUMPET

☼ ♦ ↔ 10 ft (3 m) ↑ 15 ft (4.5 m)

From southeastern Brazil. Leaves soft, dark green. Single flowers, calyx green, corolla white, narrowly funnelform, with 3 pale green ribs. Fruits narrowly ellipsoidal, green, smooth. Zones 10–12.

BRUNFELSIA

Found from Central America to subtropical South America, this genus in the nightshade (Solanaceae) family includes some 40 species of mainly evergreen shrubs and trees. Most have fragrant, large, simple, long-tubed, 5-petalled flowers, notable for their progression of color changes. White, mauve, and purple are the usual colors. The leaves are usually simple pointed ovals in lush, deep green tones. All species contain potent toxic alkaloids.

CULTIVATION: While very frost tender, *Brunfelsia* presents no cultivation difficulties in mild climates. Any sunny or partly shaded position with moist well-drained soil will do. They are not drought tolerant but grow well in containers if watered routinely. Indoor potted specimens are prone to mites and mealybugs. Propagate from soft or half-hardened tip cuttings.

Brunfelsia americana

LADY OF THE NIGHT

☼ ♦ ↔ 4–7 ft (1.2–2 m) ↑ 15 ft (4.5 m)

Large shrub or small tree from Central America and West Indies. Flowers scented at night. White when first open, with hint of purple, ageing through cream to yellow, in summer. Zones 10–12.

Brunfelsia pauciflora

syn. *Brunfelsia calycina*

☼/☀ ♦ ↔ 5 ft (1.5 m) ↑ 8 ft (2.4 m)

Heavy-flowering semi-deciduous shrub from Brazil and Venezuela. Large flowers purple-blue then age through pale mauve to white. Cultivars include 'Floribunda' ★ and 'Macrantha'. Zones 10–12.

Brunfelsia pauciflora

BUCKINGHAMIA

There are 2 species of this genus in the protea (Proteaceae) family, both from Queensland, Australia. They are fast-growing, tropical rainforest trees that resemble grevilleas in foliage and flower. *B. celsissima* is frequently grown as a street tree and is appreciated for its abundant flowers.

CULTIVATION: These plants prefer warm sheltered spots but they will also tolerate cool frost-free conditions. They prefer moist well-drained loam in either full sun or partial shade. Initial directional pruning can be beneficial, but pruning is not required once the tree's framework is established. They are propagated from ripe seed in autumn.

Buckinghamia celsissima

Buckinghamia celsissima

IVORY CURL TREE

☼ ♦ ↔ 12 ft (3.5 m) ↑ 30 ft (9 m)

Evergreen tree from northeastern Queensland, Australia. Leaves dark green, shiny, pale below, lobed when juvenile. Creamy flowers on long recurved inflorescences on short stems in autumn. Woody fruits follow. Zones 10–12.

BUDDLEJA

The name of this genus of deciduous, semi-deciduous, and evergreen plants from the Americas, Asia, and South Africa can be spelt buddleja or buddleia. The genus, a member of the foxglove (Scrophulariaceae) family, consists of about 100 species, of which a few shrubby or tree-like ones are garden grown. There are also some decorative cultivars that are grown for their profuse, small, fragrant flowers that are held in large panicles. The leaves are, with the exception of *B. alternifolia*, paired and opposite. The plants are tough, undemanding, quick growing, and salt tolerant. They are also sun loving and vigorous and, if given shelter, can be grown in climates considerably cooler than those found in their native habitats.

CULTIVATION: Basic requirements include sunlight, good drainage, fertile soil, and, from the gardener's point of view, regular pruning. Some plants show a mild preference for chalky and limy soils. Propagate from half-hardened cuttings in summer.

Buddleja alternifolia ★

FOUNTAIN BUDDLEJA

☼ ❄ ↔ 15 ft (4.5 m) ↑ 15 ft (4.5 m)

Deciduous shrub native to northwest China. Leaves small, green above, whitish beneath. Flowers fragrant, misty mauve, attract butterflies, in late spring–early-summer. 'Argentea', mauve flowers, fine growth of silvery hairs on leaves. Zones 5–9.

Buddleja colvilei

SUMMER LILAC

☼ ❄ ↔ 20 ft (6 m) ↑ 20 ft (6 m)

Large upright shrub from eastern Asia. Branches arching. Leaves dark gray-green, long, pointed, heavily veined, white woolly beneath. Flowers large, bell-like, cherry pink to rosy red, in spring. 'Kewensis', rich raspberry red flowers. Zones 8–11.

Buddleja davidii 'Black Knight'

Buddleja × weyeriana

Buddleja davidii
BUTTERFLY BUSH

☼ ❋ ↔ 17 ft (5 m) ↑ 10–17 ft (3–5 m)

Tough deciduous plant native to rocky riversides in central and western China. Quick vigorous growth, bushy habit, arching stems. Long pointed leaves, dark green above, woolly white beneath. Fragrant mauve flowers in panicles. Can be invasive. *B. d.* var. *nanhoensis*, to 5 ft (1.5 m) tall and wide. *B. d.* 'Black Knight', royal purple flowers; 'Dartmoor', red-purple flowers on fan-like stems; 'Empire Blue', steely violet-blue flowers, orange eye; 'Harlequin', cream-edged leaves; 'Nanho Blue', lavender-purple flowers; 'Nanho Purple', rich purple flowers; 'Royal Red', purple-red flowers; White Profusion', white flowers, golden eye. Zones 4–10.

Buddleja globosa
ORANGE BALL TREE

☼ ❋ ↔ 10 ft (3 m) ↑ 10–20 ft (3–6 m)

Semi-evergreen tree native to Argentina and Chile. Leaves dark green above, wrinkled, woolly white beneath; young stems silvery white. Flowers scented, orange-yellow, in clusters, in late spring– early summer. Zones 7–9.

Buddleja salviifolia
SOUTH AFRICAN SAGEWOOD, WINTER BUDDLEJA

☼ ❋ ↔ 15 ft (4.5 m) ↑ 12–25 ft (3.5–8 m)

Dense shrub or small tree from South Africa. Leaves long, narrow, pointed, felted, sage gray, lightly crinkled, on short stalks. Flowers in heavy plumes, scented, smoky mauve, in late autumn–winter. Zones 8–10.

Buddleja × weyeriana
☼ ❋ ↔ 12 ft (3.5 m) ↑ 15 ft (4.5 m)

Deciduous hybrid between *B. davidii* and *B. globosa*. Leaves dark, lance-shaped. Flowers bobble-like clusters, scented, orange-yellow shaded with lilac. 'Golden Glow', soft purple buds, apricot flowers in open panicles; 'Honeycomb', pale yellow flowers; 'Sungold', dense heads of bright yellow flowers with orange centers. Zones 6–9.

BURCHELLIA

This genus from South Africa contains a single species in the madder (Rubiaceae) family. It is named for William Burchell, a botanical explorer in South Africa. Not often seen in gardens, despite its attractive foliage and bright flowers.

CULTIVATION: *Burchellia* prefers a light, fertile, and well-drained soil with plenty of summer moisture, in a warm area not subject to heavy frosts. It tolerates full sun and filtered shade. Trim occasionally to maintain shape. Propagate from seed sown in late winter or spring or from half-hardened cuttings in late summer or autumn.

Burchellia bubalina
syn. *Burchellia capensis*
SOUTH AFRICAN POMEGRANATE

☼ ❀ ↔ 8 ft (2.4 m) ↑ 10 ft (3 m)

Evergreen shrub found from Cape of Good Hope to Tropic of Capricorn. Leaves simple, dark green and shiny above, bright green beneath. Inflorescence is terminal head of 10 to 12 flowers, bright orange-red to scarlet, in spring–summer. Zones 9–11.

Burchellia bubalina

BUXUS
BOX

A member of the family Buxaceae, this genus has most of its 50 or so species in the West Indies and Central America; there are also species through eastern Asia, the Himalayas, Africa, and Europe. All are evergreen shrubs or trees with simple smooth-edged leaves arranged in opposite pairs. Small greenish or yellowish flowers are borne in the leaf axils. Fruits are small capsules. The leaves and twigs are poisonous to livestock.

CULTIVATION: The smaller-leafed species are popular in cool-climate gardens. They are valued for their dense fine-textured foliage, hardiness, and ability to take frequent trimming and shaping. They grow in most soil types, including chalk, as long as there is reasonable drainage. Propagate from cuttings, but seed also germinates readily.

Buxus microphylla
CHINESE BOX, JAPANESE BOX, KOREAN BOX

☼ ❋ ↔ 7 ft (2 m) ↑ 8 ft (2.4 m)

East Asian species with many forms and cultivars differing in frost tolerance. Wild forms have slightly brownish green leaves, ¾ in (18 mm) long. Flowers greenish yellow, in spring. *B. m.* var. *japonica*, dense upright shrub, slow growing to 8 ft (2.4 m) high; 'Green Beauty', deep green foliage; 'Morris Midget', low-growing with yellow-green leaves. Other popular cultivars include *B. m.* 'Compacta', 'Curly Locks', 'Faulkner', 'Green Jade', and 'Green Pillow'. Zones 6–10.

Buxus sempervirens

COMMON BOX, ENGLISH BOX

☼ ❄ ↔5–15 ft (1.5–4.5 m) ↕5–30 ft (1.5–9 m)
Widespread in Europe, western Asia, and
northwestern Africa. Native to British Isles.
Leaves to 1 in (25 mm) long; leaf apex pointed,
blunt, or slightly notched. Greenish cream
flower clusters in late spring. '**Argenteovariegata**'
(syn. 'Argentea'), delicate gray-green leaves
with narrow cream margin; '**Elegantissima**',
mid-green leaves with creamy white margins;
'**Graham Blandy**', narrow columnar growth
habit; '**Handsworthiensis**', unusually large
leaves; '**Latifolia Maculata**', pale gold juvenile leaves, yellow-variegated when mature;
'**Marginata**', misshapen leaves with yellowish
band around upper margin; '**Memorial**', symmetrical form, grows to 2 ft (0.6 m); '**Suffruti-
cosa**', dense erect habit, small leaves; '**Vardar Valley**' ★, dense
mound-forming shrub, mid- to dark green leaves. Zones 5–10.

Buxus, Sheridan Hybrid, 'Green Mountain'

Buxus, Sheridan Hybrids

☼ ❄ ↔18–24 in (45–60 cm) ↕18–24 in (45–60 cm)
From North America, cultivars from crosses between *B. semper-*
virens and *B. microphylla* var. *koreana*. Dense compact shrubs.
'**Green Gem**', globular form, rich green foliage;
'**Green Mountain**', darker foliage. Zones 5–10.

Buxus sinica

CHINESE BOX, KOREAN BOXWOOD

☼/◐ ❄ ↔2–12 ft (0.6–3.5 m) ↕3–20 ft (0.9–6 m)
Shrub or small tree from eastern China and
Korea, once regarded as variety of *B. microphylla*.
Occurs in many varieties covering wide size
range. Glossy light green leaves to 1¼ in (30 mm)
long. *B. s.* var. *insularis* (syn. *B. microphylla* var.
koreana), slow growing, with small but fragrant
green-yellow flowers; '**Justin Brouwers**', dense
mound with small, narrow, deep green leaves;
'**Pincushion**' (syn. *B. microphylla* 'Cushion'),
dwarf cushion-forming shrub with dull green
rounded leaves; '**Tide Hill**', dwarf to 12 in (30 cm)
tall; '**Winter Gem**' (syn. *B. microphylla* 'Winter
Gem'), hardy, foliage remains green during winter. Zones 6–10.

CAESALPINIA

Occurring in the tropics and many warm-temperate regions (mainly
in the Americas), *Caesalpinia* belongs to the cassia subfamily of
the legume (Fabaceae) family, and consists of around 150 species
of evergreen and deciduous trees, shrubs, and scrambling climbers.
Caesalpinia species all have bipinnate leaves, with numerous leaflets. Hooked prickles on branches and leaves are common, mainly
on the climbers. Flowers are in spikes, terminating the branches.
Many species have yellow flowers; most have 5 petals, and protruding stamens of often contrasting color. The pods can be flattened and smooth, or swollen and spiny, containing hard seeds.

CULTIVATION: These plants are readily cultivated in warm climates.
Many caesalpinias tolerate exposed seashores, arid climates, or
poorly drained soil. Some of the ornamental shrub and tree species prefer deeper well-drained soils and a sunny but sheltered
position. Propagation is usually from the seed, pre-treated to
penetrate the hard coat. *C. gilliesii* can be grown from cuttings.

Caesalpinia ferrea

BRAZILIAN IRONWOOD, LEOPARD TREE

☼ ◑ ↔20 ft (6 m) ↕50 ft (15 m)
Long-lived tree native to eastern Brazil. Deciduous, smooth creamy bark dappled with gray.
Foliage bright green. Flowers pale gold panicles
in summer. Zones 10–12.

Caesalpinia gilliesii

syn. *Poinciana gilliesii*

BIRD-OF-PARADISE SHRUB

☼ ◑ ↔4–8 ft (1.2–2.4 m) ↕10 ft (3 m)
From northern Argentina and Uruguay. Evergreen or may be deciduous in dry winter climate. Ferny leaves, numerous small leaflets.
Flowers pale yellow, in erect spikes. Showy red
stamens to 3 in (8 cm) long. Zones 9–11.

Caesalpinia ferrea

Caesalpinia pulcherrima

syn. *Poinciana pulcherrima*

BARBADOS PRIDE, PEACOCK FLOWER

☼ ✿ ↔6–12 ft (1.8–3.5 m) ↕10 ft (3 m)
Of uncertain origin, from tropical America or Asia. Long-stalked
showy flowers, bright scarlet to pink, gold or pale yellow, or may
be red and gold, all year. Stamens like cat's whiskers. Zones 11–12.

CALLIANDRA

This genus in the mimosa subfamily of the legume (Fabaceae)
family consists of around 200 species, the majority occurring in
South and Central America and the West Indies. Mostly shrubs
or small trees, they have bipinnate leaves, and long-stamened

flowers in globular heads or elongated spikes. Flower colors range from white and pink to crimson. Seed pods are rigid and flattened. CULTIVATION: Most calliandras come from regions that are warm but dry, or have a pronounced dry season. Many species are frost tender. Where the climate is suitable, they tolerate hard dry soils and moderately exposed positions. Most species adapt well to clipping and can be used for hedges. Propagate from seed, or from cuttings taken in winter from short lateral branches.

Calliandra haematocephala
BLOOD-RED TASSEL FLOWER, POWDERPUFF TREE
☼/◐ ꕔ ↔ 20 ft (6 m) ↑ 10 ft (3 m)
From northern South America. Flowers pink to scarlet or deep red, densely crowded into globular heads at branch tips, most of year, autumn–winter in cooler areas. Zones 10–12.

Calliandra surinamensis
PINK-AND-WHITE POWDERPUFF
☼ ꕔ ↔ 10 ft (3 m) ↑ 10 ft (3 m)
From northern South America. Showy powderpuff flowerheads, white to pale mauve, most of year. Vase-shaped habit, with arching branches, and small clustered leaves. Drought tolerant. Zones 10–12.

Calliandra tweedii ★
syn. *Inga pulcherrima*
RED TASSEL FLOWER
☼ ꕔ ↔ 6 ft (1.8 m) ↑ 6 ft (1.8 m)
Native to Uruguay and southern Brazil. Multi-stemmed fresh green foliage has tiny crowded leaflets. Deep scarlet flowerheads in spring–autumn. Can be trimmed to dense hedge. Zones 9–11.

CALLICARPA
BEAUTY BUSH
This genus has about 140 species of trees and shrubs, both deciduous and evergreen, in the mint (Lamiaceae) family. They occur from the tropics to warm-temperate regions around much of the globe. They have simple, conspicuously veined, and toothed leaves, and spring-borne heads of tiny flowers. Individual drupes that ripen in late summer and autumn are often small but distinctively colored; massed together they create a long-lasting display. CULTIVATION: Hardiness varies with the species; some tolerate little or no frost, while others are very tough. They thrive in any moist well-drained soil in sun or partial shade. Prune the plants after the fruit has fallen, and propagate from half-hardened cuttings.

Callicarpa americana
AMERICAN BEAUTY BERRY, AMERICAN BEAUTY BUSH
☼/◐ ✽ ↔ 7 ft (2 m) ↑ 10 ft (3 m)
Found in southern USA and parts of West Indies. Leaves to 8 in (20 cm) long, downy below. Violet flowers. Densely clustered magenta drupes last well into winter. Zones 5–10.

Callicarpa bodinieri
☼/◐ ✽ ↔ 8 ft (2.4 m) ↑ 10 ft (3 m)
From central and western China. Deciduous. Toothed leaves to 8 in (20 cm) long, turn golden in autumn. Lilac flowers. Drupes violet-purple, small but profuse. *C. b.* var. *giraldii* and its cultivar, 'Profusion' ★, are more commonly cultivated. Zones 6–9.

Callicarpa japonica
JAPANESE BEAUTY BERRY, JAPANESE BEAUTY BUSH
☼ ✽ ↔ 5 ft (1.5 m) ↑ 6 ft (1.8 m)
Deciduous shrub native to China and Japan. Leaves to 8 in (20 cm) long, finely toothed margins, tapering to point. Flowers pale pink, fruit pink to violet-purple. 'Leucocarpa', white fruit. Zones 7–10.

CALLICOMA
Found in coastal eastern Australia, usually near streams or rivers, the single species in this genus is a large evergreen tree in the Cunoniaceae family. Although the name wattle has become synonymous with Australian acacias, the early European settlers first gave the name to this tree in a completely different plant family but sharing similar fluffy flowerheads. CULTIVATION: Apart from intolerance of heavy frosts, black wattle is easily cultivated. It prefers a cool root run with moist, humus-enriched, well-drained soil. Prune to shape when young and thin out any weak branches as the tree matures. Propagate from seed.

Callicoma serratifolia
BLACK WATTLE
☼ ꕔ ↔ 10 ft (3 m) ↑ 12–30 ft (3.5–9 m)
Leaves glossy, heavily veined, serrated edges, downy beneath, to 5 in (12 cm) long. Young stems downy. Round heads of filamentous creamy white flowers at branch tips, in spring–summer. Zones 9–11.

Calliandra surinamensis

Callicarpa americana

Callicoma serratifolia

CALLISTEMON

BOTTLEBRUSH

This Australian genus of about 30 species of evergreen shrubs and small trees in the myrtle (Myrtaceae) family has a large range of hybrids and cultivars. The leathery, linear or lanceolate leaves are arranged spirally around the stem. Often new growth is richly colored, usually pink or bronze. Blooming in spring, summer, and autumn, the showy long-stemmed flowers, massed together in terminal spikes, form cylindrical bottlebrush-like heads. Round woody seed capsules crowd into a cylindrical group along the stem. Nectar-feeding birds are attracted to the flowers.
CULTIVATION: Most callistemons prefer moist, well-drained, slightly acid soil in a sunny position; some are only marginally frost tolerant. All respond well to pruning in the final days of flowering to promote bushier growth. Propagate species from seed. Selected forms and cultivars are grown from half-hardened tip cuttings.

Callistemon citrinus

syn. *Callistemon lanceolatus*
SCARLET BOTTLEBRUSH
☀ ❄ ↔ 10 ft (3 m) ↑ 10 ft (3 m)
From eastern Australia. Shoots pink and silky. Bright red flowers in spring–autumn. Tolerates moderate coastal exposure and poor drainage.
'Burgundy', dark red bottlebrush flowers; 'Jeffersii', dwarf to 6 ft (1.8 m) tall, red-purple flowers, lemon-scented leaves; 'Splendens' (syn. 'Endeavour'), broader leaves, masses of large, brilliant red flowers; 'White Anzac', white bottlebrush flowers. Zones 8–11.

Callistemon phoeniceus

LESSER BOTTLEBRUSH
☀ ❄ ↔ 5 ft (1.5 m) ↑ 10 ft (3 m)
From southern Western Australia. Sturdy, slightly weeping shrub. Leaves narrow, thick, gray-green. Flower spikes bright scarlet in early spring–summer. 'Pink Ice', pink flowers. Zones 9–11.

Callistemon viminalis 'Wild River'

Callistemon salignus

PINK TIPS, WHITE BOTTLEBRUSH
☀ ❄ ↔ 15–20 ft (4.5–6 m) ↑ 15–30 ft (4.5–9 m)
From moist locations of coastal eastern Australia. Small tree, weeping habit, white papery bark. Bright pink silky new foliage. Flower spikes creamy white, in spring–early summer. 'Eureka' ★, bushy form, purplish red new shoots, vivid pink flowers. Zones 9–11.

Callistemon viminalis

WEEPING BOTTLEBRUSH
☀ ❄ ↔ 7–10 ft (2–3 m) ↑ 25 ft (8 m)
Tall shrub or small tree from coastal eastern Australia. Heavily weeping crown of light green narrow leaves, brilliant red bottlebrush flowers in spring–summer. Cultivars include 'Captain Cook', 'Dawson River Weeper', 'Hannah Ray', and 'Wild River'. Zones 9–12.

Callitris rhomboidea

Callistemon Hybrid Cultivars

☀ ❄ ↔ 5–10 ft (1.5–3 m) ↑ 6–20 ft (1.8–6 m)
Propagate callistemon hybrids from tip cuttings to retain characteristics of selected clone. 'Harkness', light green leaves, brilliant red flowers; 'Injune', gray-green leaves, light pink flowers; 'Little John' ★, dwarf to 3 ft (0.9 m) high, blue-green leaves, dark red flowers; 'Mauve Mist', narrow leaves, spikes of mauve-pink flowers; 'Reeve's Pink', to 10 ft (3 m) high, with pink flowers. Zones 9–11.

CALLITRIS

AUSTRALIAN CYPRESS PINE

This Southern Hemisphere conifer genus of the cypress (Cupressaceae) family consists of 19 species of small to medium-sized trees, 2 found only in New Caledonia, the 17 remaining species in Australia. The fine thread-like twigs are clothed in tiny scale-like leaves, arranged in whorls of 3 rather than in opposite pairs as in *Cupressus*. The cones likewise have scales arranged in whorls of three. The pollen cones are tiny, while the seed cones, borne on the same tree, are more or less globular, their gray outer surfaces smooth or dotted with warty resin blisters.
CULTIVATION: *Callitris* species are light-loving, and occur on sandy or stony soils. Most species adapt very readily to being cultivated in warm-temperate climates; species from semi-arid regions prefer a warm dry summer. Grow in deep well-drained soils. They tolerate trimming and can be grown effectively in groups or closely spaced as hedges. They should be propagated from seed.

Callitris rhomboidea

syns *Callitris cupressiformis, C. tasmanica*
OYSTER BAY PINE, PORT JACKSON CYPRESS PINE
☀ ❄ ↔ 10–15 ft (3–4.5 m) ↑ 50 ft (15 m)
Native to mainland southeastern Australia, Tasmania, and central Queensland. Variable, sometimes broadly conical, sometimes columnar. Leaves fine, olive green; turn brownish in cold winters. Cones small and woody, in tight clusters beneath leaves. Useful for screens and hedges. Zones 8–11.

CALLUNA

There is only one species in this genus belonging to the erica (Ericaceae) family. It is found from north and western Europe to Siberia, Turkey, Morocco, and the Azores. The height of this small shrub is 24 in (60 cm) on average, but this can vary greatly in some of the 500 or more cultivars. The leaves grow in overlapping pairs, arranged oppositely, along the stems, and look more like scales. The leaves are dark green, usually turning reddish or tinged with purple in winter. *Calluna* differs from *Erica* in that the corolla is hidden by the calyx.

CULTIVATION: This plant prefers acid soil in an open well-drained position in full sun. Layer stems in spring and detach once rooted, or take cuttings of half-hardened wood in mid-summer.

Calluna vulgaris

syn. *Erica vulgaris*

HEATHER, LING

☼ ❋ ↔ 30 in (75 cm) ↑ 24 in (60 cm)

Native to acid heathland. Flowers are tubular or bell-shaped racemes, single or double, ranging from white to pink to purple in mid-summer–late autumn. '**Beoley Gold**', yellow foliage, single white flowers on shorter racemes; '**Blazeaway**' ★, red foliage in winter; '**Dark Beauty**', double dark crimson-red flowers; '**Firefly**', rust-colored summer foliage, turning dull dark red in winter; '**Gold Haze**', light gold foliage, white flowers; and '**Silver Queen**', silver-gray foliage, pale mauve-tinted white flowers. Other cultivars include '**Con Brio**', '**County Wicklow**', '**Darkness**', '**Kinlochruel**', '**Multicolor**', '**Radnor**', and '**Wickwar Flame**'. Zones 4–9.

CALOCEDRUS

This genus of 2 or 3 evergreen species, in the cypress (Cupressaceae) family, is native to Thailand, Vietnam, Myanmar, southwest China, and western North America. The overlapping leaves are arranged in crossed pairs in 2 rows along the stems. Male cones are borne singly and female cones are up to 1 in (25 mm) long, and have 6, sometimes 8, scales in pairs; only the center pair is fertile. The crown shape varies with climatic conditions. The timber is used for shingle tiles.

CULTIVATION: These plants are best suited to moderately fertile soil in full sun, although they will tolerate partial shade. Half-hardened cuttings can be taken in summer, and seed should be grown in containers with protection from winter frosts.

Calocedrus decurrens

INCENSE CEDAR

☼ ❋ ↔ 30 ft (9 m) ↑ 120 ft (36 m)

Native to western North America. Bark flakes off as it ages. Leaves glossy dark green with triangular tip, closely pressed to stem. Cylindrical cones ripen to red-brown. '**Aureovariegata**', smaller than other cultivars of species, foliage marked with yellow blotches; '**Compacta**' ★, globe-shaped, sometimes columnar, and very densely branched. In winter its branches turn brown. Zones 5–9.

Calluna vulgaris 'Con Brio'

CALODENDRUM

This genus comprising a single evergreen species in the rue (Rutaceae) family is from the coastal region of South Africa. It has a spreading crown and is often used in parks and large gardens or as a street tree in the more temperate regions of the Southern Hemisphere and warmer regions of North America.

CULTIVATION: *Calodendrum* prefers an open full-sun position where its crown can develop unhindered. Grow in a fertile, well-composted, and well-drained position where water is assured, especially in its initial growth period. Hardy to light frost when mature, it requires protection in early years when grown in marginal areas.

Calodendrum capense

CAPE CHESTNUT

☼ ⊰ ↔ 30 ft (9 m) ↑ 30 ft (9 m)

Bright mid-green leaves dotted with oil glands. Flowers in pink clusters, protruding stamens, recurved petals dotted with oil glands, in spring–summer. Zones 9–11.

CALOTHAMNUS

CLAW FLOWER, NET BUSH

One of the many Australian myrtle (Myrtaceae) family genera, these 40 species of evergreen shrubs are native to Western Australia. They are notable for their one-sided flower spikes and flowers with stamen filaments fused into broad straps. The flowers usually occur in late winter and spring.

Calodendrum capense

The leaves are needle-like, varying in length with the species.

CULTIVATION: Net bushes need a light, gritty, well-drained soil. They are drought tolerant and hardy to light frosts once established, needing moisture and shelter when young. Propagate from seed or soft to half-hardened tip cuttings, preferably from non-flowering stems.

Calothamnus quadrifidus

COMMON NET BUSH, ONE-SIDED BOTTLEBRUSH

☼ ⊰ ↔ 8 ft (2.4 m) ↑ 8 ft (2.4 m)

Upright, heavily branched shrub. Flattened needle-like leaves to 1¼ in (30 mm) long. Flower spikes bright red, with stamens in bundles of 4, to 8 in (20 cm) long. Zones 9–10.

Calothamnus validus

BARRENS CLAW FLOWER

☀ ✵ ↔ 8 ft (2.4 m) ↑8 ft (2.4 m)

Easily grown, vigorous, upright or rounded shrub; can become a weed. Leaves narrow, aromatic; essential oils used in homeopathy and aromatherapy. Flowers large, crimson, in small clusters below leaves. Zones 9–11.

CALYCANTHUS

Resembling magnolias, but in the allspice (Calycanthaceae) family, the aromatic deciduous shrubs of this temperate East Asian and North American genus of up to 6 species have similar characteristics. They grow to around 10 ft (3 m) tall with a considerable spread, and have large elliptical leaves and strappy, many-petalled flowers in late spring and summer. Although the flowers are sometimes small and have rather dull colors, they are borne on the new growth and stand out well. CULTIVATION: Although difficult to propagate from cuttings (layering or seed being preferred), allspices are not difficult to grow. They prefer cool moist soil with ample summer water in sun or half-sun. The flowers do not last well in low humidity.

Calothamnus validus

Calycanthus floridus

CAROLINA ALLSPICE, STRAWBERRY SHRUB

◐/◑ ✵ ↔ 7 ft (2 m) ↑10 ft (3 m)

Native to southeastern USA. Leaves large, oval, dull mid-green. Bright red to dark red-brown fragrant flowers, up to 2 in (5 cm) wide, in spring–summer. Zones 5–9.

Calycanthus occidentalis ★

CALIFORNIAN ALLSPICE, SPICE BUSH

◐/◑ ✵ ↔ 7 ft (2 m) ↑10 ft (3 m)

From California. Reddish flowers fade to yellow with age. Large-flowered forms, with blooms up to 3 in (8 cm) wide, most often seen in garden centers. Zones 7–10.

Camellia japonica 'Elegans'

CAMELLIA

A member of the Theaceae family, this genus has nearly 300 species, native to the coast and mountain regions of east Asia. They are evergreen shrubs or small trees, bearing short-stalked flowers that bloom during the colder months. A number of flower forms, sizes, and subtle and more flamboyant petal markings are recognized. Petal colors range between shades of white, yellow, pink, rose red, dark red, scarlet, purple-red, and puce. Camellias are suitable for planting in formal or woodland settings, and for hedging, edging, topiary, and espalier. CULTIVATION: While it is usual to choose and plant camellias in late autumn and winter, it is important to withhold nutrition and additional water during this time. Acid to neutral well-drained soils, shaded or semi-shaded positions, plus dry winters and wet summers suit the majority. Propagation is by grafting, or from cuttings in late summer to winter.

Camellia grijsii

◑ ✵ ↔ 8 ft (2.4 m) ↑10 ft (3 m)

From eastern and central China. Leaves oval, dark green, finely toothed. Flowers fragrant, small, white, lobed petals, yellow stamens. Resembles *C. sasanqua*, but flowers in winter and early spring. Zones 8–10.

Camellia japonica

COMMON CAMELLIA

◑ ✵ ↔ 25 ft (8 m) ↑30 ft (9 m)

Shrub or small tree found on several Chinese, Korean, Taiwanese, and Japanese islands. Single flowers, red or puce-pink, mildly scented. Leaves broadly oval, pointed, very glossy above; paler, duller, lightly spotted beneath. Variable-sized fruit. Appearance and tolerance variable in wild. Well-known variation is apple camellia, *C. j.* var. *macrocarpa*, with large, red, apple-like fruit.

Cultivars of *C. japonica* are most popular; over 2,000 display different flower forms, colors, petal markings, growth habits, preferences, and tolerances. Leaves glossy, neat, and elliptical. Most grow into neat dense shrubs and, ultimately, small trees. They flourish in suitable climates and soils, in shaded or semi-shaded positions, and sheltered in cold climates. Well-draining neutral to acid soil is essential. 'Adolphe Audusson', semi-double dark red flowers; 'Alba Plena', double with snow white, symmetrical, overlapping petals; 'Akashigata' (syn. 'Lady Clare'), semi-double rich rose pink flowers; 'Alexander Hunter', rich crimson flowers; 'Berenice Boddy', large, semi-double, pink flowers; 'Bob Hope', dark red semi-double flowers with yellow stamens; 'Bob's Tinsie', small, bright red, anemone-form flowers; 'Bokuhan' (syn. 'Tinsie'), miniature anemone-form flowers, red outer petals, dense boss of white petaloids, moderately sun tolerant; 'Brushfield's Yellow', anemone-form, pale creamish white flowers; 'Coquettii', formal double, or incomplete double, red flowers; 'Debutante', large, pale rose, informal double flowers; 'Dona Herzilia de Freitas Magalhaes', purple-violet flowers; 'Elegans' (syn. 'Chandleri Elegans'), pink flowers; 'Elegans Champagne', big creamy petals; 'Elegans Supreme', deep pink ruffled flowers; 'Elegans Variegated', pink flowers with white blotches; 'Gloire de Nantes', semi-double to

Camellia japonica 'Alba Plena'

Camellia nitidissima

Camellia pitardii

incomplete double mid-pink flowers; '**Grand Prix**', semi-double vivid red flowers; '**Janet Waterhouse**', white, double, symmetrical flowers; '**Jupiter**', formal double red flowers; '**Lady Loch**', veined, whitish pink, peony-form flowers; '**Lavinia Maggi**', white petals, streaked light and dark pinkish red; '**Masayoshi**' (syn. 'Donckelaeri'), rich pinkish red double flowers, whitish blotches on petals; '**Miss Charleston**', intense red flowers; '**Mrs D. W. Davis Descanso**', semi-double flowers of softest pink; '**Nuccio's Cameo**', coral pink flowers; '**Nuccio's Carousel**', medium-sized, semi-double, pink flowers; '**Nuccio's Gem**', early blooming; '**Nuccio's Jewel**', formal double, star-shaped flowers, shaded pink petals; '**Nuccio's Pearl**', blush white petals tipped in shades of orchid pink; '**Roma Risorta**', pink and red striped petals; '**Rubescens Major**', glowing rose red, veined petals, dark glossy leaves; '**Tama-no-ura**', dark red, petals edged in white, upright yellow stamens; '**Tomorrow**', prize-winning early blooming American plant with large informal double flowers, pink petals and petaloids with deeper pink markings; '**Tricolor**', with semi-double flowers, white petals with rose-red markings; and '**Twilight**', with large light blush pink flowers that fade to silvery white. The **Higo Group** camellias, a popular Japanese form of *C. japonica*, are not a separate species; they have flat flowers, with profuse flared stamens, gold, pink, or red, and come in single and semi-double forms. Petals solid, blotched, or striped. Zones 8–10.

Camellia nitidissima
syn. *Camellia chrysantha*
GOLDEN CAMELLIA
☀ ☼ ↔ 8 ft (2.4 m) ↑ 10 ft (3 m)
From northern Vietnam and southwestern China. Pale bark; leaves leathery, large, conspicuously veined, pale green, with bronze new growth. Flowers golden yellow, in winter–spring. Zones 9–11.

Camellia pitardii
☀ ❅ ↔ 12 ft (3.5 m) ↑ 20 ft (6 m)
Native to southern China. Leaves lance-shaped, saw-toothed. Flowers in shades of delicate pale pink, rose pink, or white, with conspicuous bright red-pink stamens that fade to white. Cultivars include '**Fairy Bouquet**', soft pink flowers; '**Gay Pixie**', rich pink

flowers; '**Moonbeam**', upright habit, pink flowers; '**Snippet**', pale pink notched petals, used as an edging plant or bonsai specimen; '**Sprite**', attractive flowers with soft salmon pink petals. Zones 8–10.

Camellia reticulata
☼ ☼ ↔ 15 ft (4.5 m) ↑ 30 ft (9 m)
Tough open species, originating in western China. Flowers rose pink, in noticeably velvety bracts. Leaves net-veined and toothed, and duller, darker, and narrower than those of *C. japonica*. This long-lived plant can adopt tree-like form and grow to 30 ft (9 m), but is usually shorter in cultivation. Many cultivars carry distinctive leaves of parent plant and can develop parent's tree-like stance, size, and open habit. Today cultivars of *C. reticulata* sometimes referred to as Yunnan camellias. *C. r.* f. *simplex* is wild form. *C. r.* '**Arch of Triumph**', huge, peony-form, loose flowers, rose red petals, glowing yellow stamens; '**Bright Beauty**', soft light red blooms; '**Captain Rawes**', irregular, semi-double, carmine flowers; '**Change of Day**', semi-double pale pink flowers, yellow stamens; '**Cornelian**', large white-blotched red flowers, leaves can

Camellia reticulata 'Bright Beauty'

be variegated; '**Dark Jewel**', rich red peony-form flowers; '**Dayinhong**' (syn. 'Shot Silk'), prolific, large, peony-form flowers with wavy ruby pink petals; '**Highlight**', semi-double scarlet blooms, yellow stamens; '**Ida Cossom**', attractive pink blooms; '**Mandalay Queen**', dark green foliage, pinkish red flowers; Narrow-leafed Shot Silk/'**Liuye Yinhong**' somewhat willowy appearance and narrower leaves; '**Nuccio's Ruby**', semi-double flowers of ruby red; '**Otto Hopfer**', dark pink flowers, stamens tipped with gold; '**Red Crystal**', scarlet flowers, golden stamens; '**Zipao**' (syn. 'Purple Gown'), old Chinese cultivar, bears deep purple buds, opening into large wine red flowers, pin-striped in red. Zones 9–11.

Camellia saluenensis
☀ ❅ ↔ 4–15 ft (1.2–4.5 m) ↑ 4–15 ft (1.2–4.5 m)
Native to southwestern China. Open, branching. Crowded, elongate, oval leaves, dark green with blunt tips. Flowers single; white, sugar pink, or red, wavy lightly lobed petals, in late winter–early spring. Zones 7–10.

Camellia sasanqua 'Mikunikô'

Camellia sasanqua

☀ ❋ ↔ 5 ft (1.5 m) ↕ 10–25 ft (3–8 m)

Straggling, woodland, tree-like shrub from Japan. Leaves very shiny, dark green. Flowers scented, single, white or pale pink, in autumn. 'Cotton Candy', tall, spreading, free-flowering plant with soft, clear pink, semi-double flowers and ruffled petals; 'Crimson King', blooms early, deep pink-red semi-double flowers; 'Jean May', upright habit, double pink flowers; 'Mikunikô', early bloomer, single rose pink flowers with mauve tonings; 'Mine-no-yuki', early bloomer, snow white flowers; 'Misty Moon', upright habit, large, wavy, rounded petals of pale lavender-pink; 'Narumigata', white petals with curled pinkish red edges. Australia has produced **Paradise Series** of sasanqua camellias, with profuse, fluffy, small to medium-sized informal double flowers. Zones 8–11.

Camellia sinensis

syn. *Thea sinensis*

TEA

☀ ❋ ↔ 10 ft (3 m) ↕ 8–20 ft (2.4–6 m)

Probably originating in China, grown commercially for tea production for centuries. Flowers small, single, long-stalked, often in pairs, pronounced yellow stamens, usually rounded white flowers. Most tea drunk in Western world made from *C. s.* var. *assamica* (Assam tea), with smooth-edged, thin, tapering leaves. *C. s.* var. *sinensis* (Chinese tea), from which unfermented green teas are made, has long, narrow, crinkly leaves and bushy appearance to about 20 ft (6 m). *C. s.* 'Blushing Bride' is attractive cultivar. Zones 7–12.

Camellia × williamsii

☀ ❋ ↔ 4–10 ft (1.2–3 m) ↕ 7–15 ft (2–4.5 m)

These hybrids of *C. japonica* and *C. saluenensis* first developed in UK in 1930s. Said to be the most easily grown and free flowering of all camellias. Leaves duller, paler than *C. japonica*. Flowers occur mostly in shades of silvery sugary pink. Award-winner 'Anticipation', deep pink flowers to 4 in (10 cm) across; 'Brigadoon', semi-double

pink flowers; 'Donation', light pink with darker pink-veined petals; 'Elsie Jury', created in New Zealand, large frilly pale pink blooms to 5 in (12 cm) in diameter; 'Francis Hanger', single white flowers; 'George Blandford', early flowering, with semi-double flowers of lavender-pink; 'Golden Spangles', single red flowers, variegated leaves; 'J. C. Williams', pink flowers over long flowering season; 'Joan Treharne', mid-pink double flowers; 'Jubilation', informal double pink flowers with long golden stamens; 'Jury's Yellow', white outer petals around dense boss of creamy yellow petaloids; 'Margaret Waterhouse', vigorous plant with well-formed, sugar pink, semi-double flowers that have rounded petals; 'Mary Christian', rich pink petals surrounding mass of golden stamens; 'Saint Ewe', single vivid pink flowers, lustrous leaves; 'Shocking Pink', tall bushy shrub, with bright pink, irregular, ruffled petals in irregular semi-double formation; 'Water Lily', upright shrub, formal double rose pink flowers with pointed petals. Zones 8–10.

Camellia Hybrid Cultivars

☀ ❋ ↔ 3–20 ft (0.9–6 m) ↕ 3–20 ft (0.9 m–6 m)

Most popular hybrids bred to withstand particular conditions, notably cold wet winters, exposure to sunlight, or marginal soil conditions, as well as for attractive appearance. 'Adorable', upright habit, formal double pink flowers; 'Fragrant Pink Improved', miniature, deep pink, fragrant flowers, open spreading habit, long flowering season, red new growth; 'Francie L', semi-double pink to red flowers; 'Freedom Bell', upright habit, semi-double red flowers; 'Inspiration', abundant semi-double pink flowers, petals sometimes with ruffled edges; 'Ole', dark pink buds open to salmon pink flowers; 'Salutation', notched silvery pink petals, long yellow stamens, large semi-double flower formation; 'Satan's Robe', up-

Camellia × williamsii 'Francis Hanger'

right glossy shrub, flowers large, semi-double carmine petals, golden stamens; 'Snow Drop', small distinctive gray-green leaves, with miniature white flowers occasionally flushed with pale pink. **Winter Series**, blooming during colder months, bred in Maryland, USA, to withstand cold conditions. 'Winter's Charm', upright shrub, medium-sized semi-double flowers with orchid pink petals and petaloids; 'Winter's Fire', single, open, puce-pink petals surrounding pronounced yellow stamens; 'Winter's Rose', palest of pink serrated petals arranged in semi-double fluffy-looking formation. Australian-bred **Wirlinga Series** produces amazing number of miniature, often clustered flowers over prolonged periods. 'Wirlinga Belle', single, soft pink, medium-sized flowers, and open growth habit; 'Wirlinga Cascade', seedling from 'Wirlinga Belle', bears single pink flowers; 'Wirlinga Gem', abundant tiny pale pink flowers. Zones 8–10.

CANTUA

This South American genus, of the phlox (Polemoniaceae) family, is mainly Peruvian. It includes about 6 species of evergreen or semi-deciduous shrubs; all have, at one time or another, been used as garden plants. The flowers are long tubes with widely flared throats, carried in pendulous clusters, usually at branch tips.

CULTIVATION: *Cantua* is best grown in moist, humus-enriched, well-drained soil. A position in full sun will yield the best flower display, though if necessary the shrub will tolerate light shade and still flower satisfactorily. Regular pruning will result in more compact growth and also encourages heavier flowering and better foliage cover next season. Propagate from tip cuttings or fresh seed, which germinates well at around 65°F (18°C).

Cantua buxifolia ★

MAGIC FLOWER, SACRED FLOWER OF THE INCAS

☼ ⚘ ↔ 8 ft (2.4 m) ↑ 12 ft (3.5 m)

From mountains of Peru, Bolivia, and northern Chile. Flowers 3 in (8 cm) long, deep pink to purple, in early spring or in warm areas year round. 'Hot Pants', North American cultivar. Zones 9–11.

CARAGANA

PEA SHRUB, PEA TREE

This genus of around 80 species of often hardy deciduous trees and shrubs from central and eastern Asia belongs to the pea-flower subfamily of the legume (Fabaceae) family. They are wiry branched, and sometimes thorny. The pinnate leaves are made up of several tiny leaflets. The small pea-flowers are nearly always yellow, borne singly or in small clusters in spring and summer. They are followed by small brownish seed pods.

CULTIVATION: Naturally adapted to a temperate continental climate with cool to cold winters and hot summers, these are tough, easily grown plants that adapt to most temperate climates with distinct seasons. They generally perform best on neutral to slightly alkaline soils. Trim to shape but avoid hard pruning because the old wood can be slow to reshoot. Propagation is usually from seed; cultivars are cutting-grown or grafted depending on the growth form.

Caragana arborescens

SIBERIAN PEA SHRUB, SIBERIAN PEA TREE

☼ ❄ ↔ 4 ft (1.2 m) ↑ 10 ft (3 m)

Widely cultivated tree from Siberia and northeastern China. Leaves have bristle-tipped leaflets; young stems covered with very fine

hairs. Clusters of light yellow flowers in spring. 'Nana', dwarf form, short twisted branches; 'Pendula' ★, weeping growth; 'Sericea', covering of fine silky hairs. Zones 2–9.

Caragana frutex

RUSSIAN PEA SHRUB

☼ ❄ ↔ 8 ft (2.4 m) ↑ 10 ft (3 m)

Found from southern Russia to Siberia. Suckering shrub, thicket-forming with age. Leaves comprise 4 deep green leaflets on thorny rachis. Yellow flowers, in clusters of 1–3 blooms. 'Globosa', rounded form; 'Macrantha', large flowers. Zones 2–9.

CARICA

The 22 species in this South American and southern Central American genus are thick-stemmed shrubs and trees with large deeply lobed leaves and long, pulpy-fleshed, usually edible fruits; the best known is the common papaya. Leaves commonly have a snowflake shape with a long stalk. Separate male and female flowers are white or cream to green. Larger female flowers quickly develop into fruit once fertilized.

CULTIVATION: These plants need steady warm temperatures, not necessarily tropical, for the fruit to ripen well. Species from higher altitudes can even withstand very light frosts. They are best in rich, moist, well-drained soil with ample humus, in a position that receives at least a half-day of sun. The plants fruit heavily from a very young age, but often lose their fruiting vigor just as quickly, so keep a stock of strong young plants to ensure a steady supply of fruit. Propagate from seed, cuttings, or grafts.

Carica × heilbornii

syn. *Carica pentagona*

BABACO, MOUNTAIN PAPAYA

☼ ⚘ ↔ 10 ft (3 m) ↑ 6–12 ft (1.8–3.5 m)

Natural self-fertile hybrid between *C. pubescens* and *C. stipulata*. Leaves 18 in (45 cm) wide. Fruit to 12 in (30 cm) long. Fruits sterile; new plants raised from cuttings. Zones 10–11.

Camellia, Hybrid Cultivar, 'Ole'

Caragana arborescens

Carica × heilbornii

Camellia, Hybrid Cultivar, 'Wirlinga Gem'

CARISSA

This genus of around 20 species of evergreen shrubs and small trees, in the dogbane (Apocynaceae) family, is found throughout tropical and subtropical Africa, Asia, and Australia. Many are densely branched and spiny; they have glossy green foliage, and clusters of fragrant, pure white, 5-petalled, long-tubed flowers. Fruit is edible. CULTIVATION: Usually drought tolerant once established, most species prefer to be moist throughout the growing season. They thrive in warm frost-free areas in a position with well-drained soil and full sun. Prune to shape as necessary, or shear hedges after flowering or after fruiting if the fruit is required. Propagate from seed or cuttings. The stems yield a milky sap when cut, and cuttings should be allowed to dry before inserting in the soil mix.

Carissa edulis
SMALL NUM-NUM
☼ ⁂ ↔ 5 ft (1.5 m) ↕ 5 ft (1.5 m)
Spreading spiny shrub found in Africa and Middle East. Leaves rounded, dark green on red stems. Fruit tasty, round, purple-red to black. Excellent cascading container plant. Zones 10–11.

Carissa macrocarpa
AMATUNGULA, NATAL PLUM
☼ ⁂ ↔ 10 ft (3 m) ↕ 7–10 ft (2–3 m)
Widely cultivated species from South Africa, with forked spines. Leaves rounded, deep glossy green, leathery, redden in bright light. Flowers white, to 2 in (5 cm) wide. Red to purple-red fruit. 'Boxwood Beauty' ★, compact habit. Zones 10–12.

CARMICHAELIA
syns *Chordospartium, Notospartium*
Part of the pea-flower subfamily of the legume (Fabaceae) family, this genus of about 23 almost leafless small trees and shrubs is native to New Zealand, with a species from Lord Howe Island, Australia. They grow in a wide range of habitats, from shaded river valleys to coastal and alpine areas, varying in form from tall to prostrate. Juvenile plants have very small leaves, generally absent in mature specimens. Leafless branchlets are flattened or very slender and reed-like. Many small pea-flowers, often fragrant, are carried on short racemes in shades of pinkish mauve to purple and white in spring or summer. CULTIVATION: Most species are only half-hardy, needing greenhouse protection in cool-temperate areas. They prefer sunny well-drained situations, tolerating dry and poor soils but repaying better conditions with profuse flowering. Propagate from seed, or half-hardened cuttings in summer.

Carissa edulis

Carmichaelia odorata ★
NEW ZEALAND SCENTED BROOM, SCENTED BROOM
☼ ⁂ ↔ 6 ft (1.8 m) ↕ 6 ft (1.8 m)
Found along streamsides and forest edges in New Zealand's North Island. Bushy shrub, with slightly weeping branchlets. White and mauve flowers, lightly scented, in spring–summer. Zones 8–10.

Carpenteria californica

Carmichaelia stevensonii
syn. *Chordospartium stevensonii*
☼ ⁂ ↔ 10 ft (3 m) ↕ 12 ft (3.5 m)
From New Zealand's South Island. Graceful weeping branches but can look straw-like and lifeless for several years when young as it has no juvenile leaves. Flowers in summer. Zones 8–10.

CARPENTERIA
This genus contains a single species of evergreen shrub from the hydrangea (Hydrangeaceae) family, which has a very limited natural range in central California on rocky mountain slopes. It has narrow glossy green leaves, lightly felted beneath. The fragrant white flowers resemble those of *Philadelphus*. CULTIVATION: It requires a sunny site and a light, moisture-retentive, well-drained soil. It can be pruned to maintain a more compact form. Propagate from seed in spring or autumn, or cuttings that can be difficult to root.

Carpenteria californica
TREE ANEMONE
☼ ⁂ ↔ 8 ft (2.4 m) ↕ 8 ft (2.4 m)
Flowers pure white with 5 to 7 overlapping petals, prominent yellow stamens, to 2½ in (6 cm) across, in early summer. Zones 6–10.

CARPINUS
HORNBEAM
This genus in the birch (Betulaceae) family contains about 35 deciduous trees and shrubs found throughout the temperate regions of the Northern Hemisphere. Commonly known as hornbeams, they are appealing trees at all times of year. The leaves have prominent parallel veining and color well in autumn. In spring they bear pendulous yellow male catkins and separate female catkins, which are erect at first. The fruiting clusters in autumn are surrounded by leafy bracts and in winter an attractive branch pattern is revealed.

CULTIVATION: Hornbeams will grow in most soils. *C. betulus* is a popular species for pleaching and hedging. Hornbeams are propagated from seed sown in autumn; cultivars are grafted.

Carpinus betulus
COMMON HORNBEAM, EUROPEAN HORNBEAM

☀ ❋ ↔ 60 ft (18 m) ↑ 80 ft (24 m)

From Turkey to southeastern England. Trunk gray, fluted. Pointed oval leaves, serrated margins, prominent veins, turn orange in autumn. 'Fielder's Tabular', light green leaves. Zones 5–9.

Carpinus caroliniana
AMERICAN HORNBEAM, BLUE BEECH, IRONWOOD, MUSCLEWOOD

☀ ❋ ↔ 40 ft (12 m) ↑ 40 ft (12 m)

Native to moist woods and riverbanks in eastern North America. Similar to *C. betulus* but often shrubby. Leaves turn to deep shades of orange and scarlet in autumn. Zones 5–9.

CARYA (see page 356)

Carya cordiformis
syns *Carya amara*, *Juglans cordiformis*
BITTERNUT HICKORY, SWAMP HICKORY

☀ ❋ ↔ 50 ft (15 m) ↑ 80 ft (24 m)

From eastern North America. Smooth pale gray bark; narrow, deep, scaly ridges with age. Buds yellow, flattened, hairy, in winter. Leaves have up to 9 pinnate leaflets, 5 large terminal leaflets. Zones 4–9.

CARYOPTERIS

This genus in the mint (Lamiaceae) family occurs in eastern Asia, from the Himalayas to Japan, and contains 6 species of deciduous flowering shrubs with slender cane-like stems. Most species have opposite, simple, toothed leaves, often aromatic and grayish. The flowers, borne in late summer, are mainly blue, mauve, or white in axillary or terminal panicles. The fruit is winged and nut-like. CULTIVATION: Species prefer an open sunny position and thrive in cool-temperate regions, ideally in a fibrous loamy soil with free drainage. They flower on the current season's growth and should be pruned moderately in late winter or early spring. Propagate from soft-tip or firm leafy cuttings between spring and early autumn; dormant hardwood cuttings from winter prunings can also be used.

Caryopteris × clandonensis
BLUE MIST SHRUB, BLUE SPIRAEA

☀ ❋ ↔ 5 ft (1.5 m) ↑ 5 ft (1.5 m)

Hybrid of *C. incana* and *C. mongolica*. Slender vase-shaped shrub. Leaves downy, serrated. Deep blue to violet flowers, in dense cymes, in late summer. 'Arthur Simmonds', purple-blue flowers. Zones 5–9.

Caryopteris incana
syn. *Caryopteris mastacanthus*
BLUE SPIRAEA, BLUEBEARD

☀ ❋ ↔ 5 ft (1.5 m) ↑ 5 ft (1.5 m)

Small shrub native to China and Japan. Grayish, serrated, pointed leaves, slender arching stems. Heads of spiraea-like powder-blue flowers in tiers along stems in late summer. Zones 7–10.

CASSIA

Once a very large genus, *Cassia* has been revised and is now a far more consistent group of over 100 species in the cassia subfamily of the legume (Fabaceae) family. Found in tropical areas of the world, the mainly evergreen shrubs and trees have pinnate, sometimes hairy leaves, and yellow or pink flowers, borne singly, in small clusters or in panicles. Flowers are followed by bean-like seed pods. CULTIVATION: Few species tolerate repeated frosts. They prefer a mild climate, moist well-drained soil, and full or half-sun. Propagate from seed, which should be soaked in warm water prior to sowing; some cassias will grow from half-hardened cuttings.

Cassia fistula
GOLDEN SHOWER TREE, INDIAN SENNA

☀ ❂ ↔ 20 ft (6 m) ↑ 60 ft (18 m)

Native to tropical Asia. Deciduous to semi-evergreen. Smooth gray bark. Leaves pinnate, leaflets in 3–8 pairs. Flowers yellow, scented, pendulous racemes, in summer. Dark brown seed pods. Zones 10–12.

Cassia javanica
syn. *Cassia nodosa*
PINK SHOWER, RAINBOW SHOWER

☀ ❂ ↔ 10 ft (3 m) ↑ 50 ft (15 m)

From Southeast Asia. Pinnate leaves composed of up to 34 long, narrow, drooping leaflets. Flowers over 2 in (5 cm) wide in racemes, color variable, buff through pink to crimson. Zones 11–12.

Carpinus betulus 'Fielder's Tabular'

Caryopteris × *clandonensis* 'Arthur Simmonds'

Cassia fistula

Cassia × *nealiae* ★
RAINBOW SHOWER

☼ ≀ ↔ 20–30 ft (6–9 m) ↕ 25–50 ft (8–15 m)

Deciduous flowering tree, hybrid between yellow-flowered *C. fistula* and pink-flowered *C. javanica*. Flowers vary from cream to orange and red. Most common cultivars are pale yellow-white '**Queen's Hospital White**' and '**Wilhelmina Tenney**', odorless yellow flowers. '**Lunalilo Yellow**', fragrant yellow flowers. Zones 10–12.

CASSIOPE
This genus of 12 species of small evergreen shrubs is closely related to the heaths and heathers (Ericaceae). Found mainly in northern Europe and northern Asia with outliers in the Himalayas and western North America, they are very much cool-temperate to cold climate plants, with a few species ranging into the Arctic. They seldom exceed 8 in (20 cm) high and have tiny leaves arranged in 4 distinct rows on wiry whipcord stems. The flowers, which appear mainly in spring, are small, usually bell-shaped, and carried singly, though often in large numbers, on fine stems.
CULTIVATION: Cassiopes prefer moist well-drained soil that is rich in humus and slightly acidic. They are not drought tolerant plants and need ample summer moisture. Very frost hardy, they prefer a climate with distinct seasons with a cool moist summer. They are best shaded from the hot summer sun. Trim lightly if necessary. Propagate from self-layered stems or by taking cuttings.

Cassiope lycopodioides
☼ ❋ ↔ 10 in (25 cm) ↕ 3 in (8 cm)

Native to mountains of Japan, northeastern Asia, and Alaska. Flat sprawling habit, minute leaves. Flowers, nodding, around ¼ in (6 mm) wide, carried on 1 in (25 mm) long stems. Zones 3–8.

Cassiope lycopodioides

Cassiope mertensiana
☼ ❋ ↔ 10 in (25 cm) ↕ 6–12 in (15–30 cm)

Upright or spreading shrub from mountainous regions of western North America. Leaves tightly pressed to stem. Small, white, bell-shaped flowers in spring. '**Gracilis**', mound-forming. Zones 5–9.

CASTANOSPERMUM
The sole species in this genus in the pea-flower subfamily of the legume (Fabaceae) family is a rainforest tree from northeastern Australia and New Caledonia. Developing slowly into a beautifully shaped tree with a dense rounded crown of lush deep green foliage, it is prized not only as a specimen tree, but also for its timber, which is a warm deep brown color. The summer floral display is also attractive, though the flowers are often largely hidden within the foliage. Very large seed pods follow the flowers in autumn.
CULTIVATION: Considering its origins, *C. australe* is surprisingly hardy. Although best grown in warm areas, it does well in any reasonably mild, frost-free garden and will even tolerate light frosts—with some foliage loss. The soil should be humus rich, moist, and free draining. Young trees will tolerate light shade. Propagation is from seed.

Castanospermum australe
MORETON BAY CHESTNUT, QUEENSLAND BLACK BEAN

☼ ≀ ↔ 40 ft (12 m) ↕ 40 ft (12 m)

Deep green pinnate leaves made up of 11 to 15 leaflets. Flowers pea-like, in racemes, yellow, ageing orange-red. Seed pods to 12 in (30 cm) long, containing 1 to 5 large black seeds. Zones 10–12.

CASUARINA
This is a small genus in the she-oak (Casuarinaceae) family containing approximately 17 species from Australia and the Pacific Islands. In 1982 the genus was subdivided into 4 genera, with most Australian species now classified as *Allocasuarina*. All *Casuarina* species have distinctive, dark green or gray-green, slender, wiry branchlets, modified to function as leaves. The true leaves are reduced to tiny teeth-like scales in whorls at regular intervals along the branchlets. The minute, pollen-bearing, rusty red, male flowers form at the tips of branchlets. Female flowers, small and tassel-like, produce the next season's fruiting cones. Casuarinas are fast growing and may be planted singly or grouped for shade, shelter, and screening purposes. As they will withstand harsh windy conditions they are ideal for wind protection.
CULTIVATION: Grow casuarinas in full sun in any soil as long as it is well drained. Water well during the establishment period and dry hot weather. Propagate from seed.

Castanospermum australe

Casuarina cunninghamiana
RIVER OAK, RIVER SHE-OAK

☼ ⁑ ↔ 25 ft (8 m) ↑ 100 ft (30 m)

Stately tree, common on riverbanks in eastern Australia. Upright trunk. Dark green, slightly drooping branchlets near ground level. Useful for windbreaks. Prefers open moist position. Zones 9–11.

Casuarina equisetifolia
AUSTRALIAN PINE, BEACH SHE-OAK

☼ ⁑ ↔ 20 ft (6 m) ↑ 60 ft (18 m)

From subtropical and tropical eastern Australia, Pacific Islands, and Malaysia. Spreading tree, open branching crown, weeping branchlets. *C. e.* subsp. *incana,* weeping silvery green branchlets. Zones 10–12.

Casuarina glauca
SWAMP OAK, SWAMP SHE-OAK

☼ ⁑ ↔ 20 ft (6 m) ↑ 70 ft (21 m)

Native to east coast Australia. Upright tree, weeping dark green branchlets with waxy coating. Forms dense thickets in saline swamps. Withstands quite dry conditions. Zones 9–12.

CATALPA

This genus of 11 species of small to medium deciduous trees, belonging to the trumpet-vine (Bignoniaceae) family, occurs in North America, the West Indies, and southwestern China. They are attractive trees, with a tropical appearance from their large long-stalked leaves. They bear upright panicles of 2 in (5 cm) long, bell-shaped flowers, followed by hanging bean-like seed capsules up to 30 in (75 cm) in length.

CULTIVATION: *Catalpa* make excellent specimen trees and are good for street planting. They should be sheltered from wind to protect the large leaves. A sunny site with rich, moist, well-drained soil provides the most suitable conditions. Young trees may require protection from late frosts and should be trained to a single trunk. The species are propagated from seed sown in autumn and the cultivars from softwood cuttings taken in late spring or early summer.

Catalpa bignonioides
BEAN TREE, INDIAN BEAN TREE, SOUTHERN CATALPA

☼ ❋ ↔ 40 ft (12 m) ↑ 50 ft (15 m)

Found at streamsides and in low woods in south-eastern USA. Leaves large, heart-shaped bases, unpleasant smell when crushed. Large erect panicles of bell-shaped white flowers, marked with yellow and purple, in summer. Large bean-like pods. 'Aurea' ★, fine form with velvety golden leaves; 'Nana', small shrub to 6 ft (1.8 m) high, seldom bears flowers. Zones 5–10.

Catalpa bungei

☼ ❋ ↔ 25 ft (8 m) ↑ 30 ft (9 m)

Small tree native to northern China. Leaves triangular, with long central tip. Flowers rosy pink to white with purple spots, in summer. Seed capsule up to 20 in (50 cm) in length. Zones 5–10.

Casuarina equisetifolia subsp. *incana*

Catalpa speciosa
NORTHERN CATALPA, SHAWNEE WOOD, WESTERN CATALPA

☼ ❋ ↔ 90 ft (27 m) ↑ 120 ft (36 m)

From riverbanks, damp woods, and swamps of central southern USA. Like *C. bignonioides,* but has larger leaves. White flowers are larger, less dense, appearing a few weeks earlier. Zones 5–10.

CEANOTHUS
CALIFORNIAN LILAC

This genus of about 50 species of mostly evergreen, ornamental, flowering shrubs is a member of the buckthorn (Rhamnaceae) family. Mainly native to western North America, some are found in eastern USA, and from Mexico south to Guatemala. They range from low, spreading, ground-cover plants to tall shrubs. Most are quick growing but they may also be short lived. The flowers range from powder blue to deep purple, some having white or cream flowers, and appear mainly in early summer.

CULTIVATION: *Ceanothus* will grow in most soils, preferring a position in sun. They tolerate drought, heat, and cold if the soil is free draining. Most prefer dry-summer climates and are quite wind-tolerant. Tip prune young plants; adult plants require little pruning apart from removing spent flowerheads and wayward shoots. *Ceanothus* resent disturbance. Species can be propagated from the seed, and soft tip or firm hardwood cuttings can be taken between spring and early autumn.

Catalpa speciosa

Ceanothus arboreus
CATALINA MOUNTAIN LILAC, TREE CEANOTHUS

☼ ❋ ↔ 12 ft (3.5 m) ↑ 20 ft (6 m)

From southern Californian coast. Vigorous, wide-spreading, smaller in cultivation. Leaves ovate, downy beneath, larger than in other species. Flowers pale blue, fragrant, in abundant panicles, in spring. 'Mist' ★, paler gray-blue flowers; 'Trewithen Blue', large panicles of fragrant deep blue flowers. Zones 7–9.

Ceanothus × *delileanus* 'Gloire de Versailles'

Ceanothus × *delileanus*

☼ ❈ ↔ 5 ft (1.5 m) ↑ 5 ft (1.5 m)

Strong-growing, deciduous shrub, hybrid between *C. americanus* and *C. coeruleus*. Broadly oval bright green leaves. Panicles of soft blue flowers throughout summer. Cultivars include '**Gloire de Versailles**' and '**Topaze**'. Zones 6–9.

Ceanothus diversifolius

PINE-MAT

☼ ❈ ↔ 3–6 ft (0.9–1.8 m) ↑ 4–12 in (10–30 cm)

Evergreen shrub from California. Long flexible branches form low clumps. Small pale bluish green leaves, hairy beneath. Tiny heads of white to pale blue flowers in spring–early summer. Zones 8–10.

Ceanothus gloriosus

POINT REYES CREEPER

☼ ❈ ↔ 12 ft (3.5 m) ↑ 12 in (30 cm)

Occurs naturally on central Californian coast. Prostrate shrub with dark green, glossy, toothed leaves. Clusters of lavender-blue flowers in spring. *C. g.* **var.** *exaltatus*, erect shrub to 6 ft (1.8 m) high. *C. g.* '**Anchor Bay**', very dense foliage, mauve-blue flowers. Zones 7–9.

Ceanothus griseus

CARMEL CEANOTHUS

☼ ❈ ↔ 10 ft (3 m) ↑ 10 ft (3 m)

Shrub native to hills of central California. Dark green leaves, gray beneath. Pale lilac-blue flowers in spring. New growth arching. *C. g.* **var.** *horizontalis*, low-growing form with spreading habit; '**Diamond Heights**', produces golden leaves blotched with dark green; '**Hurricane Point**', fast growing, light blue flowers; '**Yankee Point**' ★, bright blue flowers. Another form, *C. g.* '**Kurt Zalnik**', discovered clinging precariously to eroding cliff face, has extremely dark blue blooms, height to 3 ft (0.9 m), spread of 15 ft (4.5 m). '**Santa Ana**', spreading habit, deep blue flowers. Zones 8–10.

Ceanothus hearstiorum

☼ ❈ ↔ 6 ft (1.8 m) ↑ 12 in (30 cm)

Prostrate, spreading, evergreen shrub from California. Previously called a hybrid, now a species. Small puckered leaves. Mid- to violet-blue flowers in small clusters in late spring–early summer. Zones 8–10.

Ceanothus impressus

SANTA BARBARA CEANOTHUS

☼ ❈ ↔ 10 ft (3 m) ↑ 10 ft (3 m)

Spreading, hardy, evergreen shrub. Leaves small, deeply veined. Flowers deep blue, in small thin clusters, in spring. Zones 8–10.

Ceanothus prostratus

MAHALA MATS, SQUAW CARPET

☼ ❈ ↔ 8 ft (2.4 m) ↑ 3 in (8 cm)

From mountainous areas of Oregon and California, USA, differing from other ceanothus in being subalpine. Creeping evergreen shrub makes dense mat, stems often rooting as they grow. Leaves toothed, dark green; flowers pale lavender-blue, in spring. *C. p.* **var.** *occidentalis*, wavy-edged wedge-shaped leaves. Zones 8–10.

CEDRUS

TRUE CEDAR

Cedrus species come from widely separated regions in northwest Africa, Cyprus, Turkey, Lebanon, and the western Himalayas. They are large long-lived trees from the pine (Pinaceae) family, with needle-like leaves arranged spirally on the leading shoots at the branch tip, crowding on the short lateral shoots to form neat rosettes. Both the male and female cones are large and conspicuous; the seeds have papery wings. All the cedars are somewhat similar in appearance, and are sometimes treated as varieties or subspecies of a single species, or as 2 or 4 separate species. CULTIVATION: Cedars are fairly frost hardy but cannot be grown in the more severe northern climates. They adapt to a range of soil types, if the soil is of moderate depth and fertility, and there is subsoil moisture available. These trees do not normally require pruning. Planting out is best done when still at a small size. Propagate from seed except for the cultivars, which must be grafted.

Cedrus atlantica

syn. *Cedrus libani* **subsp.** *atlantica*

ATLANTIC CEDAR, ATLAS CEDAR

☼ ❈ ↔ 30 ft (9 m) ↑ 80 ft (24 m)

From Atlas and Rif Mountains of Morocco and Algeria. Young trees conical with stiff erect leading shoots, ageing to broad-headed. Needles crowded on short shoots into tight neat rosettes. Foliage

Cedrus atlantica

Cedrus deodara

varies from rather bluish to green. 'Aurea', distinctive golden yel-low-tipped foliage. 'Glauca Pendula' ★, requires support of long branches from which foliage sweeps to ground. 'Pendula', all growths completely pendulous, forming curtain of bluish gray foliage, hanging down to 10 ft (3 m) or more. Zones 6–10.

Cedrus deodara
DEODAR, DEODAR CEDAR
☼ ❄ ↔ 30 ft (9 m) ↕ 200 ft (60 m)
Native to western Himalayas from Afghanistan to western Nepal. Largest of cedars. Spire-like crown with lower branches resting on ground. Leading shoots drooping with soft green needles. Seed cones barrel-shaped. 'Aurea', pale yellowish new growth, changing to darker lime green. Zones 7–10.

Cedrus libani
CEDAR OF LEBANON
☼ ❄ ↔ 90 ft (27 m) ↕ 150 ft (45 m)
From Mt Lebanon in Lebanon. Young trees narrowly conical, with stiff leading shoots and grayish green leaves. Old trees massive hori-zontally spreading limbs. 'Golden Dwarf' (syn. 'Aurea-Prostrata'), dwarf form. Zones 5–10.

CEIBA
syn. *Chorisia*
About 10 species of tropical American deciduous trees make up this genus in the mallow (Malva-ceae) family. They are tall stout-trunked trees with smooth bark often armed with large con-ical prickles. Leaves are compound with leaf-lets radiating from the end of the leaf stalk.
Flowers are cream to yellow, pink, or red, and carried in loose pan-icles toward branch tips. The fruit is a large green capsule enclosing seeds buried in cottonwool-like hairs called kapok.
CULTIVATION: They thrive in lowland tropics or in subtropical regions; they are best in climates with a summer rainfall and a dis-tinct dry season, in deep, well-drained, alluvial soils and a reason-ably sheltered position. Early growth is fast, with the full height attained in only 10 to 20 years. Propagate from freshly gathered seed or half-hardened cuttings in summer.

Ceiba insignis
PINK FLOSS-SILK TREE
☼ ❁ ↔ 40 ft (12 m) ↕ 60 ft (18 m)
Widespread in tropical South America. Ornamental yellowish green trunk, thickest near ground; crown of broadly spreading limbs. Pink to reddish pink flowers in late summer–early winter. Zones 9–11.

Ceiba pentandra
syn. *Eriodendron anfractuosum*
KAPOK TREE
☼ ➳ ↔ 80 ft (24 m) ↕ 230 ft (70 m)
From South America. High open canopy. Cream to dull yellow or pink flowers on pendent stalks from bare branch tips before new leaves. Elongated pods about 6 in (15 cm) long. Zones 11–12.

CELTIS
Occurring in all continents and many larger islands, the large, mainly tropical and mainly evergreen genus *Celtis* consists of over 100 species. Belonging to the hemp (Cannabaceae) family, the genus has the characteristic leaf shape with usually toothed edges and an asymmetric base. Flowers are greenish and inconspicuous, with male and female separate on the one tree. Small berry-like fruit has thin but sugary flesh that conceals a hard stone; in most species they ripen to black or dark brown, and are greedily eaten by birds. Some species become troublesome weed trees when cul-tivated outside their native lands.
CULTIVATION: Vigorous growers, they adapt well to tough environ-ments such as urban streets and parks, tolerating a wide range of soil conditions. The deciduous species make excellent shade trees. Propagate from seed, which in the case of temperate species should be cold-stratified for 2 to 3 months before sowing in spring; ger-mination is often erratic.

Celtis australis

Celtis australis
EUROPEAN NETTLE-TREE
☼ ❄ ↔ 60 ft (18 m) ↕ 60 ft (18 m)
Found throughout southern Europe, north-west Africa, and eastern Mediterranean region. Deciduous, rounded canopy, smooth gray-barked trunk. Leaves have saw-toothed edges with slender point, dense short hairs beneath. Berries ripen bright orange to dark brown in summer. Can be invasive. Zones 8–11.

Celtis laevigata
syn. *Celtis mississippiensis*
SUGAR HACKBERRY, SUGARBERRY
☼ ❄ ↔ 60 ft (18 m) ↕ 80 ft (24 m)
Native to southeastern USA. Deciduous species with smooth dark gray bark. Leaves thin, hairless, very one-sided at base, finely tapered at apex, with teeth in upper part. Fruit orange, ripening to purple-black, in autumn. Zones 6–11.

Ceiba insignis

Celtis occidentalis

AMERICAN HACKBERRY

☀ ❄ ↔ 60 ft (18 m) ↑ 60 ft (18 m)

From northern USA. Deciduous, low-branching; smooth, gray, bark, develops rows of corky pustules, becomes dark and furrowed with age. Leaves broad, toothed, pale yellow in autumn. Fruit ripens red to dark purple in autumn. 'Prairie Pride', dense bushy crown. Zones 3–10.

Celtis reticulata

syn. *Celtis douglasii*

NETLEAF HACKBERRY

☀ ❄ ↔ 25 ft (8 m) ↑ 25 ft (8 m)

Deciduous species from mountains of western USA and Mexico, similar to *C. occidentalis*. Pea-sized orange-red fruits. Zones 6–10.

CEPHALOTAXUS

PLUM YEW

This interesting genus of conifers consists of 6 or more species, mostly found in China. In foliage features they resemble the yews *(Taxus)* but on female plants the ovules and the plum-like seeds that develop from them are crowded onto stalked head-like cones. On male plants the pollen cones are likewise crowded into small knob-like heads. The genus is now placed in a separate family, Cephalotaxaceae. All species are shrubs or small trees with flaky brown or reddish bark, often multi-stemmed and suckering from ground level.

CULTIVATION: Tough flexible plants that adapt to a wide range of soils and climates, they tolerate exposed positions as well as partial shade, preferring a climate with adequate steady rainfall throughout the year. They are excellent for hedging as they withstand frequent trimming. Propagate from cuttings, preferably taken from leading shoots. Cold stratification is used to germinate seed.

Cephalotaxus fortunei

FORTUNE'S PLUM YEW

☀ ❄ ↔ 10 ft (3 m) ↑ 20 ft (6 m)

Whorled branches; linear, gently curved, finely pointed leaves, 2 white bands beneath, arranged in 2 rows. Oval seeds ripen to glossy purplish brown. Zones 7–10.

Celtis occidentalis

Cephalotaxus harringtonia

JAPANESE PLUM YEW

☀ ❄ ↔ 10 ft (3 m) ↑ 15 ft (4.5 m)

Spreading shrub, sometimes small tree. Branches occur alternately. Olive green leaves, arranged in 2 rows, narrowed at tip. *C. h.* var. *drupacea* ★, short stiff leaves, rows arranged in neat V-shape. *C. h.* 'Fastigiata', erect branches densely crowded into column. Zones 6–10.

CERATONIA

This genus of the cassia subfamily of the legume (Fabaceae) family consists of 2 species of evergreen tree native to the Arabian Peninsula and Somalia. The leaves are pinnate with large leathery leaflets; the flowers are small and arranged in dense branched spikes emerging from the trunk and branches. The sexes are variably distributed on each tree. The fruits are plump brownish pods with shiny seeds embedded in a sweet, floury, edible pulp.

CULTIVATION: Only *C. siliqua* (carob) is known in cultivation. It prefers a hot dry summer, moderately wet winter, and permanent deep soil moisture. It likes a position in full sun, though it will tolerate part-shade. If only one tree can be grown it should be a variety that bears male and female flowers together. Propagate from seed, or from green branch cuttings in late summer.

Ceratonia siliqua

CAROB, ST JOHN'S BREAD

☀ ❄ ↔ 25 ft (8 m) ↑ 40 ft (12 m)

Thick gnarled trunk, broad low canopy. Flowers pale greenish purple, with rank smell, in autumn. Abundant curved pods mature in early winter. Pulp used as chocolate substitute. Zones 9–12.

CERATOPETALUM

This genus of 5 evergreen species, in the Cunoniaceae family, is from east-coastal Australia and New Guinea. Small white flowers are followed by swollen reddened calyces lasting for weeks. Leaf size differs with the species: some are open lightly foliaged shrubs, others are tall densely clothed trees. Most grow in moist forests or rainforest habitats along the eastern coastline.

Cephalotaxus fortunei

Ceratopetalum gummiferum

Ceratostigma willmottianum

CULTIVATION: All species are easy to grow, but require adequate water and well-drained soil. Organic fertilizers like mulch or compost are preferred over chemical fertilizers. Partial shade will suit but better coloring will occur in full sun. Propagate from seed.

Ceratopetalum gummiferum
NEW SOUTH WALES CHRISTMAS BUSH
☼/◑ ❄ ↔6 ft (1.8 m) ↑15 ft (4.5 m)
Erect growing shrub, dainty trifoliate leaves, shallow toothed edges. Bright red calyces follow small white flowers in summer. Popular with florists at Christmas in New South Wales, Australia. Zones 9–11.

CERATOSTIGMA
From the leadwort (Plumbaginaceae) family, this is a genus of 8 species of herbaceous perennials or small evergreen or deciduous shrubs, all but one native to the Himalayas or China. They are grown for their intense blue, 5-petalled, flat flowers, borne in terminal clusters during summer into autumn, when the small-leafed foliage becomes red or bronze depending on the intensity of the colder weather.
CULTIVATION: These low-growing frost-tender plants are best grown in moist well-drained soil in full sun. Lightly prune to promote a dense compact bush—but remember, they flower on the current season's growth. They will re-shoot if killed back by winter frosts.

Ceratostigma plumbaginoides ★
syn. *Plumbago larpentiae*
☼ ❄ ↔12 in (30 cm) ↑18 in (45 cm)
Slender upright stem. Spreads from rhizomes. Cornflower blue flowers at ends of red stems, in summer–autumn. Leaves turn red with colder weather. Zones 6–9.

Ceratostigma willmottianum
CHINESE PLUMBAGO
☼ ❄ ↔5 ft (1.5 m) ↑3 ft (0.9 m)
Deciduous shrub with open low-branching habit. Mid-green leaves. Pale to bright blue flowers throughout summer–autumn. Foliage turns rich bronze tones in autumn. Forest Blue/'Lice', elliptical leaves, deep blue flowers. Zones 7–10.

CERCIDIPHYLLUM
The sole member of the Cercidiphyllaceae family, and closely allied to the magnolia family, this genus is represented by 2 species, and includes the largest deciduous native tree species in China and Japan. A distinctive elegant habit of horizontally held branches and heart-shaped leaves that color well—red, pink, and yellow—in autumn are the most notable characteristics of the species. Commonly it is found with the trunks forked low to the ground, which makes it vulnerable to damage in strong winds.
CULTIVATION: A sheltered position is essential to avoid disfigurement from drying winds and late spring frosts. Regular summer moisture is required and preferably rich soils. Propagate from seed after first subjecting to cold. Cuttings are readily struck in late spring to early summer in cool and moist conditions.

Cercis canadensis

Cercidiphyllum japonicum
KATSURA TREE
☼ ❄ ↔35 ft (10 m) ↑60 ft (18 m)
Elegant horizontal branch structure, vibrant autumn foliage. Leaves bluish green (reddish when unfolding), change to smoky pink, yellow, red in autumn, exude pungent aroma reminiscent of burnt sugar. *C. j.* var. *sinense,* velvety hairs beneath leaves. *C. j.* f. *pendulum* ★, weeping branches. Zones 6–9.

CERCIS
This small genus of 6 or 7 deciduous trees and shrubs in the cassia subfamily of the legume (Fabaceae) family, found in North America, eastern Asia, and Europe, is grown for the showy spring flowers. Leaves are alternate and mostly broadly ovate; flowers are pea-flower-like, with 5 petals in a squat calyx, usually borne on bare stems before or with the early leaves. The fruit is a flat legume with a shallow wing.
CULTIVATION: Frost hardy, plants prefer a moderately fertile soil that drains well, and exposure to the sun for most of the day. Shape to select a main leader but little regular pruning is required after that. Propagate from pre-soaked fresh seed. Take half-hardened cuttings in summer or autumn.

Cercidiphyllum japonicum

Cercis canadensis
EASTERN REDBUD, REDBUD
☼ ❄ ↔30 ft (9 m) ↑30 ft (9 m)
From USA. Variable with short main trunk, or multi-stemmed, rounded crown. Flowers dark red-brown sepals, rose pink petals, in late winter–early spring. Fruits reddish brown, in summer. 'Alba,' white flowers. 'Forest Pansy', burgundy foliage. Zones 5–9.

Cercis siliquastrum
JUDAS TREE
☼ ❄ ↔35 ft (10 m) ↑35 ft (10 m)
Native to Mediterranean region. Heart-shaped to kidney-shaped leaves. Flowers rosy purple, on bare branches, in early spring. *C. s.* f. *albida*, white flowers; 'Bodnant', deep purple-red flowers. Zones 6–9.

CESTRUM

This genus, belonging to the nightshade (Solanaceae) family, consists of around 180 species all from tropical America. They are evergreen or deciduous woody shrubs or small trees, and have mostly simple alternate leaves, usually narrow with smooth margins. The tubular to funnel-shaped flowers are borne in clusters; and they are often very fragrant and in some species are night-scented. The flowers are followed by small mostly blackish or reddish berries. All parts of the plant are poisonous. Some species have been classified as weeds.
CULTIVATION: Most grow easily in full or half-sun and moderately fertile soil with adequate watering in summer. Where frosts occur, grow these plants against a sunny wall for protection. In colder areas they may be grown in a green-house. Plants respond well to pruning; pinch back to encourage bushy growth. Propagate from soft-tip cuttings.

Chaenomeles japonica

Cestrum aurantiacum

ORANGE CESTRUM

☼ ❄ ↔ 6 ft (1.8 m) ↑ 10 ft (3 m)

Evergreen or semi-deciduous rambling shrub native to tropical America. Requires regular pruning. Smooth light green leaves, slightly hairy new growth, unpleasant smell when crushed. Flowers orange, in clusters at ends of stems, in spring–summer. Fleshy white berries. Zones 8–12.

Cestrum × cultum

PURPLE CESTRUM

☼ ❄ ↔ 6 ft (1.8 m) ↑ 10 ft (3 m)

Cross between *C. elegans* and *C. parqui*. Ovate to lance-shaped leaves. Densely flowering terminal panicles, similar to *C. elegans*; single tubular flowers resemble *C. parqui*, although pink to violet in color. Zones 8–12.

Cestrum elegans

syn. *Cestrum purpureum*

☼ ❄ ↔ 8 ft (2.4 m) ↑ 10 ft (3 m)

Strong-growing shrub from Mexico. Arching branches. Ovate-oblong to lance-shaped, hairy, olive green leaves give off disagreeable odor when crushed. Tubular-shaped red to purple flowers, in dense panicles, in summer–autumn.

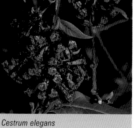

Cestrum elegans

Succulent, globular, purple-red berries. 'Smithii', orange-red flowers. Can be invasive. Zones 8–12.

Cestrum 'Newellii'

RED CESTRUM

☼ ❄ ↔ 10 ft (3 m) ↑ 10 ft (3 m)

Arching branches. Dark green leaves, narrowly ovate to elliptical, hairy, unpleasant smell when crushed. Rich crimson unscented flowers most of year. Berries small, round, dark red. Zones 8–11.

Cestrum nocturnum

NIGHT-SCENTED JESSAMINE

☼ ❄ ↔ 10 ft (3 m) ↑ 10 ft (3 m)

Evergreen shrub from West Indies. Pale greenish yellow tubular flowers give off strong night fragrance in summer–late autumn. No scent in daylight. Ovoid berries ripen green to white. Leaves somewhat succulent, bright green, paler on reverse. Zones 9–12.

CHAENOMELES

FLOWERING QUINCE, JAPANESE QUINCE, JAPONICA

This genus, which belongs to the rose (Rosaceae) family, has 3 species of spiny deciduous shrubs native to the high-altitude wood-lands of Japan and China. Their early red, pink, or white flowers appear before the leaves on last year's wood. The leaves are alternate, serrate, oval, and deep green. The flowers, which usually have 5 petals, unless double, are cup-shaped and appear from late winter to late spring, singly or in small clusters. The roughly apple-shaped, rounded, green fruit turns yellow when ripe; it is aromatic and used in jams and jellies.
CULTIVATION: Generally, well-drained moderately fertile soil, in sun or half-sun, will give best results. Grow plants against a south wall in colder climates. Good ornamental plants, they can also be used as hedging plants. Half-hardened cuttings can be obtained in summer or later in autumn. Seed can be sown in autumn in containers with protection from winter frosts or in a seed bed in the open ground.

Chaenomeles × californica

☼/◐ ❄ ↔ 5 ft (1.5 m) ↑ 6 ft (1.8 m)

Hybrid between *C. cathayensis* and *C. × superba*. Leaves mid-green, lance-shaped, 3 in (8 cm) long. Flowers 2 in (5 cm) in diameter, pink to pale red, in spring. Fruit 2½ in (6 cm) long. Zones 5–10.

Chaenomeles japonica

JAPANESE FLOWERING QUINCE

☼/✿ ❋ ↔ 6 ft (1.8 m) ↑ 3 ft (0.9 m)

From Japan. Open twiggy habit with spiny branchlets. Flowers orange-scarlet, prominent cream stamens, in late winter–early spring. Fruit fragrant, ripens green to dull yellow. Zones 6–9.

Chaenomeles speciosa

syns *Chaenomeles lagenaria, Cydonia speciosa*

CHINESE FLOWERING QUINCE, FLOWERING QUINCE, JAPONICA

☼/✿ ❋ ↔ 15 ft (4.5 m) ↑ 10 ft (3 m)

Native to China. Thicket forming, spiny suckering stems. Showy flowers in winter. Aromatic fruit ripens to green-yellow. 'Geisha Girl', apricot double-flowered form. Some cultivars are hybrids with *C. japonica*, including 'Nivalis', snow white flowers; 'Phylis Moore', pale pink flowers; 'Toyo-nishiki', pink and white flowers on same branch, sometimes produces branch of red flowers. Zones 6–9.

Chaenomeles × superba

☼/✿ ❋ ↔ 6 ft (1.8 m) ↑ 5 ft (1.5 m)

Hybrid of *C. japonica* and *C. speciosa*, garden origin. Leaves 2½ in (6 cm) long, oval to oblong-shape, lustrous mid-green. Spring flowers, white, pink, orange to orange-scarlet. Fruit to 3 in (8 cm) long, aromatic when ripe. 'Cameo' ★, fleshy pink flowers; 'Glowing Embers', orange-red blooms; 'Nicoline', large dark red flowers, 'Rowallane', bright red with yellow anthers. Zones 6–10.

CHAMAECYPARIS

This genus in the cypress (Cupressaceae) family consists of some 8 species from North America and eastern Asia. It is distinguished from true *Cupressus* by its small cones and short branches which have small leaves arranged in pairs and flattened to the stems of the branchlets. Leaves become more scale-like as it ages. Pollen and seed cones are borne on the same tree. Rice-grain-sized pollen cones appear in huge numbers; seed cones ⅓ in (8 mm) or less in diameter release small winged seeds as soon as they mature (in contrast to *Cupressus*, in which unopened seed cones may persist for years). Contact with the foliage can cause skin allergies. CULTIVATION: This genus is lime and air-pollution tolerant but will grow better in neutral to acid soil. Propagate from half-hardened cuttings taken in summer or seed sown in autumn or spring. Early trimming is necessary. Named cultivars should be grafted in late winter or early spring.

Chamaecyparis lawsoniana

LAWSON CYPRESS, OREGON CEDAR, PORT ORFORD CEDAR

☼ ❋ ↔ 10–15 ft (3–4.5 m) ↑ 100 ft (30 m)

Native to western North America. Foliage bright green to blue-green; some cultivars have yellow foliage. Red male flowers in early spring. Grayish cones ripen to rusty brown. 'Chilworth Silver', slow growing, bluish gray juvenile foliage; 'Columnaris', narrow pale gray leaves, grows to 30 ft (9 m) high; 'Intertexta', slightly weeping branches, gray-green foliage; 'Nana', yellow foliage, grows to 6 ft (1.8 m); 'Pembury Blue', silver-blue foliage; 'Stardust', medium-sized slow-growing conical tree. Other cultivars include 'Ellwoodii' ★, 'Gnome', 'Lanei Aurea', and 'Stewartii'. Zones 4–9.

Chamaecyparis obtusa

syn. *Cupressus obtusa*

HINOKI CYPRESS

☼ ❋ ↔ 20 ft (6 m) ↑ 60 ft (18 m)

Slow-growing tree native to Japan. Bark thick, rusty colored. Leaves opposite, deep green above, striped silvery white beneath. Foliage aromatic when crushed. Male cones yellow in spring. Rounded seed cones ripen to orange-brown. 'Crippsii' (syn. 'Crippsii Aurea'), golden yellow foliage; 'Coralliformis', to 8 ft (2.4 m) tall, dark green leaves; 'Nana Aurea', golden foliage; 'Nana Gracilis', to 10 ft (3 m) high; 'Spiralis', lush bright green foliage. Zones 5–10.

Chamaecyparis pisifera

syn. *Cupressus pisifera*

SAWARA CYPRESS

☼ ❋ ↔ 15 ft (4.5 m) ↑ 75 ft (23 m)

Native to southern Japan. Rusty brown bark. Foliage mid-green, white markings beneath. Male cones very small, tawny; seed cones round, black-brown. 'Boulevard', to 30 ft (9 m) tall, blue-green foliage; 'Filifera Aurea', golden yellow leaves; 'Filifera Aurea Nana', dwarf form; 'Squarrosa' (syn. 'Squarrosa Veitchii'), soft young foliage, deep green to blue-green. Other cultivars include 'Gold Spangle', 'Golden Mop', 'Nana Variegata', 'Plumosa Aurea Nana', 'Plumosa Juniperoides', and 'Squarrosa Sulphurea'. Zones 5–10.

Chamaecyparis thyoides

ATLANTIC WHITE CEDAR, COAST WHITE CEDAR, WHITE CYPRESS

☼ ❋ ↔ 12 ft (3.5 m) ↑ 50 ft (15 m)

From east coast USA. Bark gray-brown. Leaves pointed, dark green, fan-shaped sprays. Small yellow male cones; seed cones purplish black. 'Andelyensis', blue-green foliage; 'Ericoides', purplish brown winter foliage; 'Heatherbun' ★, dwarf form. Zones 4–9.

Chamaecyparis lawsoniana, in the wild, Oregon, USA

CHAMAECYTISUS

This genus includes some 30 species of trees, shrubs, and subshrubs from Eurasia and the Canary Islands in the pea-flower subfamily of the legume (Fabaceae) family. Some are ornamental, others are cultivated as quick-growing shelter and fodder. All have trifoliate leaves and pea-like flowers, usually in white, yellow, or pink shades. CULTIVATION: Though often short lived, species tolerate nitrogen-poor soils. Good drainage is important, and most prefer to be kept on the dry side except when in flower. A full-sun position is best. Propagate from seed or half-hardened cuttings.

Chamaecytisus purpureus ★

☼ ❀ ↔ 24 in (60 cm) ↑ 18 in (45 cm)

Native to southeast Europe and Balkans. Deciduous species, densely branched. Flowers pale pink to crimson, with dark central blotch, in late summer–spring. *C. p. f. albus,* white flowers. Zones 6–10.

CHAMELAUCIUM

One of Australia's best-known cut flowers, this genus, which belongs to the myrtle (Myrtaceae) family, comprises 23 species, all from the south-western regions of the continent where they grow in well-drained gravelly soil in somewhat dry conditions. They are tough evergreen shrubs with fine needle-like leaves and masses of white or pink flowers with a wax-like texture that bloom during winter. CULTIVATION: Chamelauciums have a reputation for being finicky. However, when grown in well-drained soil in a sunny situation where water and humidity can be controlled, they do well, though they can be short lived. Propagate from seed or half-hardened cuttings.

Chamelaucium uncinatum

GERALDTON WAX

☼ ❁ ↔ 8 ft (2.4 m) ↑ 8 ft (2.4 m)

From West Australian coast. Grown in gardens and for florists' trade. Flowers pink, purple, or red. Prune to keep compact. 'University', purple-red flowers; 'Vista' ★, pink flowers. Zones 10–11.

CHILOPSIS

Belonging to the trumpet-flower (Bignoniaceae) family, this genus consists of a single species of evergreen shrub or small tree native to arid regions of southwestern USA and western Mexico. It has brittle cane-like branches and narrow leaves. Short sprays of showy trumpet-shaped flowers terminate the branches, each flower 2-lipped at its mouth. Fruits are thin pendulous capsules packed with winged seeds. CULTIVATION: *Chilopsis* comes from a warm climate with a very hot dry atmosphere and although fairly frost hardy, will not thrive in cool humid climates. A warm sunny position and deep, well-drained, sandy soil suit it best. Propagate from cuttings or seed.

Chilopsis linearis

Chilopsis linearis

DESERT WILLOW

☼ ❀ ↔ 8 ft (2.4 m) ↑ 10–20 ft (3–6 m)

Downy twigs, grayish green leaves to 4 in (10 cm) or longer. Flowers 1½ in (35 mm) long, almost as wide, deep rose pink to white, darker spots in throat. 'Burgundy' ★, red-purple flowers; 'Hope', white flowers with light yellow center. Zones 8–11.

CHIMONANTHUS

There are 6 species in this deciduous or evergreen genus from China within the allspice (Calycanthaceae) family. Their scented flowers can be used dried, like lavender. Leaves are arranged opposite in pairs and appear after the flowers in spring. CULTIVATION: In colder areas they benefit from a sheltered position, which protects early flowers from frost damage. In less cold areas they can be grown in the open garden, needing full sun in fertile free-draining soil. Propagate from cuttings in summer. Sow seed in a position protected from winter frost as soon as it is ripe, but seed-raised plants will take 5 to 10 years or more to flower.

Chimonanthus praecox

syns *Chimonanthus fragrans, Meratia praecox*

JAPANESE ALLSPICE, WINTERSWEET

☼ ❀ ↔ 10 ft (3 m) ↑ 12 ft (3.5 m)

Deciduous shrub native to China. Lance-shaped leaves, glossy green, rough surface, turn pale yellow in autumn. Fragrant flowers on second-year bare wood, sulfur yellow to pale yellow, purple or brown stain on inner petals, in winter. 'Grandiflorus' ★, flowers to 2 in (5 cm) wide. 'Parviflorus', small flowers. Zones 6–10.

CHIONANTHUS

This genus in the olive (Oleaceae) family includes over 100 species of evergreen and deciduous trees and shrubs mostly from tropical regions of the world but with a few in eastern Asia and eastern USA. Leaves are smooth-edged and opposite each other on the branches. The white 4-petalled flowers are borne in terminal panicles, and are followed in autumn by a purple-blue fruit with a single seed.

Chimonanthus praecox

Choisya ternata

CULTIVATION: Some species tolerate alkaline soil; others prefer a neutral or acid soil and a position in full sun. Wood must be ripened by the sun for a good flower set. Sow seed when ripe in autumn, protecting it from frosts. Germination takes up to 18 months.

Chionanthus retusus ★
CHINESE FRINGE TREE
☼ ❋ ↔ 10 ft (3 m) ↕ 15–30 ft (4.5–9 m)
Native to China and Taiwan. Bark deeply grooved or peeling. Glossy, bright green, egg-shaped leaves, white downy undersides. Panicles of fragrant white flowers in summer. Blue-black fruit. Zones 6–10.

Chionanthus virginicus
FRINGE TREE
☼ ❋ ↔ 10 ft (3 m) ↕ 12–25 ft (3.5–8 m)
Native to eastern USA. Leaves egg-shaped, dark green, glossy, to 8 in (20 cm) long. Fragrant white flowers in pendent panicles. Blue-black fruit. 'Angustifolius' ★, narrower leaves. Zones 4–10.

CHOISYA
This genus within the rue (Rutaceae) family has about 8 species of evergreen shrubs that are native to southwest USA and Mexico. These are attractive ornamental shrubs with aromatic palmate leaves and scented, white, star-shaped flowers.
CULTIVATION: Most grow well in full sun in fertile well-drained soil. Propagation is from half-hardened cuttings rooted in summer.

Choisya 'Aztec Pearl'
☼ ❋ ↔ 8 ft (2.4 m) ↕ 8 ft (2.4 m)
Hybrid of C. arizonica and C. ternata. Strongly aromatic shrub, lush dark green foliage, fine narrow leaflets. Abundant white flowers open from pale pink buds in spring–early summer. Zones 8–10.

Choisya ternata
MEXICAN ORANGE, MEXICAN ORANGE BLOSSOM
☼ ❋ ↔ 6 ft (1.8 m) ↕ 6 ft (1.8 m)
Evergreen Mexican shrub. Glossy 3-lobed leaves. White, starry, fragrant flower clusters in spring; second flush in late summer.

Good drainage essential. Sundance/'Lich' ★, pale gold foliage, becoming more greenish on ageing, needs light shade. Zones 8–10.

CHORIZEMA
A genus of 18 species, all but one native to southwest Australia, Chorizema consists of evergreen shrubs or twiners. They are part of the pea-flower subfamily of the legume (Fabaceae) family, with massed short racemes of pea-flowers, often in contrasting colors. Leaves are heart-shaped, narrow, or lobed, and sometimes aromatic.
CULTIVATION: Chorizema species generally prefer light well-drained soil and a position in full sun or partial shade. While prolonged wet conditions are not tolerated, these plants will appreciate an occasional deep watering in summer. Propagate from seed, which needs to be soaked before sowing, or from half-hardened cuttings.

Chorizema cordatum ★
HEART-LEAFED FLAME PEA
☼/◐ ❋ ↔ 4 ft (1.2 m) ↕ 4 ft (1.2 m)
From southern Western Australia. Foliage heart-shaped, with small teeth. Flowers orange and yellow standard, deep pink to red keel. Best in well-drained soil, with a little shade. Zones 9–11.

CHRYSOPHYLLUM
This tropical genus from the sapodilla (Sapotaceae) family includes some 80 species of evergreen shrubs and trees. It is widespread in the tropics, particularly the Americas. They have medium to large-sized smooth-edged leaves, often with brown or golden yellow hair on the undersides. Flowers are small, white to cream with purple markings, in small clusters. The large fleshy berries are edible.
CULTIVATION: These trees need a warm humid climate free of frosts and cold winds. They prefer fertile, moist, well-drained, humus-enriched soil and regular feeding. Any pruning or trimming can be carried out as the fruit is harvested or, if the fruit is not required, after flowering. Propagate from seed or grafting. Seedlings take 8 to 12 years to fruit; grafted plants will crop well in 4 to 5 years.

Chrysophyllum cainito
STAR APPLE
☼ ✦ ↔ 15 ft (4.5 m) ↕ 50 ft (15 m)
Native to Central America. Leaves deep green, elliptical, yellow-brown felting beneath. Small, starry, creamy white flowers. Rounded, 4 in (10 cm) wide fruit ripens to purple. Zones 11–12.

Chorizema cordatum

Chrysophyllum cainito

Cistus albidus

Cistus ladanifer

Cistus × pulverulentus

CINNAMOMUM

This is a genus of about 250 usually evergreen trees and shrubs in the family Lauraceae, with aromatic leaves, wood, and bark. They are native to warm-temperate to subtropical regions from eastern and southeastern Asia to Australia. Panicles of inconspicuous flowers appear in summer. The fleshy berry-like fruit is grown for its spicy flavoring and for use in traditional medicine. The timber is used for making utensils and furniture, for building construction, and as fuel. Ornamentally, *Cinnamomum* species are valued both for the appearance of their foliage and as shade trees. Cinnamon is derived from the bark of *C. verum*, which is grown commercially.
CULTIVATION: These plants are best grown in full sun or part-shade, in well-drained fertile soil, preferably in a sandy loam medium. They tolerate regular pruning. Propagation is from seed sown in autumn or from cuttings of half-hardened softwood taken in spring.

Cinnamomum camphora
CAMPHOR LAUREL, CAMPHOR TREE
☼ ❄ ↔ 30 ft (9 m) ↕ 60 ft (18 m)
Evergreen shade and screen tree from China, Taiwan, and Japan. Leaves aromatic, shiny, pink-red at first, turning light green. Cream flower clusters in spring. Oval, shiny, black berries. Camphor extracted from timber. Weed in subtropical Australia. Zones 9–11.

CISTUS

A genus of about 20 species in the rock-rose (Cistaceae) family, all are small to medium-sized, evergreen, flowering shrubs found throughout the Mediterranean region. They grow on sun-baked stony hillsides. In cultivation they become very adaptable long-flowering ornamentals, ideal for difficult dry sites. The leaves are opposite, mostly dark green or whitish, and in some species they exude a sticky resin called ladanum or labdanum, which is used in incense and perfume. The flowers, which are individually short lived, have 5 broad petals in either white, pink, mauve, or reddish purple, often blotched, and with prominent yellow stamens.
CULTIVATION: All *Cistus* species revel in a hot sunny position and will grow in most soils provided drainage is good. They thrive in all climates of the Mediterranean type. Young plants should be tip pruned; pinch back older plants after the flowering period. Seeds can be sown in spring. Short cuttings from non-flowering sideshoots can be taken in autumn.

Cistus albidus
☼ ❄ ↔ 4 ft (1.2 m) ↕ 3 ft (0.9 m)
Widely distributed through southwestern Europe and North Africa. Dense shrub. Leaves whitish, white downy twigs. Flowers pale rose-lilac with yellow center. Zones 7–9.

Cistus creticus
syn. *Cistus incanus* subsp. *creticus*
HAIRY ROCK ROSE, ROCK ROSE
☼ ❄ ↔ 3 ft (0.9 m) ↕ 3 ft (0.9 m)
Found in eastern Mediterranean region from Corsica and Italy eastward. Stems hairy; leaves whitish green beneath. Flowers purple, flushed yellow at petal base. *C. c.* subsp. *incanus* (syn. *C. incanus*), less wavy margins, no yellow on petal bases. Zones 7–9.

Cistus ladanifer
GUM CISTUS
☼ ❄ ↔ 5 ft (1.5 m) ↕ 5 ft (1.5 m)
Native to North Africa and southwestern Mediterranean region. Leaves dark green, whitish, furry beneath, exuding ladanum. Flowers up to 4 in (10 cm) wide, white with brownish crimson blotch, bright yellow stamens. *C. l.* subsp. *sulcatus*, previously called *C. palhinhae*, low-growing, compact, shiny sticky leaves, white flowers. *C. l.* 'Blanche', deep green glossy leaves, grayish beneath, white flowers; 'Paladin', glossy green leaves, paler beneath, large white flowers with dark red basal blotches; 'Pat', large flowers, to 5 in (12 cm) across, white with maroon basal blotches. Zones 8–10.

Cistus × pulverulentus
☼ ❄ ↔ 6 ft (1.8 m) ↕ 2 ft (0.6 m)
Hybrid between *C. albidus* and *C. crispus*, often sold as 'Sunset' ★. Dwarf compact shrub bearing gray-green leaves with undulating margins. Bright pink flowers in spring–early autumn. Zones 8–10.

Cistus salviifolius
SAGE-LEAFED ROCK ROSE
☼ ❄ ↔ 30 in (75 cm) ↕ 30 in (75 cm)
Leaves slightly aromatic, wrinkled, rough, downy, dark gray-green upper surface, whitish gray undersurface. Flowers borne singly or in groups of 2 or 3, with crepe-like white petals, suffused with yellow at their base. 'Prostratus', prostrate form. Zones 7–10.

Cistus Hybrid Cultivars

☼ ❄ ↔ 3–6 ft (0.9–1.8 m) ↕ 2–5 ft (0.6–1.5 m)

Hybrid cultivars that cannot readily be assigned names such as *C. × dansereaui, C. × pulverulentus*, and *C. × purpureus* include '**Grayswood Pink**', with pink flowers; and '**Snow Fire**', vigorous and hardy, with white flowers bearing deep red blotches. Zones 7–9.

CITRUS (see page 358)

Citrus trifoliata

syn. *Poncirus trifoliata*

TRIFOLIATE ORANGE

☼ ❄ ↔ 15 ft (4.5 m) ↕ 15 ft (4.5 m)

Dense fast-growing shrub from north China and Korea. Deciduous; dark green trifoliate leaves turn yellow in autumn; branches deep green in winter. Solitary fragrant white flowers, on second-year wood, in late spring–early summer. Fruit green, ripens to orange. Zones 5–11.

CLADRASTIS

Native to China, Japan, and eastern USA, these 5 species of deciduous trees in the pea-flower subfamily of the legume (Fabaceae) family are cultivated for their flowers, which are carried in wisteria-like racemes from early summer, followed by flat seed pods. The pinnate leaves have fine hairs on the undersides of the leaflets.

CULTIVATION: Species tolerate a range of soils with good drainage; they hate drought or waterlogging. Grow in sun, protected from strong winds. Propagate from seed or winter hardwood cuttings.

Cladrastis kentukea

syn. *Cladastris lutea*

YELLOWWOOD

☼ ❄ ↔ 30 ft (9 m) ↕ 25–40 ft (8–12 m)

Native to eastern USA. Bright green leaves, 7 to 11 oval leaflets, golden yellow in autumn. Fragrant white flowers, 12 in (30 cm)

Cladrastis kentukea

long racemes, in early summer. Narrow, 3 in (8 cm) long, brown seed pods. Zones 3–9.

CLEMATIS

LEATHER VINE, TRAVELLER'S JOY, VIRGIN'S BOWER

This genus of over 200 species, in the buttercup (Ranunculaceae) family, encompasses a huge range of forms. *Clematis* species are mainly climbing or scrambling but sometimes shrubby or perennial, deciduous or evergreen, flowering at any time in any color, occurring in both northern and southern temperate zones and at higher altitudes in the tropics. Leaves may be simple or pinnate. Flowers have 4 to 8 petal-like sepals. Fluffy seed heads follow.

CULTIVATION: Foliage should be in the sun while the roots are kept cool and moist. Incorporate plenty of humus-rich compost before planting, and water well. Clematis wilt disease is a problem in many areas. Propagate from cuttings or layers. Species may be raised from seed; sex will be undetermined before flowering.

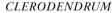
Clerodendrum bungei

Clematis heracleifolia

☼/◗ ❄ ↔ 2–5 ft (0.6–1.5 m) ↕ 3–6 ft (0.9–1.8 m)

Woody-based species from central and northern China. Lightly downy trifoliate leaves, irregularly toothed leaflets, to 2½ in (6 cm) long. Clusters of dusky, purple-blue, tubular flowers, with 4 flared and reflexed sepals, in summer–autumn. '**New Love**', dark purple-blue flowers, lighter inside, fragrant. Zones 3–9.

CLERODENDRUM

GLORY BOWER

This genus of about 400 evergreen and deciduous small trees, shrubs, and climbers is in the mint (Lamiaceae) family. They are found mostly in tropical and subtropical regions of Asia and Africa. Their simple leaves are opposite or whorled. They are grown for their summer terminal panicles of showy violet or red flowers. The fruit is a drupe or berry.

CULTIVATION: They prefer light to medium well-drained soils, rich in humus, in a protected partly shaded to sunny position. Water freely in the growing season. Stems of young plants may require support, and sucking insects can pose a problem. Propagate from seed in spring or half-hardened cuttings in winter or summer.

Clerodendrum bungei

GLORY FLOWER

☼/◗ ❄ ↔ 8 ft (2.4 m) ↕ 8 ft (2.4 m)

Evergreen aromatic shrub from south China and north India. Leaves triangular, toothed-edged, dark green, purple overtones. Flowers strongly scented, pale pink to purple-red, in summer. Zones 8–10.

Clerodendrum trichotomum

◗ ❄ ↔ 15 ft (4.5 m) ↕ 15 ft (4.5 m)

From China and Japan. Downy leaves. Heads of long-tubed, white, scented flowers in late summer. Flowers backed by pink calyces, darkening as fruit matures. Purplish blue drupes. Zones 8–10.

Clethra barbinervis

Clianthus puniceus

CLETHRA

This genus of about 60 species of deciduous small trees or shrubs in the family Clethraceae is widely distributed from southern USA to Central and South America and Asia, with one species native to Madeira. They are grown for their white fragrant flowers, often borne in long racemes or panicles, which resemble lily-of-the-valley flowers. Some of the species have attractive peeling bark, and the flowers are followed by numerous tiny seed capsules. CULTIVATION: Being closely related to the erica family, clethras like a lime-free soil and a moist sheltered spot, with some shade from taller trees. They can be propagated from seed, cuttings, or layers.

Clethra acuminata
CINNAMON CLETHRA, WHITE ALDER

☀ ❄ ↔ 12 ft (3.5 m) ↑ 12 ft (3.5 m)

Large shrub from southeastern USA. Racemes of scented creamy white flowers in late summer. Mid-green elliptical leaves have attractive golden tones in autumn. Zones 6–9.

Clethra alnifolia
SUMMERSWEET CLETHRA, SWEET PEPPER BUSH

☀ ❄ ↔ 6 ft (1.8 m) ↑ 6 ft (1.8 m)

Native to eastern North America. Fragrant white flowers, in erect terminal racemes to 6 in (15 cm) long, in late summer. 'Rosea' ★, buds and flowers tinged with pink. Zones 4–9.

Clethra arborea
LILY-OF-THE-VALLEY TREE

☀ ∄ ↔ 20 ft (6 m) ↑ 25 ft (8 m)

From Madeira, densely foliaged. Long terminal panicles of scented white flowers. Needs mild conditions to thrive. 'Flora Plena', double flowers. Zones 9–10.

Clethra barbinervis
JAPANESE CLETHRA

☀ ❄ ↔ 10 ft (3 m) ↑ 10 ft (3 m)

From mountainous woodlands of Japan. Peeling rusty brown bark. Dark green leaves, veined, attractive autumn color. Scented white flowers in terminal racemes in summer–autumn. Zones 8–9.

CLIANTHUS

This genus consists of just one (or possibly two) New Zealand species. *Clianthus*, a member of the pea-flower subfamily of the legume (Fabaceae) family, grows into a sprawling evergreen shrub, with pinnate leaves and large red flowers in early summer. CULTIVATION: When grown in cool-temperate climates it needs the protection of a sunny wall or greenhouse to prosper. In warmer areas it should be grown in sun or partial shade where protection is available from strong winds and heavy frosts. It requires well-drained soil and should be watered during dry periods. Light pruning will encourage bushier growth. Snails and slugs find the foliage very appealing and are serious pests. Propagation is from seed sown in spring or half-hardened cuttings taken in summer.

Clianthus puniceus ★
KAKA BEAK, PARROT'S BILL

☼/◐ ❄ ↔ 6 ft (1.8 m) ↑ 6 ft (1.8 m)

Rare in native habitat, northern North Island of New Zealand. Branches clothed with attractive fern-like leaves. Red flowers, shape reminiscent of beak of kaka (native parrot). Easy to propagate, fast growing, can be short lived. 'Albus', attractive white-flowering form that grows true from seed. Zones 8–11.

CLUSIA

This genus of over 140 species from the rainforests of the American tropics and subtropics belongs to the St John's wort (Clusiaceae) family. They often start life as epiphytes, but form such a thicket of aerial roots that they eventually swamp or strangle their host tree, grow down to the ground, and form a trunk of their own. Most species have thick, leathery, deep green leaves that are roughly oval in shape. Although both male and female flowers appear on the same plant, they are separate. Both occur in 3-flowered clusters and have 4 to 9 rounded petals, but the males are larger and have numerous stamens. Near-spherical leathery seed capsules follow. CULTIVATION: Most *Clusia* species require tropical warmth. They also need moist, well-drained, humus-rich soil and will not

Clusia major

withstand drought, frost, or even prolonged cool conditions. Prune to shape when young. Propagate from cuttings or aerial layers.

Clusia major
syn. *Clusia rosea*
COPEY
☼ ✦ ↔ 50 ft (15 m) ↑ 50 ft (15 m)
Shrub or tree with spreading, densely foliaged crown. Several trunks from thickened aerial roots. Flowers 3 in (8 cm) wide, pale pink with darker markings, in summer. Pale green fruit. Zones 11–12.

COCCOLOBA
A genus of about 150 mostly evergreen trees, shrubs, or vines in the knotweed (Polygonaceae) family from tropical and subtropical America, they have alternate, smooth-edged, leathery leaves, often quite large. The immature leaves are normally a different shape to the mature leaves. Spikes or racemes of small greenish white flowers are followed by a fleshy grape-like fruit, which is technically a small nut enclosed in the swollen floral remains.
CULTIVATION: Light or sandy well-drained soils are preferable, in an open sunny position, with ample watering, particularly in dry weather. Pruning is unnecessary except to maintain shape. Propagation is from seed, cuttings of ripe wood in spring, or of half-hardened wood in autumn, or by layering.

Coffea arabica

Coccoloba uvifera
JAMAICAN KING, PLATTER LEAF, SEA GRAPE
☼ ❦ ↔ 10 ft (3 m) ↑ 20 ft (6 m)
Native of tropical America. Erect, branching, evergreen tree. Leaves mid-green, leathery, heart-shaped, with reddish veins. Racemes of fragrant white flowers in summer, followed by edible fruit. Zones 10–12.

CODIAEUM
This genus belonging to the euphorbia (Euphorbiaceae) family consists of 6 species of evergreen perennials, shrubs, and small trees, native to tropical Asia and the western Pacific region. The leathery leaves are often variegated or marked and are the main ornamental attraction. Small, star-shaped, usually yellow flowers, carried in axillary racemes, appear in spring. They make good indoor plants.
CULTIVATION: They do best in fertile, well-drained, moist soil, but need to be fed and misted regularly throughout the growing season. In tropical areas they can be grown in shade. In cool climates, where they are grown under cover, they need maximum light but can suffer scorching in direct sunlight through glass. Propagate by air layering in spring or taking softwood cuttings in summer. Contact dermatitis may occur as a result of handling these plants.

Codiaeum variegatum 'Philip Geduldig'

Codiaeum variegatum
CROTON
☼/☀ ✦ ↔ 2–4 ft (0.6–1.2 m) ↑ 3–12 ft (0.9–3.5 m)
Native to tropical Asia and Australia. Small tree with numerous cultivars, varying quite widely in leaf color and pattern. Leaves may be smooth-edged, lobed, or twisted into a spiral, and are linear or egg-shaped, sometimes deeply cut to midrib, variegated red, white, and yellow on green. 'Elaine', stiff erect leaves; 'Grusonii', narrow greenish yellow leaves, flushed red on edges; 'Petra' ★, leaves variously colored yellow, green, and orange; 'Philip Geduldig', leaves turn rich orange to purple with pinkish veins. 'Evelyn Chilcot' and 'Lady Balfour' are also popular. Zones 11–12.

COFFEA
COFFEE
Renowned as the source of coffee beans, this tropical African and Asian genus in the madder (Rubiaceae) family includes some 40 species of evergreen shrubs and small trees. The species most often grown for commercial coffee production is *C. arabica*, though *C. canephora* is also popular. These are quite ornamental plants with lush deep green foliage. They bear clusters of attractive, white, fragrant flowers in the leaf axils. The flowers are followed by colorful berries, in which is found the coffee bean.
CULTIVATION: Coffee requires warm temperatures to crop well, but when grown as an ornamental it will survive in most frost-free gardens. It also adapts well to container cultivation and life as a house plant. The soil should be moist, humus enriched, and well drained. A position in light shade is best. Commercial crops are subject to attack by several pests and diseases, but these are seldom a problem in gardens. Propagate from seed, which should be fresh.

Coffea arabica ★
ARABIAN COFFEE
☀/☼ ❦ ↔ 10 ft (3 m) ↑ 10 ft (3 m)
Widely cultivated commercially, originally from Ethiopia. Large shrub or small tree. Lustrous, wavy-edged, glossy, deep green leaves. Clusters of small, fragrant, funnel-shaped, white flowers in autumn. Round berries ½ in (12 mm) in diameter, ripen to yellow, red, or purple. Zones 10–11.

COLEONEMA

All of these 8 species of evergreen shrubs in the rue (Rutaceae) family are native to South Africa, most of them confined to Western Cape Province. All have small heath-like leaves on fine twigs and small starry flowers in winter and spring, sometimes repeating in summer. The foliage is slightly aromatic. They make useful small hedges if pruned regularly after flowering when young and brought slowly to the required height. They are often referred to as *Diosma*, which is a separate but related genus.
CULTIVATION: A position in full sun is preferred, with a free-draining rather sandy soil. Avoid exposure to strong winds, as they tend to dislodge the surface roots and blow the plants over. These species are not recommended for cold climates. Seeds germinate freely, but may result in plants of uncertain flowering quality; soft-tip cuttings taken in late summer or autumn give true results.

Coleonema pulchellum
syn. *Coleonema pulchrum* of gardens
☼ ❆ ↔ 3–4 ft (0.9–1.2 m) ↑ 2–5 ft (0.6–1.5 m)
From South Africa. Well-foliaged shrub, slender branches. Soft, needle-like, aromatic leaves. Masses of tiny, starry, pink flowers in late winter–spring. Number of dwarf forms. 'Pinkie', compact, very floriferous, dark pink flowers, darker pink center stripes on petals; 'Sunset Gold' ★, pale yellow foliage intensifies to deep golden yellow in late summer–autumn if grown in semi-exposed position. Other cultivars include 'Compactum' and 'Nanum'. Zones 9–11.

COLLETIA
ANCHOR PLANT
This genus of 17 thorny shrubs in the buckthorn (Rhamnaceae) family, covered in spines and often with thickened and flattened branches, is native to temperate regions of South America. They are cultivated for their ornamental value, their spines making them particularly useful for boundary planting. Leaves are non-existent or very small and short-lived, while the small, scented, bell-shaped or tubular, usually yellowish or white flowers appear singly or in clusters, normally from summer to early autumn. The fruit is a leathery 3-lobed capsule.
CULTIVATION: They prefer light to medium, sandy, well-drained soil in a protected but sunny position. Propagation is from seed or from cuttings of half-hardened wood taken in autumn.

Colletia hystrix
syn. *Colletia armata*
☼ ❆ ↔ 10–15 ft (3–4.5 m) ↑ 10–15 ft (3–4.5 m)
Large prickly shrub from Chile and Argentina. Leaves tiny, inconspicuous, deciduous; gray-green, rounded, spine-tipped stems perform most photosynthesis. Produces tiny, scented, tubular, white flowers in late summer–autumn. Zones 8–11.

Colletia paradoxa
syn. *Colletia cruciata*
ANCHOR BUSH
☼ ❆ ↔ 8 ft (2.4 m) ↑ 6 ft (1.8 m)
Slow-growing deciduous shrub from Uruguay and southern Brazil. Flattened triangular spines instead of leaves. All parts bluish green. Fragrant yellowish white flowers in summer–early autumn. Zones 8–9.

COLUTEA

The 30-odd species of leguminous deciduous shrubs and small trees in this genus in the pea-flower subfamily of the legume (Fabaceae) family occur naturally in Africa and Europe eastward to Central Asia. They are wiry-stemmed, sometimes spiny, and have pinnate or trifoliate leaves, usually composed of very small leaflets. The small racemes of yellow to orange pea-like flowers appear from spring to autumn and are quite attractive. The pods become very inflated and balloon-like and may be colored, translucent, glossy, or hairy. They are worth growing as novelties; children love the pods because of the noise they make when burst by squeezing.
CULTIVATION: Most *Colutea* species are moderately to very frost hardy and grow in a wide range of soils with good drainage. They thrive in inland gardens and grow well near the coast. Plant in full sun for the best flower and pod production. Regular tip pinching and thinning will help to keep plants compact. Propagate from seed or from cuttings taken in summer.

Colutea arborescens
BLADDER SENNA
☼ ❆ ↔ 10 ft (3 m) ↑ 15 ft (4.5 m)
Native to southern Europe. Leaves 6 in (15 cm) long, 5 to 7 pairs of leaflets. Small yellow and orange-red flowers in late spring. Pods to 3 in (8 cm) long, bright green, developing red tints, translucent when mature. 'Bullata', compact form. Zones 5–10.

Coleonema pulchellum

Colletia paradoxa

Colutea arborescens

COMBRETUM

Widespread in the tropics, with the exception of Australia, this genus in the family Combretaceae consists of around 250 species of mainly evergreen and a few deciduous trees and shrubs, some of which are scrambling climbers. The paired leaves are usually a simple, pointed, oval to lance shape. The deciduous species, from South Africa, may have bright foliage in autumn. The flowers are small and may be petal-less, but are brightly colored and carried in racemes or panicles at the stem tips and in the leaf axils. Long-lasting 4- or 5-winged seed pods follow the flowers.

CULTIVATION: Primarily a genus of the seasonal rainfall tropics, most of these species prefer constantly warm conditions. Some of the South African species will tolerate light frosts provided the soil is dry in winter. Soil must be well-drained. Plant in full sun and propagate from seed or half-hardened cuttings.

Combretum kraussii

☼ ❄ ↔ 15 ft (4.5 m) ↑ 40 ft (12 m)

Deciduous tree from eastern South Africa. Leaves elliptical, dark glossy green, silvery white beneath. New leaves change color from green-white in spring to green-red by autumn. Creamy white flowers with new leaves in late winter–late spring. Zones 9–11.

COPROSMA

This genus belongs to the large family Rubiaceae. It comprises about 90 species of evergreen shrubs and small trees from Australia, New Zealand, and the Pacific region. There is a wide variation in habit from erect to creeping; leaves range from minute to large. Inconspicuous male and female flowers grow on separate plants. The berries on the female can give a pretty display in summer and autumn.

CULTIVATION: Adaptable plants tolerating a wide range of situations and soils, *Coprosma* species are usually best in full sun and well-drained conditions. Some are suited to harsh coastal conditions; others are useful for ground cover, hedging, and shelter. In cool-temperate climates they are barely hardy and require overwintering in the greenhouse. If a display of berries is required, male and female plants must be grown together. Propagation is from seed, which is best sown fresh, or from half-hardened cuttings taken in autumn.

Combretum kraussii

Coprosma 'Coppershine'

☼ ❄ ↔ 3–4 ft (0.9–1.2 m) ↑ 3–5 ft (0.9–1.5 m)

New Zealand raised hybrid. Compact shrub, densely foliaged, with small very glossy leaves, green with bronze overtones. Zones 8–10.

Coprosma × kirkii

☼ ❄ ↔ 7 ft (2 m) ↑ 3 ft (0.9 m)

May be natural hybrid between *C. acerosa* and *C. repens*. Variable plant, mounding or prostrate. Small, narrow, glossy leaves, inconspicuous flowers. Erratic crop of red-flecked, translucent, cream to white berries. Tolerates coastal gardens. '**Variegata**', popular cultivar with silvery, cream-edged, sage green leaves. Zones 9–10.

Coprosma repens 'Variegata'

Coprosma repens

MIRROR BUSH, TAUPATA

☼ ❄ ↔ 12 ft (3.5 m) ↑ 20 ft (6 m)

From New Zealand coastal areas. Very glossy, thick, dark green, oblong leaves. Berries orangey red. Excellent plant for warm coastal gardens. '**Marble Queen**' ★, leaves speckled white; '**Painter's Palette**', very glossy leaves of red, cream, yellow, green, and chocolate brown; '**Picturata**', glossy leaves variegated cream; '**Variegata**', cream-edged, shiny green leaves; '**Yvonne**', glossy dark green and chocolate brown leaves, intensifying color in winter. Zones 9–11.

Coprosma rugosa

☼ ❄ ↔ 6 ft (1.8 m) ↑ 6 ft (1.8 m)

From New Zealand. Reddish brown branches, needle-like leaves. Berries range from pale to dark blue. '**Clearwater Gold**', selected male form, attractive golden coloring. Zones 8–10.

CORDIA

This genus in the family Boraginaceae comprises about 300 deciduous or evergreen trees or shrubs that are native to tropical regions of Central and South America, Africa, and Asia. They have terminal flowerheads or spikes of bell-shaped or tubular white or orange flowers, and alternate simple leaves; the fruit is a drupe.

CULTIVATION: They like moist, well-drained, peaty soils, in an open sunny position. Pruning is not usually needed. Propagate in winter to spring from ripe seed, or from cuttings.

Cordia boissieri

TEXAS OLIVE

☼ ❄ ↔ 8 ft (2.4 m) ↑ 8 ft (2.4 m)

Found in Texas and New Mexico, USA, and nearby parts of Mexico. Evergreen shrub, with leaves elliptical to ovate, dull green on upper surface, downy on underside. Large, white, yellow-centered flowers in summer. Will not tolerate prolonged wet, cold conditions. Zones 8–11.

Cordyline australis, in the wild, New Zealand

CORDYLINE

This small group of about 15 species of erect, palm-like, evergreen shrubs in the family Ruscaceae is found in Australasia, the Pacific region, and one in tropical America. They are usually sparingly branched or suckering with fibrous stems tipped with a tuft of strap-like pointed leaves. Masses of small flowers with 6 spreading segments are produced in large panicles, followed by red, black, or whitish berry-like fruit.
CULTIVATION: In warmer areas grow in well-drained organically rich soil with regular water during the warmer months. Most prefer a protected partially shaded position, although *C. australis* will thrive in full sun. If multiple trunks and a clumping effect are required, cut the main stem at any height. Propagate from seed, stem cuttings, or by division.

Cordyline australis
syn. *Dracaena australis*
NEW ZEALAND CABBAGE TREE
☼/◐ ❄ ↔ 8 ft (2.4 m) ↕ 20 ft (6 m)
Erect palm-like tree from New Zealand. Usually an unbranched stem, developing broad crown of spreading, sword-like, pointed leaves. In late spring–summer, mature trees bear broad panicles of sweet-scented, creamy white, starry flowers. Clusters of white or bluish berries. 'Albertii', smaller variegated form; **Purpurea Group ★**, leaves suffused bronze to purple. Zones 8–11.

Cordyline fruticosa
syn. *Cordyline terminalis*
TI PLANT
◐ ☙ ↔ 4 ft (1.2 m) ↕ 10 ft (3 m)
From Southeast Asia, northern Australia, and many Pacific islands. Erect sparingly branched species, with thin-textured, distinctly stalked, lance-shaped leaves. White, mauve, or purplish flowers; clusters of bright red berries. 'Glauca', slender green leaves, blackish reverse, hint of purple on new growth, small starry flowers in spring. Colorful foliage forms include 'Kiwi' and 'Rubra'. Zones 10–12.

Cordyline fruticosa 'Kiwi'

Cordyline rubra
PALM LILY
◐ ☙ ↔ 3–7 ft (0.9–2 m) ↕ 10–15 ft (3–4.5 m)
From subtropical eastern Australia. Leaves 6–20 in (15–50 cm) long. Lilac flowers in summer, followed by scarlet-red berries. Zones 10–11.

Cordyline stricta ★
SLENDER PALM LILY
☼ ☙ ↔ 3 ft (0.9 m) ↕ 15 ft (4.5 m)
From subtropical forests of eastern Australia. Erect multi-stemmed clumps. Leaves narrow, drooping, toothed margins. Small purple or violet flowers in spring–summer. Glossy black berries. Zones 10–12.

CORNUS
DOGWOOD
There are about 65 species of deciduous and evergreen trees, shrubs, and herbs in this genus of the family Cornaceae, nearly all from eastern Asia, North America, and Europe. A few are ornamental, garden-grown for their autumn leaf color, colored winter stems, or their branches covered in blankets of "flowers," composed of large petals or wide decorative bracts surrounding small insignificant flowers. Other species are bractless. The simple oval leaves are usually opposite. The fleshy fruits have stones.
CULTIVATION: They need sun or part-shade, good drainage, and a fertile neutral to acid soil. Those grown for their winter stem color are best grown in full sun and cut back in early spring. Propagate the multi-stemmed species by layering of sucker growths, from hardwood cuttings taken in summer or autumn, or from seed cleaned and cold-stratified for at least 3 months. The large-bracted species can be raised from seed (also stratified), from half-hardened cuttings in summer, or by grafting.

Cornus alba
RED-BARKED DOGWOOD, TARTARIAN DOGWOOD
☼/◐ ❄ ↔ 10 ft (3 m) ↕ 10 ft (3 m)
Deciduous spreading shrub, native to eastern Asia. Forms dense thickets. Blood red young stems in winter. Dark green oval leaves, colorful autumn tones. Clusters of creamy flowers in late spring. Small, white, blue-tinted fruits. 'Argenteomarginata', cream- to white-edged leaves; 'Aurea', light greenish gold foliage; 'Gouchaltii', white and red variegations; 'Kesselringii', black-purple stems, red-and-purple autumn leaves; 'Sibirica' ★, glowing coral red stems; 'Sibirica Variegata', deep green leaves edged with creamy white. Zones 4–9.

Cornus capitata
BENTHAM'S CORNEL, HIMALAYAN DOGWOOD
☼/◐ ❄ ↔ 30 ft (9 m) ↕ 30 ft (9 m)
Bushy evergreen or semi-evergreen tree from China and Himalayas. Leathery, oval, gray-green leaves, paler underneath. Minute flowers, cream to lemon yellow sky-facing bracts in late spring–early summer. Pendent, rose to apricot, pink-tinted fruits. Zones 8–10.

Cornus controversa
GIANT DOGWOOD, TABLETOP DOGWOOD

☼ ❅ ↔ 50 ft (15 m) ↑ 60 ft (18 m)

Large deciduous tree native to Japan and China. Horizontally spreading branches, well-separated tiers. Oval pointed leaves, glossy dark green above, downy beneath, turn red and purple in autumn. White, upturned, flattish flowerheads. Fruits blue-black. Zones 5–8.

Cornus 'Eddie's White Wonder'
☼ ❅ ↔ 15 ft (4.5 m) ↑ 15 ft (4.5 m)

Hybrid between *C. florida* and *C. nuttallii*. Deciduous upright tree or shrub, pendulous outer branches. Large white flowers in spring. Autumn foliage brilliant orange, red, and purple. Zones 5–9.

Cornus florida
FLOWERING DOGWOOD

☼/◐ ❅ ↔ 25 ft (8 m) ↑ 30 ft (9 m)

Tree native to eastern and central USA. Leaves slightly twisted, oval, pointed, dark green, paler undersides; orange, red, yellow, and purple in autumn. Bracts white to pink in late spring–early summer. Berries red, persist through winter. Zones 5–9.

Cornus kousa
CHINESE DOGWOOD, JAPANESE FLOWERING DOGWOOD, KOUSA DOGWOOD

☼ ❅ ↔ 15 ft (4.5 m) ↑ 25 ft (8 m)

From Japan, China, and Korea. Deciduous. Glossy wavy-edged leaves, pointed oval, turn bronze-crimson in autumn. Profuse green flowers in summer. Creamy white bracts, edged red. Pink- or red-tinted fruits. *C. k.* var. *chinensis* ★, paler leaves. Zones 5–8.

Cornus mas
CORNELIAN CHERRY

☼ ❅ ↔ 20 ft (6 m) ↑ 25 ft (8 m)

Native to southern Europe. Short-stemmed leaves, oval, pointed, shiny, deeply veined, mid-green, turn reddish purple in autumn. Flowers yellow, on previous year's bare wood, from mid-winter to early spring. Kidney-shaped fruit. Zones 5–9.

Cornus nuttallii
CANADIAN DOGWOOD, MOUNTAIN DOGWOOD

☼ ❅ ↔ 40 ft (12 m) ↑ 60 ft (18 m)

From northwestern USA and adjacent Canada. Oval leaves, dark green, turn yellow and scarlet in autumn. Flowers small; large, flat, irregular, white bracts, flushed pink, in late spring–early autumn. Orange-red fruits. 'Gold Spot', yellow splotched leaves. Zones 7–9.

Cornus capitata

Corokia buddlejoides

Cornus controversa

Cornus sanguinea
BLOODWING DOGWOOD, COMMON DOGWOOD, EUROPEAN DOGWOOD

☼ ❅ ↔ 10 ft (3 m) ↑ 15 ft (4.5 m)

Deciduous shrub native to Europe. Red-green shoots. White scented flowers in loose clusters; blue-black fruit. Red-purple autumn foliage. 'Winter Beauty' ★, red shoots in winter. Zones 6–9.

COROKIA

This is a small genus of 4 evergreen shrubs in the family Grossulariaceae. Three are native to New Zealand; the fourth is a rare Australian species. The species are variable, but all bear small starry flowers in early summer, followed by orange, yellow, or red berries. CULTIVATION: These shrubs will grow in sun or part-shade and in soils with a reasonable level of fertility. The site should be well drained. *C. cotoneaster* tolerates dry conditions. Light pruning will maintain a compact shape. Propagate species from fresh seed, or from half-hardened spring cuttings, cultivars from cuttings only.

Corokia buddlejoides
KOROKIO

☼/◐ ❅ ↔ 7 ft (2 m) ↑ 10 ft (3 m)

From northern North Island of New Zealand. Erect slender habit. Leaves lance-shaped, leathery, olive green above, silvery gray below. Small yellow flowers. Berries bright red to almost black. Zones 8–10.

Corokia cotoneaster
WIRE NETTING BUSH

☼/◐ ❅ ↔ 10 ft (3 m) ↑ 10 ft (3 m)

From New Zealand. Tangled wiry branches, silvery when young. Sparse foliage. Starry yellow flowers. Red to yellow berries. Zones 8–11.

Corokia × virgata
☼ ❅ ↔ 6 ft (1.8 m) ↑ 6 ft (1.8 m)

Natural hybrid of *C. buddlejoides* and *C. cotoneaster*. Cultivars form well-branched shrubs, with different leaf colors, more showy displays of berries. 'Bronze King', bronze foliage; 'Frosted Chocolate', chocolate brown leaves; 'Red Wonder' ★ and 'Yellow Wonder', starry yellow flowers and red or yellow berries. Zones 8–10.

Correa, Hybrid Cultivar, 'Mannii'

Corylopsis spicata

CORREA

A member of the rue (Rutaceae) family, this is an Australian genus of 11 species, all of which hybridize readily. Handsome evergreen shrubs, *Correa* species respond well to cultivation. Most species flower from winter to spring. Some have bell-shaped flowers; others are tubular with protruding stamens.

CULTIVATION: Often found in cool, moist, shaded positions, some species are also able to tolerate coastal situations in full sun. They prefer friable, well-drained, fertile loams, and are not recommended for hot humid summer climates. Tip pruning immediately after flowering will improve plant form and density.

Correa alba

☼/◐ ❄ ↔ 6 ft (1.8 m) ↕ 3 ft (0.9 m)
From coastal southern Australia. Vigorous evergreen shrub. Leaves green, round, fragrant, furry undersurface. Small, white, starry flowers in winter–spring. Zones 8–10.

Correa backhouseana

☼ ❄ ↔ 6 ft (1.8 m) ↕ 6 ft (1.8 m)
Dense evergreen shrub from Tasmania, Australia. Leaves oval, dark green. Cream-green flowers with golden brown edges, in winter–spring. Zones 8–9.

Correa pulchella ★

☼/◐ ❄ ↔ 3 ft (0.9 m) ↕ 3 ft (0.9 m)
Small evergreen shrub from South Australia. Leaves smooth, elliptical to lance-shaped. Tubular red, salmon pink, or pink flowers in autumn–spring. Zones 8–10.

Correa reflexa

NATIVE FUCHSIA

☼/◐ ❄ ↔ 1–7 ft (0.3–2 m) ↕ 2–6 ft (0.6–1.8 m)
Tidy but variable shrub from Queensland and southern Australia. Leaves oval, narrow, or heart-shaped; smooth to hairy. Flowers tubular, pendulous, red with green or yellow tips, in spring. 'Fat Fred' ★, inflated red flowers with greenish yellow tips. Zones 8–10.

Correa Hybrid Cultivars

☼ ◐ ↔ 2–4 ft (0.6–1.2 m) ↕ 18 in–6 ft (45 cm–1.8 m)
Several cultivars and hybrids of uncertain origin have become popular with gardeners. Compact and heavy flowering. 'Dusky Bells' ★, deep dusky pink to soft red flowers; 'Ivory Bells', white to cream flowers; 'Mannii', long, tubular, red flowers; 'Marian's Marvel', pendulous clusters of pink flowers, green base. Zones 9–10.

CORYLOPSIS

Native to the eastern Himalayas, China, Taiwan, and Japan, this genus in the family Hamamelidaceae contains about 10 species of deciduous shrubs and small trees. The young branches are downy; the egg-shaped blunt-toothed leaves are light to dark green and appear in spring after the fragrant yellow flowers. The fruit, a woody capsule about ½ in (12 mm) wide, contains 2 shiny black seeds. CULTIVATION: All species prefer acid soil and need moist, fertile, well-drained woodland conditions. Propagate from freshly ripened seed in autumn, protected against winter frosts, or take softwood cuttings in summer.

Corylopsis sinensis ★

syn. *Corylopsis willmottiae*

CHINESE WINTER-HAZEL

☼ ❄ ↔ 15 ft (4.5 m) ↕ 15 ft (4.5 m)
Erect spreading shrub native to China. Oblong or slightly egg-shaped leaves, green above, blue-green below, to 5 in (12 cm) long. Pendent racemes of yellow flowers, velvety bracts, in mid-spring–early summer. *C. s.* var. *clavescens* f. *veitchiana* (syn. *C. veitchiana*), more upright, smooth leaf stems, broader pale lemon flowers. Zones 6–9.

Corylopsis spicata

SPIKE WINTER-HAZEL

☼ ❄ ↔ 10 ft (3 m) ↕ 6 ft (1.8 m)
Spreading shrub native to Japan. Egg-shaped tapering leaves, dark green above, grayish below. Pendent racemes of bright yellow flowers, red anthers, felted floral bracts, in spring. Zones 6–9.

Corymbia ficifolia

CORYMBIA

This newly named genus of 110 or more species of evergreen trees belongs to the myrtle (Myrtaceae) family. It contains many of the eucalypts (*Eucalyptus* species) traditionally known as bloodwoods and ghost gums. Many outstanding flowering species belong to this group, including the red-flowering gum *(C. ficifolia)*. They are grown for their fine straight trunks and attractive bark. The urn-shaped fruiting capsules are fairly large and often very ornamental. The genus occurs mostly across the northern half of Australia, as well as in temperate eastern Australia and southwest Western Australia. A few species occur in New Guinea.

CULTIVATION: Most species are fast growing and long lived, and many are grown as specimen plants. They are easy to grow provided the correct species is chosen for a given area. They prefer full sun; frost hardiness varies, as does the preference for moist

Corymbia citriodora

or dry conditions. Propagation is from seed, which germinates readily. Flower color may not always come true from seed.

Corymbia citriodora
syn. *Eucalyptus citriodora*
LEMON-SCENTED GUM
☼ ⚐ ↔ 35 ft (10 m) ↑ 100 ft (30 m)
Deciduous tree native to tropical Queensland, Australia. Slender straight trunk, smooth powdery white to gray bark. Long narrow leaves exude lemon fragrance. White flowers in summer–autumn. More southern *C. c.* subsp. *variegata* characterized by variegated foliage and lack of lemon scent. Zones 9–12.

Corymbia ficifolia
syn. *Eucalyptus ficifolia*
RED-FLOWERING GUM
☼ ⚐ ↔ 15 ft (4.5 m) ↑ 30 ft (9 m)
Native to southwestern corner of Western Australia. Large densely foliaged crown, short trunk, dark rough bark. Flowers scarlet, crimson, pink, or orange, in terminal clusters, in summer. Urn-shaped fruit to 1½ in (35 mm) long. Zones 9–10.

CORYNOCARPUS
The 4 species of this genus in the family Corynocarpaceae are tall, evergreen, forest trees. They are found on some western Pacific islands and in New Zealand and Australia. Their simple leathery leaves

are arranged alternately on the branches, and they bear tiny flowers in terminal panicles followed by smooth-skinned plum-like fruits.
CULTIVATION: The New Zealand species, *C. laevigata*, is the one that is usually seen in cultivation. It requires a warm site in a rich soil with adequate moisture, particularly when it is young. It should be propagated from seed, which is best sown fresh.

Corynocarpus laevigata
KARAKA
☼ ⚐ ↔ 25 ft (8 m) ↑ 50 ft (15 m)
Forest tree found on both islands of New Zealand. Densely foliaged. Leaves large, leathery, oblong, glossy, dark green. Oval orange fruits ripen in autumn. Kernels of fruits poisonous. Zones 9–11.

COTINUS
SMOKE BUSH
This genus contains 3 species of deciduous trees or shrubs found in North America and across southern Europe to central China. It belongs to the same family (Anacardiaceae) as *Rhus* and, like members of that genus, has been known to cause contact dermatitis. *Cotinus* are valuable garden plants, and have a long season of interest. In summer many tiny flowers are borne on long panicles, giving a hazy effect to the plant; hence the common name of smoke bush. In autumn their broadly oval leaves deepen in color to shades of red, yellow, and orange.
CULTIVATION: Smoke bushes will grow in a wide range of soils and climatic conditions but are best in a well-drained site in full sun. As with many trees from cool-temperate climates, richer autumn colors are achieved in areas where winters are cold. Prune to remove dead wood or to shorten long straggly branches. Propage from seed sown in autumn or from hardwood cuttings taken in late summer.

Cotinus coggygria
syn. *Rhus cotinus*
EURASIAN SMOKEBUSH, SMOKE BUSH, VENETIAN SUMACH
☼ ✳ ↔ 15 ft (4.5 m) ↑ 15 ft (4.5 m)
Rounded bush from southern Europe to central China. Broadly oval leaves. Numerous plume-like panicles, tiny bronze-pink flowers, fading to grayish purple in summer. 'Royal Purple' ★, dark red-purple leaves; 'Velvet Cloak', deep reddish purple leaves, turning entirely red in autumn. Zones 6–10.

Cotinus 'Grace'
☼ ✳ ↔ 15 ft (4.5 m) ↑ 20 ft (6 m)
Hybrid of *C. coggygria* 'Velvet Cloak' and *C. obovatus*. Reddish purple leaves, flower plumes grayish, enhancing hazy smoke-like effect. Zones 5–10.

Cotinus obovatus
syns *Cotinus americanus, C. cotinoides, Rhus cotinoides*
AMERICAN SMOKE TREE, CHITTAMWOOD
☼ ✳ ↔ 20 ft (6 m) ↑ 30 ft (9 m)
Native to central and southern USA. Foliage colors brilliantly in autumn. Similar to *C. coggygria*. Tree-like, broad conical form. Zones 5–10.

Cotinus 'Grace'

COTONEASTER

From the rose (Rosaceae) family, a genus of about 200 species of evergreen, semi-evergreen, or deciduous shrubs and trees from the northern temperate areas. Leaves are rounded to lance-shaped, simple, smooth-edged, and arranged alternately. Small flowers are white, sometimes flushed pink or red, with 5 petals, and are borne singly or in cymes. They are followed by red-black or red fruits with rather dry flesh and 2 to 5 nutlets. Grown for their profuse flowers and fruit, they can also be used as hedging plants and as attractive specimens.
CULTIVATION: Cotoneasters grow well in moderately fertile well-drained soil. Dwarf evergreens and deciduous plants fruit better in full sun, while taller evergreens grow well in part-shade. In exposed situations they may need protection from cold drying winds. Propagate by taking half-hardened cuttings of evergreen species in late summer, and of deciduous species in early summer.

Cotoneaster dammeri

syn. *Cotoneaster humifusus*

☼ ❈ ↔ 6 ft (1.8 m) ↕ 8 in (20 cm)

Prostrate evergreen shrub native to Hubei region of China. Leaves shiny green, oblong, strongly veined. White flowers, solitary or grouped in cymes, in early summer, followed by scarlet fruit in autumn. Zones 5–10.

Cotoneaster franchetii

☼ ❈ ↔ 10 ft (3 m) ↕ 10 ft (3 m)

Evergreen, sometimes semi-evergreen, erect shrub native to western China. Lustrous, bright green, oval leaves with felty undersides. Generous cymes of pink-tinted white flowers in summer. Egg-shaped orange-red fruit. Zones 6–10.

Cotoneaster frigidus

HIMALAYAN TREE COTONEASTER

☼ ❈ ↔ 30 ft (9 m) ↕ 30 ft (9 m)

Deciduous large shrub or small tree native to Himalayas. Peeling bark. Egg-shaped dull green leaves, wavy edges. Sprays of profuse white flowers in summer. Red fruit. 'Cornubia' (syn. *C.* × *watereri* 'Cornubia'), dark green lance-shaped leaves turn rich bronze in winter; 'Fructu Luteo', creamy yellow fruit; 'Notcutt's Variety', large dark green leaves. Zones 6–9.

Cotoneaster horizontalis

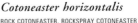

ROCK COTONEASTER, ROCKSPRAY COTONEASTER

☼ ❈ ↔ 5 ft (1.5 m) ↕ 3 ft (0.9 m)

From western China. Deciduous, herringbone-like branching. Elliptical to rounded tiny leaves, dark green, glossy, color in autumn. Flesh pink flowers in late spring. Scarlet fruit. Zones 4–9.

Cotoneaster lacteus

syn. *Cotoneaster parneyi*

☼ ❈ ↔ 12 ft (3.5 m) ↕ 12 ft (3.5 m)

Evergreen shrub from China. Arching branches. Leathery oval leaves, dark green above, felty beneath, deep veins. Creamy white flowers in summer. Red fruit persist in winter. Zones 6–11.

Cotoneaster microphyllus

☼ ❈ ↔ 3 ft (0.9 m) ↕ 3 ft (0.9 m)

Native to Himalayas. Prostrate evergreen shrub, dense mound. Thick leaves, egg-shaped, glossy deep green, hairy coating beneath when young. Tiny white flowers in spring–summer. Crimson fruit. Zones 5–10.

Cotoneaster salicifolius

syn. *Cotoneaster floccosus* of gardens

☼ ❈ ↔ 15 ft (4.5 m) ↕ 15 ft (4.5 m)

Naturally occurring in China. Variable species with slim, grace-ful, bowed branches. Lance-shaped deeply veined leaves, pointed, white felty undersides. Large corymbs in summer. Round, red, persistent fruit. 'Exburyensis', white flowers in early summer, fol-lowed by pinkish yellow fruit in winter; 'Herbstfeuer' (syn. 'Autumn Fire'), low spreading habit, red fruit; 'Repens', prostrate form; 'Rothschildianus' (syn. *C.* × *watereri* 'Rothschildianus'), vigorous, evergreen, spreading shrub, clusters of white flowers in summer, followed by lemon yellow fruit. Zones 6–10.

Cotoneaster simonsii

☼ ❈ ↔ 6 ft (1.8 m) ↕ 8 ft (2.4 m)

Deciduous or semi-evergreen shrub found naturally in northern India and eastern Himalayas. Egg-shaped deep green leaves, paler with bristly hair on undersurfaces. Pink-tinged white flowers, single or in cymes, borne throughout summer. Orange-red fruit follow flowers. Zones 5–9.

Cotoneaster franchetii

Cotoneaster horizontalis

Cotoneaster lacteus

Cotoneaster × watereri

☼ ❀ ↔ 15 ft (4.5 m) ↕ 15 ft (4.5 m)

Of garden origin, 3-way cross between *C. frigidus, C. salicifolius,* and *C. rugosus.* Evergreen shrub or small tree, bowed branches. Leaves egg-shaped, dark green, veined upper surface, felty underside. White flowers in cymes in summer. Round, red, persistent fruit. '**John Waterer**', original clone with numerous cultivars. Zones 6–10.

COUROUPITA

From the jungles of tropical South America comes this genus of 4 species of large evergreen trees belonging to the brazilnut (Lecythidaceae) family. Although these trees are fairly rare in cultivation, one species—the cannonball tree, *C. guianensis*—is grown in tropical gardens and parks for its spectacular and remarkable fruits, which emerge and dangle on long stems directly from the tree trunk. The pincushion-like flowers are large and complex in structure, usually with 6 fleshy petals.

CULTIVATION: In subtropical and tropical areas *Couroupita* species are grown in well-drained organically rich soil in a sunny position. Propagation is from seed.

Couroupita guianensis

CANNONBALL TREE

☼ ✦ ↔ 15 ft (4.5 m) ↕ 100 ft (30 m)

Evergreen tree from tropical South America. Rosettes of large elliptical leaves at branch tips. Large flowers, 6 in (15 cm) across, on long drooping branches that emerge directly from trunk, with red spreading petals and hundreds of yellow stamens. Brownish ball-like capsules mature to red pulp; they have disagreeable odor. Zones 11–12.

Couroupita guianensis

CRATAEGUS

HAWTHORN

This genus within the rose (Rosaceae) family contains around 200 species from temperate Eurasia and North America. Most are large thorny shrubs or small trees. The deep green leaves are alternate, simple or lobed, and some are toothed. The white to pink flowers, carried singly or in corymbs, have 5 sepals and/or petals. Nutlets with a fleshy edible covering follow the flowers. These fruit can be black, yellow, or bluish green, but the majority are red. *C. laevigata* and *C. monogyna* have both been used as hedging plants for centuries.

CULTIVATION: Grow species in sun or partial shade in any soil. Bud cultivars in summer or graft them in winter. Sow seed when ripe in a position that is protected from winter frosts. Germination may take up to 18 months.

Crataegus 'Autumn Glory'

☼ ❀ ↔ 10 ft (3 m) ↕ 10 ft (3 m)

Possible hybrid of *C. laevigata.* Deciduous shrub. Glossy leaves with 3 to 5 rounded blunt-toothed lobes. Produces clusters of large white flowers in early summer, followed by oval red fruit in autumn, persisting into winter. Zones 5–10.

Crataegus crus-galli

Crataegus crus-galli

COCKSPUR THORN

☼ ❀ ↔ 35 ft (10 m) ↕ 30 ft (9 m)

Native to eastern USA. Small flat-topped tree with long curved thorns. Shiny, dark green, egg-shaped leaves. Foliage turns red in autumn. Large corymbs of small white flowers in spring. Deep red fruit persist throughout winter. *C. c.* var. *salicifolia,* narrow leaves. Zones 5–9.

Crataegus laciniata

syn. *Crataegus orientalis*

☼ ❀ ↔ 20 ft (6 m) ↕ 20 ft (6 m)

Thorny shrub or tree native to southeastern Europe and western Asia. Leaves deeply lobed, dark green, to 2 in (5 cm) long, with covering of silvery white hairs. Clusters of white flowers in summer, followed by large red fruit. Zones 6–9.

Crataegus laevigata

syn. *Crataegus oxyacantha* of gardens

ENGLISH HAWTHORN, MAY, WHITE THORN

☼ ❀ ↔ 25 ft (8 m) ↕ 25 ft (8 m)

Thorny tree native to most of Europe and far northwest of Africa. Leaves egg-shaped, glossy mid-green, lobed, toothed, paler green undersides. White or pink flowers in corymbs in spring, followed by red fruit. Often grown as hedge. '**Paul's Scarlet**' ★, double deep pink flowers; '**Plena**,' double white flowers, becoming pink-tinged with age; '**Rosea Flore Pleno**', double pink flowers. Zones 5–9.

Crataegus × lavalleei

syn. *Crataegus carrierei*

LAVALLEE HAWTHORN

☼ ❀ ↔ 20 ft (6 m) ↕ 20 ft (6 m)

Of garden origin, from France. Cross between *C. crus-galli* and *C. pubescens.* Semi-evergreen in warmer climates. Leaves elliptical to oval in shape, toothed, glossy green; develop good autumn color. White flowers, red stamens, in early summer. Long-lasting red fruit. Zones 6–10.

Crataegus monogyna
HAWTHORN, MAY, QUICKTHORN
☼ ❋ ↔ 25 ft (8 m) ↕ 25 ft (8 m)
Native to Europe. Leaves broadly egg-shaped, dark green upper surface, paler green downy underside. Small clusters of white flowers, pink-tinged. Dark red, single-seeded fruit. '**Biflora**', Glastonbury thorn, flowers in mid-winter, second time in spring; '**Stricta**', columnar habit, spreads to 12 ft (3.5 m). Zones 4–9.

Crataegus persimilis 'Prunifolia'
syn. *Crataegus × prunifolia*
☼ ❋ ↔ 25 ft (8 m) ↕ 20 ft (6 m)
Large deciduous shrub or small tree. Dense foliage, thorny branches. Serrated-edged oval leaves to 3 in (8 cm) long, bright red tones in autumn. Flowers white, pink anthers, in corymbs. Red fruit. '**Prunifolia Splendens**', larger leaves and flower clusters. Zones 5–9.

Crataegus phaenopyrum
syn. *Crataegus cordata*
WASHINGTON HAWTHORN
☼ ❋ ↔ 30 ft (9 m) ↕ 30 ft (9 m)
Thorny tree from southeast USA. Leaves sharply toothed, broadly egg-shaped, lobed, shiny green, autumn color. White flowers in summer; red fruit in spring. '**Fastigiata**', narrow, upright. Zones 5–10.

Crataegus punctata
DOTTED HAWTHORN
☼ ❋ ↔ 30 ft (9 m) ↕ 30 ft (9 m)
Thorny tree native to eastern USA. Broadly egg-shaped, dark green leaves, toothed, downy underside. White flowers, pale pink anthers, in hairy corymbs. Red fruit with pale speckles. '**Ohio Pioneer**' ★, brick red fruit. Zones 4–9.

CRESCENTIA
This genus in the trumpet-vine (Bignoniaceae) family has 6 species of evergreen trees and vines. They are found in the Americas from Mexico to Brazil, including the West Indies. They have simple oval to paddle-shaped or trifoliate leaves and tubular flowers with widely flared lobes, usually in shades of yellow to tan. The bat-pollinated flowers grow straight out of the branches, rather than forming in the leaf axils or stem tips. The spherical to ovoid fruit can be very large, with a hard woody shell and a pulpy flesh. CULTIVATION: These plants demand a warm, humid, tropical climate with ample moisture during the fruiting period. They thrive in moist, humus-enriched, well-drained soil in full sun or partial shade, but will tolerate drought. Pruning or trimming is seldom necessary. Propagate from seed or half-hardened cuttings.

Crescentia cujete
CALABASH TREE
☼/◐ ☀ ↔ 20 ft (6 m) ↕ 30 ft (9 m)
Found in Mexico and Central America. Paddle-shaped, deep green leaves to 10 in (25 cm) long. Flowers single, on old wood, light

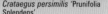
Crataegus persimilis 'Prunifolia Splendens'

Crescentia cujete

yellow-brown, purple interior. Yellow-green fruit, to 12 in (30 cm) long, tough shell, often hollowed and used as gourd. Zones 11–12.

CROWEA
This small Australian genus in the rue (Rutaceae) family is closely related to the genus *Eriostemon*. Of its 3 evergreen shrubs, the 2 species from southeastern Australia are the showiest and are the parents of several cultivars. These small rounded shrubs have linear gray-green leaves and star-shaped flowers in white or shades of pink. CULTIVATION: *Crowea* species grow naturally as understory shrubs in light dappled shade, but can withstand full sun provided they are planted in reasonably moist, well-drained, open soil with a mulch of leaf litter or similar organic matter. A light tip prune after flowering will ensure compact growth.

Cryptomeria japonica 'Nana'

Crowea exalata ★
◐ ⚘ ↔ 12–60 in (30–150 cm) ↕ 18–36 in (45–90 cm)
Extended flowering period, from spring into winter. Starry 5-petalled flowers, white to deep pink. Many forms selected, hybrids bred for cultivation, including prostrate or low spreading varieties. Zones 9–10.

Crowea saligna
◐ ⚘ ↔ 3 ft (0.9 m) ↕ 3 ft (0.9 m)
Rounded shrub. Leaves small, linear, slightly recurved margins, prominent midrib. Flowers star-like, pink, to 1½ in (35 mm) across, in autumn–winter. Good cut flower. Zones 9–10.

CRYPTOMERIA
This single-species genus belonging to the cypress (Cupressaceae) family has numerous attractive cultivars, which are also prized as garden plants. An evergreen species from Japan and China, it is a densely clothed conifer with reddish brown fibrous bark and a straight trunk that forms buttresses as it matures. The pollen-bearing male cones, held in clusters at the tips of the branches, release their pollen in spring, while the persistent female seed-bearing cones, held further along the branches, can take up to 10 months to ripen.

CULTIVATION: This long-lived species prefers deep, moist, rich soil in a full-sun position. It can be propagated from fresh seed, but cultivars need to be grown from cuttings.

Cryptomeria japonica
JAPANESE CEDAR, SUGI

☼ ❄ ↔ 20 ft (6 m) ↑ 90 ft (27 m)

Narrow, conical shape. Dense adult foliage in forward-growing spirals. Branches tiered, outer branchlets slightly pendulous. 'Compressa', dwarf form with purple-brown winter foliage; 'Elegans' ★, purplish winter foliage; 'Nana', low growing; 'Yoshino', to 50 ft (15 m) high. Zones 7–11.

CUNNINGHAMIA
This genus belonging to the cypress (Cupressaceae) family includes just 2 species, one from central China, the other from Taiwan. They are evergreen conifers that can grow to 150 ft (45 m) tall, though they seldom reach that height in cultivation. The narrow leaves are flattened and sharply pointed, deep green above but with bluish white bands on the undersides, and arranged in double rows along the branchlets. The bark is fibrous and red-brown.
CULTIVATION: Both species are rather frost tender for conifers, *C. lanceolata* being the hardier. They are not fussy about soil type as long as it is reasonably fertile and the drainage is good. Young plants will tolerate light shade and eventually grow to see the sun. Propagate from seed or cuttings.

Cunninghamia lanceolata

Cunninghamia lanceolata
CHINA FIR, CHINESE CEDAR

☼ ❄ ↔ 20 ft (6 m) ↑ 70 ft (21 m)

From central to southern China. Spirally arranged deep green leaves, to 3 in (8 cm) long. Cones sticky while green, to 1½ in (35 mm) in diameter, at branch tips. 'Glauca' ★, blue-tinted foliage. Zones 7–10.

CUNONIA
This genus of the family Cunoniaceae contains 15 species of evergreen shrubs and trees from New Caledonia, and one species in South Africa. They have lustrous, deep green, pinnate leaves in opposite pairs, with striking spoon-shaped stipules sheathing the growing tips. The bottlebrush-like racemes of fragrant white to cream or red flowers can turn an unsightly brown as they die, and are best removed at this time.
CULTIVATION: Although most species are frost tender, they are not difficult to grow. They prefer moist, fertile, well-drained soil and a position in full sun. If necessary they will tolerate poor soil and, once established, can withstand considerable periods of drought. Prune young plants to a single trunk to make

them tree-like; otherwise, a light trim after flowering will keep them compact. Propagate from seed or half-hardened tip cuttings.

Cunonia capensis
BUTTERKNIFE BUSH, SPOON BUSH

☼ ❧ ↔ 15 ft (4.5 m) ↑ 50 ft (15 m)

South African species. Often large shrub. Foliage deep green, bronze-tipped new growth, pinnate leaves of 5 to 7 leaflets, each up to 4 in (10 cm) long. Racemes of cream flowers in late summer–autumn. Zones 9–11.

CUPANIOPSIS
From Australia, New Guinea, and some Pacific islands, this genus in the soapberry (Sapindaceae) family consists of some 60 species of tropical and subtropical evergreen trees. All have divided leathery leaves, small yellow or greenish flower clusters on the branch ends, and fruit capsules that split into 3 compartments, each with a large seed and a bright fleshy attachment.
CULTIVATION: Many species adapt to difficult sites with poor soils and polluted air. Training to a single stem and early removal of side shoots is desirable. Summer mulching is useful, especially on sandy soils. Regular application of fertilizer promotes vigorous growth. Propagate from fresh seed.

Cupaniopsis anacardioides
TUCKEROO

☼ ❧ ↔ 15–30 ft (4.5–9 m) ↑ 50 ft (15 m)

Occurs along eastern and northern coasts of Australia. Leathery, shiny, divided leaves. Large clusters of small yellow flowers. In summer, yellow-orange, 3-part, capsular fruit ripen. Regarded as threatening weed in Florida, USA. Zones 9–11.

Cunonia capensis

CUPHEA

This large genus in the loosestrife (Lythraceae) family consists of about 250 species of annuals, evergreen perennials, and low-growing shrubs from Central and South America. They have flexible leafy stems and small opposite or whorled leaves. They are grown for their masses of irregularly shaped tubular flowers, produced over a long period—almost the whole year.
CULTIVATION: Species are fairly frost tender, but in warm climates they are easy to grow in average garden conditions. They do best in full sun or light shade, in well-drained moist soil, with protection from strong winds. Occasional tip pruning from an early age will encourage compact growth. Propagate from seed or from tip cuttings.

Cuphea hyssopifolia

FALSE HEATHER, MEXICAN HEATHER
☼ ⁑ ↔ 15 in (38 cm) ↕ 18 in (45 cm)
Small rounded shrub native to Mexico and Guatemala. Small, dark green, narrow, pointed leaves, on thin stems with soft hairs. Purplish pink or white 6-petalled flowers, in small axillary racemes, in late spring–summer. Can be invasive. Zones 9–12.

Cuphea ignea

CIGAR FLOWER, CIGARETTE PLANT, FIRECRACKER PLANT
☼ ⁑ ↔ 30 in (75 cm) ↕ 24 in (60 cm)
Bushy subshrub from Mexico and Jamaica. Leaves bright green, oval, pointed. Thin, orange-red, tubular flowers, tipped white, touch of black, almost year-round, peak in late spring–autumn. Zones 10–12.

Cuphea micropetala

☼ ⁑ ↔ 30 in (75 cm) ↕ 30 in (75 cm)
Rounded shrub from Mexico. Bright green lance-shaped leaves. Terminal racemes of narrow tubular flowers, golden yellow to orange-red, tipped with greenish yellow, in summer–autumn. Zones 9–11.

Cuphea × purpurea

☼ ⁑ ↔ 18 in (45 cm) ↕ 18 in (45 cm)
Bushy subshrub, garden hybrid of *C. llavea* and *C. procumbens*. Dark green, lance-shaped, pointed leaves. Narrow, tubular, deep pink to purplish red flowers, in late spring–autumn. Zones 9–11.

CUPRESSUS

CYPRESS
Originating in the warmer temperate regions of the Northern Hemisphere, this genus in the cypress (Cupressaceae) family comprises about 13 species of evergreen coniferous trees or shrubs. They are cultivated in mild climates for their dense compact crowns and bold symmetrical outlines. The tiny, scale-like, closely overlapping leaves vary in character and color; they may be soft to the touch or rather coarse, and are often aromatic. The small female cones have woody scales, are rarely over 1¾ in (4 cm) long, and are persistent.
CULTIVATION: These plants grow well in any well-drained fertile soil, preferably in full sun. Place each in a well-spaced position to enable it to develop its symmetrical shape and to avoid fungal disease. Propagate from seed in spring or from cuttings in late summer.

Cupressus arizonica

ARIZONA CYPRESS
☼ ❄ ↔ 15 ft (4.5 m) ↕ 40 ft (12 m)
Evergreen conifer from Arizona, USA, and Mexico. Densely conical at first, becomes broadly columnar. Bark gray-brown and stringy. Blue-green foliage, white markings beneath. Cones up to 1 in (25 mm) in diameter. Drought tolerant. *C. a.* var. *glabra*, smooth bark; 'Blue Ice' ★, silvery blue foliage. *C. a.* var. *stephensonii*, smooth, reddish, peeling bark, blue-green foliage. Zones 7–9.

Cupressus cashmeriana

BHUTAN CYPRESS, KASHMIR CYPRESS
☼ ⁑ ↔ 20 ft (6 m) ↕ 30 ft (9 m)
From Bhutan. Narrowly conical habit, ascending branches, long pendulous sprays of aromatic blue-gray branchlets. Unstable, prone to wind damage. Prefers warm sheltered site, regular moisture. *C. c.* var. *darjeelingensis*, soft silvery green foliage. Zones 9–11.

Cupressus funebris

syn. *Chamaecyparis funebris*
CHINESE WEEPING CYPRESS, COFFIN CYPRESS
☼ ❄ ↔ 25–30 ft (8–9 m) ↕ 70–80 ft (21–24 m)
Conical tree from China, timber used to make coffins. Gray-green foliage, pendulous branchlets, shoots all in one plane. Zones 8–10.

Cuphea micropetala

Cupressus cashmeriana var. *darjeelingensis*

Cupressus sempervirens 'Swane's Gold'

Cupressus lusitanica

CEDAR OF GOA, MEXICAN CYPRESS

☼ ❄ ↔ 20 ft (6 m) ↑ 40 ft (12 m)

From mountains of western Mexico. Vigorous conifer with spreading habit. Red-brown bark, peeling in strips. Broad crown of pendulous deep green foliage. Good tree for windbreaks. Cones round, blue-gray. '**Brice's Weeping**', attractive cultivar with weeping branches. Zones 8–10.

Cupressus macrocarpa

MONTEREY CYPRESS

☼ ❄ ↔ 35 ft (10 m) ↑ 100 ft (30 m)

Fast-growing evergreen conifer from Monterey, California, USA. Rare in wild. Spreading open habit. Thick red to brown or gray bark. Leaves small, scaly, yellowish green, aromatic. Tolerates strong winds and salt-laden air. '**Brunniana Aurea**', upright conical tree, golden foliage, lemon verbena scent; '**Coneybearii Aurea**', fine, drooping, golden leaves; '**Donard Gold**', upright, conical tree, gold-tipped leaves; '**Greenstead Magnificent**', dense, low, almost prostrate mound of blue-gray foliage becomes even bluer in shade; '**Horizontalis**', large horizontally spreading tree, grown for hedging, especially gold form '**Horizontalis Aurea**'. Zones 7–9.

Cupressus sempervirens

MEDITERRANEAN CYPRESS, PENCIL PINE

☼ ❄ ↔ 15 ft (4.5 m) ↑ 50 ft (15 m)

From Mediterranean region and southern Europe. Strongly upright habit. Fast growing when young, forming attractive spires of dark green. Persistent cones shining green, ripening red-brown to dull gray with age. **Stricta Group**, very narrow form; '**Swane's Gold**' ★, Australian cultivar, golden foliage. Zones 8–10.

Cupressus torulosa

BHUTAN CYPRESS, HIMALAYAN CYPRESS

☼ ❄ ↔ 15 ft (4.5 m) ↑ 60 ft (18 m)

From below 9,000 ft (2,700 m) in Himalayas. Strongly upright conical habit, broadly spreading at base in cool climates, narrower in warm areas. Cones small, purplish, marble-like. Suited for windbreak. '**Nana**', dwarf form, bright green foliage. Zones 8–9.

× *CUPROCYPARIS*

This group of hybrids between *Xanthocyparis* and *Cupressus* within the cypress (Cupressaceae) family are fast-growing, evergreen, coniferous trees. Fine dark green branchlets are arranged in flattened sprays. Egg-shaped male cones are yellow, the round female cones at first green, turning brown as they ripen. The crosses were made in the late nineteenth century, and 5 of the 6 have been named. They are probably the most frequently planted shelter belt trees in Britain and northern Europe, and will grow to a height of 70 ft (21 m) or so over a period of 25 years.
CULTIVATION: They are best grown in deeply dug, fertile, well-drained soil in full sun, but can be grown in partial shade. As hedging,

Cussonia spicata

trim back early in establishment, ideally 2 or 3 times a year. Propagate by taking cuttings in late summer from half-hardened wood.

× *Cuprocyparis leylandii*

syns × *Cupressocyparis leylandii*, *Cupressus leylandii*

☼ ❄ ↔ 15 ft (4.5 m) ↑ 120 ft (36 m)

Cross between *Cupressus macrocarpa* and *Xanthocyparis nootkatensis* features flattened, slightly drooping sprays of dark green leaves with gray sheen. '**Castlewellan**' ★ (syn. 'Galway Gold'), young foliage golden yellow, bronze-green with age; '**Harlequin**' (syn. 'Variegata'), creamy white variegations on leaves; '**Naylor's Blue**,' blue-gray foliage; '**Stapehill**', dense columnar tree. Zones 5–10.

CUSSONIA

Found in tropical and southern Africa and the Comoros Islands, this genus in the ivy (Araliaceae) family has 20 species of evergreen and deciduous shrubs and trees. They are characterized by large snowflake-shaped compound leaves, in spiral rosettes at the branch tips. They produce large candelabra-like heads of small white to yellow blooms and small, soft, red to black drupes.
CULTIVATION: Most species need a warm frost-free climate and ample moisture in summer. Plant in a sheltered position in full sun in moist well-drained soil. *Cussonia* species also grow well in containers, but can be very top-heavy, and are inclined to tip over. Propagate from seed.

Cussonia spicata

COMMON CABBAGE TREE

☼ ❄ ↔ 12 ft (3.5 m) ↑ 30 ft (9 m)

Native to southern and eastern Africa and Comoros Islands. Widely grown species. Thickened rather succulent trunk, develops multiple trunks with age. Much-divided leaves, carried on heavy stems. Large flowerheads in spring–summer. Zones 9–11.

× *Cuprocyparis leylandii*

CYTISUS

BROOM

This genus of about 50 species from the pea-flower subfamily of the legume (Fabaceae) family consists of mainly evergreen shrubs. They are native to Europe, with a few in western Asia and North Africa. All *Cytisus* species have typical pea-flowers; the main flowering season is late spring or summer. The plant's broom-like twiggy growths are sometimes almost leafless. The fruit is a flattened legume with small hard-coated seeds.

CULTIVATION: Brooms need a free-draining soil that is slightly acidic and fairly low in fertility. A sunny position gives the best flowers. Spent flowers and shoots should be removed after flowering, plus some of the older shoots, to encourage new growth from the base. The typical arching habit of the plant should be maintained. Most *Cytisus* species can be propagated from short-tip cuttings of ripened current year's growth, taken in late autumn or early winter.

Cytisus ardoinoi

☀ ❋ ↔ 10–24 in (25–60 cm) ↕ 10–24 in (25–60 cm)
Native to maritime Alps in southern France. Low, mat-forming, alpine shrub, arching stems, leaves deciduous, trifoliate. Bright yellow flowers in leaf axils in spring–summer. Zones 6–9.

Cytisus × kewensis

☀ ❋ ↔ 5 ft (1.5 m) ↕ 18 in (45 cm)
Hybrid between *C. ardoinoi* and *C. multiflorus*. Semi-prostrate habit, trailing stems. Masses of creamy yellow flowers in early summer. Zones 6–9.

Cytisus multiflorus

syn. *Cytisus albus*
PORTUGUESE BROOM, WHITE SPANISH BROOM
☀ ❋ ↔ 8 ft (2.4 m) ↕ 10 ft (3 m)
Erect shrub native to Spain, Portugal, and parts of North Africa. Leaves simple, narrow in upper part of plant, trifoliate lower down. Clusters of white flowers in early to mid-summer. Zones 6–10.

Cytisus × kewensis

Cytisus × praecox

☀ ❋ ↔ 5 ft (1.5 m) ↕ 5 ft (1.5 m)
Group of hybrids between *C. multiflorus* and *C. purgans*. Compact habit, profusion of flowers. 'Albus', white flowers; 'Warminster', to 5 ft (1.5 m) tall, deciduous, stems arching outward, flowers held in long sprays on outer stems, heavily perfumed. Zones 6–9.

Cytisus scoparius

COMMON BROOM, SCOTCH BROOM
☀ ❋ ↔ 7 ft (2 m) ↕ 7 ft (2 m)
Medium-sized shrub. Almost leafless. Golden yellow flowers, mostly solitary, in upper leaf axils in early summer. Brownish streaks on standards, keels yellow, anthers orange-red. Can be invasive. 'Cornish Cream', creamy white flowers. Zones 5–9.

Cytisus Hybrid Cultivars

☀ ❋ ↔ 3–6 ft (0.9–1.8 m) ↕ 3–8 ft (0.9–2.4 m)
Usually originating from *C. × praecox* or *C. scoparius*. Many sizes and flower colors. 'Boskoop Ruby', small rounded shrub, abundant red flowers; 'Burkwoodii' ★, vigorous, pink flowers, crimson wings yellow-edged; 'Firefly', yellow standards, wings stained bronze; 'Fulgens', late flowering, orange-yellow flowers, deep crimson wings; 'Hollandia', cream flowers, backs of standards and wings pink, late spring–mid-summer; 'Lena', compact free-flowering shrub, red standards, red wings yellow-edged, pale yellow keels; 'Luna', creamy yellow red-tinted flowers, wings yellow, keels lemon yellow; 'Minstead', mauve-tinged white flowers, wings flushed deeper mauve; 'Porlock', racemes of fragrant creamy yellow flowers in spring. Zones 5–9.

DABOECIA

There is only 1 species of evergreen, low-growing, spreading shrub in this genus within the heath (Ericaceae) family. Native to western Europe and the Azores, its habitat covers heathland from coastal cliffs to mountains. The roughly ovate leaves are green on the upper surface and silver on the underside. The small urn-shaped flowers are carried in racemes clear of the foliage.

CULTIVATION: Plants grow well in full sun in lime-free or neutral soil; some cultivars tolerate part-shade. Cut back after flowering. If grown indoors, feed and water freely during the growing season; these plants need good light but in direct sun young growth can be scorched. Propagate by sowing seed in spring or take half-hardened cuttings, especially of cultivars, in summer.

Daboecia cantabrica

syn. *Daboecia polifolia*
ST DABEOC'S HEATH
☀ ❋ ↔ 26 in (65 cm) ↕ 15 in (38 cm)
Native to western Europe. Variable habit, erect to very prostrate and straggling. Narrowly elliptic leaves, dark green, shiny. Flowers pale to pinkish violet in mid-summer–mid-autumn. *D. c.* subsp. *azorica* (syn. *D. azorica*), from Azores, flowers pale to deep ruby red, not frost tolerant. *D. c.* subsp. *scotica*, compact, flowers white to pink and crimson; 'Jack Drake', rich red flowers; 'Silverwells',

Daboecia cantabrica

Dacrydium cupressinum, in the wild, New Zealand

white flowers, light green foliage; '**William Buchanan**' ★, floriferous with purple-red flowers. *D. c.* '**Alba**', white flowers; '**Atropurpurea**', deep red-purple flowers; '**Bicolor**', mid-green leaves, dark red, pink, and white flowers, sometimes striped, on same plant or raceme; '**Creeping White**', low-growing spreading habit, white flowers; '**Praegerae**', mid-green leaves, pinkish red flowers; '**Purpurea**', bright purple-pink flowers; '**Snowdrift**', white flowers; '**Waley's Red**' (syn. 'Whally'), deep magenta flowers. Zones 6–9.

DACRYDIUM

Native to Southeast Asia, the western Pacific, and New Zealand, this genus within the plum-pine (Podocarpaceae) family contains around 30 species of evergreen coniferous shrubs and trees with scale-like leaves. The small cones consist of a fleshy receptacle from which 1 to 3 seeds project. They are valued for their timber. CULTIVATION: They like cool, moist, deep, rich peaty soils with plenty of moisture, in a protected sunny position. They resent root disturbance caused by transplanting. Propagate from cuttings or from seed sown in autumn.

Dacrydium cupressinum

NEW ZEALAND RED PINE, RIMU

☼ ❄ ↔ 30 ft (9 m) ↕ 90–200 ft (27–60 m)

Slow-growing evergreen tree native to New Zealand. Tiny leaves on pendulous bronzy green branchlets. Resents transplanting. Its growth slow, up to 12 in (30 cm) per year,

with nursery stock often collected from bush. Drought tender, and producing tiny nut-like seeds. Zones 8–10.

DAIS

This genus consists of 2 species of evergreen or semi-deciduous shrubs or small trees belonging to the daphne (Thymelaeaceae) family. They are found in South Africa and on the island of Madagascar where they grow in the moist frost-free margins of wooded regions. One species is widely grown in warmer climate gardens as an evergreen; it is commonly known as the pompon tree for its showy clusters of small pink flowers. CULTIVATION: Mature plants can withstand light frost, but are best planted in a sunny position with some protection from surrounding shrubs. They thrive in well-drained fertile loam covered with an organic mulch to retain moisture during the summer months. Propagate from seed in spring or from half-hardened cuttings.

Dais cotinifolia ★

POMPON TREE

☼ ❄ ↔ 10 ft (3 m) ↕ 10 ft (3 m)

Found in South Africa and Madagascar. Compact, rounded, evergreen shrub. Deciduous in cooler situations. Reddish bark, slightly scented pink flowerheads on tips of branches in summer. Blue-green foliage. Zones 9–11.

DAPHNE

Renowned for its fragrance, this popular genus in the daphne (Thymelaeaceae) family includes 50 or so evergreen and deciduous shrubs, extending from Europe and North Africa to temperate and subtropical Asia. Forming neat compact bushes, many of them make excellent rockery plants. The leaves are usually simple, smooth-edged, blunt-tipped, elongated ovals, either thin and dull green or thick, leathery, and slightly glossy. Individually flowers are small, usually in shades of white, cream, yellow, or pink, but they are carried in showy rounded heads that are sometimes highly scented. Drupes follow the flowers and are sometimes colorful. CULTIVATION: *Daphne* species generally prefer moist, cool, humus-rich, well-drained, slightly acid soil. If camellias and rhododendrons do well in your garden, so should daphnes. Once they are established, daphnes resent disturbance, so avoid damaging the surface roots by cultivation. Use mulch to suppress weeds. Small-leafed species prefer bright conditions; those with larger leaves are happier shaded from the hottest sun. Propagate from seed, cuttings, or layers.

Dais cotinifolia

Daphne bholua

PAPER DAPHNE

☼ ❄ ↔ 4 ft (1.2 m) ↕ 10 ft (3 m)

Native to eastern Himalayas. Deciduous and evergreen forms available. Strongly scented white flowers, tinged with pink, develop from deep pink buds, in winter–spring. Drupes ripen to black. Known as paper daphnes as paper and ropes were once made from bark. '**Gurkha**', both hardy and deciduous. Zones 7–10.

Daphne genkwa

Daphne cneorum

GARLAND DAPHNE, GARLAND FLOWER, ROCK DAPHNE, ROSE DAPHNE

☀ ❊ ↔ 24 in (60 cm) ↑ 8 in (20 cm)

Near-evergreen, dense, twiggy, Eurasian shrub. Massed heads of small, fragrant, bright pink flowers in spring. Requires excellent drainage, shelter from hot sun, some winter chilling. 'Eximia' ★, sturdier than species; 'Ruby Glow', rich red flowers. Zones 4–9.

Daphne genkwa

LILAC DAPHNE

☀ ❊ ↔ 5 ft (1.5 m) ↑ 5 ft (1.5 m)

Deciduous shrub from China. Young foliage coppery, new stems covered in fine down. Large, lavender, slightly fragrant, delicate flowers in spring. Zones 5–9.

Daphne gnidium

☀ ❊ ↔ 4 ft (1.2 m) ↑ 6 ft (1.8 m)

Evergreen shrub from Eurasia, North Africa, and Canary Islands. Sparse glossy leaves. Small, fragrant, creamy white to pale pink flowers, densely clustered in panicles, in late spring–early summer. Red drupes. Zones 8–10.

Daphne laureola

SPURGE LAUREL

☀ ❊ ↔ 5 ft (1.5 m) ↑ 5 ft (1.5 m)

Tough, adaptable, Eurasian native. Dark green evergreen foliage. Flowers fragrant, small, pale green, in late winter–spring. Zones 7–10.

Daphne mezereum

FEBRUARY DAPHNE, MEZEREON

☀ ❊ ↔ 3 ft (0.9 m) ↑ 4 ft (1.2 m)

European species, most common of deciduous daphnes, similar to *D.* × *burkwoodii*. Flowers on bare wood, in late winter–early spring. White- and pink-flowered fragrant forms, singles and doubles available. *D. m.* f. *alba*, white flowers, yellow fruit. Zones 4–9.

Daphne odora

WINTER DAPHNE

☀ ❊ ↔ 5 ft (1.5 m) ↑ 5 ft (1.5 m)

Evergreen shrub native to China and Japan. Deep green leaves. Fragrant clusters of fleshy, pale pink flowers from mid-winter. Not long lived. *D. o.* f. *rosacea,* white and pink flowers; 'Rubra', dark red-pink flowers, less fragrance. *D. o.* var. *variegata* 'Aureomarginata', yellow-edged leaves, hardier and easier to grow than species. Zones 8–10.

Daphne pontica

☀ ❊ ↔ 5 ft (1.5 m) ↑ 5 ft (1.5 m)

Evergreen shrub native to Balkans and western Asia. Glossy, deep green, leathery leaves. Flowers fragrant, sometimes very pale pink to white, but usually light green. Zones 6–10.

Daphne tangutica

☀ ❊ ↔ 5 ft (1.5 m) ↑ 6 ft (1.8 m)

Evergreen shrub native to northwestern China. Small gray-haired leaves. Densely crowded clusters of small, fragrant, rosy purple flowers, reminiscent of lilac *(Syringa),* in spring–summer. Small red fruit. **Retusa Group**, dark green leaves. Zones 6–9.

DARWINIA

This genus of around 45 species in the myrtle (Myrtaceae) family is endemic to Australia; many are from Western Australia. Most are small evergreen shrubs, with small crowded leaves often marked with numerous oil glands. The tiny tubular flowerheads have long protruding styles and fall roughly into 2 groups: those clustered into pincushion-like flowers and those enclosed by large colorful bracts giving the flowerhead a bell-like appearance. The flowers of most species are rich in nectar and will attract birds.

CULTIVATION: They are suited to growing in containers, and this is recommended in frost-prone areas. They require a light well-drained soil with some moisture and a little dappled shade. Good mulch around the root area will conserve soil moisture during summer. Prune lightly after flowering to maintain a compact shape. Propagate from half-hardened tip cuttings at the end of summer.

Darwinia citriodora

LEMON-SCENTED DARWINIA

☀ ❊ ↔ 5 ft (1.5 m) ↑ 5 ft (1.5 m)

Widely cultivated, compact, rounded shrub from far southwestern Western Australia. Small, neatly arranged, blue-green, oblong leaves, sometimes with reddish tints, in autumn–winter, aromatic when crushed. Small clusters of flowers, prominent orange and green leaf-like bracts, in winter–summer. Zones 9–11.

DAVIDIA

The only species in this genus of the dogwood (Cornaceae) family, a deciduous tree, was introduced from China by the French missionary Armand David in the 1890s and the genus was subsequently named after him. *D. involucrata* is native to southwestern China

where it grows in damp mountain woods. It has a broadly conical outline and attractive foliage, flowering bracts, and fruit.
CULTIVATION: *D. involucrata* makes an excellent specimen tree although it does have a tendency to branch at a low level so corrective pruning should be carried out to ensure a good straight trunk develops. It requires deep, rich, moist soil and a sheltered site. It flowers when the tree is about 10 years old. Propagate from fresh seed, as dry seed has a much-reduced germination rate.

Davidia involucrata ★
DOVE TREE, GHOST TREE, HANDKERCHIEF TREE
☼ ❄ ↔ 30 ft (9 m) ↑ 60 ft (18 m)
Leaves aromatic, toothed margins, heart-shaped bases, downy beneath, taper to long point. Spherical heads of tiny true flowers surrounded by 2 large, white, ornamental bracts of unequal size, in late spring, with new leaves. Plum-like fruit ripens to purple-brown. *D. i.* var. *vilmoriniana*, leaves smooth beneath. Zones 6–9.

DELONIX
This small genus comprising 10 species of tropical deciduous, semi-evergreen, or evergreen trees in the cassia subfamily of the legume (Fabaceae) family includes the spectacular poinciana, *D. regia*. The wide umbrella-like canopies provide good summer shade. Large, terminal, orchid-like flower clusters smother the tree crown, and appear after deciduous and semi-evergreen species shed their leaves.
CULTIVATION: For the first few years, vigorous growth should be promoted in a humus-enriched well-watered soil. A sturdy trunk should be encouraged by removing the side shoots, thus lifting the canopy above head height. These trees require ample space to spread and are tolerant of all soil types except for heavy clay. They are easily propagated from seed or cuttings, but the seedlings take 10 years or longer to flower. The flower color from the seedlings may be disappointing.

Delonix regia
FLAMBOYANT TREE, ROYAL POINCIANA
☼ ✦ ↔ 30 ft (9 m) ↑ 30 ft (9 m)
Deciduous shade tree from Madagascar. Bright green feathery leaves mature to deep green; shed prior to flowering. Large orange-scarlet

flower clusters form in profusion on branch ends in summer. Huge flattened pods harden in autumn. Zones 11–12.

DENDROMECON
This genus contains just one species of evergreen shrub, native to California in the USA, and Mexico where it grows on the dry rocky chaparral. It belongs to the poppy (Papaveraceae) family, and the relationship can be seen in the single yellow flowers borne in summer.
CULTIVATION: These plants require winter protection in climates with severe frosts. When grown outdoors, they will not survive severe winters and must be given a warm sheltered site in a well-drained, gritty soil that is not too rich. The shrub dislikes root disturbance and care should be taken at planting time to reduce transplant shock. Propagation is from half-hardened cuttings taken in summer, but these can be quite difficult to strike.

Dendromecon rigida

Dendromecon rigida
TREE POPPY
☼ ❄ ↔ 10 ft (3 m) ↑ 10 ft (3 m)
Stiff gray-green leaves. Pure yellow, 4-petaled poppy flowers of simple beauty, in summer. *D. r.* subsp. *harfordii*, thicker stems and leaves than species, and slightly smaller yellow flowers. Zones 8–10.

DESFONTAINIA
This genus, belonging to its own family, Desfontainiaceae, comprises a single species of evergreen shrub, found growing throughout the Andes from Colombia to Tierra del Fuego. In the north it grows in cool mountain forests, while further south it is found at sea level. It has brilliant orange and yellow flowers that stand out against dark glossy foliage.
CULTIVATION: *Desfontainia* needs a cool moist climate and an acid soil that is moisture retentive and rich in humus. It should have a partially shaded, sheltered position; water well in dry spells. Propagate from seed or half-hardened cuttings in summer.

Desfontainia spinosa ★
◐ ❄ ↔ 10 ft (3 m) ↑ 10 ft (3 m)
Bushy slow-growing shrub. Tubular flowers scarlet to orange with yellow tips, in summer–autumn. Cherry-sized fruit. Zones 8–9.

Davidia involucrata

Delonix regia

DEUTZIA

Widely cultivated for its ornamental members, this genus of the hydrangea (Hydrangeaceae) family contains 60 species of deciduous and evergreen shrubs, mainly from temperate Asia with a toehold in Central America. Most commonly grown deutzias are spring flowering and deciduous. They have pointed oval to lance-shaped leaves in opposite pairs, often with serrated edges, and heads of small, starry, 5-petalled, white, cream, or pink flowers usually held clear of the foliage.
CULTIVATION: Most species are very frost hardy, and are the mainstay of temperate gardens. Shelter from strong winds. Prune and thin after flowering to maintain a framework of strong branches. Propagate from seed or half-hardened summer cuttings.

Deutzia × elegantissima

☀ ✽ ↔ 5 ft (1.5 m) ↕ 5 ft (1.5 m)
Derived from *D. purpurascens* and *D. sieboldiana,* of garden origin. Ovate to oblong-ovate leaves, uneven sharp teeth. Cymes of pink flowers in early summer. 'Fasciculata', white to pale pink flowers, deep pink in bud; 'Rosealind' ★, compact white flowers with pink tinge. Zones 5–9.

Deutzia gracilis

SLENDER DEUTZIA
☀ ✽ ↔ 3–6 ft (0.9–1.8 m) ↕ 3–6 ft (0.9–1.8 m)
One of main parents of hybrid deutzias, from Japan. Spreading shrub, mounded form. Slender erect shoots arch at ends. Narrow leaves bright green, ovate to lance-shaped, pointed at ends. Narrow panicles of white flowers in mid-spring–early summer. Zones 5–9.

Deutzia × kalmiiflora

☀ ✽ ↔ 5 ft (1.5 m) ↕ 5 ft (1.5 m)
Hybrid between *D. parviflora* and *D. purpurascens,* of garden origin. Open shrub with arching branches. Finely toothed, mid-green,

narrowly oval leaves. Upright panicles of cup-shaped flowers, deep pink outside, paler inside, in early to mid-summer. Zones 5–9.

Deutzia × magnifica

☀ ✽ ↔ 7 ft (2 m) ↕ 6 ft (1.8 m)
Of uncertain parents, possibly *D. crenata* and *D. longifolia,* hybrid shrub with strong upright growth. Ovate to oblong-shaped leaves, finely toothed margins, gray and felt-like beneath. Dense panicles of single or double white flowers in early summer. Zones 5–9.

Deutzia × rosea

☀ ✽ ↔ 3 ft (0.9 m) ↕ 3 ft (0.9 m)
Dwarf shrub, hybrid of *D. gracilis* and *D. purpurascens.* Ovate to oblong, lance-shaped, finely serrated, dark green leaves. Short terminal panicles of flowers, pale pink inside, purplish outside. 'Campanulata', white flowers in dense panicles. Zones 5–9.

Deutzia scabra

FUZZY DEUTZIA
☀ ✽ ↔ 7 ft (2 m) ↕ 10 ft (3 m)
Native to Japan and China. Arching shoots; broadly ovate, rough, dark green leaves. Dense cylindrical panicles of honey-scented, white or pink-tinged, bell-shaped flowers terminate branches, in early to mid-summer. Peeling brown to orange bark. 'Candidissima', white double flowers; 'Pride of Rochester', very large, double white flowers tinged pinkish purple. Zones 5–9.

DILLENIA

This genus of about 60 evergreen trees and shrubs of the family Dilleniaceae is distributed throughout tropical Asia, the islands of the Indian Ocean, and tropical Australia. Leaves are large, lustrous, and simple; flowers are borne in terminal panicles, in spring and summer. Fleshy star-shaped fruit comprises 5 to 8 segments.
CULTIVATION: Drought and frost tender, *Dillenia* species prefer well-drained soils with heavy mulching and watering, and a protected sunny position. Propagate from seed or cuttings.

Dillenia alata

QUEENSLAND RED BEECH
☀ ⚘ ↔ 12 ft (3.5 m) ↕ 25 ft (8 m)
Broadly spreading tree from Queensland and Northern Territory, Australia. Loose, bright reddish brown, papery bark. Thick, glossy, egg-shaped leaves. Large, showy, yellow flowers in spring–summer. Red fruit, fleshy part edible, used by Aboriginal Australians to stop swelling. Zones 10–12.

Dillenia indica

CHULTA, ELEPHANT APPLE, INDIAN DILLENIA
☀ ⚘ ↔ 12 ft (3.5 m) ↕ 30–50 ft (9–15 m)
Evergreen shrub or tree from India to Java. Erect stems, roughly textured bark. Large leaves, deeply ribbed. White magnolia-like flowers. Fruit up to 4 in (10 cm) across. Zones 10–12.

Deutzia × magnifica

Dimocarpus longan

Disanthus cercidifolius

and orange in autumn. Curious, inconspicuous, deep purple flowers, spidery petals, in late autumn. Zones 7–9.

DODONAEA

A genus in the soapberry (Sapindaceae) family, it has about 70 species of evergreen shrubs or small trees found in tropical and temperate regions, mostly in Australia, quite often in arid and semi-arid areas. It is commonly known as hopbush, as early European settlers substituted fruits of some species for hops in brewing. Male and female flowers are mostly on separate plants. Flowers are small and insignificant; it is the highly colored, inflated, winged capsules that form the attraction of these plants. CULTIVATION: Frost tender, they do best in a moderately fertile well-drained soil in full sun. Some species withstand extended dry periods. Tip pruning will maintain bushy growth. Propagate from tip cuttings taken in summer.

Dodonaea viscosa
HOPBUSH

☼/☀ 🌢 ↔ 5 ft (1.5 m) ↑ 10 ft (3 m)

Fast-growing evergreen tree from Australia, New Zealand, Pacific islands, tropical America, and southern Africa. Shiny, light green, sticky foliage. Masses of green winged fruit capsules in summer, hardening to papery light brown. 'Purpurea' ★, sought-after form distinguished by its purple-red foliage and capsules. Zones 9–11.

DOMBEYA

This is a large genus of about 225 species occurring from Africa to the Mascarene Islands, with 190 species in Madagascar alone. It is a member of the mallow (Malvaceae) family. All are evergreen, deciduous, or semi-deciduous shrubs or trees with simple, alternate, broad, often lobed leaves, and often with conspicuous stipules at the base of the leaf stalk. Flowers, in axillary or terminal panicles, often densely packed, are 5-petalled, white, pink, or red in color. The fruit is a small and often hairy capsule.

CULTIVATION: Only a few species from southern Africa are cultivated, in warm-temperate and subtropical areas with adequate moisture in summer. A well-drained, fertile soil in full sun or part-shade is required. Some species are only just frost hardy for short periods. Propagate from seed in spring, or cuttings in summer.

DIMOCARPUS
syn. *Euphoria*

This is a small genus of 5 species in the soapberry (Sapindaceae) family closely allied to *Litchi* (lychee), occurring from Southeast Asia to Australia. All are trees with large pinnate leaves, a heavy crown, and small flowers borne in large dense terminal panicles. A characteristic is the fleshy edible aril surrounding the seeds inside the almost leathery skin of the fruit, which is smooth.

CULTIVATION: Rich sandy loams and protection from frost are preferred. Propagation is from seed sown soon after hardening since the seeds lose viability quite quickly.

Dimocarpus longan
syn. *Euphoria longan*
LONGAN

☼ 🌢 ↔ 20 ft (6 m) ↑ 40 ft (12 m)

Native to Southeast Asia. Cultivated for its fruit. Heavily foliaged branches, alternate pinnate leaves. Flowering in spring, fruit ripens in summer. *D. l.* subsp. *malesianus* varies little from species. Zones 11–12.

DISANTHUS

This genus belonging to the witchhazel (Hamamelidaceae) family contains a single deciduous shrub, with alternate leaves and inconspicuous flowers, that is native to China and Japan. The fruit is a dehiscent capsule.

CULTIVATION: Frost resistant but drought tender, *Disanthus* prefers a cool, moist, rich, acid or peaty soil in a protected sunny position, in conditions similar to rhododendrons and azaleas. Propagate from seed, which takes 2 years to germinate, or from cuttings taken in summer and struck under glass, or by layering.

Dombeya cacuminum

Dombeya cacuminum

☀ 🌢 ↔ 20 ft (6 m) ↑ 40 ft (12 m)

Upright, evergreen tree native to open woodlands of Madagascar. Large leaves, maple-like, shiny. Flowers large, in pendent clusters, deep pink to red. Zones 10–12.

Disanthus cercidifolius ★

☀ ❅ ↔ 10 ft (3 m) ↑ 20 ft (6 m)

From mountainous areas of China and Japan. Long leaf stalks; luxuriant, heart-shaped, bluish green leaves, turning maroon, red,

Dombeya tiliacea
FOREST DOMBEYA, NATAL WEDDING FLOWER

☀ 🌢 ↔ 12 ft (3.5 m) ↑ 25 ft (8 m)

Small evergreen tree from Eastern Cape and KwaZulu Natal in South Africa. Flowers white, in few-flowered pendulous clusters, in late summer–autumn; fruit in autumn–winter. Zones 9–11.

Dracaena draco

DRACAENA

This genus in the family Ruscaceae contains about 60 evergreen perennials, shrubs, or trees, mostly from Africa but with species in most tropical regions, plus 2 endemic to the Canary Islands. Leaves are smooth, glossy, sword-like, and often variegated; terminal panicles of flowers are short lived. Some species have a spiky growth habit, others are softer and more shrubby. The fruit is a berry.
CULTIVATION: In gardens, species prefer rich, moist, well-drained soil in a protected sunny position, or a standard potting mix in diffused sunlight or full shade. Propagate from stem or tip cuttings, or root cuttings, preferably with bottom heat, or from seed sown in spring.

Dracaena draco ★
DRAGON'S-BLOOD TREE, DRAGON TREE
☼ ❅ ↔ 12 ft (3.5 m) ↑ 30 ft (9 m)
Slow-growing palm-like tree from Canary Islands. Trunk upright, many branched. Canopy of stiff gray leaves bunched at branch ends. Insignificant flowers, orange berries, in summer. Requires free-draining soil, warmth, sun. Suitable for containers. Zones 10–12.

Dracaena fragrans
syn. *Pleomele fragrans*
HAPPY PLANT
☼/◐ ❅ ↔ 6 ft (1.8 m) ↑ 10–30 ft (3–9 m)
Variable species from tropical West Africa to Malawi. Glossy, sword-like, pale green leaves. Clusters of fragrant yellow flowers. **Deremensis Group** (syn. *D. deremensis*) cultivars have dark red flowers: '**Longii**', leaves with broad white central stripe; '**Warneckei**', leaves greenish white with bright green edging. *D. f.* '**Massangeana**', bright green leaves striped with cream to yellow down center. Zones 9–11.

Dracaena marginata ★
☼/◑ ❅ ↔ 3–10 ft (0.9–3 m) ↑ 7–17 ft (2–5 m)
Upright branching shrub or small tree from Réunion and Mauritius. Good structural upright form. Long, lance-shaped, green leaves cover tips of thin erect branches. Adapts well to indoor and outdoor cultivation. Prefers fertile moist soils. Zones 9–12.

Dracaena reflexa
☼ ❀ ↔ 3 ft (0.9 m) ↑ 8 ft (2.4 m)
Native of Madagascar and Mauritius, but now linked with plants from tropical Africa, merged as *D. reflexa*. Tangle of wiry stems, lance-shaped dark green leaves. Flowers cream, sweet-smelling at night, in spring. Bright red berries, in early summer. '**Song of India**', variegated, broad creamy white marginal stripes. Zones 10–12.

Dracaena sanderiana
RIBBON PLANT
☼ ❅ ↔ 16–32 in (40–80 cm) ↑ 5 ft (1.5 m)
From Cameroun. Upright narrow shrub, only few branches from base. Rich dark green, lance-shaped leaves edged in white. Zones 9–11.

Dracaena reflexa 'Song of India'

DRIMYS

This genus is one of 5 that make up the small family Winteraceae, the origins of which date back to the earliest evolution of flowering plants in the age of dinosaurs. It consists of 6 species of evergreen shrubs and small trees occurring in South America and higher mountains of Mexico and Central America. Another 20 to 40 species from Australasia and Southeast Asia have often been included in *Drimys*, but most recent evidence supports their being separated into the separate genus *Tasmannia*. Simple leathery leaves, without teeth or lobes, are arranged spirally and clustered toward the end of the season's growth, with new leaves often red. Star-shaped white or cream flowers are carried in umbel-like clusters in spring. The bark is aromatic, with a hot pepper-like taste. From its first discovery by Europeans it was believed to be an effective treatment for scurvy.
CULTIVATION: Most species are not fully frost hardy and at best tolerate down to 14°F (–10°C) for short spells. They thrive in a sheltered position; grow them in sun or partial shade in moist but well-drained fertile soil. Propagate by taking half-hardened cuttings in summer or sowing seed into pots as soon as it is ripe in autumn, with protection against winter frosts.

Drimys winteri ★
syn. *Wintera aromatica*
WINTER'S BARK
☼/◐ ❅ ↔ 30 ft (9 m) ↑ 50 ft (15 m)
Aromatic tree from Mexico, Chile, and Argentina. Lustrous, dark green, lance-shaped leaves, pale blue-white beneath. Fragrant flowers, creamy white, in umbels of 20 individual blossoms, in spring–early summer. Zones 8–9.

DRYANDRA

These beautiful flowering evergreen shrubs, numbering about 60 species, are native to Western Australia. They belong to the protea (Proteaceae) family and are related to banksias, and in many respects closely resemble that genus. They are grown for their decorative lobed or toothed leaves and richly colored, yellow, gold, or bronze, rounded flowerheads. Some species flower during the winter months. The flowers are most attractive to nectar-feeding birds.

CULTIVATION: Dryandras come from warm regions with winter rainfall and a pronounced dry summer season, and are frost tender. Many species will grow well in containers. Excellent drainage is essential, in full sun or part-shade. They prefer dry neutral or acid soil and low levels of nitrates or phosphates. Tip prune while young, and lightly after flowering to promote compact growth. Propagate from seed in spring.

Dryandra formosa
SHOWY DRYANDRA
☼ ⚘ ↔ 7 ft (2 m) ↑ 10 ft (3 m)

From far southern coastal regions of Western Australia. Prized for its cut flowers. Slender dark green leaves, with prickly triangular lobes, whitish underside. Rounded, almost metallic, golden flowerheads, in winter–spring. Zones 9–11.

Dryandra quercifolia
OAK-LEAF DRYANDRA
☼ ⚘ ↔ 10 ft (3 m) ↑ 10 ft (3 m)

From Esperance, far southern Western Australia. Felty new growth, dark green leaves prickly lobed. Flowerheads iridescent yellow and green, in winter–spring. Zones 9–11.

DURANTA
A genus in the vervain (Verbenaceae) family, it comprises 30 or so species of hard-wooded shrubs from southern USA to Mexico and Brazil. Evergreen, except in cold climates, they have blue, white, or violet flowers, in racemes or panicles, followed by decorative but poisonous fruit in autumn and winter. CULTIVATION: They will grow in most subtropical and frost-free temperate areas in fertile well-drained soil and full sun. They can be grown as small trees on a single trunk. Propagate from soft-tip cuttings in spring, or from firm-wood leafy cuttings in autumn.

Duranta erecta
syns *Duranta plumieri, D. repens*
GOLDEN BEAD TREE, GOLDEN DEW DROP, PIGEON BERRY
☼ ⚘ ↔ 8 ft (2.4 m) ↑ 15 ft (4.5 m)

Small evergreen species from tropical America. Drooping branches, sharp spines. Inflorescence 5–12 racemes, up to 30 lavender-blue

Drimys winteri

flowers, purplish calyx, in mid-autumn. Fruit enclosed in persistent calyx, hardens glossy yellow in early autumn. 'Alba', white flowers; 'Variegata', leaf margins creamy yellow. Zones 9–12.

Duranta stenostachya
BRAZILIAN SKY FLOWER
☼ ⚘ ↔ 4–5 ft (1.2–1.5 m) ↑ 4–6 ft (1.2–1.8 m)

Evergreen shrub from tropical Brazil. Oblong to sword-shaped leaves, slightly toothed. Clusters of fragrant, tubular, medium, blue-lilac to purple flowers in summer. Contrasting orange-yellow berries. Zones 9–11.

EDGEWORTHIA
This genus of 2 or 3 rather similar species in the daphne (Thymelaeaceae) family is named for Michael Pakenham Edgeworth (1812–81), a part-time botanist, plant collector, and employee of the East India Company. They are heavily wooded shrubs with large, elongated oval, mid-green leaves; when young the leaves have prominent midribs and a felty coating. The bark contains a very strong fiber and is naturally papery, and has been used for the production of paper pulp. The structure and fragrance of the flowerheads, which open in late winter to spring, reveal the close relationship between this genus and *Daphne*. CULTIVATION: *Edgeworthia* are best suited to moist, well-drained, humus-enriched soil in part-shade. They are moderately frost hardy plants, but are likely to be severely damaged if struck by a late frost after the young foliage has started to develop. Propagate from half-hardened cuttings, by air-layering, or from seed.

Edgeworthia chrysantha ★
PAPER BUSH
◐ ❋ ↔ 6 ft (1.8 m) ↑ 8 ft (2.4 m)

Native to China. Deciduous shrub with sparse growth and very heavy branches, which produces attractive new foliage. Globose heads of short, fragrant, tubular flowers are bright yellow, ageing to creamy white, at end of winter, and are followed by dry drupes. Some botanists regard *E. papyrifera* and *E. chrysantha* as the one species. Zones 8–10.

Dryandra quercifolia

Duranta erecta

Edgeworthia chrysantha

ELAEAGNUS

This genus of 30 to 40 species of deciduous and evergreen shrubs or small trees belonging to the oleaster (Elaeagnaceae) family is from Asia and southern Europe; North America has a single species. Valuable as hedges and windbreaks, especially in coastal areas, some species have spiny branches. Leaves may be simple or alternate, green or variegated, often covered beneath and sometimes above with silvery or brown scales. Tubular or bell-shaped flowers are borne on the lower

Elaeagnus pungens 'Aurea'

side of the upper twigs. Flowers are small, whitish or cream, sometimes strongly fragrant. The red, brown, or yellowish fruit is edible.
CULTIVATION: These plants tolerate a wide range of soil types, the exception is shallow chalk soils, and they like adequate summer water and a position in full sun. They should be pruned lightly to promote a dense leafy habit; hedges should not be close-clipped. Propagate from seed sown as soon as ripe, or from soft-tip or semi-hardwood cuttings; cultivars should be grown from cuttings.

Elaeagnus × ebbingei

☼ ❋ ↔ 12 ft (3.5 m) ↑ 12 ft (3.5 m)
Hybrid of garden origin between *E. macrophylla* and *E. pungens*. Dense, fast-growing, hardy, evergreen shrub. Glossy dark green leaves, silvery beneath, to 4 in (10 cm) long. Silver-scaled, fragrant, creamy white flowers in autumn. Orange-red fruit with silver freckles follow in spring. 'Gilt Edge' ★, deep green leaves with bright golden yellow margin; 'Limelight', silvery young leaves becoming light green with golden yellow variegation in center, though many revert as plant grows older. Zones 6–9.

Elaeagnus macrophylla

☼ ❋ ↔ 12 ft (3.5 m) ↑ 10 ft (3 m)
Large spreading shrub from Korea and Japan. Broadly ovate leaves covered in silvery scales on both surfaces, upper surface becoming green. Fragrant silvery flowers in autumn. Red scaly fruit. Zones 7–10.

Elaeagnus umbellata

Elaeagnus multiflora

☼ ❋ ↔ 10 ft (3 m) ↑ 10 ft (3 m)
Evergreen wide-spreading shrub from China and Japan. Leaves green on upper surface, silvery beneath. Fragrant creamy white flowers, on red-brown new shoots, in spring. Most attractive in mid- to late summer when covered with oblong, oxblood red, edible fruit. Zones 5–9.

Elaeagnus pungens

SILVERBERRY
☼ ❋ ↔ 20 ft (6 m) ↑ 15 ft (4.5 m)
Evergreen shrub, suitable for hedging, from Japan. Main branches spiny and horizontal. Leaves oval, glossy green above, silvery white beneath, with scattered, brown, glandular dots. Small clusters of creamy white flowers with brown dots in autumn. Fruit reddish brown with silvery white spots. 'Aurea', leaves with bright yellow margin of irregular width; 'Goldrim', deep glossy leaves with bright yellow margin; 'Maculata', large, yellow, central patch on each leaf and dark green margin, though it can revert; 'Variegata', large shrub, leaves with thin creamy yellow margin. Zones 7–10.

Elaeagnus umbellata

syn. *Elaeagnus crispa*
AUTUMN OLIVE
☼ ❋ ↔ 30 ft (9 m) ↑ 30 ft (9 m)
Strong-growing shrub from China, Korea, and Japan. New shoots golden brown, thorny. Leaves soft green, wavy-edged, silvery beneath. Fragrant yellow-white flowers in late spring–early summer. Small, rounded, silvery bronze fruit ripens to pale red speckled with white in autumn. Zones 3–9.

ELAEOCARPUS

Species in this genus of about 60 evergreen shrubs and trees, in the family Elaeocarpaceae, occur throughout the Indo-Pacific region, from tropical East Asia and India to New Zealand. The leaves are usually simple, deep green, elongated ovals, often with markedly serrated edges. The flowers are small, often white and fragrant, with fringed edges. They are carried in small, sometimes rather pendulous, racemes, and followed by unusually colored drupes.
CULTIVATION: Hardiness varies, but most species tolerate only light frosts, if any. They prefer moist, well-drained, fairly fertile soil with a position in sun or part-shade; they are not drought tolerant. Unless complete rejuvenation is required, restrict pruning to trimming to shape. Propagate from half-hardened cuttings or from seed that has been soaked before sowing.

Elaeocarpus hookerianus

POKAKA
☼ ❁ ↔ 15–30 ft (4.5–9 m) ↑ 40–80 ft (12–24 m)
Evergreen tree from New Zealand. Densely interwoven branches. Leaves usually narrow and irregularly lobed when young, become broader with toothed edges and more clearly defined pointed tip with age. Small sprays of pale green to greenish white flowers in spring–summer. Purple-red drupes. Zones 9–10.

Embothrium coccineum

Elaeocarpus reticulatus

BLUEBERRY ASH

↔ 15 ft (4.5 m) ↑ 15–30 ft (4.5–9 m)

From Australia. Pruned to shrub in cultivation. Leaves to 6 in (15 cm) long, with toothed edges. Short racemes of creamy white to pale pink flowers in spring–summer. Deep blue drupes. Zones 9–11.

EMBOTHRIUM

This genus in the protea (Proteaceae) family is represented by a single species, with regional forms, from Chile and the adjacent Andean region of Argentina. The rather upright tree is spectacular when in flower in late spring and early summer; its profusion of orange-scarlet tubular flowers are best appreciated from above.

CULTIVATION: An open sunny position with free-draining soil will reduce this plant's inclination to legginess. Protect from frost. With plentiful moisture, it grows quickly, producing flowers within a decade, but its life expectancy may not exceed 25 years. It can be propagated from seed, cuttings, or basal suckers.

Enkianthus campanulatus

Embothrium coccineum

CHILEAN FIRE BUSH

↔ 20 ft (6 m) ↑ 40 ft (12 m)

Upright evergreen tree native to Chile. Glossy leathery leaves. Orange-scarlet flowers. In cultivation, treat as tall shrub. **'Ñorquincó'** ★, hardy; flower clusters crowded on branches. Zones 9–10.

EMPETRUM

Exposed windswept sites across the cool-temperate regions of the Northern Hemisphere (and also the southern Andes and the Falkland Islands in the South Atlantic) are home to this genus of 2 heath-like, intricately branched, evergreen shrubs belonging to the family Ericaceae, low growing and carpeting in habit. Very small solitary flowers appear in the leaf axils, and the fruit is a small, juicy, edible, berry-like drupe containing up to 9 hard white seeds.

CULTIVATION: They prefer moist lime-free soil in an open sunny position, and are ideal for the rock garden in cooler climates. Propagate from seed sown in spring or from cuttings.

Empetrum nigrum

BLACK CROWBERRY, CRAKE BERRY, CURLEW BERRY, MONOX

↔ 15 in (38 cm) ↑ 12 in (30 cm)

From USA, northern Europe, and Asia. Spreading, heath-like, evergreen shrub resembling miniature fir tree. Decumbent branches. Short needle-like leaves on stems with long woolly hairs. Loose clusters of purplish red flowers in late spring–early summer. Edible fruit, glossy, blackish purple. Zones 3–8.

ENKIANTHUS

This genus from the heath (Ericaceae) family consists of about 10 species of mainly deciduous, rarely evergreen, shrubs found from the Himalayas to Japan. The leaves are elliptical or ovate. The plants flower from mid-spring through to early summer, producing umbels or racemes of white, pink, or red urn- or bell-shaped flowers at the ends of the branches.

CULTIVATION: These shrubs grow on the edge of woodlands or in woodland conditions, preferring full sun or light shade and moist, well-drained, humus-rich, acid to neutral soil. Propagate from half-hardened cuttings taken in summer, by air-layering in autumn, or from seed sown in winter or early spring. The best propagation medium is peat with lime-free sharp sand.

Enkianthus campanulatus

REDVEIN ENKIANTHUS

↔ 15 ft (4.5 m) ↑ 15 ft (4.5 m)

From mountains of Honshu in Japan. Deciduous species with whorled branches. Leaves dull green and elliptic with sharp tip and toothed margins, turning deep red in autumn. Flowers in drooping corymb-like racemes of creamy bells with red or pink veining in late spring–early summer. ***E. c.* var. *palibinii,*** dark red flowers. ***E. c.* 'Albiflorus'**, cream flowers; **'Donardensis'**, larger red flowers than species; **'Red Bells'** ★, to 10 in (25 cm) tall, red autumn leaves, red flowers in pendent clusters. Zones 6–9.

Enkianthus cernuus

↔ 8 ft (2.4 m) ↑ 8 ft (2.4 m)

Deciduous shrub from Honshu in Japan. Bright green leaves, ovate to elliptic, with toothed margins, pointed tips, and brown downy veins beneath. Good autumn color. Pendent racemes of white flowers in late spring–summer. ***E. c.* f. *rubens,*** deep red flowers. Zones 6–9.

Enkianthus perulatus

↔ 7 ft (2 m) ↑ 7 ft (2 m)

From Japan. Produces attractive shiny red young shoots. Oval toothed leaves with downy midribs beneath, mid-green, turning bright red in autumn. Small drooping umbels of white flowers in mid-spring. Zones 6–9.

EPACRIS

From the heath (Ericaceae) family, this genus comprises approximately 40 species of shrubs or subshrubs. The majority are native to heathland or sandy soils in southeastern Australia, including Tasmania, where they do not dry out because of the moisture from creeks. Foliage is mostly prickly, gray-green to deep green, with a coarse texture. Many flower for months or in regular flushes all year, but their lifespan is short to medium, even under ideal conditions. CULTIVATION: They prefer filtered light. To maintain density and improve longevity, trim lightly after flowering. Mulch to retain moisture; gravels are ideal. Propagate from half-hardened cuttings in summer. Their fine root systems make transplanting difficult.

Epacris impressa
COMMON HEATH, PINK HEATH

☀ ❄ ↔ 30 in (75 cm) ↕ 3 ft (0.9 m)

Floral emblem of State of Victoria, Australia. Straggly shrub. Tubular pendulous flowers from white through pink to red. Spot flowers throughout year, with winter–spring flush. Zones 8–10.

Epacris longiflora
FUCHSIA HEATH

☀ ❄ ↔ 3 ft (0.9 m) ↕ 3 ft (0.9 m)

Straggly but adaptable shrub found on poor sandstone-derived soil in New South Wales and Queensland, Australia. Flowers sporadically with flushes of tubular flowers, red with white tips, producing major flush in spring. Zones 9–10.

EPHEDRA
JOINT FIR, JOINT PINE, MEXICAN TEA

The 40 or so curious shrubs or climbing plants in this genus, the only one of the joint-fir (Ephedraceae) family, have slender, rush-like, jointed, green branches resembling horsetails, becoming woody with age, and very reduced, opposite, scale-like leaves. Small yellow flowers, to ½ in (12 mm) across, appear in cone-like clusters, followed by fleshy, red, berry-like fruit. Species are native to dry or desert regions across southern Europe, North Africa, Asia, and the mountains of both North and South America. CULTIVATION: These plants prefer sandy soil in a sunny position; they are ideal rock-garden plants in drier areas. Propagate by dividing clumps, separating suckers, or air-layering, or from seed.

Ephedra distachya
EUROPEAN JOINT PINE

☼ ❄ ↔ 3 ft (0.9 m) ↕ 3 ft (0.9 m)

From southern Europe to Siberia; cultivated from sixteenth century. Low evergreen shrub with creeping stems forming mats. Slender erect branches. Scale-like leaves. Red fruit in summer. Zones 4–9.

Ephedra viridis
GREEN JOINT FIR, MORMON TEA

☼ ❄ ↔ 3 ft (0.9 m) ↕ 4 ft (1.2 m)

From western USA. Erect evergreen shrub. Thin vivid green branches and awl-like leaves. Zones 6–10.

EPIGAEA

A genus of 3 small, prostrate, evergreen shrubs in the heath (Ericaceae) family, their distribution is interesting, with one species each from North America, Japan, and Turkey. They make great additions to a rockery in a cool-temperate climate. The leaves are pointed ovals with a heart-shaped base, usually deep green and glossy, sometimes red-tinted in winter. Clusters of tiny, bell-shaped, erica-like flowers appear in spring at the branch tips and in the leaf axils. CULTIVATION: Although requiring some sunlight to flower well, these cool-climate plants need shade from the hottest sun. Plant in cool, moist, humus-rich soil in dappled sunlight and water well in summer. Unless seed is required, remove spent flowers and trim lanky shoots to keep the plant tidy. Propagation can be from seed, which is very fine, or from small tip cuttings, and also by air-layering.

Epigaea repens
MAYFLOWER, TRAILING ARBUTUS

☀ ❄ ↔ 12–24 in (30–60 cm) ↕ 4–8 in (10–20 cm)

Native to North America, with low spreading habit. Leaves 1–3 in (2.5–8 cm) long and half as wide. Racemes, ½ in (12 mm) long, of 4 to 6 sweetly scented white to pale pink flowers. Zones 2–9.

ERANTHEMUM

Native to tropical regions in Asia and within the acanthus (Acanthaceae) family, this genus consists of about 30 shrubby perennial herbs and evergreen shrubs with opposite simple leaves. They produce dense branched spikes or panicles of flowers with slender tubular corollas in spring.

Epacris longiflora

Ephedra viridis

Eranthemum pulchellum

CULTIVATION: All species thrive in light, rich, medium loams in a part-shaded or protected position provided they have ample moisture. Propagate from cuttings of younger wood taken in spring.

Eranthemum pulchellum

syn. *Eranthemum nervosum*

BLUE SAGE

☀ ✦ ↔ 3 ft (0.9 m) ↕ 4 ft (1.2 m)

Evergreen shrub from India. Slightly toothed, prominently veined, glossy, green leaves, 4–8 in (10–20 cm) long. Feathery flower spikes, about 3 in (8 cm) long, bear tubular vivid blue flowers, with deep purple throats and green, papery, pointed bracts. Zones 10–12.

EREMOPHILA

This genus of about 200 species belongs to the boobialla (Myoporaceae) family and is native to mainland Australia, with most species occurring in semi-arid and arid areas. They are evergreen shrubs or small trees, often with felted or resinous leaves, stems, and floral parts. The 2-lipped tubular flowers, on short to long stalks emerging from the leaf axils, are variously lobed and may be white, yellow, violet, purple, pink, or red, and sometimes have a spotted interior. The fruit is a berry-like drupe, the seed enclosed in a tough corky or fibrous layer.

CULTIVATION: Marginally frost hardy, most species do not like moist humid conditions. They prefer a position with excellent drainage in an open sunny area with plenty of air movement. Regular light pruning encourages vigorous growth. These plants are propagated most readily from half-hardened cuttings.

Eremophila maculata

SPOTTED EMU BUSH

☼ ☘ ↔ 3–10 ft (0.9–3 m) ↕ 3–8 ft (0.9–2.4 m)

Occurs across mainland Australia. Compact dense shrub, gray-green leaves to 2 in (5 cm) long; young leaves often downy. Red, purple, pink, or yellow flowers, often spotted with darker blotches, in autumn–spring. 'Aurea', compact habit to about 3 ft (0.9 m), with light green leaves, yellow flowers; 'Carmine Star', low shrub, to 20 in (50 cm) high, purplish young branches, carmine flowers, insides paler and with prominent carmine spots; 'Pink Beauty', 10–12 ft (3–3.5 m) tall, profuse bluish pink flowers, 1½ in (35 mm) across, in late winter. Zones 9–11.

Eremophila nivea

☼ ☘ ↔ 5 ft (1.5 m) ↕ 5 ft (1.5 m)

Silvery gray shrub from Western Australia's "wheatbelt," east of Perth. Erect stems covered in dense white hairs. Small, velvety gray, linear leaves. Tubular lilac flowers, in upper leaf axils, in winter–spring. Dislikes humidity; excellent container plant. Zones 9–11.

ERICA

HEATH, HEATHER

This large genus gives its name to the heath (Ericaceae) family. It consists of about 750 evergreen species, ranging from small

Eremophila maculata

subshrubs to shrubs and trees, the great majority endemic to the Cape region of South Africa, the remainder scattered throughout East Africa, Madagascar, the Atlantic Islands, the Mediterranean region, and Europe. Habitats include wet and dry heathland and moorland. Most are only half-hardy; the European species are more frost hardy. The small leaves are linear with rolled edges, whorled, rarely opposite. The flowers are bell-shaped or tubular, in all colors except blue. Briar pipes are made from the woody root burls of *E. arborea*. Some species yield a yellow dye.

CULTIVATION: The winter-flowering heathers are lime tolerant and will grow in neutral and alkaline soil, while the summer-flowering ones like acid soil; both grow in neutral soil. Feed container-grown plants monthly during the growing season and give them plenty of water, reducing both feed and water during the dormant season. Propagation is from half-hardened cuttings taken from mid- to late summer or by air-layering in spring. The successful germination of some of the South African Cape heaths is helped by smoke treatment.

Erica arborea

BRUYERE, TREE HEATH

☼ ❋ ↔ 10 ft (3 m) ↕ 15 ft (4.5 m)

Upright shrub native to southwest Europe, through Mediterranean region, and in higher mountains of east Africa. Dark green leaves, grooved beneath. Pyramidal racemes of gray-white, scented, bell-shaped flowers in late spring. *E. a.* var. *alpina,* smaller, dense cylindrical racemes of white flowers; *E. a.* 'Albert's Gold', golden leaves year round, white flowers; 'Estrella Gold', young growth bright yellow, white flowers. Zones 7–10.

Erica canaliculata

☼ ❋ ↔ 4 ft (1.2 m) ↕ 6 ft (1.8 m)

Erect shrub from Western and Eastern Cape in South Africa. Mid-green linear leaves in whorls; undersurface paler green, hairy. Whorls of 3 white to pale pink flowers at ends of branchlets in winter–spring. Zones 8–10.

Erica canaliculata

Erica cerinthoides

Erica lusitanica

Erica regia

Erica carnea

syn. *Erica herbacea*

ALPINE HEATH, SNOW HEATH, WINTER HEATH

☼/◐ ❋ ↔ 22 in (55 cm) ↑ 12 in (30 cm)

Low-spreading shrub from Alps, northwest Italy, northwest Balkans, and eastern Europe. Dark green linear leaves in whorls of 4. Purple-pink flowers in winter–spring. 'Ann Sparkes', rose pink flowers, golden foliage with bronze tips; 'Challenger', green foliage, magenta flowers; 'December Red', deep pink flowers turn red; 'Foxhollow', lime green leaves, pinkish white flowers; 'Kramer's Rubin', blackish green foliage, dull deep pink flowers; 'March Seedling', flowers into late spring; 'Myretoun Ruby' (syn. 'Myreton Ruby'), pink flowers deepening to crimson; 'Pink Spangles', deep pink flowers; 'Pirbright Rose', rose pink flowers; 'R. B. Cooke', pink flowers turn mauve; 'Springwood White', bright green foliage, abundant white flowers; 'Winter Beauty', deep pink flowers. Zones 5–9.

Erica cerinthoides

☼ ◔ ↔ 3 ft (0.9 m) ↑ 2–5 ft (0.6–1.5 m)

From Limpopo to Eastern Cape in South Africa, also Swaziland and Lesotho. Whorls of erect, hairy, gray-green leaves. Small umbels of tubular flowers, to 1½ in (35 mm) long, bright scarlet, occasionally pink or white, at branch tips, in winter–spring. Zones 9–10.

Erica cinerea

BELL HEATH

☼ ❋ ↔ 30 in (75 cm) ↑ 24 in (60 cm)

Compact low-growing shrub from western Europe. Bottle green leaves with rolled-under edges in whorls of 3. Racemes of urn-shaped flowers, white to pink to purple, at stem tips, in summer–early autumn. 'Alba Major', mid-green foliage, white flowers; 'Alba Minor', dense habit, profuse white blooms; 'Alice Ann Davies', vigorous spreader, long spikes of dark pink blooms; 'Altadena', chartreuse foliage; 'Atrorubens', profuse bright rose purple flowers; 'Atrosanguinea', bright reddish purple flowers; 'C. D. Eason', broadly spreading low shrub, erect sprays of rose purple flowers; 'Cindy', dwarf, almost prostrate, tight clusters of rose purple flowers; 'Fiddler's Gold', leaves turn from gold to red in winter, lilac-pink flowers; 'Flamingo', bright rose pink flowers; 'Golden Drop', mat-like, lilac-pink flowers; 'Katinka', dark green foliage, black-purple flowers; 'Mrs E. A. Mitchell', fine dark green foliage, dark red flowers; 'Pink Ice', dwarf, soft rose pink flowers; 'Plummer's Seedling', mound-forming, deep pinkish red flowers; 'Prostrate Lavender', semi-prostrate, lavender-pink flowers fade to white; 'Purple Beauty', dwarf, rose-purple flowers; 'Startler', bright rose flowers; 'Vivienne Patricia', lax spreader, mauve-pink flowers; 'Wine', spreading, dense spikes of rose pink blooms. Zones 5–9.

Erica × darleyensis

DARLEY DALE HEATH

☼ ❋ ↔ 24 in (60 cm) ↑ 12 in (30 cm)

Cross between *E. carnea* and *E. erigena*, of garden origin. Vigorous bushy shrub. Mid-green lance-shaped leaves. Racemes of various-colored flowers, in winter–early spring. 'Darley Dale', pink flowers and cream-tipped leaves in spring; 'Ghost Hills', light green cream-tipped leaves; 'Jenny Porter', pinkish white flowers, pale cream-tipped foliage; 'Kramers Rote', bronze-green foliage, magenta flowers; 'Margaret Porter', lilac-pink flowers, long season; 'Silberschmelze', silver-white flowers, foliage tinged red in winter. Zones 6–9.

Erica erigena

syns *Erica hibernica*, *E. mediterranea*

IRISH HEATH

☼ ❋ ↔ 3 ft (0.9 m) ↑ 8 ft (2.4 m)

An upright shrub with brittle stems found in Ireland, southwest France, Spain, Portugal, and Tangiers in northwest Africa. Dark green linear leaves. Racemes of urn-shaped, honey-scented, lilac-pink flowers in winter–spring. 'Golden Lady', golden yellow foliage, white flowers; 'Irish Dusk', gray-green foliage, rose pink flowers in late autumn–spring; 'Superba' ★ (syn. 'Mediterranea Superba'), mid-green foliage, strongly scented pale pink flowers; 'W. T. Rackliff', mid-green foliage, white flowers in spring. Zones 7–9.

Erica lusitanica

syn. *Erica codonodes*

PORTUGUESE HEATH, SPANISH HEATH

☼ ❋ ↔ 3 ft (0.9 m) ↑ 5–10 ft (1.5–3 m)

Found from west of Iberian Peninsula to southwest France. Naturalized in southern England, New Zealand, and Australia. Whorls of 3 or 4 mid-green linear leaves. Racemes of tubular flowers, pink in bud, opening to white, in winter–spring. Can be invasive. 'George Hunt', yellow leaves, white flowers. Zones 8–10.

Erica mammosa

☼ ❄ ↔6 ft (1.8 m) ↑5 ft (1.5 m)
From Western Cape, South Africa. Dark green lance-shaped leaves in whorls of 4. Tubular flowers, white or green through to pink and dark red, in spring–summer. '**Jubilee**', pink flowers. Zones 9–10.

Erica manipuliflora

syn. *Erica verticillata* of gardens
☼ ❄ ↔3 ft (0.9 m) ↑3 ft (0.9 m)
Found in southeastern Italy and Balkans. Mid-green, linear, pointed leaves in whorls of 3. Rose pink flowers, in irregular racemes on previous year's wood, in summer–autumn. '**Aldeburgh**', scented lilac-pink flowers; '**Korcula**', pink-tinged white flowers. Zones 8–10.

Erica melanthera

☼ ❄ ↔18 in (45 cm) ↑24 in (60 cm)
Erect shrub from Western Cape, South Africa. Tiny dark green leaves in whorls of 3. Pendent pale pink to deep red blooms, black anthers extend outside cup, in spring–early summer. Zones 8–10.

Erica regia

ELIM HEATH
☼ ❄ ↔3 ft (0.9 m) ↑3 ft (0.9 m)
Erect much-branched shrub from Western Cape, South Africa. Gray-green leaves in whorls of 6 on hairy branches. Smooth, tubular, waxy flowers, small spreading lobes, in spring. Color: upper red part separated from lower white part by purple band. Zones 9–10.

Erica scoparia

BESOM HEATH
☼ ❄ ↔3 ft (0.9 m) ↑6 ft (1.8 m)
Erect shrub from southwest France, Spain, Canary Islands, north Africa. Dark green linear leaves in whorls of 3 or 4. Racemes of bell-shaped flowers, brown-red tinged green, in summer. Zones 8–10.

Erica tetralix

CROSS-LEAFED HEATH
☼ ❄ ↔20 in (50 cm) ↑12 in (30 cm)
From UK, France, and Iberian Peninsula. Gray-green lance-shaped to linear leaves, silver below, whorls of 4. Umbels of pale pink urn-shaped flowers, at stem tips, in summer–autumn. '**Alba Mollis**', silvery foliage, white flowers; '**Con Underwood**', gray-green leaves, purple-red flowers; '**Pink Star**', dark pink flowers. Zones 3–9.

Erica vagans

CORNISH HEATH, WANDERING HEATH
☼ ❄ ↔30 in (75 cm) ↑30 in (75 cm)
From UK, Ireland, western France, and Spain. Dark to mid-green linear leaves in whorls of 4 or 5. Racemes of cylindrical or bell-shaped flowers, white to pink and mauve, in mid-summer–mid-autumn. '**Lyonesse**', white flowers with light brown anthers, bright green foliage; '**Mrs D. F. Maxwell**', compact habit, vivid

rose pink flowers; '**Saint Keverne**', bright pink flowers; '**Valerie Proudley**', yellow foliage, white flowers. Zones 5–9.

Erica ventricosa

☼ ❄ ↔20 in (50 cm) ↑20 in (50 cm)
Compact shrub from Western Cape, South Africa. Dark green leaves, dark green hairy margins, in whorls of 4. Clusters of pinkish red, waxy, tubular flowers, at branch tips, in spring. '**Grandiflora**', larger than species, with pink-mauve flowers. Zones 9–11.

Erica × williamsii

☼ ✳ ↔18 in (45 cm) ↑30 in (75 cm)
Cross between *E. tetralix* and *E. vagans* that occurred in wild in Cornwall, UK. Racemes of rose pink bell-shaped flowers in summer–late autumn. '**P. D. Williams**', yellow-tipped new growth, pink flowers. Zones 5–9.

ERIOSTEMON

As now understood, following a recent revision, this genus of evergreen shrubs in the rue (Rutaceae) family consists of only 2 species from coastal eastern Australia. Other species formerly included in *Eriostemon* have now been reclassified under *Philotheca*. Growing in stunted forest heathland in poor sandy soil, they have simple spirally arranged leaves and rather conspicuous flowers with 5 waxy pink petals, borne singly in leaf axils, in late winter to spring, giving massed displays for long periods.
CULTIVATION: Species prefer light to medium, well-drained, slightly acid to neutral soil in an open position in sun or part-shade. Prune lightly to preserve shape. Propagate from tip cuttings; seed is difficult to germinate.

Eriostemon australasius

syn. *Eriostemon lanceolatus*
PINK WAX FLOWER, WAX PLANT
☼/◐ ❄ ↔3 ft (0.9 m) ↑6 ft (1.8 m)
Erect shrub from eastern New South Wales and southeastern Queensland, Australia. Leaves narrow-elliptical. Massed, shell pink, mauve, or white flowers, to 1½ in (35 mm) across. Zones 9–10.

Eriostemon australasius, New South Wales, Australia

ERYTHRINA

CORAL TREE

A member of the pea-flower subfamily of the legume (Fabaceae) family, this genus of over 100 mainly tropical deciduous or semi-evergreen trees, perennials, and shrubs is distributed globally in warm-temperate to tropical regions. Stems, branches, and even the leaflet midribs may be armed with conical or curved prickles. The compound leaves have 3 broad leaflets and inflorescences are erect to drooping racemes of showy tubular to bell-shaped flowers with the upper petal longer than the other petals. Flowers in deciduous species usually precede leaves. The fruits are elongated pods, narrowed between the seeds. Some species have medicinal properties; others may be poisonous.

CULTIVATION: Species of *Erythrina* prefer a warm dry climate and thrive in sandy, moist, but well-drained soils in sunny exposed positions in coastal environments. They are easily propagated from seed sown in spring and summer, and from cuttings of growing wood; the rootstock of herbaceous species may be divided. While fairly free of pests, mites can be a problem in drier weather.

Erythrina acanthocarpa

TAMBOOKIE THORN

☼ ❄ ↔ 6 ft (1.8 m) ↕ 6 ft (1.8 m)

Deciduous stiff shrub with many thorny stems from Cape region of South Africa. Bluish green leaflets from large underground root. Clusters of showy, pea-flower-like, scarlet blooms, tipped green, in late spring–early summer. Prickly bean-like pods. Zones 9–11.

Erythrina × bidwillii ★

HYBRID CORAL TREE

☼ ❄ ↔ 10 ft (3 m) ↕ 12 ft (3.5 m)

Originated in Australia as garden hybrid between *E. crista-galli* and *E. herbacea*. Deciduous shrub suited to drier gardens. Pale to mid-green trifoliate leaves, to 4 in (10 cm) long, on prickly stems. Striking dark red flowers with upper petal to 2 in (5 cm) long, in 3s, in spring–early summer. Zones 9–11.

Erythrina crista-galli

COCKSPUR CORAL TREE, COMMON CORAL TREE

☼ ❄ ↔ 12–40 ft (3.5–12 m) ↕ 30 ft (9 m)

Native to Brazil. Deciduous species sometimes found as gnarled old tree with considerable character. If lopped annually, very large red flower clusters appear in spring–summer. Can be grown as potted greenhouse plant in cooler climates; it should be pruned heavily in late autumn. Zones 9–11.

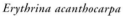

Erythrina crista-galli

Erythrina humeana

DWARF ERYTHRINA, NATAL CORAL TREE

☼ ❄ ↔ 7 ft (2 m) ↕ 12 ft (3.5 m)

Native to eastern South Africa and Mozambique. Deciduous shrub or small tree with light gray prickly bark and dark green shiny leaflets. Slender dense racemes, to 20 in (50 cm) long, of scarlet-red, tubular, pea-flower-like blooms, borne at branch tips, in summer. Bean pods black or purple. Zones 9–11.

Erythrina × sykesii

syn. *Erythrina indica* of gardens

CORAL TREE

☼ ❄ ↔ 30 ft (9 m) ↕ 50 ft (15 m)

Deciduous tree of uncertain origin, first appearing in Australia and New Zealand. Squat trunk with ascending branches armed with hooked prickles. Large scarlet pea-flowers in winter–spring. Very brittle; sheds limbs when windy. Tolerates poor soil and salt-laden air. Easily grown from branches or even wood chips. Zones 9–11.

Erythrina variegata

syn. *Erythrina indica*

CORAL TREE, INDIAN CORAL BEAN, TIGER'S CLAW

☼ ✦ ↔ 30 ft (9 m) ↕ 30–60 ft (9–18 m)

Widespread along coastlines of tropical Asia, Indian Ocean, and western Pacific. Deciduous tree with thick large-prickled branches, grayish green furrowed bark. Large heart-shaped leaflets. Dense clusters of scarlet or crimson pea-flowers, occasionally white, at branch tips, in winter. 'Parcellii', leaves variegated with light green and yellow. Zones 11–12.

ESCALLONIA

A genus of about 60 species of mostly evergreen shrubs and small trees in the gooseberry (Grossulariaceae) family, they are native to temperate regions of South America, and found mainly on hill slopes or exposed coasts in the Andes region. Free flowering over a long season, they bear panicles or racemes of small white to pink or red flowers with 5 separate petals, though these are usually pressed together in the lower half to form an apparent tube. Leaves are usually small and toothed, sometimes glandular and aromatic. The fruits are small globular capsules that shed fine seed.

Erythrina acanthocarpa

CULTIVATION: Not all species are hardy in cold inland areas but most can be grown successfully in exposed coastal gardens. These plants are lime tolerant and drought resistant, and they thrive in almost any well-drained soil in full sun. Prune immediately after flowering, but in cold climates delay this until early spring. Propagate from soft-tip cuttings in spring or semi-hardwood tips in autumn.

Escallonia bifida
syn. *Escallonia montevidensis*
WHITE ESCALLONIA
☼ ❄ ↔ 10–20 ft (3–6 m) ↑ 15–30 ft (4.5–9 m)
Small tree from Uruguay and southern Brazil. Leaves finely toothed, larger than most species; whitish midrib, dark green and slightly shiny on upper surface, paler beneath. Panicles of honey-scented white flowers, at branch tips, in early–mid-autumn. Zones 8–10.

Escallonia × exoniensis
☼ ❄ ↔ 12 ft (3.5 m) ↑ 15–20 ft (4.5–6 m)
Hybrid of Chilean species *E. rosea* and *E. rubra*. Strong erect shoots from base. Glandular young stems. Leaves dark lustrous green above, paler beneath. Loose panicles of blush pink to white flowers at branch tips in mid-spring–late autumn. 'Frades', crimson flowers. Zones 8–10.

Escallonia rubra
syns *Escallonia microphylla, E. punctata*
☼ ❄ ↔ 15 ft (4.5 m) ↑ 15 ft (4.5 m)
Variable shrub from Chile. Aromatic leaves. Loose panicles of deep pink to red flowers in mid-summer. *E. r.* var. *macrantha*, rose-crimson flowers, glossy aromatic leaves; 'C. F. Ball', grows to 10 ft (3 m) tall, large aromatic leaves, crimson flowers. *E. r.* 'Crimson Spire' ★, erect habit, bright crimson flowers; 'Woodside', low-growing, small leaves, good rock-garden plant. Zones 8–10.

Escallonia Hybrid Cultivars
☼ ❄ ↔ 6–12 ft (1.8–3.5 m) ↑ 5–10 ft (1.5–3 m)
Most popular hybrids derived from *E. rubra* and *E. virgata;* originated in UK and Ireland in first half of twentieth century. Most raised in Slieve Donard Nursery in County Down, Ireland. 'Apple Blossom', suitable for hedging, to 8 ft (2.4 m), short racemes of pink and white flowers; 'Donard Beauty', rich rose red flowers, free flowering, large leaves aromatic when crushed; 'Donard Radiance', bushy plant, rounded, glossy, dark green leaves to 1¾ in (40 mm) long, clusters of rich pink tubular flowers in summer; 'Donard Seedling', vigorous, slightly arching, with oval, deep green, glossy leaves to 1 in (25 mm) long, clusters of pink-stained white flowers in summer; 'Iveyi', upright shrub, good for hedging, very dark green glossy leaves to 2½ in (6 cm) long, dense clusters of white flowers in summer; 'Langleyensis', large spreading shrub, oval dark green leaves to 1 in (25 mm) long, masses of almost flat bright cerise flowers in summer; 'Peach Blossom', medium-sized, similar in habit to 'Apple Blossom', clear peach pink flowers; 'Pride of Donard', racemes of brilliantly rose-colored, somewhat bell-shaped flowers, larger than those of most other species, borne at branch tips, from mid-summer onward; and 'Slieve Donard', medium-sized, compact, very hardy, with small leaves and panicles of apple-blossom-pink flowers. Zones 8–10.

Escallonia, Hybrid Cultivar, 'Pride of Donard'

EUCALYPTUS
Most of the approximately 800 species of this large genus of evergreen trees are endemic to Australia; a few are found in New Guinea and southeastern Indonesia, with one *(E. deglupta)* restricted to the southern Philippines and eastern New Guinea. This genus belongs to the myrtle (Myrtaceae) family and is noted for its aromatic leaves dotted with oil glands. Species vary in size from immense forest trees to the small multi-stemmed shrubs collectively called mallees. The distinctive bark types of these plants give rise to many of the common names. Most species have 2 distinctive types of foliage: opposite juvenile leaves and alternate adult leaves. The flowers have numerous fluffy stamens, which may be white, cream, yellow, pink, or red; in bud the stamens are enclosed in a cap known as an operculum, which is composed of the fused sepals or petals or both. As the stamens expand, the operculum is forced off, splitting away from the cup-like base of the flower; this is one of the main features that unites the genus. The fruit is a woody capsule. Eucalypt flowers are rich in nectar; some species are among the world's finest honey plants. In a recent reclassification over 100 species have been split off from *Eucalyptus* to form the genus *Corymbia,* including the Western Australian red-flowering gum and the lemon-scented gum.
CULTIVATION: The great majority of species are fast growing and long lived, and once established require very little artificial watering or fertilizer. They are best suited to semi-arid or warm-temperate regions. Frost hardiness varies between species, as does the need for moist or dry conditions. Some of the Western Australian mallees dislike summer humidity. Most species can be shaped by pruning or cut back heavily if desired. Propagation is from seed, which germinates readily.

Eucalyptus bicostata
syn. *Eucalyptus globulus* subsp. *bicostata*
EURABBIE
☼ ❄ ↔ 25–50 ft (8–15 m) ↑ 120 ft (36 m)
From southeastern Australia. Smooth white or blue-gray bark, shedding in long ribbons. Juvenile leaves silvery blue, heart-shaped; adult, deep glossy green, to 24 in (60 cm) long. Creamy white flowers in spring–summer. Fruit ribbed and bell-shaped. Zones 8–10.

Eucalyptus caesia

GUNGURRU

☼ ⚘ ↔ 15 ft (4.5 m) ↑ 20 ft (6 m)

From Western Australia. Mallee or small tree with weeping branches and fairly open crown. Stems, buds, and capsules have powdery white appearance. Smooth reddish brown bark, shedding in long curling strips. Pendent clusters of large red or pink flowers in late spring–early autumn. Urn-shaped capsules. *E. c.* subsp. *magna,* red bell-shaped flowers, waxy, white, bell-shaped fruit. Zones 9–11.

Eucalyptus camaldulensis

RIVER RED GUM

☼ ⚘ ↔ 50 ft (15 m) ↑ 150 ft (45 m)

Found along watercourses of inland Australia. Single or multiple, often massive, trunk with smooth attractively mottled bark. Rich green pendent leaves. Profuse white flowers in late spring–summer. Grown worldwide for its timber, and as fuel wood. Zones 9–12.

Eucalyptus cinerea

ARGYLE APPLE, SILVER DOLLAR TREE

☼ ❄ ↔ 30 ft (9 m) ↑ 50 ft (15 m)

From southeastern Australia. Fairly short trunk. Dense spreading crown. Juvenile leaves circular, silvery gray; adult leaves often absent. Small white flowers in early summer. Moderately fast growing; retains lower branches to near ground level. Zones 8–11.

Eucalyptus erythrocorys ★

ILLYARRIE, RED-CAP GUM

☼ ⚘ ↔ 10 ft (3 m) ↑ 25 ft (8 m)

From Western Australia. Mallee shrub or small tree with smooth, gray to white, deciduous bark. Bright green leathery leaves. Unusual, large, 4-lobed, scarlet bud caps open to reveal bright yellow flowers in summer–autumn. Flowers followed by attractive, broad, bell-shaped, woody seed capsules, to 1½ in (35 mm) long. Zones 9–11.

Eucalyptus forrestiana

FUCHSIA GUM

☼ ⚘ ↔ 12 ft (3.5 m) ↑ 15 ft (4.5 m)

From Western Australia. Dense dark green canopy. Smooth gray bark peels in long strips in late summer. Bright red 4-sided flower buds, to 2 in (5 cm) long, open to reveal short yellow stamens in summer–autumn. Conspicuous red fruit. Zones 9–11.

Eucalyptus glaucescens

TINGIRINGI GUM

☼ ❄ ↔ 20 ft (6 m) ↑ 20–70 ft (6–21 m)

From mountains in southeastern Australia. Short stocking of fibrous bark at trunk's base; smooth white, gray, or greenish bark above, peeling in short ribbons. Adult leaves narrow, gray-green; juvenile broader, glaucous. White flowers in autumn. Zones 8–9.

Eucalyptus globulus

BLUE GUM, TASMANIAN BLUE GUM

☼ ⚘ ↔ 40 ft (12 m) ↑ 180 ft (55 m)

Large forest tree mostly from Tasmania, Australia. Straight trunk. Smooth dark gray bark, shed in summer–autumn. Young leaves blue-gray, rounded; adult deep green, leathery, sickle-shaped. Single, creamy white, stalkless flowers in spring. Zones 9–11.

Eucalyptus grandis

FLOODED GUM

☼ ⚘ ↔ 30–50 ft (9–15 m) ↑ 200 ft (60 m)

From coastal districts of eastern Australia. Straight shaft-like trunk, short stocking of persistent fibrous bark at base, smooth powdery white bark above. Adult leaves narrow, dark green. Clusters of small white flowers in winter. Fast-growing tree. Zones 9–12.

Eucalyptus gunnii

CIDER GUM

☼ ❄ ↔ 25 ft (8 m) ↑ 80 ft (24 m)

Found in highlands of Tasmania, Australia. Smooth gray-pink to reddish brown bark shed in late summer. Juvenile leaves glaucous, gray-green, rounded, stem-clasping. Adult leaves narrow, stalked. Small creamy white flowers in spring–summer. Zones 7–9.

Eucalyptus leucoxylon

SOUTH AUSTRALIAN BLUE GUM, YELLOW GUM

☼ ⚘ ↔ 20–40 ft (6–12 m) ↑ 100 ft (30 m)

Woodland tree from southeastern South Australia and western Victoria. Single straight trunk with smooth creamy yellow or bluish gray bark, shedding in irregular flakes. Narrow gray-green adult leaves hang vertically. Profusion of white, cream, pink, or red flowers, hang in pendulous clusters of 3, in late autumn–spring; attractive to nectar-feeding birds. Pink- and red-flowered forms often sold under name 'Rosea'. Zones 9–11.

Eucalyptus caesia subsp. *magna*

Eucalyptus cinerea

Eucalyptus forrestiana

Eucalyptus pauciflora, in the wild, Victoria, Australia

Eucalyptus pauciflora
SNOW GUM, WHITE SALLY

☼ ❋ ↔ 20 ft (6 m) ↑ 60 ft (18 m)

From mountains of southeastern Australia. Short trunk with smooth, mottled, light gray, white, or yellowish bark, shedding in irregular patches. Adult leaves shiny, leathery, blue-green, to 8 in (20 cm) long. Profuse, nectar-rich, white blossoms in spring–summer. *E. p.* subsp. *niphophila* (syn. *E. niphophila*), commonly known as alpine snow gum; occurring at elevations above 5,000 ft (1,500 m) in Snowy Mountains of New South Wales and Victoria; low-branching habit; attractive bark that sheds to leave smooth white or gray surface with patches of orange, red, yellow, and olive green; shiny blue-green leaves; glaucous buds and fruit. Zones 7–9.

Eucalyptus perriniana
SPINNING GUM

☼ ❋ ↔ 10–20 ft (3–6 m) ↑ 20–40 ft (6–12 m)

Mallee-like small tree from subalpine areas of southeastern Australia. Bark sheds to leave smooth whitish gray surface with pale brown and green patches. Juvenile leaves powdery gray, fused into disk around twig; adult leaves dull gray-green, lance-shaped. Profuse creamy white flowers in summer. Juvenile leaves popular as cut foliage for floral arrangements. Zones 7–9.

Eucalyptus macrocarpa
MOTTLECAH

☼ ❄ ↔ 12 ft (3.5 m) ↑ 6–12 ft (1.8–3.5 m)

Mallee shrub from Western Australia. Stems, new bark, and buds powdery gray. Leaves broadly ovate, silvery gray, thick-textured, stem-clasping. Showy deep pink to red flowers in late winter–spring. Woody seed capsules, to 4 in (10 cm) wide. Zones 9–10.

Eucalyptus mannifera
BRITTLE GUM

☼ ❋ ↔ 30 ft (9 m) ↑ 70 ft (21 m)

Widespread in southeastern Australia. Powdery white, cream, or gray bark, smooth to ground level, turning reddish before shedding in patches. Open canopy of narrow, gray-green, drooping leaves. Clusters of small white flowers in summer–autumn. Zones 8–10.

Eucalyptus microcorys
TALLOWWOOD

☼/◑ ❄ ↔ 40 ft (12 m) ↑ 60–180 ft (18–55 m)

From eastern Australia. Distinctive soft, fibrous, reddish brown bark. Dense spreading crown. Thin-textured dark green leaves. Showy clusters of creamy white flowers in winter–early summer. Excellent shade and shelter tree. Zones 10–12.

Eucalyptus nicholii
NARROW-LEAFED BLACK PEPPERMINT

☼ ❋ ↔ 20–40 ft (6–12 m) ↑ 50 ft (15 m)

From eastern Australia. Fast growing. Relatively short trunk, fibrous brown bark. Compact crown. Pendulous, fine, sickle-shaped, blue-green leaves. Small white flowers in autumn. Zones 8–11.

Eucalyptus leucoxylon 'Rosea'

Eucalyptus polyanthemos
RED BOX

☼ ❋ ↔ 20 ft (6 m) ↑ 25–80 ft (8–24 m)

From southeastern Australia. Short trunk. Large, often irregular crown. Oval to almost circular bluish gray leaves, pendent on slender stalks. Bark variable: may be rough, gray, and persistent on smaller branches or may shed annually, leaving tree smooth-barked. Small white flowers in spring. Zones 8–11.

Eucalyptus pulverulenta

☼ ❋ ↔ 12 ft (3.5 m) ↑ 15–30 ft (4.5–9 m)

Small tree or mallee shrub from mountains of southeastern New South Wales, Australia. Circular silvery blue juvenile leaves; rarely produces adult leaves. Attractive smooth bark, often pale brown or coppery, peels in long strips. Buds and fruit both have silvery waxy bloom. Small white flowers produced in spring. Used by florists for cut foliage. Zones 8–10.

Eucalyptus regnans
MOUNTAIN ASH

☼ ❋ ↔ 30–60 ft (9–18 m) ↑ 320 ft (96 m)

From cool mountain forests in southeastern Australia. Straight trunk with fibrous persistent bark on lower part; rest of bark sheds to reveal smooth whitish or gray-green surface. Narrow open crown. Lance-shaped leaves. Produces small white flowers in summer. *E. regnans* is recognized as tallest hardwood species in world. Zones 8–9.

Eucalyptus rhodantha
ROSE MALLEE

☼ ⸎ ↔ 10 ft (3 m) ↑ 10 ft (3 m)

Spreading mallee from southwestern Australia. Smooth pale brown bark. Powdery whitish gray branchlets. Juvenile and adult leaves rounded to heart-shaped, thick-textured, powdery gray. Solitary red flowers, on pendent stalks, in spring–autumn. Zones 9–11.

Eucalyptus urnigera
URN GUM

☼ ❊ ↔ 15–30 ft (4.5–9 m) ↑ 40 ft (12 m)

From Tasmania, Australia. Smooth-barked. Olive green leaves, to 4 in (10 cm) long. Creamy white flowers, in clusters of 3, in late summer–autumn. Urn-shaped seed capsules. Zones 8–9.

Eucalyptus viminalis
CANDLEBARK, MANNA GUM, RIBBON GUM

☼ ❊ ↔ 35 ft (10 m) ↑ 80–180 ft (24–55 m)

Forest tree from eastern Australia. Bark smooth or with stocking of rough bark on lower trunk; upper bark sheds, revealing smooth white bark. Many small white flowers in summer. Zones 8–10.

EUCRYPHIA

Found in Chile, eastern mainland Australia, and Tasmania, this genus includes 7 species of evergreen or semi-evergreen shrubs and trees, 2 of them recently discovered in Queensland, Australia. Although previously placed in a family (Eucryphiaceae) of its own, *Eucryphia* is now regarded as a member of the family Cunoniaceae. The leaves are simple or pinnate, with oblong to elliptical leaflets, and are dark green above and much lighter below, usually with a fine downy covering that wears away from the upper surfaces. The flowers, which resemble small single roses, have 4 or 5 petals that are white, cream, or occasionally pale pink. They open from late spring to autumn, and are often slightly scented.
CULTIVATION: These plants tolerate only light to moderate frost but are easily cultivated in a mild climate. The general preference is for a relatively humid atmosphere; a moist, humus-enriched, well-drained soil; and a position in sun or partial shade. In areas with hot dry summers, provide shade from the hottest sun.

Eucryphia glutinosa
HARDY EUCRYPHIA, NIRRHE

☼ ❊ ↔ 20 ft (6 m) ↑ 30 ft (9 m)

From dry mountainous areas in central Chile. May drop foliage in cold winters. Leaves pinnate, 2 in (5 cm) long, composed of elliptical leaflets, serrated edges. Large white flowers, 2½ in (6 cm) across, with red-brown anthers, in summer. **Plena Group** cultivars have semi-double or double flowers. Zones 8–9.

Eucryphia × intermedia

☼ ❊ ↔ 15 ft (4.5 m) ↑ 30 ft (9 m)

Hybrid between *E. glutinosa* from Chile and *E. lucida* from Tasmania, Australia. Simple and trifoliate leaves, also a few pinnate

Eucryphia × intermedia

leaves. Although evergreen, may drop some foliage over winter. Leaves light green with hint of blue on undersides. Pure white flowers. '**Rostrevor**' ★, named after Irish garden where cross originated, most common form. Zones 8–9.

Eucryphia lucida
PINKWOOD, TASMANIAN LEATHERWOOD

☼ ❊ ↔ 15 ft (4.5 m) ↑ 25 ft (8 m)

Upright tree from Tasmania, Australia. Trifoliate leaves of young plants change to simple, narrow, oblong leaves with age. Pendulous, usually white flowers, to 2 in (5 cm) across, in summer. '**Ballerina**', flowers 1¼ in (30 mm) across, pale pink petals edged darker pink, red stamens; '**Leatherwood Cream**', cream-edged leaves. Zones 8–9.

Eucryphia × nymansensis

☼ ❊ ↔ 15 ft (4.5 m) ↑ 30 ft (9 m)

Hybrid between 2 Chilean species—*E. cordifolia* and *E. glutinosa*—appeared around 1914 at Nymans in Sussex, England. '**Mount Usher**', semi-double flowers. Most commonly grown form, '**Nymansay**', is densely foliaged, strongly upright, and evergreen, bearing both simple, glossy, elliptical leaves and compound leaves with 3 serrated-edged leaflets. White flowers, to 3 in (8 cm) across, with clearly separated petals. Zones 8–9.

EUGENIA
STOPPER

This genus in the myrtle (Myrtaceae) family has about 550 species of evergreen trees or shrubs widely spread across tropical to subtropical regions in the Americas, with scattered species in Africa, Asia, and the Pacific Islands. They have firm, opposite, glossy, simple leaves. Conspicuous flowers, with numerous stamens, may be solitary, in panicles, or in racemes, and usually appear in spring or summer. The fruit is a drupe-like yellow, purple, red, or black berry and is sometimes edible. This genus is grown for the ornamental value of its flowers, fruit, and foliage; for hedging and screening; and some species for their edible fruit.

Eucalyptus urnigera

CULTIVATION: Easily grown in tropical and subtropical areas in sun or part-shade, they do best in well-drained sandy loam. Propagate from seed in summer or from half-hardened cuttings in autumn.

Eugenia uniflora
BRAZILIAN CHERRY, FLORIDA CHERRY, PITANGA, SURINAM CHERRY

☼ ✤ ↔ 8 ft (2.4 m) ↕ 10–30 ft (3–9 m)

Shrub or small tree from Brazil. Dull green narrow leaves, to 2½ in (6 cm) long. Fragrant, fluffy, white flowers, ½ in (12 mm) across, solitary or in groups, in summer. Red, 8-ribbed, edible fruit, 1¼ in (30 mm) in diameter. Can be invasive. Zones 10–12.

EUONYMUS

This genus belonging to the spindle-tree (Celastraceae) family consists of over 175 species of evergreen, semi-evergreen, or deciduous shrubs, trees, and climbers native to Asia, Europe, North and Central America, and the island of Madagascar; there is also a single Australian species. Not all are frost hardy. Stems and branches are often 4-sided. The leaves may be toothed or smooth-edged. The small flowers may be yellow, green, white, or red-brown, and are borne singly or in cymes in the leaf axils from late spring to early summer. The fruit is a distinctive capsule with 3, 4, or 5 compartments, each containing one large seed surrounded by a usually red or orange aril. The capsule splits open to reveal a paler, often pink, interior that contrasts with the brightly colored aril. Parts of the plant can cause stomach upsets or even poisoning if they are eaten.
CULTIVATION: They tolerate all types of soil, but *E. alatus* is especially good in alkaline soil. Grow in well-drained soil in sun or part-shade. Evergreen species need shelter from drying cold winds and slightly more moisture in the soil. Variegated forms perform better in full sun. Propagation is from seed, or from nodal cuttings taken from deciduous plants in summer or from evergreen plants in early summer to mid-autumn.

Euonymus alatus
BURNING BUSH, CORKBUSH, WINGED SPINDLE TREE

☼ ❄ ↔ 10 ft (3 m) ↕ 6 ft (1.8 m)

Euonymus fortunei 'Emerald Gaiety'

Dense, deciduous, bushy shrub found from northeastern Asia to central China and Japan. Corky wings on branches. Leaves ovate to elliptical, dark green, toothed margins, turn brilliant red in autumn. Pale green flowers in summer. Fruit pale red, 4-lobed, bright orange seeds. 'Compactus', dwarf compact shrub, winged corky branches, scarlet to purple foliage in winter; 'Nordine', large orange leaves in winter, abundant fruit; 'Timber Creek', vigorous, with arching branches and broad recurving leaves that color brilliant scarlet in autumn. Zones 3–9.

Euonymus americanus
STRAWBERRY BUSH, WAHOO

☼ ❄ ↔ 6 ft (1.8 m) ↕ 8 ft (2.4 m)

Deciduous upright shrub from eastern USA. Leaves deep green, ovate to lance-shaped, scalloped margins, somewhat wrinkly, last well into late autumn. Red-tinged green flowers in summer. Pink 3- to 5-lobed fruit with yellow-tinged white seeds. Zones 6–9.

Euonymus europaeus
EUROPEAN EUONYMUS, EUROPEAN SPINDLE TREE, SPINDLE TREE

☼ ❄ ↔ 8 ft (2.4 m) ↕ 20 ft (6 m)

Deciduous shrub or small tree found from Europe to western Asia. Green branches. Leaves elliptic, scalloped, pointed tips. Small cymes of 5 to 7 yellow to green flowers in spring. Pink to red 4-lobed fruit with white seeds and orange arils. *E. e.* f. *albus*, white fruit. *E. e.* 'Aucubifolius', white variegated foliage; 'Red Cap', bright red fruit, persisting on bare winter branches; 'Red Cascade' ★, often small tree, good autumn color, persistent orange-red fruit. Zones 3–9.

Euonymus fortunei
syn. *Euonymus radicans*
WINTERCREEPER EUONYMUS

☼ ❄ ↔ 3–10 ft (0.9–3 m) ↕ 1–10 ft (0.3–3 m)

From China. Evergreen ground-cover shrub or root-clinging climber; as climber, can reach 15 ft (4.5 m) high. Green branches with fine warts. Leaves oval or elliptic, toothed, pointed tips. Greenish yellow flowers in summer. White fruit, orange arils. *E. f.* var. *vegetus*, spreading, bushy, stiff branches, thick dull green leaves. *E. f.* 'Canadale Gold', marginal bands of yellow on leaves; 'Coloratus', green foliage turns purple-red in winter; 'E.T.', prostrate form, rounded leaves with pinkish cream margins; 'Emerald Gaiety', green leaves with white margins tinged pink in winter; 'Emerald 'n' Gold', leaves with yellow margins tinged pink in winter; 'Harlequin', leaves grayish green, streaked and marbled with cream or white, frequently throwing entirely cream leaves; 'Kewensis', prostrate form, tiny leaves; 'Minims', procumbent, rooting along branches, 2 in (5 cm) high; 'Niagara Green', deep green leaves, new growth lime green; 'Sheridan Gold', yellowish green young foliage; 'Silver Queen', bushy shrub or spreading climber, leaves with broad white margins tinged pink in winter; 'Sunspot', semi-prostrate, weak arching branches, leaves with large cream or yellow blotch mainly on basal half; 'Variegatus' older variegated cultivar. Zones 5–10.

Euonymus alatus 'Timber Creek'

Euonymus japonicus

EVERGREEN EUONYMUS

❁ ❄ ↔6–12 ft (1.8–3.5 m) ↑12 ft (3.5 m)

Found in Korea, China, and Japan. Evergreen, dense, bushy shrub or small tree, grows larger in wild than in cultivation. Leaves dark green, oval to oblong, tough, leathery. Flattened cymes of green flowers in summer. Rounded pink fruit contain white seeds and orange arils. 'Albomarginatus', dark green leaves with narrow white margins; 'Bravo', leaves deep green streaked gray-green with broad yellow margins; 'Emerald 'n' Gold', dwarf form with compact foliage, pale yellow leaves with green central zone; 'Microphyllus Aureovariegatus', deep green leaves with narrow yellow margins; 'Ovatus Aureus', leaves blotched and streaked yellow. Zones 7–10.

EUPHORBIA

This large genus of about 2,000 species of annuals, perennials, shrubs, and trees, both evergreen and deciduous, is distributed throughout the world. It gives its name to the large and diverse family Euphorbiaceae. *Euphorbia* plants range from spiny and succulent cactus-like species occurring mainly in hot dry areas to leafy perennials from cool-temperate climates. All species contain a poisonous milky sap which can cause severe skin irritation and temporary blindness. The true flowers are tiny, with separate male and female forms attached to a smooth cup-like structure, or cyathium. Cyathia are generally accompanied by bracts, which may be larger and are often colored, such as the scarlet bracts of poinsettia *(E. pulcherrima)*. These cyathia and bracts may be arranged in repeatedly branched inflorescences and sometimes form large flowerheads. The flowering times of many species are rainfall dependent; in temperate climates with even rainfall, the likely flowering time is from late spring to mid-summer.
CULTIVATION: In cool-temperate climates most succulent and sub-tropical species will require greenhouse protection; some will grow in dry rock gardens. Avoid the toxic sap when pruning and disposing of branches. Some species can only be propagated from seed, others can be grown from stem-tip cuttings or by division.

Euphorbia pulcherrima

Euptelea pleiosperma

Euphorbia fulgens ★

SCARLET PLUME

❁ ⚘ ↔30 in (75 cm) ↑5 ft (1.5 m)

Arching well-branched shrub from Mexico. Leaves deciduous, lance-shaped, on long stalks. Rounded bright red floral bracts in winter. 'Alba', cream bracts; 'Albatross', bluish green leaves, white bracts; 'Purple Leaf', burgundy foliage, orange bracts. Zones 10–11.

Euphorbia pulcherrima ★

syn. *Poinsettia pulcherrima*

POINSETTIA

❁ ⚘ ↔7 ft (2 m) ↑10 ft (3 m)

Straggly deciduous shrub from Mexico. Inconspicuous yellow flowers surrounded by large brilliant red floral bracts in winter–spring. Potted poinsettias have huge commercial market. 'Henrietta Ecke', double form; 'Rosea', one of a number of named pink varieties. Other forms have cream, white, or marbled floral bracts. Zones 9–11.

EUPTELEA

Native to Japan, China, and the eastern Himalayas, this genus consists of only 2 species of smallish deciduous trees, valued in temperate-climate gardens for their sharply toothed leaves, which quiver gracefully on slender stalks in slight breezes and take on pretty tints in autumn. Small bisexual flowers appear in globular clusters along the twigs just before the leaves, followed by small winged fruit. *Euptelea*, the only genus in the family Eupteleaceae, is one of a group of primitive

Euryops pectinatus

flowering plant families that includes the planes and the beeches.
CULTIVATION: A cool moist climate, a sheltered but sunny position, and deep, moderately fertile soil produce the best growth. Little maintenance is required, apart from trimming away basal suckers from time to time. Propagate from freshly collected seed or by air-layering of suckers or low branches.

Euptelea pleiosperma

❁ ❄ ↔15 ft (4.5 m) ↑15–30 ft (4.5–9 m)

Occurs wild from central and western China to northeastern India and Bhutan. Leaves shallowly toothed, underside whitish, turning red in autumn. Pinkish green flowers with red anthers in spring. Small brown fruit, usually with more than one seed. Zones 6–9.

EURYOPS

There are about 100 species of evergreen shrubs, perennials, and annuals in this genus, a member of the large daisy (Asteraceae) family. The majority are native to South Africa. They are attractive plants with lobed or finely divided green to grayish green leaves and bright yellow daisy flowers borne over a long period.
CULTIVATION: Easily grown in a wide range of conditions, *Euryops* species can withstand some frost, are drought tolerant, and are suitable for planting in coastal gardens. Deep free-draining soil in full sun is best. Grow against a warm wall or in a greenhouse in cool-temperate climates. Prune after flowering for a compact form. Propagate from seed or half-hardened or softwood cuttings.

Euryops acraeus

syn. *Euryops evansii*

☼ ❄ ↔ 36 in (90 cm) ↕ 12–36 in (30–90 cm)

Compact plant with small, narrow, silvery gray leaves. Bright yellow daisies, to 1½ in (35 mm) across, in spring–summer. Short-lived plant in damp climates; requires perfect drainage. Zones 7–10.

Euryops chrysanthemoides

syn. *Gamolepis chrysanthemoides*

PARIS DAISY

☼ ❄ ↔ 5 ft (1.5 m) ↕ 4 ft (1.2 m)

Easily grown, particularly in warm climates. Well foliaged with deeply lobed dark green leaves. Yellow daisies, 2 in (5 cm) across, on slender stalks above foliage, in winter–spring. Zones 9–11.

Euryops pectinatus

GOLDEN DAISY BUSH, GRAY-HAIRED EURYOPS

☼ ❄ ↔ 5 ft (1.5 m) ↕ 4 ft (1.2 m)

Fern-like foliage, deeply cut, downy, gray leaves. Bright yellow daisies held well above foliage, in spring–summer. Seldom without flowers in warm climates. Zones 8–11.

EXOCHORDA

PEARL BUSH

This genus consists of 4 or 5 species of deciduous shrubs, within the rose (Rosaceae) family, native to northeast and central Asia. Some botanists now prefer to combine these into a single variable species, for which the name *E. racemosa* takes priority. They are all attractive spring-flowering shrubs, many with arching branches that become festooned with waxy white flowers, which are borne in racemes in the leaf axils or at the branch tips. The leaves are simple and alternate.

CULTIVATION: They prefer moderately fertile well-drained soil in a cool-temperate climate with well-defined seasons, and a sheltered position in full sun. They may become chlorotic in chalk soils. Prune basal shoots by one-third in late winter; remove spent flower clusters after flowering. Seeds germinate readily when sown in spring in a warm humid atmosphere. Soft-tip or half-hardened cuttings taken in summer or autumn can be rooted under cover; or use hardwood cuttings from winter pruning.

Exochorda giraldii

☼ ❄ ↔ 10 ft (3 m) ↕ 10 ft (3 m)

Large free-flowering shrub from northwestern China. Arching, spreading habit. Green leaves, red veins. White flowers in late spring. *E. g.* var. *wilsonii*, more upright. Zones 5–9.

Exochorda × *macrantha*

PEARL BUSH

☼ ❄ ↔ 10 ft (3 m) ↕ 7 ft (2 m)

Strong-growing hybrid of *E. korolkowii* and *E. racemosa* closely resembles *E. racemosa*. Abundant racemes of pure white flowers

Exochorda racemosa

Fabiana imbricata

in late spring. 'The Bride' ★, compact shrub, to 6 ft (1.8 m) high, with slightly weeping habit and arching branches covered with large white flowers in spring. Zones 5–9.

Exochorda racemosa

syn. *Exochorda grandiflora*

COMMON PEARL BUSH, PEARL BUSH

☼ ❄ ↔ 10 ft (3 m) ↕ 10 ft (3 m)

Shrub of northeastern China. Dense spherical shape when mature, with many erect arching shoots from base. Flower buds like miniature white pearls, open to pure white, waxy, slightly fragrant flowers. Zones 4–9.

FABIANA

This genus belongs to the nightshade (Solanaceae) family and contains about 25 shrubs from warm-temperate parts of South America, especially Chile and Argentina. They have small, overlapping, needle-like to narrow, triangular leaves, usually deep green. The light-colored flowers are tubular, like those of some ericas. They open in summer, and are usually white to pale pink.

CULTIVATION: Most species tolerate light to moderate frosts but prefer mild winters. They are not fussy about soil requirements, provided the winter drainage is good. These shrubs are easily propagated from half-hardened cuttings.

Fabiana imbricata

PICHI

☼ ❄ ↔ 7 ft (2 m) ↕ 8 ft (2.4 m)

Chilean species. Leaves dark green, covered with fine down when young. Upper third of stems smothered with tubular, white to pale pink flowers in summer. *F. i.* f. *violacea*, mauve to light purple flowers. *F. i.* 'Prostrata', low-growing cultivar. Zones 8–10.

Fagus grandifolia

× Fatshedera lizei

FAGUS

BEECH

This genus gives its name to the family Fagaceae, which also includes oaks and chestnuts. The genus consists of about 10 species of deciduous trees, native to Europe and the British Isles, and also found through temperate Asia and North America, China, and Japan, with branches to ground level and smooth light green leaves. Horizontally held limbs produce layers of foliage that protect the smooth silvery gray trunks from sunburn. In late autumn to winter, leaves turn golden brown or coppery red before falling. Buds are distinctly sharp-pointed, held at an angle to the stem. Prickly fruits release 2 triangular nuts.
CULTIVATION: Grow in well-drained reasonably fertile soil in wind-sheltered gardens. Summer moisture is necessary until trees become established. They handle moderate air pollution. Propagate from seed sown when fresh, or use grafted cultivars.

Fagus crenata

JAPANESE BEECH

☼ ❋ ↔ 20 ft (6 m) ↑ 30 ft (9 m)
From Japan, important deciduous tree of temperate areas. Bark gray. Leaves oval, pale green on underside, wavy furry margins when young. Veins beneath, also furry. Zones 6–9.

Fagus grandifolia

AMERICAN BEECH

☼ ❋ ↔ 35 ft (10 m) ↑ 80 ft (24 m)
From eastern USA and Canada. Deciduous straight-trunked tree, develops spreading crown when grown in open. Does not perform well in cooler summers. Often produces suckers. Zones 4–8.

Fagus japonica

JAPANESE BLUE BEECH

☼ ❋ ↔ 25 ft (8 m) ↑ 80 ft (24 m)
Deciduous tree from mountains of Honshu, Shikoku, and Kyushu in Japan. Persistent soft hairs on underside of oval leaves. Both surfaces furry on young leaves. Zones 6–8.

Fagus sylvatica

COMMON BEECH, EUROPEAN BEECH

☼ ❋ ↔ 50 ft (15 m) ↑ 100 ft (30 m)
Deciduous tree from Europe and southern England. Strongly veined foliage, provides dense shade. Trunk straight, smooth gray bark. Autumn foliage gold to orange to brown. Prickly fruits. *F. s.* f *fastigiata*, leaves deep green with gold; *F. s.* f. *heterophylla* 'Aspleniifolia', narrow long-pointed leaves; *F. s.* f. *pendula*, weeping beech, pendulous thick branches; *F. s.* f. *tortuosa*, twisted branches. *F. s.* 'Albomarginata', variegated leaves; **Cuprea Group**, copper colored; 'Dawyck', upright tree resembling Lombardy poplar; 'Dawyck Gold', gold-tipped foliage; 'Dawyck Purple', purplish foliage; **Purpurea Group** ★, soft green turning purple; 'Purpurea Pendula', weeping foliage; 'Quercina', prickly pale copper nuts; 'Riversii' ★, color intensifies to almost black; 'Tricolor', slow growing, pink margins, white-blotched green leaves. Zones 5–9.

× FATSHEDERA

Originating in France, this is a cross between Atlantic ivy *(Hedera hibernica)* and Japanese fatsia *(Fatsia japonica)* and belongs to the ivy (Araliaceae) family. It is an unusual, sprawling, evergreen shrub, sometimes climbing. Flowers are insignificant and sterile.
CULTIVATION: It is easily grown in moist well-drained soil in partial or full shade, and tolerates neglect provided the plant remains moist. With a somewhat rangy habit, × *Fatshedera* needs regular pinching back to keep it compact and a support to keep it upright. As it is sterile it must be propagated from cuttings, though it sometimes self-layers.

× Fatshedera lizei

☼/❂ ❂ ❋ ↔ 8 ft (2.4 m) ↑ 6 ft (1.8 m)
Multi-stemmed shrub. Leaves deeply lobed, hand-shaped, bright glossy green. Small heads of greenish white flowers in autumn. 'Annemeike', yellow leaves; 'Variegata', cream-edged leaves. Zones 7–11.

FATSIA

Fatsia japonica

This genus within the ivy (Araliaceae) family contains only 3 evergreen species of large-leafed small trees and shrubs from moist coastal woodlands of South Korea, Japan, and Taiwan. They tend to sucker from the base, producing a fuller shrub; unwanted stems can be removed. They are good indoor and conservatory plants with ornamental leaves, and good specimen plants for courtyards and terraces.
CULTIVATION: They are tolerant of pollution and salt spray, and are moderately frost hardy; variegated cultivars are less frost tolerant. They like moisture-retentive soil in sun or part-shade. In warm climates they can be grown under trees. In shade, they tolerate dry nutrient-deficient soil, but do better in more fertile soil. In colder areas, they need the protection of a wall or similar shelter. Under glass and in pots, they need a loam-based compost, regular feeding, and watering during the growing season. Propagate from seed sown in autumn, from cuttings, or by air-layering.

Fatsia japonica

syns *Aralia japonica, A. sieboldii*

FATSIA, JAPANESE ARALIA

☼/◐ ❄ ↔6–12 ft (1.8–3.5 m) ↑6–12 ft (1.8–3.5 m)

Native to South Korea and Japan. Leaves dark green, glossy, 7 to 11 lobes, mostly toothed, palmately lobed. Rounded flowerheads of creamy white flowers in late summer–autumn. Fruit green, ripening black by spring. Cultivars include '**Aurea**', '**Marginata**', '**Moseri**' ★, and '**Variegata**'. Zones 8–11.

FICUS

FIG

Although this genus is in the mulberry (Moraceae) family, its flower and fruiting stages differ from those of the rest of this family. Fig species come in many variations, from climbers and creepers to large shrubs and very large trees. Many fig species of tropical forests display the "strangler" growth habit, some also develop "curtains" of aerial roots, or even the "banyan" growth form. *Ficus* species have a milky sap, and a large stipule enclosing the tip of each twig and leaving a ring-like scar when it falls. Leaves vary from tiny to huge, with variable shape. Many species shed their leaves in the tropical dry season. The variable-sized "fruits" (figs) are edible.

CULTIVATION: Some species tolerate light frosts only if protected when small. Figs are vigorous, and will quickly outgrow a small garden. Propagate from seed, from cuttings, or by air-layering. *F. carica*, the edible fig, is the most easily propagated species.

Ficus benghalensis

BANYAN

☼ ✦ ↔75–400 ft (23–120 m) ↑30–40 ft (9–12 m)

Southern Asian fig, widespread in India. Vastly spreading; single tree may produce hundreds, sometimes thousands, of trunks, creating its own mini forest. Broad, stiff leaves, shiny deep green; stalkless figs, ripen to orange. Sacred tree of Hinduism. '**Krishnae**', similar proportions, inrolled cup-shaped leaves. Zones 11–12.

Ficus benjamina

BENJAMIN FIG, BENJAMIN TREE, WEEPING FIG

☼ ◧ ↔50 ft (15 m) ↑80 ft (24 m)

Tropical Asian species. Small glossy leaves, pointing downward, narrowing abruptly at apex. Figs deep reddish tan. *F. b.* var. *nuda* (syn. *F. b.* var. *comosa*), broad-spreading limbs, non-drooping branchlets, leaves narrowed at tip, orange figs. *F. b.* '**Exotica**' ★, thinner, more finely pointed leaves; '**Golden Princess**', leaves tinged lemon yellow; '**Pandora**', small thin leaves, wavy margins; '**Starlight**', leaves cream-edged, gray-green flecked. Zones 10–12.

Ficus elastica

INDIA-RUBBER TREE, RUBBER TREE

☼ ✦ ↔40–100 ft (12–30 m) ↑40–100 ft (12–30 m)

Tropical Asian fig. Large tree, numerous aerial roots draped from branches. '**Decora**' ★, broad, glossy, bronze-tinted leaves, large reddish buds at apex; '**Doescheri**', leaves irregularly edged cream,

center marbled gray; '**Schrüveriana**', leaves peppered dark green, new leaves flushed red; '**Variegata**', variegated leaves. Zones 11–12.

Ficus lyrata

FIDDLE-LEAF FIG

☼ ◧ ↔30 ft (9 m) ↑30 ft (9 m)

From rainforests of central Africa and tropical west Africa. Bushy-crowned erect tree; large stiff leaves resemble violin body. Green figs, hidden under leaves. Popular pot plant. Zones 9–12.

Ficus macrophylla

MORETON BAY FIG

☼ ◧ ↔130 ft (40 m) ↑80–100 ft (24–30 m)

From Australia's east coast. Rapid growth, dramatic trunk buttresses, large canopy. Large dark green leaves, glossy, thick. Purple figs. *F. m* subsp. *columnaris*, from Lord Howe Island, forms spreading canopy over endemic palm, *Howea forsteriana*. Zones 9–11.

Ficus microcarpa

syns *Ficus nitida, F. retusa*

BANYAN FIG, INDIAN LAUREL FIG

☼ ◧ ↔20–50 ft (6–15 m) ↑40–70 ft (12–21 m)

Native to southern China, Southeast Asia to northern Australia. Evergreen tree, upright branchlets, often forms aerial roots. Gray to reddish bark, small horizontal flecks. Dense foliage; small, oval, dark green leaves alternate along stems. *F. m.* var. *hillii* (syn. *F. hillii*) (Hill's weeping fig), popular park tree, open habit, high sweeping limbs, drooping branchlets. Zones 10–12.

Ficus macrophylla subsp. *columnaris*, in the wild, Lord Howe Island, Australia

Ficus religiosa

BO TREE, PEEPUL TREE, SACRED FIG

☼ ◧ ↔25 ft (8 m) ↑30–40 ft (9–12 m)

Native to mountains of Southeast Asia and Himalayan foothills. Strangling fig, normally deciduous in monsoonal climates. Pale gray-barked trunk, spreading branches. Leaves heart-shaped, apex drawn out into long slender point. Zones 9–12.

Ficus benghalensis

Ficus rubiginosa
PORT JACKSON FIG, RUSTY FIG

☼ ◈ ↔ 35–70 ft (10–21 m) ↕ 30–80 ft (9–24 m)
From east coast of Australia. Evergreen tree, forms broad dome. Massive buttressed trunk, smooth gray limbs, sprouting aerial roots. Thick, leathery, oval leaves, dark green with rusty or pale olive felted reverse. Figs yellowish green, warty, ripen in autumn. Gold-variegated form available. Zones 9–11.

FIRMIANA
A genus of 9 mostly deciduous trees or shrubs in the mallow (Malvaceae) family, it is found in tropical Southeast Asia, with one species from eastern Africa. They have smooth-edged or palmate leaves and racemes or panicles of stalk-like flowers, with no petals but a colored calyx. The curious fruit consists of 4 or 5 papery, leaf-like follicles, each containing round wrinkled seeds on its margins.
CULTIVATION: Adaptable to most soil types and easily transplanted, they prefer some protection from wind. Propagate from seed in warmer months, or from cuttings of lateral shoots in early spring.

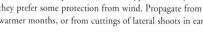
Firmiana simplex

Firmiana simplex ★
syn. *Firmiana platanifolia*
CHINESE PARASOL TREE, JAPANESE VARNISH TREE

☼ ❊ ↔ 35 ft (10 m) ↕ 60 ft (18 m)
Deciduous tree native to China and eastern Asia, from Ryukyu Islands to Vietnam. Smooth green bark; large, maple-like, palmate leaves divided into 3 to 7 lobes. Calyx lemon yellow, seed follicles hairy. 'Variegata', green leaves mottled with white. Zones 7–10.

FORSYTHIA
This small genus of about 7 species of deciduous shrubs is a member of the olive (Oleaceae) family. They occur mainly in eastern Asia, with one in southeastern Europe. Simple opposite leaves color in autumn. Yellow flowers appear before, or with, the new leaves in spring. Semi-pendulous species can be trained over a support.

Forsythia ovata 'Tetragold'

CULTIVATION: They are frost hardy and easy to cultivate in well-drained fertile soil in an open sunny position, with adequate water in summer, and winter temperatures below freezing to induce flowering. Flowers are borne on overwintered year-old shoots; remove older shoots after flowering to make room for new shoots from the base of the plant. Propagate from soft-tip cuttings in summer, or hardwood cuttings in winter. Some species are self-layering and can be increased in this way in late winter.

Forsythia × intermedia
BORDER FORSYTHIA

☼ ❊ ↔ 7 ft (2 m) ↕ 15 ft (4.5 m)
Shrub with erect spreading habit; hybrid between *F. suspensa* var. *sieboldii* and *F. viridissima*. Single basal trunk, ascending arching branches. Leaves oval, sharply toothed on upper half, with reddish stalks. Flowers lemon yellow, solitary or in 2- to 6-flowered racemes, on 1- and 2-year-old branches, in spring. 'Arnold Giant', large, nodding, rich yellow flowers; 'Goldzauber', brilliant yellow flowers before leaves; 'Lynwood', prolific large flowers, broad petals; 'Spectabilis', upright, outwardly arching shrub, flowers large, golden yellow. Zones 5–9.

Forsythia ovata
EARLY FORSYTHIA, KOREAN FORSYTHIA

☼ ❊ ↔ 8 ft (2.4 m) ↕ 5 ft (1.5 m)
Compact, bushy, early-flowering species from Korea. Leaves dark green, ovate. Golden yellow flowers in early spring. 'Tetragold', raised in Holland, dense habit, earlier larger flowers. Zones 5–9.

Forsythia suspensa
GOLDENBELLS, WEEPING FORSYTHIA

☼ ❊ ↔ 10 ft (3 m) ↕ 12 ft (3.5 m)
From China. Slender drooping branches. Autumn foliage dull yellow. Flowers solitary or in small clusters, golden yellow, in spring. *F. s.* var. *fortunei*, vigorous form, more upright habit; *F. s.* var. *sieboldii*, almost prostrate, rarely taller than 3 ft (0.9 m). Zones 4–9.

Forsythia viridissima
GOLDEN BELLS, GREEN STEM FORSYTHIA

☼ ❊ ↔ 10 ft (3 m) ↕ 10 ft (3 m)
From China. Cane-like branches grow from base into hemispherical bush. Leaves long, narrow, smooth, dark green, rather shiny, maroon in autumn. Clusters of yellow flowers in leaf axils before leaves, calyx purple shaded. 'Bronxensis', dwarf form. Zones 5–9.

Forsythia Hybrid Cultivars
☼ ❊ ↔ 10 ft (3 m) ↕ 5–10 ft (1.5–3 m)
Hardy and colorful. 'Arnold Dwarf' ★, light green foliage; 'Happy Centennial', bright yellow flowers; 'Maluch', profuse flowers with new leaves; Marée d'Or/'Courtasol', heavily branched dwarf, prolific yellow-gold flowers; 'Meadow Lark', heavy flowering, hardy buds; 'New Hampshire Gold', yellow flowers in early spring; 'Northern Gold', shiny bright green leaves, golden yellow flowers; 'Northern Sun', strong-growing shrub. Zones 4–9.

Fothergilla major

FOTHERGILLA

Mainly from southeastern USA, this genus of 2 deciduous shrubs belongs to the witchhazel (Hamamelidaceae) family. Spikes of petal-less flowers appear in spring before the leaves, their long white stamens creating a bottlebrush effect. Autumn foliage is colorful. CULTIVATION: Slow growing, they need moist, well-drained, humus-rich soil. Full sun gives best autumn color. Propagate from seed, best sown fresh, from softwood cuttings in summer, or by layering.

Fothergilla gardenii ★
DWARF FOTHERGILLA
☼ ✿ ↔ 3 ft (0.9 m) ↕ 3 ft (0.9 m)
Southeastern USA, from North Carolina to Alabama. Spreading shrub, oval leaves, irregularly toothed, fragrant white flowers. 'Blue Mist', glaucous blue foliage. Zones 5–9.

Fothergilla major
LARGE FOTHERGILLA
☼ ✿ ↔ 6 ft (1.8 m) ↕ 5–10 ft (1.5–3 m)
From Allegheny Mountains of eastern USA. Slow-growing. Leaves dark green above, glaucous beneath. Good autumn color. Fragrant white flower spikes, pinkish tinge, in late spring–early summer. 'Mount Airy', scented white flowers, red autumn foliage. Zones 5–9.

FRANKLINIA

This is a monotypic genus in the camellia (Theaceae) family. The species has not been seen in the wild for over 200 years. *Franklinia* is closely related to *Gordonia*, with which it is sometimes merged, but differs in being deciduous, and having almost stalkless flowers. The fruit is a large woody capsule containing two flattened seeds.
CULTIVATION: *Franklinia* will tolerate a slightly alkaline soil, but likes plenty of organic material; a sheltered aspect with some morning sun is preferred. Propagate from fresh seed.

Franklinia alatamaha ★
FRANKLIN TREE, FRANKLINIA
☼ ✿ ↔ 12 ft (3.5 m) ↕ 20 ft (6 m)
From Altahama River region in Georgia, USA. Attractive, small, upright, deciduous tree. Glossy bright green leaves color scarlet in autumn. Single camellia-like flowers, pure white with central bunch of yellow stamens, in late summer–autumn. Zones 7–10.

FRAXINUS
ASH
This genus in the olive (Oleaceae) family consists of 65 species. Most *Fraxinus* species are deciduous trees, but the genus also includes a few evergreens. They are mainly from temperate Europe, Asia, and North America, although a few species are found in the tropics. Their leaves are opposite and pinnate. Racemes of small, usually insignificant flowers are borne terminally or in the leaf axils, appearing before the leaves, in spring; flowers are unisexual or bisexual. They harden into single-seeded winged fruits.
CULTIVATION: Most grow well in moist loam and make good specimen trees in large gardens. They tolerate coastal salt air, exposed positions, urban pollution, alkaline soil, and heavy clay. Most species prefer alkaline soil. Propagate by sowing seed after stratifying. Cultivars can be grafted in spring, or they may be budded onto seedling stock of the same species in summer.

Fraxinus americana
WHITE ASH
☼ ✿ ↔ 50 ft (15 m) ↕ 80 ft (24 m)
Columnar tree with spreading crown native to eastern North America. Leaves pinnate, dark green, with 5 to 9 lance-shaped leaflets. 'Autumn Blaze', purple color in autumn; 'Autumn Purple' ★, autumn foliage colored red to deep crimson; 'Rose Hill', dark green leaves, turning bronze-red in autumn. Zones 4–10.

Fraxinus americana 'Autumn Purple'

Fraxinus angustifolia
syn. *Fraxinus rotundifolia*
NARROW-LEAFED ASH
☼ ✿ ↔ 40 ft (12 m) ↕ 80 ft (24 m)
Closely allied to *F. excelsior*, occurs wild in Mediterranean region and western Asia. Typical race (*F. a.* subsp. *angustifolia*) is restricted to southern Europe and northwestern Africa. Vigorous tree, ascending branches, darkish furrowed bark. Leaves have 7 to 13 rather narrow leaflets, arranged in whorls of 3. Winter buds large and dark brown. *F. a.* subsp. *oxycarpa* (syn. *F. oxycarpa*) occurs in southeastern Europe and Caucasus region, only 5 to 7 leaflets per leaf, bands of hairs on underside; *F. a.* subsp. *syriaca* (syn. *F. syriaca* 'Desert Ash'), occurs in Turkey, Syria, and Iran, smaller bushier tree, blackish bark, very thick knobbly twigs, leaves in whorls of 3 or 4, grows well in semi-arid climates. *F. a.* 'Elegantissima', small tree, light green leaves; 'Lentiscifolia', leaflets more widely spaced on longer common stalk; 'Raywood', dark wine red autumn foliage. Zones 6–10.

Fraxinus chinensis   Fraxinus uhdei

Fraxinus chinensis

☼ ❄ ↔ 25 ft (8 m) ↑ 80 ft (24 m)

Native to Korea and China. Yellow hairless young growth. Leaves with 8 leaflets, invertly egg-shaped, dark green above, slightly downy underneath. Flowers on new growth in terminal panicles. Winged fruits in summer. Zones 6–9.

Fraxinus excelsior

COMMON ASH, EUROPEAN ASH

☼ ❄ ↔ 60 ft (18 m) ↑ 100 ft (30 m)

Native to Europe. Gray branches, prominent black buds in winter. Dark green leaves with 11 pairs of leaflets, turn bright yellow in autumn. Flower panicles before leaves in spring. Fruits winged, pendent, remaining after leaves fall. *F. e.* f. *diversifolia*, leaves usually single large leaflet. *F. e.* 'Aurea Pendula', pendulous golden branches; 'Eureka', bright green leaves, serrated edges; 'Jaspidea', yellow shoots in winter; 'Pendula', weeping branches. Zones 4–10.

Fraxinus nigra

BLACK ASH, SWAMP ASH

☼ ❄ ↔ 25 ft (8 m) ↑ 50 ft (15 m)

Upright deciduous tree native to North America. Leaves dark green, 11 stalkless leaflets, lance-shaped, small-toothed edges, curved upward, downy brown veins, underside paler green. Fruit oblong, winged. 'Fallgold', non-fruiting, yellow autumn color. Zones 7–10.

Fraxinus ornus

FLOWERING ASH, MANNA ASH

☼ ❄ ↔ 40 ft (12 m) ↑ 50 ft (15 m)

Native to southern Europe and southwestern Asia. Leaves with 7 leaflets, paler beneath, hairy midribs. Dense panicles of fragrant white flowers in late spring. Fruit narrow, winged. Damaged bark secretes sugary substance. 'Arie Peters', creamy flowers. Zones 6–10.

Fraxinus pennsylvanica

GREEN ASH, RED ASH

☼ ❄ ↔ 70 ft (21 m) ↑ 70 ft (21 m)

Robust tree from North America. Olive green leaves, 9 lance-shaped leaflets, smooth or toothed edges, pointed tip, sunken midrib.

Flowers on old wood, followed by winged fruit. 'Marshall's Seedless', non-fruiting, dark green leaves; 'Patmore', strongly erect, glossy leaves, oval crown, does not fruit; 'Summit' ★, pyramidal when young, becoming upright, autumn leaves deep yellow. Zones 4–10.

Fraxinus uhdei

EVERGREEN ASH, SHAMEL ASH

☼ ❄ ↔ 15 ft (4.5 m) ↑ 25 ft (8 m)

Semi-evergreen to evergreen upright tree from Mexico and Central America. Leaves dark green, lance-shaped to oblong, toothed, hairless, 7 leaflets. Flowers in dense panicles. 'Tomlinson', small upright tree, reaches 12 ft (3.5 m) in 10 years. Zones 8–11.

Fraxinus velutina

ARIZONA ASH, DESERT ASH, VELVET ASH

☼ ❄ ↔ 30 ft (9 m) ↑ 30 ft (9 m)

Native to southwestern USA and northwestern Mexico. Dull green leaves, 7 lance-shaped to oval, toothed leaflets, leathery, hairy felting beneath. *F. v.* var. *coriacea,* leaves thicker and almost hairless; *F. v.* var. *glabra*, doubtfully distinct from *F. v.* var. *coriacea*; *F. v.* var. *toumeyi*, longer-stalked, narrower leaflets, gray-green upper surface stays velvety until late summer. *F. v.* 'Fan-Tex', handsome tree, larger dark green leaves, non-fruiting. Zones 7–10.

FREMONTODENDRON

FLANNEL BUSH

There are 3 species of evergreen shrubs in this genus from southwestern North America, which is a member of the cacao (Sterculiaceae) family. Flannel bushes have showy golden yellow to orange blooms of 5 petal-like sepals. The stems, flower buds, and seed capsules, and the underside of the leaves, are covered with fine bronze bristles that give rise to the common name of flannel bush. CULTIVATION: These shrubs require a warm, sunny, sheltered site, and in cool-temperate climates should be grown under the protection of a wall, although they will withstand some frost. Poor dry soils suit them best, as rich soils produce an excess of foliage rather than flowers and can be a factor in reducing the plant's life span. Too much moisture and root disturbance are other reasons why flannel bush plants are fairly short lived. Propagate from seed, or from softwood or half-hardened cuttings.

Fremontodendron californicum

FLANNEL BUSH, FREMONTIA

☼ ❄ ↔ 15 ft (4.5 m) ↑ 12–25 ft (3.5–8 m)

Found in Sierra Nevada range of California, USA. Leaves variable, almost round to pointed oval shape, dull green, roughened by tiny hairs. Flowers in flushes in spring–summer, bright yellow, often with orange tones on their backs. Zones 8–10.

Fremontodendron mexicanum

MEXICAN FLANNEL BUSH, MEXICAN FREMONTIA, SOUTHERN FLANNEL BUSH

☼ ❅ ↔ 12 ft (3.5 m) ↑ 20 ft (6 m)

Native to Mexico's Baja California Peninsula and San Diego area, USA. Grows in chaparral and woodland. More tender than *F. californicum*. Golden yellow flowers, partly hidden by foliage, over many months, from spring. Zones 9–11.

Fremontodendron Hybrid Cultivars

❊ ❊ ↔ 10–15 ft (3–4.5 m) ↑ 12–20 ft (3.5–6 m)

Hybrids between *F. californicum* and *F. mexicanum* have largely proved superior to either of their parents, being more vigorous, with heavier crop of larger flowers. '**California Glory**', vigorous shrub, large yellow flowers; '**Ken Taylor**' low grower, bright orange-yellow flowers; '**Pacific Sunset**', vigorous, almost tree-like, bright yellow flowers with elongated petal tips. Zones 8–10.

FUCHSIA

There are about 100 species of small or medium-sized trees and spreading or climbing shrubs in this genus, which is a member of the evening primrose (Onagraceae) family. Almost all species are from South and Central America, but a few are native to New Zealand and Tahiti. They are evergreen or deciduous, with foliage growing in whorls, alternate or opposite. Flowers bloom in terminal clusters or from leaf axils and are usually tubular and pendent, often bicolored. The flowers are followed by edible berries, usually with many seeds. In their native habitat, the American species are pollinated by hummingbirds.

Fremontodendron, Hybrid Cultivar, 'California Glory'

CULTIVATION: Most fuchsias are frost tender, and even the few fully hardy forms may die down to ground level in a severe winter. Fuchsias planted in the garden do best in fairly fertile moist soil with good drainage in full sun or partial shade. Feed regularly during flowering. Propagate species from seed and cuttings; raise cultivars from cuttings only, using softwood cuttings in spring or half-hardened cuttings in late summer.

Fuchsia arborescens

TREE FUCHSIA

❊/❊ ❊ ↔ 5 ft (1.5 m) ↑ 6 ft (1.8 m)

Native to Mexico and Central America. Leaves opposite or in whorls of 3 or 4, elliptical with pointed tip, shiny, dark green upper surface, paler green underneath. Flowers in panicles of pink-purple sepals and tubes with pale mauve corolla, in summer. Fruit purple, becomes wrinkled when ripe. Zones 10–12.

Fuchsia boliviana

❊ ❊ ↔ 3–4 ft (0.9–1.2 m) ↑ 12 ft (3.5 m)

Erect shrub or small tree occurring naturally in South America from northern Argentina to Peru; has become naturalized in Colombia and Venezuela. Dark green leaves in whorls of 3, pale gray felty veining on underside. Terminal flowers, tubes pale to dark pink, sepals pale pink to red, scarlet petals, in summer–autumn. Fruit small, red-purple, edible, sweetly flavored. *F. b.* var. *alba* ★, white tubes, sepals with light red marks at base. Zones 9–11.

Fuchsia coccinea

❊/❊ ❊ ↔ 4 ft (1.2 m) ↑ 5–20 ft (1.5–6 m)

Climber or erect shrub native to Brazil. Older branches lose bark in long strips. Leaves in groups of 2, 3, or 4, egg-shaped, pointed tip, matt light green above, paler underneath, hairless or slightly hairy. Deep pink to red flowers grow from leaf axils in summer. Zones 8–11.

Fuchsia fulgens ★

❊/❊ ❀ ↔ 30 in (75 cm) ↑ 5 ft (1.5 m)

Native to Mexico. Toothed heart-shaped leaves, red above, underside paler, flushed with red. Small flowers with red sepals tinged yellow-green toward tips and bright red corolla. Fruit oblong, deep purple. Zones 11–12.

Fuchsia magellanica

LADIES' EARDROPS

❊/❊ ❊ ↔ 6 ft (1.8 m) ↑ 10 ft (3 m)

Originating in Chile and Argentina, naturalized elsewhere. Erect vigorous shrub; older branches have flaking bark. Leaves elliptical to egg-shaped and tinted red underneath. Flowers red tubes, dark red sepals, purple corolla, in summer–late autumn. Fruit oblong, crimson in color. Makes colorful hedge in mild winter areas. *F. m.* var. *gracilis* (syn. *F. m.* var. *macrostemma*), small leaves, abundant, very pendent, small flowers, deep scarlet calyx, purple petals; *F. m.* var. *molinae*, name used for pale pink-flowered variants in cultivation; *F. m.* var. *pumila*, to 12 in (30 cm) high, red and blue flowers. *F. m.* '**Riccartonii**', commonly used for hedging in Ireland and islands around Britain; '**Versicolor**', gray-green leaves, tinted silver, small deep red flowers. Zones 7–10.

Fuchsia arborescens

Fuchsia procumbens
TRAILING FUCHSIA

☼/◐ ❀ ↔ 3 ft (0.9 m) ↑ 6 in (15 cm)

Evergreen, prostrate, spreading shrub native to New Zealand. Leaves small, heart-shaped. Small upward-facing flowers, greenish to pale orange tubes, purple-tipped green sepals, no petals, in summer. Fruit bright red, persistent. Good rock-garden plant. Zones 9–11.

Fuchsia splendens
☼/◐ ❀ ↔ 3 ft (0.9 m) ↑ 8 ft (2.4 m)

Terrestrial or epiphytic shrub from Mexico to Costa Rica. Leaves heart-shaped, toothed edges, green above; paler, flushed red, and veined beneath. Flower tube rose pink, sepals green with red base, petals olive green. Fruit green to purple, warty. Zones 8–11.

Fuchsia thymifolia
☼/◐ ❀ ↔ 20 in (50 cm) ↑ 36 in (90 cm)

From Mexico to northern Guatemala. Leaves oval to egg-shaped, sometimes with toothed edge, finely hairy both above and underneath. Flowers solitary, tube green-white to pink, sepals and petals same color, ageing to dark purple, in summer–autumn. Zones 8–11.

Fuchsia triphylla
HONEYSUCKLE FUCHSIA

☼/◐ ✤ ↔ 2 ft (0.6 m) ↑ 6 ft (1.8 m)

Native to West Indies. Leaves opposite, in whorls of 3 or 4; oval or lance-shaped, sometimes finely toothed, dull dark green upper surface, paler undersurface often tinged silvery purple. Flowers orange to coral red; fruit shiny reddish purple. 'Billy Green', rose pink flowers, light green leaves. Zones 11–12.

Fuchsia Hybrid Cultivars
☼/◐ ❀ ↔ 18–36 in (45–90 cm) ↑ 1–7 ft (0.3–2 m)

Over 8,000 fuchsia cultivars have been recorded, with about 2,000 still in cultivation. Most are derived from *F. magellanica, F. fulgens,* and *F. triphylla.*

"Hardy" types withstand winter in Zone 7, and include 'Abbé Farges', semi-double flowers, cherry red tube and sepal, rose-lilac corolla; 'Constance', tube and sepals pale pink, green-tipped corolla; 'Hawkshead', tube and sepals white with green, corolla white; 'White Pixie', red tube and sepal, corolla white, veined deep pink.

Other hybrids include 'Brookwood Belle', prolific, double medium-sized flowers, deep cerise tube, sepals and corolla white, flushed pale pink; 'Coachman', coral pink sepals, reddish orange corolla; 'Display', large flowers, pink-red calyx, corolla deeper rose pink, long stamens; 'Golden Marinka', later flowering form, trailing habit, variegated red-veined leaves, medium-sized single blooms, rich red tube and sepals, darker red corolla; 'La Campanella', semi-double, white tube, white sepals tinted pink, corolla imperial purple; 'Marcus Graham', trailing habit, large double pink flowers; 'Prosperity', medium-sized double flowers, crimson tube, crimson sepals, pink corolla, veined rose red; 'Rading's Inge', tiny flowers, rose pink tube, cream sepals, orange corolla; and 'Ri Mia', pale lilac tube, sepals, corolla. Zones 9–11.

GARCINIA

This genus in the St John's-wort (Clusiaceae) family containing 200 tropical species is found mostly in Asia and Africa. They are densely foliaged evergreen trees and shrubs with highly scented flowers that open at night. The fleshy fruits of some are edible, notably those of *G. mangostana*. Male and female flowers are separate, usually on different plants, sometimes on the same plant. Damaged branches and twigs secrete a yellow sap reputed to have medicinal qualities. CULTIVATION: Plants require a rich soil and plenty of water and are very frost sensitive, being suitable only for tropical and warmest subtropical regions. Propagation is generally from fresh seed, although some species have been successful using cuttings and air-layering.

Garcinia mangostana
MANGOSTEEN

☼ ✤ ↔ 15 ft (4.5 m) ↑ 50 ft (15 m)

Native to Malaysia and Indonesia, slow-growing (15 years before fruit), evergreen tree cultivated for delicious fruit. Large glossy leaves, heavy crown. Male and female flowers on separate trees, females generally produce seedless fruit, to 4 in (10 cm) in diameter, thick skin, rich purple color when ripe. Zones 11–12.

GARDENIA

This genus from the madder (Rubiaceae) family consists of around 250 species from tropical Africa, Asia, and Australasia. Mostly evergreen shrubs or small trees, they have opposite or whorled, shiny, simple, deep green leaves. Fragrant large flowers, tubular

Fuchsia procumbens

Fuchsia, Hybrid Cultivar, 'Marcus Graham'

Garcinia mangostana

to funnel-shaped, white or yellow, are produced singly or in few-flowered cymes. The fruit is a leathery or fleshy berry.
CULTIVATION: Most are fairly adaptable plants tolerant of sun or part-shade, and do best in a well-drained, humus-rich, acidic soil. Gardenias are surface rooted, responding well to regular mulching with good-quality compost, fertilizer, and adequate summer watering. In cool climates grow in a heated greenhouse. Propagate from seed or leafy tip or half-hardened cuttings in late spring and summer.

Gardenia augusta
syn. *Gardenia jasminoides*
CAPE JASMINE, COMMON GARDENIA
☼/◐ ✱ ↔ 5 ft (1.5 m) ↕ 5–8 ft (1.5–2.4 m)
Native to southeastern China and Japan. Bushy habit; elliptic to obovate, glossy, dark green leaves. Flowers strongly fragrant, white, wheel-shaped, in summer. Double-flowered cultivars include 'August Beauty', lush green foliage, white flowers; 'Florida' ★, to 3 ft (0.9 m) tall, white flowers; 'Grandiflora', larger leaves and pure white flowers; 'Magnifica', semi-double creamy white flowers; 'Radicans', spreading low growth, smaller leaves, plentiful semi-double white flowers; and 'Veitchii', upright yet compact shrub with small, highly scented, double white flowers. Zones 10–11.

Gardenia thunbergia
STARRY GARDENIA
☼ ❀ ↔ 7 ft (2 m) ↕ 12 ft (3.5 m)
Occurs in humid forests of South Africa. Upright shrub or small tree. Smooth gray bark. Glossy dark green leaves with wavy margins. Fragrant, white or cream, solitary flowers, spoke-like petals at end of long tube, in summer. Zones 9–11.

GARRYA
This genus of about 18 evergreen trees or shrubs belongs to the silk-tassel (Garryaceae) family. They are grown for their tough leathery leaves and distinctive pendulous catkins of inconspicuous flowers without petals. Male and female flowers are borne on separate plants from winter to early summer, while the fruit of the female plant consists of clusters of round, dry, dark, 2-seeded berries, borne from summer to autumn. Native to western North America and the West Indies, they are valued for their durability in warmer climates.
CULTIVATION: Well suited to salty coastal environments and tolerant of pollution, *Garrya* species prefer a sunny sheltered position but can cope with a wide range of soil types. Most dislike humid summers. Avoid transplanting. They are propagated from cuttings of half-hardened wood, or by layering, and from seed.

Garrya elliptica ★
CATKIN BUSH, COAST SILKTASSEL, SILKTASSEL BUSH
☼ ❀ ↔ 6 ft (1.8 m) ↕ 8–12 ft (2.4–3.5 m)
Native to southwestern USA, from Oregon to California. Glossy, oval, gray-green to matt green leaves, undulating margins, dense woolly coating beneath. Long grayish green male catkins in winter–spring. Smaller female catkins, abundant clusters of oval-shaped

Gardenia augusta 'Magnifica'

dark purple fruit. 'Evie', catkins to 12 in (30 cm) long; 'James Roof', male form, larger leaves and catkins than species. Zones 8–10.

Garrya fremontii
FEVER BUSH, FREMONT SILKTASSEL, QUININE BUSH, SKUNK BUSH
☼ ❀ ↔ 6 ft (1.8 m) ↕ 7–10 ft (2–3 m)
Native to western USA, from California to Oregon. Leathery, glossy, hairy, dark green leaves, smooth above, woolly underneath. Terminal clusters of male catkins, to 8 in (20 cm) long, in spring. Woolly female catkins, to 2 in (5 cm) long, in late summer–autumn. Dark purple oval-shaped fruit. Zones 7–10.

Garrya elliptica

GAULTHERIA
SNOWBERRY, WINTERGREEN
This genus contains some 170 species of evergreen shrubs, ranging from the Americas to Japan and Australasia. Belonging to the heath (Ericaceae) family, these tough bushes have leathery foliage and prefer temperate to cool climates. They are often found in mountainous areas, where their bright, relatively large fruits stand out among the short alpine vegetation. Flowers tend to be bell-shaped and pendulous. Fruit may be small and fairly dry or a fleshy berry. Many species are quite aromatic, often highly so, especially the fruit.
CULTIVATION: Frost hardiness varies with the species, the toughest being among the large broadleafed evergreens. They prefer moist, well-drained, humus-rich, slightly acidic soil with ample summer moisture. The exposure preference also varies with the species, though few do well in full shade. Propagate from seed, or from half-hardened cuttings or layers, which will often form naturally where the stems remain in contact with the ground.

Gaultheria depressa
☼/◐ ❀ ↔ 10 in (25 cm) ↕ 4 in (10 cm)
Near-prostrate, wiry-stemmed shrub from rocky or boggy ground in mountains of New Zealand. Tiny, leathery, serrated leaves, reddish stems. Small white to pale pink flowers, carried singly, in summer. White to deep pink berries. Zones 8–9.

Gaultheria mucronata

syn. *Pernettya mucronata*

☼/◐ ✱ ↔48 in (120 cm) ↑18–60 in (45–150 cm)

Native to Argentina and Chile. Strongly branched suckering shrub, young stems often bright pinkish red, densely covered with small deep green leaves, sharp pointed tips. White or pale pink flowers in late spring. Fruit large, white, shades of pink and red. **'Alba'**, white fruit; **'Bell's Seedling'**, crimson fruit; **'Coccinea'**, scarlet fruit; **'Crimsonia'**, crimson fruit; **'Mulberry Wine'**, maroon to purple fruit; Snow White/ **'Sneeuwwitje'**, red-speckled white fruit; **'Wintertime'**, long-lasting white fruit. Zones 6–10.

Gaultheria × *wisleyensis*

Gaultheria procumbens

CHECKERBERRY, TEABERRY, WINTERGREEN

☼/◐ ✱ ↔36 in (90 cm) ↑6 in (15 cm)

Attractive shrub from eastern North America. Deep green glossy leaves to 2 in (5 cm) long. Racemes of white to pale pink flowers in summer. Red fruit, to ½ in (12 mm) wide; source of pungent liniment used for muscle or joint problems. **'Macrocarpa'**, compact form, abundant fruit. Zones 4–9.

Gaultheria shallon

SALAL, SHALLON

☼/◐ ✱ ↔5 ft (1.5 m) ↑5 ft (1.5 m)

Found in western North America, from California to Alaska. Spreading shrub takes root along prostrate branches. Broad oval leaves to 4 in (10 cm) long. Tiny white to deep pink flowers, in conspicuous red-stemmed racemes near stem tips, in late spring. Red fruit ripens to black. Zones 5–9.

Gaultheria × *wisleyensis*

syn. × *Gaulnettya wisleyensis*

☼/◐ ✱ ↔3 ft (0.9 m) ↑3 ft (0.9 m)

Hybrid between North American *G. shallon* and *G. mucronata* of South America. Low spreading shrub forms small thickets of suckering stems. Several cultivars with leaves of varying sizes, up to 1½ in (35 mm) long. Flowers white or various shades of pink to light purple. Purplish red fruit. Zones 6–9.

GEIJERA

A member of the rue (Rutaceae) family, this genus contains 8 species from New Guinea, eastern Australia, and New Caledonia. Of the 5 endemic Australian species, 2 occur in rainforests and the other 3 in various habitats, even relatively arid regions. All are small to medium trees reaching 80 ft (24 m) tall when growing in rainforests. The flowers are small, no more than ¼ in (6 mm) across, and they are borne in terminal panicles. They are followed by small brown fruits of 2 to 4 compartments, each containing a glossy black seed. CULTIVATION: The different species come from natural habitats ranging from semi-arid inland plains to drier types of coastal rainforest, but the inland species adapt well to moister climates. All prefer reasonably fertile soil. Propagation is from fresh seed, which may germinate quite erratically.

Geijera parviflora ★

WILGA

☼ ❄ ↔35 ft (10 m) ↑40 ft (12 m)

Small tree occurring in drier inland regions of all Australian States except Tasmania and Western Australia. Pendulous narrow leaves. Creamy white flowers in spring. Propagation not easy, as seed often difficult to obtain. Zones 8–11.

GENISTA

syns *Chamaespartium, Echinospartium*

About 90 species belong to this genus within the pea-flower subfamily of the legume (Fabaceae) family. Most are deciduous but some appear evergreen because of their flat green branchlets. Native to Europe and the Mediterranean to western Asia, these shrubs or small trees mostly grow on rocky hillsides. Leaves are alternate, simple, or consist of 3 leaflets; branches can be nearly leafless. CULTIVATION: Full sun is necessary and not all plants are fully frost hardy. Grow half-hardy plants in a well-ventilated greenhouse. They tolerate all soils but need a light well-drained soil to flower well. Propagate from ripe seed in autumn or spring, and protect from winter frosts, or half-hardened cuttings in summer.

Genista aetnensis

MOUNT ETNA BROOM

☼ ❄ ↔25 ft (8 m) ↑25 ft (8 m)

Shrub native to Sardinia and Sicily. Weeping branches; narrow leaves only on young shoots, fall off as branches age. Fragrant, yellow, pea-like flowers on pendent shoots in summer–autumn. Zones 8–10.

Genista lydia

DWARF GENISTA, GENISTA

☼ ❄ ↔36 in (90 cm) ↑24 in (60 cm)

Native to eastern Balkans. Deciduous prostrate shrub, smaller in wild. Blue-green leaves, long and narrow or elliptic in shape.

Genista sagittalis

Short racemes of golden yellow flowers appear in late spring–early summer. Flat non-hairy fruit. Zones 7–9.

Genista sagittalis
WINGED BROOM
☼ ❄ ↔ 36 in (90 cm) ↑ 6 in (15 cm)
Prostrate shrub native to southern and central Europe. Winged branchlets. Leaves lance-shaped, hairy below. Golden flowers in terminal racemes in late spring–early summer. Silky fruit. Zones 4–9.

Genista × spachiana
syns Cytisus fragrans, C. × spachiana, Genista fragrans
☼ ❄ ↔ 17 ft (5 m) ↑ 10–20 ft (3–6 m)
Vigorous, evergreen, arching shrub, cross of G. stenopetala and G. canariensis. Dark green leaves with 3 oval leaflets, ¼–¾ in (6–18 mm) long, silky underneath. Long slender clusters of fragrant golden yellow flowers, ½ in (12 mm) across, in winter–early spring. Zones 9–11.

Genista tinctoria
COMMON WOADWAXEN, DYER'S GREENWEED
☼ ❄ ↔ 3 ft (0.9 m) ↑ 3 ft (0.9 m)
Deciduous spineless shrub native to Europe and western Asia. Bright green leaves, elliptic or lance-shaped. Golden flowers on upright racemes in summer. 'Flore Pleno', dwarf, double flowers; 'Golden Plate', clear yellow flowers, spreading compact shape, weeping branches; 'Royal Gold', more erect, flowers carried in panicles. Zones 2–9.

GINKGO
A primitive genus containing a single species and given its own family, Ginkgoaceae, Ginkgo is different from all other conifers. Fossil records show it to be ancient. Now unknown in the wild, it was certainly grown in China in the eleventh century; some specimens are believed to be well over 1,000 years old. The foliage resembles that of the maidenhair fern. Pollination is achieved by motile spores, a feature unknown among the higher plants, but normal among ferns. Male and female organs are carried on separate trees. The fruit is edible and nutritious.
CULTIVATION: This tree prefers hot summers and tolerates a range of conditions, including air pollution. Plant in well-drained soil in full sun. Propagate from seed or half-hardened summer cuttings.

Ginkgo biloba
GINKGO, MAIDENHAIR TREE
☼ ❄ ↔ 25 ft (8 m) ↑ 100 ft (30 m)
Deciduous, very long lived, crown only developing fully after first 100 years. Fronds fan-shaped, parallel veins spreading out from stalk. Male flowers pendulous short-stalked catkins. Fruit yellow-green, unpleasant odor when decaying. Foliage turns golden yellow in autumn. 'Aurea', yellow leaves in summer; 'Autumn Gold' ★, broadly conical, leaves turn gold in autumn; 'Fastigiata', grows to 30 ft (9 m) in height; Pendula Group members have nodding branches; 'Princeton Sentry', narrow growth habit, yellow autumn coloring; 'Saratoga', dense rounded form, with deeply cut leaves;

Ginkgo biloba

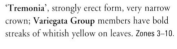
Gleditsia triacanthos f. inermis 'Halka'

'Tremonia', strongly erect form, very narrow crown; Variegata Group members have bold streaks of whitish yellow on leaves. Zones 3–10.

GLEDITSIA
LOCUST
There are 14 species of deciduous trees in this genus from the cassia subfamily of the legume (Fabaceae) family, native to North and South America, central and eastern Asia, Iran, and parts of Africa. All have fern-like, pinnately or bipinnately arranged leaves, and stout, sometimes branching, thorns on the trunk and branches. Flowers are insignificant and followed by seed pods that sometimes contain a sweet pulp.
CULTIVATION: Plants grow best in sun, in moderately fertile soil that is moisture retentive, and may require frost protection when young. However, they are generally very tough, tolerating a range of soils and climates and are pollution resistant. Species are propagated from seed sown in autumn, while cultivars are grafted or budded.

Gleditsia triacanthos
HONEY LOCUST, THORNLESS HONEY LOCUST
☼ ❄ ↔ 70 ft (21 m) ↑ 150 ft (45 m)
Native to central and eastern USA. Fern-like foliage bright green, turning bright yellow in autumn. Thorns up to 12 in (30 cm). G. t. f. inermis is thornless—nearly all cultivars of honey locust derived from it. 'Elegantissima', very compact, almost shrub-like, fine foliage, very slow growing, rarely exceeds 15 ft (4.5 m) tall; 'Emerald Cascade', weeping tree, dark emerald green foliage turns bright yellow in autumn; 'Halka', fast-growing selection, narrow crown; fine yellow color in autumn; 'Marando', dwarf with spreading twisted branches; 'Moraine' ★, tall, shapely, thornless tree, broadly spreading lower branches, dense ferny foliage; 'Rubylace', dark red young foliage, bronzing as it ages; 'Shademaster', broad-crowned upright tree, deep green leaves persisting late in autumn; 'Skyline', symmetrical outline, broadly conical crown, dark green leaves, golden yellow in autumn; 'Sunburst', bright yellow young leaves become lime green as season progresses. Zones 3–10.

GLYPTOSTROBUS

There is just a single species in this genus, allied to *Taxodium*, within the cypress (Cupressaceae) family. This tree is grown in China and northern Vietnam at the edges of riverbanks and rice paddies to stabilize the banks.
CULTIVATION: Ideal for planting in wet sites, beside water features, and riverbank planting, *Glyptostrobus* needs moist marshy soil and will even grow in shallow water. When green wood is damaged by frost, multiple stems can be produced. In moist warm climates with long, hot, humid summers it can be grown from seed. In acid soil, cuttings can be taken or it should be grafted onto *Taxodium*. The graft should be below water or soil level to encourage root growth.

Glyptostrobus pensilis
CHINESE SWAMP CYPRESS

☼ ❄ ↔ 20 ft (6 m) ↑ 80 ft (24 m)

Deciduous tree originally native to southeastern China and northern Vietnam, probably extinct in wild. Conical or columnar in shape, with irregular open canopy. Gray bark. Fine, pale green, new spring leaves, turn red-brown in autumn. Male cones form clusters of tassels; female cones erect, pear-shaped. Zones 8–11.

GORDONIA

Found in East Asia and the warmer temperate parts of North America, this genus of some 70 species of evergreen trees and shrubs is from the camellia (Theaceae) family. They are impressive plants with lush deep green foliage and beautiful flowers. Some species provide the added bonus of flowering in winter, though frost may destroy the flowers. Their flowers are usually white or cream with golden stamens, resembling the blooms of a single-flowered camellia.
CULTIVATION: The large deep green leaves suggest a preference for shade, but, as with camellias and rhododendrons, they need some sun to flower well. Shade from the midday summer sun is best. The soil should be humus-rich, friable, slightly acidic, and well drained—in other words, a woodland soil. Gordonias are not drought tolerant and need ample summer moisture. Prune lightly or tip-pinch after flowering. Propagate from seed or half-hardened cuttings.

Gordonia axillaris ★
☼ ❄ ↔ 12 ft (3.5 m) ↑ 12–20 ft (3.5–6 m)

Large shrub or small tree. Leaves leathery, dark green, to 6 in (15 cm) long, smooth-edged, slightly lobed or shallowly toothed. Creamy white flowers, conspicuous stamens, 5 or 6 petals, 4 in (10 cm) wide, from mid-winter to spring. Feed regularly. Zones 8–10.

Gordonia lasianthus
LOBLOLLY BAY

☼ ❄ ↔ 30 ft (9 m) ↑ 50 ft (15 m)

Native to southeastern USA. More commonly grows to around 25 ft (8 m) tall in cultivation. Narrow upright habit and shallowly serrated, deep green, glossy leaves. Although technically evergreen,

Gordonia axillaris

older leaves develop red tones before finally falling. Flowers white, to 3 in (8 cm) wide, in summer. Zones 9–11.

GRAPTOPHYLLUM

Occurring in Australia, New Guinea, and the southwestern Pacific, this is a genus of 10 species of tall shrubs or small trees in the acanthus (Acanthaceae) family, several of which are popular as house plants. It has a tropical and subtropical distribution in a range of habitats from rainforest margins to rocky hillsides. All have curved tubular flowers in shades of red, as well as opposite glossy leaves; some species have unfriendly spines on the stems or leaves.
CULTIVATION: These plants will grow in sun or part-shade on a range of well-drained soils, but flower better in full sun. They are mostly frost tender and need a warm climate if grown out-doors. Propagate from fresh seed, if obtainable, or from cuttings of 2- to 3-year-old shoots.

Graptophyllum pictum
CARICATURE PLANT

☼ ✦ ↔ 30 in (75 cm) ↑ 6 ft (1.8 m)

From New Guinea. Leaves elliptical, glossy, deep green. Flowers red to purple, in terminal spikes, in summer. Various color forms include leaves all purple-bronze, others green marked with white, yellow, pink, or purple, in blotches or stripes of many shapes and sizes. Propagate cultivars from cuttings to ensure color. Zones 10–12.

GREVILLEA

This genus in the protea (Proteaceae) family is represented by around 340 species. Most are native to Australia, with some from New Guinea, New Caledonia, Vanuatu, and Sulawesi. Naturally occurring Australian forms have been selected and hybrid cultivars developed with huge horticultural potential. They range from prostrate ground covers to tall trees. Distinctive colorful flower clusters come in 3 basic forms—spider-like, toothbrush-like, and large brushes. Many are rich in nectar, which makes them attractive to insects, birds, and animals (especially Australian marsupials), all of which are pollinators. They are found in a wide climatic

Glyptostrobus pensilis

range and are tolerant of extremes. Some are short lived but spectacular, others have unique flower clusters, and some have flowers with a strong sweet fragrance.

CULTIVATION: Most grevilleas prefer an open sunny position and free-draining loams, and many perform best in phosphorus-deficient soils. Propagate from half-hardened cuttings; seed also germinates well but is often difficult to obtain. Some of the species that are difficult to grow have responded well to grafting onto stocks of vigorous species such as *G. robusta*; this technique has also been used to produce weeping standard specimens.

Grevillea aquifolium

HOLLY GREVILLEA

☼ ❄ ↔ 6 ft (1.8 m) ↑ 6 ft (1.8 m)

From southeastern Australia. Variable habit, prostrate and suckering, or rounded dense shrub. Holly-like leaves, thick sharp-pointed lobes, hairy underside. Toothbrush flowers, red, pink, or dull orange, in winter–summer. Zones 8–10.

Graptophyllum pictum

Grevillea banksii

BANKS'S GREVILLEA, RED SILKY OAK

☼ ❄ ↔ 7 ft (2 m) ↑ 10–30 ft (3–9 m)

Variable dense shrub or slender tree native to coastal Queensland, Australia. Long leaves, very deeply divided, smooth, silky both sides, prominent midvein. Large nectar-rich brush flowers, red or white, with pink and apricot forms, long flowering period, spring peak. Annual light pruning, avoid old wood. *G. b.* var. *forsteri*, silvery leafed shrub to 10 ft (3 m), red or cream flowers over long period. Zones 9–11.

Grevillea curviloba

syn. *Grevillea biternata* of gardens

☼ ❄ ↔ 4 ft (1.2 m) ↑ 6 ft (1.8 m)

Spreading informal shrub native to southwest Western Australia. Leaves rich bright green, deeply lobed. Fragrant white flower clusters in spring. Long-lived dense ground cover. *G. c.* subsp. *incurva*, form most widely grown, much narrower, slightly curved leaf lobes. Prostrate to more erect, often grown under wrong name, *G. biternata*. Zones 8–10.

Grevillea × gaudichaudii

☼ ❄ ↔ 10 ft (3 m) ↑ 4 in (10 cm)

Vigorous naturally occurring hybrid between *G. acanthifolia* and *G. laurifolia*. Handsome divided leaves, reddish at tips. Clusters of burgundy toothbrush flowers in spring–summer. Zones 8–10.

Grevillea juniperina

JUNIPER-LEAF GREVILLEA, PRICKLY SPIDER FLOWER

☼ ❄ ↔ 7 ft (2 m) ↑ 8 ft (2.4 m)

Dense spreading shrub found in eastern New South Wales, Australia. Leaves dark green, needle-like. Spider flower clusters, commonly red, but can be yellow, apricot, or orange, in spring–summer. Long-lived hardy plants, excellent shelter for small birds. **'Lunar Light'** (syn. *G.* 'Australflora Lunar Light'), yellow leaf-margin variegation; **'Molonglo'**, spreading habit, pale apricot flowers. Zones 8–10.

Grevillea lanigera ★

WOOLLY GREVILLEA

☼ ❄ ↔ 4 ft (1.2 m) ↑ 5 ft (1.5 m)

Native to southeastern Australia. Variable shrub, sometimes prostrate and suckering. Narrow, occasionally fleshy leaves, soft silvery felting. Flowers all year, with flush of spider clusters of pink, red, orange, or yellow in winter–spring. Zones 7–10.

Grevillea lavandulacea

LAVENDER GREVILLEA

☼ ❄ ↔ 3 ft (0.9 m) ↑ 3 ft (0.9 m)

Compact shrub from southern Australia, parent of several hybrid cultivars. Gray-green needle-like leaves, plentiful spider flower clusters of pink-red. Variations in leaf texture, habit, and flower color common. Do not crowd, avoid summer watering. Zones 8–10.

Grevillea robusta

SILK OAK, SILKY OAK

☼ ❄ ↔ 30 ft (9 m) ↑ 60 ft (18 m)

Largest of all grevilleas, semi-deciduous. Valued timber and shade tree from southeastern Queensland, Australia. Large, golden, nectar-laden flower brushes in spring–summer; fern-like foliage. Rapid growing; prefers rich, well-drained, heavy loam. Zones 8–12.

Grevillea banksii

Grevillea lavandulacea

Grevillea robusta

Grevillea rosmarinifolia

Grevillea, Hybrid Cultivar, Banksii Group, 'Misty Pink'

Grevillea, Hybrid Cultivar, Rosmarinifolia Group, 'Canberra Gem'

Grevillea rosmarinifolia

ROSEMARY GREVILLEA

☼ ❋ ↔ 6 ft (1.8 m) ↑ 6 ft (1.8 m)

Variable, dense or open shrub from southeastern Australia. Dark green needle-like leaves. Abundant spider flower clusters, cream to pale or deep pink, in winter–summer. Zones 8–10.

Grevillea thelemanniana

HUMMINGBIRD BUSH, SPIDER-NET GREVILLEA

☼ ❁ ↔ 6 ft (1.8 m) ↑ 3 ft (0.9 m)

Dense shrub from southwestern Western Australia. Leaves linear or divided, dark green. Red spider flower clusters in winter–spring. Prefers moist but well-drained sandy loam. Zones 9–11.

Grevillea victoriae

ROYAL GREVILLEA

☼ ❋ ↔ 6 ft (1.8 m) ↑ 6 ft (1.8 m)

Hardy adaptable shrub from southern Australia. Leaves simple, oval or narrowly so, leathery texture, shiny above, silky below. Pendent spider-like flower clusters of red, orange, yellow, or pink in spring–summer. Reliable feature or screen plant. Zones 8–10.

Grevillea Hybrid Cultivars

☼/◐ ❁ ↔ 4–15 ft (1.2–4.5 m) ↑ 6 in–20 ft (15 cm–6 m)

Most hybrids fall into one of 3 groups, each derived from a limited range of parent species but with none shared between the groups. A few hybrids can be placed in a "miscellaneous" group.

BANKSII GROUP

Main parent is *G. banksii* from east coast of Australia, but cultivars can be subdivided into 2 groups: those whose other parent is *G. bipinnatifida*, and those bred from taller-growing tropical and subtropical species such as *G. pteridifolia* and *G. sessilis*. All have leaves dissected into narrow segments and dense bottlebrush-like spikes of flowers, crowded toward upper side of spike. 'Coconut Ice', shrub to 7 ft (2 m) tall, bright green foliage, red-pink flowers; 'Honey Gem', shrub to 15 ft (4.5 m) tall, dark green fern-like leaves, prolific orange or yellow flower clusters; 'Mason's Hybrid' (syn. 'Ned Kelly'), fast-growing hardy shrub to 6 ft (1.8 m), ferny light green foliage, orange-red flower clusters all year; 'Misty Pink', silvery shrub to 10 ft (3 m) tall, long pink flower clusters with cream tips; 'Moonlight', upright shrub to 10 ft (3 m) tall, ferny olive green foliage, long creamy flower clusters; 'Parfait Crème',

dense shrub to 10 ft (3 m) high and wide, creamy yellow to caramel flowers; 'Robyn Gordon'—most widely planted grevillea—shrub to 6 ft (1.8 m) tall, ferny foliage, clusters of bright pinkish red flowers; 'Sandra Gordon', shrub to 15 ft (4.5 m) tall, bright yellow flowers; 'Superb', apricot-pink tint to flowers; 'Sylvia', shrub to 10 ft (3 m) tall, rosy pink flower clusters with cream tips; 'Winter Sparkles', winter-flowering shrub to 20 ft (6 m) tall. Zones 9–12.

ROSMARINIFOLIA GROUP

Most of earliest hybrids belonged to this group, derived from *G. rosmarinifolia*, *G. juniperina*, and allies with small smooth-edged leaves and flowers in characteristic spider flower clusters. Includes most Clearview and Poorinda hybrids. Some cultivars in this group hybridize freely and may become invasive. 'Canberra Gem', 6 ft (1.8 m) tall shrub, dark green needle leaves, cerise flowers; 'Clearview David', dense shrub to 8 ft (2.4 m) tall, prickly leaves, bright red spider flowers; 'Clearview Robyn', shrub to 6 ft (1.8 m) tall, blue-green needle leaves, vibrant cerise spider flowers; 'Crosbie Morrison', dense shrub to 5 ft (1.5 m) tall, gray-green leaves, pink-red spider flowers; 'Evelyn's Coronet', erect shrub to 6 ft (1.8 m) tall, silvery, woolly, pink spider flowers; 'Noellii', may be compact form of *G. rosmarinifolia*, neat bushy growth habit; 'Penola', gray leaves, abundance of red and cream blooms; 'Poorinda Beauty', 3 ft (0.9 m) tall shrub, needle leaves, dense clusters of orange-red flowers; 'Poorinda Constance', dense shrub 8 ft (2.4 m) high, soft foliage, red flowers; 'Poorinda Firebird', shrub to 6 ft (1.8 m) high, abundant scarlet spider flower clusters; 'Poorinda Leane', dense soft-foliaged shrub to 8 ft (2.4 m) tall, orange flowers; 'Poorinda Rachel', shrub to 3 ft (0.9 m) tall, oval leaves, orange-red flowers; 'Poorinda Stephen', shrub to 3 ft (0.9 m) tall, silvery oval leaves, large dark red spider flower clusters; and 'Poorinda Vivacity', shrub to 3 ft (0.9 m) tall, broad oval leaves, tight orange-red spider flower clusters. Other cultivars include 'Poorinda Queen', 'Poorinda Rondeau', 'Poorinda Tranquillity', and 'Scarlet Sprite'. Zones 8–12.

TOOTHBRUSH GROUP

These hybrid cultivars derived from large group of species, mainly from southeastern Australian, with "toothbrush" type of flower spike: flowers densely crowded and all turned upward to form elongated brush; often bent sharply backward as well. Leaves range from simple and smooth-edged to toothed, lobed, or dissected into narrow segments. Plants range from prostrate to tall and erect. 'Boongala Spinebill' ★, adaptable spreading shrub to 8 ft (2.4 m) tall, cascading branches, new ferny foliage coppery red, deep crimson toothbrush flower clusters; **'Bronze Rambler'**, vigorous, spread of 15 ft (4.5 m), dissected leaves, bronze tint on new growth, purplish flowers; **'Brookvale Letitia'**, tall shrub to 15 ft (4.5 m) high, orange and red hairy flowers; **'Fanfare'** (syn. 'Australflora Fanfare'), prostrate, spreading to 17 ft (5 m), spring to summer inflorescences dark red, pink styles; **'Ivanhoe'** ★, dense foliage, vigorous growth to 10 ft (3 m) tall and 15 ft (4.5 m) wide, red flowers. Zones 9–12.

MISCELLANEOUS GROUP

This group includes **'Granya Glory'**, to 2 ft (0.6 m) high, creamy and rosy flowers; **'Long John'**, shrub to 10 ft (3 m) tall, red and pink flowers; **'Merinda Gordon'**, to 10 ft (3 m) tall, deep pink to red flowers; **'Orange Marmalade'**, to 8 ft (2.4 m) tall, leaves smooth-edged and silky hairy on undersurface, flowers orange; **'Pendant Clusters'** (syn. 'Australflora Pendant Clusters'), creamy yellow flowers, deep red styles; **'Poorinda Ensign'**, less than 3 ft (0.9 m) tall, leaves smooth edged, densely clustered bright pink flowers; **'Sid Reynolds'**, shrub to 8 ft (2.4 m) tall, pale reddish pink flowers; and **'Winpara Gem'**, shrub to 7 ft (2 m) tall, reddish flowers. Zones 9–12.

GREWIA

This genus from the mallow (Malvaceae) family includes about 150 species of shrubs, trees, and climbers found in Africa, Asia, and Australia. Although often attractive plants, very few are cultivated and only one species, *G. occidentalis*, is at all common. Most species have oval leaves with finely toothed edges. The flowers are starry, with 5 narrow petals and a conspicuous group of stamens at the center; they are followed by small drupes.
CULTIVATION: Best suited to warm-temperate and subtropical climates, few species will tolerate any but the lightest frosts. They prefer a sunny position with moist well-drained soil and should be pinched back to keep the growth compact. If necessary, old overgrown plants can often be rejuvenated by heavy pruning. Propagate from seed or half-hardened cuttings.

Griselinia littoralis

Grewia occidentalis

FOUR CORNERS
☼ ❄ ↔ 10 ft (3 m) ↕ 10 ft (3 m)
Southern African shrub. Bright green foliage. Flowers around 1½ in (35 mm) wide, mauve to pale purple, sepals same length as petals, creating double-flowered effect, in spring–summer. Purple-red 4-lobed fruit. Zones 9–11.

GREYIA

This South African genus of 3 species of deciduous shrubs gives its name to the family Greyiaceae. The leaves resemble those of a regal pelargonium, being rounded, lobed, and around 3 in (8 cm) wide. They occur mainly at the tips of heavily wooded branches and redden before dropping in autumn. Flowers are bright red and comprise 5 petals fused to a fleshy central disc, with 10 long stamens. They are clustered in racemes up to 6 in (15 cm) wide.

CULTIVATION: Best grown in a hot sunny position, *Greyia* species prefer mild climates but will tolerate light frosts. Soil should be fairly fertile and well drained. Water well in summer but allow plants to dry off as they approach winter dormancy. Propagate from seed or half-hardened cuttings in late spring or summer.

Greyia sutherlandii

NATAL BOTTLEBRUSH
☼ ❄ ↔ 7 ft (2 m) ↕ 15 ft (4.5 m)
Large shrub; branches very heavy at base. Bright red flowerheads at tips of bare branches in late winter–early spring. Deeply lobed leaves follow in summer, coloring in autumn. Zones 9–11.

GRISELINIA

This is a genus of 7 evergreen trees and shrubs from the dogwood (Cornaceae) family, 5 of which are native to Chile and southeastern Brazil and 2 to New Zealand. Generally plants of coastal areas, they have large, glossy, leathery leaves. The tiny yellow-green flowers are unisexual, with male and female flowers borne on separate trees.
CULTIVATION: *Griselinia* species are grown for their shiny foliage and are useful for providing screens, shelter, and hedging. They are invaluable in coastal areas, being very tolerant of salt winds, and will grow in most well-drained soils in sun or part-shade. In very cold areas they are best given a warm sheltered site or grown in a conservatory. Pruning should be carried out in summer. Propagation is easiest from half-hardened cuttings in autumn, as seed can be difficult to germinate.

Griselinia littoralis

BROADLEAF, KAPUKA, PAPAUMA
☼ ❄ ↔ 15 ft (4.5 m) ↕ 25 ft (8 m)
Found in New Zealand. Leathery oval leaves, very glossy, bright green. Panicles of tiny flowers in spring. Small purplish fruits on female trees. Attractive cultivars with foliage variegated creamy yellow include **'Dixon's Cream'** and **'Variegata'**. Zones 8–11.

Greyia sutherlandii

GYMNOCLADUS

A member of the cassia subfamily of the legume (Fabaceae) family, this genus of 2 to 5 deciduous trees allied to *Gleditsia* occurs across warm-temperate regions of North America and eastern Asia. They have bipinnate leaves and separate male and female plants with flowers in short terminal panicles. The fruit is a large woody pod containing flat, hard, glossy seeds. The fruit of *G. dioica* was used by early American settlers as a substitute for coffee.
CULTIVATION: Adaptable to most soil types in an open sunny position, these trees are drought and frost tolerant. Propagation is from seed.

Gymnocladus dioica ★
CHICOT, KENTUCKY COFFEE TREE
✺ ❋ ↔ 12 ft (3.5 m) ↑ 75 ft (23 m)
Native to central and eastern North America. Coarsely textured bark, thick branchlets, young twigs light gray, almost white. Large bipinnate leaves, 8 to 14 oval leaflets, pink, turning yellow in autumn. Dull greenish white flowers, in racemes, in summer. Thick, succulent, reddish brown or maroon fruit. *G. d.* var. *folio-variegata*, variegated foliage. *G. d.* 'Variegata', variegated cream foliage. Zones 4–8.

HAKEA

There are about 140 species in this genus of evergreen Australian plants of the protea (Proteaceae) family, mostly shrubs or small trees. Many are grown for their ornamental foliage, particularly the silky new growth. Leaves vary in shape. The nectar-rich bird-attracting flowers are borne in short axillary clusters, tight pincushion-like heads, or showy spike-like racemes. Large and decorative woody fruit usually persist on the plant until dried or burnt and then split open into 2 valves to release 2 winged seeds.
CULTIVATION: Most species are frost tender, especially when young. Hakeas prefer full sun and good drainage and dislike high-phosphorus fertilizers. Many are from Western Australia and can usually tolerate periods of dryness during the summer months. Light or moderate pruning will stimulate a compact shape, healthy regrowth, and plant vigor. Some prickly species will trim into a fine impenetrable hedge. Propagation is usually from seed.

Gymnocladus dioica

Hakea bucculenta
RED POKERS
✺ ❧ ↔ 7 ft (2 m) ↑ 8 ft (2.4 m)
From Western Australia. Shrub with erect open habit. Flat, leathery, narrow-linear leaves to 8 in (20 cm) long. Red flowers, in spike-like racemes to 6 in (15 cm) long, in late winter–spring. Ornamental, bird-attracting species. Does best away from summer humidity. Zones 9–10.

Hakea laurina

Hakea cristata
✺ ❧ ↔ 8 ft (2.4 m) ↑ 12 ft (3.5 m)
Medium upright shrub from Western Australia. Gray-green leaves, prickly toothed edges. White flowers in small clusters, in upper leaf axils, in winter. Dislikes excessive humidity. Zones 9–11.

Hakea laurina
PINCUSHION HAKEA, PINCUSHION TREE, SEA URCHIN
✺ ❧ ↔ 8 ft (2.4 m) ↑ 25 ft (8 m)
Ornamental shrub or small tree from southern sandplains of Western Australia. Long, narrow, leathery, prominently veined leaves. Nectar-rich creamy white and bright crimson flowers, in ball-like clusters, in autumn–winter. Dislikes strong winds, excessive humidity. Zones 9–11.

Hakea microcarpa
SMALL-FRUITED HAKEA
✺ ❋ ↔ 6 ft (1.8 m) ↑ 6 ft (1.8 m)
Shrub found at higher altitudes of southeastern Australia. Leathery needle-like leaves. Creamy white flowers, in small clusters, in late winter–spring. Small leathery fruit. Zones 8–10.

Hakea myrtoides
MYRTLE HAKEA
✺ ❧ ↔ 15 in (38 cm) ↑ 18 in (45 cm)
Low spreading shrub from Western Australia. Leaves crowded, small, broad, with long points. Small clusters of deep pink flowers toward branch ends in winter–early spring. Zones 9–11.

Hakea purpurea
✺ ❧ ↔ 6–10 ft (1.8–3 m) ↑ 6–10 ft (1.8–3 m)
East Australian shrub. Dark green cylindrical leaves, prickly segments. Red flowers in clusters along stems in winter–spring. Zones 9–11.

Hakea salicifolia

syn. *Hakea saligna*

WILLOW HAKEA

☀ ❄ ↔ 12 ft (3.5 m) ↑ 20 ft (6 m)

Eastern Australian shrub or small tree. Flat deep green leaves, may be bronze-colored when young. Masses of creamy white scented flowers in axillary clusters in spring. Small woody fruit. Zones 8–9.

HALESIA

SILVERBELL

This is a genus of 4 or 5 species of deciduous shrubs or small trees in the storax (Styracaceae) family, indigenous to China and eastern North America. Predominantly found in moist deciduous woodlands, these plants have graceful and attractive spring flowers. Individually the flowers are simple, small, white bells, but massed together, moving on the breeze, they have an instant appeal. The leaf is usually a simple mid-green ellipse, to 5 in (12 cm) long. Winged fruit appear in autumn. CULTIVATION: At home in a moist humid environment sheltered from strong winds, they are cool-climate plants but need a hot summer for the best display of flowers. Soil should be well drained and slightly acidic. Confine pruning to trimming the plant to shape. Propagate from seed or summer cuttings.

Halesia carolina

syn. *Halesia tetraptera*

CAROLINA SILVERBELL, SILVERBELL, SNOWDROP TREE

☀ ❄ ↔ 25–30 ft (8–10 m) ↑ 25 ft (8 m)

From southeastern USA. Spreading crown. Most commonly cultivated species. Heavy flowering, in spring, with tree smothered in pendulous clusters of white or pink-flushed bells which, by autumn, develop into 4-winged fruit. Foliage develops yellow tones in autumn. Zones 3–9.

Halesia monticola

MOUNTAIN SILVERBELL, MOUNTAIN SNOWDROP TREE

☀ ❄ ↔ 20 ft (6 m) ↑ 30 ft (9 m)

From southern Appalachian mountains of eastern USA. Larger in wild. Wide-spreading crown. White flowers in clusters of 2 to 5 blooms, followed by 4-winged fruit. *H. m.* f. *rosea*, pale pink flowers. Some botanists now treat this species as subspecies of *H. carolina*. Zones 4–9.

× *HALIMIOCISTUS*

This grouping of intergeneric hybrids between *Halimium* and *Cistus* includes some that occur naturally in their Mediterranean homelands and others of garden origin. These members of the rock-rose (Cistaceae) family are small evergreen shrubs intermediate in form between the parent genera, with small downy leaves, often gray-green to slightly glaucous, and flowers similar to *Cistus* but smaller and with the addition of yellow to their palette. Most flower in summer. CULTIVATION: Tolerating hardy to moderate frosts and easily grown in any sunny position with light well-drained soil, these are vigorous shrubs well suited to large rock gardens or general planting with other sun-lovers. They can be trimmed after flowering, though tidying is often best left until spring, when winter damage can be removed. Propagate from half-hardened tip cuttings in late summer or autumn.

× *Halimiocistus wintonensis*

☀ ❄ ↔ 30 in (75 cm) ↑ 24 in (60 cm)

Originating in Hillier's Nursery, chance hybrid between *Halimium ocymoides* and *Cistus salviifolius*. Grayish leaves. Large, 2 in (5 cm) wide flowers, pearly white, feathered zone of crimson-maroon, contrasting with yellow stains at petal base. '**Merrist Wood Cream**', flowers pale milky yellow, maroon basal spot. Zones 8–9.

HALIMIUM

There are about 12 species of evergreen shrubs and subshrubs in this genus of the rock-rose (Cistaceae) family. They are native to the Mediterranean region and western Asia in dry open forest thickets and sandy and rocky scrubland. These gray-leafed plants resemble *Cistus* (rock rose), for which they are often mistaken. CULTIVATION: Mild winters and warm summers are the ideal conditions for cultivation. *Halimium* species grow in full sun in sandy, moderately fertile soil with protection from cold and drying winds. For best results, grow in pots or a rock-garden border. In areas with wet winters, extra sharp drainage needs to be provided or the plants need to be protected from over-saturation. Grow from seed in spring in a heated tray or take half-hardened cuttings in late summer.

Halimium halimifolium

☀ ❄ ↔ 3 ft (0.9 m) ↑ 3 ft (0.9 m)

From southwestern Europe and North Africa. Leaves oblong to lance-shaped, gray-green, silver scales. Cymes of yellow flowers, red-brown blotch at petal base, in late spring–early summer. Zones 8–9.

Halesia carolina

× *Halimiocistus wintonensis* 'Merrist Wood Cream'

Halimium lasianthum ★

syn. *Halimium formosum*

☼ ❄ ↔ 4 ft (1.2 m) ↑ 3 ft (0.9 m)

Bushy erect shrub from Spain and Portugal. Gray foliage. Clusters of yellow flowers, dark red basal spot, from leaf axils, in spring–early summer. *H. l.* subsp. *alyssoides*, egg- to lance-shaped leaves, dark green above, white hairy underside. *H. l.* subsp. *formosum*, slightly larger flowers with rust red basal spot. *H. l.* 'Concolor', no basal spot; 'Sandling', bright maroon basal spot. Zones 8–9.

Halimium Hybrid Cultivars

☼ ❄ ↔ 3 ft (0.9 m) ↑ 3 ft (0.9 m)

Shrubs with spreading habit. 'Sarah', bright yellow blooms with brown center; 'Susan', compact habit, broader leaves, semi-double yellow flowers in summer. Zones 8–9.

HALLERIA

Belonging to the foxglove (Scrophulariaceae) family, this genus contains 4 species from southern Africa and Madagascar. All are evergreen trees or shrubs with curved, tubular, nectar-rich flowers that attract many birds, particularly sunbirds. Fruits are fleshy and black when ripe; long style persists at maturity. CULTIVATION: These plants are frost hardy and drought resistant and prefer a fertile light soil and full sun in a warm climate. Propagate from seed or cuttings. Fruit contain a germination inhibitor so the flesh must be removed and the seeds air-dried in shade before sowing. Seedlings take 4 to 8 weeks to appear.

Halimium lasianthum

Halleria lucida

TREE FUCHSIA

☼ ❄ ↔ 12 ft (3.5 m) ↑ 35 ft (10 m)

Evergreen tree, larger in wild, from Ethiopia to southern tip of Africa. Leaves glossy green above, paler below, broadly lance-shaped

Hamamelis japonica

to oval, tapering tip, finely toothed edges. Flowers tubular, orangey red, in clusters in leaf axils or borne on branches or trunk or stems, in winter–spring. Edible fleshy black fruit. Zones 8–10.

HAMAMELIS

This small genus of 5 or 6 species of deciduous winter-flowering shrubs or small trees in the witch hazel (Hamamelidaceae) family is found in eastern North America and eastern Asia. They are characterized by spider-like, yellow or reddish, perfumed flowers, with crinkled strap-shaped petals, clustered on the bare branches from mid-winter to early spring. Foliage often provides attractive autumn color. Fruit is a horned capsule containing 2 shiny black seeds. CULTIVATION: They grow mainly in the shade of light woodland, prefer some shade from the midday sun, and like a cool moist climate. The best flowers are borne on strong, young, 1- to 3-year-old shoots that have not been shortened. Cutting for indoor decoration makes way for new shoots. Seeds can be collected before they are discharged and sown at once, but germination may take a year or more. Layers can be put down in winter and lifted the following winter.

Hamamelis × *intermedia*

HYBRID WITCH HAZEL

☼ ❄ ↔ 12 ft (3.5 m) ↑ 12 ft (3.5 m)

Hybrid between *H. japonica* and *H. mollis*, large shrub. Leaves to 6 in (15 cm) long, turn yellow in autumn. Flowers creamy, red, and apricot crimped petals. 'Arnold Promise' ★, dense clusters of dark yellow flowers; 'Diane', red flowers, leaves color well in autumn; 'Jelena', vigorous spreading habit, large broad leaves, flowers yellow suffused copper red, foliage turns orange, red, and scarlet; 'Pallida', clear sulfur or lemon yellow flowers with no trace of other colors. Zones 4–9.

Hamamelis japonica

JAPANESE WITCH HAZEL

☼ ❄ ↔ 12 ft (3.5 m) ↑ 15 ft (4.5 m)

Large spreading shrub or small tree. Short stout trunk, rigid branches. Leaves shiny and smooth when mature. Flowers small to medium, with crimpled petals. 'Sulphurea', large spreading shrub, ascending branches, flowers small to medium, pale sulfur yellow. Zones 4–9.

Hamamelis mollis

CHINESE WITCH HAZEL, WITCH HAZEL

☼ ❄ ↔ 12 ft (3.5 m) ↑ 15 ft (4.5 m)

Native of central and eastern China. Leaves mid-green, downy above, gray-green beneath, turn deep golden yellow in autumn. Perfumed flowers in axillary clusters, golden yellow straight petals, calyx yellow-brown, 4 spreading sepals chocolate brown inside. Zones 4–9.

Hamamelis virginiana ★

syn. *Hamamelis macrophylla*

COMMON WITCH HAZEL, WITCH HAZEL

☼ ❄ ↔ 8–12 ft (2.4–3.5 m) ↑ 12–15 ft (3.5–4.5 m)

Native to northeastern USA down to Lawrence Valley and into Virginia. Leaves dark green, shiny above, paler beneath. Flowers borne in small clusters in upper axils, yellow in color, in autumn before leaves fall, sometimes partly obscured. Zones 7–9.

HARPEPHYLLUM

One species makes up this genus from South Africa which, though its common name suggests it is a type of plum, is a member of the cashew (Anacardiaceae) family. An evergreen, it is widely planted as a street or park tree in warmer climates or on the west side of houses for shade. However, in a garden situation it may be difficult to grow plants under it due to the dense shade it provides. CULTIVATION: Although tolerant of a wide range of soils, it needs a frost-free situation where its low branching habit has room to form a dense crown. Propagation is from seed, which is only produced by the female tree if a male tree is nearby.

Harpephyllum caffrum
SOUTH AFRICAN WILD PLUM, WILDEPRUIM
☼ ❁ ↔ 25 ft (8 m) ↑ 30 ft (9 m)
Densely foliaged tree, broad crown deep green, shiny compound leaves. White flowers insignificant. Plum-sized fruit follows, ripening to orange-red, used for jam. Zones 9–11.

HEBE

There are about 100 species of evergreen shrubs in this genus allied to *Veronica* in the figwort or foxglove (Scrophulariaceae) family, mostly native to New Zealand, with a handful from southern South America and New Guinea. They grow in a wide range of habitats from coastal to alpine regions. There are 2 distinct foliage groups: those with oval to lance-shaped leaves, and the "whipcord" hebes, which have compressed scale-like leaves resembling conifers. Flower spikes of small tubular flowers range in color from white through pink to deep purple and crimson. CULTIVATION: Most hebes prefer a sunny situation, tolerating a wide range of soil conditions. They vary in degree of frost hardiness, bigger-leafed species being more tender. Whipcord species dislike heat and humidity, requiring a gritty well-drained soil. Some are suitable for coastal planting. Leaf spot and downy mildew can be a problem in humid areas. Prune after flowering to maintain a compact shape. Propagation is from seed or half-hardened cuttings in late summer, cultivars from cuttings only.

Hebe albicans
☼ ❁ ↔ 27 in (70 cm) ↑ 18–24 in (45–60 cm)
Compact shrub found in rocky mountain areas of northern South Island, New Zealand. Attractive glaucous leaves, closely packed on stout branchlets. Small white flowers, crowded on short racemes, in summer–autumn. '**Red Edge**', dark red margins around grayish green leaves, in winter becoming suffused with maroon; '**Sussex Carpet**', opposite pairs of blue-green leaves. Zones 8–10.

Hebe × *andersonii* ★
☼ ❁ ↔ 4 ft (1.2 m) ↑ 3–7 ft (0.9–2 m)
Hybrid of *H. speciosa* and *H. stricta*. Well-branched shrub, broadly lance-shaped leaves to 4 in (10 cm) long. Violet flowers on spikes to 4 in (10 cm) long, in summer–autumn. '**Andersonii Variegata**', leaves dark green, grayish green, and creamy white. Zones 9–11.

Hebe × *andersonii* 'Andersonii Variegata'

Hebe armstrongii
☼ ❋ ↔ 3 ft (0.9 m) ↑ 3 ft (0.9 m)
Whipcord species, erect well-branched shrub. Very rare in wild, found in few mountain areas of central South Island, New Zealand. Yellowish green color of branches intensifies in winter. Small white flowers, secondary to foliage effect. Zones 8–10.

Hebe cupressoides
WHIPCORD HEBE
☼ ❋ ↔ 3 ft (0.9 m) ↑ 3 ft (0.9 m)
Whipcord species native to subalpine regions of South Island, New Zealand. Attractive conifer-like appearance, densely branched. Well-spaced scale-like leaves, branchlets bright green. Pale blue flowers, borne sparingly, of secondary importance. '**Boughton Dome**', to 30 in (75 cm) tall, gray-green branchlets covered in small scale-like leaves. Zones 8–10.

Hebe diosmifolia
☼ ❋ ↔ 24 in (60 cm) ↑ 36 in (90 cm)
Variable species from northern North Island, New Zealand. Well-branched shrub, narrow glossy green leaves. Covered with small flowerheads of tiny white to lavender flowers in spring. Zones 8–11.

Harpephyllum caffrum

Hebe pinguifolia 'Pagei'

Hebe speciosa

Hebe, Hybrid Cultivar, 'Marjorie'

Hebe elliptica

☼ ❀ ↔ 4 ft (1.2 m) ↕ 3–7 ft (0.9–2 m)

Found in southern South America as well as New Zealand. Well-branched; small, leathery, dark green leaves. White to lavender flowers, bigger than most species, in late spring–autumn. Tolerant of salt spray, suitable for seaside gardens. Zones 8–11.

Hebe × *franciscana*

☼ ❀ ↔ 4 ft (1.2 m) ↕ 3 ft (0.9 m)

Older hybrid, cross between *H. elliptica* and *H. speciosa*. Rounded habit, dark green leaves. Pinkish purple flowers, on spikes to 3 in (8 cm) long, in summer–autumn. **'Blue Gem'**, bluish purple flowers, often seen, useful for coastal areas; **'Variegata'** (syn. *H.* 'Waireka'), mottled leaves with yellow margins. Zones 7–11.

Hebe odora

syn. *Hebe buxifolia*

☼ ❀ ↔ 4 ft (1.2 m) ↕ 3 ft (0.9 m)

Variable in wild, rounded bush in cultivation. Small dark green box-like leaves. Conical heads of white flowers, at branch tips, in spring–late summer. **'Patty's Purple'**, popular American cultivar; **'New Zealand Gold'**, strong grower, new leaves can be bright yellow. Zones 7–10.

Hebe pinguifolia

VERONICA

☼ ❀ ↔ 30 in (75 cm) ↕ 10 in (25 cm)

From drier eastern ranges of South Island of New Zealand. Variable habit in wild. Cultivated plants usually low growing. Stout branches, small thick bluish gray leaves with red margins. Small white flowers, in dense heads near branch tips, in spring–autumn. **'Pagei'**, excellent rock-garden plant, spreading to 3 ft (0.9 m) wide, with very glaucous leaves and dark purplish branchlets. Zones 6–10.

Hebe salicifolia

KOROMIKO

☼ ❀ ↔ 7 ft (2 m) ↕ 8 ft (2.4 m)

Found throughout South Island of New Zealand and also in Chile. Well-branched spreading shrub. Attractive willow-like leaves. Drooping racemes of white to pale lilac flowers in summer. Zones 7–10.

Hebe speciosa

SHOWY HEBE

☼ ❁ ↔ 3 ft (0.9 m) ↕ 3 ft (0.9 m)

Rare in wild, in some coastal areas of North Island, New Zealand. Rounded shrub. Glossy dark green leaves, oval, reddish margins. red midrib. Racemes of purplish red flowers in summer–autumn. **'Variegata'**, leaves with yellow variegation, red margins. Zones 9–11.

Hebe topiaria

☼ ❀ ↔ 3 ft (0.9 m) ↕ 3 ft (0.9 m)

Compact, ball-shaped. Good for foliage contrast. Small, almost overlapping, bluish green leaves. Small white flowers between leaves in summer. Zones 8–11.

Hebe Hybrid Cultivars

☼ ❀ ↔ 12 in–5 ft (30 cm–1.5 m) ↕ 12 in–5 ft (30 cm–1.5 m)

Many attractive *Hebe* cultivars available. **'Alicia Amherst'**, to 5 ft (1.5 m) tall, deep purple flowers densely packed on spikes up to 2½ in (6 cm) long, in autumn; **'Amy'**, rounded compact shrub 3–5 ft (0.9–1.5 m) tall, leaves deep purplish bronze when young, erect spikes of purple flowers in late summer; **'Autumn Glory'** ★, low bushy shrub to 24 in (60 cm) tall, violet flowers on short crowded spikes in mid-summer–autumn; **'Carnea'**, dense spreading shrub to 5 ft (1.5 m) tall, rosy purple summer flowers on racemes to 3 in (8 cm) long; **'Edinensis'**, to 12 in (30 cm) high, 18 in (45 cm) wide, tiny vivid green leaves, white flowers slightly tinted mauve; **'Emerald Green'** (syns 'Emerald Gem', 'Green Globe'), fresh green compact bun shape 8–12 in (20–30 cm) high, small white flowers in summer; **'Fragrant Jewel'**, 5 ft (1.5 m) high, masses of large, fragrant, lavender-purple flowers; **'Inspiration'**, 3 ft (0.9 m) high, deep purple flowers for long periods, main flush in summer; **'Loganioides'** (syn. *H. selaginoides*), to 10 in (25 cm) tall, white flowers; **'Margret'**, 16 in (40 cm) tall, sky blue flowers fade to white in late spring–early summer; **'Marjorie'**, to 5 ft (1.5 m) tall, large mauve-blue flowers fade to white; **'Midsummer Beauty'** (syn. *H.* × *andersonii* 'Midsummer Beauty'), to 6 ft (1.8 m) tall, plum-colored new growth, lilac-purple flowers fade to white; **'Mrs Winder'** (syns 'Waikiki', 'Warleyensis'), to 3 ft (0.9 m) high, leaves flushed red at base, reddish purple in winter, violet flowers in summer; **'Orphan Annie'**, to 3 ft (0.9 m) tall, narrow cream and green variegated leaves, pink early summer flowers; **'Pink Elephant'**, 2 ft (0.6 m) tall, yellow-edged pink-tinged new growth, white summer flowers; 'Temptation', to 12 in (30 cm) tall, pink flowers fade to white; 'Wardiensis', to 8 in (20 cm) tall, white summer flowers; 'Wiri Charm', 30 in (75 cm) high, rosy purple flowers in summer; 'Wiri Dawn', to 18 in (45 cm) high, light olive green leaves, pale pinkish white flowers; 'Wiri Grace', to 5 ft (1.5 m), long spikes of light purple flowers in summer; 'Wiri Image', vigorous, to 3 ft (0.9 m) tall, long racemes of violet flowers in early summer; 'Youngii' (syn. 'Carl Teschner'), 8 in (20 cm) tall, branchlets purplish, deep violet flowers on short spikes in summer. Zones 8–11.

HELIANTHEMUM

ROCK ROSE, SUN ROSE

Related to *Cistus*, the 110 or so evergreen and semi-evergreen shrubs and subshrubs in this genus, in the rock-rose (Cistaceae) family, are less widely grown but have a wider natural range: Eurasia, North Africa, and the Americas. Relatively low-mounding, short-lived plants, foliage is often hairy, giving it a gray-green color. Flowers resemble tiny roses, and are individually short lived but appear through late spring and summer. They are in shades of yellow, orange, red, or pink, with bright yellow stamens massed at the center. CULTIVATION: They need full sun for their flowers to develop, and suit sunny borders, rock gardens, or large containers. Soil should be rather gritty and free draining. Keep moist in summer, dry in winter. Trim lightly after flowering to shape and encourage vigor. Propagation is from seed; hybrids and cultivars should be propagated from cuttings or by removing rooted pieces from established plants.

Helianthemum croceum

☼ ✳ ↔ 16–20 in (40–50 cm) ↕ 12–14 in (30–35 cm)

From southern Europe and northern Africa. Slightly fleshy leaves to ¾ in (18 mm) long. Flowers up to ¾ in (18 mm) wide in shades of yellow, white, or apricot. Zones 7–10.

Helianthemum, Hybrid Cultivar, 'Rhodanthe Carneum'

Helianthemum nummularium

syn. *Helianthemum chamaecistus*

COMMON SUN ROSE, SUN ROSE

☼ ✳ ↔ 24 in (60 cm) ↕ 20 in (50 cm)

Leaves dark green above, gray-green, felted below. Flowers bright yellow, orange, or red shades, any color except purple or blue, in late spring–summer. *H. n.* subsp. *glabrum* (syn. *H. nitidum*), from central and southwest Europe, fewer leaf hairs, slightly downy margins, orange-yellow flowers. Zones 5–10.

Helianthemum Hybrid Cultivars

☼ ✳ ↔ 18–36 in (45–90 cm) ↕ 6–12 in (15–30 cm)

Alpine and rock-garden enthusiasts have produced many hybrids in broad color spectrum. Most have *H. nummularium* in background. 'Ben Heckla', bronze-gold flowers; 'Ben Hope', light foliage, red flowers with orange center; 'Ben Ledi', dark green leaves, deep rose flowers; 'Ben Vane', terracotta flowers; 'Ben Vorlich', orange flowers; 'Butter and Eggs', creamy yellow; 'Dazzler', dark green foliage, deep red flowers; 'Fire Dragon', gray-green leaves, orange-red flowers; 'Golden Queen', large bright yellow flowers; 'Henfield Brilliant' ★, gray-green leaves, dark red flowers; 'Jubilee', double primrose yellow flowers; 'Mrs C. W. Earle', double scarlet flowers; 'Orange Surprise', orange flowers; 'Raspberry Ripple', deep reddish pink flowers tipped white; 'Rhodanthe Carneum', silvery gray leaves, orange-centered pink flowers; 'Rose Queen', rose pink flowers; 'Sudbury Gem', grayish green leaves, deep pink flowers with red center; 'The Bride', silver-gray foliage, white flowers; 'Wisley Pink', silver-gray foliage, light pink flowers; 'Wisley Primrose', gray-green foliage, primrose yellow flowers; 'Wisley White', gray foliage, white flowers. Zones 6–10.

HEPTACODIUM

This genus, in the woodbine (Caprifoliaceae) family and allied to *Abelia* and *Kolkwitzia*, consists of 1 species of deciduous shrub from central and eastern China. It has large glossy leaves with 3 longitudinal veins, in opposite pairs on the twigs. Small white flowers are borne in large panicles at branch ends. As the small dry fruits develop, the sepals, inconspicuous in flower, enlarge and turn deep pink, making a display that lasts several months. CULTIVATION: This plant likes woodland conditions with moist acid soil and shelter, though not too much shade. Lower twiggy growth should be thinned out in winter. Propagation should be from hardwood cuttings in autumn or half-hardened tip cuttings in summer, from basal suckers, or from seed.

Heptacodium miconioides ★

syn. *Heptacodium jasminoides*

CHINESE HEPTACODIUM, SEVEN SON FLOWER

☼ ✳ ↔ 7–10 ft (2–3 m) ↕ 10–15 ft (3–4.5 m)

Chinese deciduous shrub or small tree, dark green elliptical leaves. Heads of fragrant white flowers, from late summer to first frosts. Calyces of flowers turn rosy red to purple in autumn. Zones 5–9.

Heptacodium miconioides

HETEROMELES

CALIFORNIA HOLLY, CHRISTMAS BERRY, TOLLON, TOYON

This genus comprises a single species, a native of California that is an evergreen shrub closely related to *Photinia*. Fruit, which may be red or yellow, small or large, develop from heads of small creamy white flowers and, as the name "Christmas berry" suggests, it ripens around Christmas, or mid-winter, in its home range.
CULTIVATION: Any well-drained soil with a sunny or partly shaded aspect will do. Heat and drought resistant, this species will tolerate poor soils. The bush is usually a neat grower and needs trimming to shape only occasionally. It may be propagated from half-hardened cuttings or seed.

Heteromeles arbutifolia

☼ ❈ ↔ 12 ft (3.5 m) ↕ 12 ft (3.5 m)

Native to Sierra Nevada foothills of coastal California, USA, to Baja California, Mexico. Simple, oval, mid-green leaves, finely serrated edges. Flowerheads nectar-rich, with honey-like scent, in summer. Compact tough plant. Zones 8–10.

HIBBERTIA

GOLDEN GUINEA FLOWER

This mostly Australian genus in the Dilleniaceae family contains around 120 species of small, evergreen, shrubby plants or climbers grown for their profuse, usually bright yellow or sometimes orange flowers. Flowering is mostly during spring and early summer, though with some species it also occurs sporadically throughout most of the year. Though there is variation in growth habit, it is mostly the low spreading species and climbers that have become well known to horticulture. These are ideal rock-garden, container, and ground cover plants.
CULTIVATION: Easy to grow, they enjoy moderately fertile well-drained soil that does not dry out too quickly. In hotter areas partial shade is best. Marginally frost hardy, they

Hibbertia miniata

need protection in colder regions, especially when young. To keep their shape, prune tips from an early age and after flowering. Propagate from half-hardened tip cuttings taken in late summer.

Hibbertia miniata

◑ ⚘ ↔ 8 in (20 cm) ↕ 15 in (38 cm)

Small erect shrub, rare in wild, confined to jarrah forests of Western Australia. Broad gray-green linear leaves. Showy orange flowers, dark purple anthers, in spring–summer. Zones 9–11.

Hibbertia stellaris

ORANGE STARS

◑ ⚘ ↔ 30 in (75 cm) ↕ 30 in (75 cm)

Small dense shrub from coastal areas of Western Australia, growing at edges of swamps. Soft fine green foliage, red stems. Small starry apricot flowers in spring–autumn. Often difficult to grow, and is short lived. Zones 9–11.

HIBISCUS

GIANT MALLOW, MALLOW, ROSE MALLOW

This genus of over 200 annual or perennial herbs, shrubs, or trees in the mallow (Malvaceae) family is widely distributed throughout warm-temperate, subtropical, and tropical regions of the world. They are grown mostly for their large dramatic flowers, borne singly or in terminal clusters, usually lasting for just a day. The open bell-shaped flowers appear in a wide variety of colors, and are characterized by a prominent staminal column and a darker coloring in the center. The alternate simple leaves are usually palmate. The fruit is a capsule.
CULTIVATION: Most species of *Hibiscus* are drought tender and rather frost tender, and prefer a position in full sun in a rich and moist soil. Many will tolerate hard pruning after flowering to maintain shape. Perennials are propagated from seed or by division, while annuals are best grown from seed in the growing position. Shrub types can be propagated from cuttings, by grafting, or from seed sown in containers for later transplanting.

Hibiscus coccineus

SCARLET HIBISCUS, SCARLET ROSE MALLOW, SWAMP HIBISCUS

☼ ❈ ↔ 2–3 ft (0.6–0.9 m) ↕ 7 ft (2 m)

From southern USA. Shrub-like herbaceous species with 5-petalled crimson flowers, 6–8 in (15–20 cm) across, in early to mid-summer, followed by attractive papery green fruit. Vigorous grower in good conditions. '**Davis Creek**', robust cultivar. Zones 7–11.

Hibiscus heterophyllus

AUSTRALIAN NATIVE ROSELLA, SCRUB KURRAJONG

☼ ⚘ ↔ 6–10 ft (1.8–3 m) ↕ 10–20 ft (3–6 m)

Evergreen shrub or small tree native to eastern Australia. Prickly branches, narrow pointed leaves, deeply lobed. Flowers white with purple eye. **H. h.** subsp. *luteus*, yellow flowers usual in northern parts of range. Zones 10–12.

Heteromeles arbutifolia

Hibiscus moscheutos

COMMON ROSE MALLOW, SWAMP ROSE MALLOW

☼ ❋ ↔ 40 in (100 cm) ↑ 8 ft (2.4 m)

Woody perennial shrub from eastern North America. Lobed leaves 2–6 in (5–15 cm) long. Flowers large, trumpet-shaped, pink and white, in spring–summer. '**Lord Baltimore**', large, single, crimson red flowers, to 12 in (30 cm) across; '**Southern Belle**', compact, to 40 in (100 cm), deep pink flowers. Zones 5–9.

Hibiscus mutabilis

CONFEDERATE ROSE, COTTON ROSE

☼ ❋ ↔ 6–8 ft (1.8–2.4 m) ↑ 10–15 ft (3–4.5 m)

Small, spreading, deciduous shrub, or erect, branch-ing, small tree native to China. Large palm-shaped leaves, 7 serrated lobes. Double or single flowers, white or pink with darker base and staminal col-umn. '**Plena**', rounded double flowers. Zones 8–9.

Hibiscus pedunculatus

DWARF PINK HIBISCUS

☼ ❧ ↔ 5 ft (1.5 m) ↑ 4–6 ft (1.2–1.8 m)

Native from Mozambique to South Africa. Leaves have 3 to 5 rounded lobes. Nodding solitary flowers, staminal column and 2 in (5 cm) long petals, pale or deep rose purple or lilac. Zones 10–12.

Hibiscus rosa-sinensis

CHINA ROSE, CHINESE HIBISCUS, HAWAIIAN HIBISCUS, ROSE OF CHINA, SHOE BLACK

☼ ❧ ↔ 5 ft (1.5 m) ↑ 8–30 ft (2.4–9 m)

Erect, branching, evergreen shrub, or small tree to 30 ft (9 m) high. Solitary flowers, variable in color, normally red to dark red, in summer–winter. Oval-shaped, serrated, glossy, deep green leaves. Hybrid cultivars include '**Agnes Galt**' ★, tall vigorous shrub, large rose pink flowers; '**Aurora**', blush pink pompon-shaped flowers; '**Bridal Veil**', large pure white flowers with crape texture; '**Cooperi**', small, rose pink, single flowers, narrow variegated leaves, olive green marbled with red, pink, and white, good container plant; '**Crown of Bohemia**', bushy shrub, medium double flowers, gold with bright orange throat; '**D. J. O'Brien**', medium, double, orange-apricot flowers; '**Eileen McMullen**', large deep yellow flowers heavily flushed with crimson; '**Moon Beam**', bright yellow flowers, crimson throat, strongly reflexed petals. Zones 9–11.

Hibiscus schizopetalus

CORAL HIBISCUS, FRINGED HIBISCUS, JAPANESE HIBISCUS, JAPANESE LANTERN

☼ ❧ ↔ 6 ft (1.8 m) ↑ 10 ft (3 m)

Evergreen to semi-deciduous shrub native to tropical east Africa. Arching, slender, weeping habit, clusters of small, oval, serrated leaves. Flowers ragged, fringed margins, petals pink or brilliant red, long staminal column, in summer–autumn. Zones 10–12.

Hibiscus heterophyllus subsp. *luteus*

Hibiscus syriacus

BLUE HIBISCUS, ROSE OF SHARON, SHRUB ALTHEA, SYRIAN HIBISCUS

☼ ❋ ↔ 6–10 ft (1.8–3 m) ↑ 8–20 ft (2.4–6 m)

Shrub or small tree native to warm-temperate areas of China. Smooth gray branches; leaves with 3 narrow, coarsely toothed, triangular lobes. Single or double flowers, petals white, reddish purple, or bluish lavender with crimson base and staminal column. Blue Bird/'**Oiseau Bleu**', gentian blue flowers, lilac-purple center, grows to 5 ft (1.5 m); '**Diana**', single pure white flowers, grows to 5 ft (1.5 m); '**Hamabo**', large, light pink, single flowers with red center that radiates at edges into fine red streaks; '**White Supreme**', semi-double white flowers with crimson center, rose pink on outside of petals; '**Woodbridge**', wine red flowers with darker center, grows to 6 ft (1.8 m). Other cul-tivars include '**Aphrodite**', '**Boule de Feu**', '**Lady Stanley**', '**Lohen-grin**', '**Minerva**', and '**Red Heart**'. Zones 5–9.

Hibiscus tiliaceus

COAST COTTONWOOD, MAHOE, MANGROVE HIBISCUS, MAU

☼ ❧ ↔ 10–20 ft (3–6 m) ↑ 25 ft (8m)

Evergreen shrub or small tree widespread across tropical regions of world. Smooth gray bark, gnarled picturesque trunk. Rounded, smooth, leathery green leaves, hairy beneath. Solitary yellow or white flowers, with red to brown throat and staminal column, in summer. Salt tolerant and drought resistant. Zones 10–12.

Hibiscus trionum

FLOWER-OF-AN-HOUR

☼ ❧ ↔ 12 in (30 cm) ↑ 12–24 in (30–60 cm)

From warmer regions of Africa, Asia, and Australia. Hairy stems and lobed leaves. Yellow flowers, crimson-black eye. Zones 10–12.

Hibiscus moscheutos 'Lord Baltimore'

Hibiscus schizopetalus

Hibiscus trionum

Hoheria lyallii

HOHERIA

LACEBARK, RIBBONWOOD

This New Zealand genus of 5 species of deciduous and evergreen trees is in the mallow (Malvaceae) family. Leaves usually have pointed tips and serrated margins. White 5-petalled flowers are profuse in summer or autumn. The name "lacebark" is due to the lace-like fibrous layer under the surface bark.
CULTIVATION: These trees are suitable for specimen or woodland planting. They are fast growing and most will tolerate a wide range of conditions in sun or part-shade. In cold climates they need the protection of a warm wall, and in such areas the deciduous species are more hardy. Plants can be pruned if necessary. Propagation is from seed sown in autumn, or half-hardened cuttings.

Hoheria lyallii

MOUNTAIN RIBBONWOOD, NEW ZEALAND LACEBARK
☼ ❄ ↔ 10 ft (3 m) ↕ 7–12 ft (2–3.5 m)
Found on drier east coast of New Zealand's South Island. Leaves bright green, often turn yellow in autumn. White flowers. Zones 8–10.

Hoheria sexstylosa

RIBBONWOOD
☼ ❄ ↔ 20 ft (6 m) ↕ 15–25 ft (4.5–8 m)
Variable species. Leaves toothed leaves, long, narrow. Flowers small, scented. Branches tend to weep, with graceful appearance. Zones 8–11.

HOLMSKIOLDIA

This mint (Lamiaceae) family genus from the Himalayan region contains a single variable species of sprawling evergreen shrub. Leaves are opposite, simple, and oval, with a variable covering of fine hairs, and finely serrated edges. The flowers occur in small panicles or racemes and are very interestingly shaped, with a narrow tubular corolla backed by a flattened, widely flared calyx.
CULTIVATION: Quite frost tender, these shrubs are best grown in a light well-drained soil that stays moist through the warmer months. Plant in full sun or partial shade and provide a trellis or other

support to keep the growth upright. Regular pinching back will prevent the stems becoming too elongated. Propagate from seed or half-hardened cuttings.

Holmskioldia sanguinea

CHINESE HAT PLANT, CUP AND SAUCER PLANT
☼/◑ ❄ ↔ 6 ft (1.8 m) ↕ 3–6 ft (0.9–1.8 m)
Found in Himalayan lowlands. Shallowly serrated leaves to 3 in (8 cm) long. Flowers orange to scarlet with brick red calyces, in dense clusters, in warmest months. Zones 10–11.

HOLODISCUS

This genus in the rose (Rosaceae) family consists of 8 species of deciduous shrubs. Growing in dry woodland, they are found in western North America and as far south as Colombia. These plants bear airy panicles of small flowers, sometimes with red buds; flowers open to a creamy white.
CULTIVATION: Tolerant of sun or part-shade, they need moist, fertile, humus-rich soil that does not dry out. Most are easily increased by layering, or heel cuttings of half-hardened wood in a peat-sand mixture; they may need mist propagation. They can be difficult to root.

Holodiscus discolor

CREAMBUSH, OCEAN SPRAY
☼/◑ ❄ ↔ 12 ft (3.5 m) ↕ 12 ft (3.5 m)
Native to western North America. Leaves broadly egg-shaped, with 4 to 8 lobes, scalloped margins, deep green above, white felty below. Flowers in plume-like creamy panicles in summer. Zones 4–10.

HOMALOCLADIUM

This genus in the knotweed (Polygonaceae) family consists of 1 curious evergreen shrub from the Solomon Islands, often grown as a container plant. Leafless at flowering time, it has flat, ribbon-like, jointed stems and tiny flowers in spring. The fruit is enclosed by a fleshy red to purple berry. Some botanists consider it to be no more than a bizarre species of *Muehlenbeckia*.

Holmskioldia sanguinea

CULTIVATION: Easily grown and tolerant of light frosts, *Homalocladium* prefers a light, rich, moist, well-drained soil or a regular potting mix in a protected, partially shaded position. Propagation is either from fresh seed sown in spring or from cuttings taken in summer.

Homalocladium platycladum

syn. *Muehlenbeckia platyclada*
CENTIPEDE PLANT, RIBBON BUSH, TAPEWORM PLANT
◑ ❄ ↔ 6 ft (1.8 m) ↕ 6–10 ft (1.8–3 m)
Unusual evergreen shrub. Distinctive, flat, green, ribbon-like, jointed stems. Whitish green flowers, in small clusters at joints of branches, in spring; narrow green leaves. Zones 10–12.

HYDRANGEA

There are about 100 species of deciduous and evergreen shrubs, trees, and climbers in this Hydrangeaceae family genus, native to eastern Asia, and North and South America. Leaves are usually large and oval with serrated edges. Flowerheads comprise very small fertile flowers surrounded by larger, 4-petalled, sterile florets, conical, flat-topped (lacecap), or rounded (mophead). Colors range from white through to red, purple, and blue.

CULTIVATION: Hydrangeas grow in a wide range of conditions. However, they will do better in good soil with compost and light feeding. Grow in sun or dappled shade, ensuring they have ample moisture. Grow *H. macrophylla* cultivars to suit the soil pH. Color can be changed by dressing with aluminium sulphate for blue and with lime for red. Prune in late winter, and remove old wood. Propagate species from seed in spring, tip cuttings in late spring, or hardwood cuttings in winter; propagate cultivars from cuttings only.

Hydrangea arborescens
SMOOTH HYDRANGEA

❀ ❁ ❄ ↔ 8 ft (2.4 m) ↕ 3–12 ft (0.9–3.5 m)

Native to North America, from moist shady sites. Deciduous shrub, open habit, often spreading from suckers. Flat creamy white flowerheads, in summer, numerous tiny fertile flowers surrounded by a few sterile florets. *H. a.* subsp. *radiata*, deep green leaves. *H. a.* 'Annabelle' ★, large white mophead flowerheads; 'Grandiflora', slightly uneven mopheads of pure white sterile flowers. Zones 3–10.

Hydrangea aspera
syn. *Hydrangea villosa*

❀ ❁ ❄ ↔ 10 ft (3 m) ↕ 10 ft (3 m)

Variable deciduous species native to eastern Asia. Lacecap flowers, held above foliage, to 10 in (25 cm) wide, pale mauve sterile florets, tiny bright purplish blue fertile flowers in center. *H. a.* f. *kawakamii*, pink-veined leaves. *H. a.* subsp. *sargentiana*, large leaves, velvety above, bristly beneath; flat-topped flowerheads, pinkish white sterile florets surrounding mauve fertile flowers. *H. a.* 'Mauvette', mauve dome-shaped flowerheads to 6 in (15 cm) across; 'Peter Chappell', large downy leaves, flat-topped flowerheads of white sterile florets surrounding creamy pink fertile flowers. Zones 7–10.

Hydrangea heteromalla

❀ ❁ ❄ ↔ 10 ft (3 m) ↕ 10–15 ft (3–4.5 m)

Deciduous species from China and Himalayas. Leaves usually broadly lance-shaped, downy beneath in some forms. Lacecap flowers, white to pink sterile florets, greenish white fertile flowers, in summer. 'Jermyn's Lace', pink-tinged greenish white flowers. Zones 6–9.

Hydrangea macrophylla
syn. *Hydrangea hortensis*

BIGLEAF HYDRANGEA, FLORIST'S HYDRANGEA, GARDEN HYDRANGEA, HORTENSIA

❀ ❁ ❄ ↔ 8 ft (2.4 m) ↕ 10 ft (3 m)

Long-cultivated species from coastal areas of Japan. Deciduous shrub, large shiny leaves, pinkish blue flat-topped flowers. Cultivars

usually grow 3–6 ft (0.9–1.8 m) high, divided into two groups: mophead (hortensias) and lacecap. More than 500 mophead cultivars, with globular heads of showy sterile florets; suitable for coastal gardens. About 20 lacecap cultivars, with flat-topped formation of outer sterile florets, central fertile flowers.

MOPHEAD CULTIVARS

'Alpenglühen' ★, medium-sized robust plant, maintaining rosy red color even in slightly acid soil; 'Ami Pasquier', rich crimson to purple flowers all summer, leaves turn red in autumn; 'Enziandom' (syn. 'Gentian Dome'), compact shrub to 5 ft (1.5 m) tall, needing acid soil to produce gentian blue flowers; 'Hamburg', large serrated petals of deep rose to purple or blue, depending on soil pH; 'Madame Emile Mouillère', grows to 6 ft (1.8 m), one of best white mopheads; 'Nigra', distinctive black stems, small flowerheads from pink to blue depending on soil pH; 'Nikko Blue' ★, growing to 5 ft (1.5 m), blue flowers; 'Pia', very dwarf form; 'President Doumer', rich cherry red flowers in small clusters on top of small, dark green, serrated leaves; and 'Soeur Thérèse', growing up to 6 ft (1.8 m) tall, pure white variety. Other cultivars include 'Altona', 'Amethyst', 'Générale Vicomtesse de Vibraye', 'Miss Belgium', 'Montgomery', and 'Parzifal'.

LACECAP CULTIVARS

'Fireworks Pink', double, star-shaped, pink florets around outer edge of each flowerhead; 'Hobella', soft pink flowers ageing to green, then to cherry red; 'Libelle', stunning heads of white sterile florets surrounding deep blue fertile flowers; 'Love You Kiss', large white flowerheads, each petal with red margin, red-tinted leaves; and 'Mariesii', pale pink to light blue flowers. Other cultivars include 'Geoffrey Chadbund', 'Lanarth White', 'Lilacina', and 'Sea Foam'. Zones 5–11.

Hydrangea macrophylla, Mophead, 'Enziandom'

Hydrangea arborescens 'Annabelle'

Hydrangea 'Preziosa'

Hydrangea paniculata

PANICLE HYDRANGEA

☼/◑ ❋ ↔ 10 ft (3 m) ↑ 6–20 ft (1.8–6 m)

Deciduous species from Japan and southeastern China. Conical flowerheads, densely packed, creamy white sterile and fertile flowers, often in arching shape, in late summer–autumn. '**Grandiflora**', creamy white sterile flowers on panicles up to 18 in (45 cm) long; '**Kyushu**', smaller bush, panicles of creamy white sterile and fertile flowers; '**Praecox**', early flowering; '**Tardiva**', late flowering; '**Unique**', round-ended panicles larger than those of 'Grandiflora'. Zones 3–10.

Hydrangea 'Preziosa'

☼/◑ ❋ ↔ 5 ft (1.5 m) ↑ 5 ft (1.5 m)

Erect shrub with distinctive reddish stems, red-flushed leaves. Small globular flowerheads change from creamy white through shades of pink to reddish purple. Zones 6–10.

Hydrangea quercifolia

OAK-LEAFED HYDRANGEA

☼/◑ ❋ ↔ 8 ft (2.4 m) ↑ 3–8 ft (0.9–2.4 m)

Deciduous shrub from southeastern USA. Large, lobed, green leaves turn crimson in autumn. Creamy white flowers, on conical panicles to 10 in (25 cm) long, in summer, become pinkish in autumn. '**Snow Flake**', double flowers; '**Snow Queen**', exceptional autumn foliage colors. Zones 5–10.

Hydrangea serrata

syn. *Hydrangea macrophylla* subsp. *serrata*

☼/◑ ❋ ↔ 5 ft (1.5 m) ↑ 3–6 ft (0.9–1.8 m)

Deciduous species from Japan and Korea, closely related to *H. macrophylla*. Flat-topped flowerheads, sterile florets of white, pink, or blue surrounding white or blue fertile flowers, in summer, color changing with age. '**Bluebird**', neat shrub, blue lacecap flowers, carried for long time, foliage turns red in autumn; '**Grayswood**', flowerheads with bluish purple fertile flowers surrounded by sterile florets, changing color to white, pink, and crimson. Zones 6–10.

HYMENOSPORUM

Consisting of a single evergreen tree species, this genus in the pittosporum (Pittosporaceae) family is from subtropical areas of Australia's east coast where grows in rainforests. Cultivated for many years for its creamy white flowers, which turn yellow as they age, it is a slender, often open tree with mid-green shiny foliage. CULTIVATION: Though it likes a spot in full sun, it can grow in part-shade but may not flower as profusely. Moist humus-enriched soil will suit this plant as it does not like to be deprived of moisture when conditions are dry. Propagate from seed or cuttings.

Hymenosporum flavum

NATIVE FRANGIPANI

☼ ❊ ↔ 12 ft (3.5 m) ↑ 30 ft (9 m)

Slender tree. Light foliage coverage, widely spaced horizontal branches bear shiny deep green leaves. Fragrant cream blossoms, ageing to yellow, in spring. Zones 9–11.

HYPERICUM

Belonging to the St John's-wort (Clusiaceae) family, this genus has more than 400 species of deciduous, semi-evergreen and evergreen annuals, herbaceous perennials, shrubs, and trees. They occur worldwide in various habitats, and have simple smooth-edged leaves in opposite pairs and usually yellow 5-petalled flowers with a central bunch of many stamens. Some are used locally as medicinal plants. CULTIVATION: Most will thrive in sun or partial shade in good garden soil. *H. calycinum* takes root along its prostrate branches in dry shade, but also does well in partial shade. *H. olympicum* is a good rock-garden plant, and needs sharp drainage. Most North American species prefer damper conditions. Evergreen species are best sheltered from cold drying winds. Propagate from seed in autumn, though it may not come true. Take softwood cuttings in spring, half-hardened cuttings in summer.

Hypericum balearicum

☼ ❋ ↔ 10 in (25 cm) ↑ 10 in (25 cm)

From Balearic Islands. Evergreen, densely branched shrub. Warty glandular stems and leaves. Leaves oblong to egg-shaped, wavy edges. Solitary, starry, golden yellow flowers in summer. Zones 7–9.

Hypericum beanii

☼ ❋ ↔ 6 ft (1.8 m) ↑ 2–6 ft (0.6–1.8 m)

Vigorous, evergreen, bushy shrub native to Yunnan and Guizhou Provinces in China. Mid-green leaves, elliptic to lance-shaped, with pale underside. Golden yellow flowers, bowl- to star-shaped, in summer. Zones 7–10.

Hymenosporum flavum

Hypericum calycinum

AARON'S BEARD, CREEPING ST JOHN'S WORT, ROSE OF SHARON

◑ ❋ ↔ 5 ft (1.5 m) ↑ 8–24 in (20–60 cm)

Native to parts of Bulgaria and Turkey. Evergreen or semi-evergreen shrub, rooting branches. Elliptic or oblong leaves, dark green above, paler below. Bright yellow flowers in mid-summer–autumn. Good ground-cover plant for dry shade. Zones 6–9.

Hypericum empetrifolium

☼ ❄ ↔ 3 ft (0.9 m) ↕ 2 ft (0.6 m)

Native to southeastern Europe, Turkey, and Libya. Dwarf, cushion-forming, evergreen shrub. Narrow leaves mid-green in whorls of 3. Cylindrical cymes of up to 40 golden yellow star-shaped flowers in summer. *H. e.* subsp. *oliganthum* (syn. *H. e.* var. *prostratum* of gardens), 2 in (5 cm) tall. Zones 8–9.

Hypericum 'Hidcote'

☼ ❄ ↔ 4 ft (1.2 m) ↕ 4 ft (1.2 m)

Likely cross between *H.* × *cyathiflorum* 'Gold Cup' and *H. calycinum*. Dense evergreen or semi-evergreen shrub. Leaves dark green, lance-shaped. Large, bowl-shaped, deep yellow flowers in summer–autumn. Zones 7–10.

Hypericum lancasteri

☼ ❄ ↔ 3 ft (0.9 m) ↕ 3 ft (0.9 m)

Native to China. Deciduous shrub, purple-red young growth. Leaves oblong to triangular lance-shaped, mid-green. Cymes of yellow bowl- or star-shaped flowers in summer. Zones 7–10.

Hypericum × *moserianum*

☼ ❄ ↔ 24–32 in (60–80 cm) ↕ 12–16 in (30–40 cm)

Attractive, arching, semi-deciduous. Lance-shaped leaves to 2 in (5 cm) long. Flowers yellow, to 2½ in (6 cm) wide, in summer and autumn. 'Tricolor', variegated form. Zones 7–10.

Hypericum × *moserianum*

Hypericum olympicum

☼ ❋ ↔ 15 in (38 cm) ↕ 10 in (25 cm)

Dwarf deciduous shrub native to Greece and southern Balkans. Oblong, elliptic, gray-green leaves, glaucous underside. Cymes of 5 golden yellow star-shaped flowers in summer. Zones 6–10.

Hypericum prolificum

☼ ❋ ↔ 5 ft (1.5 m) ↕ 6 ft (1.8 m)

Loosely branched shrub from central and eastern USA and southern Canada. Leaves narrow, oblong, elliptical or lance-shaped, leaf edges sometimes recurved, underside features pale waxy bloom. Golden yellow flowers borne in summer. Zones 4–9.

Hypericum 'Rowallane'

☼ ❄ ↔ 4 ft (1.2 m) ↕ 6 ft (1.8 m)

Semi-evergreen shrub, chance hybrid between *H. leschenaultii* and *H. hookerianum* 'Charles Rogers'. Leaves egg-shaped or oblong to lance-shaped, dark green above, paler green and crinkly below. Rich golden flowers, in small cymes, in late summer–autumn. Zones 8–10.

HYPOESTES

An acanthus (Acanthaceae) family genus of 40 perennials, subshrubs, and shrubs from open woodland regions of Africa, Madagascar, Arabia, tropical Asia, and Australasia, some decoratively foliaged species are used as indoor plants or grown as annuals in cooler areas; others are valued for their autumn flowers. Evergreen leaves are held opposite on upright stems and in some species are velvety to touch. CULTIVATION: Grow in humus-rich well-drained soil. Water freely in summer but keep drier in the cold months. These plants do well in part-shade with protection from drying winds. Propagate in spring from seed, or from stem cuttings taken in spring to summer.

Hypoestes aristata

RIBBON BUSH

☼ ❄ ↔ 26 in (65 cm) ↕ 3 ft (0.9 m)

From southern Africa. Evergreen shrubby plant, upright stems. Downy mid-green leaves. Masses of small purple flowers, in upper leaf axils, in autumn. Zones 9–11.

Hypoestes phyllostachya

POLKA-DOT PLANT

☼ ❄ ↔ 30 in (75 cm) ↕ 3 ft (0.9 m)

Subshrub from Madagascar, widely used as indoor plant in cold areas. Pink-speckled green leaves. Soft tender stems, becoming woody near base. 'Splash', larger pink markings. Zones 10–12.

Hypericum calycinum

Hypoestes aristata

IDESIA

WONDER TREE

The sole species in this genus in the governor's-plum (Flacourtia-ceae) family is a medium-sized deciduous tree found naturally in Japan, Korea, Taiwan, and nearby parts of China. Its large foliage makes it an excellent shade tree. Bright red berries hang in large pendulous clusters long after the foliage has fallen. The flowers are unisexual but the plants are debatably dioecious: so-called female plants often bear fruit without the presence of male plants, though fruiting is better with a cross-pollinator.

CULTIVATION: Although reasonably frost hardy, *Idesia* can be severely damaged by late spring frosts that arrive after the foliage has expanded. It prefers a climate with a warm summer, a long autumn, and a short winter without late frosts. While the soil should be well drained, the tree will cope with most soil types. Prune foliage to shape when young, otherwise trim lightly after the fruit has fallen. Propagate from seed or from half-hardened cuttings.

Idesia polycarpa

☀ ❄ ↔ 35 ft (10 m) ↑ 50 ft (15 m)

Upright tree with rounded crown. Deep green leaves, heart-shaped, to 8 in (20 cm) long, red leaf stalks. Flowers tiny, in large sprays, yellow-green, fragrant. Red berries on bare branches. Zones 6–10.

ILEX

HOLLY

This widely distributed genus, belonging to the holly (Aquifolia-ceae) family, contains more than 400 species of evergreen or deciduous trees, shrubs, and climbers. Used for its foliage and berries since Roman times, holly has long been associated with Northern Hemisphere festivals celebrating the winter solstice and Christmas. Wood of some species is used for veneers and musical instruments; leaves are used as tea substitutes or in tisanes. Male and female flowers usually grow on separate trees, thus plants of both sexes are required for the production of berries.

Idesia polycarpa

CULTIVATION: North American hollies prefer neutral to acid soils, while the Asian and European species will grow in most soils that are moderately fertile, well drained, and humus-rich. Green hollies will also grow in part- or full shade (but not deep shade). Variegated hollies require a position in full sun for best effect. Propagate from half-hardened cuttings in late summer or early autumn. Seed germination may take 2 or 3 years. Tender species need greenhouse protection in winter in colder climates.

Ilex × altaclerensis

HIGHCLERE HOLLY

☀ ❄ ↔ 20 ft (6 m) ↑ 70 ft (21 m)

Hybrid group of evergreen trees or shrubs of garden origin, cross between *I. aquifolium* and *I. perado*. More robust than *I. aquifolium*, with larger broader leaves. Berries mostly red. 'Camelliifolia', stems with purple hue, and red berries; 'Golden King', dark green leaves edged yellow; 'Hendersonii', vigorous tree, brown-red berries; 'Lawsoniana', compact female shrub with yellow-streaked stems, gold and green markings in center of leaves, brownish red berries; 'Platyphylla', broad, glossy, dark green, spine-toothed leaves; 'Purple Shaft', columnar, vigorous, fruits profusely. Zones 6–10.

Ilex aquifolium

COMMON HOLLY, ENGLISH HOLLY

☀ ❄ ↔ 25 ft (8 m) ↑ 40–80 ft (12–24 m)

Occurs over southern and western Europe, North Africa, and western Asia. Glossy dark green leaves, elliptic, spine-toothed edges. Male and female flowers usually borne on separate trees. Berries red, sometimes yellow or orange. 'Amber', female cultivar, to 20 ft (6 m) tall, bright green leaves, amber berries; 'Argentea Marginata', female cultivar, dark green leaves edged creamy white; 'Argentea Marginata Pendula' (syn. 'Argentea Pendula'), weeping female tree with spiny, cream-margined, elliptic leaves; 'Ferox Argentea', spiny leaves with cream margins; 'Handsworth New Silver', female, with elongated, spiny, cream-edged leaves, dark purple stems; 'J. C. van Tol', broad female tree, dark green leaves, scarlet berries; 'Madame Briot', vigorous female form, egg-shaped dark green leaves with gold margins, vivid red fruit; 'Pyramidalis', self-fertile cultivar, yellowish green stems, spiny bright green leaves; 'Pyramidalis Fructu Luteo', female conical shrub or small tree, yellow berries; 'Silver Milkmaid', female cultivar, pale green to yellow stems, spiny mid-green leaves with silver-white markings. Other popular cultivars include 'Aurifodina', 'Bacciflava', 'Gold Flash', 'Golden Milkboy', and 'Silver Queen'. Zones 6–10.

Ilex × aquipernyi

☀ ❄ ↔ 12 ft (3.5 m) ↑ 20 ft (6 m)

Evergreen tree or shrub of garden origin, hybrid between *I. aquifolium* and *I. pernyi*. Elongated glossy green leaves, strong spines. Red berries. 'San Jose' ★, female form, green leaves with up to 9 spines. Red fruit. Zones 6–10.

Ilex cassine

Ilex crenata

Ilex × koehneana

Ilex cassine

DAHOON HOLLY

☼ ❋ ↔ 15 ft (4.5 m) ↑ 40 ft (12 m)

Evergreen tree native to Cuba and southeastern USA. Pointed or rounded, glossy, dark green leaves with pronounced midrib, leaf edges either smooth or toothed near apex. Yellow or red berries. Zones 6–10.

Ilex cornuta

CHINESE HOLLY, HORNED HOLLY

☼ ❋ ↔ 6–12 ft (1.8–3.5 m) ↑ 6–12 ft (1.8–3.5 m)

Dense, evergreen, rounded shrub native to China and Korea. Oblong dark green leaves, variable spines. Large red berries, long-lasting. **'Burfordii'**, free-fruiting female form, red berries, leaves with terminal spines; **'Dwarf Burford'**, to 8 ft (2.4 m) high, dense habit, dark red berries. Zones 6–10.

Ilex crenata

JAPANESE HOLLY

☼ ❋ ↔ 12 ft (3.5 m) ↑ 15 ft (4.5 m)

Evergreen shrub or small tree from Korea, Japan, and Sakhalin Island. Small deep green leaves, minutely scalloped. Flowers white; fruit mainly glossy black, sometimes white or yellow. **'Convexa'** (syn. 'Bullata'), female, purple-green stems, abundant black fruit; **'Golden Gem'**, compact female, to 3 ft (0.9 m) high, golden yellow leaves, prefers full sun; **'Helleri'**, spreading female shrub, dark green leaves, black fruit; **'Ivory Tower'**, female, late-ripening white fruit; **'Mariesii'** (syns *I. c.* var. *nummularioides*, *I. mariesii*), very slow-growing cultivar, dark green leaves, black fruit; **'Shiro Fukurin'** (syns 'Fukarin', 'Snow Flake'), upright female, rounded leaves with cream markings, black fruit; and **'Sky Pencil'**, narrowly columnar female. Zones 6–10.

Ilex decidua

POSSUMHAW, WINTERBERRY

☼ ❋ ↔ 6–15 ft (1.8–4.5 m) ↑ 6–20 ft (1.8–6 m)

Native to southeastern and central USA. Upright deciduous shrub, rarely a tree. Mid-green leaves, sprout in late spring, oval or egg-shaped, scalloped, crowded on short lateral spurs. Berries orange or red, sometimes yellow, last well into winter. Zones 6–10.

Ilex glabra

GALLBERRY, INKBERRY

☼ ❋ ↔ 10 ft (3 m) ↑ 10 ft (3 m)

Erect evergreen shrub from eastern North America. Glossy dark green leaves, almost smooth-edged, slightly toothed near apex. Berries round, black. Shallow rooting. *I. g.* f. *leucocarpa,* white fruit; **'Ivory Queen'**, popular form. *I. g.* **'Compacta'** ★, to 4 ft (1.2 m) high, denser foliage than species, black berries. Zones 3–10.

Ilex × koehneana

☼ ❋ ↔ 12 ft (3.5 m) ↑ 20 ft (6 m)

Evergreen shrub or tree, hybrid between *I. aquifolium* and *I. latifolia*. Strongly resembles *I. latifolia*, but more spiny; sometimes wrongly sold as that plant. Zones 7–10.

Ilex × meserveae

BLUE HOLLY, HYBRID BLUE HOLLY, MESERVE HOLLY

☼ ❋ ↔ 10 ft (3 m) ↑ 6–15 ft (1.8–4.5 m)

Of garden origin, hybrid of *I. aquifolium* and *I. rugosa*. Small, often blue-green leaves. Red berries on female plants. **'Blue Angel'**, compact female shrub, slow growing, to 12 ft (3.5 m) high, royal purple stems, blue-green leaves, least hardy; **'Blue Boy'**, male, grows to 10 ft (3 m) high; **'Blue Girl'**, female, red berries; **'Blue Maid'**, dense female shrub, red berries; **'Blue Prince'**, male, lustrous bright green leaves; **'Blue Princess'**, female shrub, prolific red berries. Zones 6–10.

Ilex mitis

CAPE HOLLY

☼ ❋ ↔ 20 ft (6 m) ↑ 30 ft (9 m)

Thick-trunked evergreen tree from wet regions of south and east Africa. Smooth-edged leaves, oblong to lance-shaped; juvenile leaves red. White flowers in spring–summer. Red berries. Zones 8–11.

Ilex opaca

AMERICAN HOLLY

☼ ❋ ↔ 35 ft (10 m) ↑ 50 ft (15 m)

From USA. Leaves oblong to elliptic, smooth-edged or spiny, matt green above, yellow-green beneath. White flowers. Red, orange, or yellow berries. **'Hedgeholly'**, hardy, compact; **'Morgan Gold'**, golden fruit; **'Old Faithful'**, large berries, less hardy. Zones 5–9.

Ilex, Hybrid Cultivar, 'Nellie R. Stevens'

Ilex pedunculosa

☼ ❋ ↔ 20 ft (6 m) ↑ 30 ft (9 m)

Evergreen tree from China, Japan, and Taiwan. Leaves glossy, dark green, egg-shaped, pointed tips, smooth-edged, spineless. White flowers; red fruit. Zones 5–9.

Ilex pernyi

PERNY'S HOLLY

☼ ❋ ↔ 12 ft (3.5 m) ↑ 30 ft (9 m)

From Gansu and Hubei Provinces in China. Evergreen shrub, smaller in cultivation. Leaves almost stalkless, dark green, triangular to rectangular. Yellow flowers in late spring. Red berries. Zones 5–10.

Ilex serrata

FINETOOTH HOLLY, JAPANESE WINTERBERRY

☼ ❋ ↔ 10 ft (3 m) ↑ 15 ft (4.5 m)

Native to Japan and China. Bushy deciduous shrub, purple new twigs. Finely toothed, oval, dark green leaves, downy coating on both surfaces. Pink flowers, small red berries. Zones 5–10.

Ilex verticillata

BLACK ALDER, WINTERBERRY

☼ ❋ ↔ 15 ft (4.5 m) ↑ 15 ft (4.5 m)

Deciduous shrub from eastern North America. Bright green leaves, obovate or lance-shaped, toothed, fine downy below. White flowers; red, yellow, or orange berries. *I. v.* f. *aurantiaca*, orange berries. *I. v.* 'Winter Red' ★, female, dark green leaves, red berries. Zones 3–9.

Ilex vomitoria

CAROLINA TEA, YAUPON

☼/◐ ❋ ↔ 12 ft (3.5 m) ↑ 20 ft (6 m)

Evergreen shrub or small tree native to southeastern USA and Mexico. Glossy dark green leaves, elliptic to egg-shaped, scalloped

edges. White flowers, red berries. 'Nana', to 3 ft (0.9 m) high; 'Pendula', lax branches, clear red fruit. Zones 6–10.

Ilex Hybrid Cultivars

☼ ❋ ↔ 5–15 ft (1.5–4.5 m) ↑ 8–20 ft (2.4–6 m)

Hollies extensively hybridized. 'China Boy', very hardy, male, grows quickly to 8 ft (2.4 m); 'China Girl', very hardy, evergreen female, masses of bright red berries; 'Ebony Magic', evergreen female, leaves with wavy margin and up to 22 spines, leaf stems almost black, orange-red berries; 'John T. Morris', male, dark evergreen foliage, 'Nellie R. Stevens', evergreen female, orange-red berries; 'September Gem', evergreen female, narrow dark green leaves, red berries; 'Sparkleberry', deciduous female, bright red berries. Zones 6–10.

ILLICIUM

This genus of over 40 evergreen shrubs and trees in the star-anise (Illiciaceae) family is found in moist shaded areas of India, East Asia, and the Americas. Leaves and flowers are fragrant, and members of the genus supply aromatic oils used in some perfumes. *I. verum* is the source of the Chinese spice star-anise. These trees were originally included in the same genus as magnolias because of their resemblance to them. Flowers range in color from cream to reddish purple and are followed by star-shaped fruit. The genus name comes from the Latin for "allurement," in reference to the perfume of some species. CULTIVATION: *Illicium* species will survive in full sun but do best in a sheltered position out of direct sunlight, in a moist, well-drained, acid soil. Propagate from half-hardened cuttings taken in summer or by layering in autumn.

Illicium floridanum, fruit

Illicium anisatum

ANISE SHRUB, JAPANESE ANISE, JAPANESE STAR-ANISE

◐ ❋ ↔ 20 ft (6 m) ↑ 25 ft (8 m)

Conical evergreen shrub from China, Taiwan, and Japan. Aromatic wood, leaves, bark. Greenish yellow flowers in mid-spring. Fruit woody, poisonous. Variegated form available. Zones 7–11.

Illicium floridanum

FLORIDA ANISE TREE, POLECAT TREE, PURPLE ANISE

◐ ❋ ↔ 8 ft (2.4 m) ↑ 10 ft (3 m)

Aromatic, bushy, evergreen shrub from southeastern States of USA. Slightly furrowed, smooth, dark brown trunk. Slender, leathery, deep green leaves. Showy, star-shaped, reddish purple flowers in late spring–early summer. 'Album', white flowers; 'Variegatum', variegated leaves; 'Woodland Ruby' ★, red-pink flowers. Zones 8–11.

INDIGOFERA

The source of the purple-blue dye indigo, this genus in the pea-flower subfamily of the legume (Fabaceae) family includes some 700 species of perennials, shrubs, and trees that are widespread in the tropics and subtropics. Leaves vary, but they are typically pinnate, often made up of many small leaflets. The flowers are primarily in pink, mauve, and purple shades, carried in long racemes or spikes. They usually open in summer but may occur year-round in mild climates. Small seed pods follow.

CULTIVATION: The shrubby species are usually neat bushes, often deciduous, that vary in hardiness depending on their origins. They generally grow best in full sun with light well-drained soil and ample summer moisture. If necessary, prune after flowering or in late winter. Propagate from seed or half-hardened cuttings. Many species produce suckers that can be replanted.

Indigofera australis
AUSTRALIAN INDIGO
☼ ✿ ↔ 6 ft (1.8 m) ↑ 6 ft (1.8 m)
Evergreen from Australia. Leaves pinnate, 9 to 21 blue-green leaf-lets, to 1 in (25 mm) long, hairy underside. Racemes of mauve-pink to magenta-red flowers in summer. Brown seed pods. Zones 9–11.

Indigofera decora ★
☼ ✤ ↔ 4 ft (1.2 m) ↑ 30 in (75 cm)
Widely cultivated, deciduous, spreading, suckering shrub from China and Japan. Leaves to 8 in (20 cm) long, 25 to 40 leaflets. Large racemes of light pink flowers in summer. Zones 6–10.

Indigofera heterantha
syn. *Indigofera gerardiana*
☼ ✤ ↔ 8 ft (2.4 m) ↑ 8 ft (2.4 m)
Deciduous shrub from northwestern Himalayas, smaller in culti-vation. Densely twiggy plant, short pinnate leaves. Massed racemes of bright pink to light red flowers in summer. Zones 7–10.

Indigofera kirilowii
☼ ✤ ↔ 3–6 ft (0.9–1.8 m) ↑ 2–5 ft (0.6–1.5 m)
Deciduous shrub from Korea, nearby parts of China, and Kyushu, Japan. Leaves pinnate, bright green, 13 leaflets. Smothered in short racemes of rose pink flowers in spring–early summer. Zones 5–10.

Indigofera potaninii
☼ ✤ ↔ 4 ft (1.2 m) ↑ 3–5 ft (0.9–1.5 m)
Sometimes sold as *I. amblyantha*. True species is deciduous shrub from southwestern China. Differs from *I. amblyantha* in shorter leaves, fewer leaflets, densely hairy below. Larger flowers, usually mauve, in summer–autumn. Zones 5–9.

IOCHROMA
These large-leafed evergreen shrubs from Central America and Andean South America have a rather lax habit with long brittle branches. Although there are around 15 species within this genus, only 5 or 6 are generally used in horticulture. The soft foliage of most species is a downy mid-green. In common with other mem-bers of the nightshade (Solanaceae) family, the late summer flowers, usually held in clusters of drooping tubular blooms, are in shades of purple, orange, red, or white.
CULTIVATION: These plants need a sunny position with wind protec-tion to ensure their quick-growing soft-stemmed branches are not

Illicium anisatum

damaged. Plant in well-drained moisture-retentive soil and ensure they are given ample water during summer. Suitable for pot cul-ture in cooler areas, they can be pruned to shape in early spring without undue loss of blossom. Propagate from cuttings or seed.

Iochroma coccineum
☼ ✿ ↔ 6 ft (1.8 m) ↑ 10 ft (3 m)
Soft-stemmed shrub from Central America. Soft, gray-green, felty leaves. Small clusters of tubular scarlet flowers with yellow throat in summer. Zones 9–11.

Iochroma cyaneum
syn. *Iochroma tubulosum*
☼ ✤ ↔ 5 ft (1.5 m) ↑ 10 ft (3 m)
Quick-growing shrub from northwestern South America. Large felty leaves, sometimes partly obscuring purple tubular flowers held in large pendent clusters in summer. Zones 8–11.

Iochroma grandiflorum
☼ ✿ ↔ 6 ft (1.8 m) ↑ 8 ft (2.4 m)
From Ecuador. Downy green leaves. Large purple flowers, in clus-ters of 5 or 6, in summer–autumn. Zones 9–11.

Indigofera decora

Iochroma grandiflorum

ISOPOGON

The majority of the 35 species in this southern Australian genus of the protea (Proteaceae) family are found in Western Australia. They are attractive evergreen shrubs with tough dissected foliage and showy flowers that form dense globular heads, generally in shades of yellow and pink. The rounded or egg-shaped cone-like fruiting heads are usually borne terminally and persist for a long time, giving some members of the genus the common names of cone bush or drumsticks.

CULTIVATION: These plants like full sun and light well-drained soil. Some species are best suited to winter rainfall areas, especially those from Western Australia. Pruning is not usually necessary, except when young to form the basis of a well-branched shrub. Most species will tolerate occasional light frosts. Propagate from cuttings or from seed, which may be slow to germinate.

Isopogon formosus   Itea ilicifolia

Isopogon dubius

☼ ❄ ↔ 5 ft (1.5 m) ↑ 5 ft (1.5 m)

Bushy upright shrub from Western Australia. Flat, grayish green, prickly leaves, divided into 3 segments. Rose pink flowers, in terminal heads, in late winter–spring. Zones 9–11.

Isopogon formosus ★

ROSE CONE FLOWER

☼ ❄ ↔ 6 ft (1.8 m) ↑ 6 ft (1.8 m)

Erect or spreading shrub from Western Australia. Narrow prickly leaves divided into short cylindrical segments. Mauve-pink flowers in cone-like heads, 2½ in (6 cm) wide, in winter–spring. Zones 9–11.

ITEA

SWEETSPIRE

Very attractive but not widely cultivated, the 10 evergreen and deciduous shrubs and small trees in this genus present an interesting combination of foliage and flowers. Although they are members of the gooseberry (Grossulariaceae) family, their foliage is often more reminiscent of members of the holly (Aquifoliaceae) family. Found naturally in Asia, with a sole eastern North American representative, the evergreens offer dark lustrous leaves throughout the year, while the deciduous species have brilliant autumn foliage color. The catkin-like racemes are not colorful and are really more of a novelty for their contrast with the foliage.

Isopogon dubius

CULTIVATION: Frost hardiness varies, but the commonly grown species are reasonably tough and will thrive in most well-drained soils with a position in full sun or partial shade. They are, however, not drought tolerant and need ample summer moisture. Propagate from seed or from half-hardened cuttings.

Itea ilicifolia

HOLLYLEAF SWEETSPIRE

☼ ❄ ↔ 10 ft (3 m) ↑ 15 ft (4.5 m)

Widely cultivated evergreen shrub from western China. Narrow erect habit. Deep green holly-like leaves, 2–4 in (5–10 cm) long, edged with small spines. Cream to pale yellow flowers, on racemes to 15 in (38 cm) long, honey scented, in summer. Zones 7–10.

Itea virginica

SWEETSPIRE, VIRGINIA WILLOW

☼ ❄ ↔ 5 ft (1.5 m) ↑ 4–10 ft (1.2–3 m)

Deciduous clump-forming shrub from eastern North America. Arching stems, 2–4 in (5–10 cm) long, serrated-edged leaves, develop vivid red and orange tones in autumn. Racemes of tiny, honey-scented, cream flowers, 2–6 in (5–15 cm) long, erect rather than pendulous. 'Henry's Garnet', well-known cultivar. Zones 5–9.

IXORA

JUNGLE FLAME

Common throughout the wet tropics, this genus of about 400 evergreen shrubs and small trees belongs to the madder (Rubiaceae) family. The genus name is from the Portuguese name for the Hindu deity, Siva, to whom the blooms are dedicated. The flowers are usually produced in showy clusters, ranging from scarlet, pink, or yellow to white, and are sometimes fragrant. Attractive glossy leaves and a compact habit make them suitable for containers or massed plantings. The 1- or 2-seeded drupe, mostly red, ripens to black.

CULTIVATION: Frost tender, many species will not tolerate a temperature much below 55°F (13°C), and prefer bright indirect sun. The soil should be friable, with added sharp sand and leaf mold. Pinch out the tips when young to encourage branching, and prune older plants after flowering. Propagate from seed in spring, or from half-hardened cuttings, taken from non-flowering shoots, in summer.

Ixora chinensis

☼ ✤ ↔ 5 ft (1.5 m) ↕ 6 ft (1.8 m)

Small, rounded, evergreen shrub from tropical parts of East Asia, particularly China and Taiwan. Glossy deep green leaves. Flowers in very large, showy, terminal clusters, to 4 in (10 cm) across, bright orange, in late spring–autumn. '**Nora Grant**', coral red flowers; '**Prince of Orange**' ★, prolific orange-red flowers. Zones 10–12.

Ixora coccinea

FLAME OF THE WOODS

☼ ✤ ↔ 8 ft (2.4 m) ↕ 8 ft (2.4 m)

Bushy rounded shrub from tropical Asia. Leaves glossy, dark green. Small brilliant orange-red flowers, in large round clusters, most of year in tropics. Zones 11–12.

Ixora Hybrid Cultivars

☼ ✤ ↔ 1–3 ft (0.3–0.9 m) ↕ 1–6 ft (0.3–1.8 m)

Numerous *Ixora* hybrid cultivars, most derived from *I. coccinea*. '**Exotica**', bright red flowers fade to orange, creating two-toned flowerhead; '**Frances Perry**', deep yellow flowers; '**Fraseri**', vivid salmon pink flowers; '**Herrera's White**',

Ixora chinensis 'Prince of Orange'

white flowers; '**Orange Glow**', bright orange flowers; '**Rosea**', rose pink flowers; '**Sunkist**', dwarf shrub to 3 ft (0.9 m), small glossy leaves, flowers of apricot-yellow, age to brick red; '**Sunny Gold**', orange-amber flowers; '**Thai King**', orange-red flowers. Zones 11–12.

JACARANDA

The genus comprises about 50 species of deciduous and evergreen trees and shrubs belonging to the trumpet-vine (Bignoniaceae) family. They are native to the drier areas of tropical and subtropical Central and South America and have elegant, fern-like, bipinnate leaves, some pinnate or simple. Mauve-blue, rarely pink or white, funnel- or bell-shaped flowers in terminal or axillary panicles appear in spring–summer. CULTIVATION: Jacarandas will grow quickly in fertile well-drained soil in full sun. Protect from wind and frost when young. They are relatively frost hardy once established. Pruning is not necessary for outdoor specimens. Water freely in the growing season and sparingly in winter. They are shallow-rooted heavy feeders, and shrubs planted nearby may suffer. Propagate from seed in late winter or early spring, and from half-hardened cuttings in summer.

Jacaranda cuspidifolia

☼ ⚘ ↔ 30 ft (9 m) ↕ 15–40 ft (4.5–12 m)

Native to Brazil, Argentina, Bolivia, and Paraguay. Large leaves with up to 20 pairs of leaflets on each pinna. Large bright blue-violet flowers in big clusters. Fruit nearly spherical, white to pale brown. Zones 10–11.

Jacaranda mimosifolia

BLUE HAZE TREE, BRAZILIAN ROSEWOOD, FERN TREE, JACARANDA

☼ ⚘ ↔ 20–35 ft (6–10 m) ↕ 25–50 ft (8–15 m)

Fast-growing deciduous tree from drier areas of South America. Mid-green bipinnate leaves may turn rich yellow in late winter

before falling. Terminal clusters of hanging, bell-shaped, mauve-blue flowers on mostly leafless branches in late spring–early summer. '**White Christmas**', white flowers. Zones 10–11.

JASMINUM

JASMINE

Famed for the fragrance of its flowers, this genus, which belongs to the olive (Oleaceae) family, is native to Africa, Europe, and Asia (with a single American species). The genus includes some 200 species of deciduous, semi-deciduous, and evergreen shrubs and woody-stemmed climbers. The foliage is usually pinnate or less commonly trifoliate and varies greatly in color and texture. The flowers, in clusters at the branch tips and leaf axils, are tubular with 5 widely flared lobes. Most commonly white, white flushed with pink, or yellow, and can be scentless to overpoweringly fragrant. CULTIVATION: Jasmines vary greatly in their hardiness, depending on their origins, though few will tolerate repeated severe frosts. They are averse to drought, preferring moist, humus-rich, well-drained soil and a position in full sun or partial shade. In suitable climates most species grow rapidly and some can become rather invasive. They are readily propagated from seed, cuttings, or layers, which with some low-growing species may form naturally, making them difficult to contain.

Jasminum humile

ITALIAN JASMINE, ITALIAN YELLOW JASMINE

☼/◐ ❄ ↔ 12 ft (3.5 m) ↕ 12 ft (3.5 m)

Evergreen or semi-evergreen shrub from Middle East to China. Short pinnate leaves, up to 7 leaflets. Clusters of yellow flowers in summer. '**Revolutum**', fragrant, with large leaves. Zones 8–10.

Jacaranda mimosifolia

Jasminum nudiflorum

Jatropha multifida

Jasminum mesnyi

PRIMROSE JASMINE, YELLOW JASMINE

☀/◐ ❋ ↔ 10 ft (3 m) ↑ 10 ft (3 m)

Evergreen sprawling shrub native to western China. Clump of arching cane-like stems. Leaves trifoliate, semi-glossy, bright green. Flowers unscented, bright yellow, semi-double, in summer. Zones 8–10.

Jasminum nudiflorum

WINTER JASMINE

☀/◐ ❋ ↔ 10 ft (3 m) ↑ 10 ft (3 m)

Sprawling deciduous shrub from northern China. Mass of slightly arched, whippy, green canes, dark green trifoliate leaves. Bright yellow blooms, in winter, when all else is bare. Zones 6–9.

JATROPHA

This variable genus of the euphorbia (Euphorbia-ceae) family comprises some 170 species of succulent perennials and evergreen or deciduous shrubs, rarely trees. All species contain a milky latex that may irritate the skin. They are found in tropical to warm-temperate regions of the world, mainly Central and South America. Leaves are usually palmately lobed, though some are lobeless. Small clusters of purple, yellow, scarlet, or red flowers occur in summer. All plant parts are poisonous. CULTIVATION: These plants appreciate a fertile, well-drained, sandy soil and full sun, but most will tolerate part-shade. Frost tender, in temperate zones they can be grown in a greenhouse. Place half-hardened cuttings in cool shade to allow the cutting ends to dry before rooting, or propagate from seed in spring or summer.

Juglans cinerea

Jatropha integerrima

syns *Jatropha hastata, J. pandurifolia*

PEREGRINA, SPICY JATROPHA

☀ ❧ ↔ 4–8 ft (1.2–2.4 m) ↑ 10–20 ft (3–6 m)

Spreading evergreen tree native to Cuba, Hispaniola, and Puerto Rico. Leaves 3-lobed to fiddle-shaped, rich green, bronze underside. Small, funnel-shaped, 5-petalled, rose red flowers throughout year, but mostly in warm weather. Seeds and sap poisonous. Zones 10–12.

Jatropha multifida

CORAL PLANT, PHYSIC NUT

☀ ❧ ↔ 10 ft (3 m) ↑ 12 ft (3.5 m)

Large evergreen shrub or small tree from Mexico to Brazil. Rounded leaves, deeply divided into 7 to 11 blades, dark green above, whitish below. Small scarlet flowers on green or red stalks, above foliage, in summer. Egg-shaped fruit contains up to 3 seeds. Zones 10–12.

JUGLANS

The walnuts, a genus of the Juglandaceae family, comprise about 20 species of deciduous trees. They are distributed over the temperate zones of the Americas, southeastern Europe, and Southeast Asia. They have alternate compound leaves and monoecious flowers, borne in spring. The fruit is a hard-shelled nut enclosed in a fleshy green drupe, the kernels being prized as food. CULTIVATION: They thrive on deep, alluvial, well-drained soil with a high organic content, and an assured water supply, in a cool humid climate. Severely prune after 1 year to force strong single-trunk growth, then stop at 12 ft (3.5 m) or so to induce lateral branches. Seed can be collected as soon as it is ripe in early autumn and stored in cool conditions until it is sown in early spring.

Juglans ailanthifolia

syn. *Juglans sieboldiana*

JAPANESE WALNUT

☀ ❋ ↔ 40 ft (12 m) ↑ 50 ft (15 m)

Upright tree from Japan. Leaves 11 to 17 leaflets, covered in dark red fine hairs. Bark striped pale and dark gray. Male catkins 6–12 in (15–30 cm) long, female flowers deep red. Fruits covered in adhesive down. Zones 4–9.

Juglans californica

☀ ❋ ↔ 30 ft (9 m) ↑ 30 ft (9 m)

Native of southern California, USA. Large shrub or small tree, attractive leaves composed of 11 to 15 lance-shaped leaflets. Zones 7–10.

Juglans cinerea

BUTTERNUT, BUTTERNUT WALNUT, WHITE WALNUT

☀ ❋ ↔ 50 ft (15 m) ↑ 60 ft (18 m)

From New Brunswick, Canada, to Georgia, USA. Fast-growing species, usually smaller in cultivation.

Juglans ailanthifolia

Shoots sticky. Leaves oblong, notched edges, hairy, yellow-green. Fruit solitary or in clusters. Can be short lived. Zones 4–9.

JUNIPERUS

This genus consists of some 60 generally slow-growing evergreen trees and shrubs in the cypress (Cupressaceae) family, occurring in the Northern Hemisphere. All species are long lived, performing particularly well on alkaline soils. Juvenile leaves are awl-shaped (needle-like), and adult leaves are scale-like and stem-clasping. When crushed, the leaves of most species are aromatic. The small, fleshy, berry-like fruit are actually cones that ripen to blue-black or reddish. Usually separate male and female plants are found. CULTIVATION: Although drought tolerant and tough, these plants are susceptible to fungal attack, needing an open airy situation. Well-drained soils are essential. Regular light pruning maintains shape, but do not cut bare wood. Propagation from fresh seed is best, although named cultivars should be either grafted or grown from a cutting in winter.

Juniperus chinensis
CHINESE JUNIPER

☼ ❋ ↔ 15 ft (4.5 m) ↑ 30 ft (9 m)
Native to China and Japan. Variable species in habit and size. Blunt-tipped adult leaves, prickly juvenile leaves, both on lower branches and within tree. Berries small, round, blue-green. *J. c.* var. *sargentii*, low growing. *J. c.* 'Aurea', golden adult leaves, yellowish green juvenile leaves, to 20 ft (6 m); 'Blaauw', vigorous shrub to 5 ft (1.5 m); 'Expansa Variegata', dwarf spreading shrub to 3 ft (0.9 m); 'Femina', good bonsai subject; 'Kaizuka', large upright shrub or small tree, spreading branches; 'Keteleeri' ★, distinctive spiralled habit of blunt-tipped closely held scales; 'Mountbatten', dense columnar habit, gray-green awl-shaped leaves; 'Oblonga', inner leaves dark green, awl-shaped, prickly, outer leaves scale-like; 'Olympia', small conical tree; 'Parsonii', dwarf shrub eventually mounding to 3 ft (0.9 m) in center; 'Shoosmith', conical tree, bright green foliage; 'Spartan', columnar form, dark green foliage; 'Variegata', mostly juvenile leaves on long branchlets when young, then progressively develops adult leaves, at all stages irregularly flecked with creamy yellow or white. Zones 4–9.

Juniperus communis 'Pendula'

Juniperus osteosperma, in the wild, Utah, USA

Juniperus communis
COMMON JUNIPER

☼ ❋ ↔ 3–15 ft (0.9–4.5 m) ↑ 20 ft (6 m)
Variable evergreen shrub or small tree widespread in Northern Hemisphere. Narrow-columnar in mild areas, tendency to spread in colder climates. Silver-backed leaves, needle-like, prickly; fruit green ripening to glossy black with whitish bloom. *J. c.* var. *montana* (syn. *J. c.* 'Nana'), slow-growing ground cover. *J. c.* 'Compressa', compact, narrow, slow-growing column to 3 ft (0.9 m); 'Depressa Aurea' ★, wide-spreading ground cover to 2 ft (0.6 m) high, foliage dense, brownish green, becoming more bronze in winter; 'Depressed Star', rounded spreading habit, light green foliage; 'Hibernica' (syn. 'Stricta'), slender column to 10 ft (3 m) high, dense foliage, prominent silvery reverse; 'Pendula', graceful weeping branches. Zones 2–8.

Juniperus conferta
SHORE JUNIPER

☼ ❋ ↔ 5–8 ft (1.5–2.4 m) ↑ 2 ft (0.6 m)
From Japan and Russian island of Sakhalin. Wide-spreading, fast-growing, prostrate, salt tolerant. Light green to blue-green foliage, very prickly and dense. Small berry-like fruit ripen to brown. 'Blue Lagoon' and 'Blue Pacific', bluer foliage; 'Emerald Sea', gray-green foliage; 'Sunsplash', green and gold variegated foliage. Zones 5–9.

Juniperus deppeana
ALLIGATOR JUNIPER, CHEQUERBOARD JUNIPER

☼ ❋ ↔ 7 ft (2 m) ↑ 20 ft (6 m)
Broad gray-barked tree from Arizona and New Mexico, USA, and northern Mexico. Blue-green leaves. *J. d.* var. *pachyphlaea*, sometimes sold as 'Conspicua', conical, coarse-textured, Mexican tree, silvery gray leaves, distinctive red-brown bark in square plates. Foliage of adult type. Performs best in cool dry conditions. Zones 7–9.

Juniperus horizontalis
CREEPING JUNIPER, HORIZONTAL JUNIPER

☼ ❋ ↔ 12 ft (3.5 m) ↑ 18 in (45 cm)
From northern North America, found on coastal cliffs and stony hillsides. Vigorous ground-hugging shrub with long trailing branches. Leaves gray-green or bluish, often with purplish tinge in winter. 'Bar Harbor', mat forming, blue-green foliage, tips turn mauve in winter; 'Blue Chip', blue-green leaves, variegated gold; 'Douglasii', prostrate to 2 ft (0.6 m) high, blue-green foliage turns purplish in autumn–winter; 'Prince of Wales', mat forming; 'Repens', blue-green leaves; 'Wiltonii', blue-foliaged, prostrate, trailing. Zones 4–10.

Juniperus osteosperma
UTAH JUNIPER

☼ ❋ ↔ 20 ft (6 m) ↑ 12–20 ft (3.5–6 m)
From eastern California to Montana, and New Mexico, USA. Short thick trunk, forking low, broad irregular crown. Dull olive-green foliage, small red-brown cones. Zones 4–9.

Juniperus sabina

Leaves awl-shaped on young plants, scale-like on adult. Fruit small, ovoid, blue-black berry with whitish bloom, with 1 to 3 seeds. **'Calgary Carpet'**, low-growing form; **'Skandia'**, mid-green foliage; **'Tamariscifolia'**, spreading, green to blue-green foliage. Zones 4–9.

Juniperus scopulorum
ROCKY MOUNTAINS JUNIPER

☼ ❄ ↔ 15 ft (4.5 m) ↕ 30 ft (9 m)

From western North America and Texas, USA. Small tree or shrub with sturdy spreading branches; tightly held, scale-like leaves, light to blue-green. Small round fruit. **'Blue Arrow'**, pencil-shaped, blue-green foliage; **'Blue Heaven'**, blue-green foliage; **'Horizontalis'**, spreading, blue-green foliage; **'Mountaineer'**, bright green foliage; **'Repens'**, prostrate, blue-green foliage; **'Skyrocket'**, very narrow columnar form to 10 ft (3 m) tall, silvery blue foliage, arguably narrowest of all conifers; **'Tabletop'**, spreading, blue-green foliage; **'Tolleson's Blue Weeping'**, pendulous; **'Wichita Blue'**, conical, blue-gray foliage. Zones 5–9.

Juniperus squamata
HOLLYWOOD JUNIPER, SINGLESEED JUNIPER, SQUAMATA JUNIPER

☼ ❄ ↔ 15 ft (4.5 m) ↕ 2–20 ft (0.6–6 m)

Extremely variable species from central Asia and China. May be mound-like shrub, small shrubby tree, or prostrate ground cover. Bark red-brown and flaky. Dense, juvenile-type, awl-shaped leaves, grayish green to silvery blue-green, upper surface marked pale green or white. **'Blue Carpet'**, spreading form, blue-green foliage; **'Blue Star'**, rounded shrub, very blue, small, dense; **'Chinese Silver'**, medium to large, dense, multi-stemmed shrub, leaves strongly silvery blue; **'Meyeri'**, open vase shape, leaves very blue when young, turning dark green with age. Zones 4–9.

Juniperus × *pfitzeriana*
syn. *Juniperus* × *media*

☼ ❄ ↔ 5–15 ft (1.5–4.5 m) ↕ 4–10 ft (1.2–3 m)

Collection of garden hybrids derived mainly from *J. chinensis*. Adult and juvenile leaves usually present simultaneously. Adult leaves stem-clasping scales; juvenile leaves triangular, sharp, protruding. Branches wide spreading, lifted just above horizontal. Dull green, adult, scale-like leaves release unpleasant scent when crushed. Many have white or blue-black fruit, globular to rounded. **'Golden Sunset'**, low-growing shrub; **'Pfitzeriana Aurea'**, greenish yellow foliage; **'Wilhelm Pfitzer'**, vigorous, spreading, shade-tolerant shrub with sturdy ascending branches and pendulous tips, leaves mostly green and scale-like. Zones 4–10.

Juniperus procumbens
BONIN ISLAND JUNIPER, CREEPING JUNIPER, JAPANESE GARDEN JUNIPER

☼ ❄ ↔ 12 ft (3.5 m) ↕ 30 in (75 cm)

From western China. Stiff and wiry habit, prickly blue-green leaves. Small berry-like cones, brown-green, each contains 2 or 3 seeds. **'Nana'**, smaller leaves, softer texture, more conical habit. Zones 4–9.

Juniperus recurva
COFFIN JUNIPER, DROOPING JUNIPER, HIMALAYAN JUNIPER

☼ ❄ ↔ 15 ft (4.5 m) ↕ 30 ft (9 m)

From southwestern China, Myanmar, and Himalayas. Weeping sprays of aromatic foliage, in whorls of 3 needle-like gray-green leaves. Bark peels off in reddish brown strips. Fruit small, round, fleshy, berry-like, ripens to glossy blue-black. *J. r.* var. *coxii,* slow growing, with smaller leaves. Zones 7–9.

Juniperus sabina
SAVIN JUNIPER

☼ ❄ ↔ 15 ft (4.5 m) ↕ 12 ft (3.5 m)

Variable, spreading, self-layering species from southern and central Europe. Dark green foliage with disagreeable odor when crushed.

Juniperus × *pfitzeriana* 'Golden Sunset'

Juniperus virginiana
EASTERN RED CEDAR, PENCIL CEDAR, RED CEDAR

☼ ❄ ↔ 12–20 ft (3.5–6 m) ↕ 40 ft (12 m)

From central and eastern North America. Upright tree, becoming more open with age. Bark reddish brown, peels in long strips. Small, adult, closely held scale leaves with pointed tip, glaucous green, purplish in winter. Fragrant timber traditionally used for casings of lead pencils. **'Burkii'** ★, narrowly pyramidal habit, blue-foliaged shrub becoming steel-blue in cold winters; **'Manhattan Blue'**, popular pencil-shaped cultivar. Zones 2–8.

JUSTICIA
syns *Adhatoda, Beloperone, Drejerella, Jacobinia, Libonia*

This largely tropical and subtropical American genus of the acanthus (Acanthaceae) family encompasses more than 400 species of perennials, subshrubs, and shrubs. The shrubby species are evergreen, their leaves usually simple pointed ovals in opposite pairs, sometimes hairy or with a velvety surface. The flowers are clustered, sometimes in upright panicles at the branch tips, or in looser, more open heads. The true flowers are often small, the flowerheads made colorful and showy by large bracts.

CULTIVATION: A feature of gardens in warm climates and popular house and greenhouse plants elsewhere, most justicias do not tolerate severe frosts. Some tolerate being frosted to the ground, reshooting in spring, but most need mild winter conditions. Justicias prefer moist well-drained soil in sun or partial shade with shelter from strong winds. Water regularly during the growth period. Keep compact by regular tip pinching or a light trimming after flowering. Propagate from seed or half-hardened cuttings.

Justicia adhatoda
syn. *Adhatoda vasica*
ADHATODA, MALABAR NUT, PHYSIC NUT
☀/◑ ⚬ ↔ 3–5 ft (0.9–1.5 m) ↑ 6–8 ft (1.8–2.4 m)
Evergreen shrub, native to southern India and Sri Lanka. Erect growth habit; mid-green lance-shaped leaves. Flowers white, red to purple veining, in summer. Powder-coated leaves, flowers, roots, and seed pods used in Indian medicine. Zones 10–12.

Justicia aurea
◑ ⚬ ↔ 3 ft (0.9 m) ↑ 3–5 ft (0.9–1.5 m)
From Mexico and Central America. Similar to better-known *J. carnea*, but foliage slightly lighter green; heads of yellow flowers rather than pink of *J. carnea*. Flowers in late summer–autumn. Often reshoots if foliage cut back by frost. Zones 9–12.

Justicia brandegeeana
syns *Beloperone guttata, Drejerella guttata*
SHRIMP PLANT
☀/◑ ⚬ ↔ 26 in (65 cm) ↑ 36 in (90 cm)
Evergreen shrub from Mexico. Curved array of overlapping pink and yellow bracts enclose small white flowers with red markings. Elliptical downy leaves, to 3 in (8 cm) long. 'Fruit Cocktail', yellow-green bracts. Zones 9–11.

Justicia carnea
BRAZILIAN PLUME
☀/◑ ⚬ ↔ 3 ft (0.9 m) ↑ 3–6 ft (0.9–1.8 m)
Evergreen shrub from northern South America. Leaves velvet-textured, conspicuously veined. Plume-like spikes of deep pink flowers, at branch tips, throughout year, especially late summer. Pinch back when young to keep compact. Zones 10–12.

Justicia rizzinii
syns *Jacobinia pauciflora, Libonia floribunda*
☀/◑ ⚬ ↔ 10–22 in (25–55 cm) ↑ 10–22 in (25–55 cm)
Hardy, densely twiggy shrub from Brazil. Small, leathery, oval leaves, often with bronze tints in winter, also main flowering season. 'Firefly', heavier flowering, scarlet red flowers with glowing golden yellow tips, flared tubes, 1 in (25 mm) long. Zones 9–11.

Justicia spicigera
syn. *Justicia ghiesbreghtiana*
MEXICAN HONEYSUCKLE, MOHINTLI
☀/◑ ⚬ ↔ 5 ft (1.5 m) ↑ 6 ft (1.8 m)
Found from Mexico to Colombia. Upright shrub, deeply veined oval leaves to 6 in (15 cm) long. Leaves with fine down on underside, smooth upper surface. Flowers to 1½ in (35 mm) long, in warmer months, in bright shades of orange to red. Zones 10–12.

KALMIA
A genus of 7 species of shrubs in the heath (Ericaceae) family, most are evergreen. They are native to northeastern USA; a single species occurs in Cuba. They are grown for their attractive foliage and their showy flowers, ranging in color from pale pink to deep red. Leaves are smooth, opposite or alternate, sometimes found in whorls, deep green above, paler beneath, occasionally stalkless. Flowers are generally carried in terminal corymbs. The fruit is a small capsule containing very small seeds.
CULTIVATION: Kalmias are at home in slightly acid, peaty soil but resent clay and lime in any form. Adequate water is needed on hot summer days. Dappled shade under tall deciduous trees in a cool moist climate is ideal. Little pruning is necessary apart from the removal of spent flowers. Propagate from seed. Firm tip cuttings taken in late summer through to winter may be struck; alternatively, simple layers can be set down in autumn and severed a year later.

Kalmia angustifolia
SHEEP LAUREL
◑ ❀ ↔ 5 ft (1.5 m) ↑ 3 ft (0.9 m)
From northeastern USA. Dwarf shrub, slowly spreading to dense bush. Leaves smooth, ovate-oblong, to ¾ in (18 mm) long. Pinkish red flowers in mid-summer. All plant parts poisonous. 'Rubra', flowers over long period; 'Rubra Nana', dwarf form. Zones 2–9.

Justicia carnea

Justicia rizzinii 'Firefly'

Kalmia angustifolia

Kalopanax septemlobus

Kerria japonica 'Pleniflora'

Koelreuteria bipinnata

Kalmia latifolia

CALICO BUSH, MOUNTAIN LAUREL

☀ ❋ ↔ 10 ft (3 m) ↑ 10 ft (3 m)

Dense shrub from eastern Canada to Gulf of Mexico. Leaves dark green, smooth above, paler beneath, to ½ in (12 mm) long. Flower buds crimped on edge; open to shell pink, purplish markings inside. '**Carousel**', mid-pink flowers; '**Clementine Churchill**', rosy pink flowers; '**Elf**', dwarf with faded pink flowers; '**Minuet**', pink flowers with purplish margins; '**Myrtifolia**', pale pink blooms; '**Nipmuck**', dark red buds open to almost white; '**Olympic Fire**', rich crimson flowers; '**Ostbo Red**' ★, vivid red buds open to faded pink; '**Pink Charm**', crimson flowers; '**Silver Dollar**', white flowers with red anthers; '**Snow Drift**', white blooms. Zones 3–9.

Kalmia polifolia

EASTERN BOG LAUREL, SWAMP LAUREL

☀ ❋ ↔ 3 ft (0.9 m) ↑ 2 ft (0.6 m)

Dwarf shrub from northeastern America. Thin leaves, dark glossy green above, silvery gray beneath. Vivid pinkish purple flowers, in large terminal clusters, in early spring. Zones 3–9.

KALOPANAX

This genus of the ivy (Araliaceae) family contains a lone species of tree native to the cool deciduous forests of eastern Asia. It has scattered stout prickles on the trunk and branches, especially on the young new growth. The leaves are large and palmately lobed. The flowerheads of small white flowers are followed by ornamental clusters of bluish black berries.
CULTIVATION: Despite its tropical appearance, this hardy species should be grown in deep, moist, fertile soil. It will grow in sun or part-shade and makes an attractive specimen or shade tree. Propagation is from seed or half-hardened cuttings taken in summer.

Kalopanax septemlobus

syn. *Kalopanax pictus*

CASTOR ARALIA, HARA-GIRI, TREE ARALIA

☀ ❋ ↔ 10–30 ft (3–9 m) ↑ 20–60 ft (6–18 m)

Round-headed, sparingly branched tree. Leaves on long stalks, 5 to 7 pointed palmate lobes, finely toothed margins, dark green above, lighter below. Large rounded clusters of small flowers in late summer. *K. s.* var. *maximowiczii*, lance-shaped leaf lobes. Zones 5–10.

KERRIA

This genus with a single species in the rose (Rosaceae) family is native to China and Japan. Leaves are alternate, toothed, egg-shaped, and dark green. It is a low, suckering, deciduous shrub with bright yellow 5-petalled flowers, 2 in (5 cm) across, and graceful cane-like stems with rather sparse but attractive foliage.
CULTIVATION: It will grow in any moderately fertile soil with free drainage, preferring a sunny or lightly shaded position and a cool moist climate. Several of the older flowering shoots should be removed at the base after flowering each year to make room for new shoots; no further pruning is necessary. It is easily propagated; soft-tip or half-hardened cuttings taken in spring or summer strike readily, or stems can be layered and lifted a year later.

Kerria japonica

◐/◑ ❋ ↔ 5 ft (1.5 m) ↑ 6 ft (1.8 m)

Found in mountains of Japan and in southwestern China. Bright green leaves, simple and alternate, 2–4 in (5–10 cm) long, prominent veins, downy beneath, turn yellow in autumn. Deep yellow flowers, on short terminal and axillary spurs, in early–late spring. '**Pleniflora**' (syn. 'Flore Pleno'), double flowers, taller, more vigorous; '**Simplex**', single flowers, arching; '**Variegata**', creamy white variegated foliage, low-spreading habit. Zones 5–10.

KIGELIA

This genus within the trumpet-vine (Bignoniaceae) family consists of a lone species. A tropical to subtropical evergreen tree, it is a native of central and southern Africa characterized by long pendent racemes of striking red to orange flowers, often reaching 6 ft (1.8 m) in length. The flowers are followed by large, brownish gray, woody fruit, up to 18 in (45 cm) in length, on very long stalks.
CULTIVATION: *Kigelia* will grow in any rich and well-drained soil, in a warm climate and in a protected sunny position. Water regularly during the growing season. Propagate from seed.

Kigelia africana

syn. *Kigelia pinnata*

SAUSAGE TREE

☀ ◗ ↔ 12 ft (3.5 m) ↑ 40 ft (12 m)

From central and southern Africa. Evergreen tree; pinnate leaves with 7 to 9 leaflets. Reddish orange bell-shaped flowers in summer, open at night with disagreeable odor that attracts pollinating bats. Fruit large, woody, resemble sausage, inedible. Zones 10–12.

KOELREUTERIA

There are only 3 species of deciduous small trees in this genus within the soapberry (Sapindaceae) family. Their natural habitat is dry woodland in open valleys in China, Korea, and Taiwan, 1 species also in Fiji. Best suited to warm climates with an extended growing season, they are moderately frost hardy and are widely grown as ornamentals for the beauty of their flowers and seed heads. Flowers are used medicinally and as a source of yellow dye in China.

CULTIVATION: Koelreuterias prefer a quite fertile, well-drained soil and thrive in full sun. Propagation is from root cuttings taken in late winter or from seed sown in autumn in sheltered conditions. Seed can also be stratified in the refrigerator and sown in spring. Plants grown from seed are very variable and root cuttings from a good tree are preferable.

Koelreuteria bipinnata
syn. *Koelreuteria integrifoliola*
CHINESE FLAME TREE, PRIDE OF CHINA
☼ ❄ ↔ 25 ft (8 m) ↑ 30 ft (9 m)
Native to Yunnan Province in southwestern China. Bipinnate leaves, elliptical to oblong leaflets, finely toothed, mid-green, turn gold in autumn. Yellow flowers, red spot at petal base, in large panicles, in summer–autumn. Red seed heads. Zones 8–11.

Koelreuteria paniculata ★
CHINA TREE, GOLDEN RAIN TREE, VARNISH TREE
☼ ❄ ↔ 30 ft (9 m) ↑ 30 ft (9 m)
Spreading tree from China and Korea. Leaves pinnate, sometimes bipinnate, leaflets elliptical-oblong, scalloped edges. Young foliage turns red to green with age, yellows in autumn. Panicles of small yellow flowers in summer. Fruit capsules rosy pink or red when ripe. *K. p.* var. *apiculata*, bipinnate leaves, light yellow flowers. *K. p.* 'Fastigiata', columnar habit. Zones 6–10.

KOLKWITZIA

There is just one species in this genus within the woodbine (Caprifoliaceae) family—a deciduous shrub occurring in the wild among rocky outcrops in the mountainous areas of Hubei Province, China. It is grown in gardens for its floriferous spring show.

CULTIVATION: *Kolkwitzia* grows in full sun in well-drained fertile soil. When planted in very cold areas it needs protection from cold spring winds, but in general it is frost hardy. Propagation is from cuttings taken from young wood in late spring or early summer or from suckers, which can be removed and grown on. Prune after flowering to retain a tidy shape.

Kolkwitzia amabilis
BEAUTY BUSH
☼ ❄ ↔ 12 ft (3.5 m) ↑ 12 ft (3.5 m)
Bushy deciduous shrub; long, upright or arching shoots. Leaves opposite, broadly egg-shaped, tapered, rounded tip. Corymbs of

bell-shaped flowers, white to pink, yellow throat, in late spring–early summer. 'Pink Cloud' ★, slightly larger flowers. Zones 4–9.

KUNZEA

This genus of the myrtle (Myrtaceae) family, containing about 35 species of evergreen shrubs, is endemic to Australia, except for *K. ericoides*, which also occurs in New Zealand. Kunzeas have small, aromatic, heath-like leaves, and are cultivated mainly for their profuse honey-scented flowers with masses of protruding stamens that give them a fluffy appearance. The flowers appear mostly in spring, attracting honeyeaters and insectivorous birds.

CULTIVATION: They prefer a mild winter climate, full sun or part-shade, and a well-drained soil. Prune lightly from an early age and after flowering to encourage compact bushy growth. Propagate from seed or half-hardened tip cuttings taken in early summer.

Kunzea ambigua
TICK-BUSH
☼ ❄ ↔ 12 ft (3.5 m) ↑ 12 ft (3.5 m)
Evergreen shrub from eastern Australia. Arching branches; small crowded leaves, dark green, narrow-linear. Masses of small creamy white flowers, in upper leaf axils, in spring–early summer. Zones 9–11.

Kunzea ambigua

Kunzea baxteri
SCARLET KUNZEA
☼ ❄ ↔ 8 ft (2.4 m) ↑ 8 ft (2.4 m)
Many-stemmed spreading shrub from Western Australia. Crowded linear leaves. Crimson flowers, in dense spikes, in late winter–spring. May be grown in coastal gardens. Zones 9–11.

Kunzea parvifolia
VIOLET KUNZEA
☼ ❄ ↔ 5 ft (1.5 m) ↑ 5 ft (1.5 m)
Open twiggy shrub from southeastern Australia. Minute, heath-like, downy leaves. Masses of fluffy deep mauve flowers, in small terminal clusters, in late spring–early summer. Zones 8–10.

Kolkwitzia amabilis

Laburnum alpinum

Kunzea pulchella

☼ ❄ ↔ 6 ft (1.8 m) ↕ 6 ft (1.8 m)

From semi-arid regions in southern Western Australia. Spreading or arching branches. Gray-green, silky hairy leaves. Bright red flowers in terminal spikes. Bird-attracting plant, suited to dry-summer climate. Pinch out tips lightly after flowering. Zones 9–11.

+ LABURNOCYTISUS

This is a hybrid between the genera *Laburnum* and *Cytisus*, the + sign indicating a graft hybrid. This particular hybrid arose in the French nursery of M. Jean-Louis Adam around 1825. Adam had been grafting the purple broom, *Cytisus purpureus,* onto stems of the common laburnum, *Laburnum anagyroides,* with the object of producing a long-stemmed broom. Most of the resulting plants turned out as expected, but one produced a branch with flowers of a curious brownish color and foliage intermediate between that of the broom and the laburnum. Adam propagated from this plant, producing plants with characteristics of both the parents, which were then named after him to acknowledge his work.

CULTIVATION: Cultivation requirements are the same as for *Laburnum.* The plants grow well in a cool-temperate climate, preferably with uniform annual rainfall. They require moderately fertile soil with good drainage. Seeds germinate readily if they are soaked in warm water for 24 hours before sowing.

+ Laburnocytisus adamii

☼ ❄ ↔ 15 ft (4.5 m) ↕ 25 ft (8 m)

Variable tree, some branches producing yellow flowers of laburnum, others with clusters of purple broom flowers, and yet others with muddy beige flowers, in short racemes. Leaves 3-palmate and dark green; leaflets about 2 in (5 cm) long. Pea-like flowers borne in late spring. Zones 5–9.

LABURNUM

This is a genus of only 2 species of small deciduous trees, allied to *Genista* in the pea-flower subfamily of the legume (Fabaceae) family, found natually in central and southern Europe. The leaves are trifoliate and alternate. The plants are widely grown for their long drooping racemes of yellow pea-flowers, which are produced in spring and early summer. All parts of the plant, especially the seeds, are poisonous.

CULTIVATION: Laburnums grow well in a cool-temperate climate, preferably with uniform annual rainfall; any moderately fertile soil with good drainage will suit them. It may be necessary to carry out some early shaping by way of removing competing leaders, but otherwise very little pruning is required. In larger gardens laburnums are popularly planted to form an arch of foliage. The seeds germinate readily if they are soaked in warm water for 24 hours before sowing. Position the plants where they will be sheltered from winter frosts.

Laburnum alpinum

SCOTCH LABURNUM

☼ ❄ ↔ 25 ft (8 m) ↕ 25 ft (8 m)

Small spreading tree from mountain regions of Europe. Leaflets deep shiny green on upper surface, paler and hairy on lower surface. Racemes of yellow flowers borne in mid-summer. Seed pods flattened, smooth, shiny. Popular cultivars include 'Pendulum', slow-growing form with pendulous branches; 'Pyramidale', upright branches. Zones 3–9.

Laburnum × watereri 'Vossii'

Laburnum anagyroides

COMMON LABURNUM, GOLDEN CHAIN TREE

☼ ❄ ↔ 25 ft (8 m) ↕ 25 ft (8 m)

Small tree. Leaves dull green to gray-green, oval to elliptic, to 3 in (8 cm) long, hairy on undersurface. Drooping racemes of vivid yellow flowers, crowded along branches, in late spring–early summer. 'Pendulum', slender drooping branches. Zones 3–9.

Laburnum × watereri

GOLDEN CHAIN TREE, LABURNUM

☼ ❄ ↔ 25 ft (8 m) ↕ 25 ft (8 m)

Hybrid between *L. alpinum* and *L. anagyroides,* which resembles *L. alpinum,* but has leaves and pods that are more densely hairy. Yellow flowers occur in packed racemes. Best-known clonal form, 'Vossii' ★, similar habit to parent but is more prolific, with longer flower racemes, to 2 ft (0.6 m). Zones 3–9.

LAGERSTROEMIA

CRAPE MYRTLE

A favorite genus in the loosestrife (Lythraceae) family, consisting of 53 species of evergreen or deciduous, small to large trees, it occurs from southern and eastern Asia to northern Australia. The plants have attractive, often peeling bark and simple, variable, usually opposite leaves that in many species provide brilliant autumn color. In summer they famously bear showy panicles of flowers with crinkled petals and a crape-like texture in differing shades of pink, mauve, and white. For all these reasons, these trees are a popular inclusion in many gardens. The fruit is a capsule. The timber of some species has been used to manufacture bridges, furniture, and railway sleepers.

CULTIVATION: These trees are generally easy to grow, as they adapt to a wide variety of soil types. They grow best in well-drained soil in a sunny position and some tolerate light frosts. Propagate from seed or half-hardened cuttings in summer, or from hardwood cuttings in early winter. Powdery mildew can be a problem in older plants, but newer cultivars are more disease resistant.

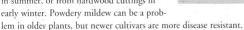

Lagunaria patersonia

Lagerstroemia floribunda

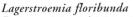

☼ ✦ ↔ 15 ft (4.5 m) ↑ 40 ft (12 m)

Native to Myanmar, southern Thailand, and Malay Peninsula. Trunk with gray bark; open crown. Leaves broad, somewhat glossy. Mauve-pink flowers, to 2 in (5 cm) across, occur in few-flowered sprays. Zones 11–12.

Lagerstroemia indica

CRAPE MYRTLE

☼ ❄ ↔ 20 ft (6 m) ↑ 20 ft (6 m)

From China and Japan. Often forms multi-stemmed deciduous tree, with wide-spreading, flat-topped, open habit when mature. Bark smooth, pinkish gray, mottled. Leaves small, dark green, turn orange-red in autumn. White, pink, mauve, purple, or carmine flowers with crimped petals, in panicles to 8 in (20 cm) long. For cultivars often included here, see *Lagerstroemia* Hybrid Cultivars entry. Zones 7–11.

Lagerstroemia indica

Lagerstroemia speciosa

syn. *Lagerstroemia flos-reginae*

PRIDE OF INDIA, QUEEN CRAPE MYRTLE

☼ ✦ ↔ 30 ft (9 m) ↑ 30–50 ft (9–15 m)

From India and China to Australia. Deciduous tree with mottled, smooth, gray-yellow, peeling bark. Leaves dark green, shiny, duller beneath, turn coppery red in autumn. Erect panicles of white, mauve, purple, or pink flowers in summer–autumn. Zones 10–12.

Lagerstroemia Hybrid Cultivars

CRAPE MYRTLE

☼ ❄ ↔ 8–25 ft (2.4–8 m) ↑ 15–25 ft (4.5–8 m)

In recent decades US National Arboretum, Maryland, has released series of hybrids between *L. indica* and Japanese species *L. faurei*, combining flower size of first with hardiness, mildew resistance, and bark color of second. 'Natchez', to about 25 ft (8 m) high, cinnamon bark often mottled with cream, white flowers; 'Tuscarora', fast growing, to 25 ft (8 m), dark coral pink flowers. An older group of hybrids originated in Australia, reportedly as back-crosses of *L. indica* × *L. speciosa* onto *L. indica*; these are upright and bear large panicles of deep heliotrope flowers. Zones 7–11.

LAGUNARIA

This genus comprising a single species in the mallow (Malvaceae) family, native to Norfolk and Lord Howe Islands, off eastern Australia, and a small stretch of coastal Queensland, Australia, was named after Andres de Laguna, a sixteenth-century Spanish physician and botanist. It is an evergreen tree growing to 50 ft (15 m) or more; there are, however, several distinct geographic forms, differing mainly in the quantity of soft downy hairs occurring on the simple alternate leaves. The flowers are hibiscus-like, with a conspicuous staminal column; the fruit is a leathery capsule. It is useful for park and street planting, especially in coastal areas, as it can withstand salt-laden winds.

CULTIVATION: This tree grows best in well-drained fertile soil in a warm-temperate or subtropical climate. It requires little or no pruning. Propagate from seed sown in spring: they germinate readily in warm humid areas.

Lagunaria patersonia

syn. *Hibiscus patersonius*

NORFOLK ISLAND HIBISCUS, WHITE OAK

☼ ❄ ↔ 15 ft (4.5 m) ↑ 25–50 ft (8–15 m)

Species named after William Paterson, who was second Lieutenant Governor of New South Wales, Australia. Solitary rosy to mauve-pink flowers with golden yellow anthers, borne in upper axils, in summer. Contact with kidney-shaped seeds, enclosed by fine sharp hairs, can cause skin irritation. 'Royal Purple', shiny green leaves and crimson flowers. Zones 10–11.

LANTANA

A small genus of about 150 species of evergreen shrubs within the vervain (Verbenaceae) family, these plants are mostly found in tropical America. They have scrambling, somewhat prickly stems, simple opposite leaves that are rough on both surfaces, and small flowers grouped in dense flattened or hemispherical heads, with the youngest flowers at the center.
CULTIVATION: Lantanas will tolerate quite harsh conditions but are at their best in light fertile soils with free drainage. They flower freely in a sunny open position in a frost-free climate, and although they are generally suitable for coastal areas, they should be given some protection from salt-laden winds. Regular tip pruning when the plants are young will help the formation of a compact shape, but in later years little or no pruning is necessary. Propagate from seed sown in spring or from half-hardened cuttings taken in summer. Soft-tip cuttings can be taken at any time of the year.

Lantana camara

LANTANA

☀ ⚑ ↔ 8–30 ft (2.4–9 m) ↕ 4–12 ft (1.2–3.5 m)

Evergreen shrub native to West Indies and Central America. Flowers in shades ranging from creamy white through yellow, orange, and pink to brick red, heads often appearing bicolored owing to florets ageing to another color. Wild forms are particularly invasive colonizers, and proclaimed as noxious weeds in some warm-climate countries, including some States of Australia. Sterile or near-sterile forms available. *L. c.* var. *crocea*, golden yellow to orange flowers. *L. c.* 'Chelsea Gem', mainly scarlet flowers, some orange; 'Orange Carpet', trailing habit, orange flowers; 'Patriot Dove Wings', cascading habit, pale yellow flowers soon turning white; 'Patriot Rainbow', compact, about 16 in (40 cm) wide and high, bicolored florets from deep pinkish red to creamy yellow; 'Schloss Ortenburg', multi-colored florets from yellow to orange or pink; 'Variegata' (syn. 'Lemon Swirl'), pale green cream-edged leaves, yellow flowers. Zones 9–12.

Lantana camara

Lantana montevidensis

syn. *Lantana sellowiana*
TRAILING LANTANA

☀ ⚑ ↔ 10 ft (3 m) ↕ 3 ft (0.9 m)

Evergreen trailing shrub native to central eastern region of South America. Leaves dark green, oblong to lance-shaped, roughly toothed. Flowers rosy lilac, 1 in (25 mm) across, bright yellow flush in throat, slightly fragrant, in winter and throughout year. 'Alba', white-flowered cultivar popular in USA. Zones 9–11.

LARIX

The larches, members of the pine (Pinaceae) family, comprise the largest genus of deciduous conifers; they are found in north Europe, over much of Asia from Siberia to as far south as the mountains of northern Myanmar, and in northern North America. They are among the earliest trees to come into leaf in spring, the leaves being carried on both long and short shoots. The upright summer-ripening cones, borne on the shorter shoots, persist on the tree for some time. With age, branches tend to droop in a graceful manner. The leaves are needle-like and usually vivid green, sometimes blue-green in summer, turning butter yellow to old gold in autumn. Some species yield valuable timber that is strong and heavy.
CULTIVATION: Larches are adaptable to most soils, though wet soils are best avoided for all but 1 or 2 species. All larches need plenty of light. Species hybridize readily, both in the wild and in cultivation. Propagate from seed.

Larix decidua

syn. *Larix europaea*
EUROPEAN LARCH

☀ ❄ ↔ 12–20 ft (3.5–6 m) ↕ 165 ft (50 m)

Native to mountains of central and eastern Europe, introduced to Britain around 1600. Conical crown becoming broader with age, with some wide-spreading horizontal as well as erect branches. Bark smooth gray, fissured on old trees, coarsely ridged. Leaves tender light green; mature cones yellowish. 'Corley', dwarf spreading tree; 'Pendula', strongly weeping habit. Zones 2–8.

Larix kaempferi

syn. *Larix leptolepis*
JAPANESE LARCH

☀ ❄ ↔ 12–20 ft (3.5–6 m) ↕ 100 ft (30 m)

Common in Japan. Long low branches sweeping out and up, upper branches sweeping upward; scaly rusty brown bark. Leaves gray-green; female flowers pink or cream; cones brown. 'Pendula' ★ and 'Stiff Weeping' both have pendulous branches. Zones 4–9.

Larix laricina

AMERICAN LARCH, EASTERN LARCH, TAMARACK LARCH

☀ ❄ ↔ 12–20 ft (3.5–6 m) ↕ 60 ft (18 m)

Found across most of northern North America, growing in sphagnum bogs and swamps. Crown open, often with twisted hooped

Larix decidua

Larix laricina, in the wild, Ontario, Canada

branches. Bark pink to reddish brown, finely flaking, not fissured. Leaves short, soft, needle-like, turn yellow in autumn. Zones 2–8.

Larix × *marschlinsii*
syn. *Larix* × *eurolepis*
DUNKELD LARCH, HYBRID LARCH
☼ ❋ ↔ 20 ft (6 m) ↑ 90 ft (27 m)
Hybrid between *L. decidua* and *L. kaempferi*. Intermediate between parents, differing in having yellow, slightly waxy-bloomed shoots and conical cones. Leaves thin, gray-green, to 1½ in (35 mm) long. '**Varied Directions**', pendulous branches. Zones 2–9.

Larix occidentalis
WESTERN LARCH
☼ ❋ ↔ 15 ft (4.5 m) ↑ 180 ft (55 m)
Native to North America. Bark purplish gray, fissured; crown open, narrowly conical. Leaves bright green. Cones rich purple in summer; orange and yellow bracts ripen purple-brown. Zones 3–9.

LAVANDULA
LAVENDER
The 28 species of evergreen aromatic shrubs and subshrubs in this genus belong to the large mint (Lamiaceae) family. They occur mainly around the Mediterranean, with a few in western Asia and the Canary and Cape Verde Islands. Their natural habitat is dry and exposed rocky areas. The narrow leaves are usually grayish green, often toothed or in some species pinnately divided. The spikes of small purple flowers vary in their intensity of color and perfume. Cultivated species belong to 3 groups: the hardy **Spica** (English lavender) **Group**, with mostly basal smooth-edged leaves and long slender flower spikes; the slightly more tender **Stoechas Group**, with flower spikes terminating in a "top-knot" of colored bracts; and the tender **Ptero-stoechas Group**, with pinnately divided leaves. Some of the Spica Group lavenders are cultivated commercially for their aromatic foliage and flowerheads, distilled to produce the lavender oil widely used in perfumes, toiletries, and air fresheners. CULTIVATION: Lavenders are excellent for hot dry sites, containers, hedging, and positions where they can be brushed against to release their aroma. They need well-drained soil that is not too fertile. Hardy species are pruned after flowering. All lavenders can be propagated from seed, or from tip cuttings in spring or half-hardened cuttings in autumn.

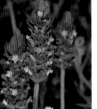
Lavandula dentata 'Ploughman's Blue'

Lavandula × *allardii*
HYBRID LAVENDER
☼ ❋ ↔ 3 ft (0.9 m) ↑ 3 ft (0.9 m)
Thought to be cross between *L. dentata* and *L. latifolia*. Vigorous grower. Leaves gray, relatively wide, roundly toothed. Long narrow spikes of dark purple flowers, carried well above foliage, in summer. Zones 8–11.

Lavandula angustifolia, Provence, France

Lavandula angustifolia ★
syns *Lavandula officinalis*, *L. spica*, *L. vera*
ENGLISH LAVENDER
☼ ❋ ↔ 4 ft (1.2 m) ↑ 2–3 ft (0.6–0.9 m)
Spica Group species native to Mediterranean region. Bushy shrub, with narrow, gray, slightly downy leaves. Fragrant deep purple flower spikes in early summer. '**Alba**', white flowers; '**Beechwood Blue**', low-growing; '**Folgate**', light gray-green foliage, bright blue flowers; '**Hidcote**', densely packed spikes of purple flowers; '**Imperial Gem**', narrow gray leaves, deep purple flowers; '**Loddon Blue**', to 20 in (50 cm) tall, bright silvery gray foliage; '**Martha Roderick**', compact mounding habit, bright lavender flowers; '**Munstead**' ★, dwarf, popular for edging; '**Princess Blue**', pale lavender flowers; '**Rosea**', pink flower spikes; '**Royal Purple**', deep purple flowers. Zones 5–10.

Lavandula dentata
TOOTHED LAVENDER
☼ ◑ ↔ 5 ft (1.5 m) ↑ 3–5 ft (0.9–1.5 m)
Stoechas Group species native to Mediterranean region, Madeira, and Cape Verde Islands. Leaves narrow, grayish green, bluntly toothed; stems slightly downy. Pale purple flower spikes on long stems above foliage. *L. d.* var. *candicans*, grayer in appearance, with flowers deeper purple. *L. d.* '**Ploughman's Blue**', lilac flower spikes on long stems to 12 in (30 cm), good for hedging and tubs. Zones 9–11.

Lavandula × *intermedia*
☼ ❋ ↔ 3 ft (0.9 m) ↑ 3 ft (0.9 m)
Various hybrids between *L. angustifolia* and *L. latifolia* known by this name. Characteristics intermediate between 2 species, flowers paler than *L. angustifolia*. Frequently grown for cut flowers and oil production. '**Gray Hedge**', attractive silvery gray foliage, purple flowers, popular as hedging plant; '**Grosso**' ★, most commonly grown for oil production, fine-leafed, long dark purple flowers; '**Provence**' ★, attractive cultivar popular in USA; '**Seal**', vigorous, very free flowering, with pale purple flower spikes. Zones 7–10.

Lavandula lanata

WOOLLY LAVENDER

☼ ❄ ↔ 3 ft (0.9 m) ↕ 3 ft (0.9 m)

Native to mountains of southern Spain. Leaves different from other species in Spica Group: wider, and covered in whitish gray down. Spikes of purple flowers, held well above foliage, in summer. Dislikes humidity. Zones 7–10.

Lavandula latifolia

SPIKE LAVENDER

☼ ❄ ↔ 4 ft (1.2 m) ↕ 3 ft (0.9 m)

Native to western Mediterranean region. Rather like *L. angustifolia*, but with broader grayish green leaves and purple flower spikes carried on long stalks, which are frequently in 3 branches. Flowers later in summer than *L. angustifolia.* Zones 7–10.

Lavandula pinnata

CANARY ISLAND LAVENDER

☼ ❄ ↔ 3 ft (0.9 m) ↕ 3 ft (0.9 m)

Native to Canary Islands. Pterostoechas Group species, lightly covered in fine short hairs. Leaves green to gray, pinnate, with broad lobes. Flowerheads of soft purple spikes, usually branched into 3, in summer. 'Sidonie', hybrid thought to have *L. pinnata* as parent; free flowering in warm climates, bearing deep purple flower spikes on long branching stalks for most of year from late winter. Zones 9–11.

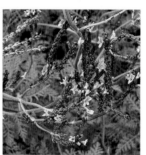
Lavandula pinnata

Lavandula stoechas

FRENCH LAVENDER, ITALIAN LAVENDER, SPANISH LAVENDER

☼ ❄ ↔ 24 in (60 cm) ↕ 24 in (60 cm)

Variable species from Mediterranean region. Leaves fine grayish green. Plump flower spikes of deep purple topped by prominent petal-like bracts in summer. Can become invasive. *L. s.* subsp. *pedunculata*, fatter and rounder spikes with longer bracts. *L. s.* 'Alba', dull white flower spikes; 'Avonview', fast growing,

Lavatera olbia

24–32 in (60–80 cm) tall, sterile bracts long and pink, bracts of fertile heads purple with fine green mid-stripe; 'Helmsdale', compact, with burgundy-purple flowers; 'Kew Red', to 10 in (25 cm) tall, pink flowers; 'Major', flowering profusely with spikes of deepest intense purple; 'Marshwood', slightly bigger, to 3 ft (0.9 m), large plump spikes of purple flowers topped with very long mauve bracts; 'Otto Quast', popular American cultivar; 'Regal Splendour', deep purple flowers, lavender bracts; 'Willow Vale', unusual wavy-edged and crinkled purple bracts. Zones 8–11.

Lavandula viridis

GREEN LAVENDER

☼ ❄ ↔ 30 in (75 cm) ↕ 36 in (90 cm)

Stoechas Group species from southern areas of Portugal and Spain and island of Madeira. Aromatic plant. Green foliage; stems covered in fine hairs. Unusual whitish green flower spikes in summer. Zones 8–11.

LAVATERA

TREE MALLOW

There are 25 species of evergreen or deciduous annuals, biennials, perennials, and softwooded shrubs in this genus within the mallow (Malvaceae) family found from the Mediterranean to the northwestern Himalayas, and in parts of Asia, Australia, California (USA), and Baja California (Mexico). The leaves are usually palmately lobed and slightly downy, and most species have attractive hibiscus-like flowers with prominent staminal columns, in colors ranging from white to a rosy purple. *Lavatera* is closely related to *Malva*, and following recent botanical studies several of its species have been reclassified as *Malva* species.

CULTIVATION: Shrubby mallows are suitable for planting in mixed borders, where they will bloom abundantly throughout summer. They should be grown in full sun in light well-drained soil. Too rich a soil will result in an excess of foliage at the expense of flowers. Prune after flowering to prevent legginess. Mallows tend to be short lived; softwood cuttings taken in spring or early summer strike readily and are the usual method of propagation for shrubby species.

Lavatera olbia

TREE LAVATERA, TREE MALLOW

☼ ❄ ↔ 5 ft (1.5 m) ↕ 6 ft (1.8 m)

From western Mediterranean region. True form of *L. olbia* is rarely cultivated; plant sold under that name is usually *L.* × *clementii.* Evergreen shrub. Bristly stems; downy lobed leaves; reddish purple flowers. Zones 8–10.

LEPTOSPERMUM

This genus in the myrtle (Myrtaceae) family is made up of about 80 species of evergreen shrubs or small trees with small narrow leaves that are often aromatic, occasionally lemon-scented, when crushed. Mostly Australian, 1 species is widespread in New Zealand and 2 are found in Southeast Asia. They are collectively known as tea-trees; the leaves of some species were used as a tea substitute by Captain James Cook's crew when they landed in Australia in

Leptospermum rotundifolium

Leptospermum spectabile

Leptospermum squarrosum

1770 and later by early settlers in Australia. The flowers are small and open with a wide nectar cup and 5 petals that are mostly white or shades of pink and occasionally red. Small woody capsules often persist for a long period. They are sometimes used as cut flowers.
CULTIVATION: Tolerating an occasional light frost, they are best suited to well-drained soil in full sun; some species will tolerate wet conditions and nearly full shade. Light feedings with slow-release fertilizers in spring are beneficial. Prune regularly after flowering to retain bushiness. Propagate from seed or half-hardened cuttings in summer; propagate cultivars from cuttings to retain characteristics.

Leptospermum laevigatum
COAST TEA-TREE
☼ ❄ ↔ 10–15 ft (3–4.5 m) ↑ 10–20 ft (3–6 m)
Widespread in eastern coastal areas of Australia. Tall dense shrub or small tree with deciduous flaky bark. Leaves small, gray-green, with rounded tip. Conspicuous white flowers in spring. Considered weed in South Africa. 'Reevesii', compact form. Zones 9–11.

Leptospermum nitidum
☼ ❄ ↔ 6 ft (1.8 m) ↑ 8 ft (2.4 m)
Rounded shrub endemic to wet heaths in Tasmania, Australia. Leaves small, crowded, glossy; new growth silky-hairy, often copper-colored. Masses of small white flowers in summer. Zones 8–10.

Leptospermum petersonii
LEMON-SCENTED TEA-TREE
☼ ❄ ↔ 10 ft (3 m) ↑ 20 ft (6 m)
From east coast of Australia. Shrub or small tree with slightly weeping habit. Leaves narrow-lanceolate, lemon-scented when crushed. Small white flowers in early summer. Popular street tree. Needs additional water during dry periods. Zones 9–11.

Leptospermum rotundifolium
syn. **Leptospermum scoparium** var. *rotundifolium*
ROUND-LEAFED TEA-TREE
☼ ❄ ↔ 10 ft (3 m) ↑ 6 ft (1.8 m)
From southeastern Australia. Leaves dark green, almost round. Attractive flowers, 1¼ in (30 mm) across, in shades of pink, mauve, or more rarely lavender, in spring. Persistent glossy capsules.

Prefers well-drained soil. 'Julie Ann', to about 12 in (30 cm) high, spreading habit, showy pale mauve flowers. Zones 8–10.

Leptospermum scoparium
MANUKA, TEA-TREE
☼ ❄ ↔ 6 ft (1.8 m) ↑ 6 ft (1.8 m)
Native of New Zealand, Tasmania (Australia), and southeastern corner of mainland Australia. Small prickly leaves. Showy white flowers, to 1¼ in (30 mm) across, in spring–summer. Fast growing; requires pruning to shape after flowering. 'Apple Blossom', pink-flushed white flowers; 'Autumn Glory', deep pink single flowers, bright green foliage; 'Big Red', covered in striking red flowers; 'Burgundy Queen', deep red double flowers, bronze-colored foliage; 'Gaiety Girl', dark-centered, pink, semi-double flowers, and reddish new growth; 'Helene Strybing', pink flowers, popular in USA; 'Kiwi', dwarf form with single light red flowers in late spring–early summer; 'Lambethii', large, dark-centered, single pink flowers; 'Nanum Kea', profuse pink flowers; 'Pink Cascade' ★, weeping branches, white flowers with pink flush; 'Pink Pearl', pink flowers, popular in USA; 'Ray Williams', white flowers streaked pink; 'Red Damask', dark green to bronze foliage, double crimson flowers; 'Ruby Glow', purple-red semi-double flowers. Zones 8–10.

Leptospermum spectabile
BLOOD-RED TEA-TREE
☼ ❄ ↔ 6 ft (1.8 m) ↑ 10 ft (3 m)
Rare shrub from small area near Sydney, New South Wales, Australia, growing along banks of Colo River. Narrow pointed leaves. Showy flowers, about 1 in (25 mm) across, with smallish deep red petals around very large receptacle glistening with nectar, in late spring. Zones 8–11.

Leptospermum squarrosum
syn. **Leptospermum persiciflorum**
PEACH-FLOWERED TEA-TREE
☼ ❄ ↔ 5 ft (1.5 m) ↑ 6 ft (1.8 m)
Erect open shrub from southeastern Australia, growing on poor sandstone soils around Sydney. Tiny, dark green, pointed leaves. Large white to bright pink flowers, on older thicker branches, in autumn. Requires good drainage. Zones 8–11.

Leschenaultia biloba

LESCHENAULTIA

syn. *Lechenaultia*

This Australian genus belonging to the Goodeniaceae family comprises about 26 species, the majority occurring in southwestern Western Australia, but with 3 in central Australia and 2 in far northern Australia, one of which also occurs in New Guinea. The genus includes perennials, subshrubs, and shrubs, with leaves that are usually small and very narrow. The flowers are the striking feature; although small and sometimes borne singly, they are profuse and in some species are very intensely colored. The flowers have 5 petals, which are fused at the base, each with a smooth central band and a broad crinkled margin; in some species they are spread in a hand-like form, in others they form more of a tube. CULTIVATION: Perfect drainage and light gritty soils give the best results when growing these plants, and few species will survive, let alone thrive, where the soil stays cold and wet over winter. These plants tolerate light frosts and will withstand more cold if kept dry during winter. They prefer a position in full sun; water occasionally during the growing season. Other than a little tidying up after flowering, trimming is seldom needed. Propagate from seed or half-hardened tip cuttings of non-flowering stems.

Leschenaultia biloba

☼ ❄ ↔ 24 in (60 cm) ↑ 24 in (60 cm)
Best-known leschenaultia, found in Perth region of Western Australia. Leaves sparse, rather dull gray-green. Magnificent sprays of gentian blue flowers in winter. Lighter colored and white-flowered forms available. Zones 10–11.

Leschenaultia formosa

☼ ❄ ↔ 24 in (60 cm) ↑ 12 in (30 cm)
From southern Western Australia. Similar to *L. biloba*, but leaves slightly larger. Distinctive flowers, usually vivid red, sometimes tending toward orange; borne singly, they smother bush in late winter. Zones 9–11.

LEUCADENDRON

This genus is a member of the protea (Proteaceae) family, and comprises approximately 80 diverse evergreen shrubs and small trees. All species are naturally found in South Africa's Western Cape province and the far west of Eastern Cape, except for 3 species, which are isolated in eastern KwaZulu-Natal. Borne on separate male and female plants in winter to spring, the flowers are produced in dense heads, the females commonly concealed among rather woody scales, the males in rather looser cone-like structures. The longer bracts surrounding both male and female flowerheads are often colorful, giving each head the appearance of a single "flower." They are much-sought after as cut flowers because of their long vase life. The leaves are simple, often leathery in texture, and spirally arranged. Most species are insect pollinated but a few are wind pollinated. The cone-like fruits yield seed that ripens in summer. CULTIVATION: The vast majority of species require perfect drainage, preferring humus-rich, acid, basaltic or sandy loams low in phosphorus. They generally prefer an open, sunny, frost-free position with good air circulation. Propagate from seed sown in autumn, from cuttings, or by grafting or budding.

Leucadendron argenteum

SILVER TREE
☼ ❄ ↔ 6–20 ft (1.8–6 m) ↑ 20–30 ft (6–9 m)
Rare in wild, occurring on slopes of Table Mountain, South Africa. Beautiful tree; trunk with whorled branches, smooth gray bark with distinctive horizontal leaf scars. Leaves lance-shaped, to 6 in (15 cm) long, silvery, silky, with glistening sheen. Female flowers, in silvery cone-like heads with pinkish tinge, occur in summer. Produces silvery cone-like fruit. Zones 9–10.

Leucadendron eucalyptifolium

☼ ❄ ↔ 8 ft (2.4 m) ↑ 20 ft (6 m)
Shrub with somewhat eucalyptus-like leaves, long, narrow, bright green, each with distinctive twist. Flowerhead bracts turning bright yellow; fragrant flowers in winter–spring. Persistent cone-like fruit. Popular with florists. Responds to pruning. Zones 8–10.

Leucadendron salicifolium

☼ ❄ ↔ 6 ft (1.8 m) ↑ 10 ft (3 m)
Vigorous evergreen shrub, growing from sea level to high altitudes in moist acid soils along stream banks. Leaves green, smooth, narrow, sharply pointed, with twist. Light green-yellow bracts in winter–early spring. Very popular species with florists. Zones 8–10.

Leucadendron sessile

Leucadendron sessile

☼ ❄ ↔ 3 ft (0.9 m) ↑ 5 ft (1.5 m)
From mountains east of Cape Town, South Africa. Tolerates heavy clay; requires constant moisture, depends on sea mists in its native habitat. Leaves green, elliptical, smooth. Yellow flowerhead bracts, turning red with age, in winter. Zones 8–10.

Leucadendron, Hybrid Cultivar, 'Superstar'

Leucadendron tinctum

☼ ❊ ↔ 4 ft (1.2 m) ↑ 4 ft (1.2 m)

Low shrub from Western Cape, South Africa. Leaves oblong, gray-green, rounded tip, held close to stems. Distinctive pink-flushed flower bracts in winter. Fragrant cones. Zones 8–10.

Leucadendron Hybrid Cultivars

☼ ⧫ ↔ 4–8 ft (1.2–2.4 m) ↑ 4–8 ft (1.2–2.4 m)

Hybrids have large showy bracts, compact growth habit, interesting foliage. '**Cloudbank Jenny**' (syn. 'Cloudbank Ginny'), cream bracts, orange cones; '**Duet**', red-edged yellow bracts, yellow cones; '**Pisa**', yellow bracts, silvery green cones; '**Safari Sunset**' ★, vivid red bracts; '**Silvan Red**', slim bracts; '**Sundance**', bright yellow to gold bracts; '**Superstar**', small red and yellow bracts. Zones 9–11.

LEUCAENA

Part of the mimosa subfamily of the legume (Fabaceae) family, the 20-odd species of evergreen trees and shrubs in this genus range from southern Texas, USA, and Mexico to South America. All have feathery foliage and fluffy globular heads of white flowers. The leaves are bipinnate, with many small leaflets or fewer larger ones. Dark brown pods hang in drooping clusters from the branches. CULTIVATION: These fast-growing plants thrive in a wide range of soils; routine care is minimal. They respond to pruning or coppicing, which quickly produces regrowth. Widely planted in tropical and subtropical areas as screen or shade trees, in cool-temperate climates they may be grown under glass. Propagate from seed, which needs soaking in warm water for 24 hours to soften it before planting, or from half-hardened cuttings.

Leucaena leucocephala

syn. *Leucaena glauca*

LEAD TREE, WHITE POPINAC

☼ ✿ ↔ 15 ft (4.5 m) ↑ 30 ft (9 m)

Vigorous, fast-growing, evergreen tree; abundantly naturalized in tropical areas. Gray-green bipinnate leaves; young stems deep copper color. Fluffy balls of creamy white flowers, on short stalks, borne in spring. Drooping clusters of dark brown, broad, flat pods borne during summer months. Zones 10–12.

LEUCOPHYTA

The sole species in this genus in the daisy (Asteraceae) family is an evergreen shrub native to the coasts of southern Australia. Rather reminiscent of lavender cotton *(Santolina chamaecyparissus)*, it develops into a dense mound of wiry stems clothed in tiny, almost scale-like, silver-gray leaves. In summer and autumn small, knob-like, white to creamy yellow flowerheads lacking ray florets open from silvery buds. CULTIVATION: Very much a coastal plant and highly resistant to salt spray, it adapts well to cultivation and can be trimmed as a low border or hedge, good for accenting darker foliage. It dislikes hot humid conditions and appreciates full sun and good air movement. The soil should be light and well drained. While tough and drought resistant, it is short lived and will eventually die out from the center; hard pruning will not rejuvenate it. Light pinching back year round can keep it more compact and vigorous. Propagate from half-hardened tip cuttings.

Leucophyta brownii

syn. *Calocephalus brownii*

CUSHION BUSH

☼ ⧫ ↔ 3 ft (0.9 m) ↑ 3 ft (0.9 m)

Intricately branched dome of bright silvery foliage. Inconspicuous yellowish flowerheads, to ½ in (12 mm) across. Western Australian race has longer leaves, to ½ in (12 mm). Zones 9–11.

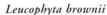

Leucophyta brownii

LEUCOSPERMUM

PINCUSHION

Unlike many plants in related genera of the protea (Proteaceae) family, leucospermums, often referred to as pincushion proteas, owe their beauty to their flowers, in roundish pincushion-like heads with long conspicuous styles. There are approximately 50 species, all evergreen shrubs, and all from a narrow coastal belt in South Africa's Western Cape province, except for a handful in eastern South Africa, one extending to Zimbabwe. The majority are compact shrubs, which flower abundantly in spring. The thick leaves are generally broadest near the tip, which usually has several rather blunt teeth. CULTIVATION: All require well-drained soil in an open sunny situation. Some species tolerate light frosts; all prefer a dry summer with low humidity. Winter watering is desirable. Pruning is usually unnecessary apart from cutting flowers. Propagate from seed or cuttings or by grafting, which is used for many of the hybrid cultivars.

Leucospermum bolusii

BOLUS PINCUSHION, GORDON'S BAY PINCUSHION

☼ ❊ ↔ 5–6 ft (1.5–1.8 m) ↑ 5–6 ft (1.5–1.8 m)

Evergreen shrub with stout, erect, branching stems. Leaves greenish gray, sword- to oval-shaped, notched at tip. Yellow to apricot pincushion-like flowers, 4 in (10 cm) in diameter, produced in spring. Zones 8–10.

Leucospermum cordifolium ★

syn. *Leucospermum nutans*

NODDING PINCUSHION

☼ ❄ ↔6 ft (1.8 m) ↑6 ft (1.8 m)

Shrub with open habit; some cultivars almost prostrate. Gray-green foliage. Apricot, pink, orange, or red flowers in spring. Tolerant of clay soils; frost tender when young. '**Aurora**', apricot-yellow flowers; '**Fire Dance**', scarlet flowerheads; '**African Red**', florets with distinctive red striping and yellow styles. Zones 8–10.

Leucospermum tottum

FIREWHEEL PINCUSHION

☼ ❄ ↔5 ft (1.5 m) ↑5 ft (1.5 m)

Dense evergreen shrub. Leaves narrow-elliptical, gray-green, covered with fine hairs. Rounded scarlet flowers with creamy styles in spring–summer. Several hybrid cultivars available, some extending flowering season into mid-summer. '**Scarlet Ribbon**', compact rounded habit, to 5 ft (1.5 m), frosted appearance, scarlet flowers in late spring. Zones 8–10.

Leucospermum 'Veldfire'

☼ ❄ ↔5 ft (1.5 m) ↑5 ft (1.5 m)

L. glabrum hybrid. Yellow-orange flowers, often age to crimson-red, with bright orange styles, in mid-spring–summer. Zones 8–10.

LEUCOTHOE

Found mainly in eastern Asia and the USA, this genus belonging to the heath (Ericaceae) family, as now understood, consists of only 6 species of evergreen and deciduous shrubs. Many more species formerly included in it are now separated as the genus *Agarista*. They usually have simple leathery leaves, dark green with toothed edges; some show a tendency to produce variegated foliage. The deciduous species often color well in autumn. The flowers are small, bell- or urn-shaped, and usually cream to pink. Opening in spring to early summer in racemes or panicles, they can be quite showy.
CULTIVATION: Most species prefer shade from the hottest sun and should be grown in cool, moist, humus-rich soil that is open and well drained. Other than light trimming to shape, pruning is seldom necessary. Propagation from seed is usually slow, so air-layering or half-hardened cuttings are more often used. Some species produce suckers that can be grown on.

Leucothoe fontanesiana

syns *Leucothoe catesbaei, L. walteri*

SWITCH IVY

☼ ❄ ↔7 ft (2 m) ↑6 ft (1.8 m)

From southeastern USA. Evergreen shrub with arching stems. Leaves long-pointed, to 4 in (10 cm) long, glossy upper surface, toothed edges; red-tinted new growth. White lily-of-the-valley-like flowers, in short racemes, in spring. '**Rainbow**' ★ (syn. 'Girard's Rainbow'), foliage variegated green, cream, and pink. Zones 5–10.

Leucothoe racemosa

FETTER BUSH, SWEET BELLS

☼ ❄ ↔5 ft (1.5 m) ↑3–8 ft (0.9–2.4 m)

Deciduous shrub from eastern USA. Leaves to 2½ in (6 cm) long, finely toothed edges; autumn foliage develops intense yellow, orange, and cherry red tones. Short racemes of white to cream flowers in spring–summer. Zones 5–9.

LEYCESTERIA

This genus in the woodbine (Caprifoliaceae) family consists of 6 species of deciduous or semi-evergreen shrubs from western China and the Himalayas as far west as Pakistan.

Leucothoe racemosa

They have small tubular flowers, borne over a long period, with colored bracts. The soft berries mature so quickly that they are often carried at the same time as the flowers. In favorable climates these plants may become invasive weeds.
CULTIVATION: Grow in moderately fertile soil in a sunny or part-shade location, though the flower bracts and fruit color better in full sun. Less hardy species can be overwintered in a greenhouse in colder climates. Propagate from seed in autumn or spring or by taking softwood cuttings in summer.

Leycesteria formosa

HIMALAYAN HONEYSUCKLE

☼ ❄ ↔6 ft (1.8 m) ↑6 ft (1.8 m)

Native to Himalayas and western China. Leaves long, dark green, slightly heart-shaped at base, smooth-edged or slightly toothed, undersurface paler and downy. Whitish flowers with purple bracts, on pendent spikes, in summer–autumn. Fruit ripening deep red-purple to black. Weed in Australia and New Zealand. Zones 7–10.

LIBOCEDRUS

This genus of 6 species of coniferous trees in the cypress (Cupressaceae) family is found in wet forest areas of New Caledonia, New Zealand, and southwestern South America, with 2 further species from New Guinea sometimes placed in the genus *Papuacedrus*. They are cypress-like trees with bright green foliage that has distinct adult and juvenile forms. Bark peels in stringy vertical strips, and male and female cones, borne on the same tree, are very small.

Leucospermum cordifolium

Libocedrus plumosa, in the wild, New Zealand

CULTIVATION: The New Zealand and South American species can be grown outdoors in moderately frosty climates but the others may require greenhouse cultivation. Outdoors these conifers will grow in any reasonable deeply worked soil; some shade should be given when young. Water well in dry spells. Propagation is usually from seed, which is best sown fresh. Cuttings are difficult to strike.

Libocedrus plumosa ★

KAWAKA

☼ ❅ ↔ 10 ft (3 m) ↑ 40 ft (12 m)

From New Zealand. Pyramidal form, maintained for many years. Slow growing in cultivation, reaching only about 8 ft (2.4 m) after 10 years. Branchlets compressed, flattened, giving soft feathery appearance; leaves rich green, scale-like. Zones 8–11.

LIGUSTRUM

PRIVET

This genus of about 50 species of both deciduous and evergreen trees and shrubs is part of the olive (Oleaceae) family. Most are found in the Himalayas and eastern Asia, with one in Europe and North Africa. All have simple opposite leaves with smooth edges and bear panicles of scented white flowers at the branch or stem tips, followed by small blue-black drupes. In warmer climates the seed is produced in large quantities and is popular with birds, which has resulted in several species becoming weeds. *L. japonicum* and *L. ovalifolium* are weeds in the USA and New Zealand; *L. lucidum* and *L. sinense* have become pests in eastern Australia. Varieties with colored foliage can be grown with less risk but are apt to revert.

CULTIVATION: They are not particular about soil or exposure to the sun. Seed can be sown as soon as ripe; colored forms are best propagated from firm tip cuttings taken in late spring or summer.

Ligustrum japonicum

JAPANESE PRIVET

☼ ❅ ↔ 8 ft (2.4 m) ↑ 10 ft (3 m)

From Japan and Korea. Compact, very dense, evergreen shrub. Leaves camellia-like, shiny, olive green. Large panicles of white flowers in late summer–early autumn. Zones 5–10.

Ligustrum lucidum

BROAD-LEAFED PRIVET, GLOSSY PRIVET, WAXLEAF PRIVET

☼ ❅ ↔ 30 ft (9 m) ↑ 30 ft (9 m)

Large evergreen shrub or small tree from China. Leaves pointed, shiny, deep green, to 6 in (15 cm) long. Large panicles of white flowers in autumn. 'Excelsum Superbum', pale green leaves edged yellow; 'Tricolor', narrow deep green leaves, predominantly marked with gray-green, edged with pale creamy yellow. Zones 7–11.

Ligustrum ovalifolium

CALIFORNIA PRIVET, OVAL-LEAFED PRIVET

☼ ❆ ↔ 12 ft (3.5 m) ↑ 12 ft (3.5 m)

Cultivated for hedging. Leaves shiny, deep green, falling in very cold climates. White flowers in mid-summer. 'Argenteum', leaves with creamy white margins; 'Aureum', the golden privet, green-centered leaves with wide yellow margins, or all yellow. Zones 5–10.

LINDERA

This genus in the laurel (Lauraceae) family consists of about 80 species of deciduous and evergreen trees and shrubs, all from East Asia except for 3 from North America. They have an open habit and aromatic alternate leaves, smooth-edged or 3-lobed. The leaves color in autumn on deciduous species. Heads of star-shaped yellow flowers appear in the leaf axils during spring, followed by clustered berry-like fruit.

CULTIVATION: Suitable for a woodland or other informal garden, in a shady position when young, all species transplant well and will survive in ordinary, somewhat acidic, soil. Established trees require little or no care but may be pruned if they become ungainly. Propagate from seed sown when fresh; if the seed must be stored, do not allow it to dry. Otherwise propagate from cuttings taken in summer or by air-layering.

Lindera obtusiloba

☼ ❆ ↔ 25 ft (8 m) ↑ 30 ft (9 m)

From East Asia. Branches gray-yellow, sometimes flushed purple. Aromatic leaves turn pale gold in autumn. Tiny, yellow-green, star-shaped flowers, in umbels on previous year's growth, in early spring, before leaves. Fruit glossy dark red to black. Zones 6–9.

Ligustrum lucidum 'Excelsum Superbum'

Lindera obtusiloba

Liquidambar formosana

Liquidambar orientalis

Liquidambar styraciflua

LIQUIDAMBAR

SWEET GUM

In the witchhazel (Hamamelidaceae) family, this genus comprises 4 species of tall deciduous trees found in North and Central America, East Asia, and Turkey. The meaning of the name is much as it appears: it refers to the resin, known as storax, exuded by the winter buds. The trees have an attractive conical or rounded form, and the palmately lobed leaves are similar to those of maples but arranged spirally on the twig instead of in opposite pairs. In autumn the foliage changes color dramatically to shades of orange, red, and purple. Spring flowers are greenish and inconspicuous, in small spherical heads, but the brown fruiting heads that follow are spiky and decorative.

CULTIVATION: These are large trees requiring plenty of room to develop; their site should be chosen carefully, as they dislike being transplanted. They require a sunny site in deep rich soil with plenty of moisture. Propagate from seed in autumn or softwood cuttings in summer, or by air-layering.

Liquidambar formosana

CHINESE LIQUIDAMBAR, FORMOSAN GUM

☼ ❄ ↔ 30 ft (9 m) ↑ 60 ft (18 m)

From mountains of east, central, and southern China, Taiwan, northern Vietnam, Laos, and South Korea. Straight trunk, gray-white bark, fissures with age. Leaves broad, 3-lobed, serrated margins, downy below. Inconspicuous greenish yellow flowers; spiky fruit. Zones 8–11.

Liquidambar orientalis

ORIENTAL SWEET GUM, TURKISH LIQUIDAMBAR

☼ ❄ ↔ 15 ft (4.5 m) ↑ 25–50 ft (8–15 m)

From southwestern Turkey. Broad crown; bark thick, orangey brown, cracking into small plates. Leaves 5-lobed, smaller than other species, turn orange in autumn. Zones 8–11.

Liquidambar styraciflua

LIQUIDAMBAR, SWEET GUM

☼ ❄ ↔ 35 ft (10 m) ↑ 70 ft (21 m)

Native to eastern USA, highlands of southern Mexico, and Central America. Bark dark grayish brown, deeply furrowed. Leaves

large, 5 to 7 tapering lobes, coloring brilliantly in shades of orange, red, and purple in autumn. Cultivars selected for their autumn colors include 'Burgundy', deep red; 'Festival', yellow, peach, pink; 'Lane Roberts', deep reddish purple; 'Palo Alto', orange and red; and 'Worplesdon', orangey yellow and purple. Other cultivars include 'Aurea', yellow-striped leaves; 'Golden Treasure', leaves with yellow margins; 'Gumball', dwarf form with rounded shape; 'Rotundiloba' ★, leaves with rounded lobes; and 'Variegata', leaves splashed with yellow. Zones 5–11.

LIRIODENDRON

This genus belonging to the magnolia (Magnoliaceae) family was believed to consist of just a single species naturally found in North America, until a second similar species was found in central China in 1875. Both species form quite tall, fast-growing, deciduous trees with long straight trunks and unusually shaped 4-lobed leaves that turn a delightful translucent yellow in autumn. The greenish bell-shaped flowers have a tangerine tint at the petal bases. They somewhat resemble a tulip, hence the common name of tulip tree. Capsule-like fruit follow the flowers. Hybrids between the 2 species are now in cultivation.

Liriodendron tulipifera

CULTIVATION: Liriodendron species grow best in a fertile soil, in a cool climate in partial shade, with protection from drying winds. Some shaping of the plant in the early stages of growth to establish a single trunk may be necessary. Propagate from seed sown in a position protected from winter frosts. Cultivars may be apical-grafted in early spring onto 1- or 2-year-old seedling understocks.

Liriodendron tulipifera

NORTH AMERICAN TULIP TREE, TULIP TREE

☼ ❄ ↔ 40 ft (12 m) ↑ 100 ft (30 m)

Found east of Mississippi River, USA, from Gulf States up to St Lawrence River and Great Lakes. Leaves quite large. Solitary flowers, 6 petalled, yellow-green with orange-yellow blotch at base, in spring. 'Aureomarginatum', yellow-edged leaves; 'Fastigiatum' ★, upright columnar habit, growing to only about half height of species. Zones 4–10.

LITHODORA

A genus in the borage (Boraginaceae) family of 7 species of low hairy shrubs or subshrubs, it is native to western and southern Europe, North Africa, and Asia Minor. Plentiful, deep dark green, simple leaves are about 1 in (25 mm) long and evergreen when grown within the zone range, though they are susceptible to frost burn. Covered with many small vibrant blue or purple flowers in late spring or early summer, their low-growing habit makes them ideal for ground covers, rockeries, and borders.
CULTIVATION: Grow in well-drained acid soil in full sun to part-shade; they can become leggy in too much shade. Propagate from seed in spring or tip cuttings in mid- to late summer.

Lithodora diffusa

syn. *Lithospermum diffusum*

☼ ◑ ❄ ↔ 24–36 in (60–90 cm) ↑6–12 in (15–30 cm)
From France, Spain, and Portugal. Green linear leaves; blue flowers in mid-spring–early summer. With age, it tends to cease producing foliage and flowers in center. 'Grace Ward', low-creeping form, bright azure flowers; 'Heavenly Blue' ★, petals edged with brilliant white; 'Star', petals edged with clear white, giving them starry appearance. Zones 7–9.

LOMATIA

There are 12 species in this genus of the protea (Proteaceae) family, 9 from eastern Australia and 3 from South America. All are shrubs or small trees, with a few reaching 60 ft (18 m) in rainforests. Leaves vary from smooth-edged to toothed to deeply divided. Small flowers, white, cream, yellow, or rarely pink, are borne on spikes in leaf axils or at branch tips. The fruit is leathery, with 2 rows of winged seeds.
CULTIVATION: Some require a sheltered, moist, frost-free position, others tolerate some dryness and some frosts. Generally, acid well-drained soils give best results. Propagate from fresh seed or cuttings taken in mid-summer from young growth that is not too soft.

Lomatia ferruginea

Lomatia ferruginea

☼ ❅ ↔ 15 ft (4.5 m) ↑30 ft (9 m)
From rainforests of Argentina and Chile. Evergreen tree with divided, dark green, fern-like leaves on brown felty stems. Clusters of red and yellow flowers, in leaf axils, in summer. Cultivated in warmer parts of UK since mid-nineteenth century. Zones 9–10.

Lomatia polymorpha

☼ ❄ ↔ 5 ft (1.5 m) ↑6–12 ft (1.8–3.5 m)
From Tasmania, Australia. Leaves narrow, deep green to yellow-green. Large cream flowers in late spring. Zones 8–10.

LONICERA

HONEYSUCKLE

Honeysuckles, belonging to the woodbine (Caprifoliaceae) family, are often regarded as somewhat untidy second-class climbers, but in the right place they are among the easiest and most rewarding plants. Occurring widely throughout the Northern Hemisphere though chiefly in temperate Eurasia, the 180-odd species in the genus encompass climbers, ground covers, and shrubs, both evergreen and deciduous, most of them very hardy. The foliage usually consists of opposite pairs of smooth-edged leaves, often somewhat leathery. The flowers, sometimes highly fragrant, vary in size; most are tubular at the base but divided at the mouth into 5 petals that are frequently arranged in 2 lips, an upper lip of 4 fused petals and a lower lip of a single petal. The fruit is an ornamental berry relished by birds, usually backed or partially enclosed by bract-like calyces that may color slightly.
CULTIVATION: Although honeysuckles are tough adaptable plants that will thrive in most conditions, they are generally best grown in rich, moist, humus-enriched, well-drained soil in full sun to partial shade. They can be raised from seed, though most are easily grown from layers or half-hardened cuttings. Cultivars and hybrids must be propagated from cuttings.

Lonicera fragrantissima

WINTER HONEYSUCKLE

☼ ❄ ↔ 8 ft (2.4 m) ↑6 ft (1.8 m)
Naturally found in China. Leaves dull green. Small, strongly scented, cream flowers, in pairs in leaf axils, in winter–spring. Red fruit. Zones 5–9.

Lithodora diffusa 'Star'

Lonicera involucrata

TWINBERRY

☼ ❄ ↔ 3 ft (0.9 m) ↕ 3 ft (0.9 m)

Deciduous shrub from Mexico, western USA, and southern Canada. Leaves to 5 in (12 cm) long. Short-tubed yellow to red flowers in spring. Deep purple berries with large purple-red bracts. Zones 4–10.

Lonicera maackii

☼ ❄ ↔ 15 ft (4.5 m) ↕ 15 ft (4.5 m)

Deciduous shrub native to East Asia. Leaves 3 in (8 cm) long, purple-stemmed. Fragrant white flowers, ageing to yellow, in spring–summer. Tiny dark red to black berries. Zones 2–9.

Lonicera nitida

syn. *Lonicera ligustrina* subsp. *yunnanensis*

BOX HONEYSUCKLE

☼ ❄ ↔ 10 ft (3 m) ↕ 12 ft (3.5 m)

Shrubby evergreen from central and southwestern China. Leaves tiny, dark green, purple toned in winter. Small cream flowers in spring. Purple-black berries. Dense bushy habit. Zones 7–10.

Lonicera × *purpusii*

☼ ❄ ↔ 8 ft (2.4 m) ↕ 10 ft (3 m)

Semi-deciduous hybrid between winter-flowering *L. fragrantissima* and *L. standishii*. Fragrant creamy white flowers, in clusters of 2 to 4, in winter–early spring. 'Winter Beauty', red berries. Zones 6–9.

Lonicera syringantha

☼ ❄ ↔ 7 ft (2 m) ↕ 10 ft (3 m)

From China and Tibet. Deciduous shrub with upright stems, graceful arching habit. Leaves blue tinted. Small, paired, fragrant, soft lilac flowers in spring–summer. Red berries. Zones 4–9.

Lonicera tatarica

TATARIAN HONEYSUCKLE

☼ ❄ ↔ 7 ft (2 m) ↕ 10 ft (3 m)

From central Asia and southern Russia. Deciduous shrub; parent of many hybrids and available in wide range of cultivars. Leaves with blue-gray underside. Flowers in white and pink shades, in spring–summer. Pale orange to red fruit. Zones 3–9.

LOPHOMYRTUS

This genus native to New Zealand belongs to the myrtle (Myrtaceae) family and is closely allied to *Myrtus* itself. It consists of 2 species of small evergreen trees or shrubs, which are grown primarily for their interesting foliage, though with age they also develop attractive dappled or streaked smooth bark. The species hybridize freely. CULTIVATION: Grow in full sun for the best leaf coloration, in reasonably fertile well-drained soil. In cool-temperate climates they are best given a warm sheltered site and protection in winter. Prune for hedging or to maintain a dense shrubby form, or to a single trunk as a small tree. Species can be propagated from seed in spring but are usually propagated from half-hardened cuttings in autumn. *L.* × *ralphii* and its cultivars can only be propagated from cuttings.

Lophomyrtus bullata ★

RAMARAMA

☼ ❂ ↔ 8 ft (2.4 m) ↕ 8–12 ft (2.4–3.5 m)

Small tree. Leaves small, oval, puckered surface, greener in shade, develop bronzy purplish tones in sun. Small fluffy cream flowers in summer. Dark reddish purple berries. Zones 9–10.

Lophomyrtus × *ralphii*

☼ ❂ ↔ 5 ft (1.5 m) ↕ 6 ft (1.8 m)

Hybrid with characteristics intermediate between parent species, *L. bullata* and *L. obcordata*. Leaves more rounded than those of *L. bullata* and much less puckered; flowers for longer period over summer. 'Gloriosa' (syn. *L.* × *ralphii* 'Variegata'), leaves variegated cream and tinged pink; 'Indian Chief', dark reddish brown leaves; 'Kathryn', purplish red, glossy, oval leaves with puckered surface; 'Pixie', bronze-green leaves, chocolate-purple when young. Zones 9–11.

LOPHOSTEMON

This genus is a member of the myrtle (Myrtaceae) family, which includes important plants such as the eucalypts. Its 6 species of evergreen trees are native to Australia and New Guinea. The leaves are spirally arranged and crowded toward the end of the branchlets. The white flowers, with 5 petals and 5 showy feather-like groups of fused stamens, are grouped in short cymes in the upper leaf axils. The fruit is a woody capsule like that of some *Eucalyptus* species, though *Lophostemon* is not closely related to *Eucalyptus*.

Lonicera maackii

Lophomyrtus × *ralphii*

Lophostemon confertus

CULTIVATION: These trees should be planted in fertile free-draining soil. They will survive outdoors in regions with very light winter frosts in a warm sheltered site but in cool-temperate climates need greenhouse protection. Propagate from seed in spring or autumn. Variegated cultivars are propagated by budding or grafting.

Lophostemon confertus
syn. *Tristania conferta*
BRUSH BOX
☼ ☙ ↔ 30 ft (9 m) ↑ 130 ft (40 m)
Found in east-coast Queensland and northeast New South Wales, Australia. Densely foliaged tree, pink-brown peeling bark. Leaves long-pointed, elliptical, dark green above, olive green below. White flowers, 1 in (25 mm) wide, fluffy stamens, in summer. Zones 10–12.

Luma apiculata

LOROPETALUM
Currently this genus is believed to comprise a single species of evergreen dome-shaped shrub or small tree from the woodland regions of the Himalayas, China, and Japan. One of the witch-hazel (Hamamelidaceae) family, it is grown for its distinctive flowers and its horizontal branching habit. Leaves are alternate, simple, and smooth-edged, and the small flowers, borne in tight heads of 3 to 6 flowers in the leaf axils, each have 4 twisted strap-like petals. The fruit is a small nut-like capsule containing 2 seeds.

Luculia gratissima

CULTIVATION: This trouble-free plant grows best in fertile, humus-rich, well-drained soil in full sun. As it flowers on the last season's wood, prune after flowering, and only to enhance the shape. Propagate from cuttings taken in summer.

Loropetalum chinense
FRINGE FLOWER
☼ ❄ ↔ 8 ft (2.4 m) ↑ 6–15 ft (1.8–4.5 m)
Bushy shrub. Leaves small, dull green, oval. Slightly perfumed, creamy white, fringed flowerheads in spring. *L. c.* f. *rubrum,* bronze-foliaged form sometimes sold as 'Burgundy'. *L. c.* 'Plum Delight', purple-red foliage and flowers; 'Sizzling Pink', red spring foliage and bright pink flowers. Zones 8–11.

LUCULIA
This genus in the madder (Rubiaceae) family comprises 5 species of deciduous flowering shrubs and small trees found in elevated forest regions of the Himalayas, from northern India to western China. They are prized both for their attractive foliage and prolific clusters of pink, red, or white flowers in the form of a slender tube opening to a broad 5-lobed disc. The fruit is a capsule with 2 chambers containing flattened seeds. Although technically deciduous, there is no long period of leaflessness, as the new foliage appears at about the same time as the old leaves are dropping.
CULTIVATION: Tolerating only mild frosts, they prefer a moderate summer temperature and grow well in moderately fertile, moist, well-drained soil with humus. They need protection from the wind and do not like competition from other roots. Plant in part-shade or sun; provide adequate water and fertilize regularly from spring to

autumn. Prune back old flowering shoots after flowering. In frost-prone areas, grow them in a greenhouse. Propagate from seed in spring or from half-hardened cuttings in summer.

Luculia grandifolia
☼/◐ ☙ ↔ 7 ft (2 m) ↑ 12–20 ft (3.5–6 m)
From Bhutan. Leaves large, deep green, elliptic to ovate; reddish purple veins, stalks, margins. Large clusters of 16 to 20 very fragrant, white, tubular flowers in summer. Zones 9–10.

Luculia gratissima
☼/◐ ☙ ↔ 10–15 ft (3–4.5 m) ↑ 10–20 ft (3–6 m)
Large shrub or small tree native to Himalayas. Leaves ovate-oblong to lance-shaped, dark green. Large trusses of fragrant, slender, rosy pink flowers in autumn–mid-winter. Egg-shaped fruit. Zones 9–10.

LUMA
This genus, found in Argentina and Chile, includes just 4 species of densely foliaged, round-headed, evergreen shrubs and trees. In the myrtle (Myrtaceae) family and closely allied to *Myrtus,* they have small aromatic leaves and 4-petalled white flowers with a central mass of stamens. The flowers usually open in spring and early summer, and are followed by dark berries. The bark can also be an attractive feature, as in some species it peels and is a warm cinnamon tone on the outside and white to pink underneath.
CULTIVATION: Species are easily cultivated in any mild climate with adequate rainfall, preferring moist well-drained soil and a position in sun or light shade. Although usually neat growers, they benefit from being lightly trimmed to shape; if allowed to become overgrown, they can be rejuvenated with heavy pruning, best done over 2 or 3 seasons. Propagate from seed or half-hardened tip cuttings.

Luma apiculata ★
syns *Myrtus apiculata, M. luma*
PALO COLORADO, TEMU
☼/◐ ☙ ↔ 20 ft (6 m) ↑ 20 ft (6 m)
Large shrub or small tree. Flaking warm brown bark. Leaves deep olive green, glossy. Small white flowers, each with over 150 stamens, in spring–summer. Small dark purple-red fruit. Zones 9–10.

LUPINUS

LUPIN, LUPINE

There are about 200 species of annuals, perennials, and evergreen shrubs in this genus in the pea-flower subfamily of the legume (Fabaceae) family. They are native to North and South America, southern Europe, and northern Africa, usually found in dry habitats. Many have ornamental flowers, borne in showy terminal panicles or racemes. The leaves are palmate, with 5 to 15 leaflets, and the stems are often covered in fine soft down.

CULTIVATION: Although these generally tolerate poor dry conditions, they are best grown in full sun in moderately fertile well-drained soil. Propagate from seed or cuttings. The seedlings should be planted out when small, as these plants dislike root disturbance.

Lupinus arboreus

TREE LUPIN, YELLOW BUSH LUPINE

↔4–8 ft (1.2–2.4 m) ↑3–7 ft (0.9–2 m)

Bushy evergreen shrub native to central coastal California, USA, mostly on seashores. Leaves grayish green, smooth above, woolly hairs beneath. Loose racemes of flowers, usually bright yellow, occasionally blue or lavender, in spring–summer. ***L. a.* var. *eximius***, hairier stems and leaves, yellow and blue flowers. Zones 8–10.

Lupinus arboreus

MACKAYA

This single-species genus is a member of the acanthus (Acanthaceae) family, which also includes the well-known perennial bear's breeches, *Acanthus mollis.* Native to southern Africa, it is an evergreen shrub that grows as an understory plant in forests, often along stream banks. Leaves are very deep green with soft wavy edges. Flowers are tubular with wide-open petals, usually mauve. They occur at the ends of branches from spring to autumn.

CULTIVATION: Grow in moist well-drained soil in full sun or part-shade in a sheltered position. Propagate from seed or from half-hardened cuttings in spring.

Mackaya bella ★

↔4 ft (1.2 m) ↑8 ft (2.4 m)

Develops spreading habit over time. Glossy deep green leaves, wavy edges. Tubular flowers, 5 flaring petals, mauve with darker veining, in loose spikes at ends of branches, in spring–autumn. Zones 9–11.

MACLURA

Notable for their spiny branches, dye-bearing flowers, and interesting fruit, this genus from the mulberry (Moraceae) family contains 12 species of evergreen or deciduous shrubs, trees, and climbers. It occurs worldwide in warm-temperate to tropical regions. There are separate male and female trees. They usually have simple, pointed, ovate leaves, sometimes with a downy underside. Male and female flowers are similar in color (yellow to green shades); female flowers occur in larger clusters. The fruit is spherical, maturing to yellow or orange.

Mackaya bella

Maclura pomifera

CULTIVATION: Frost hardiness and drought tolerance varies. Most are easily grown in any moist well-drained soil in full sun or part-shade. Brighter positions usually result in more fruit, while shade promotes foliage; thus male trees are best planted with a little shade, while females do better in sun. Prune in winter after the fruit falls, but if winter frost damage is likely, delay pruning until spring. Propagate from seed, from half-hardened cuttings in summer, or from hardwood cuttings in winter.

Maclura pomifera

OSAGE ORANGE

↔30 ft (9 m) ↑50 ft (15 m)

Deciduous tree from Arkansas to Texas, USA. Lustrous leaves, 2–6 in (5–15 cm) long, bright yellow tones in autumn. Tiny green flowers in early summer. Fruit glossy, wrinkled. Zones 6–10.

MAGNOLIA

Comprising around 100 evergreen and deciduous species and countless cultivars, this genus within the magnolia (Magnoliaceae) family occurs naturally throughout Asia and North America. The flowers are primitive, and many are fragrant. They are pollinated largely by beetles. The flowers are often seen to advantage on bare limbs before the foliage appears. Fruit are often cone-like showy clusters, pink or red with colorful seeds, these sometimes suspended on fine threads.

CULTIVATION: Although some species will tolerate lime, most do better in well-drained acid soils rich in manure and humus. Generally fast growing, their fleshy surface roots are easily damaged by cultivation. For this reason they are best left undisturbed. Wind and late frosts can also damage the large flowers. Light shade is generally ideal. Propagate by taking cuttings in summer or sowing seed in autumn. Grafting should be carried out in winter.

Magnolia acuminata

CUCUMBER TREE

↔30 ft (9 m) ↑100 ft (30 m)

Deciduous tree from eastern North America. Large oval leaves, blue-green below, hairy. Flowers metallic green to yellow-green, upright petals, in summer. Unripe fruit resemble cucumbers. Zones 4–9.

Magnolia campbellii

CAMPBELL'S MAGNOLIA, PINK TULIP TREE

☼ ❄ ↔ 30 ft (9 m) ↑ 100 ft (30 m)

Tree from Himalayan forests in southwest China to eastern Nepal. Large oval leaves, bronze when young, paler reverse. Huge slightly fragrant flowers, pale to deep pink, before leaves, in late winter–early spring. Seedlings take 30 years to flower, grafted varieties 5 years, using understock of *M. × soulangeana*. **M. c.** subsp. *mollicomata*, flowering younger, earlier in season, slightly larger flowers, more cold hardy; '**Lanarth**', huge cyclamen-purple flowers. **M. c.** '**Charles Raffill**', deep rose pink buds opening to rose-purple outside, white-flushed rose-purple inside; '**Darjeeling**' dark rose-purple flowers. Zones 7–9.

Magnolia denudata

JADE ORCHID, LILY TREE, YULAN

☼ ◗ ❄ ↔ 30 ft (9 m) ↑ 30 ft (9 m)

Deciduous tree or shrub native to central China. Leaves alternate, green underside. Flowers white, fragrant, chalice-shaped, symbol of purity, emerge on bare wood before foliage appears, in summer. An exquisite magnolia, plant flowers within 3 years. Zones 6–9.

Magnolia fraseri

EAR-LEAFED MAGNOLIA, FRASER'S MAGNOLIA

◗ ❄ ↔ 30 ft (9 m) ↑ 40 ft (12 m)

Broadly spreading, open-branched, deciduous tree from southeast USA. Young bronze foliage becomes pale green. Fragrant flowers, vase-shaped becoming saucer-shaped, creamy white, green flush to outer petals, in late spring–early summer. Zones 6–9.

Magnolia grandiflora

Magnolia grandiflora

BULL BAY, GREAT LAUREL MAGNOLIA, SOUTHERN MAGNOLIA

◗ ❄ ↔ 35 ft (10 m) ↑ 35 ft (10 m)

Evergreen tree found from central Florida to North Carolina and west to Texas, USA. Leaves stiff, leathery, deep glossy green, rusty-furry underside. Large, creamy white, saucer-shaped flowers, fragrant, in early summer. Woody fruit. '**Exmouth**', glossy green leaves, rusty-felted beneath, huge fragrant flowers borne from early age; '**Ferruginea**', erect form, dense habit, leaf

underside richly red-felted; '**Goliath**', many huge globular flowers in mid-summer; '**Little Gem**', smaller leaves, slightly smaller flowers appear when young. Zones 6–9.

Magnolia kobus

KOBUS MAGNOLIA

☼ ❄ ↔ 30 ft (9 m) ↑ 40 ft (12 m)

From Japan and Korea. Oval leaves dark green, smooth, paler underside. Lightly fragrant, creamy white flowers, streaked pink at base, in early spring, before foliage. Species considered by some to be represented by forms now named *M. × loebneri* and *M. stellata*. **M. k.** var. *borealis*, more vigorous, larger leaves, sparser flowers. Zones 4–8.

Magnolia liliiflora

syn. *Magnolia quinquepeta*

LILY-FLOWERED MAGNOLIA

☼ ❄ ↔ 15 ft (4.5 m) ↑ 10 ft (3 m)

Small deciduous tree or large shrub found naturally throughout central China; smaller than other species. Fully hardy. Oval dark green leaves, paler and downy on reverse. Purplish pink, waxy, goblet-shaped, lily-like flowers, to 3 in (8 cm) wide, appear with foliage, in spring–summer. '**Nigra**', wine purple flowers, paler purplish inside. Zones 6–11.

Magnolia × loebneri

LOEBNER MAGNOLIA

☼ ❄ ↔ 20 ft (6 m) ↑ 30 ft (9 m)

M. kobus and *M. stellata* hybrid. Deciduous tree or shrub. Leaves narrow, dark green, long oval-shaped. Flowers large, white, often pink beneath, in spring–summer. '**Leonard Messel**', spreading tree; '**Merrill**' ★, white flowers. Zones 4–8.

Magnolia macrophylla

BIGLEAF MAGNOLIA, UMBRELLA TREE

◗ ❄ ↔ 30 ft (9 m) ↑ 50 ft (15 m)

Deciduous tree from moist forests of southeast USA. Leaves large, oval, thin-textured, downy reverse. Cup-shaped creamy yellow flowers in early–mid-summer. Round pink fruit cluster. Zones 4–8.

Magnolia grandiflora

Magnolia kobus

Magnolia liliiflora 'Nigra'

glossy. Flowers erect, white to rose pink, with deeper color beneath, in spring–summer, before foliage, even on young trees. '**Alexandrina**', large erect flowers, white inside, flushed rosy purple outside, darker veins; '**Brozzonii**', very large, elongated, white flowers, pink-purple veins at base; '**Burgundy**', purple-pink flowers; '**Lennei**', globular flowers, very concave, thick fleshy petals magenta-purple outside, creamy white inside; '**Lennei Alba**', ivory white; '**Picture**', deep maroon to burgundy, fading to white at petal tips; '**Rustica Rubra**', deep rosy pink petals outside, fading to pink-white inside. Zones 4–9.

Magnolia stellata 'Royal Star'

Magnolia sprengeri

SPRENGER'S MAGNOLIA

☀ ❄ ↔ 25 ft (8 m) ↕ 40 ft (12 m)

Deciduous spreading tree from China. Leaves dark green, oval, felty underside when young. Flowers fragrant, pink, before foliage, in spring. *M. s.* var. *diva*, white flowers. Zones 7–9.

Magnolia salicifolia

WILLOW-LEAFED MAGNOLIA

☀ ❄ ↔ 20 ft (6 m) ↕ 40 ft (12 m)

Shrub or deciduous tree found along streams in Japan. Narrow pale green leaves, glaucous below; lemon-anise scent from leaves, bark, and wood when bruised. Flowers white, fragrant, before foliage, in spring. '**Wada's Memory**', popular cultivar. Zones 6–9.

Magnolia sargentiana

☀ ❄ ↔ 25 ft (8 m) ↕ 60 ft (18 m)

Deciduous tree from China. Leaves deep green, glossy, underside grayish. Flowers purplish pink to white, in spring. *M. s.* var. *robusta*, larger, more shrubby plant, earlier flowers. Sometimes regarded as form of *M. dawsoniana*. Zones 7–9.

Magnolia sieboldii

OYAMA MAGNOLIA, SIEBOLD'S MAGNOLIA

☀ ❄ ↔ 25 ft (8 m) ↕ 20 ft (6 m)

Large, spreading, deciduous shrub from Japan, Korea, and southern China. Leaves felty-white beneath. Spot-flowering, pure white, fragrant, nodding blooms, in late spring–late summer. Small pinkish fruit. *M. s.* subsp. *sinensis*, broadly oval leaves, felty underside; flowers white, cup-shaped, pendulous, strongly lemon-scented, in late spring, with leaves; large pink fruit. Zones 6–9.

Magnolia, Hybrid Cultivar, 'Judy'

Magnolia × soulangeana

SAUCER MAGNOLIA, TULIP MAGNOLIA

☀ ❄ ↔ 20 ft (6 m) ↕ 20 ft (6 m)

Deciduous low-branched tree or large shrub from cross between *M. denudata* and *M. liliiflora*. Leaves short, oval, dark green,

Magnolia stellata

STAR MAGNOLIA

☀ ❄ ↔ 10 ft (3 m) ↕ 15 ft (4.5 m)

Deciduous rounded shrub from highlands of Honshu Island, Japan. Leaves dark green, oval. Clusters of fragrant ivory white flowers, strap-like with curved reflexed petals, in late winter before foliage. Regarded by some as variety of *M. kobus* of garden origin. '**Chrysanthemiflora**', double flowers, white petals, reverse flushed pink; '**Pink Star**', pale pink almost white flowers; '**Rosea**', petals pale pink reverse; '**Royal Star**', abundant, double, snow white flowers; '**Waterlily**' ★, larger, more abundant, pale pink petals. Zones 5–9.

Magnolia × veitchii

VEITCH'S MAGNOLIA

☀ ❄ ↔ 15 ft (4.5 m) ↕ 100 ft (30 m)

Hybrid of *M. denudata* and *M. campbellii*. Leaves bronze-purple to dark green. Flowers upright, fragrant, pink at base, suffusing to white, in mid-spring before foliage. Zones 6–9.

Magnolia virginiana

SWAMP LAUREL, SWEET BAY

☀ ❄ ↔ 20 ft (6 m) ↕ 30 ft (9 m)

From coastal swamps in USA. Evergreen or deciduous. Glossy leaves, silvery below. Lemon-scented cream or white cup-shaped flowers in late summer. Zones 6–9.

Magnolia wilsonii

WILSON'S MAGNOLIA

☀ ❄ ↔ 20 ft (6 m) ↕ 20 ft (6 m)

Spreading deciduous shrub from western China. Narrow, elliptical, dark green leaves, paler felty reverse. White flowers, fragrant, saucer-shaped, pendent, in spring–early summer. Zones 6–9.

Magnolia Hybrid Cultivars

☼ ✻ ↔ 20–30 ft (6–9 m) ↕ 20–40 ft (6–12 m)

Since success of first *M. × soulangeana* hybrids, breeders have focused on producing bigger brighter magnolias. Notable are De Vos & Kosar's Eight Little Girls, Gresham hybrids from America, and those by Jury family of New Zealand. '**Ann**', deep pink base fades to pale pink on tips; '**Apollo**', rosy pink buds, rosy red flowers, in spring; '**Betty**', petals deep rose; '**Charles Coates**', scented, creamy white flowers in spring; '**Elizabeth**', primrose yellow fragrant flowers in late spring, dark green leaves; '**Freeman**', dark green, leathery, glossy leaves, fragrant white flowers in summer; '**Galaxy**', soft pink flowers with creamy white interior, upright, medium-sized to large, tulip-shaped, before foliage, in early spring; '**George Henry Kern**', small, strappy-petalled, white to pale pink flowers with mauve petal reverse; '**Gold Star**', yellow flowers; '**Heaven Scent**', one of Gresham hybrids, beautiful free-flowering, scented, narrow, deep pink, cup-shaped blooms in early spring; '**Iolanthe**', very large-flowered Jury hybrid; '**Jane**', deep pink flowers with deeper vein, in early spring; '**Judy**', small flowers, sometimes scented; '**Manchu Fan**', velvety cream flowers; '**No. 4**', pink flowers fade to white at tips, erect petals, turned back at tips; '**Pink Alba Superba**', deep pink cup-shaped flowers, in spring; '**Pinkie**', petals pink underneath, white on top; '**Randy**', very deep pink underside, triangular shrub or small tree; '**Ricki**', pale pink flowers, deeper pink underside, very erect petals; '**Rouged Alabaster**', creamy flowers, flushed with rose pink; '**Royal Crown**', flowers dark red to violet with white interior, outside tepals reflexed to resemble crown, in spring; '**Susan**', pale pink flowers deepening near center, faint ribbing; '**Vulcan**', cyclamen pink flowers; '**Yellow Lantern**', yellow flowers. Zones 6–9.

MAHONIA

This genus from the barberry (Berberidaceae) family of some 70 species of evergreen shrubs is found in Asia and North America, some species extending into Central America. Leaves are often very spiny and may be trifoliate or pinnate with relatively large leaflets; leaves may be carried alternately, or in whorls, with several changes of color during maturation. Sprays of small yellow flowers, often scented, appear between spring

Mahonia fremontii

and early winter. Fruit is usually blue-black edible berries with a grape-like powdery bloom. Botanists have long debated whether *Mahonia* should be maintained as a genus distinct from *Berberis*. Most British and Continental botanists have recognized both genera, while there is a strong school in North America, where the characteristics distinguishing the two groups tend to break down, that prefers to place all species in a broadly defined *Berberis*. Recent studies have given support to the latter classification, and *Mahonia* is recognized here only pending a more comprehensive survey.
CULTIVATION: Mahonias vary in hardiness. Most commonly grown species are temperate-zone plants tolerant of moderate to hard frosts, while some tropical Asian species withstand only light frosts. They prefer moist, well-drained, fertile soil rich in humus. Protect from the summer sun. Pruning is seldom necessary. Propagate from cuttings, or rooted suckers that grow at the base of established plants.

Mahonia aquifolium

OREGON HOLLY GRAPE

☽ ✻ ↔ 8 ft (2.4 m) ↕ 6 ft (1.8 m)

Suckering clump-forming shrub from western North America. Pinnate leaves composed of 5 to 13 spiny holly-like leaflets, dark green in summer, strong red tints in winter. Erect racemes of yellow to golden yellow flowers in late winter. Purple-black fruit. '**Compacta**', tiny, round, yellow flowers; '**Green Ripple**', green rippled leaves. Zones 5–10.

Mahonia fortunei

☽ ✻ ↔ 3 ft (0.9 m) ↕ 7 ft (2 m)

Chinese shrub, notable foliage. Leaves to 10 in (25 cm) long; dark green leaflets, 4 in (10 cm) long, pale underside. Leaflets bronze when young, toothed rather than spiny. Short racemes of bright yellow flowers in autumn. Zones 7–10.

Mahonia fremontii

DESERT MAHONIA

☼ ✻ ↔ 7 ft (2 m) ↕ 12 ft (3.5 m)

Drought-tolerant shrub from southwestern USA and Mexico. Open branching habit. Leaves pale green, strongly glaucous in best forms, 3 to 7 spiny toothed leaflets. Clusters of soft yellow flowers in summer. Deep yellow to red fruit. Zones 8–11.

Mahonia 'Golden Abundance'

☼ ✻ ↔ 3 ft (0.9 m) ↕ 6–8 ft (1.8–2.4 m)

Often listed as cultivar of *M. aquifolium*, but is probably hybrid. Densely foliaged, glossy, holly-like leaves. Golden yellow flowers, in large clusters, in summer. Purple-blue berries. Zones 6–9.

Mahonia japonica

☽ ✻ ↔ 10 ft (3 m) ↕ 6 ft (1.8 m)

Spreading shrub native to Japan; cultivated in China and Taiwan. Long leathery leaves, with 19 spiny dark green leaflets. Fragrant bright yellow flowers, in upright or arching racemes, in late winter. Small blue-black fruit. **Bealei Group**, upright shrubs, native to western China, deep olive green leaflets, scented pale yellow flowers in late winter. Zones 6–10.

Mahonia aquifolium

Mahonia lomariifolia

◗ ❄ ↔ 8 ft (2.4 m) ↑ 10 ft (3 m)

Upright shrub from Myanmar and western China. Leaves bronze ageing to dark green, 20 to 40 spiny leaflets. Erect spikes of fragrant yellow flowers in autumn–spring. Purple-blue fruit. Zones 7–10.

Mahonia × media

◗ ❄ ↔ 12 ft (3.5 m) ↑ 15 ft (4.5 m)

M. japonica and *M. lomariifolia* hybrid. Vigorous upright plant, foliage reddens in winter. Erect racemes of yellow flowers in summer. 'Arthur Menzies', bright yellow flower spikes; 'Buckland', fragrant flowers, long arching racemes; 'Charity', tall, flowers in winter; 'Winter Sun', horizontal racemes in autumn. Zones 7–10.

Mahonia repens

CREEPING MAHONIA

◗ ❄ ↔ 36 in (90 cm) ↑ 18 in (45 cm)

Suckering shrub from northwest North America. Blue-green leaves, reddening in winter, to 10 in (25 cm) long, 5 leaflets, very spiny. Flowers deep yellow, fragrant, in spring. Blue-black fruit. 'Denver Strain', dark green leaves. Zones 6–9.

Mahonia repens

MALPIGHIA

Found in tropical America and the islands of the Caribbean, this genus encompasses 45 species of evergreen shrubs and trees from the self-named Malpighiaceae family. They bear opposite pairs of sometimes hairy, rounded to lance-shaped leaves that may be smooth-edged or conspicuously toothed. Flowers are very distinctive because of the long-stemmed petals held clear of the central staminal cluster. The flowers may be borne singly or in small corymbs and are followed by small brightly colored drupes. CULTIVATION: These tropical plants will not tolerate frosts or prolonged cool conditions, but are otherwise easy to grow, provided they are given moderately fertile well-drained soil, occasional feeding, and water during dry periods. Most species can be trimmed back quite hard if necessary. Propagate from seed or cuttings.

Mahonia × media

Malpighia coccigera

BARBADOS HOLLY, MINIATURE HOLLY, SINGAPORE HOLLY

◗ ∤ ↔ 30 in (75 cm) ↑ 30 in (75 cm)

Small shrub native to West Indies. Glossy deep green leaves, 1 in (25 mm) long, deeply toothed. Covered with pink to mauve flowers in summer. Red drupes. Zones 10–12.

Malpighia glabra

ACEROLA, BARBADOS CHERRY

◗ ∤ ↔ 4 ft (1.2 m) ↑ 10 ft (3 m)

Shrub from southern Texas (USA), Caribbean, Central America, and northern areas of South America. Leaves glossy, smooth-edged, 4 in (10 cm) long. Pale to deep pink or red flowers in summer, followed by small, round, red, edible fruit. Zones 9–12.

MALUS

APPLE, CRABAPPLE

This well-known genus is found in temperate regions right around the Northern Hemisphere. The apples and crabapples comprise a large genus of around 30 species of ornamental and fruiting, small to medium-sized, deciduous trees belonging to the rose (Rosaceae) family. Nearly all have soft green leaves. The fruits are pomes; not all crabapples are edible, some being too bitter for the human palate. The cultivated apple is one of the most widely grown of all edible fruits, and the many species and cultivars of crabapple are valued as ornamental trees. CULTIVATION: *Malus* will grow in all cool-temperate regions. Apples and crabapples flower in spring and most cultivated varieties of apple require a cross-pollinator in order to produce fruit. While cultivated apples require careful winter pruning, crabapples, being largely ornamental, need less attention. Propagate by grafting onto an apple rootstock, some of which produce a dwarfed plant.

Malus baccata

SIBERIAN CRABAPPLE

☼ ❄ ↔ 40 ft (12 m) ↑ 40 ft (12 m)

Rounded erect tree from Siberia. Buds pinkish, open to single, white, fragrant flowers. Fruit red, sometimes yellow, on long thin stems. Resistant to most apple diseases. *M. b.* var. *mandshurica*, from Japan and northeast China, lightly serrated leaves, underside initially downy, single white flowers, red fruit; 'Midwest', larger creamy white flowers. *M. b.* 'Jackii', spreading habit, stouter branches; 'Spring Snow', drooping white flowers. Zones 2–9.

Malus coronaria

AMERICAN CRABAPPLE, AMERICAN SWEET CRABAPPLE

☼ ❄ ↔ 30 ft (9 m) ↑ 30 ft (9 m)

Large wide-limbed tree from eastern USA. Buds dark pink, single flowers, fragrant, pale pink to pink-white or salmon pink. Green fruit unpalatable. Susceptible to scab and rust diseases. *M. c.* var. *angustifolia*, short trunk, spreading branches, highly fragrant rose-colored flowers, susceptible to disease. *M. c.* var. *dasycalyx*, leaves paler beneath, woolly calyx; 'Charlottae', apricot to deep pink buds, light pink semi-double to double flowers. Zones 4–9.

Malus × gloriosa

Malus × micromalus

Malus × purpurea

Malus floribunda

JAPANESE FLOWERING CRABAPPLE

☀ ❈ ↔ 20 ft (6 m) ↑ 12 ft (3.5 m)

From Japan. Leaves green, serrated, tapered. Buds dark pink to red, opening to single light pink or nearly white flowers in late spring. Fruit yellow and red, ½ in (12 mm) in diameter. May be affected by powdery mildew. Long cultivated. Zones 4–9.

Malus × gloriosa

☀ ❈ ↔ 7–10 ft (2–3 m) ↑ 10 ft (3 m)

Hybrid shrub of *M. pumila* 'Niedzwetzkyana' and *M. × scheideckeri*. Heavily toothed leaves, red-tinted when young. Purple-red flowers, 1½ in (35 mm) wide. Yellow fruit, ½ in (12 mm) wide, in spring. 'Oekonomierat Echtermeyer', pendulous bronze foliage. Zones 4–9.

Malus halliana

☀ ❈ ↔ 10 ft (3 m) ↑ 15 ft (4.5 m)

Small tree with loose open habit, from China. Leaves oblong, dark green, often purple-tinted. Red stalks. Flowers bright rose, nodding, in late spring. Fruit purplish, ripening late. Disease resistant. **M. h. var. *spontanea***, shorter, smaller whitish flowers, greenish yellow fruit. **M. h. 'Parkmanii'**, bronze-green glossy leaves, flowers double or semi-double, flesh-pink; fruit red to red-purple. Zones 4–9.

Malus hupehensis

HUPEH CRABAPPLE, TEA CRABAPPLE

☀ ❈ ↔ 25 ft (8 m) ↑ 15 ft (4.5 m)

Open spreading tree from China and India. Leaves deep green, violet when young. Buds pink, open to single, white, fragrant flowers in spring. Fruit green-yellow, slight red cheek. Zones 4–10.

Malus ioensis

IOWA CRABAPPLE, PRAIRIE CRABAPPLE

☀ ❈ ↔ 20 ft (6 m) ↑ 20 ft (6 m)

Native to midwest USA. Leaves dark green, deeply serrated, yellowish green underside. Flowers white tinged with pink, fragrant, in spring. Fruit shiny green. Highly susceptible to disease, several resistant clones produced. 'Plena', fully double pink flowers; 'Prairifire' ★, dark pink buds and flowers. Zones 2–9.

Malus × micromalus

☀ ❈ ↔ 15 ft (4.5 m) ↑ 15 ft (4.5 m)

Small Japanese tree, hybrid between *M. baccata* and *M. spectabilis*. Dark brown stems, waxy serrated leaves taper to fine point. Pink blooms, in clusters of 3 to 5 flowers, in spring. Yellow somewhat pointed fruit, ½ in (12 mm) wide. Zones 4–9.

Malus × purpurea

☀ ❈ ↔ 25 ft (8 m) ↑ 20 ft (6 m)

Very early flowering, hybrid of *M. × atrosanguinea* and *M. pumila* 'Niedzwetzkyana'. Deep green leaves. Dark flowers fade to pale mauve, in late spring. 'Aldenhamensis', blooms up to 3 times per season, leaves red-green to bronze-green, single and semi-double pinkish red flowers; 'Eleyi', deep red-purple foliage, purple to red flowers, subject to leaf diseases; 'Lemoinei', red flowers. Zones 4–9.

Malus sargentii

SARGENT'S CRABAPPLE

☀ ❈ ↔ 15 ft (4.5 m) ↑ 6 ft (1.8 m)

Densely branched. Leaves broadly oval, sharp-tipped, heavy, bright green, lobed, serrated edges. Flowers white, single, fragrant, in spring. Fruit tiny, crimson to purple. Blooms in alternate years. 'Rosea', deep red-pink buds, white flowers, dark red fruit. Zones 4–9.

Malus × scheideckeri

☀ ❈ ↔ 8 ft (2.4 m) ↑ 15 ft (4.5 m)

Slow-growing, small, upright tree, hybrid of *M. floribunda* and *M. prunifolia*. Coarsely serrated leaves. Flowers faded rose pink, usually semi-double, in thick clusters on branches, in late spring. Fruit slightly ribbed, yellow-orange. Tolerates pruning. 'Exzellenz Thiel', pale pink to white flowers; 'Red Jade', drooping red fruit. Zones 4–9.

Malus sieboldii

Malus sieboldii

☀ ❈ ↔ 10 ft (3 m) ↑ 15 ft (4.5 m)

Slow-growing, small to medium-size, rounded tree from Japan. Lobed or simple leaves. Buds red to carmine, open to single white flowers in spring. Fruit very small, red. Disease resistant. *M. s.* **var. *arborescens***, larger leaves, white flowers, reddish fruit. Zones 4–9.

Malus, Hybrid Cultivar, 'Red Sentinel'

Malus sylvestris
COMMON CRABAPPLE, WILD CRABAPPLE

☼ ❄ ↔ 10 ft (3 m) ↑ 30 ft (9 m)

From Europe. Small tree with dense rounded crown, dark bark. Some branches thorny. Flowers white or pink, followed by sour yellow-green or reddish fruit. Zones 3–9.

Malus tschonoskii
☼ ❄ ↔ 20 ft (6 m) ↑ 40 ft (12 m)

From Japan. Sturdy upright habit. Green leaves turn purple, orange, bronze, yellow, and crimson in autumn. Flowers white with pink hue, in spring. Fruit insignificant. Susceptible to most apple diseases. Zones 6–10.

Malus × *zumi*
☼ ❄ ↔ 10 ft (3 m) ↑ 15 ft (4.5 m)

Small downy-stemmed tree, pyramidal habit. Natural Japanese hybrid of *M. baccata* var. *mandshurica* and *M. sieboldii*. Leaves taper to fine point, scalloped to lobed edges. Pink buds, in spring, open to white flowers, 1¼ in (30 mm) wide. Small red fruit. *M.* × *z.* var. *calocarpa*, smaller flowers, leaves smooth-edged on fruiting spurs, lobed elsewhere. Zones 5–9.

Malus Hybrid Cultivars
☼ ❄ ↔ 5–25 ft (1.5–8 m) ↑ 10–40 ft (3–12 m)

Numerous crabapple cultivars raised, many in USA. Most grown for floral display, some for decorative fruit, and larger fruit of some eaten fresh or as preserves. Parent with most influence is *M. pumila* 'Niedzwetzkyana', originating from single tree with red flowers and purple-red new foliage, discovered in central Asia before 1900. 'Adirondack', 12 ft (3.5 m) high, white flowers with traces of pink, fruit red to orange-red; 'Almey', deep reddish pink flowers, small fruit; 'Beverly', 20 ft (6 m) high, white single flowers, red fruit; 'Brandywine', 20 ft (6 m) high, double fragrant flowers of rose pink, yellow-green fruit; 'Butterball', 25 ft (8 m) high, pinkish white flowers, orange-yellow fruit; 'Chilko', single purple-pink flowers, red to crimson fruit; 'Christmas Holly' ★, 15 ft (4.5 m) high, single white flowers, fruit holly-like, bright red; 'Dolgo', white flowers, 15 ft (4.5 m) high, single white flowers, fruit coral to orange-gold; 'Golden Hornet', single white flowers, fruit lime-yellow; 'Gorgeous', single white flowers, fruit crimson to orange-red; 'Harvest Gold', single white flowers, golden fruit, disease resistant; 'John Downie', single white flowers, fruit orange with red cheeks, disease resistant; 'Madonna', 20 ft (6 m) high, flowers large, double, fragrant, white; 'Mary Potter', 20 ft (6 m) high, bright pink flowers, deep red to purple-red fruit; 'Narragansett', 12 ft (3.5 m) high, single white flowers, pink hue, shiny cherry red fruit, disease resistant; 'Pink Perfection', sterile, pink and white double flowers; 'Profusion', 20 ft (6 m) high, deep rose pink single flowers, fruit maroon to blood red; 'Red Sentinel', early white flowers, red fruit; 'Royalty', 15 ft (4.5 m) high, purple-red flowers and fruit; 'White Angel' (syn. 'Inglis'), white flowers, small red fruit; 'White Cascade', 15 ft (4.5 m) high, single white flowers, green-yellow fruit, disease resistant; 'Winter Gold', 20 ft (6 m) high, single white flowers, fruit bright lemon yellow. Zones 4–9.

MALVAVISCUS

This genus consists of 3 species of Central and South American evergreen shrubs from the mallow (Malvaceae) family. Their broad downy leaves are often lobed. They have unusually shaped flowers, borne singly in the leaf axils or in small clusters at the ends of branches. They are bright orange-red and usually held upright.

Malvaviscus penduliflorus

The long petals stay partly furled, never really opening fully, and from their center emerges a long hibiscus-like column. Small red berries follow the flowers.

CULTIVATION: Although able to withstand the very lightest frosts, these shrubs are best grown in warm subtropical to tropical areas. They thrive in moist, humus-rich, well-drained soil and can be grown in sun or part-shade. Their branches have a tendency to die back and are often attacked by boring grubs, so some pruning, thinning, and trimming is necessary. Propagate from seed or half-hardened cuttings.

Malvaviscus arboreus
TURK'S CAP, WAX MALLOW

☼ ❄ ↔ 10 ft (3 m) ↑ 12–15 ft (3.5–4.5 m)

Shrub from southern Texas and Florida, USA, to Peru and Brazil. Velvety ovate to heart-shaped leaves, may be 3-lobed. Long-stemmed rich red flowers, face upward or slightly bent, in summer. *M. a.* var. *drummondii*, brilliant reddish orange hibiscus-like flowers, swirled petals never fully open, in late summer–autumn. Zones 8–12.

Malvaviscus penduliflorus
syn. *Malvaviscus arboreus* var. *penduliflorus*

CARDINAL'S HAT, SLEEPING HIBISCUS

☼ ⚘ ↔ 10 ft (3 m) ↑ 12–15 ft (3.5–4.5 m)

Mexican shrub, similar to *M. arboreus*. Less hairy leaves. Larger, pendulous rather than upright, red flowers in summer. Zones 11–12.

MAYTENUS

This genus of the spindle-tree (Celastraceae) family, with more than 200 species, occurs in southern Europe, Africa, tropical and eastern Asia, Central and South America, and Australia. Trees, shrubs, or scrambling shrubs, all are evergreen, some with rhizomes. Leaves are simple, smooth-edged or toothed. The small, usually whitish flowers can be bisexual; there may be separate males and females on the same plant or on different plants. The leathery or woody fruit are 2- to 5-celled capsules; in a few species they are fleshy, the seeds partly or wholly surrounded by a fleshy aril. Extracts from some species have been locally used for medicinal purposes. CULTIVATION: Frost hardiness varies. All species should be grown in a sunny position in well-drained soil. Propagate from seed sown while as fresh as possible, or from cuttings.

Maytenus boaria ★

MAITEN, MAYTEN

☼ ❄ ↔ 30 ft (9 m) ↑ 70 ft (21 m)

Tree or large shrub from forests in Chile, Argentina, Bolivia, Paraguay, and southern Brazil. Glossy dark green leaves with finely toothed edges. Small, greenish, separate male and female flowers in spring. Fruit 3- to 5-celled, orange-red, aril red. Zones 8–11.

MEGASKEPASMA

The sole species in this genus from the acanthus (Acanthaceae) family is an evergreen shrub from Venezuela. It is a lushly foliaged plant with flowers that are striking in both color and shape. These appear throughout most of the year. This plant is a must for any warm-climate garden; it is also useful as a plant for large conservatories and greenhouses. CULTIVATION: This shrub needs warmth, moisture, and humidity to do well. Given the right climate, a humus-rich soil, and regular feeding, it is the very epitome of a luxuriant tropical plant. Because its stems are soft and pliable it can be espaliered against a sheltered wall in cooler zones. Propagate from seed or half-hardened cuttings.

Megaskepasma erythrochlamys

BRAZILIAN RED CLOAK

☼ ❄ ↔ 4 ft (1.2 m) ↑ 10 ft (3 m)

Evergreen shrub from Venezuela. Heavily veined, semi-glossy, mid-green leaves. White or pale pink flowers, on upright red spikes, almost enclosed by red bracts; held above foliage. Zones 10–12.

MELALEUCA

There are approximately 220 species in this genus of evergreen shrubs and trees, mostly native to Australia, from the myrtle (Myrtaceae) family. Some species are known as paperbarks for their ornamental, papery-textured, creamy white or pale brown bark that peels off in layers, but the majority have non-papery bark. The nectar-rich flowers, with numerous stamens united into 5 bundles, are grouped into dense spikes or heads and range in color from white, yellow, and orange to pink, red, and purple. Small woody seed capsules often persist on the branches. CULTIVATION: Most melaleucas are easily grown in full sun or part-shade in acidic well-drained soil. Fast-growing and adaptable plants, they can withstand pollution, some degree of coastal exposure, and moist poorly drained soil. Most species will withstand light frosts if given full sun; some species will tolerate heavy frosts. Shrubby species respond well to clipping after flowering and can be used for hedges and screens. Propagate from seed or cuttings.

Melaleuca armillaris

BRACELET HONEY MYRTLE

☼ ❄ ↔ 12 ft (3.5 m) ↑ 25 ft (8 m)

Tall shrub or small tree from southeastern coastal Australia. Spreading canopy of narrow dark green leaves. White flowers, in small cylindrical heads, in late spring–summer. Zones 9–11.

Melaleuca bracteata

BLACK TEA-TREE, RIVER TEA-TREE

☼ ❄ ↔ 20 ft (6 m) ↑ 30 ft (9 m)

Variable shrub or small tree from tropical and central Australian watercourses. Soft, linear, bright green leaves. Profuse creamy white flowers, in heads at branch ends or in short spikes. in spring. 'Golden Gem', to 6 ft (1.8 m) high, rich golden yellow leaves, colorful in early spring; 'Revolution Gold', reddish young stems, golden foliage, bushy upright habit, to 12 ft (3.5 m) high; 'Revolution Green', to 10 ft (3 m) high, fine bright green foliage. Zones 9–12.

Melaleuca fulgens

SCARLET HONEY MYRTLE

☼ ❄ ↔ 6 ft (1.8 m) ↑ 10 ft (3 m)

Erect shrub from semi-arid Western Australia. Narrow linear leaves. Spikes of red, orange, or pink flowers, on older stems, in spring–summer. *M. f.* subsp. *steedmanii*, leaves obovate, flat. Zones 8–11.

Maytenus boaria

Megaskepasma erythrochlamys

Melaleuca fulgens

Melaleuca quinquenervia, in the wild, New Caledonia

Melaleuca hypericifolia

HILLOCK BUSH

☼ ❧ ↔15 ft (4.5 m) ↕15 ft (4.5 m)

Tall, often spreading shrub from southeastern Australia. Slightly pendulous branches, oblong leaves in opposite pairs. Showy orange-red flowers, in cylindrical spikes, to 2 in (5 cm) long, in late spring–mid-summer. Tolerates exposure to salt-laden winds. Zones 9–11.

Melaleuca incana

GRAY HONEY MYRTLE

☼ ❋ ↔10 ft (3 m) ↕10 ft (3 m)

Dense weeping shrub from southwest Western Australia, grows naturally in wet situations. Gray-green linear leaves, often softly hairy, prominent oil glands. Creamy yellow flowers, in oval spikes, at branch ends, in early spring–mid-summer. Zones 8–11.

Melaleuca lateritia

ROBIN REDBREAST BUSH

☼ ❧ ↔3 ft (0.9 m) ↕6 ft (1.8 m)

Multi-stemmed shrub from Western Australia. Light green linear leaves, aromatic when crushed. Spikes to 3 in (8 cm) long of orange-red flowers, in spring–summer, other times sporadically. Zones 9–11.

Melaleuca leucadendra

CAJEPUT, WEEPING PAPERBARK

☼ ❧ ↔30 ft (9 m) ↕90 ft (27 m)

Spreading tree, pendulous branches and foliage, from tropical northern Australia. White to pale brown papery bark. Curved, thin-textured, lance-shaped leaves. Nectar-rich creamy white flowers, in spikes, in autumn–winter. Zones 10–12.

Melaleuca linariifolia

FLAX-LEAFED PAPERBARK, SNOW IN SUMMER

☼ ❋ ↔10 ft (3 m) ↕20 ft (6 m)

Bushy tree from eastern Australia. Creamy papery bark. Soft dark green foliage. Masses of creamy white flowers, in spikes, to 1½ in (35 mm) long, in early summer. 'Snowstorm' ★, prolific-flowering, to 5 ft (1.5 m) tall. Zones 8–11.

Melaleuca pulchella

☼ ❋ ↔6 ft (1.8 m) ↕6 ft (1.8 m)

Spreading shrub from southern coastal heathland of Western Australia. Small, crowded, oblong leaves. Mauve-pink flowers, large, curved claw-like stamens, in late spring–summer. Zones 8–11.

Melaleuca quinquenervia

BROAD-LEAFED PAPERBARK

☼ ❧ ↔20 ft (6 m) ↕30–50 ft (9–15 m)

Found in swampy areas in coastal eastern Australia, New Guinea, and New Caledonia. Thick, creamy, papery bark. Leathery lance-shaped leaves. Spikes of nectar-rich creamy white flowers, at ends of branches or in leaf axils, in late spring. Zones 10–12.

Melaleuca radula

GRACEFUL HONEY MYRTLE

☼ ❋ ↔6 ft (1.8 m) ↕6 ft (1.8 m)

Spreading, rather open shrub from Western Australia. Leaves narrow, linear, with raised oil glands. Pink to purple flowers, in long loose spikes, on older wood, in winter–spring. Zones 8–11.

Melaleuca thymifolia

THYME HONEY MYRTLE

☼ ❋ ↔3 ft (0.9 m) ↕3 ft (0.9 m)

Small, spreading, aromatic shrub from damp places in eastern Australia. Slender branches, small narrow-elliptic leaves. Fringed, claw-like, mauve-purple flowers, in irregular clusters, 1½ in (35 mm) long, on older wood, throughout year. 'Cotton Candy', mauve flowers; 'White Lace', white flowers. Zones 8–11.

MELASTOMA

This genus of around 70 species of tropical and subtropical shrubs from the melastoma (Melastomataceae) family is allied to the similar *Tibouchina*, and occurs primarily in tropical Asia. These plants have attractive heavily veined leaves that are often bristly above, with a downy underside. The leaves are oblong to lance-shaped with smooth edges, their size varying with the species. The flowers, borne in small heads at the ends of branches, are 5-petalled, usually in pink to soft purple shades, and are sometimes scented; they appear from 2 small bracts and have bristly calyces. Small, usually inconspicuous berries follow. CULTIVATION: These tender warm-climate shrubs are best grown in reasonably fertile, moist, humus-rich, well-drained soil in sun or part-shade. They can be pruned after flowering, or in spring in cooler climates, to remove any winter damage. Propagation is usually from half-hardened cuttings taken in summer.

Melastoma malabathricum

Melastoma malabathricum

☼ ❧ ↔5 ft (1.5 m) ↕6–8 ft (1.8–2.4 m)

Shrub from India and Southeast Asia, where its red berries are used medicinally. Scaly branches; 3- to 5-veined, velvety, broad, lance-shaped leaves. Up to 5 mauve to purple flower-heads, almost year-round. Zones 10–12.

MELIA

This small genus of 3 species in the mahogany (Meliaceae) family is native to southern Asia, Australasia, and tropical Africa. All are deciduous trees with alternate bipinnate leaves and showy flowers in long panicles. They are valued for their rapid growth and adaptability to a range of soils and climates, including dry conditions. CULTIVATION: These trees need good drainage. Severe frost will defoliate them, but is unlikely to do permanent damage. Pruning is not normally necessary, apart from the removal of competing leaders in the early stages. Propagate from seed in spring.

Melia azedarach

PERSIAN LILAC, WHITE CEDAR

☼ ❄ ↔ 25 ft (8 m) ↑ 20–80 ft (6–24 m)

Fast-growing tree from southwest Asia to China and Japan and south to Australia. Variable species. Pointed mid-green leaflets. Fragrant lilac flowers, in loose panicles, in summer. Clusters of persistent, rounded, yellow, bead-like fruit, toxic to animals and young children, but not to birds. Zones 8–12.

MELIANTHUS

This genus of 6 species of often leggy shrubs native to South Africa is a member of the honey-flower (Melianthaceae) family. *M. major* is naturalized in India. Small flowers borne in erect bracted racemes produce a large quantity of nectar. Vigorous growers, they are often treated like perennials, being cut back severely to shoot again and inhibit their straggling tendencies. CULTIVATION: Not frost hardy, they grow well in full sun or part-shade in free-draining but moisture-retentive soil. Propagate from seed in spring, softwood cuttings in spring and summer, or rooted suckers in spring.

Melianthus major

HONEY FLOWER

☼/◐ ❄ ↔ 3 ft (0.9 m) ↑ 6–10 ft (1.8–3 m)

Shrub native to hilly grasslands of South Africa. Large, decorative, pinnate leaves, 20 in (50 cm) long, up to 17 oval leaflets, toothed, gray-green. Racemes of brick red tubular flowers in spring–mid-summer. Used in folk medicine. Can be invasive. Zones 8–11.

METASEQUOIA

A genus of a single species of conifer in the cypress (Cupressaceae) family, this plant was long thought to be extinct, known only from fossil remains found in China. In 1941 a Chinese botanist visited a village between Hubei and Sichuan and noticed a deciduous conifer known locally as *shuiskan*. It was found that the tree was identical to the fossil remains. Seed was collected in 1947 and sent to the Arnold Arboretum in the USA, from where it was distributed to botanic gardens throughout the world. Finally named and described in 1948, it has become a popular ornamental tree both in and outside China. The bark is reddish brown, darkening with age. The leaves are green and flattened and turn reddish brown in autumn.

Melianthus major

Melia azedarach Metasequoia glyptostroboides

CULTIVATION: *Metasequoia* species grow rapidly, particularly in a moist but well-drained soil, and have proved hardy and relatively resistant to atmospheric pollution. It is highly regarded as an ornamental for large gardens and parks in cool-temperate areas. Propagate from seed.

Metasequoia glyptostroboides ★

DAWN REDWOOD

☼ ❄ ↔ 20 ft (6 m) ↑ 70 ft (21 m)

Vigorous, quick-growing, deciduous conifer. Cinnamon brown bark. Flattened linear leaves, on short branchlets, turn tawny pink and old gold in autumn. Pendulous dark brown cones on long stalks. Zones 5–10.

METROSIDEROS

This genus is a member of the large myrtle (Myrtaceae) family, which includes *Eucalyptus* and *Psidium* (guava). It is found in South Africa, the Pacific Islands, Australia, and New Zealand. *Metrosideros* contains 50 species of evergreen shrubs, trees, and woody climbers with simple, opposite, often leathery leaves that can be aromatic. Flowers consist of numerous stamens and are crowded into rounded heads, usually in shades of red, pink, or white. CULTIVATION: *Metrosideros* species are best suited to warmer climates, but will grow in any reasonably fertile well-drained soil. *M. excelsa*, in particular, will grow in dry soils of lower fertility and in very exposed coastal conditions. It can be pruned for hedging and used as shelter. In cool climates, plants can be grown in pots, overwintered in a greenhouse and placed outdoors for summer. Propagate from seed sown in spring, or half-hardened cuttings taken in summer.

Metrosideros excelsa ★

NEW ZEALAND CHRISTMAS TREE, POHUTUKAWA

☼ ⚘ ↔ 25 ft (8 m) ↑ 15–50 ft (4.5–15 m)

Shrubby coastal tree from New Zealand. Thick, leathery, oval leaves, dark green above, gray felted below. Red-crimson bottle-brush-like flowerheads in early summer. Young trees susceptible to frost. 'Fire Mountain', orangey scarlet flowers. Zones 9–11.

Metrosideros polymorpha

Michelia yunnanensis

Microbiota decussata

Metrosideros kermadecensis

KERMADEC POHUTUKAWA

☼ ⟶ 15 ft (4.5 m) ↑ 20 ft (6 m)

Native to Kermadec Islands, New Zealand. Similar to *M. excelsa*, but smaller leaves and flowers. Blooms spasmodically year-round. 'Variegatus', wide creamy yellow margin on leaves. Zones 9–11.

Metrosideros polymorpha

OHI'A LEHUA

☼ ⟶ 20 ft (6 m) ↑ 20–50 ft (6–15 m)

Low prostrate shrub or tree from Hawaiian Islands. Bark rough, fissured. Oval to rounded leaves, felted beneath. Bottlebrush-like flowerheads, red to pink and yellow, in spring–summer. Zones 11–12.

MICHELIA

This genus of about 45 species of mostly evergreen trees and shrubs in the magnolia (Magnoliaceae) family is native to tropical and subtropical regions of Asia. All have simple leaves and solitary flowers in leaf axils that are strongly perfumed, especially after nightfall. Oils from some species are extracted for use in perfumes. CULTIVATION: *Michelia* species grow best in a reasonably fertile, well-drained, and lime-free soil in a sunny position with shelter from strong winds. They are not reliably frost hardy. Pruning is seldom necessary apart from the removal of competing leaders. Propagate from seed sown as soon as it is hardened in a warm and humid atmosphere.

Michelia champaca

CHAMPACA

☼ ⟶ 10 ft (3 m) ↑ 100 ft (30 m)

Erect evergreen tree from eastern Himalayan foothills. Leaves bright green, shiny above, dull beneath. Cup-shaped flowers, deep yellow-ish cream, heavily perfumed, in mid-summer–mid-autumn. Fruit pale yellow-green, spotted brown. Zones 10–11.

Michelia doltsopa

☼ ⟶ 20 ft (6 m) ↑ 30 ft (9 m)

Mostly evergreen tree native to western China and eastern Himalayas. Pendulous dark green leaves. Cup-shaped flowers, white to deep cream, greenish hue at base, heavily perfumed, in late winter–spring. 'Silver Cloud' ★, profuse white flowers. Zones 9–11.

Michelia figo

BANANA SHRUB, PORT-WINE MAGNOLIA

☼ ⟶ 10 ft (3 m) ↑ 15 ft (4.5 m)

Medium to large shrub from southeastern China. Small, dark green, glossy leaves. Small purple-brown flowers in spring–summer. Fragrance resembles bananas and vintage port. Zones 9–11.

Michelia yunnanensis

☼ ⟶ 7 ft (2 m) ↑ 15 ft (4.5 m)

Slow-growing shrub or small tree native to China. Brownish velvety covering on young leaves and buds. Leaves variably sized, shaped. Flowers yellow-white, little scent, in late winter–spring. Zones 10–11.

MICROBIOTA

RUSSIAN CYPRESS, SIBERIAN CARPET CYPRESS

This conifer genus in the cypress (Cupressaceae) family contains just one species, commonly found in the mountains of southeastern Siberia above the timber line. It is a small shrub with male and female cones borne on separate plants. CULTIVATION: This shrub is quite adaptable to cultivation in milder climates in moist soil. Propagate from seed or cuttings of half-hardened shoots taken in summer.

Microbiota decussata ★

RUSSIAN CYPRESS

☼ ❄ ⟶ 5 ft (1.5 m) ↑ 2 ft (0.6 m)

Flattened short branches with tiny, scale-like, almost triangular, overlapping leaves. Cones at ends of short branches in summer; females egg-shaped. Foliage turns bronze in cold winters. Zones 3–9.

MILLETTIA

There are about 90 species in this tropical genus of trees, shrubs, and climbers from Africa and southern Asia. They are members of the pea-flower subfamily of the legume (Fabaceae) family. The leaves are alternate and compound, with a terminal leaflet and a pronounced swelling where the leaf stalk joins the stem. Flowers, in large spikes or panicles, are pink, mauve, red, or shades of these colors. Pods are often large, splitting in halves to release round seeds. CULTIVATION: These plants require rich moist soil and ample water in summer. Propagate from seed only, and the seed must be very fresh. Soak overnight in hot water prior to sowing.

Millettia grandis

SOUTH AFRICAN IRONWOOD

☼ ❧ ↔ 30 ft (9 m) ↑ 20–40 ft (6–12 m)

Medium-sized tree from low-altitude coastal eastern South Africa; briefly deciduous in early summer. Leaves compound, 6 to 7 pairs of oblong leaflets, undersurface with silky hairs. Purple pea-flowers, upright spikes, in summer. Fruit large, woody, flat pods. Zones 9–11.

MIMOSA

Allied to *Acacia*, this genus in the mimosa subfamily of the legume (Fabaceae) family consists of some 480 species of herbs, vines, shrubs, and trees. Most are from South and Central America, southern USA, Asia, and Africa. They have bipinnate leaves and often spiny stems. The tiny flowers are white, pink, or lilac, and have long multiple stamens and 4 or 5 petals. They are borne singly or in stalked rounded heads, or in spikes or racemes. The prickly flat seeds split open when mature. Some species are invasive. CULTIVATION: They are best suited to well-drained moderately fertile soil in a sunny frost-free site. Propagate from seed, usually pre-soaked in hot water, or cuttings taken from young growth.

Mimosa pudica

SENSITIVE PLANT

☼ ❧ ↔ 3 ft (0.9 m) ↑ 3 ft (0.9 m)

Native to tropical America. Prickly branching stems. Leaves make "sleep-movements" at night. Leaflets fold together when touched, stalks droop. Light pink to lilac flowers in summer. Zones 10–12.

MONTANOA

In the daisy (Asteraceae) family, this genus from tropical America comprises about 20 species of vines and shrubs. They are erect species with short branches and square stems. The hand-shaped leaves are large and covered with fine hairs. The flowers resemble dahlias, are white with a yellow center, are borne in clusters, and appear throughout summer and into autumn. Reddish brown seeds are borne in the old flowerheads, which have a papery feel. CULTIVATION: Grown for both foliage and flower display, these frost-tender plants need a warm full-sun position in fertile well-watered soil. Once the flowers have finished, the long canes can be hard pruned. Propagate from seed or from root cuttings.

Montanoa bipinnatifida

MEXICAN TREE DAISY

☼ ❧ ↔ 7 ft (2 m) ↑ 10–20 ft (3–6 m)

Evergreen shrub, sometimes tree-like, from southern Mexico. Sparse deeply dissected leaves, on fast-growing brittle canes. Masses of single white daisy flowers in autumn. Zones 10–12.

MORELLA

WAXBERRY

This genus consists of deciduous and evergreen shrubs and trees in the family Myricaceae, all until recently treated as species of *Myrica*. The 40 or so *Morella* species are mostly tropical, mainly from Africa and the Americas, but there are several from cooler areas as well. All have dark gray or brown, slightly rough bark; leaves are simple, arranged spirally on the twigs, mostly narrow and tapering to the

Mimosa pudica

Montanoa bipinnatifida

base, often toothed. Flowers are small and of different sexes, which may be on different plants. Fruit are small globular drupes, rough-surfaced and often wax-coated, in many small clusters. CULTIVATION: Species vary in hardiness, but are not difficult to cultivate in suitable climates and will thrive in well-drained soil that is not strongly alkaline or prone to prolonged drought. Plant in sun to half-day shade, water well in sun, and trim to shape if necessary. Propagate from seed, layers, or half-hardened cuttings.

Morella cerifera

syn. *Myrica cerifera*

WAX MYRTLE

◑ ✽ ↔ 15 ft (4.5 m) ↑ 30 ft (9 m)

Large evergreen shrub or small tree native to most of Central America, West Indies, southern Mexico, and southeastern USA; thrives in shade of other trees. Broad-based lance-shaped leaves. Flowers small, pale yellow-brown, in summer. Tiny fruit. Zones 6–11.

Morella pensylvanica

syn. *Myrica pensylvanica*

BAYBERRY, CANDLEBERRY

☼ ✽ ↔ 4 ft (1.2 m) ↑ 6–10 ft (1.8–3 m)

Semi-evergreen to deciduous shrub, native to coastal eastern North America. Spreading suckering growth habit. Lance-shaped leaves, smooth or toothed edges. Tiny pale gray fruit in summer. Zones 2–8.

Millettia grandis

MURRAYA

This small genus in the rue (Rutaceae) family is related to *Citrus* and consists of 4 species from tropical Asia to Australia. They are shrubs or trees with pinnate dark green leaves, and white perfumed flowers in large panicles. Fruit are small globe- to egg-shaped berries. CULTIVATION: Most are adaptable, but grow best in well-drained mulched soil with added moisture and fertilizer during the growing season. They tolerate full sun to part-shade and perform best in a warm frost-free climate. Propagate from seed or cuttings.

Murraya paniculata

COSMETIC BARK, JASMINE ORANGE, ORANGE JESSAMINE

☼ ⊰ ↔ 10 ft (3 m) ↑ 10 ft (3 m)

Globe-shaped shrub from Southeast Asia to Australia, many branches. Pinnate leaves pale green, maturing to dark glossy green. Orange blossom-like flowers, white, sweetly perfumed, in spring. Orange to red berries. Zones 10–12.

MUSSAENDA

This genus contains about 100 species of evergreen subshrubs, shrubs, and climbers native to tropical areas of Africa and Asia. It belongs to the madder (Rubiaceae) family. They have pointed elliptical leaves, opposite or in whorls. Small tubular flowers borne throughout the year are of secondary importance to the colorful enlarged sepals that accompany them. CULTIVATION: Plant in a tropical greenhouse in temperate climates. They require direct sunlight and should be watered well in the growing season. In warmer climates they can be grown outdoors in sun or part-shade, in rich well-drained soil. Propagate from seed sown in spring, or half-hardened cuttings taken in summer.

Mussaenda erythrophylla

ASHANTI BLOOD

☼ ✦ ↔ 5 ft (1.5 m) ↑ 10 ft (3 m)

Evergreen shrub native to tropical Africa. Erect or climbing, slightly downy, reddish stems. Flowers in dense, slightly drooping panicles,

Murraya paniculata

Mussaenda, Hybrid Cultivar, 'Queen Sirikit'

cream to pink and red, brilliant red sepals, in spring. 'Flamingo', bright pink sepals; 'Pink Dancer', salmon pink sepals. Zones 11–12.

Mussaenda Hybrid Cultivars

☼ ✦ ↔ 5–7 ft (1.5–2 m) ↑ 10 ft (3 m)

Hybrids often placed under *M. philippica* but may have originated from crosses between *M. erythrophylla* and *M. frondosa*. 'Aurorae', bushy shrub to 10 ft (3 m) high, yellow flowers, sepals large, white, pendulous; 'Queen Sirikit', salmon pink sepals. Zones 11–12.

MYOPORUM

This genus in the boobialla (Myoporaceae) family contains around 30 species, the majority from Australia, others from Mauritius, eastern Malaysia, New Zealand, and Hawaii, USA. Mostly small to medium-size shrubs, sometimes trees, and a few ground covers, they have simple variably shaped leaves, often leathery or succulent, and often resinous vegetative parts. The small, somewhat bell-shaped, white, sometimes pinkish, flowers occur in clusters or singly along the branches. They are followed by mainly small, often succulent fruit favored by birds. CULTIVATION: Most species are fairly adaptable, requiring good drainage and full sun or part-shade. Many will tolerate alkaline soils, medium to heavy frosts, and lengthy dry periods. Prune lightly to maintain shape. Propagate from fresh seed, cuttings, or by division of layered stems for ground covers.

Myoporum floribundum

WEEPING BOOBIALLA

☼ ⊰ ↔ 8 ft (2.4 m) ↑ 10 ft (3 m)

Native of New South Wales and Victoria, Australia. Spreading habit, weeping branches. Leaves narrow, dark green, aromatic when crushed. White, rarely mauve, perfumed flowers, in massed clusters of false spikes, in winter–summer. Zones 9–11.

Myoporum laetum

NGAIO

☼ ⊰ ↔ 10 ft (3 m) ↑ 15–30 ft (4.5–9 m)

Large shrub or small tree from New Zealand. Green fleshy leaves, lance-shaped to oblong or obovate, sticky shoot tips. White bell flowers, purple spots, in cymes, in summer. Maroon fruit. Zones 9–11.

MYRICA

syn. *Gale*

As now understood (following the removal of most species to *Morella*), this genus consists of only 2 species, one widespread in northern Europe, Asia, and North America, the other restricted to the lower slopes of California's Sierra Nevada. It gives its name to the Myricaceae family. The plants are deciduous low shrubs spreading by suckers, occurring in the wild in boggy ground and along stream banks. Leaves are small, toothed near their tip, aromatic when crushed, and arranged spirally on the reddish twigs. Flowers are small, in groups of catkins appearing before the leaves, and of

Myoporum floribundum

Myrtus communis

Nageia nagi

different sexes on different plants but the plants may switch sexes. Fruit are small, dry, flattened drupes with tiny resin dots.
CULTIVATION: Occasionally planted in woodland gardens for their fragrant foliage, they tolerate wet ground but grow equally well in well-drained soil as long as moisture is adequate. Propagate from seed, which should be cold-stratified, or by division of clumps.

Myrica gale
syns *Gale belgica*, *G. palustris*
BOG MYRTLE, SWEET GALE
☼/◐ ❂ ❄ ↔ 4 ft (1.2 m) ↕ 3–6 ft (0.9–1.8 m)
Deciduous shrub found from Europe to Japan and North America. Leaves 1–2½ in (2.5–6 cm) wide, toothed. Buff-yellow fruit, in massed spikes, in summer. Grows well in damp soil. Zones 3–9.

MYRTUS
Although *Myrtus* was once a large genus in the myrtle (Myrtaceae) family, the Southern Hemisphere species have now been classified under other genera, leaving only 2 species, both native to the Mediterranean region. These are evergreen shrubs with simple, opposite, dark green leaves and small, fragrant, white flowers in summer.
CULTIVATION: Grow these shrubs in a moderately fertile well-drained soil in a mild climate. Normally self-shaping into a rounded bush, they will respond to light tip-pruning in late winter, which produces denser foliage and a more compact habit. They prefer a position sheltered from cold drying winds. Propagate from half-hardened cuttings taken any time between spring and early winter.

Myrtus communis
COMMON MYRTLE, TRUE MYRTLE
☼ ❄ ↔ 10 ft (3 m) ↕ 10 ft (3 m)
Shrub from Mediterranean region. Leaves dark green above, paler beneath, aromatic when crushed. Flowers solitary, in upper axils, white, reddish pink shading on reverse; conspicuous stamens, in spring. Oval purplish berries. 'Citrifolium', cream flowers; 'Variegata', leaves with cream margin. Zones 8–11.

NAGEIA
This conifer genus in the plum-pine (Podocarpaceae) family consists of 6 species and occurs in

the south of India, China, and Japan, in Thailand, the Malay Peninsula, the Philippines, Indonesia, New Guinea, and New Caledonia. They are evergreen trees with broad, lance-shaped, multi-veined leaves, unusual in conifers.
CULTIVATION: Only *N. nagi* is cultivated, requiring well-drained soil and water during dry periods. Propagate from seed or cuttings.

Nageia nagi
syn. *Podocarpus nagi*
NAGI
❂ ❄ ↔ 15 ft (4.5 m) ↕ 70 ft (21 m)
Native to Japan, China, and Taiwan. Smooth dark brown bark, ageing to gray; almost horizontal branches. Leaves oval or oblong, glossy deep green, paler underside, parallel veins. Seed cones occur singly, bluish green, globular, ripen in late autumn. Zones 8–10.

NANDINA
HEAVENLY BAMBOO, SACRED BAMBOO
Just a single species of small evergreen shrub is contained in this genus. Despite its common name, this plant is a member of the barberry (Berberidaceae) family. It is grown for its colorful foliage and the bright red berries it bears in autumn. Plants are either male or female; some hermaphroditic cultivars are now available.
CULTIVATION: *Nandina* is easily grown in a rich soil that is moist but well drained. Leaf color is more intense when planted in full sun. For the best berry crops, make a group planting to ensure cross-pollination. Leggy older stems can be cut back to the base in summer. Propagate from cuttings taken in summer, as seed can be quite difficult to germinate.

Nandina domestica

Nandina domestica
HEAVENLY BAMBOO
☼ ❄ ↔ 4 ft (1.2 m) ↕ 7 ft (2 m)
Native from India to Japan. Leaves bipinnate or tripinnate, lance-shaped, soft, tinted pinkish red when young, green and glossy with age; yellow, red, and purplish hues in winter. Small creamy white flowers in summer. Popular cultivars include 'Filamentosa', 'Firepower', 'Gulf Stream', 'Harbor Dwarf', 'Nana' (syn. 'Pygmy'), 'Nana Purpurea', 'Richmond', and 'Woods Dwarf'. Zones 7–10.

NEILLIA

This genus in the rose (Rosaceae) family contains 10 deciduous species that are closely related to *Spiraea* and are found in Asia, from the eastern Himalayas to the western side of the Malay Peninsula. They are arching shrubs with prominently veined 3-lobed leaves that color to yellow in autumn. In winter their attractive form, with a zigzag pattern of twigs, is revealed. Slender panicles or racemes of small bell-shaped flowers are borne in spring or summer.

CULTIVATION: Although not widely grown, these shrubs are easily cultivated in all but the driest soils, in full sun or part-shade. After flowering, cut out old stems at ground level to encourage new growth and retain the arching habit. Propagate from seed, from cuttings in summer, or by the removal of suckers in autumn.

Neillia thibetica

Neillia sinensis ★

☼ ❄ ↔ 7 ft (2 m) ↑ 10 ft (3 m)

Native to central China. Upright habit. Smooth brown branchlets, bark exfoliates. Lobed leaves, serrated edges, purplish bronze when young. Short terminal racemes of white to pale pink bell-shaped flowers in spring–summer. Zones 6–10.

Neillia thibetica

syn. *Neillia longiracemosa*

☼ ❄ ↔ 6 ft (1.8 m) ↑ 6 ft (1.8 m)

Native to western China. Deciduous shrub with upright habit. Branchlets covered in fine down. Serrated-edged leaves prominently veined, downy beneath. Slender racemes, to 6 in (15 cm) long, of pale pink bell-shaped flowers in summer. Zones 6–10.

NERIUM

OLEANDER

This genus of a single species from North Africa, the Middle East, northern India, and southern China belongs to the dogbane (Apocynaceae) family. It is a long-flowering evergreen shrub or small tree, with simple, smooth-edged, narrow leaves, and yellow, white, pink, and tangerine flowers. Petals are fused into a narrow tube but flaring from the end into a disc or a shallow cup, and the flowers are borne in terminal clusters.

CULTIVATION: Tolerant of salt-laden winds and dry sandy soils, it can be invasive. It will grow in almost any type of soil except wet, but likes full sun, and tolerates light frosts if given a sheltered position. For a dense shrubby habit, remove flowering shoots and prune well-established plants in winter every 3 years. As these plants are extremely poisonous, wear protective clothing when pruning and dispose of prunings carefully (do not burn). Propagate from half-hardened cuttings taken in autumn, or seed in spring.

Nerium oleander

☼ ❄ ↔ 8 ft (2.4 m) ↑ 10 ft (3 m)

Evergreen shrub. Many erect shoots from base. Leaves dark green above, paler below. Flowers in late spring–early autumn, and sporadically until early winter. Many single- and double-flowered cultivars in range of colors. Double cultivars have petals crimped,

waved on outer edge. 'Casablanca', faded pink flowers, almost white; 'Delphine', single dark purplish red flowers; 'Docteur Golfin', single, mauve tinged, cherry red flowers; 'Splendens', deep rose pink double flowers; 'Splendens Giganteum Variegatum', creamy yellow edge to leaves. Zones 8–11.

NEVIUSIA

Related to *Kerria*, this genus consists of a single species of deciduous shrub in the rose (Rosaceae) family. It is a threatened species in its native Alabama, USA. It increases in width by means of rooted branches. The white flowers are petal-less, with many prominent stamens.

CULTIVATION: This shrub is suitable for the border or woodland edge. It grows in moderately fertile soils and should be watered well in periods of drought. After flowering, the old and dead wood should be cut out at the base. Propagate from seed or cuttings, or by division.

Neviusia alabamensis

ALABAMA SNOW WREATH

☼/❉ ❄ ↔ 5 ft (1.5 m) ↑ 5 ft (1.5 m)

From State of Alabama in southern USA. Suckering plant, forms wide multi-stemmed shrub. Leaves have serrated edges, downy beneath. Small flowers, with fluffy mass of white stamens, in spring. Zones 5–9. ❄

NOTHOFAGUS

SOUTHERN BEECH

There are approximately 35 species in this genus, native to temperate South America, New Zealand, New Guinea, New Caledonia, and southeastern Australia including Tasmania. Members of the beech (Fagaceae) family, all are evergreen or deciduous forest trees, with straight trunks and light lacy foliage. In native habitats, they are more stunted and more sparsely foliaged at higher altitudes. Leaves are dark green, or occasionally red, with mostly toothed edges, and commonly arranged in more or less a single plane. Tiny flowers are followed by nutlets. The timber is fine grained and valued for cabinetwork.

Neviusia alabamensis

CULTIVATION: A moderately rich and well-drained acid soil is preferred with shelter from salt-laden winds. They require regular watering until established. Propagate from fresh seed in autumn, from hardwood cuttings in summer, or by layering.

Nothofagus antarctica
ANTARCTIC BEECH, NIRRE
☼ ❅ ↔ 20 ft (6 m) ↑ 40 ft (12 m)

From Chile. Fast-growing deciduous tree, open habit, often with twisted trunk and main limbs. Leaves small, dark green, glossy, rounded to heart-shaped, irregularly toothed margins, turn yellow in autumn. Zones 8–9.

Nothofagus cunninghamii
MYRTLE BEECH, TASMANIAN BEECH
☼ ❅ ↔ 8–30 ft (2.4–9 m) ↑ 5–100 ft (1.5–30 m)

From cool-temperate forests in Tasmania and Victoria, Australia. Evergreen straight-trunked tree, variable habit. Dark green crown; small, shiny, toothed leaves in fan-like fronds. Young foliage reddish tinge. Best grown on basaltic soils. Zones 8–9.

Nothofagus fusca
NEW ZEALAND RED BEECH, RED BEECH
☼ ❅ ↔ 25 ft (8 m) ↑ 100 ft (30 m)

From New Zealand. Bark dark rusty brown to almost black, furrowed, flaking on old trees. Coarsely serrated oval leaves, turn bright red on young trees in winter, remain green on older trees before falling. Zones 8–9.

Nothofagus menziesii
NEW ZEALAND SILVER BEECH
☼ ❅ ↔ 30 ft (9 m) ↑ 60 ft (18 m)

Native to New Zealand. Evergreen tree, can develop massive trunk. Distinctive, horizontally banded and flaking, gray bark. Dense dark green leaves, tiny, oval to round, coarsely serrated. New spring foliage light green. Zones 8–9.

Nothofagus solanderi
BLACK BEECH, MOUNTAIN BEECH, NEW ZEALAND BEECH
☼ ❅ ↔ 25 ft (8 m) ↑ 60 ft (18 m)

From hilly and mountain habitats in New Zealand. Evergreen tree, distinctive black bark. Leaves shiny, bronze-green, small, oblong, paler on reverse, in fan-like sprays. Masses of small red-brown flowers in spring. Timber valued for construction. *N. s.* var. *cliffortioides*, oval leaves, more sharply pointed. Zones 8–9.

NYSSA

This is a small genus that includes about 5 species of deciduous trees from North America and eastern and southeastern Asia. It is a member of the dogwood (Cornaceae) family. They are all noted for their spectacular foliage in autumn, which ranges in color from soft green to pale yellow, gold, orange, and brown. Most species

Nothofagus solanderi var. *cliffortioides,* in the wild, New Zealand

inhabit moist land on the edges of streams, lakes, and swamps, and are rarely successful on dry soils. The leaves are simple, the flowers are inconspicuous, and the fruit are small and bluish.

CULTIVATION: These plants prefer well-drained, moist, fertile soil in full sun or part-shade. Little pruning is required, apart from the removal of competing leaders in the early stages. Propagate from seed collected as soon as it is ripe in autumn. Sow immediately, before it dries out. Alternatively, species can be propagated from half-hardened cuttings in mid-summer.

Nyssa aquatica
COTTON GUM, TUPELO GUM, WATER TUPELO
☼ ❅ ↔ 15 ft (4.5 m) ↑ 50 ft (15 m)

Native to southeastern USA, rare in wild. Erect stems, dome-shaped crown. Leaves ovate-oblong, downy underneath, serrated. Flowers greenish white, in axillary clusters, in summer. Fruit deep mauve. Zones 5–10.

Nyssa sinensis
CHINESE TUPELO
☼ ❅ ↔ 30 ft (9 m) ↑ 40 ft (12 m)

Nyssa sinensis

Rare species from China, beautiful small tree or large shrub, open habit. Leaves narrowly ovate, to 6 in (15 cm) long, juvenile foliage red. Leaves turn to almost every shade of red and yellow in autumn. Zones 7–10.

Nyssa sylvatica ★
BLACK GUM, BLACK TUPELO, SOUR GUM, TUPELO
☼ ❅ ↔ 30 ft (9 m) ↑ 50 ft (15 m)

Native to North America, from Canada to Gulf of Mexico. Deciduous tree with predominantly horizontal branches. Smooth-edged leaves, shiny dark green, paler beneath; turn shades of orange, scarlet, and purplish red in autumn. Small bluish black fruit. 'Sheffield Park', leaves start to color 2 to 3 weeks earlier than species; 'Wisley Bonfire', symmetrical form. Zones 3–10.

Ochna kirkii, fruitlet

Odontonema schomburgkianum

Olea capensis

OCHNA

There are around 80 species of deciduous and evergreen trees and shrubs included in this genus, a member of the family Ochnaceae, all occurring in Africa and Asia. The leaves of all species are simple, alternate, and have toothed margins. The flowers are borne singly or in clusters, with 5 to 10 petals that fall soon after the flower opens. In the fruit, the 5 sepals and the floral receptacle become swollen and brightly colored, with 3 or more fleshy 1-seeded fruitlets attached, usually contrasting in color when ripe.
CULTIVATION: These plants are marginally frost hardy, so they need shelter from frosts in their early years, but otherwise they can be grown in a range of well-drained soils in either full sun or part-shade in tropical and subtropical climates. Propagation is from seed or cuttings.

Ochna kirkii

☼ ❄ ↔ 7 ft (2 m) ↑ 10 ft (3 m)
From Mozambique, found along streamsides. Leaves thick, leathery, oblong to elliptic, heart-shaped base, with toothed margins. Yellow flowers, borne in terminal clusters, in spring. Bright red calyx. Zones 10–11.

Ochna serrulata

CARNIVAL BUSH, MICKEY MOUSE PLANT
☼ ❄ ↔ 7 ft (2 m) ↑ 12 ft (3.5 m)
Small tree from eastern South Africa. Bark smooth, brown. Leaves elliptic, glossy, dark green, paler undersurface, toothed margins. Fragrant yellow flowers in spring–early summer. Fleshy bright red calyx, fruitlets globular, black when ripe. Serious environmental weed in some areas. Zones 9–11.

ODONTONEMA

Native to the tropical regions of America, this genus in the acanthus (Acanthaceae) family consists of some 25 species of evergreen perennial herbs and shrubs with opposite pairs of simple, glossy green, smooth-edged leaves. They are grown for their delightful, waxy-textured, 2-lipped or 5-lobed, tubular flowers in colors of red, yellow, or white that are carried in upright terminal spikes or, in some species, drooping sprays.
CULTIVATION: Frost tender, these warm-climate plants need rich soil and regular watering. They like well-drained soil in full sun

or bright filtered light in a spot that is sheltered from the wind. Keep them neat and bushy by pinching out the growing tips. Propagate from cuttings in summer.

Odontonema callistachyum

syn. *Odontonema strictum*
FIRESPIKE
☼ ❄ ↔ 3–6 ft (0.9–1.8 m) ↑ 6 ft (1.8 m)
Evergreen shrub native to Central America. Upright growth habit, with glossy, wavy-edged, oblong leaves tapering to fine point. Showy inflorescences of waxy-textured crimson flowers, borne at branch tips, through most of year. Excellent container plant for large conservatories. Zones 10–12.

Odontonema schomburgkianum

☼ ❄ ↔ 2 ft (0.6 m) ↑ 6 ft (1.8 m)
Erect sparsely branched shrub from Colombia. Pale green leaves, lance-shaped to oblong, to 8 in (20 cm) long. Waxy crimson to scarlet flowers, in slender drooping racemes to 3 ft (0.9 m) long, in spring. Zones 10–12.

OLEA

OLIVE
This famous genus, which belongs to the olive (Oleaceae) family, includes some 20 species of evergreen shrubs and trees with a wide distribution throughout the warm-temperate areas of the world (excluding the Americas). With age, the branches become wonderfully gnarled and twisted, adding an interesting dimension to the garden. Each leaf is usually a simple narrow ellipse, deep green above and greenish white below. The flowers are massed in panicles. They are followed by the familiar fleshy drupes, each of which contains a hard pit or stone.
CULTIVATION: Olives vary in hardiness, though none are very frost tolerant, especially when the plants are young. If grown for their fruit, olives require a climate with distinct seasons. Flowering, cropping, and ripening are invariably best on trees grown in full sun with relatively mild winters and long hot summers that gradually decline into autumn. Olives are tolerant of most soil types and are very drought tolerant once they are established; fertile well-drained soil will yield a better crop. Propagate from seed, heel cuttings, or suckers.

Olea capensis

BLACK IRONWOOD

☼ ⚘ ↔ 15 ft (4.5 m) ↑ 50 ft (15 m)

South African species. Glossy deep green leaves. White flowers in spring. Small black fruit, edible after appropriate treatment but seldom used. Heartwood is very hard, sometimes used for producing small items such as bowls, utensils, and handles. Zones 9–11.

OLEARIA

syn. *Pachystegia*

There are about 180 species of evergreen shrubs and small trees in this genus, of the daisy (Asteraceae) family. Most are native to Australia, with some from New Zealand, New Guinea, and Lord Howe Island. The leaves are sometimes aromatic and vary in size but are usually leathery with gray, white, or buff, tiny, soft hairs on the underside. Daisy flowers range in color from white to pink, blue, and purple and are often borne so profusely that they smother the foliage. CULTIVATION: Most species grow in well-drained moderately fertile soil in either full sun or part-shade. In cool-temperate climates the majority are not reliably hardy below about 23°F (–5°C) and need the protection of a warm wall. Prune after flowering to maintain the plant's bushy habit. Some are suitable for hedging and shelter planting, tolerating strong winds, including coastal conditions. Propagate from seed or from half-hardened cuttings taken in summer and autumn.

Olearia furfuracea

Olearia albida

DAISY BUSH, TANGURU

☼ ❊ ↔ 7 ft (2 m) ↑ 10 ft (3 m)

Vigorous species found in coastal forests of New Zealand's North Island. Erect shrub or small tree with oblong leaves, downy white underside. Large panicles of white daisy flowers in summer–autumn. Zones 8–10.

Olearia furfuracea

☼ ❊ ↔ 7 ft (2 m) ↑ 8–15 ft (2.4–4.5 m)

Native to New Zealand's North Island. Well-branched shrub or small tree. Dark green oblong leaves, buff hairy coating beneath, wavy margins. Large clusters of small white daisy flowers in summer. Zones 8–11.

Olearia insignis

syn. *Pachystegia insignis*

MARLBOROUGH ROCK DAISY

☼ ⚘ ↔ 3–7 ft (0.9–2 m) ↑ 3–7 ft (0.9–2 m)

Spreading shrub from New Zealand. White or brown down on stems and underside of leathery oval leaves. Large, glistening, white daisy flowers with yellow center, open from felted drumstick-like heads, in summer. Zones 9–11.

Olearia macrodonta

☼ ❊ ↔ 7 ft (2 m) ↑ 7 ft (2 m)

New Zealand species similar to mountain holly (*O. ilicifolia*). Wider grayish green leaves, toothed, musky aroma when crushed. Large rounded clusters of white daisy flowers in summer. Zones 8–11.

Olearia phlogopappa

DUSTY DAISY BUSH

☼ ❊ ↔ 7 ft (2 m) ↑ 8 ft (2.4 m)

Extremely floriferous species, native to eastern Australia from New South Wales to Tasmania. Variable species with narrow oblong leaves, deep green to bluish green above, white or gray hairy coating beneath. Terminal clusters of showy daisy flowers, white, pink, mauve, or blue, in spring. *O. p.* var. *subrepanda*, lower growing shrub of sub-alpine vegetation, generally under 3 ft (0.9 m) in height, leaves only ½ in (12 mm) long. Many selections for flower color have been made, with cultivar names such as *O. p.* 'Blue Gem', 'Comber's Mauve' ★, and 'Rosea'. Zones 8–10.

Olearia × *scilloniensis*

☼ ❊ ↔ 8 ft (2.4 m) ↑ 10 ft (3 m)

Originated in an English garden; parents believed to be *O. phlogopappa* and *O. stellulata*. Well-branched shrub. Dark green wavy-edged leaves, paler underside. Crowded panicles of white daisy flowers in spring. Zones 8–10.

Olearia traversii

CHATHAM ISLAND AKEAKE

☼ ❊ ↔ 10 ft (3 m) ↑ 15 ft (4.5 m)

Shrub or small tree native to Chatham Islands of New Zealand. Attractive, pale, deeply furrowed bark. Broadly oval leaves, shiny dark green above, white hairy coating beneath. Insignificant summer flowers. Grown for attractive foliage; used as hedging, particularly in coastal areas. Zones 8–11.

Olearia phlogopappa

ONCOBA

The 39 species of shrubs and small trees in this genus are native to tropical and southern Africa. This genus is a member of the governor's-plum (Flacourtiaceae) family. Their evergreen leaves may be leathery or thin and are alternately arranged; some species are armed with spines. The fragrant flowers are borne for long periods and may be red, white, or orange. They have spreading petals with prominent stamens.

CULTIVATION: In cool-temperate climates these are greenhouse plants, but in warm frost-free areas they can be grown outside where the spiny species can make an effective barrier hedge. Grow in full sun in a fertile well-drained soil. Propagate from seed.

Oncoba spinosa

SNUFF BOX TREE

☼ ❀ ↔ 6 ft (1.8 m) ↑ 6–10 ft (1.8–3 m)

Spiny shrub from eastern and central Africa and southern Arabia. Narrow serrated-edged leaves. Fragrant white flowers, mass of yellow stamens, which fall as flower ages, resemble camellia. Round fruit with hard, shiny, brown shell. Used to make snuff boxes and rattles in Africa. Zones 9–12.

OPLOPANAX

Related to ginseng, this genus of 2 species of prickly, deciduous, semi-prostrate or erect shrubs in the ivy (Araliaceae) family is native to temperate areas of the Northern Hemisphere. The tan bark is covered with slender stiff prickles. The green leaves are deeply lobed. The flower panicles, which appear in late spring to mid-summer, are white or greenish white and are followed by red flat berries, which are inedible.

CULTIVATION: Grow in a very moist shaded area in acidic soil. Propagate from seed (which can take as long as 18 months to germinate), or from suckers and root cuttings. Layering is also an effective method of propagation. Pruning with great care.

Oncoba spinosa

Oplopanax horridus

DEVIL'S CLUB

☀/❀ ❄ ↔ 5 ft (1.5 m) ↑ 3–10 ft (0.9–3 m)

Found from Michigan to Oregon and southeast Alaska, USA. Deciduous shrub with spiny branches. Leaves similar to maple. White flowers, in pyramidal clusters, in late spring–early summer. Shiny red berries. Zones 4–9.

ORPHIUM

Named after Orpheus, a character from Greek mythology, this genus contains a single species native to coastal regions of southwestern South Africa, and is a member of the gentian (Gentianaceae) family. It is a small softwooded shrub that is grown for its glistening pink to mauve saucer-shaped flowers, up to 2 in (5 cm) across, that are carried at the tips of the branches in summer.

CULTIVATION: Marginally frost hardy, this plant will grow in a sunny position in any well-drained soil, provided it is watered regularly in dry periods. Tip prune in spring to encourage a compact habit. Propagation is from cuttings in late summer.

Orphium frutescens

Orphium frutescens

STICKY FLOWER

☼ ❀ ↔ 18 in (45 cm) ↑ 24 in (60 cm)

Small evergreen shrub from South Africa's southwestern coast. Rather succulent, pale green, stem-clasping leaves, to 2 in (5 cm) long. Slightly sticky, 5-lobed, satiny flowers, in summer. Withstands moderate coastal exposure. Zones 9–11.

OSMANTHUS

This genus of about 15 species of slow-growing evergreen shrubs and small trees in the olive (Oleaceae) family is native to East Asia, except 1 or 2 species in the USA and 1 in the Caucasus. All have simple opposite leaves, some with spiny margins, and small, 4-petalled, white or yellow flowers, often strongly perfumed. The round fruit is dark blue.

CULTIVATION: The plants prefer moderately fertile well-drained soil in full sun, and a cool moist climate. Propagate from half-hardened cuttings.

Osmanthus × burkwoodii ★

syn. × Osmarea burkwoodii

☼ ❄ ↔ 10 ft (3 m) ↑ 10 ft (3 m)

Hybrid between O. delavayi and O. decorus; resilient thick-set shrub. Leaves dark glossy green, leathery, finely toothed. Flowers white, very fragrant, produced in profusion, in late spring. Zones 6–9.

Osmanthus delavayi

☼ ❄ ↔ 8 ft (2.4 m) ↑ 8 ft (2.4 m)

Slow-growing shrub from western China. Strong arching branches. Leaves smooth, dark green above, paler beneath. Flowers white, highly perfumed, in terminal, occasionally axillary, clusters of 5 or 6, in late winter–spring. Purplish black fruit. Zones 7–9.

Osmanthus × fortunei

☼ ❄ ↔ 10 ft (3 m) ↑ 10 ft (3 m)

Hybrid between O. fragrans and O. heterophyllus; compact robust shrub. Leaves large, prominently veined on upper surface, edged with sharp teeth, sometimes smooth-edged on mature plants. Small, fragrant, white flowers in autumn. '**San Jose**', cream to orange flowers. Zones 7–11.

Osmanthus fragrans
FRAGRANT OLIVE, SWEET OLIVE, SWEET OSMANTHUS

☼ ❄ ↔ 20 ft (6 m) ↑ 20 ft (6 m)

Evergreen species from China and Japan. Leaves smooth, dark green above, paler underneath. Flowers tubular, pure white, very fragrant, in late winter–mid-summer. *O. f.* f. *aurantiacus*, smooth-edged leaves, orange flowers. Zones 7–11.

Osmanthus heterophyllus
HOLLY OSMANTHUS

☼ ❄ ↔ 12 ft (3.5 m) ↑ 12 ft (3.5 m)

Evergreen shrub or small tree found in Taiwan and on main islands of Japan. Leaves oppositely arranged, smooth, dark glossy green. Small, fragrant, pure white flowers, carried in clusters, in autumn–early winter. '**Aureomarginatus**', leaves margined and splashed with broad patches of pale yellow; '**Aureus**', yellow-edged leaves; '**Goshiki**', cream and red-brown variegated leaves; '**Purpureus**', deep purple-green leaves; '**Variegatus**', leaves irregularly margined, marked with creamy white. Zones 7–11.

Osmanthus delavayi

OSTRYA
HOP HORNBEAM

This genus in the birch (Betulaceae) family contains about 10 species of deciduous trees related to *Betulus* and *Carpinus*. They grow throughout temperate Northern Hemisphere regions in open woodland. The alternate leaves have conspicuous veining and toothed edges, and are often hairy. The male catkins resemble the flowers of hornbeams *(Carpinus)*. The female flowers, on the same tree, develop into catkins that look like those of hops *(Humulus)*, with overlapping bracts.

CULTIVATION: These slow-growing trees are not commonly seen in cultivation, but they do make good specimen trees. They prefer well-drained fertile soil in either sun or shade. Propagate in spring from fresh seed, in pots protected from frosts. Seed which has

dried out must be stratified to break its dormancy. Graft cultivars onto *Carpinus betulus* rootstocks in the colder months.

Ostrya carpinifolia
HOP HORNBEAM

☼ ❄ ↔ 70 ft (21 m) ↑ 70 ft (21 m)

Native to southern Europe and Turkey. Shoots with fine growth of hairs. Green leaves with pointed tip and doubly toothed edges, turning golden to pale yellow in autumn. Female flower clusters creamy white at first, turning brown in autumn. Zones 6–9.

Ostrya virginiana ★
EASTERN HOP HORNBEAM, IRONWOOD

☼ ❄ ↔ 35 ft (10 m) ↑ 50 ft (15 m)

From eastern North America. Dark brown bark. Leaves dark green above, paler underside, lance-shaped, double-serrated edges. Yellow male catkins in spring; female fruit clusters white at first, ripening to brown. Zones 4–9.

OXYDENDRUM

The single species of deciduous shrub or small tree in this genus is native to North America, and belongs to the heath (Ericaceae) family. It has a slender trunk, which is sometimes multi-stemmed, with rusty red fissured bark. Small white flowers appear in summer, and in autumn the leaves color vividly before they fall.

CULTIVATION: This plant is suitable for growing as a specimen or in open woodland. Grown in full sun, flowering is better and the autumn colors more intense. It needs an acid soil that is moist but well drained. Plants are slow growing and take time to become established. Propagate from seed in autumn or spring, or softwood cuttings in summer.

Oxydendrum arboreum ★
SORREL TREE, SOURWOOD

☼ ❄ ↔ 10 ft (3 m) ↑ 6–10 ft (1.8–3 m)

From eastern USA. Pointed glossy leaves, finely toothed; shades of red, purple, and yellow in autumn. Fragrant white flowers, on slender spreading racemes at branch tips, in summer. Zones 5–9.

Ostrya carpinifolia

Ostrya virginiana

Oxydendrum arboreum

Pachira aquatica

Pachystachys lutea

Paeonia delavayi var. lutea

PACHIRA

Native to regions throughout tropical America, this genus of about 20 species of evergreen or deciduous trees in the mallow (Malvaceae) family are cultivated as ornamentals for their handsome palmately lobed leaves and large flowers with a conspicuous tassel-like group of stamens fused into a tube at the base. Flowers last for a very short time and in some species are often hidden among thick foliage which is fully developed at the time of flowering. The woody fruiting capsules contain many kidney-shaped seeds embedded in a fleshy pulp.
CULTIVATION: Frost tender, these plants require a warm climate and a well-drained moist situation in full sun. Propagate from seed or cuttings taken in autumn.

Pachira aquatica
SHAVING BRUSH TREE
☀ ⚡ ↔ 10 ft (3 m) ↑ 20 ft (6 m)
Evergreen tree native from Mexico to northern South America. Large compound leaves, 5 to 9 leaflets. Large creamy white or greenish flowers, red-tipped stamens, in summer. Brown fruiting capsules; edible seeds are roasted like chestnuts. Zones 10–12.

PACHYSTACHYS

The 12 species of evergreen perennials and shrubs in this genus, a member of the acanthus (Acanthaceae) family, are native to tropical America. They are closely related to *Justicia,* with similar showy terminal flower spikes. The tubular flowers are 2-lipped and have large overlapping bracts. The opposite leaves are quite large with a rather wrinkled surface due to their prominent veining.
CULTIVATION: In cool climates these are treated as indoor or greenhouse plants, but in warm humid areas they can be grown outside. They require a fertile, moist, but well-drained soil in a partially shaded situation. Propagation is best done from softwood cuttings taken in summer.

Pachystachys lutea
GOLDEN CANDLES
☀ ⚡ ↔ 20 in (50 cm) ↑ 36 in (90 cm)
Native to Peru. Shorter narrower leaves than other species. Long flowering season, with terminal spikes of showy golden yellow bracts that hold white tubular flowers. Zones 10–12.

PAEONIA
PEONY

There are 30 or so species in this genus belonging to the peony (Paeoniaceae) family. While most of the species are herbaceous perennials native to temperate parts of the Northern Hemisphere, the genus also contains shrubs and subshrubs known as tree peonies, which have persistent woody stems, brilliantly colored flowers, and highly decorative foliage.
CULTIVATION: *Paeonia* species are best suited to deep fertile soils of basaltic origin, heavily fed annually with organic matter; soils should not be allowed to dry out in summer. Protect from strong winds, scorching sun, and early spring frost. Prune spent flower-heads and dead or misplaced shoots. Propagation is from seed, which can be slow and difficult, or by division of herbaceous peonies, or by apical grafting of tree peonies, with the graft union being buried 3 in (8 cm) below soil level.

Paeonia delavayi
MAROON TREE PEONY
☀/◐ ❄ ↔ 5 ft (1.5 m) ↑ 7 ft (2 m)
Deciduous suckering shrub from western China. Leaves large, deeply cut, dark green above, bluish green below. Flowers saucer-shaped, dark red, deep gold anthers, in spring. Pod-like fruit with colored sepals. *P. d.* var. *lutea* (syn. *P. lutea*), lemon yellow single flowers in mid-spring. *P. d.* var. *ludlowii* (syn. *P. lutea* var. *ludlowii*), larger than *P. d.* var. *lutea*, less divided leaves, more open flowers. Zones 6–9.

Paeonia × lemoinei
☀/◐ ❄ ↔ 6 ft (1.8 m) ↑ 6 ft (1.8 m)
Crosses between *P. delavayi* var. *lutea* and *P. suffruticosa,* inheriting strong yellow coloring of *P. delavayi* var. *lutea,* usually flushed red in center or colors blended giving shades of orange. 'Souvenir de Maxime Cornu' (syns 'Kinshe', 'Souvenir de Professeur Maxime Cornu'), soft orange at flower center, red margins. Zones 6–9.

Paeonia rockii
syn. *Paeonia suffruticosa* 'Joseph Rock'
ROCK'S VARIETY
☀ ❄ ↔ 3 ft (0.9 m) ↑ 7 ft (2 m)
From northern Sichuan, southern Gansu, and Qinghai Provinces, China. Woody stems. Coarsely toothed, bipinnate, bright green

leaves. Single white flowers, with notched petals, distinguished by deep purple central blotch. 'Fen He', pink flowers. Zones 7–10.

Paeonia suffruticosa
MOUTAN, TREE PEONY

☼/◐ ❄ ↔ 7 ft (2 m) ↑ 7 ft (2 m)

Upright shrub from northwestern China west to Bhutan. Smooth mid-green leaves variously cut and lobed, with bluish green below. Large, sometimes double, white, pink, yellow, or red flowers, solitary, petals fluted, frilled on edges, in mid-spring. 'Godaishu', white flowers, semi-double; 'Hiro-no-yuki', large, semi-double, white flowers; 'Louise Mouchelet', pale pink flowers; 'Mountain Treasure', white flowers, purplish blotches at petal bases; 'Shin-Shium-Ryo', yellow flowers; 'Zenobia', rich magenta blooms. Zones 4–9.

PANDANUS

The evergreen screw pines, with about 700 species in the family Pandanaceae, are found in east Africa, Madagascar, tropical Asia, the Pacific Islands, and northern Australia. Most are tree-like, often with trunks supported by stilt roots. Stems are commonly branched with terminal rosettes of long, leathery, strap-like, spiny-toothed, parallel-veined leaves arranged in distinct spirals. Male and female flowers are borne in dense spikes on separate plants. Resembling a pineapple, the woody or fleshy fruiting heads of compound drupes, many edible after cooking, can be red, pink, or yellow.
CULTIVATION: These plants need full sun and moist well-drained soil in warm humid environments. Propagation is from seed, which must be soaked for 24 hours before sowing, or from offsets or rooted suckers.

Pandanus tectorius
syns *Pandanus odoratissimus, P. pedunculatus*
BEACH SCREW PINE, PANDANG

☼ ⚘ ↔ 10–20 ft (3–6 m) ↑ 12–25 ft (3.5–8 m)

From coasts and islands of Pacific and Indian Oceans, as far as Hawaii (USA) to east, Sri Lanka

to west, Okinawa (Japan) to north, and New South Wales (Australia) to south. Short trunk, supported by strong stilt roots and broadly spreading branches. Leaves spiny edges, midribs on underside. Male flowers cream, sweetly scented, in dense spikes among large white bracts, at various times of year. Fruiting heads up to 8 in (20 cm) long, segments usually with grooved sides, ripening deep red. 'Baptistii' (syn. *P. baptistii*), to 3 ft (0.9 m) tall, arching spineless leaves with yellow stripes; 'Sanderi' (syn. *P. sanderi*), to 12 ft (3.5 m) tall, leaves small, fine striping of paler green and gold; 'Variegatus', leaves with broad gold stripes, purple-brown spines; 'Veitchii' (syn. *P. veitchii*), leaves striped cream, spines green to yellow. Zones 10–12.

PARASERIANTHES

A member of the mimosa subfamily of the legume (Fabaceae) family, this genus of 4 species occurs from Indonesia to tropical Australia and the Solomon Islands. All species were previously included in the genus *Albizia*. *P. moluccana* holds the record for the world's fastest growing tree—just over 35 ft (10 m) in 13 months. These shrubs or trees are found in lowland rainforests and in moist areas.
CULTIVATION: Propagate from seed, which germinates readily without pre-treatment, unlike most members of this subfamily. They are fast-growing plants in well-drained acid soils in full sun.

Paraserianthes lophantha
syn. *Albizia lophantha*
CAPE LEEUWIN WATTLE

☼ ⚘ ↔ 10 ft (3 m) ↑ 25 ft (8 m)

From Indonesia, and naturalized in Australia. Fast-growing small tree, leaves bipinnate, many small leaflets. Small creamy flowers, inconspicuous petals, long prominent stamens, in spring. Long, flat, brownish pods; many black seeds. Can become invasive; considered a weed in South Africa and parts of Australia. Zones 9–10.

Paraserianthes lophantha

PARMENTIERA

From Mexico and Central America, this small genus of less than 10 species of evergreen shrubs or trees, often with spines, belongs to the trumpet-vine (Bignoniaceae) family. Bell-shaped or funnel-like, white or greenish flowers are borne singly or in small clusters. The opposite compound leaves are made up of 3 leaflets. The linear or narrow cylindrical fleshy fruit bears a similarity to candles.
CULTIVATION: Frost tender, they can be cultivated in tropical and subtropical gardens where they prefer fertile, moist, but well-drained soil in sun. Propagate from seed or half-hardened cuttings in summer.

Parmentiera cereifera
CANDLE TREE

☼ ⚘ ↔ 10 ft (3 m) ↑ 20 ft (6 m)

Small tree native to Panama. Elliptic to almost diamond-shaped leaflets, 2 in (5 cm) long. Waxy, greenish white, tubular flowers, to 3 in (8 cm) long. Greenish yellow fruit. Zones 10–12.

Pandanus tectorius (tree at rear), Queensland, Australia

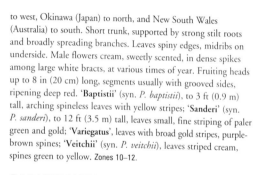

PARROTIA

This genus of a single species in the witchhazel (Hamamelidaceae) family is native to northern Iran and Azerbaijan, where it is found in the forests south and southwest of the Caspian Sea. It was named after Dr F. W. Parrot, a German plant collector who travelled through the Middle East in the early nineteenth century. It is grown mainly for its beautiful leaf color, especially in spring and autumn. It is a useful small tree for street planting and a very suitable species for parks and gardens in cool climates, where the foliage colors brilliantly.

CULTIVATION: Any moderately fertile soil with free drainage is suitable, including chalk soils; exposure to full sun is desirable. Propagation is usually from seed, which should be collected just before being expelled from the capsules, and sown immediately, taking up to 18 months to germinate. Softwood cuttings taken in summer are sometimes used.

Parrotia persica

Paulownia tomentosa

Parrotia persica

IRON TREE, PARROTIA, PERSIAN IRONWOOD, PERSIAN WITCH HAZEL

☼ ✳ ↔ 20 ft (6 m) ↑ 25–40 ft (8–12 m)

Small deciduous tree, short trunk with flaking bark. Leaves simple, alternate, leathery, shallowly toothed, pale lettuce-green; crimson, scarlet, orange, and yellow tones in autumn. Flowers small, bright red stamens, green calyx, enclosed in bract of dark brown hairy scales, in late winter–spring. 'Pendula' ★, drooping branches, slowly develops into dome-shaped mound. Zones 5–9.

PAULOWNIA

This is a genus of about 6 species in the foxglove (Scrophulariaceae) family, native to East Asia. All are deciduous trees with handsome leaves that in some species are very large in the juvenile stage, and bear large panicles of flowers in spring. Paulownias have been cultivated in China for more than 3,000 years, both for their strong light timber, and for their attractive flowers; the bark, wood, leaves, flowers, and fruit all have medicinal uses. They are characterized by their extremely rapid growth rate.

CULTIVATION: Paulownias do best in a moderately fertile and free-draining soil with adequate summer water. Protection from wind is important, especially in the early stages when the large leaves are easily damaged. Although quite hardy, dormant flower buds can be damaged by late frosts. The young trees are sometimes pruned back to 2 or 3 basal buds in order to encourage the vigorous growth of a single trunk. Propagation is from seed or root cuttings.

Pavonia hastata

Paulownia fortunei

POWTON, WHITE-FLOWERED PAULOWNIA

☼ ✳ ↔ 40 ft (12 m) ↑ 60 ft (18 m)

Found mainly in Yangtze delta area of China. Tall tree, straight-trunked, with rounded crown. Flowers open before leaves appear, in upright terminal panicles, 4 in (10 cm) long, white to cream, mauve or soft violet. Zones 6–10.

Paulownia tomentosa

EMPRESS TREE, HAIRY PAULOWNIA, PRINCESS TREE

☼ ✳ ↔ 30 ft (9 m) ↑ 50 ft (15 m)

Native to northern and central China, Korea, and Japan. Medium-sized tree, broad spreading crown. Pinkish lilac flowers in upright terminal panicles, 50 to 60 flowers in each panicle. Heart-shaped leaves downy, pale green maturing darker green, turning yellow-brown in autumn. 'Lilacina', lilac-purple flowers, hairy on outside, pale lemon yellow on inside; 'Sapphire Dragon', prominent clusters of creamy buff flowers. Zones 5–10.

PAVONIA

Found in the tropics and subtropics, especially in the Americas, this genus of the mallow (Malvaceae) family is composed of around 150 species of perennials, subshrubs, and shrubs. Easy-care plants, they are suitable for tropical gardens or can be grown as house or greenhouse plants elsewhere. The leaves may be simple or lobed, with serrated or toothed edges. The flowers vary in color and most often occur singly in the leaf axils but may be in terminal clusters or panicles. The petals fold back to reveal a hibiscus-like central column of stamens. Dry seed capsules follow.

CULTIVATION: All species are sensitive to frost and most cannot tolerate prolonged exposure to cool conditions. They respond well to container cultivation. Plant in moist well-drained soil in sun or partial shade and provide some protection from strong winds as the foliage is easily damaged. Propagate from seed or half-hardened tip cuttings.

Pavonia × gledhillii

☼ ✴ ↔ 3 ft (0.9 m) ↑ 5 ft (1.5 m)

Hybrid between Brazilian species P. makoyana and P. multiflora. Upright shrub. Deep green lance-shaped leaves, serrated edges. Flowers with bright red ring of narrow epicalyx bracts around dull purplish calyx, tubular purple corolla, in leaf axils, at branch tips, much of year. 'Rosea', dark pink flowers. Zones 10–12.

Pavonia hastata

☼ ☱ ↔ 2 ft (0.6 m) ↑ 3 ft (0.9 m)

Native to southern Brazil, Uruguay, Paraguay, and Bolivia, naturalized in southeast USA and Australia. Subshrub or shrub reshoots
if cut to ground by frost. Lance-shaped leaves, toothed edges. Flowers
usually red, may be white with red basal spotting. Zones 9–12.

PELTOPHORUM

Consisting of 8 species of evergreen or deciduous trees from the
cassia subfamily of the legume (Fabaceae) family, this genus occurs
in the tropical savannah and coastal forests of Africa, Asia, the
Americas, and northern Australia. Some species have been harvested
for timber, others widely planted as ornamentals. The glossy green
leaves are bipinnate, up to 18 in (45 cm) long, the ultimate leaflets being in 15 pairs, each about ½ in (12 mm) long. Prominent
terminal panicles up to 24 in (60 cm) long bear many fragrant
yellow flowers, with crinkly edges to the petals. Brown fruit pods
contain several seeds.
CULTIVATION: These plants are only suitable for gardens in the
tropics. Young plants require some shelter when first planted,
but when established, full sun and well-drained moist soil are
necessary. Like most legumes, propagation is from seed which
requires pre-treatment such as soaking in boiling water or scari-
fication of the seed coat.

Peltophorum pterocarpum

YELLOW FLAME TREE

☼ ✦ ↔ 30 ft (9 m) ↑ 50 ft (15 m)

Found in tropical India, Southeast Asia, Malay Archipelago,
New Guinea, and Australia's "Top End." Medium-sized tree,
with spreading branches. Leaves consist of bipinnate leaflets,
10 to 20 pairs. Terminal panicles of numerous fragrant yellow
flowers in summer. Flat, brown, leathery pods. Zones 11–12.

PERSOONIA

This is an Australian genus of about 90 species
of evergreen shrubs, or sometimes small trees,
in the protea (Proteaceae) family, named for
the eighteenth-century German botanist and
mycologist Christian Hendrik Persoon. They
have very attractive bright green leaves with
smooth edges, and masses of almost stalkless,
small, tubular, yellow flowers that have 4
rolled-back segments when they open. The
flowers are followed by succulent yellow or
green fruit, sometimes produced in large
heavy clusters. These plants are commonly
called geebungs, a version of the Dharuk
Aboriginal word *jibbong*, referring to the
edible fruit of some species.
CULTIVATION: They are best suited to full sun
or part-shade, light acidic soil, and very good
drainage. They respond well to pruning or
regular clipping. Propagation is from heat-
treated seed or from young tip cuttings
(which are notoriously difficult to strike).

Persoonia pinifolia

PINELEAF GEEBUNG

☽ ☱ ↔ 10 ft (3 m) ↑ 10–15 ft (3–4.5 m)

From eastern Australia. Erect shrub with slightly drooping branchlets and soft pine-like foliage. Profuse golden yellow flowers, in
leaf axils at branch tips, in late summer–autumn. Small, pale
green, succulent fruit. Zones 9–11.

PHELLODENDRON

This is a genus of 10 species of deciduous trees from temperate
East Asia, which belongs to the rue (Rutaceae) family. Notable
for their aromatic foliage and corky bark, these trees have large
pinnate leaves composed of broad leaflets that are often glossy.
The flowers are small and yellow-green in color and are carried
in panicles, followed by small, black, fleshy fruit. The autumn
foliage, however, is often bright yellow and can be quite spectacular in some years.
CULTIVATION: Most species in this genus need a climate with seasons
that are well differentiated, and a cool winter is important to ensure
proper dormancy. On the other hand, they handle hot summers
and harsh sun with ease, though the foliage is easily damaged by
strong winds. They seem to thrive in any well-drained soil with
a position in full sun. Plants may be propagated from seed, from
cuttings, by layering, or by grafting.

Phellodendron amurense ★

AMUR CORK TREE

☼ ✳ ↔ 40 ft (12 m) ↑ 50 ft (15 m)

Found in northern China. Corky pale gray bark. Strongly aromatic
leaves composed of 9 to 13 broad leaflets, dark glossy green upper
side, blue-green underside, turning yellow in autumn. Panicles of
small yellow-green flowers in early summer. Clusters of fruit held
erect above foliage. Zones 3–9.

Phellodendron amurense

PHILADELPHUS

MOCK ORANGE

Occurring within the hydrangea (Hydrangeaceae) family, this genus from temperate regions of Central and North America, southeast Europe, the Himalayas, and Asia includes 60 or so species of mainly deciduous shrubs. They usually have peeling bark. They are frequently grown for ornamental purposes, but are also cultivated for their scented double or single flowers, as specimen shrubs in woodland, or in a shrub border. CULTIVATION: They grow well in full sun or partial shade, or in deciduous open woodland in moderately fertile well-drained soil, but flower better in full sun. If grown in pots, a loam-based compost is best, and regular feeding and watering are necessary throughout the growing season. Propagate from softwood cuttings taken in summer or hardwood cuttings taken in autumn and winter.

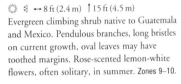

Philodendron bipinnatifidum

Philadelphus coronarius

SWEET MOCK ORANGE, SYRINGA

☼ ✽ ↔ 8 ft (2.4 m) ↑ 10 ft (3 m)

Native to southern Europe and western Asia. Deciduous upright shrub, peeling bark. Egg-shaped leaves have irregular shallow toothing, with down on main veins. Very fragrant almost white flowers, on short terminal racemes, in early summer. 'Aureus' ★, compact growth, golden leaves turn lime green with age, fragrant flowers, best in part-shade; 'Bowles' Variety', leaves with white margins; 'Variegatus', leaves have wide white margins. Zones 5–9.

Philadelphus inodorus

☼ ✽ ↔ 4 ft (1.2 m) ↑ 10 ft (3 m)

Native to eastern USA. Arching shrub, bark peels in second year. Leaves variable in size, shape, and amount of hair on either side, faintly toothed or smooth-edged. Several white flowers, in cymes, in summer. Zones 5–9.

Philadelphus, Hybrid Cultivar, 'Manteau d'Hermine'

Philadelphus lewisii

INDIAN ARROWWOOD, LEWIS MOCK ORANGE, LEWIS SYRINGA

☼ ✽ ↔ 10 ft (3 m) ↑ 10 ft (3 m)

State flower of Idaho, USA. Arching shrub native to west of North America. Leaves bright green, egg-shaped, margins occasionally finely toothed. Racemes of 5 to 11 mildly scented flowers in early summer. Zones 5–9.

Philadelphus mexicanus

MEXICAN MOCK ORANGE

☼ ❂ ↔ 8 ft (2.4 m) ↑ 15 ft (4.5 m)

Evergreen climbing shrub native to Guatemala and Mexico. Pendulous branches, long bristles on current growth, oval leaves may have toothed margins. Rose-scented lemon-white flowers, often solitary, in summer. Zones 9–10.

Philadelphus Hybrid Cultivars

☼ ✽ ↔ 6–8 ft (1.8–2.4 m) ↑ 30 in–10 ft (75 cm–3 m)

Most early hybrid cultivars created by French plant breeder Pierre Lemoine; crosses of *P. coronarius* and *P. microphyllus*, often grouped as *P.* × *lemoinei*. Influence of *P. inodorus* and *P. insignis* prompted new hybrid names *P.* × *cymosus* and *P.* × *polyanthus*, respectively. Crosses between earlier hybrids and *P. coulteri* grouped under *P.* × *purpureomaculatus*. Finally, group emerged in which *P. pubescens* showed influence, under name *P.* × *virginalis*. 'Avalanche', early Lemoine hybrid, to 6 ft (1.8 m) tall, scented white flowers; 'Beauclerk', later English hybrid, large, fragrant, single, cup-shaped, white flowers, pink-tinged center, in early–mid-summer; 'Belle Etoile', *P.* × *purpureo-maculatus* hybrid, purple-red central splash on flowers, pineapple fragrance; 'Boule d'Argent', *P.* × *polyanthus* hybrid, compact slightly arching shrub to 5 ft (1.5 m) tall, double or semi-double flowers in summer; 'Buckley's Quill', to 6 ft (1.8 m), fragrant double flowers in early–mid-summer, up to 30 quill-like petals per flower; 'Dame Blanche', Lemoine hybrid, cream colored semi-double flowers; 'Fimbriatus', Lemoine hybrid, compact fine-cut petal edges; 'Glacier', *P.* × *virginalis* hybrid, compact shrub to 5 ft (1.5 m) in height and spread, fragrant double white flowers in mid-summer; 'Innocence', Lemoine hybrid, to 10 ft (3 m), yellow foliage, fragrant white flowers in summer; 'Manteau d'Her-mine', Lemoine hybrid, to 30 in (75 cm) high, creamy double flowers in summer. Other *P.* × *virginalis* types include 'Minnesota Snowflake', double white flowers; 'Rosace', *P.* × *cymosus* hybrid, semi-double flowers; 'Schneesturm', *P.* × *virginalis* hybrid, pure white double flowers; 'Sybille', *P.* × *purpureomaculatus* hybrid, purple patches in center of single white flowers; 'Virginal', *P.* × *virginalis* hybrid, fragrant double white flowers. Zones 5–9.

PHILODENDRON

A genus in the arum (Araceae) family, it is made up of around 500 species from tropical America and the West Indies. They are mainly epiphytic clinging vines with aerial roots, but the genus also has some shrub-like and almost tree-like species. The large glossy leaves may be smooth-edged, variously lobed, or deeply divided in a feather-like pattern. Flowers are insignificant and without petals; held on a flower spike. Plant parts are poisonous, and contact with the sap may cause skin irritation. Suitable species can make attractive landscape plants in warm climates. Many are used as indoor plants. CULTIVATION: Best in the tropics and subtropics, in a moist, well-drained, humus-rich soil with generous watering in growth phase. Many species tolerate low light, grow them in dappled shade. Propagate from seed, from cuttings, or by layering.

Philodendron bipinnatifidum
syn. *Philodendron selloum*
TREE PHILODENDRON
☼/☽ ❉ ↔ 10 ft (3 m) ↑ 10 ft (3 m)
Native to southeastern Brazil. Large tree-like shrub with stout aerial roots. Spectacular, shiny, deep green leaves, to 3 ft (0.9 m) long, deeply divided, lobed, broadly ovate, somewhat arrow-shaped at base; leaf stalks as long as leaves. Spathes green to purplish red on outside, red-edged cream on inside. Zones 10–12.

PHLOMIS
This genus of about 100 low-growing shrubs, subshrubs, and herbs in the mint (Lamiaceae) family is found through Europe and Asia, from the Mediterranean regions to China. Most have felted leaves and tubular flowers in whorls along the stems. The yellow, cream, pink, mauve, or purple flowers have 2 lips at the tips. CULTIVATION: Most are quite frost hardy, and best planted in exposed sunny positions. Drought tolerant, they generally resent receiving too much water in summer. Propagate from seed or tip cuttings from non-flowering shoots.

Phlomis chrysophylla
☼ ❉ ↔ 3 ft (0.9 m) ↑ 4 ft (1.2 m)
Small evergreen subshrub native to Lebanon. Erect branching stems. Broad oval leaves, covered in golden down when young and fade to yellowish gray when mature. Bright golden yellow flowers, in whorls in leaf axils, in summer. Zones 7–10.

Phlomis fruticosa
JERUSALEM SAGE
☼ ❉ ↔ 30 in (75 cm) ↑ 30 in (75 cm)
Evergreen shrub from Mediterranean region. Leaves green and felty; bright yellow flowers in summer. Tolerates coastal conditions. Prune vigorously, to half its size, in autumn. Zones 7–10.

Phlomis fruticosa

PHOTINIA
This genus in the rose (Rosaceae) family consists of around 60 species of evergreen and deciduous shrubs and trees, most from the Himalayas to Japan and Sumatra, Indonesia. The leaves are often strikingly colored when young, especially in spring. The flowers are small, mostly white, with 5 petals, and grow in dense, flattish, clustering panicles along shoots or at their tips. The fruit are small pomes, usually red. Evergreen species are popular plants for hedging; deciduous species are more reliable than evergreens in flowering.

Photinia villosa

CULTIVATION: Most species are adaptable; good drainage is the key. For best results, plant in a well-drained fertile soil in sun. Prune to promote dense growth. Propagate from seed or cuttings.

Photinia davidiana
syn. *Stransvaesia davidiana*
☼ ❉ ↔ 20 ft (6 m) ↑ 25 ft (8 m)
Large evergreen shrub or small tree from western China. Leaves leathery, elliptical to inversely lance-shaped, dark green; older leaves may color red in autumn. Clustering panicles of small white flowers in summer. Small, red, hanging, persistent fruit. Zones 7–10.

Photinia × fraseri
FRASER PHOTINIA
☼ ❉ ↔ 15 ft (4.5 m) ↑ 15 ft (4.5 m)
Hybrid between *P. glabra* and *P. serratifolia*, developed in USA. Large shrub, many stems, leathery dark green leaves, finely serrated margins, new leaves bronze to bright red. Small white flowers, in panicles, in spring. 'Red Robin' ★, compact cultivar from New Zealand with shiny red new growth; 'Robusta', widely grown for its flushes of brilliant red new growth, encouraged by repeated trimming. Zones 8–10.

Photinia glabra
JAPANESE PHOTINIA
☼ ❉ ↔ 12 ft (3.5 m) ↑ 15 ft (4.5 m)
From Japan. Small tree with narrow-domed crown, bright red new leaves mature to green. Small white flowers, in clustering panicles, in summer. Small, fleshy, red drupes ripen to black. Zones 7–10.

Photinia villosa
syn. *Pourthiaea villosa*
ORIENTAL PHOTINIA
☼ ❉ ↔ 15 ft (4.5 m) ↑ 15 ft (4.5 m)
Native to China, Korea, and Japan. Deciduous tree or large shrub. Downy young shoots. Elliptical to obovate dark green leaves, serrated, bronze when young; yellow, orange, and red in autumn. Panicles of small white flowers in spring. Red fruit. Zones 4–9.

PHYGELIUS

This genus of evergreen subshrubs from South Africa is in the foxglove (Scrophulariaceae) family. It consists of only 2 species, which have been crossed to produce hybrids. They are often grown as herbaceous perennials where winters fall below freezing. Soft green leaves grow on erect stems; pendent tubular flowers in warm tones appear in late summer. When grown as a perennial, the suckering or running rootstock can form attractive clumps 3 ft (0.9 m) wide.
CULTIVATION: Given fertile, moist, humus-enriched soil, these plants will thrive in a morning sun position in warmer climates, but need the protection of a wall or a similar warm spot to minimize frost damage in cold climates. They are fleshy-leafed plants that dislike dry conditions, so they should be well watered throughout summer. Propagate from cuttings taken in summer.

Phygelius aequalis

◑ ❊ ↔ 3 ft (0.9 m) ↕ 3 ft (0.9 m)
South African suckering shrub. Upright stems, soft bright green foliage, dusky pink tubular flowers. Sensation/'Sani Pass', cerise to mauve flowers; 'Trewidden Pink', soft flesh pink flowers; 'Yellow Trumpet', larger leaves and flowers. Zones 8–10.

Phygelius capensis ★

CAPE FIGWORT, CAPE FUCHSIA
◑ ❊ ↔ 22 in (55 cm) ↕ 6 ft (1.8 m)
Well-clothed suckering shrub. Soft green leaves, lance-shaped. Masses of orange tubular flowers, distinctive recurved lobes. Zones 8–10.

Phygelius × rectus

◑ ❊ ↔ 4 ft (1.2 m) ↕ 4 ft (1.2 m)
Cross between *P. aequalis* and *P. capensis*. Compact suckering shrub. Dark green leaves, upright stems. Masses of pendent tubular flowers. 'African Queen', pale red flowers; 'Moonraker', creamy yellow flowers; 'Salmon Leap', deeply lobed orange blooms. Zones 8–10.

PHYLICA

Primarily native to South Africa, this genus in the buckthorn (Rhamnaceae) family has around 150 species of evergreen shrubs. A few are cultivated for their flowerheads, long lasting when cut. Leaves are dark green with a lighter underside, usually with a coating of silky silvery hairs. The true flowers are often petal-less or with fine filamentous petals, and are usually nearly enclosed by large feathery bracts or surrounded by white woolly hairs.
CULTIVATION: Plant in light, gritty, well-drained, slightly acidic soil and full sun. They tolerate high humidity, but their foliage suffers in prolonged rain. Coastal conditions suit them. Added humus and water will give lusher foliage, but a looser habit and fewer flowers. Prune by removing spent flowers and general tidying. Propagate from seed or half-hardened cuttings from non-flowering stems.

Phygelius × rectus 'Moonraker'

Phylica plumosa

syn. *Phylica pubescens*
FLANNEL FLOWER
❈/◐ ❊ ↔ 3 ft (0.9 m) ↕ 3–6 ft (0.9–1.8 m)
South African shrub densely covered with fine hairs. Tiny white flowers; hairy buff bracts. Deep green foliage. Flowerheads in early winter. Zones 9–11.

PHYLLOCLADUS

CELERY PINE
A genus of 5 or 6 coniferous trees or shrubs in the family Podocarpaceae, it comes from the Philippines and Malay Peninsula to New Zealand and Tasmania, Australia. Its "leaves" are flattened extended stems (phylloclades) resembling celery leaves. Male and female cones are on the same or different trees.
CULTIVATION: Grow in moist well-drained soil in sun or part-shade, watering during dry spells. Propagate from seed or half-hardened cuttings taken in autumn; the cuttings can be difficult to strike.

Phyllocladus glaucus

TOA TOA
❈/◐ ❊ ↔ 10–15 ft (3–4.5 m) ↕ 35–50 ft (10–15 m)
From New Zealand. Whorls of large, gray-green, compound phylloclades. Thick branches radiate in whorls up trunk. Fruiting body looks like pine cone. Rare in wild. Zones 10–11.

Phyllocladus trichomanoides

NEW ZEALAND CELERY-TOP PINE, TANEKAHA
◑ ❊ ↔ 20 ft (6 m) ↕ 70 ft (21 m)
New Zealand native, faster growing than other species, smaller in cultivation. Conical in shape, symmetrical whorled branches;

Phylica plumosa

Phyllocladus glaucus

Physocarpus opulifolius

attractive, gray-brown, mottled bark. Bright green leathery phylloclades resemble small celery leaves. Zones 8–11.

PHYSOCARPUS
NINEBARK

From North America and temperate northeastern Asia, the 10 deciduous shrubs in this genus in the rose (Rosaceae) family have showy flowerheads, foliage that is attractive in spring, sometimes in autumn, and flaking bark. Most have conspicuously veined and lobed leaves. Flowers are white or pale pink, small, and massed in rounded corymbs. Inflated fruit with 3 to 5 lobes ripen in late summer.
CULTIVATION: They are best grown in full sun in fertile well-drained soil that is moist in summer. They are not fussy, but dislike lime; foliage exposed to drought becomes desiccated and brown. Plants form thickets of stems; thin these and cut back the remaining growth after flowering. Propagate from seed or half-hardened cuttings.

Physocarpus monogynus
MOUNTAIN NINEBARK
❉ ✳ ↔ 4 ft (1.2 m) ↑ 4 ft (1.2 m)
From central USA. Thicket of arching stems. Toothed rounded leaves to 2 in (5 cm) long, 3 to 5 lobes. Flat heads of small white flowers, around 2 in (5 cm) wide, in spring–summer. Zones 5–9.

Physocarpus opulifolius
COMMON NINEBARK, NINEBARK
❉ ✳ ↔ 15 ft (4.5 m) ↑ 10 ft (3 m)
From central and eastern North America. Leaves usually 3-lobed, light green, toothed margins. Corymbs of flowers, mostly white, but may be pink-tinged or entirely pink, in late spring–early summer. *P. o.* var. *intermedius* (syn. *P. intermedius*), compact form, slightly smaller leaves, more densely packed flowerheads. *P. o.* 'Dart's Gold' ★, golden yellow foliage; 'Diabolo', burgundy foliage; 'Luteus', golden new growth, ageing to deep green, then bronze; 'Nanus', dense covering of small deep green leaves. Zones 2–9.

PHYTOLACCA

From temperate, warm-temperate, and subtropical regions, this genus in the pokeweed (Phytolaccaceae) family comprises 35 species of perennials, subshrubs, and deciduous or evergreen shrubs and trees, usually upright, with simple, often large leaves that can develop vivid colors in autumn. Their petal-less flowers are followed by conspicuous berries that in many species are poisonous.
CULTIVATION: Apart from variable frost hardiness and an intolerance of drought, most species are easily grown in moist, moderately fertile, well-drained soil in sun or part-shade. Prune at any time, but winter is often best as it will not affect the flower and fruit production or the autumn color. Propagate from seed, from rooted basal shoots, or from cuttings taken during the growing season.

Phytolacca dioica
BELLA SOMBRA TREE, OMBU
❉ ⚘ ↔ 30 ft (9 m) ↑ 50 ft (15 m)
Evergreen tree native to South America; buttressed multi-stemmed trunk. Leaves leathery, 4 in (10 cm) long, purple midrib. Racemes of tiny white flowers; golden berries ripen to black. Zones 10–11.

Picea engelmannii, in the wild, Colorado, USA

PICEA
SPRUCE

About 45 species make up this genus of resinous evergreen conifers in the pine (Pinaceae) family, from cool latitudes or high altitudes in the Northern Hemisphere. Most are large symmetrical trees, favoring deep, rich, acidic, well-drained soils in mountainous areas. The foliage is green, blue, silver, or gray, and consists of needle-like leaves on short, persistent, peg-like projections from the shoots. The cones are pendulous at maturity.
CULTIVATION: Some are slow growing, but all are wind-firm, and taller species make good windbreaks in large gardens. They tolerate a range of soils and climates, but dislike mild areas or polluted atmospheres. Smaller cultivars are suitable bonsai subjects. Propagation is from seed or, for cultivars, firm cuttings or grafting.

Picea abies
COMMON SPRUCE, NORWAY SPRUCE
❉ ✳ ↔ 20 ft (6 m) ↑ 200 ft (60 m)
Native to southern Scandinavia and other parts of northern Europe. Columnar habit, slow growing, smaller in cultivation. Thick reddish brown bark, spreading branches, 4-sided dark green leaves. Light brown cones, erect at first, becoming pendulous, to 8 in (20 cm) long. 'Clanbrassiliana', dwarf to 5 ft (1.5 m) tall, spread of 8 ft (2.4 m); 'Cupressina', 60 ft (18 m) tall; 'Echiniformis', dwarf, long prickly foliage; 'Gregoryana', rounded dwarf to 30 in (75 cm) wide; 'Humilis', dwarf to less than 18 in (45 cm) tall; 'Nidiformis' (bird's nest spruce), branches form nest-shaped central depression; 'Pendula', drooping branches; 'Reflexa', mat-forming to 12 ft (3.5 m) wide; 'Tabuliformis', prostrate branches. Other cultivars include 'Cranstonii', 'Gracilis', 'Little Gem', 'Maxwellii', 'Procumbens', 'Pumila', 'Pyramidalis', and 'Repens'. Zones 2–9.

Picea engelmannii
ENGELMANN SPRUCE
❉ ✳ ↔ 15 ft (4.5 m) ↑ 150 ft (45 m)
North American evergreen; dense columnar-pyramidal habit. Leaves sharp-pointed, 4-angled, gray-blue. Cylindrical pendulous cones, green flushed with purple. Zones 1–8.

Picea glauca
DWARF ALBERTA SPRUCE, WHITE SPRUCE
☼ ❋ ↔ 12–20 ft (3.5–6 m) ↑ 80 ft (24 m)
Slow-growing evergreen conifer from Canada, grown commercially for paper making. Bright green shoots in spring; 4-angled, aromatic, needle-like leaves, on drooping branchlets. Small narrow cones. *P. g.* var. *albertiana* 'Alberta Globe', mound-forming conifer, to 12 ft (3.5 m) tall; 'Conica' ★, slow growing to a perfect conical form, fine blue-green foliage, deepening with age to gray-green, widely regarded as one of best dwarf conifers, reaching only 6 ft (1.8 m) in height. *P. g.* 'Alberta Blue', blue-green foliage; 'Densata', slow-growing form, blue-green needle-like leaves; 'Echiniformis' and 'Nana', dwarf forms; 'Rainbow's End', conical form, attractive yellow young growth. Zones 1–8.

Picea jezoensis
YEZO SPRUCE
☼ ❋ ↔ 25 ft (8 m) ↑ 120 ft (36 m)
From Japan and northeast Asia. Branches with upturned tips sweep to ground level. Gray bark fissured with age, shed in plates. Flat dark green leaves, glaucous beneath. Small cylindrical cones crimson when young, maturing to rich brown. Zones 8–10.

Picea mariana
AMERICAN BLACK SPRUCE
☼ ❋ ↔ 10 ft (3 m) ↑ 60 ft (18 m)
Pyramidal evergreen conifer from USA. Whorled branches, narrow, blue-green, blunt-tipped leaves. Many small persistent purple-brown cones. Distinctive densely hairy shoots. 'Doumetii', broader-leafed than species; 'Nana', more rounded dwarf form. Zones 1–8.

Picea omorika
SERBIAN SPRUCE
☼ ❋ ↔ 20 ft (6 m) ↑ 100 ft (30 m)
From Bosnia and Serbia. Elegant, evergreen, narrow pyramidal form. Fast-growing drooping branches upturned at ends. Flattened, blunt-tipped, needle-like, bright green leaves, grayish beneath. 'Nana', dwarf form, rounded to conical. Zones 4–9.

Picea orientalis
CAUCASIAN SPRUCE
☼ ❋ ↔ 20 ft (6 m) ↑ 100 ft (30 m)
From sheltered sites in Caucasus and Turkey. Upright, pyramidal, slow-growing, evergreen conifer. Pendulous branches to ground level. Short glossy green leaves. Short, pendulous, purplish cones. Brick red flower catkins in spring. 'Aureospicata', upward-curving branches; 'Connecticut Turnpike', shorter denser cultivar. Zones 3–9.

Picea pungens
COLORADO BLUE SPRUCE
☼ ❋ ↔ 20 ft (6 m) ↑ 100 ft (30 m)
Evergreen pyramidal conifer from western USA. Gray bark. Horizontal branches bear stiff, sharp, needle-like, blue-green leaves. Most cultivars fall into Glauca Group with paler blue-gray foliage, such as 'Compacta', silvery green foliage; 'Glauca Compacta', silvery blue foliage. Other Glauca Group cultivars include 'Globosa', 'Hoopsii', 'Koster', and 'Moerheimii'. Zones 2–10.

Picea sitchensis
ALASKA SPRUCE, SITKA SPRUCE
☼ ❋ ↔ 25 ft (8 m) ↑ 100 ft (30 m)
From west coast of North America. Broadly conical evergreen conifer, planted for timber. Narrow stiff leaves, green above, silvery beneath, tips sharply pointed. Favored Christmas tree. Zones 4–8.

Picea smithiana
syn. *Picea morinda*
WEST HIMALAYAN SPRUCE
☼ ❋ ↔ 20 ft (6 m) ↑ 75 ft (23 m)
Pyramidal evergreen conifer from north India. Horizontal branches, cascading foliage. Needle-like, finely pointed, dark green leaves surround branches. Pendulous, shiny, brown-purple cones. Zones 6–8.

PIERIS
This genus belonging to the heath (Ericaceae) family comes mainly from subtropical and temperate regions of the Himalayas. Widely cultivated, the best known of the 7 species are popular evergreen shrubs for gardens in temperate climates, but the genus also includes a vine and some shrubby species from the eastern regions of the USA and from the West Indies. Typically, the leaves are simple pointed ellipses, often with serrated edges, and the flowers are bell-shaped, downward-facing, and carried in panicles. They usually open in spring, and are sometimes scented.
CULTIVATION: Like most members of the erica family, *Pieris* species prefer cool, moist, well-drained soil with ample humus. A position in full sun yields more flowers; light shade results in lusher foliage. Heavy pruning is seldom required as the plants are naturally tidy; light trimming and pinching back is all that is necessary. Propagate from half-hardened cuttings or by layering.

Pieris floribunda
FETTER BUSH
☼ ❋ ↔ 7 ft (2 m) ↑ 6 ft (1.8 m)
From southeastern USA. Pointed serrated-edged leaves to 3 in (8 cm) long. Flowers white, ¼ in (6 mm) long, carried in showy

Picea omorika

Picea pungens

Pieris japonica

PIMELEA

This genus consists of about 100 species in the daphne (Thymelaeaceae) family. Evergreen shrubs or subshrubs of Australasian origin, they are valued for their spectacular spring flowering. Some species, known as rice flowers, are highly valued as cut flowers. Flower color is variable within a species, ranging from white to deep pink; some species produce yellow or purple flowers. Terminal starry flowers with open reflexed tubes appear in showy heads, sometimes surrounded by prominent colored bracts. Fruit are small, and dry or fleshy.
CULTIVATION: They prefer well-drained acidic soils enriched with organic matter, and full sun or part-shade. They are tolerant of wind and salt-laden air, but dislike heavy frost. They respond to regular light pruning. Life expectancy is usually short. Propagate from tip cuttings in late spring to summer, or seed when it can be obtained. Germination may be slow.

panicles, in spring. Flowerheads differ from those of Asian species, being stiffer and held more erect. Zones 5–9.

Pieris 'Forest Flame'
☼ ❄ ↔ 6 ft (1.8 m) ↕ 12 ft (3.5 m)
Hybrid between *P. formosa* 'Wakehurst' and *P. japonica*. Strongly upright shrub, kept compact by pruning. Panicles of white flowers in spring. Young foliage bright red, changing to pink, then cream, then pale green, then dark green. Zones 6–9.

Pieris formosa
☼ ❄ ↔ 7 ft (2 m) ↕ 10–20 ft (3–6 m)
Native to Himalayan region. Leaves slightly glossy with finely serrated edges. Flower panicles mainly erect but with tendency to droop, flowers white or sometimes pink-tinted. *P. f.* var. *forrestii*, vivid red new growth, fragrant white flowers in drooping panicles; *P. f.* 'Wakehurst', leaves ageing from red to pink to green. Zones 6–10.

Pieris japonica
syn. *Pieris taiwanensis*
JAPANESE PIERIS, LILY-OF-THE-VALLEY BUSH
☼ ❄ ↔ 8 ft (2.4 m) ↕ 8–10 ft (2.4–3 m)
Species now includes *P. taiwanensis*, found in Japan, Taiwan, and eastern China. Leaves pink to bronze when young, ageing to dark green. Floral racemes erect or drooping, flowers usually white, in spring. 'Bert Chandler', light pink new growth turns yellow, then green; 'Christmas Cheer', early white and pink flowers; 'Karenoma', red-brown new growth; 'Little Heath', dwarf form, white-edged leaves; 'Mountain Fire' ★, reddish new leaves; 'Robinswood', green leaves, yellowish green edges, bright red new growth; 'Valley Valentine', purple-red flowers; 'Variegata', cream and green foliage, young leaves pink-tinted; 'Whitecaps', white flowers. Zones 6–10.

Pimelea physodes

Pimelea ferruginea
ROSY RICE FLOWER
☼ ❄ ↔ 3 ft (0.9 m) ↕ 3 ft (0.9 m)
Commonly seen species from Western Australia. Tolerant of salt spray. Oval leaves, shiny green, pointed, arranged along stems. Clusters of pink, open, tubular flowers, on branch tips, in spring, and intermittently at other times. 'Bonne Petite', profuse clusters of pink flowers. Zones 8–10.

Pimelea nivea
WHITE COTTON BUSH
☼ ❄ ↔ 3 ft (0.9 m) ↕ 6 ft (1.8 m)
Sometimes straggly evergreen shrub from Tasmania, Australia. White, or occasionally pink, star-shaped flowers, in large heads, in summer. White hairs cover plant, except upper surface of small, round to oval, glossy, dark green leaves. Zones 8–9.

Pimelea physodes
QUALUP BELLS
☼ ❄ ↔ 2 ft (0.6 m) ↕ 3 ft (0.9 m)
From Western Australia. Small hanging flowers surrounded by large red bracts. Popular cut flower. Thrives in harsh silica soil of Stirling Ranges. Can be difficult to cultivate outside its natural range. Zones 9–10.

Pimelea prostrata
NEW ZEALAND DAPHNE
☼ ❄ ↔ 36 in (90 cm) ↕ 6 in (15 cm)
From New Zealand. Evergreen prostrate shrub, dense foliage. Leaves tiny, blue-gray, along wiry stems, in 4 rows. Small white flowers in summer. Small white berries. Excellent embankment and spillover plant. Zones 8–10.

Pinus bungeana

Pinus densiflora

Pinus halepensis, in the wild, Spain

PINUS

PINE

This very variable genus of conifers in the pine (Pinaceae) family has around 110 species, found throughout Europe, Asia, north-western Africa, North and Central America, and the West Indies. They grow in a range of climates and conditions, from tropical equatorial forests to the extreme cold at the edge of the Arctic Circle. Predominantly large trees, only a couple of species are shrubs. The leaves are needle-like, and may be quite small to as long as 18 in (45 cm). They are generally found in bundles of 3 or 5, with never more than 8 in a group. The seed cones vary in shape, color, and dimension. The genus includes some of the world's most important timber species.
CULTIVATION: Most can easily withstand cold and extended dry periods, and also tolerate a range of soils, although they must have full sun. Some species are popular for bonsai. Propagation of the species is from seed; the cultivars are grafted.

Pinus banksiana

JACK PINE

 ❂ ❋ ↔ 20 ft (6 m) ↑ 60 ft (18 m)

Native to southern Canada and northeastern USA. Straight tree, irregular in outline, short twisted leaves growing in pairs. Light brown cones slightly curved. Grown and harvested for pulpwood, power poles, and railway ties, and planted for land rehabilitation and for trade in Christmas trees. Zones 2–8.

Pinus bungeana

LACEBARK PINE

❂ ❋ ↔ 20 ft (6 m) ↑ 60 ft (18 m)

Multi-trunked tree from northwestern China. Stiff leaves give off smell of turpentine when crushed. Cones small and egg-shaped. Gray-green peeling bark, splotched white and brown. Zones 5–9.

Pinus canariensis

CANARY ISLAND PINE

❂ ❀ ↔ 25 ft (8 m) ↑ 130 ft (40 m)

From Canary Islands. Straight solid main trunk, dense oval crown of 6–12 in (15–30 cm) needles that tend to droop. Attractive dark reddish brown bark, shiny brown cones. Naturalized in Australia and South Africa. Zones 9–11.

Pinus cembra

AROLLA PINE, SWISS STONE PINE

❂ ❋ ↔ 15 ft (4.5 m) ↑ 30 ft (9 m)

From central Europe. Narrow-conical to almost columnar, branching from ground. Densely foliaged with stiff 3 in (8 cm) needles, dark green, twisted. Small cones on very old trees. Zones 4–8.

Pinus contorta

LODGEPOLE PINE, SHORE PINE

❂ ❋ ↔ 25 ft (8 m) ↑ 75 ft (23 m)

Tree native to western North America, from Alaska to Mexico. Variable in habit, generally tall, straight, conical. Dense, stiff, dark green needles; small, asymmetrical, orange-brown cones. Zones 5–9.

Pinus coulteri

BIG-CONE PINE, COULTER PINE

❂ ❋ ↔ 30 ft (9 m) ↑ 100 ft (30 m)

From dry mountain slopes of California, USA. Fast-growing conifer. Long, stiff, glaucous green needles in bundles of 3. Huge, spiny, brown cones. Tolerates wind and drought. Zones 8–10.

Pinus densiflora

JAPANESE RED PINE

❂ ❋ ↔ 20 ft (6 m) ↑ 70 ft (21 m)

Tree from Japan, Korea, and China. Open irregular crown. Green leaves 5 in (12 cm) long, in tufts at ends of branches. Bark reddish brown, cones dull brown. 'Pendula' ★, vigorous, semi-prostrate; 'Umbraculifera', slow growing, shaped like umbrella. Zones 4–9.

Pinus halepensis

ALEPPO PINE

❂ ❀ ↔ 20 ft (6 m) ↑ 60 ft (18 m)

Mediterranean tree, low branches, flattened top. Leaves 4 in (10 cm) long, curved, twisted. Medium-sized cones persist for years. Naturalized in Australia, South Africa, and New Zealand. Zones 8–11.

Pinus heldreichii

BOSNIAN PINE

❂ ❋ ↔ 20 ft (6 m) ↑ 60 ft (18 m)

Found on western Balkan Peninsula southward to Greece. Sometimes shrubby tree. Irregular outline, open habit. Leaves stiff and sharp. Cones in clusters of 2, 3, or 4, opening when ripe. *P. h.* var. *leucodermis*, used as ornamental; '**Compact Gem**', dwarf. *P. h.* '**Smidtii**', compact dwarf, bright green needles. Zones 6–9.

Pinus lambertiana
SUGAR PINE

☼ ❄ ↔ 20 ft (6 m) ↑ 150 ft (45 m)

Occurs from central Oregon, USA, to northern Baja California, Mexico. Narrow irregular crown. Needles stiff, sharp, bluish. Pendulous cones, 20 in (50 cm) long, on long stalks. Zones 7–9.

Pinus longaeva
ANCIENT PINE, GREAT BASIN BRISTLECONE PINE

☼ ❄ ↔ 15 ft (4.5 m) ↑ 60 ft (18 m)

From dry subalpine peaks of western USA. Famous for its longevity with ages of over 5,000 years recorded. Small stiff leaves, medium-sized cones. Often crooked in form. Zones 5–8.

Pinus merkusii
SUMATRAN PINE

☼ ❄ ↔ 20 ft (6 m) ↑ 150 ft (45 m)

Only species found south of equator, in Sumatra, Indonesia, and also in Philippines. Conical to rounded crown, stiff needles 8 in (20 cm) long. Cones single or pairs. Zones 9–12.

Pinus monticola
WESTERN WHITE PINE

☼ ❄ ↔ 20 ft (6 m) ↑ 100 ft (30 m)

From northwestern North America. Large tree, narrow crown, solid straight main trunk. Foliage dense, leaves to 4 in (10 cm) long. Narrow cylindrical cones. Zones 4–9.

Pinus mugo
DWARF MOUNTAIN PINE, MUGO PINE, SWISS MOUNTAIN PINE

☼ ❄ ↔ 12 ft (3.5 m) ↑ 25 ft (8 m)

From mountains of central Europe. Small tree, often shrub-like, windswept habit. Long, bright green, needle leaves in pairs. Cones small, dark brown. '**Green Candles**', dense shrub; '**Honeycomb**', very compact rounded form, yellowish foliage; '**Paul's Dwarf**', tiny needle-like leaves; '**Slowmound**', tiny needle-like leaves; '**Tannenbaum**', very erect symmetrical form; '**Teeny**', dwarf. Zones 2–9.

Pinus nigra
AUSTRIAN PINE, BLACK PINE, CORSICAN PINE

☼ ❄ ↔ 25 ft (8 m) ↑ 120 ft (36 m)

Variable species, naturally occurring in southern Europe. Straight central trunk, silvery gray. Stiff needles 6 in (15 cm) long, cones light brown, glossy. Naturalized in New Zealand and parts of USA. '**Hornibrookiana**', dwarf forming compact mound. Zones 4–9.

Pinus palustris
LONG-LEAF PINE, PITCH PINE

☼ ❄ ↔ 15 ft (4.5 m) ↑ 100 ft (30 m)

Naturally found in southeastern USA. Open crown, straight trunk. Long leaves to 18 in (45 cm) in length, clustered at branch tips.

Brown cones have short thorns. Seedlings look much like tuft of grass before traditional tree trunk develops. Zones 7–10.

Pinus parviflora
JAPANESE WHITE PINE

☼ ❄ ↔ 20 ft (6 m) ↑ 80 ft (24 m)

From Japan. Smaller in cultivation; slow growing. Dense rounded crown; stiff, curved, blue-green leaves. Oval to cylindrical red-brown cones. '**Adcock's Dwarf**', to 30 in (75 cm). Zones 4–9.

Pinus patula
MEXICAN PINE, PATULA PINE, WEEPING PINE

☼ ❄ ↔ 30 ft (9 m) ↑ 50 ft (15 m)

From mountains of Mexico. Broadly conical; horizontal branches; stout trunk; weeping foliage. Long pale green needles in groups of 3. Clusters of 2 to 5 brown, conical, curved cones. Zones 8–10.

Pinus parviflora

Pinus pinaster
CLUSTER PINE, MARITIME PINE

☼ ❄ ↔ 30 ft (9 m) ↑ 100 ft (30 m)

From Mediterranean; world's main source of resin. Long, stiff, shiny, gray-green needles, in pairs. Bark with deep red-brown fissures between gray plates. Orange-brown cones. Zones 7–10.

Pinus pinea
ROMAN PINE, STONE PINE, UMBRELLA PINE

☼ ❄ ↔ 20 ft (6 m) ↑ 80 ft (24 m)

From southern Europe and Turkey. Flat-topped conifer; leaning trunk; fissured reddish gray bark. Needles bright green, in pairs. Rounded cones, shiny, brown, resinous. Large edible seeds known as "pine nuts." Drought tolerant once established. Zones 8–10.

Pinus ponderosa
PONDEROSA PINE, WESTERN YELLOW PINE

☼ ❄ ↔ 20 ft (6 m) ↑ 130 ft (40 m)

From western North America. Conical open crown; solid straight trunk; fissured pale yellow bark. Stiff pointed leaves to 10 in (25 cm) long. Prickly brown cones to 6 in (15 cm) long. Zones 3–9.

Pinus ponderosa, in the wild, California, USA

Pinus resinosa, in the wild, Minnesota, USA

Pinus sylvestris, in the wild, Scotland

Pinus wallichiana

Pinus radiata

syn. *Pinus insignis*

MONTEREY PINE, RADIATA PINE

☼ ❄ ↔ 25 ft (8 m) ↑ 100 ft (30 m)

From coastal central California, USA, and Guadalupe and Cedros Islands off Mexico. Tall tree; straight trunk, irregular open crown. Leaves 3–6 in (8–15 cm) long. Cones asymmetrically conical, 5 in (12 cm) long. Very important timber tree in Australia, New Zealand, and Chile. Zones 8–10.

Pinus resinosa

RED PINE

☼ ❄ ↔ 20 ft (6 m) ↑ 100 ft (30 m)

From northeastern USA and southeastern Canada. Trunk straight, crown narrow oval. Reddish brown bark. Sharp pointed leaves to 5 in (12 cm) long. Symmetrical oval to conical cones. Zones 2–8.

Pinus roxburghii

CHIR PINE, HIMALAYAN LONG-LEAF PINE

☼ ❄ ↔ 15 ft (4.5 m) ↑ 100 ft (30 m)

Broad-crowned tree from Himalayan foothills. Mottled gray and light brown bark. Sharp-pointed pendulous leaves. Cones 8 in (20 cm) long. Zones 6–11.

Pinus strobus

EASTERN WHITE PINE, WHITE PINE

☼ ❄ ↔ 20 ft (6 m) ↑ 165 ft (50 m)

From southeastern Canada and northeastern USA. Straight trunk, irregular crown of horizontal branches. Leaves blue-green; pendulous cones. 'Banzai Nana', bright green foliage; 'Fastigiata', upcurved branches; 'Horsford', compact foliage; 'Pendula', weeping branches; 'Prostrata', low spreading habit; 'Radiata', dwarf form. Zones 3–9.

Pinus sylvestris

SCOTCH PINE, SCOTS PINE

☼ ❄ ↔ 20 ft (6 m) ↑ 100 ft (30 m)

From Europe and northern Asia. Round-crowned tree, straight trunk, smaller in cultivation. Pairs of bluish green leaves. Gray-green symmetrical cones, 2½ in (6 cm) long. *P. s.* var. *lapponica*, smaller leaves and cones; *P. s.* var. *mongolica*, leaves up to 4 in (10 cm) long. *P. s.* 'Argentea' (syn. 'Edwin Hillier'), silver-blue foliage; 'Fastigiata', narrow erect habit, to 25 ft (8 m) tall; 'Moseri', dwarf form, yellowish needles; 'Saxatilis', low growing, dark green leaves; 'Troopsii', appealing foliage; 'Watereri', bluish leaves, slow growing, can be invasive in cool high-rainfall areas. Zones 2–9.

Pinus taeda

LOBLOLLY PINE

☼ ❄ ↔ 25 ft (8 m) ↑ 100 ft (30 m)

Leading timber tree, southeastern USA. Dense oval crown, straight trunk, lower half often free of branches. Twisted bright green leaves; oval to conical cones, 4 in (10 cm) long. Zones 7–11.

Pinus thunbergii

JAPANESE BLACK PINE

☼ ❄ ↔ 20 ft (6 m) ↑ 130 ft (40 m)

Tall tree from Japan and South Korea. Irregular outline, single main trunk often curved. Dense dark green leaves, small oval cones. 'Majestic Beauty' and 'Tsukasa', both compact and hardy. Zones 5–9.

Pinus wallichiana

BHUTAN PINE, BLUE PINE, HIMALAYAN PINE

☼ ❄ ↔ 20 ft (6 m) ↑ 150 ft (45 m)

Very tall tree with conical crown from Himalayas. Blue-green leaves to 8 in (20 cm) long, frequently arching or drooping. Cones very long, thin and cylindrical, hanging from branch tips. Zones 6–9.

PIPER

Belonging to the pepper (Piperaceae) family, this large genus of about 2,000 species of shrubs, trees, and woody-stemmed climbers is widely distributed in tropical regions. Smooth-edged, alternate, prominently veined leaves are often aromatic. Tiny flowers, borne in a dense axillary spike or raceme, are followed by small, single-seeded fruit. *P. nigrum* is the source of the black and white pepper used throughout the world as a seasoning.

CULTIVATION: All species are frost tender. In temperate climates, they make decorative indoor plants, climbing species needing some support structure. Indoors they are best suited to humid conditions and good light. Outdoor plants require a protected position in moist, fertile, well-drained soil in full sun or part-shade. Propagate from seed, half-hardened cuttings or by division.

Piper aduncum
COW'S FOOT, FALSE KAVA, FALSE MATICO, JOINTWOOD, SPIKED PEPPER

☼ ⚘ ↔ 8–17 ft (2.4–5 m) ↑ 17–25 ft (5–8 m)

Multi-branched shrub or small tree native to Central America and northern South America. Trunk to 4 in (10 cm) or more in dia-meter. Erect branches; smooth gray bark. Cord-like flexible flower spikes grow from stems. Leaves opposite, alternate, elliptical, to 10 in (25 cm) long, tapered pointed tip. Berry with small black seeds. All plant parts have peppery taste and odor. Plant used medicinally as aromatic stimulant, to prevent gonorrhea and hemorrhoids, for relief of ulcers. Zones 10–12.

PISTACIA

This small genus in the cashew (Anacardiaceae) family consists of around 9 species from the Mediterranean region, eastern and southeastern Asia, Central America, and southern USA. They are mainly deciduous trees with compound, mostly pinnate leaves terminated by a pair of leaflets, and panicles of small-petalled flowers. The flowers are followed by peppercorn-like fruit produced on the female plants; male plants are separate. Some species are important for their oils and edible seeds.
CULTIVATION: Most species originate in dry, warm-temperate regions, and are fairly adaptable. They grow best in a well-drained moderately fertile soil in full sun. Propagate from seed, cuttings, bud-ding, or grafting.

Pistacia chinensis
CHINESE PISTACHIO

☼ ❀ ↔ 15 ft (4.5 m) ↑ 25–50 ft (8–15 m)

Deciduous tree from China and Taiwan. Mostly pinnate leaves, 10 to 12 leathery dark green leaflets, turn shades of orange, red,

Pistacia chinensis

and yellow in autumn. Panicles of inconspicuous reddish flowers in summer. Small bluish fruit. Popular shade tree. Zones 7–10.

Pistacia lentiscus
LENTISCO, MASTIC TREE

☼ ❀ ↔ 12 ft (3.5 m) ↑ 12 ft (3.5 m)

Native of Mediterranean region. Aromatic evergreen tree or shrub. Pinnate leaves of 2 to 7 pairs of glossy, leathery, dark green leaflets, terminated by pair of leaflets. Panicles of small flowers in spring. Small black fruit. Zones 8–11.

PITTOSPORUM

This genus consists of about 200 species of evergreen trees and shrubs in the family Pittosporaceae. They are found in Africa, southern and eastern Asia, Australia, New Zealand, and the Hawaiian Islands, USA. The foliage is usually glossy with leaves arranged alternately or in whorls. The small flowers, 5-petalled, may be cup-shaped or reflexed, single or in clusters, and some have a sweet fragrance. Capsules contain seeds with a sticky coating. Some species are useful for shel-ter, hedging, borders, or containers. They can be clipped for formal situations and to keep the foliage dense.
CULTIVATION: Most species will grow in sun or part-shade in any well-drained soil. In cool-temperate climates they may require the protec-tion of a sunny wall, or they can be grown in the conservatory or greenhouse. Propagation is from seed, which germinates erratically, or from half-hardened cuttings taken in summer or autumn. Cultivars are propagated from cuttings only.

Pittosporum eugenioides

Pittosporum crassifolium
KARO

☼ ☽ ↔ 8 ft (2.4 m) ↑ 10–20 ft (3–6 m)

Robust New Zealand species, withstands coastal conditions. Dark green leaves, thick and leathery, white hairy coating beneath. Flowers small, dark red, noticeably fragrant in evening, in early summer. Down-covered fruit, shiny black seeds. Zones 9–11.

Pittosporum eugenioides
LEMONWOOD, TARATA

☼ ❀ ↔ 12 ft (3.5 m) ↑ 40 ft (12 m)

From New Zealand, smaller in cultivation. Glossy, light green, oval leaves, distinct pale midrib and wavy edges, release lemony aroma when crushed. Small creamy yellow flowers, honey-scented, in spring–summer. Popular for hedging and specimen planting. '**Variegatum**', features irregularly marked creamy edges to its leaves. Zones 8–11.

Pittosporum 'Garnettii'

☼ ❀ ↔ 7 ft (2 m) ↑ 7–10 ft (2–3 m)

Hybrid between *P. tenuifolium* and *P. ralphii*. Attractive oval leaves, creamy white variegations flushed pink. Solitary dark purple flowers, along branches, in spring. Zones 8–11.

Pittosporum tenuifolium
KOHUHU

☼ ❄ ↔ 15 ft (4.5 m) ↑ 15–20 ft (4.5–6 m)

Variable species, native to New Zealand, usually large shrub. Dense foliage; thin, slightly leathery, oblong leaves with wavy edges. Small flowers, reflexed petals, dark red, almost black, in spring, strong honey fragrance. Capsules turn black on maturity. 'Deborah', grayish green leaves with creamy margins flushed with pink; 'Eila Keightley' (syn. 'Sunburst'), rounded leaves with central yellow variegations; 'Irene Paterson', slower-growing form with almost white leaves speckled with pale green; 'James Stirling', blackish red branchlets, silvery green leaves; 'Marjory Channon', popular cultivar in USA; 'Tom Thumb', dwarf variety, foliage ages to dark purple; 'Variegatum', cream-edged green leaves; 'Warnham Gold', light green leaves change to creamy yellow and gold. Zones 8–11.

Pittosporum tobira
JAPANESE PITTOSPORUM, TOBIRA

☼ ❂ ↔ 7 ft (2 m) ↑ 20 ft (6 m)

Erect bushy shrub native to China and Japan. Leathery oblong leaves, dark glossy green, rolled edges. Orange-scented flowers, flaring petals creamy white, lemony yellow with age, in spring–early summer. 'Nanum', bright green leaves; 'Variegatum', leaves have irregularly marked white margin; 'Wheeler's Dwarf', compact miniature to 24 in (60 cm) high. Zones 9–11.

Pittosporum undulatum
SWEET PITTOSPORUM, VICTORIAN BOX

☼ ❂ ↔ 20 ft (6 m) ↑ 15–40 ft (4.5–12 m)

Native to eastern Australia. Vigorous species. Shiny, dark green, pointed, oval leaves, wavy edges. Creamy white flowers, sweetly scented, in terminal clusters, in spring. Orangey brown capsules. Has become weed outside its natural forest habitat. Zones 9–11.

PLATANUS
PLANE TREE

This genus in the plane (Platanaceae) family consists of about 8 species from the northern temperate zone, including Eurasia, North America, and Mexico. These deciduous trees have inconspicuous spring flowers; globe-shaped fruit on hanging stalks; large, alternate, palmately lobed, simple leaves; and ornamental, flaking, mottled bark. They are useful large shade trees. Many species are highly tolerant of compacted soils and air pollution and will grow well in both temperate and cool climates.

CULTIVATION: Most species are adaptable, as can be seen by the many cases of street trees in less than optimal conditions, but they perform best on deep, productive, alluvial soils with a consistent water source, such as a permanent stream, in full sun. Pruning is not essential, though it is desirable in the early years if a single trunk is to be established. Propagate from seed, cuttings, or by layering.

Platycladus orientalis

Platanus × *hispanica*
syns *Platanus* × *acerifolia*, *P*. × *hybrida*
LONDON PLANE

☼ ❄ ↔ 60 ft (18 m) ↑ 100 ft (30 m)

Believed to be hybrid between *P. occidentalis* and *P. orientalis*. Rounded pyramidal form. Gray to light brown bark, variable bright green leaves, usually 5-lobed. Fruit small. Tolerates heat, drought and pollution. 'Pyramidalis', upright cultivar with coarse bark, leaves 3-lobed, often slightly toothed. Zones 4–9.

Platanus occidentalis
AMERICAN PLANE, BUTTON-BALL, BUTTONWOOD, SYCAMORE

☼ ❄ ↔ 70 ft (21 m) ↑ 150 ft (45 m)

Native to USA and Canada. Very tall deciduous tree, broad open crown, spreading branches. Attractive flaking bark, 3 to 5 bright green shallow-lobed leaves. Single hanging nutlets, sometimes in pairs. Timber used for furniture and pulp. Zones 4–9.

Platanus orientalis
ORIENTAL PLANE

☼ ❄ ↔ 70 ft (21 m) ↑ 100 ft (30 m)

Large, spreading, deciduous tree from southeastern Europe to western Asia. Huge trunk with mottled, brown, gray, and greenish white bark. Dark green leaves, palmately lobed. Inconspicuous flowers in early spring. Clusters of 2 to 6 globe-shaped fruit. *P. o.* var. *insularis*, bright green leaves, toothed lobes; hairy fruit. Zones 5–9.

Platanus racemosa
ALISO, CALIFORNIA PLANE, CALIFORNIA SYCAMORE, WESTERN SYCAMORE

☼ ❄ ↔ 75 ft (23 m) ↑ 100 ft (30 m)

Large, strong-growing, deciduous tree naturally found from southern California, USA, to Mexico. Dark green leaves, 3 to

Platanus × *hispanica*

5 deep lobes, downy underside. Clusters of 2 to 7 bristly hanging fruit turn brown when mature. Zones 7–10.

PLATYCLADUS

At times put in the genus *Thuja*, this genus, within the cypress (Cupressaceae) family, is now considered distinct. It contains only 1 species, an evergreen coniferous tree featuring flattened spray-like branchlets of lightly aromatic foliage. Native to Korea, China, and northeastern Iran, it is rarely seen outside eastern Asia in its typical form, but rather as one of its numerous cultivars. These generally have a more rounded low-branching habit and are highly ornamental and dependable. Many are suitable for hedging. Dwarf varieties are excellent in rock gardens or containers and as a low border.
CULTIVATION: Grow this fully hardy genus in a moist well-drained soil in a sunny position protected from strong winds. Prune lightly in spring. Propagate from seed or cuttings.

Platycladus orientalis
syn. *Thuja orientalis*
CHINESE ARBOR-VITAE
☼ ❄ ↔ 15 ft (4.5 m) ↑ 40 ft (12 m)
Small conical tree, upward-curving branches. Small, mid-green, scale-like leaves in flattened vertical sprays. Fleshy, ovoid, female cones, ripen to waxy silvery sheen. 'Aurea Nana' ★, dense oval shape to 3 ft (0.9 m) high, creamy yellow foliage darkens to rich green in autumn–winter; 'Balaton', soft light green foliage; 'Elegantissima', compact conical bush to 15 ft (4.5 m) tall, golden yellow foliage develops bronze tones in winter; 'Meldensis', dwarf rounded bush to 3 ft (0.9 m), with soft blue-green foliage, purplish toning in winter; 'Rosedalis', to 5 ft (1.5 m) tall, fine soft foliage, changes from bright yellow in spring to sea green in summer, has purplish tones in winter. Zones 6–11.

PLUMBAGO

LEADWORT
There are about 15 species of annuals, perennials, and shrubs in this genus, which is a member of the leadwort (Plumbaginaceae) family. They are widely distributed throughout the tropical and subtropical regions of the world. They have simple light to mid-green leaves and can become rather sparsely foliaged and twiggy if they are not regularly trimmed. Their main attraction is their flowers, which appear throughout the warmer months. Carried on short racemes, they are very narrow tubes tipped with 5 relatively large lobes. The flowers come in white or various shades of pink and blue.
CULTIVATION: The taller shrubby species can be trained as climbers if they are grown against a wall. The shorter forms do well in containers. Plumbagos are not fussy about soil, as long as it is moist and well drained. Prune the plants in late winter to thin out the summer's congested growth and remove any wood that has been damaged by frost. Plant in full sun; propagate from seed, half-hardened cuttings, or layers.

Plumeria obtusa

Plumbago auriculata
syn. *Plumbago capensis*
CAPE LEADWORT, PLUMBAGO
☼ ⚘ ↔ 7 ft (2 m) ↑ 15 ft (4.5 m)
Native to South Africa. Tough vigorous shrub with long arching stems. Profuse pale blue flowers in warmer months. 'Alba', white flowers; 'Escapade Blue', light blue flowers; 'Royal Cape' ★, darker blue flowers. Zones 9–11.

Plumbago auriculata

Plumbago indica
☼ ✿ ↔ 3 ft (0.9 m) ↑ 5 ft (1.5m)
Sprawling shrub or subshrub from Southeast Asia. Long spikes of deep pink, pale red, or purple-red flowers in warmer months, intermittently at other times. Zones 10–12.

PLUMERIA

This small genus in the dogbane (Apocynaceae) family contains about 8 species from tropical America. Mostly deciduous or semi-evergreen shrubs and small trees, they have simple smooth-edged leaves arranged alternately or spirally toward the ends of fleshy branches, which have a poisonous milky sap. They are grown for their fragrant flowers, which have 5 petals arranged in a propeller-like form and joined at the base into a narrow tube, produced in clusters on the ends of branches.
CULTIVATION: Easily cultivated in a warm humid climate in a sunny position protected from strong cold winds, in cooler climates they require a warm frost-free position in a well-drained moderately fertile soil. Propagate from stem cuttings; these are most successful if taken in late winter when the plant is dormant. Allow the cut end to seal before inserting it into the growing medium.

Plumeria obtusa
PAGODA TREE, WHITE FRANGIPANI
☼ ✿ ↔ 12 ft (3.5 m) ↑ 25 ft (8 m)
Native to Bahamas and Greater Antilles. Evergreen in tropical climates. Leaves rounded or blunt tip. Fragrant flowers, white with yellow center. 'Singapore White' ★, popular cultivar. Zones 10–12.

Podocarpus latifolius

Plumeria rubra ★

FRANGIPANI

☼ ✦ ↔ 15 ft (4.5 m) ↑ 25 ft (8 m)

From Central America, Mexico, and Venezuela. Deciduous tree, spreading branches, broad rounded shape. Leaves large, dark green, shiny. Strongly fragrant funnel-shaped flowers, variable in color, in summer–autumn. *P. r.* var. *acutifolia*, panicles of yellow-centered white flowers with wide petals. *P. r.* 'Bridal White', 3 in (8 cm) wide, mildly scented, white to creamy white flowers with small yellow center and long deep green leaves with red edges; 'Celandine', golden yellow flowers; 'Dark Red', rich red flowers; 'Rosy Dawn', yellow flowers tinged pink; 'Starlight', flowers to 4 in (10 cm) wide, white with apricot to yellow center. Zones 10–12.

PODALYRIA

Containing some 25 species of evergreen shrubs and trees, this South African genus is in the pea-flower subfamily of the legume (Fabaceae) family. It is notable for its downy foliage and young growth, and for the attractive pea-flowers, which are usually in shades of pink and mauve. The leaves are simple smooth-edged ellipses with a covering of fine hairs, which gives them a silvery or pale golden sheen. The flowers, carried singly or in pairs in the leaf axils, open from similarly downy buds and are lightly scented.

CULTIVATION: These plants prefer light well-drained soil and a sunny position. They are drought tolerant once established and thrive in coastal conditions. Prune lightly after flowering to keep them compact. Propagate from seed, half-hardened cuttings, or layers.

Podalyria calyptrata

SWEET PEA BUSH

☼ ❈ ↔ 12 ft (3.5 m) ↑ 12 ft (3.5 m)

Large shrub or small tree. Dark green leaves, silvery sheen from coating of short fine hairs. Pale pink to lavender flowers, 1¼ in (30 mm) wide, in spring–early summer. Zones 9–10.

Podalyria calyptrata

PODOCARPUS

Widely distributed in warm-temperate areas of the Southern Hemisphere to tropical zones of eastern Asia and Japan, this genus in the plum-pine (Podocarpaceae) family consists of around 100 species of evergreen trees and shrubs. They have simple, usually spirally or alternately attached leaves that are mostly flat and narrow. The male and female plants are usually separate. Female flowers turn into round drupe-like fruit, often on a fleshy red or purple receptacle.

CULTIVATION: Most *Podocarpus* species prefer a well-drained soil in a sunny position protected from cold strong winds. Once established, they will tolerate extended dry periods. Propagate from seed, preferably fresh, or from cuttings.

Podocarpus elatus

BROWN PINE, PLUM PINE

☼ ❈ ↔ 20 ft (6 m) ↑ 50 ft (15 m)

Native to Queensland and New South Wales, Australia. Tall shrub or tree. Deep green leathery leaves, oblong to linear. Single greenish fruit. Especially suited for bonsai and hedging. Zones 9–12.

Podocarpus latifolius

YELLOWWOOD

☼ ✦ ↔ 15 ft (4.5 m) ↑ 90 ft (27 m)

Large evergreen shrub or tree native to Africa, from Sudan south to KwaZulu-Natal, South Africa. Smooth dark gray bark, peeling in long strips; leaves rigid, dark green, narrowly elliptical, 1¼–4 in (3–10 cm) long, tinged blue above. Male and female cones resemble small pine cones, female cone developing into small, fleshy, berry-like fruit, red tinged with purple. National tree of South Africa. Zones 10–11.

Podocarpus lawrencei

MOUNTAIN PLUM PINE

☼ ❈ ↔ 4 ft (1.2 m) ↑ 12 ft (3.5 m)

Very variable species, dwarf to tall shrub. Deep green linear leaves, bluish tinge above, paler below. Seed greenish on enlarged, pinkish red, fleshy stalk. Low-growing variants used as ground covers. Zones 7–10.

Podocarpus macrophyllus

KUSAMAKI, LOHAN PINE

☼ ❈ ↔ 20 ft (6 m) ↑ 60 ft (18 m)

Native to China and Japan. Outer branches droop. Dark green, leathery, linear to lance-shaped leaves, bluish green below. Fruit on succulent purplish red stalk. 'Maki', smaller leaves. Zones 7–11.

Podocarpus totara

TOTARA

☼ ❈ ↔ 25 ft (8 m) ↑ 80 ft (24 m)

Long-lived New Zealand tree. Dense rounded crown, giant trunk, timber highly prized, resistant to marine borers. Linear, leathery, dark green leaves. Single seeds on ends of reddish fleshy stalks. 'Aureus', grows to 10 ft (3 m) tall, with narrow conical form and yellow foliage. Zones 8–11.

POLYALTHIA

This genus of around 100 species of shrubs or trees belongs to the custard-apple (Annonaceae) family. It is widespread in tropical regions, particularly in Southeast Asia, with a few species occurring in Australia. They have large glossy leaves that have very fine oil dots and are aromatic when crushed. Borne singly or in clusters on older leafless wood, the open star-like flowers have 6 to 8 petals. Decorative clusters of succulent berry-like fruit follow.
CULTIVATION: All species demand warm frost-free conditions. They prefer moist, humus-rich, well-drained soil in full sun or part-shade. Water during dry periods. Propagate from fresh seed or cuttings.

Polyalthia longifolia
INDIAN WILLOW
☀ ✦ ↔ 3–10 ft (0.9–3 m) ↑ 50 ft (15 m)
From Sri Lanka. Columnar form, short side branches down to base. Pendulous, bright green, elliptic leaves. Small greenish yellow flowers, in axillary clusters, in summer. Zones 11–12.

POLYGALA

Covering over 500 species of almost every growth form, except tall trees, this genus, a member of the milkwort (Polygalaceae) family, is very widespread. The foliage ranges from small and linear to large and oval but is usually simple with smooth edges. The flowers have a pea-flower-like structure with distinct wings and a keel, which usually has a feathery tuft unique to polygalas. The flowers, carried in clusters or racemes, come in a range of colors, with purple and pink dominant, and are followed by small seed pods.
CULTIVATION: While frost hardiness varies, most prefer a light well-drained soil with a position in sun or part-shade. European and American alpine species are ideal subjects for pots or troughs. Shrubby species can be trimmed or pruned to shape in spring. Propagate from seed, layers, or cuttings.

Polygala × dalmaisiana
☀ ❈ ↔ 3 ft (0.9 m) ↑ 3–10 ft (0.9–3 m)
Evergreen shrub, hybrid between *P. oppositifolia* and *P. myrtifolia;* compact if trimmed occasionally. Mid-green, 1 in (25 mm) long leaves. Magenta to pale purple flowers, most of year. Zones 9–11.

Polygala myrtifolia
☀ ❈ ↔ 3–6 ft (0.9–1.8 m) ↑ 6 ft (1.8 m)
South African evergreen shrub. Elliptic to oblong, mid-green leaves, often develop purplish tints in winter. Small clusters of pale-tufted purple-pink flowers most of year. Trim to keep compact. Zones 9–11.

POLYSCIAS

This genus of around 150 species of evergreen shrubs to large trees is part of the ivy (Araliaceae) family. It is found in tropical and subtropical regions of Africa, Southeast Asia, Australia, and the Pacific Islands. They have alternate compound leaves that are pinnate to tripinnate and tend to be spirally arranged toward the ends of the branches. Very small greenish white or purplish flowers are produced in terminal racemes, which are often prominent and profuse. The fruit is a rounded or slightly compressed berry that turns purplish black when ripe.

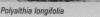

Polyalthia longifolia	*Polygala myrtifolia*

CULTIVATION: Most species are only suited to warm-temperate to tropical climates and prefer well-drained acidic soils in sun to part-shade. Provide extra water during extended dry periods. Propagate from fresh seed, cuttings in summer, or by division of root suckers.

Polyscias elegans
CELERY WOOD
◑ ❈ ↔ 15 ft (4.5 m) ↑ 100 ft (30 m)
Tree native to east Australia and New Guinea. Bipinnate leaves, glossy dark green leaflets, celery fragrance. Tiny purple flowers, in terminal panicles, in autumn–winter. Purple-black fruit. Zones 9–12.

Polyscias filicifolia
FERN-LEAF ARALIA
◑ ✦ ↔ 4 ft (1.2 m) ↑ 15 ft (4.5 m)
Shrub native to Pacific Islands. Deeply dissected leaves, many small, bright green, toothed leaflets, prominent purple veining. Tiny star-shaped flowers in summer. Zones 11–12.

Polyscias guilfoylei
GERANIUM ARALIA
◑ ✦ ↔ 8 ft (2.4 m) ↑ 20 ft (6 m)
Shrub native to eastern Malay Peninsula, northern Australia, and Polynesia. Pinnate leaves, leaflets toothed, white margins. Yellowish green flowers in summer. Tiny purplish black fruit. Zones 11–12.

Polyscias elegans, in center

POPULUS
ASPEN, POPLAR

There are about 35 species in this genus, comprising deciduous trees that range over much of the temperate Northern Hemisphere. They are in the willow (Salicaceae) family. Many poplars have deltoid-shaped leaves, but leaf shapes, sizes, and textures vary widely. Tiny flowers on pendulous catkins appear before the foliage. Small capsules follow the flowers, often filled with cotton-like down. Male and female catkins are usually on separate trees.
CULTIVATION: Poplars prefer a position in full sun in deep, moist, well-drained soil. Short-lived, they seldom exceed 60 years. They have vigorous invasive root systems and some can sucker heavily, which makes them a problem near drains and paving. Prune to shape; propagate from winter hardwood cuttings.

Populus alba
BOLLEANA POPLAR, SILVER POPLAR, WHITE POPLAR

☼ ❋ ↔ 40 ft (12 m) ↑ 80 ft (24 m)

Vigorous tree from Europe and North Africa to central Asia. Can become weed. Young stems and leaves have downy white hairs, upper surface ages to deep green. Leaves broad-based, egg-shaped, coarsely toothed edges. '**Nivea**', chalky white; '**Pendula**', weeping branches; '**Raket**' (syn. 'Rocket'), upright form. Zones 3–10.

Populus balsamifera
BALSAM POPLAR, TACAMAHAC

☼ ❋ ↔ 25 ft (8 m) ↑ 80 ft (24 m)

Northern North American and Russian species. Fragrant resin coats young twigs, buds, and new foliage; gives bronze coloration. Leaves roughly egg-shaped. Zones 3–8.

Populus × *canadensis*
CANADIAN POPLAR, CAROLINA POPLAR, HYBRID POPLAR

☼ ❋ ↔ 35 ft (10 m) ↑ 80 ft (24 m)

Hybrid between *P. deltoides* and *P. nigra*. Leaves egg-shaped to triangular, sparsely toothed edges, leaf stalks red. '**Aurea**', new growth golden; '**Eugenei**', tall columnar habit, new growth bronze;

Populus nigra 'Italica'

'**Robusta**', dense foliage, strongly upright columnar habit; '**Serotina**', male form, conical habit, comes into leaf late. Zones 4–9.

Populus deltoides
COTTONWOOD, EASTERN COTTONWOOD

☼ ❋ ↔ 60 ft (18 m) ↑ 100 ft (30 m)

From eastern half of North America. Leaves deltoid, coarse-toothed edges. Buds, new shoots, and leaves covered in balsam-scented resin. Zones 2–10.

Populus fremontii
ALAMILLO, FREMONT COTTONWOOD, WESTERN COTTONWOOD

☼ ❋ ↔ 40 ft (12 m) ↑ 100 ft (30 m)

Western North American tree. Stocky trunk. Yellow-green, broad-based, deltoid leaves, tapering to point, toothed. Female trees shed masses of seed "cotton." Zones 7–10.

Populus grandidentata
BIGTOOTH ASPEN

☼ ❋ ↔ 30 ft (9 m) ↑ 60 ft (18 m)

From eastern North America. Leaves on shorter older twigs very sharply toothed, on younger longer shoots, more ovoid, with wavy rather than toothed edges. Short branches form narrow rounded crown. Zones 3–9.

Populus lasiocarpa
CHINESE NECKLACE POPLAR

☼ ❋ ↔ 35 ft (10 m) ↑ 50–80 ft (15–24 m)

From southwestern China. Rounded crown, young stems initially have woolly coating. Glossy gray-green leaves, very large, egg- to heart-shaped, downy underside. Zones 5–10.

Populus nigra
BLACK POPLAR, THEVES POPLAR

☼ ❋ ↔ 60 ft (18 m) ↑ 100 ft (30 m)

Native to Europe, North Africa, and western Asia. Round-headed, with thick trunk, deeply fissured, knotted and gnarled, gray bark. Triangular to diamond-shaped leaves, brilliant yellow tones in autumn. '**Italica**', broadly columnar, orange young twigs, more intense autumn color; '**Lombardy Gold**', bright golden yellow foliage in summer–autumn. Zones 2–10.

Populus simonii

☼ ❋ ↔ 25 ft (8 m) ↑ 80–100 ft (24–30 m)

From northwestern China. Narrow crown, pendulous branch tips. Young twigs and leaf stalks red. Leaves fresh green, can exceed 4 in (10 cm) in length. '**Pendula**', weeping branches. Zones 2–9.

Populus tremuloides ★
AMERICAN ASPEN, QUAKING ASPEN, TREMBLING ASPEN

☼ ❋ ↔ 30 ft (9 m) ↑ 50 ft (15 m)

North American tree. Slender, upright; yellow-gray bark. Leaves broad, glossy, dark green, serrated edges, turn yellow in autumn. Zones 1–9.

Populus fremontii, in the wild, Arizona, USA

Posoqueria latifolia

Potentilla fruticosa 'Ochraleuca'

Pouteria cainito

Populus trichocarpa

BLACK COTTONWOOD

☼ ❄ ↔ 35 ft (10 m) ↑ 80–120 ft (24–36 m)

Native to western North America; furrowed dark gray bark, brittle branches. Leaves leathery, shallowly toothed, dark glossy green above, pale brown to nearly white beneath, turn yellow in autumn. 'Fritz Pauley', male cultivar. Zones 7–10.

POSOQUERIA

This genus of some 12 species of evergreen shrubs or trees in the madder (Rubiaceae) family comes from tropical America and the West Indies. Long, tubular flowers are very fragrant, white or red, and each have 5 spreading petal lobes. They are borne in large crowded clusters at branch tips in spring. Large glossy leaves are smooth-edged and arranged in opposite pairs. The fruit is a plum-sized, fleshy, yellow berry with several seeds.

CULTIVATION: Frost tender, they require a humus-enriched well-drained soil in a warm sheltered position in full sun or part-shade. Propagate from half-hardened cuttings taken in late summer.

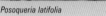

Populus tremuloides

Posoqueria latifolia

BRAZILIAN OAK

☼ ✦ ↔ 15 ft (4.5 m) ↑ 6–20 ft (1.8–6 m)

From Mexico to South America and West Indies. Glossy green leaves, prominent veins. Pure white, perfumed, tubular flowers, in dense terminal clusters, in spring. Edible yellow fruit. Zones 10–12.

POTENTILLA

This is a large genus of some 500 species in the rose (Rosaceae) family from the Northern Hemisphere. While most are herbaceous perennials, the shrubby species are very hardy, thriving in most soils, in sun and in partial shade. The flowers are like small single roses, and are produced over a long period, from spring throughout summer and, in some species, well into autumn.

CULTIVATION: These plants prefer a fertile well-drained soil. Cultivars with orange, red, or pink flowers fade in strong sunshine and should be positioned where they receive shade in the hottest part of the day. Propagate from seed in autumn or cuttings in summer.

Potentilla fruticosa

CINQUEFOIL, POTENTILLA, SHRUBBY CINQUEFOIL

☼ ❄ ↔ 5 ft (1.5 m) ↑ 5 ft (1.5 m)

Dense shrub from Northern Hemisphere. Yellow flowers in summer–autumn. Small palmately arranged leaves with 5 to 7 narrow leaflets. *P. f.* var. *dahurica*, white, sometimes yellow, disc-shaped flowers. *P. f.* 'Daydawn', yellow flowers tinged pink; 'Katherine Dykes', lemon yellow flowers; 'Ochraleuca', lemony white flowers; 'Tangerine' ★, orange flowers. Zones 3–9.

POUTERIA

A genus of evergreen trees in the sapodilla (Sapotaceae) family, they are found in tropical and subtropical Asia, Australasia, and South America. Trees have a milky sap and alternately arranged, paper or leathery, ornamental leaves. The small tubular flowers are green or white to yellow, borne along branches, and followed by often edible fruit.

CULTIVATION: Species with edible fruit require greenhouse cultivation outside warm subtropical areas. They grow in a range of soils but must have good drainage and light feeding. Propagate from fresh seed; graft fruit species.

Pouteria cainito

syns *Lucuma caimito*, *Pouteria caimito*

ABIU

☼ ✦ ↔ 15 ft (4.5 m) ↑ 35 ft (10 m)

Native to northern South America. Oblong leaves 4–8 in (10–20 cm) long. Flowers greenish white. Oval, smooth, pale yellow, edible fruit, sweet pulp eaten fresh or used in ice creams. Zones 10–11.

Pouteria campechiana

syns *Lucumis campechiana*, *L. nervosa*

CANISTEL, EGGFRUIT, SAPOTE BORRACHO

☼ ✦ ↔ 25 ft (8 m) ↑ 60 ft (18 m)

Found in Central America from Mexico to Panama. Papery leaves arranged in spirals. Small greenish white flowers. Yellow to greenish brown fruit. Orangey yellow pulp, edible, sweet. Zones 10–11.

PRINSEPIA

Native to northern China, Taiwan, and the Himalayas, and part of the rose (Rosaceae) family, this is a genus of about 4 species of deciduous thorny shrubs grown for their ornamental glossy leaves, attractive arching branches, and fragrant, yellow or white, blossom-like flowers. Crowded bright green leaves, smooth-edged or sparsely toothed, are arranged alternately along the stems. The pendent, cherry-like, edible fruit is at first yellow, ripening to red or purple. CULTIVATION: Frost hardy, *Prinsepia* species grow best in a well-drained moderately fertile and moist soil in full sun or part-shade. They must have room to spread, so position them where the thorny branches will not be a nuisance. Propagate from seed or cuttings.

Prostanthera lasianthos

Prinsepia sinensis ★

CHERRY PRINSEPIA

☼ ❈ ↔ 6 ft (1.8 m) ↑ 6 ft (1.8 m)

Spreading, rather open shrub from northeastern China. Bright green lance-shaped leaves to 3 in (8 cm) long. Fragrant flowers, bright yellow, 5-petalled, along entire stem length, in spring. Edible red cherry-like fruit. Zones 5–9.

Prinsepia uniflora

☼ ❈ ↔ 6 ft (1.8 m) ↑ 5 ft (1.5 m)

Arching shrub from northwest China. Sharp spines; narrow, dark green, oblong leaves to 2½ in (6 cm) long. Fragrant white flowers, along stems, in early spring–summer. Red to purplish black cherry-like fruit. Zones 5–9.

Prosopis glandulosa var. torreyana

PROSOPIS

Native mainly to tropical and warmer arid parts of North and South America, with a few in Africa and Asia, this genus of some 40 species of shrubs and trees is closely related to *Mimosa* and belongs to the mimosa subfamily of the legume (Fabaceae) family. They have spiny branches and bipinnate leaves with numerous pairs of tiny olive green leaflets. Fragrant, nectar-rich, greenish white to dull yellow flowers are borne in axillary spike-like catkins. The elongated, pale yellow, bean-like pods are a valuable source of food. The pods and young shoots are also valued as livestock feed in hot climates with very little rainfall. The aromatic timber gives off a slightly sweet smoke and is used for barbecues and smoking foods. CULTIVATION: These fast-growing, tough plants are easily grown in a warm dry climate. They prefer deep well-drained soil in full sun. Although most species tolerate only light frosts, they are extremely drought-resistant and provide welcome shade in arid regions. Propagate from seed or half-hardened cuttings.

Prosopis glandulosa

HONEY MESQUITE

☼ ❈ ↔ 25 ft (8 m) ↑ 30 ft (9 m)

Deciduous shrub or small tree from southern USA and northern Mexico. Spiny stems, bipinnate leaves. Fluffy yellow flowers, nectar-rich, in racemes, in spring–summer. Pale yellow linear pods. Prohibited plant in some countries. *P. g.* var. *torreyana* (syn. *P. juliflora* var. *torreyana*), smaller with shorter leaves. Zones 8–11.

Prosopis velutina

syn. *P. glandulosa* subsp. *velutina*

VELVET MESQUITE

☼ ❈ ↔ 15–40 ft (4.5–12 m) ↑ 15–40 ft (4.5–12 m)

Large shrub or medium-sized tree from southwest USA and northwest Mexico. Smooth dark brown bark; spine-covered velvety branches. Narrow, dull green, compound leaves with 2 to 3 leaflets, each with 15 to 20 pairs of minor leaflets with finely hairy surfaces. Clusters of small pale yellow to yellow-green flowers in late spring–early summer, sometimes again in autumn. Slender brown pods. Zones 8–11.

PROSTANTHERA

This Australian genus of around 100 species of evergreen shrubs belongs to the mint (Lamiaceae) family. Most have aromatic opposite leaves on squarish stems and produce masses of spring and summer flowers in shades of blue, mauve, or purple, sometimes white or red, rarely yellow. The tubular flowers are usually 2-lipped and 3-lobed, often in clusters around the upper part of the stem. CULTIVATION: Fast-growing but short-lived, they require a warm climate, excellent drainage, and a sheltered position. They can be planted beneath the light overhead cover of trees with open foliage. Tip prune from an early age and after flowering to ensure compact bushy growth. Propagate from half-hardened tip cuttings in summer.

Prostanthera cuneata

ALPINE MINT BUSH

☼/◑ ❈ ↔ 5 ft (1.5 m) ↑ 3 ft (0.9 m)

From southeastern Australia. Dense, very aromatic shrub. Thick oval leaves along stems, dotted with oil glands. Large white or pale mauve flowers, purple blotches in throat, in summer. Zones 8–9.

Prostanthera lasianthos ★

VICTORIAN CHRISTMAS BUSH

◑ ❈ ↔ 12 ft (3.5 m) ↑ 15 ft (4.5 m)

Tall shrub or small tree of southeastern Australia. Toothed lance-shaped leaves to 5 in (12 cm) long. Sprays of white to pale mauve flowers, purple and orange spots in throat, in summer. Zones 8–10.

Prostanthera nivea

SNOWY MINT BUSH

☼/◐ ◖ ↔ 7 ft (2 m) ↑ 12 ft (3.5 m)

Erect bushy shrub native to eastern Australia. Softly hairy branches, narrow-ovate leaves to 1½ in (35 mm) long. Abundant, white to pale mauve flowers, yellow-spotted throat, in spring. Zones 9–11.

Prostanthera ovalifolia

PURPLE MINT BUSH

◐ ◖ ↔ 6 ft (1.8 m) ↑ 6 ft (1.8 m)

Shrub from eastern Australia. Aromatic oval leaves, 1½ in (35 mm) long. Mass of purple or mauve flowers, darker spotted throat, in spring. 'Variegata', leaves with yellow edges. Zones 9–11.

PROTEA

Proteas belong to the family Proteaceae. The 100 or so evergreen trees and shrubs in *Protea* are all indigenous to Africa. They have bisexual flowers in cone-like heads with colored leaf-like bracts at the base, and are greatly valued for floristry because of their beauty and long vase life. Most flower between autumn and late spring.
CULTIVATION: Undemanding once established, they are fairly specific in requirements—an open sunny situation and very free-draining, gravelly, sandy, or basaltic loam, generally acid, and a climate with most rainfall in winter. They will not tolerate fertilizers rich in phosphorus. Light frosts are tolerated once established. Summer mulching is desirable but cultivation of the soil surface is resented. Good air circulation discourages fungal diseases. Regular flower removal encourages less straggly growth. Propagate from seed, cuttings, or grafting. Hybrid cultivars are usually grown from cuttings.

Protea aurea

☼ ❊ ↔ 10 ft (3 m) ↑ 10 ft (3 m)

Evergreen sprawling shrub. Foliage soft silvery when young, becoming leathery with age, leaves oval-shaped. Flowers cream, pink, or red, in autumn–winter, spot flowering at other times. Zones 8–10.

Protea cynaroides ★

GIANT PROTEA, KING PROTEA

☼ ❊ ↔ 7 ft (2 m) ↑ 7 ft (2 m)

Floral emblem of South Africa. Evergreen shrub. Bluntly oval leathery leaves and numerous, wide, bowl-shaped flowers with silky white hairs and pointed pink bracts, in mid-winter–early summer. Sought-after by florists worldwide. Zones 8–10.

Protea eximia

syn. *Protea latifolia*

DUCHESS PROTEA, RAY-FLOWERED PROTEA

☼ ❊ ↔ 10 ft (3 m) ↑ 10 ft (3 m)

Evergreen upright shrub from South Africa's Cape region. Gray-green broadly oval to heart-shaped leaves. Large pink to dark crimson flowers, with dark crimson center, at any time, but with winter flush. Zones 8–10.

Protea grandiceps

PEACH PROTEA, PRINCESS PROTEA, RED SUGARBUSH

☼ ❊ ↔ 5 ft (1.5 m) ↑ 5 ft (1.5 m)

Evergreen protea native to South Africa's Cape region. Leathery, oval, gray-green leaves. Large light peach-pink bracts, fringed reddish purple, white stamens, in late winter–early summer. Zones 8–10.

Protea lacticolor

☼ ❊ ↔ 7 ft (2 m) ↑ 7–15 ft (2–4.5 m)

Evergreen shrub or slender tree native to Cape region of South Africa. Blue-green foliage stiff and thick. Narrow spring buds open to cream flowers, with shell pink bracts, in autumn–early winter. Zones 8–10.

Protea magnifica

BEARDED PROTEA, QUEEN PROTEA

☼ ❊ ↔ 5 ft (1.5 m) ↑ 5 ft (1.5 m)

Variable evergreen shrub from South Africa's Cape region. Flowers vary from cream to pink or red with fringe of white or black at center, bracts also fringed with white. Regular pruning establishes pleasing shape. Zones 8–10.

Protea neriifolia

BLUE SUGARBUSH, OLEANDER-LEAFED PROTEA, PINK MINK

☼ ❊ ↔ 7 ft (2 m) ↑ 7 ft (2 m)

Erect evergreen shrub from south coast of South Africa's Cape region. Foliage resembles oleander. Long fluffy flowerheads from cream and pink to crimson, black feathery "beards" to bracts, in autumn–spring. 'White Brow', light crimson flowers. Zones 8–10.

Protea aurea

Protea cynaroides

Protea neriifolia

Protea repens

HONEY PROTEA, SUGARBUSH

☼ ❄ ↔ 7 ft (2 m) ↑ 8 ft (2.4 m)

Open, erect shrub from slopes of coastal mountains in Western Cape, South Africa. Nectar-rich flowers, greenish white to pale pink or claret red, with white or yellowish pink-tipped bracts, waxy appearance, in early autumn–winter. Zones 8–10.

Protea scolymocephala

GREEN BUTTON PROTEA, GREEN PROTEA, MINI PROTEA

☼ ❄ ↔ 3 ft (0.9 m) ↑ 3 ft (0.9 m)

From western mountain ranges of South Africa's Cape region. Small evergreen shrub, irregular spiky growth. Tiny flowers, around 1½ in (35 mm) wide, yellowy green or red with pink-tipped bracts, in early winter–spring. Zones 8–10.

Protea speciosa

BROWN-BEARDED SUGARBUSH

☼ ❄ ↔ 3 ft (0.9 m) ↑ 3 ft (0.9 m)

Found in South Africa's Western Cape province. Multi-stemmed shrub from group commonly known as bearded sugarbushes. Leaves gray-green, usually oblong. Flowerheads pink, or sometimes cream, in summer–autumn. Now classed as endangered species. Zones 9–10.

Protea venusta

☼ ❄ ↔ 8 ft (2.4 m) ↑ 30 in (75 cm)

Low-growing hardy shrub, at elevations up to 6,000 ft (1,800 m), sometimes covered in snow. Oval blue-green leaves. Held face-upward, small white flowerheads surrounded by pink-tipped rounded bracts in summer–autumn. Zones 8–10.

Protea Hybrid Cultivars

☼ ❄ ↔ 10 ft (3 m) ↑ 5–8 ft (1.5–2.4 m)

Most widely used parent species is *P. neriifolia*. 'Clark's Red', to 7 ft (2 m) tall, glaucous oval leaves, bright red flowerheads in mid-summer; '**Frosted Fire**', bright rosy red flowers, waxy white-fringed bracts, in late autumn–late winter; '**Pink Ice**' ★, bright pink flowerheads with silvery white fringed bracts, giving frosted appearance; '**Pink Mink**', deep pinkish red bracts, tipped black; '**Polar Blush**', pink flowers, white frilled bracts, in autumn; '**Satin Mink**', pink bracts, tipped black; '**Silvertips**', deep reddish bracts with profuse silvery white wool toward their tips. Zones 8–10.

PRUNUS

This widely grown genus is naturally widespread throughout the northern temperate regions of the world and mountain parts of Africa and includes a range of shrubs and trees, mostly deciduous. A rose (Rosaceae) family member, it is best known for the edible stone fruits (cherries, plums, apricots, peaches, and nectarines) and their ornamental flowering cousins. The leaves are usually simple pointed ellipses, often with serrated edges, and sometimes have brilliant autumn colors. Flowers are 5-petalled, carried singly or in clusters, and range in color from white through to dark pink, followed by fleshy fruit with a single seed enclosed in a hard stone. CULTIVATION: Although hardiness varies with the species, most need some winter chilling to flower and fruit properly. Wind protection is important. Most species prefer cool, moist, well-drained soil that is both fertile and rich in humus. Correct pruning techniques are important for the fruiting varieties. Propagate the species from seed, the fruiting forms by grafting, and the ornamentals by grafts or, in some cases, from cuttings.

Prunus × *amygdalo-persica*

FLOWERING ALMOND

☼ ❄ ↔ 20 ft (6 m) ↑ 20 ft (6 m)

Hybrid of *P. dulcis* and *P. persica*. Ornamental flowers; inedible green fruit. 'Pollardii', typical form, large bright pink flowers in late winter before foliage expands. Zones 4–9.

Prunus × *blireana*

DOUBLE PINK FLOWERING PLUM

☼ ❄ ↔ 15 ft (4.5 m) ↑ 15 ft (4.5 m)

Cross between *P. cerasifera* cultivar and form of *P. mume*. Small deciduous tree, drooping branch tips, bronze new growth. Large, bright pink, double flowers. '**Moseri**', small-flowered cultivar with red-tinted foliage. Zones 5–10.

Prunus campanulata

TAIWAN CHERRY

☼ ❄ ↔ 25 ft (8 m) ↑ 30 ft (9 m)

Deciduous tree from Taiwan and south Japan. Leaves large, doubly serrated, color in autumn. Flowers deep cerise, pendulous in clusters, open before foliage. Small purple-black fruit. Winter flowers in mild climates. Zones 7–10.

Protea repens

Prunus caroliniana

CAROLINA LAUREL-CHERRY, WILD ORANGE

☼ ❄ ↔ 20 ft (6 m) ↑ 40 ft (12 m)

Evergreen tree found in southern USA. Glossy, elliptical, smooth-edged leaves. Cream flowers, densely massed in racemes, in spring. Small, shiny, black fruit. Used for hedging. Zones 7–11.

Prunus cerasifera

CHERRY PLUM, FLOWERING PLUM, MYROBALAN

☼ ❄ ↔ 30 ft (9 m) ↑ 30 ft (9 m)

Eurasian species found in many cultivated varieties. Deciduous large shrub or small tree. Leaves bronze tinted, fairly small, veins on underside, hairy. White flowers; small yellow to red fruit. *P. c.* subsp. *divaricata*, lax habit, smaller yellow flowers. *P. c.* 'Hessei', shrubby, light green foliage, snow white flowers; 'Lindsayae', reddish young foliage maturing to green, pale pink flowers; 'Newport', shrubby in habit, bronze foliage, small white to pale pink flowers; 'Nigra', deep purple-black foliage; 'Pendula', weeping growth habit; 'Pissardii', red to purple leaves, white flowers opening from pink buds, plum-red fruit; 'Thundercloud', tall cultivar, deep bronze foliage, pink flowers. Zones 4–10.

Prunus glandulosa

DWARF FLOWERING ALMOND

☼ ❄ ↔ 5 ft (1.5 m) ↑ 5 ft (1.5 m)

Lovely deciduous shrub from China and Japan. Densely branched, rather narrow leaves, finely serrated edges. Smothered in deep pink to red flowers in spring. Dark red fruit. Prune to near ground level after flowering to encourage strong growth, with heavy flowering next season. 'Alba Plena', white double flowers; 'Sinensis', large leaves, pink double flowers. Zones 4–9.

Prunus ilicifolia

HOLLY-LEAFED CHERRY, ISLAY

☼ ✿ ↔ 20 ft (6 m) ↑ 25 ft (8 m)

Densely branched evergreen shrub or small tree native to California, USA. Leathery, glossy, green, holly-like leaves, spiny edges. Small creamy white flowers in racemes. Red or yellow fruit. Zones 9–11.

Prunus cerasifera

Prunus maackii   *Prunus padus*

Prunus incisa

FUJI CHERRY

☼ ❄ ↔ 15 ft (4.5 m) ↑ 15–20 ft (4.5–6 m)

Deciduous tree from Japan. White to pale pink flowers, incised petals, in spring, on bare wood. Serrated-edge leaves yellow, orange, and red tones in autumn. Fruit small, purple-black. Zones 6–9.

Prunus laurocerasus

CHERRY LAUREL, LAUREL CHERRY

☼ ❄ ↔ 30 ft (9 m) ↑ 20 ft (6 m)

Evergreen Eurasian shrub or small tree. Lustrous deep green leaves. Racemes of tiny creamy white flowers in spring. Small black fruit. 'Etna', finely toothed shiny leaves; 'Zabeliana', low-growing to 3 ft (0.9 m) high, narrow pale green leaves. Zones 7–10.

Prunus lusitanica

PORTUGAL LAUREL

☼ ❄ ↔ 30 ft (9 m) ↑ 20 ft (6 m)

Native to Iberian Peninsula. Evergreen with large, glossy, deep green leaves. Racemes of cream flowers. Fruit deep purple to near-black. *P. l.* subsp. *azorica*, Azores cherry laurel, shrubby, rarely exceeding 12 ft (3.5 m) tall, smaller leaves, shorter racemes. Zones 7–10.

Prunus maackii ★

AMUR CHOKE CHERRY, MANCHURIAN CHERRY

☼ ❄ ↔ 25 ft (8 m) ↑ 50 ft (15 m)

From Korea and nearby parts of China, smaller in cultivation. Small cream flowers, in racemes, in spring. Purple-tinted leaves, peeling papery bark, light orange-red shade. Small black fruit. Zones 2–9.

Prunus padus

BIRD CHERRY, EUROPEAN BIRD CHERRY, MAYDAY TREE

☼ ❄ ↔ 25 ft (8 m) ↑ 30–50 ft (9–15 m)

Found from Europe to Japan. Deciduous tree, often shorter in cultivation. Drooping branch tips. Racemes of numerous white flowers in spring. Tiny black fruit. 'Aucubifolia', yellow-speckled leaves; 'Colorata', pink flowers, purple-tinted young branches; 'Pendula', strongly drooping branches; 'Plena', semi-double flowers; 'Stricta', strongly erect racemes. Zones 3–9.

Prunus, Sato-zakura Group, 'Kiku-shidare'

Prunus pensylvanica

PIN CHERRY, RED CHERRY

☼ ❋ ↔ 30 ft (9 m) ↑ 30 ft (9 m)

Deciduous North American tree. Conspicuously toothed leaves to 4 in (10 cm) long. Tiny white flowers, in clusters of up to 8 blooms, in spring. Tiny red fruit. Zones 2–9.

Prunus sargentii

SARGENT CHERRY

☼ ❋ ↔ 35 ft (10 m) ↑ 50 ft (15 m)

Native to Japan, smaller in cultivation. Red-toothed leaves, 4 in (10 cm) long. Clusters of large, frilly, dusky pink flowers. Small red cherries. Zones 4–9.

Prunus, Sato-zakura Group

JAPANESE FLOWERING CHERRY

☼ ❋ ↔ 30 ft (9 m) ↑ 20–40 ft (6–12 m)

Large group, composed mainly of hybrids, probably derived from *P. serrulata*, ornamentals grown for early–mid-spring flower display. 'Alborosea', white to pink double flowers; 'Kanzan' (syn. 'Sekiyama'), strongly upright growth when young, clusters of bright pink double flowers, vivid autumn foliage; 'Kiku-shidare' (syn. 'Cheal's Weeping Cherry'), pendulous growth, pink double flowers; 'Okumi-yako' (syn. 'Shimidsu-sakura'), flat-topped tree with large, white, double flowers from pink buds; 'Shirotae' (syn. 'Mt Fuji'), massed, large, single to semi-double, white flowers, golden autumn foliage; 'Ukon', pale green semi-double flowers. Zones 5–9.

Prunus serotina

BLACK CHERRY, CAPULIN, RUM CHERRY

☼ ❋ ↔ 30 ft (9 m) ↑ 100 ft (30 m)

Deciduous tree found in North America. Glossy, mid-green, finely serrated leaves, lighter undersurface, over 3 in (8 cm) long. White flowers, in short pendulous racemes, in spring. Small near-black fruit. Zones 3–9.

Prunus spinosa

BLACKTHORN, SLOE

☼ ❋ ↔ 15 ft (4.5 m) ↑ 20 ft (6 m)

Deciduous shrub or small tree found in Eurasia and North Africa, covered in sharp spines. Small white flowers, prune-like black fruit. Recorded in hedgerows from ancient times. Zones 4–10.

Prunus × *subhirtella*

SPRING CHERRY

☼ ❋ ↔ 25 ft (8 m) ↑ 50 ft (15 m)

Broad deciduous tree from Japan, smaller in cultivation. Serrated leaves to 3 in (8 cm) long. Flowers small, white or pink, before foliage. Tiny purple-black fruit. 'Autumnalis', early flowering, white flowers with hint of pink; 'Autumnalis Rosea', pink flowers; 'Fukubana', early flowering, double pink flowers; 'Pendula', long lived, weeping habit; 'Pendula Rosea', weeping habit, pink flowers; 'Stellata', clusters of starry, single, pink flowers. Zones 5–9.

Prunus tenella

DWARF RUSSIAN ALMOND

☼ ❋ ↔ 5 ft (1.5 m) ↑ 5 ft (1.5 m)

Deciduous Eurasian shrub, similar in habit to flowering quince (*Chaenomeles*). Leaves larger, dull yellow fruit smaller. Deep pinkish red flowers. Zones 2–9.

Prunus triloba

DWARF FLOWERING ALMOND, FLOWERING PLUM, ROSE TREE OF CHINA

☼ ❋ ↔ 12 ft (3.5 m) ↑ 12 ft (3.5 m)

From China. Pale pink flowers, semi or fully double, before or with leaf buds. Leaves 2½ in (6 cm) long, often 3-lobed. Red fruit with downy skin. 'Multiplex', soft pink flowers. Zones 5–9.

Prunus × *yedoensis*

TOKYO CHERRY, YOSHINO CHERRY

☼ ❋ ↔ 30 ft (9 m) ↑ 40 ft (12 m)

Hybrid between *P.* × *subhirtella* and *P. speciosa*. Upright tree with spreading crown. Deep green serrated leaves, turn vivid orange and red in autumn. Racemes of scented white flowers in spring. Tiny black fruit. 'Shidare-yoshino' ★, weeping branches, profuse snow white flowers. Zones 5–9.

PSEUDERANTHEMUM

From tropical regions, this genus of the acanthus (Acanthaceae) family contains about 60 species of small evergreen perennials, shrubs, or subshrubs. They are grown for their often prominently veined leaves and white flowers flecked or flushed red or mauve.

Prunus triloba 'Multiplex'

CULTIVATION: Suited to warm-climate gardens, the frost-tender members of this genus need well-drained soil enriched with organic matter in a protected, partially shaded position. Outside the tropics they are best grown as greenhouse or conservatory plants. They prefer bright filtered light and regular water and fertilizer during the growing season. Tip prune from an early age to encourage a bushy habit or, if the plants become leggy, cut back hard in spring. Propagate from half-hardened cuttings or by division.

Pseuderanthemum atropurpureum
☼ ✈ ↔ 3 ft (0.9 m) ↑ 4 ft (1.2 m)
Erect evergreen shrub from Polynesia. Showy, deep purple, ovate, pointed leaves, marked with pink or green along veins. Tubular white flowers with purple markings in center, in dense terminal spikes, in summer. Zones 11–12.

Pseuderanthemum reticulatum
☼ ✈ ↔ 3 ft (0.9 m) ↑ 3 ft (0.9 m)
Evergreen bushy shrub from Vanuatu. Golden stems, bright green ovate leaves, wavy margins, network of creamy yellow lines. White tubular flowers, cerise markings in throat, in terminal panicles, in summer. 'Andersonii', yellow blotches on foliage. Zones 11–12.

Pseuderanthemum reticulatum 'Andersonii'

PSEUDOLARIX
The sole species in this genus, part of the pine (Pinaceae) family, is a larch-like deciduous conifer from eastern China, with leaves larger and strappier than true larches. Young foliage is bright green but changes to fiery hues of yellow, orange, and red-brown before falling with the first hard frosts.
CULTIVATION: Although hardy to quite severe frosts, young plants may be damaged by very early or late freezes. This tree prefers deep, fertile, humus-rich, well-drained soil with a position in sun or morning shade. Trees that are too shaded will develop poor autumn color. Naturally upright and conical, this tree needs little pruning, other than to lightly shape or tidy the branches. Propagation is usually from seed.

Pseudolarix amabilis

Pseudopanax ferox

Pseudolarix amabilis
GOLDEN LARCH
☼ ✳ ↔ 25 ft (8 m) ↑ 100 ft (30 m)
Upright conifer. Deeply fissured, warm red-brown bark. Leaves to 2 in (5 cm) long, in whorls on short sideshoots. Female cones purplish, to 3 in (8 cm) long, persist on tree after shedding their seed. 'Nana' ★, 3 ft (0.9 m) tall, with spreading habit, one of several dwarf cultivars. Zones 6–9.

PSEUDOPANAX
syns *Neopanax*, *Nothopanax*
There are about 20 species of evergreen shrubs or small trees in this genus of the ivy (Araliaceae) family. Most are native to New Zealand and the rest are found in Chile and Tasmania, Australia. They have ornamental and interesting foliage, which in several species undergoes a distinct metamorphosis from juvenile to mature stages. The leaves are simple or palmate and may have toothed edges. Tiny, greenish, male or female flowers are borne in large clusters, sometimes on separate trees, and the small fruit that follow are often black.
CULTIVATION: Cultivated for their attractive foliage and, in species such as *P. crassifolius*, for their striking form, members of this genus will grow in any fertile well-drained soil in sun or part-shade. Most will tolerate at least light frost, but should be given a warm sheltered site in cool areas or grown in a greenhouse or conservatory. Propagate from seed or from half-hardened cuttings taken in autumn.

Pseudopanax arboreus
FIVE-FINGER
☼ ✦ ↔ 15 ft (4.5 m) ↑ 10–20 ft (3–6 m)
Rounded tree native to New Zealand. Leathery palmate leaves, 5 to 7 leaflets, deep shiny green with serrated edges. Tiny flowers in winter. Small purplish berries on female trees. Zones 9–11.

Pseudopanax ferox
TOOTHED LANCEWOOD
☼ ✦ ↔ 7 ft (2 m) ↑ 15 ft (4.5 m)
Native to New Zealand. Distinct juvenile and adult stages. Grown for its dramatic juvenile form. Narrow leathery leaves to 20 in (50 cm) long; large coarse-toothed edges. Dark green with bronze tones, orangey-red midrib. Zones 9–11.

Pseudopanax lessonii
HOUPARA
☼ ✦ ↔ 7 ft (2 m) ↑ 12 ft (3.5 m)
Attractive foliage shrub native to New Zealand's North Island. Thick, glossy, dark green leaves, 3 to 5 broadly oval leaflets, shallowly toothed near tips. 'Cyril Watson', slow growing, very bushy, displays 2 leaf forms on same plant, 3 to 5 short broad lobes, coarsely toothed, or simple with shallowly toothed margins, very thick, leathery, glossy fresh green; 'Gold Splash', dark green leaves with bright yellow splashed along veins and midribs. Zones 9–11.

PSEUDOTSUGA

DOUGLAS FIR

There are 6 to 8 species of coniferous trees within this genus in the pine (Pinaceae) family. All are evergreen forest trees from western North America, Mexico, Taiwan, Japan, and China. They are major timber trees used for power poles, railway sleepers, plywood, and wood pulp and are also a source of Oregon balsam. Some trees reach 300 ft (90 m) in height in their native habitat, but this is rare in cultivation. The foliage and cones are frequently used as Christmas decorations, as the foliage sheds its needles less readily than other species. The linear leaves grow radially on the shoots. The female cones have 3-pronged bract scales protruding from between the cone scales; the cylindrical male cones are smaller.
CULTIVATION: These hardy trees prefer colder climates and will grow in any well-drained soil in full sun. Propagate the species from seed in spring, or graft cultivars in late winter.

Pseudotsuga menziesii

syns *Pseudotsuga douglasii, P. taxifolia*
DOUGLAS FIR
☼ ❄ ↔ 15–30 ft (4.5–9 m) ↑ 80–150 ft (24–45 m)
Native to North America, from British Columbia to California. Fast growing, long lived. Bark has corky plates, deep fissures developing with age. Narrow leaves, dark blue-green above, 2 white bands beneath, juvenile foliage apple-green in spring. Female cones produced on mature trees. *P. m.* var. *glauca*, glaucous blue leaves, smaller cones. *P. m.* 'Densa' and 'Fletcheri' are dwarf forms. Zones 4–9.

PSIDIUM

This tropical American genus, in the myrtle (Myrtaceae) family, contains about 100 species of evergreen shrubs or trees, several of which are grown for their edible fruit. They branch freely, almost to the ground, and have thick opposite leaves, some with prominent veins.

Pseudotsuga menziesii, in the wild, Utah, USA

The white 5-petalled flowers have numerous stamens. The fruit is a rounded or pear-shaped berry ripening to red or yellow.
CULTIVATION: Members of this genus need a warm to hot climate, moist but well-drained soil with protection from strong winds, and regular watering during summer. They are pruned to tree form, and after fruiting to retain a compact shape. Propagate from seed or cuttings, or by layering or grafting.

Psidium cattleianum

CHERRY GUAVA, STRAWBERRY GUAVA
☼ ❄ ↔ 8 ft (2.4 m) ↑ 10–20 ft (3–6 m)
Red-barked, dense, evergreen shrub. Elliptic, shiny, green leaves. Flowers white, solitary, to 1 in (25 mm) wide. Small, round, dark red or yellow fruit, dark red flesh, rich in vitamin C. Zones 9–11.

PSORALEA

As now understood, this is a genus of around 20 species of evergreen shrubs and subshrubs from southern Africa in the pea-flower subfamily of the legume (Fabaceae) family. Many other species were formerley included in *Psoralea* but are now distributed among at least 4 other genera. Leaves are mostly small and crowded, simple or compound (trifoliate or pinnate), and dotted with tiny black glands. Flowers are borne prolifically, in short dense spikes, and are mostly blue, purplish, or white; small grayish pods follow.
CULTIVATION: Cold-hardiness varies, though few will tolerate any but the lightest frosts. They prefer light but reasonably moist well-drained soil, and will flower best in full sun. Propagate from seed or half-hardened cuttings.

Psoralea pinnata

AFRICAN SCURF-PEA, BLUE PEA BUSH
☼ ❄ ↔ 7 ft (2 m) ↑ 6–10 ft (1.8–3 m)
South African shrub. Leaves with 5 to 11 narrow deep green leaflets, often with fine hairs. Clusters of violet to bright blue flowers, with white wings, in late spring–summer. Has become weed in parts of southern coastal Australia. Zones 9–11.

PTELEA

Despite looking rather more like lilacs than oranges, and bearing sycamore-like fruit, the 11 deciduous shrubs or small trees in this North and Central American genus are *Citrus* relatives, and belong to the rue (Rutaceae) family. This is only apparent in the aromatic oil glands of the leaf, which is usually trifoliate, with a dominant central leaflet flanked by a smaller one on each side. The leaves often become bright yellow in autumn. The small cream to pale green flowers are scented and clustered together in conspicuous cymes. They appear first in spring or early summer, then sporadically later. Small, 2-seeded, winged fruit, a little like hop seeds, follow.
CULTIVATION: Species from southern USA and northern Mexico are a little tender. Otherwise, most are adaptable and easily grown in any well-drained soil in sun or part-shade. In areas with hot summers, some shade from the afternoon sun is advisable. Propagate from seed, layers, or grafts.

Psoralea pinnata

Ptelea trifoliata

Pterocarpus indicus

Pterostyrax hispida

Ptelea angustifolia

WESTERN HOP TREE

☼ ❈ ↔ 12 ft (3.5 m) ↑ 12 ft (3.5 m)

Shrub from northern Mexico and southern USA. Fine hairs on young foliage and new stems. Mature leaves usually smooth, blue-green below. Flowers in early summer. Fruit rounded. Zones 8–10.

Ptelea trifoliata

COMMON HOP TREE

☼ ❈ ↔ 12 ft (3.5 m) ↑ 25 ft (8 m)

From eastern and central USA. Leaves mid-green, 3 leaflets, semi-glossy, paler below, slightly notched edges. Pale green flowers in early summer. Fruit to 1 in (25 mm) wide. 'Aurea', yellow-green foliage; 'Glauca', blue-green foliage. Zones 5–10.

PTEROCARPUS

This genus, in the pea-flower subfamily of the legume (Fabaceae) family, contains some 20 species of tropical trees or climbers highly regarded for their ornamental timber. They have wide graceful crowns and large pinnate leaves, and are usually deciduous in the dry season. Racemes of scented yellow to orange pea-flowers are borne just before, or with, new leaves. Flat rounded pods follow, their edges often extended into parchment-like wings.
CULTIVATION: These plants need a warm frost-free climate, moist well-drained soil, and full sun. Propagate from seed or cuttings.

Pterocarpus indicus

BURMESE ROSEWOOD

☼ ⚘ ↔ 35 ft (10 m) ↑ 80 ft (24 m)

Broadly spreading tree widespread in tropical Asia, from India to Philippines. Pinnate leaves, leaflets to 4 in (10 cm) long. Sprays of yellow scented flowers in spring. Wood is rose-scented. Zones 11–12.

PTEROCARYA

There are 10 deciduous trees in this genus, which belongs to the walnut (Juglandaceae) family, and these are found from the Caucasus to the temperate areas of East Asia and Southeast Asia. The leaves are pinnate and can be quite large, sometimes with more than 20 leaflets up to 4 in (10 cm) long. The foliage seldom shows much autumn color. In spring, long bract-studded catkins of tiny

green flowers open, developing into strings of winged nutlets with hard shells that become brown as they ripen.
CULTIVATION: Most species are tolerant of quite severe frosts and will thrive in any reasonably fertile, moist, well-drained soil with a position in full sun. Propagate from seed, suckers, or cuttings.

Pterocarya fraxinifolia

CAUCASIAN WINGNUT

☼ ❈ ↔ 60 ft (18 m) ↑ 80 ft (24 m)

Found from the Caucasus to northern Iraq. Dark deeply furrowed bark, leaves to 15 in (38 cm) long, with 11 to 21 leaflets. Catkins yellow-green shade. Zones 7–9.

Pterocarya stenoptera

☼ ❈ ↔ 40 ft (12 m) ↑ 70 ft (21 m)

Chinese species notable for leaves to 15 in (38 cm) long with up to 23 leaflets; new foliage downy. Fine tan down covers young twigs. Catkins often longer than leaves. Zones 7–9.

PTEROSTYRAX

The 3 species of deciduous shrubs or trees in this genus, belonging to the storax (Styracaceae) family, are native to eastern Asia. Leaves are alternately arranged, with serrated edges; numerous long open panicles of small flowers are borne in spring or summer.
CULTIVATION: These quick-growing plants prefer deep, rich, acid soil in a sheltered position in sun or part-shade. Prune after flowering to retain their shape. Propagate from seed or half-hardened cuttings.

Pterostyrax corymbosa

☼ ❈ ↔ 20 ft (6 m) ↑ 40 ft (12 m)

Spreading shrub or tree from Japan. Dark green leaves, bristly toothed margins. Small, fragrant, white, bell-shaped flowers, in panicles, in spring. Zones 6–10.

Pterostyrax hispida ★

EPAULETTE TREE

☼ ❈ ↔ 20 ft (6 m) ↑ 25 ft (8 m)

From Japan and China. Large leaves, finely serrated edges. Panicles of fragrant creamy white flowers, to 8 in (20 cm) long, in summer. Small, green, bristly fruit. Zones 6–10.

PYCNOSTACHYS

Native to tropical and southern Africa, these 40 or so species of perennials and softwooded shrubs are grown for their dense terminal spikes of 2-lipped deep blue flowers. Members of the mint (Lamiaceae) family, they have squarish stems and opposite or whorled leaves that are often aromatic when bruised.
CULTIVATION: These plants need a warm frost-free climate and are best suited to fertile, moist, but well-drained soil in full sun. In cool areas they are grown in the greenhouse or conservatory, with a plentiful supply of water during the growing season. Propagate from seed or cuttings.

Pycnostachys urticifolia
☼ ✝ ↔ 4 ft (1.2 m) ↑ 8 ft (2.4 m)
Shrub with erect branching stems. Oval leaves, 5 in (12 cm) long, toothed edges. Tubular deep blue to purple flowers, in dense terminal spikes to 4 in (10 cm) long, in summer–autumn. Zones 9–12.

PYRACANTHA

FIRETHORN

This small genus in the rose (Rosaceae) family consists of 9 species of mostly spiny shrubs, from eastern Asia and southeast Europe. They have simple leaves that are often toothed on the margins, and whitish flowers in corymbs are produced at the ends of branches. The flowers are followed by masses of red, orange, or yellow fruit, which persist into winter. Most species perform best in cool moist climates, where they are useful landscape subjects for the shrubbery or used as espalier specimens or for hedging. *Pyracantha* species can naturalize in favorable areas.
CULTIVATION: Most species are fairly adaptable shrubs tolerating exposed sites in full sun. They perform best in a fertile well-drained soil. Pruning is not essential but may be helpful to control size; hedges can be pruned from early to mid-summer. Watch for fireblight, scab, and wilt problems. Propagate from seed or cuttings.

Pyracantha angustifolia
NARROW-LEAFED FIRETHORN, ORANGE FIRETHORN
☼ ❄ ↔ 12 ft (3.5 m) ↑ 12 ft (3.5 m)
Native to southwest China. Spiny bushy shrub, horizontal branches. Dark green shiny leaves, gray and furry beneath. Dense corymbs of small white flowers in mid-summer. Yellow to deep orange berries. Zones 7–10.

Pyracantha coccinea
EUROPEAN FIRETHORN, SCARLET FIRETHORN
☼ ❄ ↔ 15 ft (4.5 m) ↑ 15 ft (4.5 m)
Dense shrub from southern Europe, Turkey, and Caucasus. Shiny, dark green, ovate to lance-shaped, toothed leaves, new growth finely downy. Small white flowers. Attractive scarlet berries on downy stalks. 'Lalandei' ★, strong growth habit, to 20 ft (6 m) tall, glossy bright orange-red fruit. Zones 5–9.

Pyracantha crenulata
HIMALAYAN FIRETHORN
☼ ❄ ↔ 12 ft (3.5 m) ↑ 15 ft (4.5 m)
Spiny shrub or small tree from southern slopes of Himalayas. Rusty downy new shoots. Glossy dark green leaves, notched margins. Corymbs of up to 30 small white flowers. Dark red berries. Zones 7–10.

Pyracantha koidzumii
TAIWAN FIRETHORN
☼ ❄ ↔ 12 ft (3.5 m) ↑ 12–15 ft (3.5–4.5 m)
Many-branched species native to Taiwan. Reddish downy young stems become smooth and purplish with age. Leaves dark green, glossy above, paler below. Small white flowers, in corymbs, in summer. Berry variable colors, sometimes orange-scarlet. Zones 7–10.

Pyracantha rogersiana
ROGERS FIRETHORN
☼ ❄ ↔ 12 ft (3.5 m) ↑ 12 ft (3.5 m)
Shrub from China; develops broad bun shape with age. Midgreen glossy leaves to 1½ in (35 mm) long. Small white flowers, in corymbs, mostly from 2-year-old branches, in spring. Yellow to orange-red berries. 'Flava', yellow berries. Zones 8–10.

Pyracantha Hybrid Cultivars
☼ ❄ ↔ 6–10 ft (1.8–3 m) ↑ 5–10 ft (1.5–3 m)
Spreading shrubs; good for hedges and shrub borders. 'Golden Charmer', vigorous arching shrub, rounded orange-yellow fruit; 'Harlequin', pink-flushed leaves, cream margins; 'Mohave', dark green leaves, masses of persistent bright orange-red fruit; 'Shawnee', spiny shrub, masses of white flowers, yellow to light orange fruit; 'Sparkler', leaves strikingly mottled; 'Watereri', compact yet vigorous shrub, bright red fruit. Other cultivars include 'Golden Dome', 'Orange Charmer', and 'Orange Glow'. Zones 5–9.

Pycnostachys urticifolia

Pyracantha angustifolia

Pyracantha crenulata

Pyrus calleryana

PYRUS
PEAR

Widely distributed through Europe and Asia, this genus of about 20 species is related to the apple (Malus) and belongs to the rose (Rosaceae) family. It comprises mostly deciduous trees of small to medium size, some thorny, with simple leaves that sometimes color to yellow and red in autumn. Flowers are mostly white, and are followed by fruit, edible in some species, that vary in size and shape. CULTIVATION: Pears will grow in most moderately fertile soils and prefer cool-temperate climates. Ornamental species are deep-rooted, drought tolerant, and reasonably tolerant of atmospheric pollution; pruning is seldom necessary. Fruiting forms require a cross-pollinator to set fruit. Pyrus species can be propagated from very fresh seed, but clonal forms are propagated by grafting to keep them true to type.

Pyrus calleryana
CALLERY PEAR
☼ ❄ ↔ 40 ft (12 m) ↑ 40 ft (12 m)
From southeastern China, Korea, Japan, and Taiwan. Ornamental tree, branches thorny. Glossy green leaves turn red in late autumn. Flowers white, unpleasant scent. Small pitted brown fruit on slender stalks. 'Bradford', non-thorny, flowers heavily in spring; Chanticleer/'Glen's Form' ★, scarlet autumn color, similar but narrower in form. Zones 5–10.

Pyrus nivalis
SNOW PEAR
☼ ❄ ↔ 20 ft (6 m) ↑ 30 ft (9 m)
Native to southern Europe. Small tree, thornless. Smooth-edged oval or egg-shaped leaves. White flowers, in racemes as young leaves open, in spring. Fruit small, round, yellowish green. Zones 5–9.

Pyrus salicifolia
SILVER PEAR, WILLOW-LEAFED PEAR
☼ ❄ ↔ 15 ft (4.5 m) ↑ 25 ft (8 m)
From Caucasus. Small graceful tree with slender drooping branches. Narrow willow-like leaves, silvery when young, age to grayish

green shiny upper surface. Flowers creamy white. Small, brown, pear-shaped fruit. 'Pendula', smaller, with fully pendulous branches; 'Silver Cascade', silvery gray foliage. Zones 4–9.

Pyrus ussuriensis
MONGOLIAN PEAR, USSURIAN PEAR
☼ ❄ ↔ 20 ft (6 m) ↑ 50 ft (15 m)
From northeastern China, Korea, and northern Japan. Yellowish green leaves ovate or rounded, bristle-toothed, crimson-bronze in autumn. Broad corymbs of white flowers in early spring. Fruit greenish brown, ripen in autumn–winter. Zones 4–9.

QUERCUS
OAK

This large genus of some 600 species, both evergreen and deciduous, is a member of the beech (Fagaceae) family. Most are trees, a few are shrubs, widely distributed throughout the Northern Hemisphere. Many are large trees that live to a great age. Fruit (acorns) are partly enclosed in a cup. All have simple leaves, often toothed or deeply lobed, some turning to spectacular tones of red or yellow-brown in autumn. Male and female flowers are carried on separate catkins on the same tree, usually in early spring. CULTIVATION: Oaks grow well in deep alluvial valley soils; only some of the Mediterranean and western North American species are tolerant of poor dry soil. Most enjoy cool moist conditions. Some early pruning may be needed to help establish a single straight trunk. Seed, sown as soon as ripe in summer or autumn, will germinate readily; cultivars and sterile hybrids are usually grafted in late winter or early spring.

Quercus agrifolia

Quercus acutissima
JAPANESE CHESTNUT OAK, JAPANESE OAK
☼ ❄ ↔ 40 ft (12 m) ↑ 80 ft (24 m)
Deciduous tree native to Japan, Korea, China, and Himalayas. Dark gray bark, roughly ridged and fissured. Narrow, oblong, chestnut-like leaves, polished green, edged with bristle-tipped teeth, persist until winter. Oval acorns half-enclosed in cups. Zones 5–10.

Quercus agrifolia
CALIFORNIA LIVE OAK, COAST LIVE OAK
☼ ❄ ↔ 35 ft (10 m) ↑ 40 ft (12 m)
From California and Mexico. Evergreen tree or large shrub, branched almost to ground. Smooth black bark, roughens with age. Leaves oval or rounded, hard-textured, edged with spine-tipped teeth, smooth underside. Acorns half-enclosed in cups. Zones 8–10.

Quercus alba
AMERICAN WHITE OAK, STAVE OAK, WHITE OAK
☼ ❄ ↔ 100 ft (30 m) ↑ 100 ft (30 m)
Large deciduous tree from southeastern Canada and eastern USA. Straight, often massive trunk, spreading branches. Bark dark gray. Oval leaves deeply and irregularly lobed, green when young, purple-crimson in autumn. Acorns in shallow scaly cups. Zones 3–9.

Quercus bicolor
SWAMP WHITE OAK

☼ ❋ ↔ 40 ft (12 m) ↑ 80 ft (24 m)

Found growing naturally in southeastern Canada and eastern USA. Matures into well-developed trunk, with ascending branches. Bark pale gray with thick ridges that are blackish gray. Leaves egg-shaped, shallowly lobed, shiny green, grayish and felted on underside. Acorns in clusters. Zones 4–10.

Quercus canariensis
ALGERIAN OAK, CANARY OAK, MIRBECK'S OAK

☼ ↔ 40 ft (12 m) ↑ 80 ft (24 m)

Semi-deciduous fast-growing tree from North Africa, southern Portugal, and Spain. Leaves large, egg-shaped or oval, shallowly lobed, dark shiny green on upper surface, paler on underside. Hemispheric acorns. Succeeds in heavy clay or shallow chalky soil. Zones 7–10.

Quercus bicolor

Quercus castaneifolia
syn. *Quercus afares*
CHESTNUT-LEAFED OAK

☼ ❋ ↔ 60 ft (18 m) ↑ 100 ft (30 m)

Found in Caucasus, Iran, and Algeria. Deciduous tree, develops broadly domed crown. Leaves oblong or narrowly oval, tapered at both ends, with coarse teeth, shiny dark green on upper surface, grayish downy on underside. Acorns dark brown. 'Green Spire', broadly columnar form with compact habit. Zones 6–10.

Quercus cerris
TURKEY OAK

☼ ❋ ↔ 75 ft (23 m) ↑ 100 ft (30 m)

Large, fast-growing, deciduous tree from southern Europe and Middle East. Slender crown when young, becoming broad-domed. Bark dull gray, roughly fissured. Leaves oval or oblong, shallowly lobed, coarsely toothed. Stalkless acorns enclosed in mossy cups. 'Argenteovariegata' (syn. 'Variegata'), leaves with conspicuous creamy white margin; 'Laciniata', leaves with narrow spreading lobes. Zones 7–10.

Quercus chrysolepis
CANYON LIVE OAK, MAUL OAK

☼ ❋ ↔ 30 ft (9 m) ↑ 70 ft (21 m)

From southwestern USA and Mexico. Variable, slow-growing, evergreen tree or large shrub, with generous spreading crown. Bark rather thick, smooth, gray-brown tinged with red. Leaves oval or ovate, spine-toothed, downy. Acorns almost stalkless. Zones 7–10.

Quercus coccinea
SCARLET OAK

☼ ❋ ↔ 40 ft (12 m) ↑ 70 ft (21 m)

From eastern and central USA. Deciduous tree with wide-spreading branches. Leaves oblong or elliptic, shiny dark green above, paler beneath, few leaves turn bright deep red, later whole crown colors in autumn. Acorns in shallow cups. 'Splendens', larger leaves, more reliable autumn color. Zones 2–9.

Quercus dentata
DAIMYO OAK

☼ ❋ ↔ 30 ft (9 m) ↑ 50 ft (15 m)

Deciduous tree naturally found in Japan, Korea, and China. Horizontal branches arise from short sinuous bole. Leaves like those of giant form of *Q. robur*, up to 15 in (38 cm) long and 8 in (20 cm) wide; most leaves turn brown and remain on tree during winter. Scaly cups half-enclose egg-shaped acorns. Zones 7–9.

Quercus douglasii
BLUE OAK

☼ ❋ ↔ 20 ft (6 m) ↑ 70 ft (21 m)

Native to California. Deciduous large shrub to medium-sized tree, rounded crown. Bark thin, gray, scaly. Leaves bluish with lobed margins. Small cone-shaped acorns in shallow hairy cups. Zones 6–11.

Quercus falcata
SOUTHERN RED OAK, SPANISH OAK

☼ ❋ ↔ 35 ft (10 m) ↑ 80 ft (24 m)

Deciduous tree from southern USA. Bark thick, nearly black, deeply furrowed. Leaves egg-shaped to ovate, shallowly 3-lobed or deeply 5- to 7-lobed, dark green above; pale gray-green and woolly beneath. Acorns nearly stalkless. *Q. f.* var. *pagodifolia*, bark smoother, becoming scaly with age, larger leaves. Zones 8–10.

Quercus frainetto
FARNETTO, HUNGARIAN OAK

☼ ↔ 60 ft (18 m) ↑ 100 ft (30 m)

Native to southern Italy, Balkans, and Hungary. Large, fast-growing, deciduous tree, broad-domed and wide-spreading. Bark pale gray, closely fissured. Leaves egg-shaped and deeply lobed. Acorns egg-shaped, half-enclosed in cups. 'Hungarian Crown', with erect habit. Zones 7–10.

Quercus coccinea

Quercus ilex

Quercus gambelii

GAMBEL OAK, ROCKY MOUNTAIN WHITE OAK

☼ ❄ ↔ 25 ft (8 m) ↕ 30 ft (9 m)

Deciduous tree from central west USA. Shrubby in harsh winters; underground runners form clumps. Leaves with 3 to 6 deep lobes on each side, fine hairs beneath. Acorns ovoid. Zones 4–9.

Quercus garryana

OREGON OAK, OREGON WHITE OAK

☼ ❄ ↔ 15 ft (4.5 m) ↕ 15 ft (4.5 m)

Deciduous tree from western USA. Short stout trunk, spreading crown. Leaves oval, deeply cut, shiny dark green above, paler and slightly hairy beneath. Acorns stalkless or nearly so. Zones 5–10.

Quercus × hispanica

SPANISH OAK

☼ ❄ ↔ 25 ft (8 m) ↕ 100 ft (30 m)

Natural cross between *Q. suber* and *Q. cerris*. Variable tree, sometimes nearly evergreen. Bark has thick fissures. Dark green lobed leaves. Acorns oblong to egg-shaped. '**Lucombeana**', tall, resembles *Q. cerris*, pale gray shallowly fissured bark, long leaves. Zones 6–10.

Quercus ilex

HOLLY OAK, HOLM OAK

☼ ❄ ↔ 60 ft (18 m) ↕ 70 ft (21 m)

Found naturally in southern Europe and North Africa. Large evergreen tree, broad-domed crown, branching close to ground. Bark brownish or black. Leaves leathery, glossy, smooth-edged or toothed, dark green above, grayish and downy below. Pointed acorns held in cups with many rows of small fluted scales. Zones 7–11.

Quercus kelloggii

CALIFORNIAN BLACK OAK

☼ ❄ ↔ 40 ft (12 m) ↕ 60–90 ft (18–27 m)

From California and Oregon, USA. Medium-sized to large deciduous tree with large, open, globe-like crown. Bark thick, divided

Quercus macrocarpa

by deep furrows into wide ridges. Leaves deeply lobed, bristle-toothed, shiny yellow-green above, paler, usually hairy beneath. Acorns carried on short stalks. Zones 7–10.

Quercus laurifolia

LAUREL OAK

☼ ❄ ↔ 60 ft (18 m) ↕ 60 ft (18 m)

Semi-evergreen tree from eastern USA. Bark thick, nearly black, furrowed. Leaves glossy green, oblong or egg-shaped, smooth-edged, can be shallowly lobed. Acorns stalkless or nearly so. Zones 6–11.

Quercus lyrata

OVERCUP OAK

☼ ❄ ↔ 30 ft (9 m) ↕ 60 ft (18 m)

Deciduous tree from southeastern USA with open crown and large crooked branches. Leaves oblong to egg-shaped, deeply and irregularly lobed, dark green above; paler, smooth or white-hairy beneath. Acorns stalkless or nearly so. Zones 8–10.

Quercus macrocarpa

BURR OAK, MOSSYCUP OAK

☼ ❄ ↔ 40 ft (12 m) ↕ 120 ft (36 m)

Found in northeastern and central North America. Large deciduous tree, massive trunk, spreading branches. Bark coarsely ridged, scaly, gray-brown. Leaves egg-shaped, conspicuously lobed. Young shoots and leaf undersurface covered in pale down. Acorns large, cups with long recurved scales. Zones 4–9.

Quercus mongolica

MONGOLIAN OAK

☼ ❄ ↔ 40 ft (12 m) ↕ 100 ft (30 m)

From Japan, Korea, northeastern China, Mongolia, and eastern Siberia. Deciduous tree with thick smooth branches. Leaves short, oval to oblong, strongly lobed, in clusters at branch ends. Egg-shaped acorns. Zones 4–9.

Quercus gambelii (golden foliage), in the wild, Colorado, USA

Quercus muehlenbergii

CHINQUAPIN OAK, YELLOW CHESTNUT OAK, YELLOW OAK

☼ ❋ ↔ 40 ft (12 m) ↑ 100 ft (30 m)

Deciduous tree found in central and southern USA. Grayish bark fissured vertically. Leaves oblong to lance-shaped, coarsely toothed, yellow-green above, pale and downy beneath; turn to rich reds and crimsons in autumn. Acorns half-enclosed in scaly cups. Zones 5–9.

Quercus nigra

WATER OAK

☼ ❋ ↔ 40 ft (12 m) ↑ 50 ft (15 m)

Broad-domed deciduous tree native to southern USA. Bark dark gray, develops scaly ridges. Leaves egg-shaped, variously lobed, glossy deep green, persist until winter, on slender stalks. Acorns enclosed in shallow cups. Zones 6–10.

Quercus palustris

PIN OAK, SWAMP OAK

☼ ❋ ↔ 60 ft (18 m) ↑ 100 ft (30 m)

Native to southeastern Canada and eastern USA. Large, dense, deciduous tree, slender branches droop at their extremities. Bark silver-gray becoming purplish gray with age. Leaves deeply lobed, shiny green; turn scarlet in autumn, persist until winter. Acorns in shallow hairy cups. Zones 3–10.

Quercus petraea

syn. *Quercus sessilis*

DURMAST OAK, SESSILE OAK

☼ ❋ ↔ 75 ft (23 m) ↑ 150 ft (45 m)

Found naturally in central and southeastern Europe. Spreading deciduous tree, similar to *Q. robur* but with stalkless acorns and more upright branches. Bark gray, deeply fissured. Leaves large, usually downy on underside. 'Columna', erect compact habit; 'Longifolia', exceptionally long leaves. Zones 5–9.

Quercus phellos

WILLOW OAK, WILLOW-LEAFED OAK

☼ ❋ ↔ 40 ft (12 m) ↑ 100 ft (30 m)

Large deciduous tree, slender branches, native to eastern USA. Bark smooth, gray, becomes fissured with age. Leaves narrow, willow-like, glossy green above, turn yellow and orange in autumn. Small acorns enclosed in shallow cups. Zones 5–10.

Quercus robur

COMMON OAK, ENGLISH OAK, PEDUNCULATE OAK

☼ ❋ ↔ 70 ft (21 m) ↑ 100 ft (30 m)

Large, long-lived, deciduous tree native to Europe, western Asia, and North Africa. Bark pale gray, closely fissured into short, narrow, vertical plates. Leaves shallowly lobed. Long-nosed acorns in shallow cups. May be invasive in cool climates. *Q. r.* subsp. *pedunculiflora,* leaves with fewer lobes, bluish underside. *Q. r.* f. *fastigiata,*

Quercus suber

Quercus robur

columnar habit. *Q. r.* 'Concordia' (golden oak), leaves suffused with golden yellow; 'Pendula', drooping branches. Zones 3–10.

Quercus rubra

syn. *Quercus borealis*

NORTHERN RED OAK, RED OAK

☼ ❋ ↔ 70 ft (21 m) ↑ 100 ft (30 m)

Deciduous tree from eastern Canada to Texas, USA. Broad head, horizontal branches. Bark smooth, silvery gray, can become brown-gray with age. Leaves large, oval to egg-shaped, lobed, turn red then red-brown to yellow and brown on old trees before falling. Dark red-brown acorns, on short stalks, in shallow scaly cups. 'Schrefeldii', more deeply lobed leaves, lobes overlapping. Zones 3–9.

Quercus shumardii

SHUMARD OAK

☼ ❋ ↔ 40 ft (12 m) ↑ 100 ft (30 m)

Native of prairie States of central USA. Large deciduous tree, wide-spreading crown. Bark thick, furrowed. Leaves 5- to 7-lobed, toothed, dark green above, paler below; turn red or golden brown in autumn. Acorns in thick shallow cups. *Q. s.* var. *schneckii,* smoother bark, less deeply lobed leaves. Zones 5–9.

Quercus suber

CORK OAK

☼ ❋ ↔ 70 ft (21 m) ↑ 70 ft (21 m)

Native to southwestern Europe and North Africa. Short-stemmed, wide-spreading, evergreen tree. Thick rugged bark provides cork. Leaves leathery, broadly toothed, shiny green above, grayish green and felted below. Egg-shaped acorns in scaly cups. Zones 8–10.

Quercus texana
syn. *Quercus buckleyi*
SPANISH OAK
☼ ❄ ↔ 50–70 ft (15–21 m) ↑ 50–70 ft (15–21 m)
From Texas and Oklahoma, USA. Broad deciduous tree, often branching close to ground. Leaves with 2 or 3 pairs of lobes, up to 5 in (12 cm) long, mature to yellow-green. Acorns ripen in second year; only base held in cup. Zones 7–10.

Quercus velutina
BLACK OAK, YELLOW BARK OAK
☼ ❄ ↔ 75 ft (23 m) ↑ 100 ft (30 m)
Large deciduous tree found in central and southern USA. Bark dark gray, smooth, deeply fissured with age. Leaves large, deeply lobed, glossy dark green above, downy below. Acorns half-enclosed in scaly cups. Zones 3–9.

Quercus virginiana
LIVE OAK
☼ ❄ ↔ 35 ft (10 m) ↑ 70 ft (21 m)
From southeastern USA, Mexico, and Cuba. Wide-spreading evergreen. Bark charcoal gray, fissured. Twigs downy, leaves elliptic or oblong, leathery, smooth-edged, glossy dark green above, grayish to whitish hairs below. Acorns singly or in clusters. Zones 7–11.

Quercus wislizeni
INTERIOR LIVE OAK
☼ ❄ ↔ 35 ft (10 m) ↑ 80 ft (24 m)
Large evergreen shrub or rounded tree from Mexico and California, USA. Bark thick, nearly black, deeply furrowed with scaly ridges. Leaves holly-like, oblong to ovate, slender spiny teeth. Acorns mature in first autumn. Zones 8–10.

QUILLAJA
There are about 3 species in this genus of evergreen shrubs or trees from South America, which is the only member of the family Quillajaceae. They have shiny, bright green, thick, and leathery leaves and white hairy flowers that appear in clusters of 3 to 5 blooms in spring. The fruit comprises 5 leathery follicles that open out into a star shape. The bark of some species is used as soap and for medicinal purposes.
CULTIVATION: These plants need a warm climate and a moist fertile soil that is well drained. Grow in a protected part-shaded position. Propagate from seed or cuttings.

Quillaja saponaria
SOAPBARK TREE
☼ ❄ ↔ 15–25 ft (4.5–8 m) ↑ 50–60 ft (15–18 m)
Evergreen tree native to Peru and Chile. Shiny, short-stalked, oval leaves. Purple-centered white flowers in spring. Thick dark bark contains saponin, lathers in water, used as soap substitute. Zones 8–10.

RADERMACHERA
This genus in the trumpet-vine (Bignoniaceae) family is made up of around 15 species, mostly trees or shrubs, from tropical Southeast Asia. The compound leaves may be bipinnate or tripinnate. The tubular to trumpet-shaped flowers, often fragrant and in shades of orange, green-yellow to yellow, pink, and white, are borne in loose panicles, mostly at the ends of branches. The capsular fruit contain flat seeds that are winged at each end. Some species are used for timber in their native regions.
CULTIVATION: Most species are fairly adaptable, but give the best results in a well-drained fertile soil in full sun to part-shade. Protection from strong winds is necessary, as is moderate irrigation during the growing period. Prune after flowering to maintain a bushy habit. Propagate from seed or cuttings, or by aerial layering.

Radermachera sinica
ASIAN BELL
☼ ✦ ↔ 15 ft (4.5 m) ↑ 30 ft (9 m)
Shrub or small tree from Southeast Asia. Dark green, glossy, bipinnate leaves, 8 ovate to lance-shaped leaflets. Scented deep yellow or white flowers, open at night, in spring–summer. Popular indoor foliage plant in cooler climates. Zones 10–12.

REHDERODENDRON
This is a small genus of 9 species of deciduous shrubs and small trees in the storax (Styracaceae) family, native to the woods of China and northern parts of Vietnam. Only *R. macrocarpum* is in cultivation, being valued for its masses of delightfully fragrant, drooping, white, bell-shaped flowers in spring. The flowers are followed by large winged seeds and richly colored leaves in autumn.
CULTIVATION: These plants grow well in deep humus-rich soil that doesn't dry out, in a sheltered site among other trees or facing into the morning sun. Propagation is from seed, which can be quite slow to germinate, or from half-hardened cuttings taken in summer and given bottom heat.

Rehderodendron macrocarpum
☼ ❄ ↔ 15–17 ft (4.5–5 m) ↑ 25–35 ft (8–10 m)
From mountains of western China. Small tree with flat layers of branches. Leaves up to 6 in (15 cm) long, color well before they shed. White, scented, bell-shaped flowers, to 2½ in (6 cm) across, held in drooping clusters, in spring. Ridged seed pods. Zones 8–10.

Quillaja saponaria

Radermachera sinica

REINWARDTIA

This small genus of 1 or 2 species of subshrubs with softwooded stems in the flax (Linaceae) family is named after Professor Kaspar Reinwardt, one-time director of the Leiden Botanic Gardens in the Netherlands. They are evergreen only in warm climates, with simple alternate leaves and slender, yellow, tubular flowers with 5 spreading petals.

CULTIVATION: They are best grown in a light fibrous soil with free drainage, in a warm position sheltered from wind. Pruning should be severe, almost to half-height, in late winter in order to encourage suckering from the base; this should be followed by a good mulching and deep watering. Propagate from soft-tip cuttings, which may be taken from the young growths in early spring.

Reinwardtia indica
YELLOW FLAX BUSH

☼ ☀ ↔ 2 ft (0.6 m) ↑ 3 ft (0.9 m)

From northern India, mostly in foothills of Himalayas. Soft erect stems sucker to form large clump. Smooth soft-textured leaves, elliptic to oval, bright green above, duller underneath. Bright butter yellow flowers in late autumn–spring. Zones 9–11.

Reinwardtia indica

RETAMA

Once included among other broom genera such as *Genista,* the 4 shrubby brooms that make up this genus, which is a member of the pea-flower subfamily of the legume (Fabaceae) family, are found in the Mediterranean region and the Canary Islands. While they are usually leafless when mature, as the chlorophyll-bearing green stems perform the functions of foliage, young plants often carry small linear leaves which sometimes also appear on adult plants in spring. Often rather untidy and wiry-stemmed, these shrubs are at their best in spring when smothered with flowers. These may be white or yellow, sometimes with purplish markings, and are often scented. The flowers are followed by conspicuous, somewhat inflated seed pods that are sometimes downy.

Retama monosperma

CULTIVATION: Best grown in full sun, and drought tolerant once established, these tough shrubs prefer a reasonably fertile, light, well-drained soil. They can be trimmed after flowering, but could never be called neat. Propagate from seed, which should be soaked before sowing, or from summer cuttings.

Retama monosperma
syn. *Genista monosperma*
SILVER BROOM

☼ ☀ ↔ 10 ft (3 m) ↑ 10 ft (3 m)

Native to Spain and northern Africa. Upright near-leafless plant with slender arching branches, silvery and downy when young, becoming grayish green as plant matures. Short racemes of small, white, fragrant pea-flowers, backed by purplish calyces, in spring. Zones 9–11.

RHAMNUS

There are more than 125 species within this genus in the buckthorn (Rhamnaceae) family. Mostly prickly evergreen or deciduous shrubs or trees, they are found throughout the Northern Hemisphere, as well as Brazil, eastern Africa, and South Africa, in woodland and heathland areas. The simple dark green leaves can be smooth-edged or toothed. The flowers are insignificant; some are fragrant. Green, blue-green, and yellow dyes are made from some species, while others are used medicinally, or wood is used commercially for turning. They are also cultivated for their ornamental foliage and berries.

CULTIVATION: Depending on the species, these shrubs or trees prefer moist to very dry conditions in full sun or part-shade, in moderately fertile soil. Some species tolerate alkaline soil and coastal sites. Propagate by sowing seed in autumn, as soon as it is ripe, giving protection from winter frosts; or from softwood cuttings of deciduous species in early summer. Half-hardened cuttings can be taken from evergreen species in summer, and layering can be done in either autumn or spring.

Rhamnus alaternus
ITALIAN BUCKTHORN

☼ ❊ ↔ 12 ft (3.5 m) ↑ 15 ft (4.5 m)

Evergreen shrub native to Mediterranean and Caucasus regions. Leaves leathery, dark green, shiny. Small yellow-green flowers in late spring–early summer. Fruit ripens to black in late summer. Tolerates dry soil conditions, pollution, and salt-laden air. 'Argenteovariegata' (syn. 'Variegata'), slightly less hardy than species, leaves with marbled grayish green center and white edges. Zones 7–10.

Rhamnus californica
COFFEEBERRY

☼ ❊ ↔ 10 ft (3 m) ↑ 12 ft (3.5 m)

Evergreen to semi-evergreen upright shrub from western USA. Red new growth, shiny green leaves. Clusters of pale greenish yellow flowers in late spring–early summer. Round red berries ripen to black. Zones 7–10.

Rhamnus californica

Rhamnus imeretina

Rhaphiolepis indica

Rhamnus cathartica
BUCKTHORN, COMMON BUCKTHORN

☼ ❄ ↔ 15 ft (4.5 m) ↑ 20 ft (6 m)

Deciduous, thorny, thicket-forming shrub from temperate Asia, Europe, and Africa. Green leaves elliptic to oval, finely toothed edges, turn yellow in autumn. Yellow-green flowers in late spring to early summer. Red fruit ripens to black. Zones 3–9.

Rhamnus crocea
REDBERRY

☼ ❄ ↔ 7 ft (2 m) ↑ 6 ft (1.8 m)

Native to Baja California, Mexico, and north to southwest Oregon, USA. Evergreen spreading shrub with thorny twigs. Leaves glossy, egg-shaped to elliptic, slightly toothed edges. Small flower clusters followed by red fruit. Zones 7–11.

Rhamnus frangula
ALDER BUCKTHORN

☼ ❄ ↔ 15 ft (4.5 m) ↑ 15 ft (4.5 m)

Deciduous shrub from North Africa, Europe, and parts of Russia. Shiny, dark green, oval leaves, paler beneath, turn red in autumn. Axillary clusters of small, greenish, hermaphroditic flowers in spring to summer. Fruit ripens from red to black. Zones 3–9.

Rhamnus imeretina

☼ ❄ ↔ 15 ft (4.5 m) ↑ 10 ft (3 m)

Deciduous shrub native to Black Sea region. Oval to oblong leaves, prominent veins, dull green above, felty lighter underside, turn dark brownish purple in autumn. Axillary clusters of unisex greenish flowers in summer. Fruit ripens to black. Zones 6–9.

Rhamnus prinoides
SOUTH AFRICAN DOGWOOD

☼ ❄ ↔ 15 ft (4.5 m) ↑ 25 ft (8 m)

From mountains of eastern South Africa and tropical Africa. Evergreen leaves leathery, deep green above, paler olive below. Cream flowers in spring–early summer. Red berries ripen black. Zones 9–11.

RHAPHIOLEPIS

There are up to 10 species of evergreen shrubs in this genus of the rose (Rosaceae) family, allied to *Photinia*. Originating in East and Southeast Asia, these plants do not bear spines or thorns; they have leathery deep green leaves and clusters of white or pink flowers in spring, often blooming again in autumn. Flowers are followed by blue-black berries that are highly attractive to some birds, which distribute the seeds.

CULTIVATION: Considered tough low-maintenance plants that are suitable for seaside planting, these shrubs can withstand quite hard pruning, which makes them ideal for hedges. Plant them in full sun in reasonable soil topped up with an organic mulch into which branches can be layered to produce further plants. The soil should be forked over as little as possible as the plants resent root disturbance. In addition to layering, the plants can be propagated from either cuttings or seed.

Rhaphiolepis × delacourii
HYBRID INDIAN HAWTHORN

☼ ❄ ↔ 8 ft (2.4 m) ↑ 6 ft (1.8 m)

Name applied to plants intermediate in character between parents *R. indica* and *R. umbellata*. First were deliberate crosses made by M. Delacour at Cannes shortly before 1900. Cultivars from these crosses include 'Coates' Crimson', slow growing, glossy green leaves, dark pink flowers in spring–summer; 'Spring Song', light pink flowers held for long time; and 'White Enchantress', dwarf form with small white flowers. Zones 8–11.

Rhaphiolepis indica
INDIAN HAWTHORN

☼ ❄ ↔ 8 ft (2.4 m) ↑ 8 ft (2.4 m)

From southern China. Leaves leathery, serrated, narrow, pointed, dark green above, olive green beneath. Pinkish brown new growths. Pink-tinted white flowers in clusters, at ends of branches, in spring. Invasive in warm-temperate climates. 'Ballerina', pink flowers; Springtime/'Monme', small flowers, bronzy new growth. Zones 8–11.

Rhaphiolepis umbellata

☼ ❄ ↔ 7 ft (2 m) ↑ 6 ft (1.8 m)

Dense mound-like shrub from coastal areas of southern Japan and Korea. Broad, thick, grayish green leaves, rounded tip, recurved edges. Bunches of white perfumed flowers in spring–early summer, spasmodically into winter in warmer areas. Blue-black berries. 'Minor' ★, dwarf form, smaller leaves and flowers. Zones 8–11.

Rhododendron albrechtii

Rhododendron alutaceum

Rhododendron arboreum

RHODODENDRON

syn. *Ledum*

AZALEA, RHODODENDRON

This very diverse genus of 800 or more species of mostly evergreen and some deciduous shrubs is widely distributed across the Northern Hemisphere, with the majority growing in temperate to cool regions. Particular concentrations occur in western China, the Himalayas, and northeastern Myanmar, while the Vireya rhododendrons grow mostly at higher altitudes throughout tropical southeastern Asia, as far south as the northern tip of Australia, with more than 200 species occurring on the island of New Guinea alone. Deciduous azalea species are scattered across cooler Northern Hemisphere climates, notably in Europe, China, Japan, and North America.

Rhododendrons vary in form from tiny, ground-hugging, prostrate and miniature plants adapted to exposed conditions, to small trees, often understory species in the forests of mountainous areas. Many species grow at altitudes of 3,000 ft (900 m) or more, and some can grow in the branches of trees or on rock faces. As members of the heath (Ericaceae) family, they are closely related to heathers (*Erica* and *Calluna* species) and have similar growing requirements. Some rhododendrons have solitary flowers but most bear terminal racemes, known as "trusses," of up to 24 or more blooms, in a wide palette of colors including white, pink, red, yellow, and mauve, excluding only shades of pure blue. Flowers may be a single color but are often multi-colored, with spots, stripes, edging, or a single blotch of a different color in the throat of the flower. With the exception of some Vireya species and hybrids, fragrant rhododendrons are always white or very pale pink. Blooms vary in size and shape but are generally bell-shaped, with a broad tube ending in flared lobes, and usually single. Flowers with double petals do occur, particularly among evergreen azaleas, which may also be "hose-in-hose," when the calyx is enlarged and the same color as the petals.

Most rhododendrons flower from early spring (early season) to early summer (late season), although some bear spot flowers briefly in autumn, and Vireya rhododendrons can flower at various times during the year, often in winter. Deciduous azaleas flower in spring on bare branches, usually before new leaf growth starts to emerge. The fruit is a many-seeded capsule, normally woody but sometimes soft, and sometimes bearing wings or tail-like appendages.

The genus is divided into 2 botanically distinct groups known as lepidotes and elepidotes, and these groups are subdivided further into the various rhododendron types. Plants from one group may not breed with plants from the other, thus limiting the options for hybridizers. The leaves, and sometimes the flowers and other parts, of lepidote rhododendrons are covered with scales, thought to aid transpiration. This group includes many cool-climate evergreen plants, such as the Vireya rhododendrons. The rest of the genus, the elepidote rhododendrons, with no scales on leaf or flower parts, includes the remaining cool-climate evergreen plants and the evergreen and deciduous azaleas. Azaleas were originally classified as a separate genus but are now regarded as botanically part of *Rhododendron*. Vireya rhododendrons can be grown in just about any climate as long as protection from frost is provided. Many are well suited to growing in hanging baskets and containers. The nectar of some species and some flower parts is poisonous.

CULTIVATION: Establishing an ideal growing environment before planting is the key to success with rhododendrons. Many of the problems likely to afflict them in the home garden can be minimized by maintaining soil quality and ensuring adequate ventilation. All prefer acidic soils between pH 4.5 and 6, high in organic matter and freely draining. A cool root run is essential; apply a deep mulch of organic material, which will also help to reduce moisture loss and control weed growth, while minimizing disturbance of the delicate roots. Many rhododendrons, particularly those with larger leaves, prefer a shaded or part-shaded aspect. They are ideally suited to planting under deciduous trees. While most prefer some protection from wind, sun, and frost, many others are tolerant of these conditions and some are well suited to exposed rock gardens.

Evergreen rhododendrons may be propagated by taking tip cuttings of new growth in spring, while deciduous azaleas are best grown from hardwood cuttings in winter. Plants may be grown from seed but germination and development is slow, and hybrids grown from seed are unlikely to be the same as the parent. Layering enables new plants to be created from low-hanging branches pinned to the ground and covered in a moist organic medium such as sphagnum moss. Plants which are difficult to propagate and establish by other means can be grafted onto the roots of stronger plants with more vigorous root systems. Regular pruning of rhododendrons is not necessary other than as required to control size, maintain shape, and to remove any damaged or diseased material; some species and hybrids actually resent pruning. Cultivated rhododendrons are compact and attain only about half the height of similar plants growing in the wild. The growing habit of all species and hybrids is related to the amount of shade the plant receives.

Rhododendron aberconwayi

◑ ❋ ↔4 ft (1.2 m) ↕6 ft (1.8 m)

Upright evergreen shrub from western China. Thick, smooth, glossy, dark green, elliptic leaves. Delicate, saucer-shaped, pale rose flowers, to 1½ in (35 mm) long, crimson or purple spots, in trusses of 5 to 12 blooms, in late spring–early summer. Zones 7–9.

Rhododendron albrechtii

◑ ❋ ↔4 ft (1.2 m) ↕7 ft (2 m)

Deciduous azalea native to central and northern Japan. Compact shrub. Whorls of 5 finely toothed leaves, gray hairy coating below. Openly bell-shaped, reddish purple flowers, in trusses of 3 to 5 blooms, in mid- to late spring. Zones 5–8.

Rhododendron alutaceum

◔/◑ ❋ ↔5–12 ft (1.5–3.5 m)
↕7–15 ft (2–4.5 m)

Large bushy shrub found in southwestern China. Broad, leathery, lance-shaped leaves, 2–6 in (5–15 cm) long, dense tan to red-brown hairs on underside. Trusses of up to 12 white to pale pink, funnel-shaped, red-spotted flowers, to 1½ in (35 mm) long, in early spring. Zones 7–10.

Rhododendron campylogynum

Rhododendron arborescens

◑ ❋ ↔8 ft (2.4 m) ↕10 ft (3 m)

Deciduous azalea native to woodlands of Appalachian region of eastern USA. Fragrant flowers white or pink, funnel-shaped, open with or after bright green obovate leaves. Zones 4–8.

Rhododendron arboreum

◑ ❋ ↔15 ft (4.5 m) ↕60 ft (18 m)

Slow-growing tree species common in Himalayan rhododendron forests, also in southern India, western China, and Thailand. Leaves

Rhododendron calophytum

tough, broad, green above; hairy brown coating below. Flowers fleshy, narrowly bell-shaped, 2 in (5 cm) wide, white or pink to blood red, in trusses of 15 to 20 blooms, in spring. *R. a.* subsp. *cinnamomeum*, leaves with reddish brown hairs beneath. *R. a.* subsp. *delavayi*, red-flowered form. Zones 7–9.

Rhododendron arizelum

◑ ❋ ↔6–25 ft (1.8–8 m) ↕6–25 ft (1.8–8 m)

Variable evergreen shrub or small tree from northeastern Myanmar, northeastern India, and western China. Bell-shaped flowers yellow, cream, or deep rose pink, in trusses of 12 to 25 blooms, mid- to late season. Oval-shaped leaves, velvety coating beneath. Zones 8–9.

Rhododendron augustinii

◑ ❋ ↔2–10 ft (0.6–3 m) ↕3–20 ft
(0.9–6 m)

Compact, freely flowering, variable, evergreen shrub from China. Elliptic leaves, hairy beneath. Flowers mauve-blue to purple, greenish spots; funnel-shaped, in trusses of 2 to 6 blooms, mid- to late season. Zones 6–9.

Rhododendron austrinum

FLORIDA AZALEA

◑ ❋ ↔10 ft (3 m) ↕10 ft (3 m)

Rarely grown, freely flowering, deciduous azalea from southeastern USA. Fragrant, funnel-shaped, creamy yellow to golden yellow, orange, or red flowers, with distinctive long protruding stamens, bloom before or as downy leaf shoots open. Zones 6–9.

Rhododendron calophytum

◑ ❋ ↔20 ft (6 m) ↕15 ft (4.5 m)

Native to China. Evergreen small tree, shorter in cultivation. Long, dark green, smooth leaves curl and droop in colder weather. White or pink bell-shaped flowers, with distinct purple basal blotch, early to mid-season. Zones 6–9.

Rhododendron campanulatum

◑ ❋ ↔15 ft (4.5 m) ↕15 ft (4.5 m)

From Himalayas. Shrub or small tree, varies widely in form and height. Smooth leaves, underside densely covered with brown woolly hairs. Bell-shaped flowers, lavender-blue or white to pale mauve, with purple spots, in trusses of 6 to 12 blooms, in spring. Zones 5–8.

Rhododendron campylogynum

◑ ❋ ↔30 in (75 cm) ↕18 in (45 cm)

Creeping evergreen shrub from eastern India and northeastern Myanmar. Dark green leaves, white or silvery hairy underside. Nodding creamy white or bright pink flowers, in delicate trusses of 1 to 3 blooms, in late spring–summer. Zones 7–9.

Rhododendron concinnum

Rhododendron canescens
FLORIDA PINXTER AZALEA, PIEDMONT AZALEA, SWEET AZALEA

☼ ❄ ↔ 8 ft (2.4 m) ↕ 15 ft (4.5 m)

Deciduous azalea native to eastern USA, from North Carolina southward and west to Oklahoma. Oblong to lance-shaped leaves. Scented pink flowers, funnel-shaped, before or with leaves, in spring. White- or magenta-flowered forms occur. Zones 6–10.

Rhododendron catawbiense ★
CATAWBA RHODODENDRON, MOUNTAIN ROSEBAY

☼ ❄ ↔ 10 ft (3 m) ↕ 10 ft (3 m)

From eastern USA; robust evergreen similar in form to *R. ponticum*. Glossy dark green leaves, broadly elliptic to obovate. Funnel-shaped faintly spotted flowers, lilac-purple, in compact trusses of 15 to 20 blooms, in late spring–early summer. Important parent of many frost-hardy hybrids. Zones 4–9.

Rhododendron ciliatum
☼ ❄ ↔ 6 ft (1.8 m) ↕ 6 ft (1.8 m)

Evergreen species from Himalayas. Young shoots and upper surface of elliptic leaves distinctively bristly. Bell- to funnel-shaped flowers, white or white flushed with pink, in trusses of 2 to 4 blooms, in spring. Zones 7–9.

Rhododendron cinnabarinum
☼ ❄ ↔ 7 ft (2 m) ↕ 10 ft (3 m)

Evergreen species from Himalayas and north Myanmar. Roundish, glaucous, green leaves. Waxy, red to orange, narrowly bell-shaped flowers, in trusses of 3 to 9 blooms, mid- to late season. Zones 6–9.

Rhododendron concinnum
☼ ❄ ↔ 6–10 ft (1.8–3 m) ↕ 6–20 ft (1.8–6 m)

Vigorous evergreen shrub or small tree from western China. Smooth dark green leaves, scaly above, gray-brown scales underneath. Purple or red-purple funnel-shaped flowers, scaly on outside, in trusses of 2 to 8, in mid- to late spring. **Pseudoyanthinum Group**, ruby red flowers. Zones 7–9.

Rhododendron dauricum
☼ ❄ ↔ 8 ft (2.4 m) ↕ 8 ft (2.4 m)

From northern latitudes in East Asia, from eastern Siberia to Japan. Evergreen straggly shrub, scaly young shoots, densely scaly dark green leaves, hairy beneath. Widely funnel-shaped flowers, pink or violet-pink, singly or in pairs, early season. Zones 5–8.

Rhododendron decorum
☼ ❄ ↔ 8 ft (2.4 m) ↕ 20 ft (6 m)

Native to western China, northeastern Myanmar, and Laos. Evergreen shrub or small tree. Large smooth leaves to 8 in (20 cm) long. Scented, white to pale pink, funnel-shaped flowers, in trusses of 8 to 12 blooms, late in season. **R. d.** subsp. *diaprepes,* larger leaves and flowers. Zones 7–9.

Rhododendron degronianum
☼ ❄ ↔ 7 ft (2 m) ↕ 8 ft (2.4 m)

Evergreen species from central and southern Japan. Shiny, dark green, deeply veined leaves, fawn-colored felt-like hairs underneath. Pink, rose, reddish, or white bell-shaped flowers, in trusses of 6 to 15 blooms, mid- to late season. **R. d.** subsp. *yakushimanum* (syn. *R. yakushimanum*), slow- and low- growing spreading form, glossy dark green leaves, distinctive recurved margins, compact trusses of 8 to 12 rose-colored buds and pink flowers. Zones 7–9.

Rhododendron edgeworthii
☼ ❄ ↔ 6 ft (1.8 m) ↕ 6 ft (1.8 m)

Evergreen species from Himalayas, upper Myanmar, and southwestern China. Deeply textured, wrinkled leaves, brown hairy coating, scales beneath. Fragrant, white, funnel-shaped flowers, occasionally flushed with pink, in trusses of 2 to 3 flowers, midseason. Zones 9–10.

Rhododendron falconeri
☼ ❄ ↔ 30 ft (9 m) ↕ 40 ft (12 m)

Native to Himalayas. Evergreen with brown flaking bark. Large, wrinkled, dark mat green leaves, white with reddish hairy coating underneath. Fragrant, creamy white to pink or pale cream, bell-shaped flowers, in large trusses of 12 to 25 blooms, mid- to late

Rhododendron falconeri

Rhododendron fortunei

season. *R. f.* subsp. *eximium,* more persistent hairy coating under leaves, regarded by some as separate species, *R. eximium.* Zones 9–10.

Rhododendron flammeum

FLAME AZALEA

☀ ✦ ↔ 3 ft (0.9 m) ↑ 6 ft (1.8 m)

Freely flowering deciduous azalea from eastern states of USA, from Georgia to South Carolina. Compact shrub, slender branches. Scarlet flowers open with leaves in late spring to early summer. Rare in cultivation. Zones 10–11.

Rhododendron forrestii

☀ ❄ ↔ 48 in (120 cm) ↑ 4 in (10 cm)

Creeping, prostrate, evergreen shrub native to western China and northeastern Myanmar. Leaves leathery, dark green, purple-red beneath. Bright scarlet tubular-campanulate flowers, singly or in pairs, mid- to late season. Used in breeding programs. *R. f.* subsp. *papillatum,* narrow leaves, light brown beneath; 'Scarlet Runner', scarlet flowers. *R. f.* Repens Group, dwarf forms with creeping habit, leaves extensively veined, red flowers; 'May Day', scarlet flowers. Zones 8–9.

Rhododendron fortunei

☀ ❄ ↔ 8 ft (2.4 m) ↑ 15 ft (4.5 m)

Widespread in its native eastern China. Evergreen, broadly upright, sometimes spreading shrub or tree. Rough grayish brown bark; reddish, bluish, or purplish leaf stalks. Fragrant, pale pink, rose, lilac to white, bell-shaped flowers, in trusses of 6 to 12 blooms, late in season. *R. f.* subsp. *discolor,* abundant pink flowers, late season; *R. f.* Houlstonii Group, soft pink to light purple flowers, mid-season. Zones 6–9.

Rhododendron griffithianum

☀ ❄ ↔ 10 ft (3 m) ↑ 60 ft (18 m)

Himalayan evergreen tree species with open habit. Flaking peeling bark; smooth oblong leaves. Fragrant flowers, white, shades of pale pink, or even yellowish, in trusses of 3 to 6 blooms, mid- to late season. Zones 8–9.

Rhododendron haematodes

☀ ❄ ↔ 5 ft (1.5 m) ↑ 5 ft (1.5 m)

Evergreen shrub naturally found in western China and northeastern Myanmar. Young shoots densely bristly; mature leaves matted with fawn to reddish brown hairs underneath. Fleshy, tubular to bell-shaped, scarlet to deep crimson flowers in late spring–early summer. *R. h.* subsp. *chaetomallum,* bristly young shoots and leaf stems. Zones 7–9.

Rhododendron impeditum

☀ ❄ ↔ 12 in (30 cm) ↑ 12 in (30 cm)

Compact ground-covering evergreen from western China. Dense, shiny, dark green, scaly foliage. Violet to purple funnel-shaped flowers, in small trusses of 1 to 3 blooms, mid-season. Zones 4–8.

Rhododendron impeditum

Rhododendron jasminiflorum

Rhododendron indicum

INDIAN AZALEA, JAPANESE EVERGREEN AZALEA

☀ ❄ ↔ 2 ft (0.6 m) ↑ 3 ft (0.9 m)

Variable evergreen species from southern Japan. Densely branched; low, sometimes prostrate habit. Mass of shiny dark green leaves. Red broadly funnel-shaped flowers, singly or in pairs, in spring. 'Balsaminiflorum', dwarf form, salmon red double flowers; 'Macranthum', compact shrub, orange-red flowers. Zones 6–9.

Rhododendron intricatum

☀ ❄ ↔ 5 ft (1.5 m) ↑ 5 ft (1.5 m)

Fast-growing, delicately branched, evergreen shrub from western China. Small, mat, smooth, grayish green leaves, densely scaly below. Tiny flowers, pale lavender to dark purple-blue, short stamens, in compact trusses of 2 to 10 blooms, mid- to late season. Zones 5–8.

Rhododendron jasminiflorum

☀ ✦ ↔ 22 in (55 cm) ↑ 22 in (55 cm)

Vireya species found in Malay Peninsula, Philippines, and Sumatra. Leaves have scaly undersides. Trusses of 6 to 12 tubular flowers, white, sometimes flushed pink, in winter. Used in hybridizing. Spreading habit makes it ideal for hanging baskets. Zones 10–11.

Rhododendron kaempferi

KAEMPFER AZALEA

☀ ❄ ↔ 4 ft (1.2 m) ↑ 4 ft (1.2 m)

Densely branched shrub native to Japan; deciduous in cool climates. Red-brown bristles on young shoots. Salmon or brick red, funnel-shaped flowers, in trusses of 2 to 4 blooms, in late spring. Zones 5–8.

Rhododendron kiusianum

KYUSHU AZALEA

☀ ❄ ↔ 3 ft (0.9 m) ↑ 3 ft (0.9 m)

Parent of Kurume Group of azaleas. Evergreen species from Kyushu, Japan; deciduous at higher altitudes. Much-branched, often prostrate shrub with small hairy leaves. Funnel-shaped flowers, rose-purple, purple, red, pink, or white, in trusses of 2 to 3 blooms, in late spring. 'Mountain Gem', rose-purple flowers. Zones 6–9.

Rhododendron konori

⬕ ✣ ↔ 6 ft (1.8 m) ↕ 12 ft (3.5 m)

Vireya species from New Guinea. Large leaves, mat green, bluish tinge, reddish brown hairy coating underneath. Fragrant white or pinkish flowers, in trusses of 5 to 8 blooms, in winter. Zones 10–11.

Rhododendron lacteum

⬕ ✣ ↔ 12 ft (3.5 m) ↕ 12 ft (3.5 m)

Evergreen shrub or small tree found in western China. Leaves have hairy underside. Large, bell-shaped, cream flowers, sometimes flushed pink, to 2 in (5 cm) long, in large compact trusses of 15 to 30 blooms, in spring. Prefers well-sheltered position. Zones 7–9.

Rhododendron laetum

⬕ ✣ ↔ 4 ft (1.2 m) ↕ 10 ft (3 m)

Vireya species native to northwestern New Guinea, more compact in cultivation. Broad elliptic leaves. Large funnel-shaped flowers of pure golden yellow, ageing to red, orange, or salmon, in open trusses of 6 to 8 blooms, in autumn–spring. Zones 10–11.

Rhododendron leucaspis

⬕ ✣ ↔ 4 ft (1.2 m) ↕ 4 ft (1.2 m)

Compact, rounded, evergreen shrub from western China. Hairy elliptic leaves. Flowers bell-shaped, milky white, often tinged pink, singly, in 2s or 3s. Protect from late winter frosts. Zones 7–9.

Rhododendron lochiae

AUSTRALIAN RHODODENDRON

⬕ ✣ ↔ 2 ft (0.6 m) ↕ 3 ft (0.9 m)

Slow-growing, compact, bushy Vireya species from northeastern tip of Australia. Scaly young shoots, dark green broadly obovate leaves, scaly underneath. Bright scarlet funnel-shaped flowers, in loose trusses of 2 to 7 blooms, in winter. Zones 10–11.

Rhododendron luteiflorum

syn. *Rhododendron glaucophyllum* var. *luteiflorum*

⬕/⬕ ✣ ↔ 18–32 in (45–80 cm) ↕ 12–36 in (30–90 cm)

Alpine species from northern Myanmar. Aromatic, pointed oval to lance-shaped, olive green leaves, around 1 in (25 mm) long. Nodding, yellow-green to yellow, 1 in (25 mm) long flowers, in trusses of 3 to 6 blooms, in mid-spring. Zones 6–9.

Rhododendron lutescens

⬕ ✣ ↔ 15 ft (4.5 m) ↕ 20 ft (6 m)

From western China, straggly habit, gray or brown flaking bark. Bright bronze-red young foliage in spring, show of color in autumn. Small, delicate, pale yellow, funnel-shaped flowers, long stamens, in trusses of 1 to 3 blooms, in late winter–early spring. Zones 7–9.

Rhododendron luteum

PONTIC AZALEA

⬕ ✣ ↔ 8 ft (2.4 m) ↕ 12 ft (3.5 m)

Widely grown deciduous azalea from eastern Europe, used extensively in breeding programs. Foliage colors red, orange, and purple in autumn. Tubular, funnel-shaped, clear yellow flowers, in trusses of 7 to 12 blooms, before leaves in spring. Zones 5–9.

Rhododendron macgregoriae

⬕ ✣ ↔ 7 ft (2 m) ↕ 15 ft (4.5 m)

Shrub or small tree, most widespread of New Guinea's Vireya rhododendrons. Leaves with scaly underside. Flowers light yellow to dark orange or red, narrow corolla tube, in trusses of 8 to 15 flowers, in winter. Zones 10–11.

Rhododendron macrophyllum

⬕ ✣ ↔ 12 ft (3.5 m) ↕ 12 ft (3.5 m)

Evergreen shrub from western North America. Dark green leaves, paler underside, smooth-edged. Bell-shaped flowers, white to pink, yellow spots, in trusses of 9 to 20 blooms, late in season. Zones 6–9.

Rhododendron maddenii

⬕ ✣ ↔ 8 ft (2.4 m) ↕ 25 ft (8 m)

From Himalayas, southwestern China, Myanmar, and Vietnam. Leaves smooth, thick, brownish, hairy below, heavy scaling. Large funnel-shaped flowers, white, often flushed pink or purple, yellow basal blotch, in trusses of 1 to 11 blooms, in late spring. Zones 9–10.

Rhododendron mallotum

⬕ ✣ ↔ 12 ft (3.5 m) ↕ 20 ft (6 m)

Evergreen shrub or small tree from western China and northeastern Myanmar. Young leaf shoots and thick, stiff, leathery leaves have gray or brown hairy coating. Trusses of up to 20 tubular bell-shaped, red or crimson flowers in early spring. Zones 7–9.

Rhododendron lacteum

Rhododendron lutescens

Rhododendron luteum

Rhododendron nuttallii

Rhododendron occidentale

Rhododendron orbiculatum

Rhododendron maximum

GREAT LAUREL RHODODENDRON, ROSEBAY RHODODENDRON

☀ ❉ ↔ 7 ft (2 m) ↑ 6 ft (1.8 m)

Compact, spreading, evergreen shrub from eastern North America. Smooth leaves, fine hairy coating underneath. Bell-shaped flowers, white to pinkish purple, with yellow-green spots, in late spring–early summer. 'Summertime', white flowers, tips of petals flushed reddish purple. Zones 3–8.

Rhododendron megeratum

☀ ⚘ ↔ 15 in (38 cm) ↑ 15–30 in (38–75 cm)

Very early-flowering, evergreen, prostrate species found in north-eastern India, northeastern Myanmar, and western China. Leaves small, almost circular, whitish hairy coating below. Broad, bell-shaped, creamy white to yellow flowers. Zones 9–10.

Rhododendron minus

☀ ❉ ↔ 3–5 ft (0.9–1.5 m) ↑ 3–5 ft (0.9–1.5 m)

Small evergreen from North America. Pointed elliptic leaves, densely scaly below. Flowers usually scaly, white to pink or mauve, in trusses of 6 to 12 blooms, in mid-spring. Carolinianum Group, pink or pale rose-purple flowers in summer. Zones 4–9.

Rhododendron molle

DECIDUOUS AZALEA

☀ ❉ ↔ 4 ft (1.2 m) ↑ 4 ft (1.2 m)

Small deciduous azalea native to eastern China. Funnel-shaped flowers golden yellow or orange color, large greenish blotch, in trusses of 6 to 12 blooms, with or before mid-green leaves, in mid-spring. *R. m.* subsp. *japonicum* (syn. *R. japonicum*), from Japan, yellow or orange flowers, one parent of Mollis hybrids. Zones 7–9.

Rhododendron mucronulatum

KOREAN RHODODENDRON

☀ ❉ ↔ 3 ft (0.9 m) ↑ 6 ft (1.8 m)

Straggly deciduous shrub from eastern Russia, northern and central China, Mongolia, Korea, and Japan. Elliptic to lance-shaped leaves. Funnel-shaped bright mauve-pink flowers, protruding stamens, blue anthers, in spring, before foliage. 'Alba', white flowers; 'Cornell Pink' ★, large clear pink flowers; 'Crater's Edge', deep pink flowers; 'Mahogany Red', wine red flowers tinged bronze. Zones 4–8.

Rhododendron neriifolium

◑/☀ ❉ ↔ 6–12 ft (1.8–3.5 m) ↑ 10–20 ft (3–6 m)

Large shrub or small tree from western China to northern Myanmar. Long, pointed elliptic to lance-shaped, dark green leaves, waxy pale blue below. Tubular bell-shaped flowers, in trusses of up to 12 blooms, usually bright red to deep pink, rarely yellow. Zones 7–10.

Rhododendron nuttallii

☀ ⚘ ↔ 20 ft (6 m) ↑ 35 ft (10 m)

Evergreen large shrub or small tree from Himalayas, western China, northern Myanmar, and northern India. Purplish brown bark, crimson-purple young growth. Creamy white bell-shaped flowers, yellow throat, in trusses of 7 blooms, in mid- to late spring. Zones 9–10.

Rhododendron × obtusum

KURUME AZALEA

☀ ❉ ↔ 3 ft (0.9 m) ↑ 3 ft (0.9 m)

Natural hybrid between *R. kiusianum* and *R. kaempferi*, from Japan. Twiggy, sometimes prostrate shrub. Densely bristly brown leaf shoots; bright green leaves. Bright red, scarlet, or crimson funnel-shaped flowers, in trusses of 1 to 3 blooms, in late spring. Zones 6–9.

Rhododendron occidentale

WESTERN AZALEA

☀ ❉ ↔ 5 ft (1.5 m) ↑ 5 ft (1.5 m)

Variable deciduous azalea from western USA. Bright green foliage turns bronze, then scarlet, crimson, or yellow in autumn. Fragrant, white or light pink, funnel-shaped flowers, deep yellow blotch, in mid-spring. Zones 6–9.

Rhododendron orbiculare

☀ ❉ ↔ 10 ft (3 m) ↑ 10 ft (3 m)

Evergreen from western China. Rounded bright green leaves, deeply notched bases. Rose to deep red bell-shaped flowers, up to 2½ in (6 cm) long, in trusses of 7 to 10 blooms, in spring. Zones 6–9.

Rhododendron orbiculatum

☀ ⚘ ↔ 3 ft (0.9 m) ↑ 3 ft (0.9 m)

Compact Vireya rhododendron from Borneo. Thick rounded leaves. Large, orchid-like flowers, white or silvery pink, in loose trusses of up to 5 blooms. Good specimen for hanging baskets. Zones 10–11.

Rhododendron periclymenoides

coating on young shoots; dark green leaves. Large trusses of 20 to 30 bell-shaped creamy white flowers, flushed rose, in late winter–early spring. Protect in cooler areas. Zones 9–10.

Rhododendron quinquefolium
FIVE-LEAF AZALEA

☼ ❄ ↔ 4–8 ft (1.2–2.4 m) ↕ 8–25 ft (2.4–8 m)

Deciduous azalea from central Japan. Oval-shaped leaves, in whorls of 4 to 5, at ends of branches. Pure white flowers, with green spots, in late spring. 'Five Arrows', white flowers spotted with olive green. Zones 6–8.

Rhododendron racemosum

☼ ❄ ↔ 5 ft (1.5 m) ↕ 5 ft (1.5 m)

Variable evergreen shrub from western China. Smooth leathery leaves. Funnel-shaped flowers, white to pale pink, in trusses of up to 6 blooms, in spring. 'Forrest', dwarf form, palest pink flowers; 'Glendoick', taller, deep pink flowers; 'Rock Rose', bright purplish pink flowers. Zones 5–8.

Rhododendron pachysanthum

☼ ❄ ↔ 3 ft (0.9 m) ↕ 4 ft (1.2 m)

Compact, rounded, evergreen shrub from Taiwan. Dark green leaves, dense brownish hair on underside. New growth felted all over with pale brownish hairs. Trusses of 8 to 10, sometimes 20, bell-shaped white flowers, densely spotted with crimson, in spring. Zones 7–9.

Rhododendron periclymenoides
syn. *Rhododendron nudiflorum*
PINXTERBLOOM AZALEA

☼ ❄ ↔ 8 ft (2.4 m) ↕ 10 ft (3 m)

Deciduous azalea from eastern North America. Trusses of 6 to 12 fragrant funnel-shaped flowers, white, pale pink, or violet-red, with distinctive long stamens and long corolla tube, open just before or with bright green leaves, in late spring. Zones 3–9.

Rhododendron ponticum
PONTIC RHODODENDRON

☼ ❄ ↔ 20 ft (6 m) ↕ 25 ft (8 m)

Native to Mediterranean region. Vigorous evergreen shrub or small tree with smooth leaves. Compact trusses of 10 to 15 pale mauve or lilac-pink funnel-shaped flowers, to 2 in (5 cm) long, in mid- to late spring. Makes useful hedge or windbreak, but can become invasive weed. 'Silver Edge', similar to 'Variegatum', which has creamy white and green variegated leaves; less vigorous and invasive than species. Zones 6–9.

Rhododendron protistum

☼ ❄ ↔ 15 ft (4.5 m) ↕ 100 ft (30 m)

Evergreen species from western China and northern Myanmar; usually tall shrub in cultivation. Dense, yellowish gray, hairy

Rhododendron ponticum

Rhododendron reticulatum

☼ ❄ ↔ 4 ft (1.2 m) ↕ 4 ft (1.2 m)

Freely flowering, hardy, evergreen azalea from Japan. Leaves hairy initially, become smooth. Reddish purple to magenta bell-shaped flowers, to 2 in (5 cm) wide, carried singly or in pairs, in mid- to late spring. Zones 6–9.

Rhododendron rubiginosum

☼ ❄ ↔ 20 ft (6 m) ↕ 30 ft (9 m)

Evergreen species from west China and northeast Myanmar. Smooth aromatic leaves. Bell-shaped flowers, pink, rose, or lilac shades, in trusses of 4 to 8 blooms, in spring. Zones 7–9.

Rhododendron schlippenbachii
ROYAL AZALEA

☼ ❄ ↔ 15 ft (4.5 m) ↕ 15 ft (4.5 m)

Deciduous azalea from Korea and far eastern Russia. Light green leaves, in whorls at ends of branches, turn bronze in autumn. Funnel-shaped star-like flowers, pale pink or white, open with or shortly after leaves, in late spring. Zones 4–8.

Rhododendron scopulorum

☼ ❄ ↔ 8 ft (2.4 m) ↕ 15 ft (4.5 m)

Native to southwestern China. Dark green grooved leaves; pale green, scaly below. Fragrant, white or pink, widely funnel-shaped flowers, in trusses of 2 to 7 blooms, mid- to late season. Zones 9–10.

Rhododendron sinogrande

☼ ❄ ↔ 30 ft (9 m) ↕ 50 ft (15 m)

Evergreen understory tree from western China and northern Myanmar. Long, dark green, heavily wrinkled leaves; silvery white, pale brown, or tan coating underneath. Creamy white or yellow flowers, in trusses of 15 to 30 blooms, in mid-spring. Zones 8–9.

Rhododendron spinuliferum

☀ ❋ ↔ 8 ft (2.4 m) ↑ 10 ft (3 m)

Evergreen shrub native to western China. Smooth, dark purple-brown bark. Juvenile leaves hairy, mature leaves smooth. Narrow tubular flowers, crimson, brick red, or orange, in trusses of 1 to 5 blooms, in mid-spring. Zones 8–9.

Rhododendron stamineum

☀ ❧ ↔ 10 ft (3 m) ↑ 10 ft (3 m)

Evergreen shrub or small tree from western China. Smooth leaves. Trusses of 1 to 3 funnel-shaped blooms, white with yellow blotch, stamens longer than corolla, in mid- to late spring. Zones 9–10.

Rhododendron thomsonii

☀ ❋ ↔ 2–20 ft (0.6–6 m) ↑ 2–20 ft (0.6–6 m)

Evergreen species from Himalayas. Red-brown, fawn, or pink bark. Thick, leathery, rounded leaves. Bell-shaped flowers, red or crimson, darker spots, in trusses of 6 to 13 blooms, in spring. Zones 6–9.

Rhododendron tomentosum

syn. *Ledum palustre*

CRYSTAL TEA, MARSH LEDUM, WILD ROSEMARY

☀/◑ ❋ ↔ 3 ft (0.9 m) ↑ 1–4 ft (0.3–1.2 m)

Evergreen shrub from northern and central Europe, northern Asia, and northern North America. Red-brown hairs on young shoots; dark green leaves with incurved edges. Clusters of white flowers, at branch tips, in late spring–early summer. Zones 2–8.

Rhododendron trichostomum

☀ ❋ ↔ 3 ft (0.9 m) ↑ 5 ft (1.5 m)

Variable evergreen shrub from western China; normally compact, tiny, twiggy, intricately branched, miniature bush. Aromatic, stiff, narrow, leathery, dark green leaves. Tiny flowers white, pink, or rose, in spherical trusses of 8 to 20 blooms, in late spring. Zones 7–9.

Rhododendron veitchianum

☀ ❧ ↔ 8 ft (2.4 m) ↑ 8 ft (2.4 m)

Spreading evergreen shrub from Laos, Myanmar, Thailand, and Vietnam, often grows epiphytically. Smooth, peeling, reddish

Rhododendron schlippenbachii

brown bark. Dark green leaves, paler below. Large, highly fragrant, pure white, funnel-shaped flowers, yellow blotch, in trusses of up to 5 blooms, in late spring–early summer. **Cubittii Group**, bristle-edged leaves, fragrant pink flowers. Zones 9–10.

Rhododendron viscosum

SWAMP AZALEA, SWAMP HONEYSUCKLE

☀ ❋ ↔ 8 ft (2.4 m) ↑ 8 ft (2.4 m)

Deciduous azalea native to eastern and central North America. New leaf growth yellowish or grayish brown. Dark green leaves, paler below. Funnel-shaped white flowers, spicy fragrance, in trusses of 4 to 9 blooms, in late spring–early summer. Zones 4–9.

Rhododendron wardii

☀ ❋ ↔ 15 ft (4.5 m) ↑ 25 ft (8 m)

Evergreen shrub from western China. Grayish brown bark. Leaves leathery, dark green, rounded; pale green, glaucous below. Saucer-shaped pale yellow or bright yellow flowers, in loose trusses of 5 to 14 blooms, in late spring. Zones 7–9.

Rhododendron williamsianum

☀ ❋ ↔ 4 ft (1.2 m) ↑ 5 ft (1.5 m)

Evergreen shrub native to western China. Bristly young shoots, rounded leaves, reddish glands beneath. Bell-shaped flowers, pale pink with darker spots, in 2s or 3s, in spring. Zones 7–9.

Rhododendron yedoense

KOREAN AZALEA, YODOGAWA AZALEA

☀ ❋ ↔ 3 ft (0.9 m) ↑ 3 ft (0.9 m)

Deciduous or semi-deciduous azalea from Korea. Compact densely branched shrub, foliage turns rich orange and crimson in autumn. Fragrant, double, funnel-shaped, lilac-purple flowers, in trusses of 2 to 4 blooms, in late spring. Originally named from this double-flowered cultivated form, wild plants subsequently named *R. y.* var. *poukhanense* ★, feature single pale to deep pink flowers. Zones 5–8.

Rhododendron zoelleri

☀ ✛ ↔ 3 ft (0.9 m) ↑ 6 ft (1.8 m)

Vireya rhododendron from New Guinea and Moluccas. Elliptic leaves. Large flowers of pinkish orange to yellow, in open trusses of up to 8 funnel-shaped blooms, in autumn–spring. Zones 10–11.

Rhododendron spinuliferum

Rhododendron williamsianum

Rhododendron, Hybrid Cultivar, Hardy Small, 'Chrysomanicum'

Rhododendron, Hybrid Cultivar, Hardy Medium, 'Purple Splendor'

Rhododendron, Hybrid Cultivar, Hardy Tall, 'Lem's Cameo'

Rhododendron Hybrid Cultivars

Rhododendron hybrids are cultivated as ornamental plants, valued for their masses of colorful flowers and year-round foliage in a great diversity of form; some are also sought-after for their attractive textured bark and rich flower fragrance.

HARDY SMALL HYBRIDS

☀ ❄ ↔ 12–40 in (30–100 cm) ↕ 12–40 in (30–100 cm)

Variable group, ranging from those derived from tiny alpine species, to dense mounding bushes with large leaves and upright flower trusses. 'Blue Tit', small leaves, abundant grayish blue flowers; 'Bric-à-Brac', small, rounded, downy leaves, small white flowers with faint pink markings on upper lobes, contrasting chocolate-colored anthers; 'Carmen', dwarf form, less than 12 in (30 cm) high, deep red bell-shaped flowers, in trusses of 2 to 5 blooms, early to mid-season; 'Chevalier Félix de Sauvage', medium-sized coral rose flowers with dark blotch in center, in trusses of 12 blooms, early to mid-season; 'Chikor', soft yellow flowers, delicate foliage turns red in winter; 'Chrysomanicum', bright buttercup yellow flowers, in trusses of 8 blooms, very early in season; 'Cilpenense', shiny deep forest green foliage, blush pink bell-shaped flowers with deeper pink shading, early in season; 'Creeping Jenny' (syn. 'Jenny'), bright red funnel-campanulate flowers, in large loose trusses of 5 to 6 blooms, early to mid-season; 'Curlew', abundant soft yellow flowers with green-brown markings; 'Dora Amateis', pure white fragrant flowers, lightly spotted green, in trusses of 3 to 6 blooms, early to mid-season; 'Elizabeth', bright red funnel-campanulate flowers, in loose trusses of 6 to 8 blooms, early to mid-season; 'Ginny Gee', dark pink flowers shading to shell pink, with white stripes, in trusses of 4 to 5 blooms, early to mid-season; 'Jingle Bells', orange flowers with red throat that fade to yellow, mid-season; 'May Day', cerise or light scarlet funnel-shaped flowers, in loose trusses of 8 blooms, early to mid-season; 'Ptarmigan', delicate foliage, densely scaly underneath, broadly funnel-shaped white flowers, in terminal clusters of several trusses of 2 to 3 blooms, early to mid-season; 'Ramapo', pinkish violet flowers, early to mid-season, almost circular leaves with distinctive deep metallic hue in winter; 'Scarlet Wonder', bright cardinal red bell-shaped flowers with wavy edges, in trusses of 5 to 7 blooms, mid-season; 'Snow Lady', dark green hairy leaves, white flowers with dark anthers, early to mid-season. Zones 6–9.

HARDY MEDIUM HYBRIDS

☀ ❄ ↔ 2–6 ft (0.6–1.8 m) ↕ 3–6 ft (0.9–1.8 m)

Plants best suited to general cultivation; encompasses hundreds of beautiful plants that bloom in full color range over entire flowering season. 'Blue Diamond', deep lilac-blue flowers, early to mid-season; 'Bow Bells', cup-shaped light pink flowers, in loose trusses of 4 to 7 blooms, early to mid-season; 'Creamy Chiffon', salmon-orange buds, creamy yellow double flowers, mid- to late season; 'Fabia', scarlet flowers, shading to orange in tube, in drooping trusses of bell-shaped blooms, mid-season; 'Furnivall's Daughter', bright pink flowers with cherry blotch, in conical trusses of 15 blooms, mid-season; 'Goldflimmer', striking variegated foliage, mauve flowers, late in season; 'Helene Schiffner', pure white flowers with faint yellow to brown markings, in upright dome-shaped trusses; 'Hotei', canary yellow bell-shaped flowers with darker throat, in round trusses of 12 blooms, mid-season; 'Humming Bird', deep pink to red bell-shaped flowers, in loose trusses of 4 to 5 blooms, early to mid-season; 'Lady Clementine Mitford' (syn. 'Lady C. Mitford'), glossy green leaves covered with silver hairs when young, soft peach pink flowers, darker at edges, slight yellow eye, mid- to late season; 'Markeeta's Prize', leathery dark green leaves, scarlet-red flowers, in trusses of 12 blooms, mid-season; 'Mrs A. T. de la Mare', large, white, upright flowers with faint green blotch, in large dome-shaped trusses of 12 to 14 blooms, mid-season; 'Mrs Furnivall', widely funnel-shaped light rose pink flowers, paler at center, with conspicuous deep sienna blotch, in large trusses, mid- to late season; 'President Roosevelt', strongly variegated leaves, frilled flowers, white flushed red with bold red edging, in medium-sized conical trusses, early to mid-season; 'Purple Splendor', very dark purple flowers, with blackish blotch, in dome-shaped to spherical trusses, mid- to late season; 'Sappho', medium-sized, white, widely funnel-shaped flowers with striking deep maroon-black blotch, in large conical trusses, mid- to late season; 'The Hon. Jean Marie de Montague' (syn. 'Jean Mary Montague'), thick emerald green leaves, large bright scarlet flowers, in dome-shaped trusses of 10 to 14 blooms, mid-season; 'Vanessa Pastel', brick red flowers, changing to apricot then to deep cream, with bronze-yellow throat, in trusses, mid- to late season; 'Winsome', reddish winter buds open to rosy cerise flowers, mid-season; 'Yellow Hammer', small, light green, scaly leaves, very deep yellow tubular flowers, in trusses of 3 blooms, early to mid-season. Zones 6–9.

HARDY TALL HYBRIDS

☀ ❋ ↔ 5–17 ft (1.5–5 m) ↕ 6–35 ft (1.8–10 m)

After many years, taller hybrids eventually become tree-like and demand more space. 'Anna Rose Whitney', large mid-green leaves, upright trusses of deep pink flowers; 'Betty Wormald', pastel pink flowers, paler center and light purple spotting, in huge dome-shaped trusses, late season; 'Crest' (syn. 'Hawk Crest'), bright primrose yellow flowers, slightly dark around throat, in large dome-shaped trusses, mid-season; 'Cunningham's White', white flowers, yellowish green at center; 'David', deep red bell-shaped flowers, frilly margins, in loose trusses, early to mid-season; 'Fastuosum Flore Pleno', medium-sized, semi-double, mauve flowers, in loose trusses, mid- to late season; 'Gomer Waterer', white flowers open from slightly pink-tinged buds, mid- to late season; 'Lem's Cameo', widely bell-shaped, apricot-cream and pink flowers, with small scarlet blotch, in large dome-shaped trusses of about 20 blooms, mid-season; 'Loder's White', slightly fragrant flowers, white, edged pale lilac, yellow tinge in throat, in large conical trusses, mid-season; 'Mrs Charles E. Pearson', pale pinkish mauve flowers edged lavender, heavy chestnut spotting, in large conical trusses, mid- to late season; 'Mrs G. W. Leak', bright pink flowers, deep reddish carmine blotch, crimson markings, in large, compact, conical trusses, early to mid-season; 'Scintillation', pastel pink flowers, yellowish brown flare in throat, in large trusses of about 15 blooms, mid-season; 'Sir Charles Lemon', white flowers faintly spotted in throat, in large round trusses, early to mid-season; 'Souvenir de Doctor S. Endtz', rose pink buds open to pink funnel-shaped flowers, marked with crimson ray, in domed trusses of 15 to 17 blooms, mid-season; 'Susan', lavender flowers fade to nearly white, dark margins, purple spots, in rounded trusses of about 12 blooms, mid-season; 'Taurus', large trusses of bright red flowers, faint black spotting. Zones 6–9.

TENDER HYBRIDS

☀/☀ ✴ ↔ 3–10 ft (0.9–3 m) ↕ 3–17 ft (0.9–5 m)

Lowland southern Asian hybrids intolerant of heavy or repeated frosts; large colorful flowers, often also heavy fragrance and lush foliage. 'Countess of Haddington' (syn. 'Eureka Maid'), fragrant white flowers flushed rose, in loose trusses, mid- to late season; 'Fragrantissimum', large, perfumed, white, trumpet-shaped flowers, tinged pink, in loose trusses, early to mid-season; 'Princess Alice' (syn. 'Caerhays Princess Alice'), fragrant white flowers, flushed pink, in loose trusses, early to mid-season. Zones 9–10.

VIREYA HYBRIDS

☀/☀ ✴ ↔ 12–60 in (30–150 cm) ↕ 18–72 in (45–180 cm)

Hybrids of tropical Southeast Asian species, featuring vivid coloration, fragrant flowers, non-seasonal flowering. 'Bold Janus', very large, lightly perfumed, apricot flowers, edged pink; 'Coral Flare', large coral pink flowers, in trusses of 3 to 7 blooms, throughout year; 'Cristo Rey', orange flowers, yellow center; 'Dresden Doll', waxy, heavily veined, lime green leaves, deep salmon pink flowers with cream throat; 'Littlest Angel', petite, waxy, deep red flowers, in trusses of 4 blooms; 'Ne Plus Ultra', bright red, tubular, funnel-shaped flowers, in trusses of 8 to 14 blooms, waxy foliage; 'Popcorn', trusses of 10 to 14 pale cream flowers, with white lobes; 'Princess Alexandra', open trusses of tubular, medium-sized, slightly flared white flowers, sometimes with blush of pale pink. Zones 10–12.

YAK HYBRIDS

☀ ❋ ↔ 2–5 ft (0.6–1.5 m) ↕ 1–6 ft (0.3–1.8 m)

Hybrids in which dominant parent is *R. degronianum* subsp. *yakushimanum*. Low growing, very hardy, attractive foliage; abundant flowers, usually in combinations of pink and white. 'Bashful', camellia pink flowers, deeper shades of rose, reddish brown blotch, early in season; 'Doc', rose pink flowers with deeper rims and spots on upper lobes, in rounded trusses of 9 blooms, mid-season; 'Dopey', glossy, red, bell-shaped flowers, paler toward edges, dark brown spots on upper lobes, in spherical trusses of 16 blooms, mid-season; 'Golden Torch', soft yellow flowers, in compact trusses of 13 to 15 blooms, mid- to late season; 'Grumpy', orange buds open to creamy flowers tinged pink, in rounded trusses of 11 blooms, mid-season; 'Hoppy', white flowers with greenish speckling, in ball-shaped trusses of 18 blooms, mid-season; 'Hydon Dawn', flowers with pink frilled petals fading toward edges, with reddish brown spots, in large, compact, rounded trusses of 14 to 18 blooms, mid-season; 'Percy Wiseman', pink funnel-shaped flowers fade to white, with pale yellow center and orange spots, in trusses of 14 blooms, mid-season; 'Peste's Blue Ice', deep purplish pink flowers fade to very pale purple, lightly spotted green, in trusses of 21 blooms, mid-season; 'Polaris', abundant pinkish purple flowers, lighter shading at center; 'Renoir', deeply bell-shaped rose pink flowers with white throat and crimson spots, in rounded trusses of 11 blooms, mid-season; 'Surrey Heath', rose pink flowers with lighter center, mid-season; 'Titian Beauty', turkey red flowers, mid-season. Zones 7–9.

Rhododendron, Hybrid Cultivar, Tender, 'Countess of Haddington'

Rhododendron, Hybrid Cultivar, Vireya, 'Cristo Rey'

Rhododendron, Hybrid Cultivar, Yak, 'Grumpy'

DECIDUOUS AZALEA HYBRIDS

Deciduous azaleas are multi-stemmed from the ground, never forming a central trunk. The leaves are thin, and the large, often sticky, winter buds contain both the flowers and the spring foliage flush. Flowers are trumpet-shaped, flaring from a narrow tube, and are mostly in shades of cream to salmon, yellow, orange, and scarlet. Deciduous azaleas bloom in spring with or before the new leaves; if they are to flower well, they need a climate with fairly cold winters.

GHENT HYBRIDS

☼ ❋ ↔ 3–6 ft (0.9–1.8 m) ↕ 5–8 ft (1.5–2.4 m)

Very hardy hybrids; large bushes flower in late spring–early summer, with large trusses of small blooms, up to 2 in (5 cm) wide, often fragrant, with long tubes, mostly single, but occasionally double. 'Coccineum Speciosum', bright orange-red flowers; 'Daviesii', fragrant white flowers with yellow flare; 'Narcissiflorum', double yellow flowers, shaded darker at center and on petal reverse; 'Vulcan', deep red flowers with orange blotch. Zones 5–9.

ILAM AND MELFORD HYBRIDS

☼/◐ ❋ ↔ 4–7 ft (1.2–2 m) ↕ 4–10 ft (1.2–3 m)

Bred in New Zealand; Knap Hill and Exbury hybrids crossed with *R. calendulaceum*, *R. viscosum*, and *R. molle* to create larger fragrant flowers. 'Galipoli', apricot flowers with orange markings; 'Ilam Ming', orange flowers with yellow flare; 'Yellow Beauty', golden yellow flowers with faintly spotted orange blotch. Zones 5–9.

KNAP HILL AND EXBURY HYBRIDS

☼/◐ ❋ ↔ 4–7 ft (1.2–2 m) ↕ 4–10 ft (1.2–3 m)

Large bushy shrubs; leaves of most turn bronze then red or yellow before falling in autumn. Large, open, sometimes fragrant, richly colored flowers, up to 4 in (10 cm) wide, in large trusses of up to 30 blooms. 'Berryrose', fragrant orange-red flowers with vivid yellow blotch; 'Cannon's Double', low-growing cultivar, creamy yellow flowers; 'Gibraltar', bright orange-red flowers; 'Homebush', semi-double crimson-pink flowers; 'Hotspur Red', deep orange flowers, almost red; 'Klondyke', deep golden orange flowers with orange-yellow blotch; 'Satan', brilliant red flowers; 'Silver Slipper', snow white flowers, flushed pink, with yellow flare. Zones 5–9.

Rhododendron, Hybrid Cultivar, Deciduous Azalea, Mollis, 'Christopher Wren'

MOLLIS HYBRIDS

☼/◐ ❋ ↔ 5–7 ft (1.5–2 m) ↕ 5–8 ft (1.5–2.4 m)

Ghent hybrids crossed with *R. molle* and *R. molle* subsp. *japonicum*; large hardy shrubs, with single sometimes fragrant flowers to 2 in (5 cm) wide, from mid-spring, in creams, yellows, oranges, and reds. Difficult to propagate from cuttings; buy seedlings when in flower. 'Christopher Wren', large yellow flowers with strong orange blotch; 'Doctor M. Oosthoek', vivid reddish orange flowers, lighter blotch; 'Spek's Orange', deep orange buds open to orange-red flowers; 'Winston Churchill', orange-red flowers. Zones 6–9.

OCCIDENTALE HYBRIDS

☼/◐ ❋ ↔ 6–10 ft (1.8–3 m) ↕ 6–10 ft (1.8–3 m)

Mollis hybrids crossed with *R. occidentale*; usually forming broad spreading shrub with white or pale pink fragrant flowers, to 3 in (8 cm) wide, open after leaves in mid-spring. Deep yellow blotch on flowers. Slow growing; most heat-, drought-, and humidity-tolerant of all deciduous azaleas. 'Delicatissimum', pink-flushed white to cream flowers, orange flare; 'Exquisitum', frilled, fragrant, pale pink flowers, orange flare, darker reddish buds; 'Magnificum', white to yellow flowers flushed pink, yellow flare. Zones 7–10.

EVERGREEN AZALEA HYBRIDS

Evergreen azalea hybrids are multi-stemmed plants. Leaves are of 2 types: spring leaves surround flowerheads and are crowded at the ends of the previous year's shoots; the summer growth flush produces longer leaves, more widely spaced on the branchlet. Flowers are widely funnel-shaped, in shades from white to pink, red, and purple, often bicolored. Most of these azaleas flower well in warmer temperate climates where winter frost is mild or even absent.

BELGIAN INDICA HYBRIDS

☼/◐ ❋ ↔ 3–6 ft (0.9–1.8 m) ↕ 2–5 ft (0.6–1.5 m)

Hybrids using *R. simsii*; damaged by repeated frosts. Compact heavy-flowering plants, among most widely grown azaleas. 'Advent Bells' (syns 'Adventglocke', 'Chimes'), strong purple-red, semi-double, cup-shaped flowers; 'Comtesse de Kerchove', soft pink, medium-sized, double flowers edged white; 'Eri Schaume', coral pink double flowers edged white; 'Helmut Vogel', long-flowering shrub, purplish red semi-double or double flowers; 'James Belton', white to pale pink flowers, darker pink stamens; 'Leopold Astrid', large, frilled, double, white flowers bordered rose red; 'Red Wings', ruffled hose-in-hose deep red blooms, long flowering, compact sun-tolerant shrub. Zones 8–11.

RUTHERFORD INDICA HYBRIDS

☼/◐ ❅ ↔ 4–8 ft (1.2–2.4 m) ↕ 3–8 ft (0.9–2.4 m)

Larger than Belgian hybrids, many have hose-in-hose flowers with ruffled or frilled petals, in reddish orange, pinks, purples, and white. 'Firelight', bright red flowers; 'Gloria USA', semi-double hose-in-hose flowers, salmon pink or white, red throat, white petal margins; 'Purity', white flowers; 'Rose Queen', deep purplish pink, semi-double, hose-in-hose flowers, white throat, darker blotch; 'White Gish', to 3 ft (0.9 m) high, white, semi-double, hose-in-hose flowers, greenish yellow markings; 'White Prince', white, semi-double, hose-in-hose flowers, red throat, sometimes flushed pink. Zones 9–11.

SOUTHERN INDICA HYBRIDS

☼/◖ ❋ ↔ 6–12 ft (1.8–3.5 m) ↕ 5–10 ft (1.5–3 m)

Vigorous sun-tolerant plants, hardier than Belgian hybrids. Early flowering, usually with single flowers, 2 in (5 cm) wide, in shades of pink, red, and dark purple; flowers sometimes striped. No hose-in-hose forms in this group. 'Alphonse Anderson', pale pink flowers, darker blotch; 'Brilliantina' (syn. 'Brilliant'), deep pink flowers, purple-red blotch; 'Duc de Rohan', salmon flowers, rose throat; 'Exquisite', fragrant lilac-pink flowers; 'Glory of Sunninghill', large, single, orange-red flowers; 'Pride of Dorking', carmine or deep pink flowers, bronze-red and orange forms available; 'Redwing', cerise flowers; 'Snow Prince', rounded bush, abundant flowers, mostly white; 'Splendens', salmon pink flowers. Zones 8–11.

KAEMPFERI OR MALVATICA HYBRIDS

☼/◖ ❋ ↔ 3–7 ft (0.9–2 m) ↕ 2–8 ft (0.6–2.4 m)

Late spring- or early summer-flowering hybrids from cross between hardy *R. kaempferi* and *R.* 'Malvaticum'. Large flowers mostly single, occasionally double or hose-in-hose, and tend to fade in full sunlight. 'Blue Danube', strong purplish pink flowers, deep purplish red midrib, deep red blotches; 'Cleopatra', upright shrub, deep pink flowers; 'Double Beauty', pink hose-in-hose flowers, mid-season; 'Fedora', deep purplish pink flowers; 'John Cairns', orange-red flowers; 'Othello', red flowers; 'Orange King', reddish orange flowers; 'Sunrise', reddish orange flowers. Zones 6–10.

Vuyk Hybrids

☼/◖ ❋ ↔ 3–7 ft (0.9–2 m) ↕ 2–8 ft (0.6–2.4 m)

Developed from original Kaempferi hybrids; very similar to them but more compact. Some Mollis azalea parentage initially suggested, now seems unlikely. 'Palestrina', snow white flowers, light green throat; 'Vuyk's Rosyred', deep pink-red flowers; 'Vuyk's Scarlet', vivid red flowers. Zones 6–10.

R., HC, Evergreen Azalea, Southern Indica, 'Alphonse Anderson'

R., HC, Evergreen Azalea, Kaempferi, Vuyk, 'Palestrina'

KURUME HYBRIDS

☼/◖ ❋ ↔ 2–4 ft (0.6–1.2 m) ↕ 2–4 ft (0.6–1.2 m)

Large, normally single flowers, in shades of pink or white, appear early to mid-season in wide range of strong colors, including pinks, reds, and purples; occasionally striped or "freckled," sometimes hose-in-hose, flowering abundantly. Hardy, slow growing; best planted in fully exposed positions. 'Fairy Queen' (syn. 'Aioi'), small, semi-double, hose-in-hose, almond-blossom pink flowers; 'Hatsugiri', vivid reddish purple flowers, pink spotting in throat; 'Hinomayo', strong purplish pink flowers; 'Irohayama', white flowers, pale lavender at edges; 'Kasane-kagaribi' (syn. 'Rositi'), shrub with low, dense, spreading growth, yellowish to salmon pink flowers; 'Kure-no-yuki', white hose-in-hose flowers; 'Mother's Day', dense low-growing bush, abundant cherry red colored flowers; 'Seikai' (syn. 'Madonna'), white, semi-double, hose-in-hose flowers; 'Takasago' (syn. 'Cherryblossom'), white hose-in-hose flowers, flushed with deep red or pale pink, dark spots; 'Vida Brown', pink-red hose-in-hose flowers; 'Ward's Ruby', blood red flowers, less hardy than other Kurume azaleas. Zones 7–10.

Rhododendron, HC, Evergreen Azalea, Belgian Indica, 'Eri Schaume'

SATSUKI HYBRIDS

☼/◖ ❋ ↔ 24–48 in (60–120 cm) ↕ 12–36 in (30–90 cm)

Late-flowering, low-growing, spreading plants cultivated for centuries in Japan, most likely originate from crosses between *R. indicum* and *R. eriocarpum* or *R. simsii*. Valued in Japan for their landscaping qualities and were also traditionally used for bonsai and container cultivation. Gumpo series of dwarf plants useful in rockeries. 'Banzai', white flowers flushed with pink; 'Gumpo', large white flowers with petals wavy-edged; 'Gumpo Lavender', large, single, lavender flowers; 'Gumpo Pink', ruffled, single, pink flowers edged with white; 'Gumpo Salmon', ruffled salmon pink flowers; 'Gumpo Stripe', white flowers with mauve-red stripes and flecks; 'Gumpo White' pretty frilly white flowers; 'Gyoten', single flowers, up to 3 in (8 cm) across, pale pink with white edges, yellowish blotch and often with random red or white stripes; 'Hitoya-no-Haru', large lilac-pink flowers, olive green spotting in throat; 'Kunpu', pale pink, wavy-edged, single flowers, 2½ in (6 cm) in diameter; 'Mansaku', salmon pink flowers, rounded wavy petals; 'Nani-Wagata', abundant white flowers; 'Osakazuki', smallish, deep pink, single blooms, darker blotch in throat; 'Otome', white and pink flowers; 'Shin-Kyo', light salmon pink flowers, 'Shinnyo-no-Hikari', white flowers with green throat; 'White Shiko', white flowers with green blaze. Zones 7–11.

AZALEODENDRON HYBRIDS

☼/◖ ❋ ↔ 2–7 ft (0.6–2 m) ↕ 2–8 ft (0.6–2.4 m)

Group of hybrids lies between deciduous azaleas and other (evergreen) rhododendrons; usually semi-evergreen, flowering in summer, sometimes have fragrant flowers. 'Broughtonii Aureum', yellow flowers; 'Dot', salmon pink flowers; 'Glory of Littleworth', cream flowers, flushed orange; 'Govenianum', deep mauve fragrant flowers; 'Hardijzer Beauty', purplish pink flowers; 'Martine', soft pink flowers; 'Ria Hardijzer', deep pink-red flowers. Zones 8–10.

RHODOLEIA

There is some doubt about the number of species in this genus, in the witchhazel (Hamamelidaceae) family. Some authorities consider that there is just a single variable species in several countries, from southern China to Indonesia, others have recognized up to 7 species. Most, if not all, of the plants in cultivation seem to have originated from material collected in Hong Kong. The range of variability within the species is not evident and the "other" species are not at all well known. All the forms are very similar: they are small evergreen trees with thick dark green leaves that are paler on the underside, and pendent bunches of reddish flowers surrounded by reddish bracts during spring.
CULTIVATION: These plants are somewhat frost tolerant and should be grown in a well-drained, acid, sandy soil to which plenty of organic matter has been added. Conditions should be the same as for azaleas and camellias. Propagate from seed or cuttings.

Rhus lancea

Rhodoleia championii
☀ ❋ ↔ 12 ft (3.5 m) ↕ 20 ft (6 m)
Variable species from southern China to Indonesia. Forms small tree. Thick oval leaves, whitish underside. Stems and leaf stalks yellowish red. Pendent bunches of pinkish red flowerheads in late winter–early spring. Zones 8–11.

RHUS
SUMAC

There are about 200 species of deciduous or evergreen trees, shrubs, and climbers in this genus within the cashew (Anacardiaceae) family. Widely distributed throughout the temperate and subtropical regions of the world, they are used to produce laquer, dyes, tannin, wax, and drinks. *Rhus* species are mainly grown in the garden for their good autumn color, interesting foliage, and fruit, which can persist on the tree into winter and often drop off only when the new leaves appear.
CULTIVATION: They grow in full sun in moderately fertile, moist, but free-draining soil with shelter from wind. Propagate from root cuttings in winter, half-hardened stem cuttings in late summer, or divided root suckers when the plant is dormant. Sow seed in autumn. Feed and water well in the growing season; do not feed in winter.

Rhodoleia championii

Rhus aromatica
FRAGRANT SUMAC, LEMON SUMACH, POLECAT BUSH
☀ ❋ ↔ 5 ft (1.5 m) ↕ 3–5 ft (0.9–1.5 m)
Suckering deciduous shrub native to eastern North America. Palmate leaves, oval toothed leaflets, aromatic. Small yellow flowers, in panicles, in spring. Round red fruit. 'Gro-Low' ★, to 2 ft (0.6 m) high, fragrant deep yellow flowers. Zones 3–9.

Rhus chinensis
CHINESE GALL, NUTGALL
☀ ❋ ↔ 15 ft (4.5 m) ↕ 20 ft (6 m)
Erect deciduous tree native to Japan and China. Leaves compound, mid-green, 3 to 7 oblong leaflets, scalloped edges, turn red in autumn. White conical clusters of flowers appear in late summer–early autumn. Rounded scarlet fruit. Zones 8–11.

Rhus copallina
DWARF SUMAC, MOUNTAIN SUMAC, SHINING SUMAC
☀ ❋ ↔ 5 ft (1.5 m) ↕ 5 ft (1.5 m)
Erect deciduous shrub from eastern North America. Dark green pinnate leaves, 15 lance-shaped leaflets, winged stalks. Yellowish green flowers, on upright panicles, in summer. Rounded red fruit. Foliage turns red in autumn. Zones 5–9.

Rhus glabra
SCARLET SUMAC, SMOOTH SUMAC, VINEGAR TREE
☀ ❋ ↔ 8 ft (2.4 m) ↕ 8 ft (2.4 m)
Bushy deciduous shrub from North America and Mexico. Bronze-colored stems, whitish bloom. Pinnate leaves, deep blue-green leaflets, turn rich red in autumn. Dense upright panicles of greenish red flowers in summer. Round, crimson, hairy fruit. Zones 2–9.

Rhus lancea
KAREE, WILLOW RHUS
☀ ⚘ ↔ 25 ft (8 m) ↕ 25 ft (8 m)
Evergreen tree native to South Africa. Leaves dark green above, paler below, 3 lance-shaped leaflets. Tiny yellow-green flowers in late summer. Fruit glossy brown. Zones 9–11.

Rhus lucida
☀ ⚘ ↔ 12 ft (3.5 m) ↕ 12 ft (3.5 m)
Evergreen tree or shrub from South Africa. Leaves 3 shiny dark green leaflets. Off-white flowers in spring. Small, glossy, brown fruit. Zones 9–11.

Rhus microphylla
CORREOSA, DESERT SUMAC, SCRUB SUMAC
☀ ❋ ↔ 4–6 ft (1.2–1.8 m) ↕ 6–10 ft (1.8–3 m)
Rounded deciduous shrub from southern USA and northern Mexico. Compound leaves with up to 9 leaflets; usually evergreen but can

Ribes sanguineum

shed leaves in cold or dry conditions. Tight spikes of tiny white flowers in spring. Tiny orange-red fruit. Zones 8–11.

Rhus pendulina

syn. *Rhus viminalis*

☼ ⚘ ↔ 15 ft (4.5 m) ↑ 15 ft (4.5 m)

Evergreen South African tree or shrub, willow-like in habit. Trifoliate leaves, lance-shaped leaflets. Light green flowers in summer. Small oblong fruit. Zones 9–11.

Rhus typhina

STAGHORN SUMAC, STAG'S HORN SUMAC

☼ ✳ ↔ 15 ft (4.5 m) ↑ 15 ft (4.5 m)

Deciduous tree or shrub from eastern North America. Can reach 30 ft (9 m) high in wild. Pinnate leaves, up to 31 dark green leaflets, turn flame red in autumn. Green-yellow flowers in summer. Felty red fruit. '**Dissecta**', finely divided leaves. Zones 3–9.

RIBES

CURRANT

Mainly from the northern temperate regions, with some species native to South America, this genus of around 150 species of shrubs is in the gooseberry (Grossulariaceae) family. Some are ornamental; others are grown for their fruit. They are usually deciduous, with twiggy or wiry stems. Usually with 3 to 5 lobes, the leaves often have scalloped or toothed edges and bristly hairs. The flowers are small, sometimes in racemes, followed by often bristly, many-seeded, frequently edible berries. Some species are important commercial or home garden crops.

CULTIVATION: Some species are not self-fertile and must be planted in groups to ensure good fruiting. Apart from this, and the need for some winter chilling, most *Ribes* plants are quite easily grown, requiring little more than a well-drained soil, moisture in summer, and some shade from the very hottest summer sun. Both rust and mildew can cause problems with some species, but disease-resistant cultivars are often available. Propagation is from seed or cuttings, or by layering.

Ribes alpinum

ALPINE CURRANT, MOUNTAIN CURRANT

☼ ✳ ↔ 3 ft (0.9 m) ↑ 3–6 ft (0.9–1.8 m)

Deciduous shrub found in Europe and extending to North Africa. Smooth purple-red stems, leaves usually 3-lobed. Erect racemes of tiny yellow-green flowers in spring. Bitter red fruit. '**Aureum**', yellow-green young growth; '**Green Mound**', non-fruiting low-growing form; '**Pumilum**', low and spreading with small leaves; '**Schmidt**', slower growing, smaller than species. Zones 2–9.

Ribes aureum

GOLDEN CURRANT, GOLDEN FLOWERING CURRANT

☼ ✳ ↔ 6 ft (1.8 m) ↑ 6 ft (1.8 m)

Deciduous bush from western USA and northwestern Mexico. Leaves 3-lobed, coarsely toothed. Pendent racemes of strongly scented yellow flowers in spring. Fruit purple-black. *R. a.* var. *gracillimum*, unscented red flowers. Zones 2–9.

Ribes fasciculatum

CLUSTERED REDCURRANT

☼ ✳ ↔ 4 ft (1.2 m) ↑ 5 ft (1.5 m)

Deciduous shrub from temperate East Asia. Leaves rounded, downy, 3 to 5 lobes, toothed edges. Yellow flowers in spring; females scented. Smooth red fruit, yellow flesh. Plants of both sexes required for cropping. *R. f.* var. *chinense*, larger, leaves to 4 in (10 cm) long. Zones 5–9.

Ribes speciosum

Ribes magellanicum

☼ ✳ ↔ 6 ft (1.8 m) ↑ 6–8 ft (1.8–2.4 m)

Deciduous shrub from southern parts of Argentina and Chile. Leaves with 3 to 5 lobes. Drooping racemes of creamy yellow flowers, age to soft gold tone, in spring. Fruit red-black. Zones 8–10.

Ribes sanguineum

FLOWERING CURRANT, WINTER CURRANT

☼ ✳ ↔ 10 ft (3 m) ↑ 10 ft (3 m)

Deciduous shrub from western USA. Branches warm red-brown. Leaves dark green, 3 to 5 lobes, downy beneath. Pendent racemes of soft pink to red flowers in spring, before leaves. Fruit deep blue-black with white bloom. *R. s.* var. *glutinosum*, leaves less downy than species. *R. s.* '**Brocklebankii**', clear pink scented flowers; '**Claremont**', almost white flowers, ageing to deep pink; '**Elk River Red**' ★, blooms bright rose red, very early in season, can become weedy; '**Inverness White**', greenish white flowers in long sprays; '**King Edward VII**', compact, with deep pink flowers; '**Plenum**', red double flowers; '**Pulborough Scarlet**', red flowers; '**Spring Showers**', pink flowers; '**Tydeman's White**', white flowers. Zones 6–10.

Ribes speciosum

FUCHSIA-FLOWERED CURRANT

☼ ✳ ↔ 10 ft (3 m) ↑ 12 ft (3.5 m)

Evergreen bushy upright shrub from California, USA. Thorny stems, small smooth leaves, 3 to 5 lobes, toothed edges. Flowers bright red, pendulous, with long red stamens; singly, pairs, or groups of 3, in summer. Fruit bristly and red. Zones 8–10.

Robinia × slavinii

Robinia viscosa

RICINOCARPOS

This genus, a member of the euphorbia (Euphorbiaceae) family, contains 16 species, 1 from New Caledonia, the others from eastern and southern Australia. All are woody shrubs that grow to 10 ft (3 m) tall, often less. Male and female flowers are separate, but appear in groups of a few males and 1 female. Male flowers have 5 white or pink petals with a bunch of united stamens in the center. Female flowers have smaller petals with a 3-celled ovary in the center. The fruit is relatively large, over ½ in (12 mm) wide. CULTIVATION: All species grow in acid sandy soils in various habitats. Frost hardiness varies, with western Australian species being the most tolerant. Propagation has been achieved using seed and cuttings. Treating seed with smoke or water may improve the rate of germination.

Ricinocarpos pinifolius

Ricinocarpos pinifolius

WEDDING BUSH

☀ ❄ ↔ 3 ft (0.9 m) ↑ 3 ft (0.9 m)

Evergreen shrub occurring in all eastern States of Australia. Narrow leaves, margins rolled under. White flowers, to 1 in (25 mm) in diameter, in spring. Prefers soil that is extremely free-draining and acidic. Zones 9–11.

RICINUS

This single-species genus, a member of the euphorbia (Euphorbiaceae) family, comes from northeastern Africa, but has naturalized throughout the tropical regions of the world. Although it is technically a shrub, it is considered a prized annual in many cold-climate gardens (but a weed in warmer regions), and is grown for its deeply lobed and often colored leaves. CULTIVATION: *R. communis* requires fertile soil with ample organic matter added to ensure moisture retention and free drainage. This plant's brittle stems need to be protected from winds and frost. When grown from seed, care must be taken as the seed coats and other parts of the plant are extremely toxic.

Ricinus communis

CASTOR BEAN PLANT, CASTOR OIL PLANT

☀ ❄ ↔ 3 ft (0.9 m) ↑ 5–15 ft (1.5–4.5 m)

Fast-growing evergreen shrub from northeastern Africa; can grow to 40 ft (12 m) high in wild. Somewhat brittle stems; distinctive, lobed, green leaves. Smaller-growing cultivars include 'Cambodgensis', purple-black stems, dark purple leaves; 'Red Spire', red stems, bronze-green foliage; and 'Zanzibarensis', taller, with large, white-veined, green leaves. Zones 9–12.

ROBINIA

The 20 or so species of deciduous trees and shrubs in this genus, in the pea-flower subfamily of the legume (Fabaceae) family, are found mainly in eastern USA. They bear pendulous racemes of white, cream, pink, or lavender pea-flowers, followed by flat seed pods. The leaves are pinnate, and are often quite large; some species have vivid yellow autumn colors. Stems may have fierce thorns. CULTIVATION: These tough adaptable plants grow quickly and tolerate most soil types provided they are well drained. They are, however, rather brittle, with branches that are prone to break or tear in strong winds. It is best to prune when young to establish a strongly branched structure. Some species sucker freely and the suckers can be used for propagation, otherwise they are propagated from stratified seed or cuttings. Special growth forms are usually grafted.

Robinia hispida

ROSE ACACIA

☀ ✳ ↔ 10 ft (3 m) ↑ 10 ft (3 m)

Large shrub from southeastern USA; dense and bushy, suckering. Branches covered in red bristles. Leaves with 7 to 15 leaflets, dark green above, gray-green below, bristles at tips. Flowers magenta to purple, in small racemes, in late spring. Zones 5–9.

Robinia pseudoacacia

BLACK LOCUST, FALSE ACACIA

☀ ✳ ↔ 35 ft (10 m) ↑ 50 ft (15 m)

Most widely grown robinia, parent of many cultivars, native to eastern and central USA. Thorny stems, red-tinted when young. Leaves with 19 bright green leaflets. White to cream flowers, in racemes, in summer. 'Appalachia', narrowly erect form; 'Aurea', greenish yellow spring foliage; 'Bessoniana', thornless rounded form; 'Coluteoides', very rounded, compact, with closely crowded leaflets; 'Frisia', bright golden foliage, thornless, few flowers; 'Inermis', thornless form, upright habit; 'Tortuosa', twisted branches; 'Umbraculifera', rounded form, dense foliage. Zones 3–10.

Robinia × slavinii

☀ ✳ ↔ 10 ft (3 m) ↑ 15 ft (4.5 m)

Shrubby hybrid between *R. kelseyi* and *R. pseudoacacia*. Leaves deep green and pinnate; rose pink racemes in spring. 'Hillieri', tree-like growth habit, pink flowers with distinct mauve tint. Zones 5–9.

Robinia viscosa

CLAMMY LOCUST

☼ ❋ ↔ 20 ft (6 m) ↕ 30 ft (9 m)

Deciduous tree native to southeastern USA. Sticky, dark brown, young stems with thorns. Leaves composed of 13 to 25 dark green leaflets, gray hairs beneath. Flowers pink with yellow markings, in tightly packed racemes, in late spring. Zones 3–10.

ROELLA

This genus, a member of the bellflower (Campanulaceae) family, consists of about 30 species, all from the Cape region of South Africa. They are perennials or small evergreen shrubs, mostly with slender branchlets clothed in small leaves, and attractive bell-shaped flowers borne singly or in short spikes at the branch tips.
CULTIVATION: At least 1 species was introduced to greenhouse cultivation in Europe by the late eighteenth century, part of the fad for Cape plants that continued to the mid-nineteenth century. Their requirements are similar to those of the Cape ericas, namely a gritty acid soil with perfect drainage, and a constant supply of moisture. Propagate from seed or tip cuttings.

Roldana petasitis

Roella ciliata

☼ ⚶ ↔ 2 ft (0.6 m) ↕ 3 ft (0.9 m)

Slender erect shrub native to South Africa's Western Cape. Small pointed leaves, bristle-haired edges. Large bell-shaped flowers, violet-blue petals, much darker blue zone in throat, at end of branches, in late spring–early summer. Zones 9–10.

ROLDANA

This genus of bushy daisies from Central America includes some 50-odd species and is a member of the daisy (Asteraceae) family. While many are annuals or perennials, the genus also includes a few shrubs. The leaves are usually large and rounded to hand-shaped with shallow lobes, dark green on top and often considerably lighter on the underside. The leaves and young stems are covered with fine hairs that can sometimes be dense enough to become felted. The flowers, which are most commonly bright yellow, are carried in corymbs and occur throughout the year if the climate is mild enough.
CULTIVATION: Many species are frost tender, though the hardiest of them will withstand light frosts and relatively cool winters. They prefer moist, well-drained, fertile soil and flower best if grown in sun. Foliage is often more luxuriant with a little shade. Propagate from seed or cuttings in general, but in some cases by division.

Roldana petasitis

syn. *Senecio petasitis*

☼ ⚶ ↔ 6–10 ft (1.8–3 m) ↕ 6–10 ft (1.8–3 m)

Native to Central America. Leaves with 7 or more pointed lobes, densely felted beneath. Yellow daisy flowers in flat-topped corymbs or in spikes, in winter. Zones 9–11.

RONDELETIA

This small genus of evergreen shrubs and small trees in the madder (Rubiaceae) family, from Central America, is named for Professor Guillaume Rondelet, a sixteenth-century French naturalist. These shrubs and trees have opposite leaves and terminal or axillary inflorescences of red, yellow, pink, or white tubular flowers that are rich in nectar.
CULTIVATION: *Rondeletia* species need a warm position in full sun, and may be damaged by frost. A light friable soil that drains freely is ideal. Pruning should be moderately severe after flowering, with flowering shoots cut back to within several nodes of the previous season's growth. Propagation is from half-hardened leafy tip cuttings, 2–4 in (5–10 cm) long, which can be taken during spring.

Rondeletia amoena

☼ ⚶ ↔ 8 ft (2.4 m) ↕ 10 ft (3 m)

Native to Mexico and Central America. Evergreen shrub, many erect stems rising from base. Dense foliage, leaves pale bronze-green, ageing to dark glossy green above, hairy below. Small salmon pink flowers, in terminal cymes, faint perfume, in spring. Zones 10–12.

Rondeletia odorata

FRAGRANT RONDELETIA

☼ ⚶ ↔ 3 ft (0.9 m) ↕ 5 ft (1.5 m)

From Panama. Small evergreen shrub; upright, vase-shaped. Leaves elliptic-ovate, dark velvety green above, reddish green below. Flowers in terminal clusters, orange-scarlet to crimson, bright yellow throat, sweetly fragrant, in late summer–autumn. Zones 11–12.

Rondeletia odorata

ROSA

ROSE

Rosa is one of the most widely grown and best loved of all plant genera. It belongs to the large rose (Rosaceae) family, which includes favorite fruiting plants such as apples, plums, and strawberries as well as ornamentals. Since ancient times roses have been valued for their beauty and fragrance as well as for their medicinal, culinary, and cosmetic properties. There are 100 to 150 species of rose, ranging in habit from erect and arching shrubs to scramblers and climbers. Most species are deciduous and have prickles or bristles. They are found in temperate and subtropical zones of the Northern Hemisphere; none are native to the Southern Hemisphere.

The pinnate leaves are usually comprised of 5 to 9, sometimes more, serrated-edged leaflets. Flowers range from single, usually 5-petalled, blooms to those with many closely packed petals. They are borne singly or in clusters. Many are intensely fragrant. Most species and old garden roses flower only once, but many modern cultivars are repeat-blooming. Rose fruit (hips or heps) are rich in vitamin C. They are usually orangey red, but can be dark. They may be small and in clusters or single large fruits.

Roses have been bred for many centuries and are divided into recognized groups. Old garden roses were originally bred from a handful of species and include groups such as Gallica and Alba. In the late eighteenth century the repeat-flowering China rose *(R. chinensis)* arrived in Europe and subsequent cross-breeding extended the number of Old Rose groups further. The Tea Roses, also repeat-flowering, followed in the nineteenth century, and 50 years later a Frenchman bred the first Large-flowered Rose, heralding the start of modern rose breeding. Large-flowered, Polyantha, Cluster-flowered, and Shrub Roses proliferated in the twentieth century. While most of the species and Old Roses are in shades of pink, red, purple, or white, modern rose-breeding programs have seen the color range increase to include shades of yellow and orange.
CULTIVATION: Roses can be grown in separate beds or mixed borders, as ground covers, climbing up arches and pergolas, scrambling up trees, as hedging, and in containers. Roses generally require a site that is sunny for most of the day, as shade inhibits flowering. They should not be overcrowded and there should be good air movement around the plants, factors that help reduce the risk of disease. Roses will grow in most well-drained medium-loamy soils in which compost or organic manure has been incorporated. When planting, the point at which the plant is grafted should be about 1 in (25 mm) below the soil. Granular or liquid rose fertilizer can be applied once or twice a year from spring. Plants should be watered well in dry periods and a mulch will help to conserve moisture in summer.

Prune roses to maintain healthy growth, a good shape, and to let light into the plant. Various pruning regimes are promoted for different rose groups, but recent research has shown that a simple "tidying up" of dead wood may be just as effective. Most pruning is done when the plants are dormant in winter. Repeat-flowering roses should be deadheaded to encourage further blooms.

Fungal diseases such as rust, black spot, and mildew can be a problem, particularly in humid areas. Insect pests can also be troublesome, the most common being aphids. Others include spider mites, thrips, leafhoppers, froghoppers, and scale. Fungicidal and insecticidal sprays, both chemical and organic, are available to combat these problems. Roses planted in a position previously occupied by another rose can suffer rose sickness—to prevent this, replace a generous amount of the old soil with a fresh supply.

Most roses are very hardy and indeed benefit from a period of winter cold, but some of the old Tea Roses are a little tender and are better suited to warm-temperate climates. In warm areas often grow much larger than their cool-climate counterparts and can be more prone to problems caused by mild winters not killing off pests and diseases. Propagation in commercial quantities is usually from budding, but the gardener can take hardwood cuttings in autumn or softwood cuttings in summer. While hybrid plants will not come true from seed, the species can be propagated in this way. Seed will need to be stratified before planting.

Rosa acicularis

☼ ❋ ↔ 4 ft (1.2 m) ↑ 6 ft (1.8 m)
Widespread species, found throughout northern areas of Europe, Asia, and America. Lax shrub, densely packed bristles of varying lengths, grayish green foliage. Mildly fragrant, single, deep pink flowers in summer. Hips bright red, pear-shaped. Zones 2–9.

Rosa beggeriana

☼ ❋ ↔ 8 ft (2.4 m) ↑ 8 ft (2.4 m)
Deciduous shrub from central Asia. Grayish green leaves. Small white flowers, in clusters of 8 or more at end of new shoots, in mid-summer. Small, round, reddish hips. Zones 4–9.

Rosa canina

Rosa davurica

Rosa eglanteria

Rosa blanda
HUDSON BAY ROSE, MEADOW ROSE, SMOOTH ROSE

☼ ❄ ↔ 3 ft (0.9 m) ↕ 3–7 ft (0.9–2 m)

Brown-stemmed shrub from eastern and central North America, similar to *R. canina*. Few prickles near base; dull green leaves. Mildly fragrant, single, mid-pink flowers in summer. Ovoid to pear-shaped red hips. Zones 3–9.

Rosa californica

☼ ❄ ↔ 6 ft (1.8 m) ↕ 7 ft (2 m)

From west of Sierra Nevadas in USA south to Baja California, Mexico. Stout prickles on stems; leaves mid-green. Single, slightly fragrant, pink flowers, in clusters, in summer. Round orange-red hips. *R. c. plena*, flowers deeper pink than species. Zones 5–10.

Rosa gallica

Rosa canina
COMMON BRIAR, DOG ROSE

☼ ❄ ↔ 10 ft (3 m) ↕ 10 ft (3 m)

Vigorous suckering shrub native to UK and Europe. Prickly stems; leaves with 5 to 7 leaflets. Scented flowers, single, pale or blush pink, occasionally white, in summer. Orangey red hips. Zones 3–10.

Rosa chinensis
CHINA ROSE

☼ ❄ ↔ 8 ft (2.4 m) ↕ 20 ft (6 m)

Variable species from China. Lustrous leaves, 3 to 5 leaflets. Single red, pink, or white flowers in summer. Hips greenish brown to scarlet. Zones 7–10.

Rosa cinnamomea plena
syn. *Rosa majalis*

CINNAMON ROSE, MAY ROSE

☼ ❄ ↔ 5 ft (1.5 m) ↕ 6 ft (1.8 m)

Deciduous shrub from central northeastern Europe. Purplish stems, downy grayish green leaves. Single to double flowers, mid- to purplish pink, in early summer. Elongated hips, dark red. Zones 6–10.

Rosa davurica

☼ ❄ ↔ 4 ft (1.2 m) ↕ 3–5 ft (0.9–1.5 m)

Deciduous shrub found in northeastern Asia and northern China. Small leaves, straight prickles. Groups of 1 to 3 pink flowers in summer. Small, oval, red hips. Zones 5–9.

Rosa ecae

☼ ❄ ↔ 4 ft (1.2 m) ↕ 4 ft (1.2 m)

Much-branched suckering shrub native to Afghanistan and Pakistan. Very prickly stems. Small, fern-like, aromatic leaves. Buttercup-sized yellow flowers in spring. Shiny red-brown hips. Zones 7–10.

Rosa eglanteria
syn. *Rosa rubiginosa*

BRIAR ROSE, EGLANTINE, SWEET BRIAR

☼ ❄ ↔ 10 ft (3 m) ↕ 10 ft (3 m)

Deciduous shrub from Europe and western Asia. Arching prickly stems, apple-scented leaves. Small, single, pink, fragrant flowers

Rosa foetida persiana

in summer. Ovoid orangey red hips. Considered weed in Australia, New Zealand, and North America. Zones 4–10.

Rosa elegantula
syn. *Rosa farreri*

☼ ❄ ↔ 8 ft (2.4 m) ↕ 3–7 ft (0.9–2 m)

Dense suckering shrub from northwestern China. Fern-like foliage, grayish green, turns purple and crimson shades in autumn. Small single flowers, white to rose pink, in summer. 'Persetosa', stems thickly covered in red bristles. Zones 6–10.

Rosa foetida
AUSTRIAN BRIAR, AUSTRIAN YELLOW

☼ ❄ ↔ 6 ft (1.8 m) ↕ 3–10 ft (0.9–3 m)

Erect shrub native to Asia. Large blackish thorns, bright green leaves. Single flowers, deep yellow with prominent stamens, unpleasant aroma, in summer. Round red hips. *R. f. bicolor* (Austrian copper rose), coppery orange flowers; *R. f. persiana* (Persian yellow rose), double yellow flowers. Zones 4–10.

Rosa gallica
FRENCH ROSE, RED ROSE

☼ ❄ ↔ 4 ft (1.2 m) ↕ 4 ft (1.2 m)

Low suckering shrub native to southern, central, and eastern Europe. Lightly bristled, leathery, dark green leaves. Mildly fragrant flowers, usually single, soft to deep pink, prominent light yellow stamens. Small ovoid hips, brick red. *R. g. officinalis* ★ (apothecary's rose, Provins rose), slightly smaller, with quite large, semi-double, heavily perfumed, crimson flowers, can become weedy. *R. g. versicolor* (syn. 'Rosa Mundi'), sport of *R. g. officinalis*, identical except for its striped white, pink, and crimson flowers. Zones 5–10.

Rosa gigantea

☼ ❄ ↔ 20–40 ft (6–12 m) ↕ 30–60 ft (9–18 m)

Near-evergreen native to northeastern India, upper Myanmar, and western China. Thorny stems, glossy deep green leaves. Flowers cream, white, or pink, in early summer. Large red hips. Zones 8–11.

Rosa laxa

Rosa moyesii fargesii

Rosa pendulina

Rosa glauca
syn. *Rosa rubrifolia*
REDLEAF ROSE
☼ ❋ ↔6 ft (1.8 m) ↑6 ft (1.8 m)
Deciduous shrub native to Europe. Arching stems dark purplish red when young, leaves bluish gray. Flowers deep pink fading to white near center, in summer. Ovoid hips, purplish red. Zones 3–10.

Rosa hemisphaerica
SULFUR ROSE
☼ ❋ ↔7 ft (2 m) ↑7 ft (2 m)
Well-branched shrub from southwestern Asia. Stiffly upright stems with scattered thorns, leaves grayish green. Double flowers cupped, deep sulfur yellow, in summer. Round dark red hips. Zones 6–10.

Rosa hugonis
syn. *Rosa xanthina* f. *hugonis*
☼ ❋ ↔6 ft (1.8 m) ↑7 ft (2 m)
Chinese species; very similar to *R. xanthina*. Differs from *R. xanthina* in having broader leaflets and primrose yellow flowers to well over 2 in (5 cm) wide. Zones 5–10.

Rosa laxa
☼/◗ ❋ ↔5–10 ft (1.5–3 m) ↑7–8 ft (2–2.4 m)
Shrub from Siberia and northwestern China. Arching stems, bristly, some large recurved thorns. Leaves up to 9 leaflets, to nearly 2 in (5 cm) long, toothed, underside can be sparsely hairy. Clusters of 1 to 6 white to pale pink flowers in summer. Red fruit. Zones 5–9.

Rosa macrophylla
☼ ❋ ↔10 ft (3 m) ↑10 ft (3 m)
Native to Himalayas. Dark red stems almost thornless, leaves purplish green. Cerise-pink single flowers in summer. Orangey red bristly hips. Zones 7–10.

Rosa marginata
syn. *Rosa jundzillii*
☼ ❋ ↔8 ft (2.4 m) ↑3–8 ft (0.9–2.4 m)
Suckering shrub native to eastern Europe. Moderately thorny, with thorns few in number, slender and scattered. Dark green leaves, can be downy on underside. Slightly fragrant, single, pale to bright pink flowers in summer. Red hips, round or ovoid. Zones 5–10.

Rosa minutifolia
☼/◗ ❅ ↔4 ft (1.2 m) ↑4 ft (1.2 m)
Near-evergreen small bush from California, USA, and Baja California, Mexico. Hairy; dense covering of fine red-brown spines. Pinnate leaves, under 1 in (25 mm) long, leaflets under ¼ in (6 mm) long. Purple-pink or white single flowers in summer. Zones 9–11.

Rosa moyesii
☼ ❋ ↔10 ft (3 m) ↑10 ft (3 m)
Deciduous shrub from western China. Stout erect stems, scattered thorns, dark green leaves. Single deep red flowers in summer. Pendulous, flagon-shaped, orange-red hips. *R. m. fargesii*, reddish pink flowers. Zones 5–10.

Rosa multiflora
JAPANESE ROSE
☼ ❋ ↔10 ft (3 m) ↑10–15 ft (3–4.5 m)
Robust shrub from eastern Asia and Japan. Prickly stems, leaves with 7 to 9 leaflets. Clusters of small, single, creamy white flowers in summer. Small, rounded, red hips. *R. m. carnea*, white to pale pink flowers. *R. m. cathayensis*, single rosy pink flowers. Zones 5–10.

Rosa nitida
☼ ❋ ↔4 ft (1.2 m) ↑3 ft (0.9 m)
Suckering shrub native to eastern North America. Slender prickly stems, small fern-like leaves, turning crimson in autumn. Small, single, fragrant, deep pink flowers in summer. Dark scarlet hips. Suitable for ground cover. Zones 3–10.

Rosa nutkana
☼ ❋ ↔7 ft (2 m) ↑6–10 ft (1.8–3 m)
Vigorous rose native to western North America. Almost thornless purplish brown stems, dark grayish green leaves. Fragrant single flowers, medium pink, in summer. Small, round, red hips. *R. n. hispida*, fragrant pink flowers. Zones 4–10.

Rosa pendulina
☼ ❋ ↔5 ft (1.5 m) ↑2–7 ft (0.6–2 m)
Deciduous shrub from mountains of central and southern Europe. Arching reddish purple stems, almost thornless. Leaves dark green. Deep pink or purplish pink single flowers, prominent yellow stamens, in summer. Red elongated hips, often pendulous. Zones 5–10.

Rosa pisocarpa

CLUSTER ROSE

☼ ✼ ↔ 4 ft (1.2 m) ↕ 3–7 ft (0.9–2 m)

Deciduous shrub from western North America. Arching stems, small leaves, bristly at base. Small single flowers in clusters, rosy pink, in summer. Small, bright red, shiny hips. Zones 6–10.

Rosa primula

AFGHAN YELLOW ROSE, INCENSE ROSE

☼ ✼ ↔ 5 ft (1.5 m) ↕ 5–10 ft (1.5–3 m)

Species native to central Asia and China. Deciduous shrub, erect branching habit, thorny brown stems. Aromatic fern-like foliage. Perfumed single flowers, primrose yellow, prominent stamens, in spring. Smooth, rounded, reddish maroon hips. Has been confused with *R. ecae* in cultivation. Zones 5–10.

Rosa roxburghii

BURR ROSE, CHESTNUT ROSE

☼ ✼ ↔ 7 ft (2 m) ↕ 7 ft (2 m)

Deciduous shrub native to western China. Branches angular, bark peels with age. Leaves with 15 small light green leaflets. Double pink flowers, prickly calyx and receptacle, fragrant, in summer. Yellowish green hips covered in short prickles. *R. r. normalis,* single flowers. Zones 5–10.

Rosa roxburghii normalis

Rosa rugosa

BEACH ROSE, JAPANESE ROSE, RAMANAS ROSE

☼ ✼ ↔ 5–8 ft (1.5–2.4 m) ↕ 5–8 ft (1.5–2.4 m)

Vigorous deciduous shrub native to Japan and eastern Asia. Stout prickly stems. Dark green leaves, wrinkled surface. Scented single flowers, light to deep pink, in summer–autumn. Round rich red hips. *R. r. alba*, pink buds, large white flowers, large tomato red hips; *R. r. rubra*, single deep pink-purple flowers. Zones 2–10.

Rosa sempervirens

EVERGREEN ROSE

☼ ✼ ↔ 20–35 ft (6–10 m) ↕ 1–6 ft (0.3–1.8 m)

Semi-evergreen shrub native to south Europe. Scrambling or trailing stems. Mid- to dark green foliage. Fragrant, white, single flowers, in clusters, in early summer. Small orange-red hips. Zones 7–10.

Rosa sericea

MALTESE CROSS ROSE

☼ ✼ ↔ 8 ft (2.4 m) ↕ 10 ft (3 m)

From western China and Himalayas. Vigorous. Stout erect branches, large hooked thorns, fern-like foliage. Single, white, 4-petalled flowers in spring. Pear-shaped bright red hips. *R. s. omeiensis* (syn. *R. omeiensis*), large wedge-shaped thorns. Zones 6–10.

Rosa setipoda

☼ ✼ ↔ 5 ft (1.5 m) ↕ 8 ft (2.4 m)

Deciduous shrub from western China. Shrubby branching habit, stout stems, thick well-spaced thorns. Foliage aromatic when crushed. Large clusters of single flowers, pale pink, prominent yellow stamens, in summer. Bristly, flagon-shaped, deep red hips. Zones 6–10.

Rosa spinosissima

syn. *Rosa pimpinellifolia*

BURNET ROSE, SCOTCH BRIAR

☼ ✼ ↔ 4 ft (1.2 m) ↕ 3–7 ft (0.9–2 m)

Suckering rose from Europe and Asia. Prickly stems, coarse fern-like leaves. Single creamy white flowers in spring. Small, round, black, shiny hips. *R. s. altaica*, pure white flowers. Zones 4–10.

Rosa stellata

DESERT ROSE

☼ ✼ ↔ 3 ft (0.9 m) ↕ 3 ft (0.9 m)

Deciduous shrub from hot southwestern areas of USA. Forms dense spiny thicket. Light green wedge-shaped leaflets, small, slightly hairy. Single pink flowers in mid-summer. Soft spines on flower buds and red hips. *R. s. mirifica*, flowers pink to purplish red. Zones 6–10.

Rosa sweginzowii

☼ ✼ ↔ 15 ft (4.5 m) ↕ 12 ft (3.5 m)

Native to northern and western China. Large thorns, bristly reddish stems. Light to mid-green leaves, heavily toothed, rounded leaflets. Small clusters of deep pink flowers, in mid-summer. Bottle-shaped orange-red hips. Zones 6–10.

Rosa virginiana

VIRGINIA ROSE

☼ ✼ ↔ 5 ft (1.5 m) ↕ 5 ft (1.5 m)

Sometimes suckering shrub native to eastern North America. Leaves shiny green, color in autumn. Single deep pink flowers, yellow stamens, in mid-summer. Round red hips. Zones 3–10.

Rosa wichurana

syn. *Rosa luciae* var. *wichurana*

MEMORIAL ROSE

☼ ✼ ↔ 20 ft (6 m) ↕ 6 ft (1.8 m)

Dense spreading shrub or short climber from eastern Asia. Stout thorns on trailing stems; glossy green leaves almost evergreen. Clusters of single, fragrant, white flowers in summer. Small, dark red, oval hips. Regarded by some as not distinct from *R. luciae*. Zones 5–10.

Rosa spinosissima

Rosa willmottiae

MISS WILLMOTT'S ROSE

☼ ❆ ↔ 5 ft (1.5 m) ↑ 6 ft (1.8 m)

Deciduous shrub native to China. Arching habit, grayish green fern-like foliage. Single light purplish pink flowers, prominent yellow stamens, in summer. Small, ovoid, orangey red hips. Zones 6–10.

Rosa woodsii

WESTERN WILD ROSE

☼ ❆ ↔ 5 ft (1.5 m) ↑ 3–7 ft (0.9–2 m)

Stiffly branching shrub native to North America. Stems purplish brown when young, very prickly. Foliage colors in autumn. Mid-pink single flowers, in small clusters, in summer. Bright red hips. *R. w. ultramontana*, smaller flowers than species. Zones 4–10.

MODERN ROSES

The term "Modern Roses" is misleading, as a number of them were developed in the latter half of the 1800s, at the same time as some of the Old Rose groups. Modern Roses are famous for their repeat-flowering qualities, floriferousness, and availability of yellow and orange flower colors. Large-flowered (Hybrid Tea) Roses crossed with Polyanthas resulted in Cluster-flowered (Floribunda) Roses; others have followed. A breeding program initiated by the Canadian Department of Agriculture in the early 1900s produced some very hardy roses, some tolerant to Zone 1. Modern Roses are divided into Bush, Shrub, Climbing, Miniature, and Ground Cover Roses.

BUSH ROSES

Bush Roses usually grow no more than 5 ft (1.5 m) tall. They have a long flowering season and are suitable for flowerbeds and borders. Complex crossings of the various groups make classification difficult, with some Large-flowered Roses bearing flowers in large clusters, and taller-growing Cluster-flowered Roses being more shrub-like.

Rosa, Modern Rose, Cluster-flowered, 'Chinatown'

Cluster-flowered (Floribunda) Roses

☼ ❆ ↔ 3–6 ft (0.9–1.8 m) ↑ 4–7 ft (1.2–2 m)

Result of cross between small cluster-flowered Polyantha Roses and Large-flowered Roses. Individual blooms usually smaller than those of Large-flowered Roses, in large crowded clusters, flowers usually flatter when fully open, mostly double or semi-double. 'Amber Queen', large, cup-shaped, clear amber-yellow flowers; 'Apricot Nectar', cupped golden-apricot flowers, well-scented; 'Betty Boop' ★ (syn. 'Centenary of Federation'), highly fragrant single blooms, creamy white to yellow, shading to red toward petal edges; 'Brass Band' ★, lightly scented blooms, apricot shades; 'Chinatown', long-stemmed fragrant blooms, bright yellow with pink highlights at petal edges; 'City of Belfast', large clusters of scarlet-red blooms; 'City of London', very fragrant, cupped, double flowers, soft pink fading to blush; 'Dearest', very fragrant, large, salmon pink flowers, prominent yellow stamens; 'Dicky' (syn. 'Anisley Dickson'), lightly scented, orange-pink, double flowers; 'Elizabeth of Glamis' (syn. 'Irish Beauty'), named for UK's Queen Mother, very fragrant well-shaped flowers, clear salmon pink; 'Fragrant Delight', strong perfume, large flowers, soft salmon-orange shades; 'Frensham', deep red semi-double flowers; 'Gavnø' (syn. 'Buck's Fizz'), soft orange blooms; 'Glad Tidings', velvety dark red blooms; 'Gold Badge' ★, large, rich yellow, double flowers; 'Hannah Gordon' (syn. 'Raspberry Ice'), creamy white petals suffused deep pink at edges; 'Iceberg' ★ (syns 'Fée des Neiges', 'Schneewittchen'), large clusters of pure white flowers; 'Lilac Charm', almost-single rose, large petals of pale lilac, red stamens; 'Lilli Marleen', large, velvety, deep red flowers; 'Livin' Easy' ★ (syn. 'Fellowship'), fiery orange-red blooms; 'Ma Perkins', large cupped flowers, pink and salmon; 'Margaret Merril', very fragrant, large, white flowers with hint of pink at center; 'Mariandel' ★, red semi-double flowers with mild fragrance; 'Matangi', so-called "hand-painted" rose, appears to be brushed with secondary colors, bright orangey vermilion with silvery white central eye and petal reverse; 'Matilda' (syn. 'Seduction'), large, white, double flowers, petals delicately edged with pink; 'Picasso', "hand-painted" rose, flowers brushed with deep pink, carmine, and silvery white; 'Prima' (syn. 'Many Happy Returns'), semi-double flowers of palest pink; 'Queen Elizabeth', long pointed buds open to large, high-centered, clear pink blooms; 'Radox Bouquet' (syn. 'Rosika'), very fragrant cupped blooms, soft rose pink; 'Rosemary Rose', camellia-like flowers, deep pinkish red, in large clusters with distinctive maroon foliage; 'Sexy Rexy' ★, large clusters of soft salmon pink camellia-like flowers; 'Sheila's Perfume' ★, very fragrant yellow flowers edged red; 'Southampton' (syn. 'Susan Ann'), apricot flowers flushed orange and red; 'Sunsprite' (syns 'Friesia', 'Korresia'), rounded buds open to very fragrant double flowers of bright yellow; 'Sweet Dream' ★, double blooms, soft apricot-orange; 'Trumpeter', brilliant scarlet-orange flowers. Zones 4–10.

Rosa, Modern Rose, Large-flowered, 'Fragrant Cloud'

Large-flowered (Hybrid Tea) Roses

☼ ❊ ↔ 3–6 ft (0.9–1.8 m) ↕ 5–8 ft (1.5–2.4 m)

Most popular of all roses; thousands have been bred. Generally sturdy plants, with upright bushy habit and mid- to dark green, often glossy leaves. Very large flowers usually double or semi-double, borne singly or in clusters. Elegant long-pointed buds; when open retain high center, to varying degrees, as outer petals reflex. Large-flowered Rose usually acknowledged as first is 'La France', bred in 1867. Only very small selection of vast numbers available included here. 'Abbeyfield Rose', rich deep pink double flowers; 'Alec's Red', plump black-red buds open to double well-perfumed flowers; 'Alexander', lightly scented, double, vermilion blooms; 'Brandy', large, sweetly perfumed, apricot flowers; 'Carina', fragrant double blooms of rosy pink; 'Congratulations', high-centered clear rose pink flowers on long stems; 'Dainty Bess', large single flowers of silvery rose pink, prominent golden-brown stamens; 'Deep Secret' (syn. 'Mildred Scheel'), very dark, deep crimson-red flowers, velvety-textured, very fragrant; 'Double Delight', very fragrant creamy pink flowers, darkening to cherry red at edges; 'Elina' ★ (syn. 'Peaudouce'), lemony yellow flowers fading to cream at edges; 'Fragrant Cloud' (syns 'Duftwolke', 'Nuage Parfumé'), highly perfumed coral red flowers; 'Indian Summer', fragrant double blooms in orange shades; 'Ingrid Bergman' ★, named for actress, deep red velvety blooms, long lasting, good for picking; 'Irish Gold' (syn. 'Grandpa Dickson'), very prickly plant, elegant lemony yellow flowers; 'Just Joey' ★, large coppery orange flowers that pale to soft pink at edge of petals; 'La France', high-centered, well-perfumed, silvery pink flowers; 'Lady Rose', high-centered bright salmon and orange flowers emerge from long pointed buds; 'Love', high-centered scarlet flowers, silvery white reverse on petals; 'Lovely Lady', fragrant, double, rosy pink flowers emerge from long buds; 'Loving Memory' (syns 'Burgund 81', 'Red Cedar'),

high-centered bright crimson blooms on long stems; 'Mme Butterfly', very fragrant soft pink flowers emerge from long buds; 'Mrs Oakley Fisher', single deep buff-yellow flowers, prominent amber stamens; 'Moonstone' ★, lightly scented, large, white flowers, highlighted with shades of soft pink; 'National Trust', large, high-centered, bright red flowers; 'New Zealand' ★ (syn. 'Aotearoa New Zealand'), soft pink fragrant flowers open from long pointed buds; 'Olympiad' ★, brilliant red, velvety, double flowers, delicately scented; 'Pascali', considered one of best whites, long, nearly thornless stems topped with ivory white flowers; 'Paul Shirville' (syn. 'Heart Throb'), perfumed, high-centered, pink flowers with hint of salmon; 'Peace', probably most famous and popular Large-flowered Rose of all, large pale yellow flowers suffused with creamy pink; 'Perfume Delight', cupped deep pink flowers, very fragrant; 'Pot o' Gold', bright yellow blooms touched with gold, very fragrant; 'Precious Platinum' (syns 'Opa Pötschke', 'Red Star'), bright red high-centered flowers with velvety sheen; 'Pristine', long pointed buds open to reveal large, shapely, white flowers flushed with pale pink; 'Remember Me', coppery orange flowers; 'Royal William', large, rich red, velvety blooms; 'Savoy Hotel', fully double soft pink flowers, deeper colored on petal reverse, lightly scented; 'Shot Silk', globular silky-petalled blooms of salmon pink with yellow base; 'Silver Jubilee', silvery pink and apricot flowers with deeper colored reverse; 'Sunblest' (syn. 'Landora'), rich yellow flowers emerge from slim buds; 'Sutter's Gold', deep yellow flowers flushed with orange and pink; 'Touch of Class' (syn. 'Maréchale LeClerc'), long-stemmed high-centered flowers in shades of cream, coral, and salmon pink; 'Valencia' ★, fragrant, apricot-yellow, double blooms; 'White Lightnin', vigorous plant, well-scented pure white flowers; 'White Wings', long pointed buds open to large, single, white flowers, prominent chocolate brown stamens. Zones 4–10.

Rosa, Modern Rose, Patio, 'Queen Mother'

Patio (Dwarf Cluster-flowered) Roses

☼ ❊ ↔ 18–36 in (45–90 cm) ↕ 18–30 in (45–75 cm)

More recent group, result of much cross-breeding between Polyantha Roses, Miniature Roses, and Cluster-flowered Roses; classification can be difficult because of this. Usually bushier and slightly taller than Miniatures; most resemble Cluster-flowered Roses with all parts proportionately smaller. Suitable for beds and borders as well as for patios and growing in containers. Some popularly grown examples of this group are 'Anna Ford', which bears long pointed buds opening to cup-shaped deep orange flowers with yellow eye; 'Boys' Brigade', single crimson flowers with paler eye; 'Brass Ring' (syn. 'Peek-a-Boo'), deep peachy orange buds opening to peach and pale apricot, fading to pink at edges; 'Dainty Dinah', soft coral red flowers on spreading plant; 'Festival', carrying clusters of striking deep red flowers, semi-double; 'Queen Mother' ★, delicate pink semi-double flowers; and 'Rexy's Baby', offspring of Cluster-flowered (Floribunda) Rose 'Sexy Rexy', which produces pale pink flowers deepening to salmon pink at center. Zones 4–11.

Rosa, Modern Rose, Polyantha, 'Gloire du Midi'

Polyantha Roses

☀ ❋ ↔ 2–3 ft (0.6–0.9 m) ↕ 2–4 ft (0.6–1.2 m)

Only a few of these small roses still available. Very hardy, withstanding winter cold of northern Europe, very free flowering, with small pompon-like flowers covering plants for months. **'Baby Faurax'**, small, amethyst-violet, pompon flowers; **'Cameo'**, semi-double blooms in shades of salmon and coral pink; **'Gloire du Midi'**, orange-red blooms; **'Mlle Cécile Brünner'**, profuse shell pink flowers open from long pointed buds; **'Mevrouw Nathalie Nypels'**, pink semi-double flowers, sweet fragrance; **'Nypels Perfection'**, semi-double blooms in shades of pink; **'Pinkie'**, cupped, semi-double, very fragrant rosy pink flowers; **'The Fairy'**, large crowded clusters of small, very double, clear pink flowers smother plant constantly throughout summer; **'White Cécile Brünner'**, slightly fragrant, double, white flowers with yellow center; **'White Pet'** (syn. 'Little White Pet'), sometimes classed as Cluster-flowered Rose, small, pompon-like, white flowers, with pink tint in bud; **'Yesterday'**, purple-pink double blooms emerge from dark buds. Zones 3–10.

SHRUB ROSES

Shrub Roses, usually bigger and more vigorous than Bush Roses, range from 4–10 ft (1.2–3 m) in height. Flower formation varies considerably and some cultivars flower only once in the season. Suitable for specimen or shrubberies and mixed borders, some can be trained as small climbers or pillar roses.

Hybrid Rugosa Roses

☀ ❋ ↔ 5–10 ft (1.5–3 m) ↕ 2–7 ft (0.6–2 m)

Distinctive group with stout bristly branches and coarse wrinkled leaves that often color to buttery yellow in autumn. Tough and healthy plants, many have very fragrant flowers; blooms range from single to double, in shades of pink and crimson, with a few white and yellow. As group they span eras of Old and Modern Roses, with plants being bred from late 1800s to present day. **'Agnes'**, dense bush, bearing very fragrant, creamy yellow, double flowers; **'Blanc Double de Coubert'**, vigorous plant with heavily perfumed semi-double flowers of purest white; **'Dr Eckener'**, very

large, heavily perfumed, semi-double flowers in soft shades of pale yellow and coppery rose, fading to pale pink; **'Fimbriata'** (syns 'Dianthiflora', 'Phoebe's Frilled Pink'), small, white, double flowers, frilled petal edges resembling *Dianthus*; **'Frau Dagmar Hartopp'**, large, single, silvery pink flowers, sometimes darker; **'Hansa'**, fragrant, double, pink-purple flowers; **'Henry Hudson'** (one of Explorer Series), hardy to Zone 1, fragrant white flowers, tinged with pink; **'Martin Frobisher'** (Explorer Series), hardy to Zone 1, fragrant soft pink flowers; **'Roseraie de l'Haÿ'**, dense and vigorous bush, with large, semi-double, extremely fragrant flowers of rich crimson-purple; **'Scabrosa'**, modern introduction with large, single, cerise flowers; **'Souvenir de Philémon Cochet'**, fully double flowers, white with pale pink center; **'Thérèse Bugnet'**, large fragrant flowers, up to 4 in (10 cm) in diameter, opening reddish pink, maturing to light pink; **'Vanguard'**, large, double, apricot-pink to salmon flowers, highly aromatic. Zones 3–10.

Rosa, Modern Rose, Hybrid Rugosa, 'Scabrosa'

Modern Shrub Roses

☀ ❋ ↔ 4–8 ft (1.2–2.4 m) ↕ 4–8 ft (1.2–2.4 m)

Plants bred from variety of different parents; various sizes and growth habits, flowers in all colors and from single to double. **'Adelaide Hoodless'**, hardy to Zone 1, semi-double clear red flowers in clusters of up to 35 blooms; **'Anna Zinkeisen'**, double flowers of ivory white, lemon tones at base; **'Berlin'**, semi-double flowers of rich red, paling at center, prominent yellow stamens; **'Bonica'** ★ (syn. 'Bonica 82'), double light pink flowers, rather frilled petals; **'Canary Bird'** (syn. *R. xanthina* 'Canary Bird'), fragrant, single, canary yellow flowers, prominent stamens; **'Cantabrigiensis'** (syn. *R. × cantabrigiensis*), large pale primrose flowers; **'Cerise Bouquet'**, semi-double deep pink-red flowers; **'Champlain'** (from Explorer Series), slightly fragrant, dark red, velvety flowers, hardy to Zone 2; **'Eddie's Jewel'**, repeat-flowering form; **'Flower Carpet'** ★, semi-double rich pink flowers with light scent; **'Fred Loads'**, large, almost-single, bright salmon pink flowers on large trusses; **'Fritz Nobis'**, once-flowering shrub, large double flowers of light pink to soft salmon; **'Geranium'** ★, more compact habit, good display of larger hips; **'Golden Wings'**, single

Rosa, Modern Rose, Modern Shrub, English, 'Golden Celebration'

pale primrose yellow flowers, prominent gold stamens; '**Goldstern**', large golden yellow blooms emerge from elegant, long, pointed buds; '**J. P. Connell**', hardy to Zone 2, clusters of 3 to 8 lemon yellow flowers fade to cream; '**Lavender Dream**', clusters of flattish lilac-pink flowers, may be slightly fragrant; '**Nevada**', almost-single white flowers, up to 4 in (10 cm) across, prominent yellow stamens; '**Phantom**', slightly fragrant saucer-shaped flowers, rich deep red petals, bright yellow stamens; '**St John's Rose**' (syns *R.* × *richardii, R. sancta*), dark green leaves, single flowers, mildly fragrant, clear delicate pink; an ancient hybrid, flowers have been found in Egyptian tombs; '**Sally Holmes**' ★, large, creamy white, single flowers open from soft apricot-pink buds; and '**Westerland**', fragrant, apricot, double blooms.

English Roses (also classed as Modern Shrub Roses). In early 1960s Englishman David Austin began breeding program that crossed Old and Modern Roses. Combines flower forms and fragrance of Old Roses with growth habits, repeat-flowering ability, and wider color range of Modern Roses. '**Abraham Darby**' ★, large, orange-pink, fully double flowers; '**Charles Rennie Mackintosh**', fragrant blooms open rose pink, age to lilac-pink; '**Constance Spry**', large, cupped, soft pink flowers, myrrh-like fragrance, in late spring–summer; '**Gertrude Jekyll**', very fragrant, rich pink, very double flowers; '**Golden Celebration**' ★, highly fragrant, deep yellow, double flowers in summer–autumn; '**Graham Thomas**', long-stemmed, rich yellow, double flowers, sweetly scented; '**Jude the Obscure**', strongly scented yellow blooms; '**Mary Rose**', rich rose pink flowers; '**Winchester Cathedral**', fragrant white blooms; '**Windrush**', large semi-double flowers, pure soft lemon, prominent yellow stamens, very sweetly perfumed.

Hybrid Musk Roses. Although placed in Modern Shrub Roses, group often thought of as "Old." First introduced in 1913 by Rev. Joseph Pemberton; most of group bred by him. Name relates to fragrance, inherited very indirectly from musk rose (*R. moschata*). Shrubby habit, often with dark green leaves and purplish stems, long flowering season, clusters of single to double flowers. Good specimen or shrubbery plants. '**Belinda**' ★, mid-pink flowers,

Rosa, Modern Rose, Modern Shrub, Hybrid Musk, 'Cornelia'

often highlighted with white at petal base; '**Buff Beauty**', double apricot blooms age to buff-yellow; '**Cornelia**', small, double, very pale pink flowers with orange base, musk-like fragrance; '**Danaë**', double blooms open yellow, age to white; '**Erfurt**', fragrant, semi-double, pink blooms, shaded yellow toward petal base; '**Moonlight**', one of first Hybrid Musk Roses, clusters of almost-single creamy white flowers, prominent yellow stamens; '**Mozart**', large white eye accents pink single flowers; '**Penelope**', semi-double blooms of palest pink, age to white; '**Prosperity**', large clusters of double white flowers on long arching stems. Zones 4–10.

MINIATURE ROSES

Among the more recent large groups to be developed, Miniature Roses of the style we know today first appeared in the late 1930s. Their tiny flowers are perfect replicas in miniature of those of the large rose bushes. What they lack in scent, they more than make up for in intricate beauty.

Miniature Roses

☼ ❄ ↔ 12–18 in (30–45 cm) ↕ 8–24 in (20–60 cm)

Perfect miniature replicas of Bush Roses, with tiny leaves and dainty buds and flowers. Useful for edging borders; make very good container plants. Some roses classed as Miniatures are somewhat taller, but bear small flowers and leaves. '**Air France**' (syns '**American Independence**', '**Rosy Meillandina**'), double flowers of clear rose pink; '**Autumn Splendour**' ★, light fruity fragrance, large, double, yellow-orange flowers, deeper coloring at petal edges intensifies with age; '**Baby Darling**', double apricot flowers; '**Baby Love**' ★, small, single, buttercup yellow flowers, prominent stamens; '**Cachet**' ★, large, unscented, white blooms; '**Cider Cup**', rich apricot double blooms, lightly scented; '**Cinderella**', pearly white flowers lightly flushed with pink; '**Fairy Tale**', small, delicately perfumed, pink flowers, mature to pale pink; '**Gentle Touch**', small, soft pink, double flowers, lightly scented; '**Gourmet Popcorn**' ★, lightly scented, semi-double, snow white flowers; '**Holy Toledo**', double flowers of apricot-orange; '**Hot Tamale**', striking pink-orange flowers, either singly or in clusters; '**Hula Girl**', long pointed buds open to deep salmon pink flowers; '**Irresistible**' ★, fragrant double blooms, almost pure white, becoming pink-tinged toward center; '**Little Red Devil**', well-perfumed, double, deep red flowers; '**Loving Touch**', long pointed buds open to fragrant high-centered flowers in apricot tones; '**Magic Carrousel**' ★, double flowers, creamy white, petals red-edged; '**My Valentine**', high-centered deep red flowers; '**Party Girl**' ★, fragrant, soft apricot-yellow, double blooms; '**Pride 'n' Joy**', profuse orange blooms, fruit-like perfume; '**Red Ace**' (syns '**Amanda**', '**Amruda**'), velvety deep red blooms; '**Rosina**' (syns '**Josephine Wheatcroft**', '**Yellow Sweetheart**'), semi-double blooms of clear yellow; '**Rosmarin**', slightly fragrant double flowers range in color from pale pink to pale red, depending on air temperature; '**Snow Carpet**', small, very double, white flowers; '**Sweet Magic**', orange semi-double blooms; '**Tapis Jaune**', profuse, double, yellow, small flowers. Zones 4–11.

Rosa, Modern Rose, Miniature, 'Rosmarin'

OLD (HERITAGE) ROSES

Under the umbrella term "Old Roses" fall a number of groups containing roses that, through deliberate breeding, have similar characteristics to each other. Some of the oldest groups, such as Gallica, contain roses that have been cultivated for centuries, while other groups, like Bourbon, are the product of nineteenth-century breeding. The term "Old Rose" is a misnomer, as some Old groups contain plants bred more recently, and the term is often used in reference to shrubs such as the Hybrid Musks (included here under Modern Roses), which are of twentieth-century origin. Many people consider that it is a rose's attributes rather than its date of introduction that earn it the title of "Old." Some of the Old Rose groups, such as the Teas, include climbing plants, and there are also Old groups of climbers and ramblers, like the Noisettes.

OLD NON-CLIMBING ROSES

For as long as roses have been cultivated, gardeners have been improving on the wild species. Old Non-climbing Roses, which include groups such as the China Roses and Damask Roses, may be once-flowering and limited in color range, but they more than make up for those failings with delicate tones, unusually shaped flowers, and fragrance that combine to conjure up a bygone era.

Alba Roses

☼ ❁ ↔ 6–10 ft (1.8–3 m) ↕ 2–8 ft (0.6–2.4 m)

Very hardy group. Light bluish green foliage; very fragrant pale-colored flowers, usually double or semi-double, blooming once, in mid-summer. '**Alba Maxima**' (syns 'Bonnie Prince Charlie's Rose', 'Jacobite Rose', 'White Rose of York'), large, pure white, double flowers; '**Félicité Parmentier**', flat double flowers, salmon pink, fade to pale pink; '**Königin von Dänemark**' ★ (syn. 'Queen of Denmark'), smaller double flowers of deeper pink than other Albas; '**Mme Plantier**', rather flat, double, white flowers, buds often tinged reddish pink; '**Maiden's Blush**' fragrant, creamy white to very light pink, double flowers. Zones 4–10.

Bourbon Roses

☼ ❁ ↔ 5–8 ft (1.5–2.4 m) ↕ 4–7 ft (1.2–2 m)

First Bourbon Rose was hybrid between *R. chinensis* and a Damask Rose; occurred naturally on Ile de Bourbon. Highly perfumed, many with repeat-flowering characteristics. Flowers semi-double

or double, often cupped or with quartered arrangement of petals. Susceptible to fungal diseases in humid areas. '**Boule de Neige**', globular, double, white blooms, sometimes with reddish purple tinge on petal edges; '**Honorine de Brabant**', light pink cupped flowers, faint rose spotting on inner surface; '**Louise Odier**', very double rose pink flowers; '**Mme Isaac Pereire**', heavily perfumed, large, double flowers, magenta-rose; '**Mme Pierre Oger**', cupped, double, translucent silvery pink flowers; '**Reine Victoria**', cupped double flowers, silky texture, lilac-pink; '**Souvenir de la Malmaison**', double flowers, flattened and quartered, flesh pink, quickly pulped by wet weather. Its sport, '**Souvenir de St Anne's**', semi-double form, yellow stamens, survives bad weather. '**Zéphirine Drouhin**', no thorns, rich pink, semi-double, fragrant flowers. Zones 6–10.

Centifolia Roses

☼ ❁ ↔ 4–8 ft (1.2–2.4 m) ↕ 2–8 ft (0.6–2.4 m)

Centifolia means "one hundred leaves," refers to crowded petals on large flowers. Flowers in shades of pink, white, and occasionally purplish magenta. Generally flower only once, in early summer. Bush often prickly, coarse, quite lax growth. '**Fantin-Latour**', fragrant, soft pink, double blooms; '**Petite de Hollande**', small, scented, double, rose pink blooms; '**Petite Lisette**', small, fragrant, pink pompon flowers; '**Reine des Centfeuilles**', fragrant pink flowers, to 2½ in (6 cm) across; '**Rose de Meaux**', small, pink, slightly frilly flowers, resemble *Dianthus;* '**The Bishop**', flowers slightly earlier than most, purplish magenta blooms; '**Tour de Malakoff**', tall lax bush, fragrant purplish magenta blooms fade to lilac. Zones 5–10.

China Roses

☼ ❁ ↔ 3–6 ft (0.9–1.8 m) ↕ 3–6 ft (0.9–1.8 m)

Low growing with airy, often spindly growth; sparsely foliaged. Repeat-blooming flowers, usually quite small and lightly fragrant, semi-double or double, in shades of pink, with some crimson and flame tints. '**Archduke Charles**', pink to crimson flowers mature to deeper shade, banana-scented; '**Comtesse du Caÿla**', loosely semi-double, scented flowers in flame shades; '**Gloire des Rosomanes**', hardy rose, large, cup-shaped, semi-double, pink to crimson flowers, in spring–autumn; '**Green Rose**' (syn. 'Viridiflora'), green leaf-like sepals with red-brown serrated edges, rather than colored petals; '**Le Vésuve**', large slightly fragrant flowers, pink or red, depending on whether grown in sun or shade; '**Louis XIV**', almost-double

Rosa, Old Rose, Alba, 'Alba Maxima'

Rosa, Old Rose, Bourbon, 'Souvenir de la Malmaison'

Rosa, Old Rose, Centifolia, 'Petite Lisette'

Rosa, Old Rose, Hybrid Perpetual, 'Baron Girod de l'Ain'

Rosa, Old Rose, Moss, 'William Lobb'

Rosa, Old Rose, Portland, 'Rose du Roi'

scented flowers, deep crimson, yellow stamens; '**Mutabilis**' ★, taller, single yellow flowers open from buff red-streaked buds, change in color through shades of pink and soft crimson; '**Old Blush**' (syns 'Common Monthly', 'Parsons' Pink'), semi-double silvery pink flowers; '**Sophie's Perpetual**', few thorns, scented mid-pink flowers, darker pink shading on some outer petals. Zones 7–10.

Damask Roses

☼ ❋ ↔ 5–8 ft (1.5–2.4 m) ↕ 3–7 ft (0.9–2 m)

Crusaders returning from Middle East took first Damask Roses to Europe. Often untidy bushes, prickly, downy grayish leaves; majority flower only once, in spring or summer. Flowers double or semi-double, pale shades of pink and white, most fragrant. '**Autumn Damask**' (syn. 'Quatre Saisons'), fragrant mid-pink blooms; '**Blush Damask**', profuse flowers in summer, mid-pink in center, lighter pink toward outer petals; '**Celsiana**', clusters of semi-double clear pink flowers; '**Gloire de Guilan**', double flowers, flattened and quartered when fully open; '**Ispahan**', longer flowering, intensely perfumed, clear pink, double flowers; '**Mme Hardy**', double white flowers, petals arranged around green "button" eye; '**Rose de Rescht**', deep pink double flowers; '**Summer Damask**', clusters of very fragrant, semi-double, pink flowers; '**York and Lancaster**', semi-double flowers white, blush pink, or 2-toned. Zones 5–10.

Gallica Roses

☼ ❋ ↔ 4–6 ft (1.2–1.8 m) ↕ 4–6 ft (1.2–1.8 m)

Mostly compact plants. Foliage usually dark green, not very prickly. Sweetly perfumed double or semi-double flowers in shades of pink or magenta-purple. Flower only once, in spring or summer. '**Belle de Crécy**', fragrant, rich pink and purple, double blooms; '**Belle Isis**', double flowers, flattened when fully open, flesh pink, fade to white near edges; '**Cardinal de Richelieu**', scented, dark red-purple, double flowers; '**Charles de Mills**' ★, fragrant, rich purple, double flowers; '**Complicata**', large single flowers, bright pink, paler at center, large stamens; '**Duc de Guiche**', fragrant, deep pink-purple, double blooms; '**Duchesse d'Angoulême**', semi-double to double, mid-pink flowers, fragrant, in summer; '**Duchesse de Montebello**', small, double, fragrant, pink flowers; '**Président de Sèze**', scented double flowers, magenta to cerise at center, shade to lilac-pink at outer petals; '**Tuscany**', purple-red double flowers, yellow stamens; '**Tuscany Superb**', fragrant purple-red flowers. Zones 5–10.

Hybrid Perpetual Roses

☼ ❋ ↔ 3–6 ft (0.9–1.8 m) ↕ 4–7 ft (1.2–2 m)

Complex parentage involving several rose groups, including Bourbons and Chinas. Repeat flowering. Large, double, usually fragrant blooms in shades of pink to red. '**Baron Girod de l'Ain**', crimson flowers, petals edged white; '**Baronne Prévost**', deep pink flowers, flattened when open; '**Comtesse Cécile de Chabrillant**', fragrant pink flowers; '**Frau Karl Druschki**' (syns 'Reine des Neiges', 'Snow Queen', 'White American Beauty'), globular white blooms; '**Général Jacqueminot**', fragrant, purple-red, double blooms on long stems; '**Henry Nevard**', red, highly fragrant, double flowers, up to 30 petals each; '**Marchesa Boccella**' ★, fragrant double flowers, pink, almost white on outer petals; '**Maurice Bernardin**', clusters of large, red, fragrant blooms; '**Paul Neyron**', mid-pink, cupped, fragrant flowers, up to 50 petals each; '**Reine des Violettes**', sweetly scented purple to violet flowers; '**Souvenir du Docteur Jamain**', deep ruby red semi-double flowers, full sun will scorch petals; '**Sydonie**', quartered mid-pink flowers; '**Ulrich Brunner Fils**', fragrant, cupped, pinkish red flowers open from rich red buds. Zones 5–10.

Moss Roses

☼ ❋ ↔ 5–8 ft (1.5–2.4 m) ↕ 3–7 ft (0.9–2 m)

First Moss Rose occurred as sport of a Centifolia. Named for mossy growth on stems and buds. Degree and type of mossing varies, some hard and prickly, others soft and downy. Large, double, fragrant blooms, flowering once, in spring or summer. '**Catherine de Würtemberg**', slightly scented, rich pink flowers; '**Comtesse de Murinais**', flattened double flowers opening soft pink, fading to white; '**Gloire des Mousseux**', large light pink flowers; '**Henri Martin**', deep pink-red semi-double blooms; '**Mme Louis Lévêque**', pink silky-petalled flowers, double, cupped; '**William Lobb**', semi-double purplish magenta flowers. Zones 5–10.

Portland Roses

☼ ❋ ↔ 3–5 ft (0.9–1.5 m) ↕ 2–4 ft (0.6–1.2 m)

Small group closely allied to Damasks and Gallicas, foliage usually resembles one or other. Most bear fragrant, double, repeat-blooming flowers in shades of pink to red. '**Duchess of Portland**' (syn. 'Portland Rose'), single or semi-double cerise-red flowers; '**Mme Knorr**', large, heavily perfumed, rich pink, double flowers; '**Rose du Roi**', heavily scented, rich red, double flowers. Zones 5–10.

Rosa, Old Rose, Tea, 'Monsieur Tillier'

Scots Roses

☼ ❄ ↔ 5–8 ft (1.5–2.4 m) ↑ 3–7 ft (0.9–2 m)

Group became prominent early in nineteenth century when breeding program began from seedlings of malformed *R. spinosissima*. Quite tough plants, with fern-like foliage and prickly stems. Flowers range from single to double in white and cream shades to yellow, and from light to deepest pink and red. Most flower only once, in spring or summer. Hips all unusually dark in color, blackish maroon when fully ripe. '**Aïcha**', large, semidouble, fragrant, yellow flowers, vigorous grower; '**Andrewsii**' (syn. 'Andrew's Rose'), large, semi-double to double, mid-pink flowers, often cream toward petal base; '**Double White Burnet**', highly fragrant white flowers, can be semi-double to double in form; '**Dunwich Rose**', soft yellow single flowers, with prominent yellow stamens; '**Falkland**', fragrant, semi-double, cupped blooms of lilac-pink fading to white; '**Karl Förster**', lightly scented, creamy white, double flowers, prominent stamens when fully open, and repeat flowering; '**Single Cherry**', thorny stems, deep red single flowers, bright yellow stamens; '**Stanwell Perpetual**', arching bush, grayish green foliage, very fragrant double flowers of soft pink (paler with age), long flowering season; '**William III**', fragrant semi-double flowers of rich maroon, becoming lighter with age. Zones 4–10.

Sweet Briar Roses

☼ ❄ ↔ 5–10 ft (1.5–3 m) ↑ 4–8 ft (1.2–2.4 m)

Apple-scented foliage of this group inherited from its *R. eglanteria* parent and is its main distinguishing feature. Majority are large, rather untidy bushes, which are best suited for planting in hedgerows or wild gardens. Flowers are usually single or semi-double, and occur in shades of pink to deep red and white. '**Amy Robsart**', prolific flower bearer, almost-single, highly fragrant, deep pink blooms; '**Lady Penzance**', most strongly scented foliage of group, single coppery pink flowers, prominent stamens; '**Magnifica**', dense scented foliage that can be pruned to form hedge, with crimson semi-double flowers; '**Manning's Blush**', densely foliaged, large, fully double, white flowers flushed with pink; '**Meg Merrilies**', extremely vigorous and prickly rose bush, deep pink to bright crimson, semi-double, scented flowers. Zones 4–10.

Tea Roses

☼ ❄ ↔ 3–6 ft (0.9–1.8 m) ↑ 3–7 ft (0.9–2 m)

Tea Roses arrived in Europe from Asia in early nineteenth century. Name thought to come from being shipped on boats that were also carrying tea rather than for any particular tea scent from leaves or flowers. With their repeat-flowering ability and yellow coloring of some blooms, they, together with Chinas, revolutionized rose breeding. Foliage large and glossy. Double flowers often have long pointed buds. Flower color varies from creamy yellows and white through to pretty shades of pink and red. They grow better in warmer climates. '**Agnes Smith**', free-flowering, flowers rose pink in cooler weather, turning paler pink in hotter months; '**Catherine Mermet**', high-pointed buds opening to light salmon pink; '**Duchesse de Brabant**' (syns 'Comtesse de Labarthe', 'Comtesse Ouwaroff'), free-flowering, cupped, double, pink flowers; '**Francis Dubreuil**', velvety, dark red, double flowers; '**Freiherr von Marschall**', rich red, ageing to deep pink, fragrant, double flowers; '**Lady Hillingdon**', long, pointed, deep yellow buds open to loose, semi-double, buff-yellow flowers; '**Mme de Tartas**', lightly scented double blooms in delicate shade of blush pink; '**Mrs Reynolds Hole**', fragrant, rich purple-pink, double flowers; '**Monsieur Tillier**', rosy pink with salmon tonings, double flowers with darker shading; '**Niphetos**', double white flowers opening from creamy buds; '**Perle des Jardins**', very double, often quartered, sulfur yellow flowers; '**Rosette Delizy**', light pink to pale yellow petals, darker pink veins; '**Souvenir d'un Ami**', double flowers in varying shades of deep rose pink to salmon. Zones 7–11.

Miscellaneous Old Garden Roses

☼/◐ ❄ ↔ 20–48 in (50–120 cm) ↑ 2–6 ft (0.6–1.8 m)

In some instances parentage of Old Roses is hard to establish or plants simply do not seem to fit any particular category. This miscellaneous group is mixed lot, though that in no way lessens their beauty. '**Duplex**' (syn. 'Wolley Dodd's Rose'), repeat-flowering, semi-double blooms; '**Dupontii**', plentiful grayish green leaves, sweetly perfumed single flowers, petals clear creamy white; '**Empress Josephine**', grayish green leaves, fragrant double flowers, dark pink with darker veining, flushed with lilac and purple; '**Fortuniana**', of garden origin in China, dark green leaves, large, scented, double flowers creamy white; '**Harison's Yellow**' (the yellow rose of Texas), of garden origin in USA, said to have been carried west by pioneers and planted wherever they stopped, small double flowers, deep clear yellow; '**Mermaid**', fragrant, single, pale yellow blooms; '**Polliniana**', white flowers, sometimes flushed palest of pink; '**The Garland**', scented semi-double blooms in shades of pink, light yellow, and white. Zones 6–9.

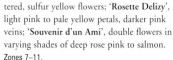

Rothmannia globosa

ROTHMANNIA

This is a genus of about 20 evergreen shrubs or small trees in the madder (Rubiaceae) family that are cultivated largely for their glossy foliage, which is often strongly veined, and their bell-shaped or tubular flowers, which are often fragrant. They are native to Africa, Madagascar, and Asia. Fruit are brown pods containing seeds. CULTIVATION: Although adaptable to most soils, *Rothmannia* species prefer well-composted neutral or slightly acid soil in a protected and sunny position. They are frost and drought resistant. Propagate from seed in spring or half-hardened cuttings in early summer.

Rothmannia globosa
syn. *Gardenia globosa*
BELL GARDENIA, CAPE JASMINE, SEPTEMBER BELLS, TREE GARDENIA
☼ ❄ ↔ 6–10 ft (1.8–3 m) ↕ 12–20 ft (3.5–6 m)
Native of South Africa. Evergreen shrub, similar to gardenia. Textured, glossy green, veined, elliptic to narrow leaves. Fragrant, white, bell-shaped flowers, singly or in cymes, in spring. Zones 9–11.

RUBUS

There are more than 250 species of shrubs, often with prickles on stems and leaves, within this genus from the rose (Rosaceae) family. Found throughout the world, some are cultivated for their ornamental value and as a useful food source, others are regarded as weeds. Most species have biennial stems or canes, which means they produce fruit only on second-year wood; leaves on first and second year's growth are often a different shape. CULTIVATION: The wide distribution of this genus means it has a variety of habitats. Most species thrive in fertile, humus-rich, moist, free-draining soil. Many grow in full sun to light shade, and some grow in deeper shade under deciduous trees. Propagate by dividing suckering species in spring or take half-hardened cuttings from evergreen species, or softwood or hardwood cuttings from deciduous species, or layer. Grow from stratified seed in spring.

Rubus crataegifolius

Rubus biflorus
☼ ❄ ↔ 10 ft (3 m) ↕ 10 ft (3 m)
Deciduous shrub from China and Himalayas. Prickly erect stems, white bloom on bare young stems. Leaves pinnate, 3 to 5 leaflets, dark green, white downy underside. Flowers white, singly or in small clusters, in summer. Yellow edible fruit. Zones 7–9.

Rubus cockburnianus
☼ ❄ ↔ 8 ft (2.4 m) ↕ 8 ft (2.4 m)
Deciduous Chinese shrub. Prickly stems, white bloom in colder months. Dark green leaves, 9 egg-shaped leaflets, furry white underside. Saucer-shaped pale purple flowers, in racemes, in summer. Unappetizing black fruit. Zones 6–10.

Rubus crataegifolius
KOREAN RASPBERRY
☼ ❄ ↔ 5 ft (1.5 m) ↕ 8 ft (2.4 m)
Deciduous shrub from temperate East Asia. Leaves deeply lobed, good color in autumn. Small white flowers. Large, juicy, bright red fruit. Zones 5–9.

Rubus fruticosus
BLACKBERRY
☼ ❄ ↔ 10–25 ft (3–8 m) ↕ 3–6 ft (0.9–1.8 m)
Prickly scrambling shrub, variable in leaf shape and plant form, from temperate Northern Hemisphere. Arching entangling stems, up to 25 ft (8 m) long; savage backward-pointing thorns. Stout, branching, creeping underground roots. Compound leaves, 3 to 5 toothed oval leaflets, prickly stalks and midribs. Many-flowered clusters of white to pink, 5-petalled flowers in spring–summer. Red berries turn black when ripe. Can become invasive. Zones 4–7.

Rubus odoratus
PURPLE-FLOWERING RASPBERRY, THIMBLEBERRY
☼ ❄ ↔ 8 ft (2.4 m) ↕ 8 ft (2.4 m)
From eastern North America. Deciduous erect shrub, vigorous arching stems, peeling bark. Toothed leaves, 5 lobes, hairy underside. Fragrant lilac-pink flowers in summer–autumn. Flat reddish orange fruit. 'Albus', white flowers. Zones 3–9.

Rubus pentalobus
syns *Rubus calycinoides*, *R. fockeanus* of gardens
☼ ❄ ↔ 3–7 ft (0.9–2 m) ↕ 4 in (10 cm)
Taiwanese, evergreen, low-growing, spreading shrub. Dark green, 3- to 5-lobed leaves, wrinkled edges, heart-shaped base, paler and often woolly underside. Solitary white flowers in summer. Round red fruit. Zones 8–11.

Rubus biflorus

Rubus thibetanus

☀ ❉ ↔ 6–8 ft (1.8–2.4 m) ↕ 6–8 ft (1.8–2.4 m)

Native to western China. Thicket-forming deciduous shrub, prickly stems with white bloom in winter. Leaves fern-like, dark green above, felty white below. Red-purple flowers, solitary or in small terminal racemes, in summer. Round black fruit. Zones 6–10.

Rubus tricolor

☀ ❉ ↔ 8–15 ft (2.4–4.5 m) ↕ 2 ft (0.6 m)

Native to western China. Low-growing evergreen or semi-evergreen shrub, bristly stems. Shiny dark green leaves, 3-lobed, felty white beneath. White saucer-shaped flowers, singly or in sparse terminal racemes, in summer. Edible red fruit. Zones 7–9.

Rubus ursinus

☀ ❉ ↔ 3–10 ft (0.9–3 m) ↕ 20–36 in (50–90 cm)

Evergreen shrub native to California, USA. Upright or prostrate habit. Leaves with 3 to 5 leaflets, hairy above, felty white underneath. Male and female flowers on separate plants, white, in prickly corymbs, in spring–summer. Black hairy fruit. Zones 7–9.

RUELLIA

Mostly from tropical and subtropical regions, with a few species in temperate North America, this is a genus containing some 150 species of evergreen perennials and soft-stemmed shrubs, belonging to the acanthus (Acanthaceae) family. They are grown for their showy funnelform flowers, usually red, pink, or mauve, that may occur singly, or in dense terminal panicles or axillary clusters. The smooth-edged, oblong lance-shaped leaves have prominent veins.
CULTIVATION: Although some species from temperate America are quite frost hardy, most need a warm climate and a fertile, moist, well-drained soil in partial shade. In cooler areas they are grown indoors or in a greenhouse. Water potted specimens adequately during the growing season and keep just moist during winter. Trim excess growth regularly and especially after flowering to maintain density of foliage. Propagation is from seed or softwood cuttings in spring.

Ruellia macrantha

CHRISTMAS PRIDE

☀❉ ↔ 20 in (50 cm) ↕ 6 ft (1.8 m)

Short-lived species native to Brazil. Erect stems, rounded crown of hairy, dark green, oval to lance-shaped leaves. Large, deep pink, trumpet-shaped flowers, darker veins, in winter. Zones 10–12.

RUSPOLIA

The 4 species of evergreen shrubs in this genus, which is a member of the acanthus (Acanthaceae) family, are native to Africa. They have oval opposite leaves and bear spikes or panicles of flowers in shades of red or yellow with flaring petal lobes.
CULTIVATION: In cool climates, species of *Ruspolia* make attractive flowering shrubs for the conservatory or greenhouse, where they

should be shaded during the hottest part of the day. In very warm and tropical climates, grow outdoors in a humus-rich soil. Propagate from softwood cuttings taken in late spring.

Ruspolia hypocrateriformis

☀ ❉ ↔ 3 ft (0.9 m) ↕ 3 ft (0.9 m)

Small shrub from tropical and southern Africa; semi-trailing habit. Smooth leaves, to 3 in (8 cm) long. Flowers deep reddish pink, tubular, with darker throat, in showy terminal panicles, appear over many months. Zones 10–12.

RUSSELIA

This genus of about 50 evergreen subshrubs and shrubs found from Mexico to Colombia is a member of the foxglove (Scrophulariaceae) family. The commonly grown species has arching stems, but *Russelia* species vary in habit and may be erect, arching, or spreading. They also vary in foliage, some species having much-reduced, scale-like leaves, others having heart-shaped leaves up to 4 in (10 cm) long. The flowers, however, are more distinctive, being flared pendulous tubes that appear through much of the year.
CULTIVATION: These plants are marginally frost tender and perform best in a mild climate. They flower most heavily when grown in full sun, and they prefer a gritty well-drained soil that can be kept moist in the warmer months. Trim lightly to encourage a neat bushy habit. Propagation is usually either from cuttings or by removing self-rooted layers.

Ruellia macrantha

Russelia equisetiformis

CORAL PLANT

☀ ❉ ↔ 8 ft (2.4 m) ↕ 5 ft (1.5 m)

Native to Mexico. Arching weeping stems, leafless or nearly so, leaves reduced to small scales, closely held to wiry green stems. Small, bright red, tubular flowers, throughout year. Zones 9–12.

RUTTYA

This genus in the acanthus (Acanthaceae) family contains just 3 species of evergreen shrubs that are native to tropical areas of

Ruspolia hypocrateriformis

Russelia equisetiformis

eastern Africa. They have oval opposite leaves and bear colorful tubular flowers on short spikes.
CULTIVATION: In tropical and subtropical climates these plants are easily grown in a fertile well-drained soil. In cooler climates they make attractive flowering plants for the greenhouse or conservatory. Young plants should be pinched out to encourage bushiness. Propagation is from seed or from half-hardened cuttings.

Ruttya fruticosa
JAMMY-MOUTH
☼ ⚡ ↔ 5 ft (1.5 m) ↕ 12 ft (3.5 m)
Bushy shrub native to eastern Africa. Oval leaves. Flowers orangey red, petals fused into 2 lips, lower lip marked with dark brown blotch, in terminal spikes, appear over several months. 'Scholesii' ★, yellow flowers, lower lip marked with black blotch. Zones 10–12.

SALIX
OSIER, WILLOW
This large genus in the willow (Salicaceae) family consists of around 400 species, most from cold and temperate Northern Hemisphere regions. They range from trees to creeping shrublets, mostly deciduous, with leaves often lance-shaped and toothed. The small flowers are usually insect-pollinated and are borne in a catkin; male and female flowers often appear on separate trees. The capsular fruit contain wind-dispersed hairy seeds. Many willows are widely grown for their timber, used for basketry and cricket bats. The bark is used medicinally, as it contains salicin, from which aspirin is derived.
CULTIVATION: Most are fairly adaptable if they are adequately watered during the growing season and the soil is well drained, not swampy. Propagate from seed, by layering, or from cuttings, which root easily even up to branch size.

Salix alba, New Zealand

clone. Long vertically pendulous branches; leaves tapering to long fine point, finely toothed, smooth, bluish-gray beneath. Non-weeping ancestral Chinese trees named *S. b.* f. *pekinensis* (syn. *S. matsudana*); they include 'Crispa', slow-growing, leaves twisted or spirally curled; 'Navajo' (syn. *S. matsudana* 'Navajo'), broad, umbrella-shaped dense crown, very large; 'Tortuosa' (syn. *S. matsudana* 'Tortuosa'), contorted shape, upright in habit, twigs twisted and curled, used in floristry; 'Umbraculifera' (syn. *S. matsudana* 'Umbraculifera'), broad rounded habit. Zones 5–10.

Salix alba
WHITE WILLOW
☼ ❋ ↔ 30 ft (9 m) ↕ 80 ft (24 m)
Broadly columnar tree native to western Asia and Europe. Drooping branch tips, dark gray deeply fissured bark. Narrow lance-shaped leaves, silky and white when young; dark green above, bluish green beneath with age. Thin catkins, with leaves, in spring. 'Vitellina', bright yellow young shoots prominent in winter. Zones 2–10.

Salix amygdaloides
PEACH-LEAFED WILLOW
☼ ❋ ↔ 25 ft (8 m) ↕ 70 ft (21 m)
Tree from western North America. Young growth smooth, yellow or reddish brown. Oval to lance-shaped leaves, serrated margins, bluish or grayish green beneath, downy when young. Female catkins to 4 in (10 cm). Zones 5–10.

Salix babylonica
PEKING WILLOW, WEEPING WILLOW
☼ ❋ ↔ 35 ft (10 m) ↕ 40 ft (12 m)
Native to northern China; brought to Middle East via trade routes, then to Europe in 1700s. Most planted trees belong to single female

Salix caprea

Salix 'Boydii'
☼ ❋ ↔ 2 ft (0.6 m) ↕ 3 ft (0.9 m)
Natural hybrid found in 1870s in Scotland. Slow-growing dwarf shrub, twigs persistently downy, gnarled appearance. Round gray leaves also downy. Small dark gray catkins, rarely produced. Zones 5–9.

Salix caprea
FLORIST'S WILLOW, PUSSY WILLOW
☼ ❋ ↔ 10–20 ft (3–6 m) ↕ 15–35 ft (4.5–10 m)
Small tree or shrub from Europe to northeastern Asia. Elliptical to oblong leaves, slightly glossy, dark green above, gray and felted below, dull yellow in winter. Plump silky male catkins in spring. 'Pendula' (Kilmarnock willow), weeping branches, yellow-brown shoots, gray male catkins. Zones 5–10.

Salix cinerea
GRAY WILLOW
☼ ❋ ↔ 8 ft (2.4 m) ↕ 10 ft (3 m)
Shrubby species found from UK and continental Europe to western Asia. Covered in fine gray down, remaining on twigs through second season. Narrow leaves dull green above, gray beneath. Silky catkins appear before leaves. Zones 2–9.

Salix fragilis

Salix daphnoides

VIOLET WILLOW

☀ ❄ ↔ 20 ft (6 m) ↑ 35 ft (10 m)

Vigorous erect tree or shrub, native to Europe and central Asia to Himalayas. Plum-colored bloom on young shoots. Long narrow leaves, glossy dark green above, bluish green below. Small, broad, silky male catkins in late winter–spring. Zones 5–10.

Salix discolor

AMERICAN PUSSY WILLOW

☀ ❄ ↔ 15 ft (4.5 m) ↑ 25 ft (8 m)

Shrub or small tree native to North America. Purplish brown shoots, downy at first. Oval leaves, bright green above, bluish gray beneath. Catkins appear before leaves, in late winter–spring. Zones 2–9.

Salix elaeagnos

HOARY WILLOW, ROSEMARY WILLOW

☀ ❄ ↔ 20 ft (6 m) ↑ 20 ft (6 m)

Shrub or small tree native to central Europe, Turkey, and southwestern Asia. Twigs gray and downy, becoming smooth, reddish yellow to brown. Dark green leaves, long, narrow, felted white beneath. Catkins appear before leaves, in spring. *S. e.* subsp. *angustifolia*, creeping stems, thin narrow leaves. Zones 4–9.

Salix fargesii

☀ ❄ ↔ 10 ft (3 m) ↑ 10 ft (3 m)

Chinese shrub. Large red winter buds. Leaves serrated edges, glossy dark green above, silky dull green below. Long slender catkins, with leaves, in spring. Zones 6–10.

Salix 'Flame'

FLAME WILLOW

☀ ❄ ↔ 20 ft (6 m) ↑ 20 ft (6 m)

Large shrub or round-headed small tree, most likely hybrid of *S. alba*. Young branches bright red. Leaves lance-shaped, downy when young, turn bright yellow, in autumn, contrasting with red twigs. Prune in spring to encourage bright new growth. Zones 5–9.

Salix fragilis

BRITTLE WILLOW, CRACK WILLOW

☀ ❄ ↔ 35 ft (10 m) ↑ 50 ft (15 m)

Broadly spreading tree native to Europe and northern Asia. Dark gray bark, deeply fissured, twigs break easily at joints. Long narrow leaves, silky, becoming dark green above, bluish green below. Slender catkins appear with leaves. Zones 6–10.

Salix gracilistyla

ROSEGOLD PUSSY WILLOW

☀ ❄ ↔ 10–15 ft (3–4.5 m) ↑ 10–15 ft (3–4.5 m)

Shrub native to eastern Asia. Oblong leaves. Catkins before leaves, in late winter; male catkins red, later orange, then yellow, female catkins silky gray. 'Melanostachys' ★ (syn. *S. melanostachys*), male form; black catkins with red-tipped yellow stamens. Zones 6–10.

Salix hastata

HALBERD WILLOW

☀ ❄ ↔ 7 ft (2 m) ↑ 5 ft (1.5 m)

Dense erect shrub native to mountainous areas of central Europe and northeastern Asia. Twigs become purple in second year. Leaves variable, oblong to slightly rounded, dull green above, glaucous beneath. Small plump catkins appear with leaves, in spring. 'Wehrhahnii', attractive silvery catkins. Zones 6–9.

Salix helvetica

SWISS WILLOW

☀ ❄ ↔ 3 ft (0.9 m) ↑ 2–5 ft (0.6–1.5 m)

Shrub from European alpine regions. Forms small spreading mound of densely interlaced twigs, larger in cultivation than species. Red-brown stems. Leaves glossy green, serrated edges, downy underside. Smothered in small silver-gray catkins in spring. Zones 5–9.

Salix nigra

Salix integra

DAPPLED WILLOW, JAPANESE WILLOW

☀ ❄ ↔ 12 ft (3.5 m) ↑ 10–15 ft (3–4.5 m)

Slender shrub from Japan and Korea; like *S. purpurea,* but leaves lighter shade of green. Drooping, purplish branches. Slender catkins before leaves. 'Hakura Nishiki', pink leaf buds and stems. Zones 6–10.

Salix lanata

ARCTIC WILLOW, WOOLLY WILLOW

☀ ❄ ↔ 6 ft (1.8 m) ↑ 2–4 ft (0.6–1.2 m)

Slow-growing shrub native to northern areas of Europe. Stout branchlets, densely woolly, gnarled with age. Oval to rounded leaves covered in silvery silky hairs, becoming dull green on upper surface. Bright golden catkins, after leaves, in spring. Zones 2–9.

Salix lindleyana

☀ ❄ ↔ 30 in (75 cm) ↑ 2 in (5 cm)

Alpine species found in Himalayas. Forms dense mats of small, green, rosemary-like leaves on reddish stems. Leaves turn attractive yellow in autumn. Tiny catkins appear with leaves. Zones 5–10.

Salix repens

Salix reptans

Salix magnifica

☼ ❄ ↔ 10 ft (3 m) ↑ 20 ft (6 m)

Tree native to China. Magnolia-like foliage, smooth purplish shoots and buds. Blunt oval leaves, grayish green, yellowish green midrib and veining. Female catkins appear in spring with leaves. **Zones 7–10.**

Salix nakamurana

☼ ❄ ↔ 36 in (90 cm) ↑ 12 in (30 cm)

Slow-growing dwarf shrub native to Japan. Stout arching stems eventually form mound. Leaves large in relation to plant size, almost round, light green, silvery hairs. Catkins also silvery. **Zones 6–10.**

Salix nigra

BLACK WILLOW

☼ ❄ ↔ 15 ft (4.5 m) ↑ 10–30 ft (3–9 m)

North American large shrub or small tree. Rough bark, yellowish twigs. Narrow, pointed, pale green leaves with finely serrated margins. Catkins on short downy shoots, with leaves, in spring. **Zones 4–10.**

Salix purpurea

ALASKA BLUE WILLOW, ARCTIC WILLOW, PURPLE OSIER WILLOW

☼ ❄ ↔ 15 ft (4.5 m) ↑ 15 ft (4.5 m)

Shrub or small tree found from Europe to northern Africa, central Asia, and Japan. Arching purplish shoots, narrow oblong leaves, bluish green above, paler beneath. Red catkins, becoming purplish black, appear in spring before leaves. 'Nana' (syn. *S. purpurea* f. *gracilis*), gray-green leaves, thin shoots; 'Pendula', thin pendulous branches. **Zones 5–10.**

Salix repens

CREEPING WILLOW

☼ ❄ ↔ 5 ft (1.5 m) ↑ 8 in–5 ft (20 cm–1.5 m)

Creeping shrub from Europe, Turkey, southwestern Asia, and Siberia. Downy shoots become smooth. Small tapering leaves, green above, silvery below. Small catkins in spring. **Zones 5–10.**

Salix reptans

ARCTIC CREEPING WILLOW

☼ ❄ ↔ 18–36 in (45–90 cm) ↑ 2 in (5 cm)

Dwarf from far northern Asia and Russia. Reddish brown branches. Leaves green, dense long hairs, wrinkled above, paler bluish beneath. Erect catkins, long-haired black-tipped scales. **Zones 2–8.**

Salix reticulata

NET-LEAFED WILLOW

☼ ❄ ↔ 15 in (38 cm) ↑ 6 in (15 cm)

Dwarf shrub from northern Europe, North America, and Asia. Oval to rounded leaves, dark green, wrinkled above, white beneath. Small, erect, mauve-tipped catkins, after leaves, in spring. **Zones 1–8.**

Salix × rubens

☼ ❄ ↔ 25 ft (8 m) ↑ 35 ft (10 m)

Natural hybrid of *S. alba* and *S. fragilis*, native to central Europe. Olive twigs tinged yellow or red. Lance-shaped leaves, bright green above, glaucous beneath. Cylindrical catkins. **Zones 6–10.**

Salix × sepulcralis

☼ ❄ ↔ 40 ft (12 m) ↑ 40 ft (12 m)

Hybrid between *S. alba* and *S. babylonica*, of garden origin. Habit and foliage similar to but slightly less weeping than *S. babylonica*. Fissured bark. Slender catkins similar to *S. alba*. **Zones 6–10.**

Salix taxifolia

☼ ❄ ↔ 7–10 ft (2–3 m) ↑ 10–15 ft (3–4.5 m)

Shrub from southern North America and Mexico. Narrow leaves, branches slightly furry. Tiny male and female catkins. **Zones 8–10.**

Salix viminalis

COMMON OSIER, HEMP WILLOW

☼ ❄ ↔ 15 ft (4.5 m) ↑ 8–20 ft (2.4–6 m)

Shrub from Europe to northeast Asia and Himalayas. Long flexible shoots, thick gray hair when young. Narrow leaves dull green above, silvery silky below. Catkins before leaves, in spring. **Zones 4–10.**

Salix × sepulcralis, UK

SALVIA

SAGE

The largest genus in the mint (Lamiaceae) family, *Salvia* contains
annuals, perennials, and softwooded evergreen shrubs. They grow
in habitats ranging from coastal to alpine; over half the 900 or
so species are native to the Americas. The leaves are opposite and
carried on squared hairy stems, and are aromatic when crushed.
The flowers are tubular, with the petals split into 2 straight or
flaring lips. Colors may be shades of blue to purple and pink to
red, as well as white and some yellows.

CULTIVATION: The shrubby sages grow in a range of soil types, but
dislike heavy wet soil. Most do best in full sun; all require a well-
drained situation. Prune in spring to remove straggly, bare, and
frost-damaged stems. Propagate most shrubby species from softwood cuttings taken throughout the growing season. Seed of all
species can be sown in spring.

Salvia apiana

BEE SAGE, CALIFORNIA WHITE SAGE

☼ ❄ ↔ 3 ft (0.9 m) ↑ 4 ft (1.2 m)

Shrub from southwestern California, USA. Silvery covering of fine
hairs. Leaves very aromatic. White or pale lavender flowers, in loose
whorls above foliage, in spring. Zones 9–11.

Salvia aurea

syn. *Salvia africana-lutea*

BEACH SAGE, BROWN SALVIA, GOLDEN SAGE

☼ ❄ ↔ 3 ft (0.9 m) ↑ 3–5 ft (0.9–1.5 m)

Stiff well-branched shrub from coastal areas of South Africa. Small,
aromatic, grayish green leaves. Whorls of large yellow flowers,
fading to orangey brown, in summer–autumn. Prominent greenish brown calyces. 'Kirstenbosch', dwarf cultivar to 3 ft (0.9 m)
high and wide, aromatic silvery leaves. Zones 9–11.

Salvia canariensis

CANARY ISLAND SAGE

☼ ❄ ↔ 3 ft (0.9 m) ↑ 4–7 ft (1.2–2 m)

Shrub native to Canary Islands. Stems covered in dense white hairs.
Leaves soft, arrowhead-shaped, grayish green, hairy. Lilac-pink
flowers, showy purplish red calyces, in spring–summer. 'Alba',
pink calyces, white flowers. Zones 9–11.

Salvia clevelandii

CALIFORNIA BLUE SAGE, CLEVELAND SAGE

☼ ❄ ↔ 15–26 in (38–65 cm) ↑ 24–48 in (60–120 cm)

Shrub from California, USA. Aromatic, oval to lance-shaped, gray-
green leaves, toothed edges, wrinkled upper surface. Whorls of
fragrant, lavender-blue, rarely white, flowers, on erect flower spikes,
in summer. 'Winifred Gilman' ★, drought-tolerant. Zones 8–10.

Salvia fruticosa

GREEK SAGE, TRILOBA SAGE

☼ ❄ ↔ 2 ft (0.6 m) ↑ 3 ft (0.9 m)

Evergreen shrub from east Mediterranean region. Rough gray-green
leaves. Spikes of small 2-lipped flowers, pink or mauve, at stem
ends. May develop cherry-sized galls from insect sting. Zones 8–10.

Salvia × jamensis

☼ ❄ ↔ 27–40 in (70–100 cm) ↑ 27–40 in (70–100 cm)

Shrubby hybrid between *S. microphylla* and *S. greggii*. Glossy green
oval leaves. Flowers in range of solid colors, including reds, pinks,
oranges, apricots, and yellows, also some bicolored forms, in summer–autumn. 'Cinega de Oro', pale yellow flowers. Zones 9–11.

Salvia karwinskii

KARWINSKI'S SAGE

☼ ❄ ↔ 4 ft (1.2 m) ↑ 8 ft (2.4 m)

Shrubby species from Central America. Large felted leaves. Abundant, large, showy heads of red-pink flowers in winter. Zones 10–11.

Salvia leucophylla

CHAPARRAL SAGE, GRAY SAGE, PURPLE SAGE

☼ ❄ ↔ 3 ft (0.9 m) ↑ 5 ft (1.5 m)

Well-branched shrub native to hot, dry, stony hillsides of California,
USA. Whitish gray, hairy leaves. Whorls of pinkish purple flowers,
on pinkish stems, in autumn. 'Figuero', smaller, silvery foliage;
'Point Sal Spreader' ★, prostrate form, grayer leaves. Zones 8–11.

Salvia mexicana

MEXICAN SAGE

☼ ❄ ↔ 7 ft (2 m) ↑ 10 ft (3 m)

Vigorous grower native to Mexico. Smooth to slightly hairy leaves,
almost heart-shaped, mid-green to grayish green. Spikes of deep

Salvia clevelandii

Salvia fruticosa

Salvia leucophylla

purple flowers, from large green calyces, held well above foliage, in autumn. 'Limelight', chartreuse stems and calyces. Zones 9–11.

Salvia regla
MOUNTAIN SAGE

☼ ⊰ ↔ 3 ft (0.9 m) ↕ 4 ft (1.2 m)

Shrub found in Texas, USA, and Mexico. Erect woody habit, upper stems dark red-brown. Leaves triangular with wavy edges. Large bright scarlet-red flowers in autumn. 'Royal', tubular orange flowers; 'Huntington', orange-red flowers. Zones 9–10.

SAMBUCUS
ELDER, ELDERBERRY

This genus from the world's temperate areas encompasses around 25 species of perennials, shrubs, and small trees that are mostly deciduous, from the woodbine (Caprifoliaceae) family. Some are ornamental, others invasive weeds. Elders have pinnate leaves, and the umbel-like heads of small white to creamy yellow flowers develop into quick-ripening berries, usually red to black.
CULTIVATION: Elders are not difficult to grow, and some species are only too easily cultivated. They are not fussy about soil type as long as the ground remains fairly moist in summer, nor are they worried by brief periods of water-logging in winter. Most species are very frost hardy, and will reshoot even when cut to the ground by frost. Prune trees to shape as necessary, and propagate from seed or cuttings.

Sambucus canadensis

Sanchezia speciosa

Sambucus canadensis
AMERICAN ELDER, AMERICAN ELDERBERRY, SWEET ELDER

☼ ✳ ↔ 12 ft (3.5 m) ↕ 8–12 ft (2.4–3.5 m)

Deciduous shrub from eastern North America, sometimes suckering. Leaves have 7 leaflets with serrated edges, smooth or woolly below. Cream flowers in summer, tiny purple-black berries. 'Goldfinch', reddish young leaves. Zones 3–9.

Sambucus ebulus
DANE'S ELDER, DANEWORT, DWARF ELDER

☼ ✳ ↔ 3–7 ft (0.9–2 m) ↕ 5–7 ft (1.5–2 m)

From southern Europe through northern Africa to Iran. Leaves divided, up to 9 leaflets to 6 in (15 cm) long. Tiny flowers in flat-tish heads to 4 in (10 cm) wide, followed by black berries, in summer. Zones 5–10.

Sambucus nigra
BLACK ELDER, EUROPEAN ELDER

☼ ✳ ↔ 10–20 ft (3–6 m) ↕ 8–30 ft (2.4–9 m)

Deciduous shrub or small tree from Europe, North Africa, and western Asia. Self-sows and suckers freely. Weed in many areas, but cultivated for edible flowers and fruit. Leaves have 3 to 9 dark green leaflets with serrated edges. Large heads of scented white flowers in spring–early summer. Purple-black berries. 'Aurea', golden yellow foliage; 'Aureomarginata', paler variegated foliage, berries grow on pink stems; 'Guincho Purple', deep green leaves turn very dark purple; 'Laciniata', deeply dissected leaflets; 'Marginata', gold- to cream-edged foliage; 'Pulverulenta', musk-scented flowers; 'Viridis', pale green flowers and fruit. Zones 5–10.

Sambucus racemosa
EUROPEAN RED ELDER, RED ELDERBERRY

☼ ✳ ↔ 12 ft (3.5 m) ↕ 12 ft (3.5 m)

Deciduous shrub found in most of temperate Eurasia. Leaves with 5 leaflets, coarsely serrated edges. Panicles of pale green to cream flowers in spring–early summer, followed by clusters of very small red berries. 'Plumosa Aurea', dissected yellow foliage; 'Tenuifolia', dwarf, deeply cut foliage, purple new growth. Zones 4–9.

SANCHEZIA

Named after Josef Sanchez, an early Spanish professor of botany, this genus of about 20 species of soft-stemmed shrubs, climbers, and perennials from the acanthus (Acanthaceae) family is native to tropical America. *Sanchezia* species are grown for their attractive leaves, which are carried in opposite pairs, and for their tubular flowers, each with 5 lobes, and often with conspicuous colorful bracts. Fruit are oblong capsules containing 6 to 8 seeds.
CULTIVATION: Frost tender, these are warm-climate plants that need good soil and regular watering. They prefer well-drained soil, in full sun or bright filtered light, in a position sheltered from wind. Water potted specimens adequately during the growing season, and keep just moist at other times. Plants can be kept neat and bushy by pinching out the growing tips. Propagate from cuttings taken in spring or summer.

Sanchezia speciosa
syn. *Sanchezia nobilis*

☼ ⊱ ↔ 5 ft (1.5 m) ↕ 5 ft (1.5 m)

Bushy evergreen shrub from South America. Large, leathery, dark green, oblong-ovate leaves, yellow or white veins. Tubular yellow flowers, bright red bracts, on ends of spikes, in summer. Zones 10–12.

Santolina rosmarinifolia

SANTALUM

This genus of around 25 species of evergreen shrubs and small trees of the sandalwood (Santalaceae) family comes from Southeast Asia, Australia, and some Pacific Islands. It includes a number of trees noted for their scented wood and oils. Some Australian species bear edible fruit, and have been researched as commercial food crops. They usually rely on the roots of other plants to supply their water and nutrients. The host may be another tree, a shrub, a dense ground-covering plant, or a well-established lawn with a vigorous root system.

CULTIVATION: Grow in warm low-rainfall areas with full sun and light well-drained soil. Species will tolerate saline soils and periods of dryness, but they resent root disturbance and poor drainage. They may be propagated from seed, but early growth is often slow, and grafted plants are preferred for orchard crops.

Santalum acuminatum

QUANDONG, SWEET QUANDONG

↔ 12 ft (3.5 m) ↑ 20 ft (6 m)

Large shrub or small tree, widespread in inland Australia. Spindly erect trunk, open crown of pale olive green lance-shaped leaves. Panicles of small whitish cream flowers, at ends of stems, sporadically throughout year. Shiny, red, edible fruit. Zones 9–11.

Santalum lanceolatum

Santalum lanceolatum

NORTHERN SANDALWOOD

↔ 15 ft (4.5 m) ↑ 20 ft (6 m)

Tall shrub or small tree from tropical Australia. Pendulous spreading branches, lance-shaped leaves. Cream or pale green flowers, in leaf axils or in panicles at ends of branches, in spring–summer. Dark blue or purplish edible fruit. Zones 10–12.

SANTOLINA

This Mediterranean genus from the daisy (Asteraceae) family is composed of some 18 species of largely similar evergreen shrubs that form low hummocks. The slender stems are crowded with narrow leaves that have finely toothed or lobed margins. They are often clothed in silvery hairs, as are the leaf stalks. Clusters of button-like flowerheads, usually bright yellow, appear in summer.

CULTIVATION: Fully to moderately frost hardy, these shrubs thrive in a warm sunny position and are ideal for dry banks and as border plants. They need perfect drainage and do not like overly wet winters, but are not fussy about soil type as long as it is reasonably loose and open. Species respond well to regular trimming to keep the bushes neat and compact. It is also advisable to remove the dead flowerheads, as they are not attractive once they have dried. Propagate from small cuttings or by removing self-rooted layers.

Santolina rosmarinifolia

GREEN SANTOLINA

↔ 36 in (90 cm) ↑ 12–24 in (30–60 cm)

Bushy shrub native to southwestern Europe. Sparsely downy linear leaves, fine narrow teeth, closely spaced. Clusters of ¾ in (18 mm) wide bright yellow flowerheads in mid-summer. **'Morning Mist ★'**, compact form; **'Primrose Gem'**, light lemon flowers. Zones 7–10.

SAPINDUS

There are about 13 species in this tropical and subtropical genus, most from the Americas and Asia. These evergreen and deciduous trees, shrubs, and climbers belong to the soapberry (Sapindaceae) family. They are grown mostly as ornamental and shade trees. They have alternate simple or pinnate leaves, which in some species color attractively to shades of yellow in autumn. They bear clusters of small 5-petalled flowers with prominent hairy stamens in summer, and these are followed by a crop of fleshy berry-like fruit. These berries are rich in saponins (glycosides that foam in water), and are used to yield a soap substitute in some countries.

CULTIVATION: Most species are fairly adaptable, and will tolerate poor soil as long as it is well drained. They prefer a sheltered position that is in full sun. Propagation is either from seed or cuttings.

Sapindus drummondii

WESTERN SOAPBERRY, WILD CHINA TREE

↔ 30 ft (9 m) ↑ 50 ft (15 m)

Deciduous tree from southern USA and Mexico, occupying harsh dry habitats. Pinnate leaves, 18 mid-green leaflets, turning golden yellow in autumn. Small white flowers, in panicles at ends of branches, in summer. Rounded orange-yellow fruit. Zones 8–10.

Sapindus mukorossi

CHINESE SOAPBERRY

↔ 20 ft (6 m) ↑ 40–80 ft (12–24 m)

Deciduous tree found from India eastward through China to Japan. Large pinnate leaves. White flowers, in panicles at ends of branches, in summer. Yellow to orange-brown fruit used as soap substitute; black seeds used for beads. Zones 8–11.

Sapindus saponaria

FALSE DOGWOOD, SOAPBERRY, WING-LEAFED SOAPBERRY

☼ ⚘ ↔ 20 ft (6 m) ↑ 30 ft (9 m)

Evergreen tree from tropical America. Pinnate leaves to 12 in (30 cm) long. White flowers, in panicles to 6 in (15 cm) long, in summer. Glossy, orange-brown, saponin-rich fruit, used as soap. Zones 10–12.

SAPIUM

This is a genus of around 100 species of mainly evergreen trees and shrubs in the euphorbia (Euphorbiaceae) family, the majority from tropical America, Asia, and Africa, with a smaller number from warm-temperate regions such as South Africa. Leaves are simple and often toothed, while the flowers are small and petal-less, carried in catkin-like spikes at the ends of branchlets, with male and female flowers on different parts of the spike; the fruit is a capsule with 1 to 3 seeds. Some species are important for timber, and the latex of some has been put to various uses.
CULTIVATION: They can be grown in a frost-free climate with ample summer rainfall. Plant in full sun and in moderately fertile soil. Propagate from fresh seed, collected as the capsules shatter.

Sapium integerrimum

DUIKER-BERRY

☼ ⚘ ↔ 20 ft (6 m) ↑ 10–20 ft (3–6 m)

Native to eastern South Africa and adjacent Mozambique, often "pioneer" tree on forest margins, briefly deciduous in dry season. Branching low, irregular crown, drooping branches; oblong to elliptic leaves, shiny deep green above, pale blue-green beneath. Yellowish flowers in spring–summer. Fruit yellow-green, to 1 in (25 mm) wide, 3-seeded. Zones 10–12.

SARACA

A genus of about 70 species of small evergreen trees in the cassia subfamily of the legume (Fabaceae) family, it comes from the tropical forests of India, extending to China and Southeast Asia. The trees are grown for their dense upturned flower clusters in shades of yellow, orange, and red. Individual flowers have no petals; instead, they have 4 brightly colored sepals at the top of a tube with slender projecting stamens up to 8 in (20 cm) long. The leaves are pinnate with paired leaflets; they are pinkish, pinkish purple when young, maturing to a bright glossy green. These trees grow beneath taller trees in their natural habitat, and therefore like to be in shade, preferably that of taller trees.
CULTIVATION: Frost tender, they require a warm humid climate and a moist well-drained soil enriched with organic matter. In cooler areas, cultivate as greenhouse plants. Propagated from seed in autumn or winter.

Saraca cauliflora

syn. *Saraca thaipingensis*

☼ ⚘ ↔ 25 ft (8 m) ↑ 30 ft (9 m)

Tree from Thailand to Malay Peninsula. Compound leaves with 6 to 8 pairs of oblong leaflets, reddish when young. Night-fragrant yellow flowers, gradually deepening in color to red, at beginning and end of tropical dry season. Narrow, oblong, leguminous fruit. Zones 11–12.

SARCOBATUS

Native to western North America, this genus contains only 1 species and belongs to the rose (Rosaceae) family. It is a dense spiny shrub with arching branches and narrow fleshy leaves. Male and female flowers appear on the same plant, and both are usually small, with the male flowers forming catkin-like spikes. The enlarging calyx of the female flowers develops into a leathery fruit with a broad papery wing toward the middle.
CULTIVATION: Moderately frost hardy, this species grows best in a warm sheltered position in full sun and well-drained soil. Propagation is from seed.

Sarcobatus vermiculatus

GREASEWOOD

☼ ❋ ↔ 7 ft (2 m) ↑ 6 ft (1.8 m)

Rounded spreading shrub with arching branches. Narrow, fleshy, gray-green leaves to 1½ in (35 mm) long. Spikes of male flowers to 1¼ in (30 mm) long. Hard yellow wood used for fuel. Zones 5–10.

SARCOCOCCA

CHRISTMAS BOX, SWEET BOX

This genus in the box (Buxaceae) family consists of evergreen monoecious shrubs cultivated for their ornamental value. Their natural habitats are damp woods and dense forests in western China, the Himalayas, and the mountains of Southeast Asia. Male flowers have visible anthers; female flowers grow below the male flowers.
CULTIVATION: They grow best in neutral to alkaline soil, with plenty of humus added. Once established, they will tolerate drier conditions in shade. They can be grown in full sun, but will need more moisture. Most tolerate years of negligence and air pollution. Propagation is from seed, by division of suckering species, or by taking half-hardened cuttings in late summer. Hardwood cuttings can be taken in winter and propagated in an area protected from winter frosts.

Sarcococca confusa

☀ ❋ ↔ 7 ft (2 m) ↑ 7 ft (2 m)

Evergreen shrub. Leathery, dark green, elliptical to lance-shaped leaves, pale underside. Clusters of cream flowers, female form very fragrant, in mid-winter. Red berries ripen to black. Zones 6–10.

Sapindus mukorossi

Saraca cauliflora

Sarcococca hookeriana

☼ ❈ ↔ 6 ft (1.8 m) ↑ 5 ft (1.5 m)

Evergreen, thicket-forming, often suckering shrub native to China. Lance-shaped deep green leaves. Clusters of scented white flowers, males with deep pink anthers, in late autumn–winter. Black fruit. *S. h.* subsp. *humilis* ★, ground-cover plant, shiny bluish black fruit. *S. h.* var. *digyna*, slender leaves, white flowers with off-white anthers. *S. h.* 'Purple Stem', young magenta shoots, pink-tinted flowers. Zones 6–10.

Sarcococca ruscifolia

☼ ❈ ↔ 3 ft (0.9 m) ↑ 3 ft (0.9 m)

Thick bushy suckering shrub native to western China and Himalayas. Glossy, deep green, broadly lance-shaped leaves. Clusters of creamy white perfumed flowers throughout winter. Dark red fruit. Zones 8–10.

Sarcococca saligna

☼ ❈ ↔ 3 ft (0.9 m) ↑ 3 ft (0.9 m)

Suckering, evergreen, thicket-forming shrub native to Himalayas from Nepal to Afghanistan. Narrow, lance-shaped, pale green leaves. Male flowers green, female flowers greenish white, in winter–early spring. Egg-shaped dark purple fruit. Zones 7–10.

SASSAFRAS

This genus includes just 3 species in the laurel (Lauraceae) family. They are deciduous trees with a rather scattered distribution, occurring in temperate East Asia and eastern North America. They have been cultivated for their aromatic oils, which repel pests and so are valuable in the furniture industry. *Sassafras* leaves may be smooth-edged or lobed, are downy on their underside, and sometimes develop vivid autumn colors. Racemes of tiny, petal-less, yellow-green flowers appear in spring with the developing leaves, and are followed by blue-black drupes.
CULTIVATION: They are reasonably frost hardy. They prefer deep, fertile, well-drained soil, and will grow in either sun or part-shade. They tend to produce multiple trunks, and clever pruning can be directed to encourage this habit or to produce a single-trunked tree, as the situation dictates. Propagation is from seed, suckers, or root cuttings.

Sassafras albidum

Sassafras albidum

SASSAFRAS

☼ ❈ ↔ 30 ft (9 m) ↑ 50 ft (15 m)

North American tree, may be many-trunked. Oval leaves, up to 3 lobes, dark green, downy underside, turn gold and red in autumn. Underbark is source of sassafras oil. Zones 5–9.

SCHEFFLERA

syns *Brassaia, Dizygotheca, Heptapleurum*

This large genus in the ivy (Araliaceae) family consists of around 900 species, occurring in tropical and subtropical regions throughout the world, usually in moist environments, with the majority found from Southeast Asia to the Pacific Islands. Mostly shrubs, trees, scrambling climbers, or epiphytes, they have leaves composed of usually rounded leaflets of similar sizes and arranged in whorls held on a long stalk. Small flowers are produced in umbels, panicles, racemes, or spikes, and are followed by small black or purple fruit. Cultivated for their ornamental foliage, they are suitable for the garden in frost-free climates, or they can be used as pot plants, both indoors and outside.
CULTIVATION: Most are fairly adaptable, tolerating full sun to part-shade. They prefer well-drained moderately fertile soil with adequate moisture during growth periods. Propagate from seed, which is sown as soon as it is ripe, from cuttings, or by aerial layering.

Schefflera actinophylla

syn. *Brassaia actinophylla*

OCTOPUS TREE, QUEENSLAND UMBRELLA TREE

☼ ✦ ↔ 12 ft (3.5 m) ↑ 30 ft (9 m)

Rainforest shrub or tree from New Guinea and northern and northeastern Australia. Many trunks; glossy light green leaflets. Radiating spikes of small red flowers, on ends of branches, in late summer–early spring. Fruit reddish black. Zones 10–12.

Schefflera arboricola

DWARF UMBRELLA TREE, HAWAIIAN ELF SCHEFFLERA

☼ ✦ ↔ 3 ft (0.9 m) ↑ 3–5 ft (0.9–1.5 m)

From Taiwan. Rounded shrub with palmate leaves, 7 to 11 glossy bright green leaflets. Small yellowish flowers, on panicles near branch tips, in spring–summer. Golden berries. Popular house plant. 'Jacqueline', leaves irregularly splashed pale yellow. Zones 10–12.

Schefflera elegantissima

ARALIA, FALSE ARALIA

☼ ✦ ↔ 10 ft (3 m) ↑ 50 ft (15 m)

Tree native to New Caledonia, smaller in cultivation. Juvenile stage is unbranched and well-foliaged, leaves consisting of 7 to 11 long, narrow, deeply serrated leaflets. Lustrous dark green leaflets become wider and more broadly toothed with maturity. Black berries. Zones 10–12.

Schefflera umbellifera

BASTARD CABBAGE TREE, FOREST CABBAGE TREE

☼ ✦ ↔ 25 ft (8 m) ↑ 30 ft (9 m)

Tree native to southern and southeastern Africa. Older specimens have dense rounded crowns and fissured resinous bark. Leaves

Schefflera actinophylla

Schinus terebinthifolius

comprise 5 oblong leaflets crowded near branch tips on long stalks. Panicles of small yellowish green flowers. Black berries. Zones 10–12.

SCHIMA

There is just a single species of evergreen tree in this genus, which is a member of the camellia (Theaceae) family. Native to the area from India to Southeast Asia and Indonesia, it is a small tree with glossy leaves and single white flowers that are borne in late summer.
CULTIVATION: This tree requires a sheltered frost-free environment and a humus-rich acid soil. In cool climates it can be grown in containers in the greenhouse or conservatory. Propagate from seed or half-hardened cuttings.

Schima wallichii
☼ ❄ ↔ 20 ft (6 m) ↑ 25 ft (8 m)
Tree with dense bushy head. Large, leathery, glossy, green leaves, bronze red when young, arranged in spirals. White flowers, mildly fragrant, prominent yellow stamens, in late summer. Zones 9–11.

SCHINUS

Found in Central and South America, this genus from the cashew (Anacardiaceae) family includes some 30 species of evergreen shrubs and trees. They are notable for their attractive pinnate leaves, sometimes weeping branches, and their sprays of brown-red drupes. The fruit develop from racemes of tiny flowers—usually white, yellow-green, or pale pink—that open in spring or summer. There are separate male and female flowers, and these may occur on the same plants or on different plants.
CULTIVATION: Hardiness varies with the species, though no *Schinus* species is extremely frost tolerant and many are frost tender, preferring a warm climate. Most species are very drought tolerant once established, and are best grown in well-drained soil in full sun. Propagate from seed or cuttings.

Schinus molle
PEPPER TREE
☼ ❄ ↔ 50 ft (15 m) ↑ 50–60 ft (15–18 m)
Spreading evergreen tree, with drooping branches, naturally found in South America. Finely divided, pinnate leaves. Small yellow-white flowers in spring. Clusters of pea-sized red berries. Used as street tree in southern Europe; can become weedy in some conditions. *S. m.* var. *areira* (syn. *S. areira*), semi-weeping habit, dark green leaves have aromatic resin, pink to red-brown berries, drought and heat tolerant. Zones 9–11.

Schinus terebinthifolius
BRAZILIAN PEPPER TREE
☼ ❄ ↔ 15 ft (4.5 m) ↑ 20 ft (6 m)
Shrub or small tree from southern Brazil, Argentina, and Paraguay. Leathery pinnate leaves with light underside, covering of fine hairs when young. Small flowers open white from pale green buds. Bright red fruit. Zones 9–12.

SCHOTIA

This small genus in the cassia subfamily of the legume (Fabaceae) family consists of 4 or 5 species from southern Africa. They are deciduous or semi-evergreen shrubs or trees with alternate leaves that have an even number of leaflets. The red or pink flowers have 5 petals, and are borne in panicles that occur along or at the ends of branches or directly from older wood in spring. Fruit are pods, usually leathery, flat, and oblong; in some species the round flat seeds are high in protein and form part of the local diet. These plants come from hot, dry, tropical, and subtropical semi-desert regions, including deciduous woodland and scrub that may be rocky. They are grown for their handsome foliage and attractive flowers.
CULTIVATION: These plants perform best in warm frost-free areas in a well-drained soil and a sunny position that is protected from strong winds. Propagation is either from seed or cuttings.

Schotia latifolia

Schotia brachypetala
AFRICAN WALNUT, TREE FUCHSIA
☼ ❄ ↔ 15–25 ft (4.5–8 m) ↑ 50 ft (15 m)
Deciduous large shrub or small tree naturally found in Zimbabwe, Mozambique, and South Africa. Rough grayish brown bark. Shiny, green, pinnate leaves; leaflets reddish when young. Fragrant crimson flowers, in large, showy, dense panicles, on leafless stems, in summer. Oblong bean-like pods, edible seeds. Zones 9–12.

Schotia latifolia
BEAN TREE, ELEPHANT HEDGE
☼ ❄ ↔ 25 ft (8 m) ↑ 50 ft (15 m)
Variable-shaped tree from eastern South Africa. Leaflets in pairs, 3 to 5 per leaf, narrow rounded bases. Panicles of almost-stalkless pinkish flowers at ends of branches. Hard pods. Zones 9–12.

SCIADOPITYS

This remarkable conifer genus has its own family, Sciadopityaceae, and consists of a single species of evergreen tree endemic to the mountains of Japan. The most striking attribute of *Sciadopitys* is its foliage, as it features 2 kinds of leaves: brown scale-leaves arranged spirally on elongated intervals of stem, and long, green, leaf-like needles radiating in whorls of up to 30 at the end of each interval. Male and female cones are borne on the same tree. The seed cones are like small pine cones, and have broad thin scales at their tips.
CULTIVATION: Plants are easily grown in cool climates as long as rainfall is adequate and summers are warm and humid. They prefer a reasonably sheltered position and deep fertile soil. Growth is slow but steady. Propagate from seed, though germination is poor unless seeds are stratified and then chilled for 3 months before sowing.

Sequoia sempervirens, in the wild, California, USA

Sequoiadendron giganteum

Sciadopitys verticillata

JAPANESE UMBRELLA PINE, UMBRELLA PINE

☼ ❋ ↔ 20 ft (6 m) ↑ 70 ft (21 m)
Conifer tree. Habit neat, conical, branches to ground level. Young plants grown in shade are more elongated. Rich brown bark peels in vertical strips. Whorls of deep glossy green leaves. Zones 6–9.

SENNA

This genus has about 350 species of tropical and warm-temperate trees, shrubs, and a few climbers, most from the Americas, Africa, Australia, and Asia. It is a member of the cassia subfamily of the legume (Fabaceae) family. All species have pinnate leaves, and almost all are evergreen. Most have yellow flowers, a few have pink flowers, but all are very showy when in flower. Many are the source of chemical compounds used medicinally. Fruit are long, flat, or rounded pods. Many species have become invasive weeds in countries where they have escaped cultivation.
CULTIVATION: Many species are frost tender. Grow in well-drained soil in open sunny positions. Species that originate from low-rainfall desert regions appear to be more frost hardy. Propagation is usually from seed, which germinates readily after pre-treatment, or from cuttings.

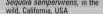

Senna didymobotrya

Senna alata

syn. *Cassia alata*

RINGWORM CASSIA

☼ ✦ ↔ 15 ft (4.5 m) ↑ 30 ft (9 m)
Shrub or tree from American tropics; naturalized elsewhere. Leaves large, 20 pairs of leaflets. Spikes of bright yellow flowers in late summer–early autumn. Winged pods age to brown. Zones 10–12.

Senna artemisioides

syn. *Cassia artemisioides*

FEATHERY CASSIA, SILVER CASSIA

☼ ⋈ ↔ 7 ft (2 m) ↑ 7 ft (2 m)
Occurs throughout arid inland of mainland Australia. Has many varied forms. Typical plant is round shrub, with silvery gray leaves,

2 to 6 pairs of narrow leaflets. Yellow flowers appear in leaf axils in spring–autumn. Narrow flat pods. *S. a.* subsp. *filifolia* (syns *S. eremophila*, *S. nemophila*), pinnate leaves, 1 to 4 pairs of very narrow leaflets, leaf stalk flattened; less frost tolerant than other forms. *S. a.* subsp. *sturtii*, bright yellow flowers year-round. Zones 9–11.

Senna corymbosa

syn. *Cassia corymbosa*

☼ ❋ ↔ 8 ft (2.4 m) ↑ 10 ft (3 m)
Native to Uruguay and Argentina; naturalized in southern USA. Shrub or small tree with spreading habit. Long, light green, pinnately divided leaves with oval leaflets. Racemes of golden yellow flowers in spring–autumn. Zones 8–11.

Senna didymobotrya

syn. *Cassia didymobotrya*

☼ ⋈ ↔ 10 ft (3 m) ↑ 10 ft (3 m)
Large evergreen shrub, originally from tropical Africa to Southeast Asia, now widely naturalized. Large leaves, leathery leaflets, downy when young. Erect flower spikes, golden yellow flowers emerging from blackish buds. Downy seed pods. Zones 10–12.

Senna multijuga

syn. *Cassia multijuga*

☼ ⋈ ↔ 20 ft (6 m) ↑ 25 ft (8 m)
Small tree native to northern South America. Found in open grasslands and forests. Leaves 12 in (30 cm) long, with 40 or more pairs of leaflets. Terminal panicles of small yellow blooms in late summer–autumn. Fruit matures to black. Zones 9–12.

Senna polyphylla

syn. *Cassia polyphylla*

☼ ✦ ↔ 12 ft (3.5 m) ↑ 25 ft (8 m)
Shrub or small tree found in Caribbean region. Stiff branches clothed with small leaves composed of 13 pairs of olive green

leaflets with slightly downy underside. Clusters of golden yellow flowers at various times throughout year, depending on climatic conditions. Pendulous flattened pods. Zones 10–12.

Senna siamea
syn. *Cassia siamea*
KASSOD TREE
※ ⚘ ↔ 35 ft (10 m) ↑ 40 ft (12 m)
Evergreen tree from Myanmar to Indonesia. Leaves pinnate, glossy dark green leaflets, young leaves often reddish. Yellow flowers, at ends of branched spikes, in spring–early summer. Long flat pods. Leaves and seeds reported to be poisonous. Zones 10–11.

Senna splendida
GOLDEN WONDER
※ ⚘ ↔ 8–12 ft (2.4–3.5 m) ↑ 10–15 ft (3–4.5 m)
Spreading shrub or small tree native to Brazil. Slender hanging branches. Glossy pinnately divided leaves with oblong leaflets. Racemes of yellow flowers in autumn. Long drooping cylindrical seed pods. Zones 10–12.

SEQUOIA
This famous genus from the cypress (Cupressaceae) family contains just a single species of coniferous tree native to the coastal areas of Oregon and California, USA. It is recognized as the tallest plant species in the world, with plants in the wild growing to over 360 ft (110 m) high.
CULTIVATION: This tree is suitable only for parks and large gardens, as it can reach 90 ft (27 m) in 20 years under ideal conditions. It does not grow well in cities as it dislikes pollution. Any good well-drained soil will suit it, but it does best in cool humid areas. It will coppice from the stump of a felled tree. Propagate from seed or from heeled cuttings.

Sequoia sempervirens
CALIFORNIA REDWOOD, COAST REDWOOD
※ ❄ ↔ 15–25 ft (4.5–8 m) ↑ 150 ft (45 m)
Tree develops conical shape. Bark deeply ridged, reddish brown, very thick, spongy, exfoliating in strips. Dark green yew-like leaves arranged in ranks along stems. Small, reddish brown, barrel-shaped cones. 'Adpressa', slow-growing dwarf cultivar, grayish green leaves, will reach 90 ft (27 m) tall in about 100 years. Two cultivars have almost horizontal branches: 'Aptos Blue', teal foliage with drooping tips, site carefully as it sets abundant seed; 'Soquel', greener foliage with curling tips. Zones 8–10.

SEQUOIADENDRON
There is just a single species of coniferous tree in this genus from the cypress (Cupressaceae) family, which was formerly included in *Sequoia*. It is found in small groves in the Sierra Nevada foothills in California, USA. This species is the largest living organism (though *Sequoia* is taller), with trees acquiring massive bulk; the biggest existing specimen is named "General Sherman," and is estimated to weigh 2,460 tons (2,500 tonnes). It is also one of the longest living trees on the planet, with specimens in the range of 1,500 to 3,000 years old.

CULTIVATION: With its great bulk, this tree is suitable only for parks and very large gardens. For planting in lines or avenues, trees should be spaced at least 70 ft (21 m) apart. They will grow in a wide range of conditions but dislike pollution. Propagate from seed or cuttings.

Sequoiadendron giganteum
syn. *Wellingtonia gigantea*
BIG TREE, GIANT SEQUOIA, SIERRA REDWOOD
※ ❄ ↔ 20–35 ft (6–10 m) ↑ 150–165 ft (45–50 m)
Often confused with *Sequoia sempervirens*. Similar conical shape, thick, reddish brown, spongy bark. Branches curve downward, then up at tip. Leaves compressed, scale-like, spirally arranged on stems. Larger cones than *Sequoia*. 'Pendulum', hanging branches. Zones 7–10.

SERRURIA
One of the many southern African genera in the protea (Proteaceae) family, *Serruria* encompasses some 55 species of evergreen shrubs, which are notable for their delicate inflorescences that often make excellent and very popular cut flowers. Most species have leaves that are very finely dissected, often so finely as to resemble needle-like foliage. A few species have simple undivided leaves. The flowerheads, which may be clustered or carried singly, are usually composed of several small hairy flowers that are largely concealed within showy bracts. Hard nut-like fruit follow.
CULTIVATION: Often tricky to cultivate outside their natural range, these species tend to be short lived. They have the typical protea requirements: low-phosphate, slightly acidic, gritty, very well-drained soil, a position in sun or part-shade, and good ventilation. If exposed to damp cool conditions in winter they tend to rot. They are also marginally frost hardy. Propagation is from seed or from cuttings, which are often slow to strike and prone to collapse.

Serruria 'Sugar 'n' Spice'
※ ❄ ↔ 4 ft (1.2 m) ↑ 4 ft (1.2 m)
Originated as hybrid between *S. florida* and *S. rosea*. Combines large flowerheads and broad bracts of first species with richer pink coloring of second. Zones 9–10.

Serruria 'Sugar 'n' Spice'

Sesbania punicea

SESBANIA

Widespread in the tropics and subtropics, this genus in the pea-flower subfamily of the legume (Fabaceae) family includes some 50 species of evergreen and deciduous leguminous herbs, shrubs, and trees. They have pinnate leaves that can be quite large, but their main feature is their racemes of pea-flowers. These develop in the leaf axils and usually open in summer. Angular seed pods follow. CULTIVATION: Demanding a warm climate, most *Sesbania* species are quick growing and short lived. They can look rather untidy unless they are kept neatly trimmed, but usually make up for it with a colorful display of flowers. They thrive in a moderately fertile, deep, well-drained soil, and a position in full sun or part-shade. Water well during the flowering season, but keep dry during the cooler months. Propagate from seed or half-hardened cuttings.

Sesbania punicea
ORANGE WISTERIA SHRUB

☼ ❊ ↔ 4 ft (1.2 m) ↑ 6 ft (1.8 m)

Shrub found in southern Brazil, Argentina, and Uruguay; naturalized in southeastern USA. Mid- to dark green leaves, 6 to 20 pairs of leaflets. Vivid orange flowers in racemes. Zones 9–11.

SHEPHERDIA

There are only 3 species of deciduous or evergreen shrubs in this genus from the oleaster (Elaeagnaceae) family. They are native to North America, where they grow on exposed slopes and dry rocky sites. They have simple opposite leaves and bear small petal-less flowers; male and female flowers are produced on separate plants. CULTIVATION: These shrubs will grow in a range of conditions, and can tolerate poor dry sites. They like full sun and free-draining soil. Propagation is from seed or cuttings.

Shepherdia argentea ★
BUFFALO BERRY, SILVER BUFFALO BERRY, SILVERBERRY

☼ ❊ ↔ 12 ft (3.5 m) ↑ 12 ft (3.5 m)

Well-branched shrub with spiny branches and silvery oblong leaves. Small yellowish white flowers in spring. Female plants produce glossy, red, pea-sized fruit. Zones 2–9.

Shepherdia canadensis
BUFFALO BERRY

☼ ❊ ↔ 8 ft (2.4 m) ↑ 8 ft (2.4 m)

Spreading shrub. Leaves dark yellowish green above, white below. Creamy yellow flowers. Yellow to red fruit. Zones 2–9.

SIMMONDSIA

This genus has only 1 species, a common shrub native to the desert regions of southwestern USA and northern Mexico. It is the sole genus of the jojoba (Simmondsiaceae) family, which is related to the box (Buxaceae) family. Sometimes cultivated in hot arid climates as an ornamental plant and for erosion control, it is more widely known and valued for its seeds, which are the source of jojoba oil, a clear waxy oil used in cosmetics and soaps. CULTIVATION: This species requires a warm to hot climate and a well-drained dry soil in full sun. It is very drought tolerant. Lightly prune regularly to shape. Propagate from seed.

Simmondsia chinensis
GOAT NUT, JOJOBA

☼ ❊ ↔ 6 ft (1.8 m) ↑ 8 ft (2.4 m)

Evergreen shrub from USA and Mexico. Hairy young stems. Small, leathery, oblong, gray-green leaves. Male and female flowers on separate plants. Clusters of cup-shaped yellow male flowers, or bell-shaped greenish female flowers, in leaf axils, in summer. Fruit capsules contain single seed. Zones 9–12.

SKIMMIA

This genus of 4 slow-growing species belonging to the rue (Rutaceae) family is native to the Himalayas and eastern Asia. They are evergreen shrubs or small trees that tolerate shade and seaside conditions in cool-temperate regions. The leaves are simple, smooth-edged, and mostly broad and glossy; they are slightly aromatic when crushed due to minute oil cavities. The small flowers are white, yellow, or pink-tinged, and borne in short dense clusters at the branch tips. Some species produce male and female flowers on different plants, so both sexes need to be grown in close proximity to ensure the production of the colorful winter-borne berries. CULTIVATION: They are easily grown in cooler climates in soil that contains plenty of organic matter and has adequate drainage. Plants can be trimmed into compact shapes or as hedges. Propagate from tip cuttings; seed can be used but the plant's sex cannot be predicted.

Skimmia × confusa

☼/❀ ❊ ↔ 4 ft (1.2 m) ↑ 2–10 ft (0.6–3 m)

Mound-forming shrub, hybrid between *S. anquetilia* and *S. japonica*. Leaves pointed, aromatic. Perfumed off-white flowers, in large clusters, in late winter. 'Kew Green', popular cultivar. Zones 7–10.

Skimmia japonica

☼ ❊ ↔ 20 ft (6 m) ↑ 20 ft (6 m)

Dense, dome-shaped, medium-sized shrub from Japan. Leathery leaves. Flowers white, fragrant, in panicles, in spring. Clusters of red globular fruit. *S. j.* subsp. *reevesiana,* white flowers, dull pink berries; 'Chilan Choice', fragrant flowers, red berries. *S. j.* 'Cecilia Brown', bright green glossy leaves, white flowers open from red buds;

'Fructo Alba', cream flowers; '**Kew White**', narrow glossy leaves, fragrant cream flowers; '**Robert Fortune**', pale leaves, dark edge; '**Rubella**' ★, male cultivar, white flowers, yellow anthers. Zones 7–10.

Skimmia laureola

☼ ❄ ↔ 3–10 ft (0.9–3 m) ↕ 2–40 ft (0.6–12 m)

Spreading shrub or erect tree from Himalayas and western China. Dark green leaves. Unisexual or both male and female flowers on same plant. Flowers creamy white, fragrant, in spring. Zones 7–10.

SOLANUM

syns *Cyphomandra, Lycianthes*

Distinguished by potato *(S. tuberosum)* in its many forms, this genus in the nightshade (Solanaceae) family includes some 1,400 species of annuals, perennials, vines, shrubs, and trees with a cosmopolitan distribution, most from tropical America. The trees and shrubs may be deciduous or evergreen, and many are armed with thorns. While variable, their flowers are all remarkably similar, being simple, small, 5-petalled structures carried singly or in clusters with a central cone of yellow stamens. Fleshy berries follow the flowers. The berries are usually somewhat poisonous and, because of their conspicuous color, may be attractive to children.
CULTIVATION: Hardiness varies: although a few species are really frost tolerant, most are tender. They are generally easily grown in any well-aerated well-drained soil; some have become serious weeds in various parts of the world. Most species prefer sun or part-shade. Propagate from seed or cuttings, or in a few cases by division.

Solanum aviculare

KANGAROO APPLE, PORO PORO

☀ ⊰ ↔ 3–12 ft (0.9–3.5 m) ↕ 3–12 ft (0.9–3.5 m)

Quick-growing evergreen shrub from Australia and New Zealand. Leaves dark green, tip end can be divided into 2 or 3 long lobes. Purple flowers. Fruit ripen green to purple to orange. Zones 9–11.

Solanum capsicastrum

FALSE JERUSALEM CHERRY

☼ ⊰ ↔ 24 in (60 cm) ↕ 12–24 in (30–60 cm)

Brazilian native, evergreen shrub. Leaves 2–3 in (5–8 cm) long, often wavy-edged. White flowers. Small, orange to red, egg-shaped fruit. Often grown as house or greenhouse plant. Zones 10–12.

Solanum giganteum

AFRICAN HOLLY

☼ ⊰ ↔ 10 ft (3 m) ↕ 12 ft (3.5 m)

Large shrub or small tree found from tropical Africa to Sri Lanka. Spiny trunks, prickle-covered silvery white branches. Leaves lance-shaped, dark green, silvery white felting beneath. Purple flowers in panicles. Small, glossy, red fruit. Zones 10–12.

Solanum mammosum

NIPPLE FRUIT

☼ ✚ ↔ 3 ft (0.9 m) ↕ 5 ft (1.5 m)

Native of tropical America, behaves as annual or shrubby perennial. Hair-covered stems whippy and spiny, with angularly lobed or toothed leaves. Inflorescences of purple flowers. Orange fruit. Zones 10–12.

Solanum pseudocapsicum

JERUSALEM CHERRY

☼ ⊰ ↔ 4 ft (1.2 m) ↕ 3–6 ft (0.9–1.8 m)

Evergreen shrub from South America. Dark green leaves, wavy edges. Small white flowers, showy bright orange fruit. Many cultivars, variably colored fruit: cream, yellow, orange, and red. Fruit eaten by birds but poisonous to humans. Zones 9–11.

Solanum pyracanthum

☼ ✚ ↔ 2–3 ft (0.6–0.9 m) ↕ 3–6 ft (0.9–1.8 m)

Shrubby biennial or perennial from tropical Africa and Madagascar. Rust-colored felted stems. Lobed leaves; eye-catching long orange spines on midrib, which provide effective protection from herbivores. Bluish violet flowers, borne in dense clusters, in summer. Zones 10–12.

Solanum rantonnetii

syn. *Lycianthes rantonnetii*

BLUE POTATO BUSH, PARAGUAY NIGHTSHADE

☼ ⊰ ↔ 7 ft (2 m) ↕ 6 ft (1.8 m)

Grown as scrambling shrub or semi-climber, long-flowering species from Argentina and Paraguay. Leaves have wavy edges. Fragrant purple to violet-blue flowers in summer. Red fruit. Trim to keep plants compact and shrubby. '**Royal Robe**', long-blooming, rich purple flowers. Zones 9–11.

Simmondsia chinensis

Skimmia × *confusa*

Solanum pseudocapsicum

Sophora davidii

Sophora japonica

Sophora tomentosa

SOPHORA

This widespread genus from the pea-flower subfamily of the legume (Fabaceae) family includes more than 50 species of evergreen, deciduous, or briefly deciduous shrubs and trees. They have pinnate leaves, often composed of many tiny leaflets. The flowers are pea-like, usually cream or yellow, and frequently have a prominent keel; they are carried in racemes or panicles. Spring is the principal flowering season, though the tropical species tend to be less seasonal in their flowering. Woody winged seed pods follow the flowers.
CULTIVATION: While hardiness varies with the species, most adapt well to cultivation and thrive in any well-drained soil with a position in sun or light shade. Propagate from seed, cuttings, or, in some cases, by grafting. The seed is particularly moisture resistant and must be soaked in warm water to soften it before sowing. Its moisture resistance allows the seed to survive prolonged exposure to seawater and this feature accounts for the rather unusual distribution patterns of some *Sophora* species.

Sophora arizonica
ARIZONA MOUNTAIN LAUREL, ARIZONA NECKLACE
☼ ❄ ↔ 8–10 ft (2.4–3 m) ↕ 10–15 ft (3–4.5 m)
Evergreen, slow-growing, spreading shrub or small tree from Arizona, USA. Silvery green pinnately divided leaves. Profuse wisteria-like bunches of fragrant violet flowers in spring, followed by bean-like seed pods, thought to be poisonous. Zones 8–10.

Sophora davidii
☼ ❄ ↔ 10 ft (3 m) ↕ 10 ft (3 m)
Deciduous shrub from China. Short leaves, up to 20 small leaflets. Flowers purple-blue with whitish tips to white, in short racemes at stem tips, in summer. Zones 6–9.

Sophora japonica
CHINESE SCHOLAR TREE, PAGODA TREE
☼ ❄ ↔ 35 ft (10 m) ↕ 50 ft (15 m)
Deciduous tree from China and Korea, long cultivated in Japan. Smaller in cultivation. Leaves light to mid-green, 16 leaflets, downy underside. Drooping panicles, 6–10 in (15–25 cm) long, fragrant creamy white flowers in mid-summer. 'Pendula', weeping habit in both flowers and foliage, usually grafted on upright standard trunk; 'Princeton Upright', to 60 ft (18 m) tall; 'Regent' ★, white flowers; 'Violacea', pale mauve-pink flowers. Zones 5–9.

Sophora microphylla
KOWHAI
☼ ❄ ↔ 20 ft (6 m) ↕ 20–30 ft (6–9 m)
Evergreen or briefly deciduous tree native to New Zealand. Fine twigs, sharp-angled nodes. Leaves small, tiny olive green leaflets. Pendulous clusters of golden yellow flowers in spring. Zones 8–10.

Sophora prostrata
DWARF KOWHAI
☼ ❄ ↔ 7 ft (2 m) ↕ 6 ft (1.8 m)
New Zealand evergreen shrub, prostrate in windswept locations. Densely interlaced branches. Small leaves, 8 tiny deep green leaflets. Flowers deep yellow to light orange, in late winter, often hidden among branches. 'Little Baby', bizarre branching habit. Zones 8–10.

Sophora secundiflora
FRIJOLITO, MESCAL BEAN, TEXAS MOUNTAIN LAUREL
☼ ❄ ↔ 15 ft (4.5 m) ↕ 30 ft (9 m)
Evergreen shrub or small tree native to Texas and New Mexico, USA, and nearby Mexico. Leaves with 3 to 5 pairs of leaflets. Racemes of fragrant violet-blue flowers in early spring. Zones 8–11.

Sophora tetraptera
KOWHAI, YELLOW KOWHAI
☼ ❄ ↔ 15 ft (4.5 m) ↕ 15–40 ft (4.5–12 m)
National flower of New Zealand, also found in Chile, evergreen. Leaves with 20 to 40 tiny leaflets. Young leaves, branches, and flower buds covered in fine brown down. Racemes of golden yellow flowers in spring. Zones 8–10.

Sophora tomentosa
SILVERBUSH
☼ ❄ ↔ 8 ft (2.4 m) ↕ 30 ft (9 m)
Large deciduous shrub or small tree from tropical Asia and Africa. Leaves with 18 leaflets. Silver-gray down on leaves and young branches. Flowers in racemes, unusual light yellow-green shade, in spring–summer. Zones 10–12.

SORBARIA

This genus, native to Asia, is a member of the rose (Rosaceae) family and is commonly called false spirea as the flowers are similar to *Spiraea*. There are 4 species of deciduous, usually suckering shrubs with pinnate leaves. They produce large panicles of small white flowers in summer followed by masses of small brownish seed capsules that often persist into winter.

CULTIVATION: They prefer a fertile moisture-retentive soil in sun or part-shade and should be planted in a position with protection from strong winds, which may damage the foliage. Cut back in early spring and remove any old weak branches at ground level. Propagate by removing suckers or from cuttings taken in summer.

Sorbaria kirilowii

syn. *Sobaria arborea*

TREE FALSE SPIREA, URAL FALSE SPIREA

⚘ ❄ ↔ 20 ft (6 m) ↑ 17 ft (5 m)

Large, deciduous, spreading, Chinese shrub with slender pointed leaflets. White flowers, on panicles to 12 in (30 cm) long, in mid-summer. Spicy fragrance. Zones 5–7.

Sorbaria sorbifolia

FALSE SPIREA

⚘ ❄ ↔ 10 ft (3 m) ↑ 10 ft (3 m)

Suckering shrub native to Asia, stiff erect stems. Pinnate leaves, finely serrated margins; colorful autumn foliage. White flowers, in large plumes, in summer. Zones 2–9.

Sorbaria tomentosa

⚘ ❄ ↔ 15 ft (4.5 m) ↑ 20 ft (6 m)

Wide-spreading, branching, Himalayan shrub. Pinnate leaves, to 21 narrow finely serrated leaflets. Yellowish white flowers, in large panicles, in summer. Zones 6–10.

SORBUS

MOUNTAIN ASH

The 100-odd species of deciduous shrubs and trees in this genus from the northern temperate zones belong to the rose (Rosaceae) family. The foliage is usually pinnate with serrated-edged leaflets, but may be simple and oval to diamond-shaped. Clusters of white or cream, sometimes pink-tinted, spring flowers, somewhat unpleasantly scented, are followed by heads of berry-like pomes that ripen through summer and autumn. Some species develop russet- to red-toned foliage in autumn.

Sorbus alnifolia

CULTIVATION: Most *Sorbus* species are very hardy and prefer a cool climate, suffering in high summer temperatures. They are best grown in moderately fertile, deep, humus-enriched soil with ample summer moisture, but adapt well to most conditions. Plant in sun or part-shade, prune to shape in autumn or winter, and propagate from stratified seed or by grafting. Fireblight can cause significant damage.

Sorbus alnifolia

KOREAN MOUNTAIN ASH

⚘ ❄ ↔ 25 ft (8 m) ↑ 50 ft (15 m)

From Japan and Korea. Leaves with heavily serrated edges; orange and red in autumn. Young stems red-brown, bright green young foliage. Flowers white; fruit red or yellow. Zones 6–9.

Sorbus americana ★

AMERICAN MOUNTAIN ASH

⚘ ❄ ↔ 20 ft (6 m) ↑ 20–30 ft (6–9 m)

Shrubby tree from central and eastern USA. Leaves with 17 bright green leaflets, gray-green underside, turn yellow in autumn. Resinous buds, white flowers, in spring. Bright red fruit. Zones 2–9.

Sorbus aria

WHITEBEAM

⚘ ❄ ↔ 25 ft (8 m) ↑ 20–40 ft (6–12 m)

Broad-crowned tree from Europe. Elliptical leaves, deep green, felty white when young. White flowers in spring. Orange-red fruit. 'Lutescens', conical growth habit, light green foliage. Zones 5–9.

Sorbus × arnoldiana

⚘ ❄ ↔ 20 ft (6 m) ↑ 15–40 ft (4.5–12 m)

Garden hybrid of temperate Eurasian *S. aucuparia* and *S. discolor*. Small dark green leaflets, gray-green beneath. Small cream flowerheads. Pink berries. 'Carpet of Gold', erect branches. Zones 5–9.

Sorbus aucuparia

EUROPEAN MOUNTAIN ASH, MOUNTAIN ASH, ROWAN

⚘ ❄ ↔ 20 ft (6 m) ↑ 15–40 ft (4.5–12 m)

Hardy tree found over much of northern Eurasia. Dark green to bronze pinnate leaves, coarsely serrated leaflets, turn orange and red in autumn. Unpleasantly scented flowers. Orange berries. Zones 2–9.

Sorbus cashmiriana

⚘ ❄ ↔ 20 ft (6 m) ↑ 30 ft (9 m)

Tree native to Kashmir region of Himalayas. Young branches red, dark green pinnate leaves, light green underside. Pink-tinted white flowers in spring. White to yellow-green fruit. Zones 5–9.

Sorbus chamaemespilus

DWARF WHITEBEAM

⚘ ❄ ↔ 3–6 ft (0.9–1.8 m) ↑ 3–6 ft (0.9–1.8 m)

Shrub from central Europe. Simple dark green leaves, finely serrated edges, sometimes felted below. Flowers deep pink. Red fruit. Zones 6–9.

Sorbus cashmiriana

Sorbus commixta

JAPANESE ROWAN

☼ ❋ ↔ 20 ft (6 m) ↑ 20–30 ft (6–9 m)

Native to Korea and Japan. Pinnate leaves, 15 leaflets, open from sticky red buds, first bronze, then light green, glaucous underside; turn yellow to red in autumn. Flowers white, fruit red. 'Embley', red autumn foliage lasts into winter; 'Jermyns', vividly colored autumn foliage, large clusters of orange-red fruit. Zones 6–9.

Sorbus decora

SHOWY MOUNTAIN ASH

☼ ❋ ↔ 15 ft (4.5 m) ↑ 30 ft (9 m)

Often small and shrubby tree found in northeastern North America. Leaves with 17 leaflets. Loose white flowerheads in spring. Clusters of small red fruit. Zones 2–8.

Sorbus esserteauiana

☼ ❋ ↔ 35 ft (10 m) ↑ 50 ft (15 m)

Tree native to western China. Leaves open from red buds, 13 bright green leaflets, downy underside, turn red in autumn. Massed panicles of white flowers. Red fruit. Zones 6–9.

Sorbus forrestii

☼ ❊ ↔ 20 ft (6 m) ↑ 25 ft (8 m)

Similar species to commonly grown *S. hupehensis*, but with larger fruit, pure white when ripe, persisting well into winter after leaves have fallen. Zones 7–9.

Sorbus × *hostii*

☼ ❋ ↔ 10 ft (3 m) ↑ 12–15 ft (3.5–4.5 m)

Hybrid between *S. chamaemespilus* and *S. mougeotii*, very similar to *S. mougeotii* except leaves a little longer, somewhat sharper teeth. Flowers pink to pale red, like those of *S. chamaemespilus*. Red fruit follow. Zones 6–9.

Sorbus hupehensis

☼ ❋ ↔ 20 ft (6 m) ↑ 30 ft (9 m)

Tree from central and western China. Pinnate leaves, dull gray-green above, lighter below, turn strong pink tones, redden then

Sorbus hupehensis

fall in autumn. White flowers in spring. Small white berries, blush pink as they ripen. *S. h.* var. *obtusa* (syn. *S. h.* 'Rosea'), up to 25 ft (8 m) tall. *S. h.* 'Coral Fire', red bark, red autumn foliage, pinkish red fruit. Zones 6–9.

Sorbus intermedia

SWEDISH MOUNTAIN ASH, SWEDISH WHITEBEAM

☼ ❋ ↔ 20 ft (6 m) ↑ 20–30 ft (6–9 m)

Usually small, sometimes shrubby, Scandinavian native. Felted young stems, simple oval leaves, small basal lobes. Densely branched heads of small flowers in spring. Orange-red berries. 'Brouwers', compact upright habit, small clusters of dark red berries. Zones 5–9.

Sorbus latifolia

FONTAINEBLEAU SERVICE TREE

☼ ❋ ↔ 20 ft (6 m) ↑ 30–50 ft (9–15 m)

Strong-growing European tree, conical growth, bronze young branches. Oak-like lobed leaves, serrated edges, dark green above, yellowish felting on underside. Woolly heads of creamy white flowers. Green fruit speckled with brown. Zones 5–9.

Sorbus megalocarpa

LARGE-FRUITED WHITEBEAM

☼ ❋ ↔ 8 ft (25 m) ↑ 30 ft (9 m)

Shrub or tree native to China. Simple wavy- to shallowly toothed-edged leaves. Creamy white flowers in dense clusters. Rusty brown pomes. Zones 6–9.

Sorbus mougeotii

☼ ❋ ↔ 15 ft (4.5 m) ↑ 40 ft (12 m)

Large shrub or small tree found in mountains of northern Europe. Simple, broad, ovate leaves, shallow lobes, pale gray down beneath. Small heads of cream flowers. Green fruit become red as they ripen. Zones 6–9.

Sorbus pohuashanensis

☼ ❋ ↔ 20 ft (6 m) ↑ 70 ft (21 m)

Round-headed tree naturally found throughout mountains of northern China, smaller in cultivation. Pinnate leaves, felted underside. Woolly clusters of cream flowers. Orange-red to red fruit. Zones 5–9.

Sorbus reducta

DWARF CHINESE MOUNTAIN ASH

☼ ❋ ↔ 6 ft (1.8 m) ↑ 15 in (38 cm)

Low shrubby species from western China and Myanmar. Clump of suckering stems, bristly young stems. Pinnate leaves, reddish stalks. Flowers not abundant; fruit cherry red. 'Gnome', smaller, compact form. Zones 6–10.

Sorbus sargentiana

SARGENT'S ROWAN

☼ ❋ ↔ 20 ft (6 m) ↑ 20–30 ft (6–9 m)

Western Chinese ornamental. Pinnate leaves, sticky buds, leaflets bright green, slightly serrated edges; lighter, downy beneath. Vivid autumn foliage. Flowers in clusters; small red berries. Zones 6–9.

Sorbus thibetica

☼ ❄ ↔ 30 ft (9 m) ↑ 50 ft (15 m)

Wild form of Chinese *S. thibetica* seldom seen cultivated. Most known as such are cultivar '**John Mitchell**' (syn. *S.* 'Mitchellii'), broad-headed tree. Simple, rounded, bright green leaves, white-felted underside. Flowers creamy white, fruit orange-red. Zones 8–10.

Sorbus × *thuringiaca*

OAK-LEAFED MOUNTAIN ASH

☼ ❄ ↔ 25 ft (8 m) ↑ 30–40 ft (9–12 m)

Hybrid between *S. aria* and *S. aucuparia*. Pinnate leaves, finely serrated leaflets. Small red fruit. '**Fastigiata**', upright growth. Zones 6–9.

Sorbus torminalis

CHEQUER TREE, WILD SERVICE TREE

☼ ❄ ↔ 25 ft (8 m) ↑ 30–50 ft (9–15 m)

From Europe, western Asia, and North Africa. Green-brown bark. Leaves bright green, simple, lobed, serrated edges, redden in autumn. Lax spring flower clusters, brown-speckled olive fruit. Zones 6–10.

Sorbus vilmorinii

☼ ❄ ↔ 15 ft (4.5 m) ↑ 20 ft (6 m)

Spreading shrub or small tree native to western China. Buds and young branches warm red-brown shade. Leaves pinnate, serrated edges, gray-green underside. Loose open flower clusters, pink or pink-flushed white fruit. '**Pearly King**', larger fruit. Zones 6–9.

Sorbus Hybrid Cultivars

☼/◐ ❄ ↔ 7–15 ft (2–4.5 m) ↑ 10–25 ft (3–8 m)

Range in size, from dwarf to tree-like forms. Foliage type and fruit color vary; all tend to be heavy cropping; often have bright foliage in autumn. '**Coral Beauty**', strong *S. aucuparia* influence, brilliant orange-scarlet fruit; '**Joseph Rock**', probable hybrid, 20–30 ft (6–9 m) tall, pinnate leaves, deeply serrated leaflets, turn orange or purple-red in autumn, flowers white, fruit ripen cream to golden yellow; '**Pearly King**', pale pearl pink fruit; '**Sunshine**', yellow fruit. Zones 6–9.

SPARMANNIA

AFRICAN HEMP, HOUSE LIME

This genus of 3 to 7 species of evergreen large shrubs or small trees comes from the linden (Tiliaceae) family, and occurs in woodland areas of southern Africa and Madagascar. Much cultivated as house plants, they will stand some neglect and continue to flower regularly in temperate climates. The simple or palmate leaves are toothed and covered in soft hairs, as are the stems. The flowers, which are produced on umbels, are usually white, or sometimes purple or pink, with prominent stamens. The seed capsule contains several seeds and is prickly on the outside. In warm climates, these are useful border plants.

Spartium junceum, France

Sparmannia africana

CULTIVATION: These plants require full sun and a rich well-drained soil, plus regular pruning to maintain their shape if grown in pots. Water very little during winter dormancy. Propagate by sowing seed or air layering in spring; half-hardened cuttings can be rooted in summer, but they require heat from beneath in cooler climates.

Sparmannia africana

AFRICAN LINDEN, CAPE STOCK ROSE

☼ ◖ ↔ 10 ft (3 m) ↑ 20 ft (6 m)

Large shrub or small tree native to South Africa. Hairy stems, light green hairy leaves, shallow lobes. White flowers, bright yellow or reddish purple stamens, in late spring–summer. '**Flore Pleno**' (syn. 'Plena'), double white flowers; '**Variegata**', variegated leaves, large white flowers. Zones 9–11.

SPARTIUM

All but 1 species in this genus of brooms from the pea-flower subfamily of the legume (Fabaceae) family have now been transferred, most of them to *Genista*. The remaining species is a deciduous shrub native to the Mediterranean region and southwestern Europe. Leafless for much of the year, but green-stemmed, it produces a few small leaves in spring, usually as it comes into bloom.

CULTIVATION: It is easily grown in any well-drained soil with a position in full sun. It can be cut back hard after flowering to encourage bushiness. Pruning also helps to prevent excessive self-sowing, which can be a problem if too many seed pods are left to ripen. Propagation is from seed or cuttings.

Spartium junceum

SPANISH BROOM

☼ ❄ ↔ 10 ft (3 m) ↑ 10 ft (3 m)

Many-stemmed shrub. Strongly scented, bright yellow pea-flowers, in large racemes on new growth, in spring–early summer, later in cool climates. Flat dark brown seed pods. Zones 8–10.

SPATHODEA

The sole species in this genus from the trumpet-vine (Bignoniaceae) family is an evergreen tree found in the warmer areas of Africa. It has a domed crown, dark green compound leaves, and large bell-shaped flowers with a spathe-like calyx. Flowers are yellow at the base on the outside, becoming bright red near the mouth. They are a bright orange inside, merging to orangey red on the lobes.
CULTIVATION: It is best grown in fertile well-drained soil with plenty of organic matter, which helps keep the soil moist during hot summers. It is frost tender and needs shelter from wind, especially salt-laden wind. The strongest leading shoot should be kept free of competition until the trunk is 7 ft (2 m) or more tall, when the crown may be allowed to develop naturally. Seed can be sown in spring in a warm environment.

Spathodea campanulata
syn. *Spathodea nilotica*
AFRICAN TULIP TREE
↔ 25 ft (8 m) ↕ 25–35 ft (8–10 m)
Evergreen tree native to tropical central and western Africa. Broad-domed crown. Leaves compound on short stalks; leaflets shiny, dark green, paler and dull underneath. Bell-shaped flowers, in racemes, in late spring–mid-summer. Fruit slender capsule. Zones 11–12.

SPIRAEA

BRIDAL WREATH, SPIREA
This genus has about 70 species of mainly deciduous, sometimes semi-evergreen, flowering shrubs in the rose (Rosaceae) family. It is valued for its flowering and foliage qualities. Leaves are simple and alternate, variously toothed and lobed. The genus is found in many northern temperate areas, mainly in eastern and southeastern Asia and in North America.
CULTIVATION: They thrive in most soils, though some grow poorly on chalk, and prefer a sunny position and cool moist conditions. They fall into 2 groups for pruning: those that flower on the current year's growth, which can be hard pruned in spring, and those that flower on the previous year's growth, which should have the old flowering shoots removed just after flowering. Propagation is from soft-tip or half-hardened cuttings during the summer months.

Spiraea 'Arguta'
BRIDAL WREATH
↔ 4 ft (1.2 m) ↕ 5–7 ft (1.5–2 m)
Dense shrub. Thin hairless branches. Inversely lance-shaped to oval leaves, smooth edges or a few teeth. Clusters of white flowers along branches in spring. Zones 4–10.

Spiraea betulifolia
BIRCHLEAF SPIREA
↔ 3 ft (0.9 m) ↕ 3 ft (0.9 m)
Dwarf shrub found in Japan and northeastern Asia. Forms mound of brown hairless shoots. Round to egg-shaped leaves. Flowers white,

Spathodea campanulata

in closely packed corymbs, in mid-summer. *S. b.* var. *aemiliana*, to 12 in (30 cm) high, broad rounded leaves. Zones 5–10.

Spiraea × billardii
↔ 7 ft (2 m) ↕ 7 ft (2 m)
Spreading shrub, hybrid between *S. douglasii* and *S. salicifolia*. Hairy upright stems. Oblong to lance-shaped leaves, sharp teeth, gray downy underside. Red flowers, in densely packed panicles, in summer. '**Triumphans**', small leaves, slightly downy underside, flowers deep pink, sometimes hint of purple. Zones 4–10.

Spiraea × brachybotrys
↔ 6 ft (1.8 m) ↕ 8 ft (2.4 m)
Vigorous shrub, hybrid between *S. canescens* and *S. douglasii*. Arching branches, egg-shaped to oblong leaves, teeth at tip, velvety gray underside. Light red flowers, in dense panicles, in summer. Zones 4–10.

Spiraea cantoniensis
REEVES' SPIREA
↔ 8 ft (2.4 m) ↕ 6 ft (1.8 m)
Deciduous or semi-evergreen shrub native to China. Arching hairless branches. Diamond-shaped leaves, glaucous underside, conspicuously toothed or 3-lobed. White flowers, in spherical clusters, in mid-summer. '**Flore Pleno**' (syn. 'Lanceata'), double flowers, most popular form of *S. cantoniensis* in cultivation. Zones 5–11.

Spiraea × cinerea
GREFSHEIM SPIREA
↔ 5 ft (1.5 m) ↕ 5 ft (1.5 m)
Garden hybrid between *S. hypericifolia* and *S. cana*. Small, rather pale green leaves. Branch tips covered with tiny white flowers, a few in leaf axils of lower branches, in spring. '**Compacta**', under 3 ft (0.9 m) tall, arching branches; '**Grefsheim**', early-flowering, slightly pendulous branches, narrower leaves. Zones 5–9.

Spiraea cantoniensis 'Flore Pleno'

Spiraea douglasii
WESTERN SPIREA

☼ ❋ ↔ 6 ft (1.8 m) ↑ 6 ft (1.8 m)

Suckering shrub from northwestern USA; naturalized in parts of Europe. Forms thicket of red shoots. Oblong leaves, downy gray below. Purplish pink flowers, in panicles, in mid-summer. Zones 4–10.

Spiraea fritschiana
KOREAN SPIREA

☼ ❋ ↔ 5 ft (1.5 m) ↑ 3 ft (0.9 m)

Mounding shrub native to Korea. Glaucous foliage, purplish tones in autumn. Large clusters of white flowers, sometimes tinged pink, in summer. Zones 4–9.

Spiraea japonica
JAPANESE SPIREA

☼ ❋ ↔ 4 ft (1.2 m) ↑ 6 ft (1.8 m)

Upright shrub from Japan, China, and Korea. Lance- to egg-shaped leaves. Pink flowers, in clusters, in summer. *S. j.* var. *albiflora*, pale green leaves, white flowers. *S. j.* 'Anthony Waterer', purplish red flowers; 'Bullata', dwarf slow-growing shrub, deep pinkish red flowers; 'Bumalda', dwarf form, leaves can be variegated pink and off-white; 'Crispa', purplish pink flowers; 'Dart's Red', bright pink flowers; 'Firelight', ovate leaves, purple-pink flowers; 'Gold Mound' ★, golden leaves turn chartreuse; Golden Princess/'Lisp', foliage ages bronze to yellow; 'Goldflame', orange autumn leaves, red flowers; 'Little Princess', pink flowers; Magic Carpet/'Walbuma', bronze-red leaves turn chartreuse, pink flowers; 'Nana', dwarf, dark pink flowers; 'Neon Flash', lance-shaped leaves, pink flowers; 'Shirobana', red buds open to deep pink and white flowers. Zones 3–10.

Spiraea nipponica
NIPPON SPIREA

☼ ❋ ↔ 6 ft (1.8 m) ↑ 6 ft (1.8 m)

Vigorous bushy shrub native to Japan. Leaves oval or inversely egg-shaped, teeth at tip. White flowers, in clusters at ends of branches, in mid-summer. *S. n.* var. *tosaensis*, smaller leaves; many sold under this name are cultivar 'Snowmound'. *S. n.* 'Halward's Silver',

Spiraea trichocarpa

Spiraea douglasii

Spiraea japonica var. *albiflora*

smaller than species, produces abundant white flowers; 'Rotundifolia', broader leaves, larger flowers than most other cultivars; 'Snowmound', green leaves, tinted blue. Zones 5–10.

Spiraea prunifolia
BRIDAL WREATH SPIREA, SHOE BUTTON SPIREA

☼ ❋ ↔ 7 ft (2 m) ↑ 7 ft (2 m)

Rounded bush native to China. Usually grown in form 'Plena', dense shrub with egg-shaped leaves, edged with very small teeth, which turn reddish orange in autumn. Double white flowers, in closely packed clusters, in spring. Zones 4–10.

Spiraea thunbergii
THUNBERG SPIREA

☼ ❋ ↔ 7 ft (2 m) ↑ 5 ft (1.5 m)

Shrub native to China, extensively naturalized in Japan. Thin hairy stems, narrow hairless leaves, toothed margins. White flowers, in small clusters, in spring. 'Okon', early flowering. Zones 4–10.

Spiraea tomentosa
HARD HACK, STEEPLEBUSH

☼ ❋ ↔ 7 ft (2 m) ↑ 7 ft (2 m)

Robust thicket-forming shrub from eastern USA. Brown velvety coating on young stems; tooth-edged leaves, downy yellow-gray underside. Crimson flowers in late summer. Zones 4–10.

Spiraea trichocarpa
KOREAN SPIREA

☼ ❋ ↔ 4 ft (1.2 m) ↑ 6 ft (1.8 m)

Shrub native to Korea. Stiff spreading branches, pointed leaves, few teeth toward tip, bluish underside. Rounded dense clusters of white flowers, crowded along outer branches, in summer. Zones 5–9.

Spiraea × vanhouttei
BRIDAL WREATH SPIREA, VAN HOUTTE SPIREA

☼ ❋ ↔ 4 ft (1.2 m) ↑ 6 ft (1.8 m)

Robust shrub, hybrid between *S. cantoniensis* and *S. trilobata*. Leaves inversely egg-shaped to diamond-shaped, lobed, toothed edges. White flowers, in dense umbels, in mid-summer. Zones 5–11.

Stachyurus chinensis

STACHYURUS

Subject to recent revisions, this genus in the family Stachyuraceae includes 6 to 10 species of deciduous shrubs and trees from the Himalayan and temperate East Asian region. While generally not spectacular plants, they have the attraction of blooming in late winter and early spring, before or just as the leaves are developing. They produce drooping racemes of small cream to pale yellow flowers at every leaf bud. The leaves are lance-shaped and are usually around 6 in (15 cm) long.
CULTIVATION: They prefer a humus-rich, well-drained, acidic soil in sun or light shade. They are not hardy in the coldest regions but thrive in areas with distinct yet relatively mild winters. Hard late spring frost may damage the flowers and young leaves. Propagate from seed or from half-hardened cuttings.

Stachyurus chinensis
☼ ❈ ↔ 8 ft (2.4 m) ↑ 8 ft (2.4 m)
Deciduous shrub native to China. Leaves 2–6 in (5–15 cm) long ovals, taper at tip. Pale yellow flowers, in racemes, in early spring. 'Magpie', light green, cream, and pink variegated foliage. Zones 7–9.

Stachyurus praecox
☼ ❈ ↔ 6–12 ft (1.8–3.5 m) ↑ 6–12 ft (1.8–3.5 m)
Shrub native to Japan. Branches tiered. Leaves 6 in (15 cm) long, color slightly in autumn. Drooping racemes of small pale yellow flowers in late winter–early spring, before foliage. Zones 7–10.

STAPHYLEA
BLADDERNUT

This genus of around 11 species of deciduous shrubs and small trees, belonging to the bladdernut (Staphyleaceae) family, is found over much of the northern temperate zone. They have large trifoliate to pinnate leaves, and long leaflets with serrated edges tapering to

a point. Panicles of pale pink to white flowers are produced at the ends of branches, mainly in spring, followed by the 2- to 3-lobed inflated seed pods that give the genus its common name. The seed pods dry and brown as they ripen. The foliage may develop attractive autumn tones.
CULTIVATION: Mostly very hardy, bladdernuts thrive in nearly all well-drained moist soils in full sun or partial shade. The bushes tend to form a thicket, or if pruned after flowering they can be thinned to one or a few main stems and made tree-like. Propagate from seed or summer cuttings; rooted suckers can sometimes be removed and grown on.

Staphylea bumalda
JAPANESE BLADDERNUT
☼ ❈ ↔ 6 ft (1.8 m) ↑ 7 ft (2 m)
Deciduous shrub native to Japan. Leaves trifoliate, lance-shaped leaflets, sharply serrated edges, down on underside veins. Panicles of white flowers in spring. Pods about 1 in (25 mm) wide, 2-lobed. Zones 4–9.

Staphylea colchica
CAUCASIAN BLADDERNUT
☼ ❈ ↔ 10 ft (3 m) ↑ 10–15 ft (3–4.5 m)
Deciduous shrub from Caucasus region. Leaves with 3 to 5 glossy green, finely toothed leaflets. Flowers to ½ in (12 mm) wide, white, fragrant. Seed pods 3-lobed, 3 in (8 cm) across. 'Colombieri', ovate, finely serrated. Zones 6–9.

Staphylea holocarpa
CHINESE BLADDERNUT
☼ ❈ ↔ 10 ft (3 m) ↑ 15 ft (4.5 m)
Chinese native, shrub or tree. Trifoliate leaves, leaflets with hairy underside. Flowers in drooping panicles, open white from pink buds. Pods around 2 in (5 cm) wide. Zones 6–9.

Staphylea pinnata

Staphylea pinnata
EUROPEAN BLADDERNUT
☼ ❈ ↔ 15 ft (4.5 m) ↑ 15 ft (4.5 m)
Temperate Eurasian shrub. Leaves with 3, 5, or 7 leaflets taper to fine point, serrated edges, glaucous underside. Flowers white, red-tipped sepals, in late spring. Seed pods 1 in (25 mm) wide. Zones 6–9.

Staphylea trifolia
BLADDERNUT, EASTERN BLADDERNUT
☼ ❈ ↔ 15 ft (4.5 m) ↑ 15 ft (4.5 m)
Shrub from eastern USA. Leaves trifoliate, 2–3 in (5–8 cm) long leaflets, finely pointed, sharply serrated edges, fine hairs beneath, change color in autumn. White flowers 1½ in (35 mm) wide, in short panicles; 3-lobed fruit. Zones 5–9.

STENOCARPUS

This genus of 25 species of evergreen trees or large shrubs, in the protea (Proteaceae) family, is from Southeast Asia, the Malay Peninsula to New Caledonia, and Australia. They feature simple alternate leaves. Tubular flowers, usually red to orange, are borne in umbels, sometimes partly hidden by the foliage. The fruit is a narrow follicle containing winged seeds.

CULTIVATION: Species need a warm site, preferably near the coast but with shelter from salt-laden winds. They prefer a light, sandy, well-drained soil with plenty of organic matter, as well as plentiful summer water. Seed sown when ripe in winter germinate readily in a warm environment; clonal varieties may be grafted on seedling understocks. These species require little or no pruning.

Stenocarpus salignus
RED SILKY OAK, SCRUB BEEFWOOD
☼ ❧ ↔ 10–15 ft (3–4.5 m) ↕ 100 ft (30 m)
Tree from northeastern Australia. Dark brown scaly bark. Leaves ovate to lance-shaped, leathery, paler beneath. Creamy white flowers, in umbels of 10 to 20 blooms, in spring–summer. Zones 9–12.

Stenocarpus sinuatus
FIREWHEEL TREE, QUEENSLAND FIREWHEEL TREE
☼ ❧ ↔ 15 ft (4.5 m) ↕ 120 ft (36 m)
Tree from eastern Australia. Gray to brown bark. Leathery leaves, shiny green above, duller beneath. Orange-scarlet flowers, in umbels of 15 to 20 blooms, in upper axils. Zones 9–12.

STEPHANANDRA
This genus of 4 species of deciduous shrubs in the rose (Rosaceae) family is native to eastern Asia. They are valued for their foliage, which often has orange autumn tones. Panicles of white or pale green flowers, shaped like tiny stars, with a profusion of stamens, are borne in summer.

CULTIVATION: They will grow in most soils in sun or part-shade, but prefer moist loam. Maintain shape by hard pruning in spring. Propagate in autumn from cuttings or by division.

Stephanandra incisa
CUTLEAFED STEPHANANDRA, LACE SHRUB
☼ ❄ ↔ 10 ft (3 m) ↕ 6 ft (1.8 m)
Shrub from Japan and Korea. Egg-shaped, deeply toothed, lobed leaves, yellow-green in autumn. Dense panicles of pale green to white flowers in mid-summer. 'Crispa' ★, dwarf. Zones 4–10.

Stephanandra tanakae
☼ ❄ ↔ 8 ft (2.4 m) ↕ 10 ft (3 m)
Shrub native to Japan. Arching branches. Deeply toothed leaves, egg-shaped to triangular, 5 lobes, pink-brown when young. Small white flowers in summer, which are not a feature. Zones 4–10.

STERCULIA
This tropical genus of around 150 species of deciduous or evergreen trees or shrubs gives its name to the family Sterculiaceae. They have broad, dark green, smooth-edged or lobed leaves. Small flowers are borne in often-pendulous racemes or panicles. Individual flowers are petal-less, but the urn-shaped calyx is usually colorful. The fruit consists of up to 5 boat-shaped woody or leathery follicles, pink to red when ripe, that open to display shiny black seeds.

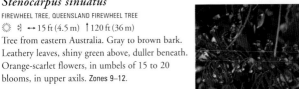

Stephanandra incisa

Stenocarpus sinuatus

CULTIVATION: These fast-growing plants need a warm climate and fertile, moist, well-drained soil. Grow in sun and protect from winds. Water regularly when young. Propagate from fresh seed.

Sterculia murex
LOWVELD CHESTNUT
☼ ❧ ↔ 10–20 ft (3–6 m) ↕ 20–40 ft (6–12 m)
South African deciduous tree. Gray-brown, nearly black, cracked bark. Compound leaves, 5 to 10 oblong to lance-shaped leaflets. Waxy yellow flowers, brown or red-pink marks, in spring. Woody fruit. Zones 9–11.

Sterculia quadrifida
PEANUT TREE
☼ ❧ ↔ 20 ft (6 m) ↕ 40 ft (12 m)
Bushy tree from northern Australia and New Guinea. Ovate to heart-shaped leaves. Scented, greenish yellow, bell-shaped flowers, in racemes, in late summer. Leathery scarlet follicles. Zones 10–12.

STEWARTIA
The 9 species of deciduous trees and shrubs from eastern North America and temperate East Asia in this genus are from the camellia (Theaceae) family. The leaves are simple and short-stemmed with serrated edges. The spring flowers, usually white, are borne singly or in clusters. The bark often flakes away to reveal a range of colors.

CULTIVATION: Generally preferring cool, moist, well-drained, humus-rich soil and a position in sun or partial shade, most species are adaptable and will grow well in any position that does not dry out in summer. If it becomes necessary, trim plants after flowering. Propagate from stratified seed or from summer cuttings.

Stewartia malacodendron
SILKY CAMELLIA, VIRGINIA STEWARTIA
☼ ❄ ↔ 10 ft (3 m) ↕ 15–30 ft (4.5–9 m)
From southeastern USA. Downy young shoots, new leaves. Leaves finely toothed edges, downy below, color in autumn. Flowers borne singly, blue-gray anthers, purplish filaments, in summer. Zones 7–9.

Stewartia monadelpha

TALL STEWARTIA

☼ ❄ ↔ 20 ft (6 m) ↑ 50 ft (15 m)

Tree from Japan and Korea. Red-brown bark sheds. Downy young shoots, leaves densely hairy on underside veins. Foliage turns pinkish red in autumn. Flowers 1½ in (35 mm) wide. Zones 6–9.

Stewartia ovata

MOUNTAIN STEWARTIA

☼ ❄ ↔ 15 ft (4.5 m) ↑ 15–20 ft (4.5–6 m)

Shrub from southeastern USA. Leaflets with sparsely toothed edges, downy underside, turn yellow in autumn. Flowers 2 in (5 cm) long. Zones 5–9.

Stewartia pseudocamellia ★

JAPANESE STEWARTIA

☼ ❄ ↔ 15 ft (4.5 m) ↑ 20–50 ft (6–15 m)

From Japan. Light reddish brown bark sheds. Leaves with serrated edges, downy underside, bright red in autumn. Flowers with frilly-edged petals, golden anthers, in spring. Zones 5–9.

Stewartia pseudocamellia

Stewartia pteropetiolata

☼ ❄ ↔ 12 ft (3.5 m) ↑ 20 ft (6 m)

Shrub or small tree native to southern China and Korea. Toothed-edged leaves, small wing-like bracts on stalks. Small flowers, jagged-edged white petals, gold anthers, in mid- to late summer. Zones 5–9.

Stewartia sinensis

CHINESE STEWARTIA

☼ ❄ ↔ 20 ft (6 m) ↑ 15–30 ft (4.5–9 m)

From China. Flaking red-brown bark. Stems and leaves downy when young, leaves taper to fine point, serrated edges, purple-red in autumn. Fragrant flowers have yellow anthers. Zones 6–9.

STRELITZIA

Native to South Africa, the 4 or 5 species in this genus are large evergreen perennials in the strelitzia (Strelitziaceae) family. Usually treated as shrubs or trees, they are clump-forming and have very long oblong to lance-shaped leaves that are borne on stout stalks. A large bud or spathe borne at the end of the stem is usually held clear of the foliage; from it opens a succession of strikingly colored flowers, each with a long projecting corolla and wing-like sepals.

CULTIVATION: They prefer full sun or part-shade, and are tender to all but the lightest frosts. Soil should be well-drained and moist, but most species will tolerate brief periods of drought once established and prefer to be kept on the dry side in winter. Roots are very strong, so take care when siting. Propagate from seed or by removing suckers. Division is possible.

Strelitzia nicolai

GIANT BIRD OF PARADISE, NATAL WILD BANANA

☼ ⬧ ↔ 15 ft (4.5 m) ↑ 30 ft (9 m)

Found in KwaZulu-Natal and Eastern Cape, South Africa. Leaves and leaf stalks often over 4 ft (1.2 m) long. Flowers light greenish to purple-blue, white projecting corolla, open from red-brown spathes, in late spring–early summer. Zones 10–12.

STREPTOSOLEN

This genus from the nightshade (Solanaceae) family is doubtfully distinct from *Browallia*. The single species is from tropical South America. It has a scrambling habit and simple alternate leaves, and is popular in warm climates for its spectacular red to orange flowers.

CULTIVATION: Plant in full sun with shelter from cold winds, in a light, fibrous, well-drained soil. It should be well watered during dry weather, and is intolerant of frost. Frequent tip pruning in the first few years will help develop a densely foliaged bush and, thereafter, regular light pruning after flowering will maintain its shape. Soft-tip cuttings can be taken in late spring or summer, half-hardened cuttings in autumn.

Streptosolen jamesonii

syn. *Browallia jamesonii*

MARMALADE BUSH, ORANGE BROWALLIA

☼ ⬧ ↔ 5 ft (1.5 m) ↑ 7 ft (2 m)

Evergreen shrub. Leaves simple, alternate, finely hairy, dark green, paler beneath. Inflorescence in 2 forms: one is mixture of yellows and reds to orange, other has pure yellow flowers, in early to late spring. Zones 9–11.

STRYCHNOS

This genus of around 150 species of woody climbers, shrubs, and small trees, from the logania (Loganiaceae) family, occurs mainly in tropical and subtropical regions of the world. Some species contain highly toxic

Strelitzia nicolai

Streptosolen jamesonii

Strychnos decussata

Styphelia tubiflora

alkaloids, most notably *Strychnos nux-vomica*, the chief source of the drug strychnine. The plants have fairly large, smooth-edged, oval leaves borne in opposite pairs at right angles to each other, with 3 to 5 major veins originating from the base of the leaf. Often spines are present in the leaf axils. The creamy white, funnel-shaped or bell-shaped flowers, borne in small clusters at the ends of branches, are often perfumed, sometimes unpleasantly. The rounded berry-like fruit has a smooth hard rind or shell and fleshy juicy pulp. CULTIVATION: Most species are suited to only warm-temperate to tropical climates and prefer well-drained acidic soils in a sunny to part-shaded position. Provide supplementary watering during extended dry periods. Propagate from seed or cuttings.

Strychnos decussata
CAPE TEAK, CHAKA'S WOOD
❂ ✤ ↔ 15 ft (4.5 m) ↑ 30 ft (9 m)
Small tree from eastern South Africa and tropical East Africa. Small leaves glossy dark green. Small greenish white flowers in spring to early summer. Globular orange or red berries. Zones 10–12.

Strychnos spinosa
NATAL ORANGE
❂ ❀ ↔ 12 ft (3.5 m) ↑ 20 ft (6 m)
Spiny shrub or small tree native to Madagascar, and tropical and southern Africa. Leathery oval leaves. Greenish white star-shaped flowers, in clusters, in spring. Yellow edible fruit. Zones 10–12.

STYPHELIA
This genus is a member of the epacris (Epacridaceae) family, with all 14 species occurring in Australia. Other species have been placed in this genus in the past, but are now correctly placed in other genera. All species are woody shrubs, often sparsely branched; some are small, some almost prostrate. Their leaves are stiff with parallel veins and a sharp point. The green, pink, or red flowers are long and tubular with the 5 petals rolled back, exposing the hairy interior and leaving the stamens protruding.
CULTIVATION: These plants require acid soils that are free draining but do not dry out. Organic matter in the soil and mulching seem to improve the chances of success. Propagation is not easy, unfortunately; cuttings do not strike readily and seed germination is often slow and erratic.

Styphelia tubiflora
❂ ❀ ↔ 30 in (75 cm) ↑ 24 in (60 cm)
Straggly shrub, occurs only in New South Wales, Australia. Leaves narrow, sharp point. Flowers red, 1 in (25 mm) long, in winter. Small berry-like fruit containing 5 seeds. Zones 8–9.

STYRAX
Found over much of the northern temperate and subtropical zones, this genus gives its name to the storax (Styracaceae) family. It has some 100 species of deciduous and evergreen shrubs and trees. Foliage usually comprises simple rounded leaves with serrated edges, obvious veins, and a pointed tip. Leaves are usually small to medium-sized, but a few species have large felted leaves. Flowers, which are usually fragrant, hang in clusters beneath the foliage of the previous season's wood. They are white, occasionally with a flush of pink, and open in spring to be followed by 1- or 2-seeded drupes.
CULTIVATION: They prefer a cool moist climate with clearly defined seasons that is not too cold in winter. Hardiness varies with the species' native range. Propagate from seed, which often needs stratification to germinate well, or by taking cuttings in summer.

Styrax americanus ★
❂ ❀ ↔ 8 ft (2.4 m) ↑ 10 ft (3 m)
Deciduous shrub from southeastern USA. Branches coated with down when young. Dark green leaves elliptical, serrated edges, pale, downy below. Pendulous clusters of flowers in late spring. Zones 6–10.

Styrax benzoin
BENZOIN
❂ ❀ ↔ 10–20 ft (3–6 m) ↑ 20 ft (6 m)
Evergreen tree from highlands of Sumatra, Indonesia. Stout trunk and main branches, heavy covering of resinous gray-brown bark. Leaves 4–6 in (10–15 cm) long, finely toothed along edges. Flower panicles carry up to 20 small white blooms. Zones 10–11.

Styrax grandifolius
BIG-LEAFED SNOWBELL
❂ ❀ ↔ 15 ft (4.5 m) ↑ 15 ft (4.5 m)
Deciduous large shrub or small tree native to southeastern USA. Leaves large, downy coating, underside gray, yellowish elsewhere. Fragrant flowers, in racemes, in spring. Zones 8–10.

Sutherlandia frutescens

Styrax japonicus
JAPANESE SNOWBELL, JAPANESE SNOWDROP TREE,
SNOWBELL TREE
☼ ❄ ↔ 15 ft (4.5 m) ↕ 20–30 ft (6–9 m)
Deciduous tree from Japan. Lightly branched.
Downy young stems. Leaves glossy dark green,
shallowly toothed edges. Short pendulous
flower clusters in late spring–early summer.
'Fargesii', vigorous cultivar with larger leaves;
'Pink Chimes', pale pink flowers. Zones 5–9.

Styrax obassia
BIG-LEAFED STORAX, FRAGRANT SNOWBELL
☼ ❄ ↔ 20 ft (6 m) ↕ 35 ft (10 m)
Tree native to Japan. Rounded oval leaves to 8 in (20 cm) long,
dark green, very fine serrations, densely downy beneath. Flowers
on 4–8 in (10–20 cm) long racemes, in late spring. Zones 6–10.

SUTHERLANDIA
BALLOON PEA
The 5 species of evergreen shrubs in this genus from the pea-flower
subfamily of the legume (Fabaceae) family are natives of South
Africa. They have pinnate leaves made up of many small finely hairy
leaflets. The red to purple pea-flowers have a large keel, and are followed by inflated bladder-like seed pods, hence the common name.
CULTIVATION: Apart from being susceptible to frost damage, *Sutherlandia* species are easily grown in light well-drained soil in full sun.
Seedlings grow quickly and often flower in their first year; in cool
winter areas with long summers the plants can be treated as annuals.
Cut back older plants to keep them compact. Propagate from seed,
soaked before sowing, or from half-hardened summer cuttings.

Sutherlandia frutescens
BALLOON PEA, CAPE BLADDER PEA, DUCK PLANT
☼ ⚘ ↔ 5 ft (1.5 m) ↕ 5 ft (1.5 m)
Found in open areas and dry woodlands of southern Africa. Softwooded shrub; drooping pinnate leaves with 13 to 21, small, finely
hairy leaflets. Pendulous clusters of orange-red flowers in late winter. Inflated pale green, sometimes red-tinged, seed pods. Zones 9–11.

SWIETENIA
MAHOGANY
From tropical regions throughout Central America and the
West Indies, this is a small genus of about 3 species of evergreen
or semi-deciduous trees belonging to the mahogany (Meliaceae)
family. Grown as shade and street trees in the tropics, they are
highly prized for their reddish brown hardwood timber, commercially known as mahogany, that is used in cabinetwork,
paneling, and ship-building. Large pinnate leaves have smooth
shiny leaflets. Small, 5-petalled, greenish white flowers are borne
in panicles in the leaf axils or at the ends of branches. Woody
capsules contain winged seeds.
CULTIVATION: Frost tender, they need a sunny protected position in
a deep well-drained soil. Provide supplementary watering during
dry periods. Propagate from seed or cuttings.

Styrax japonicus

Swietenia macrophylla
HONDURAS MAHOGANY
☼ ↰ ↔ 25 ft (8 m) ↕ 150 ft (45 m)
Tall, straight, evergreen tree native to lowland
tropical American forests, shorter in cultivation.
Pinnate leaves, 8 to 12 lance-shaped leaflets.
Large woody fruit, chestnut brown winged
seeds. Cultivated for timber. Zones 10–12.

Swietenia mahogani
WEST INDIES MAHOGANY
☼ ↰ ↔ 15 ft (4.5 m) ↕ 80 ft (24 m)
Dome-shaped West Indian tree. Pinnate leaves,
4–8 in (10–20 cm) long, 4 or 5 oval leaflets.
Small greenish yellow flowers, in clusters, in
spring. Large woody fruit, 4 in (10 cm) wide. Zones 11–12.

SYMPHORICARPOS
CORALBERRY, SNOWBERRY
Allied to the honeysuckles *(Lonicera)*, the 17 deciduous shrubs in
this genus from the woodbine (Caprifoliaceae) family are mainly
found in North and Central America, with 1 species from China.
They have opposite pairs of usually simple leaves with blunt rounded
tips. Small white or pink flowers appear in spring and may be carried
singly or in clusters. The fruit is the dominating feature of most
species. The berry-like drupes are near-spherical, and last well into
winter when they stand out clearly on the then leafless stems.
CULTIVATION: Most species are very frost hardy and prefer to grow
in a distinctly seasonal temperate climate. They are not fussy about
soil type as long as it is well drained, but will crop more freely if
fed well and watered during dry spells. Plant in sun or part-shade
and prune or trim to shape in winter after the fruit is past its best.
Propagation is most often from winter hardwood cuttings.

Symphoricarpos albus ★
COMMON SNOWBERRY, SNOWBERRY
☼ ❄ ↔ 4–6 ft (1.2–1.8 m) ↕ 4–6 ft (1.2–1.8 m)
Shrub with slightly differing varieties over most of North America.
Wiry stems, suckering habit. Clusters of small pink flowers in
spring. Berries, pale green at first, ripen to strikingly pure white.

S. a. **var.** *laevigatus* (syn. *S. rivularis*), native to western North America, upright habit, forms dense thickets, fruits more heavily than eastern forms. Zones 3–9.

Symphoricarpos × chenaultii
CHENAULT CORALBERRY

✳ ❀ ↔ 5 ft (1.5 m) ↕ 6–8 ft (1.8–2.4 m)
Garden hybrid between *S. microphyllus* and *S. orbiculatus*. Deciduous shrub, downy young stems, dark green leaves, glaucous, slightly downy beneath. Small spikes of pink flowers, near branch tips, in summer. Red-and-white spotted or mottled fruit. 'Hancock', low spreading habit, rarely exceeds 20 in (50 cm) high. Zones 5–9.

Symphoricarpos mollis
✳ ❀ ↔ 3 ft (0.9 m) ↕ 3 ft (0.9 m)
From western USA. Compact shrub, velvety new stems and young leaves. Foliage downy on underside. Inconspicuous pinkish white flowers in spring. White berries, ¼ in (6 mm) in diameter. Zones 7–9.

Symphoricarpos orbiculatus
CORALBERRY, INDIAN CURRANT

✳ ❀ ↔ 6 ft (1.8 m) ↕ 6 ft (1.8 m)
From eastern USA and Mexico. Dark green leaves, gray underside, red tints in autumn. Flowers white, flushed pink, in summer. Small berries ripen from dull white to deep red. Zones 3–9.

SYMPLOCOS
This genus gives its name to the family Symplocaceae. It consists of 250 species of trees and shrubs, some evergreen and some deciduous, occurring in woodlands throughout Asia, Australasia, and North and South America, in tropical and warm-temperate regions. Their leaves are simple and alternate. Some of the species accumulate aluminum in their tissues and these plants have yellow-green leaves and blue fruit. Other species have egg-shaped fruit that are black, purple, or white. The flowers are yellow or white and are borne in a variety of inflorescences. CULTIVATION: Well-drained, acid to neutral soils are required, in a full sun position. The species in cultivation respond well to regular feeding. Frost tolerance varies between species, depending on the climate of their original habitat. Propagation is from fresh seed or cuttings, and both methods are quite reliable.

Symplocos paniculata
SAPPHIRE BERRY

✳ ❀ ↔ 15 ft (4.5 m) ↕ 15 ft (4.5 m)
Deciduous, bushy, spreading shrub or small tree from eastern Asia and Himalayas. Oval, slightly

Syncarpha vestita, in the wild, South Africa

Swietenia macrophylla

hairy, dark green leaves, toothed margins. Small, white, sweet-smelling flowers, borne in clusters, in late spring–summer. Egg-shaped blue fruit. Zones 7–9.

SYNCARPHA
EVERLASTING

This genus of around 25 species of perennials and subshrubs endemic to the Cape region of South Africa belongs to the daisy (Asteraceae) family. They have a low shrubby habit, usually with several erect stems densely covered with thickly downy leaves that are narrowly elliptical and often semi-succulent. Showy, papery, "everlasting" flowerheads, usually white to cream with a small cluster of golden disc florets at the stem tips, can smother a small plant. Most species flower in spring or after rain. CULTIVATION: These plants are tolerant of irregular light frosts and are also drought resistant once established. Plant in a sunny position with gritty soil that provides excellent drainage. A little added humus for moisture retention will help the plants through summer. Remove spent flowerheads but otherwise trim only very lightly to shape. Propagation is usually from seed, which, as with other plants often exposed to fires, has been found to germinate better if it is smoke treated.

Syncarpha vestita
syn. *Helichrysum vestitum*
CAPE EVERLASTING

✳ ❀ ↔ 12–20 in (30–50 cm) ↕ 12–20 in (30–50 cm)
Found in rocky habitats. Clump of upright stems with mid-green leaves to 2 in (5 cm) long, densely covered with silvery white down. Abundance of creamy white flowerheads give bush overall silvery appearance. Zones 9–10.

SYNCARPIA

This genus in the myrtle (Myrtaceae) family contains 2 species found in the coastal areas of eastern Australia. Both are tall straight trees that have simple opposite leaves with noticeable venation and thick fibrous bark. From the same family as the eucalypts, they have petal-less flowers with numerous stamens and capsular fruit containing many seeds. These are important hardwood timber trees and make very good ornamental subjects for parks and large gardens. Wood from *S. hillii* was used for sidings in the building of the Suez Canal and for wharves in other countries.
CULTIVATION: These trees perform best in a moist well-drained soil in areas free from frost and protected from strong winds. Propagate from seed sown in a humid environment.

Syncarpia glomulifera, in the wild, New South Wales, Australia

Syncarpia glomulifera
TURPENTINE
☼ ◗ ↔ 25 ft (8 m) ↑ 100 ft (30 m)
Tall straight tree with dense crown, straight trunk, fibrous persistent bark. Ovate to narrow-ovate dull green leaves, whitish gray, hairy beneath, aromatic when crushed. Cream flowers, long stamens, in spring–summer. Multiple capsular fruit. Zones 9–12.

SYRINGA
LILAC
This genus, which a member of the olive (Oleaceae) family, is made up of 23 species of vigorous, deciduous, flowering shrubs, most of them native to northeast Asia, with 2 species only in Europe. Of the European species one, *S. vulgaris*, the common lilac, is known to have been grown in the gardens of western Europe since the sixteenth century; today, it is represented by more than 1,500 named cultivars. The plants have simple pointed elliptical to heart-shaped leaves in opposite pairs, and produce upright panicles of small 4-petalled flowers, usually in spring. The flowers may be single or double, and occur in conspicuous clusters. Almost all are strongly sweet smelling, although not every cultivar is noted for its fragrance. *Syringa* species are popular cool-climate shrubs.
CULTIVATION: Their main requirements are a well-drained soil and a position in sun or light shade; they thrive in a sandy gravelly soil, preferably one that is slightly alkaline, but do not do well in heavy clay. Propagate from seed, but the results may be variable. They can be grown from cuttings of the current year's growth, or by layering.

Syringa × chinensis
CHINESE LILAC
☼ ❉ ↔ 12 ft (3.5 m) ↑ 12 ft (3.5 m)
Group of hybrids between *S. laciniata* and *S. vulgaris*. Upright rounded bushes with slender branches, and oval medium to dark green leaves. Large panicles of flowers, white to pinkish lavender to reddish, highly fragrant, in late spring. 'Saugeana' ★, reddish mauve flowers. Zones 4–9.

Syringa emodi
HIMALAYAN LILAC
☼ ❉ ↔ 12 ft (3.5 m) ↑ 15 ft (4.5 m)
From western Himalayas. Upright branches, leaves oblong to elliptical, half main vein tinged purple. Flowers tinged pinkish mauve in bud, open to white, in early summer. Zones 4–9.

Syringa × hyacinthiflora
AMERICAN HYBRID LILAC, EARLY FLOWERING LILAC, HYACINTH LILAC
☼ ❉ ↔ 15 ft (4.5 m) ↑ 15 ft (4.5 m)
Hybrids of *S. oblata* and *S. vulgaris*. Ovate leaves, often red-bronze, purple-red tones in autumn. Single or double flowers in early spring. 'Blue Hyacinth', pale purple to light blue flowers; 'Charles Nordine', lilac-pink flowers; 'Laurentian', rose pink buds. Zones 4–9.

Syringa × josiflexa
☼ ❉ ↔ 7 ft (2 m) ↑ 8–10 ft (2.4–3 m)
Hybrid of *S. josikaea* and *S. reflexa*. Erect shrub, broadly lance-shaped leaves, magenta flowers in early summer. 'Anna Amhoff' and 'Elaine', both with single white flowers; 'Bellicent', perfumed pink flowers; 'Lynette', single purple flowers. Zones 5–9.

Syringa josikaea
HUNGARIAN LILAC
☼ ❉ ↔ 10 ft (3 m) ↑ 12 ft (3.5 m)
One of only 2 European lilacs, occurs in mountain regions of central to eastern Europe. Leaves leather-like, glossy green. Flowers dark blue-violet, in summer. Requires rich soil. Zones 5–9.

Syringa laciniata
CUT-LEAFED LILAC
☼ ❉ ↔ 10 ft (3 m) ↑ 12 ft (3.5 m)
From Chinese Province of Gansu, one of first oriental lilacs introduced to West. Tall shrub, smooth-edged and cut leaves. Pale lavender flowers, small clusters along branches, in spring. Zones 5–9.

Syringa × *prestoniae*

Syringa meyeri
DWARF KOREAN LILAC, MEYER LILAC
❊ ❊ ↔4 ft (1.2 m) ↑5 ft (1.5 m)
Found in garden near Beijing, China, in 1909, unknown in wild. Low compact shrub, sturdy upright branches. Flowers in small clusters, pale lilac to lilac-purple, sometimes whitish lavender, in spring, repeat late summer–early autumn. 'Palibin', smallest of all lilacs, to 4 ft (1.2 m) high, pinkish lavender flowers; 'Superba', deep pink flowers, fade with age, long flowering season. Zones 4–9.

Syringa oblata
BROADLEAF LILAC
❊ ❊ ↔10 ft (3 m) ↑12 ft (3.5 m)
Native to China and Korea, like *S. vulgaris*, but flowers in mid-spring. Loose strongly fragrant panicles. *S. o.* subsp. *dilatata*, heart-shaped leaves, fragrant pale purple flowers. Zones 5–9.

Syringa pekinensis
syn. *Syringa reticulata* subsp. *pekinensis*
CHINESE TREE LILAC, PEKING LILAC
❊ ❊ ↔12 ft (3.5 m) ↑15 ft (4.5 m)
Tall shrub or tree collected in Beijing area, China, in 1742. Dark green leaves. Tiny flowerheads, creamy white, in mid-summer. Bark peels into papery curls with age. Zones 5–9.

Syringa potaninii
syn. *Syringa pubescens* subsp. *potaninii*
❊ ❊ ↔6 ft (1.8 m) ↑6–8 ft (1.8–2.4 m)
Discovered in southern Gansu Province of China in 1885. Upright vase-like habit. Variable leaves, broad-elliptic to oblong-elliptic, downy on both surfaces. Flowers light rose-purple to whitish purple, generally fading to near-white, in late spring. Zones 5–9.

Syringa × *prestoniae*
NODDING LILAC, PRESTON LILAC
❊ ❊ ↔12 ft (3.5 m) ↑12 ft (3.5 m)
Garden hybrid between *S. reflexa* and *S. villosa*. Dark green leaves, slightly glaucous, faintly downy underside. Slightly drooping panicles of scented soft pink to light purple flowers in early summer. 'Desdemona', rich purple-pink to blue flowers; 'Elinor', purple-tinged buds open to mauve flowers; 'James MacFarlane', soft pink flowers, spreading habit to over 8 ft (2.4 m) wide. Zones 4–9.

Syringa pubescens
❊ ❊ ↔12 ft (3.5 m) ↑12 ft (3.5 m)
From China. Numerous slender branches. Flowers fragrant, buds pale purple, mature to pale lilac with pinkish wash. *S. p.* subsp. *microphylla* (syn. *S. microphylla*), slightly shorter leaves, shorter panicles of more pinkish flowers in spring and earlier summer; 'Superba', heavy-flowering, slightly darker flowers over long season. *S. p.* subsp. *patula* (syn. *S. patula*), larger leaves, purplish new growths; 'Miss Kim', darker pink buds. *S. p.* 'Excellens', white flowers, pale flesh pink buds; 'Sarah Sands', very pale mauve-pink flowers, more compact clusters. Zones 5–9.

Syringa reflexa
❊ ❊ ↔12 ft (3.5 m) ↑12 ft (3.5 m)
Found in central China in 1901, used extensively in hybridizing. Erect stems, large ovate leaves. Flower buds deep bright red, opening to pale rose, in early summer. Flower clusters sometimes pendent like those of *Wisteria* species. Zones 5–9.

Syringa reticulata
JAPANESE TREE LILAC
❊ ❊ ↔15 ft (4.5 m) ↑30 ft (9 m)
Tree lilac native to Japan. Round top. Large plumes of feathery white blooms, with protruding yellow anthers, in summer, contrast well with dark green foliage. Flowers have strong fragrance. Bark reddish brown, peels on younger branches. 'Ivory Silk', abundant ivory flowers, blooms young. Zones 3–9.

Syringa × *swegiflexa*
❊/❊ ❊ ↔5 ft (1.5 m) ↑10 ft (3 m)
Garden hybrid between *S. reflexa* and *S. sweginzowii*. Upright shrub, pointed oval leaves, downy underside. Slender, pendent, many-flowered, red to dusky pink panicles to over 6 in (15 cm) long, in late spring. Zones 6–9.

Syringa reflexa

Syringa sweginzowii
❊ ❊ ↔6 ft (1.8 m) ↑10 ft (3 m)
Neat upright shrub found in northern Sichuan Province, China, around 1893. Small leaves. Brownish red stems covered with pink florets, in open clusters, in late spring–early summer. Spicy fragrance. Zones 3–9.

Syringa tigerstedtii
❊ ❊ ↔8 ft (2.4 m) ↑8 ft (2.4 m)
Slender shrub discovered in Sichuan Province, China, in 1934. Widely spaced flower clusters, purplish pink to white, on inflorescences to around 10 in (25 cm) in length, in summer. Zones 4–9.

Syringa tigerstedtii

Syringa tomentella

☼ ❋ ↔ 10 ft (3 m) ↑ 10 ft (3 m)

Neat compact shrub, found in Sichuan Province, China, in 1891. Smooth pale gray bark. Leaves elliptic to oblong, downy underside. Pink buds, paler pink flowers fade to white, in summer. Zones 4–9.

Syringa vulgaris

COMMON LILAC, FRENCH HYBRID LILAC

☼ ❋ ↔ 20 ft (6 m) ↑ 20 ft (6 m)

One of 2 species native to Europe, with 14 subspecies reflecting geographic variations. Typical form has blue flowers, but cultivars can have deep purple and white flowers. Blooms appear in late spring–early summer.

Single-flowered cultivars include '**Andenken an Ludwig Späth**', dark reddish flowers; '**Charles X**', crimson blooms in conical panicles; '**Congo**', purple-red flowers, lighter with age; '**Maréchal Foch**', large bright purplish red flowers; '**Maud Notcutt**', panicles of white blooms; '**President Lincoln**', flowers closest to true blue; '**Primrose**', pale yellow flowers in small panicles; '**Sensation**', purplish red blooms with white margins to petals; '**Vestale**', white flowers; and '**Volcan**', dark red to purple flowers.

Double-flowered cultivars include '**Ami Schott**', medium blue flowers with deeper tones; '**Ann Tighe**', crimson-purple buds, pink flowers; '**Belle de Nancy**', purplish red buds open to pale purple-pink flowers; '**Charles Joly**', dark purple-red blooms; '**Edith Cavell**', pale yellow buds open to white flowers; '**Madame Antoine Buchner**', reddish pink to mauve flowers; '**Madame Lemoine**', pale yellow buds open to snow white flowers; '**Monique Lemoine**', late-blooming white flowers; '**Mrs Edward Harding**', deep purplish red flowers, shaded pink; '**Olivier de Serres**', large panicles of lavender-blue flowers; '**Paul Thirion**', red-purple buds becoming lovely lilac-pink flowers; '**Victor Lemoine**', thin panicles of flowers ranging from lavender-pink to lilac-blue in color; and '**William Robinson**', abundant pale pink flowers. Zones 4–9.

Syringa vulgaris 'Ann Tighe'

Syringa wolfii

syn. *Syringa formosissima*

☼ ❋ ↔ 12 ft (3.5 m) ↑ 15 ft (4.5 m)

Tall shrub from northeastern China and Korea. Bright green elliptic leaves. Large pyramidal inflorescence, 12 in (30 cm) long, lilac-colored flowers, slightly fragrant, in late spring. Color may vary from pale lavender to darker purple. Zones 4–9.

SYZYGIUM

This large genus belonging to the myrtle (Myrtaceae) family consists of around 1,000 species, the majority occurring in Southeast Asia, Australia, and Africa. Mostly evergreen trees and shrubs, they have simple opposite leaves that are often smooth and hairless. The flowers, with numerous long stamens, usually occur in panicles along or at the ends of branches; petals and sepals are smaller than the stamens. The fruit is a succulent, mostly red, purple, blue, black, or white edible berry. Mostly tropical and subtropical species, they are cultivated for ornamental and medicinal uses, as well as for food and wood; many species are popular for hedging and topiary.

CULTIVATION: *Syzygium* species perform best in moist, well-drained, deep, fertile soil in sun or shade. Propagate from seed sown as soon as ripe in spring or from cuttings in summer. In Australia, galls can disfigure the foliage. Scale may also be a problem.

Syzygium australe

syn. *Eugenia paniculata* of gardens

BRUSH CHERRY, MAGENTA CHERRY

☼ ❦ ↔ 20 ft (6 m) ↑ 25 ft (8 m)

Shrub or small tree native to Australian rainforests. Upper stems brownish green. Opposite rounded leaves, mid-green when mature. White flowers, in small dense panicles, in summer. Large, red, fleshy, edible berries. Zones 9–12.

Syzygium francisii

GIANT WATER GUM

☼ ❦ ↔ 70 ft (21 m) ↑ 80 ft (24 m)

Medium to large tree native to Australia. Prominent buttressed trunk. Bark slightly flaky.

Syzygium francisii

Tabebuia chrysantha   Tabernaemontana elegans

Glossy, dark green leaves, ovate to elliptical, wavy edges. Panicles of flowers with cream stamens in early–late summer, followed by violet-purple globe-shaped berries. Zones 10–12.

Syzygium jambos
syn. *Eugenia jambos*
ROSE APPLE
☼ ☽ ↔ 15 ft (4.5 m) ↥ 20 ft (6 m)
Large shrub or small tree from Malay Peninsula and Indonesia. Leathery, dark green, lance-shaped leaves, shiny pink when new. Large showy flowers, creamy white stamens, rich in nectar, in summer. Fragrant, pink to yellow, edible fruit. Zones 10–12.

Syzygium luehmannii
syn. *Eugenia luehmannii*
SMALL-LEAFED LILLYPILLY, RIBERRY
☼ ☽ ↔ 30 ft (9 m) ↥ 50 ft (15 m)
Tree from northeastern Australia. Leaves glossy dark green, ovate to lance-shaped, pale pink-red when young. Panicles of small creamy white flowers in summer. Pink pear-shaped fruit. Zones 9–12.

Syzygium paniculatum
syn. *Eugenia paniculata*
AUSTRALIAN BRUSH CHERRY, MAGENTA BRUSH CHERRY
☼ ☽ ↔ 20 ft (6 m) ↥ 25 ft (8 m)
Native to eastern Australia. Dense foliage, oblong to lance-shaped leaves, glossy dark green, copper-brown when young. Fluffy creamy white flowers in summer. Crimson-purple berries. Zones 9–12.

Syzygium wilsonii
POWDERPUFF LILLYPILLY
☼ ☽ ↔ 7 ft (2 m) ↥ 6 ft (1.8 m)
Scrambling shrub from Queensland, Australia. Smooth dark green leaves, narrowly oval, bronze or red new growth. Deep red flowers in spring–early summer. White berries.

TABEBUIA
GOLDEN TRUMPET TREE
This genus in the trumpet-vine (Bignoniaceae) family comprises 100 species of trees or shrubs native to tropical areas of the Americas

and Caribbean. They may be briefly deciduous or evergreen and have simple or compound, 3- to 7-fingered leaves. They produce large crowded panicles of showy, frequently fragrant, trumpet-shaped flowers in a variety of colors, followed by bean-like pods. CULTIVATION: *Tabebuia* species are best grown in the greenhouse in cool-temperate climates. In tropical and subtropical areas they make attractive specimen trees and may produce flowers sporadically throughout the year. Propagate from seed, cuttings, or air layers.

Tabebuia chrysantha
☼ ☽ ↔ 20 ft (6 m) ↥ 20–50 ft (6–15 m)
Open-crowned tree from Mexico to Venezuela. Gray bark becomes fissured, scaly. Leaves 5-fingered, slightly hairy, in pointed oblong leaflets. Yellow trumpet flowers, in large clusters, in spring, followed by long seed pods. Zones 11–12.

Tabebuia rosea
PINK POUI
☼ ☽ ↔ 30 ft (9 m) ↥ 90 ft (27 m)
Variable species from Mexico to Colombia, and Venezuela. Leaves 3- to 7-fingered, in pointed oval leaflets. Flowers white to pale pink, with yellow throat, in loose clusters, in spring. Zones 11–12.

TABERNAEMONTANA
This genus of about 100 species of evergreen shrubs and small trees belongs to the dogbane (Apocynaceae) family. Found in tropical and subtropical regions of the world, they have large

Syzygium luehmannii

glossy green leaves and waxy, usually white, funnel-shaped flowers with 5 wide-spreading curved petals. Flowers are borne throughout the warmer months and are fragrant, particularly at night. These plants have a milky sap and are recognized by the paired boat- to egg-shaped fruit joined to a common stalk. CULTIVATION: These warm-climate frost-tender plants require regular watering. They need good soil that is well-drained but moisture-retentive, in full sun or bright filtered light, and shelter from wind. Plants can be kept neat and bushy by lightly trimming. Propagate from seed or cuttings.

Tabernaemontana divaricata
syns *Ervatamia coronaria, E. divaricata*
CRAPE GARDENIA, CRAPE JASMINE, PINWHEEL FLOWER
☼ ☽ ↔ 5 ft (1.5 m) ↥ 6 ft (1.8 m)
Evergreen shrub or small tree from India to Yunnan Province, China, and northern Thailand. Leathery elliptic leaves. Large, waxy, fragrant white flowers, in small clusters, in summer. Perfume more noticeable at night. 'Flore Pleno', double flowers. Zones 11–12.

Tabernaemontana elegans
TOAD TREE
☼ ☽ ↔ 10 ft (3 m) ↥ 10–20 ft (3–6 m)
Deciduous shrub or small tree from southern Africa. Opposite, glossy, dark green, oblong leaves. Sweetly scented trumpet-shaped flowers, in small panicles, in spring–summer. Zones 9–12.

Tamarix parviflora

TAIWANIA

The single conifer species in this genus, which belongs to the cypress (Cupressaceae) family, is related to *Cryptomeria*. It is native to Taiwan, with a variety being found in southwestern China and Myanmar. It is well known for the way the bark peels off in long strips. The foliage is bluish green, forming a rather cone-shaped crown on a very tall tree. The foliage becomes scaly with age and produces male and female cones in shades of brown. On some varieties, the cones can be in shades of gray and green.

CULTIVATION: This species prefers a sheltered sunny position in an acid soil that is moist but well drained. Propagate from seed.

Taiwania cryptomerioides

Taiwania cryptomerioides

☼ ❄ ↔ 35 ft (10 m) ↑ 180 ft (55 m)

Tall tree with conical or columnar crown, much smaller in cultivation. Bark exfoliates in strips. Variable bluish green leaves, narrow and pointed on juvenile plants, scale-like on adults. Small brown male and female cones in summer. *T. c.* **var.** *flousiana*, from China and Myanmar, cones grayish green stained with maroon. Zones 8–11.

TAMARINDUS

There is one species of evergreen tree in this genus, which is a member of the cassia subfamily of the legume (Fabaceae) family. Originally from tropical Africa, it is naturalized and cultivated in many other tropical areas. It has a wide crown, often spreading. The soft green leaves resemble fern fronds. The flowers are cream or yellowish, often with a red tinge. The seed pods are long and bean-like and are a dull brown when ripe. Apart from its ornamental value, the tree has many other uses. Its bean-like pods are used in a number of culinary ways: in curries, chutneys, drinks, and sweetmeats. Parts of the tree are also used medicinally.

CULTIVATION: This species requires a sunny site in a tropical or subtropical climate. It will tolerate a range of soil types. In temperate climates it can be grown in the greenhouse but will not develop its full size. Propagate from seed or softwood cuttings.

Tamarindus indica

TAMARIND

☼ ✦ ↔ 35 ft (10 m) ↑ 90 ft (27 m)

Attractive tree originally from Africa but found in most tropical climates. Open spreading crown, fern-like bright green leaves. Racemes of small cream or orange-yellow flowers, flushed with red, in summer. Bean-like pods, to 6 in (15 cm) long, brittle and grayish brown when fully ripe. Zones 11–12.

TAMARIX

TAMARISK SALT CEDAR

This genus consists of 50 species of deciduous shrubs and small trees belonging to the tamarisk (Tamaricaceae) family, which are found in Europe, India, North Africa, and Asia. Most of the species occur on coastal flats, river estuaries, and on saline soil. They have brown, deep red, and sometimes purple bark; the main feature is the mass of attractive drooping branches covered in fine foliage. The flowers come in shades of pink and appear in drooping panicles. *Tamarix* are often used as windbreak hedging for exposed gardens near the sea; some species are also grown to stop the erosion of sand dunes. The galls of some species are used to tan leather.

CULTIVATION: In coastal areas, *Tamarix* species are happy to grow in well-drained soil in a sunny position, while in inland areas they prefer soil that is slightly moister, as well as shelter from cold drying winds. Shrubs should be pruned regularly to prevent root movement in severe winds. Propagate from just-hardened seed sown in an area that is protected from frost, or half-hardened cuttings in summer, or hardwood cuttings in winter.

Tamarix chinensis

CHINESE TAMARISK, SALT CEDAR

☼ ❄ ↔ 10 ft (3 m) ↑ 15 ft (4.5 m)

Small tree or shrub native to temperate zones of eastern Asia. Densely branched with fine drooping branchlets. Bark brown to blackish, leaves bluish green. Drooping panicles of pink flowers, on current year's wood, in summer. Zones 7–10.

Tamarix gallica

FRENCH TAMARISK, FRENCH TREE, MANNA PLANT

☼ ✳ ↔ 10 ft (3 m) ↑ 12 ft (3.5 m)

Small tree or shrub native to Mediterranean area. Bark reddish brown to purple; blue-green stalkless leaves, small and narrow. Pink flowers, in cylindrical racemes, on current year's wood, in summer. Larger in favorable conditions. Zones 5–10.

Tamarix parviflora

EARLY TAMARISK

☼ ✳ ↔ 20 ft (6 m) ↑ 15 ft (4.5 m)

Small tree or large shrub from Europe. Slender, arching, purple branches, pointed narrow leaves. Racemes of pale pink flowers, on older wood, in late spring. Zones 5–9.

Tamarix ramosissima

syn. *Tamarix pentandra*

☼ ❋ ↔ 15 ft (4.5 m) ↑ 15 ft (4.5 m)

Shrub or small tree from eastern Europe to central Asia. Upright arching branches. Leaves narrow, lance-shaped, pointed. Dense racemes of pink flowers in late summer–late autumn. '**Pink Cascade**', deep pink flowers; '**Rubra**', magenta flowers. Zones 2–10.

TAXODIUM

This group of 3 species from North America and Mexico belongs to the cypress (Cupressaceae) family. These deciduous or semi-deciduous trees are found growing in or near water. In these swampy conditions mature trees often produce aerial roots known as "knees" or pneumatophores, which allow the roots to breathe. These majestic conical trees bear foliage that resembles that of the yew *(Taxus)*, with fissured peeling bark on buttressed trunks. Both male and female cones are held on the same tree, the small male cones in pendulous groups, the females scattered along the branches. CULTIVATION: These plants will grow in either a clay or sandy soil as long as it remains relatively moist. They can withstand very low winter temperatures, where their foliage color turns to vivid rust tones before the leaves fall to reveal a fine tracery of branches. Propagate from seed, except for cultivars, which need to be grafted.

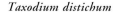

Taxodium mucronatum

Taxodium distichum

BALD CYPRESS, SWAMP CYPRESS

☼ ❋ ↔ 20 ft (6 m) ↑ 75 ft (23 m)

Fast-growing tree from North America. Deeply fissured fibrous bark exfoliates in long strips. Initially conical outline broadens, becomes irregular as tree matures. Fine leaves light green, in spring, age to deep green before turning rusty red in autumn. *T. d.* var. *imbricatum* (syn. *T. ascendens*), clasping bright green leaves; '**Nutans**', initially upright, pendulous tips with maturity. *T. d.* '**Shawnee Brave**', compact bright green leaves, ideal for hedges. Zones 6–10.

Taxodium mucronatum

MEXICAN SWAMP CYPRESS, MONTEZUMA CYPRESS

☼ ❋ ↔ 50 ft (15 m) ↑ 100 ft (30 m)

Tree from Mexico and southern Texas, USA. Evergreen in warmer climates, semi-deciduous in cooler areas. Pendulous foliage very similar to *T. distichum.* Clasping leaves, bright green turning rusty brown in autumn. Cones long, often warty. Zones 8–11.

TAXUS

YEW

This small evergreen conifer genus belonging to the yew (Taxaceae) family consists of around 7 species occurring in cool-temperate regions of the Northern Hemisphere and some more tropical mountain regions, including the Philippines and Mexico. Most are small to medium trees, with sharply pointed, linear or slightly sickle-shaped leaves, often with prominent olive green midribs.

Most species have separate male and female plants and flower in spring. The single seed found on the female plant is partly clothed in a red fleshy covering (or aril) that is sweet and edible; the rest of the plant, including the seed, is poisonous. They make useful specimen or hedge plants, and handsome topiary subjects. CULTIVATION: Slow growing but long lived, most species are fairly adaptable in cool regions, tolerating sun or shade, frost, alkaline soils, exposure, and pollution. Propagate from seed sown as soon as hardened, from cuttings, or by grafting.

Taxus baccata

COMMON YEW, ENGLISH YEW

☼ ❋ ↔ 25 ft (8 m) ↑ 50 ft (15 m)

Slow-growing tree from Europe, North Africa, and western Asia. Very long lived, dense many-branched head. Reddish brown bark, dark green linear leaves, paler yellowish green below. Male cones yellow and scaly. Female flowers on separate plants, in summer. **Aurea Group** (golden yew), golden yellow young growth turning greener with age; '**Dovastonii Aurea**', male plant, low and spreading, dense foliage; '**Dwarf White**', low and spreading, moderately dense foliage, new growth whitish but soon turning green; '**Fastigiata**' (Irish yew), female plant, dark green leaves; **Fastigiata Aurea Group** (golden Irish yew), smaller than 'Fastigiata', golden yellow leaves; '**Nutans**', to less than 20 in (50 cm) high, dark green leaves; '**Repandens**', spreading female, to 3 ft (0.9 m) high, green leaves; '**Semperaurea**', male, to 10 ft (3 m) high, ascending branches of bright yellow young growth changing to russet-yellow in winter; '**Standishii**', female, golden leaves, columnar habit. Zones 5–10.

Taxus chinensis

CHINESE YEW

☼ ❋ ↔ 15 ft (4.5 m) ↑ 20 ft (6 m)

Shrub from China. Leaves stiff, sharp, taper abruptly, glossy green, curling outward on top, gray-green below, in 2 ranks. Pollen cones yellowish maturing to brown, in summer. Zones 6–10.

Taxus baccata

Taxus cuspidata

JAPANESE YEW

☼ ❋ ↔ 20 ft (6 m) ↑ 50 ft (15 m)

Erect tree from Japan, normally seen as shrub in gardens. Horizontal or ascending branches; spirally arranged, dark green, linear leaves. New shoots red-brown, fleshy aril red when ripe, in summer. Suitable for hedging and topiary, tolerant of pollution. *T. c.* var. *nana,* low-spreading shrub with dense growth. *T. c.* 'Capitata', strong upright foliage; 'Densa', female compact form with dark green leaves; 'Densiformis', dwarf, to 3 ft (0.9 m) tall. Zones 4–9.

Taxus × media

ANGLO-JAP YEW, HYBRID YEW

☼ ❋ ↔ 20 ft (6 m) ↑ 25 ft (8 m)

Hybrid between *T. baccata* and *T. cuspidata.* Tree or shrub suitable for hedging. Linear olive green leaves, prominent white midribs beneath. Seed partly covered by scarlet aril, in summer. 'Brownii', to 10 ft (3 m) high, dark green leaves, spherical shape; 'Dark Green Spreader', shrub with very dense deep green foliage; 'Everlow', low, rounded, up to 8 ft (2.4 m) high; 'Hatfieldii', male columnar form to 6 ft (1.8 m) high; 'Hicksii', columnar, dense growth, popular for hedges; 'Nigra', compact dark green foliage. Zones 5–9.

TECOMA

syns *Stenolobium, Tecomaria*

YELLOW BELLS

There are 13 species of mostly evergreen trees and scrambling shrubs in this genus belonging to the trumpet-vine (Bignoniaceae) family. They are found from southern Arizona, USA, to Mexico and the West Indies, and as far south as northern Argentina. One species (*T. capensis),* is native to southern and eastern Africa. Pinnate leaves are borne in opposite pairs; leaflets have toothed edges. Funnel-shaped or narrowly bell-shaped flowers are borne in showy terminal clusters in yellow, orange, or red, with 5 unequal petals. The fruit is a smallish pod splitting into 2 halves.
CULTIVATION: Fine ornamentals for the tropical and subtropical garden, in cool climates they can only be grown as potted shrubs in a greenhouse or conservatory. They like a sunny but sheltered position and reasonably fertile soil with good drainage. Propagate

from fresh seed, or from tip cuttings or larger cuttings from the previous year's growth. Suckering species can be divided or layered.

Tecoma capensis

syns *Bignonia capensis, Tecomaria capensis*

CAPE HONEYSUCKLE

☼ ◗ ↔ 7 ft (2 m) ↑ 10 ft (3 m)

Adaptable shrub, partly climbing habit, from eastern and southern Africa. Glossy green pinnate leaves. Orange-red to scarlet tubular flowers, in racemes at ends of branches, in spring–autumn. Tolerates salt spray, drought, wind. 'Aurea', golden yellow flowers. Zones 9–12.

Tecoma castaneifolia

☼ ◗ ↔ 8–12 ft (2.4–3.5 m) ↑ 15–25 ft (4.5–8 m)

Evergreen species from Ecuador. Upright tree, leathery elliptic leaves, very hairy underside. Yellow flowers, 2 in (5 cm) long, in spring–autumn. Beanpod-like capsules, 5 in (12 cm) long. Zones 10–12.

Tecoma stans

syns *Bignonia stans, Stenolobium stans*

SHRUBBY TRUMPET FLOWER, YELLOW BELLS, YELLOW ELDER

☼ ◗ ↔ 10 ft (3 m) ↑ 15–30 ft (4.5–9 m)

Small tree or large open shrub native to southern USA and Central and South America. Leaves oblong, lance-shaped, toothed, bright green leaflets. Yellow flowers, funnel-shaped, in terminal racemes or panicles, in late winter–summer. Capsules ripen brown. Zones 10–12.

TELANTHOPHORA

This genus, which is a member of the daisy (Asteraceae) family, was previously included in *Senecio* and contains 14 species of small evergreen trees and shrubs native to Central America. The stems are usually downy and have few branches. Large leaves have wavy or toothed edges. Yellow flowers are daisy-like and carried in terminal clusters. They flower profusely from late spring through summer.
CULTIVATION: These are easily grown plants that tolerate a range of soils in sun or part-shade. They are frost tender and in cool-temperate climates will require greenhouse protection. Propagate from seed.

Telanthophora grandifolia

syn. *Senecio grandifolius*

☼ ◗ ↔ 12 ft (3.5 m) ↑ 20 ft (6 m)

Evergreen shrub or small tree native to Mexico. Downy stems, large oval leaves, with wavy, lobed, or toothed edges. Yellow daisies, in large showy clusters, in late summer–early spring. Zones 9–11.

TELOPEA

WARATAH

Known for their spectacular flowerheads in shades of red, there are just 5 species in this southeastern Australian genus of evergreen shrubs and small trees belonging to the protea (Proteaceae) family. They have dark green, prominently veined leaves with toothed or lobed edges and leathery pods up to 5 in (12 cm) long that contain many seeds. The flowerheads are large and waxy and have a ring of bright red bracts. The Australian Aboriginal name for *T. speciosissima* is "waratah," now the accepted common name for the genus. All species are highly ornamental garden plants.

Tecoma capensis

Telanthophora grandifolia

Telopea speciosissima, in the wild, Australia

CULTIVATION: Waratahs require a deep, well-drained, acidic soil in full sun or part-shade. They have a low resistance to alkaline soils and excessive phosphorus, and prefer not to be overfed. Frost tolerance varies with the species. Tip prune from an early age to encourage branching, and after flowering cut old flowered stems back to halfway. Propagate from seed in spring, or from cuttings.

Telopea mongaensis
☼ ❄ ↔10 ft (3 m) ↑10 ft (3 m)
Multi-branched bushy shrub from southern New South Wales, Australia. Dark green, smooth, leathery leaves, smooth-edged or broadly lobed, yellowish green when young. Large, open, crimson flowerheads, at branch ends, in late spring–early summer. Zones 8–10.

Telopea oreades
GIPPSLAND WARATAH
☼ ❄ ↔10 ft (3 m) ↑10–30 ft (3–9 m)
Found in sheltered wet forests of southeastern Australia. Smooth lance-shaped leaves often have glaucous underside. Globular deep crimson flowerheads, up to 3 in (8 cm) across, in early summer. Zones 9–10.

Telopea speciosissima ★
WARATAH
☼ ❄ ↔5 ft (1.5 m) ↑10 ft (3 m)
Erect slender shrub, floral emblem of New South Wales, Australia. Toothed leathery leaves, prominent veins. Red dome-shaped flowerheads, surrounded by ring of bright red bracts, in spring. Grown commercially for high-quality cut flowers. 'Corroboree', vigorous growth, narrow leaves, large domed flowerheads with relatively

inconspicuous bracts; '**Flaming Beacon**', large rich red bracts, red florets tipped white; '**Olympic Flame**', released to mark 2000 Sydney Olympic Games, tall grower, exceptionally large high-domed flowerheads; '**Wirrimbirra White**', creamy white flowers. Zones 9–10.

Telopea truncata
TASMANIAN WARATAH
☼ ❄ ↔10 ft (3 m) ↑10 ft (3 m)
From subalpine mountainous areas of Tasmania, Australia. Deep green smooth-edged leaves on new growth. Underside of new leaves and unopened flowers usually covered with soft brown hairs. Slightly flattened red flowerheads in late spring. Zones 8–10.

TEPHROSIA
Belonging to the pea-flower subfamily of the legume (Fabaceae) family, this genus contains about 400 species of usually evergreen perennials or shrubs native to tropical and subtropical areas of the world. They show considerable variation and may be erect or sprawling, with alternate leaves comprising 1 to 41 leaflets. The flowers are borne in pairs or clusters. They are typical of those in the pea-flower family and range in color from orange to purple. CULTIVATION: Most species are frost tender but if given a protective mulch in winter in cooler areas they should resprout from the base in spring. They prefer well-drained soil and can tolerate quite arid conditions. Propagate from seed, which requires hot water treatment.

Tephrosia grandiflora
☼ ❄ ↔3 ft (0.9 m) ↑2–5 ft (0.6–1.5 m)
Shrubby species native to South Africa. White or rusty down on stems. Pinnate leaves, 9 to 15 leaflets, white-hairy beneath. Clusters of purple-pink flowers in spring–early summer. Zones 9–11.

Tephrosia grandiflora

TERMINALIA
The name of this genus of about 200 species of evergreen or deciduous trees refers to the leaves, which are often clustered near the shoot tips. It is a member of the family Combretaceae. Found in tropical regions from Asia, India, Sri Lanka, and south to Polynesia and parts of Australia, these trees often grow near the coast and their trunks are frequently buttressed. They are grown for the ornamental qualities of their large, handsome, often leathery leaves and sprays of flowers as well as for dyes, oils, nuts, and some medicinal purposes. CULTIVATION: Terminalia species grow in any reasonably fertile soil that is well drained and in full sun. In cool areas they need to have greenhouse protection. Propagate from seed.

Terminalia arostrata
NUTWOOD
☼ ❄ ↔6–10 ft (1.8–3 m) ↑17–35 ft (5–10 m)
Semi-deciduous drought-resistant tree from northern and western Australia. Upright trunk, drooping branches, fissured bark, rounded crown. Leathery, broadly oval-shaped leaves. Spikes of tiny creamy flowers in summer. Berries dark purple or black, edible. Zones 9–11.

Tetradium ruticarpum

TERNSTROEMIA

This genus of 85 species of evergreen trees and shrubs is a member of the camellia (Theaceae) family. These plants are found in Asia, Africa, and the Americas. The large glossy leaves are leathery, sometimes with a serrated edge. The single white flowers are 5-petalled and appear in summer. The seed capsules are red.
CULTIVATION: These plants will grow well in a fertile, humus-rich, acid soil that is moisture retentive but well drained. Pinch out the shoot tips to encourage branching. Propagate from seed or from half-hardened cuttings in late summer.

Ternstroemia japonica ★
syn. *Ternstroemia gymnanthera*
☀ ❄ ↔ 10 ft (3 m) ↑ 12 ft (3.5 m)
Shrub or small tree from Japan. Thick, leathery, glossy, oval leaves. Hanging clusters of small white flowers, lightly perfumed, in summer. Round red fruit, red seeds. Zones 8–11.

TETRACLINIS

This conifer genus in the cypress (Cupressaceae) family contains 1 species, native to northwestern Africa and southeastern Spain. It is a very dense tree with a strong thick trunk that is crowded with branches; branchlets are flat and splayed with slightly brittle thin leaves. Tiny erect cones appear at the tips of the branches.
CULTIVATION: This is a frost-tender species that requires greenhouse cultivation in cool climates. In mild climates it is a good choice for dry areas, being very drought tolerant. It should be planted in well-drained soil. Propagate from seed or cuttings.

Tetraclinis articulata
ALERCE, ARAR, JUNIPER GUM PLANT
☀ ❄ ↔ 25 ft (8 m) ↑ 50 ft (15 m)
Conifer from northwestern Africa and southern Spain. Broad conical crown, thick trunk with closely packed branches. Cypress-like foliage, branchlets in flat open sprays, scale-like leaves in whorls of 4. Small, erect, glaucous cones, at branch tips, in summer. Zones 9–11.

TETRADENIA

Found in southern Africa and Madagascar, this genus of 5 deciduous or semi-deciduous aromatic shrubs belongs to the mint (Lamiaceae) family. The foliage and semi-succulent stems are often coated with a fine down. Light green to gray-green leaves are heart-shaped to rounded, usually with deeply lobed edges. Minute honey-scented flowers are massed in whorled panicles.
CULTIVATION: They tolerate only light frosts and short periods of drought, preferring a position in full sun or part-shade with well-drained soil. Water well during the growing season. Cut back after flowering for compact growth. Propagate from seed or cuttings.

Tetradenia riparia
syn. *Iboza riparia*
MOSCHOSMA, NUTMEG BUSH
☀ ❄ ↔ 8 ft (2.4 m) ↑ 8–10 ft (2.4–3 m)
Shrub from South Africa. Leaves rounded, light sage green, velvety hairs. Heads of scented pale pink to mauve flowers in winter–early spring. Leaves, young stems emit spicy aroma if crushed. Zones 10–11.

TETRADIUM

Native to the area from the Himalayas through to East and Southeast Asia, this small genus of about 9 species of deciduous and evergreen shrubs and trees belongs to the rue (Rutaceae) family. They are grown for their aromatic foliage, masses of small sweetly scented flowers, and the generous clusters of capsular fruit, which contain dark red to black seeds that are poisonous in some species.

Tetradium daniellii

CULTIVATION: Most species are very frost hardy. To thrive, they need a fertile, moist, but well-drained soil in full sun or part-shade. Prune to remove damaged foliage and spent flowerheads. Propagate from seed in autumn, or from cuttings in late winter.

Tetradium daniellii
syn. *Euodia daniellii*
KOREAN EUODIA
☀ ❄ ↔ 40 ft (12 m) ↑ 50 ft (15 m)
Large tree from southwestern China and Korea. Large pinnate leaves, 11 ovate or lance-shaped, glossy, dark green leaflets, russet in autumn. Small, white, perfumed flowers, in terminal sprays, in late summer–early autumn. Pear-shaped fruit. Zones 8–10.

Tetradium ruticarpum
syn. *Euodia ruticarpa*
☀ ❄ ↔ 15 ft (4.5 m) ↑ 30 ft (9 m)
Small tree naturally found in China and Taiwan. Leaves smooth, glossy and dark green above, greenish brown and densely hairy below. Sprays of small white or yellowish green flowers in late summer. Round red to black fruit. Zones 9–11.

TETRATHECA

BLACK-EYED SUSAN
This Australian genus is a member of the family Tremandraceae and comprises about 40 species of low-growing evergreen shrubs

with fine green leaves on slender stems. Nodding bell-like flowers are pink or purple with a black eye that is not readily seen. CULTIVATION: Give these shrubs a well-drained position in part-shade to ensure they are trouble-free in both garden and pot culture. Propagate from half-hardened cuttings.

Tetratheca thymifolia ★

◐ ❄ ↔ 2 ft (0.6 m) ↕ 2 ft (0.6 m)

Mound-forming shrub from Australia. Small green leaves held on dainty stems. Profusion of deep pink bell-like blooms in spring. White-flowering forms also available. Zones 9–11.

TEUCRIUM

GERMANDER

This genus of about 100 species of herbs, shrubs, and subshrubs is a member of the mint (Lamiaceae) family. They are found growing in warm-temperate regions, particularly around the Mediterranean. The shrubs are attractive and often colorful flowering plants. All have characteristic squarish stems with opposite leaves that are usually downy or hairy, oval to lance-shaped, and have notched or slightly toothed edges. The summer flowers are borne in whorls on loose stems and are cream, purple, or pink. CULTIVATION: These plants are mostly frost hardy, and will perform best in a sunny position with well-drained soil. While they will tolerate the dry heat of the inland, they prefer coastal conditions. Lightly prune the ends of the branchlets to remove spent inflorescences and stimulate lateral growth immediately after the summer-flowering period. Propagate from firm tip cuttings in summer.

Teucrium fruticans

BUSH GERMANDER, SHRUBBY GERMANDER

☼ ❄ ↔ 6 ft (1.8 m) ↕ 4 ft (1.2 m)

Evergreen shrub native to southern Spain, Portugal, and Italy, as well as North Africa. Dense white hairs on stems and underside of grayish leaves. Flowers pale lilac-blue, in summer. Zones 8–10.

THEVETIA

This small genus belonging to the dogbane (Apocynaceae) family includes around 8 species native to tropical America. They are trees and shrubs with simple alternate leaves spirally arranged. Their plentiful summer flowers are showy, often yellow, and funnel-shaped,

and are produced at the ends of shoots. The fruit is squat and berry-like. The genus is closely related to *Nerium,* which includes the poisonous plants commonly known as oleanders. All parts of *Thevetia* plants are highly poisonous, including the milky sap. CULTIVATION: Most members of this genus are fairly adaptable but will give the best results when planted in a mulched, well-drained, sandy soil with plenty of water during summer. They will tolerate full sun to part-shade. Propagate from seed or cuttings.

Thevetia peruviana

syn. *Thevetia neriifolia*

LUCKY NUT, YELLOW OLEANDER

☼ ❄ ↔ 8 ft (2.4 m) ↕ 15 ft (4.5 m)

Upright shrub or small tree from Central America, Peru, and West Indies. Linear to narrowly lance-shaped leaves, shiny dark green. Fragrant funnel-shaped flowers, apricot-yellow, in cymes, in summer. Fleshy fruit. All parts of plant are poisonous. Zones 10–12.

THRYPTOMENE

This genus consists of around 40 species of evergreen shrubs from Australia. It is a member of the myrtle (Myrtaceae) family, and is allied to the genus *Baeckia.* These shrubs have wiry stems and small linear leaves that are usually aromatic when crushed. Their tiny starry flowers are white, pink-tinted, or pink and are abundant on every small side shoot, coloring the plant in late winter and spring. The flowers are rich in nectar, which gives them a honeyed scent. CULTIVATION: *Thryptomene* species prefer a light well-drained soil, in full sun, and will do best if kept free from frosts. These shrubs will not tolerate prolonged wet and cold conditions, but are otherwise easily grown. They make excellent cut flowers, and one of the best ways to keep the bush compact is to trim the flowering branches for use indoors. Propagation of *Thryptomene* species is from small tip cuttings of non-flowering stems.

Thryptomene saxicola

ROCK THRYPTOMENE

☼ ❄ ↔ 5 ft (1.5 m) ↕ 3–5 ft (0.9–1.5 m)

Shrub found naturally on rocky hillside outcrops in most of southern Australia. Mass of wiry stems, sprays of small rounded leaves. White or pale pink flowers in late winter–spring. Give it a light annual trim after flowering. Prefers well-drained conditions. Zones 9–10.

Tetratheca thymifolia

Teucrium fruticans

Thryptomene saxicola

THUJA
syn. *Platycladus*

ARBORVITAE, RED CEDAR, WHITE CEDAR

This genus consists of 5 coniferous evergreen trees within the cypress (Cupressaceae) family. Their natural habitat is North America and East Asia, in high rainfall woodland or damp, cold, coastal and lowland plains. Bark is reddish brown and comes off in long vertical strips on mature trees. Leaflets are flattened and scale-like. Solitary male cones grow on the ends of branchlets, and the solitary female cones, with 6 to 12 overlapping scales, grow lower down. These are important timber trees as well as being used for hedging and in floristry. The aromatic foliage can cause skin allergies. CULTIVATION: Young trees do well in full sun in deep, moist, well-drained soil, but need shelter from cold drying winds. They will survive boggy areas that are too wet for other conifers. Propagate by sowing seed in winter in an area protected from frosts, or by rooting half-hardened cuttings in late summer.

Thuja occidentalis

AMERICAN ARBORVITAE, EASTERN ARBORVITAE, WHITE CEDAR

☼ ❊ ↔ 15 ft (4.5 m) ↑ 30–70 ft (9–21 m)

Large conifer native to eastern North America. Conical form, rounded at top with dense foliage. Bark hangs in orange-brown strips. Crowded, flattened, dull green branchlets, grayish green underside. Female cones have 8 to 10 pairs of smooth scales, in summer. 'Caespitosa', slow-growing shrub, 12 in (30 cm) high; 'Filiformis', thin pendent branchlets, grows to 25 ft (8 m) high, golden yellow leaves; 'Golden Globe', height and width of 3 ft (0.9 m); 'Nigra', grows to about 30 ft (9 m) high, narrowly conical form, branches down to ground, very dark green foliage that retains color through winter; 'Ohlendorffii', retains juvenile foliage; 'Pyramidalis Compacta', column of fairly dense, compact, bright green foliage to about 12 ft (3.5 m) high but no more than 4 ft (1.2 m) wide, tapering to pointed leader, fast-growing, good for screens and hedges; 'Rheingold', pink tints when young, turns golden bronze in cold winters; 'Silver Queen', green-yellow foliage; 'Smaragd', conical shrub, bright green foliage; 'Tiny Tim', dwarf form, rust-colored winter foliage; 'Wintergreen', broadly conical; 'Woodwardii', compact shrub with light green foliage. Zones 2–10.

Thuja plicata

GIANT ARBOR, WESTERN RED CEDAR

☼ ❊ ↔ 15 ft (4.5 m) ↑ 70–120 ft (21–36 m)

Tall columnar tree native to western North America, often with buttressed bole. Flattened horizontal sprays of leaves, mid- to dark green, pale green to gray-white below. Female cones have 4 to 5 pairs of scales, each one with tiny hook, in summer. 'Atrovirens', makes compact hedge; 'Aurea', narrow conical habit, gold-tipped shoots soon revert to yellowish green; 'George Washington', broadly conical, long leading shoot; 'Hillieri', height and spread of 6–10 ft (1.8–3 m), bluish green foliage; 'Stoneham Gold', young leaves golden, age to green; 'Sunshine', yellow-green foliage; 'Zebrina', conical, green leaves with yellow stripes. Zones 5–10.

Thuja standishii

JAPANESE ARBORVITAE

☼ ❊ ↔ 20 ft (6 m) ↑ 100 ft (30 m)

Large tree native to Japan, split reddish brown bark. Open crown, broadly conical. Flattened branchlets green above, white below. Female cones have 4 pairs of scales, in summer. Zones 6–9.

Thuja standishii

THUJOPSIS

The single species of conifer tree in this genus is a member of the cypress (Cupressaceae) family and is native to Japan. It resembles the better known *Thuja* but has broader and flatter branchlets that are almost horizontal with tips lifting. The bark is brownish, often tending to red. The deep glossy green leaves are larger than those of *Thuja* species, and have a silvery underside. CULTIVATION: Extremely slow growing, this tree should be planted in a sheltered position in moisture-retentive soil. It is very hardy but must have high humidity. Propagate from seed or cuttings.

Thujopsis dolabrata

DEERHORN CEDAR, FALSE ARBORVITAE, HIBA, HIBA CEDAR

☼ ❊ ↔ 20 ft (6 m) ↑ 100 ft (30 m)

From Japan. Conical crown, almost horizontal branches, upswept at tips. Reddish brown bark exfoliates in strips. Leaves deep glossy green, silvery underside. Slow growing, just 8 ft (2.4 m) after 5 to 10 years in garden. 'Nana', grows to about 30 in (75 cm) high. Zones 6–10.

THUNBERGIA

From tropical Asia and Africa, and also found in South Africa and Madagascar, containing around 100 species of annuals, perennials, and shrubs that are members of the acanthus (Acanthaceae) family. They form an enormously varied group with many being vigorous twining climbers, others are shrubby in habit. Their leaves are usually pointed oval to heart-shaped, sometimes lobed or toothed. Flowers occur in a wide color range, but most often yellow, orange,

Tibouchina lepidota 'Alstonville'

and purple-blue shades, borne singly or in racemes and are generally long-tubed trumpets with 5 large lobes.
CULTIVATION: These plants are mostly frost tender or tolerant only of very light frosts. Plant in a warm sheltered position in moist, humus-rich, well-drained soil. Many species are quite drought tolerant but generally perform best with frequent watering and feeding. Propagate from cuttings or seed, rarely by division.

Thunbergia erecta
BUSH CLOCK VINE, KING'S MANTLE
☀ ⬦ ↔ 7 ft (2 m) ↑ 6–8 ft (1.8–2.4 m)
Erect free-standing or twining shrub from tropical western Africa to South Africa. Toothed ovate leaves. In summer, solitary, cream-centered, violet-blue flowers follow sun. Zones 10–12.

TIBOUCHINA
syns *Lasiandra, Pleroma*
GLORY BUSH, LASIANDRA
This large genus belonging to the meadow-beauty (Melastomataceae) family consists of around 350 species, most naturally found in tropical South America. They are mostly shrubs or small trees, perennials, and scrambling climbers with large, hairy, prominently veined, simple leaves, which are oppositely arranged, often on square stems. The large, showy, 5-petalled flowers are violet, purple, pink, or white and may be borne singly or in panicles at the ends of branches. The flowers are followed by capsular fruit containing spirally curved seeds. *Tibouchina* species are generally only suitable for warm to hot areas that are frost free, although well-established plants that are properly acclimatized may tolerate light frosts. Tibouchinas make very attractive horticultural subjects, and some grow well in large pots or tubs.
CULTIVATION: Most tibouchinas are fairly adaptable to a variety of conditions, but they perform best in warm areas in a light well-drained soil with a high organic content. They prefer a situation in full sun with plentiful water during summer. Protect from strong winds and prune after flowering. Propagate from seed or cuttings taken in late spring or summer.

Tibouchina granulosa
GLORY BUSH
☀ ⬦ ↔ 10 ft (3 m) ↑ 12–35 ft (3.5–10 m)
Large shrub or small tree native to southeastern Brazil. Thick branching stems, lance-shaped to oblong leaves, shiny dark green, hairy underneath. Variable-colored flowers, violet to rose-purple or pink, in panicles at ends of branches, in autumn. 'Rosea', smaller purple to rosy magenta flowers. Zones 10–12.

Tibouchina lepidota
GLORY BUSH
☀ ⬦ ↔ 10 ft (3 m) ↑ 12 ft (3.5 m)
Bushy shrub native to Ecuador and Colombia, taller and more tree-like in its natural environment. Ovate-oblong to oblong lance-shaped leaves, dark green, paler on underside. Panicles of violet-purple flowers, with violet-purple stamens, in late summer–early winter. 'Alstonville', prolific display of vibrant purple flowers. Zones 10–12.

Tibouchina urvilleana   *Tilia americana* 'Redmond'

Tibouchina urvilleana
syns *Lasiandra semidecandra, Tibouchina semidecandra*
GLORY BUSH, PRINCESS FLOWER
☀ ⬦ ↔ 10 ft (3 m) ↑ 15 ft (4.5 m)
Fast-growing shrub from Brazil. Dense rounded form, red hairy stems. Oblong-ovate leaves, dark green, serrated edges. Purple-violet flowers, purple stamens, singly or in panicles, in summer. 'Edwardsii', similar to species, but larger flowers. Zones 9–12.

TILIA
BASSWOOD, LINDEN
Tilia has been revised down to just 45 species of deciduous trees belonging to the linden (Tiliaceae) family. They occur in eastern and central North America, Europe, as well as most of temperate Asia. They are upright single-trunked trees with a rounded to conical crown of foliage. The bark is silver-gray and smooth, and with great age it becomes fissured. The leaf shape is usually oval to heart-shaped with serrated edges, tapering to a fine point. The foliage is usually mid-green but develops vibrant yellow tones in autumn. Small, cream, scented, separate male and female flowers with large bracts are produced in small clusters from late spring. These trees produce conspicuous pale green fruit.
CULTIVATION: These very hardy trees prefer a temperate climate with 4 distinct seasons. They thrive in deep well-drained soil and should be given plenty of moisture in summer. Trim young trees to shape. Propagate from the copiously produced seed, which needs stratification; from cuttings or layers; or, for special forms, by grafting.

Tilia americana
AMERICAN LINDEN, BASSWOOD
☀ ❋ ↔ 40 ft (12 m) ↑ 100 ft (30 m)
Broad-crowned tree from central and eastern North America. Leaves up to 6 in (15 cm) long, almost as broad, serrated edges, paler green below, tapering abruptly to point. Clustered, pale yellow, fragrant flowers in mid-summer. *T. a.* var. *caroliniana* (syns *T. australis, T. caroliniana*), leaves generally smaller, more heavily serrated, blue-green on underside. *T. a.* var. *heterophylla* (syn. *T. heterophylla*), leaves white-felted on underside, sometimes sparsely. *T. a.* 'Ampelophylla', large-lobed leaves; 'Fastigiata', narrow conical habit; 'Macrophylla', very large leaves; 'Redmond', conical growth habit. Zones 3–9.

Tilia cordata
LITTLE-LEAF LINDEN, SMALL-LEAFED LIME

☼ ❀ ↔ 40 ft (12 m) ↑ 80–100 ft (24–30 m)

Wide-crowned tree found over most of temperate Europe from Wales, UK, to western Russia. Dark green rounded leaves, serrated, taper to narrow tip. Clusters of 5 to 7 fragrant cream flowers in summer. 'Greenspire' ★, strong-growing form with narrow crown; 'Rancho', conical habit, glossy leaves. Zones 3–9.

Tilia × euchlora
☼ ❀ ↔ 40 ft (12 m) ↑ 70 ft (21 m)

Hybrid most likely of *T. cordata × T. dasystyla* parentage. Arching branches, become increasingly more pendulous with age. Leaves deep glossy green, pale blue-green hairy beneath. Cream flower-heads, relatively large, attractive to bees, in summer. Zones 4–9.

Tilia × europaea
syn. *Tilia × vulgaris*
COMMON LIME, EUROPEAN BASSWOOD

☼ ❀ ↔ 40 ft (12 m) ↑ 100 ft (30 m)

T. cordata × T. platyphyllos hybrid. Tall, broad, conical crown, branches well down trunk. Leaves dark green, heart-shaped, hairy underside veins. Yellow autumn color. Cream flowers, in clusters, in summer, attractive to bees. 'Pallida', pale green leaves; 'Wratislaviensis', golden yellow leaves when young. Zones 5–9.

Tilia japonica
JAPANESE LIME

☼ ❀ ↔ 20 ft (6 m) ↑ 50 ft (15 m)

Tree found in Japan and nearby parts of China. Small pointed leaves, somewhat glaucous underside. Fragrant creamy yellow flowers in summer. Its relatively small size and upright growth habit make it attractive specimen for avenue planting. Zones 6–10.

Tilia oliveri
OLIVER'S LIME

☼ ❀ ↔ 30 ft (9 m) ↑ 100 ft (30 m)

Tall tree native to western China. Particularly large leaves, light to mid-green, silver-white underside, tend to be held horizontally.

Tilia japonica

Tipuana tipu

Clusters of 7 to 10 flowers in summer. 'Chelsea Sentinel', densely foliaged, broad, upright column with weeping branches. Zones 6–9.

Tilia platyphyllos
BROAD-LEAFED LIME

☼ ❀ ↔ 50 ft (15 m) ↑ 100 ft (30 m)

Dome-shaped tree found in various forms from western Europe to southwest Asia. Stems very hairy when young. Small clusters of pale yellow flowers in early summer. Fruit persist after leaves fall. 'Laciniata', dome shape, yellow flowers from crown; 'Orebro', shorter and broader, slightly deeper green foliage. Zones 5–9.

Tilia tomentosa
EUROPEAN WHITE LIME, SILVER LIME, SILVER LINDEN

☼ ❀ ↔ 50 ft (15 m) ↑ 80–100 ft (24–30 m)

Dense conical to dome-shaped tree from areas around Black Sea. Rounded heart-shaped leaves, very dark green, coarsely serrated edges, fine gray down below. Dull white summer flowers. 'Brabant', broadly conical; 'Nijmegen', mottled gray bark. Zones 6–9.

TIPUANA

From northern South America, this genus, which is a member of the pea-flower subfamily of the legume (Fabaceae) family, consists of a single species. It is an evergreen tree widely grown for its out-standing floral display and overall attractive appearance. It has a wide flat crown covered in dark green foliage. In spring, the tree bursts into a profusion of deep yellow flowers at the tips of the branches. It has become a favorite shade and avenue tree in sub-tropical regions of the world. In cool or dry conditions it may be deciduous, but is bare for only a short period.
CULTIVATION: This tree needs a warm climate and a fertile, moist, but well-drained soil in sun. Pruning is rarely necessary, but young specimens may be shaped in late winter. It is sensitive to frost. Propagate from scarified seed in spring, which must be pre-treated by rubbing them briefly on sandpaper and soaking in cold water.

Tipuana tipu
syn. *Tipuana speciosa*
PRIDE OF BOLIVIA, TIPU TREE

☼ ⸙ ↔ 25 ft (8 m) ↑ 100 ft (30 m)

Fast-growing slender tree from northern South America. Spreading, slightly flattened crown. Dark green pinnate leaves, composed of 11 to 21 glaucous, green, oblong leaflets. Profuse racemes of orange-yellow flowers in spring. Woody winged seed pods. Zones 9–12.

TOONA
syn. *Cedrela*

This small genus in the mahogany (Meliaceae) family consists of 4 or 5 species occurring from southern and eastern Asia to eastern Australia that were once included in the genus *Cedrela*. All are evergreen or deciduous trees with pinnate leaves. They are valuable timber trees, particularly *T. ciliata* which is suitable for temperate to tropical regions. *T. sinensis* suits cooler areas.
CULTIVATION: They are best grown in deep, well-drained, fertile soil in sun with plentiful watering. Grow them in a moist climate and protect from strong winds. Propagate from seed or suckers.

Toona ciliata

Toona ciliata
syns *Cedrela toona*, *Toona australis*
AUSTRALIAN RED CEDAR, RED CEDAR
☼ ⚘ ↔ 20 ft (6 m) ↑ 120 ft (36 m)
Beautiful deciduous tree from moist rainforests of northeastern Queensland to southeastern New South Wales, Australia. Spreading crown, glossy green pinnate leaves composed of ovate leaflets. New foliage bronzy red color, in late spring. Small, fragrant, white or pink flowers in spring. Zones 9–12.

Toona sinensis
syn. *Cedrela sinensis*
CHINESE TOON
☼ ✳ ↔ 30 ft (9 m) ↑ 40 ft (12 m)
Variable deciduous tree from China and Southeast Asia. Dark green pinnate leaves, with 8 to 12 pairs of leaflets, turn orange-yellow in autumn; rosy pink new growth. Hanging panicles of perfumed, small, white flowers in spring. 'Flamingo', suckering growth to 20 ft (6 m) high, new leaves bright pink changing to creamy yellow then green. Zones 6–11.

TORREYA

This genus consists of 7 species of evergreen coniferous shrubs or trees belonging to the yew (Taxaceae) family. It is native to North America and Asia, and is found in sheltered woodland and moist riverside situations. The species vary from shrubs to trees with a wide-open crown. The leaves are glossy, fine, sharp needles, yew-like, with a paler underside. Some of the leaves will emit a scent when crushed. The fruit is a seed, smooth or furrowed, dull green to purplish in color. The kaya nut of Japan *(T. nucifera)* is edible and the oil is used for cooking in that country. The timber of

T. taxifolia is used for fencing; however, this is an endangered species surviving in the wild in only a few small areas in the States of Florida and Georgia, USA.
CULTIVATION: These plants require shelter from cold or drying winds and grow in moist fertile soil with good drainage in full sun or part-shade. Propagate from half-hardened cuttings in late summer, or sow seed as soon as it is ripe in an area protected from frost. Label well as germination may take up to 2 years.

Torreya californica
CALIFORNIA NUTMEG, CALIFORNIA NUTMEG YEW
☼ ✳ ↔ 25 ft (8 m) ↑ 80 ft (24 m)
Tall tree native to California, USA, only species to adapt to cool seaside climates. Open crown, broadly conical. Somewhat pendulous shoots. Leaves yew-like, dark green needles, paler on underside, scented when crushed. Greenish purple female cones in summer. Zones 7–10.

Torreya nucifera
JAPANESE NUTMEG YEW, KAYA NUT
☼ ✳ ↔ 25 ft (8 m) ↑ 50–80 ft (15–24 m)
Tree or shrub native to Japan. Leaves glossy dark green above, blue-white stomatal bands beneath, scented when crushed. Olive green female cones have edible kernel. Zones 7–10.

Torreya californica

TOXICODENDRON

Widely distributed in temperate and sub-tropical regions of North America and East Asia, this is a genus of 6 to 9 species of trees, shrubs, and woody climbers belonging to the cashew (Anacardiaceae) family. It is closely related to *Rhus* and some highly noxious species that were previously included in *Rhus* have now been transferred to this genus, including the poison ivy of North America, *T. radicans*. The cultivation of a few species is prohibited in some places; however, when *Toxicodendron* species are cultivated they are grown mainly for their brilliantly colored autumn foliage and sometimes ornamental fruit. They all contain a milky or resinous sap that is highly caustic and capable of producing dermatitis or a severe allergic reaction in susceptible people.
CULTIVATION: Frost hardy, these plants all require full sun and a well-drained soil. Locate as background plants away from lawns or walkways, where people are least likely to touch them. Propagate from seed in summer, or from cuttings.

Toxicodendron diversilobum
syn. *Rhus diversiloba*
CALIFORNIAN POISON OAK, WESTERN POISON OAK
☼ ✳ ↔ 7 ft (2 m) ↑ 8 ft (2.4 m)
Erect, occasionally climbing, shrub from western USA. Compound leaves, leaflets smooth-edged or lobed, hairy underside. Panicles of greenish white flowers in summer. Creamy white fruit. Contact can produce severe dermatitis. Zones 5–10.

Toxicodendron succedaneum

Trevesia palmata

Tristania neriifolia

Toxicodendron succedaneum

syn. *Rhus succedanea*

POISON SUMAC, RHUS TREE, WAX TREE

☼ ❋ ↔ 20 ft (6 m) ↑ 30 ft (9 m)

Large deciduous shrub or small spreading tree from eastern parts of Asia. Compound leaves of 9 to 15 oval pointed leaflets, shiny green, orange-red to scarlet in autumn. Tiny pale yellow flowers in early summer. Waxy yellowish brown drupes. Highly poisonous and not recommended for small home gardens. Zones 5–10.

Toxicodendron vernix

syn. *Rhus vernix*

POISON ELDER, POISON SUMAC

☼ ❋ ↔ 10 ft (3 m) ↑ 10 ft (3 m)

Deciduous shrub or small tree from temperate eastern North America. Pinnate leaves, 7 to 13 oblong leaflets, smooth edges, color brilliantly in autumn. Small yellow flowers in early summer. May produce dermatitis on contact. Zones 3–9.

TREVESIA

The 12 species of shrubs and trees in this genus, which is a member of the ivy (Araliaceae) family, are found from the Himalayas to southern China and Southeast Asia. Often forming dense clumps, they have thick stems that may be prickly. The large palmately lobed leaves are carried in clusters near the branch tips. Large terminal clusters of small creamy flowers are borne in summer.
CULTIVATION: They require greenhouse or conservatory protection in cold climates. In humid tropical areas they will need a sheltered and partly shaded site in moisture-retentive, deep, fertile soil. Propagate from seed or softwood cuttings.

Trevesia palmata

☽ ⚘ ↔ 12 ft (3.5 m) ↑ 30 ft (9 m)

Native from India to southern China and Southeast Asia. Can grow unbranched or develop into wide-crowned shrub or tree. Stout thorny stems and unusual palmately lobed leaves. Large clusters of off-white flowers in spring. Zones 10–12.

TRIADICA

A genus of 3 species of small to medium deciduous trees in the euphorbia (Euphorbiaceae) family, from eastern and southern Asia, they were formerly included in the larger genus *Sapium*. The sap is milky; leaves are elliptical to almost circular, dark green above but paler and bluish beneath. Flowers are small and petal-less, in catkin-like spikes at branchlet tips, and are followed in summer by distinctive capsules; these shed the fruit walls at maturity to reveal 3 conspicuous round seeds, each coated with a thick layer of chalky-white wax and persisting on the tree in autumn. The wax has had many uses, including candles and soap.
CULTIVATION: Only one species has been widely cultivated, originally for its seed wax in China, later as an ornamental tree. It prefers a subtropical to warm-temperate climate with hot summers, and a sunny position in any reasonably fertile, well-drained soil. Propagate from fresh seed, or half-hardened cuttings when in leaf.

Triadica sebifera

syn. *Sapium sebiferum*

CHINESE TALLOW TREE

☼ ❋ ↔ 15–20 ft (4.5–6 m) ↑ 20–30 ft (6–9 m)

From central and southern China and southern Japan, small tree with rounded crown. Leaves long-stalked, 2–4 in (5–10 cm) long, round to almost diamond-shaped, dull dark green, turning orange to deep red in autumn even in warm climates. Yellow-green flowers in late spring–early summer; ¼ in (6 mm) wide white seeds in autumn. Has become weed in parts of southern USA. Zones 8–11.

TRISTANIA

This is a single-species genus from Australia and is a member of the myrtle (Myrtaceae) family. Several closely related species were included in this genus in the past, but have now been placed in other genera. A shrub or small tree, it has smooth sometimes flaking bark. The leaves are opposite, lance-shaped, with obvious oil glands. It blooms in summer, producing small, yellow, rather insignificant flowers that appear in bunches, giving it a more heavily flowered appearance. It produces a 3-celled fruit capsule. *Tristania* is limited in its distribution, occurring from just north of Sydney to just south and west, along the banks and beds of streams.
CULTIVATION: *Tristania* adapts particularly well to garden situations. Well-drained sandy soils, acid to neutral pH, and water during dry periods are required for good growth. It is somewhat frost tender and grows best in full sun. Propagate from seed or cuttings.

Tristania neriifolia

DWARF WATER GUM, WATER GUM

☼ ⁑ ↔ 7 ft (2 m) ↑ 15 ft (4.5 m)

Shrub or small tree from mid-coast of New South Wales, Australia. Smooth or flaking bark. Leaves opposite, narrow, lance-shaped, with numerous prominent oil glands. Small yellow flowers, in bunches in upper axils, in summer. Zones 10–11.

TRISTANIOPSIS

This genus, a member of the myrtle (Myrtaceae) family, consists of 40 species, the majority of which are found in the moist forest areas of eastern Australia, in New Caledonia, Indonesia, and parts of Southeast Asia. Most are shrubs or trees with simple alternate leaves without any obvious venation. Small clusters of cymes occur along the branches, composed of 5-petalled flowers that are yellow to white, often with many stamens. The fruit is a capsule that contains mostly winged seeds. This group of plants was once included in the closely related genus *Tristania*. Many species make useful screen or hedge plants. CULTIVATION: Most species are fairly adaptable but perform best in warmer climates in a moist well-drained soil in full sun or part-shade. Prune to shape. Propagate from seed.

Tristaniopsis laurina

syn. *Tristania laurina*

KANUKA BOX, WATER GUM

☼ ⁑ ↔ 20 ft (6 m) ↑ 60 ft (18 m)

Tall tree native to eastern Australia. Dense canopy of oblong to lance-shaped leaves, glossy dark green above, paler below. Nectar-rich, small, yellow flowers, in cymes along branches, in summer. Round fruiting capsules. Smaller in cultivation. Tolerates medium frosts and compacted wet soils. Zones 10–12.

TROCHODENDRON

This genus, a member of the family Trochodendraceae, contains a single species of evergreen tree or shrub that has attractive tiered branches and is native to Japan, Korea, and Taiwan. The leaves are glossy and bright green and grow spirally near the tips of the stems. The green and petal-less flowers are produced in upright clusters from late spring. The genus name means "wheel tree," which refers to the spoke-like arrangement of the flower stamens. In the wild this plant will often start life as an epiphyte growing on *Cryptomeria japonica*. Its wood resembles that of coniferous trees and it is thought to be a quite primitive plant. CULTIVATION: Although interesting and attractive, this species is very slow growing in cultivation. It requires a fertile moisture-retentive soil in part-shade with protection from cold winds. Propagate from seed or half-hardened cuttings.

Trochodendron aralioides

WHEEL TREE

◑ ✳ ↔ 25 ft (8 m) ↑ 70 ft (21 m)

Tall tree from Japan, Korea, and Taiwan; in cultivation it will slowly grow to about 15 ft (4.5 m) high. Tiered branches bear simple glossy green leaves in spirals near stem tips. Upright clusters of 10 to 12 small, green, petal-less flowers in late spring. Zones 8–10.

TSUGA

HEMLOCK SPRUCE

These 10 or 11 evergreen, monoecious, coniferous trees from North America and Asia belong to the pine (Pinaceae) family. They grow in mountainous areas in their southern distribution, and in wet cool coastal areas and plains in the north. Most young trees are shade tolerant. They have flattened linear leaves with whitish silver bands on the underside. The female cones become pendent as they ripen and drop off in the second year. They are grown mainly for their timber and ornamental cultivars. CULTIVATION: *Tsuga* species grow in humus-rich, slightly acid, neutral to marginally alkaline soil in shade to sun. All need moist well-drained soil and shelter from cold winds. In poor dry soil these plants make weedy specimens. Propagate by sowing seed in pots in an area protected from winter frosts, or by rooting half-hardened cuttings in late summer to autumn.

Tsuga canadensis

CANADIAN HEMLOCK, EASTERN HEMLOCK

☼ ✳ ↔ 30 ft (9 m) ↑ 80–120 ft (24–36 m)

Evergreen tree native to eastern North America, in cultivation often smaller, multi-stemmed. Gray hairy young shoots; linear leaves arranged in 2 rows. Leaves toothed, mid-green above, silver underneath. Female cones brown, grow on end of branchlets. 'Aurea', grows to 25 ft (8 m) tall, young foliage golden, turns green as it matures; 'Bennett', dwarf cultivar with lighter green leaves; 'Cole's Prostrate', low-growing ground cover that reaches up to 12 in (30 cm) tall; 'Gracilis', slow-growing dwarf; 'Jacqueline Verkade', dwarf cultivar of globular form; 'Minuta', very compact form; 'Pendula ★', mound-forming slow-growing shrub with pendent branches, reaches 12 ft (3.5 m) in height. Zones 4–9.

Tristaniopsis laurina

Trochodendron aralioides

Tsuga heterophylla, in the wild, Washington, USA

The flowers, borne singly or in small clusters, are fragrant and range from pale yellow to gold. CULTIVATION: Gorses are tough and adaptable plants that thrive under a wide range of growing conditions. Generally they prefer a moist, light, well-drained soil, but they will tolerate winter damp and grow well on sandy soils near the coast. In New Zealand, where common gorse *(U. europaeus)* is a weed, farmers often tame it and use it for roadside hedging.

Ulex europaeus
COMMON GORSE, FURZE, GORSE, WHIN

☼ ❄ ↔ 7 ft (2 m) ↑ 8 ft (2.4 m)

Associated with Scotland but found over much of west Europe. Dense many-branched shrub covered with fine hairs and ½ in (12 mm) long spines. Flowers fragrant, golden yellow, in late winter–spring. '**Flore Pleno**', sterile form, preferable for cultivation. Zones 6–10.

Tsuga heterophylla
WESTERN HEMLOCK

☼ ❄ ↔ 20–30 ft (6–9 m) ↑ 60–120 ft (18–36 m)

Large tree native to western North America. Horizontal branches have pendent tips; glossy dark green leaves. Egg-shaped female cones. Shade tolerant, needs protection from wind. Timber and bark used commercially. '**Argenteovariegata**', white young shoots; '**Laursen's Column**', dwarf, narrow and columnar. Zones 6–10.

Tsuga mertensiana
MOUNTAIN HEMLOCK

☼ ❄ ↔ 20 ft (6 m) ↑ 50 ft (15 m)

Slow-growing tree, native to western North America. Blue-green leaves, blunt tips. Young cones purple, mature to dark brown, in summer. '**Glauca Nana**', to 10 ft (3 m) high, silver-gray foliage. Zones 4–9.

Tsuga sieboldii
SOUTHERN JAPANESE HEMLOCK

☼ ❄ ↔ 25 ft (8 m) ↑ 50–100 ft (15–30 m)

Multi-stemmed tree native to southern Japan. Shiny tan young shoots; leaves with notched tips. Leaves dark glossy green above, pale green to white underside. Shiny yellowish tan young cones ripen to brown in summer. Zones 6–10.

ULEX
Cultivated as ornamentals in some areas, but among the worst of weeds in others, gorses can provoke quite extreme reactions when gardeners meet farmers. This genus from the pea-flower subfamily of the legume (Fabaceae) family is from North Africa and western Europe, and is made up of some 20 species of densely branched, fiercely spiny shrubs. Young plants have fuzzy trifoliate leaves but the foliage is reduced to a chlorophyll-bearing spine in adults.

ULMUS
ELM

There are 45 species of elms in the family Ulmaceae. Most are trees, some very large, but a few are shrubs. Although most are deciduous and very hardy, a few are semi-evergreen and not so tough. They occur in northern temperate zones and even extend into the subtropics. They are generally round-headed trees with bark often furrowed or fissured though seldom corky, except on young shoots. Leaves are usually elliptic with conspicuous veins and serrated edges. Flowers are inconspicuous, but the papery winged fruit (samaras) that follow can be showy.

CULTIVATION: In the main, elms are tough plants that adapt well to cultivation, growing successfully in a range of soils provided the drainage is good. However, in some areas populations have been decimated by Dutch elm disease, a fungal infection carried by small beetles with wood-boring larvae. Propagate from seed or by grafting.

Ulex europaeus

Ulmus americana
AMERICAN ELM, WHITE ELM

☼ ❄ ↔ 100 ft (30 m) ↑ 100 ft (30 m)

Largest of North American elms. Impressive tree, deep gray furrowed bark. Large leaves turn bright yellow in autumn. '**Augustine**', vigorous grower, columnar habit; '**Columnaris**', columnar habit. Zones 3–9.

Ulmus carpinifolia
syn. *Ulmus minor*

FIELD ELM, SMOOTH-LEAFED ELM

☼ ❄ ↔ 70 ft (21 m) ↑ 50–70 ft (15–21 m)

Native to central and southern Europe, including UK. Leaves 2–4 in (5–10 cm) long, serrated edges, golden orange autumn tones. '**Variegata**', white-speckled leaves. Zones 5–10.

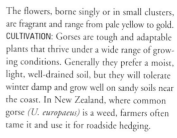

Ulmus crassifolia

CEDAR ELM

☼ ❄ ↔ 40 ft (12 m) ↑ 70–100 ft (21–30 m)

Found in southern USA. Young twigs edged with "wings" of bark. Rather stiff leaves, about 2 in (5 cm) long, toothed edges, downy underside. Zones 7–10.

Ulmus glabra

SCOTCH ELM, WYCH ELM

☼ ❄ ↔ 70 ft (21 m) ↑ 100 ft (30 m)

Large tree from northern Europe to western Asia. Deeply toothed, dark green, rounded, 2–6 in (5–15 cm) leaves sometimes lobed at base, turn yellow in autumn. Lime green fruit in spring. '**Camperdownii**' ★, low-growing, spreading crown of weeping branches; '**Exoniensis**', erect conical habit; '**Pendula**', (syn. 'Horizontalis'), horizontal spreading branches. Zones 5–9.

Ulmus × *hollandica*

DUTCH ELM

☼ ❄ ↔ 80 ft (24 m) ↑ 100 ft (30 m)

Naturally occurring hybrid between *U. glabra* and *U. carpinifolia*. Strong, heavily veined, serrated, deep green leaves turn yellow in autumn. '**Groenveldt**', disease-resistant; '**Jacqueline Hillier**', shrubby, to 8 ft (2.4 m) tall; '**Major**', wide-spreading crown, broad leaves; '**Modolina**', vase-shaped crown. Zones 5–9.

Ulmus japonica

☼ ❄ ↔ 60 ft (18 m) ↑ 100 ft (30 m)

Large broad-headed tree native to Japan and nearby parts of temperate northeastern Asia. Young stems have corky yellow-brown bark, roughly oval leaves taper abruptly to point, coarsely toothed edges. Small purplish flowers, pale green fruit. Zones 5–9.

Ulmus laevis

RUSSIAN ELM

☼ ❄ ↔ 30 ft (9 m) ↑ 70 ft (21 m)

From France to eastern Europe and Caucasus. Dark gray to brown bark, open spreading crown. Broad rough-textured leaves, 4 in (10 cm) long, gray hairs beneath. Zones 4–9.

Ulmus parvifolia

CHINESE ELM

☼ ❄ ↔ 30 ft (9 m) ↑ 70 ft (21 m)

Disease-resistant tree from Japan, Korea, and China, near-evergreen in mild climates. Round crown, smooth flaking bark, fine branches. Mature fruit in autumn. '**Frosty**', compact shrub, white-toothed leaves; '**True Green**', reliably evergreen in mild winters. Zones 5–10.

Ulmus procera

ENGLISH ELM

☼ ❄ ↔ 50 ft (15 m) ↑ 70–100 ft (21–30 m)

Stately English tree now rare due to Dutch elm disease. Leaves deep green, serrated-edged, bright yellow in autumn. Pale green fruit, most sterile, in spring. '**Argenteovariegata**', white-speckled leaves; '**Louis van Houtte**', very popular yellow-leafed cultivar, especially bright in autumn; '**Purpurea**', slight purplish tint to young foliage. Zones 4–9.

Ulmus pumila

CHINESE ELM, SIBERIAN ELM

☼ ❄ ↔ 20–30 ft (6–9 m) ↑ 20–35 ft (6–10 m)

Native to cool-temperate Asia. Coarsely textured, serrated leaves, color slightly in autumn. '**Den Haag**', disease-resistant tall form, with open crown. Zones 3–9.

Ulmus 'Sapporo Autumn Gold'

☼ ❄ ↔ 35 ft (10 m) ↑ 50 ft (15 m)

Hybrid notable for its resistance or tolerance of Dutch elm disease. Strongly upright habit when young, eventually develops broad crown. Soft yellow-green new spring foliage matures to lime green; golden yellow autumn foliage. Zones 4–9.

Ulmus 'Sarniensis'

JERSEY ELM, WHEATLEY ELM

☼ ❄ ↔ 23–25 ft (7–8 m) ↑ 75–80 ft (23–24 m)

Hybrid between *U. carpinifolia* and *U.* × *hollandica*. Very erect upright habit, with broad-based conical crown. Heavily serrated dark green leaves to 4 in (10 cm) long. Sets copious quantities of fruit, most sterile. Makes good lawn tree. Zones 7–10.

Ulmus laevis

Ulmus parvifolia

Ulmus 'Sarniensis'

Ulmus thomasii

CORK ELM, ROCK ELM

☼ ❋ ↔ 40 ft (12 m) ↑ 100 ft (30 m)

Native to eastern North America. Upright tree, narrow rounded crown. Young branches with distinctly corky bark. Leaves 2–4 in (5–10 cm) long, heavily serrated. Seldom color much in autumn. Zones 2–9.

UMBELLULARIA

Related to the laurels *(Laurus)*, the sole species in this genus from the family Ulmaceae is an aromatic evergreen tree found naturally only in Oregon and California, USA. It has tough leathery leaves and male and female flowers carried on separate flowerheads. The foliage is so strongly aromatic that crushing it in the hand and sniffing it can cause an instant though usually brief headache. It was widely used medicinally by native North Americans. Its timber is quite dense and used in woodturning for mainly ornamental objects or utensils.

CULTIVATION: Tolerant of light to moderate frosts and not particularly fussy about the soil type, California laurel grows best in deep, moist, humus-enriched, well-drained soil with a position in full sun or partial shade. Propagation is either from seed or half-hardened cuttings.

Umbellularia californica

CALIFORNIA LAUREL, HEADACHE TREE

☼ ❋ ↔ 35 ft (10 m) ↑ 50–70 ft (15–21 m)

Densely foliaged spreading crown, scaly red-brown bark. Strongly aromatic, glossy deep green, oval to lance-shaped leaves. Clusters of small yellow flowers, at branch tips, in spring. Purplish olive-like berries 1 in (25 mm) long. Zones 8–10.

VACCINIUM *(see page 372)*

Vaccinium crassifolium

CREEPING BLUEBERRY

◐ ❋ ↔ 3 ft (0.9 m) ↑ 15 in (38 cm)

From southeastern USA. Low evergreen shrub takes root as it spreads. Tiny leaves, thick and leathery, finely serrated edges. Flowers very small, white, white with pink markings, or pink, in small clusters, in late spring. Purple-black fruit. Zones 7–10.

Vaccinium nummularia

◐ ❋ ↔ 12–15 in (30–38 cm) ↑ 12–15 in (30–38 cm)

Small evergreen shrub found in Himalayas, Bhutan, and north-eastern Indian province of Sikkim. Leaves rounded, finely serrated, ¾ in (18 mm) long. Small clusters of tiny pink flowers. Berries edible, deep blue-black. Zones 7–10.

Vaccinium stamineum

DEERBERRY

◐ ❋ ↔ 3 ft (0.9 m) ↑ 5 ft (1.5 m)

Deciduous shrub found in eastern and southern USA. Leaves smooth-edged, covered with minute hairs, develop good autumn color. Sprays of small white to cream flowers borne in spring. Greenish yellow to blue-green berries. Host for blueberry maggot fly. Zones 5–9.

Vaccinium vitis-idaea

COWBERRY

◐ ❋ ↔ 2–4 ft (0.6–1.2 m) ↑ 6 in (15 cm)

Creeping evergreen shrub found over much of cool-temperate Northern Hemisphere. Tiny oval leaves deep green, with black spotting on underside; develop bronze tones in winter. Clusters of white to pink flowers in late spring. Bright red berries in autumn. Zones 2–8.

VERTICORDIA

This genus from the myrtle (Myrtaceae) family is endemic in Australia; most of its 97 species occur in the southwest of the country. All are woody shrubs. The small leaves are opposite in alternating pairs, and have oil glands. The flowers are the attractive feature, with colors ranging from white to yellow, mauve, and red, and with the calyx of each flower deeply divided and appearing feathery. The petals of some species are also divided or lobed. Habitats are generally heaths and low scrubs, on sandy or gravelly soils that have an acid pH.

CULTIVATION: The majority of species do not do well in regions where summer rainfall is high or frequent. Propagate from seed or cuttings. Seeds are few and fertility is usually low. While cuttings are not always reliable, some species do strike readily. Grafting onto rootstocks of related genera that have proved reliable in a variety of garden situations has been successful with some species.

Vaccinium vitis-idaea

Verticordia grandis, in the wild, Western Australia

Verticordia plumosa

Verticordia chrysantha

☼ ❊ ↔ 2 ft (0.6 m) ↕ 2 ft (0.6 m)

Shrub from southern sandplains of Western Australia. Small linear leaves. Feathery flowers, in dense yellow heads, in spring. Grafting onto rootstocks of *Darwinia citriodora* has been successful. Zones 8–9.

Verticordia grandis

☼ ❊ ↔ 3 ft (0.9 m) ↕ 7 ft (2 m)

From sandheaths to north of Perth in Western Australia. Straggling shrub with opposite, almost circular, grayish green leaves. Few brilliant scarlet flowers, 1 in (25 mm) across, in upper leaf axils, in spring. Zones 8–9.

Verticordia plumosa

☼ ❊ ↔ 20 in (50 cm) ↕ 20 in (50 cm)

Variable species, with gray-green leaves about ¼ in (6 mm) long. Dense terminal heads of pinkish flowers in spring. Propagation successful from seed and cuttings. Most commonly cultivated *Verticordia*. Zones 8–9.

VESTIA

The single species in this genus within the nightshade (Solanaceae) family is an evergreen shrub growing in the Chilean woodland. It is grown for its flowers and foliage; the alternate, shiny, deep green leaves emit an unpleasant smell when crushed. The yellow-green flowers are pendent. CULTIVATION: It prefers well-drained soil in a site sheltered from full sun and frost. Water and feed moderately during the growing season, and reduce watering in the dormant period. Propagate from cuttings in summer, or seed in autumn or spring.

Vestia foetida

syn. *Vestia lycioides*

◑ ❊ ↔ 5 ft (1.5 m) ↕ 6 ft (1.8 m)

Erect evergreen shrub native to Chile. Thin, glossy, green leaves. Pale yellow, tubular, pendent flowers in spring–late summer. Green seed capsules turn pale brown. Zones 9–10.

Vestia foetida

VIBURNUM

This genus in the woodbine (Caprifoliaceae) family consists of easily grown, cool-climate, deciduous, semi-evergreen or evergreen, shrubby plants that are grown for their pretty flowers, autumnal leaf color, and berries. Most have erect branching stems, paired leaves, a spread about two-thirds their height, and display their small white flowers in dense clusters. (Those plants that resemble the lace-top *Hydrangea* species bear sterile florets at the outer edges of the cluster.) The buds and petals, particularly in cultivars, may be softly colored in tints of pink, yellow, and green. CULTIVATION: Light open positions and light well-drained soils are preferred. Many are drought tender. Prune the evergreens by clipping in late spring and the deciduous species by removing entire old stems after flowering. For a good berry display grow several plants in the same area. Propagate from cuttings taken in summer, or from seed in autumn.

Viburnum × *burkwoodii*

Viburnum betulifolium

☼ ❊ ↔ 10 ft (3 m) ↕ 10 ft (3 m)

Upright, arching, deciduous shrub native to western China. Bark smooth, purple-brown. Bright green roundly oval leaves, glossy underside. Tiny white flowers, in flat-topped clusters, in early summer. Persistent, round, glowing red berries. Zones 6–8.

Viburnum × *bodnantense*

☼ ❊ ↔ 7 ft (2 m) ↕ 10 ft (3 m)

Large, upright, deciduous shrub, hybrid of *V. farreri* and *V. grandiflorum*. Long, oval, mid-green leaves, paler beneath, noticeably veined, color in autumn. Persistent, pinkish white to red, fragrant flowers, in dense clusters on bare wood, in late autumn–early spring. 'Charles Lamont', large bright pink flowers; 'Dawn', distinctive, deep pink, fragrant flowers that fade with age. Zones 7–9.

Viburnum × *burkwoodii*

BURKWOOD'S VIBURNUM

☼ ❊ ↔ 8 ft (2.4 m) ↕ 8 ft (2.4 m)

Open bushy shrub, English hybrid of *V. carlesii* and *V. utile*. Evergreen dark leaves, shiny above, felted below, bronze when young, turn yellow. Flowers in rounded clusters, intense fragrance, in early spring, pink in bud, white on opening. 'Anne Russell', deciduous, valued for its small size, neat compact habit; 'Park Farm Hybrid', red autumnal foliage. Zones 6–9.

Viburnum × *carlcephalum*

FRAGRANT SNOWBALL VIBURNUM

☼ ❊ ↔ 8 ft (2.4 m) ↕ 8 ft (2.4 m)

Deciduous shrub, garden hybrid between *V. carlesii* and *V. macrocephalum* f. *keteleeri*. Lustrous leaves redden in autumn. Pink buds, mildly scented pink flowers, in spring, lighten with age. Zones 5–9.

Viburnum carlesii

Viburnum carlesii
KOREAN SPICE VIBURNUM
☼ ❄ ↔ 7 ft (2 m) ↕ 8 ft (2.4 m)
Dense, deciduous, rounded shrub from open scrub of Korea and Japan. Mid-green leaves, paler beneath, oval shape, bronze-tinted when young, purple-red in autumn. Clustered crimson-pink buds, pink flowers fade to white. 'Aurora' ★, light green young leaves, red buds, pink flowers; 'Diana', red flowers fade to purple. Zones 9–11.

Viburnum 'Cayuga'
☼ ❄ ↔ 6 ft (1.8 m) ↕ 6 ft (1.8 m)
Hybrid of *V. carlesii* and *V. × carlcephalum*. Leaves have soft orange tones in autumn. Pink buds; flowers scented, outer flowers pink, those in center white. Fruit deep purple-red to black. Zones 8–10.

Viburnum davidii
☼ ❄ ↔ 4 ft (1.2 m) ↕ 4 ft (1.2 m)
Low-growing, dense, evergreen, mound-forming shrub from woods of western China. Glossy green leather-like leaves, 3 distinctive main veins. Small off-white flowers, in stiff well-spaced clusters, in late spring. Bright, oblong, midnight blue berries. Zones 6–8.

Viburnum farreri

Viburnum macrocephalum

Viburnum dentatum
ARROWWOOD, SOUTHERN ARROWWOOD
☼ ❄ ↔ 10 ft (3 m) ↕ 10 ft (3 m)
Dense, deciduous, bushy shrub found naturally across North America. Stems erect and branching. Leaves broadly oval, coarsely toothed, redden in autumn. Flat clusters of tiny white flowers in late spring–early summer. Dark blue oblong fruit. 'Ralph Senior', vigorous bushy habit, large leaves. Zones 2–6.

Viburnum dilatatum
LINDEN VIBURNUM
☼ ❄ ↔ 8 ft (2.4 m) ↕ 10 ft (3 m)
Deciduous bushy shrub from China and Japan. Leaves large, oval, coarse, roundish, toothed, dark green, good autumn coloring. Tiny, creamy white, star-shaped flowers, in clusters, in late spring or summer. Oval scarlet fruit persist. 'Catskill', broad low-growing habit, smaller leaves than species, good autumn coloring; 'Erie', pink fruit, rich autumn colors; 'Iroquois', shorter than species, reddish yellow fruit. Zones 5–8.

Viburnum erubescens
☼ ❄ ↔ 10 ft (3 m) ↕ 20 ft (6 m)
Deciduous to near-evergreen shrub or small tree found from Himalayan region southward to Sri Lanka. Leaves elliptic, serrated edges, downy underside. Small pendulous clusters of pink-tinted white flowers in summer. Red fruit ripen to black. Zones 6–11.

Viburnum farreri
syn. *Viburnum fragrans*
☼ ❄ ↔ 8 ft (2.4 m) ↕ 10 ft (3 m)
Upright deciduous shrub native to northern China. Leaves oval, veined, tapering, bronze when young, red when mature. Sweetly scented persistent flowers pale pink or white, before leaves, in mid-autumn–spring. Edible scarlet berries, poisonous stones. Zones 6–9.

Viburnum × globosum
☼ ❄ ↔ 3–4 ft (0.9–1.2 m) ↕ 3–4 ft (0.9–1.2 m)
Evergreen *V. davidii × V. lobophyllum* hybrid, usually seen as selected form 'Jermyn's Globe', neat rounded shrub. Lustrous, leathery, heavily veined, red-stemmed leaves. Heads of massed small white flowers open from red-tinted buds. Small dark blue fruit. Zones 7–10.

Viburnum × hillieri
☼ ❄ ↔ 7 ft (2 m) ↕ 6–8 ft (1.8–2.4 m)
English-raised hybrid, cross between *V. erubescens* and *V. henryi*. Evergreen shrub with elliptic leaves, shallowly irregularly serrated edges. Small panicles of white flowers in summer. Red fruit ripen to black. Typical form usually sold as 'Winton'. Zones 6–10.

Viburnum japonicum
☼ ❄ ↔ 8 ft (2.4 m) ↕ 8 ft (2.4 m)
Robust evergreen shrub from Japan. Leaves long, leathery, lustrous, oval, dark green above, paler beneath. Tiny, white, strongly scented flowers, in clusters, in early summer. Berries red, persist through winter. Zones 7–9.

Viburnum × juddii

JUDD VIBURNUM

☼ ❄ ↔ 7 ft (2 m) ↕ 6 ft (1.8 m)

Deciduous *V. bitchiuense* and *V. carlesii* cross. Spreading habit. Leaves elongated, oval, dull dark green. Sweetly fragrant, pink budded, white starry flowers, in rounded clusters, in spring. Zones 5–9.

Viburnum lantana

WAYFARING TREE

☼ ❄ ↔ 12 ft (3.5 m) ↕ 15 ft (4.5 m)

Robust deciduous shrub or small tree native to Europe and north-west Asia. Oblong-oval dull green leaves, can turn rusty crimson in autumn. Creamy white flowers, in terminal clusters, in late spring–early summer. Red oblong fruit mature to black. **'Mohican'** ★, darker leaves, reddish orange fruit mature to black; **'Versicolor'**, light yellow new leaves age to golden yellow. Zones 3–6.

Viburnum lantanoides

syn. *Viburnum alnifolium*

HOBBLE BUSH

☼/◐ ❄ ↔ 15 ft (4.5 m) ↕ 15 ft (4.5 m)

Deciduous shrub native to North America. Branches downy when young. Large leaves veined, broadly oval, turn yellow and red in autumn. Large white flowers, in lace-top clusters, in late spring–early summer. Oblong purple-black fruit. Zones 3–6.

Viburnum lentago

NANNYBERRY, SHEEPBERRY, WILD RAISIN

☼/◐ ❄ ↔ 10 ft (3 m) ↕ 20 ft (6 m)

Slender, branching, vigorous, deciduous shrub or small tree from North America. Broadly oval, lustrous, dark green leaves, attractive autumn hues. Creamy white fluffy flowers, in clusters, in spring–early summer. Oval bluish black berries. Zones 2–5.

Viburnum macrocephalum

CHINESE SNOWBALL BUSH/TREE

☼ ❄ ↔ 15 ft (4.5 m) ↕ 15 ft (4.5 m)

Chinese species with spreading branches. Showy pompon-like clusters of white flowers, opening from almost luminous green buds, in spring. May be semi-evergreen in mild winters. Dark green oval-oblong leaves, downy on under-side. *V. m.* f. *keteleeri*, lacecap-like flowers. *V. m.* 'Sterile', sterile and berryless. Zones 6–9.

Viburnum nudum

POSSUM-HAW VIBURNUM, SMOOTH WITHE-ROD

☼ ❄ ↔ 6 ft (1.8 m) ↕ 10 ft (3 m)

Deciduous erect shrub native to eastern USA and Canada. Oval glossy leaves, prominent veins, minutely toothed edges, turn reddish purple in autumn. Flowers white or pale yellow, in summer. Blue-black fruit. Zones 6–9.

Viburnum nudum

Viburnum opulus

COMMON SNOWBALL, EUROPEAN CRANBERRY, EUROPEAN SNOWBALL, GUELDER ROSE

☼ ❄ ↔ 15 ft (4.5 m) ↕ 15 ft (4.5 m)

Vigorous parent plant to many popular deciduous garden shrubs. Native hedgerow habitat from Siberia to Algeria. Deep green vine-like leaves, paler downy underside, redden in autumn. Lace-top clusters of white flowers in early summer. Lustrous, semi-translucent, red fruit. **'Aureum'**, bright yellow spring foliage, yellow-green in summer, easily scorched by sun; **'Nanum'**, dwarf cultivar of dense multi-stemmed habit, to 2 ft (0.6 m) tall, with small crowded leaves, rarely flowers; **'Notcutt's Variety'**, tall vigorous shrub to 12 ft (3.5 m) high, fine foliage color in autumn, large red fruit last into winter; **'Roseum'** (syn. 'Sterile'), showy, snowball-like, greenish white flower clusters in mid-spring with leaves; **'Xanthocarpum'**, white flowers, mid-green leaves, berries glossy, partly translucent, yellow. Zones 3–9.

Viburnum plicatum

syn. *Viburnum plicatum* var. *tomentosum*

DOUBLEFILE VIBURNUM, JAPANESE SNOWBALL

☼ ❄ ↔ 10 ft (3 m) ↕ 8 ft (2.4 m)

From China and Japan. Vigorous, deciduous, spreading shrub with tiered branches. Leaves pleated surface, bright green in spring, mid-green in summer, burgundy-red in autumn. Profuse flat umbels of small, cream, fertile flowers in late spring–early summer, ringed by larger, white, sterile flowers. Small red fruit. **'Fireworks'**, reddish black fruit, purple-red autumn foliage; **'Grandiflorum'**, white flowers turn pink; **'Lanarth'**, spreads to 15 ft (4.5 m); **'Mariesii'**, large flat heads of mainly sterile flowers, rarely fruiting; **'Nanum Semperflorens'** (syn. *V. watanabei*), slow-growing, small flowerheads in warmer months; **'Pink Beauty'**, white flowers age to pink; **'Roseum'**, white flowers age to deep pink; **'Shasta'**, 7 ft (2 m) tall, deep purple-red autumn foliage, large white flowers; **'Summer Snowflake'**, compact shrub, long-lasting white flowers, purple-red autumn foliage. Zones 4–9.

Viburnum lantana

Viburnum prunifolium

BLACK HAW

☼ ❋ ↔ 12 ft (3.5 m) ↑ 20 ft (6 m)

Spreading deciduous shrub or small tree from eastern North America. Leaves roundish oval, finely and sharply toothed. Reddish buds open to small, white, flat-topped clusters of flowers in spring–early summer. Yellow-green berries ripen blue-black. Zones 3–9.

Viburnum rhytidophyllum

☼ ❋ ↔ 8 ft (2.4 m) ↑ 10 ft (3 m)

Stout, upright, fast-growing, evergreen shrub. Leaves long, narrow, wrinkled, veined, leathery, dark green, gray or yellow woolly below. Terminal clusters of small, fluffy, yellowish to pinkish white flowers in early summer. Oval red fruit ripen black. '**Aldenhamense**', leaves with yellow tinge; '**Roseum**', deep pink flowers turn lighter with age. Zones 6–8.

Viburnum sieboldii

☼ ❋ ↔ 15 ft (4.5 m) ↑ 10 ft (3 m)

Spreading deciduous shrub from Japan. Young growth downy. Leaves large, veined, oblong-oval, glossy, dark green above, paler below. Panicles of tiny creamy white flowers in late spring–early summer. Red fruit ripen black. '**Seneca**', up to 30 ft (9 m) high, clusters of white flowers followed by persistent red fruit, ripening to almost black. Zones 4–8.

Viburnum tinus

LAURUSTINUS

☼ ❋ ↔ 8–10 ft (2.4–3 m) ↑ 8–10 ft (2.4–3 m)

Native to Mediterranean region. Dense evergreen shrub that has been popular for centuries as hedging plant. Leaves dark green, glossy, oblong-oval, pointed. Flattened heads of white, pink, or pinkish white flowers, strongly fragrant. Blue-black berries. Several named forms grow in sun or shade, tolerate coastal conditions, and are semi-tolerant of summer drought. '**Eve Price**', elongated leaves and light pink flowers; '**Lucidum**', particularly glossy leaves; '**Purpureum**', bronzed new growth; '**Robertson**', small whitish flowers; '**Variegatum**', leaves margined in yellow. Zones 7–9.

Viburnum tinus

Viburnum trilobum

syns *Viburnum americanum*, *V. opulus* var. *americanum*

AMERICAN HIGHBUSH CRANBERRY, CRANBERRY BUSH

☼ ❋ ↔ 10 ft (3 m) ↑ 10 ft (3 m)

Deciduous shrubby plant from North America. Dark leaves, broadly oval, deeply serrated, turn red shade in autumn. Showy, flat-topped, white flowerheads in early summer. Bright scarlet edible berries. '**Bailey Compact**' and '**Compactum**', attractive autumn foliage; '**Wentworth**', vigorous cultivar, tolerant of damp soils, very brightly colored long-lasting fruit. Zones 2–8.

Viburnum utile

☼ ❋ ↔ 5 ft (1.5 m) ↑ 6 ft (1.8 m)

From China. Evergreen, slender, open shrub with dark shiny leaves. Flowers white, in dense rounded clusters, in spring. Oval berries. Zones 7–9.

Viburnum veitchii

CHINESE WAYFARING TREE

☼ ❋ ↔ 5 ft (1.5 m) ↑ 5 ft (1.5 m)

Deciduous upright shrub from central China. Sharply toothed mid-green leaves. White flowers, in flat rayed clusters. Red berries ripen black. Zones 5–9.

VIRGILIA

This is a small South African genus of evergreen trees in the pea-flower subfamily of the legume (Fabaceae) family, named after Virgil, the classical Latin poet (70–19 BC). They are popular garden plants, chosen for their attractive fern-like foliage, showy flowers, and extremely rapid growth rate, although they have a rather short life span, especially in warm moist climates. The fruit are flat pods typical of legumes.

CULTIVATION: These trees thrive in well-drained light soil with adequate summer moisture, but are likely to fall over in heavy shallow soil. While they are adaptable to many different garden situations, they do require shelter from frost when young. Propagation is from seed, sown in spring in a position protected from winter frosts. Pre-soak the seed for a day before sowing.

Viburnum veitchii

Warszewiczia coccinea

Virgilia oroboides

syn. *Virgilia capensis*

CAPE LILAC, TREE-IN-A-HURRY

☼ ◑ ↔ 15 ft (4.5 m) ↑ 30 ft (9 m)

Erect evergreen tree, broadly conical crown, native to South Africa. Fast-growing but often short-lived species. Leaves alternate, with 11 to 31 leaflets. Lightly perfumed pea-flowers, pink-purple with dark burgundy veins, in spring–summer. Zones 9–11.

VITEX

This unusual genus that encompasses several seemingly very different species is made up of some 250 species of evergreen and deciduous shrubs in the family Verbenaceae, and has a widespread distribution in the tropical, sub-tropical, and warm-temperate zones. The foliage is usually digitately divided with up to 7 leaflets, and may be smooth-edged or toothed. The flowers are clustered in panicles, racemes, or cymes, and come in a wide range of colors. CULTIVATION: As expected of a genus with tropical members, many species of *Vitex* are frost tender, but some are quite hardy and will tolerate moderate frosts. In general, *Vitex* species prefer to avoid the extremes of soil moisture, being tolerant of neither drought nor waterlogging. Plant them in moist, fertile, well-drained soil and water them well in summer. Most grow best with at least half-sun. Hard pruning is seldom required but trim to shape as necessary. Propagation is from seed or cuttings.

Vitex agnus-castus ★

CHASTE TREE

☼ ❄ ↔ 15 ft (4.5 m) ↑ 15 ft (4.5 m)

Aromatic shrub or small tree found from southern Europe to western Asia, naturalized in mild areas. Leaves gray-green, with 5 to 9 narrow leaflets, downy underside. Dusty white buds open to scented lilac flowers in summer–autumn. Purple drupes. Zones 7–10.

Vitex lucens

PURIRI

☼ ◑ ↔ 10–15 ft (3–4.5 m) ↑ 30–50 ft (9–15 m)

Evergreen tree from New Zealand. Lustrous deep green leaves, with 3 to 5 wavy-edged leaflets. Sprays of 1 in (25 mm) long pink to red flowers in autumn–winter. Pinkish red drupes. Zones 9–11.

WARSZEWICZIA

This genus in the madder (Rubiaceae) family contains 4 species of shrubs or trees native to tropical America. They are slightly hairy plants with opposite leaves and terminal panicles of small funnel-shaped flowers with showy bracts. CULTIVATION: In cool climates grow these plants in a greenhouse. In warmer areas they can be grown outdoors in a moist well-drained soil in a sunny situation. Propagate from seed or from greenwood cuttings in spring.

Warszewiczia coccinea

☼ ✦ ↔ 10 ft (3 m) ↑ 15 ft (4.5 m)

Leaves oblong, 6–24 in (15–60 cm) long. Terminal panicles, up to 20 in (50 cm) long, of small yellow flowers, 1 or 2 calyx lobes enlarged into showy, bright red, petal-like bracts, appear year round. Zones 10–12.

Vitex agnus-castus

WEIGELA

CARDINAL BUSH, WEIGELA

The 10 or 12 species of this genus within the woodbine (Caprifoliaceae) family are deciduous long-lived shrubs native to eastern Asia, with opposite oblong to elliptic leaves. Cultivated for their bell- or funnel-shaped flowers, produced in late spring and early summer, they have pink, red, white, or sometimes yellow blooms, growing on the previous year's wood. CULTIVATION: They do well in moist but well-drained fertile soil in sun or part-shade. Remove older branches after flowering to encourage vigorous growth. Propagate by sowing seed in autumn in an area protected from winter frosts, or from half-hardened cuttings in summer. Seed may not come true, as weigelas tend to hybridize freely.

Weigela decora

☼ ✲ ↔ 5–7 ft (1.5–2 m) ↑ 10–15 ft (3–4.5 m)

Species native to Japan, with leaves 4 in (10 cm) long. In spring–early summer bears white trumpet flowers to 1½ in (35 mm) long, ageing to cerise-red. Zones 6–10.

Weigela floribunda

☼ ✲ ↔ 8 ft (2.4 m) ↑ 10 ft (3 m)

Deciduous shrub native to Japan. Slender toothed leaves slightly hairy above, white and woolly beneath. Up to 3 dark red flowers in each leaf axil, in spring–summer. Zones 6–10.

Weigela florida

bell-shaped pink to red flowers; **'Bristol Ruby'**, carmine red flowers; **'Candida'**, vivid green leaves, bell-shaped white flowers; **'Chameleon'**, around 6 ft (1.8 m) tall, finely serrated mid-green leaves, pastel pink flowers, grows in sun or part-shade; **'Eva Rathke'**, dark green leaves, funnel-shaped dark purple flowers; **'Florida Variegata'** (syn. *W. florida* 'Variegata'), cream-edged leaves, rich pink trumpet flowers to 1¼ in (30 mm) long; **'Looymansii Aurea'**, yellowish leaves, rich pink flowers with paler pink center, foliage will scorch in hot sun, and lose its color in heavy shade; **'Madame Lemoine'**, pale pink flowers fading to white; **'Minuet'**, 30 in (75 cm) high with coppery oval leaves, bell-shaped magenta flowers; **'Newport Red'** ★ (syn. 'Vanicek'), tall, very hardy, with dark red flowers; **'Praecox Variegata'** (syn. *W. praecox* 'Variegata'), slightly scented pink trumpet flowers with soft yellow center, leaves have creamy yellow margins turning white as they age; **'Red Prince'**, lushly foliaged, long-lasting dark red flowers. Zones 5–10.

Weigela florida
OLD-FASHIONED WEIGELA, WEIGELA
☼ ❄ ↔ 8 ft (2.4 m) ↑ 8 ft (2.4 m)

From East Asia, larger in wild. Oblong leaves, pointed tips, toothed margins, felty underside. Funnel-shaped dark pink to nearly white flowers in spring–summer. **'Alexandra'** (syn. 'Wine & Roses'), recent cultivar with purple spring foliage becoming almost blackish and glossy in summer, flowers bright rose red, plant compact form, under 5 ft (1.5 m) in height; **'Foliis Purpureis'**, coppery foliage with dark pink flowers, compact habit to 3 ft (0.9 m); **'Java Red'**, purple-tinged foliage, dark pink flowers. Zones 5–10.

Weigela japonica
☼ ❄ ↔ 10 ft (3 m) ↑ 10 ft (3 m)

Native to Japan, larger in wild. Leaves dark green. Spring flowers solitary or in pairs, white, turning red later. *W. j.* var. *sinica,* taller than species, light pink flowers turn deeper pink. Zones 6–10.

Weigela middendorffiana
☼ ❄ ↔ 5 ft (1.5 m) ↑ 5 ft (1.5 m)

Erect shrub from eastern Asia. Vivid green leaves. Solitary or paired flowers, bell-shaped, pale yellow with orange or red throat markings, in summer. Protect from strong winds. Zones 4–10.

Weigela praecox
☼ ❄ ↔ 7 ft (2 m) ↑ 8 ft (2.4 m)

Erect densely branched shrub native to Korea, northeastern China, and Japan. Parent of numerous early-flowering cultivars. Leaves dark green, hairy underside. Fragrant, pink, funnel-shaped flowers, with yellow throat, in late spring–early summer. Zones 5–10.

Weigela Hybrid Cultivars
☼ ❄ ↔ 5–8 ft (1.5–2.4 m) ↑ 5–12 ft (1.5–3.5 m)

Great plants for placing in borders, hybrids between number of *Weigela* species. Range of cultivars to choose from very extensive, with many color possibilities. **'Abel Carrière'**, dark green leaves,

WEINMANNIA
This genus of 150 to 190 species of evergreen shrubs and trees in the family Cunoniaceae is widespread, from Central and South America, to the Pacific region and tropical Asia. The cultivated species are grown mainly for their dense dark foliage and their wand- or bottlebrush-like racemes of flowers, which are usually white or cream. The foliage is usually pinnate and made up thick leathery leaflets that are often toothed and which may differ in size and shape between juvenile and adult plants.

Weigela middendorffiana

CULTIVATION: While hardiness varies somewhat with the species, none are extremely frost tolerant. They prefer relatively mild winter conditions and a moist, humus-rich, well-drained soil that does not dry out in summer. Plant in full sun or part-shade and trim plants lightly to shape after flowering. Propagation is either from seed or from half-hardened cuttings.

Weinmannia racemosa
KAMAHI
☼ ❂ ↔ 8–15 ft (2.4–4.5 m) ↑ 30 ft (9 m)

New Zealand shrub or tree, taller in wild. Leaves simple, dark green to bronze, serrated edges. Juvenile plants often have 3-part leaves. White bottlebrush-like flowers in summer. Very attractive to bees. Zones 9–10.

Weinmannia trichosperma
MADEN, TINEO
☼ ❂ ↔ 5–12 ft (1.5–3.5 m) ↑ 70 ft (21 m)

Large shrub or tree native to Chile and Argentina. Remains bushy for many years. Pinnate leaves, composed of 11 to 13 toothed leaflets, each 1 in (25 mm) long. Flowers creamy white, on long spikes. Zones 9–10.

WESTRINGIA
This is an Australian genus in the mint (Lamiaceae) family consisting of 25 species. All are shrubs with angled stems and foliage usually arranged in whorls of 3 to 5 small leaves. Small tubular

flowers are 2-lipped, the upper lip having 2 lobes and the lower lip 3 lobes, and are produced in the leaf axils over a long period. The fruit is divided into 4 tiny nutlets hidden in the persistent calyx. Most grow in coastal heathlands, scrublands, forests, and sandy or rocky areas. They are useful landscape subjects for regions with mild winters and are often seen as hedging or screening plants. CULTIVATION: Most are fairly adaptable in a well-drained soil with full sun, tolerating salty winds and exposed conditions. They require adequate water in summer. Prune after flowering to maintain a compact shape. Propagate from cuttings.

Westringia fruticosa
COASTAL ROSEMARY, NATIVE ROSEMARY
☼ ✤ ↔ 7 ft (2 m) ↑ 6 ft (1.8 m)

From east-coastal Australia. Leaves linear, gray above, felty white below, in whorls of 4 around stems. White flowers, lower lobe dotted brownish or purplish, for most of year. Tolerant of wind, drought, and salt. Zones 9–11.

Westringia 'Wynyabbie Gem'
☼ ✤ ↔ 5 ft (1.5 m) ↑ 4 ft (1.2 m)

Popular hybrid between *W. eremicola* and *W. fruticosa*. Bushy shrub with fine dark green foliage. Small bluish pink flowers in groups at branch tips, most of year. May not be long lived. Zones 9–11.

WIDDRINGTONIA
This is a genus in the cypress (Cupressaceae) family containing 3 species, 2 native to South Africa and 1 distributed more widely from tropical Africa south to Cape Town, South Africa. All are evergreen shrubs or trees with fragrant timber. Timber cutting and bushfires have decimated the populations of these trees. Juvenile leaves are needle-like and spirally arranged on the young twigs. The adult leaves are scale-like, arranged in an opposite or alternate pattern, and closely pressed against the stems. Male and female cones are borne on the same plant, the males are catkin-like, the females are woody. The seeds are egg-shaped with a thin wing. CULTIVATION: They do not adapt well to cultivation. Early growth is slow, and the plants sometimes languish and can fail to thrive.

Maintaining them as compact plants in a large pot may be a better option. They grow best in a humid mild climate. Propagation is from seed, which germinates readily, or from cuttings.

Widdringtonia nodiflora
MLANJE CEDAR, MOUNTAIN CEDAR, MOUNTAIN CYPRESS
☼ ✤ ↔ 6–12 ft (1.8–3.5 m) ↑ 40 ft (12 m)

Surviving in wild only in relatively inaccessible sites. Grayish bark peels in long strips. Tiny leaves. Cones ripen in early autumn, seeds black with red wing. Zones 9–11.

Widdringtonia schwarzii
WILLOWMORE CEDAR
☼ ❄ ↔ 15–30 ft (4.5–9 m) ↑ 120 ft (36 m)

Only known from small area just east of Cape Town, South Africa. Bark flaky, leaves arranged in opposite pairs. Male cones catkin-like, female cones globular, dark brown. Seeds flattish with prominent wing. Zones 8–9.

Widdringtonia schwarzii

WIGANDIA
The 5 members of this genus belonging to the waterleaf (Hydrophyllaceae) family are evergreen shrubs from Central and South America. Large, alternate, oval to oblong leaves can be up to 18 in (45 cm) long. The undersurface of the deep green leaves is covered with white hairs, often stinging. Violet-blue flowers are borne from spring to autumn in large, terminal, 1-sided panicles. CULTIVATION: These plants need moist but well-drained soil in full sun. They are frost tender, and make good container specimens. Propagation is from seed or from cuttings taken in spring.

Wigandia caracasana
syn. *Wigandia urens* var. *caracasana*
☼ ✦ ↔ 12 ft (3.5 m) ↑ 15 ft (4.5 m)

Found in jungles of Mexico, Colombia, and Venezuela. Variable species, often small spreading tree. Rough-textured deep green leaves, oval, with wavy edges and hairy white underside. Flowers violet to purple, with white throat, form in long terminal clusters. Zones 10–12.

Weinmannia trichosperma

Westringia 'Wynyabbie Gem'

Wigandia caracasana

WOLLEMIA

This genus belonging to the araucaria (Araucariaceae) family consists of a single species, endemic to the Wollemi National Park, 93 miles (150 km) northwest of Sydney, Australia. It comes from warm-temperate forests and emerges over coachwood and sassafras trees within sandstone canyons of the National Park. An extremely rare, endangered, and remarkable conifer, it has spongy nodular bark and an unusual branching pattern producing a double crown effect. The old leaves do not fall individually—instead, the tree sheds whole branches. *W. nobilis* was discovered in 1994. The chance discovery reinforces the importance of conservation areas in preserving both plant and animal species. The tree yields the anti-cancer drug taxol.

CULTIVATION: Because this genus is so new to horticulture, cultivation information is limited. It can be seen growing at the Royal Botanic Gardens in Sydney, and young plants can now be purchased from nurseries. Propagation from seed, cuttings, and tissue culture has been undertaken and research in these areas continues.

Wollemia nobilis
WOLLEMI PINE

☼ ❆ ↔ 4–10 ft (1.2–3 m) ↕ 120 ft (36 m)

Very rare majestic conifer. Fern-like juvenile leaves dark green and waxy on underside; 4-ranked adult leaves yellow-green, stiff, long, and narrow. Cylindrical male cones on separate branches to globular female cones, which contain winged seeds. Zones 9–11.

Wollemia nobilis

XANTHOCERAS

The 1 species of deciduous shrub or small tree in this genus is native to northern China and is a member of the soapberry (Sapindaceae) family. It has pinnate leaves clustered near the branch tips and bears clusters of 5-petalled flowers. Fruit are thick-walled green capsules resembling the fruit of chestnut trees.

Xanthoceras sorbifolium

CULTIVATION: Although quite hardy, this species needs a long hot growing season to flower well, so in cooler areas should be given the shelter of a warm wall. Grow in a well-drained fertile soil and prune to maintain a compact shape. Propagate from seed, cuttings, or suckers.

Xanthoceras sorbifolium ★

 ☼ ❆ ↔ 10 ft (3 m) ↕ 25 ft (8 m)

Shrub or small tree with wide rounded habit, dark green pinnate leaves, and sharply toothed leaflets. Fragrant white flowers have crimson blotch at their base, and are borne in sprays, in spring–summer. Zones 6–9.

ZANTHOXYLUM

This is a widespread genus of around 250 species of deciduous or evergreen spiny shrubs and trees with pinnate leaves and aromatic bark from North and South America, Africa, Asia, and Australia. They are members of the rue (Rutaceae) family, and are grown for their attractive habit and handsome aromatic foliage, and sometimes for their fruit, which are dried and used for spices. Some species have medicinal uses and others provide a fine timber for woodworking.

CULTIVATION: Depending on the species, they are frost hardy to frost tender. They need a fertile, moist, but well-drained soil with a position in full sun or part-shade. Pruning is rarely necessary, but young specimens may be shaped in early spring. Propagate from seed, cuttings, or rooted suckers.

Zanthoxylum americanum
NORTHERN PRICKLY ASH, PRICKLY ASH, TOOTHACHE TREE

☼ ❆ ↔ 15 ft (4.5 m) ↕ 25 ft (8 m)

Deciduous large shrub or small tree naturally found in eastern North America. Spiny stems and aromatic pinnate leaves. Very small yellow-green flowers, in clusters, before leaves, in spring. Fruit is black berry. Zones 4–10.

Zanthoxylum piperitum
JAPANESE PEPPER

☼ ❆ ↔ 10 ft (3 m) ↕ 20 ft (6 m)

Deciduous, bushy, spiny shrub or small tree native to China, Korea, and Japan. Aromatic, glossy, dark green, pinnate leaves composed of many oval leaflets, which turn yellow in autumn. Small yellow-green flowers, in small clusters, in spring. Tiny orange-colored berries. Zones 7–10.

Zanthoxylum planispinum

☼ ❆ ↔ 8 ft (2.4 m) ↕ 12 ft (3.5 m)

Deciduous shrub native to Japan, Korea, and China. Spreading prickly stems. Pinnate leaves, stem-clasping leaflets to 4 in (10 cm) long. Pale yellow flowers, in small clusters, in spring. Tiny, warty, red berries. Zones 7–10.

Zanthoxylum simulans

FLAT-SPINE PRICKLY ASH, PRICKLY ASH
☼ ❄ ↔ 7–25 ft (2–8 m) ↑ 7–25 ft (2–8 m)
Rounded, spreading, deciduous shrub or small
tree from China and Taiwan. Broad flattened
spines on finely hairy branches. Compound leaves
have 7 to 11 smooth, toothed, oval to oblong
leaflets, to 2 in (5 cm) long, with prickly midrib.
Slender cymes of reddish green flowers in mid-
summer, followed by red to black berries in
autumn. Zones 5–8.

ZELKOVA

Allied to the elms *(Ulmus)* but not troubled by
Dutch elm disease, the 5 deciduous trees in this
genus are members of the family Ulmaceae, and
are found in China, Taiwan, and Japan, as well as
in the Caucasus and Crete, Greece. They have simple, pointed,
elliptical leaves with conspicuous veins and heavily serrated edges.
The foliage often develops attractive autumn colors. In some species
the bark is an attractive feature, flaking to reveal interesting patterns
and colors. The separate male and female flowers are largely inconspicuous, as are the small nut-like fruit.
CULTIVATION: Quite frost hardy, these spreading round-headed
trees develop a better shape if sheltered from strong winds when
they are young. They also benefit from pruning to encourage a
strong single trunk. Plant in deep, fertile, well-drained soil in full
sun. Propagation is from seed, from root cuttings of the young
potted plants, or by grafting.

Zanthoxylum planispinum

Zelkova carpinifolia

CAUCASIAN ZELKOVA
☼ ❄ ↔ 25 ft (8 m) ↑ 100 ft (30 m)
Native to Caucasus. May develop several trunks. Round-headed
tree, upright gray-barked branches, weep at tips. Young stems very
downy, veins on underside of serrated leaves. Flowers pleasantly
scented. Zones 5–9.

Zelkova serrata

JAPANESE ZELKOVA
☼ ❄ ↔ 50 ft (15 m) ↑ 60–100 ft (18–30 m)
Widely cultivated; from Japan, Taiwan, and eastern China. Wide-
spreading crown, bark flakes to reveal range of colors and textures.
Heavily toothed, veined leaves, fine hairs on underside veins. Foliage turns gold and russet in autumn. 'Goblin', 3 ft (0.9 m) high
dwarf cultivar; 'Green Vase' ★, vase-shaped form, brilliant green
foliage; 'Village Green', fast-growing, rich green leaves. Zones 5–9.

ZENOBIA

The single species in this genus in the heath (Ericaceae) family is
a deciduous or semi-evergreen shrub found in southeastern USA,
on open heathland and in pine forest clearings. Notable for its
beautiful flowers and their pleasant scent, this plant's foliage sometimes develops attractive red tints in autumn.
CULTIVATION: This plant prefers cool, moist, humus-rich, acidic
soil conditions. It is very frost hardy, and prefers a situation in

part-shade. If necessary, trim the plant to shape after flowering.
Propagate from either seed or summer cuttings. Alternatively, try
removing rooted layers or suckers.

Zenobia pulverulenta ★

◐ ❄ ↔ 4 ft (1.2 m) ↑ 3–10 ft (0.9–3 m)
From southeast Virginia to South Carolina, USA.
Retains much of its foliage in mild winters, deciduous elsewhere. Narrowly elliptical leaves, light
green, covered with powdery bluish bloom. Heads
of bell-shaped, nodding, scented white flowers in
late spring. 'Quercifolia', retains shallowly lobed
foliage often seen on juvenile plants. Zones 5–10.

ZIZIPHUS

This tropical and subtropical genus consists of
80 or so species of evergreen or deciduous trees
and shrubs in the buckthorn (Rhamnaceae) family. Some have
spiny branches with double armaments—1 hooked and 1 straight
thorn at each node. They have alternate shiny green leaves, mostly
with 3 prominent veins from the base. The insignificant flowers
are greenish, white, or yellow, and arranged in axillary clusters;
they are followed by small fleshy fruit that are sometimes edible.
The genus is best known in horticulture for *Z. jujuba*, the jujube,
which has been cultivated in China since antiquity.
CULTIVATION: They are ideally grown in a deep moisture-retentive
soil that is well drained, and prefer a sunny position. Shelter from
strong winds and water regularly during the growing season. Tip
prune to maintain compact growth. Propagate from seed or root
cuttings. Improved fruiting varieties may be obtained from grafting.

Ziziphus mucronata

BUFFALO THORN
☼ ❄ ↔ 10–20 ft (3–6 m) ↑ 17–35 ft (5–10 m)
Evergreen tree from South Africa. Crooked trunk and drooping
branches, usually covered with pairs of spines, 1 curved and 1
straight. Glossy drooping leaves conspicuously 3-veined from base.
Inconspicuous yellowish flower clusters. Roundish russet-colored
fruit, dry meal-like pulp. Used in traditional medicine. Zones 7–9.

Zelkova serrata

Ziziphus mucronata, in the wild, South Africa

Fruit Trees, Nut Trees, and Other Fruits

Botanically, a fruit is a mature ovary, a home for the seed inside. It is also a delicious form of food. As we or other animals enjoy and are nourished by succulent fruits, we incidentally help disperse their seeds.

Not all botanical fruits function in the same way. Nuts are fruits whose mature ovaries are hard shells that provide protection. Other fruits ripen without any seeds at all. The seeds might be absent because they abort, as with seedless grapes, or because the ovary is able to swell and develop without the stimulus of seed development, as with seedless persimmons. These examples have been bred to be seedless.

For best-quality yields, most fruit plants need a helping hand. Fruiting demands considerable energy, so plants need to be positioned in full sunlight for maximum yields (even those plants that naturally inhabit shaded sites). Annual pruning is essential, which helps expose branches to sun and air, and fruit thinning—pinching off excess fruit—ensures good annual crops, as heavy fruiting one year leads to a reduced yield the next year.

Fruit and nut plants generally enjoy moist but well-drained fertile soils that are slightly acidic. Blueberries, cranberries, and lingonberries are notable exceptions, preferring infertile and very acidic soils.

The persimmon *(Diospyros kaki)* has been long cultivated in Japan for its edible fruit. More than 2,000 cultivars have been developed from this species.

Fruits and Nuts Finder

The following cultivation table features at-a-glance information for every species or hybrid with an individual entry in the Fruit Trees, Nut Trees, and Other Fruits chapter of this book. Simply find the plant you wish to know more about, and run your eye along the row to discover its height and spread, whether it is frost tolerant or not, the aspect it prefers, and more.

The type of plant is abbreviated to **T**, **S**, **C**, or **P**:
T – the plant is a tree.
S – the plant is a shrub.
C – the plant is a climber.
P – the plant is a perennial.

The climate(s) that each plant needs to thrive in the outdoors are given, abbreviated to **C**, **W**, or **T**:
C – the plant prefers a cool climate.
W – the plant prefers a warm-temperate or subtropical climate.
T – the plant prefers a tropical climate.

The season in which the plant produces flowers or fruit is abbreviated to **A**, **W**, **Sp**, **Su**, or **T**:
A – the plant flowers or fruits in autumn.
W – the plant flowers or fruits in winter.
Sp – the plant flowers or fruits in spring.
Su – the plant flowers or fruits in summer.
T – tropical plants with flowers and/or fruit that appear at any time of year in tropical/monsoonal areas.

Edible parts of the plant are abbreviated to **F**, **N**, **D**, or **B**:
F – the fruit is eaten.
N – the nut is eaten.
D – the drupe is eaten.
B – the berry is eaten.

Plant name	Height	Spread	Type	Climate	Deciduous	Evergreen	Flowering season	Fruiting season	Part eaten	Frost tolerant	Full sun	Half sun	Heavy shade
Actinidia arguta	20–30 ft (6–9 m)	20–30 ft (6–9 m)	C	C	◆		Su	A	F	◆	◆		
Actinidia deliciosa	35 ft (10 m)	35 ft (10 m)	C	C/W	◆		Sp/Su	A/W	F	◆	◆		
Actinidia kolomikta	20–35 ft (6–10 m)	17–20 ft (5–6 m)	C	C	◆		Sp	A	F	◆	◆		
Anacardium occidentale	40 ft (12 m)	25 ft (8 m)	T	T		◆	T	T	N		◆		
Ananas comosus	30 in (75 cm)	30 in (75 cm)	P	W/T		◆	T	T	F				◆
Annona, Atemoya Group	10–15 ft (3–4.5 m)	6–9 ft (1.8–2.7 m)	S/T	W/T		◆	T	T	F		◆		
Annona cherimola	20 ft (6 m)	10 ft (3 m)	T	W/T		◆	T	T	F		◆		
Annona muricata	20 ft (6 m)	10 ft (3 m)	T	W/T		◆	T	T	F		◆		
Annona squamosa	25 ft (8 m)	10 ft (3 m)	T	W/T		◆	T	T	F		◆		
Artocarpus altilis	50 ft (15 m)	20 ft (6 m)	T	T		◆	T	T	F		◆		
Artocarpus heterophyllus	30–50 ft (9–15 m)	20 ft (6 m)	T	T		◆	T	T	F		◆		
Asimina triloba	30 ft (9 m)	20 ft (6 m)	T	C/W	◆		Sp	A	F	◆	◆		
Averrhoa bilimbi	50 ft (15 m)	15 ft (4.5 m)	T	T		◆	T	T	F		◆		
Averrhoa carambola	20 ft (6 m)	10 ft (3 m)	T	T		◆	T	T	F		◆		
Capparis spinosa	3 ft (0.9 m)	10 ft (3 m)	S	W/T		◆	Su/A	W	Buds		◆		
Carica papaya	30 ft (9 m)	12 ft (3.5 m)	T	W/T		◆	Sp/Su	A/W	F		◆		
Carya illinoinensis	100 ft (30 m)	70 ft (21 m)	T	C/W	◆		Sp	A	N	◆	◆		
Carya laciniosa	100 ft (30 m)	35 ft (10 m)	T	C	◆		Sp	A	N	◆	◆		
Carya ovata	80 ft (24 m)	70 ft (21 m)	T	C	◆		Sp	A	N	◆	◆		
Castanea mollissima	40 ft (12 m)	35 ft (10 m)	T	C	◆		Sp	A	N	◆	◆		

Plant name	Height	Spread	Type	Climate	Deciduous	Evergreen	Flowering season	Fruiting season	Part eaten	Frost tolerant	Full sun	Half sun	Heavy shade
Castanea pumila	15 ft (4.5 m)	20 ft (6 m)	T	C	◆		Sp	A	N	◆	◆		
Castanea sativa	60 ft (18 m)	40 ft (12 m)	T	C	◆		Sp	A	N	◆	◆		
Citrullus lanatus	3–6 ft (0.9–1.8 m)	10–20 ft (3–6 m)	C	W/T	◆		Sp/Su	Su/A	F		◆	◆	
Citrus × aurantiifolia	8–15 ft (2.4–4.5 m)	10 ft (3 m)	S	W/T		◆	Sp/Su	A/W	F		◆		
Citrus × aurantium	15 ft (4.5 m)	10 ft (3 m)	S	W/T		◆	Sp/Su	A/W	F		◆		
Citrus hystrix	10 ft (3 m)	6 ft (1.8 m)	S	W/T		◆	Sp/Su	A/W	F		◆		
Citrus japonica	6 ft (1.8m)	3 ft (0.9 m)	S	W/T		◆	Sp/Su	A/W	F		◆		
Citrus × limon	10–15 ft (3–4.5 m)	10 ft (3 m)	S	W/T		◆	Sp/Su	A/W	F		◆		
Citrus × limonia	20 ft (6 m)	12 ft (3.5 m)	T	W/T		◆	Sp/Su	A/W	F		◆		
Citrus maxima	20–40 ft (6–12 m)	10 ft (3 m)	T	W/T		◆	Sp/Su	A/W	F		◆		
Citrus medica	6–15 ft (1.8–4.5 m)	8 ft (2.4 m)	S	W/T		◆	Sp/Su	A/W	F		◆		
Citrus reticulata	10–17 ft (3–5 m)	6–10 ft (1.8–3 m)	T	W/T		◆	Sp/Su	A/W	F		◆	◆	
Corylus avellana	15 ft (4.5 m)	15 ft (4.5 m)	S	C	◆		W/Sp	Su/A	N	◆	◆	◆	
Corylus maxima	30 ft (9 m)	15 ft (4.5 m)	T	C	◆		Sp	Su/A	N	◆	◆	◆	
Cucumis melo	16–28 in (40–70 cm)	7–10 ft (2–3 m)	C	W/T		◆	Sp/Su	Su/A	F		◆		
Cydonia oblonga	10–15 ft (3–4.5 m)	15 ft (4.5 m)	T	C	◆		Sp	A	F	◆	◆		
Cydonia sinensis	20 ft (6 m)	10 ft (3 m)	T	C/W	◆		Sp	A	F	◆	◆		
Diospyros kaki	50 ft (15 m)	25 ft (8 m)	T	C/W	◆		Sp	A/W	F	◆	◆		
Diospyros virginiana	50 ft (15 m)	10 ft (3 m)	T	C	◆		Sp	A/W	F	◆	◆		
Durio zibethinus	80 ft (24 m)	20 ft (6 m)	T	T		◆	T	T	F		◆		
Eriobotrya japonica	20 ft (6 m)	15 ft (4.5)	T	W		◆	A	Sp	F	◆	◆		
Ficus carica	35 ft (10 m)	15–30 ft (4.5–9 m)	T	W/T	◆		Sp	A	F	◆	◆		
Fragaria × ananassa	6 in (15 cm)	40 in (100 cm)	P	C/W		◆	Sp/A	Sp/A	B	◆	◆	◆	
Fragaria chiloensis	6 in (15 cm)	20 in (50 cm)	P	C/W		◆	Sp/Su	Su	B	◆	◆	◆	◆
Fragaria vesca	2 in (5 cm)	12 in (30 cm)	P	C		◆	Sp	Su	B	◆	◆	◆	◆
Fragaria Hybrid Cultivars	2–6 in (5–15 cm)	8–60 in (20–150 cm)	P	C/W		◆	Sp/Su	Su	B	◆	◆	◆	
Hylocereus undatus	17–30 ft (5–9 m)	15–25 ft (4.5–8 m)	C	W		◆	Sp/Su	A	F		◆		
Juglans major	50 ft (15 m)	30 ft (9 m)	T	C/W	◆		Sp	A	N		◆		
Juglans nigra	100 ft (30 m)	70 ft (21 m)	T	C/W	◆		Sp	A	N	◆	◆		
Juglans regia	40–60 ft (12–18 m)	35 ft (10 m)	T	C/W	◆		Sp	A	N	◆	◆		
Litchi chinensis	20–40 ft (6–12 m)	15 ft (4.5 m)	T	W		◆	W/Sp	Su/A	D		◆		

Plant name	Height	Spread	Type	Climate	Deciduous	Evergreen	Flowering season	Fruiting season	Part eaten	Frost tolerant	Full sun	Half sun	Heavy shade
Macadamia integrifolia	50 ft (15 m)	20 ft (6 m)	T	W		♦	W/Sp	Su/A	N		♦	♦	
Macadamia tetraphylla	40 ft (12 m)	20 ft (6 m)	T	W		♦	W/Sp	Su/A	N		♦	♦	
Malus pumila	50 ft (15 m)	20 ft (6 m)	T	C	♦		Sp	Su/A	F	♦	♦		
Mangifera indica	80 ft (24 m)	25 ft (8 m)	T	W/T		♦	T	T	D		♦		
Manilkara zapota	100 ft (30 m)	20 ft (6 m)	T	W/T		♦	Sp	A	B			♦	
Mespilus germanica	20 ft (6 m)	25 ft (8 m)	T	C	♦		Sp	A/W	F	♦	♦	♦	
Morus alba	30–50 ft (9–15 m)	30 ft (9 m)	T	C/W	♦		Sp/Su	Su/A	F	♦	♦		
Morus nigra	50 ft (15 m)	40 ft (12 m)	T	C/W	♦		Sp	Su/A	F	♦	♦		
Morus rubra	50 ft (15 m)	40 ft (12 m)	T	C/W	♦		Sp	Su	F	♦	♦		
Musa acuminata	12–20 ft (3.5–6 m)	8 ft (2.4 m)	T (P)	W/T		♦	Su	A/W	F		♦		
Musa × paradisiaca	10–20 ft (3–6 m)	8 ft (2.4 m)	T (P)	W/T		♦	Su	A/W	F		♦		
Olea europaea	20–30 ft (6–9 m)	20 ft (6 m)	T	W		♦	Su	A/W	D	♦	♦		
Opuntia ficus-indica	15 ft (4.5 m)	15 ft (4.5 m)	S	W		♦	Sp/Su	A/W	F		♦		
Passiflora alata	20 ft (6 m)	8–20 ft (2.4–6 m)	C	W/T		♦	Su	A/W	F		♦	♦	
Passiflora edulis	15 ft (4.5 m)	8–15 ft (2.4–4.5 m)	C	W/T		♦	Su	A/W	F		♦	♦	
Passiflora quadrangularis	50 ft (15 m)	10–20 ft (3–6 m)	C	W/T		♦	Su	A/W	F		♦	♦	
Persea americana	60 ft (18 m)	30 ft (9 m)	T	W		♦	Su	A/W	D		♦		
Pistacia vera	30 ft (9 m)	15 ft (4.5 m)	T	C/W	♦		Su	A	N	♦	♦		
Pouteria sapota	40 ft (12 m)	20 ft (6 m)	T	W		♦	T	T	F		♦		
Prunus americana	25 ft (8 m)	12 ft (3.5 m)	T	C	♦		Sp	Su	D	♦	♦		
Prunus armeniaca	25 ft (8 m)	15 ft (4.5 m)	T	C	♦		Sp	Su/A	D	♦	♦		
Prunus avium	50 ft (15 m)	20 ft (6 m)	T	C	♦		Sp	Su	D	♦	♦		
Prunus cerasus	20 ft (6 m)	15 ft (4.5 m)	T	C	♦		Sp	Su	D	♦	♦		
Prunus × domestica	30 ft (9 m)	15 ft (4.5 m)	T	C	♦		Sp	Su	D	♦	♦		
Prunus dulcis	20–30 ft (6–9 m)	15 ft (4.5 m)	T	C	♦		Sp	Su/A	N	♦	♦		
Prunus mume	20–30 ft (6–9 m)	25 ft (8 m)	T	C	♦		Sp	Su	D	♦	♦		
Prunus persica	8–20 ft (2.4–6 m)	6–20 ft (1.8–6 m)	S/T	C	♦		Sp	Su/A	D	♦	♦		
Prunus salicina	30 ft (9 m)	25 ft (8 m)	T	C	♦		Sp	Su	D	♦	♦		
Psidium guajava	30 ft (9 m)	15 ft (4.5 m)	T	W/T		♦	Sp	Su	B		♦		
Punica granatum	25 ft (8 m)	15 ft (4.5 m)	S/T	C/W	♦		Sp/Su	Su/A	F	♦	♦		
Pyrus communis	50 ft (15 m)	20 ft (6 m)	T	C	♦		Sp	Su/A	F	♦	♦		
Pyrus pyrifolia	50 ft (15 m)	30 ft (9 m)	T	C	♦		Sp	Su/A	F	♦	♦		

Plant name	Height	Spread	Type	Climate	Deciduous	Evergreen	Flowering season	Fruiting season	Part eaten	Frost tolerant	Full sun	Half sun	Heavy shade
Ribes gayanum	5 ft (1.5 m)	3 ft (0.9 m)	S	C/W		◆	Sp	Su	B	◆	◆		
Ribes nigrum	7 ft (2 m)	6 ft (1.8 m)	S	C	◆		Sp	Su	B	◆	◆		
Ribes odoratum	6 ft (1.8 m)	6 ft (1.8 m)	S	C	◆		Sp	Su	B	◆	◆		
Ribes rubrum	5–7 ft (1.5–2 m)	32–60 in (80–150 cm)	S	C	◆		Sp	Su	B	◆	◆	◆	
Ribes uva-crispa	36 in (90 cm)	36 in (90 cm)	S	C	◆		Sp	Su	B	◆	◆		
Rubus arcticus	6–12 in (15–30 cm)	18–24 in (45–60 cm)	P	C	◆			Su	B	◆	◆		
Rubus idaeus	5 ft (1.5 m)	4 ft (1.2 m)	S	C	◆		Sp/Su	Su	B	◆	◆		
Rubus loganobaccus	4–6 ft (1.2–1.8 m)	2–3 ft (0.6–0.9 m)	S	C	◆		Sp	Su	B	◆	◆		
Rubus occidentalis	10 ft (3 m)	10 ft (3 m)	S	C	◆		Sp	Su	B	◆	◆		
Rubus phoenicolasius	10 ft (3 m)	10 ft (3 m)	S	C	◆		Sp	Su	B	◆	◆		
Rubus Hybrid Cultivars	2–8 ft (0.6–2.4 m)	6–12 ft (1.8–3.5 m)	S	C	◆		Sp	Su	B		◆		
Solanum betaceum	10 ft (3 m)	7 ft (2 m)	S	W		◆	Sp/Su	Su/A	F		◆		
Solanum melanocerasum	24 in (60 cm)	18 in (45 cm)	S	W/T	◆		Sp/Su	Su/A	F		◆		
Solanum muricatum	36 in (90 cm)	36 in (90 cm)	S	W/T		◆	Sp/Su	Su/A	F		◆		
Solanum sessiliflorum	7 ft (2 m)	4 ft (1.2 m)	S	W/T		◆	Sp	Sp/Su	F		◆		
Sorbus domestica	30–50 ft (9–15 m)	30 ft (9 m)	T	C	◆		Sp	Sp/Su	B		◆		
Syzygium aqueum	35 ft (10 m)	20 ft (6 m)	T	W/T		◆	Sp	Su	B		◆		
Syzygium malaccense	40–80 ft (12–24 m)	15 ft (4.5 m)	T	W/T		◆	Sp	Su	F		◆		
Terminalia catappa	90 ft (27 m)	35 ft (10 m)	T	T	◆		Sp	Su/A	F		◆		
Theobroma cacao	25 ft (8 m)	10 ft (3 m)	T	T		◆	Sp	Su	F				◆
Ugni molinae	6 ft (1.8 m)	3 ft (0.9 m)	S	C/W		◆	Sp	Su/A	F	◆	◆		
Vaccinium ashei	3–15 ft (0.9–4.5 m)	7 ft (2 m)	S	C/W	◆		Sp	Su/A	B		◆		◆
Vaccinium corymbosum	3–6 ft (0.9–1.8 m)	5 ft (1.5 m)	S	C	◆		Sp	Su/A	B		◆		◆
Vaccinium macrocarpon	3 ft (0.9 m)	5–10 ft (1.5–3 m)	S	C		◆	Sp	Su/A	B		◆		◆
Vaccinium myrtillus	18 in (45 cm)	36 in (90 cm)	S	C	◆		Sp	Su/A	B		◆		◆
Vaccinium ovatum	3–5 ft (0.9–1.5 m)	4 ft (1.2 m)	S	C/W		◆	Sp	Su/A	B		◆		◆
Vaccinium parvifolium	6 ft (1.8 m)	6 ft (1.8 m)	S	C/W	◆		Sp	Su/A	B		◆		◆
Vaccinium Hybrid Cultivars	2–5 ft (0.6–1.5 m)	3–6 ft (0.9–1.8 m)	S	C	◆		Sp	Su/A	B		◆		◆
Vitis rotundifolia	100 ft (30 m)	10–20 ft (3–6 m)	C	C	◆		Sp	Su/A	F	◆	◆		
Vitis vinifera	35 ft (10 m)	15–30 ft (4.5–9 m)	C	C	◆		Su	Su/A	F	◆	◆		
Vitis 'Waltham Cross'	35 ft (10 m)	15–30 ft (4.5–9 m)	C	C	◆		Sp	Su/A	F	◆	◆		
Ziziphus jujuba	30 ft (9 m)	12 ft (3.5m)	T	C/W	◆		Sp	Su	F	◆	◆		

Actinidia deliciosa 'Hayward'

ACTINIDIA

This genus of about 60 species of evergreen and deciduous twining climbers from East Asia belongs to the family Actinidiaceae. They are grown for their handsome foliage and often scented creamy white flowers in spring. The fruit of some is edible, but both male and female plants are needed to produce these. They can be used to cover walls, pergolas, and dead or unattractive trees.
CULTIVATION: Plant in full sun to partial shade in any well-drained loamy soil that should not dry out. Prune in winter as necessary. Vines become heavy so provide support. There is little need for fertilizer. Propagate from seed sown in spring or autumn, from half-hardened cuttings, or by layering in late autumn or winter. Vines of both sexes are required for fruiting of most varieties.

Actinidia arguta

BOWER ACTINIDIA, BOWER VINE, COCKTAIL KIWI, DESSERT KIWI, HARDY KIWI, KOKUWA, SIBERIAN GOOSEBERRY, TARA VINE, YANG-TAO
☼ ❄ ↔ 20–30 ft (6–9 m) ↕ 20–30 ft (6–9 m)
Vigorous twining vine of variable habit from Japan, Korea, and northeastern China. Fragrant white flowers tinged green, purple anthers, in mid- to late summer. Leaves to 6 in (15 cm) long, oval, smooth, serrated. Fruit abundant, yellow-green, hairless, slightly acid flavor. 'Ananasnaya' (syn. 'Anna'), vigorous female cultivar, large clusters of small sweet-smelling flowers; 'Issai', self-pollinating form. Zones 4–9.

Actinidia deliciosa ★

syn. *Actinidia chinensis* of gardens
CHINESE GOOSEBERRY, KIWI FRUIT, YANTAO
☼ ❄ ↔ 35 ft (10 m) ↕ 35 ft (10 m)
Vigorous climber from China. Large, furry, green leaves to 8 in (20 cm) long. Scented cream flowers in spring, followed by tasty, brown, fuzzy fruit with green flesh and black seeds that ripen in early winter. 'Hayward', large-fruited commercial form. Zones 7–10.

Actinidia kolomikta

syn. *Trochostigma kolomikta*
☀ ❄ ↔ 17–20 ft (5–6 m) ↕ 20–35 ft (6–10 m)
Climber from East Asia, grown for its handsome leaves, green or tipped with white or pink. Variegation develops as plant grows,

rarely evident in very young plants. Not produced commercially but, if both male and female plants present, fruit edible. 'September Sun', richer variegated foliage. Zones 4–9.

ANACARDIUM

This tropical American genus of the cashew (Anarcardiaceae) family is made up of 11 species of evergreen or semi-deciduous small to medium trees with simple, smooth-edged, leathery leaves. Small flowers are borne in large panicles. Fruit, on fleshy (and edible) stems, is small, and curved like the enclosed seed, which is covered by a thin flesh containing a dangerously caustic juice.
CULTIVATION: These plants are successfully grown in a tropical monsoonal climate with a long dry season; they are prone to pests and diseases in wetter tropics. Intolerant of frost, they prefer well-drained, sandy, moderately fertile soils, and are tolerant of fierce sun or coastal salt spray. Propagate from seed. The best cultivars can be increased by grafting, cuttings, or air-layering.

Anacardium occidentale

ACAJOU, CASHEW
☼ ♣ ↔ 25 ft (8 m) ↕ 40 ft (12 m)
Origin uncertain, though southern India is largest supplier of nuts. Stalk—"cashew apple"—commonly used in refreshing drink. Zones 11–12.

ANANAS

PINEAPPLE
Currently there are 7 species in this genus of the pineapple (Bromeliaceae) family, but research by the pineapple industry has shown that there is very little difference between them. In nature they are prickly plants with many seeds and leaves. Indigenous populations in Central America and northern South America selected the better plants over hundreds of years, resulting in the seedless fruit we enjoy today. Even the leaves are without teeth on the edges in some cultivars. Known as *Ananas* in its native region for thousands of years, how it came to be called "pineapple" is not recorded.
CULTIVATION: It is good for the greenhouse or conservatory in cool-temperate areas, or outdoors in warm-temperate, subtropical, and tropical areas. Water before the potting mix is totally dry. If good-quality potting mix is to be used, extra fertilizer is not necessary. Propagate mainly by basal offset.

Ananas comosus

PINEAPPLE
☀ ◗ ↔ 30 in (75 cm) ↕ 30 in (75 cm)
Leaves narrow, triangular, gray-green, to 30 in (75 cm) long, strong teeth on edges (some forms are spineless), forming open rosette. Flower stem short and stout. Flowerhead globular to cylindrical with many small flowers. Petals blue-lavender. Cultivars include 'Abacaxi', 'Queen', 'Red Spanish', and 'Smooth Cayenne'. Zones 9–10.

ANNONA

Widespread in the tropics of Africa and America, this genus of the custard-apple (Annonaceae) family includes some 100 species of evergreen or semi-deciduous shrubs and trees. Several are important either commercially or locally, particularly the

cherimoya and the custard apple. Most of the common species have aromatic, simple, oblong leaves with pronounced veins. Flowers are unusual, having 6 thick fleshy petals and a central mass of densely packed stamens and pistils. These develop into a fruit with a pulpy center and a sometimes spiny exterior.
CULTIVATION: Species need warm subtropical or tropical conditions, and shelter from strong winds. They are best in a sunny position with moist, well-drained, humus-rich soil. Flowering and fruiting can occur any time, and the plants should not dry out too much or fruit quality will suffer. Propagate from seed or by grafting.

Annona, Atemoya Group
ATEMOYA, CUSTARD APPLE
☼ ⚡ ↔ 6–9 ft (1.8–2.7 m) ↑ 10–15 ft (3–4.5 m)
Hybrids between *A. cherimola* and *A. squamosa*. Spreading trees, large drooping leaves, many trumpet-shaped yellow flowers. Fruits with few seeds, flesh free from grainy texture. 'African Pride', dwarf, yields fruit 1–1½ lb (454–680 g) twice annually; 'Pink's Mammoth', large sweet fruit weighing up to 6½ lb (3 kg). Zones 10–12.

Annona cherimola
CHERIMOYA, CUSTARD APPLE
☼ ⚡ ↔ 10 ft (3 m) ↑ 20 ft (6 m)
Evergreen tree native to Peru and Ecuador. Leaves deep green, oval to lance-shaped, velvety beneath. Flowers fragrant, yellowish, purple spotting inside, covered in fine brown hairs. Fruit rounded, delicious fleshy pulp. 'El Bumpo', soft-skinned, sweet; 'Honeyhart', mid-sized, yellow-green; 'McPherson', mid-sized, dark green; 'Pierce', mid-sized, smooth-skinned; 'Spain', pineapple flavor. Zones 10–12.

Annona muricata
GUANABANA, SOURSOP
☼ ⚡ ↔ 10 ft (3 m) ↑ 20 ft (6 m)
Evergreen tree from Central America and West Indies. Leaves glossy with age. Flowers yellow-green. Surface of ovoid dark green fruit has soft curved spines with white flesh. Zones 10–12.

Annona squamosa
CUSTARD APPLE, SWEETSOP
☼ ⚡ ↔ 10 ft (3 m) ↑ 25 ft (8 m)
Evergreen tree native to tropical America. Scented leaves narrow, lance-shaped. Yellowish flowers with purple-spotted interiors. Fruit spherical, custard-like creamy white pulp inside. Zones 10–12.

ARTOCARPUS
This genus of around 50 species of evergreen and deciduous trees of the mulberry (Moraceae) family occurs wild in tropical Asia and the Malay Archipelago. It includes several commercially important fruits, notably breadfruit and jackfruit. The leaves may be large and simple or lobed, with large stipules at the stalk base. Separate male and female flowers are produced; males are borne in small catkins, females in large heads. Flowers are tiny, but the starchy, white-fleshed, compound fruit that follows is conspicuous and may be very large.

Annona muricata

CULTIVATION: *Artocarpus* species require constantly warm moist conditions and prefer well-drained humus-rich soil. They will fruit more reliably and heavily if fed well. Plant in full sun or partial shade with shelter from strong winds. Propagate the species from seed and the cultivars from cuttings or aerial layers.

Artocarpus altilis
syns *Artocarpus communis, A. incisus*
BREADFRUIT
☼ ⚡ ↔ 20 ft (6 m) ↑ 50 ft (15 m)
From East Asia. Broad crown of deeply lobed leaves to 30 in (75 cm) long. Spherical, 8 in (20 cm) wide, yellow-green fruit, eaten boiled or baked. Zones 11–12.

Artocarpus heterophyllus
JACKFRUIT
☼ ⚡ ↔ 20 ft (6 m) ↑ 30–50 ft (9–15 m)
From India to Malay Peninsula. Simple, dark green leaves. Ripe fruit mustard shade. Yellow to pink flesh smells unpleasant but is edible. Zones 10–12.

ASIMINA
This genus of 7 or 8 evergreen or deciduous shrubs or trees from eastern North America is in the custard-apple (Annonaceae) family. White or purple, nodding, bell-shaped flowers appear in clusters.
CULTIVATION: Generally frost hardy, most species tolerate temperatures of 5°F (–15°C) or lower. They will grow in moist well-drained soil in sun or part-shade, though they are affected by long dry periods. They respond well to pruning and shaping and can be used for hedging, though this reduces flowers and fruit.

Artocarpus heterophyllus

Asimina triloba

PAWPAW

☼ ❋ ↔ 20 ft (6 m) ↑ 30 ft (9 m)

From eastern and central North America. Leaves oval, pointed, and narrow, up to 10 in (25 cm) long. Reddish brown pendulous flowers, around 2 in (5 cm) wide, in spring. Edible fruits ripen to yellowish brown in autumn. 'Prolific', early ripening; 'Rebecca's Gold', late ripening; 'Sunflower', large, late ripening; 'Taylor', small fruit, late ripening; and 'Wells', with golden orange flesh. Zones 5–10.

AVERRHOA

East Asian genus of 2 species of evergreen trees, of the wood-sorrel (Oxalidaceae) family. Foliage is pinnate, composed of quite large leaflets. The flowers, white to red or purple with white markings, are carried in short inflorescences, followed by 5-angled edible fruit, to 5 in (12 cm) long.
CULTIVATION: Easily cultivated, other than requiring tropical or subtropical conditions. Thrive in warm sheltered positions with moist well-drained soil and high humidity. Propagate from seed, or grow fruiting cultivars from grafts or aerial layers.

Averrhoa bilimbi

Averrhoa bilimbi

BILIMBI, PICKLE FRUIT

☼ ✈ ↔ 15 ft (4.5 m) ↑ 50 ft (15 m)

Leaves composed of up to 40 leaflets, 5 in (12 cm) long. Inflorescences sprout directly from the branches. Flowers are purple to orange-red. The yellow-green fruit, shallowly angled, lacks the sweetness of *A. carambola*. Zones 11–12.

Averrhoa carambola ★

CARAMBOLA, FIVE-CORNER, STAR FRUIT

☼ ✈ ↔ 10 ft (3 m) ↑ 20 ft (6 m)

Leaflets blue-green on undersides, to 4 in (10 cm) long. They are sensitive to touch and light, folding at night or if handled. Dull red flowers appear for much of the year. The edible fruit is yellow-green to orange. Zones 11–12.

Carica papaya

CAPPARIS

This genus of around 250 species of shrubs, scrambling climbers, and small trees is from the caper (Capparidaceae) family. It contains both evergreen and deciduous plants, which grow in warm climates around the world. *C. spinosa* is the source of the edible capers used as a condiment and the only species occurring naturally in Europe. The simple leaves have paired and often hooked spines at the base. Flowers have early-shedding petals and long showy stamens, and fruit is berry-like. The species grow in a range of habitats, from dry open woodland, vine thickets, and rainforest, to rocky seashores. In some regions the foliage is eaten by the larvae of the caper white butterfly.
CULTIVATION: Needs vary, but most are sun-loving and prefer a reasonably fertile soil. Few tolerate more than very light frosts. *C. spinosa* requires hot dry summers and well-drained open soil. Propagate from freshly extracted seed or from half-hardened cuttings in summer.

Capparis spinosa

CAPER BUSH

☼ ❀ ↔ 10 ft (3 m) ↑ 3 ft (0.9 m)

From southern Europe, Africa, Asia, and northern Australia. Scrambling shrub, semi-prostrate branches. Leaves very broad, rounded, arranged in 2 rows. Flowers white, pale purple stamens, on slender stalks, in summer–autumn. Unopened buds pickled in brine as capers. Fruits elongated, strongly ribbed. Zones 9–12.

CARICA (see page 107)

Carica papaya

PAPAYA, PAWPAW

☼ ✈ ↔ 12 ft (3.5 m) ↑ 30 ft (9 m)

Native to lowlands of tropical South America. Single trunk, ringed with leaf scars. Leaves to 24 in (60 cm) wide, stalk to 36 in (90 cm) long. Fruits mature to yellow or orange, contain yellow or pinkish flesh, black seeds. Zones 11–12.

CARYA

syn. *Hicoria*

This genus, belonging to the walnut (Juglandaceae) family, consists of about 25 species, most of which come from eastern North America, with some from Vietnam and China. These large deciduous trees have both functional male and female organs on the one plant. The gray-brown bark becomes scaly with age. The pinnate leaves are alternate with serrated-edged leaflets. Male inflorescence is a pendent branched catkin; female inflorescence is a terminal spike with up to 20 individual flowers. The fruit is a drupe. Commercially valuable for pecan nuts, and hard wood. Transplanting is difficult as they resent disturbance.
CULTIVATION: Seedlings develop a long tap root very early, so plant when young into deep, fertile, humus-rich but well-drained soil. Sow seed into a seed bed as soon as it is ripe. If growing in a pot, use one that is extra deep. Use good loam with added leafmold; cultivars require winter grafting.

Carya illinoinensis

Carya ovata

Castanea mollissima

Carya illinoinensis

syns *Carya olivaeformis, Juglans illinoinensis*

PECAN

↔ 70 ft (21 m) ↑ 100 ft (30 m)

Native to the southern and central USA and northern Mexico. Grows best in deep alluvial soil. Scaly gray bark, mid-green leaves, with up to 17 lance-shaped leaflets. Pecan nuts are an important crop exported worldwide. Some 500 cultivars are available: '**Pawnee**' and '**Lucas**' are early ripeners. Zones 6–11.

Carya laciniosa

BIG SHELLBARK HICKORY

↔ 35 ft (10 m) ↑ 100 ft (30 m)

From eastern USA. Bark peels in 3 ft (0.9 m) long curving plates. Leaves reach 18 in (45 cm) long with 5 to 7 leaflets. Fruit oval, 2 in (5 cm) long. Good timber tree. Zones 4–9.

Carya ovata

syns *Hicoria ovata, Juglans ovata*

LITTLE SHELLBARK HICKORY, SHAGBARK HICKORY

↔ 70 ft (21 m) ↑ 80 ft (24 m)

From eastern USA. Gray-brown peeling bark. The leaves are mid-green, with 5 leaflets, turning golden yellow in autumn. Fruit edible, splitting when ripe. Cultivars often hybrids with *C. cathayensis* or *C. laciniosa*. Zones 4–9.

CASTANEA

Belonging to the beech (Fagaceae) family, this is a small genus of about 12 species of sweet chestnuts native to temperate regions of the Northern Hemisphere, from North America across Europe and into eastern Asia. In habit they range from low suckering shrubs to tall trees. Several species are of economic importance, being grown for their sweet-tasting edible nuts, enclosed in a spiny whorl of bracts. The taller species are also valued for their use as ornamental trees, especially for their spectacular yellowish green drooping male catkins.

CULTIVATION: Sweet chestnuts prefer a well-drained and slightly acid soil; adequate rainfall is essential. Most are frost hardy down to Zones 4 or 5. Propagation is usually from seed which should be sown as soon as it is ripe; selected clones can be reproduced by grafts onto 1- or 2-year-old understocks, in early spring.

Castanea mollissima

CHINESE CHESTNUT

↔ 35 ft (10 m) ↑ 40 ft (12 m)

Native to central and eastern China and Korea. Ovate or oblong, coarsely serrated, short-stalked leaves, coarse white hair beneath. Edible nuts. Resistant to chestnut blight. Highly valued as an ornamental. '**Pendula**', a popular cultivar. Zones 5–9.

Castanea pumila

ALLEGHENY CHINKAPIN, CHINQUAPIN

↔ 20 ft (6 m) ↑ 15 ft (4.5 m)

Large suckering shrub from eastern and southern areas of USA. Downy young shoots, young leaves white and furry on the undersides. '**Ashei**' has less densely spiny bracts. Zones 6–9.

Castanea sativa

syn. *Castanea vesca*

CHESTNUT, SPANISH CHESTNUT, SWEET CHESTNUT

↔ 40 ft (12 m) ↑ 60 ft (18 m)

Native of the high forest areas of southern Europe and western Asia. Fast-growing deciduous tree. Glossy, dark green, coarsely serrated leaves, lighter and slightly furry beneath. Yellow-green catkins, in mid-summer. Edible nuts are a delicacy, "marrons glacés." Cultivars include '**Albomarginata**' and '**Glabra**'. Zones 5–9.

CITRULLUS

An African and Asian pumpkin (Cucurbitaceae) family genus of just 3 species of annual and perennial trailers and climbers, best known as the home of the watermelon (*C. lanatus*). Stems are covered with short coarse hairs and bear simple or branched tendrils in the leaf axils. Leaves are oval to palmate but often so deeply lobed that they appear pinnate. Foliage color ranges from blue-gray to deep green, sometimes with small translucent patches. Large, 5-lobed, bell-shaped, yellow flowers appear in the leaf axils and develop into rounded to elongated fruit, usually pale green with dark striping and mottling, and ranging from golf ball to larger than soccer ball size, weighing up 60 lb (27.25 kg).

CULTIVATION: Melons need a long warm growing season and good drainage to ripen. Water well and allow to dry off as the fruit nears ripeness. Usually propagated from seed, though *C. colocynthis* will grow from cuttings or layers.

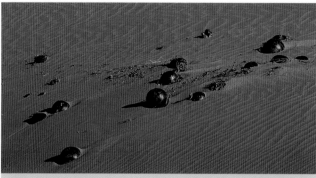

Citrullus lanatus, in the wild, South Africa

Citrullus lanatus

syn. *Citrullus vulgaris*

WATERMELON

☼/☀ ⚡ ↔ 10–20 ft (3–6 m) ↑ 36 in–6 ft (90 cm–1.8 m)

Annual climber or trailer from Namibia, naturalized elsewhere. Of indeterminate size, spreading or climbing throughout growing season. Oval, lobed, pinnate, green leaves with toothed edges and small translucent patches. Branched tendrils and pink- to red-fleshed, mottled, green fruit to over 20 in (50 cm) long. '**Candy Red**', oblong fruit weighing up to 40 lb (18 kg), ripens 85 days after petal fall; '**Dixie Queen**', bright red flesh, even round fruit to 50 lb (22.5 kg), 80-day ripening period; '**Fordhook Hybrid**', deep pink flesh, small fruit to 10 lb (4.5 kg), 74-day ripening period; '**Klondike RS57**', medium-sized fruit, pinkish red flesh, 85-day ripening period; '**New Queen**', round fruit; '**Sweet Favorite**', oblong, red-fleshed fruit to 20 lb (9 kg), 82-day ripening period; '**Triplesweet Seedless**' ★, round fruit, deep pink seedless flesh, to 20 lb (9 kg), 85-day ripening period. Zones 10–12.

CITRUS

syns *Eremocitrus, Fortunella, Microcitrus, Poncirus*

Ranging in the wild from China to India, Southeast Asia, New Guinea, and Australia, this genus comprises about 20 species of mostly evergreen shrubs and small trees and belongs to the family Rutaceae. Grown in warmer countries for their edible fruits—the oranges, lemons, limes, grapefruit, and mandarins, among others. Most cultivated citrus are ancient hybrids, derived from 3 wild species. Ornamental plants with dark glossy foliage; fragrant, starry, white flowers appear singly or in clusters at different times of the year. Twigs are often thorny; the spirally arranged leaves are jointed at the junction with the stalks, a relic of ancestral compound leaves (still compound in *C. trifoliata*). Their unique fruit structure identifies the genus: the tough skin, dotted with aromatic oil glands, encloses a white pith of varying thickness, inside which are the segments (carpels) with seeds embedded among juice-filled vesicles, or giant cells.

CULTIVATION: In frost-free conditions most species flourish in fertile well-drained soil in a sunny position protected from wind. During the growing season they need plenty of water and regular small applications of nitrogenous fertilizer to promote growth and fruit size. They need very little pruning. Propagation is by budding, or by grafting the desired cultivar onto a suitable rootstock.

Citrus × *aurantiifolia*

syn. *Limonia aurantiifolia*

LIME

☼ ✹ ↔ 10 ft (3 m) ↑ 8–15 ft (2.4–4.5 m)

This popular plant is widely cultivated in Mexico, the West Indies, and Florida, USA. It has spreading prickly branches. Small, thin-skinned, oval to round, seeded fruit, greenish yellow, acid, juicy, green pulp. Limes thrive in tropical and subtropical regions. Zones 11–12.

Citrus × *aurantium*

syns *Citrus* × *paradisi, C. sinensis, C.* × *tangelo, C.* × *tangor*

☼ ✹ ↔ 10 ft (3 m) ↑ 15 ft (4.5 m)

This name has expanded to include oranges, grapefruits, tangelos, and tangors, all of which are believed to be hybrids between the mandarin *(C. reticulata)* and the shaddock *(C. maxima)*. These major citrus types are now treated as cultivar groups.

Grapefruit Group (syn. *C.* × *paradisi*): Rounded bushy tree to 30 ft (9 m). Large oval leaves, some spines. Large, thin-skinned, yellow fruits ripen late autumn–early spring. Some varieties withstand light frosts. Frost tolerant varieties '**Duncan**' and '**Marsh**' ★ have pale straw-colored flesh. '**Red Blush**' and '**Ruby**' have pink flesh and require a hot frost-free climate to develop good color.

Sour Orange Group: The Seville orange is the only widely grown member of this group. Tough spiny tree to 30 ft (9 m), highly perfumed flowers, aromatic thick peel, bitter-tasting fruit, ripens in autumn, used for marmalade. Withstands light frosts.

Sweet Orange Group (syn. *C. sinensis*): This group comprises the common eating oranges. Attractive, medium-sized, rounded tree to 25 ft (8 m) high. Glossy dark green leaves, beautiful, fragrant, white blossoms. Fruit is deep orange in color, and has sweet juicy flesh. These plants do best in a Mediterranean cli-

Citrus × *aurantium* 'Valencia'

mate. Some varieties tolerate light frosts. **'Ruby'**, a popular "blood orange," has reddish skin, flesh, and juice; **'Valencia'** produces abundant fruit, relatively seedless. The navel subgroup of sweet oranges is normally seedless; well known **'Washington Navel'** is possibly one of the best eating oranges.

Tangelo Group (syn. *C. × tangelo*): Grows up to 30 ft (9 m), bears reddish orange fruit, pleasant acid-sweet flavor, good for juicing. Frost sensitive, needs a long hot growing season. Most ripen in spring. Best varieties are **'Minneola'**, **'Orlando'**, and **'Samson'**.

Tangor Group (syn. *C. × tangor*): to 12 ft (3.5 m) high. Fruit is intermediate in flavor and size between orange and mandarin, but more rounded than the latter. The cultivar **'Honey Murcott'**, the original cross, has 3 in (8 cm) wide, thin-skinned, yellow-orange fruit, juicy, sweet, orange flesh.

'Temple', a deep orange-red easy-to-peel variety with a sweet rich flavor, ripens in spring. Zones 9–11.

Citrus hystrix
CAFFRE LIME, LEECH LIME, MAURITIUS PAPEDA

☼ ⚘ ↔ 6 ft (1.8 m) ↑ 10 ft (3 m)

Aromatic leaves flavor Thai and Malay dishes. Unusual leaves, leaf stalk swells to almost same width as blade. Small, rough, wrinkled fruit, little juice, rind used as flavoring. Zones 10–12.

Citrus japonica
syns *Fortunella japonica*, *F. margarita*
CUMQUAT

☼ ⚘ ↔ 3 ft (0.9 m) ↑ 6 ft (1.8 m)

From southern China. Dense branches, oval leaves, small, round to oval, golden fruit. **Marumi Group**, round or flattened fruit; **'Sunstripe'**, variegated foliage and fruit. **Nagami Group** (syn. *Fortunella margarita*), elongated thin-skinned fruit. Zones 9–10.

Citrus × limon
LEMON

☼ ⚘ ↔ 10 ft (3 m) ↑ 10–15 ft (3–4.5 m)

An ancient hybrid; one parent is *C. medica*, the other uncertain. Smooth-skinned, acidic, yellow fruit, several flushes throughout the year. Best in a Mediterranean climate. **'Garey's Eureka'**, thornless, fruits year round, mostly in summer; **'Lisbon'**, vigorous, winter-bearing variety, suited to hot areas. Zones 9–11.

Citrus × limonia
RANGPUR LIME

☼ ⚘ ↔ 12 ft (3.5 m) ↑ 20 ft (6 m)

Lemon/mandarin hybrid, originating in China. Thorny, many branches. Fragrant white flowers, pinkish tinge. Rounded fruit, deep yellow-orange, ripen in winter. Zones 10–12.

Citrus × aurantium 'Washington Navel'

Citrus maxima
POMELO, SHADDOCK

☼ ⚘ ↔ 10 ft (3 m) ↑ 20–40 ft (6–12 m)

Presumed native to Southeast Asia. it produces dense, large, glossy, oval to oblong leaves. Pale yellow fruit with yellowish to pink flesh. Zones 10–12.

Citrus medica
CITRON

☼ ⚘ ↔ 8 ft (2.4 m) ↑ 6–15 ft (1.8–4.5 m)

From northern India. Shrub or small tree. Short stiff spines, large, oval, serrated leaves, purplish new growth. Large flowers, purplish outside, white within. Large wrinkled fruit, little juice, thick fragrant rind. The cultivar **'Etrog'** has a long-pointed apex. Zones 9–11.

Citrus reticulata
MANDARIN, SATSUMA, TANGERINE

☼/◑ ⚘ ↔ 6–10 ft (1.8–3 m) ↑ 10–17 ft (3–5 m)

From warm-temperate to subtropical East Asia. Small thorny tree. Lance-shaped leaves 2–4 in (5–10 cm) long, leaf stalks with small wings. Small, fragrant, white flowers, followed by oval to flattened, sweet-fleshed, golden fruit. **'Clementine'**, large, rather acidic, spherical, orange-red fruit with few seeds; **'Dancy'**, flattened orange-red fruit, good flavor, few to many seeds; **'Encore'**, upright tree, few thorns, rounded orange-yellow fruit with darker spots, good flavor but many seeds; **'Fairchild'**, round deep orange fruit, many seeds, bush near thornless, needs cross-pollination; **'Fremont'**, early fruiting, good flavor, few seeds; **'Kinnow'**, very hardy, thin leaves, flattened, orange-yellow, seedy fruit; **'Page'**, round orange fruit, often very seedy, sometimes sold as orange; **'Pixie'**, small, very sweet, seedless. Some varieties that are marketed as mandarins or tangerines are in fact tangors, which are mandarin/orange hybrids (see *C. × aurantium*). Zones 9–11.

CORYLUS

Known as filberts, hazelnuts, cobnuts, and cobs, there are about 15 species of deciduous suckering shrubs and trees in this genus in the birch (Betulaceae) family, some garden grown. The flowers, both the long flouncing male catkins ("lambs' tails") and the inconspicuous female flowers, appear on last year's bare wood, the same plant carrying both sexes. Catkins are usually visible by late winter and fluff out in spring, when the female flowers appear. The husked edible nuts ripen in autumn. **CULTIVATION:** They are easily grown in rich moist soils in full sun or part-shade. Propagate from detached suckers, mounding up soil beforehand to promote root growth. Early summer softwood cuttings are also used, treated with hormone powder. Seeds require cold stratification for about 3 months for germination. Nut production may require a different cultivar for pollination.

Citrus maxima

Corylus avellana

COBNUT, EUROPEAN HAZELNUT

☼/◑ ❄ ↔ 15 ft (4.5 m) ↕ 15 ft (4.5 m)

Native of Europe, western Asia, North Africa. Thicket-like shrub. Coarse mid-green leaves turn yellow in autumn. Long pale yellow catkins in winter on bare branches; red female flowers in early spring. Nuts half covered in ragged husks. '**Aurea**', greenish yellow leaves; '**Contorta**', dense slow-growing shrub of twisted branches. Zones 4–8.

Corylus maxima

FILBERT

☼/◑ ❄ ↔ 15 ft (4.5 m) ↕ 30 ft (9 m)

Native of southern and eastern Europe and western Asia. Vigorous bushy shrub or small tree. Leaves large, heart-shaped, mid-green, new growth covered in sticky hairs. Large brown nuts, elongated lobed husks. '**Purpurea**', young leaves coppery purple tint, fade to leathery greenish purple. Zones 5–9.

Corylus avellana 'Contorta'

CUCUMIS

CUCUMBER, MELON

This is a genus of about 25 species of trailing or climbing annuals in the pumpkin (Cucurbitaceae) family. Originating from warm to tropical areas of Africa and Asia, they are now grown worldwide. Their large, often hairy or prickly leaves can be smooth or may be lobed like a grape leaf. Separate male and female flowers are produced on the one plant and are usually yellow or orange. Fruits are generally green and either long and narrow or round, and are best eaten when young, as bitterness often develops as they mature. Skin can be smooth, bumpy, spiny, or ridged.

CULTIVATION: Cucumbers are grown from seed and like a rich soil with lots of organic matter and a constant supply of moisture during the growing period. Melons are not as demanding.

Cucumis melo

CANTALOUPE, HONEYDEW, MELON, MUSKMELON

☼ ⚘ ↔ 7–10 ft (2–3 m) ↕ 16–28 in (40–70 cm)

Annual vines found in arid regions of Africa, Arabia, southwest Asia, and Australia. Wild types may be bitter, but cultivars produce a range of generally round sweet fruit with either smooth or rough skins. **Cantalupensis Group**: Sweet fragrant melons; the skin can be smooth, scaly, grooved or rough, but not netted. Usually round. **Inodorus Group**: Round or oval sweet melons with green, white, orange, pinkish, or yellowish green flesh. **Reticulatus Group**: Netted melons or cantaloupes, assorted shapes and sizes. Skins can be ribbed, smooth, or netted. Seed cavity large in old varieties, smaller in newer varieties. Some varieties (muskmelons) have musky aroma. '**Ambrosia**', firm, luscious, extra sweet, juicy, peach-colored flesh. Zones 9–12.

Cydonia oblonga

CYDONIA

syn. *Pseudocydonia*

Genus of 2 species of long-lived, small, deciduous tree in the rose (Rosaceae) family, one from the Caucasus region and one from China. Allied to apples *(Malus)* and pears *(Pyrus)*, they bear large pome fruits with a waxy aromatic skin and hard flesh. Simple oval leaves; densely downy on new growth. White to pink flowers, almost stalkless and borne singly among leaves at ends of spring growths. Fruits ripen slowly to yellow through summer and persist well into autumn; woody seeds embedded in the flesh, which contains stone cells.

CULTIVATION: They prefer a temperate climate with well marked seasons and tolerate a range of soils. Plant in full sun; protect from wind. Can be propagated from seed or cuttings, but cultivated forms are normally grafted onto quince rootstocks. Quinces are self-fertile, so even a single tree is capable of producing fruit.

Cydonia oblonga

QUINCE

☼ ❄ ↔ 15 ft (4.5 m) ↕ 10–15 ft (3–4.5 m)

Originally from northern Iran, Turkey, and Armenia, later spread around Mediterranean, then northward through Europe. Rather crooked tree, umbrella-like rounded crown. Leaves very pale green, hairy beneath. Large, upright, white or pink flowers. Fruits round or pear-shaped, to 4 in (10 cm) long. '**Champion**', '**Lusitanica**' (syn. '**Portugal**'), and the Turkish '**Smyrna**' are 3 of the best cultivars. Zones 4–9.

Cydonia sinensis

syns *Chaenomeles sinensis*, *Pseudocydonia sinensis*

CHINESE QUINCE

☼ ❄ ↔ 10 ft (3 m) ↕ 20 ft (6 m)

Native to eastern China. Dappled bark, leaves and flowers slightly smaller than those of *C. oblonga*. Leaves brownish woolly beneath; vivid autumn coloring. Reddish pink flowers in spring. Fruit ovoid, to 7 in (18 cm) long, aromatic. Zones 5–10.

DIOSPYROS

EBONY, PERSIMMON

This genus in the ebony (Ebenaceae) family of some 475 species of evergreen and deciduous, tender and hardy, tropical and temperate shrubs and trees is quite a diverse group of plants. Some have economic importance, either for their timber or their fruit, while others are used in the garden as attractive ornamentals. Their foliage is usually quite simple and the leaves of the deciduous species can be very colorful in autumn. The flowers are unisexual, and to ensure better fruit production it helps to have several trees for cross-pollination. The fruits range from small fleshy berries to the pear-like persimmons.

CULTIVATION: With such a diverse genus it is difficult to generalize about cultivation needs. Only a few species will tolerate prolonged drought and most prefer moist well-drained soil that is reasonably fertile. Propagation is from seed or by root cuttings or grafting.

Diospyros kaki
JAPANESE DATE PLUM, PERSIMMON
☼ ❄ ↔ 25 ft (8 m) ↑ 50 ft (15 m)
Long cultivated in Japan, this species is not known in the wild. Deciduous tree, edible fruit. Choose named cultivars for fruit production where warmth is needed. 'Fuyu' ★, a low tannin variety, needs ample warmth; 'Hachiya', produces a large, tender-skinned, conical-shaped, pinkish orange fruit, not sweet, unpalatable until fully ripe and soft; 'Izu', a compact low tannin variety. Zones 8–10.

Diospyros kaki, with ripe fruit

Diospyros virginiana
AMERICAN PERSIMMON, PERSIMMON
☼ ❄ ↔ 10 ft (3 m) ↑ 50 ft (15 m)
Native to eastern USA, deciduous tree, simple oval leaves color well in autumn. Small, edible, yellow fruit. Timber used for making golf woods. 'John Rick' ★, old-established fruiting cultivar grown for superior eating qualities. Zones 5–9.

DURIO
Night-flying bats pollinate flowers of the 28 species of tall evergreen trees in this genus, placed in the mallow (Malvaceae) family, and found from Myanmar to Malaysia and Indonesia in lowland rainforest. All have simple lance-shaped leaves, shiny on upper surface, lower surface grayish and covered with small scales. Creamy white flowers in clusters on stems and trunks.
CULTIVATION: Like most tropical tree species, propagation is best from fresh seed, since viability is lost quickly. Grow in full sun or dappled shade, in moist humus-rich soil with good drainage. Apart from the durian, members of this genus are seldom grown.

Eriobotrya japonica

Durio zibethinus
DURIAN
☼ ⚘ ↔ 20 ft (6 m) ↑ 80 ft (24 m)
From Malaysia and Indonesia. Leaves lance-shaped, shining green, grayish beneath. Flowers on older wood, creamy white or pink. Fruits large, green to brown, covered in sharp spines. Zone 12.

ERIOBOTRYA
This genus from the rose (Rosaceae) family consists of about 10 species of evergreen trees and shrubs found from the eastern Himalayas to Southeast Asia and China. They are all tough plants with dull green, leathery, strongly veined leaves, felted underneath. The felted buds held at the branch tips develop into scented creamy flower clusters in the autumn. The showy, fragrant, fleshy, edible fruits are sweet, soft, and juicy at full ripeness. The best known species is the loquat, *E. japonica,* which is both edible and decorative, but attracts birds and fruit fly.
CULTIVATION: They prefer subtropical conditions; although generally drought-tolerant, they need abundant moisture in winter to produce good fruit. All except strongly alkaline soils are suitable. Seedlings are easily propagated but variable, often producing fruit with large seeds and minimal flesh, but grafted selected varieties are available. Self-sown seedlings are common.

Eriobotrya japonica
LOQUAT
☼ ❄ ↔ 15 ft (4.5 m) ↑ 20 ft (6 m)
Long cultivated in Japan but native to central China. The common name derives from the Cantonese name, *lo kwat.* An evergreen tree valued for its luscious fragrant fruit in early spring. The leaves are large, dull green, and lance-shaped, with prominent veins and woolly undersides, occurring mostly at the branch tips. The flowers, which are usually self-fertile, develop from woolly buds in autumn. Zones 8–11.

FICUS (see page 159)

Ficus carica

EDIBLE FIG

☼ ❄ ↔ 15–30 ft (4.5–9 m) ↕ 35 ft (10 m)

Cultivated over 5,000 years ago in western Asia, origins obscure. Deciduous tree, spreading rounded canopy. Smooth silvery-gray bark. Leaves 3- to 5-lobed, toothed edges. Tiny flowers. Purple-brown fruit. Used for dried figs. Prefers climates with long warm summers, dry atmosphere, on soils of low to medium fertility. 'Black Genoa' ★, large tree, dull purple fruits, sweet dark red flesh; 'Brown Turkey', pink-fleshed, brown-skinned figs, flavor sweet but slightly insipid; 'White Adriatic', tall grower, pale greenish brown figs, tasty deep pink flesh. Zones 10–12.

FRAGARIA

STRAWBERRY

This genus of 12 perennials, a member of the rose (Rosaceae) family, is found in northern temperate zones and in Chile. Many botanists now believe that the distinction between *Fragaria* and the large, diverse genus *Potentilla* is artificial, and that strawberries should be included in *Potentilla*. It is likely that this reclassification will be generally accepted in the future. Among the most widely grown of the small fruits, strawberries are tough adaptable plants that spread by runners. Leaves grow in groups of 3, and are heart-shaped to rounded, with toothed edges. Clusters of pretty, white, 5-petalled flowers precede the fruits, which may be red, white, yellow, pink, or orange. The fruits are unusual in that they carry their seeds on the outside. CULTIVATION: Hardy in temperate zones in all but the coldest winters, strawberries need moist, fertile, well-drained soil, water to swell the fruit, and sun to ripen it. Planting atop mounds ensures good drainage. Cover with netting to keep the birds away from the fruit. Propagation is usually by layering, using either natural layers or runners, pegged down until the roots establish.

Fragaria × ananassa

GARDEN STRAWBERRY

☼ ❄ ↔ 40 in (100 cm) ↕ 6 in (15 cm)

From Holland. Low-growing ground cover; parent of many of the most successful strawberries around the world. Palmate,

toothed, green leaves. White flowers with yellow centers in late spring–autumn. Medium-sized dark red fruits, in summer–autumn. 'Cambridge Rival', large, firm, sweet fruit; 'Earlisweet', popular early fruiting variety, rich flavor, medium-sized fruit; 'Eros', mid-season, large, firm, glossy, red fruit, resistant to red stele; 'Symphony', shiny, medium-sized fruit; 'Tioga', large sweet fruit, heavy cropper, disease resistant; 'Redgauntlet', vigorous growth habit, medium-sized fruit, mid-season; 'Tribute', with medium to large, flavorful, firm fruit. Zones 3–10.

Fragaria chiloensis

BEACH STRAWBERRY

☼/◐ ❄ ↔ 20 in (50 cm) ↕ 6 in (15 cm)

From North and South America. Short thick leaves, hairy undersides. White flowers, rose-colored edible fruit with white flesh. Grows naturally in coastal areas. Zones 4–10.

Fragaria vesca

WILD STRAWBERRY

☼/◐ ❄ ↔ 12 in (30 cm) ↕ 2 in (5 cm)

From European woodland regions. Compact rosettes of dark green leaves on ground-hugging plant. Flowers white; dark red, sweet, edible fruits in summer. 'Alexandra', smaller red berries, very sweet, plant habit slightly smaller than species; 'Fructo Albo' (white wild strawberry), creamy white edible fruits. Zones 5–9.

Fragaria Hybrid Cultivars

☼/◐ ❄ ↔ 8–60 in (20–150 cm) ↕ 2–6 in (5–15 cm)

These are popular mainly for their ground-covering abilities, although some do produce edible fruits. The most popular hybrid cultivars include: 'Darselect', large, firm, bright red berries; 'Lipstick', ornamental variety, dark green leaves, deep pink flowers, small fruit; Pink Panda/'Frel', dark green, heavily veined, palmate foliage, sterile pink flowers, no fruit; 'Rosie', ground-covering habit, sterile variety, rosy red flowers. Zones 5–9.

HYLOCEREUS

A genus of 18 species of climbing night-flowering cacti, in the Cactaceae family, from southern Mexico, the Caribbean, Central America, and northern South America. These clambering, climbing, or epiphytic plants produce aerial roots and may reach 35 ft

Fragaria × ananassa 'Symphony'

Fragaria chiloensis

Fragaria, Hybrid Cultivar, 'Rosie'

(10 m) wide and 7–10 ft (2–3 m) long. Usually stems have only 3 ribs, are segmented, green to bluish green, with a horny margin. Spines are absent or few, and always small. Flowers are large, nocturnal, white, rarely red. Floral tubes are strong with large naked scales. Seedpods are spherical to oval, usually red. CULTIVATION: Easily grown in a compost-rich well-drained soil. May be raised from seed but are usually propagated from cuttings dried out for a week or two. Rest in winter.

Hylocereus undatus ★
DRAGON FRUIT, QUEEN OF THE NIGHT
☼ ⦚ ↔ 15–25 ft (4.5–8 m) ↑ 17–30 ft (5–9 m)
Of uncertain origin, long cultivated as an ornamental for its spectacular flowers and delicious fruits. Sprawling, climbing, producing many stout, 3-angled, jointed stems, with a wavy horny margin. Has 1 to 3 spines, short, conical, brown to gray, 3 mm long. Flowers from sides of stems, white, 10–12 in (25–30 cm) long. Fruit spherical to oval, bright red, with large often green scales, edible. Zones 10–11.

JUGLANS
The walnuts, a genus of the Juglandaceae family, comprise about 20 species of deciduous trees. They are distributed over the temperate zones of the Americas, southeastern Europe, and Southeast Asia. They have alternate compound leaves and monoecious flowers, borne in spring. The fruit is a hard-shelled nut enclosed in a fleshy green drupe, the kernels being prized as food. Some species produce hard, beautifully grained wood, valued for furniture making; some produce juglose, which can poison apple trees. CULTIVATION: Walnuts thrive on deep, alluvial, well-drained soil with a high organic content, and an assured water supply, in a cool humid climate. Plantation trees are often severely pruned after one year to force strong single trunk growth, then stopped at 12 ft (3.5 m) or so to induce lateral branches; ornamental trees can be treated the same way. Seeds can be collected as soon as ripe in early autumn and stored in cool conditions until sown in early spring.

Juglans major
syn. *Juglans elaeopyren*
ARIZONA WALNUT, NOGAL
☼ ⦚ ↔ 30 ft (9 m) ↑ 50 ft (15 m)
New Mexico to Arizona, USA. Single upright trunk, slender crown. Leaves oblong to lance-shaped, 9 to 13 leaflets. Nuts with dark brown shells. Autumn foliage pale yellow. Zones 9–11.

Juglans nigra
AMERICAN WALNUT, BLACK WALNUT
☼ ✳ ↔ 70 ft (21 m) ↑ 100 ft (30 m)
Native of eastern and central USA and southeastern Canada. Dome-shaped crown, large leaves, 11 to 23 leaflets. Edible nuts dark brown. Grows quickly in warm areas on rich soils, usually slow elsewhere. 'Laciniata' has finely cut leaves. Zones 4–10.

Juglans major

Juglans regia
ENGLISH WALNUT, PERSIAN WALNUT, WALNUT
☼ ✳ ↔ 35 ft (10 m) ↑ 40–60 ft (12–18 m)
Native to southeastern Europe, the Himalayas, and China. Edible nuts. Bark pale gray. Smooth aromatic leaves, 7 leaflets; young leaves coppery purple turning green as they mature. Cultivars of the **Carpathian Group** are cold hardy, and popular in the USA, especially selected commercial clones 'Broadview' and 'Buccaneer'. 'Laciniata' has deeply cut leaflets. Zones 4–10.

LITCHI
Genus in the soapberry (Sapindaceae) family of just one species, from southern China and Southeast Asia. Evergreen tree. Leaves are pinnate, with up to 8 oblong leaflets. Insignificant greenish white flowers are borne in large panicles in the upper leaf axils. Globular fruit contains a large seed enclosed in an edible juicy translucent white inside a thin hard skin. CULTIVATION: Needs warm humid weather and high rainfall for vegetative growth but a cool dry spell to induce flowering, followed by warmth and humidity to ensure pollination. Hot dry winds are harmful at any time. Deep moist soil, regular watering, and protection from wind and cold provide ideal growing conditions. Remove non-fruiting flower panicles at harvest. Fruit turns bright red when ripe and is harvested immediately. Propagate by air-layering or grafting.

Litchi chinensis

Litchi chinensis
LYCHEE
☼ ⦚ ↔ 15 ft (4.5 m) ↑ 20–40 ft (6–12 m)
Spreading tree, with a thick canopy of dark green leaves reaching to the ground. Flowers in long panicles at branch tips, male and female flowers in the same panicle. Fruits round, about 1½ in (35 mm) in diameter, turning red when ripe. Zones 10–11.

Macadamia integrifolia

MACADAMIA

This genus from the protea (Proteaceae) family contains 8 species of evergreen rainforest trees, 7 from coastal eastern Australia; one from Sulawesi, Indonesia. In warm frost-free climates they grow into compact trees with large glossy leaves and long pendulous sprays of creamy white or pale pink blossoms. Self-pollinating, the round hard-shelled nuts ripen in late summer to autumn. Two species are cultivated commercially in Australia, Hawaii and California, USA.
CULTIVATION: Grow in a humus-rich well-drained soil in full sun or partial shade. They require an ample supply of water in dry periods. Propagate from seed, but trees will not bear fruit until at least 6 years old. Selected clones are commonly grafted or budded.

Macadamia integrifolia
SMOOTH-SHELLED MACADAMIA NUT
☀/◑ ❄ ↔ 20 ft (6 m) ↕ 50 ft (15 m)
From southeastern Queensland, Australia. Glossy oblong leaves, in whorls of 3, smooth, slightly wavy edges. Creamy white to pinkish flowers. Creamy white nut. Zones 9–11.

Macadamia tetraphylla
BOPPLE NUT, MACADAMIA NUT, QUEENSLAND NUT
☀/◑ ❄ ↔ 20 ft (6 m) ↕ 40 ft (12 m)
From subtropical rainforests of coastal eastern Australia. Whorls of dark green oblong leaves, prickly teeth. Long pendulous racemes of white or pinkish flowers, in winter–spring. Zones 9–11.

MALUS (see page 214)

Malus pumila
syns *Malus × domestica, Pyrus malus*
APPLE, CRABAPPLE, ORCHARD APPLE
☀ ❉ ↔ 20 ft (6 m) ↕ 50 ft (15 m)
The origins of eating apples were uncertain, but recent intensive botanical studies have virtually solved this puzzle and helped to establish correct botanical names. It was believed that apples were of ancient hybrid origin, so the name *M. × domestica* was used to distinguish them from wild species. But now DNA and other evidence has shown that only one wild species is involved, *M. pumila*, and fieldwork has revealed a large range of variation in wild populations. The wild range of *M. pumila* is from western China through mountain regions of Central Asia to Europe. Young leaves, flower stalks, and calyces vary in downiness. Pink buds open to white flowers suffused with pink. Fruits over 2 in (5 cm) in diameter. *M. p.* 'Niedzwetzkyana', the most significant parent of hybrid crabapples, has young leaves, buds, blossoms, fruit, bark, branches all purple-red.

Orchard apples run to many thousands of cultivars, some still popular after 200 years. Some can be eaten raw, some are better cooked, and a number are suitable only for cider. Apples often need a pollinator of a different cultivar to set good crops. 'Bramley's Seedling', late red fruit, best cooked; 'Cox's Orange Pippin', small, strong-flavored, orange to red fruit; 'Fuji' ★, white-fleshed red fruit with yellowish markings; 'Gala', good flavor, long-keeping, yellow-marked red fruit; 'Golden Delicious', white-fleshed, red-marked, golden yellow fruit; 'Honey Crisp', very juicy, yellow-marked red fruit, cold tolerant; 'James Grieve', yellow-fleshed red fruit, quite acidic; 'Red Delicious', deep red to black-red, strong-flavored; 'Scarlet Gala', red fruit. Recent varieties, such as 'Pacific Rose', are patent-protected. Zones 3–9.

Malus pumila 'Scarlet Gala'

MANGIFERA

Best known for the mango, *M. indica*, This genus is from the cashew (Anacardiaceae) family and consists of around 40 to 60 species originally from the tropical rainforests of India, Southeast Asia, and the Solomon Islands. Simple, leathery, smooth-edged leaves are reddish when young. Panicles of small bisexual and male flowers are produced on the same plant. The fruit is a large, fleshy, hanging drupe with a flat fibrous seed. Grown in tropical and warm-temperate countries for their handsome foliage and fruit. The timber of some species is used for floorboards and tea chests. The sap and plant parts may cause dermatitis.
CULTIVATION: They need deep well-drained soil with regular fertilizing, a warm frost-free climate, and warm dry weather to set fruit; regions with low rainfall during flowering must be selected for fruit production. Propagate from seed or by grafting.

Mangifera indica
MANGO
☀ ✦ ↔ 25 ft (8 m) ↕ 80 ft (24 m)
From Southeast Asia, especially Myanmar and eastern India. Young leaves red, ageing to shiny dark green. Yellowish or reddish flowers, in dense panicles. Fruit irregularly egg-shaped fleshy drupe. May be "alternate-bearing," fruiting heavily every 2 to 4 years. 'Campeche', deep yellow fruit with reddish pink tinge; 'Edward', medium to large fruit; 'Kensington Pride' (syn. 'Pride of Bowen'), Australian cultivar, propagated as seedling. Zones 11–12.

MANILKARA

This genus of around 70 species of evergreen trees belonging to the sapodilla (Sapotaceae) family has a wide distribution throughout the tropics. Leaves are usually simple and large with a thin, papery texture. Flowers form in the leaf axils and may be carried singly or in clusters. They are followed by fleshy berries containing only a few seeds. Some species yield a latex.
CULTIVATION: They are variable in their climatic preferences. Some come from the seasonally dry tropics but most prefer year-round warmth, moisture, and high humidity. They like well-drained humus-rich soil in part shade or full shade and can be trimmed lightly to maintain a pleasing shape. Propagate from seed or cuttings, but allow the latex that is exuded from the cut to dry before inserting the cutting into the potting mix.

Manilkara zapota

SAPODILLA

☀ ◗ ↔ 20 ft (6 m) ↑ 100 ft (30 m)

Commercially grown tree from Mexico to Costa Rica. Simple leaves, 6 in (15 cm) long. Small white flowers. Rough-skinned, egg-shaped, golden brown fruits, to 3 in (8 cm) long. Timber known as chicozapote. Zones 10–12.

MESPILUS

This genus within the rose (Rosaceae) family has one species, a deciduous tree that grows in mountain woodland and scrubland throughout southeast Europe and southwest Asia. It is a good ornamental shrub or tree with large single flowers that are usually white, sometimes with a pink flush, and good autumn foliage. It is now grown less for its fruit, which is only edible after frost, when it is described as "bletted" (slightly rotted); the high malic acid content is reduced and the sugar increased in this way.
CULTIVATION: Grows well in any good moisture-retentive soil with shelter from strong winds. Propagate from seed in autumn, or by bud-grafting in late summer. Can also be grafted onto hawthorn to form graft hybrids.

Mespilus germanica

MEDLAR

☀ ✽ ↔ 25 ft (8 m) ↑ 20 ft (6 m)

A large shrub or small tree from Europe. Thorny branchlets in the wild, but cultivated forms are usually thornless. Leaves alternate, oblong to lance-shaped, toothed, dull green above, felty underneath, red and yellow, in autumn. Profuse apple-blossom-like flowers, in spring. Round, fleshy, brown fruit, too astringent to eat until bletted. 'Breda Giant', apple-cinnamon flavored fruit; 'Dutch', ornamental tree; 'Large Russian', pink tinged flowers, spreading crown; 'Nottingham', good-flavored fruit; 'Royal', medium-sized fruit; 'Stoneless', seedless, small fruit. Zones 4–9.

MORUS

MULBERRY

There are about 12 species of deciduous trees and shrubs in this genus belonging to the mulberry (Moraceae) family. Most species are from Asia, a few are from North America and central Africa. Heart-shaped leaves with serrated edges are arranged alternately. Inconspicuous male and female flowers are borne on separate catkins, followed by fruits resembling raspberries. The black mulberry (*M. nigra*) has edible fruits; leaves of the white mulberry (*M. alba*) provide food for silkworms.
CULTIVATION: They grow in any reasonably fertile well-drained soil. Prune only in winter and keep to a minimum as the sap bleeds freely. Propagate from cuttings in spring or autumn; large pieces of branch (truncheons) up to 5 ft (1.5 m) long can be planted 20 in (50 cm) into the ground.

Mangifera indica

Morus alba

WHITE MULBERRY

☀ ✽ ↔ 30 ft (9 m) ↑ 30–50 ft (9–15 m)

Native to China. Leaves broadly oval, heart-shaped base, 2- to 3-lobed, coarsely toothed; silkworm food. Greenish male and female flowers, in separate clusters, in early summer. Fruit white, becoming pale pink then red. 'Bungeana', dense bright green foliage; 'Pendula', weeping form; 'Venosa', heavily veined mid-green leaves. Zones 4–10.

Morus nigra

BLACK MULBERRY

☀ ✽ ↔ 40 ft (12 m) ↑ 50 ft (15 m)

Deciduous tree from central or southwestern Asia. Wide dense crown, relatively short trunk, gnarled with age. Broadly oval to heart-shaped leaves, roughened uppersurface. Greenish flowers, in spring. Edible berries ripen to purplish black. Zones 5–10.

Morus rubra

RED MULBERRY

☀ ✽ ↔ 40 ft (12 m) ↑ 50 ft (15 m)

From eastern USA and southeastern Canada, rarely cultivated. Slightly heart-shaped leaves, sometimes lobed, roughened uppersurface, serrated edges. Ripe purple fruit in summer. Zones 5–10.

Mespilus germanica

Passiflora alata

MUSA

BANANA

There are about 40 species in this genus of evergreen suckering perennials found from Asia to Australia. They belong to the banana (Musaceae) family. Leaves are large, paddle-shaped, and smooth-edged. The flowers appear on a spike that can be pendent or erect. The female or hermaphrodite flowers are near the base and the male flowers are near the tip. The fruit can be long, slim, and curved, or stubby, nearly round, sausage-shaped, or cylindrical. Although usually grown for the fruit, some species are cultivated for their foliage or flowers. CULTIVATION: Species are found in woodland margins and do best in humus-rich fertile soil in full sun, with shelter from wind. In temperate areas where frosts occur, grow in a greenhouse in loam-based compost with added leafmold. Water and feed regularly during the growing months. Propagate by division of suckers, or from seed in spring.

Musa acuminata

syn. *Musa cavendishii*

BANANA

☀ ❋ ↔ 8 ft (2.4 m) ↑ 12–20 ft (3.5–6 m)

From Southeast Asia and north Queensland, Australia. Paddle-shaped leaves, mid- to gray-green. Pendent flowers, yellow, white, or cream, in summer. Edible yellow fruit. 'Dwarf Cavendish' (syn. 'Basrai'), smaller, yellow flowers and purple bracts. Zones 10–12.

Musa × paradisiaca

syn. *Musa sapientum*

BANANA, PLANTAIN

☀ ❋ ↔ 8 ft (2.4 m) ↑ 10–20 ft (3–6 m)

An *M. acuminata* and *M. balbisiana* cross, that produces both cooking and eating bananas. Leaves large, green, oblong. Fruit

yellow with pale pulp, seedless, in summer. Zones 10–12.

OLEA (see page 226)

Olea europaea

COMMON OLIVE

☀ ❋ ↔ 20 ft (6 m) ↑ 20–30 ft (6–9 m)

Evergreen tree from the Mediterranean region. Gnarled branches, fissured bark with age. Leaves leathery, silver undersides. Very long lived. Fruit is not edible off the tree, must be processed. *O. e.* subsp. *cuspidata* (syns *O. africana*, *O. cuspidata*, and *O. e.* subsp. *africana*), to 25 ft (8 m) high, makes a good shade tree, self-seeds quite freely, can become invasive; leaves not silvery, pea-sized globular fruit. *O. e.* 'Manzanillo' ★, leathery leaves, edible black fruit; 'Mission', a vigorous cold-hardy cultivar. Zones 8–10.

OPUNTIA

PRICKLY PEAR, TUNA

This genus in the cactus (Cactaceae) family contains more than 180 species that grow throughout the Americas, from southern Canada to the most southerly part of South America, and also in the West Indies and Galapagos Islands. They range widely from high-altitude to temperate-region and tropical lowland species. Stem segments are highly variable. The spring and summer, cup- or funnel-shaped flowers are followed by prickly egg-shaped fruits. Some species have become invasive. Most species have bristles that break off; these can cause irritation when they penetrate and stick in the skin. CULTIVATION: Opuntias dislike having their roots confined. Those grown outdoors do best in sandy, humus-enriched, moderately fertile, well-drained soil. Frost-hardy species need protection from too much winter wet; grow them in full sun under glass, with filtered light in hot summers. Feed regularly from spring to summer, and reduce or stop watering during winter. Propagate in spring by sowing pre-soaked seed or rooting stem segments.

Opuntia ficus-indica

Opuntia ficus-indica

syns *Opuntia engelmannii*, *O. vulgaris*

INDIAN FIG, INDIAN FIG PEAR

☀ ❋ ↔ 15 ft (4.5 m) ↑ 15 ft (4.5 m)

Native to Mexico, naturalized elsewhere. Green or bluish green, flattened, oblong or rounded segments, areoles with 1 or 2 spines. Yellow flowers, in late spring to early summer. Purple edible fruits. Zones 9–11.

PASSIFLORA

PASSIONFLOWER

Type genus for its family, Passifloraceae, the 500 or so species of passionflowers are mainly evergreen tendril-climbing vines from tropical America, though there are a few shrubby species and the range does extend to Asia and the Pacific Islands. Flowers have an unusual structure, with a tubular calyx of 5 conspicuous sepals, usually 5 petals of the same size and color as the sepals, a corona of anthers, and 3 styles on an extended central tube. Fruits of many species are mildly to quite poisonous, though others are edible. CULTIVATION: Most species are frost tender and prefer a warm climate in full or half-sun with deep, moist, humus-rich, well-drained soil. Feed and water well. Trim to shape and remove any frosted foliage in spring. Propagate from seed or cuttings, or by layering.

Passiflora alata

☼/◑ ✼ ↔ 8–20 ft (2.4–6 m) ↑ 20 ft (6 m)

Vigorous climber from Amazonian Brazil and Peru. Winged stems, simple pointed oval leaves to 6 in (15 cm) long, edges may be finely toothed. Scented flowers up to 5 in (12 cm) wide, deep red petals, purple and white banded filaments, in summer. Ovoid to pear-shaped, edible, yellow fruit to 4 in (10 cm) long. Zones 10–12.

Passiflora edulis

GRANADILLA, PASSIONFRUIT, PURPLE GRANADILLA

☼/◑ ✼ ↔ 8–15 ft (2.4–4.5 m) ↑ 15 ft (4.5 m)

Summer-flowering climber from Brazil. Glossy, 3-lobed leaves to 4 in (10 cm) long. White flowers with white and purple banded filament. Ovoid edible fruit to around 3 in (8 cm) long, becoming purple-black and wrinkled when ripe. *P. e. f. flavicarpa*, golden yellow fruit, hybrids between these 2 forms include: 'Lacey' and 'Purple Gold' ★, light purple fruit; 'Fredrick' and 'Red Rover', red fruit. *P. e.* 'Edgehill', large purple-black fruit; 'Kahuna', pale purple fruit. Zones 10–12.

Passiflora quadrangularis

GIANT GRANADILLA

☼/◑ ✼ ↔ 10–20 ft (3–6 m) ↑ 50 ft (15 m)

Climber from tropical South America. Pointed oval, leathery leaves. Flowers dusky gray-pink, with twisted blue, white, purple-red banded filaments. Bright yellow, ovoid fruit. Zones 10–12.

PERSEA

Belonging to the laurel (Lauraceae) family, this genus of around 200 species of evergreen shrubs or trees comes chiefly from subtropical and tropical America and Southeast Asia. *Persea* species have prominently veined alternate leaves, and bear panicles of small greenish flowers in the leaf axils. The fruits contain a single large stone, and may be large or small, pear-shaped or rounded; the yellowish green flesh is smooth and rich. The best-known species is the avocado *(P. americana)*, long cultivated for its fruit. CULTIVATION: Best suited to a sheltered but sunny position in a well-drained soil rich in humus. Water moderately during the growing season. Little pruning is necessary once the plants are established. Propagation is from seed or from cuttings. Plants may take up to 7 years to bear fruit; grafted plants are recommended for varieties grown for their fruits.

Persea americana

ALLIGATOR PEAR, AVOCADO

☼ ✼ ↔ 30 ft (9 m) ↑ 60 ft (18 m)

Native to Central America and the West Indies. Fast-growing; grafted trees are smaller. Leathery elliptical leaves, panicles of yellowish green flowers. Large dark green fruits, pear-shaped or rounded. 'Haas', thick-skinned cultivar. Zones 9–11.

PISTACIA *(see page 243)*

Pistacia vera

PISTACHIO

☼ ✼ ↔ 15 ft (4.5 m) ↑ 30 ft (9 m)

Native to western China; cultivated in the Mediterranean region and USA for its nut crop. Pinnate leaves; oval, shiny, paired leaflets, duller beneath. Panicles of flowers; small reddish fruit with bony shell contains the edible green or yellow seed. Zones 8–10.

POUTERIA *(see page 249)*

Pouteria sapota

syns *Calocarpum mammosum, C. sapota, Pouteria mammosa*

MAMEY SAPOTE, MARMALADE PLUM, SAPOTE

☼ ✼ ↔ 20 ft (6 m) ↑ 40 ft (12 m)

Native of Central America and northern South America. Broad oblong leaves and small flowers clustered near branch tips. Large ovoid fruits, edible pulp in shades of orangey pink, that take 1 to 2 years to ripen. 'Magana', fruit weighs up to 6 lb (2.75 kg). Zones 10–11.

Persea americana 'Haas'

PRUNUS *(see page 252)*

Prunus americana

AMERICAN PLUM, AMERICAN RED PLUM, GOOSE PLUM, HOG PLUM, WILD PLUM

☼ ✼ ↔ 12 ft (3.5 m) ↑ 25 ft (8 m)

Eastern and central North American tree with spiny branches, peeling dark brown bark. Leaves to 4 in (10 cm) long, white flowers. Small, yellow-fleshed, red to plum-blue fruit. Zones 3–9.

Pouteria sapota

Prunus armeniaca
APRICOT

☼ ❄ ↔ 15 ft (4.5 m) ↑ 25 ft (8 m)

Flat-topped tree, red-brown bark, leaves large, heavily serrated. Needs winter chilling, summer heat to produce fruit. Flowers white or pale pink, on bare wood, prone to damage from late frosts. Golden orange fruit. *P. a.* var. *ansu*, cultivated race, broader leaves, fruit's stone is rougher. Zones 5–10.

Prunus avium
GEAN, MAZZARD, SWEET CHERRY, WILD CHERRY

☼ ❄ ↔ 20 ft (6 m) ↑ 50 ft (15 m)

The main parent of edible cherries. Deciduous Eurasian tree with serrated-edged leaves. Flowers white, massed in small clusters, open before the new leaves. Purple-red fruit. 'Asplenifolia', deeply cut leaves; 'Cavalier', medium-sized to large fruit, black, produced early to mid-season; 'Plena' (syn. 'Multiplex'), peeling bark, orange-red autumn foliage, white double flowers. Zones 3–9.

Prunus cerasus
SOUR CHERRY

☼ ❄ ↔ 15 ft (4.5 m) ↑ 20 ft (6 m)

Found from southeastern Europe to India. Small, deep green, glossy leaves, finely serrated edges. Long-stemmed umbels of small white flowers. Fruit resembles sweet cherries. Zones 3–9.

Prunus × *domestica*
EUROPEAN PLUM, PLUM

☼ ❄ ↔ 15 ft (4.5 m) ↑ 30 ft (9 m)

The common plum has been grown since ancient times, a hybrid, probably between *P. spinosa* and *P. cerasifera* subsp. *divaricata*. Leaves to 4 in (10 cm) long, flowers white, soft-fleshed yellow or red-skinned fruit. 'Angelina Burdett' (syn. 'Angelina'), early fruiting, light red skin, yellow flesh; 'Bühlerfrühwetsch', purple-skinned; 'Coe's Golden Drop', mid-season, yellow skin, yellow flesh; 'Hauszwetsch' and 'Mount Royal', purple-skinned; 'President', mid- to late season, large, purplish blue skin, yellow flesh; **Reine Claude Group** (syn. Greengage Group), mid-season, greenish yellow skin, yellow flesh, largely self-fertile. Zones 5–9.

Prunus dulcis
ALMOND

☼ ❄ ↔ 15 ft (4.5 m) ↑ 20–30 ft (6–9 m)

Species native to eastern Mediterranean and North Africa. Narrow leaves with finely serrated edges, 5 in (12 cm) long. Large white to deep pink flowers, followed by edible kernels. 'Alba Plena' has white double flowers; 'Macrocarpa' has large pale pink flowers; 'Roseoplena' has pink double flowers. Zones 7–10.

Prunus mume
JAPANESE APRICOT, MEI

☼ ❄ ↔ 25 ft (8 m) ↑ 20–30 ft (6–9 m)

Early flowering deciduous tree from China. Rounded crown of leaves to 4 in (10 cm) long. Flowers, more than 1 in (25 mm) wide, soft fragrance, dusky rose pink. Yellow fruit. 'Beni-chidori', small, deep pink, double flowers; 'Dawn', large, light pink, double flowers; 'Geisha', dusky pink, semi-double flowers; 'Pendula', single pale pink flowers. Zones 6–10.

Prunus persica
syn. *Amygdalus persica*
NECTARINE, PEACH

☼ ❄ ↔ 6–20 ft (1.8–6 m) ↑ 8–20 ft (2.4–6 m)

Believed native to China. Leaves 4–6 in (10–15 cm) long; white or pink flowers. Fruiting cultivars can be subdivided as freestone or clingstone; white or yellow fleshed; early-, mid-, or late season.

Peach Group: Fuzzy-skinned fruit. 'Cresthaven' and 'Jerseyglo', late-season, yellow, freestone; 'Texstar' early to mid-season, semi-freestone, yellow. **Nectarine Group:** Smooth-skinned fruit. 'Anderhone', large late-season fruit; 'Gold Mine' and 'Lord Napier' white flesh, freestone, mid-season. **Ornamental Group:** Flowers, mostly double, white or pink to red, some flecked. 'Klara Meyer', compact, deep pink double flowers. Zones 5–10.

Prunus salicina
JAPANESE PLUM

☼ ❄ ↔ 25 ft (8 m) ↑ 30 ft (9 m)

Deciduous tree from Japan and China. New shoots red, lush dark green foliage. White flowers in pairs or small clusters. Yellow to red fruit. 'Methley', purple-skinned, yellow-fleshed fruit; 'Red Heart', large red fruit. Zones 6–10.

PSIDIUM

This tropical American genus, in the myrtle (Myrtaceae) family, contains about 100 species of evergreen shrubs or trees; several are grown for their edible fruits. They branch freely, and have thick opposite leaves. The white 5-petalled flowers have numerous stamens. Fruit is a rounded or pear-shaped berry.

Prunus persica

Psidium guajava

Pyrus communis 'Doyenné du Comice'

Ribes nigrum 'Ben Connan'

CULTIVATION: They need a warm to hot climate, moist but well-drained soil, protection from strong winds. Water regularly during summer. Prune after fruiting to retain a compact shape. Propagate from seed or cuttings, or by layering or grafting.

Psidium guajava

GUAVA

☼ ✿ ↔ 15 ft (4.5 m) ↑ 30 ft (9 m)

Dark brown scaly bark; light to mid-green oval leaves, prominent veins, downy undersides. Large white flowers, in spring. Edible fruit, pink strongly aromatic flesh. Zones 10–12.

PUNICA

This genus in the loosestrife (Lythraceae) family contains only 2 species, both small, deciduous, fruiting trees native to the Mediterranean region, North Africa, Iran, and Afghanistan. They have simple lance-shaped leaves, scarlet flowers, and reddish yellow apple-shaped fruits.

CULTIVATION: Plant in well-aerated coarsely textured soil, enriched with organic matter. Lightly prune current year's growth in late winter. Propagate from seed sown in spring, or from soft-tip or half-hardened cuttings between spring and autumn.

Punica granatum

COMMON POMEGRANATE

☼ ✽ ↔ 15 ft (4.5 m) ↑ 25 ft (8 m)

Small tree, broad domed crown, lateral shoots thorny. Leaves opposite, broadly lance-shaped, reddish in spring, then bright green; turn yellow in autumn. Flowers with 5 to 8 bright scarlet petals, many stamens, late spring–late summer. Orange-red fruit, jelly-like crimson pulp. Cultivars include 'Nana', 'Nochi Shibari', and 'Wonderful', a double-flowered form. Zones 8–11.

PYRUS *(see page 259)*

Pyrus communis

CALLERY PEAR, COMMON PEAR, GARDEN-PEAR

☼ ✽ ↔ 20 ft (6 m) ↑ 50 ft (15 m)

Medium-sized tree with rounded or oval, glossy, green leaves. Thorny branches covered in white blossoms, in spring. Large, edible fruit. Cultivated for centuries. Over 1,000 named cultivars

raised. 'Beurré d'Anjou', very old French cultivar, smooth green fruit, slight red cheek or all red; 'Cascade', heavy bearer, almost globular fruit, bright red, some yellow showing through, white juicy flesh; 'Clapp's Favourite Liebling', small fruit, juicy flavor; 'Conference', large pear, with a long neck, brown skin, yellow-green showing through, sweet juicy flesh faintly pink-tinged; 'Doyenné du Comice' ★ (syn. 'Comice'), old French pear, with many variants, fruit smooth-skinned, ripening to pale green, sweet creamy flesh; 'Gellerts Butterbirne', greenish yellow fruit, bronze-orange cheek; 'Red Bartlett', bright red fruit; 'Williams' Bon Chrétien' (syn. 'Bartlett'), bright green with a slight red cheek, ripening yellowish. Zones 2–9.

Pyrus pyrifolia

CHINA PEAR, NASHI PEAR, SAND PEAR

☼ ✽ ↔ 30 ft (9 m) ↑ 50 ft (15 m)

Native to China and Japan. Leaves oblong, serrated, in shades of orange and bronze, in autumn. Small white flowers appear just before or with emerging leaves. Small, hard, brown fruit. 'Chojuro', squat, russet brown, densely dotted fruit; 'Hosui', yellow-brown fruit; 'Nijisseiki' ★, green-yellow fruit; 'Shinko', medium-sized fruit of regular globular form. Zones 4–9.

RIBES *(see page 279)*

Ribes gayanum

CHILEAN BLACKCURRANT

☼ ✽ ↔ 3 ft (0.9 m) ↑ 5 ft (1.5 m)

Evergreen shrub from the Chilean Andes. Leaves covered in woolly down, 3 to 5 coarsely toothed lobes. Short upright racemes of yellow flowers, pleasant honey scent, in early summer. Edible black fruit has a downy coating. Zones 8–10.

Ribes nigrum

BLACKCURRANT

☼ ✽ ↔ 6 ft (1.8 m) ↑ 7 ft (2 m)

Deciduous shrub from Eurasia. Upright multi-stemmed habit. Downy pendent racemes of red-centered yellow-green flowers, in spring. 'Ben Connan', award-winning cultivar; 'Ben Lomond', late large fruit; 'Black Beauty', American cultivar; 'Boskoop Giant', large fruit; 'Jet', large dark fruit. Zones 5–9.

Ribes rubrum

Rubus, Hybrid Cultivar, 'Navajo'

Rubus idaeus 'Heritage'

Ribes odoratum

BUFFALO CURRANT, CLOVE CURRANT, GOLDEN CURRANT

☀ ❄ ↔ 6 ft (1.8 m) ↑ 6 ft (1.8 m)

From central USA. Spice-scented leaves, 3 to 5 lobes, toothed edges. Pendent racemes of sweetly scented yellow flowers. Edible black fruit. 'Xanthocarpum', orange-yellow berries. Zones 5–9.

Ribes rubrum

syns *Ribes sativum, R. silvestre, R. spicatum*

NORDIC CURRANT, REDCURRANT

☀/◐ ❄ ↔ 32–60 in (80–150 cm) ↑ 5–7 ft (1.5–2 m)

Smooth-stemmed shrub found from Scandinavia to eastern China. Leaves are 3- to 5-lobed, to 4 in (10 cm) in diameter. Upright to pendulous racemes of small red-flushed green flowers in early summer. Shiny red fruit. Cultivars include 'Red Lake', 'Macrocarpum', and 'White Grape'. Zones 3–9.

Ribes uva-crispa

GOOSEBERRY

☀ ❄ ↔ 36 in (90 cm) ↑ 36 in (90 cm)

Found through Europe to North Africa and the Caucasus region. Thorny many-branched bush. Leaves heart-shaped, green flowers. Bristly green fruit. Fruit of some ripen to yellow or red. Cultivars include: 'Crown Bob', 'Leveller' ★, and 'Roaring Lion'. Zones 5–9.

RUBUS (see page 293)

Rubus arcticus

ARCTIC BRAMBLE, CRIMSON BRAMBLE

☀ ❄ ↔ 18–24 in (45–60 cm) ↑ 6–12 in (15–30 cm)

Herbaceous rhizomatous perennial, native to boggy woods of the higher latitudes of Europe, Asia, and North America. Compound leaves with 3 to 5 oval, smooth, toothed leaflets. Clusters of 1 to 3 pink or red flowers, purple stamens, in summer. Red globular fruit. 'Kenai Carpet' (nagoonberry), pink flowers. Zones 1–7.

Rubus idaeus

RASPBERRY

☀ ❄ ↔ 4 ft (1.2 m) ↑ 5 ft (1.5 m)

Native to Europe, northern Asia, and North America. Deciduous erect shrub, prickly or bristly arching stems. Leaves pinnate, 7 oblong to egg-shaped leaflets. White spring–summer flowers on axillary or terminal racemes. Red fruit. *R. i.* subsp. *strigosus* has more bristly stems. *R. i.* 'Amity', large dark red fruit; 'Aureus', yellow fruit; 'Autumn Bliss' and 'Chilcotin', large red fruit; 'Fallgold', large, yellow fruit; 'Glen Moy', red summer fruit; 'Heritage', late-bearing cultivar; 'Taylor', red fruit. Zones 3–9.

Rubus loganobaccus

LOGANBERRY

☀ ❄ ↔ 2–3 ft (0.6–0.9 m) ↑ 4–6 ft (1.2–1.8 m)

Strongly growing herbaceous shrub developed in California in 1916 by Judge James Harvey Logan by crossing a blackberry, 'Aughinburgh', and a raspberry, 'Red Antwerp'. Vigorous prickly canes; leaves with 3 to 5 leaflets. Ruby red blackberry-shaped berries turn purplish red in early autumn when ripe. Zones 4–7.

Rubus occidentalis

BLACKCAP

☀ ❄ ↔ 10 ft (3 m) ↑ 10 ft (3 m)

Native to eastern and central North America. Deciduous shrub, prickly curved stems. Dark green leaves, 5 leaflets on non-flowering stems, 3 leaflets on flowering stems, white felty undersides. White flowers, in summer. Dark purple fruit. 'Brandywine', large purple-red fruit; 'Cumberland', 'Jewel', 'Morrison', and 'Munger', glossy black fruit; 'Sodus', purple fruit. Zones 3–9.

Rubus phoenicolasius

☀ ❄ ↔ 10 ft (3 m) ↑ 10 ft (3 m)

Native to China, Korea, and Japan. Deciduous shrub, spreading stems with red bristles. Leaves have 3 leaflets, are broadly egg-shaped, coarsely toothed and lobed, with white felty undersides. Light pink flowers in summer. Red cone-shaped fruit. Zones 5–9.

Rubus Hybrid Cultivars

☀ ❄ ↔ 6–12 ft (1.8–3.5 m) ↑ 2–8 ft (0.6–2.4 m)

Most *Rubus* hybrids have been bred for fruit production, with an emphasis on flavor and vigor. 'Benenden' ★ (syn. *R. × tridel*), white flowers, in late spring–early summer; 'Navajo', North American eating blackberry, thornless canes, smallish black fruit; 'Silvan', purple fruit; 'Tayberry', heavy yielding hybrid, sweet, fairly large, highly perfumed fruit, dark red when ripe. Zones 6–9.

SOLANUM *(see page 307)*

Solanum betaceum
syn. *Cyphomandra betacea*
TAMARILLO, TREE TOMATO
☼ ⚘ ↔ 7 ft (2 m) ↑ 10 ft (3 m)
Bushy evergreen shrub from the Andes in Peru. Large heart-shaped leaves, with an unpleasant smell. Pale pink bell-shaped flowers, in spring–summer. Fruits early autumn. Zones 9–11.

Solanum melanocerasum
GARDEN HUCKLEBERRY
☼ ⚘ ↔ 18 in (45 cm) ↑ 24 in (60 cm)
Bushy annual probably originating from western tropical Africa. Broadly oval leaves. Small white flowers. Black berries, ¾ in (18 mm) wide, through summer; edible if cooked. Zones 9–12.

Solanum muricatum
PEPINO, MELON PEAR, MELON SHRUB
☼ ⚘ ↔ 36 in (90 cm) ↑ 36 in (90 cm)
Variable plant from the Andes. Flowers purple, or white, purple markings. Juicy, melon flavored, white, green, purple, or striped, oblong to pear-shaped, edible fruit. 'Ecuadorian Gold', golden fruit, long fruiting season. Zones 9–12.

Solanum sessiliflorum
COCONA
☼ ⚘ ↔ 4 ft (1.2 m) ↑ 7 ft (2 m)
From South America. Downy stems and large, oval, scallop-edged leaves. Yellowish green flowers. Pear-shaped orangey red edible fruit, mild tomato flavor, in spring–summer. Zones 10–12.

SORBUS *(see page 309)*

Sorbus domestica
SERVICE TREE
☼ ✳ ↔ 30 ft (9 m) ↑ 30–50 ft (9–15 m)
From southern Europe, North Africa, and western Asia, pinnate leaves, serrated edges, downy undersides. White flowers. Edible large berries yellow-green, ripening to red; sometimes used in jams and jellies. Zones 6–10.

SYZYGIUM *(see page 322)*

Syzygium aqueum
WATER APPLE, WATER ROSE APPLE
☼ ⚘ ↔ 20 ft (6 m) ↑ 35 ft (10 m)
Tree from Malay Peninsula, Borneo, and New Guinea. Leathery leaves, dull light green. White, red, or dull purple flowers, in loose clusters, in summer. Glossy, pear-shaped, edible fruit, red or white. Zones 10–12.

Syzygium malaccense
syn. *Eugenia malaccense*
MALAY APPLE
☼ ⚘ ↔ 15 ft (4.5 m) ↑ 40–80 ft (12–24 m)
Native to the Malay Peninsula. Soft leathery, dark green leaves, paler undersurface, new growth wine red, then pinkish. Clusters of cream or reddish purple flowers occur on branches or trunk, in summer. Edible red, pink, or white fruit. Zones 10–12.

TERMINALIA *(see page 327)*

Terminalia catappa
INDIAN ALMOND, KOTAMBA
☼ ⚘ ↔ 35 ft (10 m) ↑ 90 ft (27 m)
Tree found in tropical Asia, parts of Polynesia, and northern Australia. Broad spreading crown, tiered horizontal branches. Semi-deciduous; large oblong leaves turn red before falling. Small white flowers in summer. Large greenish yellow and red edible fruits. Zones 11–12.

THEOBROMA
This genus from tropical America is a member of the cacao (Sterculiaceae) family and contains 20 species of evergreen trees; the best known is *T. cacao*, from which cocoa is obtained. They have alternately arranged simple leaves. Flowers arise directly from the leaf axils after the leaves have fallen and are followed by large fleshy fruits that contain many seeds.
CULTIVATION: Frost tender, they need a greenhouse in cool areas. In warm areas grow in a sheltered spot in fertile, moisture-retentive, yet well drained soil. Water and feed regularly in the growing season. Propagate from seed, sown fresh, or by air layering.

Solanum sessiliflorum

Syzygium aqueum

Terminalia catappa

Theobroma cacao

COCOA

☀ ✦ ↔ 10 ft (3 m) ↑ 25 ft (8 m)

Tree from Central and South America. Pointed oblong leaves, red when young. Clusters of small, creamy pink, slightly fragrant flowers borne directly on the trunk and thick branches, in spring. Ribbed seed pods ripen to purplish brown. Zones 11–12.

UGNI

Once included in the genus of the true myrtles *(Myrtus)*, this variable group of approximately 10 species of evergreen shrubs from the temperate Americas is now in a genus of its own within the myrtle (Myrtaceae) family. They have simple oval leaves that are usually tough, leathery, and small. Their flowers are carried singly, in the leaf axils; they have 5 petals and tend to hang downwards. Fleshy berries, sometimes edible, follow the flowers and can become very aromatic as they near ripeness.
CULTIVATION: A little frost tender when young, these plants dislike lime. Grow in cool, moist, humus-rich, well-drained soil in sun or part-shade. An annual trim, after either flowering or fruiting, will keep the growth compact. Propagate from seed, cuttings or by removing naturally formed layers.

Ugni molinae ★

CHILEAN CRANBERRY, CHILEAN GUAVA

☀ ❄ ↔ 3 ft (0.9 m) ↑ 6 ft (1.8 m)

Native to Chile and western Argentina. Wiry-stemmed shrub with glossy deep green leaves on red stems. Flowers are cream flushed with pink, with a cluster of 40 to 60 tiny stamens at the center, in spring to early summer. Red berries follow. Zones 8–10.

VACCINIUM

BLUEBERRY

This genus of around 450 species of evergreen and deciduous shrubs, small trees and vines includes the blueberries, cranberries, and huckleberries. Members of the heath (Ericaceae) family, they occur over much of the Northern Hemisphere, with a few species found in South Africa. Their main feature is the small but colorful edible fruits. Flowers are urn-shaped, carried singly or in clusters. Leaves are simple, oval to lance-shaped, often pointed at the tip and sometimes serrated around the edges.
CULTIVATION: *Vaccinium* species prefer cool, moist, humus-rich soil that is acidic and well drained, with shelter from the hottest summer sun. The conditions preferred by *Camellia* and *Rhododendron* give the best results. Prune shrubby species to shape: after flowering if the fruit is not required, or at harvest. Propagate from seed, cuttings, layers, or in some cases, by division.

Vaccinium corymbosum

Vaccinium ashei

RABBIT-EYE BLUEBERRY

☀ ❄ ↔ 7 ft (2 m) ↑ 3–15 ft (0.9–4.5 m)

Shrub from southeastern USA. Usually deciduous, sometimes near-evergreen in mild winters. Broad, serrated-edged leaves. White to light red flowers, in spring. Edible, ½ in (12 mm) wide, purple-black fruit. Zones 8–10.

Vaccinium corymbosum

BLUEBERRY, HIGHBUSH BLUEBERRY

☀ ❄ ↔ 5 ft (1.5 m) ↑ 3–6 ft (0.9–1.8 m)

Deciduous shrub from eastern USA. Lance-shaped leaves develop orange tones, in autumn. White flowers, sometimes with a red tint, in clusters, in spring. Edible, blue-black berries. 'Earliblue' is a tall vigorous cultivar with large fruit. Zones 2–9.

Vaccinium macrocarpon

CRANBERRY

☀ ❄ ↔ 5–10 ft (1.5–3 m) ↑ 3 ft (0.9 m)

Native of eastern North America and northern Asia. Low-growing evergreen shrub, takes root as it spreads. Leaves dark green, lighter undersides. Flowers mauve with stamens extending beyond the petals. Fruit is red. Zones 2–9.

Vaccinium myrtillus

BILBERRY, BLAEBERRY, WHORTLEBERRY

☀ ❄ ↔ 36 in (90 cm) ↑ 18 in (45 cm)

Semi-deciduous shrub found from Europe to the cold near-Arctic of northern Asia. The 1 in (25 mm) long leaves have finely serrated edges, and hairs on the underside veins. Flowers are borne in small clusters, opening green and turning red with age. Edible blue-black berries. Zones 3–9.

Vaccinium ovatum

BOX BLUEBERRY, EVERGREEN HUCKLEBERRY

☀ ❄ ↔ 4 ft (1.2 m) ↑ 3–5 ft (0.9–1.5 m)

Found naturally in western North America, this evergreen shrub has 1 in (25 mm) long oval leaves with finely serrated edges. Small white to pale pink flowers, tinted with red, are produced in clusters in spring. The fruit is blue-black. Zones 7–10.

Ugni molinae

Vaccinium parvifolium

RED HUCKLEBERRY, RED WHORTLEBERRY

☀ ❄ ↔ 6 ft (1.8 m) ↑ 6 ft (1.8 m)

Found from Alaska to California, USA. A deciduous shrub with small leaves, 1 in (25 mm) long. Flowers ¼ in (6 mm) wide, green with red tints, in spring. Edible, pinkish red berries. Zones 6–10.

Vaccinium Hybrid Cultivars

☀ ❄ ↔ 3–6 ft (0.9–1.8 m) ↑ 2–5 ft (0.6–1.5 m)

There are many popular hybrids and cultivars, some of indeterminate origin. 'Beckyblue', with medium-sized blue fruit; 'Elliott', to 8 ft (2.4 m) tall, with a long-lasting display of orange-red autumn color; 'Lingonberry', reddish pink tints; 'Ornablue', bright red leaves during autumn; 'Sharpeblue' ★, smallish sweet fruit. Zones 2–9.

Vitis vinifera 'Pinot Noir'

VITIS

GRAPE

This is a genus of 65 species of woody deciduous vines indigenous to the Northern Hemisphere, particularly North America, giving its name to the grape (Vitaceae) family. The vines climb by tendrils; leaves are mostly simple, toothed or lobed. Flowers are small, sometimes fragrant. Berries can be small and unpalatable or large and sweet and are often produced in bunches. There are many hundreds of cultivars, particularly of *Vitis vinifera*, the European wine grape.

CULTIVATION: These vines prefer deep, moderately fertile, well-drained, often chalky, alkaline soil. Full sun and warmth are necessary for best fruit ripening. Most commercial *V. vinifera* grapes are grafted onto *Phylloxera*-resistant American species rootstock. Propagate from hardwood cuttings in late winter; propagate *V. coignetiae* by layering or from seed.

Vitis rotundifolia

BULLACE, FOX GRAPE, MUSCADINE

☀ ❄ ↔ 10–20 ft (3–6 m) ↑ 100 ft (30 m)

From moist swampy areas in southeastern USA, this vigorous plant has tight, non-shredding bark. Its glossy, coarsely toothed, occasionally lobed, rounded leaves turn a soft yellow during the autumn months. The large, round, greenish to purplish fruit has a musky flavor. Zones 5–9.

Vitis vinifera

COMMON GRAPE VINE

☀ ❄ ↔ 15–30 ft (4.5–9 m) ↑ 35 ft (10 m)

From southern and central Europe. High-climbing. Variably sized leaves, rounded or palm-shaped, 3- to 7-lobed, toothed, heart-shaped at base. Late summer fruit. Source of most of the world's wine and table grape cultivars, including: 'Black Corinth' (syn. 'Zante Currant'), tiny seedless black fruit, tiny yields; 'Cabernet Sauvignon', small, black, and very seedy fruit; 'Chardonnay', small round fruit, used for white wines; 'Chenin Blanc', medium-sized yellow-green fruit; 'Flame Seedless' ★,

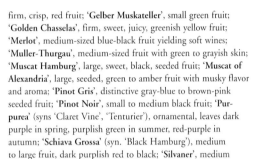

Ziziphus jujuba

firm, crisp, red fruit; 'Gelber Muskateller', small green fruit; 'Golden Chasselas', firm, sweet, juicy, greenish yellow fruit; 'Merlot', medium-sized blue-black fruit yielding soft wines; 'Muller-Thurgau', medium-sized fruit with green to grayish skin; 'Muscat Hamburg', large, sweet, black, seeded fruit; 'Muscat of Alexandria', large, seeded, green to amber fruit with musky flavor and aroma; 'Pinot Gris', distinctive gray-blue to brown-pink seeded fruit; 'Pinot Noir', small to medium black fruit; 'Purpurea' (syns 'Claret Vine', 'Tenturier'), ornamental, leaves dark purple in spring, purplish green in summer, red-purple in autumn; 'Schiava Grossa' (syn. 'Black Hamburg'), medium to large fruit, dark purplish red to black; 'Silvaner', medium sized blue to yellow-green fruit; 'Sultana' (syns 'Sultanina', 'Thompson Seedless'), small, seedless, greenish table fruit; 'Trebbiano' (syns 'Saint-Emilion', 'Trebbiano Toscano', 'Ugni Blanc'), medium-sized, golden yellow fruit, one of most widely planted grapes in the world; 'Zinfandel', reddish black to black fruit. Zones 6–9.

Vitis 'Waltham Cross'

syns *Vitis* 'Dattier', *V.* 'Lady Finger'

☀ ❄ ↔ 15–30 ft (4.5–9 m) ↑ 35 ft (10 m)

This popular, older Middle Eastern variety may be a pure *V. vinifera* cultivar. Large, oval, sweet, juicy, gold-tinted white fruit. Zones 6–9.

ZIZIPHUS (see page 347)

Ziziphus jujuba

CHINESE DATE, CHINESE JUJUBE, COMMON JUJUBE

☀ ❄ ↔ 12 ft (3.5 m) ↑ 30 ft (9 m)

Widely distributed from southern Europe to China. Fast-growing, deciduous tree. Oval to lance-shaped serrated leaves. Axillary clusters of tiny creamy flowers, in late spring. Dark red plum-like fruits, eaten fresh, dried, preserved, or candied. Zones 7–10.

Index to Plant Names

Italicized page numbers refer to a photograph on the page, while plain page numbers indicate a reference in either the text or the tables.

Acknowledgments

Proofreading Puddingburn Publishing Services

Photographers David Banks, Chris Bell, Rob Blakers, Lorraine Blyth, Greg Bourke, Ken Brass, Geoff Bryant, Derek Butcher, Claver Carroll, Leigh Clapp, Mike Comb, David Austin Roses, Grant Dixon, Heather Donovan, e-garden Ltd, Bruce Elder, Katie Fallows, Derek Fells, Stuart Owen Fox, Richard Francis, Robert Gibson, William Grant, Denise Greig, Barry Griffith, Barry Grossman, Gil Hanly, Ivy Hansen, Dennis Harding, Jerry Harpur, Jack Hobbs, Neil Holmes, Paul Huntley, Richard I'Anson, Jason Ingram, Steve Johnson, David Keith Jones, Ionas Kaltenbach, Willie Kempen, Colin Kerr, Robert M. Knight, Carol Knoll, Albert Kuhnigk, Stan Lamond, Mike Langford, Gary Lewis, Geoff Longford, Stirling Macoboy, John McCann, David McGonigal, Richard McKenna, Ron Moon, Eberhard Morell, Barry Myers-Rice, Steve Newall, Connall Oosterbrock, Ron Parsons, Luke Pellatt, Larry Pitt, Craig Potton, Janet Price, Geof Prigge, Nick Rains, Christo Reid, Howard Rice, Jamie Robertson, Tony Rodd, Rolf Ulrich Roesler, Luke Saffigna, Don Skirrow, Raoul Slater, Michael Snedic, Peter Solness, Ken Stepnell, Warren Steptoe, Angus Stewart, Oliver Strewe, J. Peter Thoeming, David Titmuss, Wayne Turville, Georg Uebelhart, Ben-Erik van Wyk, Sharyn Vanderhorst, Kim Westerskov, Murray White, Vic Widman, Brent Wilson, Geoff Woods, Gary Yong Gee, Grant Young, James Young